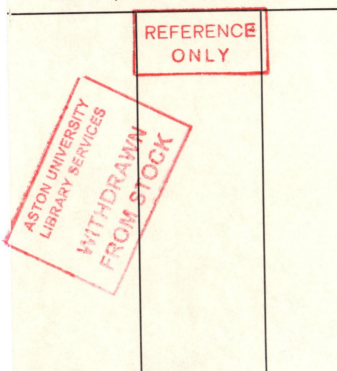

TOOL AND MANUFACTURING ENGINEERS HANDBOOK

VOLUME IV
QUALITY CONTROL AND ASSEMBLY

SOCIETY OF MANUFACTURING ENGINEERS

OFFICERS AND DIRECTORS, 1986-1987

TOOL AND MANUFACTURING ENGINEERS HANDBOOK

FOURTH EDITION

VOLUME IV
QUALITY CONTROL AND ASSEMBLY

A reference book for manufacturing engineers, managers, and technicians

Charles Wick, CMfgE
Editor-in-Chief

Raymond F. Veilleux
Staff Editor

Revised under the supervision of the SME Publications Committee in cooperation with the SME Technical Divisions

Society of Manufacturing Engineers
One SME Drive
Dearborn, Michigan

TMƎH ™

ISBN No. 0-87263-177-X

Library of Congress Catalog No. 82-60312

Society of Manufacturing Engineers (SME)

Copyright © 1987, 1976, 1959, 1949 by Society of Manufacturing Engineers, One SME Drive, P.O. Box 930, Dearborn, Michigan 48121

First edition published 1949 by McGraw-Hill Book Co. in cooperation with SME under earlier Society name, American Society of Tool Engineers (ASTE), and under title *Tool Engineers Handbook*. Second edition published 1959 by McGraw-Hill Book Co. in cooperation with SME under earlier Society name, American Society of Tool and Manufacturing Engineers (ASTME), and under title *Tool Engineers Handbook*. Third edition published 1976 by McGraw-Hill Book Co. in cooperation with SME under current Society name and under title *Tool and Manufacturing Engineers Handbook*.

Printed in the United States of America.

PREFACE

The first edition, published as the *Tool Engineers Handbook* in 1949, established a useful and authoritative editorial format that was successfully expanded and improved on in the publication of highly acclaimed subsequent editions, published in 1959 and 1976, respectively. Now, with continuing dramatic advances in manufacturing technology, increasing competitive pressure both in the United States and abroad, and a significant diversification of information needs of the modern manufacturing engineer, comes the need for further expansion of the Handbook. As succinctly stated by Editor Frank W. Wilson in the preface to the second edition: "...no 'bible' of the industry can indefinitely survive the impact of new and changed technology."

Although greatly expanded and updated to reflect the latest in manufacturing technology, the nature of coverage in this edition is deeply rooted in the heritage of previous editions, constituting a unique compilation of practical data detailing the specification and use of modern manufacturing equipment and processes. Yet, the publication of this edition marks an important break with tradition in that this volume, dedicated to quality control and assembly, is the fourth of five volumes to be published to comprise the fourth edition. Volume I, *Machining*, was published in March 1983, Volume II, *Forming*, in April 1984, and Volume III, *Materials, Finishing and Coating*, in July 1985. The final volume of this edition will be *Manufacturing Management*.

The scope of this edition is multifaceted, offering a ready reference source of authoritative manufacturing information for daily use by engineers, managers, and technicians, yet providing significant coverage of the fundamentals of manufacturing processes, equipment, and tooling for study by the novice engineer or student. Uniquely, this blend of coverage has characterized the proven usefulness and reputation of SME Handbooks in previous editions and continues in this edition to provide the basis for acceptance across all segments of manufacturing.

Subjects covered comprehensively in the Quality Control section of this volume include statistical quality control, inspection equipment and techniques, dimensional metrology and geometric conformance, and surface texture and integrity. Separate chapters are devoted to nondestructive testing and mechanical testing and balancing.

The Assembly section of this volume includes in-depth coverage of mechanical fastening, welding and cutting, brazing and soldering, adhesive bonding, and automated assembly. The mechanical fastening chapter includes details on integral, threaded, and special-purpose fasteners; rivets; eyelets; retaining rings; pins; washers; stitching and stapling; shrink and expansion fits; and injected metal assembly. Robotic and electronic assembly are discussed in the chapter on automated assembly.

In-depth coverage of all subjects is presented in an easy-to-read format. A comprehensive index cross references all subjects, facilitating quick access to information. The liberal use of drawings, graphs, and tables also speeds information gathering and problem solving.

The reference material contained in this volume is the product of incalculable hours of unselfish contribution by hundreds of individuals and organizations, as listed at the beginning of each chapter. No written words of appreciation can sufficiently express the special thanks due these many forward-thinking professionals. Their work is deeply appreciated by the Society; but more important, their contributions will undoubtedly serve to advance the understanding of manufacturing technology throughout industry and will certainly help spur major productivity gains in the years ahead. Industry as a whole will be the beneficiary of their dedication.

Further recognition is due the members of the SME Publications Committee for their expert guidance and support as well as the many members of the SME Technical Activities Board.

The Editors

SME staff who participated in the editorial development and production of this volume include:

EDITORIAL

Thomas J. Drozda
Director of Communications

Charles Wick
Editor-in-Chief

Raymond F. Veilleux
Staff Editor

Ellen J. Kehoe
Technical Copy Editor

Shirley A. Barrick
Editorial Secretary

TYPESETTING

Shari L. Smith
Administrative Coordinator

Nancy Bashi
Typesetter

GRAPHICS

Kathy J. Lake
Art Director

Thomas J. Martin
Illustrator/Keyliner

SME

The Society of Manufacturing Engineers is a professional engineering society dedicated to advancing manufacturing technology through the continuing education of manufacturing managers, engineers, and technicians. The specific goal of the Society is "to advance scientific knowledge in the field of manufacturing engineering and to apply its resources to research, writing, publishing, and disseminating information."

The Society was founded in 1932 as the American Society of Tool Engineers (ASTE). From 1960 to 1969 it was known as the American Society of Tool and Manufacturing Engineers (ASTME), and in January 1970 it became the Society of Manufacturing Engineers. The changes in name reflect the evolution of the manufacturing engineering profession and the growth and increasing sophistication of a technical society that has gained an international reputation for being the most knowledgeable and progressive voice in the field.

As a member of the World Federation of Engineering Organizations, SME is the universally acknowledged technical society serving the manufacturing community. Among SME's activities are the following:

Associations of SME—The Society provides complete technical services and membership benefits through a number of associations. Each serves a special interest area. Members may join these associations in addition to SME. The associations are:

Association for Finishing Processes of SME (AFP/SME)
Computer and Automated Systems Association of SME (CASA/SME)
Machine Vision Association of SME (MVA/SME)
North American Manufacturing Research Institute of SME (NAMRI/SME)
Robotics International of SME (RI/SME)
Manufacturing Automation Protocol & Technical and Office Protocol Users Group of SME (MAP/TOP)
Composites Group of SME (CoGSME)
Electronics Manufacturing Group of SME (EM/SME)

Members and Chapters—The Society and its associations have some 80,000 members in 70 countries, most of whom are affiliated with SME's 380-plus senior chapters. The Society also has some 8000 student members and more than 140 student chapters at colleges and universities.

Publications—The Society is involved in various publication activities encompassing handbooks, textbooks, videotapes, and magazines. Current periodicals include:

Manufacturing Engineering
Manufacturing Insights (a video magazine)
Robotics Today
Technical Digest

Certification—This SME program formally recognizes manufacturing managers, engineers, and technologists based on experience and knowledge. The key certification requirement is successful completion of a two-part written examination covering (1) engineering fundamentals and (2) an area of manufacturing specialization.

Educational Programs—The Society annually sponsors more than 200 conferences, expositions, and workshops throughout the world. It also operates the Center for Professional Development at its Dearborn, Michigan, world headquarters.

CONTENTS
VOLUME IV—QUALITY CONTROL AND ASSEMBLY

SYMBOLS AND ABBREVIATIONS

The following is a list of symbols and abbreviations in general use throughout this volume. Supplementary and/or derived units, symbols, and abbreviations that are peculiar to specific subject matter are listed within chapters.

A

A	Ampere
AAC	Air-carbon arc cutting
AAW	Air-acetylene welding
a-c	Alternating current
AGMA	American Gear Manufacturers Association
AGV	Automatic guided vehicle
AHW	Atomic hydrogen welding
AISI	American Iron and Steel Institute
Al	Aluminum
AMS	Aerospace Material Specification (of SAE)
ANSI	American National Standards Institute
AOC	Oxygen arc cutting
APAS	Adaptable-programmable assembly system
API	American Petroleum Institute
ASME	American Society of Mechanical Engineers
ASNT	American Society for Nondestructive Testing
ASQC	American Society for Quality Control
ASTM	American Society for Testing and Materials
AW	Arc welding
AWS	American Welding Society

B-C-D

BBS	Beta ray backscatter
Bhn	Brinell hardness number
BLT	Bubble emission leak testing
BMAW	Bare metal arc welding
Btu	British thermal unit
C	Celsius or Carbon
CAC	Carbon arc cutting
CAD/CAM	Computer-aided design/computer-aided manufacturing
CAW	Carbon arc welding
CAW-G	Gas carbon arc welding
CAW-S	Shielded carbon arc welding
CBLT	Chemical-based leak testing
CEW	Coextrusion welding
cfm	Cubic foot per minute
CHM	Chemical milling
CIM	Computer-integrated manufacturing
CLT	Conductivity leak testing
cm	Centimeter
CMM	Coordinate measuring machine
CNC	Computer numerical control
CO_2	Carbon dioxide
Cr	Chromium
CRT	Cathode ray tube
Cu	Copper

CW	Cold welding or Continuous wave
dB(A)	Decibel ("A" scale)
d-c	Direct current
DCEN	Direct current, electrode negative
DCEP	Direct current, electrode positive
DEC	Distance-echo correction
DFA	Design for assembly
DFW	Diffusion welding
diam	Diameter
DIP	Dual in-line package (for integrated circuits)
DNC	Direct numerical control
DPH	Diamond pyramid hardness

E-F

EB	Electron beam
EBC	Electron beam cutting
EBM	Electron beam machining
EBW	Electron beam welding
ECG	Electrochemical grinding
ECH	Electrochemical honing
ECM	Electrochemical machining
ECP	Electrochemical polishing
ECT	Electrochemical turning
EDG	Electrical discharge grinding
EDM	Electrical discharge machining
EDS	Electrical discharge sawing
EDWC	Electrical discharge wire cutting
EGW	Electrogas welding
EMR	Electromagnetic riveting
EPA	Environmental Protection Agency
EPROM	Erasable programmable read-only memory
Eq.	Equation
erg	Work or energy
esu	Electrostatic unit
ESM	Electrostream milling
ESW	Electroslag welding
ET	Eddy-current testing
eV	Electron volt
EVA	Ethylene vinyl acetate
EXW	Explosion welding
F	Fahrenheit
FCAW	Flux-cored arc welding
Fig.	Figure
FOC	Chemical flux cutting
FOW	Forge welding
fpm	Foot per minute
fps	Foot per second
FRW	Friction welding
ft or '	Foot
ft-c	Foot-candle

ft-lb	Foot pound
ft-lbf	Foot pound force
FW	Flash welding
FWDC	Full-wave rectified direct current

G-H

g	Gram
gal	Gallon
GALT	Gas absorption leak testing
GMAW	Gas metal arc welding
GPa	Gigapascal
gpm	Gallon per minute
GTAC	Gas tungsten arc cutting
GTAW	Gas tungsten arc welding
H	Hydrogen
H_2	Hydrogen gas
HAZ	Heat-affected zone
HDLT	Halogen detector leak testing
HE	Helium
HFIW	High-frequency induction welding
HFRW	High-frequency resistance welding
HIP	Hot isostatic pressing
HMPSA	Hot-melt pressure-sensitive adhesive
HNDT	Holographic nondestructive testing
H_2O	Water
hp	Horsepower
HPW	Hot pressure welding
hr	Hour
HSLA	High-strength, low-alloy
HSS	High-speed steel
HV	Vickers hardness
HWDC	Half-wave rectified direct current
Hz	Hertz

I-J-K

IACS	International Annealed Copper Standard
Ibid.	In the same place
IC	Integrated circuit
ID	Inside diameter
IEEE	Institute of Electrical and Electronic Engineers
IFI	International Fasteners Institute
IMA	Injected metal assembly
in. or ″	Inch
I/O	Input/output
ipm	Inch per minute
ipr	Inch per revolution
ips	Inch per second
IR	Infrared
IRHD	International rubber hardness degree
ISO	International Organization for Standardization
J	Joule
K	Kelvin or Potassium
keV	Kilo electron volt

kg	Kilogram
kg/lin m	Kilogram per linear meter
kHz	Kilohertz
kN	Kilonewton
kPa	Kilopascal
ksi	1000 pounds per square inch
kVA	Kilovolt-ampere

L-M

L	Liter
LAN	Local area network
lb	Pound
LBC	Laser beam cutting
lb-in.	Pound-inch (torque)
lb/lin ft	Pound per linear foot
LBM	Laser beam machining
LBW	Laser beam welding
LCD	Liquid crystal display
LED	Light-emitting diode
LMC	Least material condition
L/min	Liter per minute
LOC	Oxygen lance cutting
Loc. cit.	In the place cited
LSI	Large-scale integration
LVDT	Linear variable differential transformer
m	Meter
MAG	Metal active gas
MAP	Manufacturing Automation Protocol
max	Maximum
MEK	Methyl ethyl ketone
MeV	Mega electron volt
mg	Milligram
Mg	Magnesium
mHz	Millihertz
MIG	Metal inert gas
mil	Milli-inch (0.001 in.)
MIL	Military
min	Minimum or Minute
mL	Milliliter
mm	Millimeter
MMC	Maximum material condition
mm/rev	Millimeter per revolution
Mo	Molybdenum
moles/s	Moles per second
MOS	Metal-oxide-silicon
MPa	Megapascal
MPS	Methylacetylene-propadiene stabilized
mr	Milliroentgen
MSI	Medium-scale integration
MSLT	Mass spectrometer leak testing
MT	Magnetic particle testing

N-O-P

N	Newton or Nitrogen
N_2	Nitrogen gas
Nb	Niobium

NBS	National Bureau of Standards	RLT	Radioisotope leak testing
NC	Numerical control	rms	Root mean square
NDT	Nondestructive testing or Nil ductility transition	ROI	Return on investment
Nd:YAG	Neodymium-doped, yttrium aluminum garnet	rpm	Revolution per minute
		RPW	Resistance projection welding
Ne	Neon	RSEW	Resistance seam welding
NEMA	National Electrical Manufacturers Association	RSW	Resistance spot welding
		RT	Radiographic testing or Room temperature
NFPA	National Fire Protection Association	RTV	Room temperature vulcanizing
Ni	Nickel	RW	Resistance welding
nm	Nanometer	RWMA	Resistance Welder Manufacturers Association
N·m	Newton-meter		
No.	Number		
NRC	Nuclear Regulatory Commission	s or sec	Second
		SAE	Society of Automotive Engineers
O or O$_2$	Oxygen	SAW	Submerged arc welding
OAW	Oxyacetylene welding	SBR	Styrene-butadiene rubber
OC	Oxygen cutting	SCARA	Selective Compliance Assembly Robot Arm
OD	Outside diameter	SCR	Silicon-controlled rectifier
OFC	Oxyfuel gas cutting	SFD	Source-to-film distance
OFW	Oxyfuel gas welding	Si	Silicon
OHW	Oxyhydrogen welding	SI	International System of Units
OMFS	Optimum Metric Fastener System	sin	Sine
Op. cit.	In the work cited	SMAC	Shielded metal arc cutting
OSHA	Occupational Safety and Health Administration	SMAW	Shielded metal arc welding
		SMD	Surface-mounted device
oz	Ounce	SOT	Small outline transistor
		SPC	Statistical process control
Pa	Pascal	SPE	Society of Plastics Engineers
PAC	Plasma arc cutting	SPI	Society of the Plastics Industry
PAM	Plasma arc machining	Std cm^3/s	Standard cubic centimeter per second
Pa·m^3/s	Pascal cubic meter per second	SW	Stud arc welding
PAW	Plasma arc welding		
PC	Personal computer or programmable controller		
PCB	Printed circuit board		
PCMT	Pressure change measurement leak testing		
PEW	Percussion welding		
PGW	Pressure gas welding		
pH	Acidity measure		
PID	Proportional-integral-derivative		
PLC	Programmable logic controller		
PLT	Pressure leak testing		
POC	Metal powder cutting		
PSA	Pressure-sensitive adhesive		
psi	Pounds per square inch		

R-S

r	roentgen
R	Rockwell hardness, subscript letters indicate various scales
rad	Radiation absorbed dose or Radius
RAM	Random access memory
rbe	Relative biological effectiveness
RCC	Remote center compliance
R & D	Research and development
rem	Roentgen equivalent man
RIA	Robotic Industries Association

T-U-V-W-X

t	Metric ton
Ta	Tantalum
Temp.	Temperature
Ti	Titanium
TIG	Tungsten inert gas
TOP	Technical and Office Protocol
TTT	Time temperature transformation
TW	Thermit welding
UL	Underwriters' Laboratories
ULT	Ultrasonic leak testing
UNS	Unified Numbering System
USW	Ultrasonic welding
UT	Ultrasonic testing
UV	Ultraviolet
UW	Upset welding
V	Vanadium or Volt
VDLT	Voltage discharge leak testing
VHN	Vickers hardness number
VLSI	Very large scale integration
W	Watt or Tungsten
XRF	X-ray fluorescence

Z

Zn	Zinc
Zr	Zirconium

α	Alpha
Å	Angstrom
$\approx$	Approximately equal to
£	Coefficient of linear expansion
°	Degree
Δ or δ	Delta
ϵ	Epsilon
λ	Lambda or Wavelength
$\leq$	Less than or equal to
μin.	Microinch
μm	Micrometer
μ	Mu
Ω	Ohm or Omega
%	Percent
ϕ	Phi
π	Pi
$\pm$	Plus or minus
ψ	Psi
ρ	Rho
Σ or σ	Sigma
θ	Theta

QUALITY CONTROL

SECTION

1

ASSURANCE AND CONTROL OF QUALITY

An effective quality system within a company is both customer and user oriented. It should extend throughout all functional areas of the company associated with the product or component in question, from design through the customer/end user. The quality function is more concerned with the entire product cycle than in the past, providing confidence to management that the job is being done right. The entire organization should be concerned with continual quality improvement, finding root causes, and implementing irreversible corrective action prior to production or customer receipt.

DEFINITION OF QUALITY

Vital to the understanding of the implications of quality in a manufacturing enterprise is a perception of the meaning of quality. According to the American Society for Quality Control (ASQC), quality is the totality of features and characteristics of a product or service that bear on its ability to satisfy given needs.[1] The definition implies that the needs of the customer must be identified first because satisfaction of those needs is the "bottom line" of achieving quality. Customer needs should then be transformed into product features and characteristics so that a design and the controlling product specifications can be prepared. It should be carefully noted that it is really a composite of product features and characteristics taken as a whole that must satisfy the needs of a broad range of customers.

The product design and specifications are a translation of the product features and characteristics into performance and manufacturing terms. Assessments prior to and during the development and manufacture of the product determine if it conforms to the requirements of the design and specifications. If the needs of the customer have been properly translated, these assessments will predict whether or not the needs will be met.

To satisfy the given needs of the customer, the product must allow the customer to achieve the purposes for which it was bought. The life of the product and its dependability are also of concern.

Other considerations include safe use of the product, ease of performing maintenance, and availability of spare parts and service facilities.

Another concern is the availability of clear instructions so that the product is used correctly and misuse or misapplication will not occur to result in injury to the user, loss of performance, or premature failure.

Product designs should address an appropriate market segment of customers. For example, customers participating in a lower price market segment for appliances may not need the additional features found in appliances in the higher price market segment. For some, it may be a balance between the financially affordable and the operationally adequate; therefore, the desires of that type of customer translate into a product with fewer features. Some features are desirable to both the lower and higher price market segments; an example of this is the expected life of a product. Another very important consideration in analyzing customer needs is what is or could be offered by the competition in the same price market segment to better satisfy customer expectations.

Identifying the needs of customers is often very complex. Mail surveys to customers have been useful in mass-marketing situations, where many customers are provided with equivalent products. In contractual situations, where the customer is not the ultimate user, the needs of both the immediate customer and the ultimate user of the product should be identified. It should also be noted that the needs of customers change, requiring identification of needs to be constantly updated.

The bathtub curve is often used to illustrate failure patterns of products being used by customers

Contributor of this chapter is: William O. Winchell, Quality Consultant, C.P.C. Group, General Motors Corp.

Reviewers of sections of this chapter are: Howard B. Aaron, Ph.D., President, Q.E.D.; Howard H. Bailie, Project Advisor, Nuclear Operations Div., Westinghouse Electric Corp.; Edward H. Boyer, Manufacturing Engineering Specialist, Ford Motor Co.; William W. Chenevert, Quality Staff Engineer, Product Quality Office, Operations Support Services, Ford Motor Co.; William M. Ferguson, General Manager, Quality Control Co.; Howard P. Hansen, Director Quality Assurance, Admiral Div., Magic Chef, Inc.; Dr. H. James Harrington, Project Manager, Quality Assurance, General Products Div., IBM Corp.; Nathan D. Hollander, Manager, Manufacturing Consulting Group, Management Consulting Services, Ernst & Whinney; A. Michael Honer, Manager of Advanced Manufacturing and Quality Assurance, Precision Tools and Pump Div., Brown and Sharp Mfg. Co.; Charles M. Pelto, Supervisor Quality Assurance Planning, Quality Assurance Engineering, Williams International; William O. Winchell, Quality Consultant, C.P.C. Group, General Motors Corp.

DEFINITION OF QUALITY

(see Fig. 1-1). The time segment marked A is called the "infant mortality period" and represents failures occurring very early in the use of the product. Typically, these failures are due to manufacturing defects or are the result of misuse or misapplication.

The time segment marked B is called the "constant failure-rate period." Failures in this segment are due to design, unforeseen changes in environment, accidents during use that may be unavoidable, or accidents that may have been avoided by proper maintenance.

The time segment marked C is called the "wearout period," during which time failures occur because the parts are reaching the end of their useful life.[2]

In addition to a proper understanding of the term quality, it is important to understand the meaning of the terms quality management, quality system, quality assurance, and quality control. In the past, there has been a considerable variation in the use of these terms. Some of this variation is due to the inconsistent use of the terms in job titles. Figure 1-2 illustrates the use of these terms by the quality profession.[3]

Quality management is that aspect of the overall management function that determines and implements the quality policy.[4] The responsibility for quality management belongs to senior management. This activity includes strategic planning, allocation of resources, and related quality program activities.

A *quality system* is the collective plans, activities, and events that are provided to ensure that a product, process, or service will satisfy given needs.[5] The elements that comprise a quality system are discussed later in this chapter. It should be noted that a quality system should be as comprehensive as required to meet the objectives of the company and company contract requirements.

Quality assurance includes all the planned or systematic actions necessary to provide adequate confidence that a product or service will satisfy given needs.[6] These actions are aimed at providing confidence that the quality system is working properly and include evaluating the adequacy of the designs and specifications or auditing the production operations for capability. Internal quality assurance aims at providing confidence to the management of a company, while external quality assurance provides assurance of product quality to those who buy from that company.

Quality control comprises the operational techniques and activities that sustain a quality of product or service so that the product will satisfy given needs. It is also the use of such techniques and activities.[7] The quality control function is closest to the product in that various techniques and activities are used to monitor the process and to pursue the elimination of unsatisfactory sources of quality performance.

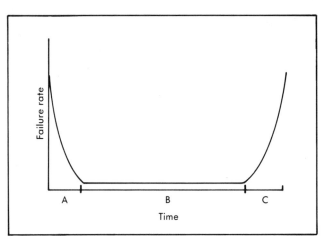

Fig. 1-1 Failure rate versus time curve.

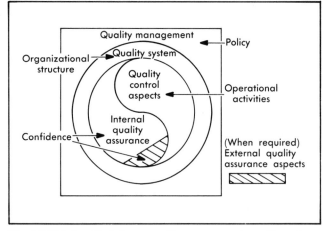

Fig. 1-2 Relationship between quality management, quality system, quality assurance, and quality control.

QUALITY CONSIDERATIONS

Many factors must be taken into consideration when developing a quality system. Some of the most important factors are the following:

- Prevention of defects.
- Customer focus.
- Standards.
- Legal liability.
- Total involvement.
- Selection and training.

PREVENTION OF DEFECTS

Many of the quality systems of the past were designed with the objective of sorting good products from bad products during the various processing steps. Those products judged to be bad had to be reworked to meet specifications. If they could not be reworked, they were scrapped. This type of system is known as a "detection/correction" system. With this system, problems were not found until the products were inspected or when they were used by the customer. Because of the inherent nature of human inspectors, the effectiveness of the sorting operations was often less than 90%. The old cliche "You can't inspect quality into your product..." was proven over and over.

Quality systems that are preventive in nature are being widely implemented. These systems prevent problems from occurring in the first place by placing emphasis on proper planning and problem prevention in all phases of the product cycle. The various elements of this type of system are described later in this chapter.

CUSTOMER FOCUS

The final word on how well a product fulfills needs and expectations is given by the customers and users of that product and is influenced by the offerings of competitors that may also be available to those customers and users. It is important to recognize that this final word is formed over the entire life of the product, not just when it was purchased.[8]

Being aware of customers' needs and expectations is very important, as was previously discussed. In addition, focusing the attention of all employees in an enterprise on the customers and users and their needs will result in a more effective quality system. For example, group discussions on product designs and specifications should include specific discussion of the needs to be satisfied. In this way, the risk that the product is viewed by employees as only an inanimate object is minimized.[9]

STANDARDS

The ramifications of not being aware of and hence not complying with applicable industry standards can be very significant to a manufacturing enterprise. Standards exist for many industrial and business areas such as design, procurement, manufacturing, quality control, marketing and distribution, and use of product, its service and ease of repair.

The subject matter or coverage of industrial standards is also very broad. Standards can cover size and strength characteristics; performance in terms of quality, reliability, and safety; assembly methods; inspection, testing, and other control procedures; packing and packaging; distribution; and documenta-tion and identification. They can also cover safe use, which would include warnings, labels, and instructions. Some standards are defined in various federal and state laws, as well as by international bodies. Many standards are set by committees under the guidance of groups such as the American Society for Quality Control, American National Standards Institute, and the International Organization for Standardization. Standards applicable to this chapter are given in Table 1-1.

Manufacturing enterprises should develop workmanship standards to be used to judge the acceptability of a product. These are especially useful when visual judgments are required and provide a means by which a comparison can be made. An example of a workmanship standard is shown in Fig. 1-3.[10]

LEGAL LIABILITY

Various theories of liability have developed over the years, permitting the purchaser or user of a product to recover damages from a manufacturer or supplier. The major theories are negligence, breach of express warranty, breach of implied warranty, and strict liability. A suit grounded on negligence generally means that reasonable and prudent care has not been taken in manufacturing the product. A breach of express warranty may exist when representations are made, often in advertisements or sales agreements, that the product does not meet. Cases of breach of implied warranty had their beginning when a disclaimer of warranty in a sales agreement by a manufacturer was ignored by the court. Strict liability can occur when a defect exists in a product that makes the product unreasonably dangerous to use and thus causes harm. Customers and users can be better protected and the risk of legal liability for a manufacturer can be minimized through a properly designed quality system that integrates product safety considerations.[11]

TOTAL INVOLVEMENT

Quality cannot be accomplished by concentrating on inspection, product design, operator education, supplier control, or reliability studies alone, important as each element may be.

TABLE 1-1
Standards for Quality Control

Standard Number	Standard Title
ANSI/ASQC A3	Quality Systems Terminology
ANSI/ASQC C1 (ANSI Z1.8)	Specifications of General Requirements for a Quality Program
ANSI/ASQC Z1.15	Generic Guidelines for Quality Systems
ANSI/ASQC E2	Guide to Inspection Planning
MIL-Q-9858A	Quality Program Requirements
MIL-I-45208A	Inspection System Requirements
MIL-STD-45662	Calibration System Requirements
ISO/DIS 8402*	Quality Assurance Vocabulary
ISO/DIS 9000*	Guide to Quality Management and Quality Assurance Standard
ISO/DIS 9001*	Quality Systems: Assurance Model for Design/Development, Production, Installation and Servicing Capability
ISO/DIS 9002*	Quality Systems: Assurance Model for Production and Installation Capability
ISO/DIS 9003*	Quality Systems: Assurance Model for Final Inspection and Test Capability
ISO/DIS 9004*	Guide to Quality Management and Quality System Elements

*At the time of this writing, these standards have not been approved and published; for current status, contact the American National Standards Institute, 1430 Broadway, New York, NY 10018; (212) 354-3300.

CHAPTER 1

QUALITY CONSIDERATIONS

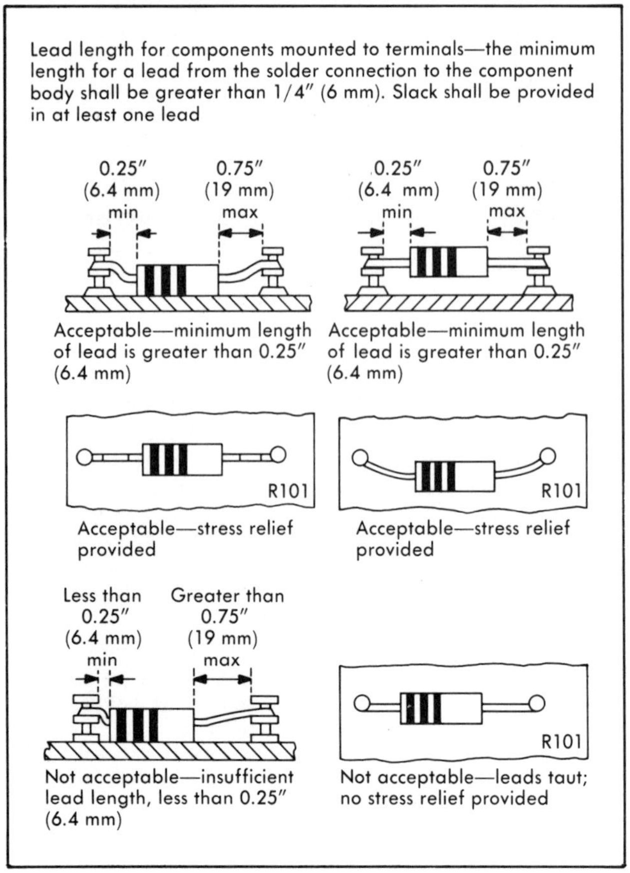

Lead length for components mounted to terminals—the minimum length for a lead from the solder connection to the component body shall be greater than 1/4" (6 mm). Slack shall be provided in at least one lead

Fig. 1-3 Workmanship standards used by a manufacturing company. (*Copyright American Society for Quality Control, Inc. Reprinted by permission.*)

Quality activities must exist in all mainline operations: marketing, design, manufacturing, accounting, as well as the others.[12] These activities must work in concert as a finely tuned network to satisfy the needs of the customers and users.

Quality can be achieved in the workplace only with the participation of all the men and women in the workforce. This extensive participation demands strong, continued operational support, not occasional quality awareness programs. Organizationally, this may mean altering the top-down form of management and tearing down the high walls between departments, which together have characterized industrial practice in some companies for a long time.[13] Participatory management approaches such as quality circles and employee involvement teams have made significant progress in this area.

The use of product development teams is a growing approach in companies. These teams are initiated early in the product development cycle and are composed of members from each of the disciplines associated with developing and manufacturing the product. As soon as suppliers are selected, representatives from the suppliers join the team. Teams have been very successful in the early identification of problems and the implementation of timely solutions prior to and during the production phase.

SELECTION AND TRAINING

An analysis of companies implementing total quality control indicates that, in a successful company, the team leader is often referred to as the "change agent." This very critical position is likely to be held by the president or general manager. The person facilitating the change must have the stature and credibility to overcome the natural resistance to change as well as entrenched ideology, teachings, and concepts. The leader must also be able to make people realize that changes must be made to stay competitive and that, maybe more important, they must be willing to change.

Another characteristic found in successful companies is the setting of specific company objectives and goals. In addition, resources in terms of people and the tools required by those people are identified as being essential to the accomplishment of the specific goals and objectives. Teams can then be formed from these people.

Once the proper team and tools have been selected, the company can start training, which may take many forms. Some larger companies have corporation-wide quality institutes. Others begin with off-site workshops conducted by noted quality professionals for management and the functional staff. In-house training by plant personnel is then started on specific subjects related to the objectives to be achieved. Other training can be given for specific topics such as statistical quality control. Training needs must be constantly reassessed and courses repeated and new courses provided.[14]

QUALITY SYSTEM

A quality system forms the framework for quality activities that directly affect the quality of the finished product. The internal and external influences on the system include the following:[15,16,17]

- Management.
- Marketing.
- Design.
- Suppliers.
- Material.
- Manufacturing.
- Customers.
- Audits.

ROLE OF MANAGEMENT

In the past, the strategy of many companies was driven by product design and technology. Inconsistent quality resulted from such things as reworked processes to match product designs that were changed when it was too late to order the needed new equipment. This strategy is changing because management now recognizes that quality must be a fundamental driving strategy for manufacturing to be competitive in today's world marketplace.

Figure 1-4 illustrates a planning model used by a company that recognizes quality as a fundamental strategy.[18] Strategic planning for this company means that the business plan must not allow quality to suffer to meet the other strategic driving forces. The answer for this company was to strategically schedule product development, manufacturing planning, and supplier commitments so they are done concurrently and not in series. Rather than solving manufacturing and vendor problems at the time the product is released for production, they are now handled at the same time that laboratory and production prototype assessments are made so all requirements can be integrated early in the production cycle. Figure 1-5 shows the investment profile that had to be followed in the business plan of this company to carry out the new strategy.[19]

A quality policy should be adopted to describe management's specific intentions with respect to quality. This policy should be approved by and released under the signature of the chief executive officer of the company. Figure 1-6 illustrates a typical quality policy.[20]

The company goals and objectives previously discussed should be established for key elements of performance. These should include field performance levels, safety requirements, internal failure levels, vendor performance, training and qualification of personnel, quality cost levels, and quality improvement projects. It is important to recognize that numerical goals set for other people, without provision for a road map to reach the goal, have effects opposite to the effects sought.[21]

An overall quality plan should be prepared to meet the quality policy, goals, and objectives of the company. This plan is really a part of the business plan. The quality plan should detail the implementation of the elements of the quality system necessary for the company. It should also address the resources required and the plans for timely deployment.

The quality policy and system should be documented in a quality manual that is readily available to all employees. This manual should contain the general quality policy, a description of the quality system, and a general description of the quality planning requirements with specifics for each product line where appropriate.

ROLE OF MARKETING

Marketing plays a critical role in quality because this is where translation of customer or user needs into a product's features and characteristics starts. A product definition should be established in a form effective for making designs and design and manufacturing specifications. Customer or user requirements should be established through customer or user surveys or contacts. Competitive offerings must also be evaluated in the market sector for the product. Elements requiring definition include performance characteristics (usage conditions), sensory characteristics (style), applicable industry standards, packaging requirements, and other quality considerations. In addition, past experience by the customer or user on similar products is invaluable so that problems are not repeated.

ROLE OF DESIGN

Many inputs are required to develop new designs and specifications. The product definition from the marketing area is a key input. Other considerations required are the quality

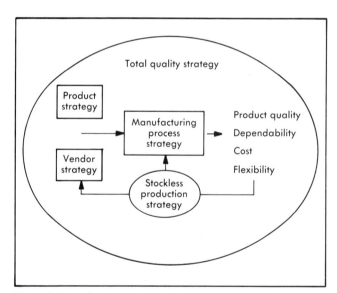

Fig. 1-4 Strategic model used by a manufacturing organization. (*Copyright American Society for Quality Control, Inc. Reprinted by permission.*)

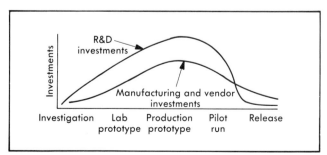

Fig. 1-5 Resource allocation for concurrent strategy. (*Copyright American Society for Quality Control, Inc. Reprinted by permission.*)

"Quality is the number one operating priority in General Motors.

"Our goal is to give quality top attention, top status, and top dedication in every decision we make, every action we take, and every move we make.

"This philosophy is to be implemented at every General Motors location by adherence to the following six quality mandates:

1. Every GM product must be the unquestioned quality leader within its market segment, as perceived by the customer.

2. Every manager in General Motors must develop a strategy and an action plan to carry out the first mandate.

3. Every member of every unit must understand that the cost of quality is the expense of doing things wrong.

4. Every GM employee must recognize that quality means total conformance to specifications and procedures that will result in satisfied customers. Well-designed and fully implemented process control systems will be a part of our procedures.

5. Top management at General Motors must become involved in the organization and the management of quality programs.

6. Every employee at General Motors must become actively involved in the implementation of a new quality ethic. Everyone on the team must be committed to quality."

Fig. 1-6 A typical quality policy of a manufacturing firm. (*Copyright American Society for Quality Control, Inc. Reprinted by permission.*)

QUALITY SYSTEM

policy, goals, and objectives of the company. The ability of the company to produce similar products should be fully explored, as well as the ability of those products to meet requirements. Past experience should be fully utilized to prevent previous problems from recurring. A detailed design and associated validation plan should be prepared to ensure that the necessary steps are taken in a timely manner.

The team composed of the product's natural working group must document agreed-on specifications on the product drawing. The use of ANSI Y14.5M, "Geometric Dimensioning and Tolerancing," is an effective tool to clearly communicate product specifications in a language that can be correctly interpreted worldwide. This standard is quickly becoming nationally recognized to ensure consistent product definition and interpretation. For more information on the measurement of geometric dimensioning and tolerancing, refer to Chapter 4, "Dimensional Metrology and Geometric Conformance," of this volume.

As the design and specifications are developed, the design validation phase occurs. In many cases, significant improvements in the product design and specifications are found during validation at key points in the development of the product. Analytical approaches include independent calculations and management review, as well as design failure mode and effects analysis (DFMEA), fault tree analysis, hazard analysis, or risk assessment. A typical form used for a DFMEA is shown in Fig. 1-7.[22]

The effect of any failure mode identified in a DFMEA may lead to a design change that will preclude the failure mode from occurring. If this cannot be done, the manufacturing process and quality procedures may be able to be designed to minimize the risk. Also, validation may take place where third-party independent evaluations are used to verify original calculations that the design is based on. Other methods of validation include the inspection and testing of prototype models to validate both performance and durability. An adequate number of samples should be inspected and tested to provide statistical confidence in the results. The tests should include the evaluation of performance and durability under expected storage and operational conditions. The tests should also be performed on models in which the intended design features and changes have been incorporated. Test results should be analyzed, and the methods for preventing problems should be identified and incorporated in subsequent design changes.

Design reviews should be scheduled regularly during the development of the design. Topics that can be covered are items pertaining to customer needs and satisfaction, product specifications, quality needs, process capability, safety, cost, standards, maintainability, and serviceability. A key objective is to ensure that all known problem areas have been properly addressed.

A market readiness review is of great importance before release for production to determine if production and field service will be ready to handle the new or redesigned product. This review should include availability of customer manuals, location of field service offices, training of field service people, availability of spare parts from production, and the advisability of pilot service programs in the field prior to full introduction of the product.

Controls must be provided so that the design and specifications released to production are "baseline" in that they represent the validated design. These controls should also provide a method for communicating changes necessary to that baseline design. The method should provide for incorporating changes at specified points, removing obsolete drawings and specifications from work areas, and verifying that the changes are made at the right times.

ROLE OF SUPPLIERS

In many companies, quality values added to the product by suppliers are greater than those added by the company. Implied in this relationship is that the success of a company is largely contingent on its suppliers and that suppliers are really an extension of the company. Selection of suppliers is critical, and the selection analysis should include on-site surveys of performance capability, quality organization and program evaluation of product samples, past quality history, and experience of other customers.

Once a supplier is selected, all engineering, production, and quality requirements should be understood and mutually agreed to by both the supplier and purchaser. These requirements must be documented in the contract specifications, drawings, and purchase orders given to the supplier.

The responsibility for the quality of the material purchased should be placed on the supplier, thereby matching responsibility with control. In some cases, suppliers have also assumed design responsibility with the accompanying "ownership" of performance and durability requirements. In many cases, the supplier is responsible early in the product cycle for furnishing prototype parts. A joint determination and agreement of the quality elements that must be implemented in the supplier's quality system should be reached before purchase order issue.

Item Part No.	Block Diagram Reference	Function	Failure Modes	Failure Mechanism (cause)	Effect On			Other Effects (interface, etc.)	Criticality		Corrective Action Implementation		
					Local	Higher Levels	End Item		Severity	Frequency	Detectability	Time Available for Corrective Action	Recommendation	Item Close Sign Off or Rationale for Other Action

Fig. 1-7 A typical form used for a design failure mode and effects analysis. (*Copyright American Society for Quality Control, Inc. Reprinted by permission.*)

The quality capability of each supplier should be periodically reevaluated by such means as source surveillance visits that are scheduled based on observed incoming quality performance. A formal vendor rating system may help in determining the degree of control required by the purchaser. Other factors to be considered in this judgment include the complexity of the item, the quantity purchased, and the requirements established in the purchase agreement. Some companies have found that a formal certification of the quality system of a supplier has been effective in maintaining high quality.

A clear agreement should also be developed with the supplier on the methods by which conformance to the requirements of the purchaser will be verified for incoming material from the supplier. In the initial stages, a special procedure may be necessary to qualify the supplier's production process. For regular shipments, verification of conformance to requirements could be based on supplier-generated quality information. Verification of this information can take many forms, such as auditing by the purchaser (certification), inspection at the supplier by the purchaser (source inspection), or inspection when received by the purchaser (receiving inspection). Agreements should also address the exchange of supplier and company inspection and test data with the objective of improving quality.

A procedure must also be established so disputes with suppliers regarding quality can be settled in a businesslike manner. Effective communication before problems occur can minimize difficulties in the later interpretation of requirements as well as inspection, testing, or sampling methods.

ROLE OF MATERIAL QUALITY

Many product quality problems can be traced to improper handling and storage. This occurs not only during the shipping of material from suppliers, but also during manufacturing of the product. The risk of this happening continues until the product is received by the user and placed into service. Many things, such as vibration, shock, abrasion, corrosion, temperature and humidity extremes, and even vandalism, could cause damage resulting in poor product quality. The risk of deterioration can be minimized through proper planning and the use of such things as special types of shipping containers, vehicles for transportation, and in-house material handling devices. A key to ensuring the effectiveness of these measures is adherence to clear and detailed written procedures for handling, packing, and storing. Provisions must also be in place to ensure that deteriorated items are not used. Also, these provisions should provide for periodic monitoring of this activity to provide confidence that the system is effectively implemented.

Products should be suitably identified on the shipping carton or container and the product itself. The marking should be legible, durable, and remain intact during the time that it will be of use. Identification, in conjunction with adequate records, helps provide traceability to the location of the product either before or after it reaches the user, in case it must be replaced, repaired, or additional instructions need to be communicated. In this way, the extent of product recalls and resulting customer and user inconvenience/dissatisfaction may be minimized. Among other things, this identification also ensures the proper usage of look-alike parts in subsequent assemblies. Certain product labeling requirements may be mandatory, such as safety warnings, symbols, and regulatory markings. Adequate controls must also be in place to ensure both the protection and identification of material.

ROLE OF MANUFACTURING

Marketing and product engineering departments identify the needs of the customer and translate these into designs and specifications. If this job is done properly, products produced to the design and specifications by manufacturing meet the needs of the customers.

To help achieve this on new or revised products or manufacturing processes, a manufacturing quality plan should be prepared. The manufacturing quality plan is a subset of the overall quality plan previously mentioned, but is specific to the product and is very detailed. The plan indicates who has the responsibility and authority for various tasks and identifies specific quality objectives, acceptance criteria, timing, processing, tools, gages, equipment, specific procedures and work instructions, process validation methods, specific testing, in-process controls, gage controls, inspection requirements, and auditing procedures. In addition, it addresses the detailed implementation of the appropriate elements of the quality system for that product. The manufacturing quality plan is designed to closely match system responsibilities with control responsibilities and accountability.

For example, the manufacturing function is generally responsible for meeting design and specification requirements. For this reason, the manufacturing function may be assigned responsibility for quality control, as defined previously in this chapter. The quality function assumes the role of quality assurance. By the same reasoning, a production operator, rather than an inspector, is assigned the responsibility for statistical process control charts because the operator can most effectively adjust or otherwise get the machine or tooling fixed.

Inputs into the manufacturing quality plan are critical. Besides the need to correlate these inputs with the overall quality plan, the plan must address those considerations identified during the design validation phase, such as preventing a potential failure mode of the product from existing. Prevention of such conditions can be minimized through the design processes, control of the processes, and automatic machine inspections. The need for preventing a potential failure mode can be identified by a design failure mode and effects analysis (DFMEA) during the design validation phase.

After doing a DFMEA, some companies use a technique known as "failure prevention analysis" (FPA) to communicate those portions of the design and specifications requiring failure mode consideration during manufacturing. Actions are then identified to prevent the failure modes from occurring. Other companies use a method known as "seriousness classification of characteristics" to establish various levels of criticality for guidance in planning manufacturing quality controls. These classifications typically fall into three or four categories. A typical classification method is shown in Table 1-2.[23]

Another valuable input into the manufacturing quality plan is the process failure mode and effects analysis (PFMEA). This technique evaluates the manufacturing process for potential failure modes and their causes. Its purpose is to identify and eliminate potential process failure modes or to minimize the risk of those that cannot be avoided. Actions that may be taken include process redesign, process control, and changes in the product for ease of manufacturing. Figure 1-8 illustrates a typical PFMEA form used by an automobile manufacturer.[24]

Another key input into the manufacturing quality plan is current capability studies on the machines and processes being considered for the product. A process capability study measures functional parameters on the product to determine whether the

TABLE 1-2
Seriousness Classification of Automotive Defects

Class	Nature	Description	Examples
A	Critical to safety; essential to vehicle function	Defects that can endanger human life or can render the vehicle inoperative in an essential functional degree	Heat treatment of kingpins; pressure resistance of hydraulic brake hose
B	General function of vehicle; function of essential parts; appearance essential to the user	Nonsafety defects that might affect primary vehicle function; essential appearance characteristics	Noisy brakes; trunk lock will not open; body finish discolored
C	Functions of minor parts; appearance not essential to user	Defects that do not affect vehicle function or appearance essential to user. Defects neither A nor B	Rust on chassis; crooked identification decals on components

(*McGraw Hill Book Co., reproduced with permission*)

process is in statistical control. These data can be invaluable in deciding the best method for meeting design and specification requirements. Decisions can be made as to where new equipment and tools are required or if existing production resources will be utilized. Process and machine capability studies are discussed in Chapter 2 of this volume.

Gage capability studies, along with a thorough knowledge of accuracy and precision requirements, will also help in deciding whether new gages are required or whether existing production resources are sufficient. A gage capability study basically determines the accuracy and repeatability of a gage. When inspection and testing equipment are part of production equipment, gage capability studies must also be performed.

Validation of the process and gages is scheduled just prior to production to ensure that the process is capable of producing the product and that the gages are capable of checking the product to the specifications. Process and gage validation is much broader in concept than process or gage capability studies

in that they may include product durability testing, product functional testing, and a thorough evaluation of the readiness of the entire quality and manufacturing system. When the process and gages have been successfully validated, production can then commence.

The control of production should proceed according to the manufacturing quality plan. The quality system should ensure that the required production operations are done in the specified manner and sequence. Documented work instructions should define what is required of each operator and also contain the criteria as to the appropriate standard of quality. When adequate controls are not provided on equipment, statistical process control charts should be used by production operators to help reduce variability on critical dimensions and characteristics. The use of process control charts is discussed in Chapter 2 of this volume.

Special processes, such as welding and chemical cleaning, may affect product characteristics in ways that cannot be easily

						Existing conditions						Resulting				
POTENTIAL FAILURE MODE AND EFFECTS ANALYSIS (PROCESS FMEA) Page ____ of ____																
Part name/ part number	Process function	Potential failure mode	Potential effect(s) of failure	▽	Potential cause(s) of failure	Current controls	Occurrence	Severity	Detection	Risk priority number (R.P.N.)	Recommended action(s) and status	Action(s) taken	Occurrence	Severity	Detection	Risk priority number (R.P.N.)	Responsible activity

Process _____ Outside suppliers affected _____ Engineer _____
Primary process responsibility _____ Model year/vehicle(s) _____ Section supervisor _____
Other div.(s) or PEO(s) involved _____ Scheduled production release _____ FMEA date: (orig.) _____ (rev.) ____

Fig. 1-8 A typical form used for a process failure mode and effects analysis. (*Ford Motor Co.*)

measured. To control quality, the periodic evaluation of the equipment used in the special process may be required. Additionally, in many cases it may be desirable to provide for operator certification. Also used in these situations are checks on the key parameters of the medium used for processing, such as solution control for pH.

It is very important to control the gages and measuring equipment. This control requires the periodic calibration of the gages and measuring equipment against certified standards that have a known valid relationship to national standards. The frequency of calibration should be such that all measuring and testing devices can be adjusted, repaired, or replaced prior to becoming inaccurate. If gages or equipment are found to be inaccurate, it may be necessary to recheck those items previously processed. The calibration procedure should also be adopted for gages and control devices that are part of production tools and equipment.

Nonconforming material is another area requiring close control. It is vital that the material be clearly marked and segregated in a designated holding area until a decision is reached as to what should be done with it. This material may be scrapped, reworked, repaired, returned to the supplier, downgraded to seconds, or used "as is." If the material is reworked or repaired, it must be reinspected prior to reintroducing it into the production process. Decisions on nonconforming material are important to the quality objectives of the company and should be made by a clearly defined body of people designated by management. In some companies, this body is called the material review board (MRB). Equally important is the effectiveness of the material review board in obtaining corrective action so that problems are not repeated.

Changes to the process or gages must be carefully controlled and documented. As a part of this, the manufacturing quality plan must be carefully evaluated as to its effect on quality and then revised to incorporate the change. Also the need for revalidation of the process or gages prior to implementation must be determined.

Inspection may be classified as receiving, in-process, or final. Testing may also be accomplished during each of these phases. As mentioned previously, receiving inspection is one of several ways of verifying how a supplier's performance meets the requirements of the manufacturer. If inspection is performed on incoming products, the use of acceptance sampling is normally the preferred method. A key consideration in acceptance sampling is the critical dimensions and characteristics selected for sampling inspection. Carefully kept records of a supplier's quality history are usually necessary to decide the level of inspection required. Tests, such as the chemical analysis of material, may also be done at this stage. In designing the receiving inspection area, quarantine areas for both unchecked and rejected material should be provided to prevent their inadvertent use in production.

In-process inspection or testing should be considered at critical spots in the production process. In general, the verification of conformance to requirements of the product design and specifications should be in close proximity to the point of making the particular characteristic. In many cases, this is done by the machine operator, and results may be used to generate statistical process control charts and keep the machine in adjustment. It may also be performed by a machine automatically. Sometimes the results of these automatic checks drive adaptive controls that control variability automatically. For more information on automatic gaging and process control,

refer to Chapter 3, "Inspection Equipment and Techniques," of this volume.

An often-used application is setup and first-piece inspection prior to starting the production run. Although diminishing, there are still applications where fixed inspection stations are placed at intervals through the process. Also, applications still exist where roving inspectors monitor specified operations.

Final inspection and testing is accomplished, as the name implies, after the product is completely processed. Acceptance inspection may be performed by examining each item produced, selecting items based on acceptance sampling plans, or selecting items based on continuous sampling plans. Many companies perform only an audit of the finished products. Some select the units for evaluation from products that are packed and ready to be shipped. Other companies perform a comprehensive final acceptance inspection and testing to ensure that all performance and quality requirements have been met prior to packaging. Still other companies use both the audit approach and the acceptance inspection and testing approach for the finished product. Results of both approaches are used to provide feedback for correction of both product and process problems.

Product testing can be either destructive or nondestructive in nature. In destructive testing, not all units can be tested because there would not be any units left to sell. Therefore, sampling plans are widely used in performing destructive testing. Mechanical testing and destructive testing is discussed in Chapter 7, "Mechanical Testing and Balancing," of this volume. This limitation does not exist with nondestructive testing (NDT), discussed in Chapter 6, "Nondestructive Testing," of this volume. Functional testing is generally nondestructive because wearout is usually insignificant. This is not true of durability testing, which is generally destructive.

Inspection and testing may also be performed by outside agencies. Those products meeting the requirements of certain industrial standards may receive a "certification" or "approval" status. Some of these approvals are used in advertisements to market products to consumers.

ROLE OF THE CUSTOMER

It is important that the customer or user not be misled by advertising or promotional literature prior to purchasing the product. If the customer or user is misled, it may be likely their needs will not be met. The quality system should provide for review of what and how information is communicated about product performance, quality, compliance to safety standards, reliability, and maintainability. The message to potential customers should be accurate, clear, and complete.

When the customer or user receives the product, it should be accompanied by material such as owners' manuals, assembly instructions, warning tags and labels, service or maintenance tags, and installation instructions to prevent misuse or misapplication. This material should communicate essential technical information in a language understandable to the user. Product revisions and other updates should be promptly incorporated in the literature. The instructions should be validated to ensure that they produce the desired results. Any special tools required for installation should be readily available and validated.

Means for adequately servicing the product should be provided. The product should be easily maintainable, and the necessary parts and materials for maintenance should be readily available to ensure a minimum of downtime for the user. A service manual, for which the procedures have been validated, should be available, as well as appropriate service facilities and

QUALITY IMPROVEMENT

parts. The product should be easily serviced to minimize inconvenience to the user. Special tools required for service should be readily available and validated so that they will perform the required functions. Measuring and testing equipment used in installation and servicing should meet the same standards and also be maintained and calibrated with the same diligence as the equipment used in production.

Timely and meaningful information on user product acceptance and field failures should be fed back to appropriate parties. A sample of users should be contacted after receiving the product to learn if their quality and performance expectations have been met. Continual feedback from users should be analyzed for collective as well as individual meanings. This means summarizing data in various ways, such as by product type, failure modes, length of use, and type of application. The information for this summary can be obtained from the failure analysis of returned materials, service contract reports, warranty claims, complaints, product acceptance surveys, and user review panels. A separate tracking system may be necessary in some cases for the evaluation of the safety performance of the product. Other feedback may be available from trade associations, government bodies, or insurance companies. Collecting this information should drive corrective action to prevent problems from recurring.

ROLE OF AUDITS

Audits must be conducted on a periodic basis to help management assess where improvements can or should be made. These audits should evaluate the effectiveness of both the quality management process and the quality system in meeting objectives. Other audits, such as audits of product quality, are regularly conducted.

QUALITY IMPROVEMENT

A basic commitment of management should be that quality improvement must be relentlessly pursued. Actions should be ingrained in the day-to-day workings of the company that recognize that quality is a moving target in today's marketplace driven by constantly rising customer expectations. Traditional efforts that set a quality level perceived to be right for a product and direct all efforts to only maintain that level will not be successful in the long haul. Rather, management must orient the organization so that once the so-called right quality level for a product has been attained, improvement efforts continue to achieve progressively higher quality levels.

To achieve the most effective improvement efforts, management should ensure that the organization also has ingrained in its operating principles the understanding that quality and cost are complementary and not conflicting objectives. Traditionally, recommendations were made to management that a choice had to be made between quality and cost—the so-called tradeoff decision—because better quality inevitably would somehow cost more and make production difficult. Experience throughout the world has shown that this is not true. Good quality fundamentally leads to good resource utilization and consequently means good productivity and low quality costs. Also significant is that higher sales and market penetration result from products that are perceived by customers to have high quality and performance reliability during use.[25]

QUALITY COST

One way of looking at quality costs is to view them as the costs that are associated with the activities and events taking place in the quality system. Four basic categories that quality costs can be placed in are the following:

- Prevention—costs incurred in planning, implementing, and maintaining a quality system that will ensure conformance to quality requirements at economical levels. An example of prevention cost is training in the use of statistical process control.
- Appraisal—costs incurred in determining the degree of conformance to quality requirements. An example of appraisal cost is inspection.

- Internal failure—costs arising when products, components, and materials fail to meet quality requirements prior to transfer of ownership to the customer. An example of internal failure cost is scrap.
- External failure—costs incurred when products fail to meet quality requirements after transfer of ownership to the customer. An example of external failure cost is warranty claims.

Each cost category contains many specific subelements that can be used as a guide in designing a quality cost report. Many companies refine the formal definitions for these categories to correspond to the particular language usage and conditions in their companies. Prevention and appraisal cost can be viewed as inputs into the quality system that are normally budgeted for and controlled by management. Based on how effectively these inputs are applied, particularly prevention, internal and external failures occur. The internal and external failures can be viewed as outputs of the system. This relationship is illustrated in Fig. 1-9.[26,27,28]

In the past, quality cost reporting was used to foster improvement, with often inadequate results. This was because the reports did not have an associated improvement effort. It is now recognized that a far more realistic objective is for quality cost reporting to support an improvement team whose effort is directed toward improving quality and productivity. Multi-discipline improvement teams can use quality cost reports to point out the strengths and weaknesses of a quality system. These improvement teams can also describe the benefits and ramifications of changes in terms that everyone can understand—dollars. Return-on-investment (ROI) models and other financial analyses can be constructed directly from quality cost data to justify proposals to management. Those on improvement teams can also use this information to rank problems in order of priority, seek out root causes, and implement the most effective irreversible corrective action. They can also track results to ensure that they are headed in the right direction. Companies who collect and report quality costs recognize the value of this information to those making improvements and also recognize that reporting will accomplish nothing without someone "making it happen."[29]

CORRECTIVE ACTION

A problem-solving approach should be followed in seeking quality improvement. The results of any improvement effort will not be permanent unless the root causes of the problems have been found so appropriate (irreversible) corrective action can be implemented.

The root cause can be defined as the real cause of a problem. This is often quite different from the apparent cause, which

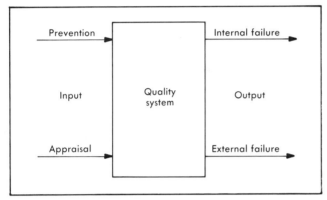

Fig. 1-9 Relationship of the basic quality cost categories. (*Copyright American Society for Quality Control, Inc. Reprinted by permission.*)

appears after a superficial investigation. A frequently asked question is how to know when the root cause is found and when the investigator is not still being deceived by the apparent cause. A meaningful answer is that if the root cause has been found, the problem is able to be turned on and off by adding or removing the cause.

Once the root cause has been found, an irreversible corrective action must be implemented so there is no foreseeable situation by which the root cause can return and so permanent improvement results.

A problem-solving approach used by one company is illustrated in Fig. 1-10.[30] This system is very effective for several reasons. First, it recognizes that it is possible that a problem may be solved by a single person when the problem is obvious after some investigation (Phase I). It also recognizes that help may be needed from others to determine potential causes and suggests brainstorming and cause-and-effect analysis by those knowledgeable about the situation (Phase II).

Another important aspect of the problem resolution system in Fig. 1-10 is that it recognizes the existence of system or management problems. Noted quality practitioners have consistently maintained that only 15-20% of problems are within the control of production operators and that the remainder can only be solved by management because they are largely system problems (Phase III and Phase IV).

A commonly used technique for cause-and-effect analysis is called an Ishikawa diagram,[31] illustrated in Fig. 1-11. This diagram enables the analysis of an effect or problem for causes by considering the many diverse and complex relationships that

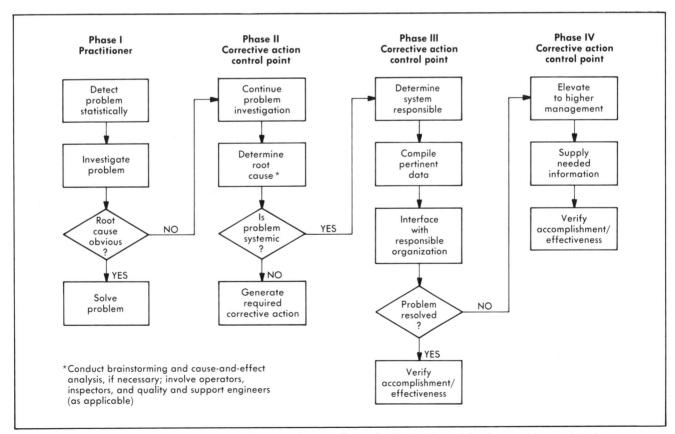

Fig. 1-10 Diagram of a problem-solving approach. (*Copyright American Society for Quality Control, Inc. Reprinted by permission.*)

REFERENCES

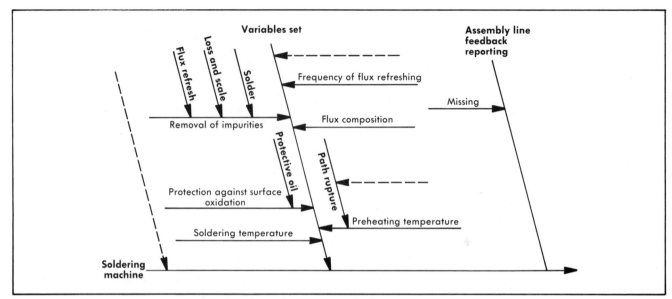

Fig. 1-11 An Ishikawa diagram of a process. (*Copyright American Society for Quality Control, Inc. Reprinted by permission.*)

exist. The weakness of this approach, as well as other approaches, is that root causes are not distinguishable among all the causes identified. Other methods must be used, such as detailed investigations, comprehensive data analysis, and design of experiments to discover the root causes. Design of experiments is discussed in Chapter 2.

References

1. "Quality Systems Terminology," ANSI/ASQC A3 (Milwaukee: American Society for Quality Control, 1978), p. 2.
2. J. M. Juran and Frank M. Gryna, Jr., *Quality Planning and Analysis* (New York: McGraw-Hill Book Co., 1980), pp. 203-205.
3. "Guide to Quality Management and Quality Assurance Standards," ISO/DP 9000. At the time of this writing, this standard has not been approved and published; for current status, contact the American National Standards Institute (ANSI), 1430 Broadway, New York, NY 10018; (212) 354-3300.
4. "Quality Assurance—Vocabulary," ISO/DP 8402. At the time of this writing, this standard has not been approved and published; for current status, contact ANSI.
5. "Quality Systems Terminology," ANSI/ASQC A3, *op. cit.*, p. 3.
6. *Ibid.*
7. *Ibid.*, p. 4.
8. Lawrence J. Utzig, "Quality Reputation—A Precious Asset," *34th Annual Quality Congress Transactions* (Milwaukee: American Society for Quality Control, 1980).
9. William O. Winchell, "Assuring Quality in Strategic Business Units," *38th Annual Quality Congress Transactions* (Milwaukee: American Society for Quality Control, 1985).
10. L. Ferris Bell, "Workmanship Standards for High Technology Products," *35th Annual Quality Congress Transactions* (Milwaukee: American Society for Quality Control, 1981).
11. Herbert E. Greenstone, "A Lawyer's View of Manufacturer's Responsibility," *34th Annual Technical Conference Transactions* (Milwaukee: American Society for Quality Control, 1980).
12. A. V. Feigenbaum, *Total Quality Control*, 3rd ed. (New York: McGraw-Hill Book Co., 1983).
13. ————, "Quality: Managing the Modern Company," *Quality Progress* (March 1985).
14. Constantine Pavsidis, "Total Quality Control: An Overview of Current Efforts," *Quality Progress* (September 1984).
15. "Generic Guidelines for Quality Systems," ANSI/ASQC Z1.15 (Milwaukee: American Society for Quality Control, 1979).
16. "Guide to Inspection Planning," ANSI/ASQC E2 (Milwaukee: American Society for Quality Control, 1984).
17. "Guide to Quality Management and Quality System Elements," ISO/DIS 9004. At the time of this writing, this standard has not been approved and published; for current status, contact ANSI.
18. Jeffery P. Kalin, "Quality, Stockless Production and Manufacturing," *38th Annual Quality Congress Transactions* (Milwaukee: American Society for Quality Control, 1984).
19. *Ibid.*
20. C. R. Davis, "Key Elements in Quality and Reliability Assurance," *37th Annual Quality Congress Transactions* (Milwaukee: American Society for Quality Control, 1983).
21. W. Edwards Deming, *Quality, Productivity, and Competitive Position* (Cambridge, MA: Massachusetts Institute of Technology, Center for Advanced Engineering Study, 1982).
22. Dev Raheja, "Failure Mode and Effects Analysis—Uses and Misuses," *35th Annual Quality Congress Transactions* (Milwaukee: American Society for Quality Control, 1981).
23. Juran and Gryna, Jr., *op. cit.*, p. 367.
24. "Potential Failure Mode and Effects Analysis for Manufacturing and Assembly Processes" (Dearborn, MI: Ford Motor Co., 1983).
25. A. V. Feigenbaum, "Quality: Managing the Modern Company," *Quality Progress* (March 1985).
26. *Quality Costs—What and How*, 2nd ed. (Milwaukee: American Society for Quality Control, 1971).
27. *Guide for Reducing Quality Costs* (Milwaukee: American Society for Quality Control, 1977).
28. *Guide for Managing Vendor Quality Costs* (Milwaukee: American Society for Quality Control, 1980).
29. William O. Winchell, "Organizing Quality Cost Efforts to Minimize Difficulties," *39th North East Quality Control Conference Transactions* (Milwaukee: American Society for Quality Control, 1985).
30. Billie Ruth Marcum, "An Updated Framework for Problem Resolution," *Quality Progress* (July 1985).
31. Edward Kindlarski, "Ishikawa Diagrams for Problem Solving," *Quality Progress* (December 1984).

Bibliography

Bader, Morton E. *Practical Quality Management in the Chemical Process Industry*. New York: Marcel Dekker, Inc., 1983.

Besterfield, Dale H. *Quality Control*. Englewood Cliffs, NJ: Prentice-Hall, Inc., 1979.

Caplan, Frank. *The Quality System: A Sourcebook for Managers and Engineers*. Radnor, PA: Chilton Book Co., 1980.

Charbonneau, Harvey C., and Webster, Gordon L. *Industrial Quality Control*. Englewood Cliffs, NJ: Prentice-Hall, Inc., 1978.

Crosby, Philip P. *Quality is Free*. New York: McGraw-Hill Book Co., 1979.

——————. *Quality Without Tears*. New York: New American Library, 1984.

Dunn, Robert, and Ullman, Richard. *Quality Assurance for Computer Software*. New York: McGraw-Hill Book Co., 1982.

Enrick, Norbert L. *Quality Control and Reliability*. New York: Industrial Press, 1978.

Furniture Quality Program Guide. Milwaukee: American Society for Quality Control, 1984.

"Guide to Software Requirements Specifications." ANSI/IEEE 830-1984. New York: American National Standards Institute, 1984.

Hagan, John T. *The Management of Quality: Preparing for a Competitive Future*. Milwaukee: American Society for Quality Control, 1985.

Hayes, Glenn E. *Quality Assurance: Management and Technology*. Encino, CA: Glencoe Publishing Co., 1983.

——————, and Romig, Harry G. *Modern Quality Control*. Encino, CA: Glencoe Publishing Co., 1982.

How to Conduct a Supplier Survey. Milwaukee: American Society for Quality Control, 1977.

How to Establish Effective Quality Control for the Small Supplier. Milwaukee: American Society for Quality Control, 1981.

How to Evaluate a Supplier's Product. Milwaukee: American Society for Quality Control, 1981.

Interlaboratory Testing Techniques. Milwaukee: American Society for Quality Control, 1978.

Ishikawa, Kaoru. *Guide to Quality Control*, 2nd ed. New York: UNIPUB, 1982.

——————. *What is Total Quality Control? The Japanese Way*. Milwaukee: Quality Press, 1985.

Jamieson, Archibald. *Introduction to Quality Control*. Reston, VA: Reston Publishing Co., Inc., 1982.

Johnson, L. Marvin. *Quality Assurance Program Evaluation*. West Covina, CA: Stockton Trade Press, Inc., 1982.

Johnson, and Weber. *Buying Quality*. Milwaukee: Quality Press, 1985.

Juran, J. M. *Managerial Breakthrough*. New York: McGraw-Hill Book Co., 1964.

Lawrence, and Aft. *Productivity Measurement and Improvement*. Reston, VA: Reston Publishing Co., 1983.

Lester, R. H.; Enrick, N. L.; and Mottley, H. E. *Quality Control for Profit*. New York: Industrial Press, Inc., 1977.

Luca, D., and Wright, R., eds. *Product Design Engineering for Quality Improvement*. Dearborn, MI: Society of Manufacturing Engineers, 1983.

Patton, Joseph D. *Maintainability and Maintenance Management*. Triangle Park, NC: Instrument Society of America, 1980.

Procurement Quality Control. Milwaukee: Quality Press, 1985.

Product Recall Planning Guide. Milwaukee: American Society for Quality Control, 1981.

The Quality Circle Process: Elements of Success. Milwaukee: American Society for Quality Control, 1982.

Quality Defect and General Defect Classification Guideline. Milwaukee: American Society for Quality Control, 1983.

Quality Engineering Workmanship Standards Manual. Maitland, FL: Martin Marietta, 1981.

Shetty, and Buehler. *Quality and Productivity Improvements*. Chicago: Manufacturing Productivity Center, 1983.

Snee; Hare; and Trout. *Experiments in Industry*. Milwaukee: Quality Press, 1985.

"Software Quality Assurance Plans." ANSI/IEEE 730-1981. New York: American National Standards Institute, 1981.

Sullivan, Charles D. *Standards and Standardization*. New York: Marcel Dekker, Inc., 1983.

Wilborn, Walter. *Compendium of Audit Standards*. Milwaukee: American Society for Quality Control, 1983.

STATISTICAL METHODS FOR QUALITY AND PRODUCTIVITY DESIGN AND IMPROVEMENT

Central to the development of quality products at low cost is the focus of attention on the product design function (the optimization of design for function) and its relationship to the manufacturing process (product and process design for improved manufacturability). The ability to use scientifically sound concepts and methods for experimentation and the use of statistical thinking and methods to study product and process performance are important factors in establishing a well-founded approach to quality planning, design, and control. In particular, emphasis on quality upstream at the product design stage has been a key to the success of the Japanese in establishing the trend of increasing shares over a broad range of consumer markets.

Pioneers such as Shewhart, Deming, and Juran made major contributions to the concepts and techniques of quality design, planning, and improvement; however, the significance of their work has not been fully understood and appreciated, by management especially, on a broad basis until recently. Currently, considerable attention is being placed on process design and improvement using statistical thinking and methods. The use of control charts discussed subsequently is well recognized as an effective means of studying process variation and, in particular, of isolating major sources of variation so that quality and productivity improvement opportunities may be revealed. Often the stability of a process (that is, a process in good statistical control) signals but the *beginning* of a major improvement effort aimed more fundamentally at determining appropriate system changes to effect overall performance improvements. In this regard, the role of statistical design of experiments in both product and process design is now becoming better understood as a tool to reveal significant opportunities for improvement of performance.

The presence of statistical control provides the condition of stability or predictability of the system under study. It provides a measure of *constancy* with respect to average performance and *consistency* in terms of variation in performance. Statistical control suggests that the process performance is free of special or sporadic variation causes and is governed only by a constant system of common or chronic causes of variation. Design of experiments concepts and methods provide a powerful approach to the discovery of improvement opportunities for already stabilized processes. The manner and extent to which a set of factors may singly or in concert influence the process mean level (location effects) and/or process variability level (dispersion effects) can be efficiently revealed using statistically designed experiments. Conversely, design of experiments techniques can be of great help in identifying the root cause(s) of special causes of variation in unstable processes so that actions may be taken to bring such processes into statistical control.

For many problems, the concept of statistical control or stability may be premature. In engineering design and prototype testing, a process may not really exist; but again, planned experimentation can provide valuable insights into the ways in which changes in important product and process design parameters can improve overall quality and cost performance. The wide-ranging applicability of design of experiments techniques for dealing with both off-line issues of quality design and on-line issues of process control and continuing improvement are only just beginning to be recognized broadly.

Over the years, many definitions and meanings have been given to the word "quality." Some of these are summarized as follows. *Quality* is:

- The degree to which a specific product satisfies the wants of a specific consumer.
- The degree to which a specific product conforms to design specifications.
- Fitness for use or function.
- The characteristic(s) that distinguishes one item or article from another.

This chapter contributed by: Dr. T.H. Chang, Associate Professor, Dept. of Industrial and Systems Engineering, University of Wisconsin-Milwaukee; *Dr. Richard E. DeVor*, Professor of Industrial Engineering, Dept. of Mechanical and Industrial Engineering, University of Illinois at Urbana-Champaign.

Reviewers of sections of this chapter are: Dr. Hans J. Bajaria, President, Multiface, Inc.; *Peter M. Belaire*, Statistical Methods Facilitator, Plastics, Paint and Vinyl Div., Ford Motor Co.; *Richard P. Copp*, Quality Assurance Supervisor, Colt Industries, Holley Automotive Div.; *Lynda M. Finn*, Jass Software Div., Joiner Associates, Inc.; *J. Stuart Hunter*, Consultant; *Tim Kramer*, Total Quality Resources Div., Joiner Associates, Inc.; *Leonard R. Lamberson*, Professor and Chairman, Industrial Engineering and Operations Research, Wayne State University; *John Lazur*, Manager of Statistical Analysis Services, Decisions Technologies Div., Electronic Data Systems; *Joseph G. Pigeon, Ph.D.*, Senior Statistician, Research Laboratories, Rohm and Haas Co.; *Richard D. Sanders*, Professor, Stokely Management Center, University of Tennessee-Knoxville; *Narendra J. Sheth*, Chief Statistician, Product Assurance, Ford Motor Co.

CHAPTER 2

STATISTICAL METHODS FOR DESIGN

Several difficulties exist with these definitions. Among these are the fact that articulations of quality in such forms do not really provide a quantitative criterion that can be used for product and process design and performance and optimization. Also, such definitions for quality are not particularly supportive of the "never-ending" improvement" principle so crucial to the enhancement of competitive position. Rather, such meanings for quality tend to promote improvement to an acceptable plateau beyond which the economics of continued improvement may seem questionable.

In recent years the concept of quality as put forth by Taguchi has been gaining broader acceptance.[1] In conceptual terms, Taguchi defines quality as the loss imparted to the customer from the time the product is shipped. As a quantitative measure, he defines quality as loss due to variation/deviation of the product's function from the desired target value as mandated by design. Although this definition may raise some questions related to more popular notions concerning engineering specifications (tolerances), it offers a fresh philosophical view that supports and encourages in principle the concept of never-ending improvement and provides a quantitative and economically grounded working definition of quality. This definition is useful for engineering design as well as manufacturing.

Figure 2-1 contrasts the two views of quality that are currently being subjected to considerable study and discussion. In the more traditional view of quality (view a), part A would be a good part, part B a bad part, and no real distinction would be

made between parts A and C; however, such an interpretation may be questionable from a functional point of view. Such an interpretation puts quality strictly on an attribute basis (view b). Although this view of quality is quite consistent with heretofore popular notions about sampling and inspection (product control), it may inhibit a person's ability to embrace the concepts of process control and quality design. In particular, this view makes it more difficult to appreciate the need to seek continual reductions in variability. Furthermore, such a view tends to treat quality as though it were a shipping criterion rather than a design criterion.

On part function grounds, if the nominal is really a true reflection of design intent, then it seems more reasonable to consider that: (1) part C must be better than part A and (2) parts A and B are not much different at all. Such an approach to the understanding of quality can be quantified through the use of the "loss function" idea shown in Fig. 2-1, view c. Under this representation of quality performance, the closer the part characteristic is to the design intent (the nominal value), the smaller will be the variation in its performance (smaller functional variation), and so the quality of the part should be considered better. It is important to note that given two products that both function at about the same level of performance, the product that performs more consistently (less variation about the nominal) is considered a better product (higher quality). This is because the product will ultimately experience less trouble in the field and exhibit longer life.

The loss function can be numerically derived and evaluated in terms that embrace the economics of the situation. The loss function may be used to establish specifications, based on the tradeoff between the consequences of field failure and the costs of remedial action at the process to prevent the field failure. Further, the loss function may be used to evaluate production actions such as tool change strategies and quantify the gain in quality and productivity precipitated by improvements in the product and process design and operation. Such improvements help improve target adherence. The loss function approach to measuring and evaluating quality will be discussed in more detail later in this chapter.

As was pointed out previously, quality is a matter of product function, and in general, the failure to meet intended function can stem from either failure to achieve the nominal performance mandated by engineering design or excessive variation about the intended nominal performance level. These two problems are graphically depicted in Fig. 2-2.

In terms of improvement strategies, these two problems have often tended to be somewhat separated both conceptually and methodologically. For example, design of experiments methods have generally focused on the "average" problem, seeking to understand the ways in which purposeful changes in design/ control factors can improve performance on the average. On the other hand, the techniques of statistical process control have emphasized the identification of sources of variation so that remedial actions can be taken to continually reduce variation.

Of course, the world is not divided into these two types of problems; in fact, producing a product on target with the smallest variation is not two separate problems, but a single twofold problem. The following example illustrates how this joint problem can be approached through the use of experimental design techniques.

To control part weight of a molded plastic product, a simple two-level factorial experiment may be conducted to determine how two molding machine parameters influence part weight.

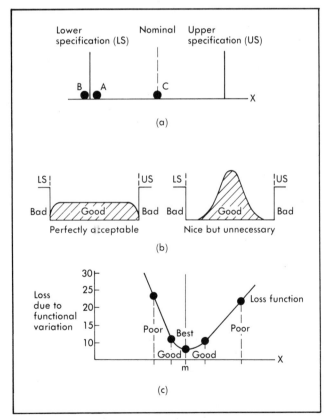

Fig. 2-1 Different views of specifications: (a) conformance to bilateral specification, (b) process performance relative to traditional views of quality needs, and (c) quality as measured by the loss function.

The experiment results are shown in Fig. 2-3. Each response weight is the average of 25 parts molded consecutively under each of the four given process conditions.

The results of the experiment seem to indicate that by manipulating control variable 1, average part weight can be controlled. Control variable 2 seems to have little effect on average part weight; that is, changing the level of control variable 2 does not cause average part weight to vary much. As a result, control variable 2 may be set according to some other process performance criterion such as minimum energy consumption.

In addition to evaluating the molding process performance "on the average," the variation in performance about the average can and should also be examined as a process response. Figure 2-4 shows the results of each test in the two-level factorial design as viewed as a time plot of the individual part weight under each machine condition. This process variation response could be summarized in a single statistic for each test such as the standard deviation or the range.

Reexamination of the experimental results reveals something important that was not apparent previously. Although control variable 2 does not affect part weight on the average, it does appear to affect variation in part weight. The complete results of the experiment indicate that not only average weight can be controlled by manipulating control variable 1, but also the variation in weight can be reduced by setting control variable 2 at its high level. In the past, it has been less common to use variation as an experimental design response and to seek ways

to reduce variation in product/process performance through designed experimentation.

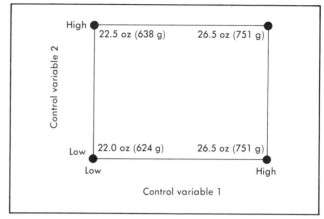

Fig. 2-3 Experimental results of molded part weights.

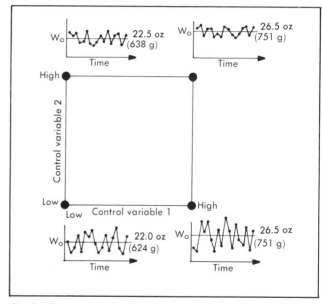

Fig. 2-4 Time plots of part weights.

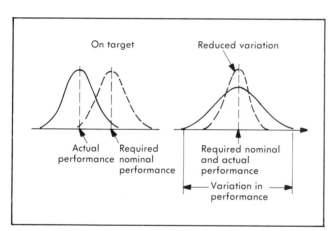

Fig. 2-2 Two problems in meeting intended functions.

SOURCES OF VARIATION AND THEIR COUNTERMEASURES

The view of quality as measured by loss due to functional variation in performance suggests that it is important to understand the meaning of functional variation—in particular the specific sources or causes of variation. Only when the basic sources of functional variation become clear is it possible to begin to formulate the quality design and improvement strategies that will serve as the countermeasures against these sources.

It has been suggested that a product's performance is influenced by three basic sources of variation or three basic types of noise factors.[2] These noise factors are outer noise, inner noise, and variational noise. Outer noise factors describe the conditions such as temperature, humidity, and material contamination operating during product use. These factors generally cannot be easily controlled and, by their presence, generally

SOURCES OF VARIATION

degrade performance through increased functional variation. Inner noise factors describe internal product change during use. An example of internal product change is deterioration as precipitated by mechanical wear, material aging, or fatigue. Variational noise refers to manufacturing imperfection and is the variation that occurs between like products manufactured to the same specifications.

The basic countermeasures required to mitigate the forces of noise/variation sources may be quite different in nature. Outer noise is clearly a design issue and can only be effectively dealt with at the engineering design stage using off-line quality control methods such as design of experiments. Inner noise is also most effectively dealt with at the design stage. Specific countermeasures against the forces of outer and inner noise that are an integral part of the engineering design process will be discussed subsequently.

Variational noise is basically a manufacturing problem and, although product design may play a significant role here, it does so from the relationship between design and the manufacturing process. Because variational noise is based on manufacturing imperfection, the techniques of statistical process control can provide an effective means to identify special and common causes of variation in the process, thus providing a sound basis for action.

Originally Shewhart and later Deming and Juran found it important to partition variational noise into two basic sources, as shown in Table 2-1. All three characterizations clearly depict the nature of the problem and suggest where the responsibility for action lies. Special causes or sporadic problems often arise in a somewhat unpredictable and erratic fashion. They are largely the result of influences external to the system and can generally be handled locally at the process level by the operator or supervisor, provided that the proper tools are given to them by management. Common causes or chronic problems, on the other hand, are sources of variation integral to the system and provide a consistent influence on the process. Such causes of variation require the attention of management to take the lead in formulating the proper corrective action and make the decisions necessary to change the system.

Another on-line quality and productivity improvement tool aimed at the manufacturing process is "Evolutionary Operation," known as EVOP.[3] Evolutionary Operation makes use of simple design of experiments concepts and tools to monitor and track process performance over time. It is a tool that enables the process to provide useful information on opportunities for improvement while maintaining an economically viable process. Evolutionary Operation recognizes that even optimized processes undergo change over time. By continually monitoring the process using methods of Evolutionary Operation, which employ simple two-level factorial designs, directions of adjustment of certain important process variables can be identified to continually improve the process on-line. As such, EVOP appears to be an on-line countermeasure against the forces of the inner noise factors surrounding a process.

TABLE 2-1
Partitioning of Variational Noise

Shewhart	Deming	Juran
Assignable Causes	Special Causes/Local Faults	Sporadic Problems
Random Causes	Common Causes/System Faults	Chronic Problems

QUALITY PERSPECTIVE IN ENGINEERING DESIGN

The disciplines of engineering have advanced considerably since the days of Euclid, Archimedes, and other early scientists and mathematicians. Although a great wealth of theory has been developed on which to build the technologies of the day, much engineering work and scientific discovery is still rooted in observation based on experimental work. Proposed designs must be tested and refined. Alternate approaches, materials, methods, and structures must be compared as to their absolute and relative performances so that the selection and refinement process can take place.

One important aspect of the study of product performance is the evaluation of the ability of the product to operate within a specified envelope of conditions for a designed life. For many products this may reduce to "normal" operation for a given number of cycles, miles, or hours without failure. The body of knowledge often referred to as reliability engineering involves basically the activities of reliability modeling and prediction and life testing. Reliability modeling encompasses the study and development of probabilistic models for predicting the probability of survival for individual components as well as complex systems of components. Life testing may be used to estimate the failure distributions and test the validity of claims or verify conformance to design requirements. Life testing may also be employed in the estimation of various reliability parameters associated with one or more failure modes.

The characteristic of reliability testing that seems to separate it from other uses of experimentation is that it examines performance over time under a fixed set of design parameters and operating conditions. Reliability testing focuses on the simultaneous operation of many identical units for the purpose of examining the probabilistic nature of failure. Physical study of failed units may give some clues to the underlying nature of the failure mechanism, but may neither pinpoint the root cause nor suggest design modifications for improvement.

In contrast, the field of design of experiments grew out of the need to efficiently evaluate alternate treatments in agricultural research. Particular attention was directed toward not only comparing the yields of competing fertilizers or hybrid seeds, but to doing so under a wide range of conditions such as soil condition, rainfall, sunlight, and drainage conditions that define the operating envelope. Later, design of experiments concepts suggested by Fisher[4] and others were adapted, extended, and refined for use in the industrial sector.[5] Many new techniques were also developed for industrial experimentation. The purpose of such experimental work was to discover those factors that govern ultimate product/process performance so that action toward improvement could be taken off-line (at engineering design) or on-line (process control). In contrast to performing many tests under fixed conditions for many cycles, an experimental strategy can be directed at performing one or a few tests at each of many combinations of design and operating variables over a number of variables for a few cycles to observe performance.

Perhaps one of the most important contributions of Taguchi in the quality and productivity improvement arena is emphasis on pushing the problem farther upstream into engineering design, well ahead of manufacturing.[6] Taguchi suggests both a conceptual framework and a set of tools and methods to improve quality through design. At the center of this framework is the interpretation of quality as measured by loss due to functional variation in the performance of a product or a process. Taguchi stresses the design process as a fundamental countermeasure against the forces of variation, in particular the forces of outer noise and inner noise.

Taguchi advocates a three-stage engineering design process that includes system design, parameter design, and tolerance design. System design is the application of the prevailing experience and technologies of the day to arrive at the most promising design alternative. Parameter design is the study and analysis of important factors or parameters of the system design to determine the optimum nominal values for those parameters. Tolerance design uses the loss function concept to develop the economic tradeoffs that give rise to the setting of tolerances for the factors identified as important during parameter design.

Taguchi places particular importance on the parameter design activity. In particular, the key elements in the method of parameter design are the following:

1. The use of simulation through mathematical modeling to optimize a design.
2. The use of design of experiments methods as a framework for performance evaluation through simulation.
3. The concept of "robust design." In this concept, levels of the parameters of the product or process are sought that minimize the functional variation in performance caused by external (environmental) variation sources, which Taguchi calls noise factors.

The concept of robust design is one that has a great deal of appeal. When a product is said to be robust it means that its function is minimally affected by outer and inner noise as well as variational noise. An automobile design may be said to be robust if, for example, the fuel mileage remains fairly constant (minimal functional variation) over a wide range of speed, road conditions, and wind velocities, all of which might be considered as outer (environmental) noise factors.

The parameter design concept counteracts the forces of noise factors on functional performance through action at the engineering design stage. To illustrate the idea, Fig. 2-5 depicts a certain product functioning in the field. Its performance is experiencing an excessive amount of functional variation. This functional variation is in part caused by a set of external noise

factors that are degrading product performance. Change(s) in the basic design is sought to reduce this functional variation, thereby improving product quality.

Traditionally, one common design strategy to combat this problem is to use more expensive raw materials. Using more expensive raw materials generally means that certain important material properties are to be held to closer tolerances (see Fig. 2-6). By tightening the performance specifications on the material properties, the amount of noise transmitted through the product is reduced. This strategy amounts to moving from system design directly to tolerance design without first optimizing the design performance using parameter design.

As an alternative to tightening the input material property specification, Fig. 2-7 indicates that the application of the same material (same input variation) at a different nominal value

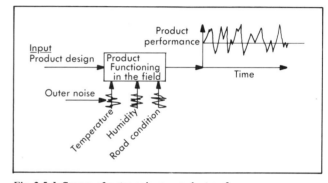

Fig. 2-5 Influence of outer noise on product performance.

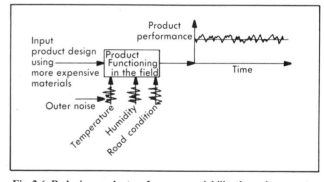

Fig. 2-6 Reducing product performance variability through parameter design.

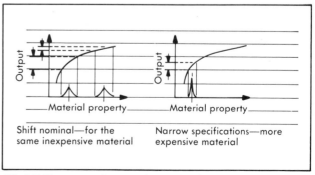

Fig. 2-7 Two approaches to variance reduction.

STATISTICAL PROCESS CONTROL

within a feasible region can also lead to a reduction in output performance variation. In this case, the nonlinearity in the design is exploited to reduce performance variation (achieve a more robust design) without the use of more expensive (tighter tolerances) raw materials. Opportunities such as the one just described are primarily discovered during parameter design.

STATISTICAL PROCESS CONTROL

For many years the primary role of the quality control function was to ensure that the manufactured product conformed to engineering specifications. The primary instrument of this function was inspection, using either ad hoc methods or plans for sampling based on statistical methods and probability theory. In either case the principal result was the assurance of a satisfactory outgoing quality level for the goods being inspected.

For years the vast majority of those in the U.S. industrial community embraced the quality control function through these methods of product control. As a result, from a productivity standpoint, inefficiency and waste were widespread and perhaps even increased over the two decades prior to 1980, but competitive balance was maintained because everyone was doing an equally poor job. This situation slowly changed through the 1970s as worldwide competition in the marketplace intensified. A competitive edge grew slowly but steadily until the problem gained alarming proportions. It soon became obvious that many world competitors of the U.S. were using a different management philosophy and a total systems approach to quality in both engineering design and manufacturing.

In his book *Quality, Productivity and Competitive Position*,[7] Deming discusses at great length his "Fourteen Obligations of Top Management." Embracing these tenets requires the emergence of a new way of thinking about how to conduct business. In particular, Deming stresses the need to place more emphasis on innovation and long-range planning, to abandon the philosophy of accepting defective products and the use of mass inspection to find them, to place more emphasis on technical training and retraining, to make maximum use of statistical concepts to find problems, and to eliminate inhibitors to never-ending improvement such as work standards or production quotas. These are but a few of the important concepts that define this new management philosophy.

Since 1980, important progress has been made in the U.S. to regain a leadership position in many markets. As techniques such as statistical process control (SPC) become better understood conceptually and then implemented across a broader and broader base, real differences are being made.

The techniques of SPC, as put forth more than 60 years ago by Dr. Walter Shewhart, employ basic probability laws and statistical methods to develop models for the behavior of the variations witnessed in the quality characteristics of manufactured goods during production.[8] Through the statistical study of these patterns of variation, it is possible to attribute certain types of variations to certain types of fault sources and hence develop a knowledge and understanding of what types of corrective actions may be required. In this regard, the most fundamental principle in the application of SPC methods is the partitioning of the total variation pattern into two major sources: (1) the system sources (chronic problems or common causes) and (2) more localized sources (sporadic problems or special causes). Because system variation comes from many ever-present sources, it appears as a stable, random, and well-behaved pattern of variation. On the other hand, sporadic problems being of external disturbance origin produce unusual patterns of variation that are visible when statistical methods are used to study the total variation pattern.

It is important to recognize the proper assignment of responsibility for corrective action of common and special causes. Because common causes are system faults, they require the attention of management. It is likely that some major breakthrough is required to affect a significant improvement in quality and productivity when common causes are involved. Only management can institute the changes required to remove major sources of common cause variability.

The roles and responsibilities of management in precipitating breakthrough are substantial because the vast majority of all the problems that must be dealt with on a continuing basis are chronic problems. Deming and Juran have often said that 80-85% of the problems encountered are system problems. Because of this, managers must become more knowledgeable in the concepts and philosophy of SPC.

Understanding the need for the pursuit of statistical control or process stability when the process is already producing parts within the specifications is essential to the continual improvement of quality and productivity. In this regard, central to the acceptance of SPC as an essential concept and manufacturing management tool is the recognition of the quality/productivity relationship. Statistical process control helps identify the fundamental product and process faults that lead to the production of defective material and helps formulate corrective actions to prevent defective materials from being made in the first place.

Every fault or source of variation not only erodes quality, but is a source of waste and inefficiency in one form or another. As a result, the elimination of each and every source of variation leads to improvements in productivity as well as in quality. It is therefore advantageous to adopt the philosophy of never-ending improvement using SPC rather than the notion of attaining and then maintaining an acceptable level of improvement. The quality/productivity relationship is a clear motivation for the continual pursuit of process stability.

A stable process is a predictable process, and hence the management of scheduling, inventory control, and maintenance management are all directly influenced by the presence (or absence) of process control. Improvements in the efficiency of production management can obviously be a tremendous force in the attainment of a positive competitive position. The lack of process control/stability will always have a deleterious effect on the ability to efficiently manage and control the total resources of a manufacturing operation.

Statistical control is also essential to the proper evaluation of process capability. Process capability is a measure of the consistent ability of the process to produce at a certain level. Consistency means stability, the ability to extrapolate performance into the future with a strong degree of belief that predictions of future performance levels will be realized. If the process is behaving in an erratic and unstable fashion, it is impossible to assess the process capability. Process data collected at different times may give totally different pictures of the process capability.

Attaining process stability is by no means sufficient to ensure high levels of quality and productivity. A process may be stable or predictable, but not at all capable in terms of its ability to produce a high percentage of acceptable product. A process in a state of good statistical control simply means that the best is being done under the present system. Because a controlled process means that the process is subject only to common causes of variation, the system will have to be changed to make any additional improvement.

The continual pursuit of variation reduction in a manufacturing process provides for still another important benefit—the existence of a quiet, low noise level system. Systems with low noise levels (high signal-to-noise ratios) are more sensitive to change and therefore provide stronger signals when either purposeful change through experimentation is introduced or when sporadic change occurs in the form of special causes of variation. In other words, the ability to efficiently and reliably reveal improvement opportunities through the techniques of statistical process control and experimental design depends strongly on the ability to continually affect noise reduction in the system.

It is not uncommon today to hear of efforts to reduce the number of defective items produced to levels that seem on the surface to defy all reason and practical judgment. If variation reduction was only done for the sake of reducing scrap from one defect per 10,000 items to one defect per 1 million items, the economic basis for continual improvement may be considered weak; clearly it is the other broad-based benefits of variation reduction that overwhelmingly support its continuance on a never-ending basis.

DATA CHARACTERIZATION

Variable measurements from a process under statistical control tend to collect themselves into a predictable pattern of variation that can be easily described by a frequency distribution. The frequency distribution serves as a model that predicts how the process will behave if it is subject to a constant set of common causes.

Occasionally, an unusual disturbance occurs that changes process performance by changing the mean of the process, or by changing the standard deviation of the process, or by changing both. Over time, a process can be subject to several kinds of disturbances (special causes) that can produce a variety of unstable behaviors with respect to either its mean level or the level of process variability or both. Figure 2-8 graphically portrays this concept of process behavior.[9]

To find out how the process is behaving in terms of an output quality characteristic, samples can be drawn from the process, and the information can be used to estimate process behavior as a whole. The whole unique process, if it exists, is often referred to in statistical terms as a population. It may be described by a set of measures called population parameters. A process (population) is said to exist if all the elements of the population are subject to a fixed set of common causes of variation. Usually a population can be adequately characterized by a few simple measures such as the mean and standard deviation and a probability distribution. These measures are defined by population parameters that are seldom known and hence are estimated by corresponding measures calculated from sample data. Because sample measures, called statistics, are based on only part of the population, they are uncertain estimates of the population parameters. Consequently, each kind of statistic follows a sampling distribution of its own, which is different from the parent population of individual measurements.

TYPES OF DATA

Data that are collected for quality design and improvement purposes are obtained by direct observation of the process and are classified as either variable data or attribute data. Variable data are characteristics that are measurable along a continuous scale. Examples of these characteristics are length, weight, resistance, temperature, and force. Attribute data are characteristics that are countable or are categorized into discrete classes. Examples of these characteristics are number of scratches and defective or nondefective items.

FREQUENCY DISTRIBUTION

Table 2-2 gives the data from 50 samples/subgroups of size $n = 5$ each, obtained by measuring soft gasket sheets from one production line over a two-week period. The table records the

TABLE 2-2
Thickness of Gasket Sheet Samples, in. x 10^{-4}

Sample Number	Observations					Avg.	Range
1	427	428	457	430	450	438.40	30
2	456	448	442	459	440	449.00	19
3	425	415	441	440	422	428.60	25
4	465	450	438	437	439	445.80	28
5	464	438	439	453	440	446.80	25
6	435	427	418	431	439	430.00	21
7	437	429	444	443	432	437.00	15
8	451	433	461	435	462	448.40	29
9	438	417	426	436	429	429.20	21
10	415	439	425	438	427	428.80	24
11	431	456	441	457	431	443.20	26
12	429	418	425	426	444	428.40	26
13	437	449	436	461	456	447.80	25
14	427	437	436	432	421	430.60	16

(*continued*)

CHAPTER 2

DATA CHARACTERIZATION

TABLE 2-2—*Continued*

Sample Number	Observations					Avg.	Range
15	423	448	435	434	446	437.20	25
16	461	446	450	437	436	446.00	25
17	435	433	443	442	437	438.00	10
18	433	427	442	420	429	430.20	22
19	435	438	431	439	432	435.00	8
20	435	442	463	437	457	446.80	28
21	434	435	457	432	436	438.80	25
22	423	432	441	431	414	428.20	27
23	425	416	439	423	441	428.80	25
24	435	436	439	462	451	444.60	27
25	437	435	457	436	438	440.60	22
26	429	438	444	433	437	436.20	15
27	456	437	436	440	458	445.40	22
28	426	456	428	443	429	436.40	30
29	442	446	447	431	441	441.40	16
30	456	435	436	463	440	446.00	28
31	429	458	439	432	442	440.00	29
32	433	437	462	457	434	444.60	29
33	430	433	429	459	431	436.40	30
34	446	444	425	434	443	438.40	21
35	430	451	457	429	450	443.40	28
36	437	440	432	415	434	431.60	25
37	447	444	443	445	449	445.60	6
38	463	439	440	441	445	445.60	24
39	437	433	432	434	440	435.20	8
40	427	427	426	456	436	434.40	30
41	433	437	423	450	440	436.60	27
42	457	448	434	433	437	441.80	24
43	440	448	433	449	432	440.40	17
44	436	449	440	448	451	444.80	15
45	436	418	444	427	440	433.00	26
46	424	450	439	456	432	440.20	32
47	443	458	456	428	433	443.60	30
48	438	441	446	434	433	438.40	13
49	430	457	442	446	453	445.60	27
50	437	423	426	447	435	433.60	24

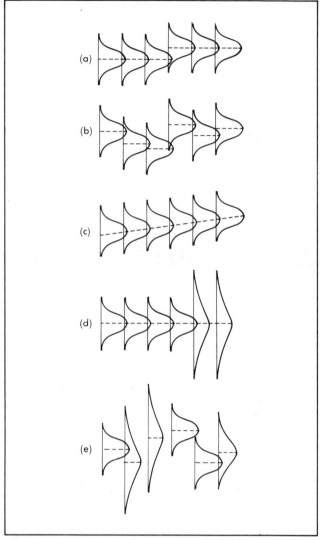

Fig. 2-8 Unstable process behaviors due to special causes: (a) stable variability, sustained shift in mean; (b) stable variability, erratic shifts in mean; (c) stable variability, trend in mean; (d) sustained increase in variability, constant mean; and (e) erratic shifts in both mean and variability.

individual thickness measurements as well as the average and range for each sample/subgroup.

When plotting a frequency histogram of the individual sheet thicknesses, the data are first grouped into cells or intervals. The frequency of observations falling within each cell is tallied (see Fig. 2-9).

To convert the tally sheet to a histogram, the number of observations within each cell is represented by the height of a rectangle; the width of the rectangle represents the cell or interval size. The histogram for the data of Fig. 2-9 is shown in Fig. 2-10. From the frequency histogram, the following three specific things can be noted about the data:

1. The data tend to cluster about a certain value (central tendency).
2. The data exhibit a spread or variation about the central value.

3. The frequencies are approximately symmetric about the center and fall off rapidly from the center.

MEASURES OF CENTRAL TENDENCY

A measure of central tendency of a distribution is a numerical value that describes the central position or location of the data. The most commonly used measure is the arithmetic average or mean value of all the data in the sample or population.

The true mean of a population (a parameter) can be calculated by the equation:

$$\mu = \sum_{i=1}^{N} X_i / N \tag{1}$$

where:

μ = true mean of the population
Σ = the sum of
N = the total number of observations in the population
X_i = the i-th value of the individual observation

In practice, however, the true mean of the population is seldom calculated because it is rarely possible and unnecessary to measure or count all items in the population. In most instances, the true mean is estimated by the sample mean or average (a statistic). The sample mean can be calculated by the equation:

$$\overline{X} = \sum_{i=1}^{n} X_i / n \tag{2}$$

where:

$\overline{X}$ = the sample mean (pronounced X-bar)
n = the total number of observations in the sample

MEASURES OF DISPERSION OR VARIABILITY

The variance is an important measure of the variability in data. It is the average of the sum of the squared deviations of the data from their mean. The true variance, σ_X^2, can be calculated by the equation:

$$\sigma_X^2 = \sum_{i=1}^{N} (X_i - \mu)^2 / N \tag{3}$$

The square root of the variance called the standard deviation, σ_X, is a more commonly used measure of variation.

In practice, both the true mean and true variance of the population are seldom known and are therefore estimated from sample data. The sample variance, s^2, can be calculated by the equation:

$$s_X^2 = \sum_{i=1}^{n} (X_i - \overline{X})^2 / (n-1) \tag{4}$$

In Eq. (4), the denominator (n-1) is often a source of confusion. Mathematically, it can be shown that the estimate of the true variance using the sample variance has desirable statistical properties and therefore is commonly used. It is important to realize that the sample observations X_1, X_2, ..., X_n are independent. In Eq. (4), there are n deviations ($X_i - \overline{X}$), but only (n-1) of them are independent.

Cell	Observed frequencies
412-414	1
415-417	11111
418-420	1111
421-423	11111 11
424-426	11111 11111 1
427-429	11111 11111 11111 11111
430-432	11111 11111 11111 11111 1
433-435	11111 11111 11111 11111 11111 11111 1
436-438	11111 11111 11111 11111 11111 11111 11111 1
439-441	11111 11111 11111 11111 11111 1111
442-444	11111 11111 11111 1111
445-447	11111 11111 1
448-450	11111 11111 11111
451-453	11111 1
454-456	11111 1111
457-459	11111 11111 1111
460-462	11111 1
463-465	11111

Fig. 2-9 Tally sheet of gasket thicknesses.

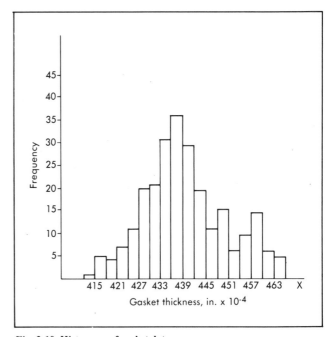

Fig. 2-10 Histogram of gasket data.

Another important measurement of variability is the range, which is the difference between the largest value and the smallest value of the data within a sample. The range is calculated by the equation:

$$R = X_l - X_s \tag{5}$$

where:

R = the range
X_l = largest value in the sample
X_s = smallest value in the sample

CHAPTER 2

DATA CHARACTERIZATION

The range is often used to obtain an estimate of the population standard deviation (σ_X). Mathematically, an exact relationship between R and σ_X has been established by the equation:

$$\sigma_X = R/d_2 \tag{6}$$

The value of d_2 varies depending on the size n of the sample/subgroup. This relationship also depends on the assumption that the observations of X come from the normal distribution. Moderate departures from this assumption, however, do not markedly erode the effectiveness of this relationship. The numerical value of d_2 for different subgroup sizes can be found in Table 2-3.

THE NORMAL DISTRIBUTION CURVE

About 200 years ago it was observed that errors of measurement seemed to follow a definite pattern with respect to their relative frequency of occurrence. For example, repeated measurements of the length of certain objects seemed to rise in a frequency sense according to a bell-shaped curve, symmetric about the mean. The frequency of these measurements also falls off rapidly beyond a distance of about one standard deviation from the mean.

This frequency distribution is referred to as the normal distribution. Mathematically, the normal distribution curve is defined by the equation:

$$f(X) = \frac{1}{\sqrt{2\pi}\,\sigma_X}\, e^{-\frac{1}{2}\left(\frac{X-\mu}{\sigma_X}\right)^2} \tag{7}$$

where:

$f(X)$ = probability density function of the random variable X

Figure 2-11 shows the appearance of the normal curve and the relationship between the shape of the curve and the parameters μ_X and σ_X. Strictly speaking, the curve stretches from minus infinity to plus infinity; however, much of it is distributed

TABLE 2-3
Factors for Computing Centerlines and Control Limits for $\overline{X}$ and R Charts

Subgroup Size, n	Chart for Averages ($\overline{X}$) Factors for Control Limits A_2	Chart for Ranges (R) Factors for Centerlines d_2	Factors for Control Limits D_3	Factors for Control Limits D_4
2	1.880	1.128	-	3.267
3	1.023	1.693	-	2.574
4	0.729	2.059	-	2.282
5	0.577	2.326	-	2.114
6	0.483	2.534	-	2.004
7	0.419	2.704	0.076	1.924
8	0.373	2.847	0.136	1.864
9	0.337	2.970	0.184	1.816
10	0.308	3.078	0.223	1.777
11	0.285	3.173	0.256	1.744
12	0.266	3.258	0.283	1.717
13	0.249	3.336	0.307	1.693
14	0.235	3.407	0.328	1.672
15	0.223	3.472	0.347	1.653
16	0.212	3.532	0.363	1.637
17	0.203	3.588	0.378	1.622
18	0.194	3.640	0.391	1.608
19	0.187	3.689	0.403	1.597
20	0.180	3.735	0.415	1.585
21	0.173	3.778	0.425	1.575
22	0.167	3.819	0.434	1.566
23	0.162	3.858	0.443	1.557
24	0.157	3.895	0.451	1.548
25	0.153	3.931	0.459	1.541

(American Society for Testing and Materials)

DATA CHARACTERIZATION

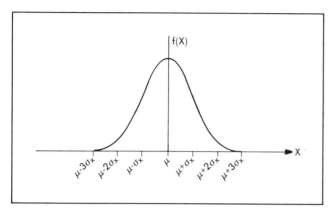

Fig. 2-11 Normal curve.

over a relatively narrow range. In a normal distribution, 68.26% of the observations fall between $\mu - \sigma_X$ and $\mu + \sigma_X$; 95.46% of the observations fall between $\mu - 2\sigma_X$ and $\mu + 2\sigma_X$; and 99.73% of the observations fall between $\mu - 3\sigma_X$ and $\mu + 3\sigma_X$.

Standard Normal Distribution

Because the mean and standard deviation of the normal distribution can take on many different values from situation to situation, it is convenient to define and work with a standardized normal distribution.

The standard normal variable is generally denoted by the letter z and the standard normal probability density function by $f(z)$. Because the standard normal distribution has a standard deviation (σ_z) equal to 1, the value for z can be interpreted as representing the number of standard deviations from the mean (μ_z), which is 0. In terms of any normal distribution with a mean (μ_X) and a standard deviation (σ_X), the z value (number of standard deviations) can be calculated by the equation:

$$z = (X - \mu)/\sigma_X \tag{8}$$

Figure 2-12 illustrates the relationship between the normal distribution curve and the standardized distribution curve. Partial areas under the standardized normal curve have been calcu-

TABLE 2-4
Areas Under the Normal Curve*

$\dfrac{X_i-\mu}{\sigma}$	0.09	0.08	0.07	0.06	0.05	0.04	0.03	0.02	0.01	0.00
-3.5	0.00017	0.00017	0.00018	0.00019	0.00019	0.00020	0.00021	0.00022	0.00022	0.00023
-3.4	0.00024	0.00025	0.00026	0.00027	0.00028	0.00029	0.00030	0.00031	0.00033	0.00034
-3.3	0.00035	0.00036	0.00038	0.00039	0.00040	0.00042	0.00043	0.00045	0.00047	0.00048
-3.2	0.00050	0.00052	0.00054	0.00056	0.00058	0.00060	0.00062	0.00064	0.00066	0.00069
-3.1	0.00071	0.00074	0.00076	0.00079	0.00082	0.00085	0.00087	0.00090	0.00094	0.00097
-3.0	0.00100	0.00104	0.00107	0.00111	0.00114	0.00118	0.00122	0.00126	0.00131	0.00135
-2.9	0.0014	0.0014	0.0015	0.0015	0.0016	0.0016	0.0017	0.0017	0.0018	0.0019
-2.8	0.0019	0.0020	0.0021	0.0021	0.0022	0.0023	0.0023	0.0024	0.0025	0.0026
-2.7	0.0026	0.0027	0.0028	0.0029	0.0030	0.0031	0.0032	0.0033	0.0034	0.0035
-2.6	0.0036	0.0037	0.0038	0.0039	0.0040	0.0041	0.0043	0.0044	0.0045	0.0047
-2.5	0.0048	0.0049	0.0051	0.0052	0.0054	0.0055	0.0057	0.0059	0.0060	0.0062
-2.4	0.0064	0.0066	0.0068	0.0069	0.0071	0.0073	0.0075	0.0078	0.0080	0.0082
-2.3	0.0084	0.0087	0.0089	0.0091	0.0094	0.0096	0.0099	0.0102	0.0104	0.0107
-2.2	0.0110	0.0113	0.0116	0.0119	0.0122	0.0125	0.0129	0.0132	0.0136	0.0139
-2.1	0.0143	0.0146	0.0150	0.0154	0.0158	0.0162	0.0166	0.0170	0.0174	0.0179
-2.0	0.0183	0.0188	0.0192	0.0197	0.0202	0.0207	0.0212	0.0217	0.0222	0.0228
-1.9	0.0233	0.0239	0.0244	0.0250	0.0256	0.0262	0.0268	0.0274	0.0281	0.0287
-1.8	0.0294	0.0301	0.0307	0.0314	0.0322	0.0329	0.0336	0.0344	0.0351	0.0359
-1.7	0.0367	0.0375	0.0384	0.0392	0.0401	0.0409	0.0418	0.0427	0.0436	0.0446
-1.6	0.0455	0.0465	0.0475	0.0485	0.0495	0.0505	0.0516	0.0526	0.0537	0.0548
-1.5	0.0559	0.0571	0.0582	0.0594	0.0606	0.0618	0.0630	0.0643	0.0655	0.0668
-1.4	0.0681	0.0694	0.0708	0.0721	0.0735	0.0749	0.0764	0.0778	0.0793	0.0808
-1.3	0.0823	0.0838	0.0853	0.0869	0.0885	0.0901	0.0918	0.0934	0.0951	0.0968
-1.2	0.0895	0.1003	0.1020	0.1038	0.1057	0.1075	0.1093	0.1112	0.1131	0.1151
-1.1	0.1170	0.1190	0.1210	0.1230	0.1251	0.1271	0.1292	0.1314	0.1335	0.1357
-1.0	0.1379	0.1401	0.1423	0.1446	0.1469	0.1492	0.1515	0.1539	0.1562	0.1587
-0.9	0.1611	0.1635	0.1660	0.1685	0.1711	0.1736	0.1762	0.1788	0.1814	0.1841
-0.8	0.1867	0.1894	0.1922	0.1949	0.1977	0.2005	0.2033	0.2061	0.2090	0.2119
-0.7	0.2148	0.2177	0.2207	0.2236	0.2266	0.2297	0.2327	0.2358	0.2389	0.2420
-0.6	0.2451	0.2483	0.2514	0.2546	0.2578	0.2611	0.2643	0.2676	0.2709	0.2743
-0.5	0.2776	0.2810	0.2843	0.2877	0.2912	0.2946	0.2981	0.3015	0.3050	0.3085
-0.4	0.3121	0.3156	0.3192	0.3228	0.3264	0.3300	0.3336	0.3372	0.3409	0.3446
-0.3	0.3483	0.3520	0.3557	0.3594	0.3632	0.3669	0.3707	0.3745	0.3783	0.3821
-0.2	0.3859	0.3897	0.3936	0.3974	0.4013	0.4052	0.4090	0.4129	0.4168	0.4207
-0.1	0.4247	0.4286	0.4325	0.4364	0.4404	0.4443	0.4483	0.4522	0.4562	0.4602
-0.0	0.4641	0.4681	0.4721	0.4761	0.4801	0.4840	0.4880	0.4920	0.4960	0.5000

DATA CHARACTERIZATION

TABLE 2-4—Continued

$\dfrac{X_i-\mu}{\sigma}$	0.00	0.01	0.02	0.03	0.04	0.05	0.06	0.07	0.08	0.09
+0.0	0.5000	0.5040	0.5080	0.5120	0.5160	0.5199	0.5239	0.5279	0.5319	0.5359
+0.1	0.5398	0.5438	0.5478	0.5517	0.5557	0.5596	0.5636	0.5675	0.5714	0.5753
+0.2	0.5793	0.5832	0.5871	0.5910	0.5948	0.5987	0.6026	0.6064	0.6103	0.6141
+0.3	0.6179	0.6217	0.6255	0.6293	0.6331	0.6368	0.6406	0.6443	0.6480	0.6517
+0.4	0.6554	0.6591	0.6628	0.6664	0.6700	0.6736	0.6772	0.6808	0.6844	0.6879
+0.5	0.6915	0.6950	0.6985	0.7019	0.7054	0.7088	0.7123	0.7157	0.7190	0.7224
+0.6	0.7257	0.7291	0.7324	0.7357	0.7389	0.7422	0.7454	0.7486	0.7517	0.7549
+0.7	0.7580	0.7611	0.7642	0.7673	0.7704	0.7734	0.7764	0.7794	0.7823	0.7852
+0.8	0.7881	0.7910	0.7939	0.7967	0.7995	0.8023	0.8051	0.8079	0.8106	0.8133
+0.9	0.8159	0.8186	0.8212	0.8238	0.8264	0.8289	0.8315	0.8340	0.8365	0.8389
+1.0	0.8413	0.8438	0.8461	0.8485	0.8508	0.8531	0.8554	0.8577	0.8599	0.8621
+1.1	0.8643	0.8665	0.8686	0.8708	0.8729	0.8749	0.8770	0.8790	0.8810	0.8830
+1.2	0.8849	0.8869	0.8888	0.8907	0.8925	0.8944	0.8962	0.8980	0.8997	0.9015
+1.3	0.9032	0.9049	0.9066	0.9082	0.9099	0.9115	0.9131	0.9147	0.9162	0.9177
+1.4	0.9192	0.9207	0.9222	0.9236	0.9251	0.9265	0.9279	0.9292	0.9306	0.9319
+1.5	0.9332	0.9345	0.9357	0.9370	0.9382	0.9394	0.9406	0.9418	0.9429	0.9441
+1.6	0.9452	0.9463	0.9474	0.9484	0.9495	0.9505	0.9515	0.9525	0.9535	0.9545
+1.7	0.9554	0.9564	0.9573	0.9582	0.9591	0.9599	0.9608	0.9616	0.9625	0.9633
+1.8	0.9641	0.9649	0.9656	0.9664	0.9671	0.9678	0.9686	0.9693	0.9699	0.9706
+1.9	0.9713	0.9719	0.9726	0.9732	0.9738	0.9744	0.9750	0.9756	0.9761	0.9767
+2.0	0.9773	0.9778	0.9783	0.9788	0.9793	0.9798	0.9803	0.9808	0.9812	0.9817
+2.1	0.9821	0.9826	0.9830	0.9834	0.9838	0.9842	0.9846	0.9850	0.9854	0.9857
+2.2	0.9861	0.9864	0.9868	0.9871	0.9875	0.9878	0.9881	0.9884	0.9887	0.9890
+2.3	0.9893	0.9896	0.9898	0.9901	0.9904	0.9906	0.9909	0.9911	0.9913	0.9916
+2.4	0.9918	0.9920	0.9922	0.9925	0.9927	0.9929	0.9931	0.9932	0.9934	0.9936
+2.5	0.9938	0.9940	0.9941	0.9943	0.9945	0.9946	0.9948	0.9949	0.9951	0.9952
+2.6	0.9953	0.9955	0.9956	0.9957	0.9959	0.9960	0.9961	0.9962	0.9963	0.9964
+2.7	0.9965	0.9966	0.9967	0.9968	0.9969	0.9970	0.9971	0.9972	0.9973	0.9974
+2.8	0.9974	0.9975	0.9976	0.9977	0.9977	0.9978	0.9979	0.9979	0.9980	0.9981
+2.9	0.9981	0.9982	0.9983	0.9983	0.9984	0.9984	0.9985	0.9985	0.9986	0.9986
+3.0	0.99865	0.99869	0.99874	0.99878	0.99882	0.99886	0.99889	0.99893	0.99896	0.99900
+3.1	0.99903	0.99906	0.99910	0.99913	0.99915	0.99918	0.99921	0.99924	0.99926	0.99929
+3.2	0.99931	0.99934	0.99936	0.99938	0.99940	0.99942	0.99944	0.99946	0.99948	0.99950
+3.3	0.99952	0.99953	0.99955	0.99957	0.99958	0.99960	0.99961	0.99962	0.99964	0.99965
+3.4	0.99966	0.99967	0.99969	0.99970	0.99971	0.99972	0.99973	0.99974	0.99975	0.99976
+3.5	0.99977	0.99978	0.99978	0.99979	0.99980	0.99981	0.99981	0.99982	0.99983	0.99983

*Proportion of total area under the curve that is under the portion of the curve from $-\infty$ to $(X_i-\mu)/\sigma$ (X_i represents any desired value of the variable X).

lated and put in tables (see Table 2-4 on page 2-11). Because Table 2-4 is left-reading, the areas associated with each value of z are for that portion of the curve from $-\infty$ to a particular value of z.

Example Calculation

Figure 2-13 graphically illustrates the diameter of shafts turned on a lathe. The diameters are normally distributed and have a mean of 1.00″ and a standard deviation of 0.01″. To determine the probability that a given shaft will have a diameter between 0.985 and 1.005″, it is necessary to find the areas under the curve denoted as areas 2 and 1; area 3 (the desired probability) is then the difference between area 2 and area 1. The calculations shown in Fig. 2-13 indicate that 62.47% of the shafts will have a diameter between 0.985 and 1.005″.

DISTRIBUTION OF SAMPLE MEANS

It has been shown that the sample mean, $\overline{X}$, provides an estimate of the population mean, μ. Because $\overline{X}$ is calculated from a sample from the population, it is an uncertain estimate of μ. That is, if a number of samples of size n are drawn from the population, each time calculating an $\overline{X}$, then these $\overline{X}$ values will vary simply because of sampling variation. The precision of $\overline{X}$ as an estimate of μ depends on the amount of process (population) variation and the size of the sample. In particular, as n increases, the sample variance of the $\overline{X}$s decreases according to the equation:

$$\sigma_{\overline{X}}^2 = \sigma_X^2 / n \qquad (9)$$

The *central limit theorem* states that sample means have a distribution that approaches the normal distribution for a sufficiently large sample size. As the sample size increases, the tendency to the normal distribution improves. Furthermore, the population from which the samples are drawn generally does not need to be normally distributed for the sample means to be approximately normal.

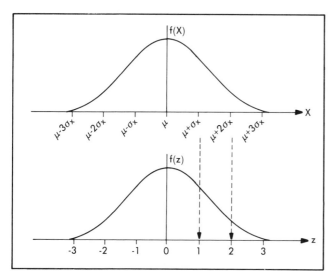

Fig. 2-12 Standardized normal curve.

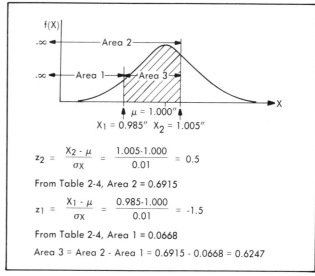

Fig. 2-13 Normal probability calculations.

CONTROL CHARTS

Collecting production performance data and keeping charts of this data over time is a common practice in industrial plants. Observation of dimensions, strengths, weights, yields, defects, and other quality characteristics can be of great utility not only in documenting performance relative to goals or targets, but more importantly in terms of the identification of ways to improve performance.

Regrettably, such data are often examined in a most cursory manner and then filed away never to be seen again. The primary reason for this apparent neglect of production data is that the data are often not conceived of, modeled, and then interpreted on a statistical basis. Many years ago, Walter Shewhart showed how such data could be developed and interpreted through the use of a very simple but profound statistical method referred to as the control chart. Shewhart's concept was that by monitoring process variations over time and modeling them statistically it would be possible to identify unusual process behaviors (out-of-control conditions) that were causing an erosion of both product quality and process productivity. The charts would indicate the presence of improvement opportunities and could lead to the appropriate remedial actions.

However, control charts were too often viewed as a tool to be used by operators on the shop floor to keep production tracking within the product specifications. If "points" showing out-of-control conditions were present, but the individual parts were within specifications, no action was usually taken. This misuse of the control chart concept was commonplace and eventually led to the abandonment of the practice.

The adoption and continuing use of control charts often requires production personnel to become accustomed to thinking about manufactured products and the associated processes in a somewhat different light. All processes are subject to variations that cause the product in terms of its quality characteristics to vary from the desired or target level. The majority of this variation comes from a multitude of sources inherent in the process and the surrounding environment. These are referred to as common, system, or chronic causes of variation. Collectively these sources result in the appearance of a natural, random scatter in the data.

Occasionally a much larger disturbance enters the system, causing a more serious departure from the targeted performance. This unnatural or chaotic variability comes from what are referred to as special or sporadic causes of variation. Examples of special causes could include the chipping of a cutting tool, failure of a machine bearing, changes in raw material composition, or substitution of an unexperienced operator.

A major objective of statistical process control is to recognize the occurrence of special causes in the presence of the constant system of common cause and to shed light on the nature of the special cause, thereby providing a basis for corrective actions.

CONTROL CHARTS

Control charts are one of the tools used to accomplish this objective.

The control chart builds a model that describes the way the process variability pattern is expected to appear when only common causes of variation are at work. Once this model is established through appropriate sampling and statistical data characterization methods, a basis is formed for identifying the occurrence of a variation that does not fit the pattern of common cause variation.

The control chart is similar to a jury in a court of law. Each piece of data from the sample is judged to determine whether it represents the forces of a special cause disturbance. Unless the evidence is overwhelmingly in favor of the occurrence of a special cause disturbance, a verdict of not guilty is entered. This means that there was no strong reason to believe that forces other than those of common causes are at work.

If a process under surveillance by periodic sampling maintains a state of good statistical control, this means that its mean level and level of variability remain constant over time. Nearly all the sample means ($\overline{X}$) would fall within a band of ± 3 standard deviations of $\overline{X}$ about the mean and would have a distribution of points that follow the normal distribution curve.

Because the chance of realizing a point outside the 3 standard deviation limits is so small if good statistical control is evident, the occurrence of such a sample result must be interpreted as signaling some special departure from the expected behavior. Figure 2-14 illustrates the presence of a special cause on a control chart for averages (X-bar chart).

While the control chart serves as a basis for action, it also indicates when to leave the process alone. If only common causes are present, any improvement of the process by simple "machine" adjustment will be difficult. Such adjustments can only lead to trouble because they may induce additional variation into the process and its products. Improvement of a stable process requires identification and removal of some common causes. In other words, it requires a fundamental change in the system.

A variety of control charts are available for monitoring and improving a production operation. The charts are generally classified according to the type of data they are based on. The charts most frequently used are presented in Table 2-5.[10]

VARIABLE CONTROL CHARTS

Generally, chaotic disturbances manifest themselves in two possible ways: (1) shifts or changes in the mean level of the process and (2) shifts or changes in the amount of process variability. Sample means ($\overline{X}$) may be used to determine when the former has occurred. The sample ranges, as well as other variability measures such as the standard deviation, can be tracked over time to detect possible changes in process consistency.

Chart Construction

Once the quality characteristic to be studied has been determined, data are collected. When collecting the data, the samples must be properly selected, which is often described by the principles of rational sampling. Rational samples are groups of measurements, the variation among which is attributable to only one system of causes. In other words, the samples should be chosen in such a way to minimize the chances of mixing within the sample measurements that reflect only common cause variations and measurements that have been contaminated by additional special cause variations. By selecting rational samples, the ability of the chart to detect special causes when they occur is enhanced.

Examples of nonrational sampling include sampling from multiple parallel machines, sampling over extended periods of time, and sampling from products of several sources. These

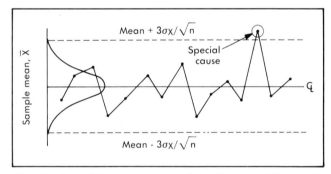

Fig. 2-14 Control chart for averages indicating a special cause of variation.

TABLE 2-5
Commonly Used Control Charts

Data Type	Chart Name	Value Charted
Variables	$\overline{X}$ and R chart	Sample averages and ranges
	$\overline{X}$ and s chart	Sample averages and standard deviations
	X and moving R chart	Individual observations and moving ranges
	Median and R chart	Sample medians and ranges
Attribute	p chart	Proportion or percent of units nonconforming (defective) per sample
	np chart	Number of units nonconforming (defective) per sample
	c chart	Number of nonconformities (defects) per inspection unit
	u chart	Average number of nonconformities (defects) per production unit

methods should be avoided. Rational sampling methods will be discussed further in the next section of this chapter.

As a good rule of thumb, 25 to 50 samples should be selected to provide a solid basis for the initiation of the control chart. Once the process is in a good state of statistical control, periodic recalculation of the control limits is necessary to update the information.

Given a set of rational samples from the process, the following six steps can be used as a guide when constructing control $\overline{X}$,R charts:

1. Calculate the average ($\overline{X}$) for each sample using Eq. (2).
2. Calculate the range within the sample using Eq. (5).
3. Calculate the grand average ($\overline{\overline{X}}$). This is the arithmetic mean of all the sample averages and is an estimate of the process mean (μ). The grand average becomes the centerline of the $\overline{X}$ control chart.
4. Calculate the average of the sample ranges ($\overline{R}$). $\overline{R}$ is the arithmetic average of the sample ranges and becomes the centerline of the R control chart.
5. Calculate the control limits for the $\overline{X}$ chart. The three standard deviation control limits are given by $\overline{\overline{X}} \pm 3\ \sigma_{\overline{X}}$. Because $\sigma_{\overline{X}}$ is equal to $\sigma_X/\sqrt{n}$, the control limits take the form:

$$UCL/LCL = \overline{\overline{X}} \pm 3\ \sigma_X/\sqrt{n} \qquad (10)$$

where:

UCL = upper control limit
LCL = lower control limit

As was shown in Eq. (6), the value for σ_X can be estimated by $\overline{R}/d_2$, and therefore Eq. (10) can be written as:

$$UCL/LCL = \overline{\overline{X}} \pm 3\overline{R}/(d_2\sqrt{n}) \qquad (11)$$

The term $3/(d_2\sqrt{n})$, which depends only on the sample size n, can be combined into a single constant, A_2. Equation (11) then changes to:

$$UCL/LCL = \overline{\overline{X}} \pm A_2\overline{R} \qquad (12)$$

Values for A_2 for varying sample sizes n are conveniently tabulated in Table 2-3.

6. Calculate the control limits for the R chart. Although the distribution of sample ranges is not normal and not symmetric, the symmetrical $\overline{R} \pm 3\ \sigma_R$ limits are conventionally used for the R chart. If the lower limit is less than 0, the lower control limit is assigned a value of 0. The control limits can be calculated by the equations:

$$UCL = D_4\overline{R} \qquad (13)$$

$$LCL = D_3\overline{R} \qquad (14)$$

Values for D_3 and D_4 have been tabulated as a function of sample size n and are also given in Table 2-3.

The following techniques should be used when plotting the charts:

- Place the R chart directly below the $\overline{X}$ chart using the same horizontal axis. This makes it easy to compare $\overline{X}$ and R results for individual samples.
- Use a heavy solid line to denote the centerline of each chart.
- Plot the individual $\overline{X}$ and R values as solid dots. Connecting these dots helps to clearly see the patterns in the data.

- Use a heavy dashed line to denote the control limits.
- Write the specific numerical values for the control limits on the charts as well as for the centerlines.
- Circle any points that indicate the presence of special causes such as points beyond the control limits.

Chart Interpretation

The purpose of the control chart is to monitor and evaluate the process performance over time. Initial chart use is directed toward identifying the presence of all special causes so that the process can be brought into a state of statistical control. Once control is established, continuing examination of the data patterns helps to indicate further opportunities for quality and productivity improvement.

When interpreting the charts, it is important to start with the R chart and get it under statistical control first because the limits of the $\overline{X}$ chart depend on the magnitude of the common cause variation of the process measured by $\overline{R}$. If some points on the R chart are initially out of control (special causes present), the limits on the $\overline{X}$ chart will be inflated.

Figure 2-15 shows $\overline{X}$ and R charts constructed from 50 samples of size $n = 5$. The charts show good statistical control because:

- No points exceed the control limits.
- The points are approximately normally distributed about the centerline on the $\overline{X}$ chart.
- The points show no evidence of trends or recurring cycles.
- The points look quite random with time. No patterns such as runs above or below the centerline are evident.

When just one subgroup average (or range) is beyond a control limit, the process is considered out of control. Further, because the distribution of $\overline{X}$ tends to be normal, serious departures from normality can signal the presence of special causes even if all points are within the control limits. Too many points near the limits or near the centerline may signal problems with the process such as overcontrol or with improper methods of sampling.

The occurrence of a trend or reoccurring cycles in the data pattern can indicate that the system is experiencing a drift or cyclical change with respect to its mean or range. Runs of points

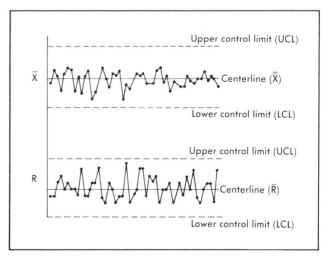

Fig. 2-15 $\overline{X}$ and R charts in good statistical control.

CONTROL CHARTS

above or below the centerline may indicate small shifts in the mean or level of variability.

Whenever an out-of-control condition is indicated, it is important to determine the basic process fault that is producing it. Some useful generic conditions to look for include the following:

Trends/cycles: Systematic changes in the process environment, worker fatigue, maintenance schedules, wear conditions, accumulation of waste material, and contamination.
High proportion of points near or beyond control limits: Overcontrol of the process, large differences in incoming raw material, and charting more than one process on a single chart.
Sudden shifts in level: New machine, die, or tooling; new worker; new batch of raw material; change in measurement system; and change in production method.

Up to this point, a number of general control chart patterns have been discussed, indicating various types of unnatural process behaviors. The unnatural patterns were fairly obvious even through the most cursory examination of the charts. Often, however, special causes of variation produce patterns that are less obvious. Therefore a more rigorous pattern analysis should generally be conducted.

Several useful tests for the presence of unnatural patterns (special causes) can be performed by dividing the distance between the upper and lower control limits into six zones; each zone is one standard deviation wide (see Fig. 2-16). The zones for the upper half of the chart are referred to as *A* (outer third), *B* (middle third), and *C* (inner third); the lower half is considered a mirror image. The probabilistic basis for the tests to be discussed using the zones is derived from the normal distribution. These tests are therefore applicable to an $\bar{X}$ chart and may be applied to the chart for individuals if it can be assumed that the data follow a normal distribution.

The various tests are illustrated in Fig. 2-17.[11] Although these tests can be considered as basic, they are not totally comprehensive. Analysts should be alert to any patterns of points that might indicate the influences of other special causes in their particular process. Tests 1, 2, 5, and 6 are separately applied to the upper and lower halves of the chart; tests 3, 4, 7, and 8 are applied to the entire chart.

When the existence of a special cause is signaled by a test, the last point should be circled. Points can contribute to more than one test. In this case, however, a point should be circled each time a test is satisfied.

SELECTION OF SAMPLES

Rational subgroups or samples are collections of individual measurements, the variation among which is attributable only to a constant system of common causes. In the development and continuing use of control charts, subgroups or samples should be chosen in a way that provides the maximum opportunity for the measurements within each subgroup to be subject only to common causes, thus providing the maximum chance for special causes arising between subgroups to be detected.

Sample Size

The size of the rational sample is governed by the following considerations:

- The sample size should be small enough to achieve the objective that all members of the sample are subject to one fixed system of variation causes. A sample that is too large may include some members that are subject to one or more different systems of causes, such as one with added variations due to special causes. If the sample size is large enough to allow this to happen often, the sensitivity of the control chart will be eroded.

- The sample size should be large enough to ensure the presence of a normal distribution for the sample means. In general, the larger the sample size, the better the $\bar{X}$ distribution is represented by the normal curve. In practice, sample sizes of 4 or more ensure a good approximation to normality.

- The sample size should be large enough to enhance the sensitivity to the detection of special causes, particularly for detecting small shifts in the mean.

When these considerations are taken into account, a sample size of 4 to 6 is likely to emerge. The most commonly used size is 5 because of the relative ease of further computations.

Sampling Methods

Consecutive sampling. The most common basis of selecting subgroups is the time order of production. One method of selecting subgroups by production time is to sample parts all produced at approximately the same time. An example of this method is as follows:

5 consecutive measurements at 9:00 a.m.,
5 consecutive measurements at 9:45 a.m.,
5 consecutive measurements at 10:30 a.m., etc.

In this example, the interval between samples is approximately 45 minutes, but each sample is randomly selected over a much smaller time period within this interval. Taking measurements of samples produced at the same time minimizes the chance for other than common cause variation within subgroups to occur and maximizes the chance for special cause variation arising between the subgroups to be detected.

Distributed sampling. If a process is subject to abrupt shifts in the mean level or variability and those shifts are sustained, then the method of consecutive sampling may be preferred. This is because the shift will be more easily seen from one sample result to another; however, if a process is subject to frequent abrupt but short-lived shifts in the mean, then a distributed sample may be preferred. Distributed sampling provides a better opportunity for detecting the shift through the *R* chart with more sensitivity than consecutive sampling. In the distributed sampling method, the various units in a sample are taken at approximately equally spaced time periods within each sampling interval. Distributed sampling can also be used to detect gradual changes in the mean because the opportunity is greater

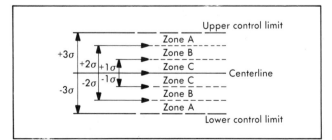

Fig. 2-16 Representation of dividing control regions into zones.

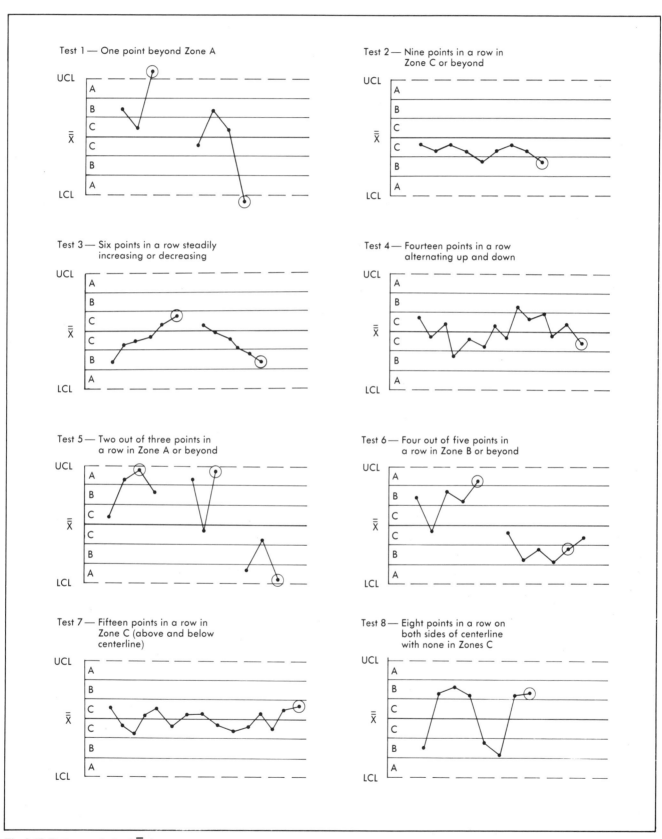

Fig. 2-17 Pattern analysis of $\overline{X}$ charts.

CONTROL CHARTS

to observe large sample ranges and more rapid changes in the sample means.

There is often a tendency to focus greater attention on the $\overline{X}$ chart and to be on the lookout for changes in process mean level. With this in mind, consecutive sampling may be preferred because it tends to have greater sensitivity to the detection of shifts in the mean. This is so because within-sample variability is a more likely reflection of only common cause variation.

Pitfalls in Sampling

In many situations, it is inviting to combine the output of several parallel and assumed identical machines into a single sample to be used in maintaining a single control chart for the product. Two variations of this approach can be particularly troublesome: (1) stratification and (2) mixing.

Stratification. In stratification, each machine contributes equally to the composition of the sample. An example of stratification is the selection of one measurement each from five parallel machines, yielding a sample of $n = 5$. When this approach is used, there will be a tremendous opportunity for special causes in the form of true differences among the machines to occur within samples.

R charts developed from stratified data will usually show very good control while the corresponding $\overline{X}$ control chart will show very wide limits relative to the plotted $\overline{X}$s and hence their control will appear almost too good. The wide limits result from the fact that the variability within subgroups is inflated due to the differences among the true means of the machines.

When serious problems do arise they will be very hard to detect because of the use of stratified samples. Stratification can be detected through the unusual nature of the $\overline{X}$ chart pattern (Test 7, Fig. 2-17) and rectified provided the concepts of rational sampling are understood.

Mixing. In certain applications, it is inviting to combine the output of several parallel machines/lines into a single stream of well-mixed product that is then sampled for the purposes of maintaining control charts. The resulting charts may show good statistical control, although special causes due to machine-to-machine differences will have been included in the sample. The mixing process creates a new population of parts, which when treated as a group (from several machines) precludes the possibility of detecting special causes attributable to problems with a single machine. This kind of sampling is difficult to detect from the appearance of the control chart. If wide differences in machine means are present, mixing tends to show some more extreme points on the $\overline{X}$ chart (Test 8, Fig. 2-17).

CHARTS FOR INDIVIDUALS

Often only a single value or measurement is meaningful for analysis. In certain situations, the notion of taking a succession of measurements to be formed into a rational subgroup of sample size n simply does not make sense. For example, process data such as temperature, pressure, voltage, humidity, conductivity, gas composition, viscosity, and results of chemical analyses consist of individual values, not averages. In these situations, the process output is fairly homogeneous, and special control charts must be used.

One pair of these special control charts is called X and R_m charts; X is the value of the individual measurements and R_m stands for the moving range. The moving range is the range of a set of consecutive individual measurements, artificially combined to form a subgroup of size n. In Fig. 2-18, the moving range is calculated for an application using three consecutive

measurements, which form the subgroups of size $n = 3$. It is important to note that the successive subgroups are overlapping. A commonly used artificial sample size is 2, in which case the moving range is comprised of the difference in two successive individual measurements.

The pattern on the X chart is analyzed in the same manner as other control charts. Points outside of the control limits are circled as well as those that indicate a nonrandom sequence. However, tests for unnatural patterns are less reliable in this situation than on $\overline{X}$ charts because the individuals charts are sensitive to the shape of the distribution of the individuals, which may be nonnormal and nonsymmetrical. At the same time, trends appear in the same way and mean the same thing as on an $\overline{X}$ chart. Checks should also be made to see whether the fluctuations are becoming narrower or wider, indicating a change in process uniformity. This can be done on the X, R_m charts.

Table 2-6 lists the process data for an example used to illustrate the construction of X and R_m control charts. The centerline of the X chart is set at $\overline{X}$. When calculating $\overline{X}$, the total of the X values is divided by 15. The $\overline{R}_m$ value is the centerline of the R_m chart and is also used for determining the upper and lower control limits of both the X and R_m charts. When calculating $\overline{R}_m$, the sum of R_m values is divided by 14 because there are 14 moving ranges for a subgroup size of 2.

The equations for determining the upper and lower control limits (UCL and LCL) are as follows:

$$UCL_X = \overline{X} + (3\ \overline{R}_m / d_2) \tag{15}$$

$$LCL_X = \overline{X} - (3\ \overline{R}_m / d_2) \tag{16}$$

$$UCL_{Rm} = D_4 \overline{R}_m \tag{17}$$

$$LCL_{Rm} = D_3 \overline{R}_m \tag{18}$$

Calculations for the control limits of this example are given in Table 2-6. The values for d_2, D_4, and D_3 are obtained from Table 2-3 for a subgroup size of 2 ($n = 2$). Figure 2-19 shows the X and R_m control charts for the data in Table 2-6.

ATTRIBUTE CONTROL CHARTS

Many quality characteristics of manufactured goods are not of the variable measurement type. Instead, they are more logically defined in a "presence of" or "absence of" sense. Examples of instances when this approach would be used include surface flaws on a sheet metal panel, cracks in drawn wire, color inconsistencies on a painted surface, voids, flash or spray on an injection molded part, or wrinkles on a sheet of vinyl. These defects or nonconformities are often simply observed visually or by some sensory device and cause a part to be classified as being defective. In these cases, it is said that the product quality is being assessed by attributes.

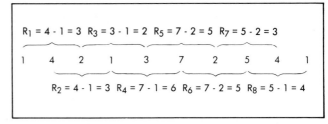

Fig. 2-18 Diagram showing how the moving range is calculated for three consecutive measurements.

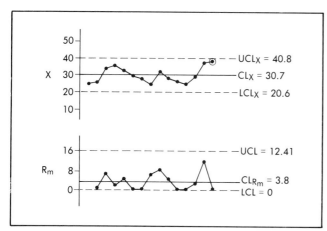

Fig. 2-19 Control charts for individuals.

TABLE 2-6
Sample Data for X and R_m Charts

Measurement	X	R_m	Range
1	25.0	—	
2	25.3	0.3	25.3-25.0
3	33.8	8.5	33.8-25.3
4	36.4	2.6	36.4-33.8
5	32.2	4.2	32.2-36.4
6	30.8	1.4	30.8-32.2
7	30.0	0.8	30.0-30.8
8	23.6	6.4	23.6-30.0
9	32.3	8.7	32.2-23.6
10	28.1	4.2	28.1-32.3
11	27.0	1.1	27.0-28.1
12	26.1	0.9	26.1-27.0
13	29.1	3.0	29.1-26.1
14	40.1	11.0	40.1-29.1
15	40.6	0.5	40.6-40.1
Total	460.4	53.6	

$$\bar{X} = \frac{460.4}{15} = 30.7 \qquad \bar{R}_m = \frac{53.6}{14} = 3.8$$

UCL_X = 30.7 + (3 x 3.8/1.128) = 40.8
LCL_X = 30.7 - (3 x 3.8/1.128) = 20.6
UCL_{Rm} = (3.267) (3.8) = 12.41
LCL_{Rm} = (0) (3.8) = 0

Sometimes a quality characteristic is inherently measurable, but measurements are not made in the interest of economy. For example, a GO/NOT-GO gage may be used to determine whether or not a variable characteristic falls within certain specifications rather than measuring the exact dimension. Parts that fail such a test are labeled "defective" or "nonconforming." Such data may be initially studied according to attributes to determine the presence of certain key factors that can be further analyzed as measurable data using $\bar{X}$ and R charts.

Two primary types of control charts exist for attribute data. The first type of chart is for nonconforming parts (defectives) and is called the p chart. The p chart is based on the binomial probability distribution. This chart plots the fraction defective in a sample over a succession of samples. A defective is a part or unit with one or more defects.

The other type of attribute control chart is for nonconformities per sample (defects). This type of chart is based on the Poisson probability distribution and is called a c chart. A defect is any fault that causes a part or unit to fail to meet specification requirements. Another closely related chart is the u chart, which is a chart for defects per unit rather than defects per sample.

The general chart construction procedures that apply to variable control charts also apply to attribute control charts.

p Chart

The p chart measures the output of a process as the number of nonconforming or defective units (d) in a subgroup of size n. Each unit is recorded as being either conforming or nonconforming even if the unit has more than one defect. The process characteristic of interest is the true process fraction defective, p'. Because of this, each sample is converted to a fraction defective using the equation:

$$p = d/n \qquad (19)$$

The data fraction defective p are the plotted quantity on the p chart.

The p chart is composed of a centerline and upper and lower control limits. The centerline (p') represents the mean value for p and the control limits are set at ± 3 standard deviations (of p) about p'. Because the mean value p' is generally not known, the trial centerline for a p chart can be calculated from the data:

$$\bar{p} = \sum_{i=1}^{k} d_i / \sum n_i \qquad (20)$$

where:

$\bar{p}$ = average fraction defective in k subgroups
d_i = number of defective units in the i-th subgroup
n_i = number of items inspected in the i-th subgroup
k = number of subgroups

The control limits for the p chart are calculated using the equations:

$$UCL_p = \bar{p} + 3\sqrt{\bar{p}(1-\bar{p})/n} \qquad (21)$$

$$LCL_p = \bar{p} - 3\sqrt{\bar{p}(1-\bar{p})/n} \qquad (22)$$

Because the binomial distribution is generally not symmetric, Eq. (22) may yield a value for the lower control limit of less than 0. When this occurs, a lower control limit of 0 is used.

Whenever possible, p charts should be used with a constant subgroup size; however, there are situations when the subgroup size varies. Because the control limits of the p chart depend on the subgroup size, some adjustments must be made to ensure that the proper interpretation of the chart is made. Some of the

CONTROL CHARTS

more common approaches used to handle variable subgroup size are the following:

1. Compute separate limits for each individual subgroup. This approach leads to a correct set of limits for each sample, but requires continual calculation of the control limits and a somewhat messy looking control chart.
2. Determine an average subgroup size and set the limits based on this size. This method may be appropriate if the subgroup sizes do not vary greatly, perhaps no more than about 20%; however, if the actual sample size is less than the average subgroup size, a point above the control limit based on that size may not be above its own true upper control limit. Conversely, if the actual subgroup size is greater than the average subgroup size, a point may not show out of control when in fact it really is.
3. A third procedure for varying subgroup size is to express the fraction defective as normalized quantity on a control chart where the centerline is 0 and the control limits are simply ±3.0. This stabilizes the plotted value even though the subgroup size may be varying.

c Chart

While the p chart monitors the fraction defective of the process, the c chart monitors the number of nonconformities (defects) per sample. A sample could only be one part, particularly if the part is an assembled item such as an automobile, a lift truck, or a washing machine. Examples of defects on a part are missing rivets on an aircraft wing and flash, splay, voids, and knit lines on an injection-molded truck grille.

Because c charts are based on the Poisson distribution, two conditions must be met to collect data and set up the control chart. First, the opportunity for the occurrence of a defect must be large. The second condition requires the probability of getting a defect at a specific point to be small. It is also important that the opportunity space for defects to occur is constant from sample to sample. Examples of a constant opportunity space are fixed length, area, and quantity.

In most applications, the centerline of the c chart is based on the estimate of the average number of defects per sample. This estimate can be calculated by the equation:

$$\bar{c} = \sum_{i=1}^{k} c_i / k \qquad (23)$$

where:

$\bar{c}$ = average number of defects per sample
c_i = observed number of defects in the i-th sample
k = number of samples

The trial control limits are determined from the equations:

$$UCL_c = \bar{c} + 3\sqrt{\bar{c}} \qquad (24)$$
$$LCL_c = \bar{c} - 3\sqrt{\bar{c}} \qquad (25)$$

u Chart

Although in most c-chart applications it is common to comprise a sample of only a single unit or item, the sample or subgroup may be comprised of several units. Further, from subgroup to subgroup, the number of units per subgroup may vary, particularly if a subgroup is an amount of production for the shift or day.

In these applications, the opportunity space for the occurrence of defects per subgroup changes from subgroup to subgroup, violating the equal opportunity space assumption on which the c chart is based. In this case, it is necessary to create some standardized statistic, and such a statistic may be the average number of defects per unit or item.

The average number of defects per unit is calculated using the equation:

$$u = c/n \qquad (26)$$

where:

u = number of defects per unit in a subgroup
c = number of defects per subgroup
n = the number of units per subgroup

When a certain number of subgroups are gathered, the centerline on the u chart is calculated using the equation:

$$\bar{u} = \sum_{i=1}^{k} c_i / \sum_{i=1}^{k} n_i \qquad (27)$$

where:

$\bar{u}$ = average number of defects per unit (centerline)

The trial control limits for the u chart are calculated using the equations:

$$UCL_u = \bar{u} + 3\sqrt{\bar{u}/n} \qquad (28)$$
$$LCL_u = \bar{u} - 3\sqrt{\bar{u}/n} \qquad (29)$$

IMPLEMENTATION OF SPC METHODS: A CASE STUDY

The following case study discussion is grounded in fact and details the experiences of a certain plant in applying statistical thinking and methods for quality and productivity improvement. Some liberties have been taken with the presentation because of space limitations and in the interest of emphasizing certain key points.

Background of the Problem

A certain plant, heavily involved in the injection molding of automobile components, was experiencing high and often erratic scrap rates on some of the products. As a result, the shipping requirements were producing a need to run with a considerable amount of overtime and often necessitated the running of backup dies on other presses to increase production quantity. Some troubleshooting activities were ongoing, and some improvement had been realized. As production orders increased during a time when automobile sales were increasing, the problem became more and more critical.

During this time period, the people in this plant were being introduced to the concepts and techniques of statistical process control, and it was decided that an excellent opportunity existed to not only attempt to solve a pressing problem using SPC, but also for those in the plant to gain some experience in implementing the techniques and gain confidence in the power and importance of their use. The product involved in this particular case study is a radiator grille.

Formulating a Strategy for Implementation

The first step taken by those in the plant was to form a group of individuals who were involved in the process. These individuals included operators, setup persons, supervisors, molding engineers, quality people, area managers, and statistical methods facilitators. They began to hold meetings to try to understand the problem and get everyone's input. It was decided to begin to collect data from the process during production and to use statistical charting to study the process variations. This required that the group address such issues as: What quality characteristics should be monitored? How should these characteristics be measured/observed? How many samples should be taken? And how often should they be taken? What other useful process information should be recorded? Other relevant questions were addressed as well. Because this was the first implementation experience in this plant, it was decided that the statistical methods facilitator and assistants would assume the primary data collection and analysis responsibilities. Ultimately such activities will become a natural part of the system as the role of inspectors, supervisors, and others slowly change under the adoption of the new way of doing business.

Prior to actually initiating the use of control charts, an orientation meeting was held for press operators and machine setup personnel to discuss the purpose of the study. At this meeting, the important role that these people would play in affecting improvement was discussed, and the management commitment to improvement was emphasized. Suggestions were sought, and as it turned out later, information obtained from press operators and setup persons was central to solving two major problems. The operators also attended an 8-hour presentation on basic control chart concepts and philosophies so they could understand the importance of using the statistical approach to problem-solving.

Operational Definitions

Perhaps the most difficult task in the entire process for the group was agreeing on what the defects were and how they were to be specifically defined. It was decided to focus on visual flaws such as scratches, black spots, and flowlines, but common agreement on what was important and what was not came slowly. The group realized the importance of writing down detailed operational definitions for defects so that all concerned were "playing by the same rules" and so the most quantitative and sensitive measures of improvement opportunities could be developed and invoked. Initially, Table 2-7 was developed to serve as a basis of observation and measurement of quality. Later, the operational definitions were modified to provide for more sensitivity in finding the root causes of the problems. For example, scratches may be acceptable in a product control sense on the nonvisual areas of the grille, but the mechanism putting the scratches on the grille puts them anywhere, depending on its random orientation at some point. Hence, all scratches should be observed and counted to increase the chart sensitivity.

Sampling Frequency and Data Collection

At the onset of the study, the occurrence of defects was rather high, and process behavior was erratic. Because of this, it was decided to collect samples rather frequently so that the clues to the causes could be developed based on defect data and information collected on other process conditions. The group spent many hours discussing potential special and common causes of variation (defect occurrence). This was deemed important to understanding what process data (temperatures, pressures, and material conditions) ought to be collected to provide a basis for doing the detective work that would ultimately lead to the root causes of the defects. Among other things, a process condition sheet was placed at the machine each

TABLE 2-7
Operational Definitions for Defects

Defect	Criteria
• Splay	Not acceptable on high surround or horizontal grille bars
• Scratches/scuffs	Not acceptable on visual surround. (Use grease pencil test)
• Flash	Not acceptable; must be repaired
• Oil	Minimal amount; should be wiped clean so that the residual amount will be removed by acid etch
• Grease	Not acceptable if it cannot be wiped clean
• Flowlines	Not acceptable in high surround. (Use grease pencil test)
	Maximum 1/4" flowline at base of surround (See sample)
	Flowline acceptable in lower rail and between vertical ribs
• Short shots	Front surface and visual ribs must be full
	Acceptable—only back rib behind paint step allowed short to 1/8" maximum (See sample)
• Burns	Unacceptable on visual surfaces
	Minimal amount acceptable on back rib surfaces
• Sinks	Unacceptable on visual surface Acceptable on bottom base rail at outer vertical ribs (See sample)
• Sprue on part	Part requires being scrapped
• Material buildup	No residue allowed
• Black spots	Unacceptable as groups on surface
	Acceptable in minimal number under surface
• Defective trim	Gouges and chatter unacceptable
	Flash standing can be repaired

Fig. 2-20 Control chart (*u* chart) for the number of defects from an injection molding process: (a) process out of control, (b) process after injection machine screw was changed, and (c) process after new vent system was installed on injection machine.

shift, and operators and setup persons were urged to jot down observations and/or thoughts they might have during the shift.

In the early stages of a study such as this, when process behavior seems erratic and the problems seem to be many, it is probably useful to collect samples quite frequently to clearly reveal the short-term and rapidly occurring changes in the process. For an attribute-based study such as this, sample sizes can be small if the occurrence of defects is great (an average of 2-3 defects per sample may be sufficient). As problems are found and solved, the process becomes more steady and defect rates fall, so less frequent sampling is in order although sample size requirements will increase.

CONTROL CHARTS

Fault Diagnosis Experience

After collecting a sufficient number of samples (25 is a bare minimum), a control chart for number of defects per item was constructed (often referred to as a u chart). Figure 2-20, view a, shows this initial u chart and indicates that a very erratic out-of-control process is present with a very high average defect rate ($\bar{u}$ = 4.5 defects/item). To begin to shed some light on the problem,

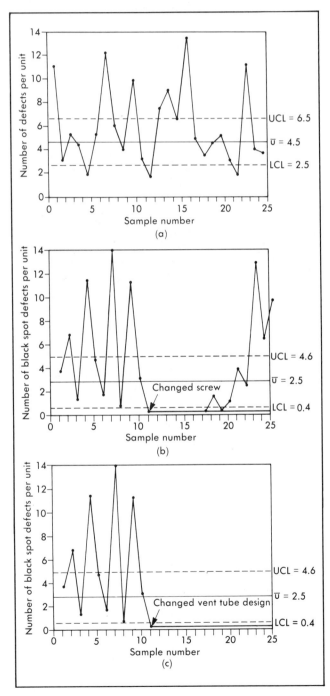

Fig. 2-20 Control chart (u chart) for the number of defects from an injection molding process: (a) process out of control, (b) process after injection machine screw was changed, and (c) process after new vent system was installed on injection machine.

a Pareto chart for defects was also constructed (see Fig. 2-21). The Pareto chart is a bar graph that indicates the relative frequencies of occurrence of the various types of defects observed and is useful in identifying major problems that may then be attacked in some precedence order. The Pareto diagram based on this initial u chart shows that black spots (degraded material at the surface of the part) constitute the vast majority of all defects at this point. The group decided to focus its attention for the time being only on this problem.

In an effort to identify the root cause(s) of the black spot defect, the group used the "fishbone" or cause-and-effect diagram. Such a diagram is shown in Fig. 2-22; the major cause categories include the human element, methods, machine, and materials. For each of these major potential cause categories, the group began to add increasing levels of detail to the diagram in an effort to reach the root cause level. For example, initial attention focused on the machine, in particular because the screw was felt to be worn out through extended processing of this raw material. It was reasoned that the material was adhering to the worn areas on the screw, which raised the temperature of the molten material to locally high levels at times, giving rise to degradation of the raw material. Particles of degraded material would then be carried along the screw and ultimately injected into the die cavity where they would appear on the surface of the part. Finally, the group recommended that a new screw be ordered and installed.

After some delay, the new screw was installed in the machine. Statistical charting was continued all during the diagnostic period and after installation of the new screw. Figure 2-20, view b, shows the u chart immediately before and after the screw was changed. Initially, black spots completely disappeared, and there was a great deal of backslapping and handshaking going around. However, a few days later the black spots returned with the same level of intensity as before the screw was changed. It was therefore evident that the root cause of black spots was not properly identified. Because charting continued as it should, this fact was clearly borne out by the u chart. This points to an important role statistical charting plays in clearly showing the short and long-term effects (if any are present) of taking a certain remedial action at the process.

The group continued to meet to discuss possible solutions to the black spot problem. It was noted that the design of the gas vent tube on the barrel of the machine was somewhat different than on most other machines and that operators complained of vent tube clogging and difficulty in subsequent cleaning. It was theorized that either material accumulated in the vent tube port became overheated and then periodically broke free and con-

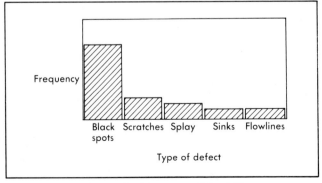

Fig. 2-21 Pareto diagram for defects on radiator grille.

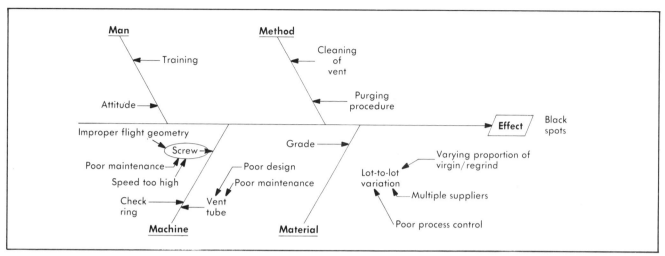

Fig. 2-22 Cause-and-effect diagram for black spot defects on radiator grille.

tinued down the barrel or was pushed back into the barrel during cleaning. A new vent tube port design was proposed to eliminate this problem. The maintenance department built the new vent system and installed it on the machine. Figure 2-20, view c, shows the u chart after the new vent system was installed and indicates the immediate and lasting effect of this process change on the occurrence of black spots.

With this major problem solved and a great deal of experience and confidence gained, the group enthusiastically continued to seek further improvement opportunities. As a result of the elimination of the black spot problem, the u chart was beginning to show signs of more stable process behavior, and the defect rate had dropped from 4.5 to slightly more than 1.0 defects per part on the average. The group prepared another Pareto diagram, which showed that scratches were now the most frequently occurring defect (see Fig. 2-23). Several theories were discussed, but the most popular was that offered by a press operator who felt that injected parts falling on the metal lacings of the press conveyor belt were causing the problem. The logical solution would be to use a continuous (vulcanized joint) belt. However, this solution was not viewed favorably because its unit cost was approximately double that of the existing belt and the installation time was also much longer.

To test the belt lacing theory, a soft latex coating was put on the metal lacings, and as sampling and charting continued, scratches disappeared completely for some time (see Fig. 2-24, view a). Eventually, the soft coating wore away and broke off with belt flexing, and scratches suddenly appeared again on the u chart. This again emphasizes the important role that continual charting plays in verifying the effect that a given remedial action may or may not have on the process. With evidence from the u chart that the belt metal lacings were causing the problem, action was taken to install a vulcanized belt on the press. As

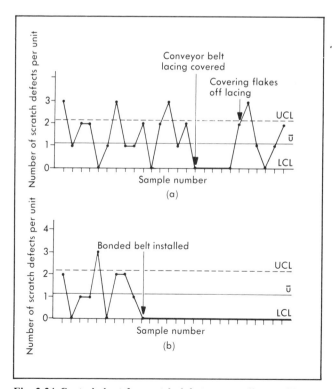

Fig. 2-24 Control chart for scratch defects on a radiator grille: (a) before and after latex coating was applied to conveyor belt and (b) after new bonded belt was installed on conveyor.

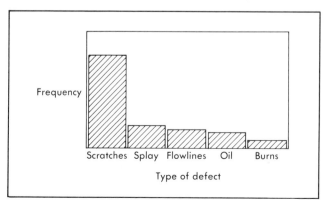

Fig. 2-23 Pareto diagram for defects on radiator grille after new vent system was installed on injection molding machine.

evidenced by Fig. 2-24, view *b*, this led to a permanent elimination of the problem of scratches.

It is important to point out that all presses in this plant had conveyor belts with metal lacings. Once this root cause was clearly demonstrated, the logical action would be to replace the belts on all the machines. This emphasizes the fact that many problems are common to a broad set of circumstances and that results from charting on a single machine can be usefully extrapolated to other machines. Although such may not always be the case, given resources and priorities, it certainly helped in thinking through the problem of being faced with putting parallel charts on perhaps hundreds of machines versus selectively charting a few key or representative processes.

With the scratch problem solved, the process defect rate had now fallen from 4.5 defects per part down to 0.17 defects per part. Scrap was noticeably reduced, overtime was eliminated, and the running of the backup die on another press was stopped. The economic implications here are obviously very

significant and need not be detailed. However, the group continued to work on further improvements and began in earnest to attack the problem of splay. The splay phenomenon was found to be quite complicated, and as a result, statistical experiments were designed and conducted to develop a better understanding of the root cause of this process defect.

As an important footnote, it should be mentioned that over the period of about 3 months after the scratch problem was solved, the defect rate fell from 0.17 to 0.08 defects per part for no apparent reason. The most logical explanation for this occurrence stems from the fact that as quality and productivity improvements were made, those involved in the process became more knowledgeable and concerned about the process. Press setup persons rarely needed to make adjustments, and management utilized the added free time at the press to perform more regular and thorough preventive maintenance on both the press and the mold. These factors undoubtedly would all give rise to improved process performance.

PROCESS CAPABILITY

Two issues need to be discussed when process data are statistically represented: (1) the ability of the process to produce parts that conform to specifications and (2) the ability of the process to maintain a state of good statistical control. These two process characteristics are linked together because it is not valid to determine process capability with respect to conformance to specifications without the process being in a state of good statistical control. Although statistical control does not imply conformance, it is a necessary prerequisite for assessing conformance.

In a statistical sense, conformance to specifications involves the process as a whole, and therefore attention must be focused on the distribution of individual measurements.

Because of the distinction between populations and samples, part specifications should not be confused with or compared to control limits. In fact, specification limits should never be placed on a control chart because the control chart monitors sample statistics such as $\bar{X}$ and R, not individual measurements. Placing specification limits on the control chart may give the impression that good conformance exists when it does not.

Occasionally parts produced by a certain process may not meet the specified production standards even though the process itself is in statistical control. One possible reason for this problem is that the process is not centered properly. This means that the actual mean value of the parts produced may be significantly different from the specified nominal value of the part. If this is the case, the machine should be adjusted to move the mean closer to the nominal value. Another possible reason for lack of conformance to specifications is that a statistically stable process may be producing parts with a high level of common cause variation.

To illustrate how a process capability study is performed, the following example will be used. For the process under study, many of the parts were being rejected when inspected using a GO/NOT-GO gage because they did not conform to the specified dimension of 0.140 ± 0.003″. It was then decided to study the capability of the process using $\bar{X}$ and R charts. Data were collected from the same machine and operator at a rate of one

sample per hour. Table 2-8 gives the results of 27 samples, each having a subgroup size of 5.

After the data were collected, $\bar{X}$ and R charts were constructed to determine whether the process was in statistical

TABLE 2-8
Data Collected from a Machine for a Process Capability Study

Sample Number	Measurement on Each Item of 5 Items Per Hour*					Average,* $\bar{X}$	Range,* R
1	140	143	137	134	135	137.8	9
2	138	143	143	145	146	143.0	8
3	139	133	147	148	139	141.2	15
4	143	141	137	138	140	139.8	6
5	142	142	145	135	136	140.4	10
6	136	144	143	136	137	139.2	8
7	142	147	137	142	138	141.2	10
8	143	137	145	137	138	140.0	8
9	141	142	147	140	140	142.0	7
10	142	137	145	140	132	139.2	13
11	137	147	142	137	135	139.6	12
12	137	146	142	142	140	141.4	9
13	142	142	139	141	142	141.2	3
14	137	145	144	137	140	140.6	8
15	144	142	143	135	144	141.6	9

(*continued*)

TABLE 2-8—*Continued*

Sample Number	Measurement on Each Item of 5 Items Per Hour*					Average,* X	Range,* R
16	140	132	144	145	141	140.4	13
17	137	137	142	143	141	140.0	6
18	137	142	142	145	143	131.8	8
19	142	142	143	140	135	140.4	8
20	136	142	140	139	137	138.8	6
21	142	144	140	138	143	141.4	6
22	139	146	143	140	139	141.4	7
23	140	145	142	139	137	140.6	8
24	134	147	143	141	142	141.4	13
25	138	145	141	137	141	140.4	8
26	140	145	143	144	138	142.0	7
27	145	145	137	138	140	141.0	8

*The values for the measurements are expressed in units of 0.001″.

control. The calculations for the centerlines and upper control limits are shown in Fig. 2-25 along with the plotted charts. The values for A_2, D_4, D_3, and d_2 are from Table 2-3 based on a subgroup size of 5.

The existence of statistical control is an essential condition for the continuation of the assessment of the process capability. If the process at this point is found not to be in control, no further meaningful statistical analysis of the individual measurements can be made. Attention should immediately be directed toward the identification of specific causes of variation.

Examining the control charts for this example indicates that the process is in statistical control; no points exceed the 3 standard deviation (3σ) limit, a reasonably normal distribution of points exists between the limits, and there are no trends or cycles in the data. The good control of the R chart indicates that the estimate of the process variation ($\sigma_X = 0.0037''$) is a reflection of the forces of common cause variation alone. Based on these results, the process can now be evaluated with respect to its conformance to specifications.

The first step in evaluating the data with respect to conformance to specifications is plotting a frequency histogram (see Fig. 2-26). Examining the histogram reveals that the data appear to be normally distributed with a mean slightly higher than the specified dimension of 0.140″.

Using the estimate of the process mean ($\overline{\overline{X}}$) and the process standard deviation ($\hat{\sigma}_X$) as well as the assumption of normality, the population distribution curve of the individual measurements can be sketched (see Fig. 2-27). The shaded area under the curve represents the probability of obtaining a part that does not meet the specifications.

To calculate the probability of a part falling below the lower specification limit and/or above the upper specification limit, the standardized normal value is calculated using Eq. (8) and

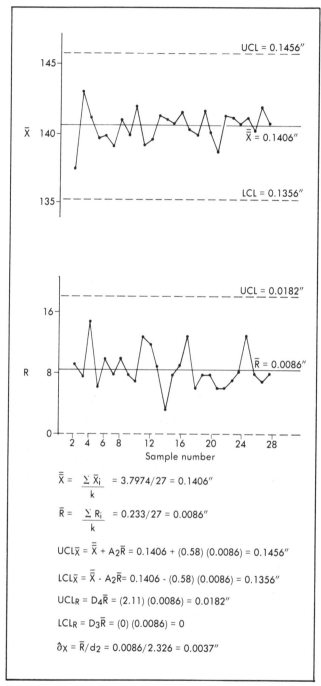

$$\overline{\overline{X}} = \frac{\Sigma \overline{X}_i}{k} = 3.7974/27 = 0.1406''$$

$$\overline{R} = \frac{\Sigma R_i}{k} = 0.233/27 = 0.0086''$$

$$UCL_{\overline{X}} = \overline{\overline{X}} + A_2\overline{R} = 0.1406 + (0.58)(0.0086) = 0.1456''$$

$$LCL_{\overline{X}} = \overline{\overline{X}} - A_2\overline{R} = 0.1406 - (0.58)(0.0086) = 0.1356''$$

$$UCL_R = D_4\overline{R} = (2.11)(0.0086) = 0.0182''$$

$$LCL_R = D_3\overline{R} = (0)(0.0086) = 0$$

$$\hat{\sigma}_X = \overline{R}/d_2 = 0.0086/2.326 = 0.0037''$$

Fig. 2-25 $\overline{X}$ and R control charts for process capability study.

the standard normal table (Table 2-4). The calculations for this example are as follows:

- Probability of a point below the lower specification limit

$$z = \frac{0.137-0.1406}{0.0037} = -0.97$$

From Table 2-4, the probability of having an individual part falling below the specified lower limit is 16.6%.

PROCESS CAPABILITY

- Probability of a point above the upper specification limit

$$z = \frac{0.143 - 0.1406}{0.0037} = 0.65$$

From Table 2-4, the probability for $z = 0.65$ is 0.7422, but this represents the area (probability) below the upper specification limit. Therefore the probability of having an individual part falling above the limit is $1 - 0.7422 = 0.2578$ or 25.78%. The total probability of nonconforming parts for this process is 42.37%. The percentage of nonconforming parts is clearly too high. Additional calculations may be made to determine the influence of recentering the process mean at 0.140″ instead of 0.1406″. These calculations are as follows:

- Probability of a point above the specification limit

$$z = \frac{0.137 - 0.140}{0.0037} = -0.81$$

From Table 2-4, the probability of having an individual part falling below the specification limit is .20.9%. Similarly, the probability of having an individual part falling above the limit is $1 - 0.791 = 0.209$ or 20.9%.

The total probability of nonconforming parts with the process recentered is 41.8%. It is evident that recentering the process does not significantly increase the probability of producing parts that conform to the specifications. Possible actions that are commonly evoked to deal with this problem include the following:

1. Continue to sort by 100% inspection.
2. Increase the tolerance on the part dimension to $0.140 \pm 0.006″$.
3. Use a more precise process to produce the parts, thereby reducing process variation.
4. Use statistical methods to identify areas where the variation could be reduced in the existing process.

Action 1 involves high costs of inspection and does not meet the real problem head-on. Action 2 may appear to solve the manufacturing problem, but product quality (functional capability) will likely suffer; the real problem is merely being passed on to others. Action 3 may prove to be necessary, but probably carries an increased price tag and should only arise if action 4 proves completely unsuccessful. Action 4 is really what this chapter is all about. It deals with the problem from both quality and productivity perspectives and hence will ultimately be proven to be the most economically rewarding action for everyone involved in the product's manufacture and use.

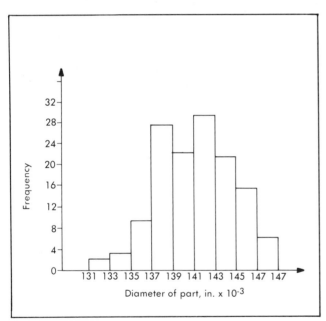

Fig. 2-26 Frequency diagram used in a process capability study.

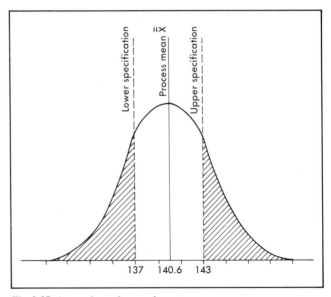

Fig. 2-27 Approximated normal curve.

ASSIGNMENT OF TOLERANCES

In previous sections, the issue of engineering specifications or tolerances arose on several occasions. In particular, the notion of transmitted variability from input variations in properties to output performance was considered. As such, this puts the issue of tolerances more directly on product function grounds rather than being simply treated as an allowance for the variations of the manufacturing process having no bearing on the performance as long as the input variation is within acceptable limits.

It is often necessary to consider how tolerances on individual components in an assembly are to be combined to determine the variations that will result in the assembled unit. Conversely, it may be necessary to partition an allowable assembly variation to assign the required tolerances to the individual components. Statistical models for variations can be very useful in approaching these problems.

STATISTICAL TOLERANCES

The following two examples illustrate some important statistical principles that will help determine how to combine or partition tolerances.

Example 1

The three-part assembly for example 1 is illustrated in Fig. 2-28.[12] Individual part tolerances for part 1, part 2, and part 3 are established to be $\pm 0.0040''$, $\pm 0.0032''$, and $\pm 0.0028''$, respectively. The nominal dimension AD of the assembly is the sum of the component nominal dimensions ($AB + BC + CD$). The processes producing the components are assumed to be in statistical control and normally distributed, and the process capability is ± 4 standard deviations ($\pm \sigma_X$); the bilateral specification for each part is therefore $8\sigma_X$ wide. This is often referred to as the natural tolerance of the process.

When the tolerance of the assembly must be determined, it is sometimes incorrectly assumed that the individual part tolerances are added together, yielding in this case an assembly tolerance of $\pm 0.010''$. However, if several assemblies were made and then measured, a smaller natural spread would be observed. When the assembly tolerance must be determined, it is necessary to take into consideration the statistical distribution of individual part measurements and the fact that the parts are assembled through random selection.

When parts in question are drawn randomly from their respective normal distributions, the chance of getting any single part with a measurement 4 standard deviations below the nominal is about 0.0005. The chance of getting all three parts having measurements at $-4\sigma_X$ is therefore extremely small (see Fig. 2-29).

Further, the additive law of variances states that for independently selected parts the square of the standard deviation of the assembly is equal to the sum of the squares of the standard deviations of the individual parts. In equation form, this law is represented by:

$$\sigma^2_{Assembly} = \sigma^2_1 + \sigma^2_2 + \ldots + \sigma^2_n \tag{30}$$

where:

$\sigma^2_{Assembly}$ = variance of the assembly

$\sigma^2_1, \sigma^2_2, \sigma^2_n$ = individual part variances

Based on this law, the standard deviation of the assembly in Fig. 2-28 is calculated to be 0.0015″. If the assembly's natural tolerance is also set at $\pm 4\sigma_X$, then virtually all assemblies will fall within $\pm 0.006''$ of the nominal assembly dimension. In fact, 99.73% of all the assemblies will fall within $\pm 0.0045''$ of the nominal assembly dimension; this value is less than one half of the value obtained by adding part tolerances.

Example 2

The reverse problem of the previous example is a problem of greater practical importance. Instead of trying to determine the assembly tolerance when individual part tolerances are given, this example will discuss how to determine individual part tolerances when an assembly tolerance is given.

The assembly tolerance of three identical parts is designated to be $\pm 0.009''$ (see Fig. 2-30). It is assumed that the natural part and assembly tolerances are $\pm 4\sigma_X$. It is also assumed that the part standard deviations are equal because they are made by the

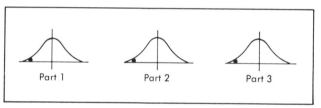

Fig. 2-29 The possibility of selecting three parts all in the far left tail of their respective distributions is small.

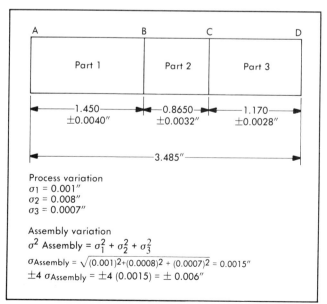

Fig. 2-28 Determining assembly tolerances.

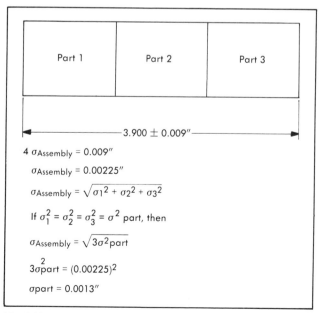

Fig. 2-30 Determining part tolerances.

same or similar processes. Based on these assumptions and the additive law of variances, the standard deviation of each part is calculated to be 0.0013″, based on given assembly standard deviation of 0.00225″. The individual part tolerance would then be ±0.0052″, which is much greater than a ±0.003″ part tolerance that would be specified using simple addition/partition.

Assigning tolerances by simple addition makes individual part tolerances too tight or overestimates assembly tolerances. If the part tolerances are too tight, the machining costs could be unnecessarily increased. Tight part tolerances may also cause individual parts to be deemed unacceptable and as a result scrapped, reworked, or downgraded unnecessarily.

LOSS FUNCTION APPROACH TO QUALITY CHARACTERIZATION

From a practical standpoint, part tolerances may need to be determined based on their cost effectiveness relative to part function (customer satisfaction). Furthermore, the economic effects of deviation from the target and/or excessive variation need to be evaluated in light of the strategies for process operation including such things as tool wear, associated tool change, die maintenance, and die repair. This is the role of tolerance design. The following example will be used to demonstrate how the concept of loss function is applied in the evaluation of process capability to the engineering specifications.[13] The quality characteristic of interest is the lever effort on a heater control. Very low efforts would cause customer complaints of flimsy feel or rattle, while very high efforts would cause customer complaints of stiffness. And in each case, the more extreme the condition, the more likely it would prompt a customer complaint. The total complaint rate is the sum of these two individual kinds of complaints. Between the extremes the net complaints from the two conditions drops low. A loss function of the sum of losses from both complaints can be developed as the curve illustrated in Fig. 2-31.

By choosing the point with the minimum loss as the target, it is possible to use the continuous loss function to give an economic interpretation to a specification limit (see Fig. 2-31). There are two possible choices at each measured part quality level X: (1) letting the part pass on to customer with an expected loss as determined by the loss function or (2) reworking or replacing the part at a cost. To minimize the total costs, the alternative with the lower cost should be chosen. The point of indifference between the two choices determines the specification limit.

Defining a Loss Function

In general, a loss function may be defined by evaluating the expected losses for several values of the quality characteristic. Assuming that a quadratic equation approximates the true loss function, then the loss function can be derived from the expected losses estimated from any two points, such as the loss at the target and the loss at one other point. The quadratic loss function together with the statistical distribution of the actual process output can be used to evaluate the expected loss per piece using the equation:

$$L(X) = k\,(\sigma_X^2 + (\mu - m)^2) \qquad (31)$$

where:

$L(X)$ = expected loss per piece of quantity X
k = loss coefficient
σ_X = standard deviation of the process
μ = the actual process mean
m = the target process mean

Centered Process

The example in Fig. 2-32 considers a process that is assumed to be in good statistical control and centered between a bilateral specification of ±1.0. The standard deviation of the process is $\sigma_X = 0.33$ so that, in terms of the traditional process capability analysis, the process is 6 σ capable. The replacement cost (k) of the part is equal to $1.00.

By applying the quadratic loss function, it is found that the $1.00 part carries with it an additional loss of about $0.11. This is a hidden loss above and beyond direct costs for materials, labor, and processing. It is experienced first by the downstream customers in terms of additional costs that they will incur or by decreased utility of the product.

The hidden loss of $0.11 could be reduced through some process improvement. Because the loss $L(X)$ is proportional to the square of the process standard deviation (σ_X), it is possible to reduce the incremental loss by reducing the process variation; that is, identify and remove one or more common causes of variability. Figure 2-33 shows the effects of reducing the process standard deviation to 0.10. The loss beyond the replacement cost of $1.00 is now only $0.01. It can be seen that a reduction in process variation by a factor of 3 has led to a reduction in the hidden loss by a factor of 11.

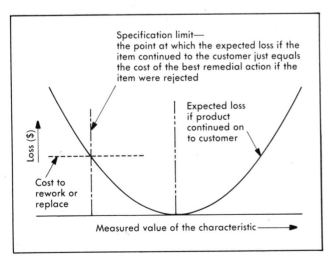

Specification limit—
the point at which the expected loss if the item continued to the customer just equals the cost of the best remedial action if the item were rejected

Expected loss if product continued on to customer

Cost to rework or replace

Loss ($)

Measured value of the characteristic

Fig. 2-31 Loss function curve.

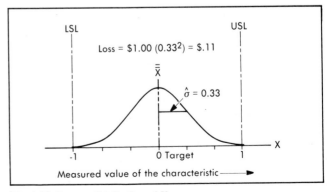

LSL   USL

Loss = $1.00 (0.33^2) = $.11

$\bar{\bar{X}}$

$\hat{\sigma} = 0.33$

-1   0 Target   1   X

Measured value of the characteristic

Fig. 2-32 Process distribution of X.

ASSIGNMENT OF TOLERANCES

Traditional manufacturing wisdom values such "better-than-necessary" performance in terms of process variability primarily because such a process can absorb some shocks from special causes of variation without generating nonconforming output. This example, however, shows that additional benefits can be gained from reduced variation even when the process is already stable, centered on the target, and has a natural spread well within the specification limits.

Noncentered Process

When a process shows a great deal more than just marginal capability, one way of capitalizing on this potential is to seek a short-term benefit by running the process toward one side of the specifications that minimizes, for example, material usage or cycle time. By taking the preceding example (standard deviation = 0.10) and locating the process mean as far to the low side as possible, Figure 2-34 shows the results of such an approach. This process, which generated only $0.01 in hidden losses when centered on the target, now causes $0.50 in customer losses when run close to the lower specification limit. Very few pieces

do not conform to specifications, and such a process would meet the explicit requirements of conventional purchase agreements. However, the loss arises because the output is consistently mediocre; in this situation, the customer suffers loss first.

It is clear that this evaluation of process performance is a global perspective and requires the understanding and appreciation of all participants in the total system. Unilateral decisions toward local optimization such as the consistent but noncentered process may appear to lead to short-term gain, but sooner or later the price for such action is paid by all participants in the system. Hence, it is important that marketing, sales, design, manufacturing, the supplier base, and the base being supplied all have a common vision and mutual understanding concerning the loss that products incur in the field because of functional variation.

Linear Drift Processes

Another common approach used to take advantage of small process variation relative to the specifications is to reduce labor or tooling costs by allowing the process to drift across the specification range. A tool change discipline that involves setting the process 3 standard deviations away from one specification limit and then letting the tool wear continue until the process is 3 standard deviations away from the other specification limit seems rational. For those who regularly must deal with the problems of tool wear, die wear, chemical solution replenishment, and the like, it appears uneconomical to think in any other terms. However, these apparent savings are not achieved without risk of hidden customer loss.

A normally distributed process with a standard deviation of 0.10 may be allowed to drift to its maximum extent, with its centers moving from -0.7 to +0.7. Figure 2-35 shows the process distributions at these extreme centers, as well as the resulting product distribution of a complete drift cycle. As can be seen, this net distribution is no longer "bell-shaped," but more "loaf-shaped."

The total hidden loss in this example is $0.17, coming mainly because the lengthy tool change interval causes marginally

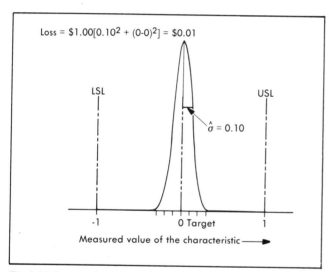

Fig. 2-33 Process distribution of X with reduced variability.

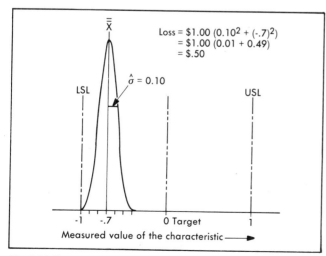

Fig. 2-34 Noncentered process.

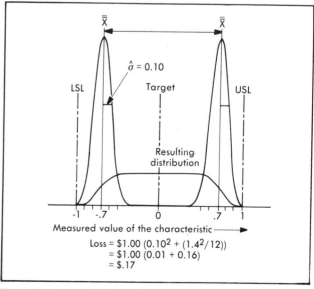

Fig. 2-35 Process with linear drift in the mean.

acceptable products to be produced near the beginning and end of each cycle. If the tool change interval was reduced by 30%, for instance, with set and change points at -0.5 and +0.5, the hidden loss would be reduced by almost half, to $0.09. It is apparent that tool change policy should really balance the economies of longer change intervals against the downstream

losses to achieve the lowest total cost. It is also apparent that when a process with relatively small variations is allowed to vary within the relatively wide specifications, rather than being maintained in statistical control near the target, this lack of shop discipline is not cost-free, but comes at the expense of the customer's and the producer's own downstream processes.

THE ROLE OF DESIGN OF EXPERIMENTS

It has been shown that bringing a process into statistical control in no way guarantees the existence of a capable process, rather only that process capability can be properly assessed. If the level of common cause variation is large in a stable process, process capability may be poor, and efforts must continue to identify the root causes of the major sources of chronic variation. Sometimes the knowledge and experience of those familiar with the process may be sufficient, when properly brought to the forefront, to identify actions that lead to improved process capability. Often, however, the underlying process mechanisms are not well understood, and hence it is necessary to build up new information to effect improvement. This new information may be obtained by experimenting with the process to determine the consequences on performance when certain changes are purposefully introduced. The field of experimental design grew out of the need to approach this problem in a valid, efficient, and meaningful way.

In the off-line pursuit of improved product and process designs or the on-line pursuit of process improvement, experiments may be run and data gathered to relate quality and productivity performance measures to key design and control factors. The purpose is to identify the best levels/settings for those factors. In fulfilling this objective, care must be exercised to ensure that the experiments conducted are valid and sensitive indicators of performance improvement opportunity and provide a comprehensive and realistic portrayal of the situation at hand. Ultimately, permanent design and improvement actions should only be taken when experimental results can be reproduced in the field. Proof of the persistence of important factor effects is the ultimate measure of the value of the decisions made.

In conducting experiments and analyzing product and process performance, difficulties may arise as a result of the environment under study or the manner in which the study is being conducted. Some simple but powerful experimental design strategies and tools may be invoked to mitigate these difficulties. It is beyond the scope and bounds of this chapter to discuss all of these issues or even some of them in any depth. However, a few key issues are briefly presented with the hope that attention to these considerations will lead to more meaningful experimental work.

CONSIDERATIONS IN EXPERIMENTAL WORK

When designing experiments, there are a number of important factors that must be considered. Some of these are involved with the forces of process variability and external noise that may cloud the experimental results if countermeasures are not properly planned for the experiments. In this section, certain key concepts in planned experimentation and the relationship between design of experiments and SPC are discussed.

Correlation Without Causation

In some situations, instead of conducting a designed experiment, data are passively gathered over time on one or more quality and/or productivity measures and on several factors that are felt to impact those measures. The data are then analyzed by techniques such as regression analysis in an effort to determine which factors are important. Unfortunately, such analyses may provide strong correlations between performance measures and product/process parameters of interest that have no basis in cause. Although such "nonsense" correlation relationships may be used for prediction purposes so long as the system does not change, they are not useful for design and control purposes.

For example, a strong correlation may exist between automobile sales and the level of Lake St. Clair, which lies between Lake Huron and the Detroit River, perhaps with a time lag of one month. Such a relationship could be useful in predicting next month's auto sales. It is doubtful, however, that sales could be controlled by pumping water in or out of Lake St. Clair. Such is too often the case in planning and designing manufacturing processes. Manufacturers passively stand idle and observe a correlative relationship, then use it actively in an attempt to improve the process, but nothing happens.

In short, there is only one way to learn how changes in a process lead to improved performance; purposeful change must be made to the process, and the effects of these changes must be observed. Such is the mission of planned experimentation.

Effects of Change

In many instances, the variables of importance are not clearly known without examination or analysis. It is desirable to be able to study several variables together, but "independently" estimate the effect of a change in each of the variables. Furthermore, it may be deemed important to know if a variable effect varies when other variables take on different levels. When such information on the interactions among the factors is sought, the arrangement of the tests becomes very important.

For example, suppose a chemical reaction is to be studied and the influence of concentration and temperature on reaction time is to be determined.[14] Two possible test arrangements are shown in Fig. 2-36.

The arrangement in view *a* is somewhat haphazard and cannot be used to observe the effect of changing temperature only because no two tests exist for which temperature changes but concentration remains fixed. When the outcome of any two trials is compared, both temperature and concentration change simultaneously. It is therefore difficult to sort out exactly what is effecting change and what is not.

DESIGN OF EXPERIMENTS

The arrangement in view *b*, however, provides for the opportunity to learn much about the relationships between the two variables and the reaction time. In particular:

1. The effect of changing either of the two variables alone can be observed.
2. It can be observed that the possibility that the effect of one of the variables altered can change as the fixed conditions of the other variable are altered. That is, variable interactions can be revealed.
3. In the case of temperature, it can be observed that the possibility that the effect of temperature can vary over the range of temperature (curvilinear behavior) for fixed levels of concentration.

The arrangement in view *b* is generally referred to as a *factorial* arrangement of test points and is particularly useful for comparison and modeling purposes.

Forces of Experiment Variation

It would be a happy state of affairs if, upon running an experiment on part shrinkage in the injection molding process, that a shrinkage result observed of, say, 3.2% could be literally interpreted. Unfortunately, if the experiment were repeated several times, different values would be observed for shrinkage each time. Although every attempt is made to carefully conduct the tests while controlling all those factors being studied directly, things are changing from one test to another. Most of these changes occur totally unknown to the experimenter. It is hoped that the many unknown factors, which are varying, collectively produce a reasonably small and randomly fluctuating error. Sometimes just one or two error factors can produce a large amount of the total experimental error. Strategies to deal with this problem will be discussed subsequently.

It is essential that an experiment is designed to provide for the opportunity to observe the amount of variation inherent in the test environment so that inferences on the magnitude and direction of variable effects can be made in light of the noise in the system. The amount of system noise can best be estimated from results of replicated experimental trials. Replication, not to be confused with repetition, is necessary to reduce risks associated with drawing a wrong conclusion from the experiment.

Replication of an experiment means that the factors under study, which define a unique trial, are separately and independently established or set on more than one occasion and the observed result is recorded in each case. Repetition, on the other hand, refers to the multiple observation of an experiment under a given set of conditions. If on two separate occasions the control settings on a machine are set to the same conditions and

a single part is made each time, two replicates exist for a given test condition. If on one occasion the machine is set to those conditions and two parts are made, we have two repetitions. In studying a process in control, for example, repetition could provide a measure of the common cause variation in the process under a given set of conditions. In trying to draw conclusions about the results of comparative experiments, however, replication is necessary to provide a realistic estimate of experimental errors resulting from errors in the settings of the independent variables and from variation due to fluctuating environmental conditions over the course of completing all experiment trials. Variation in repetitions would likely underestimate this total experimental error.

Relationship of Design of Experiments with SPC

If the phenomenon under study is already a viable and ongoing process, the pursuit of improvement opportunities through experimentation can be considerably enhanced by employing the techniques of statistical process control discussed previously. In such a way, sporadic sources of variation can be identified and then removed through remedial action. A stable process contributes to the ability of observing the effects of purposeful process change. Continued study in this fashion will further help to observe the persistence of changes that might be introduced.

Once a process is stabilized, continued attack on the common cause system leads to a progressively quieter process, further enhancing the ability to observe the forces of purposeful process change through experimentation. For example, a simple experiment can be run to see if a change in raw material viscosity has any real effect on the quality of a certain chemical product. Suppose that this change in viscosity actually does increase the average of the quality characteristic; $\bar{X}$ and R control charts are kept on the quality characteristic to monitor possible changes in mean level or amount of variability. Figure 2-37 shows two possible scenarios for this example. The time T_o is the time when the raw material viscosity is purposely changed. In view *a*, the level of common cause variation is so large that the increase in the process mean due to the change in viscosity cannot be seen on the $\bar{X}$ chart. The signal-to-noise ratio of the process is low because of excessive variation. In view *b*, however, it appears that the reduced level of common cause variation has provided the ability to detect the change in product quality (a run above the centerline is evident on the $\bar{X}$ chart).

Countering Nuisance Variation

The accommodation and treatment of sources of variation of either a more sporadic nature or of a more predictable nature has long been an issue when conducting experiments. Sir R. A. Fisher shed light on this problem and made significant contributions to improving the validity and sensitivity of experimental work.[15]

Emphasis on the fact that experiments ought to be comparative internally helps to counter the problems associated with the fact that the systems under study may not be particularly stable. Instead, their performance may drift in average level over time. For many processes under study, the notion of statistical control or stability may be of little meaning, especially when research and development work on new products and processes is being considered.

When certain factors cause a process to undergo systematic change, the technique of randomization can be used to avoid

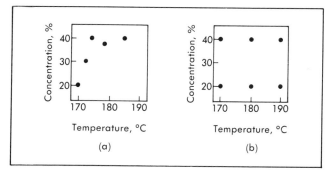

Fig. 2-36 Illustration of two test arrangements.

CHAPTER 2

DESIGN OF EXPERIMENTS

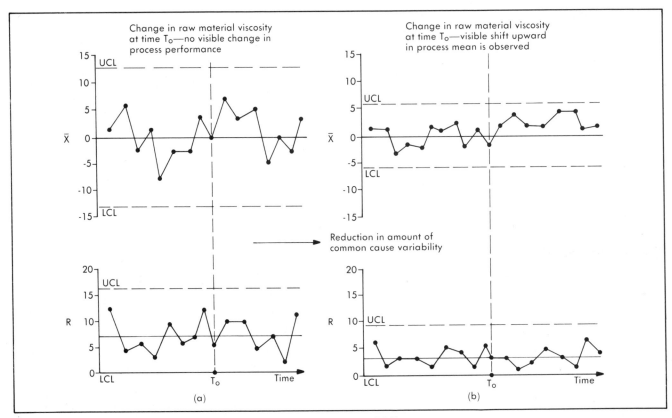

Fig. 2-37 Increased sensitivity of control charts due to reduced common cause variability.

the problems of nonsense correlation and the aliasing of the effects of factors under study with extraneous factor effects.

Fisher's work offers an important perspective on nuisance variation. A given prescribed treatment (experimental) condition could be adversely affected by the presence of variation conditions in the testing environment. Here, adversely means that variation in soil conditions, water content, amount of sunlight, or drainage conditions could cause excessive variation in performance among multiple applications of a single treatment. The variation erodes the sensitivity of the comparative experiment to the point where actual differences in average performance simply cannot be seen.

Of course, Fisher suggested that the experiment could be judiciously conducted in a series of smaller units or blocks, the conditions within which are controlled much more uniformly than the conditions from block to block. It is important that the treatment comparisons are made within the block, thereby eliminating the otherwise deleterious effect of the nuisance factor. As a result, a more sensitive comparative experiment is designed. Large variations due to differences in incoming raw materials, machine-to-machine or operator-to-operator differences, and/or large differences in ambient conditions from day to day could be examples of nuisance factors. When these factors are properly identified, they can be effectively dealt with through blocking in an experimental design strategy.

The following discussion demonstrates how the techniques of blocking and randomization may improve the sensitivity and validity of an experiment. Suppose two different methods of assembly of a certain subsystem are to be compared. The response of interest is the number of units completed per worker

per shift. Twelve assemblers across two shifts are randomly assigned to one of the two methods, six for each method. To make the comparison, an average number of units per shift is determined for the six workers for each method, and the two averages are compared.

The previously described design of experiments may constitute a valid comparison, but it may not be very sensitive because of large differences in skill level from one worker to another. A more sensitive comparison might be developed by using only six workers, each testing both methods. Comparison between methods could then be made for each worker and then averaged across all workers. The worker becomes the experimental subunit or block. Using this design, worker-to-worker variation is blocked from the comparison of methods.

Now suppose the initial experiment (12 workers) was run using the six workers on the day shift to test one of the methods and the six workers on the night shift to test the other method. Now shift-to-shift difference in overall performance due to worker skill level, level of supervision, and type of training could bias the results. The issue now is one of design validity, not simply sensitivity. In this case, shift differences would be confounded with method differences, and as a result, the comparison may not be valid. Randomization of the assignment of method type to worker across both shifts would solve this problem.

Taguchi's Approach to Extraneous Variation

Logic may dictate that comparative experiments can provide more efficient and reliable results if blocking is employed as an experiment design tool; however, there is another side to this coin. Central to Taguchi's definition of quality as loss due to functional variation in product/process performance is the notion of outer noise as a major contributor to performance variation.

Taguchi defines outer noise as sources of variation in product/process performance due to the presence of external/extraneous variables such as temperature, wind velocity, and humidity. The argument is that as these outer noise factors vary they produce functional variation in performance. In other words, they increase the amount of scatter/dispersion of the process. Outer noise factors could include incoming raw material variation, operator-to-operator differences, changing ambient conditions, or even differences in the performance of maintenance. The important things to remember are that:

- The variation sources are somewhat difficult to control or regulate.
- The variation sources are a real part of the environment in which the product/process functions.

Taguchi's approach is to employ design of experiments and often process simulation to understand how the forces of outer noise may be mitigated through the adroit manipulation of controllable variables (process/product design factors). Taguchi refers to this as the method of parameter design. It is a totally different way of thinking about extraneous/external or nuisance noise factors.

When outer noise sources can be identified and "controlled" either in a physical experiment or through simulation, Taguchi has suggested the use of inner and outer array experimental design structures. Through such experiments, adjustments in design/control factors are sought that temper the effects of outer noise factors. In other words, a robust design/process is sought. The emphasis here is on achieving more consistent performance in the face of the inevitable presence of noise in the environment in which the product/process functions. An examination of experimental design structures and how they can be used to facilitate the development of robust products and processes is discussed subsequently.

TWO-LEVEL FACTORIAL DESIGN EXPERIMENTS

When experimental programs are to be undertaken, the most fundamental question to be answered is: "What specific arrangement of test conditions should be planned to study the way in which a set of factors influence the quality and productivity measures of interest?" For example, the process might be injection molding, the part an automobile grille, the quality response could be part weight, and the factors of interest might be screw speed, material melt flow index, cycle time, and holding pressure. In setting up the experiment, it would be necessary to determine what set of varying process conditions ought to be considered as an experiment design to evaluate how these four factors influence part weight.

One common approach to the problem is to first select a range of interest for each of the factors and then run a series of experiments varying only one factor at a time. The results for tests varying only cycle time could appear as shown in Fig. 2-38. The procedure is then repeated for each of the other three factors (screw speed, melt flow index, holding pressure) and their curves developed.

Some of the problems that exist with this one-factor-at-a-time approach to experimentation are the following:

1. Too many tests required. Usually the number of levels for each factor is chosen to be many more than is reasonably required. For example, in Fig. 2-38, seven different cycle times are considered, but the resulting relationship is roughly a straight line, which could have been determined using only two cycle times. Even if the relationship was strongly curvilinear, using three or four different cycle times over the range would probably be adequate.

2. Poor long-range planning. With this approach there is a tendency to focus on one factor, study it, and, if a solution to the problem is not found, then some other factor is studied. The resulting experimental program often becomes a random walk across the product/process factor environment.

3. Failure to recognize factor interactions. Often the way in which a certain factor influences the test outcome depends

on the level/setting of one or more other factors. For example, in Fig. 2-39, increasing holding pressure increases weight when the screw speed is 20 fpm, but decreases weight when the screw speed is 50 fpm. It is difficult to clearly see these interactions when experiments are performed by varying only one variable at a time.

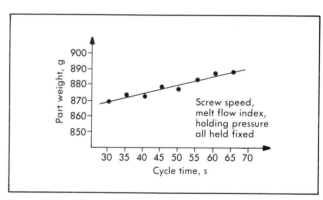

Fig. 2-38 Experiments of one factor at a time.

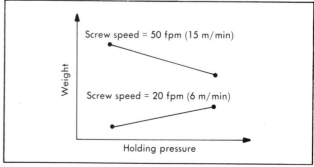

Fig. 2-39 A two-way diagram for interaction analysis.

TWO-LEVEL FACTORIALS

4. Difficult to control. When experiments are conducted in a systematic fashion, conducted over a long period of time, or when they proceed in a somewhat ad hoc fashion, it becomes difficult to deal with the presence of nuisance factors in the experimental environment such as accommodating blocking and/or randomization. Experiments involving several factors require thoughtful advance planning and a unified approach.

FEATURES OF TWO-LEVEL FACTORIALS

In an effort to overcome the problems previously discussed, a simple but powerful class of experiments commonly referred to as *two-level factorial designs* can be used. These experimental designs jointly examine a group of factors (k = the number of factors), with each factor taking on two distinct levels or settings. All possible combinations of the k factors over two levels each are considered; there are a total of 2^k unique test conditions.

Some of the advantages of two-level factorials are that they:

- Provide for the independent determination of the average effect that each factor has on the response.
- Provide a structure that can easily reveal variable interactions.
- Provide a structure amenable to the techniques of blocking and randomization.
- Do not require many tests (as long as k is not large).
- Have an appealing geometric representation that makes them simple to visualize, explain to others, and interpret.
- Constitute a basic building block for further experimentation.
- Have an associated mathematical model that explicitly relates the process response to the factors under study.

Although a 2^k factorial may have up to a k factor interaction effect, most problems only require consideration of main effects and two-factor interaction effects. The main effect is a measure of how much change occurs in the process response on the average when a given factor is varied from one level to the other level. It is the average change in the response in the sense that the individual measures of change are averaged over the high and low levels of all the other variables. The two-factor interaction effect is a measure of the extent to which the individual (main) effect of any given factor depends on the specific levels of some other factor. The two-factor interaction is also an average in that it is averaged over the two levels of all other variables.

In the effect definitions previously mentioned, consideration is given to how changes in the factor(s) influence the mean of the process (mean response). Sometimes such effects are referred to as location effects. In a subsequent section, the manner in which changes in the factors influence the variability of the process (variation response) will be discussed. These effects are referred to as dispersion effects.

TWO-LEVEL FACTORIAL EXPERIMENT EXAMPLE

High-carbon steel has been extensively used for railway track because of its high strength and low cost; however, because of its high carbon content it is not easy to weld, thus making repair and reinforcement in the field difficult. According to the code of the American Welding Society (AWS), additional steps of preheating and postheating are required to obtain good-quality welds. Several years ago the Rail Steel Bar Association sponsored a research project at the Welding Research Laboratory of the University of Wisconsin to study whether preheating and postheating were really needed.[16]

A statistical experimental design that was formulated for this study was a two-level, three-variable factorial design, simply designated as a *2^3 factorial design*. Two levels were chosen for each variable based on desired field conditions to be simulated. The high and low levels of the three variables are given in Table 2-9.

The test condition matrix in both coded and uncoded form is shown in Table 2-10. The eight sets of test conditions are given

TABLE 2-9
Data for Two-Level, Three-Variable Factorial Design

Variable	Unit	Low Level	High Level
Ambient temperature, T	°F	0	70
Wind velocity, V	mph	0	20
Bar size, B	$1/8''$	4	11

TABLE 2-10
Test Condition Matrix for a Two-Level, Three-Variable Factorial Design

Test Number	Coded Test Conditions			Actual Test Conditions		
	X_1	X_2	X_3	T, °F	V, mph	B, $1/8''$
1	-1	-1	-1	0	0	
2	1	-1	-1	70	0	4
3	-1	1	-1	0	20	4
4	1	1	-1	70	20	4
5	-1	-1	1	0	0	11
6	1	-1	1	70	0	11
7	-1	1	1	0	20	11
8	1	1	1	70	20	11

TWO-LEVEL FACTORIALS

by the eight rows corresponding to test numbers 1-8. The three factors being studied are represented by X_1, X_2, and X_3. The actual levels of the factors are coded to -1 and +1 values; a -1 represents the low level, and a +1 represents the high level. Other coding notations are also used for the test condition matrix of a two-level factorial. In place of -1, a minus sign (-) or zero (0) can be used; in place of +1, a plus sign (+) or one (1) can be used. Although the tests are written down (1-8) in a systematic order, they should be performed in a random order for the reasons previously discussed.

If the three variables are considered as three mutually perpendicular coordinate axes (X_1, X_2, and X_3), the 2^3 factorial design can be represented geometrically as a cube (see Fig. 2-40). The numbers encircled at the eight corners of the cube represent the corresponding test numbers in standard order. The eight actual test conditions are given in brackets.

Each of the eight tests performed in this example were replicated for a total of sixteen tests (see Table 2-11). The main purpose of running replicated tests is to provide for the estimation of the experimental error. The response for each of these welding experiments is the ultimate tensile strength of the welds, and the average responses for each test condition are also provided in Fig. 2-40.

Geometrically, the main effect of the ambient temperature on the ultimate tensile strength of the welds is the difference between the average test result on plane II and the average test result on plane I (refer to Fig. 2-40); therefore, the main effect equation for ambient temperature is:

$$E_1 = \left(\frac{\overline{Y}_2 + \overline{Y}_4 + \overline{Y}_6 + \overline{Y}_8}{4} \right) - \left(\frac{\overline{Y}_1 + \overline{Y}_3 + \overline{Y}_5 + \overline{Y}_7}{4} \right)$$

where:

E_1 = the main effect of temperature, ksi (MPa)
$\overline{Y}_i$ = the average response (i = 1 through 8), ksi (MPa)

Substituting the data from Table 2-11 into this equation yields main effect of temperature of +9.15 ksi (63 MPa). The interpretation of this main effect is that, on the average, increasing the ambient temperature from its low level to its high level causes an increase in ultimate tensile strength of 9.15 ksi (63 MPa). In a similar fashion, the main effects of wind velocity (X_2) and bar size (X_3) are calculated to be -5.10 ksi (-35 MPa) and 0.85 ksi (5.9 MPa), respectively. These main effects are graphically depicted in Fig. 2-40.

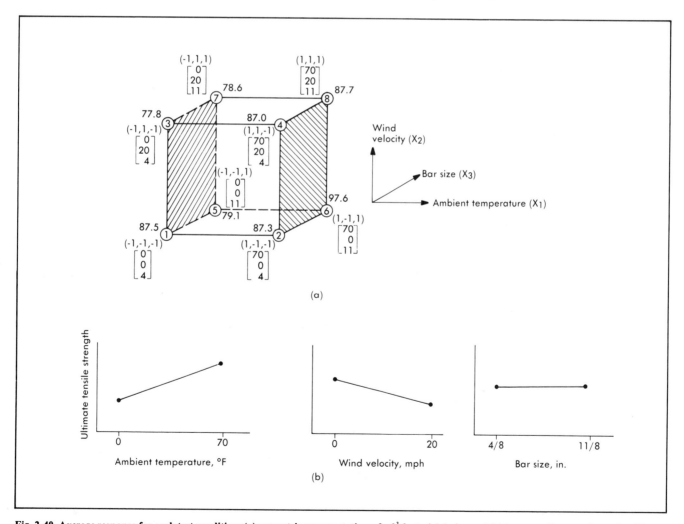

Fig. 2-40 Average response for each test condition: (a) geometric representation of a 2^3 factorial design and (b) two-way diagrams for main effects.

TWO-LEVEL FACTORIALS

TABLE 2-11
Results of the 16 Welding Experiments

Test Number	Ambient Temperature	Wind Velocity	Bar Size	Test Order for	Ultimate Tensile Strength, ksi (MPa)		Test Order for	Average Response, ksi (MPa)
(i)	X_1	X_2	X_3	Y_{ai}	Y_{ai}	Y_{bi}	Y_{bi}	$\bar{Y}_i = (Y_{ai} + Y_{bi})/2$
1	-1	-1	-1	6	84.0(579)	91.0(627)	3	87.5(603)
2	1	-1	-1	8	90.6(625)	84.0(579)	7	87.3(602)
3	-1	1	-1	1	69.6(480)	86.0(593)	5	77.8(536)
4	1	1	-1	2	76.0(524)	98.0(676)	4	87.0(600)
5	-1	-1	1	5	77.7(536)	80.5(555)	8	79.1(545)
6	1	-1	1	3	99.7(687)	95.5(658)	1	97.6(673)
7	-1	1	1	4	82.7(570)	74.5(514)	2	78.6(542)
8	1	1	1	7	93.7(646)	81.7(563)	6	87.7(605)

An alternate way to view the main effect of temperature is to compare or contrast pairs of tests that vary in ambient temperature setting, but have fixed levels of wind velocity and bar size. Such contrasts are evident in Fig. 2-40 as results are compared from left to right on the cube. The average of the four contrasts is equivalent to the main effect and the main effect of the ambient temperature would be represented by the equation:

$$E_1 = [(\bar{Y}_2 - \bar{Y}_1) + (\bar{Y}_4 - \bar{Y}_3) + (\bar{Y}_6 - \bar{Y}_5) + (\bar{Y}_8 - \bar{Y}_7)]/4$$

The main effect of wind velocity and bar size could be viewed in a similar manner.

In calculating the main effect of ambient temperature, both the amount and direction of change in weld strength with a change in temperature appeared to depend on the particular levels of wind velocity and bar size (see Table 2-12). It is therefore important to determine the interaction effects among temperature, wind velocity, and bar size.

To examine the interaction between temperature and wind velocity, it is convenient to think in terms of compressing the cube of Fig. 2-40 in the bar size direction. Compressing the cube means that the response values for given temperature and wind velocity combinations are averaged across the high and low levels of the bar size. The result is that the cube becomes a square (see Fig. 2-41). The interaction between temperature and bar size and wind velocity and bar size can also be examined in a similar manner. The calculation of these interactions is as follows:

Interaction between temperature and wind velocity:

$$E_{12} = [(87.35-78.20) - (92.45-83.30)]/2 = 0$$

Interaction between temperature and bar size:

$$E_{13} = [(92.65 - 78.85) - (87.15-82.65)]/2 = 4.65$$

Interaction between wind velocity and bar size:

$$E_{23} = [(83.15-88.35) - (82.40-87.40)]/2 = -0.1$$

A graphical summary of all the factor effects for this two-level factorial experiment is given in Fig. 2-42.

It is important to note that nothing has been said about the size of the estimated variable effects relative to the level of the experimental error. Error analysis can be based on the replication in the experiment. For this problem, it turns out that the error (standard error) of an effect estimate is about 4.11 ksi (28.3 MPa). As a result, it would appear that perhaps only the average main effect of temperature is important. Refer to the

TABLE 2-12
Change in Weld Strength as Related to Changes in Temperature

Wind Velocity	Bar Size	Effect of Temperature
0 mph	4/8″	-0.2 ksi
20 mph	4/8″	+9.2 ksi
0 mph	11/8″	+18.5 ksi
20 mph	11/8″	+9.1 ksi

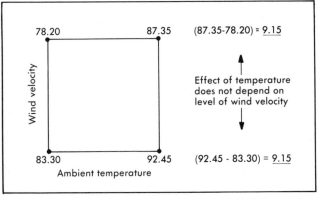

Fig. 2-41 Two-way diagram of temperature to wind velocity interaction effect.

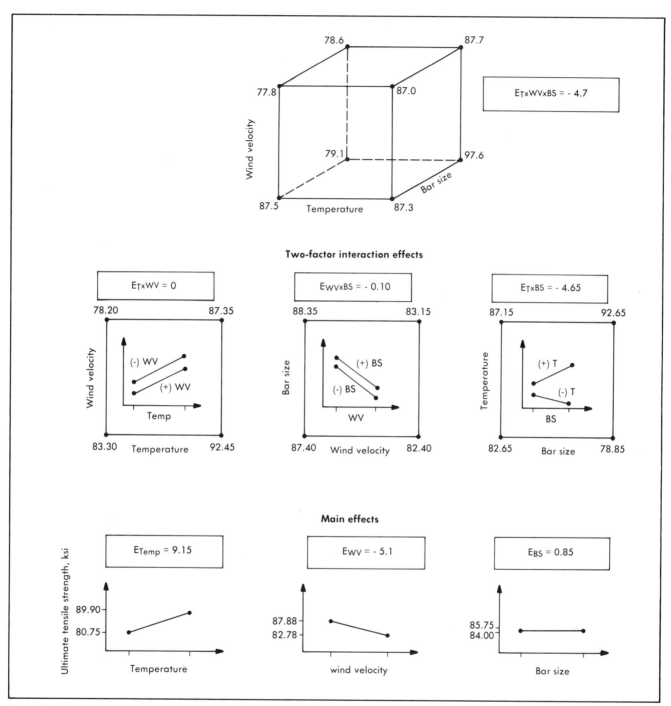

Fig. 2-42 Summary diagrams of variable effects.

reference by Box, Hunter, and Hunter for a complete discussion and analysis of the relative importance of variable effects as judged in relation to the level of inherent error in the experiment.

UNREPLICATED EXPERIMENTS

When it is not feasible or desirable to include replications in a two-level factorial experiment, it is not possible to obtain a direct measure of the experimental error for statistical analysis of the relative importance of the factor effects. In such cases, the use of normal probability plots of the effect estimates will aid in the assessment of their relative importance.[17,18]

The use of probability plots to determine the importance of the effect estimates is based on the following two facts:

1. Effect estimates tend to be normally distributed due to the central limit theorem because they represent linear combinations of the response data.

TWO-LEVEL FACTORIALS

2. Effect estimates that are small (the true effect is 0) may be thought of as arising from a normal distribution with a mean of 0 and therefore will fall about a common straight line when plotted on normal probability paper. Effect estimates that are significant have a true mean other than 0 and will fall off this line.

A coded test condition matrix is given in Table 2-13 for an experiment that was conducted to study the effect of various processing conditions on the rear edge dimension of a certain part. The values of the high and low levels for the four variables in this experiment are given in Table 2-14, and the effect estimates are given in Table 2-15. To assess the relative importance of the effects, normal probability plots can be constructed.

Calculations. To prepare a normal probability plot of the effect estimates, the following procedure is used:

1. Arrange the effect estimates in ascending order (see Table 2-16).

2. Calculate the cumulative probability associated with each effect estimate in ascending order using the equation:

$$P(i) = [(i - 0.5)/m] (100\%) \qquad (32)$$

where:

$P(i)$ = cumulative probability for the i-th estimate in ascending order, %
i = ascending order
m = total number of main effect and interaction effect estimates

The effect estimates and the cumulative probabilities may be conveniently set out in tabular form as in Table 2-16.

3. Plot cumulative probability, P(i), versus the i-th ordered effect estimate on normal probability paper (see Fig. 2-43).

Interpretation. As the plot in Fig. 2-43 is examined, many of the effect estimates fall on a nice straight line centered about 0.

TABLE 2-13
Test Condition Matrix for Unreplicated Data

Test	1	2	3	4	Rear Height, in.
1	-	-	-	-	0.375
2	+	-	-	-	0.475
3	-	+	-	-	0.500
4	+	+	-	-	0.475
5	-	-	+	-	0.534
6	+	-	+	-	0.550
7	-	+	+	-	0.600
8	+	+	+	-	0.642
9	-	-	-	+	0.342
10	+	-	-	+	0.450
11	-	+	-	+	0.558
12	+	+	-	+	0.467
13	-	-	+	+	0.500
14	+	-	+	+	0.634
15	-	+	+	+	0.642
16	+	+	+	+	0.542

TABLE 2-14
High and Low Levels of a Four-Variable Experiment with Unreplicated Data

Variable	Levels	
	-	+
1. Oven temperature, °F (°C)	374 (190)	392 (200)
2. Oven setting, bottom	50/40	70/40
3. Oven cycle time, s	80	100
4. Delay time, s	20	30

TABLE 2-15
Effect Estimates of Unreplicated Data

Effect	Estimate	Effect	Estimate	Effect	Estimate
E_1	0.023	E_{13}	0.000	E_{123}	0.015
E_2	0.071	E_{14}	-0.010	E_{124}	-0.042
E_3	0.125	E_{23}	-0.019	E_{134}	0.004
E_4	-0.002	E_{24}	0.000	E_{234}	-0.027
E_{12}	-0.067	E_{34}	0.000	E_{1234}	-0.023

TABLE 2-16
Ranking and Probability of Effect Estimates

Ascending Order, i	Effect Estimates	Identity of Estimates	$P(i)$,%
1	-0.067	12	3.3
2	-0.042	124	10.0
3	-0.027	234	16.7
4	-0.023	1234	23.3
5	-0.019	23	30.0
6	-0.010	14	36.7
7	-0.002	4	43.3
8	0.000	13	50.0
9	0.000	24	56.7
10	0.000	34	63.3
11	0.004	134	70.0
12	0.015	123	76.7
13	0.023	1	83.3
14	0.071	2	90.0
15	0.125	3	96.7

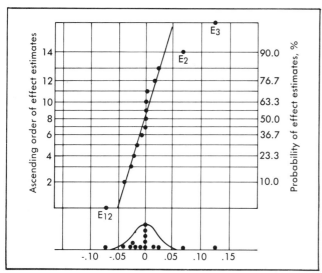

Fig. 2-43 Normal probability plot.

These effects are considered unimportant. Effect estimates 2, 3, and 12 do not follow the line. Because of this, these effects are considered important.

ALGEBRAIC REPRESENTATION

Although the geometric representation of the two-level factorial provides a useful basis for analysis and interpretation, it is not a convenient way to estimate the factor effects, particularly if four or more factors are involved. However, a simple algebraic method can be employed using a matrix representation (see Table 2-17). The first three columns (from the left, X_1, X_2, X_3) are referred to as the *design matrix*. They define the test conditions for the eight tests in this 2^3 factorial design. The next four columns (X_1X_2 through $X_1X_2X_3$) are obtained by forming all possible cross-product combinations of the first three columns. Together, all seven columns are referred to as the *calculation matrix*. Each column in the calculation matrix is used together with the data (last column) to estimate the factor effects.

To obtain the estimate of the main effect of X_1, the inner product of column X_1 and the Y column is formed, summed, and then divided by $N/2$. The calculation would appear as follows:

$$E_1 = [-Y_1 + Y_2 - Y_3 + Y_4 - Y_5 + Y_6 - Y_7 + Y_8]/4$$

The two-factor interaction effects and the three-factor interaction effects would be obtained in a similar fashion.

In general, for a 2^k factorial design:

- A total of 2^k unique test conditions exist and hence the calculation matrix will have 2^k rows.
- The calculation matrix will have 2^k-1 columns representing the k main effects and $2^k-(k + 1)$ interaction effects.
- There will be k main effects, $k!/(k-1)!1!$ two-factor interactions, $k!/(k-2)!2!$ three-factor interactions,...., and one k-factor interactions.
- The i-th effect estimate is given by $E_i = (2/n)[\pm Y_1 \pm Y_2 \pm ... \pm Y_n]$, where $n = 2^k$ and $i = 1, 2, ..., 2^k-1$.

DETERMINATION OF DISPERSION EFFECTS

In addition to location effects (effects on the process average), changes in certain variables may give rise to changes in the amount of process/product performance variation. These changes are referred to as dispersion effects (see Fig. 2-44).[19] In Fig. 2-44, it is seen that increases in X_1 cause an increase in the average performance (a location effect), while increases in X_2 cause an increase in the variation in performance (a dispersion effect).

The graphical representation of the results of a 2^3 factorial experiment are shown in Fig. 2-45. An estimate of the main effect of variable X_1 on location is obtained by calculating the average responses on planes I and II and then taking the difference ($E_1 = Y_{II} - Y_I$). However, the calculation of effects of variable X_1 on dispersion requires some thought because a significant portion of the variation in the data on plane I and in the data on plane II may be attributed to the presence of a location effect due to X_2 and/or X_3. Therefore, important location effects must be removed (filtered out) from the data before the dispersion effects are calculated. One way to accom-

TABLE 2-17
Matrix Used for Algebraic Estimation of Variable Effects

Test	X_1	X_2	X_3	X_1X_2	X_1X_3	X_2X_3	$X_1X_2X_3$	Y
1	-1	-1	-1	+1	+1	+1	-1	Y_1
2	+1	-1	-1	-1	-1	+1	+1	Y_2
3	-1	+1	-1	-1	+1	-1	+1	Y_3
4	+1	+1	-1	+1	-1	-1	-1	Y_4
5	-1	-1	+1	+1	-1	-1	-1	Y_5
6	+1	-1	+1	-1	+1	-1	-1	Y_6
7	-1	+1	+1	-1	-1	+1	-1	Y_7
8	+1	+1	+1	+1	+1	+1	+1	Y_8
Divisor	4	4	4	4	4	4	4	
Effect	E_1	E_2	E_3	E_{12}	E_{13}	E_{23}	E_{123}	

TWO-LEVEL FACTORIALS

plish this is through the mathematical model, which can be expressed in general form as:

$$Y = \hat{Y} + \epsilon \qquad (33)$$

where:

Y = data
$\hat{Y}$ = model prediction
ϵ = residual error

The model prediction, $\hat{Y}$, is an expression of all relevant location effects including the average ($\overline{Y}$), and is also the expected result in the long term (a prediction of the average response). Therefore, the residual errors ($\epsilon = Y - \hat{Y}$) constitute the data after the location effects have been removed from consideration. Any important dispersion effects, however, remain within the data.

Using the data given in Fig. 2-45, the main and interaction effects on location were determined. It was found that only E_1, E_3, and E_{23} are significant location effects. To prevent the location effects from being aliased with the dispersion effects, it is necessary to determine the model residuals based on the mathematical model. The model residuals are as follows:

$$Y - \hat{Y} = Y - (14.5 + 3.75\ X_1 + 1.0\ X_3 + 1.25\ X_2\ X_3)$$

The model residuals associated with the geometric representation of the 2^3 factorial design under consideration are shown in Fig. 2-46.

Box and Meyer have defined a main dispersion effect estimate related to a variable as the ratio of the sample variance determined for tests/data at the high level of that variable and the sample variance determined for tests/data at the low level of that variable.[20] From the data in Fig. 2-46, the sample variance for the high level of the variable is calculated using the residuals on plane II; the sample variance for the low level of the variable is calculated using the data/residuals on plane I. The dispersion effect is then given as:

$$D_1 = \frac{s^2\ (1+)}{s^2\ (1-)} = \frac{0.625}{1.125} = 0.55$$

In a similar fashion, main effects of X_2 and X_3 on dispersion may be determined. Dispersion interaction effects may also be determined in the usual fashion, but again the model residuals, not the actual observed responses, would be used as the data. Similar to the notion of a location interaction effect between two factors, no dispersion interaction is considered to exist between the factors X_1 and X_2 if the dispersion effect of X_1 is constant, irrespective of the level of X_2. In other words, the effect of going from a minus level of X_1 to a plus level of X_1 is to multiply the variance by a constant, regardless of the level of X_2.

Clearly, the notion of dispersion effects is quite consistent philosophically with the desire to identify ways to adjust/control the process or the product to produce a more consistent output (less variability about the nominal performance level).

The calculation matrix could be used to determine all of the main and interaction dispersion effects. In this case, the columns associated with the 2^k-1 variable effects (2^k rows) would be identical to those for the determination of location effects. The data, however, would be the model residuals that result from the removal of all important location effects from the data. For any effect column, the groups of $2^k/2$ minus signs and $2^k/2$ plus signs would identify the residuals used to determine $s^2(i-)$ and $s^2(i+)$, respectively. Their ratio is then the i-th dispersion effect.

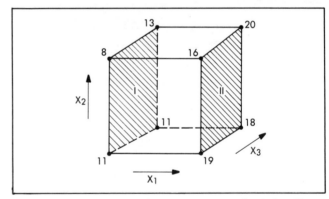

Fig. 2-45 Calculation of average response on plane I and plane II.

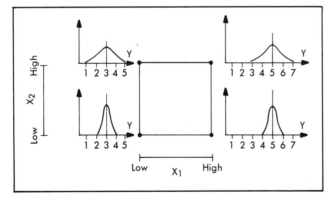

Fig. 2-44 Change in performance variations.

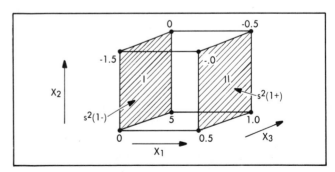

Fig. 2-46 Model residuals.

TWO-LEVEL FRACTIONAL FACTORIAL DESIGNS

Although the class of two-level factorial designs appears to be an efficient way to deal simultaneously with several factors, this efficiency seems to disappear as the number of variables to be studied grows. Because the two-level factorial requires the consideration of all possible combinations of k variables at two levels each, a 10-variable experiment would require $2^{10} = 1024$ tests. Such a test plan is obviously prohibitive in size. Furthermore, although the volume of information from the experiment may on the surface seem impressive, the practical significance of the majority of this information is in question. For example, for a 2^{10} factorial experiment the investigator could, in theory, estimate the following variable effects:

10 main effects

45 two-factor interaction effects

120 three-factor interaction effects

210 four-factor interaction effects

252 five-factor interaction effects

210 six-factor interaction effects

120 seven factor interaction effects

45 eight-factor interaction effects

10 nine-factor interaction effects

1 ten-factor interaction effect

From a practical standpoint, it is quite reasonable to assume that most of the above variable effects, particularly higher-order interactions, will be quite small. Therefore, it seems likely that fewer than 1024 tests may be used to study 10 factors in some kind of factorial arrangement.

There are basically two mechanisms at work that lead to the conclusion just described. First of all, although many variables (10) are considered to be potentially important, in the end only a few of these (perhaps no more than three or four at the most) will prove to be important. Secondly, because the relationship between the process response Y and the independent variables X_i is expected to be somewhat smooth (well behaved), interactions of higher orders will probably be very small in magnitude, and therefore can be neglected. Usually, interactions of three or more factors can be neglected without too much loss of information. These two facts define the principle of "sparsity of variable effects"[21] and lead to the conclusion that, if judiciously chosen, a greatly reduced subset of the full 2^k factorial design may be conducted and still obtain all useful and relevant information about those factor effects that are potentially important. The very powerful class of two-level fractional factorial designs serves this purpose.[22,23]

CONSEQUENCES OF FRACTIONATION

In the rail steel bar problem discussed in the section on two-level factorial design experiments, three variables were studied to determine their possible effect on the ultimate tensile strength of the welded bars. A 2^3 full factorial design was performed, and the three main effects, the three two-factor interaction effects, and the one three-factor interaction effect were all separately estimated.

Suppose now that the investigator had wished to consider the effects of the type of welding flux (a fourth variable), but the full factorial ($2^4 = 16$ tests) could not be considered; rather only eight tests could be performed.

Based on the assumption about the negligible importance of third and higher order interaction effects, the column of plus and minus signs associated with the $\underline{123}$ interaction in the calculation matrix could be assigned to the fourth variable. This should be acceptable because it is believed that the $\underline{123}$ interaction is very small in magnitude; therefore, this column can be used to define the levels of variable $\underline{4}$ for the eight separate tests. The main effect of variable $\underline{4}$ can therefore be estimated using this column.

In using the $\underline{123}$ column to introduce a fourth variable to the experiment, the new design matrix, which defines the eight tests to be conducted, is shown in Table 2-18. Expanding the design matrix in Table 2-18, the calculation matrix for all possible products of columns $\underline{1}$ through $\underline{4}$ can be obtained (see Table 2-19).

Examination of this calculation matrix reveals, however, that many of the columns are identical. The pairs of variable effects represented in the calculation matrix by the same column of plus and minus signs are:

$\underline{1}$ and $\underline{234}$	$\underline{12}$ and $\underline{34}$
$\underline{2}$ and $\underline{134}$	$\underline{13}$ and $\underline{24}$
$\underline{3}$ and $\underline{124}$	$\underline{23}$ and $\underline{14}$
$\underline{4}$ and $\underline{123}$	Avg. and $\underline{1234}$

The effects represented by the columns that have the same plus and minus signs are said to be confounded or confused; they are "aliases" of a unique column of plus and minus signs. That is, one cannot definitively assign the column estimate to one specific main effect or interaction. The tradeoff for the reduced number of tests performed in a fractional factorial experiment over the full factorial is called confounding. To minimize the practical effect of confounding, a good experimental design confounds main effects with higher-order interactions, which may be assumed to be of lesser importance and can be subsequently neglected.

DESIGN GENERATORS AND DEFINING RELATIONSHIP

In any two-level fractional factorial experiment involving n unique test conditions, there will exist only $n-1$ unique columns of plus and minus signs available for the independent estimation of effects. Therefore, if $n-1$ is less than 2^k-1, some degree of confounding among the effects will be present. For example, if five variables are studied in a two-level experiment with only eight tests, then each of the seven independent columns in the

TABLE 2-18
Design Matrix for a Two-Level Fractional Factorial Design

Test	1	2	3	123 4
1	-	-	-	-
2	+	-	-	+
3	-	+	-	+
4	+	+	-	-
5	-	-	+	+
6	+	-	+	-
7	-	+	+	-
8	+	+	+	+

TWO-LEVEL FRACTIONAL FACTORIALS

TABLE 2-19
Confounding in a Calculation Matrix When Studying Five Variables with Eight Tests

Test	1	2	3	4	12	13	14	23	24	34	123	124	134	234	1234
1	-	-	-	-	+	+	+	+	+	+	-	-	-	-	+
2	+	-	-	+	-	-	+	+	-	-	+	-	-	+	+
3	-	+	-	+	-	+	-	-	+	-	+	-	+	-	+
4	+	+	-	-	+	-	-	-	-	+	-	-	+	+	+
5	-	-	+	+	+	-	-	-	-	+	+	+	-	-	+
6	+	-	+	-	-	+	-	-	+	-	-	+	-	+	+
7	-	+	+	-	-	-	+	+	-	-	-	+	+	-	+
8	+	+	+	+	+	+	+	+	+	+	+	+	+	+	+

calculation matrix is simultaneously representing several effects. If five variables are to be studied in eight tests, which normally would accommodate only three variables as a full factorial, two additional variables need to be assigned to any two of the interaction columns $\underline{12}$, $\underline{13}$, $\underline{23}$, and $\underline{123}$ in the 2^3 calculation matrix. To illustrate this, suppose variables 4 and 5 are assigned to the $\underline{12}$ and $\underline{13}$ columns, respectively (see Table 2-20).

In the matrix of plus (+) and minus (-) signs, the first five columns (excluding I) represent the eight unique test conditions for the five variables. These five columns constitute the design matrix for the 2^{5-2} fractional factorial design. All seven $n-1$ columns, plus a column of all plus signs (column I) constitute the complete calculation matrix for this 2^{5-2} design. This means that all main and interaction effects among the five variables will be contained within these eight linear combinations of the data. The question that remains is to precisely determine which effects are confounded with each other.

Design Generators

Whenever a column heading is referred to as $\underline{1}$, $\underline{23}$, or $\underline{123}$, a column of plus (+) and minus (-) signs should be imagined directly under it. Now, if any column of plus (+) and minus (-) signs is multiplied by itself, a column of all plus signs is produced. This column is referred to as the identity column and has the heading I.

The 2^{5-2} design was generated by setting column 4 equal to column $\underline{12}$ ($4 = \underline{12}$) and column 5 equal to $\underline{13}$ ($5 = \underline{13}$). Given the definition of I, if both sides of the two equations are multiplied by 4 and 5, respectively, the result is:

$$4 \times 4 = 12 \times 4$$
$$5 \times 5 = 13 \times 5$$

which reduces to $I = \underline{124}$ and $I = \underline{135}$. These two identities are referred to as *design generators*.

Defining Relationship

As was just mentioned, columns $\underline{124}$ and $\underline{135}$ are equal to I. Because of this identity, the product of columns $\underline{123}$ and $\underline{135}$ would also be equal to I. The identity (in the current example, $I = \underline{124} = \underline{135} = \underline{2345}$), which is comprised of the design generators and their products in all possible combinations, is referred to as the *defining relationship*. The defining relationship reveals the complete confounding structure of any two-level fractional factorial design.

TABLE 2-20
Calculation Matrix for a Two-Level Fractional Factorial Design

Test	I^*	1	2	3	4 12	5 13	23	123	Y
1	+	-	-	-	+	+	+	-	Y_1
2	+	+	-	-	-	-	+	+	Y_2
3	+	-	+	-	-	+	-	+	Y_3
4	+	+	+	-	+	-	-	-	Y_4
5	+	-	-	+	+	-	-	+	Y_5
6	+	+	-	+	-	+	-	-	Y_6
7	+	-	+	+	-	-	+	-	Y_7
8	+	+	+	+	+	+	+	+	Y_8

*The column denoted I (all plus signs) is used to estimate the mean response ($\overline{Y}$).

Confounding Pattern

For the current example the calculation matrix has seven independent columns of plus and minus signs and one identity column. By letting column $\underline{4}$ equal to $\underline{12}$ and $\underline{5}$ equal to $\underline{13}$, much confounding among the variable effects has been created. To find out what are the aliases of the column headings in the example, each column heading is multiplied by every term (including I) in the defining relation. For example, in column heading 1 (main effect of variable 1) this would be as follows:

$$I(1) = (1)124 = (1)135 = (1)2345$$

Removing all I's [$(1)(1) = I$] yields:

$$1 = 24 = 35 = 12345$$

This means that the aliases of 1 are $\underline{24}$, $\underline{35}$, and $\underline{12345}$. Therefore, when the 1 column is multiplied by the Y column, summed, and divided by 4, an estimate of the sum (linear combination) of E_1, E_{24}, E_{35}, E_{12345} is obtained. This sum of confounded variable effects is denoted as l_1 (l stands for the linear combination of the effects). A summary of the confounding pattern and linear combinations of aliased effects that can be estimated from this experiment is given in Table 2-21.

TWO-LEVEL FRACTIONAL FACTORIALS

TABLE 2-21
Summary of the Confound Pattern, Linear Combinations and Aliased Effects for a 2^{5-2} Fractional Factorial Design

l_i estimates $I + 124 + 135 + 2345$
l_1 estimates $1 + 24 + 35 + 12345$
l_2 estimates $2 + 14 + 1235 + 345$
l_3 estimates $3 + 1234 + 15 + 245$
l_4 estimates $12 + 4 + 235 + 1345$
l_5 estimates $13 + 234 + 5 + 1245$
l_6 estimates $23 + 134 + 125 + 45$
l_7 estimates $123 + 25 + 34 + 145$

The five-variable, eight-test two-level experiment is referred to as a two-level fractional factorial design because it considers only a fraction of the tests defined by the full factorial. In this case, a one-fourth fraction design has been created. It is commonly referred to as a 2^{5-2} fractional factorial design. It is a member of the general class of 2^{k-p} fractional factorial designs. For such designs, k variables are examined in 2^{k-p} tests requiring that p of the variables be introduced into full factorial in $k-p$ variables by assigning them to interaction effects in the first $k-p$ variables.

2^{k-p} fractional factorial designs are very useful in screening large numbers of potentially important factors in an effort to identify those few factors that actually are important. Two-level fractional factorials may also be usefully employed sequentially, by selecting designs from the same family and combining them in a series of two or perhaps three successive experiments.[24] The idea of sequential and iterative experimentation is important from the standpoint of converging to a state of considerable knowledge and understanding about product or process performance in an efficient and reliable manner.

DESIGN RESOLUTION

Although two-level fractional factorials may be set up by using any interaction columns in a 2^m scheme ($m = k-p$) to introduce the additional p factors, some choices are much better than others. For example, to study five factors in 16 tests means that a 2^{5-1} fractional factorial is required. The fifth factor can be introduced, as well as others, by using either columns $\underline{123}$ or $\underline{1234}$ in the 2^4 structure. If the fifth factor is assigned to the $\underline{123}$ interaction, then the resulting confounding pattern among all factor effects will have main effects aliased with three-factor interactions, while two-factor interactions will be aliased with each other. However, if the fifth factor is assigned to the $\underline{1234}$ interaction, then main effects are confounded with four-factor interactions, and two-factor interactions are confounded with three-factor interactions. In the latter case, clear estimates of all main effects and two-factor interactions can be obtained if third and higher order interactions are neglected. This is not the situation in the first case.

Design resolution is an important concept that helps define what is meant by "judicious fractionation" of factorial designs. Design resolution is used to define the nature of the confounding pattern in terms of how the effects are aliased with each other. For example, if a design is of resolution III, this means that no main effect is confounded with any other main effect.

However, some main effects are confounded with two-factor interactions.

If a design is of resolution IV, this means that no main effect is confounded with any other main effect or two-factor interactions. However, some main effects are confounded with three-factor interactions, and two-factor interactions are confounded with each other.

If a design is of resolution V, this means that no main effect or two-factor interaction is confounded with any other main effect or two-factor interaction, but at least some two-factor interactions are confounded with three-factor interactions, while at least some main effects are confounded with four-factor interactions.

In the preceding example, assigning the fifth factor to column $\underline{123}$ leads to a resolution IV design, while assigning the fifth factor to column $\underline{1234}$ leads to a resolution V design. The higher the design resolution, the better the confounding pattern because it is generally assumed that the higher the order of the interactions, the more likely the interaction is to be negligible.

The resolution of a fractional factorial design can be identified by using an appropriate Roman numeral subscript. For example, 2^{4-1}_{IV} refers to a resolution IV fractional factorial design for four variables in eight tests. Box and Hunter have promoted the concept of design resolution and provide extensive recommendations on preferred two-level fractional factorial designs involving up to 11 variables in 128 tests or less.[25,26] A portion of their recommended 2^{k-p} designs are listed in Table 2-22.

ORTHOGONAL ARRAYS

In recent years, Taguchi and his colleagues have popularized the use of orthogonal arrays as efficient experimental design structures. In this section, the use of orthogonal arrays is examined. The relationship between these designs (considering only two levels for each factor) and the class of 2^{k-p} fractional factorials discussed in the last section is explained.

The use of orthogonal arrays has been widespread for some time. The theory of fractional factorial designs was first worked out by Finney and Rao.[27,28] Other orthogonal arrays were introduced by Plackett and Burman.[29] Two-level and three-level fractional factorial designs gained widespread attention and industrial application beginning in the 1950s with the publication of numerous papers on theory and applications. Papers such as "The 2^{k-p} Fractional Factorial Designs, Part I and Part II" provide much useful guidance to the practitioner in the use of these experimental design structures.[30]

To many, the most significant property of the designs being examined is orthogonality. Orthogonality is the characteristic of the designed experiment that allows the user to separate out the individual effects of each of several variables on a response of interest. Orthogonality can be thought of geometrically as each effect being mutually perpendicular to all other effects. Although some have used the words "not mixed" or "not confounded" to describe the property of orthogonality in orthogonal arrays, the use of these descriptors is incorrect. In particular, the words "not confounded" are incorrect because in this regard it is not the experiment structure itself, but rather the assumptions used in its application that can be used to justify the terminology. When anything less than a full factorial is under consideration, confounding or mixing of effects is always present by definition. Such confounding can only be removed by assumptions made about the physical system, not the experimental design.

CHAPTER 2

TWO-LEVEL FRACTIONAL FACTORIALS

Highly fractionated factorials suffer from having main effects of factors confounded with lower-order interaction effects, often with two-factor interactions. If not for the principle of redundancy and the sequential assembly of experimental designs, highly fractionated designs might be of limited utility.

Effect sparsity suggests that only a small number of variable effects will truly be important. It is associated with the phenomenon that although many variables may be initially under study, ultimately it is shown that only a very few turn out to be of importance. Sequential assembly states that judicious design selection from among similar structures (families of fractional factorials) enables a sequence of two or more experimental designs to be combined to remove some ambiguities created by the confounding patterns of the individual designs. The concepts of effect sparsity and sequential assembly are important for efficient, reliable use of fractional factorials.

It is important to point out that in applying orthogonal arrays as experimental design structures, Taguchi does not discuss or consider the concept of design resolution. Taguchi methods usually assume that all interactions may be neglected. Only those interactions that are felt a priori worthy of estimation are included in the orthogonal array structure.

The $L_{16}(2^{15})$ orthogonal array shown in Table 2-23 appears as problem 2 in the exercise section of Chapter 6 of the publication by Taguchi and Wu.[31] Column 8 was originally labeled as variable D, but has been corrected for this publication and is labeled as variable C.

In this application of the $L_{16}(2^{15})$ orthogonal array, the following assignments have been made:

- Eight (8) columns have been assigned to variable main effects (A, B, C, D, E, F, G, H).

TABLE 2-22
Two-Level Fractional Factorial Designs for k Variables in N Tests

Number of Tests	Number of Variables, k						
	$k = 5$	$k = 6$	$k = 7$	$k = 8$	$k = 9$	$k = 10$	$k = 11$
8	2^{5-2}_{III} $\pm 4 = 12$ $\pm 5 = 13$	2^{6-3}_{III} $\pm 4 = 12$ $\pm 5 = 13$ $\pm 6 = 23$	2^{7-4}_{III} $\pm 4 = 12$ $\pm 5 = 13$ $\pm 6 = 23$ $\pm 7 = 123$				
16	2^{5-1}_{V} $\pm 5 = 1234$	2^{6-2}_{IV} $\pm 5 = 123$ $\pm 6 = 234$	2^{7-3}_{IV} $\pm 5 = 123$ $\pm 6 = 234$ $\pm 7 = 134$	2^{8-4}_{IV} $\pm 5 = 234$ $\pm 6 = 134$ $\pm 7 = 123$ $\pm 8 = 124$	2^{9-5}_{III} $\pm 5 = 123$ $\pm 6 = 234$ $\pm 7 = 134$ $\pm 8 = 124$ $\pm 9 = 1234$	2^{10-6}_{III} $\pm 5 = 123$ $\pm 6 = 234$ $\pm 7 = 134$ $\pm 8 = 124$ $\pm 9 = 1234$ $\pm \overline{10} = 12$	2^{11-7}_{III} $\pm 5 = 123$ $\pm 6 = 234$ $\pm 7 = 134$ $\pm 8 = 124$ $\pm \underline{9} = 1234$ $\pm \overline{10} = 12$ $\pm \overline{11} = 13$
32		2^{6-1}_{VI} $\pm 6 = 12345$	2^{7-2}_{IV} $\pm 6 = 1234$ $\pm 7 = 1245$	2^{8-3}_{IV} $\pm 6 = 123$ $\pm 7 = 124$ $\pm 8 = 2345$	2^{9-4}_{IV} $\pm 6 = 2345$ $\pm 7 = 1345$ $\pm 8 = 1245$ $\pm 9 = 1235$	2^{10-5}_{IV} $\pm 6 = 1234$ $\pm 7 = 1235$ $\pm 8 = 1245$ $\pm \underline{9} = 1345$ $\pm \overline{10} = 2345$	2^{11-6}_{IV} $\pm 6 = 123$ $\pm 7 = 234$ $\pm 8 = 345$ $\pm \underline{9} = 134$ $\pm \overline{10} = 145$ $\pm \overline{11} = 245$
64			2^{7-1}_{VII} $\pm 7 = 123456$	2^{8-2}_{V} $\pm 7 = 1234$ $\pm 8 = 1256$	2^{9-3}_{IV} $\pm 7 = 1234$ $\pm 8 = 1356$ $\pm 9 = 3456$	2^{10-4}_{IV} $\pm 7 = 2346$ $\pm 8 = 1346$ $\pm 9 = 1245$ $\pm \overline{10} = 1235$	2^{11-5}_{IV} $\pm 7 = 345$ $\pm 8 = 1234$ $\pm \underline{9} = 126$ $\pm \overline{10} = 2456$ $\pm \overline{11} = 1456$
128				2^{8-1}_{VIII} $\pm 8 = 1234567$	2^{9-2}_{VI} $\pm 8 = 13467$ $\pm 9 = 23567$	2^{10-3}_{V} $\pm 8 = 1237$ $\pm \underline{9} = 2345$ $\pm \overline{10} = 1346$	2^{11-4}_{V} $\pm 8 = 1237$ $\pm \underline{9} = 2345$ $\pm \overline{10} = 1346$ $\pm \overline{11} = 1234567$

TWO-LEVEL FRACTIONAL FACTORIALS

TABLE 2-23
An L_{16} (2^{15}) Orthogonal Array

Test	F 1	A 2	e 3	B 4	e 5	A x B 6	E 7	C 8	H 9	e 10	B x D 11	e 12	A x D 13	G 14	D 15	Results
1	1	1	1	1	1	1	1	1	1	1	1	1	1	1	1	
2	1	1	1	1	1	1	1	2	2	2	2	2	2	2	2	
3	1	1	1	2	2	2	2	1	1	1	1	2	2	2	2	
4	1	1	1	2	2	2	2	2	2	2	2	1	1	1	1	
5	1	2	2	1	1	2	2	1	1	2	2	1	1	2	2	
6	1	2	2	1	1	2	2	2	2	1	1	2	2	1	1	
7	1	2	2	2	2	1	1	1	1	2	2	2	2	1	1	
8	1	2	2	2	2	1	1	2	2	1	1	1	1	2	2	
9	2	1	2	1	2	1	2	1	2	1	2	1	2	1	2	
10	2	1	2	1	2	1	2	2	1	2	1	2	1	2	1	
11	2	1	2	2	1	2	1	1	2	1	2	2	1	2	1	
12	2	1	2	2	1	2	1	2	1	2	1	1	2	1	2	
13	2	2	1	1	2	2	1	1	2	2	1	1	2	2	1	
14	2	2	1	1	2	2	1	2	1	1	2	2	1	1	2	
15	2	2	1	2	1	1	2	1	2	2	1	2	1	1	2	
16	2	2	1	2	1	1	2	2	1	1	2	1	2	2	1	

- Three (3) columns have been assigned to two-factor interactions (A x B, B x D, A x D).
- Four (4) columns have been assigned to the estimation of error.

Table 2-24 shows the design matrix for a 2^{8-4} fractional factorial design. This design matrix was constructed in the following way:

- Columns 1 through 4 are the columns in the $L_{16}(2^{15})$ orthogonal array assigned to variables C, B, A, and F, respectively.
- Columns 5 through 8 are the columns in the $L_{16}(2^{15})$ orthogonal array assigned to variables E, H, G, and D, respectively.

In viewing the orthogonal array of Taguchi as a 2^{k-p} fractional factorial, the $L_{16}(2^{15})$ array (as shown in Table 2-23) is actually a resolution III fractional factorial because the column 6 (factor G) is actually the negative product of columns 1 and 4 (C and F). Hence, some main effects are aliased with two-factor interactions. It is possible, however, to employ a somewhat different 2^{8-4} fractional factorial where the interactions <u>123</u>, <u>124</u>, <u>134</u>, and <u>234</u> are used to introduce variables 5, 6, 7, and 8. In such an experimental design, main effects are confounded with, at worst, three-factor interactions, which is more desirable from the standpoint of protecting the assumptions made about interactions and hence providing a stronger basis for interpretation. Again, the concept of the resolution of a fractional factorial design appears to be quite important and useful in selecting the appropriate orthogonal array.

TABLE 2-24
Design Matrix for a 2^{B-4} Factorial Design

Test	1	2	3	4	234 5	-14 6	123 7	-1234 8
1	-	-	-	-	-	-	-	-
2	+	-	-	-	-	+	+	+
3	-	+	-	-	+	-	+	+
4	+	+	-	-	+	+	-	-
5	-	-	+	-	+	-	+	+
6	+	-	+	-	+	+	-	-
7	-	+	+	-	-	-	-	-
8	+	+	+	-	-	+	+	+
9	-	-	-	+	+	+	-	+
10	+	-	-	+	+	-	+	-
11	-	+	-	+	-	+	+	-
12	+	+	-	+	-	-	-	+
13	-	-	+	+	-	+	+	-
14	+	-	+	+	-	-	-	+
15	-	+	+	+	+	+	-	+
16	+	+	+	+	+	-	+	-
	C	B	A	F	E	G	H	D*

*Letters denote variable "names" given by Taguchi and Wu in the $L_{16}(2^{15})$ orthogonal array.

ROBUST PRODUCT AND PROCESS DESIGN

In the introduction to this chapter, a model for the engineering design process put forth by Taguchi was briefly discussed. This model describes a three-stage engineering design procedure involving system design, parameter design, and tolerance design.

Of the three stages, parameter design has often been given less (or no) attention in the design process. In fact, when design improvements are needed, it can be said that tolerance design has often been used to play the dual role of both parameter and tolerance design, promoting the use of excessively tight processing and assembly tolerances, but often at a high cost of manufacturing.

VARIABLE CLASSIFICATION

An important aspect of the Taguchi philosophy is the classification of variables. Unlike other planned experimentation strategies that tend to lump all potentially influential factors into one "pile" (a single class), Taguchi classifies the important factors that govern product/process performance into signal, control, and noise factors. Such a classification recognizes the varying roles that factors may play in the system.

Signal factors are selected based on engineering knowledge to attain the desired level of performance. Examples of variables that would be classified as signal factors are the steering angle in a steering mechanism and the speed control on a fan.

Control factors constitute the product or process parameters that can be set at various levels. Control factors are specified by the designer according to some criterion such as maximizing the performance stability of the design.

Noise factors in the product/process environment are generally uncontrollable or very expensive to control, although they do influence performance. According to Taguchi, noise factors can only be described in terms of statistical characteristics. Noise factors are further broken down into outer noise, inner noise, and variational noise classifications.

Classifying the variables is extremely useful for an engineering design because it helps the engineer to think about the design in terms of what causes change/variation in performance. It also helps when considering what actions can be taken to counteract undesirable forces. It is important to recognize, however, that as circumstances and needs vary, what might appear to be a control factor could be treated as a noise factor or vice versa. Because of this, it is important to think of the degree of control, the extent to which a factor can and/or should be controlled.

All factors do not have the same effect on the response under study. Some factors may influence only the average response but not the variability, while others may have a strong effect on process variation or signal-to-noise ratio. Taguchi refers to those factors that affect average response as signal factors and those that affect signal-to-noise ratio as control factors. Others simply lump these two categories into control and design factors, but separately consider their influence on both the process mean and the process variation (location effects and dispersion effects).

The following example will help illustrate the classification of variables. In this example, an experiment is performed to study the effects of carburetor design, engine displacement, tire pressure, and speed on the fuel economy of an automobile. The objective of this experiment is to select the best levels for these factors.

It is important to realize that the notion of "best" levels does not have the same meaning for all the variables. Carburetor type and engine displacement may be rigidly controlled in the design process. Once desirable levels are identified, they will remain essentially fixed throughout the life of the product. Because the speed of a car is affected by such conditions as weather, traffic, and legal speed limits, it is unreasonable to select a best level. Tire pressure, on the other hand, may be fixed more closely by design, but will also vary with ambient temperature and driving conditions. Speed and tire pressure could be viewed as noise variables because they vary during performance and cannot be easily controlled.

DESIGN STRATEGY FOR PARAMETER DESIGN

The purpose of the parameter design (robust design) strategy is to find the nominal values of the control factors that reduce (minimize) the transmission of inner and outer noise. To demonstrate how these nominal values can be evaluated, the following hypothetical example will be used.

In this example, the objective is to select a set point for an injection molding process that minimizes part shrinkage on the average and to identify the most consistent set point. A set point is a group of settings for each of the process control variables.

The machine settings that have some influence on part shrinkage are nozzle temperature (X_1), holding pressure (X_2), hold time (X_3), mold temperature (X_4), and screw speed (X_5). These settings are referred to as control variables because they can be controlled at the machine.

Three additional factors also influence part shrinkage: (1) mold cooling water temperature (N_1), (2) proportion of virgin versus reground molding material (N_2), and (3) ambient temperature at the machine. These factors are referred to as noise factors because they can only be controlled with great difficulty and/or expense.

To assist in the selection process, two identical 2^3 factorial designs can be performed for the three noise factors at each of the two set points defined by these unique combinations of the five control variables. Table 2-25 shows the data for this hypothetical example. Set points 1 and 2 comprise what is referred to as the inner design of the experiment. The 2^3 factorials for the noise variables comprise what is referred to as the outer design. For each of the two test settings in the inner design, the average shrinkage and the variation in shrinkage about that average can be calculated based on the results of the tests that comprise the outer design. The results of the calculations for set point 1 are:

$$\overline{Y} = \frac{88}{8} = 11$$

$$s_Y^2 = \frac{6}{7} = 0.86; \text{ therefore } s_Y = 0.93$$

The results of the calculations for set point 2 are:

$$\overline{Y} = \frac{88}{8} = 11$$

TABLE 2-25
Data for Two Hypothetical 2^3 Factorial Designs

Test	N_1	N_2	N_3	Set Point 1	Test	N_1	N_2	N_3	Set Point 2
1	-	-	-	10	1	-	-	-	7
2	+	-	-	10	2	+	-	-	10
3	-	+	-	12	3	-	+	-	15
4	+	+	-	11	4	+	+	-	11
5	-	-	+	10	5	-	-	+	11
6	+	-	+	12	6	+	-	+	8
7	-	+	+	11	7	-	+	+	12
8	+	+	+	12	8	+	+	+	14

$$s_Y^2 = \frac{52}{7} = 7.43; \text{ therefore } S_Y = 2.73$$

From these results, it can be seen that the noise factor variation for set point 2 is almost three times larger than that for set point 1. This means that the process performance at set point 1 is less influenced/less contaminated than set point 2 by the noise factors surrounding the process. In short, set point 1 is a more robust process operating condition than set point 2. Therefore, the selection of this process performance is preferred. If only average shrinkage was considered in the analysis, then the two set points would have been viewed as comparable.

The example just described is used to demonstrate the principle of parameter design. The actual performance of such an experiment might be difficult in that achieving levels of the noise variables in the real process setting might be difficult, although certainly neither impossible nor implausible. However, the use of parameter design in product and/or process design is greatly facilitated through the use of mathematical models for the underlying mechanisms and the ability to use computers to evaluate such models.

SIGNAL-TO-NOISE RATIO AS A QUANTITATIVE ANALYSIS TOOL

The emphasis placed on variation and variation reduction in the methods of Taguchi suggests that the signal-to-noise ratio may be used for the evaluation of experiments containing both design/control and noise factors. The signal-to-noise ratio is commonly used in the communications field and is defined as the ratio of the average response to the root mean square variation about the average response. In simple terms, the signal-to-noise ratio (S/N) can be calculated using the equation:

$$S/N = \bar{Y}/S_Y \qquad (34)$$

where:

S/N = the signal-to-noise ratio
$\bar{Y}$ = the average response
S_Y = the root-mean-square variation

Signal-to-noise ratio as a performance measurement has several advantages. First, it allows a two-step optimization process. In the first step, an attempt is made to reduce variation due to the noise factors using the control factors. After this initial reduction, the response is brought to the desired target using the signal factors. This strategy assumes that signal and control factors are unrelated; in other words, they do not have an interaction effect. Another feature of the signal-to-noise ratio concept is its ability to examine alternate strategies for system design and improvement on more philosophical grounds.

Quantitative Use

It is sometimes useful to think of the generally unknown functional relationship that links a performance measurement to a set of signal/control variables and noise variables as composed of two parts. This relationship can be represented by the equation:

$$Y = g(X) + e(Z) \qquad (35)$$

where:

Y = the performance measurement
g = the signal (predictable)
X = the signal/control variables
e = the noise (unpredictable)
Z = the noise variables.

The larger the signal part is in relation to the noise part, the more predictable the response becomes.

Signal-to-noise ratio can also be defined as the ratio of the variances associated with the two parts of the performance measurement. It is commonly defined in the form given below:

$$S/N = 10 \log_{10}(\sigma_g^2/\sigma_e^2) \qquad (36)$$

where:

σ_g^2 = the variance of the signal
σ_e^2 = the variance of the noise

Depending on the nature of the response (to be minimized, to be maximized, to be driven to a specified target), S/N may be defined mathematically in different ways.

To illustrate how the S/N ratio can be used as a performance response in a parameter design application, the following hypothetical example will be used. In this example, the process is a face milling machining operation, and the response is the flatness of the part surface after machining. The design/control factors (inner design) under study may be the number of cutter inserts or teeth, cutter offset (relative position on the part), depth of cut, feed rate, and part structure stiffness. Noise factors (outer design) being studied might include cutter insert runout, uncut (initial) machined surface flatness, and variation of part microstructure hardness. A mathematical model for the cutting

ROBUST DESIGN

force system is available as are models for the part displacements based on both static and dynamic force loading situations.

To study the control and noise factors, all to be varied at two levels each, a 2^{5-1} fractional factorial is used for the inner design and a 2^3 factorial for the outer design. For each of the 16 test conditions in the inner design involving the five control factors, the eight tests of the outer design will be run over three noise factors; a total of 128 tests would be required (16 x 8 = 128).

After the 128 simulations are conducted (using the mathematical models for cutting forces and deflections) and the part flatness calculated for each case, the data could be analyzed in the following way:

1. For each of the 16 conditions of the inner design, the average response and signal-to-noise ratio response could be calculated in each case based on the 2^3 factorial of the outer design.
2. The main effects and two-factor interaction effects for the five inner design factors based on the 2^{5-1} fractional factorial could then be determined.
3. Based on the analysis in 2, those factors that influence S/N would be used to prescribe action(s) to reduce the effect of the noise factors. Those factors that influence the average response but not the S/N would be used to control the performance to the prescribed target.

In the context of Taguchi methods, the previously described analysis would normally proceed using analysis of variance (ANOVA).[32] However, other analysis structures such as those discussed previously could also be used that determine the effects of each factor (both main and interaction) on each response.

In any event, the key points to emphasize in Taguchi's method of experimental design are the (1) *classification of variables* in accordance with the physical roles each plays in the system, (2) the *use of signal-to-noise* ratio as a means to quantitatively evaluate the influence that certain factors may have on system variability, (3) the *use of inner and outer design* experimental design structures as a means to evaluate the relationship between noise factors and design/control factors, and (4) the method of *parameter design*, which is aimed at finding the nominal settings for the control factors that minimize the variation induced by the noise variables.

Conceptual Analysis

As attempts are made to view and to analyze the systems around us in terms of the identification of improvement oppor-

tunities, it may be quite illuminating to more broadly consider their performance as measured by signal-to-noise ratio. Whether it be communications theory, where it has its roots, or in the context of Taguchi-based methods, signal-to-noise ratio enhancement (increasing the S/N ratio) may follow two quite different paths, both philosophically and mathematically. It is perhaps the two paths thusly defined that contrast the varying views held in the past on the importance and role of quality, whether it be design, planning, control, or assurance.

There are two fundamental ways to increase the signal-to-noise ratio measure of performance of any system: (1) increase the signal or (2) decrease the noise. It is worthwhile to think of the systems that are dealt with by asking the question: Was an improvement strategy implemented based on increasing the signal or reducing the noise? The answer to this question may be somewhat humbling.

Suppose the system is a shop floor processing unit. The ratio of the production rate (number of parts per day) to (1 + failure rate/part) might be thought of as the signal-to-noise ratio. An example of this can be shown as:

$$S/N \text{ Ratio} = \frac{500 \text{ parts/shift}}{1 + 0.08} = 463 \text{ good parts}$$

If the target for production is 500 good parts, then action must be taken to increase the signal-to-noise ratio. Two choices exist for increasing the signal-to-noise ratio:

Action 1: Increase the production rate, put on a second machine or authorize overtime.

Action 2: Implement a program aimed at identifying the root cause(s) of a defective part. Techniques such as statistical process control could be useful.

Action 1 approaches the problem of increasing the S/N ratio by increasing the signal, while action 2 is directed toward reducing the noise. It is not difficult conceptually to decide which action will lead to a more permanently redeeming solution to the problem.

In an engineering design problem, a certain component may be experiencing field failures due to mechanical breakage. The problem may be diagnosed as excessive loading variation leading to more rapid fatigue failures. One approach to the problem could be to increase the strength of the material used (increase the signal). Another alternative might be to study design configuration changes that would reduce stress variation for the same general external loading conditions (reduce the noise).

RESPONSE SURFACE METHODOLOGY

In the previous section, methods based primarily on the work of Taguchi were presented as one approach to the design optimization problem. Specifically, these methods advocated the use of design of experiments (off-line quality control) to identify the particular settings of the signal and control factors that lead to being on target with the smallest variation. It is important to point out that the optimal factor levels are generally selected from among the levels used for each factor in the experiment and are selected for each factor independent of the others. Although these assumptions seem somewhat restrictive, they are often invoked in the interest of simplicity and in an

effort to quickly take a large step forward in the direction of improvement.

In this section, other design and operations optimization methods will be examined. These methods are felt by many to be simple, intuitively appealing, complementary to engineering logic and methods, and are based on a solid foundation of statistical theory. The main method that will be discussed is Response Surface Methodology (RSM), which has central to its technique a mathematical model. The mathematical model is a useful tool that enables the user to bridge the gap between the true and often unknown workings of the world being studied and the observations made on the behavior of that world. These observations are often based on judiciously selected experiments.

The purpose of RSM is to find the optimum settings for the factors under study, given a product/process response of interest and a set of factors that have been tentatively found to impact that response. These settings are found by thinking of the underlying relationships between the response and the product/process factors as represented by a smooth surface called the response surface.

Response surface methodology employs a two-stage procedure aimed at rapid advancement from the current operating point into the general region of the optimum followed by mathematical model characterization of the response surface in the vicinity of the optimum. The basic tools used to achieve these objectives are two-level and three-level factorials and linear model building, which employs simple polynomial forms and the method of least squares for model fitting.

DEFINING THE PATH OF STEEPEST ASCENT

To achieve rapid advancement toward the optimum condition, RSM analyzes the path of steepest ascent/descent. Assuming that a response surface is similar to Fig. 2-47, the objective is to identify the path on the surface that has the steepest slope at point A. This can be accomplished by considering the surface to be planar at the current point. Based on this assumption, the actual surface in this region can be characterized using the mathematical model:

$$Y = b_0 + b_1 X_1 + b_2 X_2 + \epsilon \qquad (37)$$

where:

$$\begin{aligned} Y &= \text{process response under study} \\ X_1, X_2 &= \text{control factors/variables} \\ b_0, b_1, b_2 &= \text{model parameters to be estimated} \\ \epsilon &= \text{random error} \end{aligned}$$

A two-level factorial design could be used to obtain the data to estimate the model parameters.

If the experiment results are as shown in Fig. 2-48, fitting the first-order model leads to a set of contours having constant response values that are straight lines. Moving in a direction perpendicular to these contours would be equivalent to moving along the path of steepest ascent (PSA). To find the exact

direction of steepest ascent, X_1 and X_2 must be changed (increased in this example)in proportion to their slopes.

EXPLORING THE PATH OF STEEPEST ASCENT

Once the PSA has been established, the next step is to pursue this direction by running tests along the path at appropriate intervals. These tests are continued as long as the response continues to improve (move toward the optimum). When no further progress can be realized by moving along the PSA, additional tests should be performed to redefine the path of steepest ascent. These new tests should be run at or near the point on the original path found to have the best result response value.

Figure 2-49 depicts four tests that have been run along the PSA (as previously depicted in Fig. 2-48) with results of $Y = 22$, 25, 28, and 24. Because the response started to decrease, no further testing along this path is useful. A second 2^2 factorial should probably be run at or near the point of the path that produced the experimental result of $Y = 28$. When running the second factorial, the investigator may wish to adjust the ranges of the factors (low to high) depending on the results of the first 2^2 factorial. The path of steepest ascent analysis may proceed in a fashion like that shown in Fig. 2-50. Three iterations have brought the investigation from point A, which is far away from the optimum, to point C, which is near the optimum.

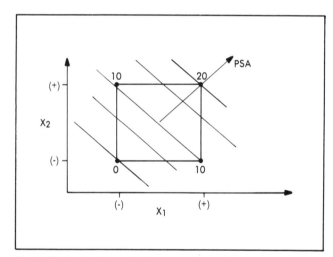

Fig. 2-48 Contour lines of a linear response surface.

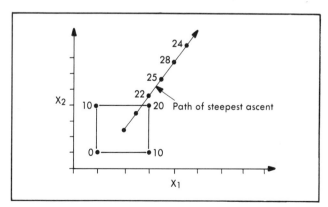

Fig. 2-49 Path of steepest ascent.

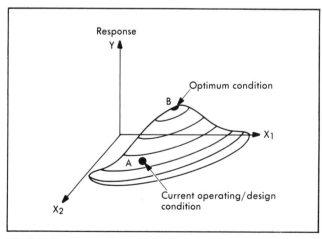

Fig. 2-47 Response surface.

RESPONSE SURFACE METHODOLOGY

MODELING OF THE NEAR-OPTIMAL REGION

As the optimum region is approached, the surface develops more curvature locally; hence the planar assumption, which stands as the means to use simple first-order models and associated experimental designs for path of steepest ascent analysis, becomes poorer and poorer (see Fig. 2-50). At some point it becomes appropriate to assume that the optimum is nearby and therefore analysis for the path of steepest ascent is abandoned. An experiment should then be set up, the data from which can be used to fit a higher order model, as an approximation to the true response surface function. Such a model form is given as follows:

$$Y = b_0 + b_1X_1 + b_2X_2 + b_{12}X_1X_2 + b_{11}X_1^2 + b_{22}X_2^2 + \epsilon \quad (38)$$

Figure 2-51 shows the relationship that may exist between the actual response surface, view a, and its representation by a fitted mathematical model of the form of Eq. (38), view b. By fitting this equation to the actual experimental data, the equation can be used to determine values of X_1 and X_2 that maximize Y. In addition, the complete nature of the response surface can be clearly visualized and explored.

Several useful design structures have been proposed to obtain data to fit models such as the second-order polynomial. Figure 2-52 illustrates the two most common designs for this purpose are the three-level factorial and the central composite design (CCD).[33]

ANALYSIS OF THE NEAR-OPTIMAL REGION

The fitted equation for the response surface may be used to study and analyze the nature of the response. Standard model checking procedures should be employed to ensure that the fitted model is an adequate representation of the true surface. Furthermore, it may be advisable to conduct a few confirmatory tests to make sure that the model predictions are reproducible at the process.

The fitted model for the surface may be used to identify the values for X_1 and X_2 that maximize the predicted response. The model may be also used to examine the relative sensitivity of the response to both X_1 and X_2. This information may be useful in understanding the controls that need to be applied to X_1 and X_2 to maintain the response at reasonably high levels. The fitted equation may also be used in conjunction with other responses under study or with other operating constraints to define appropriate operating conditions.

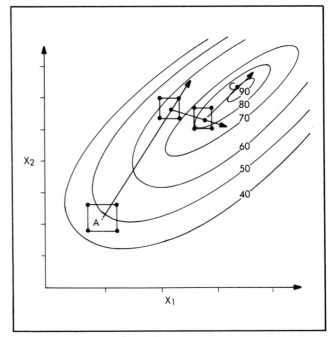

Fig. 2-50 Illustration of an RSM with true contours.

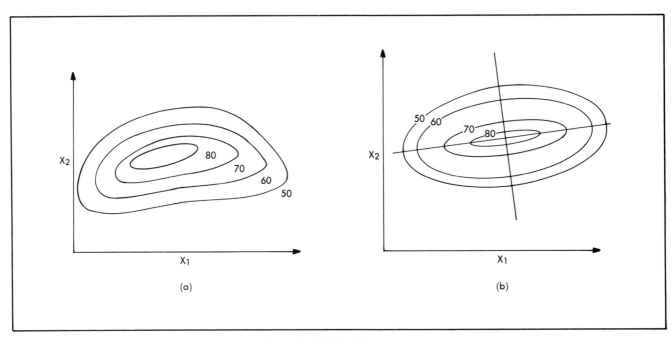

Fig. 2-51 Actual versus fitted response surface contours: (a) actual and (b) fitted.

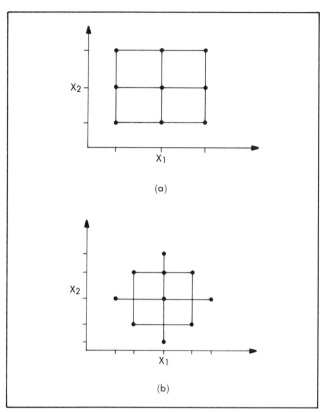

Fig. 2-52 Design structures for second-order polynomial model: (a) three-level factorial and (b) central composite design.

References

1. G. Taguchi and Y. Wu, *Introduction to Off-Line Quality Control* (Japan: Central Japan Quality Control Association, 1979).
2. *Ibid.*
3. G.E.P. Box and N.R. Draper, *Evolutionary Operation: A Statistical Method for Process Improvement* (New York: John Wiley and Sons, Inc., 1969).
4. R.A. Fisher, *The Design of Experiments*, 8th ed. (New York: Hafner Publishing Co., 1966).
5. G.E.P. Box, W.G. Hunter, and J.S. Hunter, *Statistics for Experimenters* (New York: John Wiley and Sons, Inc., 1978).
6. Taguchi and Wu, *op. cit.*
7. W. E. Deming, *Quality, Productivity, and Competitive Position* (Cambridge, MA: Massachusetts Institute of Technology, Center for Advanced Engineering Study, 1982).
8. W.A. Shewhart, *The Economical Control of Quality of Manufactured Product* (New York: McGraw-Hill Book Co., 1931).
9. E.L. Grant, *Statistical Quality Control*, 3rd ed. (New York: McGraw-Hill Book Co., 1964).
10. Jacob Frimenko, *Statistical Process Control: Fundamental Concepts*, SME Technical Paper MF84-472 (Dearborn, MI: Society of Manufacturing Engineers, 1984).
11. L.S. Nelson, "The Shewhart Control Chart—Tests for Special Causes," *Journal of Quality Technology*, vol. 16, no. 4 (1984), pp. 237-239.

12. Grant, *op. cit.*
13. P.T. Jessup, "The Value of Continuing Improvement," *Proceedings of IEEE International Communications Conference*, ICC 85, 1985.
14. Box, Hunter, and Hunter, *op. cit.*
15. Fisher, *op. cit.*
16. S.M. Wu, "Analysis of Rail Steel Bar Welds By Two-Level Factorial Design," *Welding Journal Research Supplement* (1964), pp. 179s-183s.
17. Box, Hunter, and Hunter, *op. cit.*
18. C. Daniel, *Applications of Statistics to Industrial Experimentation* (New York: John Wiley and Sons, Inc., 1976).
19. G.E.P. Box and R.D. Meyer, "Studies In Quality Improvement I: Dispersion Effects From Fractional Designs," *Technometrics* (February 1986), pp. 19-28.
20. *Ibid.*
21. *Ibid.*
22. Box, Hunter, and Hunter, *op. cit.*
23. G.E.P. Box and J.S. Hunter, "The 2^{k-p} Fractional Factorial Designs," Part I and Part II, *Technometrics*, vol. 3 (1961), pp. 331-351 and 449-458.
24. *Ibid.*
25. Box, Hunter, and Hunter, *op. cit.*
26. Box and Hunter, *op. cit.*
27. D.J. Finney, "The Fractional Replication of Factorial Arrangements," *Annals of Eugenics*, vol. 12, no. 4 (1945), pp. 291-301.
28. C.R. Rao, "Factorial Experiments Derivable From Combinatorial Arrangements of Arrays," *Journal of Royal Statistical Society*, vol. B9 (1947), pp. 128-140.
29. R.L. Plackett and J.P. Burman, "Design of Optimal Multifactorial Experiments," *Biometrika*, vol. 23 (1946), pp. 305-325.
30. Box and Hunter, *op. cit.*
31. Taguchi and Wu, *op. cit.*
32. H. Scheffe, *The Analysis of Variance* (New York: John Wiley and Sons, Inc., 1959).
33. Box, Hunter, and Hunter, *op. cit.*

Bibliography

Duncan, A.J. *Quality Control and Industrial Statistics*. Homewood, IL: Richard D. Irwin, Inc., 1974.

Hahn, G.J. "Design Of Experiments: Industrial and Scientific Applications." *Encyclopedia of Statistical Sciences*, vol. 2. New York: John Wiley and Sons, Inc., 1982.

Hayes, G.E., and Romig, H.G. *Modern Quality Control*. Encino, CA: Bruce, 1977.

Hunter, J.S. "Statistical Design Applied To Product Design." *Journal of Quality Technology*, vol. 17, no. 4 (1985), pp. 210-221.

Kackar, R.N. "Off-Line Quality Control, Parameter Design, and the Taguchi Method." *Journal of Quality Technology*, vol. 17 (1985), pp. 176-209.

Montgomery, Douglas C. *Introduction to Statistical Quality Control*. New York: John Wiley and Sons, Inc., 1985.

Morris, M.D., and Mitchell, T.J., "Two-Level Multifactor Designs For Detecting The Presence of Interactions." *Technometics*, vol. 25 (1983), pp. 345-355.

Ott, E.R. *Process Quality Control: Trouble Shooting and Interpretation of Data*. New York: McGraw-Hill Book Co., 1975.

Shewhart, W.A. *The Economic Control of Quality of A Manufactured Product*. New York: D. Van Nostrand Co., Inc., 1931.

Statistical Quality Control Handbook. Newark: Western Electric Co., Inc., 1956.

Steinberg, D.M., and Hunter, W.G., "Experimental Design: Review and Comment" *Technometrics*, vol. 26 (1984), pp. 71-130.

INSPECTION EQUIPMENT AND TECHNIQUES

Although the level of quality control is determined in large part by probability theory and statistical calculations, it is very important that the data collection processes on which these procedures depend be appropriate and accurate. The best statistical procedure is worthless if fed faulty data, and like machine processes, inspection data collection is itself a process with practical limits of accuracy, precision, resolution, and repeatability.

For example, inspection of die-cut rubber or foam plastic parts with tool steel calipers is liable to force the parts out of their true shape. Processible data will be collected from this inspection task, but it will be biased by the inspection method. Similarly, visual determination of the accuracy of a part by using an optical comparator at 10X magnification to check a dimension to 0.0005″ (0.01 mm) will not be accurate because of the limitations of the human eye, which cannot reliably discriminate a linear dimension of 0.005″ (10 x 0.0005″).

All inspection and/or measurement processes can be defined in terms of their accuracy and repeatability, just as a manufacturing process is evaluated for accuracy and repeatability. Controlled experiments can be performed, and statistical measures of the results can be made to determine the performance of a method of inspection relative to the parts to be inspected. Suitability of one or another method can be judged on the basis of standard deviations and confidence levels that apply to each approach as used in a given inspection situation.

The necessity of performing an experiment to validate the inspection approach will probably depend on the specifics of the situation. Choice of the inspection method can then be made based on the required sensitivity and chances of error as well as on tooling cost and skill level availability.

Other criteria may also enter into the choice of inspection method. The nature and quantity of inspection called for by a project are overriding considerations as is the availability of existing inspection tooling. General-purpose measuring gaging may be necessary only for the first piece produced because there may be high confidence in the integrity of the molds, dies, or other fabrication tools. In other cases gaging may be on a sampling basis or a 100% inspection basis. This could lead to a significantly increased load on the inspection resources and a search for more efficient measuring methods.

In this chapter, the available inspection equipment and techniques will be discussed with a view to obtaining valid data. The limitations of various types of inspection tooling will be pointed out, and appropriate methods will be suggested. The chapter is divided into four main sections based on the equipment classifications: (1) general-purpose measuring devices, (2) fixed gages, (3) visual reference gaging, and (4) automatic gaging. In addition, laser inspection devices, coordinate measuring machines, machine vision systems, and robotic inspection systems are also discussed. However, before discussing the equipment, it is important to have a good understanding of units of measurement and standards.

FUNDAMENTAL UNITS AND STANDARDS

Measurement is the means whereby data or information is collected about an item or event. The first basic requirement of measurement is that the measuring units be consistent. In other words, each unit should have one universal value.

Two major systems of units are in use throughout the world today, the English or Imperial system and the metric system. English units are now defined in terms of the metric units, making the latter the primary system of units; in this way,

Contributors of sections of this chapter are: B. J. Brown, President, Control Gaging, Inc.; *William E. Drews*, Marketing Manager, Rank Precision Industries, Inc.; *Don Marchand*, Director of Engineering, Autoflex, Inc.; *Craig McLanahan*, President, McLanahan & Co., Inc. and Assistant Professor, Business Administration Dept., Salem State College; *William C. Mullin*, Technical Consultant, Edmunds Gages; *Dr. Walt Pastorius*, Vice President-Marketing, Diffracto, Ltd.; *William Planick*, Techwrite; *Richard H. Searle*, Metrology Specialist, Bridgeport Machines Co.

Reviewers of sections of this chapter are: Philip E. Armitage, Product Manager, Metrology Instrumentation, Zygo Corp.; *Bill Arnold*, Engineering Manager, Gaging Systems Operations, Sheffield Measurement Div., The Warner and Swasey Co.; *Ronald W. Arriel*, President, Visual Inspection Products; *Larry J. Best*, Engineering Manager, Rank Precision Industries, Inc.; *William J. Blaiklock*, Chief Engineer, Edmunds Gages; *Hans Bostrom*, President, C.E. Johansson, Inc.; *Mel Brenner*, Technical Manager, Instrument Group, Nikon, Inc.; *B.J. Brown*, President, Control Gaging, Inc.; *Wayne R. Cannava*, Manager, Metras Div., Flexible Gauging Systems, Marposs Corporation; *William E. Drews*, Marketing Manager, Rank Precision Industries, Inc.; *Harry R. Dziedzic*, Special Applications Manager, Rank Precision Industries, Inc.;

FUNDAMENTAL UNITS AND STANDARDS

consistency of units is assured. It should be noted that the metric system, by virtue of its greater simplicity, is supplanting the English system in many countries, even in England where the system originated. At present, more than 90% of the people in the world use the metric system, and it is probable that within the next 50 years the metric system will be used universally in certain fields of measurement.

A second requirement of units is that they be of convenient and practical size. It is cumbersome, for instance, to express all length measurements in miles or even in meters. The English system employs an assortment of units such as the inch, the foot, and so on up to the mile to cover the wide range of length measurement. In the metric system there is one primary unit for each parameter. For dimensional measurement, it is the meter. Larger and smaller quantities are expressed as multiples and submultiples of the meter; the various multiples and submultiples are related by factors of 10. This decimal logic is one of the attractive features of the metric system. No such logic exists in the English system, in which a foot is 12 inches, a yard is 3 feet, a rod is 5.5 yards, a furlong is 40 rods, and so on.

Units are defined and embodied in standards. Units are the language of measurement, and standards are the hardware. For example, the meter was originally defined as the distance between two lines on a specific bar maintained at the International Bureau of Weights and Measures in Paris; that bar was the standard for the meter.

One of the primary requirements of a basic standard is that it be unchangeable. To satisfy this condition, the standard must be indestructible (or if destroyed it should be capable of exact reproduction) and it must be stable. It was this consideration of immutability that led to the adoption of the new basic standard of length, the wavelength of a certain radiation of light. The radiation is produced by a krypton lamp; the wavelength of light produced by the lamp is an atomic constant and thus never changes. The meter bar, on the other hand, is a specific bar that if destroyed could not be reproduced exactly; moreover, it is dimensionally unstable.

A second requirement for a basic standard is that it be reproducible and not singular, as is the case of the meter bar or the kilogram. Any laboratory with adequate facilities can maintain a krypton lamp, and many do. No longer are they dependent on the meter bar at Paris to define their unit of length.

Yet another requirement of standards is that of practicality. This requirement is particularly dominant in working standards used throughout industry. The popularity of gage blocks as standards of length is in no small measure due to their simplicity and practicality. It is also important that standards be as insensitive as possible to outside influences such as temperature and pressure. This requirement is particularly difficult to satisfy and has led to the adoption of standard measuring conditions.

CALIBRATION

Measurement is a comparison process whereby an unknown quantity is compared with a known quantity or standard. The comparison is made by means of an instrument that indicates the differences between the unknown and the standard. Ideally all measurements should be made directly in terms of the basic standards that define primary units. This, however, is impractical, and consequently it is necessary to establish a hierarchy of standards similar to the pyramidal organization structure of a large company.

The chain of standards ends at the shop floor. The lathe operator checks the diameter of the shaft being turned with a micrometer. The micrometer has a precision thread on the spindle and a scale engraved on the barrel or a digital readout. These combine to form the standard in terms of which the diameter of the shaft is measured. But how accurate is this standard? When the micrometer indicates a value of 0.750″ (19.05 mm), does it really mean that the dimension it is measuring is actually 0.750 (19.05 mm)? The accuracy of the micrometer is checked by using it to measure a known dimension, normally the length of a gage block. The value of the gage block is determined in turn by comparing it with a master block of higher accuracy, and so on, until the basic standard is reached.

The process of comparing one standard or measuring device against a higher-order standard of greater accuracy is known as calibration. Through the process of calibration, all measurements are related back to the primary standard. In other words, traceability is maintained to ensure that all measurements are consistent. The requirements for traceability go hand in hand with requirements for interchangeability, a feature of modern-day production. In the early days of the Industrial Revolution, mating parts were made at the same time and adjusted to give the desired fit. This mode of operation soon became impractical, and in the 1850s Eli Whitney introduced interchangeable production in the manufacture of guns. The work of Joseph Whitworth in England on screw threads led to standards for making nuts and bolts interchangeable. In recent years the requirements for consistency and compatibility have increased enormously, with components manufactured in one plant expected to mate with components from another plant in a final assembly; hardware for the space program and advanced weapons systems are prime examples.

CHARACTERISTICS OF A MEASUREMENT

In making a measurement, one of the first considerations is the resolution of the measuring instrument. Resolution refers to the minimum change in value that the instrument can reliably indicate. For instance, many dial gages are graduated in 0.001″ (0.01 mm) divisions, but can be read to 0.0005″ (0.005 mm). If it

Reviewers, cont.: John A. Gaughan, Sales Manager, Edmunds Gages; Kenneth Gibbs, Metrology Applications Engineer, Bridgeport Machines Inc.; Stephen Goff, Marketing Manager, Brown & Sharpe Manufacturing Co.; Antonio Guarini, Metrology Specialist, Digital Electronic Automation, Inc.; Prudence F. Heikkinen, Product Manager, Machine Vision International; Joseph Herbst, Vice President, Dundick Corp.; Owen Herman, Senior Project Engineer, Advanced Manufacturing Systems; Ray Hinson, Director, Manufacturing Technology Institute, Advanced Manufacturing Systems; Michael Honer, Quality Assurance Manager, Brown & Sharpe Manufacturing Co.; Irvin D. Koch, Senior Project Engineer-Group Leader, Manufacturing Engineering Dept., Fisher Guide Flint Manufacturing, Div. of GMC; Joseph Kochan, Senior Metrology Specialist, Precision Tools, Brown & Sharpe Manufacturing Co.; Edward Kornstein, President, Expert Technology, Inc.; Tushar Kothari, Director of Sales, View Engineering; Timothy J. Kusters, Sales Applications Engineer, Gage Sales Engineering Dept., Moore Products Co.; John Macfarlane, Quality Assurance Manager, The VanKeuren Co.; Dale L. Markham, Senior Staff Engineer, Flexible Machining Laboratory, Industrial Technology Institute; Darryl L. McIntosh, Director of Sales, Size Control Co.; Craig McLanahan, President, McLanahan & Co., Inc. and Assistant Professor, Business Administration Dept., Salem State College; John D. Meyer, Tech Tran Consultants, Inc.;

is necessary to measure a dimension to only 0.005" (0.15 mm), there is no advantage in using an instrument with a resolution to 0.0005" (0.015 mm); in fact it is likely to be a disadvantage. One reason for this is that with most gages there is an inverse relationship between resolution and range—the finer the resolution, the smaller the range. Another disadvantage is that the finer the resolution a gage has, the more susceptible it is to extraneous influences, particularly vibration, temperature, and dirt. This makes it difficult to get a reliable reading and can be a source of irritation to the operator. Yet another and often more serious disadvantage is that the operator tends to place too much reliance in the value indicated by the instrument. For example, if the diameter of a part is measured to be 0.9473" (2.406 mm), the last digit may be meaningless unless the geometry of the part is good and the conditions of the measurement justify faith in the last digit. Even though the operator is interested only in the diameter to within ±0.001" (0.025 mm), the temptation is there to believe that the diameter of the part is exactly 0.9473" (2.406 mm).

There is considerable confusion between the terms *repeatability* and *accuracy* as they relate to measurement. Often, too, repeatability and *resolution* are equated.

Accuracy means closeness to truth. In discussing the accuracy of a micrometer or an electronic gage, reference is to the degree to which it can measure the true size of a part. For the sake of simplicity, consider a gage block. It has a certain true length, and when it is measured, it is to ascertain that true length, but for numerous reasons, the true length can never actually be determined; it is only approximated. If the measurement shows the gage block is 1.000" (25.00 mm) long, and the measurement is known to be accurate to ±0.001" (0.025 mm), the true length of the gage block is said to lie between 0.999 and 1.001" (25.025 and 24.975 mm).

The first requirement of any measuring system is that it have adequate repeatability. For instance, if widely varying results are obtained with each measure of the length of a gage block, these results are meaningless, and the measuring system is ineffective.

The repeatability of a group of repeated measurements is the extent to which they are in agreement and is generally stated in statistical terms. Consider a number of repeat measurements of a gage block made with an electronic comparator; if the comparator has sufficient resolution, it will give a slightly different value each time. This can result from a number of things: The temperature may be fluctuating, particles of dust absent during some measurements may lodge between the stylus and the surface of the block during others, the gaging force may vary slightly, the indicating needle on the comparator may not repeat exactly, and so on. These influences are random, and the values obtained from the measurements should be random. If the

values keep increasing or decreasing with successive measurements, the system is unstable, and readings should not be accepted until the drift has disappeared.

In a normal situation, the results follow a Gaussian distribution, and they can be characterized by two parameters, the mean value and the standard deviation. The mean value is simply the arithmetic average of the results. The standard deviation, sigma (σ), is a measure of the spread of the results or their precision. The closeness of the mean value to the true value refers to the accuracy of the measurement. The magnitude of sigma is a measure of the repeatability of the measuring system. The smaller sigma is, the more repeatable the measuring system.

The difference between repeatability and accuracy is illustrated by the target analogy in Fig. 3-1, which shows that a group of measurements can be repeatable (precise) but not necessarily accurate, and vice versa. In this analogy, which compares the 10-shot groups of five marksmen, accuracy is judged by closeness to the "bull's-eye," which represents true value. The shooting of marksman A is neither accurate nor precise. Marksman B is precise (his shots are close together) but inaccurate. Marksman C is no more precise than A, but has greater accuracy. Marksmen D and E are equally precise, but E is more accurate.[1]

Various sources of error can affect the accuracy of a measurement, and various influences can affect the repeatability. There are two types of errors: fixed or systematic errors and random errors. Fixed errors, as the name implies, do not vary between one measurement and the next; they remain constant during a set of measurements. One example might be a zero error on an electronic meter. Another error of this type would be the error in a master block used for calibrating another gage block. The difference of a few degrees in the mean temperature of the two blocks during the course of the measurements is

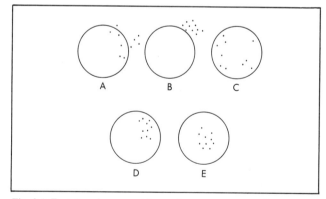

Fig. 3-1 Target analogy: precision and accuracy compared.

Reviewers, cont.: **Donald Moors**, *President, Western Gage Corp.;* **Mike Moyer**, *Senior Application Engineer, Rank Precision Industries, Inc.;* **William C. Mullin**, *Technical Consultant, Edmunds Gages;* **Carmen R. Mycroft**, *Technical Sales Specialist, Validator Coordinate Measuring Systems, Brown & Sharpe Manufacturing Co.;* **Richard C. Newton**, *Works Manager, The L.S. Starrett Co.;* **Richard G. Nolf**, *Electrical Engineering Manager, Control Gaging, Inc.;* **Kenneth Parlee**, *Vice President, Gage Master Corp.;* **Dr. Walt Pastorius**, *Vice President-Marketing, Diffracto, Ltd.;* **Leonard Pernecky**, *President, Dundick Corp.;* **Harry G. Petrohilos**, *Chief Engineer, Lasermike Div., Techmet Co.;* **William Planick**, *Techwrite;* **Gary J. Rutledge**, *Director Machine Perception, GMF Robotics Corp.;* **Richard H. Searle**, *Metrology Specialist, Bridgeport Machines Co.;* **John J. Setlock**, *Product Manager, Rank/Ferranti, Rank Precision Industries, Inc.;* **Kenneth L. Sheenan**, *Manager of Software Development, IMT Div., Carl Zeiss, Inc.;* **William Tandler**, *President, Multi-Metrics, Inc.;* **Vince Vaccarelli**, *Product Manager, Instrument Group, Nikon, Inc.;* **Ronald E. VerSchage**, *Contour Projector Product Manager, Optical Gaging Products, Inc.;* **Gary Wagner**, *Vice President of Marketing, Penn Video;* **Ken Wendt**, *Product Manager, Image Product Group, Zygo Corp.;* **Robert C. Wiebe**, *Vice President, Autoflex, Inc.;* **David R. Wiese**, *President, Selective Electronic, Inc.*

FUNDAMENTAL UNITS AND STANDARDS

another fixed error that could affect results. Fixed errors affect the accuracy of a measurement, so every effort should be made to isolate and quantify these errors. Once their magnitudes are known, the results can be corrected to allow for them.

Random errors, on the other hand, result from changing conditions during a set of measurements. The conditions under which a measurement is made, such as temperature and gaging force, should be clearly defined, and every effort should be made to maintain these conditions constant or at least reduce fluctuation to an insignificant level. It is never possible to eliminate extraneous influences completely. This is particularly true when trying to measure to the higher orders of accuracy. Consequently, a single measurement should never be relied on. Even the toolmaker using a micrometer is aware of this, for when a part is measured the second time, a slightly different value is obtained. The toolmaker also knows that something may have gone wrong the first time, so a few more readings should be taken. Three readings is a minimum, with more preferable in any type of measurement. The average value of a large number of readings is more accurate than that obtained from a small number of readings, and the standard deviation is smaller.

As measuring instruments and systems become more complex, there is normally greater opportunity for inaccuracies. A coordinate measuring machine with digital readout is an example. There are numerous sources of error that can affect the accuracy of the machine. The ways have to be straight and square to each other, and the bearings must run true. Parts loaded on the machine could cause deflections, and temperature gradients in the machine could lead to erroneous results. There is room for error in the scales and reading heads, and the electronics are not immune. There are many sources of random error, and consequently the accuracy of such a machine is quoted not simply as a plus or minus value, but in statistical terms.

Two basic types of measurement exist: absolute or direct measurement and comparative measurement. Although all measurements are comparative in nature, the term is normally reserved for situations where like or essentially like items are compared. The comparison of two 3″ (75 mm) gage blocks is a good example of comparative measurement. If the length of a gage block is measured with a micrometer, or in terms of the wavelength of light, the measurement is classified as direct. Comparative measurements have the advantage of being considerably more accurate than direct measurements. The relative size of two similar gage blocks is known with much greater accuracy than the absolute size of either. The principal reason for this is that in comparative measurement many systematic errors are eliminated.

If a gage block made of steel is compared with a similar steel block so that the temperature coefficients of expansion of the two blocks are identical, then, provided both blocks are the same temperature, it does not matter what that temperature is—the blocks will have the same relative lengths at 75° F (24° C) as they had at 68° F (20° C) because both will have expanded equal amounts. If, however, the steel block is compared with an aluminum block, it will no longer be sufficient for the two blocks to be at the same temperature; that temperature must be known. If the temperature of the blocks is 75° F (24° C), each will have expanded by different amounts from their size at the standard temperature of 68° F (20° C). This is a systematic error. It is necessary to estimate its value and to make the necessary correction to the results (see Fig. 3-2). Another systematic error

in this situation is that steel and aluminum have different moduli of elasticity, and a probe or stylus used in making the measurements penetrates to a greater depth in the aluminum block than in the steel block (see Fig. 3-3). Hence the advantages of comparing items that are alike in as many ways as possible become readily apparent.

MEASURING CONDITIONS

All measurements should be made under standard conditions. If the measurements are not made under standard conditions, results must be referenced to standard conditions by correcting for any deviations. Because all materials have different coefficients of expansion, it is not sufficient to simply say that a shaft is so many inches (millimeters) in diameter. It is necessary to know at what temperature it has that value.

It is internationally agreed that all dimensional measurements should be referenced to 68° F or 20° C. The temperature in most metrology laboratories is controlled to a nominal value of 68° F (20° C). A temperature-controlled environment eliminates the worry of temperature drifts and ensures that the test pieces and the standards are at the same temperature. In this

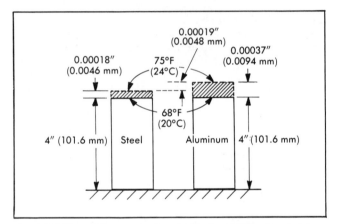

Fig. 3-2 Differential expansion in gage blocks of different materials.

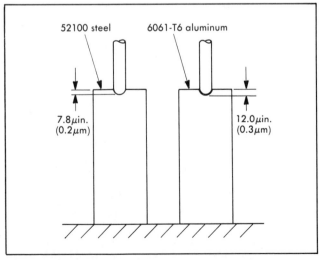

Fig. 3-3 Hardened steel spherical-pointed feeler (5/32″ diam) acted on by a 2.1 oz (0.6 N) contact force penetrates more deeply into aluminum than into steel because of the difference in elasticity of the two materials.

FUNDAMENTAL UNITS AND STANDARDS

regard, it should be mentioned that it is essential to allow sufficient time for this equilibrium state to be achieved. When a gage block or a workpiece is brought into the metrology laboratory for measurement, its temperature may be 77° F (25° C). Measurements cannot be made until the temperature of the object reaches 68° F (20° C). The time required for this will depend on the size or mass of the object and the material from which it is made.

In the shop, the temperature is not normally controlled, but shop practice does not seek the level of accuracy sought in the metrology laboratory. This, however, is no reason for complacence, particularly when part tolerances are in "tenths," ±0.0001-±0.0003″ (0.0025-0.0075 mm). It is not uncommon for the temperature in many shops to change by as much as 18° F (10° C) during the course of the day. For a 2″ (50 mm) diam steel shaft, this corresponds to a change in diameter of 0.00023″ (0.0006 mm). If the gage used to measure the part is at the same temperature as the part and has the same coefficient of expansion, the measurements are valid, and temperature corrections are not required. But if, for instance, measurements are being made of the cylinder bore of an aluminum engine block with a steel air plug, corrections or adjustments may have to be made to allow for differences in the coefficients of expansion.

Another environmental condition to be concerned with is humidity. High humidity causes rusting, and variations in humidity can cause condensation and evaporation, which affect the temperature of a part.

The wavelength of light varies with barometric pressure because of changes in the index of refraction of air. Consequently, when making measurements in terms of the wavelength of light, it is necessary to measure the barometric pressure and correct for any deviations from 760 mm of mercury, which is the international standard for barometric pressure.

Prior to measurement, part cleanliness must be ensured. Another requirement often overlooked is that of compatible geometry. It is not meaningful to report the diameter of a hole to 0.0001″ (0.0025 mm) if the hole is out of round by 0.0003″ (0.008 mm). Neither is it meaningful to measure the length of a gage block to 5 μin. (130 μm) if the two faces are out of parallel by 10 μin. (250 μm) or if either face is not flat within 5 μin. (130 μm).

All materials deform when subjected to a load. The initial deformation is elastic, and its extent is determined by the Young's modulus of the material, the geometry of the contact, and the magnitude of the load. For example, a 1/8″ (3 mm) radius steel stylus under a load of 0.5 lb (2.2 N) will cause net deformation of 16.4 μin. (415 μm) in a steel plane such as the face of a gage block. The corresponding net deformation for an aluminum surface would be almost 25 μin. (635 μm).

These are but a few of the conditions that must be taken into consideration when making dimensional measurements. In the case of low-accuracy measurements such as those at the shop floor, many of the factors discussed are insignificant. It is essential, however, to be aware of them and to make the necessary corrections when the situation calls for it.

FUTURE TRENDS IN MEASUREMENT

Reference is usually made to end standards and line standards. Typical of the first category are gage blocks, plug gages, and ring gages, each of which defines a single dimension. Line standards refer to the various types of scales and range from the simple ruler to the sophisticated light beam. Line standards can be graduated in numerous ways, and each line standard defines a multitude of lengths. With the advent of digital readout devices, there is a definite trend away from fixed gages toward line standards or direct-reading gages. Digital readout height gages and coordinate measuring machines are typical of the new generation of gages. Digital readout simplifies matters for the operator, a digital signal is ideal for processing by peripheral equipment such as computers, and a marked increase in the use of such equipment can be expected.

With more and more products being manufactured on a mass production basis, automatic gaging will assume greater importance. Sample inspection based on sound statistical principles provides, in many cases, the most economical approach to inspection. However, warranty claims and safety lawsuits, particularly in the auto industry, are now putting increased stress on quality control, necessitating 100% inspection in many cases. Automatic gaging makes this feasible. One such machine is the computer-controlled coordinate measuring machine, which features digital readout in three axes. In operation, a small computer drives the probe through a programmed inspection cycle. Measured values are stored in the computer and compared with nominal values. Actual dimensions and out-of-tolerance conditions are printed out automatically. All the operator has to do is load the part on the machine, locate the probe at the starting position, and press the button.

In the laboratory, new measuring techniques are also evolving. Chief among these is the laser for use in length measurement and alignment work. The laser is also being used in the shop along with a great variety of electronic gages. With demands for higher accuracy on more complex parts at the shop floor, it is reasonable to expect more from measuring systems. Traditionally, standards have been 10 times more accurate than the gages they check. This will become impractical, and standards three or four times more accurate will become the norm.

GENERAL-PURPOSE MEASURING DEVICES

Long the mainstay of the inspector, general-purpose measuring devices are still used in toolrooms, receiving inspection areas, and calibration labs for taking many precision measurements. They are often used in conjunction with a surface plate and are capable of measurements with accuracies of 0.001″ (0.02 mm). Instruments with high resolution permit measurements of 0.0001″ (0.002 mm) to be determined. General-purpose measuring devices are usually fabricated of hardened tool steel and are

subject to error because of mishandling and the introduction of dirt or cutting chips. It is therefore necessary to calibrate these devices periodically to ensure their integrity. When tolerances of 0.005″ (0.12 mm) are required, these devices can be relied on to give accurate results. Instruments with high repeatability may be used to calibrate the tooling on which the parts are produced because tooling tolerances are typically 10% of product tolerances.

GENERAL-PURPOSE DEVICES

Skill requirements for the use of these general-purpose precision measuring instruments is relatively high. Inspectors and/or toolmakers performing measurements of this type must know how to read drawings, how to use and read the instruments themselves, and how to perform basic trigonometric calculations to relate the physical measurements to the manufacturing requirements. Tooling costs for this type of inspection are relatively low because most instrumentation is general purpose and can be used on a wide variety of projects.

Use of these tools implies that inspection is to be done by measuring the part rather than determining if it is within specified limits. Of the two approaches, measuring is the more costly and slower because specific readings have to be taken. Determining if the part is within specified limits on a "GO/NOT-GO" basis can take much less time, but the setup of the inspection process usually requires some additional planning and tooling in the form of preset gages or visual references.

NONGRADUATED TOOLS OR INSTRUMENTS

As their name implies, nongraduated measuring tools do not have linear or angular graduations incorporated in the tool. These tools are generally used when comparing measurements, and their size must be verified by a graduated measuring device.

Calipers and Dividers

Various types of calipers and dividers are available for contact measurement. They are particularly useful for measuring distances between or over surfaces or for comparing dimensions or sizes with standards such as steel rules. Because they are sometimes used for checking work in a metal lathe, calipers should never be used when the work is turning. This could result in having the tool torn out of the user's hand.

Calipers. Calipers consist of two movable metal legs with formed contacts at one end. The legs are joined by a strong spring hinge and linked together by a screw and adjusting nut. When the contacts are pointed out, the caliper is designed for taking inside measurements and is referred to as an inside caliper. When the contacts are facing in, the caliper is designed for taking outside measurements and is referred to as an outside caliper.

A variation of the standard caliper is the hermaphrodite caliper. This type of caliper has one straight leg ending in a sharp point and one bow leg. Hermaphrodite calipers are used in layout work for scribing parallel lines from an edge or for locating the center of cylindrical work.

Dividers. Dividers are somewhat similar to calipers, but both of the legs are straight and have sharply pointed contacts. They are used for measuring distances between lines or points, transferring lengths taken from a steel rule, and for scribing circles or arcs. Dividers are restricted in range by the opening span of the legs. They become less effective for scribing and similar uses when the points are sharply inclined to the surface on which the scribing is performed.

Telescope Gages

The telescope gage is a T-shaped tool in which the shaft of the tee acts as a handle. The cross arms have hardened spherical forms on the ends to serve as contact elements. The cross arms telescope into each other and are held out by a light spring.

During use, the cross arms are compressed, placed in the hole, and then allowed to expand. A locknut on the top of the handle is turned to lock the cross arms, and then the gage is withdrawn from the hole. The distance across the arms is measured with a micrometer.

Telescoping gages are commonly furnished in sets, the smallest for 5/16 to 1/2" (8 to 12.5 mm) diam holes and the largest for 3 1/2 to 6" (90 to 152 mm) diam holes. Telescope gages are sometimes preferred to internal calipers for measuring internal diameters.

When the measurement of holes smaller than 5/16" (8 mm) is required, small-hole gages can be used. Small-hole gages consist of a small, split, ball-shaped member mounted on the end of a handle. The ball is expanded by turning a knob on the handle until the proper feel is obtained. Once the gage is withdrawn from the hole or recess, the size is measured with a micrometer. Small-hole gages are also available in sets, with each gage capable of measuring a certain range of sizes. The smallest gage can measure diameter from 1/8 to 3/16" (3 to 5 mm) and the largest from 3/8 to 1/2" (9.5 to 12.5 mm).

Straightedges and Squares

Straightedges are flat lengths of tool steel or granite finished to extremely fine tolerances. They are used for scribing straight lines and to check surfaces for straightness. Straightedges are available in lengths from 12 to 72" (300 to 1800 mm).

The steel square is one of the most accurate hand tools available for right-angle measurement. It consists of a base into which a blade is set; the blade may be beveled or nonbeveled. Precision squares are so accurate that when they are placed against a master square on a surface plate, they will shut out a vertical source of light. Precision squares are available in blade lengths from 3 to 36" (75 to 915 mm).

Surface Plates

A surface plate is a flat plane that is used as a reference surface from which final dimensions are taken. They should be inspected periodically with an autocollimator to ensure flatness. When an overall unilateral flatness of 0.00005" (0.0013 mm) or finer is required, toolmakers' flats or optical flats are used as a reference surface.

Originally, surface plates were made from cast iron and had cross-ribbed bases to reduce weight and increase resistance to warpage. Currently, however, they are made from different types of hard and homogeneous granite. The most important advantages of granite surface plates are closer tolerances and lower prices. The next most important feature is their noncorroding and nonrusting property. They are also not subject to contact interference. In addition, granite surface plates are nonmagnetic, hard, stable, long wearing, easy on the eyes, easy to clean, and have exceptional thermal stability.

Sine Bars and Plates

The sine bar is a hardened, stabilized, precision ground and lapped tool for accurate angle setting or measuring. It consists of a bar to which two cylinders are attached. When the cylinders are brought in contact with a flat surface, the top of the bar is parallel to that surface.

Sine bars are used in conjunction with gage blocks and a surface plate. The operation of the sine bar is based on known trigonometric relationships between the sides and angles of a right-angled triangle.

Sine blocks and plates are similar in design to sine bars. The primary difference is the width of the instrument and whether it has an attached base or not. Sine blocks are generally wider than 1" (25 mm) and have tapped holes in the bar for attaching parts as well as a stop to keep the parts from sliding off. Sine plates have a hardened base attached to them. Sine bars and blocks are usually manufactured in lengths of 5 or 10″ (125 or 250 mm). This length is the distance between the axes of the two supporting rolls.

GRADUATED TOOLS OR INSTRUMENTS

Graduated measuring tools have either linear or angular graduations incorporated into the measuring system of the tool. These tools are applied directly to the part being measured, and the dimension is read by the user.

Rules

The rule is a basic measuring tool from which many other tools have been developed. Because rules are so frequently used on a variety of work, a wide selection exists to suit the needs of the precision worker. They range in size from as small as 1/4″ (6 mm) in length for measuring in grooves, recesses, and key-ways to as large as 12′ (3.5 m) in length for large work.

Rules are made from carbon steel or stainless steel, and many have a satin-chrome finish and enameled graduations for ease of reading. They are graduated in the English or metric system units and sometimes scales for both systems are provided on a single rule. The graduations can be on each edge of both sides and even on the ends. English graduations are commonly as fine as 0.01″ in decimals or 1/64″ in fractions. Metric graduations are usually as fine as 0.5 mm. Most precision rules are graduated to agree with standards calibrated by the U.S. Bureau of Standards in Washington, DC. Effects of normal temperature variations are insignificant in the degree of accuracy attained in reading a rule.

Calipers

Slide calipers. Slide calipers are a refinement of the steel rule and are capable of more accurate measurements. With these tools, a head or pair of jaws is added to the rule; one jaw is fixed at the end and the other movable along the scale. Provision is made for clamping the movable jaw to lock the setting. The slide is graduated to read inside or outside measurements. The scale is graduated in increments of either 1/32 or 1/64″ for the English system and in increments of 0.5 mm for the metric system.

Vernier calipers. A typical vernier caliper consists of a stationary bar and a movable vernier slide assembly. The stationary rule is a hardened, graduated bar with a fixed measuring jaw. Vernier calipers are available in sizes ranging from 4 to 80″ (100 to 1500 mm). The size of the caliper indicates the maximum dimension that can be measured. The stationary rule frequently is graduated in increments of 0.050″ for the English system and 0.5 mm for the metric system.

The vernier slide assembly combines a movable jaw, vernier plate, clamp screws, and adjusting nut. It moves as a unit along the graduations of the bar to bring both jaws in contact with the work. The vernier plate is graduated in increments of 0.001″ for the English system and 0.02 mm for the metric system.

Caliper height gages. Like the vernier caliper, the caliper height gage consists of a stationary bar or beam and a movable slide. The graduated, hardened and ground beam is combined with a hardened, ground and lapped base. The vernier slide assembly can be raised or lowered to any position along the bar. It can be adjusted in thousandths (English system) or hundredths (metric system) by means of the vernier slide fine-

adjusting knob. Caliper height gages are available in sizes ranging from 8 to 72″ (200 to 900 mm).

The primary use of caliper height gages is in the field of surface plate work as a layout tool. It is commonly used for marking off vertical distances and for measuring height differences between steps at various levels. When marking off distances, scribers are attached to the contact jaw.

Vernier depth gage. The vernier depth gage differs slightly from the vernier caliper and the caliper height gage in that the vernier slide assembly remains fixed while the steel rule is moved to obtain the desired measurements. The vernier slide also forms the base that is held on the work by one hand while the blade is operated with the other. Vernier depth gages are available in sizes ranging from 6 to 12″ (150 to 300 mm).

Obtaining a measurement is accomplished in the same manner as with a vernier caliper gage. After the blade is brought into contact with the bottom of a slot or recess, the clamp screw adjacent to the fine-adjusting nut is tightened. Then the fine-adjusting nut is turned to obtain an exact measurement. Once the final measurement is obtained, the clamp screw next to the vernier plate is tightened.

Gear tooth vernier caliper. The gear tooth vernier caliper measures chordal thickness or thickness at the datum circle of a gear tooth to an accuracy of 0.001″ or 0.01 mm, depending on the units. It can also measure hobs and form and thread tools. Its construction combines in one tool the function of both the vernier depth gage and vernier caliper.

In use, the vertical slide is set to depth by means of its vernier plate fine-adjusting nut so that when it rests on top of the gear tooth, the caliper jaws will be correctly positioned to measure across the datum circle of the gear tooth. The horizontal slide is then used to obtain the chordal thickness of the gear tooth by means of its vernier slide fine-adjusting nut. For additional information on measuring gears, refer to Chapter 4, "Dimensional Metrology and Geometric Conformance."

Dial calipers. Similar to vernier calipers, dial calipers have a stationary bar and a movable slide assembly. The bar is graduated in increments of 0.1″ or 2 mm and is available in sizes ranging from 4 to 12″ (100 to 300 mm).

The vernier plate is replaced by a caliper dial graduated in increments of 0.001″ or 0.02 mm. A pinion gear actuates the dial hand as it moves along a rack located in the stationary bar.

Because the dial caliper is direct reading, there is no need to determine the coincident line on a vernier scale. This feature facilitates the reading of these instruments. Dial heads are also incorporated on caliper height gages and depth gages.

Digital calipers. Because gaging is a vital part of SPC, a new generation of electronic instruments has been produced. These instruments incorporate liquid crystal displays (LCD) and are capable of interfacing with a data collection device. Both inch and metric units are incorporated in one tool. The electronic feature is available on calipers, height gages, and depth gages.

Micrometers

A variety of micrometers exist for different applications. The three major types of micrometers are outside, inside, and depth. All micrometers operate based on the principle that an accurately made screw will advance a specified distance with each complete turn. Micrometers graduated in the inch system advance 0.025″ for each turn; those graduated in the metric system advance 0.5 mm for each turn.

Micrometers have both a linear and circumferential scale. The linear scale measures the axial advance of the spindle. It is

GENERAL-PURPOSE DEVICES

generally graduated in increments identical to the pitch of the micrometer screw. The circumferential scale indicates the amount of partial rotation that has occurred since the last complete revolution. For inch-based micrometers, this scale is divided into 25 equal parts, with each division representing 0.001". For metric-based micrometers, the circumferential scale is divided into 50 equal parts, with each division representing 0.01 mm. Some micrometers also have a third scale that permits the evaluation of fractions of circumferential graduations. Depending on the units, each division on this scale represents either 0.0001" or 0.002 mm.

Outside micrometers. An outside micrometer consists of a C-shaped frame with an anvil and a threaded spindle. The thread is precision ground to ensure uniform movement of the spindle toward or away from the anvil. The spindle moves as it is rotated in the stationary spindle nut. A graduated stationary sleeve and a graduated rotating thimble are the bases for determining measurement. A locking mechanism can be provided for holding an established reading. A friction thimble or ratchet stop is also available to establish a uniform feel among individual users.

Outside micrometers generally are available in a variety of sizes. Size refers to the limits of its measuring range. The most common size is 1" (25 mm), which permits measurements over a range from 0 to 1" (25 mm). Larger outside micrometers are also available in sizes up to 60" or 600 mm.

In addition to the standard outside micrometers, micrometers also exist with different anvil and spindle shapes for specialized applications. Blade micrometers are used for measuring narrow slots and grooves. The disc micrometer is used for measuring thin materials such as paper as well as for measuring the distance from a slot to an edge. Hub micrometers can be put through a hole or bore to permit the measurement of the hub thickness of a gear or sprocket. Screw thread micrometers measure the pitch diameter of screw threads.

Like calipers, outside micrometers are also available with the capability to interface with data collection devices. These micrometers have an LCD that replaces the graduations on the sleeve and thimble.

Inside micrometers. An inside micrometer consists of a micrometer head with one permanent contact. The other contact consists of accurate rods in various increments that are seated snugly in the opposite end of the head against a shoulder and securely locked in place. Inside micrometers are available with solid or tubular rods. Handles can be attached to the micrometer head for measuring into deep holes.

The smallest bore that can be measured with this type of micrometer is 2" (50 mm), and the maximum upper limit depends on the rods available. Inside micrometers with solid rods are capable of measuring bores of up to 32" (800 mm); with tubular rods, the largest bore size is 107" (2700 mm).

Another type of internal micrometer consists of a specially designed micrometer head and three self-aligning measuring points on the other end. The self-aligning property of this instrument is particularly useful when measuring deep bores.

Three-point internal micrometers are available in sizes from 0.275 to 12" (6 to 300 mm). The individual instrument has a measuring capacity varying from 0.075" (2 mm) for the smallest size to 1.0" (25 mm) for the largest size. Three-point internal micrometers are also available with digital readouts, both mechanical and electronic.

Depth gages. Depth gages consist of a hardened, ground and lapped base with a micrometer head. Measuring rods are inserted through a hole in the micrometer screw and brought to a positive seat by a knurled nut. The screw is precision ground and has either a 1" or a 25 mm movement. The rods are furnished to measure in increments of 1" (25 mm); rods are available to measure to a depth of 9" (225 mm). Each rod protrudes through the base and moves as the thimble is rotated.

Depth gages measure the depth of holes, slots, recesses, and keyways from a flat reference point. They are available with standard or digital readout.

Bench micrometer. The bench micrometer is a precision instrument ideal for bench use either in the shop or inspection laboratory. It can be used as a comparator measuring to 50 μin. (1 μm) or for direct measuring to 0.0001" (0.001 mm). It can also be adapted for electronic readout.

The anvil actuates the indicator through a motion transfer mechanism and can be retracted by a lever for repeated measurements. A heavy-duty micrometer head mounted at the right of the base reads directly in 0.0001" (0.001 mm) and has a range from 0 to 2" (50 mm). Some bench micrometers have an adjustable base permitting measurements up to 4" (100 mm).

An adjustable worktable is centered beneath the anvil and the spindle. Work can be accurately aligned between anvil and spindle by adjusting the table to the proper height and then locking it in position by a lockscrew.

Protractors

Protractors are used to directly measure angular surfaces. The tools most commonly used are the simple protractor, the protractor head, and the universal bevel protractor.

Simple protractor. A simple protractor consists of a rectangular head graduated in degrees along a semicircle with a blade pivoted on the center pin. By rotating the blade on the center pin, any angle from 0 to 180° can be set.

Protractor head. The protractor head is one of several tools on the combination square. It has revolving turrets with direct-reading double graduations a full 0-180° in opposite directions. This permits direct reading of angles above or below the blade.

Universal bevel protractor. The universal bevel protractor consists of a round body with a fixed blade on which a graduated protractor dial rotates. The turret is slotted to accommodate a 7 or 12" (180 or 300 mm) nongraduated blade. The blade and dial may be rotated as a unit to any desired position and locked in place by means of the dial clamp nut. The blade may also be independently extended in either direction from the protractor dial.

The protractor dial is graduated 360° reading 0-90°, 90-0°, 0-90°, and 90-0°. Each 10° increment is numbered, and each 5° increment is indicated by a line longer than those on either side of it. The vernier is graduated in 12 spaces, with each increment representing 5 minutes.

COMPARATIVE INSTRUMENTS

Comparative instruments compare the workpiece being measured against a master that was used to calibrate the instrument. Because these instruments are compared against a master, they are generally only capable of measuring the amount of deviation as well as the direction of deviation from the calibrated size. The range of the deviation that can be measured depends on the type of comparative gage used. The three most commonly used comparative or indicating gages are mechanical, pneumatic, and electronic.

Mechanical Indicating Gages

Mechanical indicating gages mechanically amplify or magnify variations or displacements in dimensions for the purpose of making precise observations. This magnification may be accomplished by gear trains, levers, cams, torsion strips, reeds, or a combination of these. The direction of the original displacement that can be sensed by an indicator may be in line with the instrument spindle axis or normal to the contact lever swinging over a small angle. For some applications, attachments can be also used to redirect the original displacement to the contact element of the indicator instrument.

Mechanical amplifying devices must be used in conjunction with a reference point, line, or surface to produce either a direct or comparative measurement. The combination of the mechanical amplifier or indicator and the reference comprises a gage.

Indicator types. Indicators are mechanical instruments for sensing and measuring distance variations. The mechanism of the indicator converts the axial displacement of the measurement spindle into rotational movement. This rotational movement is mechanically amplified and then displayed by a pointer rotating over the face of a circular dial with evenly spaced graduations. Some indicators have hands that can be moved around the face to indicate the permissible tolerance being measured.

Specifications for indicators are covered in ANSI Standard B89.1.10, "Dial Indicators (For Linear Measurements)." According to this standard, there are three major types of indicators. Type A indicators have the spindle parallel to the dial face, Type B indicators have the spindle at right angles to the dial face, and for Type C indicators, the measuring contact is a lever. The first two types are referred to as dial indicators and the third type as test indicators.

According to ANSI Standard B89.1.10, indicators are available in four different classes. These classes refer to the least graduation value on the indicator dial; indicators with other graduations are also available from manufacturers. Units may be either English or metric. Table 3-1 lists the four classes of indicator graduations.

TABLE 3-1
Dial Indicator Graduations

| Class | Bezel diam, in. (mm) | Smallest graduation | |
		Inches	Millimeters
1	1⅜-2	0.0001	0.005
	(35-50)	0.0005	0.01
		0.001	
2	2-2⅜	0.00005	0.001
	(50-60)	0.0001	0.002
		0.0005	0.005
		0.001	0.01
3	2⅜-3	0.0001	0.001
	(60-76)	0.0005	0.002
		0.001	0.005
			0.01
4	3-3¾	0.00005	0.001
	(76-95)	0.0001	0.002
		0.0005	0.005
		0.001	0.01

Dial indicators. The magnification of a dial-type indicator is obtained by means of a gear train. This type of indicator is most commonly used because its magnification accuracy meets the large majority of requirements. A typical dial indicator is shown in Fig. 3-4.

In operation, a sensitive contact or point is attached to a rack that transfers the motion to the rack gear. A train of three to five gears, depending on the magnification desired, magnifies and transmits the movement of the contact to the pinion gear on which the indicator hand is mounted with a hairspring and takeup gear to eliminate backlash. Some indicators are designed with a spring-loaded link at some part of the gear train to absorb the impact of a sudden shock and protect the indicator against damage.

The pressure of the sensitive contact is established by a pullback spring that exerts a downward pressure on the rack spindle, thus keeping the contact constantly in touch with the workpiece. There must always be sufficient pressure to ensure positive contact and to overcome the internal friction of the indicator itself, which measures approximately 15 to 35 g (0.5 to 1.2 oz).

The amplification of dial indicators ranges from approximately 40 to 1 to about 1500 to 1. On long-range indicators, revolution counters are used to count the revolutions of the main hand, and the effective scale length can be as much as 17' for 0.400" (5 m for 10.00 mm) in spindle motion.

Modifications combining both spirals and gears are employed to change the direction of travel of the contact point with reference to the indicator dial. This is a convenience in locating the indicator to suit certain gaging needs.

The readings on dial indicators may be consecutively graduated or balanced. For consecutively graduated dials, the graduations are normally numbered clockwise from 0 to the range included in one complete revolution of the pointer. This arrangement is best for measuring linear displacements. A revolution counter is also included on dial indicators having an extra long measuring range.

Balanced dials have the graduations numbered systematically in both directions from the starting 0. In most cases, the largest value is 180° away from the initial position. One side of the dial is marked plus (+) and the other minus (-). This arrangement is best for comparative measurements.

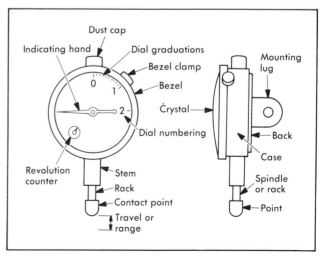

Fig. 3-4 Nomenclature used in describing dial indicator components.

GENERAL-PURPOSE DEVICES

Test indicators. Test indicators sense and measure displacements that occur in a direction perpendicular to the shaft of the contact point (see Fig. 3-5). Magnification is obtained by gears and levers. Because they are small, test indicators are particularly useful in setup inspection and toolroom work.

Reed-type indicators. In this type of indicator, the reed magnifying mechanism uses various combinations of flat steel reeds to obtain mechanical amplification (see Fig. 3-6). The sensitive spindle is mounted on a block that floats on reeds connected to a fixed block that is attached to the mounting. Extending from the top of the two blocks is a vertical member consisting of a pair of reeds, one of which is attached to each of the fixed and the floating blocks; a hand or pointer is mounted on this member. Slight motion of the sensitive contact flexes the reeds and moves the hand along a vertical arc.

The reed mechanism is capable of amplification on the order of 200 to 1, depending on the relative length of the reeds. However, this mechanism is frequently coupled with a system of lenses that project light on a graduated scale while a pointer mounted on the vertical member casts a shadow on the dial. With this combination, amplifications from 500 to 1 up to 20,000 to 1 are obtainable. The absence of inertia in the light beam and the very low friction in the reed mechanism make these instruments extremely sensitive and provide low gaging pressure. However, their range is limited because the graduated arc can be used only once instead of for several revolutions as in the case of dial indicators. Because there are no wearing parts, reed mechanisms maintain their accuracy without impairment resulting from use.

Another type of reed mechanism consists of a doubly twisted single reed of spring steel. One end of the strip is anchored to a stationary block while the other end is attached to a lever actuated by the contact point. The indicating hand is centrally mounted on the reed. Elongation of the reed causes it to unwind and thus rotate the indicating hand.

Applications. Dial indicators are designed for use on a wide range of standard measuring devices such as bench comparators, indicator plug gages, depth-indicating gages, indicator snap gages, bore indicator gages, and thread-indicating gages.

Pneumatic Indicating Gages

Pneumatic or air gaging uses the restriction of airflow between a nozzle tip and the part being tested to determine part size. Although a variety of instrument designs and modes of operation exist, a pneumatic gage cannot operate without a regulated air supply, a flow metering device, and one or more nozzles. A typical pneumatic circuit is shown in Fig. 3-7.

In operation, the air from the regulated supply flows through the restriction and then through the nozzle. When the nozzle is free and open to the atmosphere, there will be a maximum flow of air through the nozzle. In addition, there will be a minimum of pressure in the system downstream of the restriction. If a plate is moved in front on the nozzle and slowly brought toward it, the airflow will gradually be restricted until the nozzle is shut off. At this point, the airflow would be 0. When the nozzle has been completely closed off, the pressure downstream of the restriction will build up until it becomes the same as the regulated supply.

Figure 3-8 shows a plot of both airflow and air pressure versus the distance between the plate and nozzle. With the exception of the extremes of flow and pressure, the curve is virtually a straight line. Because of this linearity, the distance of the plate from the nozzle can be determined.

Advantages. Air gaging is not the answer to all gaging problems, but it does offer many advantages.[2] In the measurement of hole conditions, air gaging is unsurpassed for speed and accuracy. In addition, air gaging offers sufficient magnification and reliability to measure small tolerances. An air gage can easily determine a size difference of 5 μin. (0.13 μm) and can measure holes as small as 0.040″ (1.02 mm). The linear range and resolution of the pneumatic circuit depend on the orifice

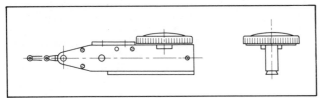

Fig. 3-5 Typical test indicator.

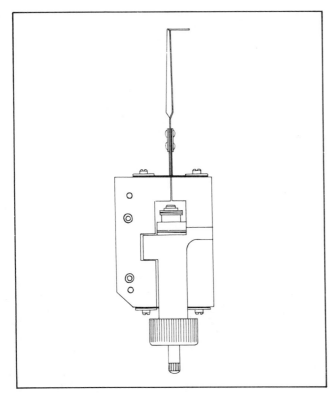

Fig. 3-6 Reed-type dial indicator.

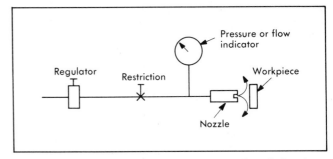

Fig. 3-7 Diagram of basic air gage components. (*Edmunds Gages*)

diameter of the air nozzle and part diameter. In general, the linear measuring range of an open air nozzle is less than 0.16 of the orifice diameter.

Simplicity is one of the biggest advantages of air gaging. Production workers do not require special training, for using an air gage is as simple as inserting the air probe into a hole and then reading the meter.

Air gages are also economical. Once the basic gage is purchased, additional tooling for a wide variety of jobs can be used with it.

The noncontact characteristic of most air gage tooling makes it particularly useful for checking soft, highly polished, thin-walled, or otherwise delicate materials. When extremely rough surfaces are involved or when bores with small interior projections must be measured, contact-type air gage tooling can be used.

Another advantage of air gaging is the cleaning effect of the air escaping from the tooling. This reduces the possibility of false readings due to oil, dirt, or coolant on the part.

Air gage systems. Air gage systems are usually divided and classified according to their operating principles. The two general types of circuits used are freeflow and back pressure. Each type of circuit has individual advantages and areas of performance. Back-pressure gaging is used with an air-to-electronic converter to generate electrical signals for control and analysis.

Flow gage system. The flow gage system is characterized by freedom from restricting orifices and mechanical wearing elements. In principle, air under constant pressure enters the bottom of an internally tapered glass column and flows to the gaging element or tooling (see Fig. 3-9, view *a*). A lightweight float moves up or down in direct ratio to the flow of air between the tooling and the workpiece.

A limitation to this type of system is that the float and tapered glass column tend to get loaded down with the oil in the shop-supplied air. This requires scheduled cleaning of the flow monitoring system.

A modification of the basic flow gage system is shown in Fig. 3-9, view *b*. In operation, air under constant pressure passes through a venturi tube into the gaging element or tooling. Each chamber of the venturi has a pressure tube connected to the opposite sides of a bellows or diaphragm. A difference in pressure existing between the two sections of the venturi tube actuates this bellows, which in turn operates a mechanical amplifier. Variations of air escaping between the tooling and workpiece effect a change in pressure differential in the venturi.

Back-pressure gage system. Several different types of back-pressure gage systems have been developed. In its basic form, the back-pressure gage system consists of air under constant

pressure passing through a controlling orifice of predetermined or adjustable size and into the gaging element or tooling (see Fig. 3-10, view *a*). A suitable pressure-indicating device inserted in the system between the controlling orifice and the tooling indicates changes in pressure resulting from the air escaping between the tooling and workpiece.

The water-column gage system was first developed to determine the size of carburetor jets (see Fig. 3-10, view *b*). This system uses the self-balancing properties of connected vessels, the constant pressure being maintained by the height of the water column. The level of the liquid in the graduated tube indicates the amount of obstruction that is facing the escaping jets in the gage head.

Another modification of the basic back-pressure circuit is the differential air gage system, which employs a parallel circuit as shown in Fig. 3-10, view *c*. In this system, air under constant pressure enters two separate channels and passes into opposite sections of a bellows cavity and housing. Air in one of the channels is allowed to escape through the gaging plug. In the other channel, air is allowed to escape through the zero setting valve. In operation, the difference between air escaping between the tooling jets and the workpiece as compared to the amount escaping when the master is in place causes a pressure differential at the bellows. The pressure differential is registered by a dial-type indicator or converted to an electrical signal using a pressure transducer.

Air gage tooling. The tooling used in air gaging is classified as either noncontact or contact.

Noncontact. Noncontact tooling, also referred to as open-jet tooling, uses the direct flow of air from the air escapement orifice to contact the part. The rate of flow depends on the diameter of the nozzle hole and the clearance between the jet and the part. Because the freeflowing air helps to blow away oil or foreign material, noncontact tooling is commonly used in automatic gaging machines if the cycle time permits. The speed of the air circuit must be considered in many applications.

A noncontact gage head may have single jets, dual jets, or multiple jets. Single-jet tooling permits simplicity in design, a minimizing of many pneumatic problems, and practical han-

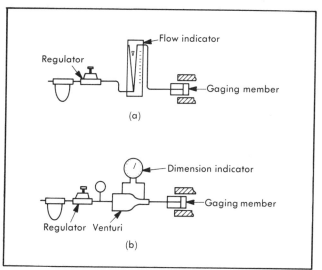

Fig. 3-9 Diagram of basic types of airflow gage systems: (a) airflow gage with rotameter tube and (b) velocity-type air gage with venturi chamber.

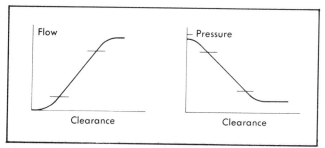

Fig. 3-8 Graph comparing airflow and air pressure with clearance between plate and nozzle. (*Edmunds Gages*)

dling by a nonspecialist. Because single-jet tooling is inherently sensitive to gage position, it is not used for inside and outside diameter applications. Figure 3-11 illustrates some of the many ways that single-jet tooling can be used.

Dual-jet tooling is used in air probes for internal diameter inspection and in air snap and air ring gages for outside diameter measurements. This type of tooling eliminates the need for precise placement of the workpiece and the use of semiskilled help. Figure 3-12 illustrates some dual-jet tooling applications.

A dual-jet probe can measure true diameter because it has diametrically opposed jets. By traversing and rotating the probe, as the hole is gaged two-point out-of-round, bellmouth, hourglass, and barrel-shape conditions can be determined.

Dual-jet ring and air snap gages are the most widely used noncontact tooling for external diameter measurement. They inspect the true and average outside diameter of a cylindrical part and reveal conditions of taper and out-of-roundness. They are manufactured in many different types, shapes, and sizes and may be designed for presenting the part to the gage or the gage to the part. Air rings and snap gages with three jets are used for diameter, taper, and cloverleaf (three-lobe) conditions.

Contact. Contact tooling has a mechanical member between the air escapement orifice and the part. This mechanical member can be freely rotating balls, a plunger, or levers. The movement of the mechanical member may be in an axial or a radial direction. Contact-type tooling is generally used for the

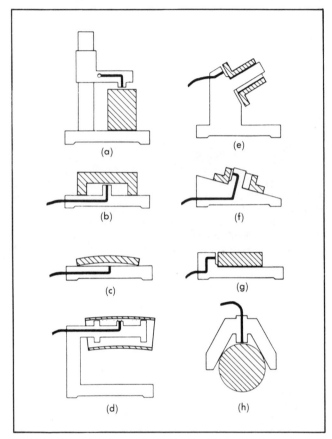

Fig. 3-11 Examples of single-jet tooling: (a) height gage; (b) depth gage; (c) flatness measurement; (d) camber or banana-shape measurement; (e), (f), and (g) squareness; and (h) outside diameter snap gage. (*Sheffield Measurement Div., Warner & Swasey*)

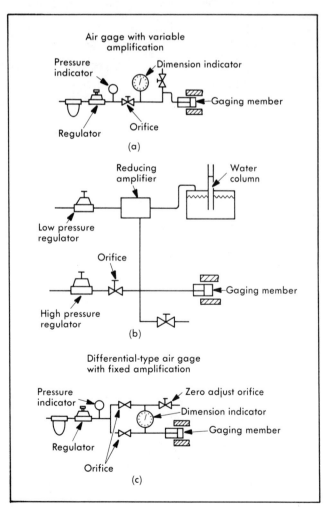

Fig. 3-10 Diagram of basic types of back-pressure gage systems: (a) air gage with variable amplification, (b) water-column gage system, and (c) differential-type air gage with fixed amplification. (*Western Gage Corp.*)

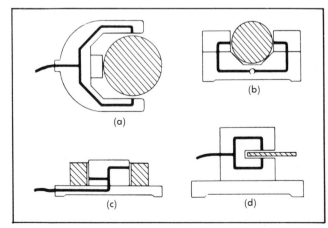

Fig. 3-12 Examples of dual-jet tooling: (a) outside diameter snap gage, (b) outside diameter V-block gage, (c) perpendicularity measurement, and (d) thickness measurement.

measurement of rough and porous surfaces or extending the linear measuring range of the air nozzle.

A typical air cartridge is shown in Fig. 3-13. It consists of a plunger that moves in a radial direction and a poppet-type air valve. Any change in the plunger position changes the airflow and the reading on the pneumatic comparator. Because the tapered plunger moves in and out of the air nozzle, the escape area of the air nozzle changes more gradually with the position of the measured surface. This allows for a linear measuring range of up to 0.080″ (2.00 mm). Some typical air cartridge applications are shown in Fig. 3-14. Air cartridges must be fixed securely on the measuring fixture before measurements are made.

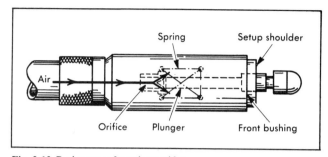

Fig. 3-13 Basic parts of an air cartridge.

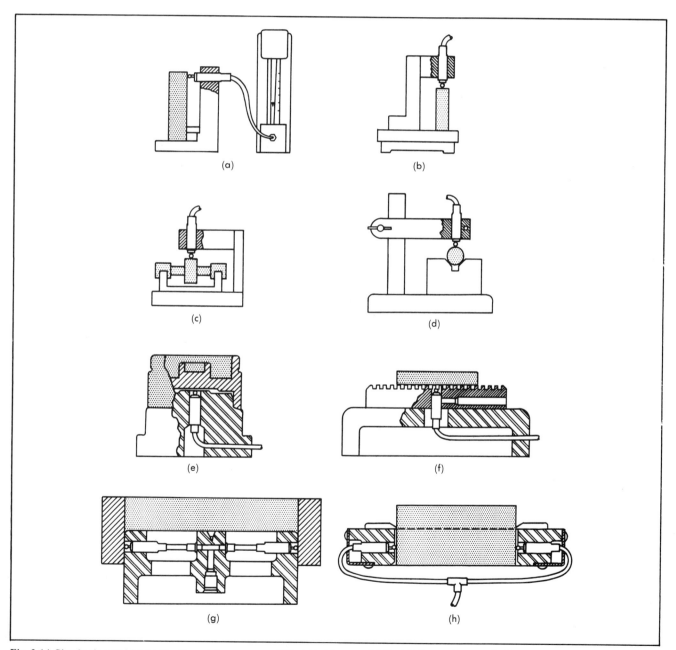

Fig. 3-14 Simple air-cartridge applications: (a) squareness, (b) height, (c) concentricity, (d) three-point outside diameter, (e) depth, (f) flatness, (g) inside diameter, and (h) outside diameter. (*Sheffield Measurment Div., Warner & Swasey*)

GENERAL-PURPOSE DEVICES

Air gage mastering. Because air gages are not direct measuring instruments, the comparator instrument and gaging member must be calibrated with a master of known size. When this calibration is achieved, a certain point on the instrument's scale indicates a particular size. Obtaining accurate data at other points also requires that the correct scale factor be established. That is, the comparator must be adjusted so that the span indicated by the display corresponds identically to a corresponding variation in workpiece size. The two methods used to ensure correct calibration of the gaging system are single master calibration and dual master calibration.

Single master calibration. In single master calibration, both the comparator and the gaging member are manufactured to predetermined pneumatic scale factors. No span adjustments are required or available to the user. Comparators designed for single master operation utilize fixed orifices for flow restriction or variable restrictors that are factory set and sealed. Precise calibration of these instruments is done at the factory before shipment using master orifice standards.

Standardized scale factors for gaging members manufactured for single master operation are obtained by precisely sizing jet holes so that the sensitivity of the gaging member specifically matches the pneumatic scale factor of the comparator with which they are operated. Using members not specifically designed for a particular model of single master comparator can result in substantial gaging error.

The use of only one master for system setup has significant advantages. The simplification of setup procedure saves time as well as reducing the skill level required of the operator. The elimination of the requirement for a second setting master has substantial cost savings when large sizes are to be gaged.

Dual master calibration. In dual master calibration, the system sensitivity (scale factor) is set by adjusting the span displayed by the comparator instrument to correspond to the difference between minimum and maximum setting masters. This method directly sets the combined sensitivity of all the components of the gaging system. Sensitivities of such items as flow restrictors, amplifiers, pressure indicators, flowmeter tubes, and gaging nozzles as well as restrictive effects of air lines are included in one overall setting. Utilizing the two-master method, stringent control of these individual components is not necessary to obtain highly accurate overall results.

The dual master setting technique permits back-pressure type comparators with variable flow restrictors to be used with virtually any practical nozzle size. By calibrating with two masters, the adjustment of the flow restrictor readily compensates for variations in nozzle sensitivity due to the use of nonstandard jet hole sizes.

Usually, product tolerance limits are selected for master dimensions; however, other limits can be satisfactorily used. Close-tolerance select fits, for example, are mastered over a range of values. In these cases, tradeoffs between accuracy and the total gaging range covered become involved, and it is best to obtain factory recommendations.

Comparison. Selection of one or the other method involves trading off the simplicity and economy of the single master system versus the accuracy and reliability of the dual master system. Because single master systems utilize comparators that have standardized scale factors, allowance must be made for possible scaling errors in both the comparator and the gaging members. Such errors increase in direct proportion to the span between the master and the point of measurement. For instance, if a measurement is made 0.0002" (0.005 mm) from the mastered dimension, a scale factor error of 5% would cause an error of 5% of the 0.0002" (0.005 mm) span or 0.000010" (0.00025 mm); if the span were extended to 0.001" (0.025 mm), this error would become 0.000050" (0.00125 mm). An error of 5% is a realistic assumption considering that accuracy of manufacture and stability with age must be allowed for in both the gaging member and the comparator. For most applications, this is an acceptable level of accuracy. Users should be aware, however, that attempting to use a master that is well outside of the tolerance zone may lead to unacceptable errors. For instance, if someone has a 0.0001" (0.0025 mm) total tolerance and attempts to use a master that is 0.001" (0.025 mm) larger, a scaling error of 0.00005" (0.00125 mm) is clearly unacceptable even though it may be within the dial range.

Machine control. Air gaging can be used on external grinders, surface grinders, and centerless grinding machines to locate parts precisely, indicate grinding wheel position if needed, measure wheel wear, and measure and control part size. Figure 3-15 shows an air cartridge mounted to the infeed slide of an external grinder. The cartridge indicates against a fixed adjustable stop attached to the stationary part of the machine. As the part is ground, infeed slide movement is shown by the falling float in the air column. When the float reaches a preset position in the column, the operator knows that the part is at final size.

In setting up the operation, the first part is ground and then gaged on a comparator or air snap gage. The stop is adjusted to position the float correctly in the column. The infeed slide wheel is next manipulated until the float is at "zero" in the tube, indicating the correct diameter size. All succeeding parts are ground till "zero" float position is reached in the column gage.

Another method of continuous grinding control is to use an air cartridge in a caliper sizing gage. This enables the operator to control stock removal accurately by watching the float action against the scale.

Electronic Indicating Gages

The three characteristics most responsible for the ever-widening use of electronic gaging equipment are its ability to sense size differences as small as 1 μin. (0.025 μm), its ability to amplify these small measurements as much as 100,000 times, and its ability to generate an electronic signal that can be

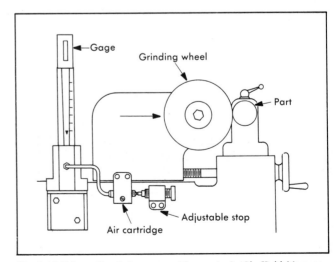

Fig. 3-15 Schematic of air gage machine control. (*Sheffield Measurement Div., Warner & Swasey*)

computer processed. Systems measuring dimensions having very tight tolerances [10 μin. (0.25 μm)] are best put to use in laboratory measuring instruments such as gage block comparators and in comparators and height gages for shop applications. Electronic gages also find their way into automatic sizing and automatic gaging and sorting systems. These applications will be discussed subsequently in the section on automatic gaging and process control.

When using an electronic comparator, the gage is first calibrated by a master to the master dimension. The workpieces are then compared with this dimension, and the variation is displayed on an indicator.

Equipment. As was previously mentioned, the most common types of electronic gaging equipment are the electronic comparator and the height gage. An electronic comparator usually consists of the gaging head(s) (transducer), the stand or support to which the head is attached, the indicator, and the amplifier. The basic difference between the comparator and the height gage is that the comparator has a built-in work support or reference surface. Height gages require a surface plate or some other reference base to support the workpiece and the stand.

Gaging head. Gaging heads transform a displacement of a measuring tip into a proportional electrical signal. They come in a variety of sizes and configurations and are built around different types of transducers.

The three most common head configurations are the lever type, cartridge type, and frictionless type[3] (see Fig. 3-16). The lever-type head, probably the most versatile, features an angularly adjustable, clutch-mounted contact finger. This allows the head to be set at the most convenient gaging angle and protects it against accidental blows. A reversing mechanism allows most of these heads to be used for measuring from above or below without turning the head upside down. Lever-type heads are most often used in height-gage setups.

The cartridge head is generally used in production gaging fixtures, snap gages, and in jobs involving space and mounting restrictions. Many of them are designed to fit into clamps normally used to hold dial indicators.

The "frictionless" head is the most accurate of these gaging heads and is used mainly in comparator setups. The spindle is suspended from two reeds, assuring virtually frictionless operation.

Of the many types of transducers used in electronic gaging heads—inductance bridge, differential transformer, strain gages, variable capacitors, piezoelectric crystals, and others—the inductance bridge, differential transformer, and strain gage are the most widely used. Both the linear variable differential transformer (LVDT) and the inductance bridge can sense small displacements over a limited range.

The gage head used in connection with an inductance bridge consists of two coils with a small iron core centered between them. When this core is in the center position, both coils have the same inductance, but when the core is displaced (as the tip contacts a workpiece), the inductance of one coil increases and that of the other decreases. This changes the current through the coils, and the change, within certain limits, is proportional to the core displacement.

The LVDT produces an electrical output proportional to the displacement of a separate movable core. It consists of three coils equally spaced on a cylindrical coil form (see Fig. 3-17). A rod-shaped magnetic core positioned axially inside this coil assembly provides a path for magnetic flux linking the coils. The secondary coils are connected in series opposition so that the two voltages in the secondary circuit are opposite in phase; the net output of the transformer is the difference of these voltages. When the magnetic core is in the central position, the output voltage is 0. This position is called the balance point or null position. As the core moves from this position, the voltage induced in the secondary coil toward which the core is moved increases. The voltage in the other secondary coil decreases. If the gage head is properly designed, this produces a differential voltage output from the transformer that varies linearly with a change in core position.

Both the inductance bridge and the LVDT depend on magnetic fields, so it is important that they be adequately shielded from external magnetic fields that would influence measure-

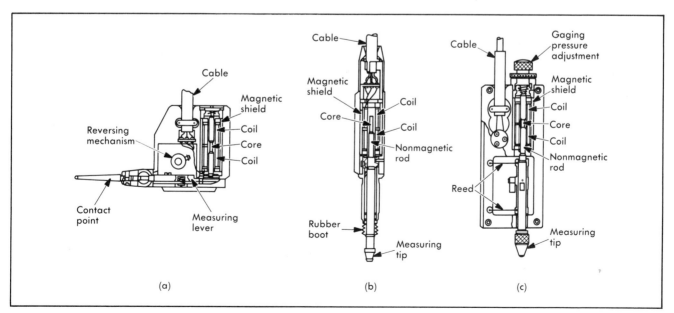

Fig. 3-16 Common gage heads used in electronic gaging: (a) lever-type, (b) cartridge type, and (c) frictionless type.

GENERAL-PURPOSE DEVICES

ment. This is especially true in shops where many different sources of magnetic fields are present—machines, power lines, and magnetic chucks, to name just a few.

Strain gages are also used as transducers in gaging heads. The strain gage principle involves the stretching of a wire. Any strain on the wire changes its length and diameter, thereby changing its resistance in proportion to the strain.

Another type of transducer used in gage heads is the capacitive transducer. Gaging heads with capacitive transducers have two steel plates separated by an air gap (see Fig. 3-18). When the gage tip moves, the gap between the plates vary, thereby changing the capacitance. The change in capacitance is a measure of tip displacement.

Linear encoders can also be used to measure dimensions on different parts. The main advantage to using linear encoders is that measurements can be taken over a very long range [up to 24″ (610 mm)] with an accuracy of ±20 μin. (0.5 μm). Different applications include camshaft lobe profile, single-flank gear lead, and length checks.

Stand. With the interest in transducers, gage head mechanisms, and the workings of electronic amplifiers, it is easy to overlook the stand, which is a very important part of the electronic gaging system. Several manufacturers have devised special stands for certain applications such as thread measurement, squareness, and ID measurement. However, most electronic gaging is done either on a comparator or with a height gage. In designing a comparator stand, the goal is maximum stability and rigidity; in designing a height gage stand, stability and rigidity are kept in mind, but the aim is range and versatility.

Amplifier. The sturdiest stand and the finest gage head are practically useless unless they are teamed up with a quality amplifier. The stability, accuracy, and drift of a gaging system depend directly on amplifier quality.

The recent growth of electronic gaging owes much to the development of the transistorized amplifier. Utilizing transistors instead of vacuum tubes and printed circuits instead of hand-wired ones, the modern electronic gaging amplifier is smaller, lighter, and more troublefree than its predecessors. Also, the operating temperature of such an amplifier is so close to room temperature that it can be used in the proximity of the comparator or height gage without affecting gage accuracy.

Power for portable amplifiers can usually be furnished by mercury cell battery packs, rechargeable batteries, or direct line power.

Applications. Most electronic gages of the comparator type are used in a manner similar to dial indicators. The major difference is that the electronic gage can read much smaller deviations because the signal is digitized.

Because electronic instruments are highly stable, they can be used as absolute measuring devices. Thin parts, up to the maximum range of the instrument, can be measured directly without the use of a master. The accuracy depends on the type of probe and gaging system. For the best accuracy, one master is always required.

Differential measurements are also commonly made with electronic gages. Two gages are connected to one amplifier, and the difference or sum of the gage head outputs is measured. This technique can be used for checking roundness, thickness, parallelism, and taper. Because two gaging operations are combined in one, time savings are considerable.

Squareness, or lack of it, can be detected to 10 μin. (0.25 μm) through use of electronic gage heads and simple fixtures. Electronic gaging is also used in ultraprecision laboratory instruments such as gage block and ring and disc comparators, roundness checkers, and other master-checking devices. Such units are seldom, if ever, found in a shop; they are operated within special controlled-environment rooms or modules.

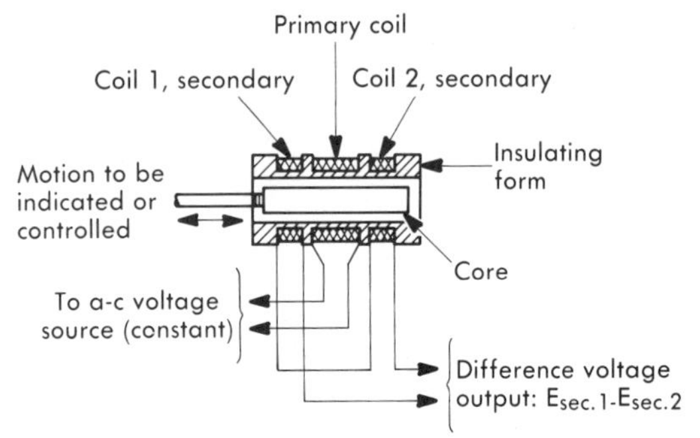

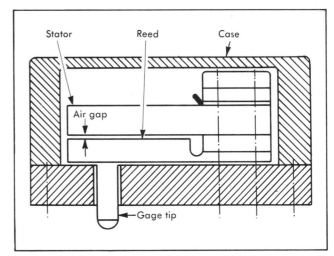

Fig. 3-17 Cross section of a linear variable differential transformer. (*Schaevitz Engineering*)

Fig. 3-18 Capacitive-type gage head.

GAGE BLOCKS

Linear measurement and size agreement of parts, tools, and gages manufactured by various companies in different locations is essential to interchangeability. Gage blocks are the master gages providing the reference standard for comparison in linear

GAGE BLOCKS

measurement. They are made of steel, carbide, or chromium-plated steel that has been stabilized for dimensional stability. The measuring surfaces of these blocks are plane, parallel, and at a specified distance apart. Common shapes for the gaging surfaces of these blocks are rectangular and square; most square blocks have a hole in the center.

Gage blocks are available individually or in sets. In the English system of units, sets contain from 5 to 88 blocks and permit a systematic progression of measurements. Attachments are available to use a combination of gage blocks for height gage measurements, length, and internal and outside diameter checking. Combinations of gage blocks can be formed in increments as small as 25 μin. (1 μm).

Gage blocks come in four different accuracy grades specified by ANSI Standard B89.1.9 (see Table 3-2). The grades determine the area in which the blocks can be used. Gage blocks are available in both English and metric units.

USING GAGE BLOCKS

When using gage blocks, it is extremely important that the individual blocks and any associated tooling be free of dirt, grease, and foreign matter. The block faces should, however, have a light film of oil on them. The complete set of blocks should be taken to the location where the inspection will be performed to minimize the potential of scratching or nicking the individual blocks. The blocks selected for a specific application should be removed from the box and placed on clean paper, cloth, or chamois.

Temperature Considerations

The universally accepted standard measuring temperature is 68° F (20° C). Each particular gage block and work material has its own coefficient of expansion. If measured and used at this temperature, these differences are not of consequence. By necessity, however, measurements are often made under uncontrolled temperature. In this case, for accurate results, the coefficient of expansion of both gages and the workpiece must be considered (see Table 3-3). Steel gage blocks used to measure a steel workpiece will usually expand a like amount and produce fairly accurate readings. Conversely, steel work blocks used to measure an aluminum workpiece would require computation of expansion differences through consideration of prevailing temperature, size of work, and coefficient of expansion for both materials. Both metals must be known to have achieved the same temperature. Suitable allowances must then be made in the readings obtained.

The errors in measurement caused by differential dimensional changes at temperatures other than the standard can be calculated by the equation:

$$C = L\,(\Delta k)\,(\Delta T) \tag{1}$$

where:

C = correction value, μin. (μm)
L = length of gage block(s) at standard temperature, in. (m)
Δk = difference in coefficient of linear expansion between the gage block and material being measured, μin./in./° F (μm/m/° C)
ΔT = temperature deviation from 68° F or 20° C, ° F (° C)

As a general rule, the correction value is added to the measured length providing the following conditions are met:

1. The coefficient of linear expansion of the part is greater than that of the gage block.
2. The temperature is greater than 68° F (20° C).

If these conditions are not met, the correction value would be subtracted from the measured value.

Forming Combinations

As was previously stated, gage blocks are produced in sets of various series. The sets are available to provide both a range of sizes that may be measured and a range of increments in which measurements may be made. It is therefore necessary to have a system by which to combine blocks to produce any desired dimension within the range of the particular set being used. The system consists of progressively eliminating the last one or two digits. This is continued until the entire dimension is duplicated in the sum of the combined block sizes.

An example of this procedure would be to select blocks to form the dimension 2.4817". The first block selected is 0.1007", which eliminates the smallest increment by subtraction, leaving 2.381". The next block selected is 0.131". This value subtracted from 2.381" leaves 2.250". A 0.250" block is then chosen, which eliminates all except 2.000", so that a 2.000" block completes the combination.

Wringing Gage Blocks

When individual gage blocks are combined to provide a specific measurement, they are assembled together using a technique known as "wringing." Wringing is achieved by sliding the mating gaging surfaces on each other until they adhere to

TABLE 3-2
Accuracy of Gage Block Grades

Grade	Former Designation	Tolerance, in. (mm)	Use
0.5	AAA	±0.000001 (±0.00003)	Basic reference standard in calibration laboratory. Referred to as grand masters
1	AA	±0.000002 (±0.00005)	Gage room reference blocks
2	A+	+0.000004, -0.000002 (+0.0001, -0.00005)	Setting and checking indicating and limit gages serving inspection and process control
3	A & B	+0.000006, -0.000002 (+0.00015, -0.00005)	Working gage blocks for use in toolroom and production areas

GAGE BLOCKS

such a degree that considerable force must be exerted to break the wring (see Fig. 3-19). A slight pressure is used when sliding the blocks together to prevent any moisture and airborne dust from being trapped between the blocks that could cause scratches and inaccurate measurements.

Blocks are usually wrung in the reverse order of selection, with the largest block on the bottom of the stack. Thin blocks should be wrung to heavier blocks to remove any deflection in the thin block. The wringing operation is repeated until all the necessary blocks needed to form the combination desired are assembled. After completing the combination, the temperature of the blocks should be allowed to stabilize. This can be aided by a cooling plate. This problem can be minimized by the use of forceps, gloves, or other insulating factors, making as little contact as possible. Avoid touching the gaging surfaces, because an overacidic condition can result in etching the steel.

Gage blocks should not be left wrung together any longer than necessary to complete the job because moisture trapped between steel blocks will cause corrosion. After the gage blocks are disassembled, they should be wiped clean with a soft cloth or chamois and a light coat of protective oil applied before return-

ing to them their individual inserts in the case. A chamois lubricated with a rust-preventive oil will usually give excellent results.

Gage Block Calibration

Because gage blocks are subject to wear, corrosion, and damage, which affect their size or measuring ability, they must be checked periodically to verify their accuracy. The frequency of this check depends on the tolerance requirements of the job, the amount of use, and the conditions under which they are used.

Calibration certificates are provided by gage block manufacturers and qualified measuring laboratories who provide traceability to the National Bureau of Standards. These certificates provide a report of the actual size of each block to a degree of accuracy compatible with the corresponding grade specifications.

TABLE 3-3
Expansion of Gage Block Materials

Gage Material	Linear Expansion, μin./in./°F (μm/m/°C)
Tool steel	6.4 (11.5)
Stainless steel (410)	5.5 (9.9)
Tungsten carbide	3.3 (5.9)
Chromium carbide	4.5 (8.1)

Fig. 3-19 Wringing gage blocks together.

FIXED FUNCTIONAL GAGES

Unlike the general measuring devices, which can be used for a variety of applications, fixed gages are designed for a specific application. The value of these gages is in their ability to check parts much faster than an inspector can measure parts using the general-purpose measuring devices. If the gage is properly designed, good parts are ensured by the interaction of the gage points and the part being inspected. However, little is known about the exact measurements of the part. The nature of the part to be inspected, its material composition, the precision desired, the number of pieces to be checked per hour or day, and the skill of the inspector all enter into the choice of this type of gage.

Fixed functional gages are the direct or reverse physical replica of the workpiece dimension being measured.[4] They are usually designed to measure a single dimension. The gage may represent the part in its nominal condition or in one of its limit conditions.

Gages manufactured to the nominal size are referred to as master gages. They are primarily used for setting up comparator-type measuring instruments. Another application of master gages is calibrating measuring tools.

Limit gages check the dimension of the workpiece at one of the specified design limits. For most dimensions checked, two separate gages are required. The GO limit gage checks the part dimension at its maximum material condition and ensures the ability of the part to be assembled. For an inside feature such as a hole, this would be the smallest diameter permissible; for outside features, this would represent the maximum size. If the gage can enter the part feature or the part feature can enter the gage, the dimension is considered acceptable.

To ensure the part's functional adequacy, the minimum material condition must also be checked. This is done with the NOT-GO gage. If the NOT-GO gage enters the part feature, the dimension is considered unacceptable.

Several different fixed functional gages are available. They can be classified on the basis of whether they are used to check outside dimensions or inside dimensions. Outside dimensions are commonly made with cylindrical ring gages and snap gages; inside dimensions are made with cylindrical plug gages. Functional gages are also used to check different geometrical shapes such as tapers, threads, and splines. Additional information on screw thread gages and spline gages can be found in Chapter 4, "Dimensional Metrology and Geometric Conformance," of this volume.

GAGE MATERIALS

The most important material properties in fixed gage applications are dimensional stability and wear resistance.[5] Modern heat treating methods, including deep freezing, when judiciously applied to properly selected steel grades, can provide a high degree of stability. In addition to advances in heat treating processes, alloying elements in steel grades currently selected for the manufacture of fixed gages substantially improve the wear resistance of the gaging members, thereby extending the useful life of the gage. Realizing the harmful effect of surface roughness on the capability of resisting frictional wear, leading gage manufacturers are using special lapping processes to produce an exceedingly fine surface finish and also to improve the geometry of the gaging members.

Although for the majority of applications fixed gage members made of alloy steels prove entirely satisfactory, there are specific applications that warrant the use of even more wear-resistant gage materials. Such conditions may exist for gages in extended use to check very tightly toleranced dimensions or for gaging parts made of materials having unusually abrasive properties.

For applications requiring a particularly high degree of wear resistance, fixed gages are also made from other kinds of materials or by using special processes. Tungsten carbide materials provide good stability and wear resistance, but their use is generally limited because of cost and sensitivity to chipping. When checking tightly toleranced parts with tungsten carbide gages, controlled environments are required because its coefficient of thermal expansion is different than steel. Another type of material providing good wear resistance is ceramic. However, the limitations for ceramic materials are greater than for tungsten carbide.

Plating the gage member with chromium increases wear resistance as well as reduces friction. It can also be used for restoring worn gages to their original size.

GAGE TOLERANCES

A fixed functional gage is a manufactured product and must be made to a manufacturing tolerance. Although the gage tolerances are small, they may consume a part of the product tolerance and should therefore be taken into consideration when selecting a gage for a particular application. In general commercial practice, tolerances for limit gages are 10% of the tolerance of the dimension being checked.

The principal gaging systems are based on either the bilateral or unilateral system, or a combination of the two. In the bilateral system, the gage tolerance is equally split and applied one-half plus and one-half minus. The bilateral system is generally used on master gages; the unilateral system is generally used on limit gages. In the unilateral system, the total tolerance is applied to either the plus or minus side of the dimension. The side to which the tolerance is applied depends on the type of gage being produced.

GO-type cylindrical plug gages have the tolerances applied to the plus side of the dimension, and NOT-GO plug gages have the tolerances applied to the minus side. GO cylindrical ring gages have the tolerances applied to the minus side, and NOT-GO ring gages have the tolerances applied to the plus side of the dimension.

In most gaging systems, it is common practice to relate the gagemakers' tolerance to the total tolerance of the component. The magnitude of the tolerance affects the cost of the gage as well as its useful function. If the tolerance of the gage is unnecessarily small, the cost may rise sharply for both the gage and its application; on the other hand, if the gage tolerance is too large it may not fulfill its intended function and may cause needless rejection of good parts. A gaging system is incomplete unless definite values are established for permissible gage tolerances and wear limitations.

Table 3-4 shows the gagemakers' tolerances for limit-type cylindrical plug and ring gages. They have been standardized in four classes according to nominal size and to the degree of accuracy required in the gaging operation. Class XX gages are precision lapped to extremely close tolerances and are used

TABLE 3-4
Gagemakers' Tolerance

Size Range		Inches			
Above	Up to and Including	Class XX	Class X	Class Y	Class Z
0.029	0.825	0.00002	0.00004	0.00007	0.0001
0.825	1.510	0.00003	0.00006	0.00009	0.00012
1.510	2.510	0.00004	0.00008	0.00012	0.00016
2.510	4.510	0.00005	0.00010	0.00015	0.00020
4.510	6.510	0.000065	0.00013	0.00019	0.00025
6.510	9.010	0.00008	0.00016	0.00024	0.00032
		Metric Equivalents			
0.74	20.96	0.00051	0.00102	0.00178	0.00254
20.96	38.35	0.00076	0.00152	0.00229	0.00305
38.35	63.75	0.00102	0.00203	0.00305	0.00406
63.75	114.55	0.00127	0.00254	0.00381	0.00508
114.55	165.35	0.00165	0.00330	0.00483	0.00635
165.35	228.85	0.00203	0.00406	0.00610	0.00813
228.85	311.40	0.00254	0.00508	0.00762	0.01016

FIXED FUNCTIONAL GAGES

chiefly for master gages and setting gages or where product tolerances are close. Class X gages are precision lapped and are used for the top grade of inspection work. Class Y gages are lapped and are used as working gages at the machine and for inspection of better class commercial work. Class Z gages are ground, polished, and lapped and are used as inspection and working gages when tolerances are fairly wide.

CYLINDRICAL PLUG GAGES

A cylindrical plug gage is a hardened and accurately ground steel pin. A typical plug gage consists of a handle and two gage members; one is the GO gage member and the other the NOT-GO (see Fig. 3-20, view a). Plug gages larger than 2 1/2″ (64 mm) usually only have one gage member attached to the handle. Another style of plug gage combines both gage members into one and is referred to as a progressive plug gage (see Fig. 3-20, view b). The front two thirds of the gage is ground to the GO size, and the remaining portion is ground to the NOT-GO size.

Cylindrical plug gages are available in sizes from 0.002 to 12.010″ (0.05 to 305.05 mm). The size is usually marked on the gage member when it is large enough. The design of the gage member and the method used to attach it to the handle depends on its size.

Plug gage members from 0.002 to 0.760″ (0.05 to 19.30 mm) in diameter are usually of the wire-type plug gage design. The gage members are usually held in the handle by a threaded collet and bushing (see Fig. 3-21, view a). This type of gage member is reversible when one end becomes worn, thus increasing the life of the gage. The threaded collets are often color coded to prevent confusion between the GO and NOT-GO gage members. Green is used for GO gage members and red for NOT-GO gage members.

Plug gage members from 0.059 to 1.510″ (1.50 to 38.35 mm) diam are usually of the taper lock design. The gage members have a taper shank on one end that fits into the end of the handle (see Fig. 3-21, view b). A drift hole in the handle permits the gage member to be removed.

Another method of mounting gage members from 0.760 to 8.010″ (19.30 to 203.45 mm) diam is the trilock design. The gage members in this design have a hole drilled through the center and are counterbored on both ends to receive a standard socket-head screw (see Fig. 3-21, view c). Three equally spaced grooves are also milled into each end of the gage member. Each end of the handle has three equally spaced prongs that engage the corresponding grooves in the gage member. A socket-head screw attaches the gage member to the handle. Like the wire-type gages, trilock gages are also reversible.

For cylindrical plug gages larger than 8.010″ (203.45 mm) diam, an annular design is used. To reduce weight, the center of

the gage is drilled. Ball handles are also threaded into the gage member to facilitate handling during the gaging process.

The GO gage member checks the minimum or low limit of a hole. The NOT-GO gage member checks the maximum or high limit of the part and also controls the looseness of fit. If the GO gage member slips through the hole, the part is considered acceptable. If it does not slip through the hole, the hole is undersize. The hole is oversize if the NOT-GO gage members slip through it. On the other hand, if a NOT-GO gage member does not slip through the hole, the part is considered in size by agreement between contractors. The hole in the part could also be out of round. This condition is undetectable by a standard cylindrical plug gage. One way of checking a hole for out-of-roundness is to have flats ground on the side of the gage member (see Fig. 3-22). This style of gage is rotated during use.

Plug gages are also available in shapes other than cylindrical. Examples of some of the shapes are square, hexagonal, octagonal, and oblong.

CYLINDRICAL RING GAGES

Cylindrical ring gages are used for checking the limit sizes of a round shaft. They are generally used in pairs—one gage checks the upper limit of the part tolerance (GO gage) while the other checks the lower limit (NOT-GO). The NOT-GO ring is distinguished from the GO ring by a groove in the outside diameter of the gage (see Fig. 3-23).

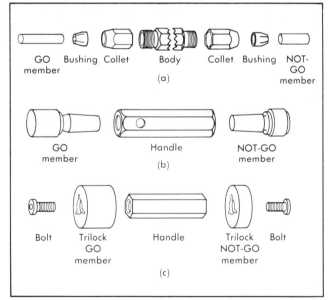

Fig. 3-21 Attachment of the gage member to the handle can be by: (a) threaded collet and bushing, (b) taper lock, or (c) trilock. (*The Van Keuren Co.*)

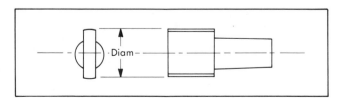

Fig. 3-22 Flats are ground on some cylindrical plug gage members to check a hole for an out-of-round condition. (*Southern Gage Co.*)

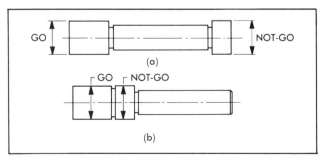

Fig. 3-20 Typical plug gage.

FIXED FUNCTIONAL GAGES

Cylindrical ring gages are available in sizes from about 0.060″ to more than 12″ (1.5 to 300 mm). The design of the gage body depends on the size of the gage. Gages used for measuring diameters up to 1.510″ (38.35 mm) are plain rings made from hardened steel. They are knurled on the outside diameter and lapped to a close tolerance on the inside diameter. In some instances, cylindrical ring gages smaller than 0.510″ (12.95 mm) have a soft steel body. A hardened steel bushing is then inserted to act as the gaging member. For rings between 1.510 and 5.510″ (38.35 and 139.95 mm), a flange is machined in the gage to reduce weight and increase rigidity. For cylindrical ring gages larger than 5.510″ (139.95 mm), two ball handles are attached to the flange to facilitate the handling of the ring during the gaging process.

Slipping the GO ring over the length of the shaft establishes that the shaft does not exceed the maximum diameter at any point. If the NOT-GO ring slips over the shaft, the part must be rejected as undersize. Failure of the GO ring to go over the shaft indicates that the part is oversize. However, if the NOT-GO ring does not slip over the shaft, it is declared in size by agreement between contractors. It is possible that a shaft could be larger on the ends than it is in the middle or it could be out of round. These conditions cannot be detected with a standard cylindrical ring gage. To check the shaft for out-of-roundness, the inside diameter of some ring gages are relieved (see Fig. 3-24). This style of ring gage is rotated during use. Snap gages are recommended to check the diameter of a shaft on the ends and in the middle.

SNAP GAGES

A snap gage is a fixed gage that has the gaging members arranged for measuring diameters, lengths, thicknesses, or widths. An external-measuring snap gage consists of a C-frame with gaging members in the jaw of the frame (see Fig. 3-25). The form of the gaging members may be selected to fit the particular part configuration. These members can usually be adjusted within a specific range to provide two gage sizes corresponding to the dimensions being measured. The outer gaging button, where the workpiece enters the gage, is set at the GO dimension. Snap gages are generally not recommended for inspecting part dimensions if the tolerance is smaller than 0.002″ (0.05 mm).

A master gage is used for setting and checking the snap gage; that is, the distance between the adjustable button and the fixed anvil must be equal to or slightly less than the maximum distance permitted by the part tolerance. The inner gaging button is set at the NOT-GO or minimum dimension.

Checking the diameter or length of a part is quick and easy. The anvil of the gage is placed on the part, and while rocking the gage back and forth, the part should pass through the GO button. If the part does not pass through the GO button, it is oversize. A part that is within tolerance will stop at the NOT-GO button. If it is not within tolerance (undersize) the part will pass through the NOT-GO button. The accuracy of the snap gage should be periodically checked with a master gage.

TAPER GAGES

Taper body forms are commonly used to achieve a precise alignment yet detachable connection between mechanical members. The critical dimensions of machine tapers are the included angle and the diameter at a specific reference level.

Taper gages are made for both internal and external tapers in the form of plug and ring gages, respectively. They are also made to inspect machine tapers with or without tangs.

THREAD GAGES

Fixed-limit thread gages are single-purpose gages in that they are made for a specific thread system, form, size, and class. Each designation is stamped or marked on the gage. These gages incorporate the essential functional dimensions of the thread and are used primarily to ensure the ability to assemble the product thread with its mating part.

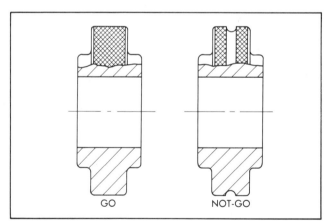

Fig. 3-23 Ring gage set used to inspect the diameter of shafts.

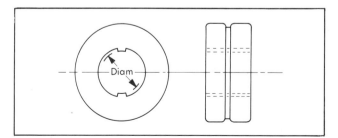

Fig. 3-24 To check a shaft for an out-of-round condition, a ring gage is used that has the inside diameter relieved. (*Southern Gage Co.*)

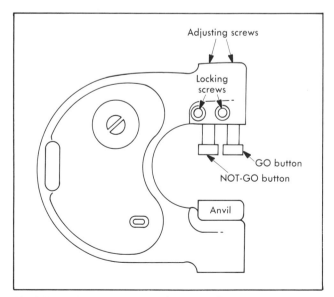

Fig. 3-25 Typical snap gage. (*Southern Gage Co.*)

FIXED FUNCTIONAL GAGES

Fixed-limit gages are generally made from tool steel that has been treated for wear resistance and dimensional stability. For extreme part tolerances or abrasive work conditions, other gage materials, such as carbides and chrome plate, are used. Because solid thread gages are subject to wear, a periodic inspection of these gages should be made; worn gages should be discarded.

The accuracy to which these gages are manufactured is determined by their intended use. Gages that directly check the product thread are made to X tolerances. Gages that are used as reference or master gages are made to W tolerances. The X tolerances are three times larger than W tolerances for most common sizes. The designated tolerances for unified inch screw threads and metric screw threads are given in ANSI B1.2 and ANSI B1.16M, respectively.

The commonly used fixed-limit gages are thread plug gages and adjustable thread ring gages. Thread snap gages can also be classified as fixed-limit gages, although some are adjustable.

Thread Plug Gages

Working thread plug gages are similar in design to cylindrical plug gages except that they are threaded. They are designed to check internally threaded products. Thread plug gages are made with either a full thread profile or with their flanks reduced by truncation. The style of the thread profile selected depends on the application.

The types of thread systems for which thread plug gages are available include unified, American National, metric, Whitworth, acme, buttress, and pipe. When thread plug gages are manufactured to W tolerances, they are used as reference or master gages for setting adjustable thread ring gages, thread snap gages, and indicating gages.

A typical thread plug gage consists of a handle and one or two thread gaging members. Depending on the gaging member size, the member can be held in the handle using a threaded collet and bushing design, a taper lock design, or a trilock design. The threaded collet and bushing design is generally used for gaging members ranging from 0.030 to 0.760" (0.76 to 19.30 mm); the taper lock design for members from 0.059 to 1.510" (1.50 to 38.35 mm), and the trilock design for members from 0.760 to 8.010" (19.30 to 203.45 mm). An annular design is used for gaging members more than 8.010" (203.45 mm).

The two members in a thread plug gage are referred to as the GO and NOT-GO members. The NOT-GO member is sometimes referred to as the HI member. The GO gaging member is generally longer than the NOT-GO member and is used to check the maximum material functional limit of the product thread. The NOT-GO member checks the NOT-GO (HI) functional diameter limit of the threaded product.

Thread Ring Gages

Thread ring gages are similar in design to cylindrical ring gages except that the internal surface is threaded. They are available in both solid and adjustable or split designs. Minor adjustments of an adjustable thread ring gage can, at times, be made by qualified shop or inspection personnel. If the user is unsure of the correct procedure and/or does not have the proper truncated setting plug, the ring should be sent to a calibration or gage house for the adjustment.

Thread ring gages are supplied in pairs as GO and NOT-GO gages. The NOT-GO ring is sometimes referred to as a LO ring gage. The GO gage checks the maximum material functional limit of the threaded part. The NOT-GO gage checks the NOT-GO (LO) functional diameter limit of the threaded part and usually has an annular groove machined on the periphery of the ring to differentiate it from the GO ring.

Thread Snap Gages

Thread snap gages have two pair of gaging elements combined in one gage. With proper gaging elements, these gages can check the maximum and minimum material limit of external product screw threads in a single pass. One style of thread snap gage is shown in Fig. 3-26.

The functional or GO portion of the gage may incorporate either functional segments or functional rolls. Rolls rotate when the part is inserted, thus reducing wear. The length of the segments or rolls is approximately equal to the applicational length of engagement of the product thread. The NOT-GO portion of the gage generally contains cone and vee profile rolls.

Snap gages may be held on a stand where the threaded product is presented to the gage, or they can be used as a handheld gage by presenting the gage to the part that may be between centers in a machine. Snap gages are available in sizes from 0.060 to 20" (1.5 to 500 mm). In most cases, snap gages are dedicated to one size or varying classes of a size. In addition, the same gage can be used for checking right and left-hand threads of the same nominal size.

SPLINE GAGES

A common way of inspecting splined workpieces prior to assembly is with fixed-limit gages. External splines are checked with internal-toothed rings, whereas internal splines are checked with external-toothed plugs.

Basically there are only two types of fixed-limit spline gages, composite and sector. Composite gages have the same number of teeth as that of the part (see Fig. 3-27, view *a*). Sector gages have only two sectors of teeth 180° apart (see view *b*). These gages are further subdivided into GO and NOT-GO gages.

The GO gages are used to inspect maximum material conditions (maximum external or minimum internal dimensions). They may be used to inspect an individual dimension or the relationship between two or more functional dimensions. In

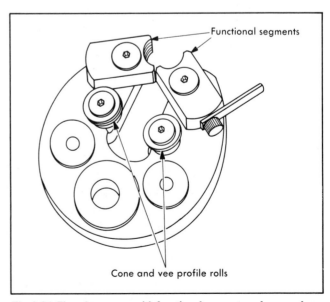

Fig. 3-26 Thread snap gage with functional segments and cone and vee profile rolls. (*The Johnson Gage Co.*)

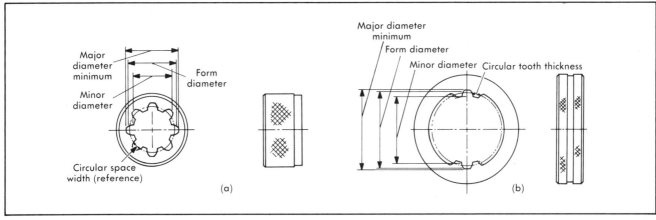

Fig. 3-27 Fixed limit spline gages: (a) GO composite ring gage and (b) NOT-GO sector ring gage. (*Society of Automotive Engineers*)

addition, they control the minimum looseness or maximum interference.

The NOT-GO gages are used to inspect minimum material conditions (minimum external, maximum internal dimensions),

thereby controlling the maximum looseness or minimum interference. Unless otherwise agreed on, a part is only acceptable if the NOT-GO gage does not enter or go on the part. A NOT-GO gage can only check one dimension.

VISUAL REFERENCE GAGING

Visual references are used in a number of gaging procedures to check parts. When part features are easy to see and feature tolerances allow wide enough latitude, overlay visual templates may be used directly with the part to gage shape without magnification. When tolerances are too tight to judge by eye alone, optical comparators or toolmakers' microscopes may be used, employing magnifications ranging from 5 to 200X. Between these extremes, overlay templates are sometimes used with supplementary magnification supplied by inspection loupes or bench magnifiers of various types.

Visual references consist of transparent materials that are dimensionally stable and can be either engraved or marked with reference lines to accurately show feature sizes and/or position; typical materials are glass and plastic. Examples of visual references are optical comparator charts, microscope reticles, and engraved plastic overlay templates. These gages can be made to show a large number of features on the same piece of glass or plastic, and even parts that are oversized for the available visual field can be "stepped" into view using precisely controlled positioning stages or fixtures.

Accurate inspection, using the visual reference approach, depends to a great degree on the repeatability required. For example, under proper light and without magnification, tolerances of 0.010" (0.25 mm) can be repeatedly judged accurately on a GO/NOT-GO basis. When this repeatability is required in the average machine shop, however, it would be better to use a magnification of 5 or 10X to ensure a valid determination. For tolerances of 0.005" (0.12 mm), a magnification of at least 10X is required, while 20X is recommended for tolerances of 0.001" (0.03 mm), 50X for 0.0005" (0.012 mm), and at least 100X for 0.0001" (0.003 mm). Below these magnifications, inspection

accuracy will be diminished because the inspector's eye is not able to resolve the small angles and displacements involved.

Whether visual references are used with magnification or not, they usually present the part profile in silhouette form with the part features outlined on the surface of the gage. A double line indicates the permissible variation of tolerance. The part can be laid out on the gage in its entire shape, if desired, or only specific features may be represented, at the option of the inspection planners or gage designers.

The advantages of visual reference gaging, together with some examples, include the following:

- Many dimensions can be checked simultaneously because they can appear together on the gage. (The inspection of gaskets, stampings, and die-cut parts benefit from this.)
- Complete contours, including irregular or mathematically defined shapes, may be checked for total form instead of probed at specific points. (Cam surfaces and form-ground parts are examples.)
- Unskilled personnel may be used as inspectors, or process operators may quickly and simply verify their own work because the part outline and associated tolerances are usually obvious on the gage. Written instructions can appear on the gage when necessary.
- Gage setup and calibration are facilitated because instructions may be incorporated into the gage, and calibration measurements may be directly verified with an optical comparator or coordinate measuring machine having a video pickup or microscope viewing head.
- Zero gaging pressure is required because contact probes are not used. (The inspection of soft and/or delicate parts

VISUAL REFERENCE GAGING

such as foamed plastic, small springs, rubber, foil, or paper parts benefits because of this feature.)

- Duplicate gages are easily fabricated for use by machine operators, quality control personnel, vendors, or customer receiving personnel.
- Changes are easily incorporated as designs are revised. (The photoengraving masters or scribing-control NC tapes or files can usually be altered or reworked and new gages issued quickly.)
- Families of similar parts may often be incorporated onto one gage, depending on part geometry. (Fasteners, spacers, washers, and brackets are examples.)

In addition to these generic advantages of visual reference gaging, specific other advantages that result from the use of overlay templates, microscopes, and optical comparator charts are discussed in the appropriate subsections that follow.

OVERLAY TEMPLATES

Overlay templates are transparent plates that are often used in the inspection of flat parts made of paper, rubber, plastic, fabric, and metal as well as other materials. They are also used to check out processes such as the registration of printing on paper and plastic, the legibility and quality of text coming off of computer printout devices, and the size and positioning of test images in photographic processes.

Overlay templates are made of a transparent material onto which is engraved or scribed the min-max profile of the part or feature to be inspected. Incorporated into the overlay may be fixturing devices such as stops, dowel pins, or other machined features to promote precise positioning of the overlay and the part being inspected.

Materials used for direct-contact overlays are usually plastic, although glass is sometimes used when extra dimensional stability is needed. Commonly used plastics include polycarbonates, acrylics, and sometimes vinyls or polyesters. When glass is used, it is usually not fitted with fixturing pins, and it is usually either tempered or laminated safety plate to protect the user from injury in case of breakage. Dimensional stability of glass is comparable to that of steel, while dimensional stability of the plastic materials is an order of magnitude less than that of steel (as measured by the thermal coefficients of expansion), while remaining high enough to suit most practical gaging operations.

Line work for the overlay templates is either photoengraved from scribed artwork masters or directly scribed or chemically etched into the surface of the template. For contrast against dark parts, line colors such as red may be used instead of the standard black. Line widths, unless otherwise specified, are usually approximately 0.004 to 0.006″ (0.10 to 0.15 mm) in width, but can be made wider for special inspection requirements. Although the most accurate overlays are usually drawn up using computer-controlled CNC engraving or photo plotting machines, it is possible to draw up overlays by hand using manual drafting materials. The accuracy and durability of these overlays needs to be carefully monitored, however, because drafting vellum expands and contracts rapidly with humidity, and the characteristics of the line produced from a pencil or handheld pen can vary widely in width and position.

The finest determination that an inspector can make using an overlay without magnification is about ±0.010″ (±0.25 mm)—a tolerance band 0.020″ (0.50 mm) wide. For finer tolerances, it is recommended that the inspection process make use of magnifica-

tion either through use of a loupe, a bench magnifier, or an optical comparator.

Major advantages of overlay templates, in addition to those for all visual reference gaging, are low cost, ready acceptance by operators and inspectors, and physical toughness, except for those made of glass. The physical toughness characteristic permits overlay templates to be used on the shop floor without extra precautions.

Hybrid fixture overlays are possible when some dimensions require control to close tolerances, while others can be checked on a visual reference basis. In this situation, the hard gaging fixture is designed to check the close tolerance features, and overlays are added to verify features that are allowed greater latitude. Specific examples are gages that verify overall assembly dimensions of large parts such as liquid quantity pickups, flow rate transducers, and thermocouple harnesses used on aircraft engines, tanks, and fuel systems. For these applications, the installation features and surfaces such as bolt holes and keyways are gaged with hard gaging techniques while the locations of connectors, junction boxes, and wiring routings are gaged using overlays permanently attached to and calibrated with the hard gages.

An example of an overlay template for final inspection of a floppy disk jacket assembly used on many personal computers is shown in Fig. 3-28. The overlay image is engraved on the back side of a 1/4″ (6 mm) thick clear plastic plate. The image is engraved on the back side of the template so that it can be in contact with the part inspected. Dowel pins are incorporated as stops on the left side of the gage. During inspection, the part is pushed lightly against these pins to locate it for checking. The allowable positioning of the features of the jacket, such as holes, notches, and edges, are incorporated into the min-max lines. The dimensions that the gage measures and measurement instructions are also incorporated on the template. In use, the

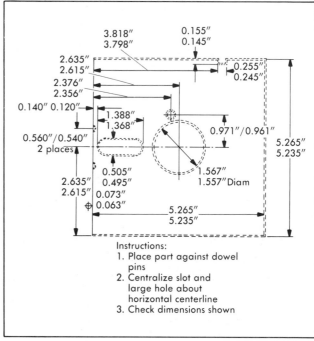

Instructions:
1. Place part against dowel pins
2. Centralize slot and large hole about horizontal centerline
3. Check dimensions shown

Fig. 3-28 Sight gaging for a floppy disk envelope. (*Visual Inspection Products*)

part is held behind the overlay, and conformance to dimensions is judged by reference to the part outline shown.

It is important to note that the min-max outline given for this part checks only the positioning of the features of the part and not feature sizes themselves. As in other gaging processes, position and size must be checked separately. In this case, feature size could be checked by another overlay showing the min-max feature sizes without regard to position, or they could be checked using functional gaging such as plug gages. Because the product is made of vinyl plastic or paper, the use of contact measuring probes such as calipers might distort the part while measurement was being attempted.

TOOLMAKERS' MICROSCOPES

The toolmakers' microscope consists of a microscope mounted to a base that carries an adjustable stage, a stage transport mechanism, and optionally supplementary lighting for the objects mounted on the stage. Micrometer barrels are often incorporated into the stage transport mechanism to permit precisely controlled movements, and digital readouts of stage positioning are becoming increasingly available. Various objective lenses provide magnifications ranging from 10 to 200X.

Engraved glass reticles, mounted in a reticle holder in the eyepiece of the microscope, can be used to measure parts or to inspect parts on a GO/NOT-GO basis just as overlay templates are used. In some microscope setups, other types of reticles can more easily be introduced into the optical path of the microscope by a light-splitting arrangement that lets the reticle be mounted outside the microscope barrel. Here, film or engraved plastic reticles may also be used to check parts.

Accessories available to users of microscopes include a full range of general-purpose fixturing devices such as vises, centers, and rotating tables. In addition, special workholding fixtures may be designed and built to speed up inspection or to make it more reliable.

Optical zooming features are incorporated in some microscopes. Although this can be a useful feature, it usually prevents the calibration of the instrument for accurate measuring work using reticles mounted in the eyepiece.

OPTICAL COMPARATORS AND COMPARATOR CHARTS

An optical comparator (sometimes also called an optical or profile projector) is basically a small parts-measuring microscope, similar in many functions to a toolmakers' microscope, but using a large projection screen instead of eyepieces. It has a stage for mounting parts to be measured and/or inspected, stage transport mechanisms, stage lighting, an optical path that is usually folded by means of mirrors within the machine itself, and a viewing and control area where the operator/inspector works. The image appears on the screen as either an inverted (reversed) or erect image where the part is seen exactly as it is staged. The comparator bounces the image off of one or more mirrors to reverse the inverted image.

Most comparators are sold in sizes of 10, 14, 20, 30, and 50" (254, 355, 508, 762, and 1270 mm) screens. The most popular screen sizes are 14 and 30" (355 and 762 mm).

Optical comparators are available with magnifications ranging from 5 to 500X, depending on the lens chosen, in fixed steps usually of 10, 20, 31.25, 50, 62.5, 100, 200, and 500X. Because a different objective lens must be used for each magnification, many comparators have several lenses mounted on a turret.

Internal lens turrets provide a constant focal point, eliminating the need to refocus when a lens is changed. External lens turrets require refocusing when the lens is changed because different power lenses have different focal lengths.

Some comparators or vision systems have recently been offered with computer-controlled readout and positioning devices for stage stepping and measuring purposes. On these machines, computer programs may be used to automatically sequence the part positioning, take data, and perform analyses of this data. Data processing allows measurement of complex parts that require many measurements with distance and angular relationships.

There are often two lighting systems in an optical comparator. One permits silhouette viewing of an outside profile of a part. A second surface illuminator permits viewing of the area within the silhouette outline. A schematic sketch of the operation of a direct-lighted optical comparator is shown in Fig. 3-29. The silhouette image is formed on the screen by placing the sample part between the light source and the objective lens. Surface illumination requires that light be projected onto the part either through the objective lens using a 1/2 reflecting mirror or from a supplementary oblique lighting system. With sufficient illumination, the objective lens can "see" the surface features of the part. The surface features can then be measured on the screen. Both types of illumination can be used simultaneously, but care should be taken to prevent the part from being subject to high temperatures when high-wattage mercury or xenon illuminators are used; special filters are available to eliminate heat.

The objective lens, together with the other optical components of the comparator, controls the magnification of the image presented to the operator. The operator sees an image enlarged precisely by the magnification factor, as long as the optical system of the machine is in calibration. Overlay charts, drawn at this magnification, can then be placed over the screen image to quickly judge the conformance of the part to the requirements. Alternatively, if part measurements are necessary, a general-purpose cross line may be placed on the screen and the stage positioning mechanisms used to measure the part to high precision. Still a third method is to have an overlay drawn of the part at its nominal contour, without any tolerance allowances, and to check the part using the stage positioners to "bring in" the part to its correct contour, noting the correcting

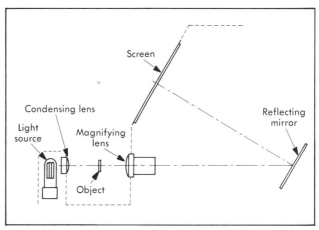

Fig. 3-29 Schematic arrangement of a horizontal shadow lighted optical comparator.

VISUAL REFERENCE GAGING

adjustments as this is done. Specific part overlays are illustrated in Fig. 3-30.

Each of these measuring methods has its own inspection tooling cost, data output, and inspection process time tradeoffs. A fully toleranced chart is more expensive to develop, but it permits rapid GO/NOT-GO inspection by unskilled operators. This type of chart is often used for checking thread pitch and other simple contour measurements. Use of the general-purpose measuring grid is simple but relatively much slower, and it requires a more skilled individual. The nominal profile chart falls somewhere between these two approaches in both development cost and inspection process time. A typical chart and fixturing setup is shown in Fig. 3-31.

To establish the effective specimen area that can be projected onto the comparator screen, the screen diameter is divided by the magnification of the lens system being used. For example, a 30″ (760 mm) comparator working at a magnification of 50X presents a viewing field of 0.600″ (15.00 mm), and a 20″ (500 mm) comparator working at 10X shows an image field of 2.000″ (50.00 mm). These fields of view, however, need not be limitations on overall part or feature size because parts may be stepped into the viewing field by means of the stage transport mechanism. Most old-style stage transports use a micrometer barrel; measurements must be read off the barrel vernier. Many stage transports have provisions for inserting gage blocks as a way of offsetting the stage a precise amount, thereby bringing a new field into view and permitting the controlled stepping of dimensions too long to measure with the motion permitted by the barrel micrometer. Electronic readout linear encoder stages are becoming more common because they eliminate operator error and increase the speed of the measuring process. These stages are able to accurately measure distances of several inches without the use of gage blocks.

Although the calculated viewing area extends across the full width of the screen, it is good practice to avoid the outer limits of the screen. When it becomes necessary to use this area, it is good practice to check the calibration of the comparator at the edges of the screen. Lenses tend to be more accurate at the center of their fields of view.

Optical Comparator Charts

The comparator chart for inspecting a specific workpiece is a very accurately scribed, magnified outline drawing of the workpiece to be gaged containing all the contours, dimensions, and tolerance limits necessary for the purpose and mounted in an appropriate way on the viewing screen. Chart gages may be made on glass, certain types of plastics, paper, or vellum and laid out by hand drafting methods, special scribing, or chart layout devices. The material and method of layout are such that the chart gage will not significantly add to or detract from manufacturing tolerances. Glass offers the greatest dimensional stability; paper or vellum is suitable only for temporary use.

Chart layout lines should be dense black, sharply defined, and about 0.006 to 0.010″ (0.15 to 0.25 mm) wide for best legibility. Dimensions are normally to the center of the lines. When maximum and minimum tolerance lines are used, the magnification should be high enough to maintain a minimum of 0.020″ (0.50 mm) spacing between the lines of the chart gage. For closer tolerance checking, special lines or "bridge" arrangements based on gaging to the edge of the lines are often used.

For contrast reasons, the dimensional lines are purposely broadened and normally appear on the chart gage as a dense black opaque line when the shadow of the part is projected on the chart screen. The operator's only concern is that some light appear between the edge of the workpiece shadow and a dimension line for GO tolerance and that it not be seen for NOT-GO tolerance (see Fig. 3-32, view a).

When bridge lines are used on the chart page, the dimension line must be widened sufficiently to produce sharp definition between the shadow of the part and the chart line itself. In

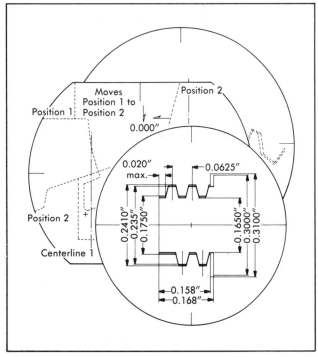

Fig. 3-30 Typical part overlay for use with an optical comparator. (*Visual Inspection Products*)

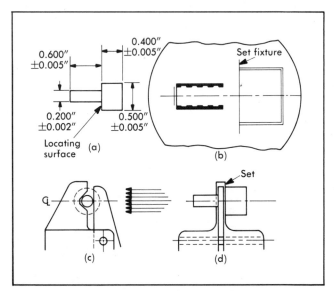

Fig. 3-31 Example of optical gaging: (a) part to be gaged, (b) chart with bridge line for clear visibility, (c) end view of workpiece located in a vee, and (d) front view of fixture with workpiece shouldered against set (reference) surface.

Fig. 3-32, view *b*, the distance from edge A to B represents the prescribed tolerance.

For inspection of individual geometric elements, standard chart gages with grids, protractors, and radii are frequently used (see Fig. 3-33). They are also sometimes employed in conjunction with the horizontal and vertical measuring attachments of the comparator.

For some applications, precision reticles may be used on the comparator stage in place of the magnified chart gage screen. Reticles are 1:1 scale precision master outlines on glass, usually made from larger layouts photographically reduced. The reticle is mounted into a special floating fixture that enables the workpiece to control the motion of the reticle so as to compare the magnified deviation between the workpiece and the projected master outline on the viewing screen. Such fixtures ordinarily explore the part by tracing or probing. By the use of such methods, parts may be checked that when magnified would be many times the screen area. Contours that normally could not be seen by direct projection can also be checked in this manner.

When the magnified layout is too large to be contained within the available screen area, one or more sections of it may be superimposed and the part shifted accordingly. When employing staging fixtures with special chart gages, set lines for coordinating the chart gage and fixture should be incorporated on the chart layout.

Measurement by Translation

Many parts can be successfully gaged on optical comparators even though the part configuration cannot be projected by the light beam. Parts having recessed contours such as actuator cam

tracks, ball sockets, and the internal grooves of ball nuts can all be gaged by means of tracer techniques. A tracer, as the term is used in projection gaging, is a one-to-one pantograph. On one arm of the pantograph is a stylus that freely traces over the part contour in a given plane. The other arm carries a follower, visible in the light path, that is projected by the light beam as it moves. Three types of followers are used (see Fig. 3-34):

1. Probe follower (view *a*)—an exact duplicate of the stylus tracer in size and shape.
2. Dot follower (view *b*)—a glass reticle having an opaque dot of the same diameter as the stylus tracer.
3. Reticle-gage follower (view *c*)—a glass reticle having an exact one-to-one actual-size reproduction of the part profile.

The choice of follower for a given gaging problem depends on the size of the path and the magnification to be used. In general, the probe or dot is used if the size of the part is less than the field of view of the projector at the given magnification. In some cases, larger parts are gaged by using two followers suit-

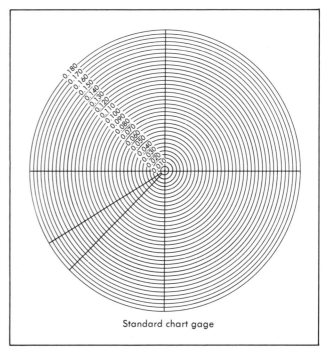

Standard chart gage

Fig. 3-33 Standard chart gage.

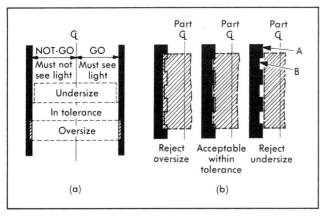

Fig. 3-32 Optical gaging for tolerance.

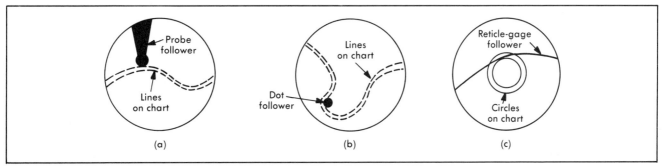

Fig. 3-34 Projector tracer followers: (a) probe type, (b) dot type, and (c) recticle-gage type.

ably spaced to correlate with a special type of chart in which one section of the contour is superimposed on another section. For some purposes, the dot follower is preferred to the probe because it provides a complete circle shadow unrestricted by the shadow of the supporting stem.

The reticle gage follower is more versatile in its application because it is not restricted by part size or magnification. Large parts can be gaged with reticle gages using high magnification. The reticle gages must be of a very high order of accuracy because any error in them shows up directly as an error in the part. To achieve the necessary accuracy, the contours should be laid out on precision scribing machines at a magnified size. Precision cameras can then be used to reduce them photographically to the one-to-one size for the reticle.

Tracer units equipped with either probe or dot followers are used with chart gages having a contour layout of the part. The layout may be a single-line profile or it may be a double-line profile showing the permissible limits of the part. As the stylus traces across the part, the projected image of the follower moves across the screen. If a single-line chart is being used, the follower shadow must stay tangent to the line throughout the transit for a part to be without error. Using the double-line chart, the edge of the follower shadow should always remain between the two lines.

A different type of chart gage is used when tracing with a reticle gage follower. This chart has a circle on it representing the diameter of the stylus tracer at the magnification being used. The projected reticle gage contour moves past this fixed circle as the part is traced and, if the part is perfect, will always remain tangent to it. If the tolerance limits on the part are uniform throughout, it is convenient to put two circles on the screen to represent the tolerance spread. The projected reticle contour then should fall between these circles as it passes across the screen. If the part tolerance varies from point to point along the contour, the tolerance lines can be put on the reticle follower and projected to a single circle on the screen.

Standard tracer units are available as accessory equipment and can be used on many projectors. Their coordinate slides operate on precision preloaded balls to provide uniform motion without play or backlash. They can be fitted with special stylus arms for specific purposes such as the tracing of internal contours and checking for concentricity. Some tracers are designed to be used with horizontal light beams and others are for use with a vertical beam. The standard units can provide coordinate movements up to 4 x 9″ (100 x 225 mm), but special tracers of considerably greater travel have been built.

MAGNIFIERS

Hand loupes fitted with measuring or toleranced GO/NOT-GO reticles are often used as "pocket comparators." A typical loupe consists of an eyepiece, magnifying lens, and a reticle in contact with the part being inspected. These devices are most often used to evaluate small parts, printing or photographic images, and details on larger parts.

Bench magnifiers add magnification and sometimes illumination to an existing inspection setup. They consist of a magnifying lens, a light source, and sometimes a transport mechanism for either the part or the lens.

Reticles for magnifiers may be either general purpose or custom designed for a specific part or measuring application; the reticles for loupes are easily changed by unscrewing a reticle holder ring. Magnifications available usually are in the 2 to 5X range, but some 10X units are available. Fields of view for loupes typically range from 0.50 to 1.50″ (1.3 to 38.0 mm) diam.

Reticles used with bench magnifiers can be almost any size within the limitations of the size of the lens and/or the transport mechanism used. With a magnification of 5X, parts can be inspected to a tolerance of ±0.005″ (0.12 mm), providing the dimensions to be checked are within the field of view and are able to be brought into focus simultaneously.

Reticles for loupes are usually fabricated of glass with the measuring or toleranced part scales etched into the lower glass surface and filled with a colored substance. Reticles for bench magnifying setups are usually visual overlays used in direct contact with the part being measured. Materials for these overlays can be either glass or a variety of plastics.

Reticle design can be on either a measuring or a GO/NOT-GO toleranced basis, as described in the section on visual overlay templates. Physical size of the pocket comparators is up to several inches long, and they weigh less than a pound, making them easily portable. Typical uses include the checking of small machined parts, electronic assemblies, and printed and photographically reproduced graphical images and the blemish evaluation of sheet metal, plastic, and fabric products.

OPTICAL FLATS

The simplest method of applying interference phenomena to metrology employs optical flats. It may provide the most advantageous combination of precision and accuracy of any readily available measurement method. Precision is sufficient for the closest tolerances. Because light waves are used for a standard, they have accuracy to match precision.

For practical application, three things are needed in addition to the part to be measured. These are the optical flat, a monochromatic light source, and a suitable surface from which to work.

The wavelength of krypton 86 is the international standard for measurement of length. For practical use, however, certain factors must be considered. One of these is the definition of the fringe bands. Other considerations are cost and convenience. The light emitted by helium gas has proved most practical when all considerations are balanced. Its wavelength is 23.2 μin. (0.59 μm).

Under a helium monochromatic light source, interference bands (fringes) are observed when an optical flat is placed on a flat or nearly flat part that has a reflective surface. These bands locate steps of 11.6 μin. (0.30 μm) from the surface being tested to the surface of the optical flat. The bands occur because the light waves reflected from the surface of the part either interfere with or reinforce the light waves reflected from the surface of the optical flat.

Optical flats are made in a range of sizes, shapes, and materials. Although they are available in sizes as large as 16″ (400 mm) in diameter or more, most are from 1 to 6″ (25 to 150 mm). Materials range from inexpensive glass to very expensive sapphire. The majority are of high optical quality fused quartz.

The measuring surface generally has one of three degrees of flatness. Working flats are 4 μin. (0.1 μm); this is a unilateral tolerance in that no point will deviate in height from any other point by more than that amount. Master flats are 2 μin. (0.05 μm), and reference flats are 1 μin. (0.025 μm). Some manufacturers also furnish a commercial grade that is 8 μin. (0.2 μm). One or both surfaces may be finished for measurement. The second finished surface adds very little additional cost. Generally, however, when one surface is worn out of tolerance, it is no longer clear. To use the other surface, the user must look through the worn surface; therefore, expectancy of double life is unrealistic.

Optical flats are available with coated surfaces at extra charge. The coating is a hard, partially reflective, thin evaporated metal, usually titanium dioxide, applied on the surface to improve fringe band contrast by increasing the reflectivity of the optical flat. The less light lost by unwanted reflection, the clearer the fringe bands. The coating is so thin that it does not affect the position of the fringe bands, but a coated flat requires even greater care than an uncoated one because scratches are more apparent on coated flats. Carbon, carbide, hard coat anodized, or hardened steel surfaces that may have sharp edges or burrs can scratch or damage an optical flat, whether coated or uncoated.

Factors That Control Accuracy

The supporting surface on which optical flat measurements are made must provide a clean, rigid platform. If the measurements consist of the changes on one surface, little more is needed. If, however, the measurement involves comparison of two surfaces, the supporting surface becomes the factor limiting the precision of the measurements.

For the latter reason, optical flats are often used as support for the part. Steel flats, known as toolmakers' flats, are also available. These are simply optical flats to which parts and gage blocks may be wrung for measurement. Glass flats should not be used to wring gage members or parts. Other precision-finished surfaces may also be used. The errors contributed by the supporting surface are of the independent type. They may combine with the measurement errors, thereby increasing the uncertainty of the overall system. Cleanliness is of tremendous importance in optical flat measurements. Even a stray particle of dust that might settle on the part before the flat is placed over it can completely destroy any chance for reliable measurement.

Temperature changes are more apparent when using optical flats than with most other kinds of measurement. Fortunately, they usually involve relatively small parts that normalize quickly. Most optical flats have a lower coefficient of thermal conductivity than the metal parts with which they are used. They are heated rapidly by handling, and once heated or cooled, the flat requires a longer time to regain the ambient temperature. Fused quartz is more stable than Pyrex.

When viewing, the more nearly perpendicular the line of sight is to the surface, the more accurate the measurement will be. To achieve maximum clarity, the measurement surface should be as close to the light source as convenient. The reflex type of monochromatic light provides this automatically. In this type, a beam-splitter mirror is used to permit both the line of sight and the monochromatic illumination to be reasonably perpendicular to the measurement surface.

A gage block will begin to wring to an optical flat almost immediately unless one of three conditions prevent it. These conditions are: (1) insufficiently flat surfaces, (2) insufficiently fine surface finish, and (3) improperly cleaned surfaces. A gage block, a part, or another flat should never be left wrung to an optical flat beyond the time required for measurement. If left overnight or longer, the flat might be broken in separating them. If they must be forced apart, a wood block should be used.

As soon as the part has begun to wring, fringe bands will appear. Continued wringing can cause the bands to run in any direction across the part. Because of wear to the optical flat and the danger of scratching, wringing should be as slight as possible to obtain the desired fringe pattern.

Optical Flat Convention

Actually, the fringe bands form in the air between the observer and the measurement surface. Therefore, to make fringe bands a practical measurement tool, a convention must be adopted. This is known as parallel-separation-planes concept. Although theoretically nonexistent, it is a great aid in actual measurement.

The convention consists of a set of imaginary planes all parallel to the working surface of the flat and one-half wavelength apart (see Fig. 3-35). The intersections of these planes and the part are the dark fringe lines. The number of fringes thus represents separation between the surfaces in units of half wavelengths. Because the two surfaces are so nearly parallel, the cosine error is in billionths of an inch.

The air-wedge configuration is easily demonstrated. After thorough cleaning, the part and the optical flat are placed together until the fringe pattern crosses the part sidewise as shown in Fig. 3-36. The five dark banks or fringes show that there is an air wedge of five half-wavelengths height separating the flat from the part. At the moment it is not known which way the wedge is facing. The open end is found by applying force to the ends. If there is no change, as in view b, the force is being

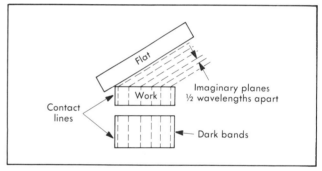

Fig. 3-35 Parallel-separation-planes concept envisions planes parallel to the working surface of the flat and one-half wavelength apart. Dark fringes occur at their intersection with the part.

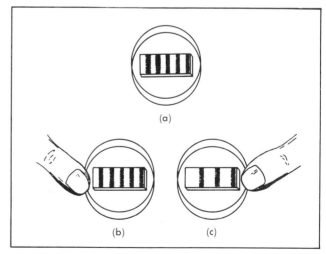

Fig. 3-36 The five fringes shown in view a represent an air wedge with a height of five half wavelengths. Pressure at the left as shown in view b does not change the pattern, but pressure at the right as shown in view c does. The broadening of the fringes shows that the wedge is being closed. Thus the open portion of the wedge is at the right.

exerted along the line of contact (wedge point). When the force causes the fringes to spread out, the open end of the wedge is being squeezed closed (view c). The situation, greatly exaggerated, is shown by comparing Fig. 3-35 with Fig. 3-37. Another method is to lower the line of sight. The bands then appear to move toward the open end of the air wedge. However, the band "value" increases as the line of sight decreases from perpendicular viewing.

The air-wedge configuration would have applied equally well if the fringes were oriented lengthwise along the part (see Fig. 3-38). After the contact has been found, the height can be determined by multiplying the number of fringes by one half the wavelength of the light used. The general relationships are: the fewer the bands, the narrower the angle; the more numerous the bands, the greater the angle. More important is the understanding that the number of bands is a measure of height difference, not of absolute height.

As in all measurement, there must be a reference from which every length is expressed. In surface inspection, the matter of reference is easy. Some part of the surface is arbitrarily chosen as the reference from which the other parts are expressed. In Fig. 3-38, the fringe pattern shows that the surface is flat because the fringe bands are straight and uniformly spaced. A sharp dropoff would have shown as a change in the pattern. Thus in Fig. 3-39 the closely spaced bands at the right show that the angle is larger along the right-hand edge of the test surface than along the other edge. The actual height change could be measured from this.

Typical configurations are demonstrated in Fig. 3-40. In view a the reference is a line R, the lower edge of the part. The bands curve toward the line of contact, showing that the surface is convex and high in the center. The reverse is the case in view b; this surface is concave and low in the center. Views c, d, and e show surfaces that are progressively more convex. View f indicates a surface that drops at the outer edges. Note the importance of the reference line—if it had been at the left, the same fringe pattern would indicate a surface that rises at the outer edges. The surface in view g has two ridges with low center trough and edges. A surface that is flat at one end but becomes increasingly convex is shown in view h. View i shows a surface that is flat near the reference line but rises above the right edge.

The two points of contact in view j, a common occurrence, show two high points surrounded by lower areas. Note that in this case there is no air wedge. The points establish the reference. The fringe pattern is a true contour map of the surface.

Once surface configurations are recognized from fringe patterns, it is easy to measure the configurations. In Fig. 3-40, view a, the surface is convex by one third of a band. The reverse is true in view b, where the surface is concave or low in the center by the same amount. The surface in view c is one-half wavelength high in the center; view d is one wavelength high, and view e is one and one-fifth wavelengths high. The edges in view f drop off one-quarter wavelength. The ridges in view g are five sixths of a wavelength higher than the center trough.

Few surfaces are as uniform as in the examples just described. Most surfaces change contour from end to end. In the example in Fig. 3-40, view h, a flat surface becomes progressively more convex toward the right. At point 1, the surface is one half a band convex. At point 2, it is one band convex. View i shows a surface that is flat near the reference line but rises at the right edge. The top right edge is about one wavelength high, while the lower right edge is about three and one-half wavelengths high.

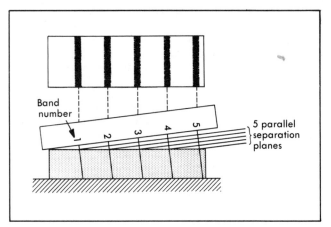

Fig. 3-37 When the wedge is closed down tighter, the number of parallel separation planes decreases.

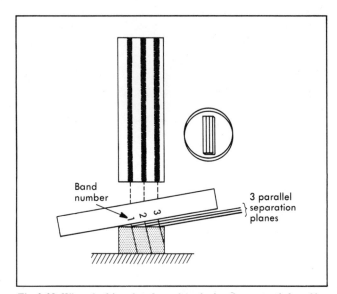

Fig. 3-38 When the fringe bands run lengthwise, the contact is found by applied force.

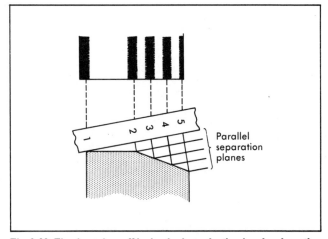

Fig. 3-39 The sharp dropoff is clearly shown by the close bands on the right.

VISUAL REFERENCE GAGING

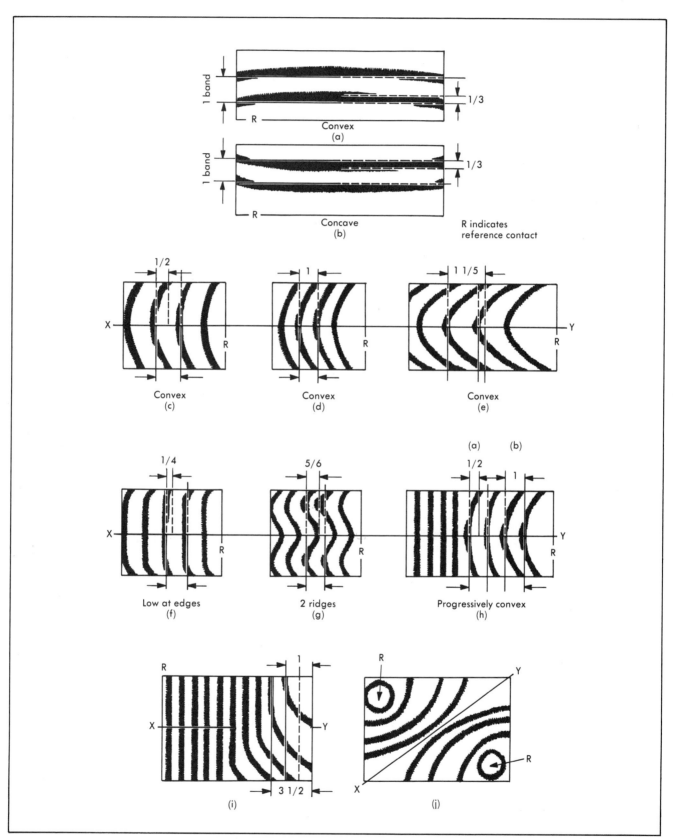

Fig. 3-40 Measurements are the deviations of bands compared with the distances between bands.

VISUAL REFERENCE GAGING

In each case, the fringe pattern could have been perpendicular to the ones chosen. These fringe patterns would have been just as useful to show the surface configuration. The reason is that the number of bands is a measure of height difference, not of absolute height. Any fringe pattern shows the surface conformation, if the contact point is known. If a change in elevation is desired, it is most easily measured by bands that cross the area in which the change takes place. Then the change can be measured by the amount that the band deviates from straightness.

The examples shown in views *a* through *i* of Fig. 3-40 demonstrate the air-wedge method. In view *j*, the contact method is shown. This typical configuration has two contact points with a low trough between them. To measure with the contact method it is only necessary to remember that it is as far uphill to one point as it is downhill from another. The bottom of this trough is approximated by the line *XY*. Note that there are four convex bands on each side of the high points. The four bands indicate that the trough is four and one-half wavelengths low at a point. To find the depth of the valley between high points, 1 is added to the number of bands and then the number of bands is divided by 2. This quotient is then multiplied by one half the wavelength of light $(n + 1)/2 \times \lambda/2$, where *n* is the number of bands and is the wavelength.

Checking Parallelism

Assume that a gage block of questionable condition is to be checked for parallelism. If this unknown block is wrung to a flat along with a known block, we then know that the wrung surface of each is parallel to the other to within the limit of flatness of the optical flat. Assuming that the known block is in calibration, its top surface is very nearly parallel to the top surface of the unknown block. The lack of parallelism may be along two of the three axes. With optical flats, the rotation about both these axes is determined simultaneously. Because the substitute reference plane is very near to the top plane of the unknown part, fringe patterns can be seen. The comparison of those on the known part with those on the unknown provides the measure of parallelism.

The example in Fig. 3-41 reveals three facts. First, the unknown surface *U* is parallel longitudinally to the known

surface *M* because it produces the same number of bands. Second, it is not parallel across the width because the bands on the unknown surface are at an angle to those on the known surface. Third, the amount that the unknown surface is out of parallel to the known surface is one-half band in one width. These differences may be measured in much the same way that the fringe patterns were read to evaluate flatness.

In the example shown in Fig. 3-41, an assumption was made that the unknown part had the same basic size as the known part. In most cases there would be a small difference in height. The effect of this is shown in Fig. 3-42. After the known and the unknown parts have been wrung tightly to a flat and are positioned alongside each other, it is necessary to determine which one is the higher. This is done by placing the second optical flat over them, orienting the fringe pattern to run lengthwise, and then applying force to a point above the center of each part. If force applied at *X* in Fig. 3-42 does not spread out the pattern but force applied at *Y* does, then the known part is the higher. In this example, the air-wedge triangles formed over each part are identical. Therefore the fringe patterns are identical. Counting the fringes across the unknown part shows that it is two bands lower than the known.

The same principle applies when the differences are very small. The method must be altered, however, because pressure at either *X* or *Y* causes the bands to spread out. When this happens, the top flat is manipulated until the band patterns run diagonally, as in Fig. 3-43. Then if the bands on the known block exactly correspond to those on the unknown, the blocks are the same height. If they do not correspond in number or do not line up, the blocks are not the same height. In view *b*, the reference line intersects band 1 on the known block and band 2 on the unknown block. Therefore, 2 bands minus 1 band multiplied by the wavelength of the light source would indicate how much lower the unknown block is from the known block. The reference line could have been anywhere else along the fringe pattern. The difference would have been the same. In view *c*, the reference line intersects the first band on the known block and then crosses the unknown half between the second and third bands. The difference is 1 1/2 bands.

These same techniques and principles apply when the surfaces being compared are not nearly as flat as they have been in these examples, but it becomes vastly more complex. Suggested practice is to sketch the surface configuration of each block before making height comparisons. Reference to the sketches will often clarify confusing patterns formed by the two blocks together.

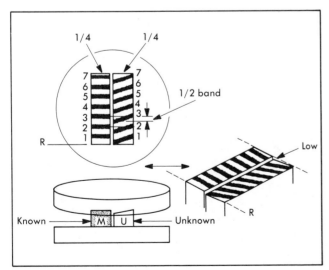

Fig. 3-41 Both surfaces have the same number of bands, but those on the unknown surface slant.

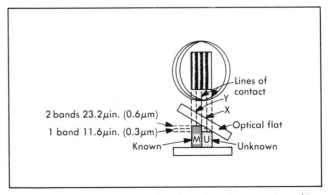

Fig. 3-42 Counting the number of bands on the unknown part provides the measurement of the height difference. Force is applied at points *X* and *Y*.

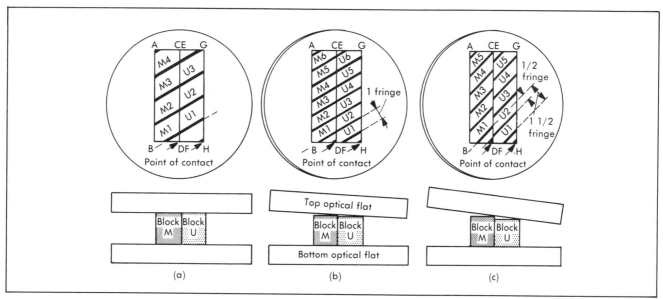

Fig. 3-43 Counting the number of bands on the unknown part provides the measurement of the height difference. Force is applied at points X and Y.

LASER INSPECTION DEVICES

The word "laser" is an acronym that stands for "Light Amplification by Stimulated Emission of Radiation." Laser light differs from ordinary light by being extremely intense, highly directional, strongly monochromatic, and coherent to a high degree. Unlike light emitted from an ordinary source, the waves of laser light are coordinated in time and space (they are coherent) and have essentially the same wavelength (they are monochromatic). Directionality results largely from the geometry of the device and the coherence of light. The intensity of the laser beam is the result of the light energy at a single wavelength in a particular direction.

There are a number of different types of lasers available. The type of laser used depends on the specific application. Manufacturing operations such as welding metals or drilling and cutting tough steels, ceramics, and diamonds employ high-energy, solid-state lasers such as pulsating ruby lasers or high-power molecular carbon dioxide lasers. For metrology, low-power lasers, usually of a continuous-wave output type, are employed; these are generally gas lasers.

As a group, gas lasers cover a wide spectrum range. Hydrogen cyanide gas lases in the far infrared region, while hydrogen gas lases in the ultraviolet region. The common helium-neon laser (neon is the lasing material) emits light in the visible spectrum. Argon gas is an ion laser with several transitions in the visible range.

The helium-neon laser, excited by an electric discharge or a high-frequency field, is more nearly perfectly monochromatic than any other source. It produces intense light at a wavelength of 6328 Å (0.6 μm) that is in phase and coherent, with an intensity that is literally 1000 times more than any other monochromatic source.

The precise wavelength of a laser is not simply a function of the lasing material employed, but is influenced somewhat by the mechanical spacing of the end resonators. For longer lasers, there are always several discrete, closely spaced wavelengths that match the spacing of the end plates. The helium-neon laser, for instance, can lase both in the visible and in the infrared ranges. Different sets of mirrors are needed for the different wavelengths. The mirrors used must have the appropriate reflectivity at the operating wavelength.

The uses of the laser in metrology arise from the characteristics of laser light that differentiate it from ordinary light. Those characteristics are the extreme intensity, the highly directional, small, collimated beam, the monochromaticity, and the coherent nature of the light.

One of the largest uses of lasers is by contractors for alignment and surveying. Here the intensity and directionality properties make the laser a natural.

These same properties are fundamental for the high-speed measuring devices that employ a scanning laser beam. The transmitter section of the gage emits a moving beam of light that scans at a regular speed. The object being measured interrupts the beam, and the detector determines the time that the beam took to traverse the part. The electronic controller converts the data into discrete dimensional readings for end use. The inherent stability of these devices have led to their being used in harsh industrial environments such as steel bar mills.

Again, the intensity and directional properties are fundamental to high-speed contour gages that measure by optical triangulation. These gages direct a small, intense beam of light onto the workpiece. A lens system and photodetector are located at a known angle with respect to the incident beam axis. As the part is moved in the Y direction, the gage determines the change in location of the spot in the X direction. To avoid the problems involved in having the image of the spot move across the detector, the gage moves the part in the X direction to the original location using a null-seeking system. The resulting data are a series of X-Y locations that can be plotted or compared to master data by the gage's computer.

The laser is used in the measurement of straightness deviation, such as in the inspection of surface plates and for machine tool alignment. Before the availability of the laser, it was necessary to use a measuring autocollimator, which requires a high degree of skill on the part of the operator. The laser autocollimator unit is much simpler and easier to use. It directs a collimated laser beam to a flat target mirror that can be at varying distances from the light source.

If the surface being examined is perfect, the reflected beam would be returned superimposed on the projected beam. Imperfections in the surface cause misalignment of the mirror and an angular offset of the return beam. The autocollimator detector array senses the offset in two axes simultaneously.

There are many applications of lasers in metrology based on the coherence of laser light. Coherence in time implies that a portion of the beam at one location has specific relationship in time to other portions of the beam. Spatial coherence is a measure of the correlation between two separated points in space at the same time.

The concept of coherence is historically related to the idea of the wave nature of light and the achievement of interference phenomena. The ability to achieve interference fringes is a measure of coherence. Thus one of the earliest uses of laser light was in interferometry. Metrology and measurement of surfaces by interferometry became possible under much less restrictive conditions.

LASER SCANNING INSTRUMENTS

For the accurate measurement of the diameter of soft, delicate, hot, or moving objects, noncontacting sensors must be used. Devices of this character include capacitive gages, eddy-current gages, air gages, and optical sensors.

Optical sensors have advantages over these other gages because of the nature of light itself. The principal advantages are the following:

1. They do not require direct mechanical contact between the sensor and the object to be measured.
2. The distance from the sensor to the object to be measured can be large.
3. The response time is limited only to that of the photodetector and its electronics.
4. Light variations or interruptions are directly converted to electrical signals.

Optical sensors used for the dimensional gaging of part profiles employ various techniques, such as shadow projection, diffraction phenomena, diode arrays, and scanning light beams. If the object to be measured is small or does not move about more than a small fraction of an inch, a dimensional gage based on diffraction phenomena or diode arrays can be used. However, if the object to be measured has a dimension of more than a small fraction of an inch, diffraction techniques and diode arrays become impractical.

A scanning laser beam is particularly suited to this latter type of measurement. The concept of using a scanning light beam for noncontacting dimensional gaging is certainly not new and predates the laser. Instruments using scanning laser beams in a variety of ways have been designed and manufactured. These instruments are increasingly utilizing the potential of this technique when precision performance is required.

System Components and Operation

A typical laser scanning instrument consists of a transmitter module, a receiver module, and processor electronics (see Fig. 3-44). The transmitter contains a low-power HeNe gas laser, a power supply, a collimating lens, a multifaceted reflector prism, a synchronizing pulse photodetector, and a protective window. In operation, the transmitter module produces a collimated, parallel, scanning laser beam moving at a high, constant, linear speed. The scanning beam appears as a line of red light and sweeps across its measurement field. When a part is placed in the field, it interrupts the beam. The receiver module collects and photoelectrically senses the laser light transmitted past the part being measured. The processor electronics process the receiver signals, converting them to a convenient form and then displaying the dimension being measured.

Applications

Laser scanning instruments can be used in a broad range of manufacturing operations and a variety of industries. Some of the potential areas of application are wire manufacturing, centerless grinding, plastic extrusion, metal product fabrication, and nuclear reactor metrology.

By modifying the techniques by which the detector output is digitized and interpreted by the processor unit, measurements can be made on translucent material such as fiber-optic cables or transparent material such as glass tubing. In addition to simple diameter measurement, product position, gap size, and multiple dimensions, measurements are possible by examining the detector output in different ways. More elaborate scanner geometries can be used to achieve dual-axis inspection. In these applications, the laser beam is alternately swept across the measurement field in two axes 90° apart. By stacking individual scanners back to back or detecting only the edge of a product and relating it to the position of a reference edge, products much larger than the range of an individual scanner can be measured. Extra-high-speed scanners, which measure at four to six times the normal rate, allow detection of smaller defects, such as lumps or neckdowns, in moving product applications.

LASER TRIANGULATION

A variety of noncontact techniques can be used for proximity or range-type measurements. These include time-of-flight techniques such as laser radars, ultrasonic and acoustic radar ranging, and a variety of optical techniques. Ultrasonic and acoustic systems have the advantage of large range, but in general are only capable of providing medium resolutions of proximity. Also, they use relatively large spot sizes or footprints on the part being measured. The large spot size is a disadvantage when the part to be measured is small or of a nonflat geometry. Laser radar devices tend to be only moderately precise and relatively expensive.

Of the many optical techniques, several procedures have been utilized. These include measurement of the width of a spot with a conical or tapered beam, measurement of the spacing between two projected spots with the input angles being selected for sensitivity, and single-spot laser triangulation. Of these three, laser triangulation is the preferred method for high-accuracy measurements. The simplicity of this method allows the development of a highly rugged, reliable, and for the most part accurate device as part of the mechanical and optical hardware design.

It is important to note that there are a number of techniques that fit under the general title of laser triangulation. These

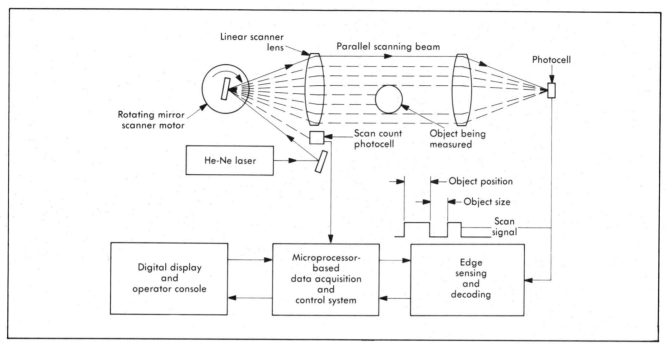

Fig. 3-44 Schematic of laser scanning instrument. (*Lasermike Division, Techmet Co.*)

include structured light, light stripe, and single-spot techniques. This discussion is limited to single-spot laser triangulation techniques.

Operating Principle

The principle of single-spot laser triangulation is illustrated in Fig. 3-45. The sensors use a small, low-powered laser. A beam of laser light from the source is projected and focused by optics to the surface of the object. This creates a spot of light on the object surface similar to shining a flashlight on a wall. At some angle relative to the axis of the projected laser light, an image of the spot falls on the detector. As shown in Fig. 3-45, the location of the centroid of the imaged spot is directly related to the standoff distance from the sensor to the object surface. A change in standoff distance results in a lateral shift of the spot centroid along the sensor array; calculation of the optical triangles, hence the name optical triangulation, is carried out by the sensor processor. The sensor processor is frequently remotely mounted from the sensor head itself. The microprocessor-controlled processor typically provides a readout of the surface standoff distance relative to the sensor or of the standoff distance variation relative to a programmable nominal.

A variety of single-spot laser triangulation sensors are available at various specifications. Typically, the nominal standoff distance of such a sensor is 2-6″ (50-150 mm). The measurement range is from ±0.02 to ±0.50″ (±0.5 to ±12.5 mm). Accuracies, proportionally, are in the region of 50 μin. to 0.003″ (1 to 75 μm). Data rates from single-spot laser triangulation sensors are typically 100-300 readings per second, with some suppliers offering sampling rates of more than 30,000 readings per second. Surfaces that are oriented at an angle to the input beam of up to 20° or larger can be measured depending on the texture and reflectivity characteristics of the surface.

For many measurement applications, particularly where flexibility is required, the sensor must be equipped with a form

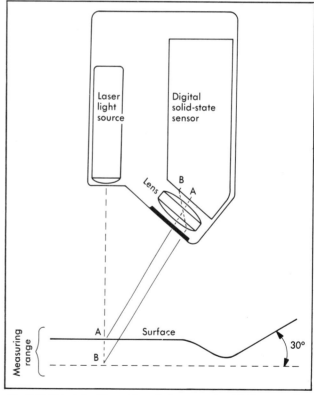

Fig. 3-45 Principle of laser triangulation operation (*Diffracto, Ltd.*)

of adaptive gain control to compensate for varying surface reflectivities. This is particularly important in a programmable system when a variety of surfaces must be inspected. Sensors are

CHAPTER 3

LASER INSPECTION DEVICES

generally equipped with an automated gain control that operates by varying the sensor sensitivity depending on the light level reflected. Typical gain control ranges from 500 to 1 in reflectivity ratio for a simple sensor to a 100,000 to 1 ratio for a complex sensor designed for a variety of surface applications. It is desirable that this gain control function be carried out automatically and not require operator intervention to set up the sensor.

Sensors

A single-spot laser triangulation sensor is sealed to withstand the heat and/or dust conditions of the industrial environment. Frequently a crash detector or contact plate is fitted to the front of the sensor to provide an indication to a measuring system controller in case the sensor contacts the part being measured. A contact plate is required if the sensor chosen for a given application has a small standoff distance and measuring angle. It is also particularly useful in flexible programmable measuring systems because it is used to stop machine motions before damage to the sensor or machine occurs. Selecting a sensor with a longer standoff distance or measuring range may negate the need for a crash alarm device.

In terms of size, most sensors are typically 6 x 3 x 2" (150 x 75 x 50 mm) and operate at a standoff distance of 2-4" (50-100 mm). The mounting post can be designed to be coaxial and concentric with the laser source, thus permitting the sensor to be mounted on a measuring machine or robot and rotated about the measuring beam. The cable between the sensor and control unit is typically 30' (9 m) or more in length. The control unit provides a two-line liquid crystal display of the proximity or proximity variation from nominal size. Readout is typically available in inch or metric units, and both RS-232 and parallel outputs are available for coupling the measured values to a higher level processor, data acquisition, or other device. A typical sensor weighs about 16 oz (450 g).

Applications

Single-spot laser triangulation sensors have found a wide number of applications in the industrial environment. One such area is in dimensional gaging of components where the sensor provides a direct replacement for a contact (LVDT) or noncontact (air or capacitance) probe. The advantage of such sensors over LVDTs include remote measurement without contact and a high data rate. Relative to air and capacitance gaging techniques, laser triangulation permits longer standoff distances, higher response, and greater resolution.

The disadvantage of a single-spot laser triangulation sensor as a direct replacement for other forms of gaging probes is that the triangulation sensor cost is currently higher than that of more traditional measuring probes. However, in many applications, the speed of the measurement, the greater resolution, and the facts that there are no contact and no moving parts in the sensor provide ready justification for their use.

Laser triangulation sensors can be used as a replacement for the touch trigger probes typically used on coordinate measuring machines. In this application, the sensor determines surface features and surface locations utilizing an edge-finding feature. However, the sensors cannot be used for probing down the depth of a bore to determine size or location. When utilized for surface measurement applications, the advantage of the use of the laser triangulation sensor on the coordinate measuring machine is a significant increase in speed of measurement.

Typically this increase over a touch trigger probe is on the order of 4 to 10 times.

This advantage stems from several factors. First, the sensor does not have to be indexed toward the surface to determine the null point. Instead, the sensor provides an active measurement of the plus or minus deviation of surface location from the nominal position used to drive the machine. Second, when indexing from measurement point to measurement point, the sensor does not need to be retracted to avoid crashing into the surface because the standoff distance provides adequate clearance for movement between measurement points. In addition, the noncontact nature of the laser triangulation sensor eliminates the potential for deformation of flexible surfaces and damage to soft or other delicate surfaces.

Laser triangulation sensors can also be used with industrial robots. The sensor provides a feedback signal to the robot controller indicating the range or proximity to an object. This can be used to assist the robot in acquiring the location of the component and to provide a vision capability for gripping of the part. In addition, such a sensor mounted on a robot can be used to create a measurement robot. The limitation in this case, however, is that the accuracy of the overall system is limited by the positioning accuracy of the robot, which generally is not adequate for measurement applications requiring total accuracies of ±0.004" (±0.10 mm) or better.

Safety

Laser triangulation sensors typically use a low-powered laser (solid-state or helium-neon) as their light source. As such, they must be certified to the appropriate class under current governmental regulations. These include mandatory warning labels and indications of the power level from such lasers. Laser power levels are typically a few thousandths of a watt. Because solid-state lasers operate in the infrared region of the electromagnetic spectrum (the beam is invisible), additional care must be exercised during their use.

AUTOCOLLIMATORS

The popularity of autocollimators rests on their ability to sense remotely, with high accuracy, the angular rotation of a flat mirror around axes that are in the plane of the mirror. With sensitivities approaching 1/10 arc second, or even less under special conditions, it has become common practice to use autocollimators not only to monitor angular tilts as such, but to convert linear displacements into angular ones so that they can be monitored with this versatile instrument.

Optically, an autocollimator is simply a special form of a telescope. It consists basically of an illuminated target pattern or reticle located in the focal plane of the telescope objective. A plane mirror perpendicular to the optical axis in front of this telescope will reflect an image of the pattern back on itself in the same plane and in focus. A rotation of the mirror by an angle about its perpendicular position causes the return image to be displaced by a specific amount. The amount of displacement can be calculated using the equation:

$$d = 2f\theta \tag{2}$$

where:

d = displacement, in. (mm)
f = focal length of the autocollimator objective, in. (mm)
θ = angular rotation of the mirror

A viewing system is required to observe the relative position of the image, which can be in the form of an illuminated slit or cross line or cross hair in an illuminated field. A simple eyepiece may serve or a compound microscope can be used as shown in Fig. 3-46. The fiducial index should be designed for maximum precision in zeroing the image; for example, a double line to frame a single line. Measurement is made by moving either the image or the index under micrometer control. Although most autocollimators measure around one axis only, a suitable target pattern and a two-axial index micrometer system are all that is required to make readings about two axes.

Mirror Characteristics

Because the reflecting mirror is part of the overall system, mirror properties such as size, flatness, and distance from the objective play a role in making measurements. A mirror smaller than the objective will send rays back through different portions of the objective, depending on where its center is located with respect to the optical axis. This causes readings to vary unless the objective is free of all aberrations, which is most unlikely. One test for quality of an autocollimator is to move a 1/8″ (3 mm) wide slit in front of the objective with the reflector mirror fixed while observing whether the image shifts noticeably.

If the mirror is not flat, it will not focus the returning image and present an undefined reference plane. Hence high-quality autocollimator mirrors are held to flatness tolerance of 1/4 fringe [2.5 μin. (0.06μm)] or better. At first glance it might seem that there should be no limit to the distance between an autocollimator and the reflecting mirror because they are separated by light that is collimated (has parallel rays). In practice, however, limitations arise from several sources. One source is that the light is never perfectly collimated. Another more direct limit is

set by simple geometry. Assume a mirror is centered on an axis a distance L away from the objective of diameter C (see Fig. 3-47). When $L = C/\theta$, no light whatsoever is returned to the autocollimator. For a 2″ (50 mm) diam objective, a mirror tilt of 10 arc seconds leads to L_{max} = 700″ (18 m). In practice, however, the mirror could not be farther away than a fraction of this amount.

It is important to remember that the air path between the mirror and the autocollimator is a real part of the optical system. Measurements to 1 arc second over distances up to 5′ (1.5 m) in a reasonably quiet environment seldom cause trouble. However, when higher resolution or longer distances, or both, are required, close attention must be paid to adequate shielding of the air path from drafts and especially temperature gradients. Even a simple cardboard tube can be helpful for shielding.

Photoelectric Autocollimators

Autocollimators that replace the judgment of the human eye with appropriate photoelectric systems have some important advantages that can outweigh their increased cost and complexity. Setting accuracy is improved and no longer differs between observers. Readings can be made remotely and monitored cotinuously when required. Such autocollimators come in sizes from 1″ (25 mm) (with null-setting sensitivity better than 0.1 arc second) to very large instruments with 10″ (250 mm) objectives. Some provide merely a photoelectric null setting without measuring capability, while others have analog or digital readout with ranges from 10 seconds to a full degree or more.

In the system shown in Fig. 3-48, the illuminated target reticle slit is imaged back in its own plane through the autocollimator objective and reflecting mirror, but displaced radially for convenience. It is then reimaged onto a vibrating slit by

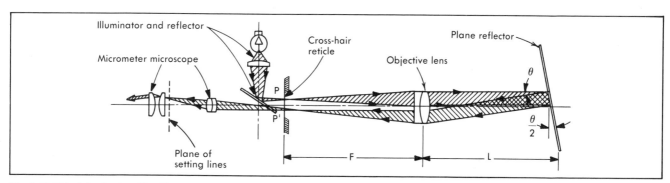

Fig. 3-46 Principle of autocollimation.

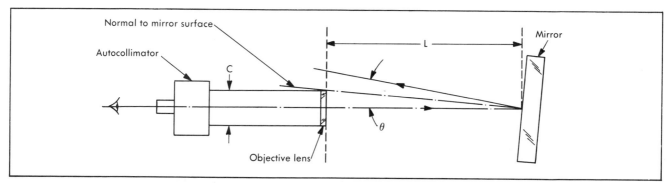

Fig. 3-47 No light is reflected back into the autocollimator when $L\theta \geq C$.

LASER INSPECTION DEVICES

means of a relay lens. Behind the slit is a photocell whose output is now modulated by the vibrating slit, which makes possible the phase discrimination required to make the amplified output sensitive to the direction as well as the amount of mirror rotation from a central null position. Such a system can be used to read mirror tilt in analog fashion on the meter. If the vibrating slit assembly is moved with a precision micrometer, a reading is obtained with the meter acting merely as a null indicator. In the latter case, the electronics need no longer behave linearly and may be simplified. A sensitivity of 0.1 arc second is readily obtainable.

A different type of system is shown in Fig. 3-49. Here an entire grid pattern is imaged back on itself by the autocollimator optics. As a result, what a photodetector sees when the

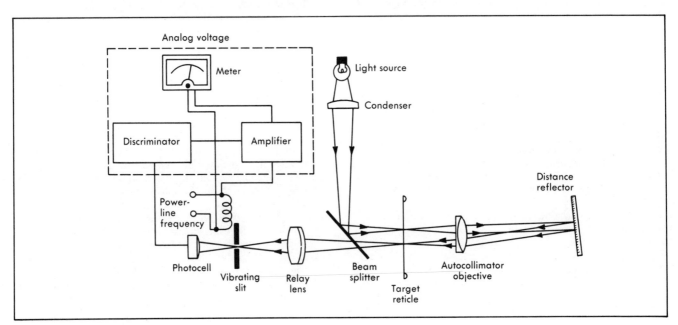

Fig. 3-48 Schematic of photoelectric autocollimator.

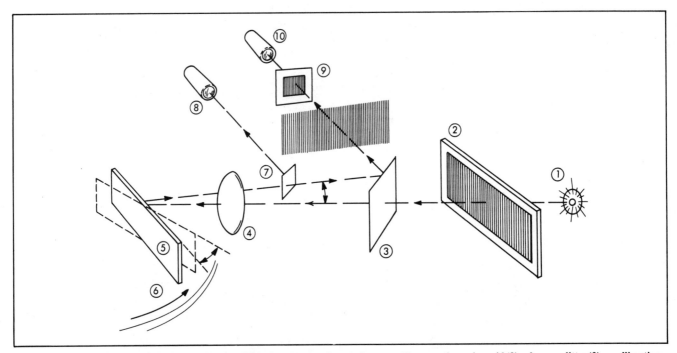

Fig. 3-49 Continuous photoelectric autocollimator. Light from a monochromatic source (1) passes through a grid (2), a beam splitter (3), a collimating lens (4), and strikes a mirror (5) mounted on the rotating specimen being tested (6). The image is reflected back into the autocollimator, where it is directed by a beam splitter (7) to the stability reference photosensor (8). The image is also reflected by beam splitter (3) through a second grid (9) to the control photosensor (10), which generates a periodic signal as mirror (5) is rotated.

mirror tilts are periodic changes in intensity; the period is a function of grid spacing and the focal length of the objective and can vary from 10 arc seconds to 10 minutes of arc. Corresponding ranges vary from 1 to 3°. Keeping track of these periods is equivalent to digitizing the angle of tilt and may be all that is required. For highest sensitivity, the analog position between periods can also be recorded. An important advantage of this approach is that a much larger part of the field is optically active, so that the systems can be made relatively compact even in applications where high sensitivity is combined with a long angular range. The illumination is much more effectively utilized, resulting in excellent signal-to-noise ratio.

Calibration

The only effective method for calibrating autocollimators is to monitor output or readings as the reference mirror is tilted through accurately controlled angles. The problem of how to generate small angles accurate to 1 arc second or better has been solved by designing special sine-bar fixtures with a precisely defined axis at one end, while at the other end a well-defined cylinder is raised or lowered with a special micrometer or with gage blocks. A fixed wedge can also be used to calibrate an autocollimator; however, a fixed wedge only gives a specific angle whereas a sine bar can give an infinite number of angles.

Checking Way Straightness

In designing for applications of an autocollimator, the central thought must be that these instruments are sensitive to angular tilts only, not to translations. In this respect, they differ from alignment telescopes. A series of measurements cannot be better than the angular stability of the surface on which the autocollimator rests. This tends to show up in such applications as the checking of a machine bed when the instrument is mounted on no more than a floor-supported tripod. A platform fastened directly to the casting involved is likely to be much more stable.

Checking the straightness and flatness of a way or equivalent surface is one of the most frequent applications of an autocollimator. The first objective is to convert deviation from straightness stepwise into successive tilts of a mirror carriage as it is moved along a straight line in increments just equal to the distance between locating pads. At each point, readings are taken from a rigidly mounted autocollimator. These readings are then converted back to a profile curve. Note that such a test says nothing about the geometry between the contact points of the mirror carriage; this requires some other type of assurance or traverses with a carriage of shorter base length. It may seem odd to go through such a double conversion to angles and back when all that is wanted is to measure straightness or flatness; manual recording of readings and subsequent graphing can be tedious and time consuming.

The photoelectric autocollimator can be interfaced to a computer that enables the time for straightness checks and calibration of surface plates for flatness to be considerably reduced. The computer with an interactive program permits three X, three Y, and two diagonal generator lines to be used with a printout of results including a straightness graph and an isometric plot of the surface plate.

INTERFEROMETERS

Interferometric testing has long been used in optical metrology. The advent of the laser has not only made interferometry more convenient to use, but has also extended its range of application. Interferometry is used as a tool in optical fabrication, precision metal finishing, microlithography, and optical and electro-optical systems alignment.

For most interferometry, the output of the test is an interference fringe pattern that can be observed in real time and photographed to produce an interferogram. The type of pattern is determined by the particular measurement configuration and by the errors in the part under test. The quantitative reduction of an interference fringe pattern is usually based on ascertaining the fractional deviation of the interference fringe pattern from some ideal, best-fitting pattern. The denominator of the fractional deviation is the measured spacing between a pair of fringes in the ideal pattern.

The quantitative usefulness of an interference pattern is dependent on having a method of data extraction and reduction. Interference pattern reduction can range in complexity from a simple visual evaluation to an elaborate reduction of the data extracted by an automatic microdensitometer with a large computer. Between these extremes there are a great variety of means for hand reduction and a number of microprocessor-based interferometer and data reduction systems.

Operating Principles

Interferometry, which came into use as a tool for scientific investigation into the nature of light prior to 1900, has been used since that time as a measuring instrument in the fabrication of modern optics. Regardless of the configuration, all interferometer systems make use of the interference phenomena of light. Light waves are useful for many types of measurement because they constitute an effective unit of measure that is very small, and they are capable of the most accurate length definition known. The wave nature of light, which makes such accurate measurement possible, is ever present, but not apparent under ordinary conditions. Only by making light waves interact with each other is the wave effect made visible and thus made useful for measuring purposes. This phenomenon of interaction is known as interference, and nearly all instruments designed to measure with interference are known as interferometers, the exception being optical flats, whose widespread and simple application has kept this method of flatness testing from being so classified in common usage.

The reason why interference is not observed generally is that it can occur only when two wavefronts, or light rays, come together in a compatible condition known as coherence. Coherence means that the two rays that meet at any given point in a field of view maintain whatever phase relationship they have for an appreciable length of time. This condition is possible only when the two rays have originated from the same point in the light source at the same time. As a result, all practical interferometers make use of some type of beam divider that splits an incoming ray into two parts that travel different paths until they are recombined, usually in the same beam divider. An exception to the above is the gas laser, whose light output under special conditions is sufficiently coherent to interfere with light from another laser.

As a general rule, the greater the difference in the optical lengths that the two beams travel between splitting and recombining, the more complex the instrument is likely to be. This path difference varies from just a few wavelengths to one million wavelengths or even more with laser light sources. Applications of interference of most interest in metrology are accurate comparison of surface geometry against a master,

LASER INSPECTION DEVICES

which can be done with or without microscopic magnifications, and the relative and absolute calibration of length.

Fizeau interference. The most common interference effects are those associated with thin, transparent films or wedges bounded on at least one side by a transparent surface. Soap bubbles, oil films on water, and optical flats fall into this category. Light is usually from an extended "white" light source, such as the sky, but for measuring purposes a single-wavelength source is preferred. Helium lamps meet this requirement reasonably well and are therefore the most widely used. The dominant wavelength is 23.4 μin. (0.59 μm), an orange color.

The mechanism by which interference takes place is most readily described in terms of an optical flat (test plate) placed over a reasonably reflecting workpiece (see Fig. 3-50). Natural irregularities or dust particles can be counted on to provide a wedge angle α, typically 1-10 arc seconds, rather than the exaggerated value shown for clarity. The observer's eye looking at a point such as C on the workpiece will see it through the transparent optical flat, illuminated by light along the ray path OABC, reflected along path CDEF. In addition, a quantity of light (typically 4%) is reflected from both surfaces of the optical flat, and some of this also finds its way to the observer's eye. Light reflected from the top surface AGE is not interesting under these conditions, but that reflected from point B via ray BGF is "coherent" with that of ray BCDEF and thus is capable of interacting with it. Coherence is obtained because the two rays BGF and BCDEF were obtained from the beam-splitting action to the glass-air interface on the single incoming ray OAB at B. When two coherent rays come together in this fashion, they interact according to wave theory, giving rise to the phenomenon of interference.

From Fig. 3-50, ray BCDEF is longer than ray BGF by an optical distance BCD. Should this distance BCD be equal to 1 or any whole number of lengths, the waves of the two interfering rays will arrive in phase with each other, which causes them to reinforce each other. On the other hand, if distance BCD should happen to be 1/2, 3/2, or, simply, 1/2 plus any whole number of wavelengths, the reverse is true. The two rays will be exactly 180° out of phase with each other, resulting in total destructive interference. Under these conditions, point C appears dark, being covered by an interference fringe. In effect, the ray reflected at the glass-air interface BD undergoes a 180° phase shift, while at the workpiece surface there is little or no such

phase shift. The result is merely to shift the fringe pattern one-half fringe parallel to itself and for that reason the effect is commonly ignored.

The workpiece surface, as it is scanned by the observer's eye, is covered by a pattern of such dark fringes (lines that may be straight or curved), each representing the locus of a constant distance BCD. A new fringe is formed everywhere that BCD increases or decreases by one wavelength, but because BC is practically 1/2 BCD, the fringes repeat every time the wedge has increased or decreased its height by one-half wavelength, commonly written $\lambda/2$.

It is important to note that an interference fringe is not an entity like a wire, which has a definite position in space. It has no existence except as the observing instrument gives it form. That this is so can readily be confirmed for the system described by moving the head with everything else unchanged. The fringes will be seen to move. How to interpret such a fringe pattern and derive from it the shape of a surface with respect to that of a reference is described in greater detail in the section on optical flats.

Multiple reflections. When the undersurface of an optical flat is given a reflecting coating (50-90% reflectivity to roughly match that of the workpiece), the rays that combine at F are no longer limited to two, but instead represent a whole series of multiple reflections (10 or even as many as 100 under special conditions). The most obvious difference to the eye is that the fringes, while still separated by the same $\lambda/2$ equivalent height, are much sharper and thus easier to interpret. This comes about because the large number of rays combine destructively only when all are exactly in opposite phase to the directly reflected ray, and this happens only over a very narrow angle of viewing.

The contrast between fringes and their background varies considerably with the reflectivity of both the surface being examined and that of the reference. The better the match between these reflectivities, the greater the fringe contrast, a statement that holds equally well for two-beam and multiple-beam interference. This explains why glass against glass gives good two-beam fringes, but glass against polished steel does not and why high-reflection coatings on the glass help in the latter case. Multiple-beam fringes demand high reflectivity on both surfaces (at least 50% is desirable), which precludes applying the technique to materials like glass unless the surface has been specially overcoated with a thin deposit of metal (silver or aluminum), which may be removed chemically after testing. Semitransparent films of silver on the reference surface are now generally replaced by multiple-layer dielectric coatings that have the advantage of absorbing very little light (less than 1%) in themselves. This high efficiency makes possible a large number of reflections.

Collimated illumination and viewing. Simple visual observation of the Fizeau fringes between two surfaces very close to each other (no more than a few wavelengths apart), as in Figs. 3-50 and 3-51, is satisfactory for most applications. However, there are some clear limitations that cannot be ignored if the surfaces are large and if the test specifications are tight.

The theoretically correct arrangement is to illuminate and observe the interference-producing wedge in parallel or collimated light (see Fig. 3-52). An additional advantage of such a system is that it is no longer necessary to have the two interfering surfaces touching, avoiding possible damage to the carefully finished reference surface as well as the component under test.

One answer to the relatively high cost of a large-aperture fringe-viewing system is to use a small system and traverse it

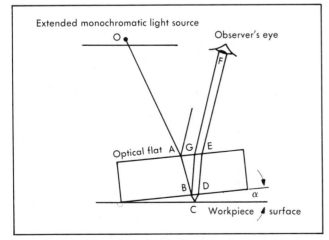

Fig. 3-50 Simple interference-fringe formation of an optical flat.

over the stationary reference and workpiece. The disadvantage of this is that it is then no longer possible to judge the shape of an entire surface in a single glance. The surface topography can be derived by networking together a series of overlapping interference patterns. The wedge angle is always adjusted so that a fringe is parallel to the direction of traverse. Multiple-beam fringes should always be viewed in collimated light to obtain the accuracy that goes with the precise, sharp fringes.

Types of Interferometers

Michelson interferometers. The basic Michelson interferometer is shown in Fig. 3-53. Light from an extended source, most often monochromatic (single wavelength), falls onto a plane-parallel plate BD, which has on its back a semitransparent layer of silver or a more efficient multilayer film. This divides the light into two rays of equal intensity, one of which is transmitted through compensating plate CP to mirror M_1 and the other of which is reflected through BD to mirror M_2. The rays are reflected back from the mirrors and reunite at the beam-splitter surface. There they are transmitted to the eye at E, where fringes can be observed.

The only purpose of the compensator plate is to introduce exactly the same amount of glass in each of the paths, which is important mainly when a white light source is used. However, so-called white light fringes can be seen only if both ray paths are exactly equal (to a few wavelengths) in total length. The path lengths themselves are not important; only their differences affect fringe formation. Monochromatic sources allow fringes to be seen over a range of path difference that may vary from a few to a million wavelengths, depending on the source.

Modern two-beam, Twyman-Green interferometers are all based on a specialization of the Michelson arrangement (see Fig. 3-54). The central rays are seen to describe the same path, but owing to the presence of a pair of collimating lenses combined with a pinhole-source diaphragm, all other rays are parallel to the central ray. In the Michelson concept, the rays describe a cone, giving rise to various types of fringe patterns that may be hard to interpret.

Fabry-Perot interferometers. Fabry-Perot interferometers, or etalons, are made up of two optical flats, flat to 1/20 fringe or better, coated with a high-efficiency, semitransparent film on the two facing surfaces. The flats must be kept exactly parallel by means of a carefully designed spacer. When illuminated, as shown in Fig. 3-55, a series of very sharply defined bright circles are seen on a screen that result from interference between rays that are multiply reflected between the two working faces of the etalon.

Although etalons are seldom used in shop metrology, they are of interest because most of the original determinations of the meter in terms of the wavelengths of light were made with this instrument, and all the recent highly accurate intercomparisons of wavelengths depend on specialized versions of the Fabry-Perot etalon. In addition, a specialized form of the Fabry-Perot etalon is used in an intracavity configuration to provide longitudinal mode operation in a number of laser systems.

Spherical interferometers. Commercially produced interferometers are capable of measuring spherical as well as planer surfaces when configured with the proper reference accessories. The spherical accessory generates a cone of light that converges to a focus point and then diverges as the focus point is passed. Within the two cones of light (converging and diverging) there are an infinite number of spherical wavefronts of different

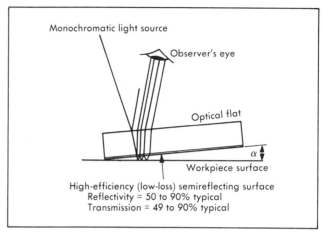

Fig. 3-51 Schematic showing rays for multiple-beam interference (all angles are exaggerated for clarity).

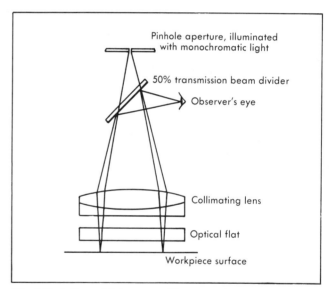

Fig. 3-52 Collimated light source—Fizeau interferometer.

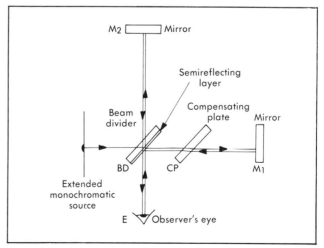

Fig. 3-53 Michelson interferometer.

LASER INSPECTION DEVICES

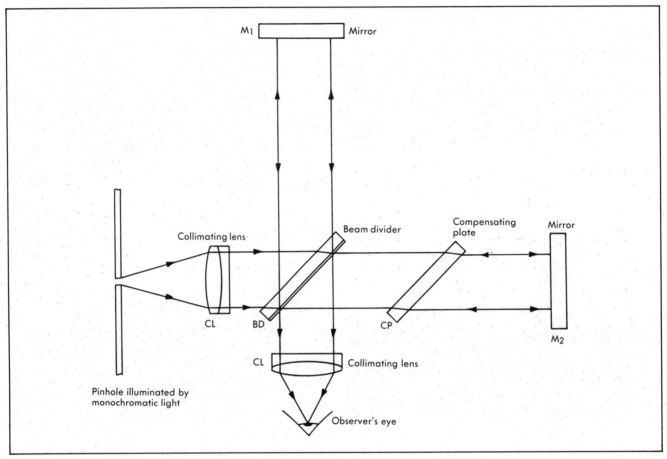

Fig. 3-54 Twyman-Green specialization of Michelson interferometer.

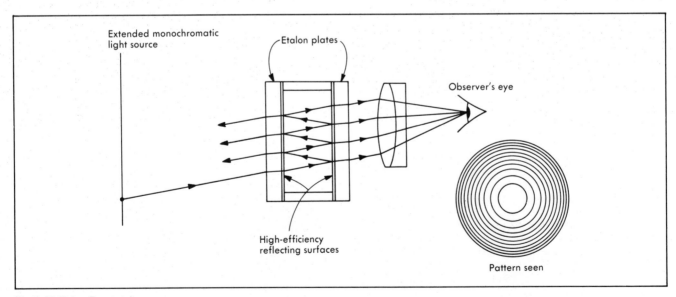

Fig. 3-55 Fabry-Perot etalon.

radius. To test a spherical part it is only necessary to place the center of curvature of the part in such a way that it is concentric with the focus of the reference. At this point, a wavefront of the same radius as the part will be reflected back into the interferometer system where it interferes with the reference wavefront producing the fringe pattern.

Fringe-counting interferometers. If in a Twyman-Green type interferometer, with both end mirrors perpendicular to the optical axis, one mirror is displaced slowly, exactly parallel to itself, the observer will note periodic changes from bright to dark in the intensity of the field being viewed. Measurement will show the intensity variation to be sinusoidal, with a period that corresponds to mirror motion of exactly half the wavelength of the light source used. If one of the end mirrors is slightly inclined to the optical axis, parallel fringes will be seen that move parallel to themselves by just one fringe for every $\lambda/2$ mirror motion. Counting of such fringes by eye, or with photo-detectors hooked up to high-speed counters, enables measurement of linear mechanical motion directly in terms of the wavelength of light (see Fig. 3-56). Accuracy of one part in one million should be attainable and has in fact been attained. A

number of conditions, however, must be met and understood before such results can be realized.

Gage block interferometers. All gage block interferometers are variations of the Fizeau or Twyman-Green (or Köster's prism equivalent) interferometers. Optical diagrams of two types are shown in Figs. 3-57 and 3-58.

Fundamentally, these interferometers measure the length of a gage block with respect to a baseplate, to which the block is wrung, by arranging the baseplate almost perpendicular to the interferometer axis and determining the number of fringes between the baseplate and the surface of the block. Multiplying this number by half the wavelength of the light used should give the length of the block. Because the number of fringes is of the order of 100,000 for a 1″ (25 mm) block and because all fringes look alike, the exact value is not immediately evident. The only quantity that is readily determined by a glance at the fringe pattern is whether the block length is an exact integral multiple of the half wavelength or whether it exceeds by some fringe fraction. Thus it is easy to tell that the block is, say, 1/3 fringe [about 3 μin. (0.08 μm)] longer than a whole number of fringes, while there is nothing to tell whether this whole number is 100,000, 99,990, 100,010, or some other multiple of $\lambda/2$. Within a range of 10 such numbers one can usually arrive at the solution by checking the block with conventional equipment and dividing this length by the known half wavelength of the light. If greater precision is required to tie down the missing information, use is made of the "exact-fraction" method. This requires observing in fairly rapid sequence the same fringe pattern as before, but at several different wavelengths, usually three to five depending on the spectral source used. The fractional displacement between the base and the gage block fringes is noted each time. Because the wavelengths bear no simple relationship to each other, only one single whole number of fringes can make up the length of the block and at the same time yield the specific fringe fractions observed for each color. Thus the length is uniquely defined.

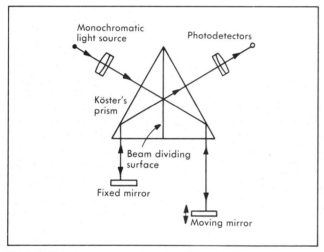

Fig. 3-56 Fringe-count system based on Köster's prism.

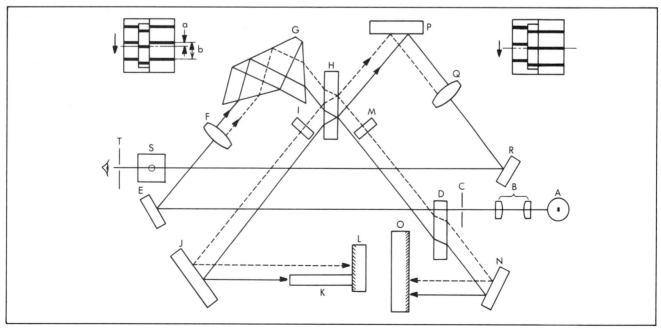

Fig. 3-57 Zeiss gage block interferometer.

LASER INSPECTION DEVICES

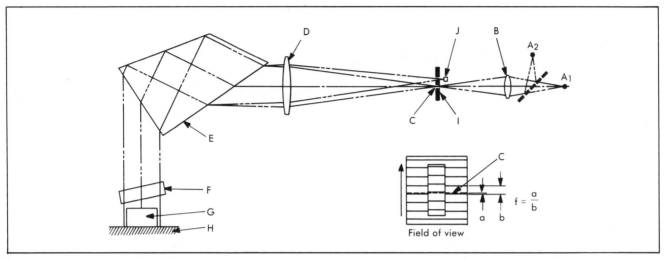

Fig. 3-58 N.P.L. gage block interferometer.

In practice, the procedure involved is simplified through the use of tables and special slide rules and computers that save all complicated arithmetic. However, corrections for atmospheric effects on wavelength must be applied; even more important, as a rule, are corrections for thermal expansion of the gage block if it is not exactly at 68° F (20° C). To measure 1 μin. (25 μm) requires that the fringe fraction of the dominant wavelength be determined to an accuracy of better than 1/10 fringe.

Interference microscopes. Checking the finish of finely polished or lapped surfaces can be done qualitatively with any good microscope equipped with proper illumination. However, when quantitative information is desired concerning scratch depth and shape, it becomes highly desirable to superimpose interference fringes over the field. Instruments designed for this purpose are called interference microscopes. Fringe patterns are interpreted exactly as in any other case.

Two basic types of interference microscopes are available. The simpler one makes use of Fizeau fringes, often the multiple-beam sharpened fringes that occur between a very small, optically flat reference surface in contact with the workpiece. The flat is not only small but thin, to make room for it in the limited space between the microscope objective and the workpiece. Most microscopes of this type are limited in magnification to 150X, sometimes up to 300X, by the presence of the reference flat. Fortunately this is enough for many purposes, but not for all. Like all such systems, monochromatic light is required, filtered mercury being preferred because very small lamps are available.

It is possible, but much more difficult, to adapt the Michelson Twyman-Green interferometer to a microscope. For very low magnifications (15X), the entire interferometer, in miniature form, fits in front of a low-magnification microscope objective. The only advantage of such a system lies in the ability to use white light fringes. When the interferometer arms are adjusted for equality, large steps can be checked and a bright picture results. For surface finish testing, it has insufficient magnification. High magnification becomes possible, in both white and monochromatic light, when suitably corrected microscope objectives are placed in both arms of the interferometer, one focused on the reference mirror and the other on the work surface. To get clear fringes, especially in white light, the two objectives have to be balanced to a very high degree. This is difficult to accomplish and, together with other optical requirements not described here, explains the relatively high price of this type of instrument.

Light Sources of Interferometry

Many light sources are used in various interferometers, with the choice based on cost, convenience, and the type of application. Nearly all modern interferometer systems use some type of laser because the longer coherence length offers distinct advantages with respect to fringe visibility, instrument flexibility, and freedom from path length restrictions.

Other nonlaser sources utilize the excitation of atoms of certain elements, which then radiate light at certain discrete wavelengths. These are generally a discharge lamp that is charged with one or sometimes two elements, and a means to electrically excite it. The commonly used types of sources are mercury, mercury 198, cadmium, krypton 86, thallium, sodium, helium, neon, and gas lasers.

AUTOMATIC GAGING AND PROCESS CONTROL

Automatic control over forming, machining, inspection, and assembly ensures greater productivity and lower costs, higher quality, and maximum use of machine capability. Control units must be accurate, have high-speed response, and be unaffected by vibration, oil, dirt, and coolant.

Practically all dimensions, conditions, or spatial relationships can be automatically inspected, including internal and external diameters, length, depth, taper, out of round, and geometrical conditions such as squareness, parallelism, concentricity, and center distance. Advances in electronic circuitry permit almost all configurations of workpieces to be inspected during all stages of the manufacturing process. Parts with large interruptions can be moved or rotated through gage fingers and measured to an accuracy of 20 μin. (0.5 μm) by damping, filtering, or by electronically detecting the interruptions and disregarding the resulting size change.

Automatic gage systems often include statistical process control features to ensure that corrections are made to the process only when the corrections are warranted. For example, if one workpiece in 100 measures oversize because of some periodic malfunction in the process, statistical controls will cause the system to disregard the measurement and not provide a correction to the workpiece.

GAGING FEASIBILITY

Among the variables to be considered in automatic gaging are part size and shape, material and finish, production rate, tolerances, part handling, cleanliness of part, type of gage element, and inspection rate. Interchangeable and adjustable tooling enable a gage to handle different parts, sizes, and tolerances. To accommodate slightly misaligned holes or locations, automatic gages are sometimes designed with floating-type gaging elements. If a part's size or shape prevents it from being gaged in one operation, it is better to inspect the close tolerances first. This prevents wasting the expense of checking the broader tolerances first only to have the part rejected later.

Usually, locating surfaces for the gaging operation should be the same as those used in the machining operation. However, for final or assembly inspection they may be based on the function or end use of the part. A large variety of part transfer devices are used in automatic gages, such as walking beam devices, endless belts, gravity feeds, or robots.

With the advent of the computer, it has become practical to design automatic gages that can separate size tolerances from location tolerances at one gaging station. To obtain increased (faster) speed, this type of gage may employ laser gaging or vision (video) gaging. These gages do not rely on a fixed location of the part, but will determine the location of the datum surfaces and inspect in relation to them. Although air, air-electric, or electronic automatic gages require interchangeable or adjustable gage heads or tooling to handle different part sizes or tolerances, video systems need only to be programmed to inspect a wide variety of parts. With tutorial, menu-driven (software), user friendly programming, video automatic systems are easy to change from one part to another. Once the program is written, it is only a matter of calling up the new program from the system memory. Flexible, programmable gaging systems using CNC logic and LVDT transducers are also available. These systems can provide higher accuracy than optical systems or coordinate measuring machines and are designed to operate in a harsh shop environment. In addition to providing totally automatic parts measurement, these systems can directly control one or more machining processes by sending statistically based compensation commands directly to the machine tool.

The computer has blurred the dividing line between manual and automatic gages. For instance, the coordinate measuring machine (CMM) was always known as a manual device because it depended on an operator to position the probe in relation to the surfaces being gaged. However, the use of the sensing or touch probe and the computer to direct the motions of the probe holder have made a semiautomatic system out of the CMM. With automatic loading, the CMM would be completely automatic in operation.

The following questions are presented as a guide to assist the manufacturing engineer in deciding on the exact type of process control to use. The questions highlight some of the distinctions used in defining the connections between the product measurement and the process correction.

1. What part variability is to be processed?
   a. Dedicated to single part.
   b. For family of parts.
   c. For batches of unrelated parts.
2. What type of machine tool is to be used?
   a. Single-purpose.
   b. Machining center.
   c. CNC lathe.
   d. Dial machine.
   e. Linear transfer line.
   f. Manufacturing cell.
   g. FMS.
3. How is part to be transferred?
   a. Into the machine tool.
   b. Into the gage.
   c. Out of the system.
4. What are the objectives of gaging and process control?
5. How timely is the correction to the process?
   a. Corrections are made on that very piece.
   b. Corrections are made on the very next piece.
   c. Corrections are made several pieces later.
   d. Corrections are made on a statistical basis.
6. When is the measuring done?
   a. While cutting the workpiece.
   b. While not cutting.
7. Where is the measuring done?
   a. On the machine tool.
   b. Off the machine tool.
8. What is the environment?
   a. Shop floor—"in-process."
   b. Clean room/QC area.
9. What is the measuring capability?
   a. Dedicated gaging—specialized for a given part.
   b. Flexible gaging—suited for a family of parts.
   c. General-purpose—suited for almost any part produced on the machine tool.
10. How good does the gage have to be?
    a. Repeatability.
    b. Accuracy.
11. How much processing is performed on the measured data?
    a. Makes a single measurement and displays it.
    b. Makes measurements of different product features and calculates their relationships.
    c. Makes many measurements and stores the readings.
    d. Measures, stores, and processes many data points statistically.
12. How is gaging information linked to the process control?
    a. Measurements are taken for historical purposes only.
    b. Measurements are taken and QC tells operations about the results.
    c. Measurements are taken by manufacturing personnel and they make corrections.

AUTOMATIC GAGING AND PROCESS CONTROL

d. Measurements are taken and automatically fed into the machine tool for correction.

TYPES OF SYSTEMS

Automatic gaging devices are usually referred to by function or position in the manufacturing process: as preprocess gages (inspection before machining), in-process gages (inspection during machining), postprocess gages (inspection after machining), final inspection gages, and assembly gages. Combinations of various types of gaging can provide fully automatic control over dimensional size from the moment the part enters the manufacturing process through assembly.

Preprocess Gaging

In preprocess gaging, the part is inspected before being loaded in the machine tool to ensure proper conditions of stock and location of machining area. Preprocess gaging helps to avoid damage to the machine and/or tooling, eliminates the expense of machining parts with insufficient stock, and extends tool life by ensuring that only correct parts are fed to the manufacturing process.

In-Process Gaging

With in-process gaging, the gage measures the part during metal removal and stops the process when the correct size is reached. With the advent of the flexible machining system concept there is more demand for in-process gaging to control the indexing and/or changing of the tooling.

Part shape and tolerances, type of machining, method of chucking, and the ability of the machine to utilize the gaging signal determine the type of in-process gaging employed. Earlier applications tended to be air or air-electric gaging. More recently, the flexibility of electronic gaging has led to it being the most commonly used system. The noncontact capabilities of electro-optical gaging and the ease with which it may be interfaced to computers and control systems have sparked interest in that approach.

Postprocess Gaging

Postprocess gaging has been the most common type of automatic gaging, with the part being gaged after the manufacturing operation is completed. Feedback signals can be sent to the producing machine to warn, adjust, or shut down the machine if faulty parts are being produced. Frequently, automatic classification and segregation of parts by dimensional size is performed by postprocess gages. The postprocess gage may also function as the preprocess gage for a subsequent operation.

Many earlier postprocess automatic gages employed air gaging or air-electric gaging; some even used fluidic logic systems. Air-electronic systems are used primarily when there are internal dimensions to be checked and high speed is required. The dominant system used today is the solid-state electronic gage, which is fast in operation, highly accurate, and readily interfaced with microprocessors and computers.

Final Inspection Gages

Final inspection gages are usually high-speed gages that inspect 100% of the output of a line of manufacturing machines. They may inspect as many as 25,000 parts per hour, but more commonly will inspect at a rate of several thousand parts per hour. Frequently they may categorize the parts by size and segregate salvageable parts from the rejects. Data may be kept relating to total throughput and individual categories.

Assembly Gaging

An automatic assembly gage may be used for preassembly gaging, selective fit assembly, or postassembly inspection. Electronic gaging circuits are normally used in automatic assembly for both pre and postassembly inspection. Parts are inspected for dimensional correctness and selective assembly.

The automatic assembly of a taper-rolling bearing illustrates how this system works. In operation, a preassembly gage checks the diameter and flange thickness of the inner race to determine the correct roller size to be assembled within a given ring. Then the gage feeds a signal to one of six preselected-size storage hoppers to release 18 rollers to the assembly station where race, rollers, and cage are assembled into a bearing of predetermined tolerance. The bearing is then inspected under a revolving-load condition for torque, noise level, and standout, the latter usually being checked with a linear displacement transducer of the LVDT type. Standout is the distance that the back face of the cone extends from the cup. Bearings are segregated as acceptable or into reject classes based on noise, torque, or standout.

GAGE TRANSDUCERS

The most common type of transducer used for automatic measurement and process control systems is the linear variable differential transformer (see Fig. 3-59). This device produces an electrical output proportional to the displacement of a separate movable core. Three coils are equally spaced on a cylindrical coil form. A rod-shaped magnetic core positioned axially inside this coil assembly provides a path for the magnetic flux linking the coils. When the primary or center coil is energized with alternating current, voltages are induced in the two outer coils.

In the wiring installation of the transformer, the outer or secondary coils are connected in series opposition so that the two voltages in the secondary circuit are opposite in phase, the net output of the transformer being the difference of these voltages. For one central position of the core, this output voltage will be essentially 0. This is called the balance point or null position (see Fig. 3-60).

When the core is moved from this balance point, the voltage induced in the coil toward which the core is moved increases while the voltage induced in the opposite coil decreases. This produces a differential voltage output from the transformer that, with proper design, varies linearly with change in core position. Motion of the core in the opposite direction, beyond the null position, produces a similar linear voltage characteristic, but with the phase shifted 180°. A continuous plot of voltage output versus core position (within the linear range limits) appears as a straight line through the origin if opposite algebraic signs are used to indicate opposite phases.

Advantages of the LVDT over other types of transducers are high sensitivity and high output level, stable zero output position, excellent linearity, mechanical simplicity, extreme ruggedness and resistance to vibration and shock, small size and weight, and durability.

PROCESS CONTROL

Gaging systems used for machine size control are most often used on external grinders, ID grinders, centerless grinders, and double disc grinders to precisely locate parts, indicate wheel infeed, measure wheel wear, and measure and control part size.

AUTOMATIC GAGING AND PROCESS CONTROL

They are also used extensively in automatic transfer lines to monitor each station and correct for size variations or to halt the process in the event that catastrophies caused by tool breakage occur.

There are two types of process control systems in use: in-process and postprocess. In-process gages are used to measure the workpiece during grinding and control the grinder wheel slide to produce workpieces within the desired tolerance limits. Postprocess gages measure the workpiece after it has been ground and provide a size offset that will apply a correction to the next workpiece to be ground.

An increasing number of gaging systems are also being used for turning applications and for automatic assembly equipment. In turning, the gage is often used to measure the location of the cutting tool in reference to the workpiece and correct for variations that occur. It is also used in postprocess applications to measure the workpiece after it has been turned, then provide any necessary correction to the cutting tool that will apply to the subsequent workpiece. Additional information on automatic gaging systems can be found in Volume I, *Machining*, of this Handbook series.

Figure 3-61, view *a*, shows a typical application of a gaging system mounted on a plunge grinder. The gage measures the workpiece while it is being ground, and the size of the workpiece is displayed continuously on the amplifier meter.

In setting up the system, either a master workpiece is used for setup or a workpiece is ground manually and then gaged with bench-type gaging equipment. The gage amplifier is then set to the correct reading on the meter while the gage fingers are positioned on the ground workpiece.

In operation, with the gage fingers measuring the diameter of the workpiece, the grinding proceeds at a fast rate until the workpiece nears final size, at which time a preset control in the gage system causes the infeed rate of the wheel slide to decrease to a slower rate. When the workpiece is within 0.001" (0.025 mm) or less from the desired size, a second gage preset control point causes an additional decrease in the infeed rate. This allows the desired size to be approached at a slow rate, which improves the finish and roundness and causes the final size to be held to a closer tolerance. When the gage system measures final size, the gage causes the wheel slide to retract to the rear position.

In production grinding, economic considerations dictate that metal should be removed as rapidly as possible. This can result in a large force buildup (workforce pressure) between the grinding wheel and the workpiece. As this force continues to

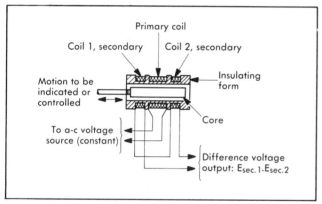

Fig. 3-59 Schematic of linear variable differential transformer. (*Schaevitz Engineering*)

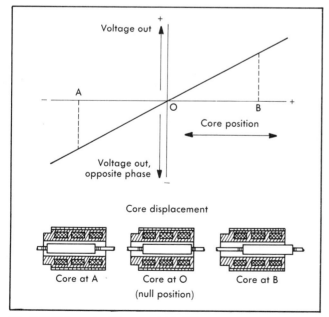

Fig. 3-60 Schematic of linear variable differential transformer operation. (*Schaevitz Engineering*)

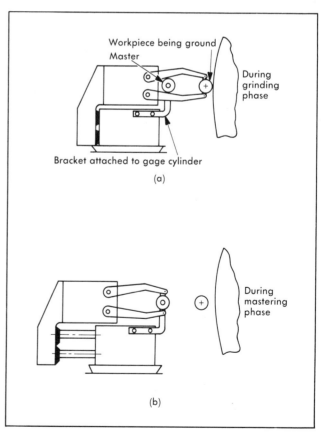

Fig. 3-61 Typical application of a gaging system mounted on a plunge grinder. (*Control Gaging, Inc.*)

COORDINATE MEASURING MACHINES

exist even when the infeed movement of the wheel is stopped, it is sometimes necessary to allow the workpiece pressure to dissipate before final size is reached. This is known as "sparkout" or "dwell" and is accomplished by stopping the wheel slide when the workpiece is approximately 0.0005 to 0.001" (0.013 to 0.025 mm) above final size and then allowing the pressure buildup of the workpiece against the grinding wheel to cause grinding to proceed until either the final size is reached or the pressure is dissipated. The grinding rate at this time is a function of the magnitude of the workpiece pressure and the sharpness of the grinding wheel. In the event that the pressure is dissipated during dwell before final workpiece size is reached, it is neces-

sary to restart the wheel slide infeed movement to attain final size and terminate the grinding cycle.

Figure 3-61, view *b*, shows a self-mastering system included in the gage that is used to maintain size of the workpiece by compensating for temperature changes, wear of the gage tips, or accidental bumping of the gage fingers. Whenever the gage is in the retracted position, the gage fingers are positioned on a master, and the gage amplifier detects and automatically resets the gage to the size of the master prior to each grinding cycle. This arrangement provides a system, generally used with automatic machine loading, that will operate unattended for extended periods of time.

COORDINATE MEASURING MACHINES

With the advent of numerically controlled machine tools, the demand has grown for a means to support this equipment with faster first-piece inspection and, in many cases, 100% dimensional inspection. To fill this need, coordinate measuring machines (CMM) were developed in the early 1960s. A few CMMs can even be used as layout machines before machining and for checking feature locations after machining. Thus the CMM plays a vital role in the mechanization of the inspection process because it is a universal measuring machine.

Since their development, CMMs have been increasingly used throughout industry; the automotive and aerospace industries are the primary sectors where CMMs are used. Although they were once considered an exotic tool for ensuring quality control, CMMs are now becoming a mandatory piece of equipment for both the large manufacturing plant and the small job shop. This is primarily due to the need for an accurate measuring instrument and detailed documentation of the components being produced.

Currently, coordinate measuring machines are being used in one of three ways in a manufacturing firm. The simplest approach is to place the CMM at the end of the production line or in an inspection area. With this approach, the CMM is used to inspect the first part of a production run to verify the machine setup. Once the setup is verified, it then measures parts on a random basis. For many applications, this permits the best approach to inspection.

Another approach is to incorporate the coordinate measuring machine between two workcenters and then measure 100% of the parts produced at the first center before any secondary operations are performed at the second workcenter. This approach is possible because CMMs are capable of measuring three-dimensional geometry and making many different measurements within a short period of time. When this approach is used, the CMM indirectly controls the production process. In this setting, however, the CMM must be "hardened" to perform in the shop environment or it must be completely enclosed to provide an optimum environment for part inspection.

A third approach integrates the CMM into the production line. This permits the CMM to directly control the production process. In operation, an integrated system would measure the workpiece, compare the measurements with required dimensions, and, if necessary, automatically adjust the machine controls so that the part is manufactured within the required specifications.

A basic coordinate measuring machine consists of four elements: (1) the machine structure, which basically is an *X-Y-Z* positioning device, (2) the probing system used to collect raw data on the part and provide input to the control system, (3) machine control and computer hardware, and (4) the software for three-dimensional geometry analysis. The measuring envelope is defined by the *X*, *Y*, and *Z* travel of the machine. A diagram of a coordinate measuring system is shown in Fig. 3-62.

Although a variety of machine designs and configurations exist, all designs incorporate the same fundamental concept of three coordinate axes. Each axis is square in its own relationship to the reference plane created by the other two axes. Each axis is also fitted with a linear measurement transducer for positional feedback. This allows position displays within the envelope to be independent of any fixed reference point.

The most common reference systems in use are stainless steel and glass scales. Both systems utilize noncontact, electro-optical reader heads for determining the exact position of the machine. Stainless steel reference systems are widely used in shop environments because the difference in the coefficient of expansion between the stainless steel scale and workpiece is minimal. Glass scale reference systems are generally used in controlled environments because of the difference in the coefficient of expansion between glass and the metal workpiece. Although glass scales can be more accurate than stainless steel scales, the advent of computer compensation all but eliminates any performance differences.

The worktable of the machine generally contains tapped holes to facilitate the clamping and locating of parts. It may be

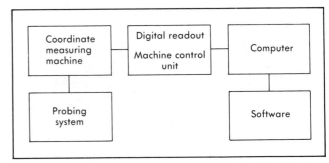

Fig. 3-62 Diagram of a coordinate measuring system. (*Multi-Metrics, Inc.*)

made from granite because of its stability in various environments. Electronic or solid probes are inserted into the probe arm, which is supported by cantilever, bridge, gantry, or column members. Probe arm movement is guided by means of frictionless air bearings or mechanical bearings.

Coordinate measuring is a two or three-dimensional process that determines the position of holes, surfaces, centerlines, and slopes. Up to six sides of a cube-shaped part may be inspected without repositioning.

In a typical operation, the part is placed on the table of the CMM at a random location; generally this is approximately central to the machine axes to access all the part surfaces to be inspected with the probe. Depending on the size of the part and the type of probes used, the part may need to be clamped to the machine table. If multiple inspections of similar parts are required, a reference location point may be established with a reference precision cube or sphere. The probe is then moved, manually or by machine control, until contact is made with desired part features. Reader heads, traveling on each axis along built-in axis measuring scales, transfer the instantaneous machine position through the digital display to the computer interface. The dimensional and geometric elements may then be calculated, compared, and evaluated, or stored, or printed out as required.

ADVANTAGES

Some of the advantages of using CMMs over conventional gaging techniques are flexibility, reduced setup time, improved accuracy, reduced operator influence, and improved productivity.[6]

Flexibility

Coordinate measuring machines are essentially universal measuring machines and do not need to be dedicated to any single or particular measuring task. They can measure practically any dimensional characteristic of virtually any part configuration, including cams, gears, and contoured surfaces. No special fixtures or gages are required; because electronic probe contact is light, most parts can be inspected without being clamped to a surface plate.

Reduced Setup Time

Establishing part alignment and appropriate reference points are very time consuming with conventional surface-plate inspection techniques. These procedures are greatly simplified or virtually eliminated through software available on computer-assisted or computer-controlled CMMs.

Such software allows the operator to define the part's orientation on the CMM, and all coordinate data are subsequently automatically corrected for any misalignment between the part reference system and the machine coordinates. A CMM with sophisticated software can inspect parts in a single setup without the need to orient the part for access to all features even when a fourth axis (rotary table) is employed.

Improved Accuracy

All measurements on a CMM are taken from a common geometrically fixed measuring system, eliminating the introduction and accumulation of errors that can result with hard-gage inspection methods and transfer techniques. Moreover, measuring all significant features of a part in one setup prevents the introduction of errors due to setup changes.

Reduced Operator Influence

The use of digital readouts eliminates the subjective interpretation of readings common with dial or vernier-type measuring devices. Operator "feel" is virtually eliminated with modern electronic probe systems. All CMMs have canned software routines for typical part features, such as bores or center distances. In the part-program-assisted mode, the operator positions the machine; once the initial position has been set, the machine is under the control of a program that eliminates operator choice. In the computer numerically controlled (CNC) mode, motor-driven machines run totally unattended by operators. Also, automatic data recording, available on most machines, prevents errors in transcribing readings to the inspection report. This all adds up to the fact that less skilled operators can be readily instructed to perform relatively complex inspection procedures.

Improved Productivity

All the factors previously mentioned help to make CMMs more productive than conventional inspection techniques. Further dramatic productivity improvements are realized through the computational and analytical capabilities of associated data handling systems, including calculators and all levels of computers.

MACHINE CONFIGURATIONS

A variety of machine configurations is available from the manufacturers of CMMs. Each configuration has advantages that make it suitable for particular applications. A total of 11 different machine configurations exist; however, some of these configurations are modifications of one of the five primary configurations: cantilever, bridge, column, gantry, and horizontal arm.

Cantilever

Cantilever-type coordinate measuring machines employ three movable components moving along mutually perpendicular guideways. The probe is attached to the first component, which moves vertically (Z direction) relative to the second. The second component moves horizontally (Y direction) relative to the third. The third component is supported at one end only, cantilever fashion, and moves horizontally (X direction) relative to the machine base. The workpiece is supported on the worktable. A typical machine of this configuration is shown in Fig. 3-63, view a. A modification of the fixed-table cantilever configuration is the moving-table cantilever CMM (see Fig. 3-63, view b).

Cantilever-type CMMs are usually the smallest in size and lowest in cost and occupy a minimum of floor space. This configuration permits a completely unobstructed work area, allowing full access to load, inspect, and unload parts that may be larger than the table. It also provides convenient, close grouping of machine controls. The single overhanging beam support for the probe head may limit accuracy if a special compensation is not built into the cantilever arm. The movement of the probe from one inspection point to another is usually performed manually by the machine operator; however, joystick and CNC machines are available.

Bridge

Bridge-type coordinate measuring machines employ three movable components moving along mutually perpendicular

COORDINATE MEASURING MACHINES

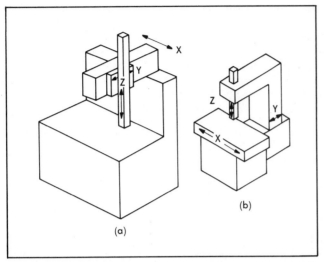

Fig. 3-63 Cantilever-type coordinate measuring machines: (a) fixed table and (b) moving table. (*Used with permission of the American Society of Mechanical Engineers*)

guideways. The probe is attached to the first component, which moves vertically (Z direction) relative to the second. The second component moves horizontally (Y direction) relative to the third. The third component is supported on two legs that reach down to opposite sides of the machine base and moves horizontally (X direction) relative to the base. The workpiece is supported on the base. A typical machine of this configuration is shown in Fig. 3-64, view a. This type of configuration is often referred to as a moving-bridge or a traveling-bridge CMM.

One modification of the moving-bridge configuration has each end of the bridge structure fixed to the machine base (see Fig. 3-64, view b). The workpiece is mounted on a separate table that moves horizontally (X direction) relative to the base. The configuration is referred to as a fixed-bridge CMM.

Another modification of the bridge configuration has two bridge-shaped components (see Fig. 3-64, view c). One of these bridges is fixed at each end to the machine base. The other bridge, which is an inverted L-shape, moves horizontally (X direction) on guideways in the fixed bridge and machine base.

A third modification of moving-bridge configuration is the central-bridge drive (see Fig. 3-64, view d). The drive forces are applied to the center of mass of the bridge assembly. This

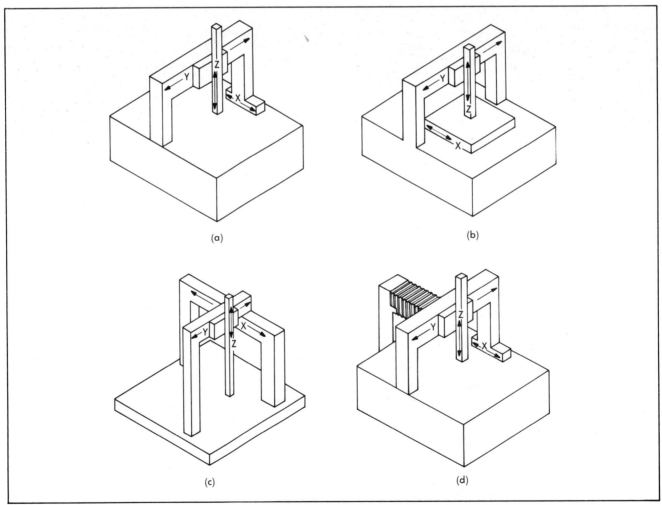

Fig. 3-64 Bridge-type coordinate measuring machines: (a) moving bridge, (b) fixed bridge, (c) L-shaped bridge, and (d) central-drive bridge. (*Used with permission of the American Society of Mechanical Engineers*)

eliminates pitching and yawing moments on the bridge assembly, allowing higher acceleration and deceleration rates.

The bridge-type CMM is the most popular configuration. The double-sided support of this type of CMM provides more support for large and medium-sized machines. The bridge can slide back on the base to give complete accessibility to the working area for safe, easy loading and unloading of parts.

Traveling-bridge CMMs have longer Y strokes for less cost than do cantilever-type CMMs. However, because of the weight of the extra support, the inertia of the moving mass is greater than in the cantilever configuration. In addition, the parts being measured with this type of CMM cannot be wider than the clearance between the two sides of the bridge.

Column

Column-type CMMs are similar in construction to accurate jig boring machines (see Fig. 3-65). The column moves in a vertical (Z) direction only, and a two-axis saddle permits movement in the horizontal (X and Y) direction.

Column-type CMMs are often referred to as universal measuring machines rather than CMMs by manufacturers and are considered gage-room instruments rather than production-floor machines.

Gantry

Gantry-type CMMs employ three movable components moving along mutually perpendicular guideways (see Fig. 3-66). The probe is attached to the probe quill, which moves vertically (Z direction) relative to a cross beam. The probe quill is mounted in a carriage that moves horizontally (Y direction) along the cross beam. The cross beam is supported and moves in the X direction along two elevated rails, which are supported by columns attached to the floor.

The gantry-type configuration was initially introduced in the early 1960s to inspect large parts such as airplane fuselages, automobile bodies, ship propellers, and diesel engine blocks. The open design permits the operator to remain close to the part being inspected while minimizing the inertia of the moving machine parts and maintaining structural stiffness.

Horizontal Arm

Several different types of horizontal arm CMMs are available (see Fig. 3-67). As is typical of all CMMs, the horizontal arm

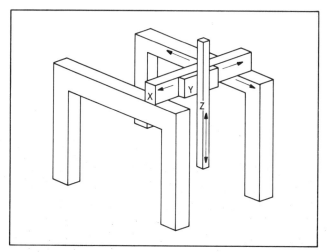

Fig. 3-66 Gantry-type coordinate measuring machines. (*Used with permission of the American Society of Mechanical Engineers*)

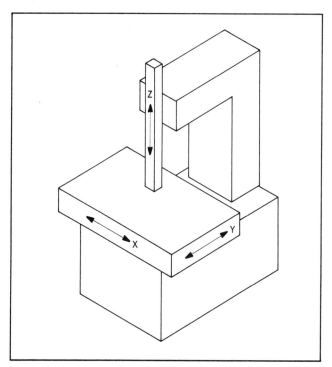

Fig. 3-65 Column-type coordinate measuring machines. (*Used with permission of the American Society of Mechanical Engineers*)

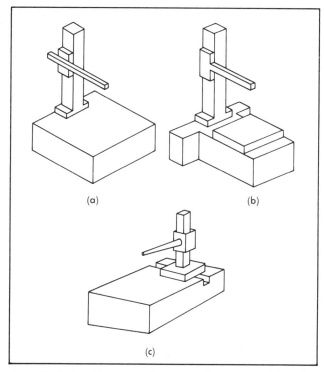

Fig. 3-67 Horizontal arm coordinate measuring machines: (a) moving ram, (b) moving table, and (c) fixed table. (*Used with permission of the American Society of Mechanical Engineers*)

COORDINATE MEASURING MACHINES

configuration employs three movable components moving along mutually perpendicular guideways. In the moving-ram design, the probe is attached to the horizontal arm, which moves in a horizontal Y direction (see view a). The ram is encased in a carriage that moves in a vertical (Z) direction and is supported on a column that moves horizontally (X direction) relative to the base.

In the moving-table design, the probe is attached to the horizontal arm, which is permanently attached at one end only to a carriage that moves in a vertical (Z) direction (see view b) on the column. The arm support and table move horizontally (X and Y directions) relative to the machine base.

In the fixed-table design, the probe is attached to the horizontal arm, which is supported cantilever style at the arm support and moves in a vertical (Z) direction (see view c). The arm support moves horizontally (X and Y directions) relative to the machine base. Parts to be inspected are mounted on the machine base. Horizontal arm CMMs are used to inspect the dimensional and geometric accuracy of a broad spectrum of machined or fabricated workpieces. Utilizing an electronic probe, these machines check parts in a mode similar to the way they are machined on horizontal machine tools. They are especially suited for measuring large gearcases and engine blocks, where high-precision bore alignment and geometry measurements are required. By incorporating a rotary table, four-axis capability is obtainable.

PROBES

The utility of a coordinate measuring machine depends largely on the nature of the probing device. Three types of probes are commonly used: (1) hard, (2) electronic, and (3) noncontact. A probe is selected according to the dimensional and geometrical requirements of the inspection process.

Hard Probes

Hard probes consist of a shaft and a probe tip mounted in various ways to the probe arm. A variety of probe tip shapes and sizes are available; the shape of the probe determines its application. Conical probes are used for locating holes; ball probes for establishing surface locations; cylindrical probes for checking slots and holes in sheet metal parts; and edge-finder probes are used for part alignment and measurement of flat surfaces or edges of parts. Hard probes can only be used in small, manually operated CMMs when inspecting simple parts of a short production run.

Electronic Probes

Electronic probes are commonly classified into one of three categories: (1) switching, (2) proportional, and (3) nulling probes. Switching probes are the most popular probes in use. This electronic probe, also called a touch probe, is an omni-directional triggering device consisting of a probe body and a stylus; multiple stylus arrangements are also available. When the stylus is brought into contact with the workpiece, a signal is sent to the computer interface, indicating the instantaneous three-dimensional location of the stylus. All probe designs allow stylus overtravel, some by as much as 0.04″ (1.0 mm) normal to probe axis and 0.08″ (2.0 mm) perpendicular to the probe axis. When the deflection force is removed, the stylus returns to its initial position. Switching-type probes suffer from lobing due to stylus bending. This lobing effect is exacerbated by high trigger forces and long stylus extensions. Electronic touch probes are used on all CMMs.

Because of their design, proportional-type probes are used exclusively on CMMs that are controlled by direct computer control (DCC). This type of probe is designed for automatic scanning of profiles contained in section planes passing through the probe axis. The probe consists of a transducer and a motor-powered, servocontrolled axis and carries on its tip a servo-assisted feeler that is kept in contact with the surface to be inspected. The feeler generates an error signal, proportional to the pressure exerted on the surface, for the control of the probe motor. During the scanning operation, the probe applies a very light contact pressure to the part and reacts with its motor to profile variations whose amplitudes are smaller than the probe axis working stroke. Longer profile variations are in turn followed by the CMM axes that are coupled to the probe axis position through the control system. A typical proportional probe stroke is ±0.5″ (±12.5 mm) from the center of probe axis stroke. Other probes with simultaneous radial and axial scanning capabilities are designed with the above concept.

Nulling probes are basically the same as the proportional probe with two major differences. First of all, it is more accurate than the proportional probe because the control system indicates the three-dimensional location of the stylus when the probe is at null condition (machine axis at rest). The second major difference is that the probe must leave the surface to proceed to the next inspection location whereas the proportional probe does not.

Noncontact Probes

Noncontact probes are used when fast, accurate measurements are required with no physical contact with the part. Several types of noncontact probes are used.

Optical probes are used when inspecting drawings, printed circuit boards, and small, fragile workpieces. When these probes are used, the basic measuring programs can still be used.

The two types of optical probes used on manual CMMs are a projection microscope and a centering microscope. On the projection microscope, the image under inspection is displayed on the screen. Part feature locations are obtained by moving the CMM to align the screen reticle to the feature. With the centering microscope, part feature locations are obtained in the same way as the projection microscope as the user looks through the eyepiece.

Another manufacturer has developed an acoustical probe that senses contact with the workpiece by the sound wave generated by the touch rather than by any physical displacement of the probe. At contact, vibration travels up the probe and is picked up by a sensitive acoustic microphone inside the head.

A third type of noncontact probe contains a laser light source that projects a small diameter spot on the part surface. A digital solid-state sensor detects the position of this spot and computes part surface location by optical triangulation. Because of the intrinsic nature of these probes, part inspeciton is generally limited to two dimensions.

ACCESSORIES

Various accessories used in conjunction with the probes enhance the capability of coordinate measuring machines.

Indexable Probe Heads

Indexable probe heads permit orienting the measuring probe in horizontal and vertical planes to keep the probe normal to the plane desired. This feature gives the CMM the capability to reach and inspect geometrical elements that are not aligned to the machine axes. In addition, the use of indexable heads is generally required when inspecting and scanning complex surfaces. Indexable probe heads, however, tend to shrink CMM measuring volume.

A microprocessor control system is usually supplied with indexable heads to operate as a power drive and intelligent interface between machine control and indexing heads. Head plane wobble during rotation is compensated for through a special software program that runs on the control system computer.

Rotary Tables

Rotary tables are especially useful when inspecting complex, multifaced parts or workpieces with a rotation axis such as cams, gears, and rotors. A variety of sizes are available to accommodate different size workpieces. Rotary tables expand CMM measuring volume.

Rotary tables can be controlled manually or automatically. When automatically controlled tables are used, special software programs interact with the machine controls to control table movement and provide misalignment compensation.

MACHINE CONTROL

Besides their physical configurations, coordinate measuring machines can also be classified according to their mode of operation: manual, manual computer-assisted, motorized computer-assisted, and direct computer controlled.[7] Manual machines have a free-floating, solid probe that the operator moves along the machine's coordinate axes to establish each measurement. Digital readouts, associated with each axis, provide the measurement values that the operator notes and records manually. In some instances, a simple digital printout device may be used to record the readings.

Manual computer-assisted CMMs use a data processing system to manipulate the measurements, which are still made by manually moving the probe through a series of measurement locations. Solid or electronic probes may be used on this type of machine. The data processing may be accomplished by a special microprocessor-based digital readout, a programmable calculator, or a full-fledged computer.

Depending on the sophistication of the data processing system and associated software, computer-assisted CMMs perform functions ranging from simple inch/millimeter conversion to automatic three-dimensional compensation for misalignment and a host of geometric and analytical measuring tasks. Storing of predetermined program sequences and operator prompting are also available to create part programs.

In effect, the computer system can carry out all the calculations and analyses required to arrive at dimensional and tolerance evaluations and can lead the operator through a prescribed series of positioning and measuring moves. Data recording is usually included with computer-assisted CMMs.

A motorized computer-assisted CMM has all the features of a computer-assisted CMM, but uses power-operated motions under the control of the operator, who uses a joystick. The part program is generated and stored in the computer, which determines the inspection sequence and compares measured results with nominal values and tolerances for automatic GO/NOT-GO decisionmaking. Most motorized CMMs also provide means for disengaging the power drive to permit manual manipulation of the machine motions. Some machines use direct-current servomotors and pneumatically operated friction clutches to reduce the effect of collisions, and all permit drive disengagement for manual movements.

Direct computer controlled (DCC) CMMs are equivalent to CNC machine tools. A computer controls all the motions of a motorized CMM. In addition, the computer also performs all the data processing functions of the most sophisticated computer-assisted CMM. Both control and measuring cycles are under program control. Most DCC machines offer various programming options, including program storage and, in some instances, off-line programming capability.

SOFTWARE

Beyond the microprocessor-based digital readouts, which were initially developed to provide basic measurement data processing capabilities for manual coordinate measuring machines, there is also a need to solve sophisticated measuring problems involving three-dimensional geometry and to provide more flexible general-purpose programming capabilities to solve special measuring problems.[8] Many CMM manufacturers offer a series of data processing equipment for such purposes, including full DCC capability.

The key to the productivity of all forms of computer-assisted CMMs lies in the sophistication and ease of use of the associated software. Software is the most important element in any coordinate measuring system because its power determines how many part features can be measured, and its ease of use determines the extent to which the machine is used.

The functional capabilities of CMM software depend on the number and type of application programs available. Virtually all CMMs offer some means of compensation for misalignment between the part reference system and the machine coordinates by probing selected points; some are limited to alignment in one plane, while most machines provide full three-dimensional alignment. Once the designated points have been taken, the program calculates the misalignment and applies the appropriate correction to all subsequent measurement readings.

Conversion between Cartesian, polar, and, in some instances, spherical coordinate systems is also commonly handled. Most systems also calculate the deviation of measurements from nominal dimensions of the part stored in memory and flag out-of-tolerance conditions.

Geometric functions handled by CMM software define geometric elements—such as points, lines, planes, circles, cylinders, spheres, and cones—from a series of point measurements and solve measurement problems dealing with the interaction of such geometric elements. Such software can determine, for example, the intersection of two circles established on the basis of a selected number of measurements or it can establish the angle of intersection of two surfaces.

Many software packages also provide a means for evaluating geometric tolerance conditions by determining various types of form and positional relationships (such as flatness, straightness, circularity, parallelism, or squareness) for single features and related groups of features.

Best-fit programs can identify the location of a part finished to size within a rough part from which it is to be made, to optimize the machining-allowance distribution; maximum material condition (MMC) programs evaluate features dimensioned according to MMC principles.

Other application programs include automatic part scanning for digitizing profiles and a variety of special programs to

MACHINE VISION SYSTEMS

handle the inspection of special shapes such as gears and cams. Statistical analysis software available provides for graphic data display, including histograms.

The accuracy of some CMMs is enhanced beyond the mechanical rigidity and stability of the machine with the aid of software geometry error compensation. A typical compensation package automatically interpolates the probe position throughout the measurement envelope. It corrects each axis for inaccuracies in pitch, yaw, scale errors, straightness, and squareness to the other axes. This software package is usually an integral part of the system software provided with the machine.

MACHINE VISION SYSTEMS

Machine vision for industry has generated a great deal of interest in the technical community over the past several years. In a machine vision process, information is extracted from visual sensors to enable machines to make intelligent decisions. It has become practical with the advent of high-speed, low-cost computers, microprocessors, and advanced sensors. In addition, the availability of low-cost memory has led the way to cost-efficient machine vision systems.

The concept of machine vision goes back many years, paralleling the development of imaging sensors.[9] In the mid-1960s, the growth of digital electronics led to experiments in electronic image processing techniques. These concepts began to capture the interest of a number of possible users for applications such as military reconnaissance, satellite image processing, medical testing, and optical character recognition. It was not until the late 1970s that shop floor applications of machine vision began to be a practical reality.

Many individuals within the industrial and research communities consider machine vision to be a subset of the larger field of artificial intelligence. Others view machine vision as a separate topic based on a number of other fields such as image processing, pattern recognition, and scene analysis. In either case, machine vision represents a relatively complex subject drawing on many technical disciplines.

To be classified as machine vision, the system must be capable of performing four primary functions.[10] The first function is image formation. In image formation, incoming light is received from an object or scene and then converted into electrical signals. In the next step, the signals are organized in a form compatible with computer processing capabilities. The third function is to analyze and measure various features or characteristics of these signals that represent the image. Finally, a machine vision system interprets the data so that some useful decisions can be made about the object or scene being studied.

This description of machine vision makes a clear distinction between several broad categories of optical sensing equipment currently used in manufacturing applications. For example, optical comparators, which are used to project silhouettes of a workpiece on a viewing screen, would not fall under this classification because they do not possess the image analysis and interpretation capability normally associated with a machine vision system. Similarly excluded would be equipment such as photocells and other light-beam equipment for measuring presence or dimensions and closed-circuit television systems where the monitors are observed by human operators for off-line inspection applications.

APPLICATIONS

Machine vision as applied to manufacturing extracts information from visual sensors to enable machines to make intelligent decisions. Such decisions are needed in quality control (detection of defects), process monitoring (prevention of defects), product routing (parts acquisition and sorting), and statistical reporting (performance evaluation).

The three main industrial application categories are inspection, identification, and machine guidance. Among the inspection tasks are the following:

- *Gaging.* Checking to make sure that dimensions fall within acceptable tolerance bands.
- *Verification.* Checking to make sure that a product is present, complete, or the right one in the proper orientation.
- *Flaw detection.* Checking for unwanted features of unknown shape anywhere on the observed portion of the product.

Among the identification tasks are the following:

- *Symbol recognition.* Deciding which one of many possible symbols is present in a given location. Examples of this application are reading serial numbers or bar codes.
- *Object recognition.* Deciding which of many possible objects is present by examining features of the object under test.

Among the guidance functions performed by machine vision are the following:

- *Object location.* Two or three-dimensional determination of position and orientation for purposes of part acquisition, transfer, and assembly.
- *Tracking.* Continuously updating the position of a feature relative to a tool to control continuous processes such as gluing or welding.

SYSTEM OPERATION

The machine vision process consists of four basic steps (see Fig. 3-68).[11] In the first step, an image of the scene is formed. The formed image is usually transformed into digital data that can be used by the computer. In the third step, the characteristics of the image are enhanced and analyzed. Finally, the image is interpreted, conclusions are drawn, and a decision is made so that some action can be taken.

Image Formation

Image formation frequently involves a combination of lenses, mirrors, and prisms that image the relevant portion of the object on the photodetector. The important parameters in image formation are lens focal length, aperture, depth of field, and magnification. In addition to these parameters, the object must be properly illuminated to provide good image contrast and properly oriented to obtain a quality image.

MACHINE VISION SYSTEMS

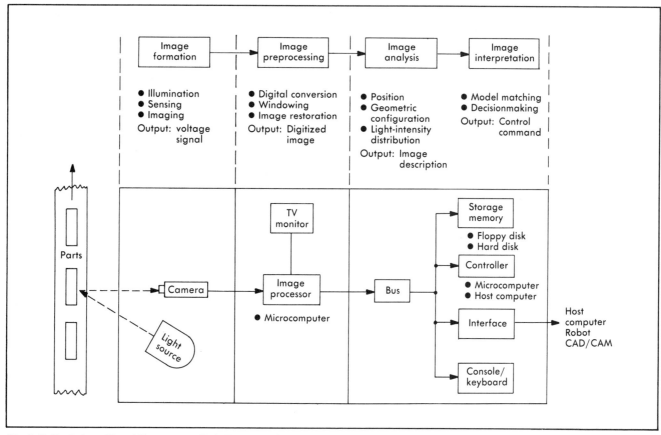

Fig. 3-68 Typical machine vision process. (*Tech Tran Consultants*)

Illumination. The image formation step begins with the lighting of the part being observed. The source of illumination must provide the vision system with the best possible images of the part under a given set of circumstances. The images should provide the system with the most contrast between the features and their backgrounds for subsequent analysis. The lighting design should also ensure that extraneous lighting around the machine will not interfere with its operation.

Light intensity, angle, wavelength, and structure are the major factors attributing to the success of an image processing installation. Typical light sources used on machine vision systems include incandescent bulbs, fluorescent tubes, fiber-optics, arc lamps, and strobe lights. In addition, laser beams and X-ray tubes are used for special imaging applications. Occasionally, polarized or ultraviolet light is used to reduce glare or increase contrast.

Three basic lighting techniques and modification of these techniques are used for machine vision systems:[12] (1) front lighting, (2) back lighting, and (3) structured lighting (see Fig. 3-69). When selecting a lighting technique for a particular application, the following factors should be considered:

- What feature on the part is to be identified?
- Is the part moving or stationary during inspection?
- In what type of environment will the application be used (oily, dusty)?
- What type of sensors are going to be used for the application?

Front lighting. In front lighting, the camera and the light are on the same side of the part. This technique should be used whenever a surface feature or texture needs to be inspected. Front lighting is the most widely used technique in machine vision applications with both gray-scale and binary systems.

Back lighting. The back lighting technique provides the vision system with the most contrast and can simplify the analysis task. However, because it only produces silhouette information, it is limited to certain applications. Examples of where back lighting is used are measurement and feature absence/presence applications.

Structured lighting. A structured light source has the shape and form of its projected beam controlled by using apertures and lenses and/or coherent light sources (lasers).

Structured lighting is sometimes used to extract three-dimensional information from a two-dimensional feature. It is also used with line scan or matrix cameras for noncontact measurement and feature analysis.

Image sensing. Sensing involves the formation of an optical image and the conversion of that image into electrical signals through the use of some photosensitive target. When selecting an electronic imaging device for a particular application, several factors should be taken into consideration. These factors are field of view, resolution, contrast, signal-to-noise ratio, spectral response, dynamic range, geometric distortion, lag, time and temperature stability, and cost.

Commercial machine vision systems employ imaging devices (cameras) that generate images in the form of two-

MACHINE VISION SYSTEMS

dimensional arrays or one-dimensional, linear arrays. Two-dimensional arrays are similar to those images formed by conventional television cameras. One-dimensional, linear arrays are used to create the image by scanning the scene one line at a time. To capture a complete two-dimensional scene, the second dimension is obtained either by motion of the object past the scanner or by mirror or prism deflectors.

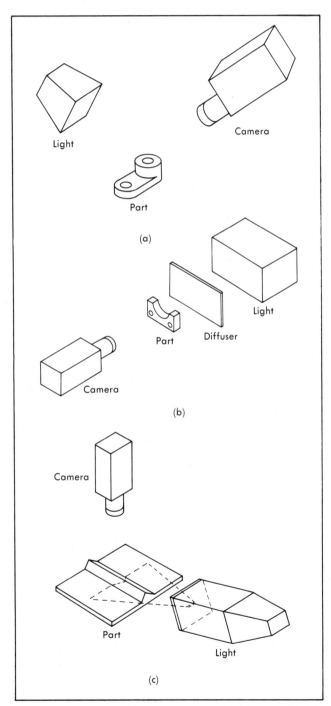

Fig. 3-69 Three primary lighting techniques used in machine vision: (a) front lighting, (b) back lighting, and (c) structured lighting. (*Penn Video*)

Vidicon cameras. The most commonly used camera in early vision systems was the vidicon camera, which is still extensively used in consumer video products. The vidicon camera has the advantage of providing a great deal of information about a scene at high speed and at a relatively low cost. An image is formed by focusing the incoming light through a series of lenses onto the photoconductive faceplate of the vidicon tube. An electron beam within the tube scans this photoconductive surface and produces an analog output voltage proportional to the variations in light intensity for each scan line in the original scene. Normally, the output signal conforms to commercial TV standards, thus the total image is represented by 525 scan lines (interlaced into two fields of 262.5 lines), which is repeated 30 times per second.

The use of vidicon cameras for industrial machine vision applications does have several drawbacks. First of all, they tend to distort the image because of nonlinearities in the scanning beam and are subject to image burn-in on the photoconductive surface. They also have limited useful lives and are susceptible to damage from vibration and shock. However, they can provide high-resolution images at low cost.

Solid-state cameras. Solid-state cameras employ charge-coupled device (CCD) or charge-injected device (CID) image sensors. The sensors are fabricated on silicon chips using integrated circuit technology. They contain matrix or linear arrays of small, accurately spaced photosensitive detector elements. When light passing through the camera lens strikes the array, each detector element converts the portion of light falling on it into an analog electrical signal. The entire image is thus broken into an array of individual picture elements, also known as "pixels." The magnitude of the analog voltage registered for each pixel is directly proportional to the intensity of light in that portion of the image. This voltage represents an "average" of the light intensity variation over the area of the pixel. CCD and CID arrays differ primarily in how the voltages are extracted from the sensors.

The type of solid-state sensor and its configuration selected for a specific application will depend on a number of factors, including the resolution required, lenses employed, lighting, and cost. Typical solid-state matrix-array cameras have 256 x 256 detector elements per array, although a number of other configurations such as 128 x 128, 240 x 320, and 380 x 490 are also popular. The output from solid-state matrix-array cameras may or may not be compatible with commercial TV standards.

Linear arrays may have from 256 to 1024 or more elements. The use of a linear array necessitates some type of mechanical scanning device, or workpiece motion, to generate a two-dimensional representation of an image.

Although solid-state cameras are more expensive than vidicon cameras, they offer several important advantages. In addition to being smaller, they are more rugged. The photosensitive surfaces do not deteriorate with use as they do in vidicon cameras. Solid-state cameras also exhibit less image distortion because of the accurate placement of the photodetectors.

Image Preprocessing

The initial sensing operation performed by the camera results in a series of voltage levels that represent light intensities over the area of the image. This preliminary image must then be processed so that it is presented to the microcomputer in a form suitable for analysis. A camera typically forms an image 30 or 60 times per second or once every 33 or 17 milliseconds. At selected time intervals, the image is captured or frozen for processing by an image preprocessor. The image preprocessor transforms the analog voltage values for the image into corresponding digital values by means of an analog-to-digital converter. The result is an array of digital numbers that represent a light intensity distribution over the image area. This digital pixel array is then stored in memory until it is analyzed and interpreted.

Depending on the number of possible digital values that can be assigned to each pixel, vision systems are classified as either binary or gray scale. Most simple commercial systems in use are binary; however, gray-scale systems are growing in popularity because they are less influenced by part-to-part reflectivity changes or lighting variations.

Binary system. In the binary system, the voltage level for each pixel is assigned a digital value of 0 or 1, depending on whether the magnitude of the signal is less than or greater than some predetermined threshold level. The light intensity for each pixel is thus considered to be either white or black, depending on how light or dark the image is. The placement of the lighting is important with the binary system because it affects the threshold values.

Gray-scale system. Like the binary system, the gray-scale system assigns digital values to pixels depending on whether or not certain voltage levels are exceeded. The difference is that a binary system allows two possible values to be assigned, while a gray-scale system typically allows 2^n different values, where n is the number of bits assigned to each pixel. For example, an 8-bit system would have 2^8 or 256 levels. In addition to white or black, many different shades of gray can be distinguished. This greatly increased refinement capability enables gray-scale systems to compare objects on the basis of such surface characteristics as texture, color, or surface orientation, all of which produce subtle variations in light intensity distributions. Gray-scale systems are less sensitive to the placement of illumination than binary systems. The major drawback with the gray-scale system is the greatly increased computer processing requirements relative to those of binary systems.

Image Analysis

The third general step in the vision sensing process is to analyze the digital image that has been formed so that conclusions can be drawn and decisions can be made. This can be performed in the system's central processing unit (CPU) or in custom hardware. The image is analyzed by describing and measuring the properties of several image features. These features may belong to the image as a whole or to regions of the image. In general, machine vision systems begin the process of image interpretation by analyzing the simplest features and then adding more complicated features until the image is clearly identified. A large number of different techniques are either used or being developed for use in commercial vision systems to analyze the image features describing the object's position, its geometric configuration, and the distribution of light intensity over the visible surface of the object.

Some simple geometric features may be area, perimeter, diameter, centroid, curvatures, or angles. More complex features may be edge gradients, spatial frequency content, projections, histograms, or convolutions.

Image Interpretation

When the system has completed the process of analyzing image features, some conclusion must be made about the find-

ings, such as the verification that a part is or is not present, the identification of an object based on recognition of its image, or the establishment that certain parameters of the object fall within acceptable limits. Based on these conclusions, certain decisions can then be made about the object or the production process. These conclusions are formed by comparing the results of the analysis with a prestored set of standard criteria. These standard criteria describe the expected characteristics of the image and are developed either through a programmed model of the image or by building an average profile of previously examined objects. The two most commonly used methods of image interpretation are feature weighting and template matching.

Feature weighting. In cases in which several image features must be measured to interpret an image, a simple factor weighting method may be used to consider the relative contribution of each feature to the analysis. For example, when identifying a valve stem from among a group of stems of several sizes, the image area may not be sufficient by itself to ensure a positive identification. The measurement of height may add some additional information, as may the determination of the centroid of the image. Each feature would be compared with a standard for a goodness-of-fit measurement. Features that are known to be the most likely indicators of a match would be weighted more than others. A weighted total goodness-of-fit score could then be determined to indicate the likelihood that the object has been correctly identified.

Template matching. In template matching, a mask is electronically generated to match a standard image of an object. When the system inspects other objects in an attempt to recognize them, it aligns the image of each object with that of the standard object. In the case of a perfect match, all pixels would align perfectly. If the objects are not precisely the same, some pixels will fall outside of the standard image. The percentage of pixels in the two images that match is a measure of the goodness of fit. A threshold value can then be assigned to test for "pass" (positive match) or "reject" (no match). A probability factor, which presents the degree of confidence that a correct interpretation has been made, is normally calculated along with the GO/NOT-GO conclusion.

Interfacing

A machine vision system is rarely used without some form of interaction with other factory equipment, such as CAD/CAM devices, robots, or host computers. This interaction is the final element of the machine vision process, in which conclusions about the image are translated into actions. In some cases, the final action may take the form of cumulative storage of information in a host computer, such as counting the numbers of parts in various categories for inventory control. In other situations, a final action may be a specific motion such as the transfer of parts into different conveyors, depending on their characteristics. The use of vision systems for control purposes is increasingly being performed through the combination of vision systems and robots. In this case, the vision system acts to greatly expand the flexibility of the robot.

For most applications, interfacing a machine vision system with other equipment is a straightforward task. Most systems come equipped with a number of input and output ports, including a standard RS-232C interface. When it comes to connecting a vision system to a robot, however, the task is much more complicated because of timing constraints, data formats, and the inability of most robot controllers to handle vision

MACHINE VISION SYSTEMS

system inputs. To overcome this problem, several robot and vision system manufacturers have developed integrated system capabilities. Robot inspection systems are discussed in the next section.

PERFORMANCE CHARACTERISTICS

The components of a vision system and the process by which these components work together to form, analyze, and interpret an image describe the basic principles of machine vision. In addition to understanding how machine vision works, it is also useful to understand the basic criteria by which machine vision systems can be evaluated and compared. These represent the basic considerations that potential users should review when deciding which vision system to select for a particular application.

In general, the ideal system is one that allows fast, accurate interpretation of a wide variety of complex images with a minimum of jigs and fixturing. Some of the more important performance characteristics that should be considered include resolution, processing speed, discrimination, and accuracy.

Resolution

The ability of a vision system to resolve, or create a recognizable image of an object or scene, is directly determined by the number of pixels in the image array and the image sensor's field of view. For an array of 256 x 256 pixels, the system can resolve portions of an object that just fit into the field of view down to approximately 1/256 of either the horizontal or vertical dimension of the object. For example, if the object is 1" (25 mm) long, the system might be able to perceive pieces of the object as small as 0.0039" (0.010 mm). For an array of 512 x 512 pixels, resolution might improve to 0.0020" (0.005 mm). Resolution for a given array can be improved by using a camera lens with a higher magnification, but the field of view will then shrink.

Processing Speed

A machine vision system should be capable of forming an image, analyzing it, and interpreting it at a speed consistent with the speed at which parts are being presented. Two categories of speed can be considered. First, image processing speed measures the number of bits of information that can be processed by the image processor. More important during an on-line application, however, is the speed at which individual items can be examined by the system. This is a difficult number to determine, because processing time is affected by many factors, such as the complexity of the image, the type of illumination, the accuracy required in interpreting an image, and whether or not windowing is employed. Typical vision systems can inspect and recognize simple parts at rates of 2-10 items per second, with some achieving speeds of 15 parts per second and higher. Solid-state CCD cameras can achieve higher speeds than vidicon cameras. The speed of a vision system will be inversely proportional to the amount of information, or number of pixels, being analyzed. For character recognition systems, which read alphanumeric characters on parts, speeds of 5-15 characters per second are typical.

Discrimination

The ability of a vision system to discriminate variations in light intensity over an image is determined by the number of intensity thresholds present in the system. A binary system, which allows two levels of intensity, provides the least discrim-

inative ability. A gray-scale system is able to perceive more subtle intensity variations, with 16-level gray-scale systems offering the highest degree of discrimination of commonly used machine vision systems. The tradeoff is that better discrimination means increased processing time along with a higher computer memory capacity.

Accuracy

A tradeoff can be made between processing speeds and the ability to correctly interpret images. A higher probability of correct interpretation can be achieved by processing more image features, which increases the processing time. Accuracy, also known as reliability or consistency, can be defined as the percentage of correct decisions made about a group of objects being examined by a vision system. This is a difficult number to estimate because it is a function of the variability of the objects, scene conditions such as illumination, the amount of teaching performed on the system, and the adequacy of the standard model used for teaching or programming as well as many other factors. An acceptable accuracy rate depends on the accuracy required by the application, as in any quality control situation.

SELECTION AND IMPLEMENTATION

During the past decade, machine vision technology has moved from the laboratory to the shop floor. Although the technology is still evolving, many practical and cost-effective manufacturing applications exist today.

In spite of many success stories, selecting and implementing a machine vision system is not easy, particularly for first-time users. Vision technology seldom represents an off-the-shelf solution to a specific problem, and considerable development or applications engineering effort is usually required for a successful application. Furthermore, first-time users rarely have the range of skills needed to apply this technology without some type of outside assistance.

To overcome these difficulties, it is important to follow a structured approach to selecting and installing a machine vision system. A three-step approach is recommended: (1) finding applications, (2) system selection, and (3) installation and use. The types of factors to be considered in each step are shown in Table 3-5.

TABLE 3-5
Factors to Consider When Selecting and Implementing Machine Vision Systems

1. Decision to use machine vision
   - Complexity of the scene to be viewed
     - Number of objects
     - Lighting characteristics
     - Degree to which objects touch or overlap
     - Shape of objects (e.g., surfaces)
   - Degree of similarity among parts
     - Area of images
     - Dimensions
     - Shapes of images
   - Degree of structure
     - Frequency of appearance of parts
     - Location of parts
     - Part orientation
     - Variations in lighting

TABLE 3-5—*Continued*

- Speed of operation
  - Number of parts per second
  - Speed of movement of parts
- Accuracy requirement of application
- Economics of machine vision
  - System cost
  - Payback period

2. Selection of machine vision system
- Capabilities of each system
  - Feature measurement capabilities
  - Image analysis capabilities
  - Performance (resolution, speed, discrimination)

- Interface/expansion capabilities
  - Number of input/output options
  - Presence of both communications port and information port
  - State-of-the-art control capability
  - Software upgrade capability
  - User-oriented system

3. Installation and implementation
- Manufacturer applications engineering capability
- User applications engineering capability
- Manufacturer servicing policies

(Tech Tran Consultants)

ROBOTIC INSPECTION SYSTEMS

Gaging systems can be broadly classified into fixed inspection and flexible inspection systems. Fixed inspection utilizes multiple contacting or noncontacting sensors mounted in a test fixture that holds the part to be inspected. This approach lends itself to the inspection of parts at high throughput rates. However, to switch from one part to another requires changing the test and inspection fixture. Flexible inspection utilizes sensors that are moved along a programmed path trajectory of the part being inspected. This approach lends itself to processing at moderate throughput rates. Changing from one part to another can be accomplished quickly by downloading to the machine controller a new path trajectory program. There are also systems available that move the part on an *X-Y* slide.

With the recent introduction of sophisticated machine vision systems into the workplace, it is now possible to expand the role of robots in flexible inspection.[13,14] Recent advances in CAD/CAM technology now make possible the integration of CAD/CAM into robotic systems.[15] This marriage of CAD/CAM with robotics significantly improves the productivity and economies of robot inspection systems.

The application areas for robotic inspection systems can be generalized as follows:

- Moderate throughput rates.
- Frequent part or model changes or model mix.
- Off-line part inspection requiring a large number of measurements.
- Large parts with complex geometry such as cavities.

ADVANTAGES AND LIMITATIONS

Robot-based inspection systems can provide the maximum in flexibility. A variety of sensors can be mounted on the robot wrist. Robots with articulated arms can reach inside of parts with cavities, such as car bodies and appliances. Robots can be programmed to measure reference datum points and planes on a part. Algorithms, using these reference point measurements, can calibrate the part coordinate system, which allows the CAD/CAM database to be integrated into the robotic measuring system. This integration eliminates the need for precision part fixturing, allows real-time adaptive robot path trajectory control, and provides off-line programming of robot path trajectories.

Inspection robots have a number of limitations. As previously pointed out, they can inspect parts only at moderate throughput rates; about 100 parts per hour would be a nominal rate. They are, therefore, not well suited for very high speed production lines where 1000 parts per hour are common. Gaging accuracy is another concern. At the present time, robot gaging systems rely on the repeatability of the robot for the gaging tolerance. Positioning repeatabilities of commercially available robots suitable for inspection applications range from ±0.001 to 0.008" (±0.025 to 0.20 mm). The sensors are typically accurate to one part in 500 to one part in 1000 of the total field of view, which is usually 2" (50 mm).

SYSTEM COMPONENTS

The main components in a robotic inspection system are the robot, sensors, part presentation device, computer/control system, and software.

Selection

In selecting a robot-based inspection system for a particular application, the following factors must be considered:

- Robot size, repeatability, resolution, and reach.
- Sensor selection.
- Accuracy requirements.
- Process inspection times.

Robot size and geometry are established by the inspection volume specified for a given application. It is important to consider design trends in the parts to be inspected so as to allow for future increases in part size and/or geometry. Sensor selection is largely dependent on the geometrical characteristics of the part features to be inspected.

Inspection accuracies that the system must provide are determined by the product specifications. In selecting equipment, it is important to consider the effects that aging and wear will have on inspection system accuracies. Process inspection times are principally governed by the number of inspection locations, length of robot path trajectories, and robot settling times. Other delays, such as vision image processing times, can be handled in parallel with other system functions using distributed data processing.

ROBOTIC INSPECTION SYSTEMS

The Robot

Robots are available in a variety of arm coordinate geometries.[16] These designs fulfill a wide range of needs in material handling and assembly applications. Refer to Chapter 12, "Automated Assembly," for additional information on the different types of robot designs.

For inspection applications, the Cartesian-style robot appears most appropriate. Because of its geometric design, the Cartesian robot can provide higher repeatable positioning accuracy than other articulated arm robot styles. Experience has shown that a five-axis robot is adequate for most inspection work. This is because coordinate transformation algorithms can be used to correct sensor limitations imposed by a five-degree-of-freedom robot.

Robot positioning accuracy is determined by the ability to match its actual position in three-dimensional space to the command position called for by the program's position instruction. The error between actual and command positions is caused by a number of factors, including servocomponent design, structural natural frequencies, bearing friction, gear backlash, and load torques. This error is a summation of static and dynamic error components. Bearing friction and steady-state load torques produce static position errors. Structural natural frequencies, inertia load torques, gear backlash, and closed-loop servo gain contribute to dynamic errors. As the robot approaches its command position, it searches for its position by dithering about the position until it stops. This is called settling time. The inspection system must wait for the robot to settle before it can make its measurement.

Robot settling time is a very important performance consideration because it causes a direct tradeoff between measurement accuracy and process inspection time. This tradeoff is shown by the data in Fig. 3-70, which compares robot positioning error distributions for two different settling times. These data were obtained with the robot executing an inspection path program representative of a typical process inspection cycle for a production application. Increasing the settling time by 117% reduced the variability in robot position by 36%; however, process inspection cycle time increased by 19%.

Vision Sensors

There are three types of sensors typically used in gaging systems: (1) one-dimensional sensors, (2) contour sensors, and (3) array sensors. One-dimensional sensors give the range or distance from the sensor to a point on the object. These sensors use triangulation techniques, where the light source is usually a single-point laser diode set at a known angle from the pickup sensor. The pickup sensor is a one-dimensional linear device, either digital (solid-state line scan) or analog (lateral effect photodiode). The range can be calculated from the position of the reflected light on the linear sensor.

A contour sensor analyzes a line of light across an object; the light is usually from a laser. The laser in the visible range (red) is a gas tube device containing helium and neon. More recently these are being replaced by solid-state lasers that operate in the near-infrared range. The laser light source provides a point source of light that is converted to a line by using a cylindrical lens or by scanning the light with an oscillating or rotating mirror. It is placed at a known angle to the pickup sensor, which is usually a solid-state array camera. Subpixel techniques are used to obtain the X, Y, and Z values of the line of light across the part to better than one part in 1000 of the total field of view in the X and Z coordinates. The measurement resolution in the Y coordinate is the scanning resolution, which is typically 240 lines. Triangulation methods are used to locate and measure surfaces, contours, and edges.

An array sensor can be used to take area images of the part for locating features such as holes. This two-dimensional information can be further enhanced by adding a range sensor to obtain Z-axis information, effectively creating a simple but limited three-dimensional device.

One-dimensional sensors can take several thousand measurements per second, while the structured light and area sensors are limited to 60 frames per second; each frame contains several hundred points. The system throughput is slowed down by the postprocessing of the data, not by the data acquisition of the sensor.

Sensor selection is determined by the geometry of the part. Range sensors can be used for point information only and cannot be used to analyze edges, holes, or contours. Structured light sensors are used for edges and contours, but are not well suited for holes. Area sensors work well on holes, but need additional information for use on surfaces and contours. Depending on the part geometry of the application, one or more sensors (either different types or different focal lengths) are mounted on the robot arm to make the measurements.

Computer/Control Systems

A robotic inspection system may be composed of two to four small computers that are required to perform different distributed processing functions. These computers are interconnected by a data communication and control network. This configuration allows a host computer to coordinate and control the robot and sensor(s). For example, a robot vision inspection system could be composed of a host computer or cell controller interconnected to a robot controller and a vision controller. Communications between the vision controller and the robot

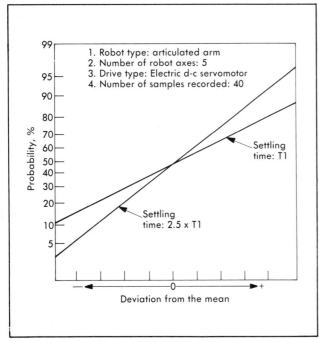

1. Robot type: articulated arm
2. Number of robot axes: 5
3. Drive type: Electric d-c servomotor
4. Number of samples recorded: 40

Fig. 3-70 Comparison of robot position repeatability for two different settling times.

controller can be direct or through the host computer, with the former most common and preferred.

The communication and control links can be either parallel or serial. Parallel links provide handshaking signals for synchronizing control activities and to handle high-speed transfer of measurement data. Serial data links provide two-way communications to allow the host computer to carry on a dialog with other processors in the system. This capability provides many advantages, and it makes possible many of the advanced control features discussed in the section on system software.

System Software

The host computer required by the robotic inspection system can range from a small microcomputer or programmable controller to a powerful minicomputer, depending on the degree of flexibility desired and level of data processing and storage required. Consequently, the system software can range from a 64-byte package for a small microcomputer to several million

bytes for a large minicomputer. Even the smallest software package should provide, as a minimum, the following functions:

- Initiate and coordinate the process inspection cycle.
- Read in and store sensor measurement data during inspection cycle execution.
- Transform measured data points into real-world coordinates and compare to desired measurement.
- Output process data results in some acceptable report format.
- Provide a limited operator interface to handle calibration and diagnostic requirements.
- Output warning and diagnostic messages to indicate system malfunction and type of error(s).

An example of the flexibility and increased system functions that can be provided by a large software package, running on a powerful minicomputer, is illustrated by the software functional diagram in Fig. 3-71. This configuration is used to

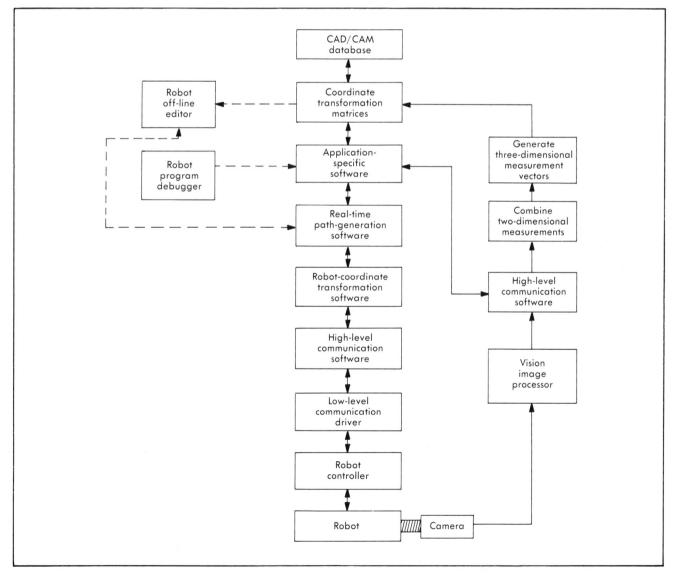

Fig. 3-71 Functional diagram of the software package needed to operate a robot inspection system using vision sensors.

operate a robot vision inspection system. In addition to the functions previously described, the software operating system provides the following functions:

- Uploading/downloading of robot path programs.
- Robot off-line programming.
- Vision off-line programming.
- Real-time robot program debugging through the computer terminal.
- Integration of the CAD/CAM database into the measuring system.
- Adaptive vision image processing.
- Adaptive real-time robot path trajectory control.
- Measurement of three-dimensional part features using a two-dimensional vision sensor.

The application-specific software can, depending on application requirements, be quite extensive. This software coordinates and controls the robot and sensor(s) to run reference point programs (required for setting up the CAD/CAM coordinate transformation system) and to run process inspection programs. Another function that it usually provides is acting as the database manager for storing processed inspection data. This manager can then retrieve selected portions of this data for outputting, in the proper report format, to a CRT terminal or hard-copy printer.

References

1. T. Busch, *Industrial Quality Control*, vol. 23, no. 1 (July 1966).
2. William M. Stocker, Jr., and Diane Heiberg, *Tools of Our Metalworking Trade* (New York: McGraw-Hill, Inc., 1982), p. 93.
3. *Ibid.*, p. 96.
4. Francis T. Farago, *Handbook of Dimensional Measurement*, 2nd ed. (New York: Industrial Press, Inc., 1982), p. 27.
5. *Ibid.*, p. 40.
6. George Schaffer, "Taking the Measure of CMMs," *American Machinist* (October 1982), pp. 146-147.
7. *Ibid.*, p. 153.
8. *Ibid.*, p. 158.
9. *Machine Vision Systems: A Summary and Forecast*, 2nd ed. (Lake Geneva, WI: Tech Tran Consultants, 1985), p. 1.
10. *Ibid.*, pp. 26-27.
11. *Ibid.*, pp. 29-66.
12. Amir Novini, "Fundamentals of Machine Vision Lighting," *Vision* (May 1986), pp. 18-20.
13. P. Villers, *Recent Proliferation of Industrial Artificial Vision Applications*, SME Technical Paper MS83-311 (Dearborn, MI: Society of Manufacturing Engineers, 1983).
14. T. Pryor and W. Pastorius, *Applications of Machine Vision to Parts Inspection and Machine Control in the Piece Part Manufacturing Industries*, SME Technical Paper MS83-312 (Dearborn, MI: Society of Manufacturing Engineers, 1983).
15. R.L. Simon, "The Marriage Between CAD/CAM System and Robotics" (Bedford, MA: Computer-Vision Corp.).
16. J.F. Engelberger, *Robotics in Practice* (New York: AMACOM, 1980).

Bibliography

Air Gaging. Data Sheet 8001. Spring House, PA: Moore Products Co., 1972.

Automation Controllers. Data Sheet 8015. Spring House, PA: Moore Products Co., 1978.

Blaiklock, W.J. *Air Gaging, Then and Now*. Farmington, CT: Edmunds Gages.

Comparator Gages. Data Sheet 8013. Spring House, PA: Moore Products Co., 1978.

"Dial Indicators (For Linear Measurements)." ANSI B89.1.10. New York: American Society of Mechanical Engineers, 1978.

Dimensional Air Gage Buyer's Guide. Catalog 86. Newbury Park, CA: Western Gage Corp., 1985.

"Gages and Gaging for Unified Inch Screw Threads." ANSI/ASME B1.2. New York: American Society of Mechanical Engineers, 1983.

"Involute Splines and Inspection, Inch Version." ANSI B92.1. Warrendale, PA: Society of Automotive Engineers, 1982.

Kennedy, Clifford W., and Andrews, Donald E. *Inspection and Gaging*, 5th ed. New York: Industrial Press, Inc., 1977.

Laser Gauging and Inspection Conference Proceedings. Held March 18-20, 1986, Dearborn, MI. Dearborn, MI: Society of Manufacturing Engineers.

"Methods for Performance Evaluation of Coordinate Measuring Machines." ANSI/ASME B89.1.12M. New York: American Society of Mechanical Engineers, 1985.

Precision Measuring Tools. Handbook No. 37. Watertown, MA: The Van Keuren Co., 1979.

Roth, Edward S., ed. *Gaging Practical Design and Application*, 2nd ed. Dearborn, MI: Society of Manufacturing Engineers, 1983.

Ryffel, Henry H., ed. *Machinery's Handbook*, 22nd ed. New York: Industrial Press, Inc., 1984.

"Screw Thread Gaging Systems for Dimensional Acceptability." ANSI B1.3. New York: American Society of Mechanical Engineers, 1979.

DIMENSIONAL METROLOGY AND GEOMETRIC CONFORMANCE

MEASUREMENT OF GEOMETRIC DIMENSIONING AND TOLERANCING

Geometric dimensioning and tolerancing can be described in its simplest terms as a means of specifying the geometry or shape of a piece of hardware on an engineering drawing.[1] It provides the designer with a clear way of expressing design intent and part requirements, which in turn enables the manufacturer to choose the proper method to produce the part. Geometric dimensioning and tolerancing also indicates how the part should be inspected and gaged, thus protecting the design intent.

Geometric dimensioning and tolerancing is rapidly becoming a universal engineering drawing language and technique that manufacturing industries and government agencies are finding essential to their operational well-being. Over the past 30 years, this subject has matured to become an indispensable tool; it assists productivity, quality, and economics in building and marketing products.

This subchapter has been designed to explain certain concepts and rules of geometric dimensioning and tolerancing that must be understood by all personnel before they can successfully interpret engineering drawings and validate parts. Additional information on geometric dimensioning and tolerancing can be found in American National Standards Institute (ANSI) standard ANSI Y14.5M, "Dimensioning and Tolerancing." This subchapter also explains the various differences existing between the three revisions of the standard (USASI Y14.5-1966, ANSI Y14.5-1973, and ANSI Y14.5 M-1982). Tolerance control is also discussed in Volume I, *Machining*, of this Handbook series.

GLOSSARY OF TERMS

The terms in this glossary are abstracted with permission from "Modern Geometric Dimensioning and Tolerancing."[2]

actual size The measured size of the feature.

angularity The condition of a surface, axis, or center plane that is at a specified angle (other than 90°) from a datum plane or axis.

basic dimension The theoretical value used to describe the exact size or location of a feature. It is used as the basis from which permissible variations are established by means of a feature control frame.

basic size That size from which limits of size are derived by the application of allowances and tolerances.

bilateral tolerance Tolerance in which variation is permitted in both directions from the specified basic size.

center plane The middle or median plane of a feature.

circularity The condition on a surface of revolution (cylinder, cone, or sphere) where all the points of the surface intersected by any plane perpendicular to an axis (cylinder or cone) or passing through a center (sphere) are equidistant from the center.

circular runout The composite control of circular elements of a surface independently at any circular measuring position as the part is rotated through 360°.

clearance fit A fit having limits of size prescribed that always results in clearance when mating parts are assembled.

coaxiality Coaxiality of feature exists when two or more features have a common axis.

concentricity The condition in which two or more features in any combination have a common axis.

contour tolerancing See profile of a line or surface.

cylindricity A condition of a surface of revolution in which all points of the surface are equidistant from a common axis.

Contributors of sections of this chapter are: Dino Emanuelli, Manager, Product Engineering, Greenfield Tap and Die, TRW; **Lowell W. Foster**, President, Lowell W. Foster Associates, Inc.; **John W. Geier**, Consultant-Instructor; **Gary K. Griffith**, Manager, Quality Planning, Quality Assurance Engineering, AiResearch Mfg. Co.; **Bill Janninck**, Technical Manager, ITW Illitron; **Stanley P. Johnson**, Executive Vice President, Johnson Gage Co.; **Max A. Kickhofel**, General Manager, Invospline, Inc.; **Richard S. Marrelli**, Mechanical Design Consultant; **George Pruitt**, Technical Documents Consultants; **Ronald M. Pruitt**, Technical Documents Consultants; **Edward S. Roth**, President, Productivity Services, Inc.; **Warner Weniger**, Product Manager, Metrology, Rank Precision Industries, Inc.; **Gary Whitmire**, Consultant, Tec/Trend.

Reviewers of sections of this chapter are: Peter Ackroyd, Assistant Product Manager, Geometry and Surface Gaging Products, Federal Products Corp.; **Hu Amstutz**, Consultant, Sheffield Measurement Div., The Warner & Swasey Co.; **David A. Bechtel**, President, Valmet, Inc.; **Michael J. Bingham**, Product Manager, Metrology Instruments, Sheffield Measurement Div., The Warner & Swasey Co.; **Dennis Cadieux**, Supervisor, Gage Engineering, Greenfield Tap and Die, TRW; **Brian Cluff**, Sales Manager, American Pfauter Corp.; **Ron Coutermarch**, Quality Control Manager, Fellows Corp.; **Bill Daniels**, Manager, Engineering Services, American Gear Manufacturers Assn.; **Paul M. Dean**, Mechanical Technology, Inc.;

GEOMETRIC DIMENSIONING AND TOLERANCING

datum A theoretically exact point, axis, or plane derived from the true geometric counterpart of a specified datum feature. A datum is the origin from which the location or geometric characteristics of features of a part are established.

datum axis The theoretically exact centerline of the datum cylinder as established by the extremities or contacting points of the actual datum feature cylindrical surface.

datum feature An actual feature of a part that is used to establish a datum.

datum plane Theoretically exact plane established by the extremities or contacting points of the datum feature (surface) with a simulated datum plane (surface plate or other checking device).

datum reference A datum feature as specified by a letter in the feature control frame.

datum reference frame A system of three mutually perpendicular datum planes or axes established from datum features as a basis for dimensions for design, manufacture, and verification. It provides complete orientation for the feature involved.

datum surface A datum surface refers to the actual part surface or feature coincidental with and/or used to establish a datum.

datum target A point, line, or small area specified on the drawing to establish corresponding contact places with the tooling.

dimension A linear or angular measurement expressed in appropriate units on the drawing.

feature The general term applied to a physical portion of a part, such as a surface, hole, pin, slot, or tab.

feature control frame A rectangular box containing the geometric characteristic symbol and the form, orientation, profile, runout, or location tolerance. If necessary, datum references and modifiers applicable to the feature or the datums are also contained in the frame.

feature of size A cylindrical or spherical surface, or a set of two plane parallel surfaces, each of which is associated with a dimension.

fit The general term used to signify the range of tightness or looseness that may result from the application of a specific combination of allowance and tolerance in the design of mating part features.

flatness The condition of a surface having all elements in one plane.

form tolerance A tolerance that states how far an actual surface or feature is permitted to vary from the desired form specified on the drawing. Expressions of these tolerances refer to flatness, straightness, circularity, and cylindricity.

full indicator movement The total movement observed with the dial indicator (or comparable measuring device) in contact with the part feature surface during one full revolution of the part about its datum axis or in traverse over a fixed noncircular shape.

full indicator reading See full indicator movement.

geometric characteristics The identifying shape of a feature or the relationship of two or more features. The ANSI standard identifies 13 shapes and relationships and assigns symbols to each of them for use on drawings.

implied datum An unspecified datum whose influence on the application is implied by the dimensional arrangement on the drawing. Implied datums are not supported by the 1982 standard.

interference fit A fit having limits of size so prescribed that an interference always results when mating parts are assembled.

interrelated datum reference frame An interrelated datum reference frame is one that has one or more common datums with another datum reference frame.

least material condition (LMC) This term implies that condition of a part feature wherein it contains the least (minimum) amount of material.

limits of size The specified maximum and minimum sizes of a feature. Limits of size specified on an engineering drawing are absolute.

line fit A fit having limits of size so prescribed that surface contact or clearance may result when mating parts are assembled.

location tolerance A location tolerance states how far an actual feature may vary from the perfect location specified by the drawing as related to datums or other features.

maximum dimension The acceptable upper limit.

maximum material condition (MMC) The condition where a feature of size contains the maximum amount of material within the stated limits of size.

median plane The middle or center plane of a feature.

minimum dimension The acceptable lower limit.

minimum material condition See least material condition.

multiple datum reference frames Multiple datum reference frames are more than one datum reference frame on one part.

nominal size The stated designation that is used for the purpose of general identification.

normality See perpendicularity.

orientation tolerance The manufacturing variation in the attitude of one feature relative to another. Orientation tolerances are perpendicularity, angularity, and parallelism.

parallelism The condition of a surface, line, or axis that is equidistant at all points from a datum surface, line, or axis.

perpendicularity The condition of a surface, axis, or line that is 90° from a datum surface, line, or axis.

position tolerance A position tolerance (formerly called true position tolerance) defines a zone within which the axis or center plane of a feature is permitted to vary from true (theoretically exact) position.

profile of a line tolerance The condition permitting a uniform amount of profile variation, either unilaterally or bilaterally, along a line element of a feature.

profile of a surface tolerance The condition permitting a uniform amount of profile variation, either unilaterally or bilaterally, over the entire surface.

Reviewers, cont.: **Omer DeSchepper**, *Dimensional Control Manager*, *CPC Div. of General Motors Corp.;* **Robert Dodge**, *Vice President*, *Pennoyer-Dodge Co.;* **Dino Emanuelli**, *Manager*, *Product Engineering*, *Greenfield Tap and Die*, *TRW;* **Lowell W. Foster**, *President*, *Lowell W. Foster Associates*, *Inc.;* **John W. Geier**, *Consultant-Instructor;* **Larry E. Gibson**, *Director of Manufacturing*, *Morse/Hemco Corp.;* **Gary K. Griffith**, *Manager*, *Quality Planning*, *Quality Assurance Engineering*, *AiResearch Mfg. Co.;* **Bill Janninck**, *Technical Manager*, *ITW Illitron;* **Stanley P. Johnson**, *Executive Vice President*, *Johnson Gage Co.;* **Dennis P. Karl**, *Unit Supervisor*, *Product Design*, *Powertrain Div.*, *Ford Motor Co.;* **Max A. Kickhofel**, *General Manager*, *Invospline*, *Inc.;* **Casimir Krulikowski**, *Product Design Senior*, *Powertrain Div.*, *Ford Motor Co.;* **John Laporte**, *Senior Project Engineer*, *Feinpruef Corp.;* **Bob Larsen**, *Technical Director*, *Klingelnberg America Corp.;* **Ed Lawson**, *Senior Applications Engineer*, *M & M Precision Systems*, *An Acme-Cleveland Co.;* **Bob Lee**, *President*, *AXIAM*, *Inc.;*

GEOMETRIC DIMENSIONING AND TOLERANCING

profile tolerance A tolerance that controls the outline or shape of a part as a total surface or planes of a part.

projected tolerance zone A tolerance zone applied to a hole in which a pin, stud, screw, or bolt is to be tightly inserted. It controls the perpendicularity of the hole to the extent of the projection from the hole and as it relates to the mating part clearance.

regardless of feature size (RFS) The condition where a specified geometric tolerance must be met irrespective of where the feature lies within its size tolerance.

roundness See circularity.

runout The composite deviation from the desired form of a part surface of revolution detected during full rotation (360°) of the part on a datum axis. Runout tolerance may be circular or total.

runout tolerance A tolerance that states how far an actual surface or feature is permitted to deviate from the desired form or position specified by the drawing during full rotation of the part on a datum axis.

size tolerance A tolerance that states how far individual features may vary from the desired size. Size tolerances are specified with either unilateral, bilateral, or limit tolerancing methods.

squareness See perpendicularity.

straightness Straightness is a condition where an element of a surface or an axis is a straight line.

symmetry The quality of being the same on both sides in size, shape, and relative position from a center plane.

tolerance The total amount by which a specific dimension may vary; thus, the tolerance is the difference between limits.

total indicator reading See full indicator movement.

total runout The composite variation of all elements, circular or straight, detected by rotating the part 360°.

transition fit A fit having limits of size so prescribed that either a clearance or an interference may result when mating parts are assembled.

true position A term used to describe the perfect (exact) location of a point, line, or size feature in relationship with a datum reference or other feature.

unilateral tolerance A tolerance in which variation is permitted in only one direction from the specified dimension.

virtual condition The collective effect of size, form, orientation, and location error that must be considered in determining the fit or clearance between mating parts or features.

PRINCIPLES

To properly understand and implement geometrics it is important to understand the principles or fundamentals of the concept of geometric dimensioning and tolerancing. Figure 4-1 illustrates the 13 basic geometric characteristic symbols that are defined in ANSI Y14.5M. These symbols are divided into five types of controls, which will be discussed subsequently. Other related symbols and terms are shown in Fig. 4-2.

TYPE OF FEATURE	TYPE OF TOLERANCE	CHARACTERISTIC	SYMBOL
Individual (no datum reference)	Form	Flatness	▱
		Straightness	—
		Circularity (roundness)	○
		Cylindricity	⌭
Individual or related	Profile	Profile of a line	⌒
		Profile of a surface	⌓
Related (datum reference required)	Orientation	Perpendicularity	⊥
		Angularity	∠
		Parallelism	//
	Location	Position	⊕
		Concentricity	◎
	Runout	Circular runout	↗
		Total runout	↗↗

Fig. 4-1 Geometric characteristic symbols. (*American Society of Mechanical Engineers*)

.605
Basic, or exact, dimension

–A–
Datum feature symbol

Ⓜ
Maximum material condition

Ⓢ
Regardless of feature size

Ⓛ
Least material condition

Ⓟ
Projected tolerance zone

∅
Diametrical (cylindrical) tolerance zone or feature

⊕ ∅ .005 Ⓜ A
Feature control frame

Ⓐ1
Datum target symbol

Fig. 4-2 Related geometric characteristic symbols and terms.

Reviewers, cont.: **Richard S. Marrelli**, *Mechanical Design Consultant;* **Craig McLanahan**, *President, Visual Inspection Products, Inc.;* **George Pruitt**, *Technical Documents Consultants;* **Alex Pryshlak**, *Product Manager, Metrology, Pneumo Precision, Inc.;* **John Rieman**, *Vice President, Engineering and Manufacturing, Stocker & Yale, Inc.;* **Mike Rose**, *Manufacturing Engineer, Southern Gage Co.;* **Edward S. Roth**, *President, Productivity Services, Inc.;* **James Schmidt**, *Chart Gage Product Manager, Optical Gaging Products, Inc.;* **Leonard J. Smith**, *Vice President and General Manager, Invincible Gear;* **Robert E. Smith**, *The Gleason Works;* **Ronald E. VerSchage**, *Contour Projector Products Manager, Optical Gaging Products, Inc.;* **Warner Weniger**, *Product Manager, Metrology, Rank Precision Industries, Inc.;* **Gary Whitmire**, *Consultant, Tec/Trend;* **Don Whitney**, *Manager of Cutter Design, Fellows Corp.*

GEOMETRIC DIMENSIONING AND TOLERANCING

Basic Dimensions

A basic dimension is a theoretical, exact dimension without tolerance. When used in conjunction with geometric tolerance specification, the basic dimension locates the exact center of the tolerance zone. The center plane or axis of an acceptable feature is allowed to vary within the basic located tolerance zone as shown in Fig. 4-3. Basic dimensions on drawings are enclosed by a rectangular box around the dimension (refer to Fig. 4-2). On older drawings, basic dimensions are identified by the word BASIC or the abbreviation BSC near the dimension.

When features are located by basic chain dimensioning on the drawing, there is no accumulation of tolerance between features (see Fig. 4-4). Basic dimensions are absolute values, and, when added together, they equal an absolute value. The basic dimensions locate the tolerance zone and not the manufactured feature. The manufactured feature can float within the perfectly located tolerance zone.

Material Condition Modifiers

The three material condition modifiers used with geometric dimensioning are maximum material condition (MMC), regardless of feature size (RFS), and least material condition (LMC). The accepted symbols for these modifiers are shown in Fig. 4-2. Material condition modifiers can only be used with size features such as holes, shafts, pins, and slots rather than surface features.

Maximum material condition. The maximum material condition is the condition in which a feature of size contains the maximum amount of material within the stated limits of size. When the MMC symbol is associated with the tolerance or a datum reference letter in the feature control frame, the specified tolerance only applies to the feature if the feature is manufactured at its maximum material condition size.

For example, a pin having a diameter of 0.500±0.010″ will only be at maximum material condition if it was manufactured at 0.510″; a 0.509″ diam pin would not be at maximum material condition. Likewise, a part with a hole 0.525±0.010″ diam would be at maximum material condition if the hole was drilled 0.515″ diam. In other words, maximum material condition is the maximum allowable shaft size or minimum allowable hole size.

Regardless of feature size. Regardless of feature size is the term used to indicate that a geometric tolerance or datum reference applies at any increment of size of the feature within its size tolerance. When the RFS symbol is selected to modify the tolerance or datum reference in the feature control frame, the specified tolerance applies to the location of the feature regardless of the feature's size.

Least material condition. Least material condition is the condition in which a feature of size contains the least amount of material within the stated limit of size. Examples of LMC are a shaft made to the smallest size and a hole drilled to the largest size.

The application of least material condition was not introduced until the approval of ANSI Y14.5M-1982. When a feature control frame references LMC to the tolerance or datum reference letter, the specified tolerance only applies when the feature is produced at the LMC size.

Feature Control Frame

The feature control frame (formerly called the feature control symbol) specifies the type, shape, and size of the geometric tolerance zone, dictates the datum surfaces and order precedence for part setup, and assigns material condition

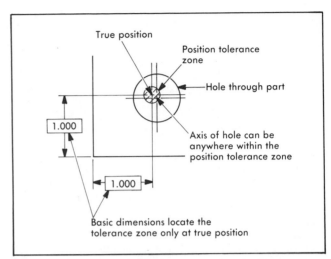

Fig. 4-3 Positional tolerance zone.

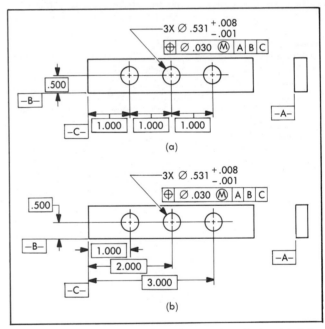

Fig. 4-4 Chain dimensioning versus baseline dimensioning: (a) chain dimensioning and (b) baseline dimensioning. The .531 diam holes can be dimensioned with chain dimensioning or baseline dimensioning and retain the identical interpretation.

modifiers to the tolerance and datum reference letters when applicable. A typical feature control frame is shown in Fig. 4-5.

The symbol Ⓜ in the feature control frame in Fig. 4-5 indicates that the 0.014″ tolerance only applies when the feature being verified is produced at its maximum material condition size. The symbol ∅ preceding the tolerance value indicates that the tolerance zone has a cylindrical shape. If no symbol precedes the tolerance value, the tolerance zone is the total area between two parallel planes or two parallel lines 0.014″ apart.

The 1966 standard required the abbreviation *DIA* for diameter tolerance zone and *R* for radius tolerance zone to be included in the feature control frame. It also required the specifications of *TOTAL* for total wide tolerance zone.

The order of specified datum reference letters in the feature control frame is very important (refer to Fig. 4-5). The primary datum reference is shown at the left; the least important datum reference is shown at the right. The datum precedence allows manufacturing and inspection personnel to determine the correct part orientation for their respective functions. The part is fixtured to allow a minimum of three points of contact on the primary datum surface, a minimum of two points of contact for the secondary datum feature, and a minimum of one point of contact for the tertiary datum feature. With respect to functional datums, these points of contact must be the highest points on the surface when brought into contact with a simulated datum plane (surface plate).

The 1966 revision of the Y14.5 standard required the datum reference letters to precede the tolerance compartment of the feature control frame, while the 1982 revision requires the datum reference letters to follow the tolerance compartment. Either method was accepted in the 1973 revision of the standard. The left-to-right datum precedence concept is identical in both methods.

Bonus and Additional Tolerances

When a tolerance or datum reference letter is modified with the MMC symbol, the specified tolerance in the feature control frame only applies if the feature is manufactured at its MMC size. As the feature departs from MMC size, the geometric tolerance increases. The amount that the feature deviates from MMC size is added to the geometric tolerance specified in the feature control frame. This extra tolerance is called *bonus* tolerance.

As shown in Fig. 4-6, the 0.014″ diam position tolerance applies when the hole is drilled at 0.515″ diam. If hole number two was drilled at 0.525″ diam, a departure of 0.010″ from the MMC size of the hole, a bonus tolerance of 0.010″ would be gained. The 0.010″ bonus tolerance is added directly to the original 0.014″ positional tolerance to give a total positional tolerance of 0.024″ for the 0.525″ diam hole. The axis of hole two must be within the 0.024″ diam tolerance zone. The total positional tolerance zone size for each hole must be determined in conjunction with the actual manufactured hole size.

An *additional* locational tolerance can be gained as a datum feature of size departs from MMC size. For example, in Fig. 4-7 a bonus tolerance of up to 0.005″ could be gained for the 0.010″ positional tolerance specification if the 0.260″ diam hole is not made at MMC. An additional tolerance of up to 0.020″ could also be gained if datum B departs from MMC. However, this additional tolerance does not add directly to the original

positional tolerance as a bonus tolerance would. The additional tolerance must be applied to the hole pattern as a group, allowing the four-hole pattern to shift off center as a group. No additional hole-to-hole tolerance gain is realized within the four-hole pattern.

The rules and principles of MMC bonus and additional tolerances also apply to tolerances and datum references that are specified at LMC. The only difference is that the bonus and additional tolerances are determined from the feature's departure from LMC size.

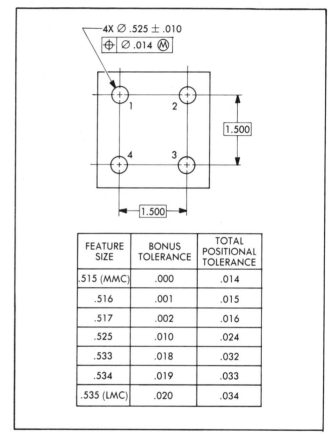

FEATURE SIZE	BONUS TOLERANCE	TOTAL POSITIONAL TOLERANCE
.515 (MMC)	.000	.014
.516	.001	.015
.517	.002	.016
.525	.010	.024
.533	.018	.032
.534	.019	.033
.535 (LMC)	.020	.034

Fig. 4-6 Application of bonus tolerances to a part.

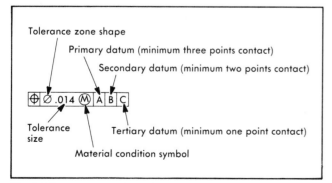

Fig. 4-5 Feature control frame for a noncylindrical part.

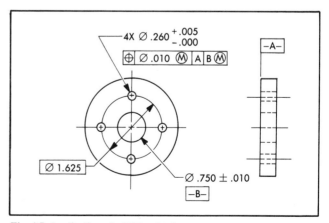

Fig. 4-7 Application of additional tolerances to a part.

GEOMETRIC DIMENSIONING AND TOLERANCING

The 1966 and 1973 revisions of ANSI Y14.5 allowed the MMC symbol to be implied by the drawing user on positional tolerances when the material condition symbol had been omitted from the feature control frame. It should be noted that this rule is contrary to international practice, which is understood to be RFS in the same situations. The 1982 revision of ANSI Y14.5 requires the position feature control frame to be completed with the appropriate material condition symbol (no implied modifier).

The above rule only applies to position feature control frames. All other geometric characteristic symbols such as straightness, parallelness, and perpendicularity are implied to apply regardless of feature size (RFS) if the material condition symbol is omitted.

Datums

Datum specification in the feature control frame is of great importance to the drawing user. Proper functional datum selection allows the part to be fixtured for manufacturing and inspection as it will be assembled as a finished product. Consistency with quality control will be ensured when manufacturing uses the specified datum features in the proper order of precedence for machining operations. Although manufacturing does not have to locate functional datums to make the part, the end result must be verified to the datums.

The 1966 and 1973 revisions of the ANSI Y14.5 standard allow the use of implied datums by not specifying datum reference letters in the feature control frame. This required the print users to make certain assumptions in the course of manufacturing and inspection; such as, which features to fixture on and in what order of precedence. Use of implied datums can lead to problems if everyone concerned does not make the same assumptions. Designers and drafters should be encouraged to specify all necessary datum references to provide uniform drawing interpretation. The 1982 revision of the standard has discontinued the use of implied datum references.

The three-plane datum reference frame is necessary to ensure correct drawing interpretation. For noncylindrical parts, the manufacturing/inspection fixture shown in Fig. 4-8 can be constructed to ensure uniformity during manufacturing and inspection operations. All related measurements of the part originate from the fixture datum planes.

For cylindrical parts, the three-plane reference frame is more difficult to visualize. The primary datum is often described as a flat surface perpendicular to the axis of the cylindrical datum feature as shown in Fig. 4-9. This axis can be defined as the intersection of two planes, 90° to each other, at the midpoint of the cylindrical feature. The tertiary datum is used if rotational orientation of the cylindrical feature is required due to interrelationship of radially located features. The tertiary datum is often a locating hole, slot, or pin. If no angular located features are involved in the hardware requirements, the tertiary datum is omitted.

The two types of datum features are datums of size and nonsize datums. Datums of size are established from features that have size tolerance, such as holes, outside diameters, and slot widths. The center plane or axis of a simulated datum contacting or representing MMC size of the feature is the actual datum. For example, a 0.250±0.005″ hole specified as a datum would be a datum feature of size. The centerline or axis of the simulated datum contacting the manufactured hole is the actual datum. Nonsize datums are established from surfaces. A datum

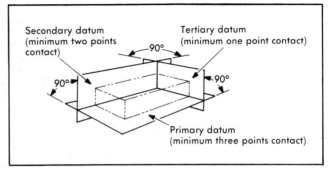

Fig. 4-8 Three-plane datum reference frame for noncylindrical features.

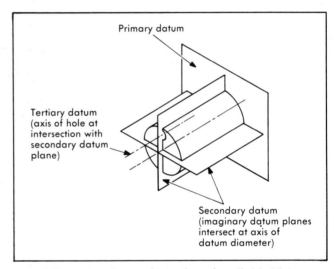

Fig. 4-9 Three-plane datum reference frame for cylindrical features.

surface has no size tolerance because it is a plane from which dimensions or relationships originate.

Screw Thread Specification

When geometric tolerancing is expressed for the control of a screw thread, or when a screw thread is specified as a datum reference, the application shall be applied to the pitch cylinder. If design requirements necessitate an exception to this rule, the notation MINOR DIA or MAJOR DIA shall be shown beneath the feature control frame or datum reference as applicable.

Gears and Splines Specification

When geometric tolerancing is expressed for the control of a gear or spline, a specific feature of the gear or spline must be designated to derive a datum axis. This information is stated beneath the feature control frame or beneath the datum feature symbol.

Separate Requirements

When more than one pattern of features such as holes and slots are located by basic dimensions from common datum features of size, and the feature control frame for each of the patterns contains the same datums in the same order of precedence and at the same material condition, all the features are considered as one single pattern. In Fig. 4-10, the two 0.221″

diam holes appear as one pattern, and the two 0.391″ diam holes are a separate pattern. Because the location feature control frame for both hole patterns contain the same datums, in the same order of precedence and at the same material condition, the patterns are considered one pattern of four holes. The parts inspector must verify the dimensional conformance of both hole patterns simultaneously. If the designer had felt this interrelationship of the four holes was not required between the two patterns of features in Fig. 4-10, a notation such as *SEPARATE REQUIREMENTS* would have been placed beneath the feature control frames. This would allow each pattern of features to shift independently in relationship to the

common datum system. The parts inspector would then verify each pattern of holes separately.

Envelope Rule

The envelope rule specifies the limit of size of an individual feature and controls variations of geometric shape (form) within the envelope created by the specified size at MMC. A feature produced at the MMC size must have perfect form (straightness, circularity, cylindricity, or flatness) to remain within the MMC size envelope as shown in Fig. 4-11.

As a feature deviates from the MMC size, the form is allowed to vary within the MMC envelope. The quality control

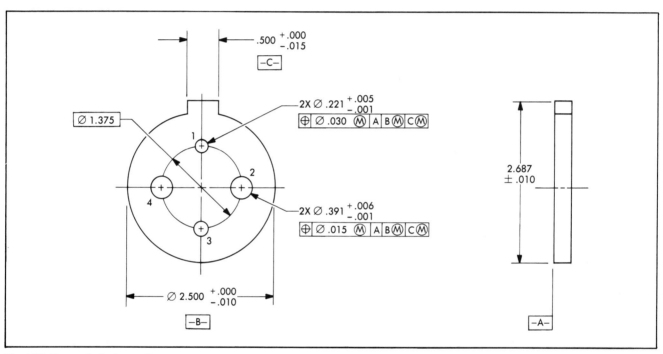

Fig. 4-10 Composite feature patterns.

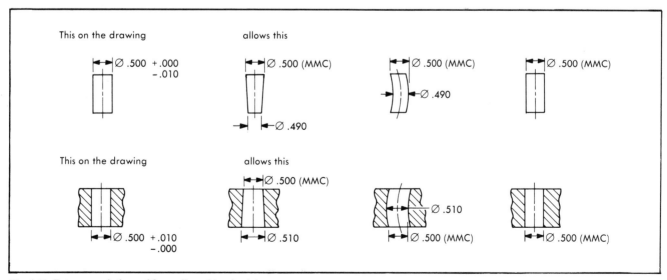

Fig. 4-11 Extreme variations of form allowed by size tolerance.

FORM CONTROL TOLERANCES

inspector is required to verify envelope rule conformance of shape when drawings are prepared in accordance with ANSI Y14.5. Caliper or hole/telescope gage measurements verify size only and do not ensure form acceptance. The boundary of perfect form at MMC can be verified by using full-form gages in conjunction with calipers or hole/telescoping gages.

Virtual Condition

Virtual condition is a size representing the worst possible assembly condition of mating parts resulting from the collective effects of size and the geometric tolerance specified to control the feature (see Fig. 4-12). Virtual condition is primarily a size used by product and tool/gage designers for calculating basic gage element size or performing tolerance analysis to ensure assembly of mating parts. The following formulas are used to determine virtual conditions:

$$\text{EXTERNAL FEATURES} =$$
$$\text{MMC SIZE} + \text{TOLERANCE OF FORM,}$$
$$\text{ORIENTATION, OR LOCATION}$$

$$\text{INTERNAL FEATURES} =$$
$$\text{MMC SIZE} - \text{TOLERANCE OF FORM,}$$
$$\text{ORIENTATION, OR LOCATION}$$

FORM CONTROL TOLERANCES

The four form control symbols—flatness, surface straightness, circularity, and cylindricity—are applied to control the shape of the finished item. These symbols tell the inspector the amount a feature can vary from the perfect shape specified on the drawing. Refer to Fig. 4-1 for the symbols used to represent these geometric characteristics.

Flatness

Flatness is the condition of a surface having all elements in one plane.[3] A flatness tolerance specifies a tolerance zone defined by two parallel planes within which the entire surface must lie. When a flatness tolerance is specified, the feature control frame is attached to a leader directed to the surface or to an extension line of the surface (see Fig. 4-13).

In Fig. 4-13, the outer limit of the 0.005″ flatness tolerance zone is established by the extremities of the manufactured surface. If the surface being verified for flatness was placed on an inspection surface plate, the high points of the surface would make contact with the surface plate, creating the outer tolerance zone limit (see Fig. 4-14). The upper limit of the tolerance would be 0.005″ above the surface plate. Every element of the surface must be within this tolerance band zone to be an acceptable part. No surface valley or peak could violate the two parallel planes that are 0.005″ apart. The flatness tolerance must be contained within the boundary of perfect form at MMC.

Another method of checking flatness requirements is shown in Fig. 4-15. In this method, the surface to be inspected is placed on three stacks of gage blocks; each stack is the same height. A test indicator is then traversed over the entire underside of the part, comparing the part's surface to that of the theoretical flat plane generated by the gage block stacks. The full indicator movement must not exceed the 0.005″ flatness tolerance specified in the feature control frame.

Occasionally an inspector will place the surface opposite of the feature to be checked for flatness on the surface plate to avoid the inconvenience of measuring flatness conformance as shown in Fig. 4-15. However, this procedure verifies parallelism rather than flatness and could result in rejecting parts that were actually within specification.

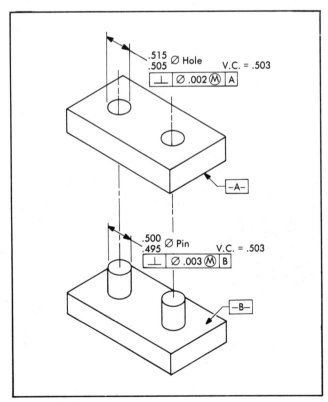

Fig. 4-12 Virtual condition of mating parts.

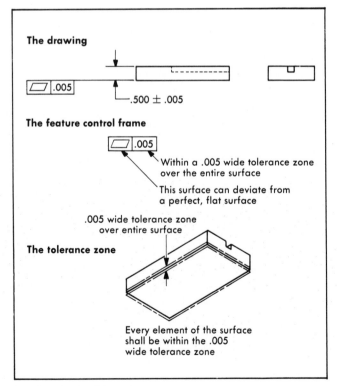

Fig. 4-13 Flatness control.

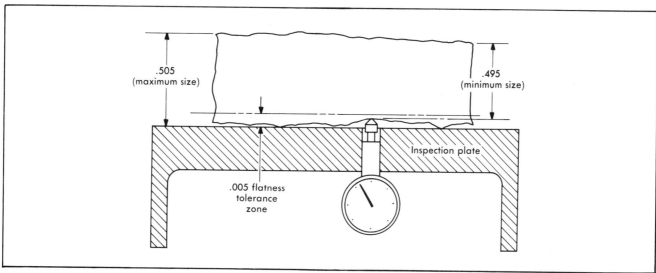

Fig. 4-14 Inspecting flatness on a surface plate.

For example, if the full indicator movement of the upper surface is within the flatness specification, the part is acceptable. But if the dial indicator reading is not within specification, the part may still be acceptable. The excessive variation may be due to the allowable part thickness tolerance of 0.010″. The upper surface could be perfectly flat, but the allowable thickness variation would mislead the inspector into believing the part was discrepant from a flatness standpoint.

When flatness must be verified on the upward side of the part due to part size or configuration, the allowable part thickness variation must be nullified. The part thickness variation can be nullified by using leveling screws as shown in Fig. 4-16. The screws are adjusted so that the upper surface extremities of the part establish the upper limit of the flatness tolerance zone. The dial indicator is then traversed over the upper surface of the part. The full indicator movement over the entire surface must not vary greater than the flatness requirement.

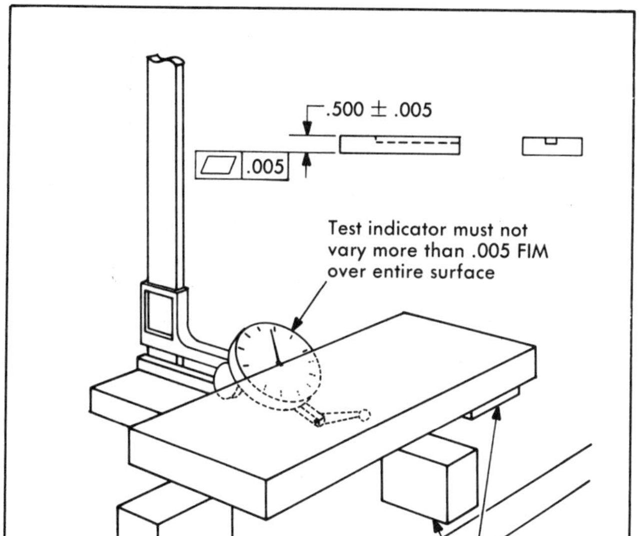

Fig. 4-15 Inspecting flatness by placing the workpiece on gage blocks and checking full indicator movement.

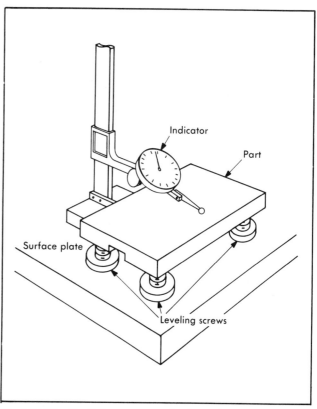

Fig. 4-16 Checking flatness on top surface by nullifying part thickness variation with leveling screws.

FORM CONTROL TOLERANCES

Straightness

Straightness is a condition where an element of a surface or an axis is a straight line.[4] A straightness tolerance specifies a tolerance zone within which the considered element or axis must lie.

Straightness specifications are divided into surface straightness and axis straightness. Surface straightness is depicted by attaching the straightness feature control frame to the surface of the part as shown in Fig. 4-17, view *a*. Axis straightness is indicated by placing the feature control frame with the feature size dimension (see Fig. 4-17, view *b*). The diameter symbol (∅) is required to precede the straightness tolerance value in the feature control frame when straightness is specified to a cylindrical feature. The person interpreting the drawing must be able to recognize which straightness requirement has been specified on the drawing.

Surface straightness. Figure 4-18 shows the surface straightness tolerance specification on an engineering drawing and then illustrates the tolerance zone for each line element of the surface. To verify surface straightness, the part is placed on two equal stacks of gage blocks that are spaced apart as far as possible (see Fig. 4-19). A test indicator is passed under and perpendicular to the shaft at a number of locations while noting the full indicator movement. For the part to be acceptable, the variation in the maximum indicator reading cannot exceed the straightness specification. This procedure is repeated as the part is rotated a sufficient number of times to ensure that the part meets the drawing requirement.

Occasionally an inspector will attempt to verify surface straightness on the upper surface of the part as shown in Fig. 4-20. When this method is used, the parts that are within tolerance are acceptable. However, the parts that are out of

tolerance may also be acceptable because the size specification (0.495-0.505″ diam) allows a full indicator movement of 0.010″. For this reason, it is recommended that the inspector use the previously described procedure to verify surface straightness.

When the straightness feature control frame is attached to a flat surface, the location of the control frame is very important. For example, in Fig. 4-21, view *a*, the feature control frame is

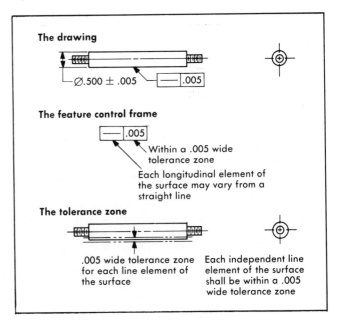

Fig. 4-18 Surface straightness tolerance.

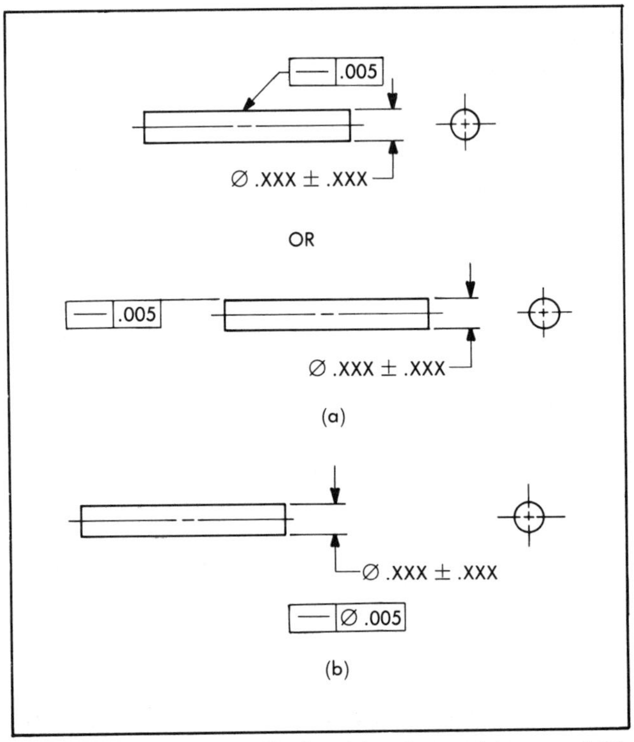

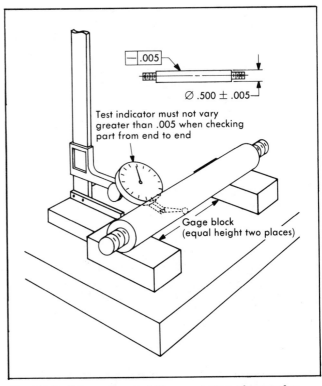

Fig. 4-17 Straightness specification: (a) surface straightness and (b) axis straightness.

Fig. 4-19 Verifying surface straightness on bottom of part surface.

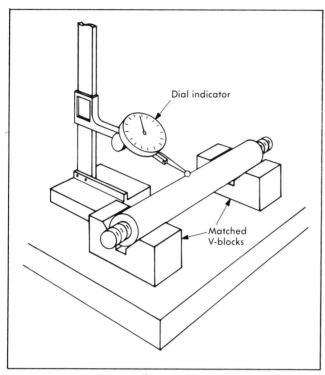

Fig. 4-20 Verifying surface straightness on top of part surface can result in rejecting parts that are within tolerance.

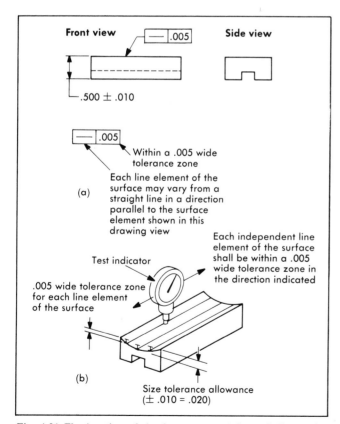

Fig. 4-21 The location of the feature control frame indicates the direction in which a flat surface should be verified.

attached to the front view, indicating that the surface straightness should be verified along the length of the part as shown in view *b*. If the feature control frame were attached to the side view, the surface straightness would be verified along the width of the part.

Axis straightness. The straightness specification in Fig. 4-22 allows the axis of the shaft to vary within a 0.005″ diam cylindrical tolerance zone. Because an axis or centerline cannot be seen on an actual part, the external surface of the feature is used to verify the axis straightness specification. To determine the axis straightness conformance, surface straightness, taper, and circularity verification methods are used.

Because the feature control frame does not designate a material condition modifier, the regardless of feature size (RFS) material condition is implied. If the maximum material condition (MMC) modifier were designated, the bonus tolerance would have to be evaluated.

In the section on principles of geometric dimensioning and tolerancing, it was stated that the envelope rule controls straightness, flatness, circularity, and cylindricity within the MMC envelope. This rule would require the shaft in Fig. 4-18 to be perfectly straight and round if it was produced at MMC size (0.505″ diam) because the surface straightness tolerance is not additive to the MMC envelope. However, when the axis straightness is applied to a shaft or hole, the feature is no longer required to meet the perfect form at MMC rule. Axis straightness is the only geometric symbol that is allowed to violate the envelope rule without special notation.

When the MMC symbol is indicated with an axis straightness tolerance, a bonus tolerance is gained as the feature departs from MMC size. An example of this condition is shown in Fig. 4-23. The part can also be functionally gaged; the gage would be at least 3.030″ long with a hole at the virtual condition of the feature (see Fig. 4-24). It should be noted that this gage can verify form only, size must be verified separately. It is also necessary to consider gage makers' tolerances and wear allowances when using functional gages.

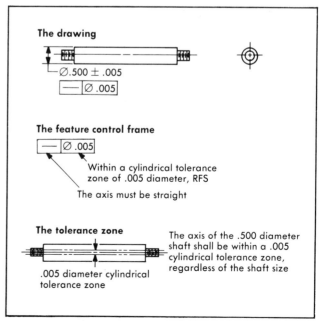

Fig. 4-22 Axis straightness control.

FORM CONTROL TOLERANCES

Circularity (Roundness)

Circularity is a condition of a surface of revolution (cylinder, cone, or sphere) where all the points of the surface intersected by any plane perpendicular to a common axis (cylinder or cone) or passing through a common center (sphere) are equidistant from the center.[5] A circularity tolerance specifies a tolerance zone bounded by two concentric circles within which each circular element of the surface must lie, and it applies independently at each cross section.

The outer tolerance zone boundary is established by the extremities of the manufactured surface of the part (see Fig. 4-25). The inner tolerance zone diameter is less than the outer tolerance zone diameter by two times the tolerance value specified in the circularity feature control frame. The tolerance value specified in the feature control frame is a radial requirement. The circularity tolerance zone applies independently at every cross section perpendicular to the common axis of the feature. Several cross-sectional checks should be made to ensure part conformance. Circularity verification is discussed subsequently under "Measurement of Circularity."

Tapered parts are also occasionally specified with circularity control. Because the circularity tolerance zone applies independently at each cross section and the outer tolerance zone limit is established by the manufactured surface, each outer tolerance zone limit will be a different size from the others. Several cross-sectional checks should be made to ensure part conformance.

Cylindricity

Cylindricity is a condition of a surface of revolution in which all points of the surface are equidistant from a common axis.[6] A cylindricity tolerance specifies a tolerance zone bounded by two concentric cylinders within which the surface must lie (see Fig. 4-26).

Cylindricity control stretches the circularity tolerance requirement over the length of the part. Cylindricity tolerance applies simultaneously to both circular and longitudinal elements of the part's surface.

Some of the common ways to verify circularity and cylindricity are with a micrometer, with a V-block and test indicator, and between bench centers. Care must be exercised when

AS MANUFACTURED SHAFT DIAMETER	STRAIGHTNESS BONUS TOLERANCE	TOTAL STRAIGHTNESS TOLERANCE
.505 (MMC)	.000	.005
.504	.001	.006
.503	.002	.007
.502	.003	.008
.501	.004	.009
.500	.005	.010
.499	.006	.011
.498	.007	.012
.497	.008	.013
.496	.009	.014
.495 (LMC)	.010	.015

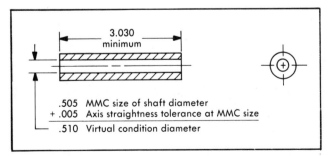

Fig. 4-23 Axis straightness control at MMC.

Fig. 4-24 Functional gage at the virtual condition of the part in Fig. 4-23.

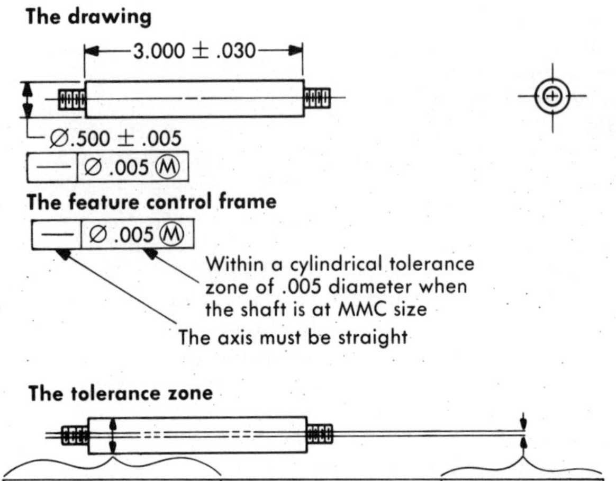

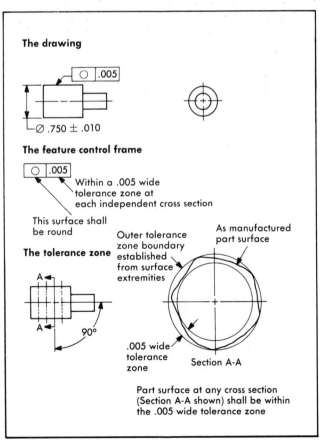

Fig. 4-25 Circularity control.

verifying cylindricity with the micrometer, with a V-block and test indicator, and between bench centers because these methods can give misleading results. For example, a part may check to be within tolerances when verifying cylindricity with a micrometer, but the parts may actually be lobed-shaped and therefore unacceptable. The most accurate method for verifying cylindricity is in a precision spindle instrument. Techniques for measuring cylindricity are discussed subsequently under the section "Measurement of Circularity."

PROFILE CONTROL TOLERANCE

Profile tolerancing is a method of controlling irregular surfaces, lines, arcs, or unusual shapes as well as regular shapes. Profiles can be applied to individual line elements (profile of a line) or to the entire surface (profile of a surface) of a part. Refer to Fig. 4-1 for the symbols used to represent these geometric characteristics.

Definition

The profile tolerance specifies a uniform boundary along the true profile within which the elements of the surface must lie.[7] Profile of surface tolerances are three-dimensional extending along the length and width of the considered feature or features. On the other hand, line tolerances are two-dimensional, extending along the length of the considered feature.

The profile tolerance zone is the distance between two boundaries shaped to the true configuration indicated on the drawing by basic dimensions. The profile tolerance specified in

the feature control frame can be applied to the drawing to indicate that the tolerance zone is divided on both sides of the true profile (bilateral tolerance). It can also be used to indicate that the tolerance zone only applies to one side of the true profile (unilateral tolerance). The two methods of indicating the profile tolerance zones are illustrated in Fig. 4-27.

Verification

Several inspection methods are commonly used to verify profile acceptance. One method uses hard tooling. In this method, the part is moved in relationship to a mastered test indicator at the specified part profile configuration from a datum reference frame.

Another method uses an optical comparator in conjunction with an overlay gage to verify profile requirements. This inspection method is limited to smaller parts that can be enlarged on the comparator screen. The part shadow must fall completely within the acceptable tolerance zone area of the overlay gage to be accepted. The image, visible on the screen, represents the maximum envelope of the part. The minimum envelope of the part should also be verified to make sure that it is within the tolerance requirements. For additional information on optical comparators and overlay gages, refer to Chapter 3, "Inspection Equipment and Techniques," of this volume. Profile tolerances can also be verified on NC, programmed coordinate, or universal measuring machines.

ORIENTATION TOLERANCES

Perpendicularity, angularity, and parallelism controls are referred to as orientation tolerances. These tolerance specifications control the orientation or attitude of a feature to a datum feature or features. Refer to Fig 4-1 for the symbols used to represent these geometric characteristics.

Perpendicularity Tolerance

Perpendicularity is the condition of a surface, median plane, or axis at a right angle to a datum plane or axis.[8] Perpendicu-

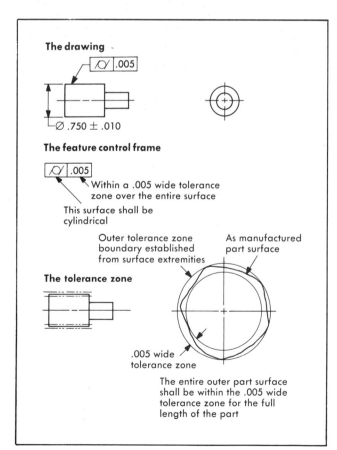

Fig. 4-26 Cylindricity control.

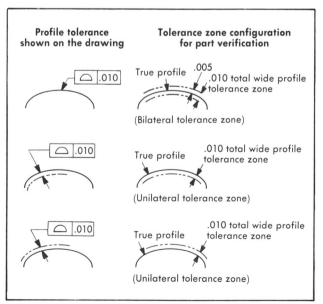

Fig. 4-27 Profile tolerance zones.

ORIENTATION TOLERANCES

larity specifications can be applied to a surface or to a feature of size. When a feature of size is controlled, the tolerance zone value applies at RFS unless the MMC symbol is included in the feature control frame. If MMC is utilized, the inspector must take into account allowable bonus tolerances as the controlled feature departs from the MMC size.

In Fig. 4-28, the end of the part is required to be square to datum surface A within a 0.005″ wide tolerance zone. The tolerance zone is exactly 90° to datum surface A. The entire end surface of the part must be within the tolerance zone to meet the drawing requirements.

Perpendicularity requirements are normally verified with a test indicator and angle plate as shown in Fig. 4-29. The datum feature is placed against the angle plate to provide proper orientation of the part for inspection, and the test indicator is traversed over the entire end surface. The perpendicularity is acceptable if the full indicator movement does not exceed the 0.005″ perpendicularity specification. Caution should be exercised when aligning the part to the angle plate to ensure that only perpendicularity error is measured.

In Fig. 4-30, a 2.000″ diam hole is controlled by a perpendicularity requirement. The axis of the hole must be square to datum surface A within a 0.005″ cylindrical tolerance zone when the hole is produced at the MMC size. As the hole departs from the MMC size, a bonus tolerance is added to the specified

perpendicularity tolerance. The bonus tolerance is equal to the amount the hole departs from the MMC size and is added directly to the perpendicularity tolerance shown in the feature control frame. If the MMC material condition symbol was not shown in the feature control frame, the RFS would be implied.

To verify the perpendicularity of the part shown in Fig. 4-30, the largest size gage pin would be fitted into the center hole and a test indicator would measure the deviation over the 2.500″ length of the gage pin; the length of the pin is the depth of the hole (see Fig. 4-31). For the part to be acceptable, the deviation should not exceed the 0.005″ perpendicularity tolerance value. Because a cylindrical tolerance zone (diameter symbol) has been designated by the feature control frame, the gage pin must be verified in other angular rotations. For example, the part should be rotated 90° and reverified.

The cylindrical tolerance zone requires a three-dimensional verification of the perpendicularity conformance. If the diameter symbol would have been omitted in the feature control frame, the tolerance zone would be between two parallel planes (two-dimensional control). The 0.005″ tolerance zone would be in the direction of the arrows dimensioning the 2.000″ diam hole.

Angularity Tolerance

Angularity is the condition of a surface or axis at a specified angle (other than 90°) from a datum plane or axis.[9] Angularity can be specified at all angles except 90°. The 90° case of angularity is perpendicularity, which was previously discussed. The tolerance zones for angularity and perpendicularity are essentially the same for surface and two-dimensional axis controls. A typical feature control frame for angularity tolerance is shown in Fig. 4-32.

When inspecting parts for angularity, the part must be placed on the datum surface(s). The specified tolerance zone limits must not be exceeded for the part to be acceptable. Common methods for verifying angularity are discussed subsequently under the section "Measurement of Angles."

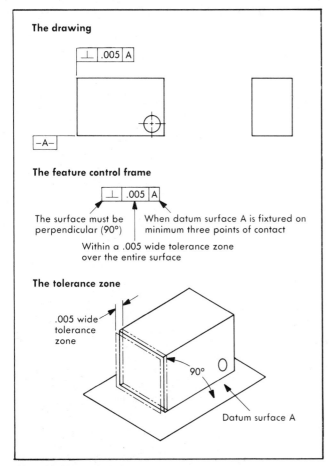

The drawing

⊥ .005 A

–A–

The feature control frame

⊥ .005 A

The surface must be perpendicular (90°)

When datum surface A is fixtured on minimum three points of contact

Within a .005 wide tolerance zone over the entire surface

The tolerance zone

.005 wide tolerance zone

90°

Datum surface A

Fig. 4-28 Perpendicularity control.

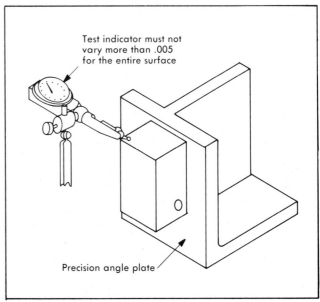

Test indicator must not vary more than .005 for the entire surface

Precision angle plate

Fig. 4-29 Verifying perpendicularity using a test indicator and a precision angle plate.

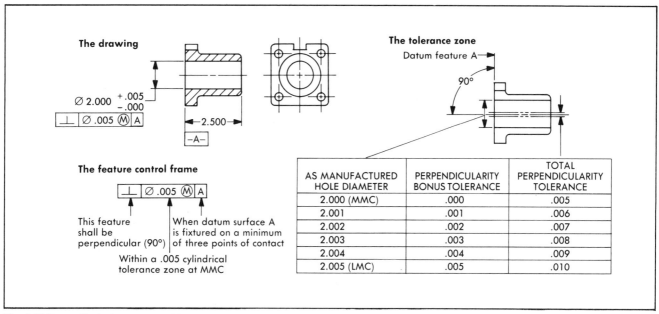

Fig. 4-30 Perpendicularity control at MMC.

AS MANUFACTURED HOLE DIAMETER	PERPENDICULARITY BONUS TOLERANCE	TOTAL PERPENDICULARITY TOLERANCE
2.000 (MMC)	.000	.005
2.001	.001	.006
2.002	.002	.007
2.003	.003	.008
2.004	.004	.009
2.005 (LMC)	.005	.010

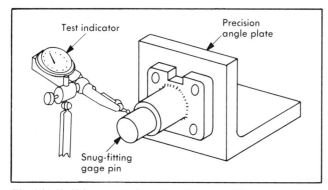

Fig. 4-31 Verifying perpendicularity with a snug-fitting gage pin and a test indicator.

Parallelism Tolerance

Parallelism is the condition of a surface equidistant at all points from a datum plane or an axis equidistant along its length to a datum axis.[10] The feature control frame in Fig. 4-33 specifies that the part surface must be parallel within a 0.001″ wide tolerance zone. The tolerance zone is parallel (equidistant) to the inspection table, which establishes datum plane A. The part thickness is allowed to vary within the part size tolerance (±0.005″). The parallelism specification refines the parallelism control allowed by the envelope rule, therefore the parallelism error allowed must be contained inside the boundary of perfect form at MMC.

Figure 4-34 shows a test indicator being used to check the parallelism specification of the part's upper surface. The lower surface, datum reference A, must make a minimum of three points of contact with the surface plate. Because datum planes exist in the manufacturing and inspection tooling and not the actual part, the real datum plane A is the surface plate. According to the ANSI definition, parallelism must be validated

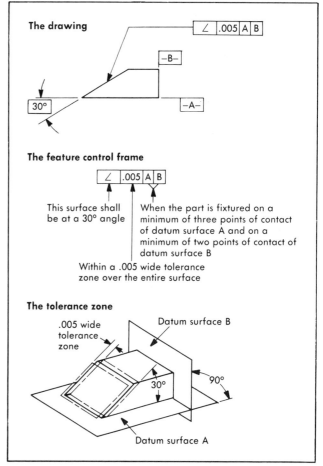

Fig. 4-32 Angularity control.

ORIENTATION TOLERANCES

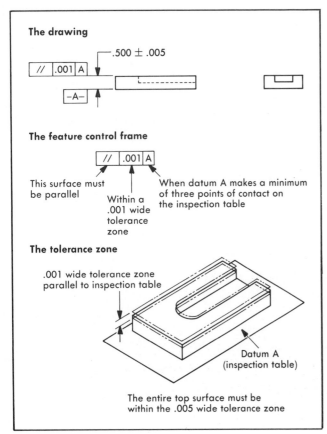

Fig. 4-33 Parallelism control.

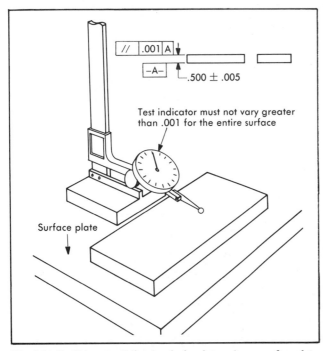

Fig. 4-34 Verifying parallelism by placing datum A on a surface plate and checking full indicator movement.

in relationship to the extremities of surface A as it contacts the surface plate or inspection table.

Parallelism control can also be applied to features of size as shown in Fig. 4-35. The axis of the small hole is specified to be equidistant to the axis of the large hole within a 0.005″ cylindrical tolerance zone. Because of the inclusion of the MMC symbol in the feature control frame, the 0.005″ parallel tolerance zone applies when the small hole is produced at 0.249″ diam. As the hole departs from MMC size, additional parallelism tolerance is allowed.

Figure 4-36 shows a standard setup to check parallelism of the part in Fig. 4-35. Snug-fitting gage pins are placed in each hole. The datum reference pin is placed in a V-block to establish datum axis A (the gage pin axis) parallel to the inspection table. Measurements are then made with the test indicator on both sides of the 0.250″ diam hole to a length on the gage pin equal to the thickness of the part.

Because the cylindrical tolerance zone feature precedes the parallelism tolerance zone value in the feature control frame, the part must be checked at several angular orientations by rotating the datum gage pin and the part together (refer to Fig 4-35). If the indicator readings do not exceed the specification in any orientation, the part is acceptable. It is important to note

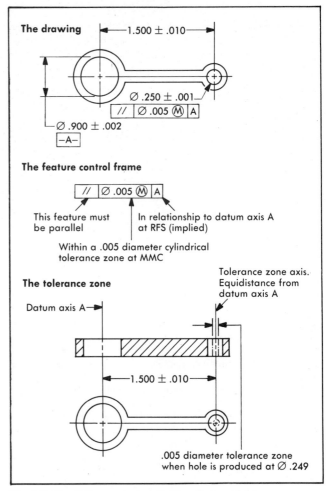

Fig. 4-35 Parallelism control applied to a feature of size.

that the cylindrical tolerance zone applies only to the portion of the gage pin within the part.

The previously described procedure did not evaluate all allowable tolerance for part conformance. Because a selective-fit gage pin was used in the small hole, the axis of the hole is established at RFS rather than the specified MMC. To compensate for this, the gage pin diameter should be measured, and the difference between this size and the MMC size should be added to the specified parallelism tolerance value.

LOCATION TOLERANCES

The two locational tolerance controls in the ANSI Y14.5M-1982 standard are position and concentricity. The 1966 and 1973 revisions of the standard also included symmetry tolerance as a location tolerance control. In the latest edition, the symmetry symbol has been replaced by positional tolerance at RFS. Refer to Fig. 4-1 for the symbols used to represent these geometric characteristics.

Positional Tolerance

A positional tolerance defines a zone within which the center, axis, or center plane of a feature of size is permitted to vary from true (theoretically exact) position.[11] Basic dimensions establish the true position from datum features and between interrelated features. A positional tolerance is indicated by the position symbol, a tolerance, and appropriate datum references placed in a feature control frame.

A positional tolerance is the total permissible variation in the location of a feature about its exact location. For cylindrical features such as holes and outside diameters, the positional tolerance is generally the diameter of the tolerance zone within which the axis of the feature must lie. The center of the tolerance zone is located at the exact center, which is called true position.

For features that are not round, such as slots and tabs, the positional tolerance is the total width of the tolerance zone within which the center plane of the feature must lie. The center of the tolerance zone is located at the exact location, which is called true position.

Positional tolerance zones are three-dimensional and apply through the thickness of the part. As shown in Fig. 4-37, a diameter position tolerance zone is 90° from the specified primary datum reference surface. It is important to note that the tolerance zone will also control perpendicularity of the feature within the position tolerance requirement.

The three methods used for verifying positional tolerances are functional gages, coordinate analysis, and graphical inspection analysis. Functional gages are three-dimensional mating parts at virtual condition and can only be used if MMC is specified. If the gage assembles to the part being inspected, then all other conforming parts will assemble. Functional gaging should be considered when any of the following conditions exist:

- The ability to be assembled must be ensured.
- A number of parts of identical configuration are to be verified for conformance.
- Production schedules require in-process acceptance gaging.
- Variables inspection data is not required. Simple GO or NOT-GO attributes are sufficient for verification.
- Part configuration does not allow efficient open setup inspection of manufactured part.

Additional information on functional gages can be found in Chapter 3, "Inspection Equipment and Techniques," of this volume. Both coordinate and graphical inspection analysis employ standard measuring instruments such as test indicators, height gages, and coordinate measuring machines to verify the X and Y-coordinate positions of the feature.

Coordinate analysis. Coordinate analysis is basically a two-step procedure used to verify the positional tolerances of a part. In the first step, the position features are measured using standard inspection instruments while the part is mounted on the specified datum surfaces. The data from these measurements

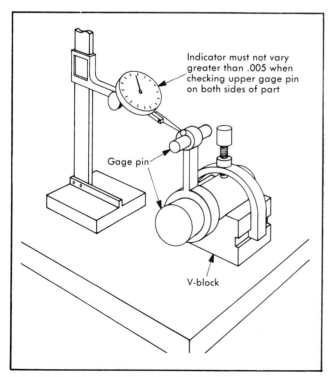

Fig. 4-36 Verifying parallelism of part in Fig. 4-35.

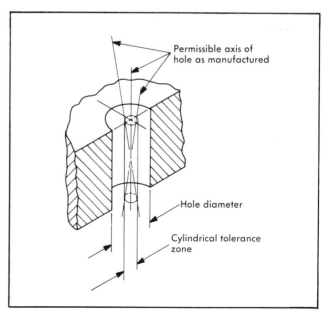

Fig. 4-37 Position tolerance cylindrical zone.

LOCATION TOLERANCES

are recorded and then analyzed to determine if the features are within the specified circular positional tolerance zones.

For example, the feature control frame for the part in Fig. 4-38 specifies the axis of the drilled hole must be within the specified cylindrical tolerance zone. As the hole departs from MMC size (0.528″ diam), bonus tolerance can be added to the 0.014″ position tolerance. When MMC is specified, the hole size must be measured to determine the allowable bonus tolerance.

From the datum precedence in the feature control frame, the part will make a minimum of three points of contact on surface A (primary datum reference), a minimum of two points of contact on surface B (secondary datum reference), and a minimum of one point of contact on surface C (tertiary datum reference). Measurements originate from the datum planes as established by the inspection tooling for both holes. When plug gages are used for determining the location of the produced holes, one half of the gage diameter must be subtracted from the measurement to establish the dimension of the hole from the datum plane.

A chart for recording the data is shown in Fig. 4-39. The location dimension is subtracted from the basic dimension specified on the drawing for each hole in both the X and Y coordinates to determine the deviations. The actual location of each hole in relationship to specified true position can be determined by inserting the hole location deviations in the following equation:

$$T_p = 2 \sqrt{D_x^2 + D_y^2} \qquad (1)$$

where:

T_p = position tolerance, in. (mm)
D_x = X-coordinate deviation, in. (mm)
D_y = Y-coordinate deviation, in. (mm)

The position tolerance of the holes can also be determined with Table 4-1. The X deviation is located on the horizontal scale and Y deviation is located on the vertical scale. The position tolerance for the hole as manufactured is found at the intersection of the two scales.

For the part to be acceptable, the values obtained by Eq. (1) or from Table 4-1 must be within the drawing requirements. Because MMC was specified in Fig. 4-38, the part as indicated by the data in Fig. 4-39 is acceptable. If RFS was specified, the part would be unacceptable because the allowable position tolerance for hole number two exceeds the specified position tolerance.

Graphical inspection analysis. Graphical inspection analysis is a four-step procedure that permits the inspector to physically see what the tolerance zones look like. It provides the benefit of functional gaging without the expense and time required to design and manufacture a close-toleranced, hardened-metal functional gage. Graphical inspection analysis is primarily suited for inspecting small lots of parts, but can also be used for large quantities.

The following five examples are provided to show how the dimensioning method affects the analysis. In general the procedure is the same for each example, except when indicated otherwise.

Example one. The part and dimensioning method for this example is shown in Fig. 4-40. The first step of the graphical inspection analysis involves plotting the basic location of the feature to be inspected in relationship to the datum features as described by the engineering drawing. This plot is called the data graph and is generally drawn on 10 x 10 graph paper at any convenient scale (configuration scale); 8 1/2 x 11″ paper can be used for simple parts, whereas larger sheets are required for complex parts.

TABLE 4-1
Conversion of Coordinate Measurements to Circular Position Tolerance Zone

Position Location, in.									
0.020	0.0400	0.0402	0.0404	0.0408	0.0412	0.0418	0.0424	0.0431	0.0439
0.019	0.0380	0.0382	0.0385	0.0388	0.0393	0.0398	0.0405	0.0412	0.0420
0.018	0.0360	0.0362	0.0365	0.0369	0.0374	0.0379	0.0386	0.0394	0.0403
0.017	0.0340	0.0342	0.0345	0.0349	0.0354	0.0360	0.0368	0.0376	0.0385
0.016	0.0321	0.0322	0.0325	0.0330	0.0335	0.0342	0.0349	0.0358	0.0367
0.015	0.0301	0.0303	0.0306	0.0310	0.0316	0.0323	0.0331	0.0340	0.0350
0.014	0.0281	0.0283	0.0286	0.0291	0.0297	0.0305	0.0313	0.0322	0.0333
0.013	0.0261	0.0263	0.0267	0.0272	0.0278	0.0286	0.0295	0.0305	0.0316
0.012	0.0241	0.0243	0.0247	0.0253	0.0260	0.0268	0.0278	0.0288	0.0300
0.011	0.0221	0.0224	0.0228	0.0234	0.0242	0.0250	0.0261	0.0272	0.0284
0.010	0.0201	0.0204	0.0209	0.0215	0.0224	0.0233	0.0244	0.0256	0.0269
0.009	0.0181	0.0184	0.0190	0.0197	0.0206	0.0216	0.0228	0.0241	0.0254
0.008	0.0161	0.0165	0.0171	0.0179	0.0189	0.0200	0.0213	0.0226	0.0241
0.007	0.0141	0.0146	0.0152	0.0161	0.0172	0.0184	0.0198	0.0213	0.0228
0.006	0.0122	0.0126	0.0134	0.0144	0.0156	0.0170	0.0184	0.0200	0.0216
0.005	0.0102	0.0108	0.0117	0.0128	0.0141	0.0156	0.0172	0.0189	0.0206
0.004	0.0082	0.0089	0.0100	0.0113	0.0128	0.0144	0.0161	0.0179	0.0197
0.003	0.0063	0.0072	0.0085	0.0100	0.0117	0.0134	0.0152	0.0171	0.0190
0.002	0.0045	0.0056	0.0072	0.0089	0.0108	0.0126	0.0146	0.0165	0.0184
0.001	0.0028	0.0045	0.0063	0.0082	0.0102	0.0122	0.0141	0.0161	0.0181
	0.001	0.002	0.003	0.004	0.005	0.006	0.007	0.008	0.009

Y Coordinate, in. (vertical axis label)

X Coordinate, in.

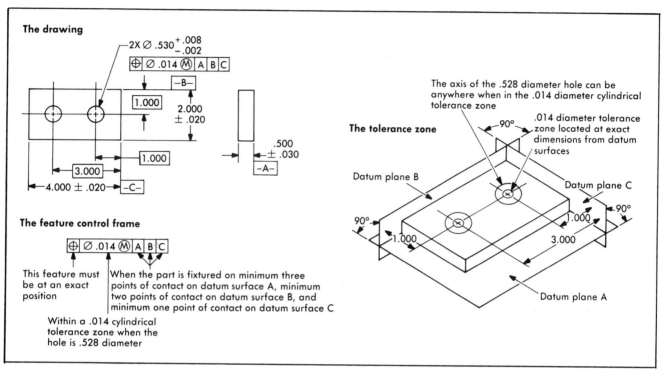

Fig. 4-38 Position tolerance.

The second step involves measuring the location features along their X and Y axes and recording the values on an appropriate chart (see Fig. 4-41). The locations of the actual inspected features are then plotted on the data graph in relationship to the basic part; because the deviations from the basic specified location are in the order of magnitude of thousandths of an inch (0.025 mm), another scale must be established on the data graph. The new scale is referred to as the deviation scale, with each grid square of the graph paper typically representing 0.001″ (0.025 mm). Figure 4-42 shows a data graph with the specified and measured hole locations of an inspected part.

TABLE 4-1—*Continued*

Position Location, in.										
0.0447	0.0456	0.0466	0.0477	0.0488	0.0500	0.0512	0.0525	0.0538	0.0552	0.0566
0.0429	0.0439	0.0449	0.0460	0.0472	0.0484	0.0497	0.0510	0.0523	0.0537	0.0552
0.0412	0.0422	0.0433	0.0444	0.0456	0.0469	0.0482	0.0495	0.0509	0.0523	0.0538
0.0394	0.0405	0.0416	0.0428	0.0440	0.0453	0.0467	0.0481	0.0495	0.0510	0.0525
0.0377	0.0388	0.0400	0.0412	0.0425	0.0439	0.0452	0.0467	0.0482	0.0497	0.0512
0.0360	0.0372	0.0384	0.0397	0.0410	0.0424	0.0439	0.0453	0.0469	0.0484	0.0500
0.0344	0.0356	0.0369	0.0382	0.0396	0.0410	0.0425	0.0440	0.0456	0.0472	0.0488
0.0328	0.0340	0.0354	0.0368	0.0382	0.0397	0.0412	0.0428	0.0444	0.0460	0.0477
0.0312	0.0325	0.0339	0.0354	0.0369	0.0384	0.0400	0.0416	0.0433	0.0449	0.0466
0.0297	0.0311	0.0325	0.0340	0.0356	0.0372	0.0388	0.0405	0.0422	0.0439	0.0456
0.0283	0.0297	0.0312	0.0328	0.0344	0.0360	0.0377	0.0394	0.0412	0.0429	0.0447
0.0269	0.0284	0.0300	0.0316	0.0333	0.0350	0.0367	0.0385	0.0402	0.0420	0.0439
0.0256	0.0272	0.0288	0.0305	0.0322	0.0340	0.0358	0.0376	0.0394	0.0412	0.0431
0.0244	0.0261	0.0278	0.0295	0.0313	0.0331	0.0349	0.0368	0.0386	0.0405	0.0424
0.0233	0.0250	0.0268	0.0286	0.0305	0.0323	0.0342	0.0360	0.0379	0.0398	0.0418
0.0224	0.0242	0.0260	0.0278	0.0297	0.0316	0.0335	0.0354	0.0374	0.0393	0.0412
0.0215	0.0234	0.0253	0.0272	0.0291	0.0310	0.0330	0.0349	0.0369	0.0388	0.0408
0.0209	0.0228	0.0247	0.0267	0.0286	0.0306	0.0325	0.0345	0.0365	0.0385	0.0404
0.0204	0.0224	0.0243	0.0263	0.0283	0.0303	0.0322	0.0342	0.0362	0.0382	0.0402
0.0201	0.0221	0.0241	0.0261	0.0281	0.0301	0.0321	0.0340	0.0360	0.0380	0.0400
0.010	0.011	0.012	0.013	0.014	0.015	0.016	0.017	0.018	0.019	0.020

X Coordinate, in.

LOCATION TOLERANCES

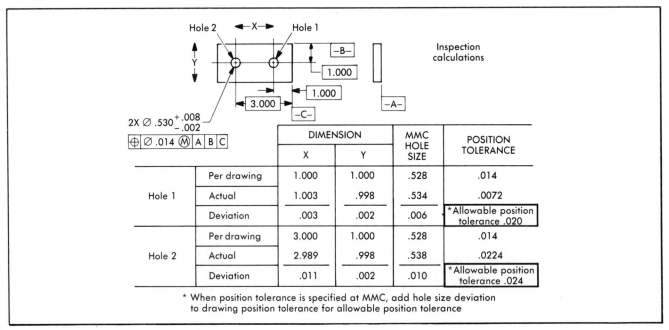

		DIMENSION		MMC HOLE SIZE	POSITION TOLERANCE
		X	Y		
	Per drawing	1.000	1.000	.528	.014
Hole 1	Actual	1.003	.998	.534	.0072
	Deviation	.003	.002	.006	*Allowable position tolerance .020
	Per drawing	3.000	1.000	.528	.014
Hole 2	Actual	2.989	.998	.538	.0224
	Deviation	.011	.002	.010	*Allowable position tolerance .024

* When position tolerance is specified at MMC, add hole size deviation to drawing position tolerance for allowable position tolerance

Fig. 4-39 Inspection report for part in Fig. 4-38.

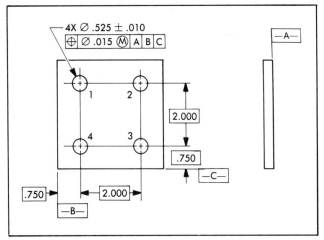

Fig. 4-40 Example part.

The third step involves producing a transparent gage, called the tolerance zone overlay gage, by placing a transparent material over the data graph and drawing the allowable position tolerance zone at each of the basic locations. The tolerance zones are drawn at the same scale (deviation scale) used to plot hole location deviations in step two. It is important to add any bonus tolerances to the specified tolerance when applicable.

In the fourth step, the tolerance zone overlay gage is superimposed over the data graph and rotated and/or translated to provide alignment with the datum feature. The part is acceptable when the location features are within their allowable position tolerance zone (see Fig. 4-43).

Example two. The zero position tolerancing concept of controlling feature locations is commonly used. Figure 4-44 shows the part from Fig. 4-40 dimensioned with the zero position concept. The maximum allowable hole size of both parts and the position tolerance at the least material condition size are identical. The only differences between the two methods

	FEATURE LOCATION						FEATURE SIZE			POSITION TOLERANCE			
	X axis			Y axis									
FEATURE NUMBER	Specified	Actual	Deviation	Specified	Actual	Deviation	Specified MMC size	Actual	Deviation	Material Condition	Specified	Bonus	Total
1	.750	.754	.004	2.750	2.751	.001	.515	.531	.016	MMC	.015	.016	.031
2	2.750	2.760	.010	2.750	2.750	.000	.515	.533	.018	MMC	.015	.018	.033
3	2.750	2.762	.012	.750	.748	.002	.515	.535	.020	MMC	.015	.020	.035
4	.750	.753	.003	.750	.749	.001	.515	.530	.015	MMC	.015	.015	.030

INSPECTION DATA

Fig. 4-41 Sample inspection data table for part in Fig. 4-40.

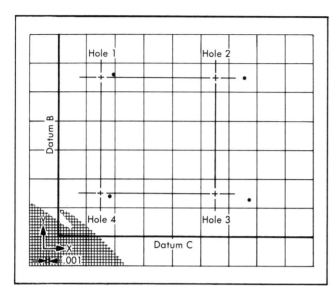

Fig. 4-42 Data graph for part in Fig. 4-40.

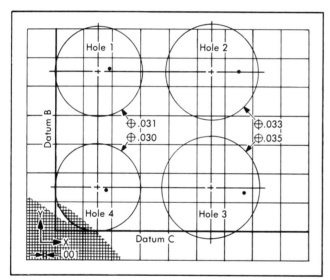

Fig. 4-43 Tolerance zone overlay gage superimposed over data graph.

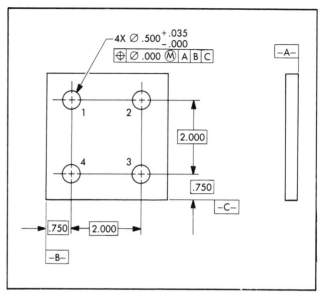

Fig. 4-44 Part dimensioned using zero positioning dimensioning method.

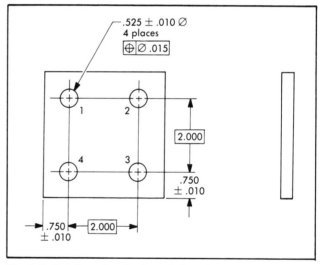

Fig. 4-45 Part dimensioned using techniques from ANSI Y14.5-1973.

of dimensioning are the minimum allowable hole size and the specified tolerance at MMC.

For example, the manufacturer of the part in Fig. 4-44 could drill the holes at 0.500″ diam, but by doing so a perfect location (zero position tolerance at MMC) would be required. Another way that the manufacturer could produce the part is by drilling the holes to 0.515″ diam, thus permitting a bonus tolerance of 0.015″ for the location requirement of the holes. As the hole increases to its maximum size, additional bonus tolerances for the hole location are permitted.

Example three. The part shown in Fig. 4-45 is dimensioned according to the 1973 edition of ANSI Y14.5, which is no longer used. In this example, datum features to be used for inspection are not specified. The surfaces from which the 0.750±0.010″ dimensions originate are implied datum surfaces, but datum precedence is not known. In addition, the 0.750″ dimension is not specified as a basic dimension. By using this dimensioning

method, the part designer has attempted to allow manufacturing more liberal location tolerances for the group of holes while maintaining a more restrictive tolerance for hole-to-hole inter-relationship. The ±0.010″ tolerance locates the centers of the positional tolerance zones and not the centers of the actual holes. Composite position tolerance is preferred over this method (see example four).

Figure 4-46 shows the data graph of a sample part with the tolerance zone overlay gage superimposed. The omission of datum reference letters in the feature control frame and the failure to provide basic dimensions to locate the position tolerance zones allow the centers of the positional tolerance zones to float anywhere within the ±0.010″ square tolerance zones. Because the overlay gage can capture all four-hole centers with the center of each position zone within the square zone, the part meets the drawing requirements.

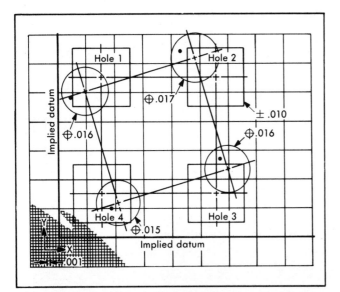

Fig. 4-46 Tolerance zone overlay gage superimposed over data graph of part in Fig. 4-45.

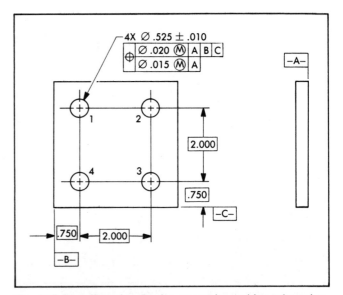

Fig. 4-47 Part dimensioned using composite position tolerancing method of dimensioning.

Example four. In Fig. 4-47, the composite position tolerancing method of dimensioning has been used to provide the same design intent as specified in Fig. 4-45. However, in this method the coordinate dimensions (the 0.750″ dimensions) are also specified as basic.

The upper entry of the feature control frame has specified selected datum features and the order of precedence for common interpretation. The lower entry is independent of any secondary or tertiary datum reference. With this dimensioning method, each entry must be verified separately. If functional receiver gages were used, verification of this part would require separate gages to be designed and manufactured for each entry.

The data table for this dimensioning method is slightly different from the previously described methods (see Fig. 4-48). The first two steps of the graphical inspection analysis are the same as the previously described procedure. For the third step, however, tolerance zone overlay gages are prepared for both

the upper and lower entry of the composite position feature control frame.

The tolerance zone overlay gage for the upper entry is aligned with the specified datum surfaces on the data graph as specified by the feature control frame. The axis of each hole must be within the overlay gage tolerance zone to meet the requirements of the upper entry. The lower entry overlay gage can float (see Fig. 4-49). The lower tolerance zone overlay gage establishes hole-to-hole locational requirements and orientation to any datum specified. The part is considered acceptable as long as the hole axes are within both overlay tolerance zones.

Example five. The part in Fig. 4-50 has the specified datums B and C as datums of size. When datums of size are specified at MMC size, it is possible to gain additional manufacturing tolerance as the datums depart from MMC size. This additional tolerance does not add to the original positional tolerance as a bonus tolerance, but allows extra locational tolerance of the

INSPECTION DATA

FEATURE NUMBER	FEATURE LOCATION						FEATURE SIZE			POSITION TOLERANCE			
	X axis*			Y axis*									
	Specified	Actual	Deviation	Specified	Actual	Deviation	Specified MMC size	Actual	Deviation	Material Condition	Specified	Bonus	Total
1	1.000	1.008	.008	1.000	1.002	.002	.515	.516	.001	MMC	.015	.001	.016
2	1.000	.991	.009	1.000	1.004	.004	.515	.517	.002	MMC	.015	.002	.017
3	1.000	1.004	.004	1.000	1.002	.002	.515	.516	.001	MMC	.015	.001	.016
4	1.000	.996	.004	1.000	1.006	.006	.515	.516	.001	MMC	.015	.001	.016
Datum B	---	---	---	---	---	---	3.510	3.504	.006	MMC	---	---	---
Datum C	---	---	---	---	---	---	3.510	3.500	.010	MMC	---	---	---

* From datum planes

Fig. 4-48 Inspection table for part in Fig. 4-47.

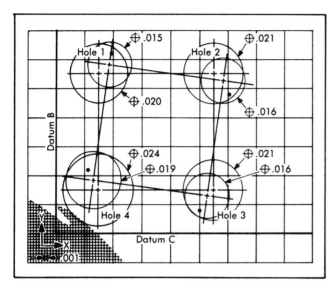

Fig. 4-49 Tolerance zone overlay gages superimposed over data graph of part in Fig. 4-47.

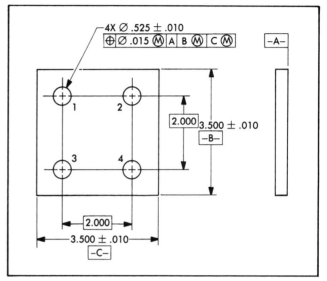

Fig. 4-50 Part having specified datums as dimensions of size.

pattern of features as a group. The additional tolerances must be included on the data graph to complete the tolerance analysis. Refer to the section on "Principles" for further explanation of the subject of additional tolerances.

When the specified datum features are datums of size, the axis or center plane of the feature is the real datum. The feature locations are measured from the center planes of the part rather than from the side as indicated by the data in Fig. 4-51.

In addition to allowable position tolerance zones at each basic location, datum center plane lines are included on the tolerance zone overlay gage to represent datums B and C (see Fig. 4-52). The lengths of the datum features are also marked on the gage.

When the tolerance zone overlay gage for an inspected part is superimposed on the data graph, holes one and two do not meet the drawing requirements (see Fig. 4-53). However, when the additional tolerance is taken into consideration and the overlay gage is rotated or shifted within this tolerance, the part meets the drawing specification (see Fig. 4-54).

Symmetry

Symmetry is the quality of being the same on both sides in size, shape, and relative position from a center plane. In the earlier editions of the standard, symmetry was represented by the symbol ⩳. As was previously mentioned, the symmetry symbol has been replaced by position tolerance at RFS in the 1982 version of the standard.

Figure 4-55 shows the notation for a part with a symmetrical feature from the earlier editions of the ANSI Y14.5M standard. According to these specifications, the center plane of the 0.500″ tab is to be within the 0.005″ wide tolerance zone at RFS.

To check for symmetry, the part is placed on the inspection table as shown in Fig. 4-56, view *a*. If the sides of the datum feature are not parallel, they must be shimmed to centralize the center plane of the datum feature. The distance from the inspection table to the top surface of the tab is measured, and the maximum value is recorded. The part is then turned over to allow the opposite side of the datum feature to rest on the

	INSPECTION DATA												
FEATURE NUMBER	FEATURE LOCATION						FEATURE SIZE			POSITION TOLERANCE			
	X axis			Y axis									
	Specified	Actual	Deviation	Specified	Actual	Deviation	Specified MMC size	Actual	Deviation	Material Condition	Specified	Bonus	Total
1	.750	.754	.004	2.750	2.757	.007	.515	.515	.000	MMC	.020	.000	.020
1										MMC	.015	.000	.015
2	2.750	2.755	.005	2.750	2.743	.007	.515	.516	.001	MMC	.020	.001	.021
2										MMC	.015	.001	.016
3	2.750	2.745	.005	.750	.743	.007	.515	.516	.001	MMC	.020	.001	.021
3										MMC	.015	.001	.016
4	.750	.746	.004	.750	.757	.007	.515	.519	.004	MMC	.020	.004	.024
4										MMC	.015	.004	.019

Fig. 4-51 Inspection data for part in Fig. 4-50.

LOCATION TOLERANCES

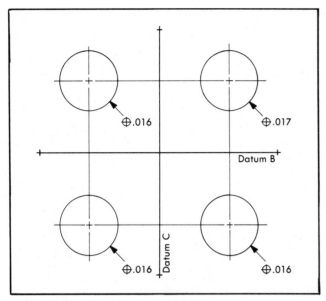

Fig. 4-52 Tolerance zone overlay gage for part in Fig. 4-50.

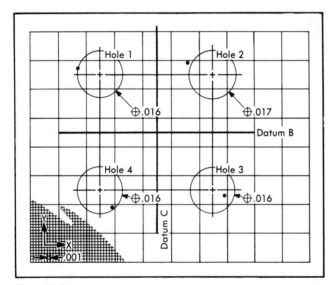

Fig. 4-53 Tolerance zone overlay gage superimposed over data graph of part in Fig. 4-50.

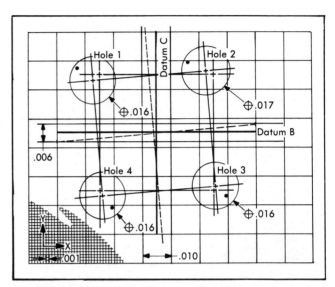

Fig. 4-54 Tolerance zone overlay gage shifted within the additional tolerance zones on the data graph.

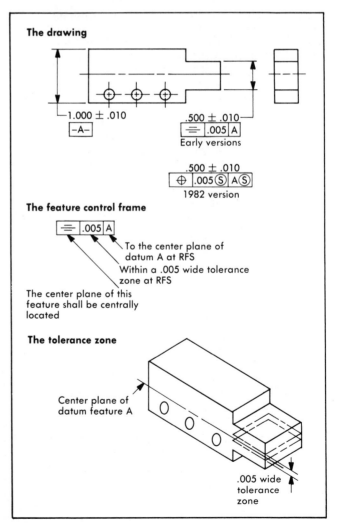

Fig. 4-55 Symmetry control.

inspection table (see Fig. 4-56, view *b*). Again the maximum distance from the inspection table to the top surface of the tab should be measured and recorded. The difference between the two recorded values is compared. Symmetry control has been met if the difference between the two recorded values does not exceed the specification.

Concentricity

Concentricity is the condition where the axes of all cross-sectional elements of a surface of revolution are common to the axis of a datum feature.[12] Figure 4-57 illustrates how concentricity control is noted on a typical drawing and explains what is required for the part to be in conformance. When concentricity is verified, the feature axis must be evaluated in relationship to the datum axis. The datum axis is established by tooling (precision chucks, collets, expanding mandrels, or gage pins) making contact with the surface of the datum feature. The axis of the controlled feature may, however, be difficult to identify because it must be established from the feature surface, which may be bowed or out-of-round in addition to being eccentric to the datum axis. To establish the true feature axis, an analysis of the surface irregularities may be required.

Concentricity can be verified (not measured) by rotating the part on the datum axis with a dial indicator in contact with the controlled feature surface (see Fig. 4-58). For the part to be in conformance, the entire feature surface must rotate within the concentricity specification. This inspection procedure actually verifies runout control. Parts that check within tolerance specifications are acceptable, but parts exceeding acceptance criteria may also be acceptable.

In addition to excessive feature axis eccentricity, failure to meet the concentricity specification can also be attributed to excessive surface irregularity. Parts having excessive surface irregularities such as out-of-roundness or bow can be within concentricity specifications. Therefore, it is necessary to nullify the surface irregularities in the inspection process.

Out-of-roundness can be nullified by inspecting the part as shown in Fig. 4-59. In view *a*, dial indicator readings are taken

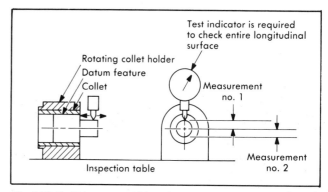

Fig. 4-58 Verifying concentricity using runout.

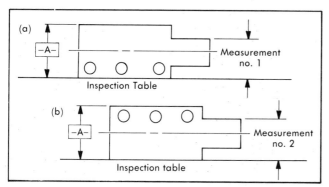

Fig. 4-56 Verifying symmetry.

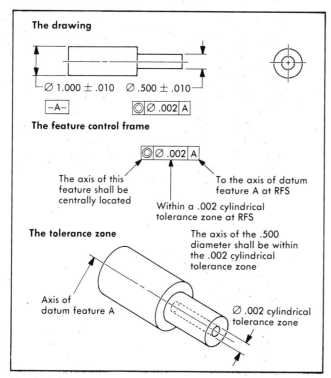

Fig. 4-57 Concentricity control.

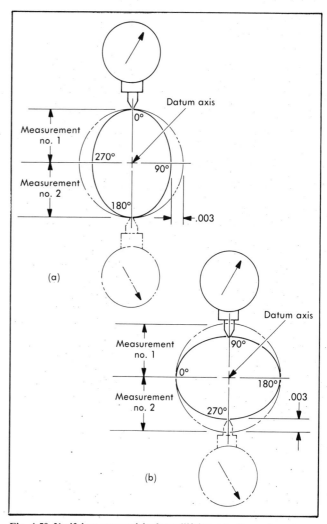

Fig. 4-59 Verifying concentricity by nullifying out-of-roundness.

RUNOUT TOLERANCE

at 0° and 180°. If the readings are equal, the feature axis is exactly coincident with the datum axis in this rotational plane. In view *b*, measurements are made at 90° and 270°. Although the readings are 0.003″ (which is greater than the specification), they are equal, indicating that the part is also concentric in this plane.

If the part were trilobed, the dial indicator readings would be verified at 120° increments. When nonsymmetrical lobing and bowing is combined, the inspection process is extremely difficult.

RUNOUT TOLERANCE

Runout tolerance is a combination of surface (form) and position (location) control. Runout can be specified to control surfaces constructed around a datum axis and surfaces perpendicular to the datum axis. Runout tolerances are always applied at RFS and cannot be applied at MMC.

The two types of runout control are circular runout and total runout. Figure 4-60 shows how the runout feature control frames have evolved with revisions of the standards. To check for runout, the part can be mounted on one or two functional diameters or on a functional face and diameter, depending on the datums specified by the control frame.

Circular Runout

Circular runout provides control of circular elements of a surface.[13] The tolerance is applied independently at any circular measuring position as the part is rotated 360°. A circular runout tolerance applied to surfaces constructed around a datum axis controls the cumulative variances of circularity and coaxiality. When it is applied to surfaces constructed at right angles to the datum axis, it controls circular elements of a plane surface. The feature control frame specifying circular runout is shown in Fig. 4-61. The tolerance indicates the amount of full indicator movement that is permitted for the feature to be acceptable.

To verify the circular runout of the part in Fig. 4-61, the datum feature is mounted in a precision rotating device to allow the part to rotate on the datum axis. A part mounted on one functional diameter is shown in Fig. 4-62. A test indicator is then placed in contact with the part surface and the part is rotated 360°. Several independent checks should be made along the part's surface to ensure that the entire feature is within

tolerance. The indicator should be reset to zero for each circular measurement. For the part to be acceptable, the full indicator movement must be within the specified tolerance.

Total Runout

Total runout provides composite control of all surface elements.[14] The tolerance is applied simultaneously to circular and longitudinal elements as the part is rotated 360°. Total runout controls the cumulative variations of circularity, cylindricity, straightness, coaxiality, angularity, taper, and profile when it is applied to surfaces constructed around a datum axis. When it is applied to surfaces constructed at right angles to a datum axis, it controls cumulative variations of perpendicularity (to limit wobble) and flatness (to limit concavity or convexity).

Total runout is verified in a similar manner as circular runout. The only difference in the inspection process is that when testing total runout, while the part is rotated, the test indicator is moved parallel to the datum axis (for circular surfaces) or perpendicular to the axis (for perpendicular plane surfaces). In addition, the indicator does not have to be reset to zero during the entire testing procedure.

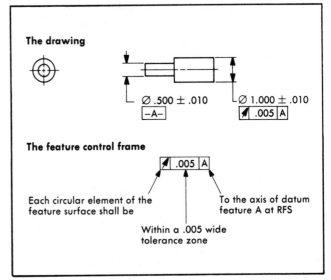

Fig. 4-61 Circular runout control.

	Circular runout	Total runout
Y14.5-1966	⤢ A .005 Circular	⤢ A .005
Y14.5-1973	⤢ A .005	⤢ A .005 Total
Y14.5M-1982	⤢ .005 A	⤢⤢ .005 A

Fig. 4-60 History of runout symbols.

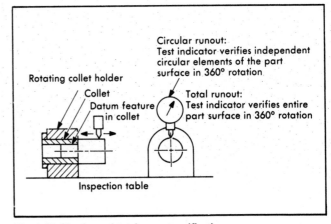

Fig. 4-62 Circular and total runout verification.

MEASUREMENT OF CIRCULARITY (ROUNDNESS)

Geometrically, a part can be said to be round (circular), in a given cross section, if there exists within the section a point from which all points on the periphery are equidistant. In practice, however, the radius of nominally round parts tends to vary from point to point around the periphery. Thus the problem encountered by the manufacturing engineer is one of displaying and assessing these variations and correctly interpreting the results.

The symbol for circularity is based on and used in accordance with the feature control criteria established in ANSI Y14.5M-1982, "Dimensioning and Tolerancing." Figure 4-63 shows the feature control frame for a round part. The control frame specifies the size of the required tolerance zone for the manufactured part. It does not specify the measuring method to use nor the method of evaluating the data obtained from the measuring method. The method of measurement is selected based on the accuracy required.

Most surfaces of circular cross section are originally generated by revolving about, or with reference to, fixed points, axes, or lines of contact in a machine tool such as centers, work spindles, steady rests, tool edges, and grinding wheel surfaces. However, the relationships of these points, axes, and lines of contact with the part are never perfect. Variable deflections and imperfect rotation occur as the surface is generated because of unbalance, erratic cutting action, inadequate lubrication, wear, defective or incorrect machine parts, and poor part geometry.

The result of these deflections is usually a deviation from circularity, referred to as out-of-roundness, in the form of lobes, waves, or undulations about the circumference of the part. The number of lobes or waves can vary from two to several hundred; two to fifteen lobes are generally generated by the manufacturing process. Out-of-roundness may also result from distortion of the part by chuck jaws, fixturing, localized heating, excessive feeds, and warped or out-of-round stock. Table 4-2 lists the typical causes for parts containing various numbers of lobes.

It is important to know the characteristics of the lobes present so that the correct measuring method can be selected. For example, the out-of-roundness of a part with an odd number of evenly spaced lobes cannot be detected by diametrical methods. Out-of-roundness is also distorted in magnitude when V-block methods are used. In addition, certain lobing patterns cannot be detected in a V-block.

Direct evaluation of a circular surface as a whole is difficult, and assessment is simplified by measuring a series of cross-sectional profiles. For most applications, this approach provides sufficient information about the form of the entire surface.

NOMENCLATURE

The following definitions are abstracted from ANSI B89.3.1 with permission from the publisher.[15]

actual profile The actual profile is the cross-sectional profile of the part feature.

concentricity The condition in which two or more features in any combination have a common axis.

filter An electrical circuit that attenuates the amplitudes of certain undulations of the actual profile.

ideal roundness Ideal roundness is the representation of a planar profile on which all points are equidistant from a center in the plane.

least squares circle (LSC) center The center of a circle from which the sum of the squares of the radial ordinates of the measured polar profile has a minimum value. It is established by mathematical analysis of the profile and generally requires a computer to be practical.

magnification The amount of enlargement in one direction.

maximum inscribed circle (MIC) center The center of largest circle that can be inscribed within the measured polar profile. It is also known as the plug-gage center and is sometimes used for internal diameters.

measured polar profile (polar chart) The measured profile that has been recorded about a center or axis of rotation wherein the central angles of the measured profile features do not differ significantly from those of the circular surface.

measured profile The representation of the actual profile obtained by a particular measurement method.

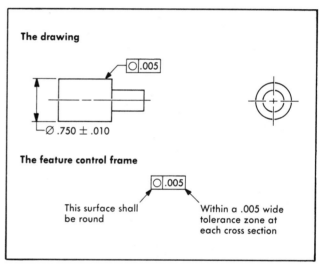

Fig. 4-63 Feature control frame of a circular part.

TABLE 4-2
Typical Causes of Lobing Conditions on Circular Parts

Number of Lobes	Causes
2	Inaccuracy in tooling (elliptical). Part not square in machine. Part not square in measuring machine
3-4	Distortion of part due to clamping in machine or measuring system. Commonly caused by three or four-jaw chuck
5-15	Machining process (centerless grinding produces an odd number of lobes)
>15	Process and material parameters. Common process parameters include vibrations, tool condition, spindle speed, feed rates, and medium to high-frequency chatter

MEASUREMENT OF CIRCULARITY

minimum circumscribed circle (MCC) center The center of smallest circle that will contain the measured profile. It is also known as the ring-gage center and is sometimes used for external diameters.

minimum radial separation (MRS) center The common center of two concentric circles that contain the profile and have a minimum radial difference. It is also known as the center for minimum total indicator reading and zone circles.

nominal profile The intended cross-sectional profile, the extent and shape of which are usually shown and dimensioned on a drawing or descriptive specification.

out-of-roundness (OOR) The radial deviation of the actual profile from ideal roundness.

out-of-roundness value The difference between the largest and smallest radius of a measured profile. The radii are measured from a defined center and the units of measurement are generally inches or millimeters.

pickup The electrical transducer that converts movement of the stylus into electrical signals. It is sometimes referred to as a probe or gage.

preferred center The center from which the out-of-roundness value is determined. It is the minimum radial separation center unless otherwise specified.

stylus The part of the instrument that contacts the part.

undulations The peaks and valleys of a profile.

MEASURING METHODS

The conditions of circularity, external and internal, demand the most attention of any form or shape measurement because this type of geometry comprises the great majority of mechanical form conditions in manufacturing operations. Two primary methods of gaging are currently being used to determine the form trueness and to measure the form irregularities of nominally circular objects. The main difference between these two methods is the datum surface from which the measurement is made. In the first method, points on the surface of the part are used as a datum. This method is commonly referred to as the intrinsic datum method. The second method uses an external member as the datum reference and is called the extrinsic datum method.

Both methods have their particular advantages and limitations. The intrinsic datum method is more widely used, while the extrinsic datum method provides information that, for most applications, is more pertinent to the functionally proper form of the part. The extrinsic datum method is generally recommended by national and international standards.

Intrinsic Datum Method

The measurement of circularity using one of the intrinsic datum methods is extensively used throughout industry. The most commonly used intrinsic datum methods are diametrical measurements, V-block measurements, and bench center measurements. However, it is important to understand that none of these methods will supply information in complete agreement with the standard specifications of circularity. These methods may be of value in comparison tests where functional or performance criteria have been related to geometric conditions based on that particular circular measuring method. Intrinsic datum methods should be regarded as a convenient, low-investment approximation of the true out-of-roundness value.

The necessary equipment for the intrinsic datum method is fairly inexpensive, is adequate for many applications, and is considered standard instrumentation in most manufacturing plants. In addition, the equipment is rugged, simple to use, and provides relatively quick measurements. Measurement of circularity with this equipment, however, is slow when compared to most size determinations.

Diametrical measurements. One of the most common methods of measuring out-of-roundness is by the comparison of diameter measurements made in a common, cross-sectional plane. Measurements are made between two contact points. Two-point measurement methods can only determine the out-of-roundness value when the part is known to have an even number of uniformly spaced and uniformly sized lobes or undulations around its periphery.

When diametrical measurements are used as an indication of out-of-roundness, the lobing condition must be taken into consideration. For parts having an odd number of lobes, the difference in diametrical measurements is generally smaller than the true radial out-of-roundness. The difference will diminish to zero for uniform, symmetrically shaped lobes. Parts having an even lobed surface will produce diametrical out-of-roundness values larger than the true value.

Some of the typical equipment used for diametrical measurements include micrometers, bore gages, air gages, and comparator stands. When using a micrometer, several measurements should be made at each cross section of the part; measurements should also be made at more than one cross section. The maximum and minimum measurements are then compared to see if the part is within specification. Parts that exceed the allotted tolerance limit are nonconforming. However, parts that are within the tolerance limit may also be nonconforming.

V-block measurements. The V-block measurement method is a three-point method suitable for measuring parts with an odd number of lobes. It is not suitable for parts with an even number of lobes because supporting the part in a V-block will conceal the out-of-roundness condition. The part is placed in the vee and then rotated slowly to keep from disturbing the V-block and gage stand while the test indicator tip is in contact with the part (see Fig. 4-64, view a). If the part is truly round with negligible irregularity, the pointer of the indicator will not move. If, however, the part is out-of-round, the irregularities or lobes will displace the plunger of the test indicator as they are passed under it.

For large parts, an inverted arrangement is sometimes used (see Fig. 4-64, view b). The indicator is mounted in a frame that can be moved around the part; the feet of the frame represent the arms of the vee. A similar arrangement can be used to check the circularity of bores (see Fig. 4-64, view c).

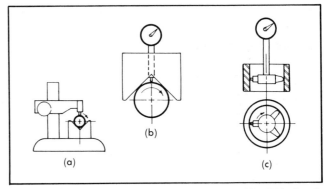

Fig. 4-64 Out-of-roundness can be checked on parts with a V-block and test indicator.

The amount that the pointer on the test indicator moves depends on the height and angular spacing of the lobes as well as the angle of the V-block. The amount of out-of-roundness is actually exaggerated so a conversion factor must be used with the measured value. To determine the angular spacing or the number of lobes on the surface of the parts, it is necessary to employ one of the extrinsic datum methods discussed subsequently. The ideal included angle of the V-block can be determined by the equation:

$$A = 180 - 360/n \qquad (2)$$

where:

A = included angle of the V-block, deg
n = number of lobes

Table 4-3 gives the conversion factor for known odd-number lobes that are checked with the proper V-block. The conversion factor is divided into the measured out-of-roundness value.

Bench center measurements. The bench center method is only suitable for parts that are manufactured with machine centers. In this method, the part to be measured is mounted between the centers of a bench center and then rotated while a test indicator (mechanical or electronic) is in contact with the surface (see Fig. 4-65).

With the bench center measurement method, parts that are within the tolerance specification are acceptable. However, parts that are not within the tolerance specification may also be acceptable because of errors inherent in this method. Out-of-roundness error can be caused by an improper alignment of the bench centers and/or center holes. The angles of the centers

TABLE 4-3
Conversion Factors for Roundness
Measurements Using V-Blocks

Number of Lobes	Included Angle of V-Block	Conversion Factor
3	60°	3.000
5	108°	2.236
7	128° 34′	2.110
9	140°	2.064

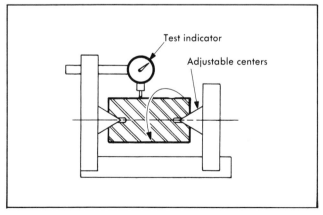

Fig. 4-65 Measurement of out-of-roundness using the bench-center method.

may also be different than the center holes. Other sources of error include out-of-round center holes and centers, inadequate surface condition of centers and center holes, and bowed parts.

Extrinsic Datum Method

In the extrinsic datum method, precision spindle instruments are used to measure part circularity. The part is mounted on either a stationary or rotating table, depending on the instrument design, with an electronic probe (stylus) contacting the surface of the part. When the part or spindle is rotated, the instrument prints an enlarged scale representation of the surface configuration on a polar graph chart. In addition to printing the surface configuration, most precision spindle instruments also print a reference circle for verification.

Measuring circularity with precision spindle instruments supplies a true image of the geometric condition of the part by selective magnification. Magnification rates and suppression of inconsequential features can be varied to enhance the most meaningful aspects of the circularity condition. The image of the part can also be evaluated by different methods of interpretation; the method selected is based on the functional requirements of the part. Continuous tracing around the entire surface in the selected plane minimizes the possibility of disregarding errors that can be missed by point-to-point measurements. In addition, the graphical representations of the circularity conditions are valuable for a thorough analysis and serve as a permanent record.

Polar graph interpretation. The trace produced by the polar graphing instrument is simply a graphical record, suitably magnified, of the displacement of the stylus of the measuring instrument. The out-of-roundness value can be assessed by the differences between the maximum and minimum radial ordinates of the profile measured from a specific center. The four methods by which this center can be located are:

1. Minimum radial separations (MRS).
2. Least squares circle (LSC).
3. Maximum inscribed circle (MIC).
4. Minimum circumscribed circle (MCC).

Minimum radial separation. In the minimum radial separation or minimum zone circles method, two concentric circles are chosen so as to have the least radial separation and yet contain between them, all of the polar trace (see Fig. 4-66, view *a*). The radial separation is the measure of the out-of-roundness value.

The proper location and size of the inscribed and circumscribed circles are most conveniently determined with engraved or printed circles on transparent templates. The radial separation can be noted from the engraved circles directly or measured from auxiliary concentric circles that can be drawn from the center located by the engraved circles.

Trial-and-error methods using a bow compass can also be used to determine the size and location of the boundary circles. However, these methods are generally slower than using transparent templates with engraved circles. Whether transparent templates or trial-and-error methods are used, at least two outer contact points and two inner contact points must occur alternately, but not necessarily consecutively, for one complete profile traverse (see Fig. 4-66, view *a*).

Least squares circle. In the least squares circle method, a theoretical circle is located within the polar profile such that the sum of the squares of the radial ordinates between the circle and the profile is a minimum. The center of this circle is then used to

MEASUREMENT OF CIRCULARITY

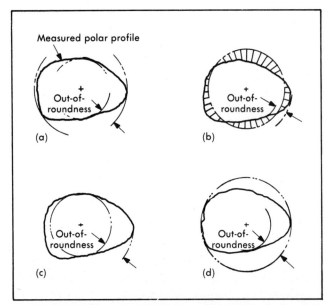

Fig. 4-66 Different methods are used for determining the center of measured profile when measuring out-of-roundness: (a) minimum radial separation, (b) least squares circle, (c) maximum inscribed circle, and (d) minimum circumscribed circle.

draw a circumscribed and inscribed circle on the profile graph (see Fig. 4-66, view *b*). The out-of-roundness value is then the radial separation of these two circles.

The least squares circle (LSC) and its center are unique because there is only one circle that meets the definition. The accuracy of the center and radial zone width depends on the number of ordinates taken. Manual graphical assessment can be tedious and time-consuming, but digital instruments and/or computers can reduce the time and effort required for LSC evaluation.

Maximum inscribed circle. In the maximum inscribed circle method, the profile center is determined by the largest circle that can be fitted inside the profile (see Fig. 4-66, view *c*). The center can be determined by trial-and-error with a bow compass or with engraved circles on a transparent template. The out-of-roundness of the part is the maximum outward departure from the inscribed circle.

Minimum circumscribed circle. In the minimum circumscribed circle method, the profile center is determined by the smallest circle that contains the measured profile (see Fig. 4-66, view *d*). From this center point, an inscribed circle fitted inside the profile is drawn. The out-of-roundness is the maximum inward departure from the circumscribed circle.

Operating parameters. In addition to graph interpretation, the out-of-roundness value is influenced by the instrument response, stylus size and geometry, and stylus force.

Circularity measurement using a precision spindle instrument is based on the coincidence of the master axis with the part axis. The master axis is represented by the axis of rotation of the instrument; the part axis is represented by an imaginary straight line at equal distance from the surface of a basically round part or feature. Before the part surface can be traced with the stylus, the center of the part and the center of the rotational movement producing the reference circle must be coincidental, which includes correcting any angular misalignment between the part axis and the master axis. Most precision spindle instruments

are equipped with provision for automatic centering and automatic axis alignment.

Instrument response. The instrument response, referred to as the cycles per revolution (CPR) response, is the sensitivity of the instrument to surface irregularities. The value of the CPR response should be selected based on the number of radial deviations required to be represented on the polar graph. If all the deviations were represented on the graph, the high-frequency surface irregularities could mask the lobing condition or the form of the profile. To suppress the representation of high-frequency radial deviations, an electrical or computerized signal filter is used. Varying the size, shape, and weight of the stylus as well as the stylus contact force also helps to suppress or filter the high-frequency deviations.

Typical CPR response values are 0, 1.67, 5, 15, 50, 150, 500, and 1500; lower values tend to smooth out the small-scale irregularities. A value of 50 is assumed if a CPR value is not specified. Figure 4-67 shows a polar graph of a part measured at four different CPR values.

Stylus size and geometry. The stylus is in direct contact with the part surface and transmits any surface profile variations to the pickup. For most applications, the tip of the stylus is ball-shaped and 1/16 to 1/8″ (1.6 to 3.2 mm) in diameter. When fine details of the profile are required, the smallest size tip radius should be used along with a high instrument response. Large radius styli should be used on materials softer than 20 R_C to prevent plastic deformation of the surface resulting from the high stylus contact force.

Stylus contact force. The appropriate stylus force to maintain adequate contact with the part surface depends on the hardness, flexibility, and maximum compressive strength of the part material; the rotational speed and mass of the stylus assembly (for rotating stylus instruments); and the stylus tip radius. To minimize surface damage from high compressive stresses, yet maintain a high contact pressure for consistent measured profiles, the maximum stylus force for each nominal

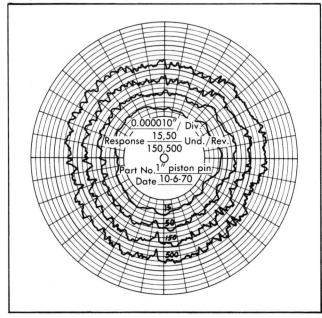

Fig. 4-67 Typical measured profile polar chart with instrument response settings of 0, 15, 50, 150, and 500.

stylus radius should be selected. The recommended stylus force with respect to the stylus radius is given in Table 4-4.

Polar graph magnification. When a single measured polar profile is to be measured for out-of-roundness, the polar graph magnification should be either the largest value available so that the profile is completely contained within the chart boundaries or the lowest value commensurate with the best assessment of the part features or tolerance. At the lowest magnification condition, the distortion arising from various systematic causes will be minimized.

When a series of measured profiles is needed, such as concentricity, taper, or other interrelated measurements, it is advisable to limit all the magnifications to the lowest value available within the series that will accomplish the measurement objectives. By doing so, profile comparisons are facilitated. Increasing the magnification often requires recentering of the part to reduce the profile miscentering distortion.

EQUIPMENT

In addition to micrometers, V-blocks, and indicators, precision spindle instruments are commonly used to measure circularity. The two types of these instruments are: (1) those in which the part rotates while the stylus and pickup remain stationary and (2) those in which the stylus and pickup rotate while the part remains stationary (see Fig. 4-68). Each type has its advantages and is more suitable for certain types of measurement; the choice depends on the measurements to be made and the size and shape of the parts being measured.

The rotary table instruments are generally used to measure circularity on small parts and with the center of rotation close to the part center because large eccentric loads can adversely affect the accuracy of the machine. These machines are also used to measure any relationships relative to the part axis such as concentricity, eccentricity, perpendicularity, parallelism, and coaxiality because changes in the pickup configuration and

TABLE 4-4
Stylus Contact Force with Respect to Stylus Radius

Nominal Stylus Radius, in. (mm)	Maximum Contact Force,* g
0.001** (0.03)	0.5
0.003 (0.08)	2.0
0.010 (0.25)	5.0
0.030 (0.76)	10.0
0.100 (2.50)	20.0

Note: A stylus radius of 0.010″ (0.25 mm) shall be assumed if no radius is specified.

* Steel or harder materials. For materials softer than R_C20, the stylus force should be selected to prevent objectionable plastic deformation of the surface, yet should be high enough to reduce stylus bounce and produce repeatable traces.

** Fine surface irregularities, such as surface roughness, may be penetrated by a stylus of this or smaller radius, which may confuse and make it difficult to interpret the measured profiles.

position do not affect the spindle to the part relationship. Rotating pickup instruments are the most accurate because the load on the spindle bearings is constant; part weight and configuration do not affect accuracy.

Operation

In operation, the stylus of the pickup is brought into contact with a point along the selected surface element of the part and adjusted to a position of zero indication.[16] The rotary displacement movement of the machine is started while the stylus remains in contact with the part surface. An uninterrupted succession of an infinite number of contact points is thus created, describing a complete circle around the surface of the part.

Variations in the distance between the axis of rotation and the contacted points along the surface element cause the stylus to deflect. These deflections produce electrical signals in the

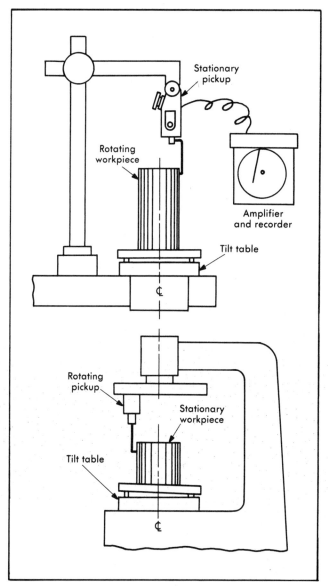

Fig. 4-68 Rotating-workpiece and rotating-pickup types of precision spindle instruments for measuring roundness.

pickup that are electronically amplified at a preset rate and then displayed on a meter or by a recorder. The recorder reproduces the deflections on a polar or linear graph. The distance between the axis of rotation and any contact point on the part surface is considered to represent the radius to the momentarily contacted surface point. The variations of the consecutive radii are the measure of departure from perfect circularity as represented by the displacement path of the stylus.

Computerization

In the 1960s, analog computers began to be applied to roundness measuring systems to evaluate the least squares center (LSC) and out-of-roundness relative to the LSC and concentricity. However, this approach was very limited in its applications and accuracies.

Since the introduction of the microprocessor, small digital computers have been used with precision spindle instruments to evaluate a wide variety of parameters. Some of the parameters that can be measured and evaluated include least squares center, maximum inscribed center, minimum circumscribed center, minimum radial separation, eccentricity, concentricity, total-indicator reading, squareness, and flatness. Three-dimensional pictures of measured parts can also be generated by the computer to provide a true picture of the part.

MEASUREMENT OF ANGLES

Angular dimensions are usually expressed in either degrees and decimal parts of a degree or in degrees, minutes, and seconds. A degree is a 360th part of the circumference of a circle. Each degree is then divided into 60 minutes and each minute into seconds. In technical measurements, angular measurements are also expressed in terms of their trigonometric functions, the sine, cosine, and tangent being the most frequently used.[17]

The wide variety of geometric conditions that are defined in angular units influence the type of angle measuring methods and equipment used for a given application.[18] In addition, angle measuring methods and equipment are influenced by the size and general shape of the part, the location and accessibility of the angular feature to be measured, the expected range of angle variations, and the required sensitivity and accuracy of the measurement.

One of the most widely used general groups of angle measurements is based on comparing the angular conditions of a part or of a feature to an angle of known size. Angular measurements can also be measured directly using an instrument that is equipped with a scale graduated in angular units. The third general group consists of devices that can be rotated in controlled angular units.

INDIRECT MEASUREMENT

In indirect measurements, the angular surface of the part is compared to an angle of known size. The comparison may be done with a fixed gage (described in Chapter 3, "Inspection Equipment and Techniques," of this volume) or with an adjustable-type gage. To determine the magnitude of discrepancy between the master and the part, additional instruments are required.

Adjustable Gages

The main gages used in this group are sine bars and sine plates. A sine bar consists of a hardened steel bar to which two support rolls are attached. The fixed distance between the two rolls is usually 5 or 10″. The sine bar is always used in conjunction with a flat surface and gage blocks.

Angles are generated by placing gage block(s) of known height under one end of the sine bar (see Fig. 4-69). The height

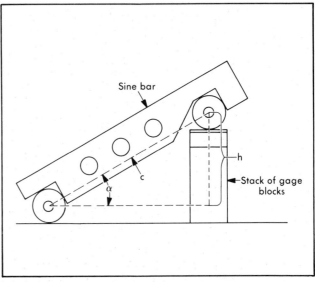

Fig. 4-69 Measuring the angular surface of a part using a sine bar and gage blocks.

of the gage blocks required for a specific angle can be determined by the equation:

$$h = \sin \alpha \times c \qquad (3)$$

where:

h = height of gage block stack, in.
α = angle to be measured, deg
c = length of sine bar between roll centers, in.

Once the angle has been established, the part to be measured is placed on the sloping surface of the sine bar. A height gage with a test indicator is then used to check if the plane of the part's top surface is parallel to the plane of the supporting surface plate. It is generally recommended that sine bars should not be used for checking angles greater than 45° because of the decrease in accuracy resulting from trigonometric relations.

The deviation from basic angle can be determined by the equation:

$$\delta = \tan^{-1}\left(\frac{e}{m}\right) \qquad (4)$$

where:

δ = angular value of deviation, deg
e = measured height difference, in.
m = length of the measured section, in.

Sine plates are wider instruments than sine bars and contain an integral base and tapped holes for the attachment of parts. Their increased width permits placing another sine bar on top to allow the generation of compound angles.

Angle Gage Blocks

Angle gage blocks are comprised of solid blocks having two flat working surfaces that are inclined to each other by a specified angle. The blocks are wrung together to produce the desired angle. Angle blocks are always used in conjunction with flat surfaces.

Once the angle has been established, the part may be placed on the blocks or vice versa. A height gage can then be used to check if the plane of the part's top surface is parallel to the plane of the supporting surface plate. The angle deviation can be determined using Eq. (4).

DIRECT MEASUREMENT

The most commonly used instrument for the direct measurement of angles is the vernier protractor. A typical protractor contains one fixed blade and another blade attached to a rotating turret or dial. The dial is graduated in degrees and a vernier is graduated in five minute increments (one-twelfth of one degree).

Because the protractor measures only the angle between its blades, contact between the blade and the part being measured must be maintained. Intimate contact can be checked by placing a light source behind the protractor. If the contact is good, there will not be any light passing through the blades and the part being measured.

ROTATIONAL MEASUREMENT

Many parts are designed with features arranged in locations that result from the division of a common reference circle.[19] The spacing of these features is determined by associating them with the pertinent radii of the reference circle and specifying the central angles that intercept the radii.

To check the correctness of the angular positions, these features must be presented to the sensing member of a measuring instrument in precise correspondence with the basic values of the specified angle spacings. Common devices for rotating the part by the required angular increments are rotary tables and dividing or indexing heads. The main difference between these two devices is the position of the rotational axis—vertical for the rotary tables and horizontal for the dividing heads. The actual measurement is taken by a mechanical or electronic indicator that references from one of the features at a point contained in a circular path common to all of the features to be inspected.

OPTICAL MEASUREMENT

The three primary methods of optical angle measurement are optical comparators, toolmakers' microscopes, and autocollimators.

Optical Comparators

The optical comparator (projector) displays magnified images on an appropriate viewing screen, with the magnified image used to measure angular relationships. An optical comparator normally contains a high-intensity light source that illuminates the objects either by forming a shadow image on the screen, or by magnifying the object's illuminated surface. An object lens then focuses the enlarged image onto the screen after reflection on one or more mirrors.

To achieve a high accuracy of measurement, the plane of measurement must be perpendicular to the optical axis of the projector. Perpendicularity can be ensured by maintaining sharp focus of all portions of the measured angle. The image should be enlarged to fill as much of the screen as possible. The angle measurement can be made using protractor rings, angular chart gages, or a rotation stage.

Protractor rings. A rotatable protractor ring is used to measure angles by aligning a reference line on the screen with one side of the measured angle and then the other side. Degree increments are usually marked directly on the rings, with associated verniers readable to one minute of arc.

Angular chart gages. In the angular chart gage method, radial lines are ruled directly on the screen or on a separate overscreen chart; the graduations are marked in degrees.

Rotation stage. In the rotation stage method, the part is placed on a rotary table and translational stages. Angular measurement is then made by rotating the part so that the enlarged image is made to coincide with the reference line on the screen. Angular measurements are made with the readout provided with the rotary table.

Toolmakers' Microscope

A toolmakers' microscope can be used in a similar manner to an optical comparator, except that the eye observes the image through a microscope instead of a screen. The eyepiece reticle is used in a similar fashion to the rear projection screen of an optical comparator. Toolmakers' microscopes are normally supplied with a goniometric eyepiece containing a reticle that can be rotated through 360°. Readout of rotation is then made by reading the circular graduations.

Autocollimators and Reflectors

An autocollimator measures, remotely, the angle of a reflector (mirror). Because of the instrument's extreme sensitivity (1/10 second of arc), it is used to measure small angles and as a nulling accessory when employed with angular gage blocks and rotary tables.

The autocollimator is a modified form of telescope that has an illuminated target or reticle located in the focal plane of an objective lens (Fig. 4-70). The illumination emanating from the autocollimator is directed to the mirror that is used to reflect the image back on itself. Any rotation of the mirror by a small angle deflects the beam by twice this angle, which in turn displaces the image of the cross hairs, as observed through the eyepiece. The motion of the image is verified using a standard driven by a micrometer and slide. The micrometer scale is graduated in 0.1 second of arc increments, with the measuring range normally

SCREW THREAD GAGING AND MEASUREMENT

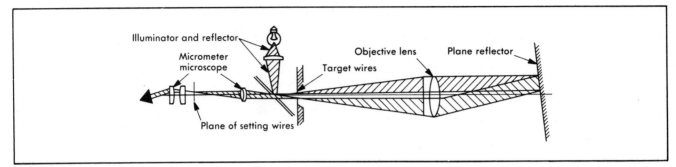

Fig. 4-70 Optical configuration of typical autocollimator.

being 10 minutes of arc. In addition to micrometer readout, electronic readouts are available that operate by photoelectrically sensing the motion of the image of the reticle. In this manner, higher sensitivity and repeatability are realized.

The autocollimator can be used to measure the angle between two surfaces by placing the mirror in contact with the first surface, and then moving it to contact the second surface. The difference between the two readings is the angle between the two surfaces. This measurement is possible only if the two surfaces are adjacent to each other (within the size of the autocollimator apertures). If this angle is larger than the small range of the collimator, then an angular gage block may be added between the mirror and measured surface to bring the

image within the operating range.

An autocollimator is capable of measuring right angles to a high order of accuracy ($\pm 1/2$ second), when used with an accessory right-angle reflector (pentaprism). The prism has the capability to bend the light beam precisely 90° and is thus used as the standard for comparison when checking orthogonal surfaces.

Laser autocollimators are similar in concept to those described above, except that the coherent light source provides a high degree of collimation and brightness. Consequently, alignment may be made rapidly because the beam is visible in full daylight. Laser autocollimators are normally supplied with photoelectric readout for direct reading of angular displacement.

SCREW THREAD GAGING AND MEASUREMENT

Screw threads are important elements of mechanical design with wide and varied applications, particularly for controlled translational motion and for fasteners providing disengageable connections.[20] The dimensional accuracy of screw threads is necessary to ensure the dependable assembly of threaded mating components, the interchangeability of the corresponding threaded parts, the consistent proportional relationship between the imparted rotational and resulting translational movements, and the mechanical strength of the threaded connection.

As is the case with all other mechanical elements, the actual sizes of screw threads on manufactured parts are not exactly identical to the pertinent design sizes. Such deviations may be within acceptable (tolerance) limits or exceed the applicable tolerances. Components with out-of-tolerance screw thread dimensions are considered defective products. For the threads to be acceptable, the dimensions of the different thread characteristics and elements must be held within specific limits. These limits are established in the standards for different thread systems and classes. Complete sets of standards are available for the commonly used thread systems such as unified, metric, acme, buttress, Whitworth, and pipe. Table 4-5 lists the standards available from the American National Standards Institute (ANSI) for these thread systems.

Although not everyone involved in thread measurement needs to become a thread expert, it is important to have a proper understanding of the nomenclature, specifications, and gaging principles to ensure the production and/or acceptance

of dimensionally conforming threaded products. This section describes the different types of gages and instruments used in screw thread measurement, as well as the procedures for measuring the various parameters of product screw threads. For information on producing screw threads, refer to Volume I, *Machining*, of this Handbook series.

THREAD NOMENCLATURE

The terms commonly applied to screw threads may be classified in four general groups: (1) types of screw threads, (2) sizes and fits of mechanical parts in general, (3) geometrical elements of both straight and taper screws, and (4) dimensions of screw threads. The following definitions are limited to those directly associated with the gaging and measurement of screw threads. A more complete listing is contained in ANSI Standard B1.7. The terms relating to screw threads are shown in Figs. 4-71, 4-72, 4-73, 4-74, and 4-75.

Terms Relating to Types of Screw Threads

classes of threads Threads of a given type are distinguished from each other by the amounts of tolerance or tolerance and allowance specified. Various combinations of these tolerances and allowances have been set in tables to form a set of standard classes.

external thread A thread on a cylindrical or conical exterior surface (see Fig. 4-71).

SCREW THREAD GAGING AND MEASUREMENT

internal thread A thread on a cylindrical or conical interior surface (see Fig. 4-71).

multiple-start thread A thread in which the lead is an integral multiple, other than one, of the pitch.

screw thread A screw thread is a ridge, usually of uniform section, and is produced by forming a groove in the form of a helix on the external or internal surface of a cylinder, or in the form of a conical spiral on the external or internal surface of a cone or frustrum of a cone. A screw thread formed on a cylinder is known as a straight or parallel thread, to distinguish it from a taper screw thread that is formed on a cone or frustrum of a cone.

single-start thread A thread having the lead equal to the pitch.

Terms Relating to Size and Fit of Mechanical Parts

allowance The prescribed difference between the design size and the basic size of a thread.

fit The general term used to signify the range of tightness or looseness that results from application of a specific combination of allowances and tolerances in mating parts.

limits of size The applicable maximum and minimum sizes.

maximum material condition (MMC) The condition where a feature of size contains the maximum amount of material within the stated limits of size. For example, the minimum internal thread size and the maximum external thread size (see Fig. 4-72).

TABLE 4-5
Screw Thread Specifications

Standard	Title
ANSI B1.1	Unified Inch Screw Threads (UN and UNR Thread Form)
ANSI B1.3	Screw Thread Gaging Systems for Dimensional Acceptability
ANSI B1.1a	Unified Inch Screw Threads (UN and UNR Thread Form)
ANSI/ASME B1.2	Gages and Gaging for Unified Inch Screw Threads
ANSI B1.12	Class 5 Interference-Fit Thread
ANSI/ASME B1.13M	Metric Screw Threads—M Profile
ANSI/ASME B1.16M	Gages and Gaging Practice for Metric M Screw Threads
ANSI B1.21M	Metric Screw Threads—MJ Profile
ANSI B1.22	Gages and Gaging Practice for "MJ" Series Metric Screw Threads
ANSI B1.5	Acme Screw Threads
ANSI B1.8	Stub Acme Screw Threads
ANSI B1.9	Buttress Inch Screw Threads
ANSI/ASME B1.20.1	Pipe Threads, General Purpose (Inch)
ANSI B1.20.5	Dryseal Pipe Threads (Inch), Gaging for

minimum material condition (least material condition, LMC) The condition where a feature of size contains the least amount of material within the stated limits of size. For example, the maximum internal thread size and the minimum external thread size.

tolerance The total amount that a specific dimension is permitted to vary. The tolerance is the difference between the maximum and minimum limits of size.

Terms Relating to Geometrical Elements of Screw Threads

axis of thread The axis of a thread is coincident with the axis of its pitch cylinder or cone.

basic form of thread The permanent reference profile from which the design forms for both external and internal threads are developed.

crest The surface of the thread that joins the flanks of the thread and is farthest from the cylinder or cone from which the thread projects (see Fig. 4-73). The crest of an external thread is at its major diameter while the crest of an internal thread is at its minor diameter.

flank The flank (or side) of a thread is either surface connecting the crest with the root. The flank-surface intersection with an axial plane is theoretically a straight line.

following flank The following (trailing) flank of a thread is the one that is opposite to the leading flank.

form of thread The form of a thread is its profile in an axial plane for a length of one pitch of the complete thread.

leading flank The flank that, when the thread is about to be assembled with a mating thread, faces the mating thread.

load flank The flank that takes the externally applied axial load in an assembly. The term is used in relation to unified, buttress, square, trapezoidal acme, and stub acme threads.

root The surface of the thread that joins the flanks of adjacent thread forms and is immediately adjacent to the cylinder or cone from which the thread projects (see Fig. 4-73). The root of an external thread is at its minor diameter, while the root of an internal thread is at its major diameter.

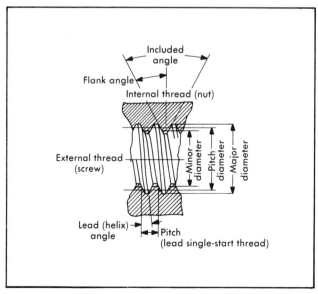

Fig. 4-71 Screw thread terms relating to types and dimensions (single-start thread; lead equal to pitch).

SCREW THREAD GAGING AND MEASUREMENT

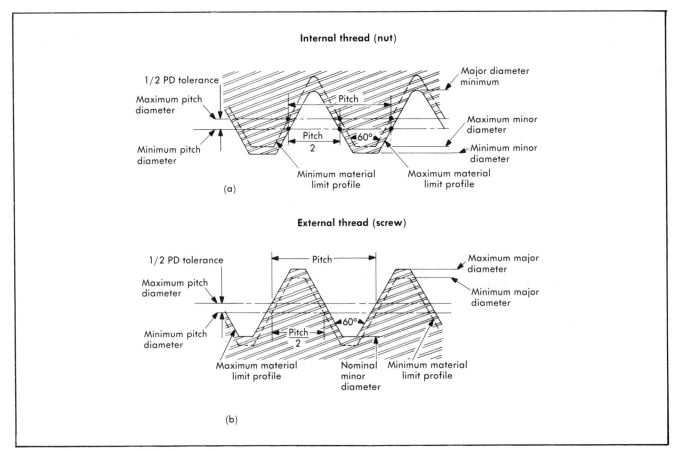

Fig. 4-72 Maximum and minimum material limit profiles for: (a) internal threads and (b) external threads.

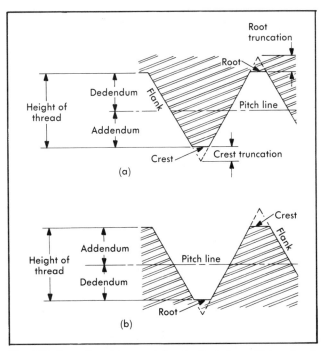

Fig. 4-73 Screw thread terms relating to dimensions of internal and external screw threads: (a) internal threads and (b) external threads.

Terms Relating to Dimensions of Screw Threads

addendum The addendum of an external thread is the radial distance between the major and pitch cylinders or cones, respectively. The addendum of an internal thread is the radial distance between the minor and pitch cylinders or cones, respectively (see Fig. 4-73).

crest truncation The crest truncation of a thread is the radial distance between the sharp crest (crest apex) and the cylinder or cone that would bound the crest (see Fig. 4-73).

dedendum The dedendum of an external thread is the radial distance between the pitch and minor cylinders or cones, respectively. The dedendum of an internal thread is the radial distance between the major and pitch cylinders or cones, respectively (see Fig. 4-73).

flank angle The flank angles are the angles between the individual flanks and the perpendicular to the axis of the thread, measured in an axial plane. A flank angle of a symmetrical thread is commonly termed the half angle of thread.

functional (virtual) diameter The functional diameter (virtual condition per ANSI Y14.5M) of an external or internal thread is the pitch diameter of the enveloping thread of perfect pitch, lead, and flank angles, having full depth of engagement but clear at crests and roots and of a specified length engagement. It may be derived by adding to the pitch diameter in the case of an external thread, or subtracting

SCREW THREAD GAGING AND MEASUREMENT

from the pitch diameter in the case of an internal thread, the cumulative effects of deviations from specified profile, including variations in lead (uniformity of helix) and flank angle over a specified length of engagement. The effects of taper, out-of-roundness, and surface defects may be positive or negative on either external or internal threads. A perfect internal or external GO-thread gage having a pitch diameter equal to that of the specified material limit and having clearance at crest and root is the enveloping thread corresponding to that limit.

height of thread The height (or depth) of thread is the distance measured radially between the major and minor cylinders or cones, respectively.

helix angle On a straight thread, the helix angle is the angle made by the helix of the thread and its relation to the thread axis. On a taper thread, the helix angle at a given axial position is the angle made by the conical spiral of the thread with the axis of the thread. The helix angle is the complement of the lead angle.

included angle The included angle of a thread (or angle of thread) is the angle between the flanks of the thread measured in an axial plane (refer to Fig. 4-71).

lead When a thread part is rotated about its axis with respect to a fixed mating thread, the lead is the axial distance moved by the part in relation to the amount of angular rotation. The basic lead is commonly specified as the distance to be moved in one complete rotation. It is necessary to distinguish measurement of lead from measurements of pitch, as uniformity of pitch measurements do not ensure uniformity of lead (see Fig. 4-74, view b). Variations in either lead or pitch cause the functional diameter of thread to differ from the pitch diameter.

lead angle On a straight thread, the lead angle is the angle made by the helix of the thread at the pitch line with a plane perpendicular to the axis. On a taper thread, the lead angle at a given axial position is the angle made by the conical spiral of the thread, with the plane perpendicular to the axis, at the pitch line.

major diameter On a straight thread, the major diameter is that of the major cylinder. On a taper thread, the major diameter at a given position on the thread axis is that of the major cone at that position (refer to Fig. 4-71).

minor diameter On a straight thread, the minor diameter is that of the minor cylinder. On a taper thread, the minor diameter at a given position on the thread axis is that of the minor cone at that position (refer to Fig. 4-71).

pitch The pitch of a thread having uniform spacing is the distance, measured parallel to its axis, between corresponding points on adjacent thread forms in the same axial plane and on the same side of the axis. Pitch is equal to the lead divided by the number of thread starts (see Fig. 4-74, view a).

pitch cylinder The pitch cylinder is one of such diameter and location of its axis that its surface would pass through a straight thread in such a manner as to make the widths of the thread ridge and the thread groove equal. On a theoretically perfect thread, the widths of each thread ridge and groove are equal to one-half the basic pitch (see Fig. 4-75).

pitch diameter On a straight thread, the pitch diameter is the diameter of the pitch cylinder. On a taper thread, the pitch diameter at a given position on the thread axis is the diameter of the pitch cone at that position. Note that when the crest of a thread is truncated beyond the pitch line, the pitch diameter, pitch cylinder, or pitch cone would be based on a theoretical extension of the thread flanks to a sharp vee at the major and minor diameters.

root truncation The root truncation of a thread is the radial distance between the sharp root (root apex) and the cylinder or cone that would bound the root (refer to Fig. 4-73).

threads per inch The number of threads per inch is the reciprocal of the pitch in inches.

MEASURING EQUIPMENT

A variety of thread gages and gaging equipment is currently being used by industry for the measurement of product screw

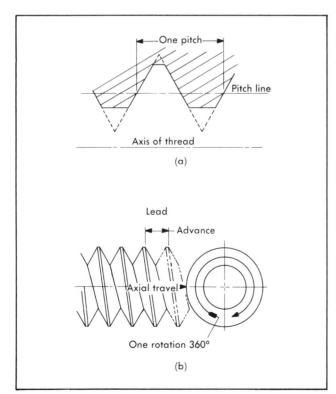

Fig. 4-74 Pitch and lead of a screw thread.

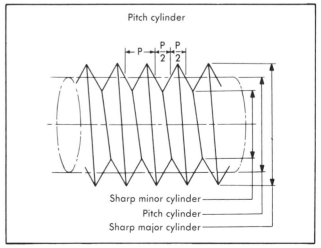

Fig. 4-75 Pitch cylinder.

SCREW THREAD GAGING AND MEASUREMENT

threads. The type of gage or equipment used depends primarily on the thread characteristics being measured and the accuracy required. Some of the commonly used gages are micrometers, fixed-limit gages, and indicating gages. Optical comparators, toolmakers' microscopes, lead testers, and helical-path analyzers are also used and are discussed in greater detail in Chapter 3, "Inspection Equipment and Techniques," of this volume.

Screw Thread Micrometers

Screw thread micrometers have a specially designed spindle and anvil so that externally threaded products can be measured. The end of the spindle of this type of micrometer is pointed to form a 60° cone, and the anvil has the form of a vee to fit over the thread (see Fig. 4-76). The sharp tip of the spindle is ground off to make sure that only the pitch diameter is measured rather than the root or minor diameter.

Flats are ground on the peaks of the vee, and the root of the vee is ground out. The anvil can be fixed in the frame or it can be free to rotate, permitting the anvil to adjust to the helix of the thread being measured. Specially designed anvils and spindles are also available for Whitworth and metric threads.

Screw thread micrometers for measuring American National and unified screw threads are available in sizes ranging from 1 to 6″ in 1″ increments. Micrometers for metric threads are available in sizes 0-25 mm and 25-50 mm.

A screw thread micrometer is generally designed to measure threads within a narrow range of pitches. To cover the whole range of pitches, several micrometers are required. One type of screw thread micrometer has replaceable anvils permitting the micrometer to measure the pitch diameter on the whole range of pitches.

Fixed-Limit Gages

Fixed-limit gages are single-purpose gages in that they are made for a specific thread system, form, size, and class. These gages incorporate the essential functional dimensions of the thread and are used primarily to ensure the ability to assemble the product thread with its mating part.

Fixed-limit gages are generally made from tool steel that has been treated for wear resistance and dimensional stability. For extreme part tolerances or abrasive work conditions, other gage materials, such as carbides and chrome plate, are used. Because solid thread gages are subject to wear, a periodic inspection of these gages should be made; worn gages should be discarded.

The accuracy to which these gages are manufactured is determined by their intended use. Gages that directly check the product thread are made to X tolerances. Gages that are used as reference or master gages are made to W tolerances. The X

tolerances are two times larger than W tolerances. The designated tolerances for unified inch screw threads and metric screw threads are given in ANSI B1.2 and ANSI B1.16M, respectively.

The commonly used fixed-limit gages are thread plug gages and adjustable thread ring gages. Thread snap gages can also be classified as fixed-limit gages although some are adjustable.

Thread plug gages. Working thread plug gages are similar in design to cylindrical plug gages except that they are threaded. They are designed to check internally threaded products. The types of thread systems for which thread plug gages are available include unified, American National, metric, Whitworth, acme, buttress, and pipe. When thread plug gages are manufactured to W tolerances, they are used as reference or master gages for setting adjustable thread ring gages, thread snap gages, and indicating gages.

A typical thread plug gage consists of a handle and one or two thread gaging members (see Fig. 4-77). Depending on the gaging member size, the member can be held in the handle using a threaded collet and bushing design (view *a*), a taperlock design (view *b*), or by a trilock design (view *c*). The threaded collet and bushing design is generally used for gaging members ranging from 0.030 to 0.760″ (0.76 to 19.30 mm); the taperlock design for members from 0.059 to 1.510″ (1.50 to 38.35 mm); and the trilock design for members from 0.760 to 8.010″ (19.30 to 203.45 mm). An annular design is used for gaging members above 8.010″ (203.45 mm).

The two members in a thread plug gage are referred to as the GO and NOT-GO members. The NOT-GO member is sometimes referred to as the HI member. The GO gaging member is generally longer than the NOT-GO member and is used to check the maximum material functional limit of the product thread. The NOT-GO member checks the NOT-GO (HI) functional diameter limit of the threaded product.

Thread ring gages. Thread ring gages are similar in design to cylindrical ring gages except that the internal surface is threaded. They are available in both solid and adjustable or split designs. Minor adjustments of an adjustable thread ring

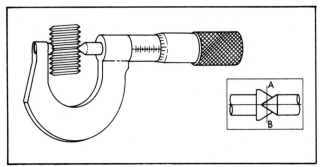

Fig. 4-76 Screw thread micrometer. (*L. S. Starrett*)

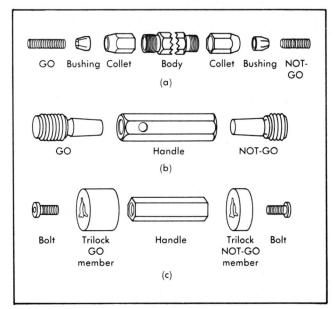

Fig. 4-77 Thread plug gages: (a) threaded collet and bushing design, (b) taperlock design, and (c) trilock design. (*The Van Keuren Co.*)

gage can, at times, be made by qualified shop or inspection personnel. If the user is unsure of the correct procedure and/or does not have the proper truncated setting plug, the ring should be sent to a calibration or gage house for the adjustment.

Thread ring gages are supplied in pairs as GO and NOT-GO gages. The NOT-GO ring is sometimes referred to as a LO ring gage. The GO gage checks the maximum material functional limit of the threaded part. The NOT-GO gage checks the NOT-GO (LO) functional diameter limit of the threaded part and usually has an annular groove machined on the periphery of the ring to differentiate it from the GO ring.

Thread Snap Gages

Thread snap gages have two pair of gaging elements combined in one gage. With proper gaging elements, these gages can check the maximum and minimum material limit of external product screw threads in a single pass. One style of thread snap gage is shown in Fig. 4-78.

The functional or GO portion of the gage may incorporate either functional segments or functional rolls. Rolls rotate when the part is inserted, thus reducing wear. The length of the segments or rolls is approximately equal to the applicational length of engagement of the product thread. The NOT-GO portion of the gage generally contains cone and vee profile rolls.

Snap gages may be held on a stand where the threaded product is presented to the gage, or they can be used as a handheld gage by presenting the gage to the part that may be between centers in a machine. Snap gages are available in sizes from 0.060 to 20″ (1.5 to 500 mm). In most cases snap gages are dedicated to one size or varying classes of a size. In addition, the same gage can be used for checking right and left-hand threads of the same nominal size.

Indicating Thread Gages

Several different designs of indicating thread gages are available for either internal or external screw thread measurement. Indicating thread gages must be set to the proper thread setting using master thread plug or thread ring gages before checking the threaded parts. Indicating thread gages for internal threads are made in sizes for measuring threads from 0.138 to 40″ (3.5 to 1000 mm) diam and for external threads in sizes from 0.06 to 20″ (1.5 to 500 mm) diam. A typical gage consists of a frame, a set of contact elements, and a dial indicator (see Fig. 4-79).

Contact elements are available for the commonly used thread systems and are identified by their nominal size and the number of threads per inch. Most indicating thread gages have either three contact elements spaced at 120° or two contact elements at 180°. Generally one, two, or three of the elements are movable to permit the threaded product to be inserted in the gage. The movable contact(s) is also connected to the dial indicator, which indicates the amount of deviation from a specified standard.

The contact element design determines the thread characteristics and elements that can be measured with a given gage. Because the elements are removable, one gage can be used for the measurement of a variety of thread characteristics, elements, and sizes.

Cone and vee segments or rolls that have thread pitch engagement at the pitch diameter line are used when measuring pitch diameter (minimum material size and limit). They can also be used to measure roundness and taper of the threaded product. Full-form segments or functional rolls can be used to measure the GO functional limit and size as well as roundness. When cone and vee contact elements are used in conjunction with full-form elements, the amount of variation of each individual thread characteristic and element can be determined. This procedure is commonly referred to as differential gaging. The position of the minor (internal threads) or major (external threads) diameter with respect to the pitch diameter, referred to as runout or eccentricity, can also be measured with a combination of plain and threaded contact elements.

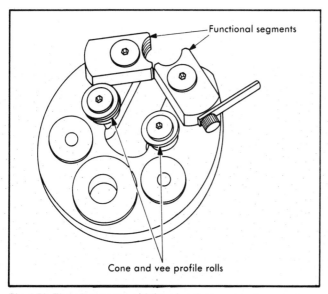

Fig. 4-78 Thread snap gage with functional segments and cone and vee profile rolls. (*The Johnson Gage Co.*)

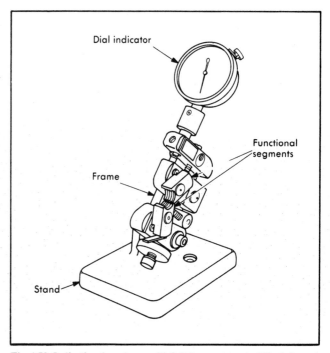

Fig. 4-79 Indicating thread gage with full-form segments. (*The Johnson Gage Co.*)

CHAPTER 4

SCREW THREAD GAGING AND MEASUREMENT

MEASURING METHODS

One of the basic fundamentals of thread gaging is to select gaging that is as consistent as possible with the requirements of the application and threading process. The proper gage selection ensures the highest degree of repeatability and reduces the probability of generating sort, scrap, rework, and selective assembly conditions.

The two primary categories of screw thread inspection are inspection by attributes and inspection by variables. Inspection by attributes involves the use of fixed-limit gages (thread plug, ring, and snap gages) and only provides for a limit check of the functional size (maximum material). Inspection by variables involves the use of comparative type instruments or gages (indicating thread gages, micrometers, precision measuring machines along with wires, optical comparator, and lead tester) to determine the extent of deviations of product threads and their individual elements in addition to determining size relative to maximum and minimum material limits.

Before measuring the threaded screw product to determine if it is dimensionally acceptable, it is advisable to visually inspect the screw threads using a magnifying glass. Some of the items to look for are dirt, chips, splinters, malformed threads, or a drunken helix. If these items are present and a fixed-limit gage is used, undue wear will occur resulting in a reduction of gage life. It is also advisable to check the thread count or pitch measurement using a rule or screw-pitch gage.

Method Selection

In the past there has been confusion over the acceptability of product screw threads. Much of the confusion has been due to the means by which federal and commercial standards have defined thread acceptability. In earlier standards, thread acceptability was based on the type of gage used for inspection rather than the actual dimensions. Recently, ANSI has developed Standard B1.3, "Screw Thread Gaging Systems for Dimensional Acceptability."[21] This presents screw thread gages and measuring equipment suitable for determining the acceptability of UN, UNR, and UNJ screw threads on externally and internally threaded products. It also establishes the criteria for screw thread acceptance when a specified gaging system is used.

Unfortunately thread standards define the maximum material functional limit (virtual condition) geometry and then allow deviations. However, the geometry of the minimum material condition is of greatest concern to the designer because failure is most likely to occur if perfect form is not assessed.

Tables 4-6 and 4-7 (see pages 4-42 and 4-44) list the gages, gaging elements, and measuring equipment that can be used in the measurement of screw threads on external and internal products, respectively. The horizontal column contains the various screw thread dimensions and the vertical column contains the gages or equipment currently being used to gage or measure product screw thread dimensions. The horizontal column is also subdivided, where appropriate, into functional limit and size columns. Functional limit refers to attributes inspection and is a qualitative assessment, which only determines if a characteristic is in conformance. Functional size refers to variables inspection and is a quantitative and qualitative assessment. The assessment is then compared with tabled values to determine if the characteristic is in conformance. The type of gage or measuring equipment that could be used to determine a specific screw thread characteristic is designated by a black dot in the body of the appropriate table.

Three levels (systems) of dimensional conformance for external and internal product screw threads are identified in ANSI B1.3 as System 21, System 22, and System 23. The difference between these systems is the level of inspection required to determine dimensional conformance. Although these three levels of dimensional conformance exist, different gages or measuring equipment are not always required for each level.

System 21 provides for interchangeable assembly with functional size control at the maximum material limits within the length of standard gaging elements. It also controls the characteristics identified as HI (internal) and LO (external) functional diameters.

System 22 provides for interchangeable assembly with functional size control at the maximum material limits within the length of standard gaging elements and also control of the minimum material size limits over the length of the full thread. Other thread characteristics such as lead, flank angle, taper, and roundness variations are confined within these material limits; however, control of their magnitude is not specified.

System 23 provides for interchangeable assembly with functional size control at the maximum material limits within the length of standard gaging elements. It also controls the minimum material size limits over the length of the full thread. The magnitude of the other thread characteristics such as lead, flank angle, taper, and roundness are further controlled within these limits.

The screw thread of a threaded product is considered acceptable when each of the thread characteristics specified in the designated gaging system are found acceptable. The gaging system used to inspect the screw thread product per ANSI B1.3 must be specified in addition to thread size designation and thread class in the product standard, procurement drawing, or purchase inquiry and order. Thread acceptability requirements may be specified by a general note on the drawing or procurement document or by showing the system number (21, 22, or 23) in parentheses following the thread tolerance class designation.

Tables 4-8 and 4-9 (see pages 4-46 and 4-47) list the dimensions that must be inspected to determine thread acceptability by the different gaging systems along with the gages and gaging equipment that can be used. The numbers in the attributes and variables columns correspond to the numbers in the thread gages and measuring equipment column of Tables 4-6 and 4-7. Gages and gaging equipment are manufactured for various thread types, sizes, and classes.

Micrometer Measurements

A screw thread micrometer with modified pitch line contacts can be used to measure the minimum material pitch diameter limit and size of an external screw thread. The screw thread micrometer can also be used to check roundness and taper of the pitch cylinder.

The zero setting of a screw thread micrometer capable of measuring 0-1" or 0-25 mm is achieved by establishing direct contact between the spindle cone and anvil vee. A checking standard is usually supplied for larger capacity micrometers. The pitch diameter is represented by the reading on the micrometer sleeve and thimble when the spindle cone and anvil vee are in contact with the thread.

When measuring the pitch diameter of threaded products with a screw thread micrometer, small errors in measurement are sometimes introduced. The errors often result from a slight variation of the anvil position on the thread because the anvil is used to measure a range of pitches. To compensate for this error, it is recommended that the pitch diameter of a known standard plug gage be measured and the difference noted. The difference between the measured value and the known value should then be added or subtracted from the values obtained for the threaded products.

Measurement Over Wires

The pitch diameter of an externally threaded product can be measured using accurately finished and hardened steel wires along with a suitable measuring device. Generally, three wires are used, but two wires are used when measuring the pitch diameter of taper pipe threads. Measuring the pitch diameter over wires is commonly used in checking the accuracy of threaded plug gages and other precision screw threads. It is not normally used to check parts in ordinary manufacturing practice because thread gages require less time and are preferable for shop measurements. The pitch diameter of internal screw threads can also be measured. For this application, three balls are used instead of wires as contact elements along with a measuring machine that has special ball-holding gaging arms.

When measuring screw threads by the three-wire method, two of the wires are placed in the thread groove on one side and one wire is diametrically opposed (see Fig. 4-80). The measurement over the wires is then made using a micrometer or other length measuring instrument. The accuracy of the pitch diameter measurement depends on the measuring instrument, the wire diameter, and the contact force.

To measure the pitch diameter of a threaded product to an accuracy of 0.0001" (0.003 mm) requires strict adherence to the following:

- The best-sized wires shall comply with the specifications listed for wires in ANSI B1.2.
- The diameter of the wires must be known to within 0.00002" (0.0005 mm).
- The measurement over the wires should be made with a measuring instrument that has flat, parallel contacts and reads directly to 0.00001" (0.0003 mm).
- The measuring instrument should have a means for directly adjusting the measuring or contact force for the various values specified.
- The wires should be free to assume their positions in the thread grooves without restraint. Holding wires in position with elastic bands can introduce error.

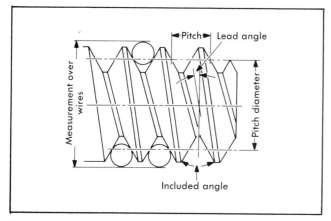

Fig. 4-80 Measuring the pitch diameter of an external thread using the three-wire method. (*The Van Keuren Co.*)

- The measured value should be given to five decimal places to ensure accurate values for pitch diameter measurement.
- Measurements should be made at 68° F (20°C).

Wire size. A set of wires consists of three wires having a hardness equivalent to a Knoop indentation number of 630 and a surface finish better than 2 μin. (50 μm) arithmetic average. The best size of wire to use is the diameter that will contact the thread flanks at the pitch line. The best-sized wire is used because the measurements of pitch diameter are least affected by errors that may be present in the flank angle of the thread.

The best-sized wire for most types of screw threads, assuming lead angle does not exceed 5°, can be approximated using the equation:

$$w = 0.5p \times \sec \alpha \qquad (5)$$

where:

w = diameter of wire, in. (mm)
p = pitch of the thread, in. (mm)
α = one half of the included angle of the thread, deg

For threads with a 60° included angle (unified and metric), Eq. (5) becomes:

$$w = 0.57735p \qquad (6)$$

For threads with a 29° included angle (acme), Eq. (5) becomes:

$$w = 0.51645p \qquad (7)$$

The best-sized wire diameter for American National buttress threads (ANSI B1.9) can be approximated using the equation:

$$w = 0.54147p \qquad (8)$$

If it becomes necessary to measure the pitch diameter with wires other than the best size, the following limitations should be adhered to:

- The minimum wire size is limited to the diameter that permits the wire to project above the crest of the thread. Care should be taken that the wire does not bottom out on the root of the thread and give an erroneous reading.
- The maximum wire size is limited to the diameter that permits the wire to rest on the flanks of the thread just below the crest.

The diameters of the best-sized, maximum, and minimum wires for unified threads are given in Table 4-10 (see page 4-48).

Measuring force. When measuring the pitch diameter of screw threads or screw thread gages by the three-wire method, variations in contact force will result in different measurement readings. The force used should be sufficient to align the wires in the thread grooves or gage without deforming the wire or threads. In general, the measuring force is dependent on the thread type and pitch as given in Table 4-11 (see page 4-48).

Pitch diameter equations. The equations in Table 4-12 (see page 4-49) can be used for computing the pitch diameter from the measurement over wires of different types of screw threads having lead angles from 0 to 5°. It is important to note that these equations neglect the effect of lead angle, thereby giving results that are slightly larger than the true condition. If the lead angles are large enough to decidedly affect the result, as in the case of multiple threads, an equation that compensates for lead angle should be used.[22, 23]

SCREW THREAD GAGING AND MEASUREMENT

TABLE 4-6
Screw Thread Gages and Equipment for External Product Thread Characteristics

Thread Gages and Measuring Equipment	Maximum Material GO Func. Limit A₁	Maximum Material GO Func. Size A₂	LO Functional Diameter Func. Limit B₁	LO Functional Diameter Func. Size B₂	Minimum Material Pitch Diameter Limit C₁	Minimum Material Pitch Diameter Size C₂	Minimum Material Thread Groove Diameter Limit D₁	Minimum Material Thread Groove Diameter Size D₂
1. Threaded rings (ANSI B47.1 split or solid): 1.1 GO	•							
1.2 LO			•					
2. Thread snap gages: 2.1 GO segments	•							
2.2 LO segments—two pitches approximately			•					
2.3 GO rolls	•							
2.4 LO rolls—two pitches approximately			•					
2.5 Minimum material—pitch diameter type—cone and vee					•			
2.6 Minimum material—thread groove diameter type—cone only							•	
3. Plain diameter gages: 3.1 Maximum plain cylindrical ring for major diameter								
3.2 Major diameter snap type								
3.3 Minor diameter snap type								
3.4 Maximum/minimum major diameter snap type								
3.5 Maximum/minimum minor diameter snap type								
4. Indicating thread gages having either two contacts each at 180° or three contacts each at 120°: 4.1 GO segments	•	•	•	•				
4.2 LO segments—two pitches approximately			•	•				
4.3 GO rolls	•	•	•	•				
4.4 LO rolls—two pitches approximately			•	•				
4.5 Minimum material—pitch diameter type—cone and vee					•	•		
4.6 Minimum material—thread groove diameter type—cone only							•	•
4.7 Major diameter/pitch diameter eccentricity gage								
4.8 Differential segment or roll**								
5. Indicating plain diameter gages: 5.1 Major diameter type								
5.2 Minor diameter type								
6. Pitch micrometer with standard contacts (approximately LO profile) cone and vee			•	•				
7. Pitch micrometer with modified contacts (approximately P.D. contact) cone and vee					•	•		
8. Thread measuring wires with suitable measuring means							•	•
9. Optical comparator/toolmakers' microscope with suitable fixturing					•	•		
10. Profile tracing equipment with suitable fixturing								
11. Lead measuring machine with suitable fixturing								
12. Helical path attachment used with GO type indicating gages								
13. Helical path analyzer								
14. Plain micrometer/calipers—modified as required								
15. Surface measuring equipment								
16. Roundness equipment								

 * Maximum minor diameter limit is acceptable when product passes GO gage.
** GO profile for one pitch in length used in combination with a GO indicating gage to yield a diameter equivalent for deviation in lead including uniformity of helix; and a minimum material indicating gage to yield a diameter equivalent for deviation in flank angle.

SCREW THREAD GAGING AND MEASUREMENT

TABLE 4-6—Continued

Oval 180° Limit E_1	Oval 180° Size E_2	Multilobe 120° Limit F_1	Multilobe 120° Size F_2	Taper of Pitch Cylinder Limit G_1	Taper of Pitch Cylinder Size G_2	Lead Including Helix Deviation H	Flank Angle Deviation I	Major Diameter Limit J_1	Major Diameter Size J_2	Minor Diameter Limit K_1	Minor Diameter Size K_2	Root Radius L	Diameter Runout Major to Pitch M	Surface Texture N
										*				
•										*				
•				•										
•										*				
•				•										
•				•										
•				•										
								•						
								•						
										•				
								•						
										•				
•	•	•	•							*				
•	•	•	•	•	•									
•	•	•	•							*				
•	•	•	•	•	•									
•	•	•	•	•	•									
•	•	•	•	•	•									
													•	
•	•	•	•	•	•	•	•							
								•	•					
										•	•			
•	•			•	•									
•	•			•	•									
•	•			•	•									
•	•	•	•			•	•	•	•	•	•	•	•	
							•							•
						•								
						•								
						•								
								•	•					
														•
•	•	•	•											

(ANSI)

SCREW THREAD GAGING AND MEASUREMENT

TABLE 4-7
Screw Thread Gages and Equipment for Internal Product Thread Characteristics

Thread Gages and Measuring Equipment	Maximum Material — GO — Func. Limit A_1	Func. Size A_2	HI Functional Diameter — Func. Limit B_1	Func. Size B_2	Minimum Material — Pitch Diameter — Limit C_1	Size C_2	Thread Groove Diameter — Limit D_1	Size D_2
1. Threaded plugs (ANSI B47.1):								
1.1 GO	•							
1.2 HI			•					
1.3 Full-form gage GO plug (UNJ only)	•							
2. Thread snap gages:								
2.1 GO segments	•							
2.2 HI segments—two pitches approximately			•					
2.3 GO rolls	•							
2.4 HI rolls—two pitches approximately			•					
2.5 Minimum material—pitch diameter type—cone and vee					•			
2.6 Minimum material—thread groove diameter type—cone only							•	
3. Plain diameter gages:								
3.1 Minimum plain cylindrical plug for minor diameter								
3.2 Major diameter snap type								
3.3 Minor diameter snap type								
3.4 Maximum/minimum major diameter snap type								
3.5 Maximum/minimum minor diameter snap type								
4. Indicating thread gages having either two contacts each at 180° or three contacts each at 120°:								
4.1 GO segments	•	•						
4.2 HI segments—two pitches approximately			•	•				
4.3 GO rolls	•	•						
4.4 HI rolls—two pitches approximately			•	•				
4.5 Minimum material—pitch diameter type—cone and vee					•	•		
4.6 Minimum material—thread groove diameter type—cone only							•	•
4.7 Minor diameter/pitch diameter runout gage								
4.8 Differential segment or roll**								
5. Indicating plain diameter gages:								
5.1 Major diameter type								
5.2 Minor diameter type								
6. Pitch micrometer with standard contacts (approximately HI profile) cone and vee			•	•				
7. Pitch micrometer with modified contacts (approximately P.D. contact) cone and vee					•	•		
8. Thread measuring balls with suitable measuring means							•	•
9. Optical comparator/toolmakers' microscope with suitable fixturing and cast replica					•	•		
10. Profile tracing equipment with suitable fixturing								
11. Lead measuring machine with suitable fixturing								
12. Helical path analyzer								
13. Plain micrometer/calipers—modified as required								
14. Surface measuring equipment								
15. Roundness equipment								

* Minimum major diameter limit is acceptable when product passes GO gage.
** GO profile for one pitch in length used in combination with a GO indicating gage to yield a diameter equivalent for deviation in lead including uniformity of helix; and a minimum material indicating gage to yield a diameter equivalent for deviation in flank angle.

SCREW THREAD GAGING AND MEASUREMENT

TABLE 4-7—Continued

Thread Characteristics														
Roundness of Pitch Cylinder				Taper of Pitch Cylinder		Lead Including Helix Variation	Flank Angle Variation	Major Diameter		Minor Diameter		Root Radius	Diameter Runout Minor to Pitch	Surface Texture
Oval 180°		Multilobe 120°												
Limit	Size	Limit	Size	Limit	Size			Limit	Size	Limit	Size			
E₁	E₂	F₁	F₂	G₁	G₂	H	I	J₁	J₂	K₁	K₂	L	M	N
								*						
								*		•				
•								*						
•				•										
•								*						
•				•										
•				•										
•				•										
										•				
								•						
										•				
								•						
										•				
•	•	•	•					*						
•	•	•	•	•	•									
•	•	•	•					*						
•	•	•	•	•	•									
•	•	•	•	•	•									
•	•	•	•	•	•									
													•	
•	•	•	•	•	•	•	•							
								•	•					
										•	•			
•	•			•	•									
•	•			•	•									
•	•			•	•									
						•	•	•				•		
							•						•	•
						•								
						•								
								•	•	•	•			
														•
•	•	•	•											

(ANSI)

SCREW THREAD GAGING AND MEASUREMENT

TABLE 4-8
Gaging Systems for External Threads

System	Dimensions Inspected	Applicable Thread Gages and Measuring Equipment			
		Attributes/Fixed Limit		Variables/Indicating	
		Control	Column	Control	Column
	For dimension/gage combinations to be used, refer to Table 4-6				
21	GO maximum material	1.1, 2.1, 2.3, 4.1, 4.3	A1	4.1, 4.3	A2
	LO functional diameter	1.2, 2.2, 2.4, 4.1, 4.2, 4.3, 4.4, 6	B1	4.1, 4.2, 4.3, 4.4, 6	B2
	Major diameter	3.1, 3.2, 3.4, 5.1, 14	J1	5.1, 14	J2
22	GO maximum material	1.1, 2.1, 2.3, 4.1, 4.3	A1	4.1, 4.3	A2
	Minimum material: Pitch diameter	2.5, 4.5, 7	C1	4.5, 7	C2
	or Thread groove diameter	2.6, 4.6, 8	D1	4.6, 8	D2
	LO functional diameter combined with mandatory examination of:	1.2, 2.2, 2.4, 4.1, 4.2, 4.3, 4.4, 6	B1	4.1, 4.2, 4.3, 4.4, 6	B2
	or Lead (including helix) and			4.8, 9, 11, 12, 13	H
	Flank angle over the length of full thread			4.8, 9, 10	I
	Major diameter	3.1, 3.2, 3.4, 5.1, 14	J1	5.1, 14	J2
	Minor diameter (UNJ only)	3.3, 3.5, 5.2, 9	K1	5.2, 9	K2
	Root profile (UNJ only)			9, 10	L
23	GO maximum material	1.1, 2.1, 2.3, 4.1, 4.3	A1	4.1, 4.3	A2
	Minimum material: Pitch diameter	2.5, 4.5, 7	C1	4.5, 7	C2
	or Thread groove diameter	2.6, 4.6, 8	D1	4.6, 8	D2
	Major diameter	3.1, 3.2, 3.4, 5.1, 14	J1	5.1, 14	J2
	Minor diameter (UNJ only)	3.3, 3.5, 5.2, 9	K1	5.2, 9	K2
	Root profile (UNJ only)			9, 10	L
	Roundness of pitch cylinder: Oval 180°	2.1, 2.2, 2.3, 2.4, 2.5, 2.6, 4.1, 4.2, 4.3, 4.4, 4.5, 4.6, 4.8, 6, 7, 8, 9, 16	E1	4.1, 4.2, 4.3, 4.4, 4.5, 4.6, 4.8, 6, 7, 8, 9, 16	E2
	Multilobe 120°	4.1, 4.2, 4.3, 4.4, 4.5, 4.6, 4.8, 9, 16	F1	4.1, 4.2, 4.3, 4.4, 4.5, 4.6, 4.8, 9, 16	F2
	Taper of pitch cylinder	2.2, 2.4, 2.5, 2.6, 4.2, 4.4, 4.5, 4.6, 4.8, 6, 7, 8	G1	4.2, 4.4, 4.5, 4.6, 4.8, 6, 7, 8	G2
	Lead including helix deviation			4.8, 9, 11, 12, 13	H
	Flank angle deviation			4.8, 9, 10	I
	Major/pitch diameters			4.7	M
	Surface texture			10, 15	N

(ANSI)

SCREW THREAD GAGING AND MEASUREMENT

TABLE 4-9
Gaging Systems for Internal Threads

System	Dimensions Inspected	Attributes/Fixed Limit Control	Column	Variables/Indicating Control	Column
	For dimension/gage combinations to be used, refer to Table 4-7				
21	GO maximum material	1.1, 1.3, 2.1, 2.3, 4.1, 4.3	A1	4.1, 4.3	A2
	HI functional diameter	1.2, 2.2, 2.4, 4.2, 4.4, 6	B1	4.2, 4.4, 6	B2
	Minor diameter	1.3, 3.1, 3.3, 3.5, 5.2, 13	K1	5.2, 13	K2
22	GO maximum material	1.1, 1.3, 2.1, 2.3, 4.1, 4.3	A1	4.1, 4.3	A2
	Minimum material: Direct method: Pitch diameter	2.5, 4.5, 7	C1	4.5, 7	C2
	or Thread groove diameter	2.6, 4.6, 8	D1	4.6, 8	D2
	Indirect method: HI functional diameter combined with control of:	1.2, 2.2, 2.4, 4.2, 4.4, 6	B1	4.2, 4.4, 6	B2
	Lead (including helix)			4.8, 9, 11, 12	H
	Flank angle			4.8, 9, 10	I
		1.3, 3.1, 3.3, 3.5, 5.2, 13	K1	5.2, 13	K2
	Roundness of pitch cylinder: Oval 180°	2.1, 2.2, 2.3, 2.4, 2.5, 2.6, 4.1, 4.2, 4.3, 4.4, 4.5, 4.6, 4.8, 6, 7, 8, 15	E1	4.1, 4.2, 4.3, 4.4, 4.5, 4.6, 4.8, 6, 7, 8, 15	E2
	Multilobe 120°	4.1, 4.2, 4.3, 4.4, 4.5, 4.6, 4.8, 15	F1	4.1, 4.2, 4.3, 4.4, 4.5, 4.6, 4.8, 15	F2
	Taper of pitch cylinder	2.2, 2.4, 2.5, 2.6, 4.2, 4.4, 4.5, 4.6, 4.8, 6, 7, 8	G1	4.2, 4.4, 4.5, 4.6, 4.8, 6, 7, 8	G2
23	GO maximum material	1.1, 1.3, 2.1, 2.3, 4.1, 4.3	A1	4.1, 4.3	
	Minimum material: Pitch diameter	2.5, 4.5, 7	C1	4.5, 7	C2
	or Thread groove diameter	2.6, 4.6, 8	D1	4.6, 8	D2
	Major diameter	1.3, 3.1, 3.3, 3.5, 5.2, 13	K1	5.2, 13	K2
	Roundness of pitch cylinder: Oval 180°	2.1, 2.2, 2.3, 2.4, 2.5, 2.6, 4.1, 4.2, 4.3, 4.4, 4.5, 4.6, 4.8, 6, 7, 8, 15	E1	4.1, 4.2, 4.3, 4.4, 4.5, 4.6, 4.8, 6, 7, 8, 15	E2
	Multilobe 120°	4.1, 4.2, 4.3, 4.4, 4.5, 4.6, 4.8, 15	F1	4.1, 4.2, 4.3, 4.4, 4.5, 4.6, 4.8, 15	F2
	Taper of pitch cylinder	2.2, 2.4, 2.5, 2.6, 4.2, 4.4, 4.5, 4.6, 4.8, 6, 7, 8	G1	4.2, 4.4, 4.5, 4.6, 4.8, 6, 7, 8	G2
	Lead including helix deviation			4.8, 9, 11, 12	H
	Flank angle deviation			4.8, 9, 10	I
	Major/pitch diameters runout			4.7	M
	Surface texture			10, 14	N

(ANSI)

SCREW THREAD GAGING AND MEASUREMENT

TABLE 4-10
Wire Sizes and Constants, Unified Threads

Threads per Inch, n	Pitch, in. $p = \dfrac{1}{n}$	$\dfrac{\text{Pitch}}{2}$, in. $\dfrac{p}{2} = \dfrac{1}{2n}$	Depth of V-Thread, in. $\dfrac{\cot 30°}{2n}$	Wire Sizes,* in. Best, 0.577350p	Maximum, 1.010363p	Minimum, 0.505182p
80	0.012500	0.00625	0.010825	0.00722	0.01263	0.00631
72	0.013889	0.00694	0.012028	0.00802	0.01403	0.00702
64	0.015625	0.00781	0.013532	0.00902	0.01579	0.00789
56	0.017857	0.00893	0.015465	0.01031	0.01804	0.00902
48	0.020833	0.01042	0.018042	0.01203	0.02105	0.01052
44	0.022727	0.01136	0.019682	0.01312	0.02296	0.01148
40	0.025000	0.01250	0.021651	0.01443	0.02526	0.01263
36	0.027778	0.01389	0.024056	0.01604	0.02807	0.01403
32	0.031250	0.01562	0.027063	0.01804	0.03157	0.01579
28	0.035714	0.01786	0.030929	0.02062	0.03608	0.01804
24	0.041667	0.02083	0.036084	0.02406	0.04210	0.02105
20	0.050000	0.02500	0.043301	0.02887	0.05052	0.02526
18	0.055556	0.02778	0.048113	0.03208	0.05613	0.02807
16	0.062500	0.03125	0.054127	0.03608	0.06315	0.03157
14	0.071429	0.03571	0.061859	0.04124	0.07217	0.03608
13	0.076923	0.03846	0.066617	0.04441	0.07772	0.03886
12	0.083333	0.04167	0.072169	0.04811	0.08420	0.04210
11	0.090909	0.04545	0.078730	0.05249	0.09185	0.04593
10	0.100000	0.05000	0.086603	0.05774	0.10104	0.05052
9	0.111111	0.05556	0.096225	0.06415	0.11226	0.05613
8	0.125000	0.06250	0.108253	0.07217	0.12630	0.06315
7	0.142857	0.07143	0.123718	0.08248	0.14434	0.07217
6	0.166667	0.08333	0.144338	0.09623	0.16839	0.08420
5	0.200000	0.10000	0.173205	0.11547	0.20207	0.10104
4 1/2	0.222222	0.11111	0.192450	0.12830	0.22453	0.11226
4	0.250000	0.12500	0.216506	0.14434	0.25259	0.12630

* These wire sizes are based on zero lead angle. Also maximum and minimum sizes are based on a width of flat with the crest equal to 1/8 x p. The use of wires of either extreme size is to be avoided.

TABLE 4-11
Measuring Force

Type of Thread	Threads per Inch	Pitch, in. (mm)	Recommended Force, lb (N)
60°	20 or less	0.05 (1.25) or larger	2 1/2 (11)
	Above 20-40	0.025-0.05 (0.64-1.27)	1 (4.4)
	Above 40-80	0.013-0.025 (0.32-0.64)	1/2 (2.2)
	Above 80-140	0.007-0.013 (0.18-0.32)	4 oz (1.1)
	Above 140 or more	0.007 (0.18) or smaller	2 oz (0.5)
Acme	Less than 8	0.125 or larger	2 1/2 (11)
	8 and greater	0.125 or smaller	1 (4.4)
Buttress	---	---	2 1/2 (11)

SCREW THREAD GAGING AND MEASUREMENT

TABLE 4-12
Equations for Calculating Pitch Diameter

Thread	Equation*	
Unified, national, metric, and straight pipe (60° included angle)	$E = M + 0.86603p - 3w$	(9)
Acme (29° included angle)	$E = M + 1.933357p - 4.9939w$	(10)
Buttress (general)	$E = M + \left[\dfrac{P}{\tan a + \tan (A - a)} \right] - \left[1 + \cos \left(\dfrac{A}{2} - a \right) \times \csc \dfrac{A}{2} \right] w$	(11)
Buttress (7°/45° single start)	$E = M + 0.890643p - 3.156891w$	(12)

where:
E = pitch diameter, in. (mm)
M = measurement over the wires, in. (mm)
p = pitch of the thread, in. (mm)
w = diameter of wire, in. (mm)
A = included angle of thread and thread groove, deg
a = angle of front face or load-resisting side, deg

* For screw threads having lead angles from 0 to 5°.

The equations in Table 4-12 are arranged to calculate the pitch diameter value when the measurement over the wires is known. This equation arrangement is useful for determining the pitch diameter of an existing thread gage or other screw thread in connection with inspection work. The equations can also be arranged to calculate the measurement over the wires based on a specified pitch diameter. This arrangement is useful in the shop or toolroom when cutting or grinding new threads because the pitch diameter is generally specified on the drawing.

Taper pipe threads. The pitch diameter of taper pipe threads can be measured using two wires as well as three wires. A two-station indicating thread gage can also be used to measure the pitch diameter of taper pipe threads. The two-wire method is more accurate than the three-wire method because it measures the actual taper of the thread. The two-wire method also simplifies the calculations.

When measuring the pitch diameter, it is necessary to locate one measuring wire at a definite position on the taper. This position may be at any convenient length, L, from the end of the thread (see Fig. 4-81).

A known position can be located with a 60° gage block accessory point as shown in Fig. 4-81. A combination of gage blocks is put together such that the cone is at a known distance above a surface plate. The threaded gage is moved into contact with the cone point and rotated until the cone point excludes light on both sides of the thread. A mark is then placed on the side of the next thread with a soft lead pencil, prussian blue dye, or similar marking device.

Two-wire method. In the two-wire method, one of the wires is located at a known distance from the end of the thread. This wire is referred to as the fixed wire. The second wire is placed opposite the first wire a half thread distance toward the small end of the taper as shown in position A of Fig. 4-82 and the measurement is recorded. Another measurement is made with

the second wire opposite the first wire a half thread distance toward the large end of the taper, location B of Fig. 4-83.

The pitch diameter of a 60° included angle, taper thread gage, having a lead angle of less than 5° and a taper of 0.0625 in./in. (mm/mm), can be calculated using the equation:

$$E = M_A - (3.00049w - 0.86603p) \qquad (13)$$

where:
E = pitch diameter, in. (mm)
M_A = average of the two measurements over wires, in. (mm)
w = diameter of wire, in. (mm)
p = pitch of the thread, in. (mm)

The actual pitch diameter is the average of the two measurements. The theoretical pitch diameter at any other point on the threaded product is obtained by multiplying the distance parallel to the axis of the thread by the taper and then adding the product to or subtracting it from the measured pitch diameter.

Three-wire method. In the three-wire method one of the wires is placed at a known distance from the end. The other two

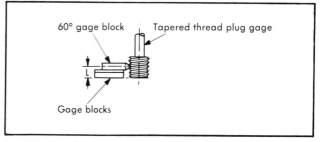

Fig. 4-81 Locating the position of the wire on a taper pipe thread.

SCREW THREAD GAGING AND MEASUREMENT

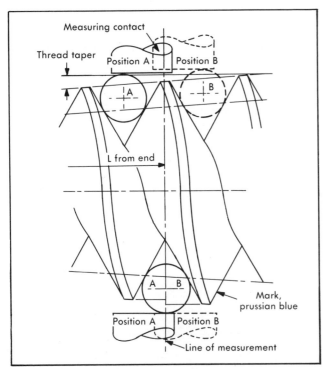

Fig. 4-82 Measurement of the pitch diameter of taper thread-plug gages by the two-wire method.

wires are placed opposite the initial wire (see Fig. 4-83). Care must be exercised when making the measurement so that the measuring contacts touch all three wires. When proper contact is made, the three wires are at an angle to the axis of the thread. The pitch diameter of a 60° included angle, taper thread gage, having a lead angle of less than 5° and a taper of 0.0625 in./in. (mm/mm), can be calculated using the equation:

$$E = 1.00049M - (3.0049w - 0.86603p) \qquad (14)$$

where:

M = measurement of the wires, in. (mm)

Thread Plug Gages

Thread plug gages are used for checking internally threaded products. They are made for all different screw thread systems, sizes, and classes, with each designation stamped or marked on the gage. Screw thread gages are made with either a full thread profile or with their flanks reduced by truncation. The style of thread profile selected depends on the application.

Two types of thread plug gages are commonly made, GO and NOT-GO (HI). Both of these gages are generally combined together in a handle. The GO gage is usually longer than the NOT-GO gage.

The GO thread plug gage checks the maximum material functional limit of the threaded part. Verifying the maximum material functional limit ensures interchangeable assembly of maximum material mating parts. For the product to be acceptable, the gage must enter and freely pass through its full-threaded length. Because the GO gage makes a cumulative check of all thread elements except the minor diameter, a GO/NOT-GO cylindrical plug gage should be used to check the minor diameter.

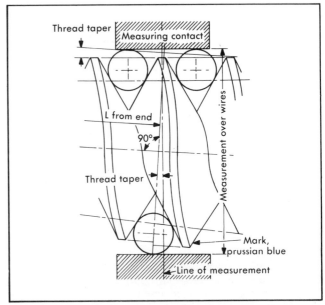

Fig. 4-83 Measurement of the pitch diameter of taper thread-plug gages by the three-wire method.

The NOT-GO thread plug gage checks the NOT-GO (HI) functional diameter limit of the threaded product. Verifying the functional diameter limit helps to ensure that there may be a sufficient amount of material for the required operational strength. For the thread to be acceptable, the gage should not enter the part or have a definite drag because of contact with product material before it enters more than three complete turns. On metric threads, a definite drag should be felt before two complete turns. The gage should not be forced into the part once a definite drag is felt. Because excessive lead and/or flank angle deviations of the screw thread can prevent the NOT-GO gage from entering the threaded opening, the major diameter of the NOT-GO gage is truncated and always smaller than that of the corresponding GO gage.

A double NOT-GO gage can also be used for checking the functional diameter limit. The double NOT-GO gage uses two NOT-GO gages with selectively truncated operating surfaces. One of the gages contacts the flanks near the major diameter, and the other gage contacts the flanks near the minor diameter of the inspected internal thread.

When using working thread plug gages, it is important to thoroughly clean the threads of dirt and chips before inserting the gage. An excess amount of dirt or chips can cause premature wear of the gage. The gage should be screwed into the workpiece except when large, double-handled gages are used. Screwing force should be limited to 2 lb (9 N); generally this is obtained by using the fingers to turn the gage rather than the forearm or a wrench.

Set thread plug gages can be used as a master for setting and checking other gages such as adjustable thread ring gages, snap gages, or indicating gages or for the direct inspection of product threads. The accuracy to which the gage is made is determined by its intended application.

Thread Ring Gages

Working thread ring gages are used for checking externally threaded products. Like thread plug gages, they are made for all

SCREW THREAD GAGING AND MEASUREMENT

different screw thread systems, sizes, and classes, with each designation stamped or marked on the gage. Thread ring gages are made as either solid rings or split (adjustable) rings and are available as GO and NOT-GO (LO) gages; they are usually supplied in pairs. The NOT-GO ring usually has an annular groove machined on the periphery of the ring.

The GO thread ring gage checks the maximum material functional limit of the threaded part, which determines whether a part will assemble in a thread of a given size. For a part to be acceptable, it must freely enter the GO thread ring gage for the entire length of the threaded portion. Because the GO makes a cumulative check of all threaded elements except the major diameter, a GO/NOT-GO plain cylindrical ring gage or a micrometer should be used to check the major diameter.

The NOT-GO thread ring gage checks the NOT-GO (LO) functional diameter limit of the threaded product. Verifying this limit helps to ensure that there may be sufficient amount of material. For the thread to be acceptable, the gage should not enter the thread or pass over the thread more than three complete turns without having a definite drag. Variations in lead or flank angle as well as a taper or out-of-round condition can increase the size of the part and prevent it from entering the gage.

Split or adjustable thread ring gages should not be adjusted any significant amount in the field. If the adjustment is altered, the ring is no longer round. The three cylindrical diameters (minor, pitch, and major) may be out-of-round, which may create a great deal of size incompatibility and inconsistency between gages that are marked and intended to be the same size. Theoretically, an adjustable thread ring gage should be relapped by the manufacturer if the setting has been altered. European manufacturing inspection standards require the use of solid thread ring gages to avoid the previously described condition and use wear limit gages to monitor size as gage is worn.

When using thread ring gages, the threaded product should be turned into the gage except with large, heavy parts. To avoid using excessive torque, only two fingers should be used to turn the part into the gage. The entire length of the product thread should be run through the gage.

Care should be taken in the handling of ring gages, as dropping or rough usage will result in improper adjustment. In addition, ring gages may load up from chips, plating, or corrosion and should be cleaned regularly. Threaded products should be lubricated before gaging to prevent loading the threads in the gage and to provide lubrication, which minimizes gage wear.

Because most product threads are usually always not formed to the maximum limit of the major diameter, they will wear steps into the flanks of the ring gage after a period of gage usage. Thread ring gages with worn flanks should be discarded or sent back to a gage house for recondition because a worn ring will accept parts larger than the master size.

Thread Snap Gages

Thread snap gages are used to check maximum and minimum material limits of external product screw threads. Before using the gage, the setting of the gaging elements should be checked using a GO and NOT-GO master set thread plug.

When using snap gages, the threaded product and the gaging elements should be clean and free from any metal particles. The part should be inserted into the GO segments or rolls from a radial direction. It should then pass through the GO elements without force and perceptible drag and come to rest on the

NOT-GO rolls. The part should be rotated 90° while in contact with the NOT-GO rolls to check for out-of-roundness. The threaded product should not pass through the NOT-GO rolls without perceptible drag. If the part does not pass through the GO elements or passes through the NOT-GO rolls, it is out of tolerance.

Indicating Gaging

Several different designs or types of indicating thread gages are available for both internal and external screw thread measurement. The type selected is determined by the thread characteristics being measured.

The GO functional limit and size, LO functional limit and size, and roundness can be measured with indicating thread gages that are equipped with either full-form segments or full-form rolls.

Indicating thread gages equipped with GO or LO full-form thread segments or GO or LO rolls are used to measure LO functional limit and size, roundness, and taper. Indicating gages with cone and vee type segments or rolls are used to measure pitch diameter size and limit, roundness, and taper. The thread groove diameter limit and size can be measured with a gage equipped with cone-type rolls. In general, the maximum minor diameter limit is acceptable when the threaded product passes the GO gage.

Indicating thread gages must be set to the proper thread setting using master plug or ring gages before checking the threaded products. The actual dimension is set at zero on the indicator and the tolerance is adjusted to either minus or plus values. For externally threaded parts, indicator flags are set zero to minus while internally threaded products are set zero to plus. The indicator reading indicates the position of the threaded product within the tolerance range.

Most indicating thread gages have a moveable contact element to permit the part to be inserted in the gage. The part should be rotated to check for out-of-roundness; the lowest or highest value represents the product size. The part should also be checked in the front, middle, and the end to check for taper.

Differential Gaging

The concept of differential gaging for product threads makes use of fundamental geometric theorems that relate directly to size, position, and form.[24] Both internal and external threads can be measured by using the appropriate indicating thread gages.

The two main characteristics measured in differential gaging are maximum material limit (GO) functional size and the minimum material limit pitch diameter size. In some instances, the thread groove diameter can be measured instead of the pitch diameter. These two measurements are equal only when the product thread has perfect position and form. Any variation in lead, flank angle, taper, or roundness of the thread will result in unequal measurements.

Differential gaging is a variables method of in-process inspection, final conformance inspection, or both that provides the actual numerical values for the GO functional and pitch diameter sizes. These are the two extreme sizes of any product screw thread. The pitch diameter is the size of the thread with essentially zero variation in all other thread elements. The GO functional size is the size of the thread with the variation effects added to the pitch diameter. The numerical value between these two sizes is called a cumulative thread element variation differential and represents the diametral effect of the total

SCREW THREAD GAGING AND MEASUREMENT

amount of variations. The inspection process that further refines the total amount of variation so that the amount of variation of each individual element becomes known is called single thread variation analysis.

Advantages.[25] Differential gaging with indicating instruments offers many potential advantages over the use of fixed-limit type gages, whether of the solid type or adjustable design. Some of the advantages include indicating capability, speed of measurement, selectiveness, dependability, versatility, economy, and adaptability to automation. However, not every thread inspection process can benefit from all or even most of these advantages.

Indicating capability. Indicating thread instruments are capable of determining, in increments of standard units of measurement, the deviation of the gaged dimension from its specified value. The numerical values are useful for the adjustment of machines and tools used in producing threaded products and for the data needed in statistical quality control or for control charts serving other purposes.

Speed. Indicating thread instruments are designed to establish gaging contact by a radial approach rather than an axial assembly, which is used for solid screw thread gages. Because these instruments use either dials with tolerance position hands or gages equipped with limit-position signaling lights, compliance to the specified limit as well as the amount of deviation can be readily obtained.

Selectiveness. Specific thread characteristics such as functional size, single-pitch diameter size, or root diameter size can be checked by equipping the indicating gage with appropriate contact elements. Other characteristics can also be checked using consecutively two indicating gages with different types of contact elements.

Dependability. Indicating thread gages are designed to establish and to maintain contact with the product thread by means of spring pressure. Once this pressure has been set, it remains uniform, thus eliminating reliance on the feel of the inspector. The pointer on the indicator dial also provides dependable information on the size condition of the gaged dimension, eliminating reliance on human judgment.

Versatility. Indicating thread gages are usually designed to be adaptable to a wide range of thread types, sizes, and classes. The measuring contacts must be exchanged only when the pitch or form of the thread are different.

Economy. Indicating thread gages are economical to use because of their versatility and their ability to compensate for wear. The contact elements must be replaced or reworked only if the wear affects their form.

Adaptability to automation. Indicating thread gages can be designed to generate signals that can trigger such actions as segregation, rejection, or even feedback signals for machine adjustment.

Procedure. A difference between the measured pitch diameter size and the GO functional diameter size will always exist unless the threads are perfect. In differential gaging, three measurements are performed on the threaded product. Two measurements are made to check the pitch diameter and one is made to check the GO functional diameter. Figure 4-84 illustrates the various measurements made on an externally threaded product with both perfect and imperfect threads.

Before any measurement is made on the actual parts, it is necessary to adjust the tolerance flags on the indicator with a master thread gage inserted in the indicating thread gage. The tolerance limit is based on the thread's class of fit. For the product to be acceptable, the indicator reading must fall within the specified tolerance limit for any given measurement.

Measurements. Pitch diameter is first measured using an indicating thread gage equipped with cone and vee segments or rolls that have one-thread pitch engagement at the pitch diameter line. A thread groove diameter type indicating gage can also be used. A measurement should be made and recorded at the front, center, and back of the part to check for taper. The part should be rotated one turn at each location to check for three-point out-of-roundness. The maximum value is the pitch diameter and is designated by X.

The GO functional diameter is then measured with an indicating thread gage equipped with functional contact segments or rolls. To check for two-point out-of-roundness, the part should be rotated one turn. The lowest value is the GO functional diameter size and is referred to as measurement Z.

If the indicated numerical difference between smallest value for the GO functional diameter size and the largest value for pitch diameter size does not exceed a specified percent of the total pitch diameter tolerance, no further analysis of thread geometry is required. Further analysis is required to determine the source of this difference if it exceeds the specified percent.

If further analysis is required, the lead/flank angle should be measured using an indicating thread gage equipped with full-form cone and vee thread segments having one-thread pitch engagement. Measurements should be made at the front, center, and back of the part to check for taper; out-of-roundness should also be checked at each location. The maximum value is the lead/angle size and is referred to as measurement Y.

Analysis. The difference in the indicator readings, Z and X, between the two gages gives the cumulative form differential reading. This reading corresponds to the pitch diameter equivalent for the combination of lead, helix, flank angle, roundness, and taper on the product thread.

The difference between the measured values, Z and Y, is the lead differential reading. This reading corresponds to the pitch diameter equivalent for the lead and helix variation on the threaded product. Dividing the lead and helix variation by 1.732 gives the exact linear lead error. If the indicated size difference exceeds the specified percent of the total pitch diameter tolerance, lead deviation is excessive.

The difference between the measured values, Y and X, is the flank angle differential reading. This reading corresponds approximately to the pitch diameter equivalent for the combined flank angle variation on the threaded product. If the indicated size difference exceeds the specified percent of the pitch diameter tolerance, the diametrical effect of angle deviation may be excessive.

Optical Gaging

Optical comparators and toolmakers' microscopes can be used to measure pitch diameter, roundness of pitch cylinder, lead (including helix deviation), flank angle deviation, major and minor diameter, root radius, and diameter runout of externally threaded products. They can also be used to measure pitch diameter, lead (including helix deviation), flank angle deviation, major diameter, and root radius of internally threaded products. For internally threaded products, however, measurements are taken on a cast replica of the part.

Both of these instruments magnify the thread form, which is then compared with appropriate linear and angular scales on the instrument and with overlay charts (optical comparator) or

SCREW THREAD GAGING AND MEASUREMENT

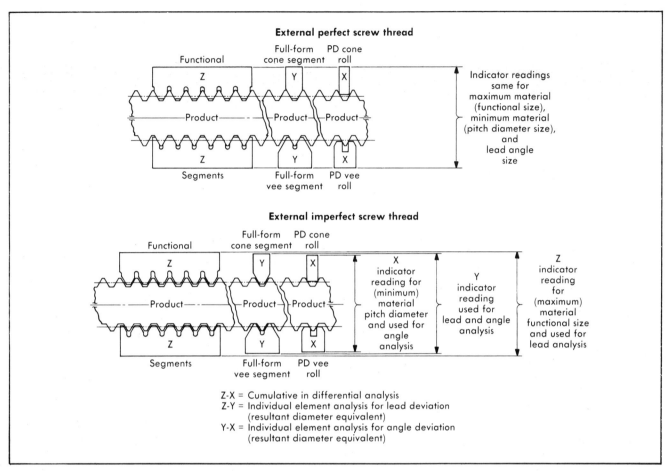

External perfect screw thread

Functional

Full-form cone segment — Y

PD cone roll — X

Z — Product — Product — Product

Z

Segments

Full-form vee segment — Y

PD vee roll — X

Indicator readings same for maximum material (functional size), minimum material (pitch diameter size), and lead angle size

External imperfect screw thread

Functional

Full-form cone segment — Y

PD cone roll — X

Z — Product — Product — Product

Z

Segments

Full-form vee segment — Y

PD vee roll — X

X indicator reading for (minimum) material pitch diameter and used for angle analysis

Y indicator reading used for lead and angle analysis

Z indicator reading for (maximum) material functional size and used for lead analysis

Z-X = Cumulative in differential analysis
Z-Y = Individual element analysis for lead deviation (resultant diameter equivalent)
Y-X = Individual element analysis for angle deviation (resultant diameter equivalent)

Fig. 4-84 Pictorial steps in differential gaging of external product screw threads. (*The Johnson Gage Co.*)

transparent reticles (toolmakers' microscope). Optical comparators are generally fitted with lenses providing magnification from 10X to 100X whereas the magnification of a toolmakers' microscope is lower. A detailed description of optical comparators and toolmakers' microscopes can be found in Chapter 3, "Inspection Equipment and Techniques," of this volume.

Standard chart gages for checking screw threads are based on specifications set up in the National Bureau of Standards

Handbook H-28.[26] The charts used are generally of the envelope type. In such charts, dimensional and manufacturing tolerances are interpreted to produce a double-line outline indicating allowable maximum and minimum conditions of the part. An example of a tolerance-outline chart for unified threads is shown in Fig. 4-85. Selection of the chart gages is based on the measurements being made, the type, size, and class of thread, the magnification rate that is used, and the orientation

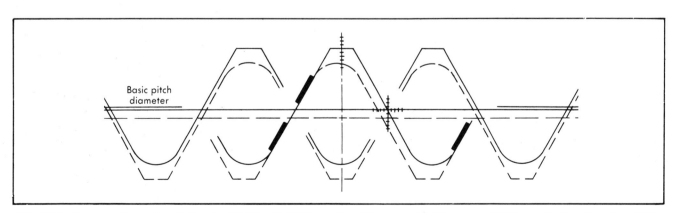

Basic pitch diameter

Fig. 4-85 Tolerance outline on thread chart for 1/2-20 unified National thread form, class 2A tolerance, at 62.5X magnification. Thread profile is shown normal to the axis; central tooth form is compensated for helix. (*Optical Gaging Products, Inc.*)

SCREW THREAD GAGING AND MEASUREMENT

of the threaded product with respect to the focal plane of the optical system.

A staging fixture supports the part in such a way that the contour to be projected is positioned in the focal plane of the optical system. In many instances, the same holding device will adequately support a number of different parts. The threaded part is oriented either normal to the axis or normal to the helix. A table that can be rotated to the helix angle is required to orient the part normal to the helix position. Table 4-13 summarizes the procedures used for measuring different thread characteristics on an optical comparator with both normal to the axis and normal to the helix orientation. The choice of approach depends on the items to be checked and the ease with which one or the other approach allows these items to be checked.

Electromechanical Gaging

The lead of threaded screw products can be checked with indicating gages and optical instruments such as optical comparators and toolmakers' microscopes. Although these instruments are adequate for certain applications, these instruments have various limitations. For example, with indicating gages (differential gaging) the effect of lead deviations on the pitch diameter is determined by assuming that variables other than lead produce only negligible interference. In optical gaging, the repeat accuracy of the visual target and the applicable rate of magnification are limiting factors.

In applications requiring an accurate measurement of lead, specially designed electromechanical instruments are used. Examples of these instruments are lead testers and helical-path analyzers. The surface roughness and roundness of externally threaded products can also be checked with the appropriate equipment.

Lead tester. The electromechanical lead tester consists of a precision, direct-reading headstock in combination with an axially movable carriage. The carriage supports a sine bar, two work-mounting centers, and an electronic thread locating head. The head has interchangeable ball-point contact elements with different radii. Selection of the ball-point elements radius is based on the pitch of the thread being measured.

When measuring the lead, the ball-point elements are moved in an out-of-the-thread groove by the operator and an attached counterweight ensures a constant contact pressure. A microammeter, located on the head, indicates when the correct measuring point is reached. Electromechanical lead testers are capable of measuring both straight and taper threads and have a measuring accuracy of 25 μin. (0.6 μm).

Helical path analyzers. Helical path analyzers measure the total deviation in helical path of a threaded product by

TABLE 4-13
Measurement of Threaded Products with an Optical Comparator

Thread Characteristic	Orientation	
	Normal-to-Helix Staging	Normal-to-Axis Staging
Thread form, major and minor diameter, crest, and root form	Only the thread at the center of screen is in critical focus, although chart gages show a tooth on either side of center. Check tooth at center of screen. To check other threads, move staging table along helix axis until tooth is in position and focus	All the threads visible across the screen diameter can be checked. Focus is limited to either the right or left flanks of the screw thread at any one time. The focus difference can usually be ignored for small diameter threads
Pitch and lead	Measured by successively positioning each tooth to the chart-gage form or moving and measuring along the helix table axis. Pitch over three teeth is foreshortened due to helix angle. Chart-gage is compensated accordingly	Measured by comparing threads to profiles shown on chart-gage or by traversing and measuring along standard table axis
Thread angle	Projected angle is foreshortened approximately 4 min depending on thread helix; the chart-gages are compensated for foreshortening of thread angle. Focus is sharp on both flanks and the image is accurately defined	Actual angle as specified on drawing is projected and can be compared to thread shown on chart-gage. Some refocusing from one flank to the other may be required, depending on helix angle of thread
Pitch diameter	Measured by first fitting thread and opposite space into thread form on chart-gage. The vertical table displacement is then measured with micrometer measuring attachment	Measured by same method as for normal-to-helix staging. Alternate method stages on special fixture coordinated to chart-gage with set master thread gage or plug
Major and minor diameter	Measured by use of vertical measuring attachment or by comparison to thread chart-gage. A staging fixture, coordinated to the chart-gage with a set master, is sometimes used	Measured by same method as for normal-to-helix staging

(Optical Gaging Products, Inc.)

combining the effects of linear lead and helical deviation. They consist of a motor-driven headstock, tailstock, electronic gaging head, sine bar, follower, pitch blocks, chart recorder, and a control panel.

The part to be measured is mounted between centers and the sine bar is set at the proper angle, which is based on the thread pitch, using the applicable pitch block. When the machine is activated, the motor rotates the part through three revolutions. At the same time, this rotary motion is transmitted to the drive of the chart recorder. Concurrently, the sine bar advances until the follower contacts the thread groove, which causes a lateral movement of the gage head at a rate corresponding to the nominal lead of the threaded product. The chart gives readings in lead variation and drunken thread variation. An example of the chart tracings are shown in Fig. 4-86.

Surface roughness. Measurement of surface roughness on screw thread flanks is usually made with an instrument that traverses a radiused stylus across the lay. The stylus displacement as a result of surface irregularities is electronically amplified and the meter readings display the arithmetical average roughness height in microinches or micrometers. Some instruments produce a chart of the traced path showing the peak-to-valley heights of the surface irregularities. Special fixturing is required to position and guide the stylus over the thread surface. For additional information on surface roughness, refer to Chapter 5, "Surface Texture and Integrity," of this volume.

Roundness equipment. The two types of precision roundness measuring instruments used are precision rotary tables and precision spindles. A special stylus coupled to an electric unit records the out-of-roundness on a circular chart as it traces around the cylindrical surface of the workpiece. The instrument provides a series of magnifications for stylus displacement, a filtering system for isolating lobing from surface irregularities, various means for centering the amplified stylus trace on the polar chart, and a selection of rotating speeds. Roundness measurement is covered in more detail in the previous section of this chapter.

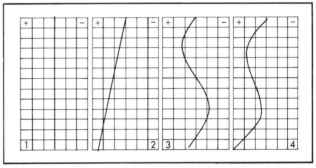

Fig. 4-86 Examples of chart tracings produced by helical path analyzer. The tracings represent different conditions of the inspected helical path, such as correct (1) and with deviations, which are progressive (2), periodic (3), or cumulative (4). The instrument has dual magnification, producing chart tracings with each chart division corresponding to 0.000020 or 0.0001". (*Colt Industries—Pratt & Whitney*)

MEASUREMENT OF GEARS AND SPLINES

Gears and involute splines are important drive elements used in a variety of machines and mechanical devices. Gears are available in various types such as spur, helical, bevel, and worm, each having individual advantages for specific applications. Applications for gears range from transmitting motion at high or low speeds under heavy or light loads to holding some elements in a fixed position. The information presented in this section covers the range of fine-pitch gearing from 120 to 20 diametral pitch, up to 12" (305 mm) diam, and coarse-pitch gearing from 19.99 to 0.5 diametral pitch, up to 200" (5080 mm) diam. The meshing teeth of practically all gears is based on the involute form.

A splined shaft is a shaft having a series of parallel keys formed integrally with the shaft and mating with corresponding grooves cut in a hub or fitting.[27] They are available in 30°, 37.5°, and 45° pressure angles and are based on the involute form. Splined shafts are commonly used for coupling shafts when heavy torques are to be transmitted without slipping; for transmitting power to gears, pulleys, and other rotating members; and for attaching parts that may require removal for indexing or changing angular position.

Gears and splines are produced using both nonmachining (forming) and machining processes. The method selected to manufacture a specific type of gear is based on a number of factors. These factors include the design of the gear or spline; type, hardness, and condition of the workpiece material; amount of stock to be removed or formed; accuracy and finish requirements; type, capability, and condition of the machine tool to be used; rigidity of the setup; production requirements; operating conditions; and tooling cost per part produced. Gear and spline production is discussed in detail in Volume I of this Handbook series.

Gears, like other mechanical components, must be subjected to some form of inspection to maintain process control and to determine how the gear will perform in continual engagement with a mating gear. The two methods of gear inspection commonly performed are analytical and functional checks. Analytical inspection involves the measurement of individual parameters of gear quality. In functional inspection, the gear being tested is rolled in tight mesh contact with a corresponding master gear of known accuracy.

This subchapter has been designed to familiarize the manufacturing engineer with the various measurements made on gears and splines. It also provides some practical information on how the measurements are made and a description of the equipment used. The material used when discussing gear inspection was abstracted with permission from the American Gear Manufacturers Association (AGMA) Standard 390.03, "Gear Handbook,"[28] The material for spline inspection was abstracted from American National Standards Institute (ANSI) B92.1, "Involute Splines and Inspection."[29]

STANDARDS AND SPECIFICATIONS

The cost of producing a gear or spline is generally directly related to the gear tooth accuracy. The specific application of the end product determines the accuracy required when producing gears and splines.

CHAPTER 4

MEASUREMENT OF GEARS

In the United States, gear tooth accuracy requirements are based on American Gear Manufacturers Association specifications. The accuracy of the gear tooth elements is related to the designated quality number for the gear being produced. Quality numbers range from 3 to 15; high quality numbers indicate that the gearing is made more precise and with closer tolerances than low quality numbers. Tolerance values for the different quality numbers can be obtained from tables or calculated from equations given in AGMA standards. The gear tooth parameters covered in the standards are runout, pitch variation, profile variation, tooth alignment (lead) variation, tooth-to-tooth composite tolerance, and total composite tolerance. Table 4-14 lists some of the AGMA standards more commonly used when inspecting gears.

Another choice for gear tolerances, popular with foreign gear manufacturers, is the West German DIN standard. The classification numbers range from 1 to 12, with the low numbers indicating high gear accuracy. Like the AGMA standard, tolerance values for the various gear tooth elements can be obtained from tables or calculated from equations in the DIN standards. Some of the DIN standards that are related to gear measurement are listed in Table 4-14.

TABLE 4-14
Commonly Used Gear and Spline Manufacturing Standards

Standard Number	Title
	AGMA Standards
112.05	Gear Nomenclature (Geometry) Terms, Definitions, Symbols and Abbreviations
120.01	Gear-Cutting Tools Fine and Coarse-Pitch Hobs
201.02	Tooth Proportions for Coarse-Pitch Involute Spur Gears
202.03	System for Zerol Bevel Gears
207.06	Tooth Proportions for Fine-Pitch Involute Spur and Helical Gears
208.03	System for Straight Bevel Gears
209.04	System for Spiral Bevel Gears
231.52	Pin Measurement Tables for Involute Spur Gears
341.02	Design of General Industrial Coarse-Pitch Cylindrical Wormgearing
370.01	Design Manual for Fine-Pitch Gearing
390.03	Gear Handbook
	DIN Standards
3962 (Part 1)	Tolerances for Cylindrical Gear Teeth; Tolerances for Deviations of Individual Parameters
3962 (Part 2)	Tolerances for Cylindrical Gear Teeth; Tolerances for Tooth Trace Deviations
3962 (Part 3)	Tolerances for Cylindrical Gear Teeth; Tolerances for Pitch-span Deviations
3967	System of Gear Fits; Backlash, Tooth Thickness Allowances, Tooth Thickness Tolerances; Principals
5480 (Part 1)	Involute Splines; Fundamental Definitions
5480 (Part 2)	Involute Splines; Summary of Data
5480 (Parts 3-13)	Involute Splines; Nominal Dimensions; Measurements, Module 0.6-10
5480 (Part 14)	Involute Splines; Side Fits; Tolerances
5480 (Part 15)	Involute Splines; Testing and Gages for Side Fit
	ANSI Standards
B92.1	Involute Splines and Inspection, Inch Version
B92.2M	Involute Splines, Metric Module
B92.2Ma	Involute Splines, Metric Module (supplement)

Standards published by ANSI control the accuracy of involute splines. The standards most commonly referred to are listed in Table 4-14.

NOMENCLATURE

The following definitions relating to the inspection of gears and gear teeth are adapted from AGMA 390.03 with permission from the publisher. For definitions of geometric terms related to gearing, refer to AGMA 112.05 (ANSI B6.14), "Gear Nomenclature."

allowable pitch variation See pitch variation, allowable.

allowable variation See variation, allowable.

axial pitch See pitch, axial.

axial runout See runout, axial.

base circle The base circle is a circle from which involute tooth profiles are derived.

base cylinder The base cylinder corresponds to the base circle and is the cylinder from which involute tooth surfaces, either straight or helical, are derived.

chordal tooth thickness The length of the chord subtending a circular-tooth-thickness arc (see Fig. 4-87).

circle, datum The datum circle is a circle on which measurements are made.

circular pitch See pitch, circular.

circular tooth thickness The length of arc between the two sides of the same gear tooth, on a specified circle (see Fig. 4-87).

composite action test A method of gear inspection in which the work gear is rolled in tight, double-flank contact with a master gear or a specified gear to determine composite variations.

composite tolerance, tooth-to-tooth (double-flank) The permissible amount of tooth-to-tooth composite variation.

composite tolerance, total (double-flank) The permissible amount of total composite variation.

composite variation (double-flank) Variation in center distance when a gear is inspected by a composite-action test.

composite variation, tooth-to-tooth (double-flank) The greatest change in center distance while the gear being tested is rotated through any angle of $360° / N$ during a double-flank composite-action test.

composite variation, total (double-flank) The total change in center distance while the gear being tested is rotated one complete revolution during a double-flank composite-action test.

datum axis of rotation The axis of the gear used as the basis for measurements.

datum tooth The designated tooth used as the starting point for measuring other teeth.

diameter, profile control The specified diameter of the circle beyond which the tooth profile must conform to the specified involute curve.

eccentricity The distance between the center of a datum circle and a datum axis of rotation.

face width The length of the gear teeth in an axial plane.

face width, functional The portion of the face width less the edge round at each end.

gear blank The material shape used for the manufacture of a gear, prior to machining or forming the gear teeth.

index variation The displacement of any tooth from its theoretical position, relative to a datum tooth. Measurements are usually linear, near the middle of the functional tooth profile. If the measurements are made normal to the tooth surface, they should be corrected to the transverse plane.

index variation, total The maximum algebraic difference between the extreme values of index variation for a given gear. Total index variation is also equivalent to total accumulated pitch variation as measured by a two-probe spacing system.

inspection chart The generated recording or trace from an inspection machine used to display a measured variation of gear geometry.

lead The axial advance of a helix for one revolution (see Fig. 4-88).

master gear A gear of known quality that is used to perform a composite-action test.

outside diameter The diameter of the addendum circle (outside) of a cylindrical gear.

pitch The distance between similar, equally spaced tooth surfaces along a given line or arc (see Fig. 4-89).

pitch, axial The pitch of a gear parallel to the axis of rotation.

pitch, base On an involute gear, the base pitch is the pitch on the base circle or along the line of action. It is equal to the

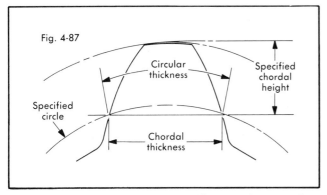

Fig. 4-87 Chordal and circular tooth thickness. (*American Gear Manufacturers Association*)

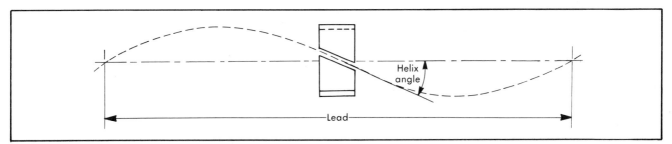

Fig. 4-88 Lead of a helical gear. (*American Gear Manufacturers Association*)

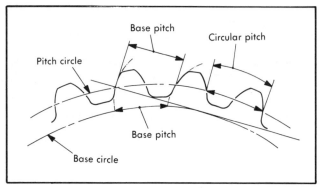

Fig. 4-89 Principal pitches on a gear. (*American Gear Manufacturers Association*)

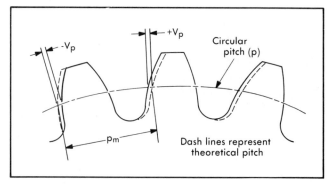

Fig. 4-90 Pitch variation. (*American Gear Manufacturers Association*)

circumference of the base circle divided by the number of teeth (see Fig. 4-89).

pitch, circular The distance along a specified pitch circle or pitch line between corresponding profiles of adjacent teeth (see Fig. 4-89).

pitch, diametral The ratio of the number of teeth to the pitch diameter in the transverse plane. It is equal to π divided by the circular pitch.

pitch, diametral, normal The ratio of the number of teeth to the pitch diameter in the normal plane of a helical gear. The normal plane and the transverse of a spur gear are coincident.

pitch variation The plus or minus difference in the transverse plane between the average measured pitch and the actual pitch measurement (see Fig. 4-90).

pressure angle, normal The angle at a point on the pitch cylinder between the line of pressure that is normal to the tooth surface and the plane tangent to the pitch cylinder.

profile One side of a tooth in a cross section between the outside circle and the root circle (see Fig. 4-91).

    profile, functional The portion of the tooth flank between the profile control diameter and the addendum circle or the start of tip round (see Fig. 4-92).

    profile variation The difference between the measured and the specified functional profile.

reference axis A specified line about which a gear is intended to rotate.

runout The maximum variation of the distance between a surface of revolution and a datum surface, measured perpendicular to the datum surface.

    runout, axial (wobble) The runout measured in a direction parallel to the datum axis of rotation.

    runout, radial The runout measured in a direction perpendicular to the datum axis of rotation.

span measurement The measurement of the distance across several teeth long a line tangent to the base cylinder. It is used to determine tooth thickness.

standard pitch circle A circle defined by the number of teeth and a specified module or circular pitch.

surface, datum The surface used as the basis for measurements. It is established by the specific measuring device used.

surface, tooth The tooth surface forms the side of a gear tooth and is sometimes referred to as the flank (refer to Fig. 4-91).

test radius A measure of functional tooth thickness.

tooth alignment The theoretical lengthwise alignment of the line of intersection between the tooth flank and the pitch cylinder.

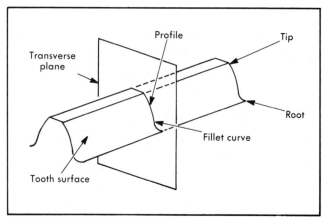

Fig. 4-91 Gear tooth profile in transverse plane. (*American Gear Manufacturers Association*)

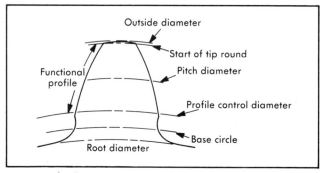

Fig. 4-92 Functional profile of a gear tooth. (*American Gear Manufacturers Association*)

tooth thickness The thickness of a gear tooth at a specified diameter or tooth height (refer to Fig. 4-87).

wobble See runout, axial.

work gear The manufactured gear being inspected.

ANALYTICAL GEAR CHECKING

From a diagnostic standpoint, the functional check cannot show the specific amount of variation that would be attributed individually to the various gear tooth parameters. Tooth-to-tooth variations revealed in the functional check are usually a combination of these different parameter variations; therefore a separate check or a series of checks is required to determine the accuracy of each parameter. The parameters commonly inspected by analytical gear checking are runout, pitch variation, accumulated pitch variation, profile variation, tooth alignment (lead) variation, and tooth thickness.

Normally, on large-lot gear production, the analytical check is used on a sampling basis to ensure that the specific parameter tolerances are being met. Analytical gear checking is also used on a troubleshooting basis to determine and correct manufacturing and production problems.

Runout

Runout is the total variation of the distance between a datum surface and an indicated surface. The datum and indicated surfaces must be specified or identified. The two commonly specified runouts are axial and radial.

Axial runout (wobble) is formed when an angle exists between the datum surface and an indicated surface. It is normally measured in a direction parallel to the axis of rotation between the indicated and datum surfaces.

Radial runout is formed by variations between the datum and indicated surfaces. It is measured in a direction perpendicular to the axis of rotation. Radial runout measurements may include the effects of eccentricity, out-of-roundness, tooth alignment variation, profile variation, pitch variation, and tooth thickness variation.

Gears can be checked for runout by measuring indicator variations in the radius dimension over pins, balls, or wedges placed in consecutive tooth spaces. With some spacing instruments, the runout can be charted automatically. Runout and spacing of wormgears can be checked in the same manner as conventional gears if measurements are taken at the center of the throat radius.

On small worms it is practical to measure runout by the projection method. In this method, a magnified shadow of the worm is compared with a template as the worm is rotated to successive positions. On worms, the runout may vary appreciably across the face width and consequently should be measured near both limits of the contact area. Appreciable differences in runout near the limits are an indication of wobble, which is more objectionable than uniform runout. Wobble is likewise objectionable on wormgears and may best be detected in the test for area of contact.

Pitch Variation

Pitch, spacing, and accumulative pitch or index variations are elemental parameters relating to the accuracy of tooth locations around a gear. Measurements for determining the variations are made (1) at or near the center of the profile, (2) in the transverse plane, or (3) relative to the gear datum axis of rotation with bench or floor-type instruments or relative to the top lands when using portable instruments.

With helical gears, the pitch measurement may be made in the normal plane. The values obtained are then divided by the cosine of the helix angle for comparison with the specified tolerances. Sequential tooth flanks in both directions of rotation should be used for pitch measurements. However, if the specific operating direction of the gear is known, only the loaded flanks need to be measured.

The two common types of devices for measuring pitch, spacing, and index variations are the two-probe device and the single-probe device. The two-probe device is used for comparison of adjacent pitches around a gear, while the single-probe device can determine the actual location of each tooth around a gear.

Two-probe device. The two-probe device has one fixed probe contacting a flank on a datum circle near the center of tooth profile. The second probe, either a mechanical or electronic indicator, contacts the adjacent tooth flank at or near the same point on the profile (see Fig. 4-93). As the gear is rotated around its datum axis, the two-probe device moves in and out on a precision slide and stop and indicates successive adjacent pitches. If the base pitch variation is to be measured, the two-probe device should be aligned along a tangent to the base circle. Two-probe devices are available as bench or floor models as well as portable models.

The pitch measurements obtained by the two-probe device are added together and then divided by the number of gear teeth, yielding the average measured pitch as shown in Table 4-15. The average measured pitch is then subtracted from each actual pitch reading to obtain the plus and minus values of pitch variation. To obtain the total accumulated pitch variation, the pitch variation values are successively summed together. The difference between adjacent values of pitch variation yields values of spacing variation.

Single-probe devices. On single-probe devices, a precision indexing device is used to index the gear exactly $360°/N$ ($N =$ number of teeth) or one pitch for each tooth. Typical indexing devices are an index plate, a circle divider, an optical or electronic encoder, and a polygon and autocollimator.

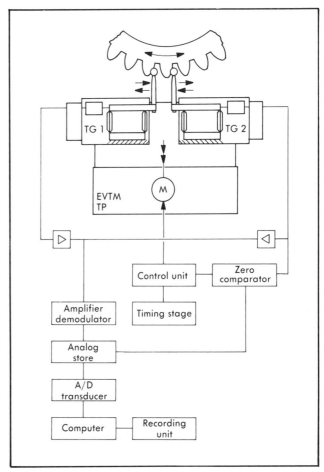

Fig. 4-93 Schematic of portable two-probe pitch testing unit. (*American Pfauter Limited*)

MEASUREMENT OF GEARS

In operation, a single probe on a precision slide mechanism is brought into contact with the first and each successive tooth flank around the gear (see Fig. 4-94). The readings from this series of measurements are recorded as the actual value of index variation as shown in Table 4-16. The difference between adjacent measurements determines the individual values of pitch variation. The difference between any two adjacent values of pitch variation is calculated to determine the spacing variation. Total accumulated pitch variation is the difference between the minimum and maximum index readings.

Profile

Profile is the shape of the tooth flank from its root to its tip (see Fig. 4-95). The functional profile is the operating portion that is in actual contact during mesh and cannot extend below the base cylinder. Profile measurements are commonly made using generative, coordinate (nongenerative), or portable involute checking instruments.

Generative instruments. The most common instruments used for profile inspection are generative involute checking instruments. These instruments measure the variation of the actual profile from a nominal involute profile that is generated by the instrument. Generating the nominal involute requires a tangential movement of a measurement probe on the involute surface in a synchronized, linear relationship with the rotational movement of a gear mounted on the instrument spindle (see Fig. 4-96).

Generative involute checking instruments may employ a master base circle or master involute cam to generate the nominal involute curve. The instruments may include a ratio mechanism that relates the actual workpiece base circle to the master base circle. They may also employ a CNC electronic drive system to generate the nominal involute curve.

TABLE 4-15
Pitch Variation Data from a Two-Probe Measuring Device

Teeth	Readings*	Pitch Variations**	Index Variation†	Spacing Variation
1-2	0	+2	+2	
				2
2-3	-2	0	+2	
				2
3-4	0	+2	+4	
				8
4-5	-8	-6	-2	
				8
5-6	0	+2	0	
				4
6-7	-4	-2	-2	
				4
7-1	0	+2	0	
	-14			

(*American Gear Manufacturers Association*)
* Average measured pitch (P_m) -14/7 = -2
** Maximum pitch variation = -6
† Total accumulated pitch variation = 4 - (-2) = 6

TABLE 4-16
Pitch Variation Data from a Single-Probe Measuring Device

Gear Tooth	Index Variation*	Pitch Variation** Gear Teeth	Value	Spacing Variation
1	0			
2	+2	(2-1)	+2	
				2
3	+2	(3-2)	0	
				2
4	+4	(4-3)	+2	
				8
5	-2	(5-4)	-6	
				8
6	0	(6-5)	+2	
				4
7	-2	(7-6)	-2	
				4
1	0	(1-7)	+2	

(*American Gear Manufacturers Association*)
* Total accumulated pitch variation = 4 - (-2) =6
** Maximum pitch variation = -6

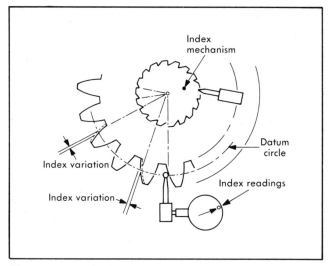

Fig. 4-94 Schematic of single-probe measuring device. (*American Gear Manufacturers Association***)**

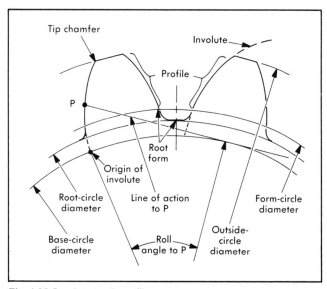

Fig. 4-95 Involute tooth profile.

In operation, the gear must be accurately mounted with its datum axis of rotation coincident with the instrument spindle axis. Additionally, the probe tip must be accurately positioned within the plane, tangent to the base circle with its zero roll position precalibrated. Probe tips may have a chisel point, or be disc or spherically shaped, as long as accurate positioning is maintained.

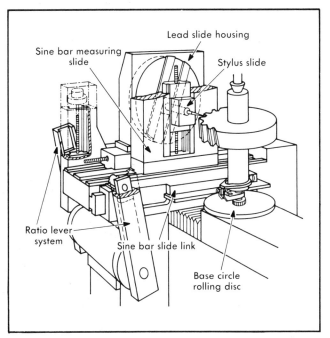

Fig. 4-96 Schematic of mechanical lead and involute checker. (*American Pfauter Limited*)

Coordinate instruments. Coordinate measurement inspection instruments indicate the tooth profile by a series of discrete points. The variation of the actual profile from the nominal profile is then determined by comparison of the stored test-point coordinates against calculated coordinates of the theoretical nominal profile.

Coordinate measurement inspection instruments may operate in two dimensions (X and Y coordinates) or three dimensions (X, Y, and Z coordinates). When using instruments operating in two dimensions, the gear must be mounted accurately and its axis must be parallel to the X-Y plane. Three-dimensional systems require alignment of the gear axis parallel to one of the three instrument axes. The alignment may be accomplished by accurately mounting the part or mathematically adjusting the instrument axis to coincide with the gear axis.

Coordinate measurement inspection instruments generally use spherically shaped probe tips. Because of this, they require a correction for shift of the probe contact point.

Portable instruments. Profile measuring instruments are generally fixed-type machines. Gears to be tested must be brought to the instrument and accurately mounted between centers or on a face plate. However, for large gears it may be preferable to use a portable involute checking instrument that can be taken to the gear. These instruments operate on a variety of generative or nongenerative (coordinate) principles.

Portable instruments must be accurately mounted at a known distance from and in alignment with the gear axis. To permit accurate mounting, the design and manufacture of the gear blank must be carefully controlled.

Profile charts. Amplified traces of profile inspection test results should be presented on charts that are calibrated for degrees of roll or rolling path length as well as magnification of measured variation (see Fig. 4-97). An unmodified profile with no variations will be charted as a straight line. Excess material on the profile is considered a plus variation, while insufficient

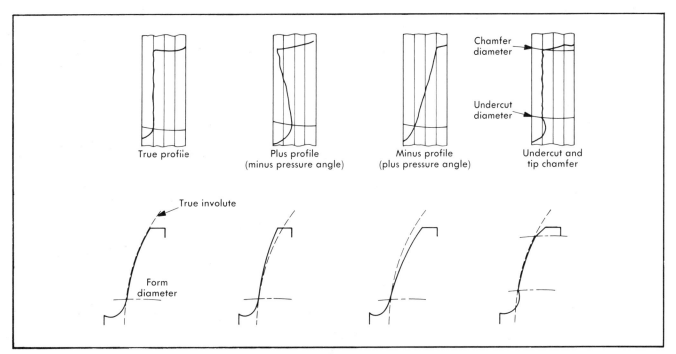

Fig. 4-97 Typical tooth profile tolerance charts. (*American Gear Manufacturers Association*)

MEASUREMENT OF GEARS

material is considered a minus variation. In addition to identifying the location and magnitude of the highest points on the profile or the maximum profile variation, these charts are valuable for determining profile characteristics such as tip round, undercut, and tip or root relief.

Other inspection methods. A shadow of the gear tooth being inspected may be optically magnified and projected on an optical comparator. The projected profile is then compared to a large-scale layout of a specified profile. This method is generally limited to small gears. However, when gears are too large to be mounted in the comparator, a thin wafer (cut simultaneously with the gear) or a mold of a gear tooth form may be used for projection. When using an optical comparator for gear inspection, two known reference surfaces are required to locate the image both radially and angularly.

The profile of a gear tooth can also be checked in an indirect way using a gear tooth caliper or wires, rolls, pins, or balls of several different diameters (see Fig. 4-98). When using a gear tooth caliper, the chordal tooth thickness and associated addendum depth for several positions are measured. These measurements are compared with computed values for the positions measured to give an indication of profile accuracy. The measurements do not indicate which profile may have an error because two flanks of a measured tooth are contacted at the same time. In addition, this method will not reveal variations that cancel each other, such as those caused by a form cutter.

Tooth Alignment

Tooth alignment is the lengthwise alignment of the tooth flank across the face from one end to the other. The theoretical tooth alignment of a spur gear is a straight line parallel to its rotating axis. On helical or herringbone gears, the tooth alignment is a helix contained on the surface of a cylinder that is concentric with the datum axis of the gear's rotation. Tooth alignment is restricted to the portion of the gear tooth that is in contact with the drive tooth when loaded. It does not include edge rounds or chamfers.

Lead, a term used for helical and herringbone gears, is the axial advance of a helix for one complete turn of the gear. The lead of a spur gear is infinite. The lead of a helical gear is

commonly specified by the angle of inclination of the helix to the axis of rotation at a specified diameter. This helix angle is normally specified at the standard pitch diameter.

Tooth alignment variation, also referred to as lead variation, is the difference between the specified and the measured tooth alignment of the gear. It is measured in a direction normal to the specified alignment (see Fig. 4-99). Tooth alignment is normally measured using generative, coordinate, or portable checking instruments. Portable instruments are generally only used for checking large gears.

An indication of tooth alignment accuracy may be derived from inspection of axial pitch on gears with sufficient helix angle and face width to have multiple axial overlaps. Although the axial pitch method of tooth alignment inspection does not provide the actual levels of tooth alignment variation, it is useful when measuring large-diameter, wide-face gears.

Generative instruments. Generative tooth alignment checking instruments are the most common instruments for checking tooth alignment. These instruments measure the variation of the actual tooth alignment from a nominal tooth alignment generated by the instrument. Generation of the nominal tooth alignment requires the axial movement of a measurement probe in a synchronized, linear relationship with rotational movement of the gear mounted on the instrument spindle. When measuring spur gears, the rotational movement is not required.

Generative tooth alignment checking instruments may employ a variety of mechanical configurations to generate the nominal tooth alignment. The gear is commonly rotated by a master disc driven by a straightedge. The tangential movement of the straightedge is translated into axial movement of the probe by a ratio mechanism. These instruments may also employ a CNC electronic drive system to generate the nominal tooth alignment trace.

During inspection, the gear must be accurately positioned with its axis of rotation coincident with the instrument spindle axis. In addition, the probe tip should be positioned to operate normal to the tooth surface at or near the pitch diameter. The most commonly used probe tips are spherical or disc-shaped.

Coordinate instruments. Coordinate measurement instruments probe the tooth lengthwise at a series of discrete points,

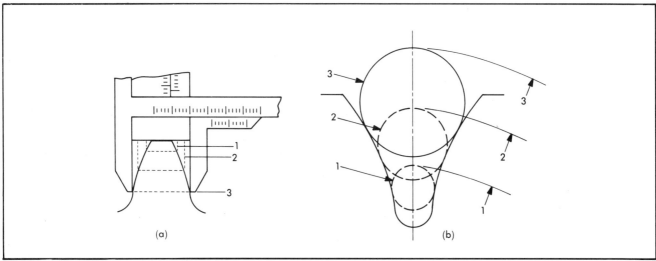

Fig. 4-98 Indirect measurement of gear tooth profile using (a) a gear tooth caliper and (b) pins or balls with a micrometer. (*American Gear Manufacturers Association*)

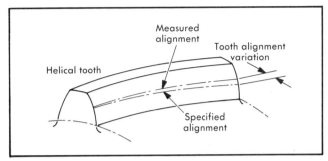

Fig. 4-99 Tooth alignment variation. (*American Gear Manufacturers Association*)

storing the rectangular coordinates of each point. The variation of the actual tooth alignment is determined by comparing the stored test-point coordinates against calculated coordinates of the theoretical, nominal tooth alignment.

Coordinate measurement instruments operate in three dimensions (*X, Y,* and *Z* coordinates) to measure tooth alignment. The gear axis must be aligned parallel with one of the three instrument axes. This alignment may be accomplished by accurately mounting the part or mathematically adjusting the instrument axis to coincide with the gear axis. Coordinate measurement instruments generally use spherically shaped probe tips. The probe tips require correction for shift of probe contact point.

Tooth alignment charts. Amplified traces of test results from tooth alignment inspection should be presented on charts (see Fig. 4-100). The charts should be calibrated for axial displacement and the magnification of the measured tooth alignment variation.

Alignment of an unmodified tooth, free of any variations, will be charted as a straight line. Excess material is considered a plus variation, while insufficient material is considered a minus variation. In addition to identifying the location and magnitude of tooth alignment variations, these charts are valuable for identifying tooth alignment characteristics such as edge chamfers, end relief, crown, and taper.

Tooth Thickness

Tooth thickness of a gear tooth can be specified in the transverse plane or in the normal plane. The methods used to determine tooth thickness are not generally direct measurements. To evaluate tooth thickness, each measuring method involves some additional characteristic of the gear. Thus when the maximum and minimum limits for tooth thickness are determined using the tolerance values in AGMA 390.03, the measurement limits must be selected to allow for additional characteristics introduced by the specific measuring method being used.

Tooth thickness can be measured using gear tooth calipers, addendum comparators, micrometers with pins, balls, or blocks, and vernier or plate micrometers. It can also be measured using functional checking techniques.

Gear tooth vernier caliper. The gear tooth vernier caliper combines in one tool the function of both a vernier depth gage and a vernier caliper (Fig. 4-101). The vertical slide is set to depth so that when it rests on top of the gear tooth, the caliper jaws will be correctly positioned to measure across the datum circle of the gear tooth. The gear tooth vernier caliper is generally used only when checking the first gear of a production

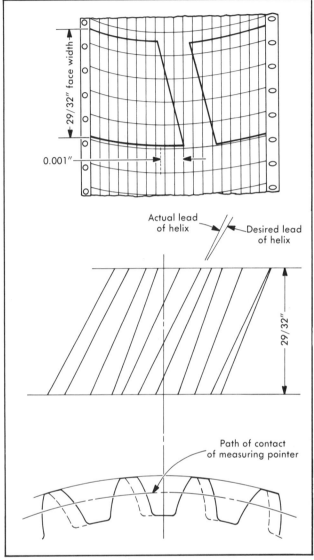

Fig. 4-100 Typical tooth alignment inspection chart.

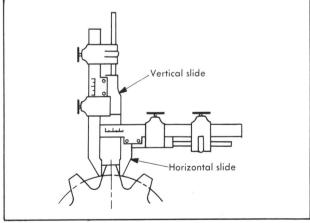

Fig. 4-101 Gear tooth caliper used in tooth thickness inspection.

MEASUREMENT OF GEARS

lot. Once the gear cutting machine has been set to size, all the other gears in the lot are cut to the same size.

Because a gear tooth vernier caliper measures on a straight or chordal line, it measures the chordal thickness rather than the circular thickness (refer to Fig. 4-87). The chordal thickness is slightly less than the arc thickness. Although this difference is frequently ignored, it becomes significant for coarse-pitch gears and gears with low numbers of teeth. In addition, significant errors can result unless the actual radius of the top land of the tooth is known and considered when setting the vertical slide.

Addendum comparator. The addendum comparator measures tooth thickness by comparing the gear addendum with that of a basic rack (see Fig. 4-102). The comparator jaws have the same angle as the normal pressure angle of the gear being inspected. Before measuring a gear, the comparator jaws are set to the proper width using a steel block that corresponds to a rack tooth of the proper normal pitch. With the block in place, the dial indicator is set to read zero for the standard addendum. Correction must be made for taper and dimensional variation of the outside diameter of the gear blank because it is used as a reference point.

When a gear is checked, a thin tooth will project further into the instrument and the dial indicator will read plus. Conversely, a thick tooth causes a minus reading. The change in tooth thickness is the difference in thickness between the gear being measured and the specified tooth thickness. This change in tooth thickness can be computed by:

$$\Delta_t = 2 \times R_c \times \tan \phi_n \qquad (15)$$

where:

Δ_t = change in tooth thickness, in. (mm)
R_c = addendum comparator reading, in. (mm)
ϕ_n = normal profile angle of the instrument, deg

Span measurement. In the span measurement method, a vernier caliper or plate micrometer is used to measure the distance across several teeth along a line tangent to the base cylinder (see Fig. 4-103). The distance measured is the sum of the base pitches of the spanned teeth minus one (n-1), plus the thickness of one tooth at the base cylinder. The number of teeth included between the vernier caliper or plate micrometer when measuring dimension M as shown in Fig. 4-103 is based on the number of teeth and pressure angle of the gear being measured. Refer to AGMA 231 for the method of computation.

The tooth thickness determined by span measurement is not affected by outside diameter variations or runout. However, span measurements are influenced by variations in tooth pitch, profile, and alignment. The measurements would be erroneous if attempted on a portion of the profile that had been modified from a true involute shape. In addition, span measurements cannot be applied when a combination of high helix angle and narrow face width prevent the caliper from spanning a sufficient number of teeth.

Measurement over pins. The pin or wire method of checking gear tooth thickness is an accurate method because the measurements are not influenced by the outside diameter or runout of the gear. Measurements are affected, however, by variations in tooth spacing and profile. Tooth thickness measurements can also be made over one pin in a proper fixture, but the result will be influenced by runout.

In practice, two or three cylindrical pins or wires of a specified diameter are placed in diametrically opposite tooth spaces for gears with an even number of teeth (see Fig. 4-104). If the gear has an odd number of teeth, the pins or wires are

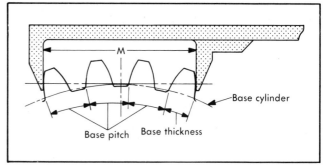

Fig. 4-103 Span-measurement tooth thickness inspection method.

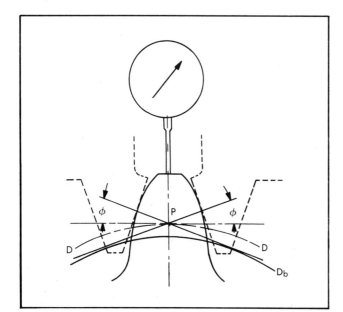

Fig. 4-102 Gear tooth comparator used in tooth thickness inspection.

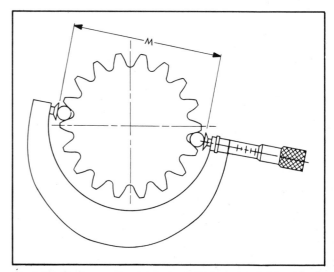

Fig. 4-104 Measurement-over-pins tooth thickness inspection method.

located as nearly opposite as possible. The overall dimension M is measured using the appropriate-sized micrometer. The pin diameter is based on the diametral pitch of the gear and whether the gear is internal or external. Formulas for determining the tooth thickness based on the measurement over pins are given in AGMA 231.

Backlash

Backlash in gears is the play between mating tooth surfaces; a single gear cannot have backlash. For purposes of measurement and calculation, backlash is defined as the amount by which a tooth space exceeds the thickness of an engaging tooth (see Fig. 4-105). The actual backlash is a function of the variations in runout, tooth thicknesses, profile, and tooth alignment. It does not include the effect of center-distance changes of the mountings and variations in bearings. Numerical values of backlash are understood to be measured at the tightest point of mesh on the pitch circle, unless otherwise specified.

The general purpose of backlash is to prevent gears from jamming together and making contact on both sides of their teeth simultaneously. A certain amount of backlash is also necessary to provide room for gear lubrication. Lack of backlash may cause noise, overloading, overheating of the gears and bearings, and even seizing and failure. In addition, unnecessarily close backlash tolerances increase the cost of producing the gear because variations in runout, pitch, profile, and mounting must be held correspondingly smaller. The amount of backlash specified is generally based on the application and size of the gear. Decreasing backlash seldom improves the quality of the gear.

One method used to measure backlash is to hold one gear solidly against rotation while permitting the other gear to rotate. An indicator is then mounted against the tooth surface of the gear that is free to rotate. The indicator axis of motion should be perpendicular to this surface (at the large end in the case of bevel gears). Normal backlash can be read on the indicator by turning the gear back and forth. The range over which the gear can be moved is the backlash. Several checks are usually necessary to determine the minimum backlash of the gear.

In spur gears, parallel helical gears, and bevel gears, it is immaterial whether the pinion or gear is held stationary for the test. In crossed helical and hypoid gears, backlash readings may vary depending on which gear is held stationary. It is therefore customary to hold the pinion stationary.

Another method of checking backlash on large gears, which are too heavy to be rotated by hand, is with feeler gages. With

this method, different-sized feeler gages are inserted between the meshing teeth in various positions around the gear to determine the backlash.

When checking backlash with a dial indicator or a feeler gage, the value obtained is backlash in the normal plane. However, backlash is generally specified in the transverse plane or plane of rotation. Backlash in the normal plane can be converted to backlash in the transverse plane by the equation:

$$B_T = \frac{B_N}{(\cos \phi)(\cos \psi)} \qquad (16)$$

where:

B_T = backlash in the transverse plane, in. (mm)
B_N = backlash in the normal plane, in. (mm)
ϕ = helix angle, deg
ψ = pressure angle, deg

On extremely fine-pitch gears, it may not be possible to measur backlash using indicating devices. For small gears, a toolmaker's microscope can be used. The best way to measure backlash on fine-pitch spur and helical gears is on a gear-rolling tester (double-flank testing).

FUNCTIONAL GEAR CHECKING

Functional or composite gear checking involves rolling two gears together and measuring the resultant motion. The gears rolled together can be either work and master gears or two work gears. The two commonly used functional checking methods are double-flank testing and single-flank testing. Another checking method related to functional checking is tooth contact or bearing pattern checking.

Functional gear checking can be divided into three categories: manual, semiautomatic, and automatic. These designations refer to the method in which the gears are loaded into the checking position and the degree of automatic classification of measurements employed.

Double-Flank Testing

In double-flank testing, the gear to be tested (work gear) is mounted on a gear-rolling tester and then run in tight mesh (double-flank contact) against a master gear (see Fig. 4-106). The work gear is constrained from all motion other than rotary while the master gear is mounted on a fixture with a variable center distance. The variations in center distance (or mounting distance) that occur as the meshed gears rotate are either recorded on a strip chart or indicated by means of a dial indicator. A typical strip chart from a double-flank test is shown in Fig. 4-107.

The information obtained from the double-flank test is a quick measure of the rolling characteristics of a gear or pair of gears. The type of gears that can be checked with this method include spur, helical, bevel, and wormgears. Gear variations evaluated by double-flank testing are total composite variation and tooth-to-tooth composite variation. In certain cases, radial runout and functional tooth thickness can also be evaluated. The type of variations being checked determines how the gear-rolling tester must be set up. Double-flank testing does not provide information regarding accumulated pitch variation or specific tooth profile characteristics.

Total composite variation is the total change in center distance that occurs when the work gear is rotated one complete revolution (refer to Fig. 4-107). It is the combination of runout

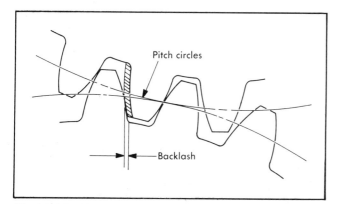

Fig. 4-105 Backlash in the plane of rotation. (*Fellows Corp.*)

MEASUREMENT OF GEARS

with tooth-to-tooth composite variation. To determine whether the work gear is acceptable, it is necessary to compensate for the total composite variation of the master gear. The work gear is acceptable if:

$$a \leq c - b \qquad (17)$$

where:

a = total composite variation reading as measured on the chart or dial indicator

b = total composite variation reading of master gear as obtained from calibration Type 1 or Type 2

c = total composite tolerance allowed on drawing

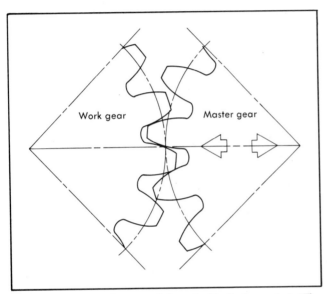

Fig. 4-106 Contact of gear teeth in a double-flank gear test. (*The Gleason Works*)

The work gear is rejected if:

$$a > b + c \qquad (18)$$

If neither of these conditions exist, the work gear is in question. In this case, the master gear should be indexed to the work gear and the test repeated. The work gear would be considered acceptable if:

$$a \leq b + c \qquad (19)$$

Tooth-to-tooth composite variation is the greatest change that occurs in center distance while the work gear is rotated through any angle of $360°/N$; N is the number of teeth on the work gear (refer to Fig. 4-107). Tooth-to-tooth composite variation includes the effects of profile, pitch, tooth thickness, and tooth alignment variations in both the work and master gears. However, it is not possible to subtract the variations in the master gear from the recorded values. For the work gear to be acceptable, the recorded variations must be within the allowable values given in AGMA 390.03.

Radial runout is measured by observing the center distance or mounting distance variation between the work and master gear. The readings (refer to Fig. 4-107) include variations of the master gear and the tooth-to-tooth composite variations in the gear being tested. The variations in each gear on the gear-rolling instrument should be taken into consideration when determining the acceptability of the gear being tested.

The functional tooth thickness is the tooth thickness of a work gear as determined by meshing with a calibrated master gear on a calibrated gear-rolling instrument. When the gear-rolling instrument is calibrated to determine size, the two limit lines as shown in Fig. 4-107 will be obtained. The trace of the tested gear must lie between the limit lines for the work gear to be acceptable. Because it is difficult to calibrate large gear-rolling instruments, it is not common practice to check the functional tooth thickness of gears over 15″ (380 mm) diam.

Operation. When performing a double-flank test, the master gear and gear-rolling fixture should be calibrated. The work

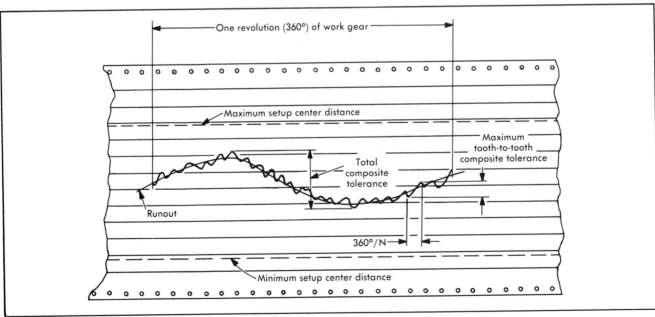

Fig. 4-107 Composite-action chart of a typical gear when run with a master gear on a gear-rolling fixture.

gear and master gear should then be mounted on their respective fixture. If mounting surfaces are specified on the drawing, they should be used. When the gears are in double-flank contact, the work gear should be rotated at least one complete revolution.

The amount of applied load is important when checking gears on a gear-rolling fixture. For example, excessive loads on fine-pitch gears of narrow face width, on gears made of soft materials, or on journal-type gears having slender shafts result in incorrect readings. The incorrect readings are caused by the deflection of the teeth or blanks. Conversely, too light a load on coarse-pitch gears of relatively wide face width results in incorrect readings caused by variations in contact between the work gear and the master gear.

The recommended loads between the work and master gears are given in Table 4-17. The values given are based on the diametral pitch and a face width of 0.1″ (2.5 mm). They also include the force of the indicating device. The recommended loads take into consideration that the movable head has antifriction mountings. For face widths less than 0.1″ (2.5 mm) the load should be decreased proportionately. It is not necessary to increase the load for a face width greater than 0.1″ (2.5 mm).

Equipment. A schematic diagram of a gear-rolling instrument is shown in Fig. 4-108. The diagram shows the kinematic and mechanical requirements of the instrument, but does not imply that this is the only acceptable construction.

For any gear-rolling instrument, provision should be made for the master gear to rotate with a minimum of runout or lateral wobble. Fixed, hardened and ground studs are generally used for master gears with bores. Hardened and ground

bushings, precision-interference ball bushings, or centers for use with shank-type master gears should be considered for more accurate use. Any clearance between the master gear bore or hub and its mounting stud or bushing will be reflected in the inspection results.

The instrument should be designed for holding the gear to be inspected on axes that are parallel to the master gear axis. Some

TABLE 4-17
Recommended Checking Load for Metallic Gears

Size, Diametral Pitch (Equivalent Module)	Load,* oz (kg, ±20%)
1-9 (2.5 to less than 25)	33-39 (1.0)
10-19 (1.25 to less than 2.5)	29-35 (0.9)
20-29 (0.8 to less than 1.25)	25-31 (0.8)
30-39 (0.6 to less than 0.8)	21-27 (0.7)
40-49 (0.50)	17-23 (0.6)
50-59 (0.40)	13-19 (0.5)
60-79 (0.30)	6-10 (0.3)
80-99 (0.25)	3-5 (0.2)
100-149 (0.16)	3-5 (0.1)
150 and finer (finer than 0.16)	3-5 (0.1)

*For metallic gears, use 1/2 of the listed value.

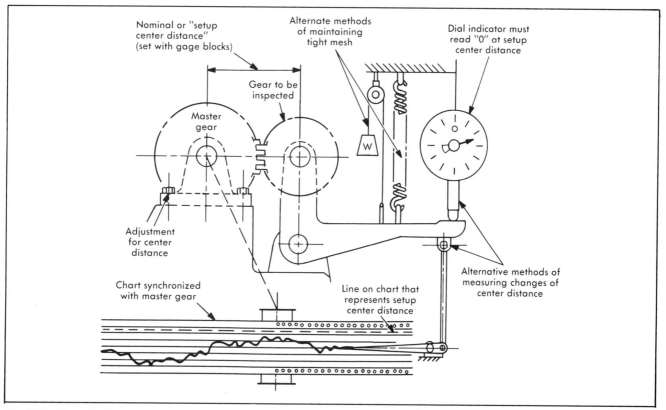

Fig. 4-108 Schematic diagram showing mechanical and kinematic requirements of a gear-rolling fixture.

MEASUREMENT OF GEARS

instruments provide a means of tilting the master gear and work gear axes in relation to each other. The gear-rolling instrument should also incorporate provisions for accurately setting the tilt angle and realigning the axis to the zero position with precision. In addition, a provision should be made for keeping a fixed angular relationship between the axis of the work gear and that of the master gear during their movement toward and away from each other.

To keep the work gear in tight mesh with the master gear, an adjustable-force mechanism should be incorporated in the design. The applied force or load should be uniform over the entire reading scale. The two main methods used to maintain the proper mesh and contact force are a weight and a spring.

The changes in meshing center distance are indicated by means of a dial indicator or a recording device. If a recording device is used, it should be capable of establishing the relationship between the position on the chart. It should also establish the circumferential position on either the work gear or master gear. An accurate method of calibrating the dial indicator or recording equipment over its working range is essential.

A typical indicating-type gear-rolling instrument is shown in Fig. 4-109. These instruments are usually manually operated and thus relatively inexpensive. They also permit quick testing. In general, indicating-type gear-rolling instruments are used to determine whether the center distance variations exceed an acceptable range. They are widely used for on-the-spot quality control at the gear-cutting machine. They are not used to analyze in detail the conditions that cause the variations.

A typical recording-type gear-rolling instrument is shown in Fig. 4-110. During testing, the master gear is driven by a variable speed motor. Recorder chart drive speed is also variable. The recorders for these instruments are either mechanical or electronic, with electronic recorders being most common. Most recording systems are capable of recording the variations in several different magnifications. The most commonly used magnification is 500 to 1, with each graduation line of the chart paper representing a 0.0002″ (0.005 mm) departure from an ideal straight line that would result in the case of zero center variations. Refer to Fig. 4-107 for a strip chart recording from a double-flank test.

Single-Flank Testing

Single-flank testing simulates the actual operating conditions of a gear pair. The mating gears roll together at their proper center distance with backlash and with only one flank in contact (see Fig. 4-111). The driven gear generally has a slight drag. Gears can be tested by pairs or with master gears. Single-flank testing is used for checking parallel axis, bevel, worm, crossed helical, and offset conical gears.

The single-flank test is run using encoders or other devices to measure rotational motion. Encoders may be attached to the input and output shafts of a special machine for testing pairs of gears. The encoders may also be used portably by attaching them directly to the input and output shafts of an actual gear box so as to inspect the quality of a complete train of gears.

Data from the encoders is processed in an instrument that shows the accuracy or smoothness of rotational motion resulting from the meshing of the gears. This data can be directly related to portions of involute or profile variations, pitch variation, runout, and accumulated pitch variation. The most important aspect of single-flank testing is that it permits measurement of profile conjugacy, which is the parameter that most closely relates to typical gear noise. Another important aspect of single-flank testing is its ability to check accumulated pitch variation.

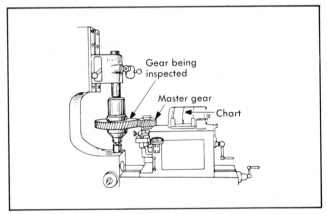

Fig. 4-110 View of system for spur and helical gear inspection. (*Fellows Corp.*)

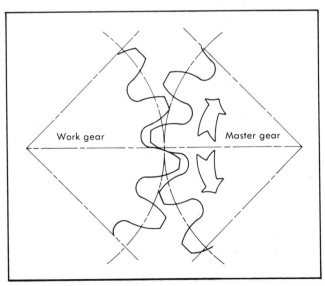

Fig. 4-111 Contact of gear teeth in a single-flank gear test. (*The Gleason Works*)

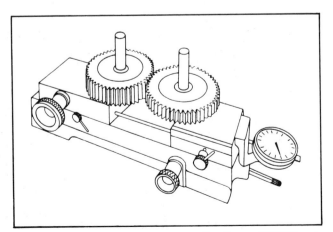

Fig. 4-109 Variable center distance gear-rolling fixture. (*ITW Illitron*)

Single-flank testing cannot measure lead or tooth alignment of spur and helical gears directly. Lead variations do, however, influence other motion transmission variations that result from profile variations, because of the influence of overlap or increased contact ratio. Lead or tooth alignment variation is best measured by elemental checks, gimbal-head double-flank composite check, or by tooth contact pattern checks.

Operation. Figure 4-112 shows schematically the operation of a single-flank measuring machine. The two motions being compared are monitored by circular optical gratings. The gratings give a train of impulses having a frequency that is a measure of the angular movements of the two shafts. Because most gear ratios are not 1:1, one or both of the trains of impulses is processed.

The phase difference of the two processed pulse trains is converted to an analog waveform proportional to variations in transmission motion. Motion variations of less than one arc second can be detected. This difference is recorded as an analog waveform and comes out of the instrument on a strip chart as shown in Fig. 4-113.

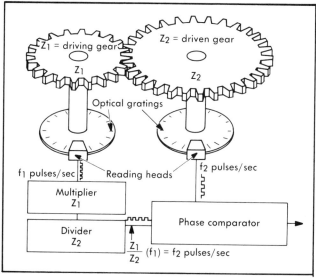

Fig. 4-112 Schematic diagram of the operating principle of a single-flank measuring machine. (*The Gleason Works*)

Data interpretation. Gears with perfect involute tooth forms roll together with uniform motion. Nonuniform motion results when pitch variations or involute modifications exist.

In some gear applications, perfect involutes are desirable. However, profiles of gear teeth are often modified to obtain a compromise between load-carrying capabilities and smoothness of roll or transmitted motion. Such modifications produce variations in the recorded data output. These variations must be considered when interpreting the graphs.

Figure 4-114 shows three typical tooth shapes and their resulting motion curves. The tooth shape and curve in view *a* is of a perfect involute. Because the teeth are perfect involutes, the motion between the teeth is smooth, resulting in an angular motion curve that is a straight line. View *b* shows a gear tooth with a profile modification. The modification is indicated by the dotted line. As the gear revolves on its center, the contact progresses from the tip to the root of one member. The lack of stock at the root and the tip results in a parabola-like motion curve. The tooth in view *c* has a pressure angle variation indicated by the dotted line. As the contact progresses from the tip to the root, the tooth form gets closer to the correct shape. This type of tooth variation results in a ramp or sawtooth type of motion curve.

Another way to show the relationship between involute shape and a single-flank graph of a spur gear is depicted in Fig. 4-115. The curves are a graphic representation of some of the types of nonuniform motion that gears are likely to transmit.

Data analysis. Much of the information about the gear teeth can be read directly from the graph described previously. However, in many cases, this data becomes complex and difficult to read. Techniques available to aid in this analysis include Fourier analysis (real-time analyzers), time history averaging, and computer-aided data analysis.

Contact Pattern Check

Contact checking is used for the inspection of mating gear sets to determine their operational compatability. It is also used for the inspection of gears that will not fit into available checking machines because of size and weight limits. Contact checking is commonly used on bevel, mill, marine, and high-speed gears.

In practice, the teeth of the gears being checked are coated with a thin film of marking compound. The mating gears are then run under a light load for a few seconds. The contact pattern

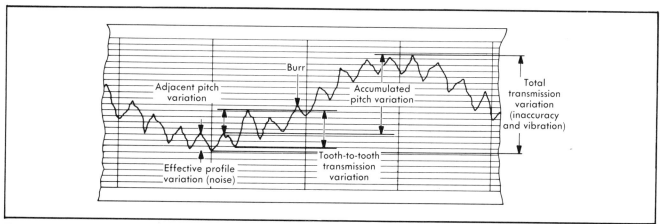

Fig. 4-113 Strip chart from single-flank measuring machine showing individual variations. (*The Gleason Works*)

MEASUREMENT OF GEARS

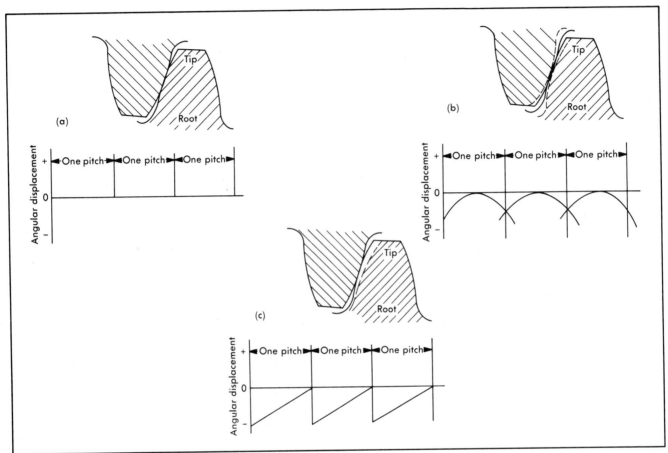

Fig. 4-114 Three typical tooth shapes and their corresponding motion curves: (a) perfect involute, (b) modified tooth shape, and (c) pressure angle variation. (*The Gleason Works*)

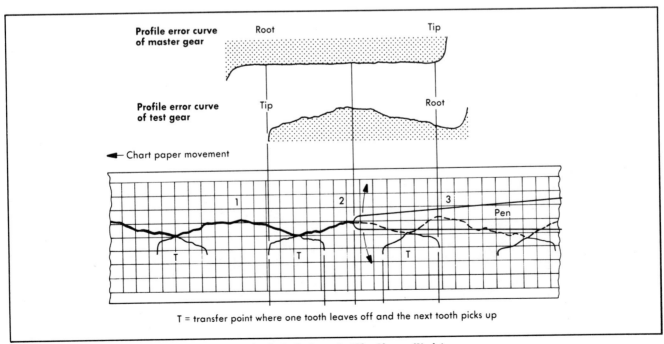

Fig. 4-115 Relationship between the involute shape and a single-flank graph. (*The Gleason Works*)

developed on the gear tooth surface is observed and then evaluated. Contact pattern acceptability is specified by defining the area in which contact may not occur, the areas in which contact should occur, and the percentage of contact required in the desired area. In most applications, a uniform contact pattern extending over the entire area of the tooth surface is desirable. Diagrams of typical contact patterns, indicating different types of errors, can be obtained from AGMA.

The reproducibility of contact pattern checks is dependent on careful control of the test conditions. A small variation in test gear locations from test to test will have a significant effect on the test results. If the gears are tested outside the housing in which they will be used, or if the assembled centers are adjustable, the gears must be mounted with their axes exactly parallel. If the test gears are being compared to a master gear, the master gear must be of known quality and of a level to ensure that errors in the master gear will not appreciably affect the results.

Various marking compounds can be used, including prussian blue, dye check developer, and proprietary compounds. It is important that the compound be controlled carefully because its viscosity and the method of application affect film thickness. Proper film thickness is critical to the interpretation of results.

Contact patterns are usually recorded by photography, sketches, or tapes. Instant-developing color film is particularly useful for recording contact patterns. Tapes are made by carefully applying transparent mending tape over the contact pattern, removing the tape, and applying the tape with adhering pattern to white paper.

MEASUREMENT OF INVOLUTE SPLINES

Involute splines provide a positive rotational coupling between a shaft with external teeth and a related outer member with internal spline teeth. The use of splines permits ease of assembly or disassembly for replacement or servicing and permits fixed or sliding connections. Splined products also permit compact assembly of parts or, by use of standardized fittings, the intercoupling of motors with gearboxes or other loads.

Because there is no rolling action between the mating members as there is between meshing gears, all of the spline teeth are expected to fit together. Although various internal and external fits are available, the final goal of involute splines is to achieve a self-centering condition with full contact bearing. The result of this would be equalized load-sharing and stress on all the teeth.

Various manufacturing-induced errors diminish this ideal equalized condition up to the point where a spline may fail to properly engage its mating member. Some typical factors that affect proper mating are tooth thickness, space width, index variations, profile variations, lead variation, and out-of-roundness. Among the manufacturing processes, the one most difficult to deal with is heat treating. Heat treating is particularly troublesome if the part is slender, thin-walled, or tubular because distortion becomes extremely likely and also irregular.

Fixed-Limit Gaging

A common way of inspecting splined workpieces prior to assembly is with fixed-limit gages. External splines are checked with internal-toothed rings whereas internal splines are checked with external-toothed plugs.

Basically there are only two types of fixed-limit spline gages, composite and sector. Composite gages have the same number

of teeth as that of the part (see Fig. 4-116, view *a*). Sector gages have only two sectors of teeth 180° apart (see Fig. 4-116, view *b*). These gages are further subdivided into GO and NOT-GO gages. Figure 4-117 illustrates the relationship between the various space width and tooth thickness limits and the main type of gages used for their inspection.

The GO gages are used to inspect maximum material conditions (maximum external or minimum internal dimensions). They may be used to inspect an individual dimension or the relationship between two or more functional dimensions. In addition, they control the minimum looseness or maximum interference.

The NOT-GO gages are used to inspect minimum material conditions (minimum external, maximum internal dimensions), thereby controlling the maximum looseness or minimum interference. Unless otherwise agreed on, a part is only acceptable if the NOT-GO gage does not enter or go on the part. A NOT-GO gage can only check one dimension.

Both of these gages require a degree of manual dexterity in use. The GO gage needs to be tried in only one angular position. Some skill is required to start the spline into or onto the gage, especially when the fit between part and gage is close. If the spline will not enter fully, it is classed as an oversize reject. Because of its limited number of teeth, a usual nonentry situation, the NOT-GO gage is more difficult to use than the GO gage. In addition, industry standards for this check are not consistent for either the number of places that constitute a reject or the force required to attain engagement.

Analytical Spline Inspection

Analytical spline inspection is the measurement of individual dimensions and variations. The variations measured are size,

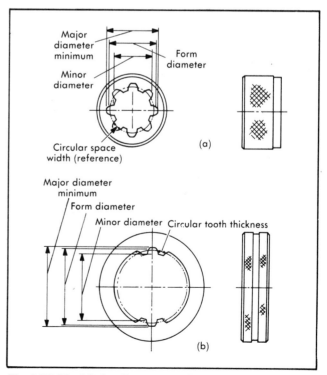

Fig. 4-116 Fixed-limit spline gages: (a) GO composite ring gage and (b) NOT-GO sector ring gage. (*Society of Automotive Engineers***)**

MEASUREMENT OF SPLINES

index, profile, lead (tooth alignment), roundness, and eccentricity. Profile inspection also covers the form diameter and tooth tip chamfer.

Analytical spline inspection is performed in the same manner as analytical gear inspection, discussed previously, and may be required:

- To supplement inspection by gages.
- To evaluate parts rejected by gages.
- For prototype parts or short runs when spline gages are not used.
- To supplement inspection by gages when each individual variation must be restrained from assuming too great a portion of the tolerance between the minimum material actual and the maximum material effective dimensions.

Measurement with pins. Actual space width and actual tooth thickness may be measured with pins. These measurements do not determine the fit between mating parts but may be used to approximate the actual space width or tooth thickness.

Measurements are made with either two or three round pins. When clearance at the major diameter cannot be obtained with round pins, flatted pins are required. Two pins are used for all external splines and some internal splines. Three pins are preferred for measuring small internal splines. A plug gage of the proper diameter must be used when measuring the distance between three pins. A micrometer is used for measuring the distance over two pins for external splines. The pin diameter used is based on the pressure angle and diametral pitch of the spline.

Total index variation. Index variations are the variations in the spacing of all corresponding tooth profiles with respect to one arbitrarily selected tooth side. The total index variation is the spread between the two greatest opposite index variations.

Profile variation. Profile is the shape of the spline tooth flank from its root to its tip. Profile variation is the difference between the measured and the specified functional profile.

Lead variation. Lead variation (tooth variation) is the variation of the direction of the spline tooth from its intended direction parallel to the reference axis. It includes parallelism and alignment variations.

Lead variation affects the fit between mating splines if all or part of the variation is because of helix or parallelism variation. It also affects the fit between mating splines if the same reference axis is used for location of a related component.

Out-of-roundness. Out-of-roundness is the variation of the spline from a true circular configuration. It is measured by taking a series of measurements using two pins placed diametrically opposite.

Eccentricity. Eccentricity occurs in splined workpieces when the spline axis and the product axis are not the same. It may be inspected by taking readings over one pin while rotating about the part axis. However, these readings include the effect of out-of-roundness and index variations.

Eccentricity may also be inspected by measuring the center distance variation when the teeth roll in tight mesh with a mating master. Because splines are not designed to roll as gears, each tooth may lose involute contact before the next tooth comes into mesh, causing abrupt center distance variations between each tooth engagement. These variations should be disregarded. Readings obtained by this method reflect index and profile variations and are sometimes used to give a general indication of spline uniformity.

Another way in which eccentricity can be checked is by using gages with straight or tapered teeth, or special gaging fixtures with solid or expanding spline members. The relation of the effective spline contour with respect to other surfaces is checked without the effect of out-of-roundness. The type of equipment used depends on the tolerances on space width, tooth thickness, and eccentricity.

Composite Spline Inspection

An automated method for involute spline inspection has been developed for high-volume spline production. Its purpose is to permit a higher percent of product inspection as a supplement to the continued use of fixed gaging. The composite

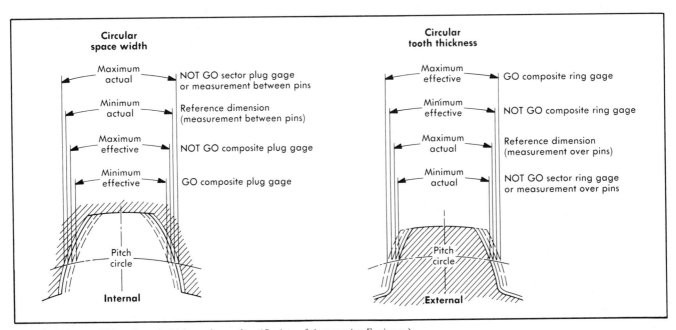

Fig. 4-117 Space width and tooth thickness inspection. (*Society of Automotive Engineers*)

spline inspection method uses a dynamic means for span measurement that duplicates the principle of a flange micrometer on block measurement.

In this method of inspection, the splined workpiece is supported on its journals in a cradle or between centers. A pair of rotating checking discs engage the spline over an appropriate span of teeth (see Fig. 4-118). One of the discs is axially fixed and keyed to its drive shaft to rotate the spline. The second keyed disc is free to slide axially on the drive shaft. It is also spring-loaded so that it will close over the spline teeth span.

As the workpiece is rotated through one full revolution, the axial movement of the second disc progressively senses the variation in spans tooth by tooth. A displacement transducer records the axial movement of the sensing disc. The transducer also provides a continuous signal that includes a succession of span readings equal to the number of teeth in the part. The output of the displacement transducer may be displayed on a video screen (oscilloscope), recorded on a strip chart, or made to trigger indicator lights. Various indicator lights light up to designate whether the workpiece is good, undersize, or oversize.

The machines used for composite spline inspection may be either semiautomatic or automatic in operation. Production rates vary for each machine depending on diametral pitch and pitch diameter of the specific spline being inspected.

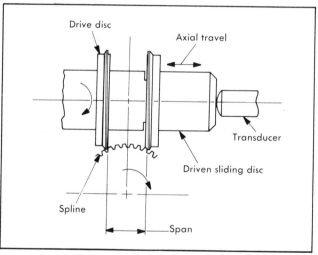

Fig. 4-118 Schematic of operating principle of a composite spline inspection machine. (*ITW Illitron*)

References

1. Lowell W. Foster, *Modern Geometric Dimensioning and Tolerancing*, 2nd ed. (Fort Washington, MD: National Tooling and Machining Association, 1982), p. 1.
2. *Ibid.*, pp. 147-153.
3. "Dimensioning and Tolerancing," ANSI Y14.5M—1982 (New York: American Society of Mechanical Engineers, 1982), p. 94.
4. *Ibid.*, p. 91.
5. *Ibid.*, p. 95.
6. *Ibid.*, p. 96.
7. *Ibid.*, p. 97.
8. *Ibid.*, p. 106.
9. *Ibid.*
10. *Ibid.*
11. *Ibid.*, p. 53.

12. *Ibid.*, p. 84.
13. *Ibid.*, p. 109.
14. *Ibid.*
15. "Measurement of Out-of-Roundness," ANSI B89.3.1 (New York: American Society of Mechanical Engineers, 1979).
16. Francis T. Farago, *Handbook of Dimensional Measurement*, 2nd ed. (New York: Industrial Press, Inc., 1982), p. 352.
17. *Ibid.*, p. 211.
18. *Ibid.*, p. 215.
19. *Ibid.*, p. 229.
20. *Ibid.*, p. 397.
21. "Screw Thread Gaging Systems for Dimensional Acceptability," ANSI B1.3 (New York: American Society of Mechanical Engineers, 1979).
22. *Precision Measuring Tools*, Handbook No. 37 (Watertown, MA: The Van Keuren Co., 1979), p. 149.
23. Henry H. Ryffel, ed., *Machinery's Handbook*, 22nd ed. (New York: Industrial Press, Inc., 1984), p. 1375.
24. "Gages and Gaging for Unified Inch Screw Threads," ANSI/ASME B1.2 (New York: American Society of Mechanical Engineers, 1983).
25. Farago, *op. cit.*, p. 409.
26. *Screw-Thread Standards for Federal Services*, Handbook H-28, Part I (Washington, DC: National Bureau of Standards, 1969).
27. Ryffel, *op. cit.*, p. 895.
28. *Gear Handbook*, Volume 1, AGMA 390.03 (Alexandria, VA: American Gear Manufacturers Association, 1980).
29. "Involute Splines and Inspection," Inch Version, ANSI B92.1 (Warrendale, PA: Society of Automotive Engineers, 1982).

Bibliography

Cluff, Brian W. "Gear Inspection and Chart Interpretation." *Gear Processing and Manufacturing*, 2nd ed. Dearborn, MI: Society of Manufacturing Engineers, 1984.

Drews, William E., and Stallard, Rodney D. *Talking Roundness.* SME Technical Paper IQ78-275. Dearborn, MI: Society of Manufacturing Engineers, 1978.

Janninck, William L., and Nielsen, John C. *Involute Spline Size Inspection*. Lincolnwood, IL: ITW Illitron, 1984.

Moderow, Robert H. "Gear Inspection and Chart Interpretation." *Gear Processing and Manufacturing*, 2nd ed. Dearborn, MI: Society of Manufacturing Engineers, 1984.

Siddal, Graham J. *High Precision Roundness Measurement*. SME Technical Paper IQ78-167. Dearborn, MI: Society of Manufacturing Engineers, 1978.

Smith, Robert E. *Single Flank Testing*. Rochester, NY: The Gleason Works, 1984.

SURFACE TECHNOLOGY

Surface technology is the activity that describes, details, and evaluates both the surface and subsurface layers of manufactured components.[1] Traditionally, surface texture has been accepted as the criterion that controls the quality of a surface. Direct relationships are widely assumed to exist between surface roughness and fatigue strength as well as other properties. However, tests have indicated that surface texture is only part of the consideration.[2] Metallurgical and other alterations below the surface, referred to as surface integrity, also have a major influence on material performance. The performance of a material becomes particularly important when high stresses or severe environments are encountered by the workpiece. Surface technology components are shown in Fig. 5-1.

SURFACE TEXTURE

Surface texture is a term used to describe the general quality of a workpiece surface. The term *surface finish* is colloquial, used widely to denote the general quality of a surface.[3] It is not specifically tied to the texture or characteristic pattern of the surface nor is it tied to the specific roughness values. However, a good "finish" implies low roughness values and vice versa.

The texture on a workpiece can be important for both cosmetic and functional performance reasons. In addition, surface texture and dimensional tolerances go hand in hand. For example, bearing surfaces and locating surfaces usually require close dimensional and surface finish control for proper operation and for ensuring that functional dimensions are maintained throughout the useful life of the workpiece.

Other surface texture requirements exist that are not related to dimensional tolerance. For example, surface texture is important for surfaces to be painted to ensure good adherence; for surfaces that are to be marked to ensure legibility; for surfaces over which gases or fluids are to flow; for surfaces having special appearance requirements; and for surfaces that have specific heat or light reflectivity requirements. In some cases, specific surface patterns must also be maintained.

In many instances relating to mechanical parts, the design engineer specifies the surface texture requirements for various workpiece surfaces. The designer must have a thorough understanding of surface quality to correctly specify the surface texture that will provide optimum properties for service, life, appearance, performance, and other desired mechanical functions. In addition, it is important to recognize the relationship between surface texture and the cost of producing parts. In general, as the quality of surface texture increases, the cost of producing the part also increases.

Manufacturing, process control, and inspection personnel must also have a good understanding of surface texture. For these individuals, a special emphasis should be made to understand the capabilities of the various manufacturing methods at their disposal and the methods available for measuring surface texture.

The purpose of this section of the chapter is to give the manufacturing engineer and those involved in manufacturing an understanding of the various parameters and how they can be used to characterize surface texture. In addition, the various methods and equipment used for checking surface texture are discussed. Specific surface qualities for a given application, however, are not recommended. Because of the widely varying conditions under which different surfaces must operate, no single set of criteria can be used to determine which surface or combination of surfaces may be best for a given purpose.

The discussion in this section is based primarily on ANSI B46.1, "Surface Texture," published by the American Society of Mechanical Engineers (ASME).[4] It is important to note, however, that most industrially developed countries have their own national standards; the approach taken in these documents is sometimes different from the one used in ANSI B46.1. In addition, there are several standards and recommendations on surface texture published by the International Organization for Standardization (ISO) that are accepted by most of the member countries. These standards describe the various surface texture parameters and the equipment and techniques used to properly measure the parameters. Therefore, the user of foreign-made equipment should be aware of these different approaches.

NOMENCLATURE

The terms referring to surface texture are commonly divided into those related to surfaces of solid materials and those related to the measurement of surface texture. These terms apply to surfaces produced by such means as abrading,

---

Contributor of sections of this chapter is: William E. Drews, Marketing Manager, Rank Precision Industries. Reviewers of sections of this chapter are: Dr. John A. Bailey, Professor and Department Head, Department of Mechanical and Aerospace Engineering, North Carolina State University; David A. Bechtel, President, Valmet, Inc.; Mike Bingham, Product Manager, Sheffield Measurement Div., The Warner & Swasey Co.;

SURFACE TEXTURE

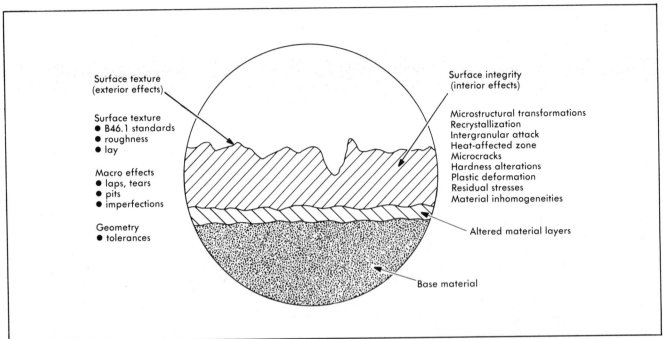

Fig. 5-1 Simulated section of the surface and surface layers of a manufactured workpiece. (*Used with permission of the Machinability Data Center*)

casting, coating, cutting, etching, plastic deformation, sintering, wear, and erosion. The definitions are abstracted with permission of ASME from ANSI B46.1.

Surfaces of Solid Materials

error of form The deviation from the nominal surface that is not included in surface texture.

flaws Unintentional, unexpected, and unwanted interruptions in the topography typical of a part surface.

lay The direction of the predominant surface pattern, ordinarily determined by the production method used.

roughness The fine irregularities of surface texture, usually including those irregularities that result from the inherent action of the production process.

surface The boundary of an object that separates that object from another object, substance, or space.

   surface, measured A representation of the surface obtained by instrumental or other means.

   surface, nominal The intended surface contour (exclusive of any intended surface roughness), the shape and extent of which is usually shown and dimensioned on a drawing or descriptive specification.

surface texture The repetitive or random deviations from the nominal surface forming the three-dimensional topography of the surface. Surface texture includes roughness, waviness, lay, and flaws.

waviness The widely spaced component of surface texture.

Measurement of Surface Texture

cutoff The electrical response characteristics of the roughness measuring instrument that is selected to limit the spacing of the surface irregularities to be included in the assessment of roughness average. The cutoff is rated in inches or millimeters.

electrical meanline The centerline established by the selected cutoff and its associated circuitry in an electric roughness measuring instrument.

graphical centerline The line about which roughness is measured. It is parallel to the general direction of the profile within the limits of the sampling length such that the sums of the areas contained between it and those parts of the profile that lie on either side are equal.

height A general term used to describe measurements of the profile taken in a direction normal to the nominal profile.

peak The point of maximum height on that portion of a profile that lies above the centerline and between two intersections of the profile and the centerline.

profile The contour of the surface in a plane perpendicular to the surface, unless some other angle is specified.

   profile, measured A representation of the profile obtained by instrumental or other means. When the measured profile is a graphical representation, it will usually be distorted through the use of different vertical and horizontal magnifications but shall be as true to the actual profile as technically possible.

Reviewers, cont.: **William E. Drews**, *Marketing Manager*, *Rank Precision Industries*; **Robert E. Fromson**, *Consultant*, *Advanced Manufacturing Technology*; **Gerry Geverdt**, *Manager of Conventional Machining Technology*, *Manufacturing Technology Lab*, *Aircraft Engine Business Group*, *General Electric Co.*; **Frank Gorsler**, *Manager-Advanced Machinability*, *Manufacturing Technology Lab*, *Aircraft Engine Business Group*, *General Electric Co.*; **John F. Kahles**, *Senior Vice President*, *Metcut Research Associates Inc.*; **Dr. Ranga Komanduri**, *Manufacturing and Materials Engineer*, *Metallurgy Laboratory*, *Corporate R & D*, *General Electric Co.*; **John LaPorte**, *Senior Project Engineer*,

profile, modified A measured profile in which filter mechanisms (including the instrument datum) are used to minimize certain surface texture characteristics and emphasize other characteristics.

profile, nominal The intended profile of the nominal surface exclusive of any intended roughness profile.

roughness average The arithmetic average of the absolute values of the measured profile height deviations taken within the sampling length and measured from the centerline.

sampling length The nominal spacing within which a surface characteristic is measured.

sampling length, roughness The sampling length within which the roughness average is determined. This length is chosen, or specified to separate the profile irregularities that are designated as roughness from those irregularities designated as waviness.

sampling length, waviness The sampling length within which the waviness height is measured.

spacing The distance between specified points on the profile measured parallel to the nominal profile.

spacing, roughness The average spacing between adjacent peaks of the measured profile within the roughness sampling length.

spacing, waviness The average spacing between adjacent peaks of the measured profile within the waviness sampling length.

traversing length The length of profile that is traversed by the stylus to establish a representative measurement.

valley The point of maximum depth on that portion of a profile that lies below the centerline and between two intersections of the profile and the centerline.

SURFACE TEXTURE COMPONENTS

The repetitive or random deviations from the nominal surface form the three-dimensional texture of the surface. This does not include errors of form, which are those components of surface topography caused by such things as warping of parts or straightness errors in the machines that produce the surface. A traditionally machined workpiece surface is composed of many surface texture components created during the manufacturing process. These components become superimposed over one another, forming a complex pattern called the profile. The common components of surface texture are roughness, waviness, and lay. They are shown individually and collectively in Fig. 5-2.

Another component of surface texture is a flaw. Flaws are unintentional, unexpected, and unwanted interruptions in the part surface. They are usually caused by nonuniformity of the material, or they may result from damage to the surface after processing, including scratches, dents, pits, and cracks. If acceptable/nonacceptable flaws are defined in advance by the buyer and seller, the workpieces should be inspected for flaws prior to performing final surface roughness measurements. If defined flaws are not present, or if flaws are not defined, then interruptions in the part surface may be included in roughness measurements.

Roughness

Roughness consists of the finer irregularities of the surface texture, usually including those irregularities that result from the inherent action of the production process. The roughness component of surface texture is generally quantified by the parameter roughness average, R_a.

Roughness average is the arithmetic average of the absolute values of the measured profile height taken within the sampling length and measured from the centerline (see Fig. 5-3). Because R_a is an arithmetic average, it only provides a general description of the actual surface. A large R_a value indicates that the actual surface is rough, and a small R_a value indicates that the actual surface is smooth.

For graphical determinations of roughness average, the height deviations are measured normal to the chart centerline. When R_a is determined from electrical averaging instruments, the cutoff selection is equivalent to the roughness sampling length. Selecting the proper cutoff length is discussed subsequently under the profile method of surface texture measurement.

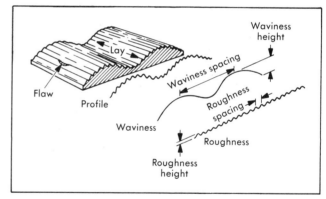

Fig. 5-2 Components of surface texture.

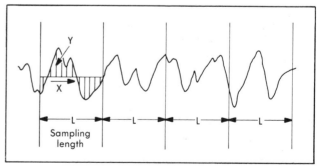

Fig. 5-3 Profile trace of roughness average measurement.

*Reviewers, cont.: Feinpruef Corp.; Randall J. Leifheit, Product Manager, Metrology, Rodenstock Precision Optics, Inc.; **Mark D. Mello**, Applications Engineer, Research and Development, Laser Fare Limited, Inc.; **Susan M. Moehring**, Manager, Machinability Data Center, Metcut Research Associates Inc.; **Roy B. Pleiman**, Product Manager, Tool and Pump Div., United Technologies Elliott; **John R. Riendeau**, Branch Manager, Federal Products Corp.; **Donald G. Risko**, Manager, Surfex Div., Extrude Hone Corp.; **Paul Rohall**, Specialist, Bearing Division, The Timken Co.; **Alexander N. Tabenkin**, Product Manager, Geometry & Surface Gaging Products, Federal Pro-ducts Corp.*

SURFACE TEXTURE COMPONENTS

Roughness range. Surfaces produced by a given type of machining or finishing operation vary widely in their roughness. This variation is due partly to factors that the operator has control over, partly to factors beyond the operator's control, and largely to differences in shop practices of the individual plants.

Figure 5-4 shows the typical range of the roughness average values that can be produced by common production methods. It is also evident from the figure that higher or lower values may be obtained under special conditions.

As was previously mentioned, the ability to produce a particular surface roughness on a part by a certain process depends on many factors in addition to characteristics of the material and condition of the machine tool. For example, in surface grinding, the final surface depends on the peripheral speed of the wheel, the speed of the traverse, the rate of feed, the grit size, bonding material and state of dress of the wheel, the amount and type of grinding fluid at the point of cutting, and the mechanical properties of the piece being ground. In turning, the surface roughness is geometrically related to the nose radius of

the tool and the feed per revolution.[5] For electrical discharge machining, the roughness level is related directly to the individual spark discharge energy level, electrode (tool) material, and electrical characteristics of the power supply. A small change in the previously mentioned factors may have a marked effect on the surface produced.

Relation of surface roughness to tolerances. Because the measurement of surface roughness involves the determination of the average deviation of the actual surface from the nominal surface, there is a direct relationship between the dimensional tolerance on a part and the permissible surface roughness. If the deviations induced by the surface roughness exceed those permitted by the dimensional tolerance, the dimension will be subject to an uncertainty beyond the tolerance.

On many surfaces, the total profile height of the surface roughness (peak-to-valley height) can vary from 4 to 10 times the measured roughness average. These values may vary somewhat with the character of the surface under consideration, but they may be used to establish approximate profile heights. Accordingly, the specified tolerance on a diameter should be at

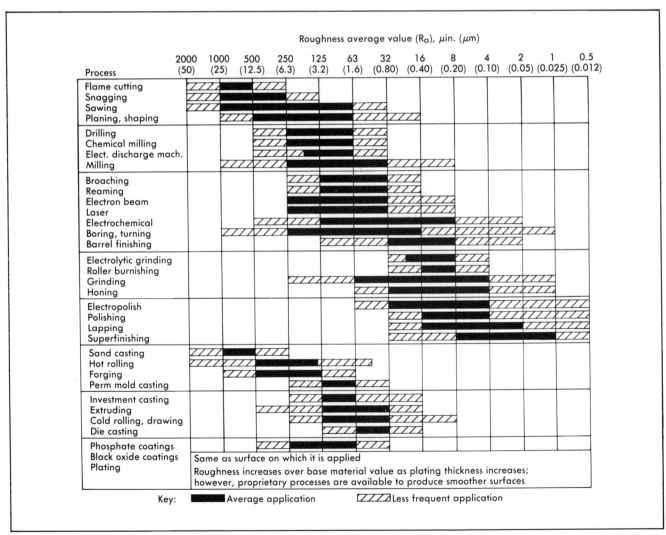

Fig. 5-4 Surface roughness produced by common production methods. (*Based on ANSI B46.1-1978; used with permission of the American Society of Mechanical Engineers*)

least 8 to 20 times the roughness average value. If the tolerance is less, the deviation in surface roughness could exceed the allowable tolerance.

Each application, however, must be evaluated on its own merit. Table 5-1 indicates the roughness average values that may be necessary when machined work must be held to close tolerance for reasons other than merely surface texture.[6] Other factors that influence tolerance control are part size, overall size of the surface being cut, and the material removal operations involved.

Waviness

Waviness is the more widely spaced component of surface texture. Unless otherwise noted, waviness includes all irregularities whose spacing is greater than the roughness sampling length and less than the waviness sampling length. Waviness may result from such factors as machine or work deflections, vibration, chatter, heat treatment, or warping strains. Roughness may be considered as superimposed on a wavy surface.

Waviness is frequently confused with profile straightness.[7] Straightness is usually specified to ensure the function of a part, whereas waviness is specified to control and limit the sources of vibration and imperfections of the machine tool and of the environment that might affect the accuracy of the machine tool.

Lay

Lay is the direction of the predominant pattern on the surface of the workpiece. These patterns are generally determined by the production method used. Processes such as turning, milling, grinding, and drawing produce a pattern that is regular and repetitive, providing an observable directionality to the surface texture pattern. The pattern from etching, electrical discharge machining, or rolling between grit-blasted rolls is irregular and random, resulting in no observable directionality. Commonly used lay symbols and their meanings are given in Fig. 5-5.

Surface Texture Parameters

A parameter is a method of assigning a numerical value to typify a surface. The most commonly used parameter for speci-

fying surface texture is roughness average, R_a. However, the value of this parameter does not always adequately indicate how the surface will function for its intended use.

Figure 5-6 shows the profile traces of two different surfaces having the same roughness average. Although the R_a readings are almost identical, the surfaces will function quite differently. It is therefore necessary to consider the function of the part when determining the surface texture parameters to be measured.

For example, if a part is being prepared for painting, the surface must be finished in such a way that the paint adheres in a smooth manner. On the other hand, a part surface that oils or wipes another surface requires a completely different surface texture.

TABLE 5-1
Guide to Surface Roughness Values for
Close-Tolerance Machine Work

Dimensional Tolerances, in. (mm)	Surface Roughness, μin. (μm)
Below 0.0002 (Below 0.005)	Below 8 (below 0.2)
0.0002-0.0005 (0.005-0.012)	8-16 (0.2-0.4)
0.0005-0.0010 (0.012-0.025)	16-32 (0.4-0.8)
0.0010-0.0020 (0.025-0.05)	32-63 (0.8-1.6)
0.0020-0.0100 (0.05-0.25)	63-250 (1.6-6.3)

(*Used with permission of the American Society for Metals.*)

Lay symbol	Meaning	Example showing direction of tool marks
—	Lay approximately parallel to the line representing the surface to which the symbol is applied	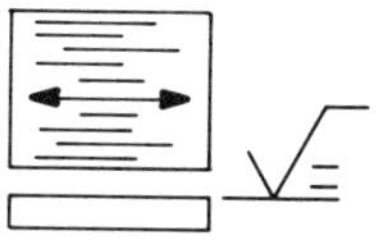
⊥	Lay approximately perpendicular to the line representing the surface to which the symbol is applied	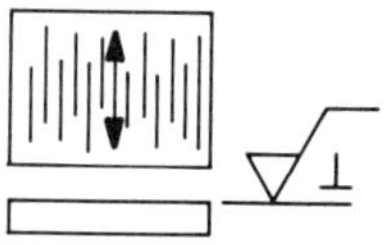
X	Lay angular in both directions to line representing the surface to which the symbol is applied	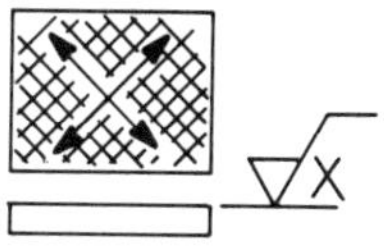
M	Lay multidirectional	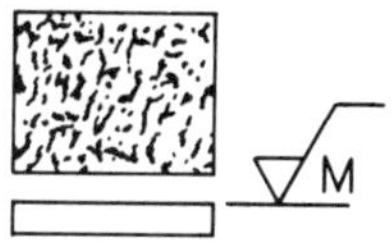
C	Lay approximately circular relative to the center of the surface to which the symbol is applied	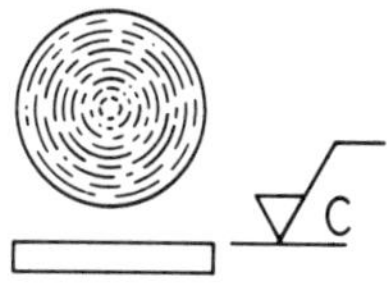
R	Lay approximately radial relative to the center of the surface to which the symbol is applied	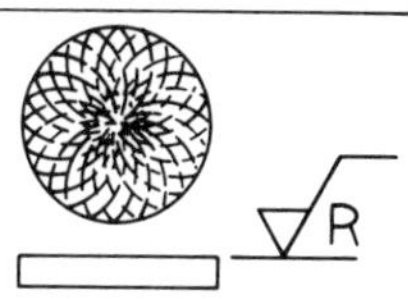
P	Lay particulate, nondirectional, or protuberant	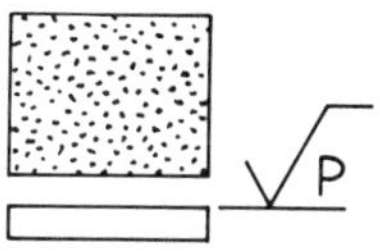

Fig. 5-5 Lay symbols. (*Based on ANSI Y14.36-1978; used with permission of the American Society of Mechanical Engineers*)

SURFACE TEXTURE COMPONENTS

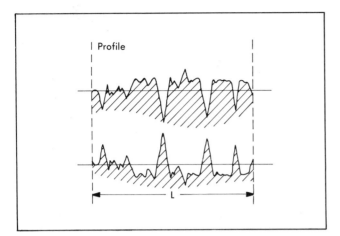

Fig. 5-6 Profile traces of two different surfaces having the same roughness average.

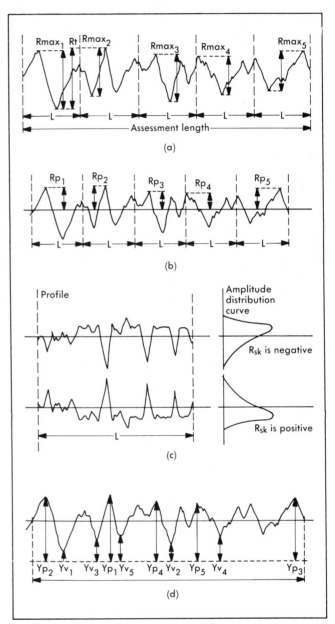

Fig. 5-7 Amplitude parameters used in the measurement of surface texture: (a) peak-to-valley height, (b) profile height, (c) skewness, and (d) ten-point height.

The type of surface texture on a part becomes more complex when the surface must satisfy more than one function. For example, in the automotive industry, the drawing performance of steel sheet in the forming process is sensitive to the surface texture. In addition, the exposed parts must also have the proper finish for paint appearance quality.

Because of the multiplicity of functions that the surface of a part must perform and an increasing push toward better quality, new surface texture parameters have been developed. In general, more than one parameter is required to adequately describe the surface texture. Currently, more than 50 parameters exist for describing surface conditions. Based on the information they provide, these parameters break down into three groups: amplitude parameters, spacing parameters, and hybrid parameters.

Amplitude parameters. Amplitude parameters are sensitive to variations in the profile height of the surface. The parameters generally included in this grouping are roughness average, geometric roughness average, peak-to-valley height, profile height, skewness, and ten-point height.

Geometric roughness average. The geometric roughness average, R_q, is an alternative to roughness average that is more sensitive to occasional highs and lows. It is defined as the root mean square (RMS) value of a profile calculated over a single sampling length. The geometric roughness average can also be expressed as the mean result of measurement over five consecutive sampling lengths.

Peak-to-valley height. The peak-to-valley height of a surface can be characterized by several different parameters. The maximum peak-to-valley height within the assessment length is represented by R_t (see Fig. 5-7, view *a*). The R_t measurement is valuable for analyzing finish to provide guidance for planning subsequent metal removal operations such as honing or lapping. This value indicates how much material can be removed before the part size reaches a particular limit. It also is useful in determining when continued processing of the part would produce little or no effect.

R_{max} or R_y represents the maximum peak-to-valley height within a sampling length L. Because R_{max} can be affected by a scratch or particle of dirt on the surface, it is more usual to use the average peak-to-valley height (R_{tm}) of five consecutive sampling lengths in the German DIN Standard, R_{tm} is designated R_z (DIN).

Profile height. Like the peak-to-valley height, the profile height is characterized by more than one parameter. The maximum profile height from the meanline within the sampling length is represented by R_p (see Fig. 5-7, view *b*). The mean value of R_p determined over five sampling lengths is R_{pm}.

Skewness. Skewness, R_{sk}, is a measure of the symmetry of the profile about the meanline (see Fig. 5-7, view *c*). It distinguishes between asymmetrical profiles having the same R_a or R_q values.

Skewness shows whether a porous sintered and cast surface will yield a meaningful R_a value. A positive skew indicates an abundance of peaks, and a negative skew indicates valleys. Skewness provides a criterion for judging bearing surfaces. A good bearing surface should have negative skew.

Ten-point height. The ten-point height, R_z (ISO), is the average height difference between the five highest peaks and the five lowest valleys (see Fig. 5-7, view *d*). It is measured over a single sampling length from a line parallel to the meanline and not crossing the profile.

The ten-point height can be combined with R_a for a more complete characterization of surface texture. Measuring R_z (ISO) is one preferred method for analyzing short surfaces.

Spacing parameters. Spacing parameters are sensitive to variations in the profile wavelength. The parameters generally included in this grouping are peak count, high spot count, and mean spacing.

Peak count. Peak count, P_c, is the number of peak-and-valley pairs per inch projecting through an arbitrarily specified band width centered about the meanline (see Fig. 5-8, view *a*). It is an important parameter for surfaces that are formed or are intended to accept a coating such as a polymer or paint. When used in conjunction with R_a, P_c provides essential information about the quality of surfaces prior to coating.

High spot count. The high spot count, HSC, is an alternative peak count (see Fig. 5-8, view *b*). It is the number of profile peaks projecting above the meanline or a line parallel to the meanline at a preset distance from it or from the highest peak. The count of the profile peaks projecting above the meanline is made over five cutoffs.

Mean spacing. Mean spacing, S_m, is the mean spacing between profile peaks at the meanline, assessed over one sampling length L (see Fig. 5-8, view *c*). It is a peak count parameter independent of amplitude.

Hybrid parameters. Hybrid parameters are sensitive to variations in the profile height of the surface as well as profile wavelength. The parameters generally included in this grouping are wavelength, slope, bearing length ratio, and bearing area.

Wavelength. Average wavelength, λ_a, or RMS wavelength, λ_q, is a measure of the spacings between local peaks and valleys. This measurement takes into account the relative peak-to-valley amplitudes and individual spatial frequencies. Being a hybrid parameter, it is more useful than a parameter based solely on amplitude or spacing for some applications.

Average wavelength provides a direct relationship with average grit size in grinding operations. By monitoring λ_a, a manufacturer can obtain information related to the effects of changes in grinding wheel makeup or obtain information to help determine when a wheel needs dressing to maintain quality.

Average wavelength also relates directly to tool feed marks in precision turning operations. If something goes wrong in a turning process, the average wavelength of the part may change dramatically even though R_a may not change significantly.

Slope. The average or RMS value of the slope of the profile throughout its length is characterized by Δ_a or Δ_q, respectively. From this value, the ratio of the actual profile length to the nominal measured length can be obtained.

The slope provides a measure of crushability of surfaces. If the slope is greater than 10°, the surface is considered elastic; the surface will recover after a load is removed. Conversely, if the slope is less than 10°, the surface is considered plastic; the surface will remain deformed.

Slope measurements are useful in describing optical surfaces. If the slope is small, the surface is a good mirror. The slope parameter can also be used to indicate friction characteristics. If the slope is large, it indicates that good contact exists. The slope parameter is also used in studying noise generated by surface roughness.

Bearing length ratio. Bearing length ratio, t_p, is the length of the bearing surface, expressed as a percentage of the assessment length L, at a depth p below the highest peak (see Fig. 5-9). It simulates wear at various cutting depths of surface. The bearing length ratio is useful whenever bearing surfaces must be analyzed and qualified for lubrication and wear properties.

The bearing length ratio is also known as the bearing area. In microprocessor-based instruments, the bearing area can be expressed quantitatively as the percent relationship of material surface area to the evaluation length of specific cutting depths.

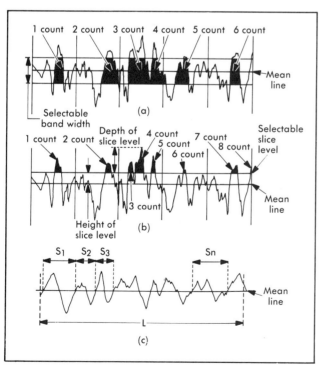

Fig. 5-8 Spacing parameters used in the measurement of surface texture: (a) peak count, (b) high spot count, and (c) mean spacing.

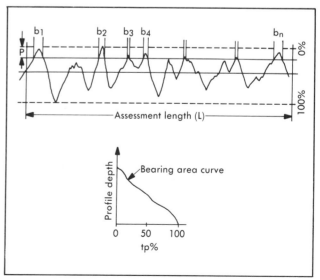

Fig. 5-9 Profile trace of bearing length ratio curve.

SURFACE TEXTURE DESIGNATION

It can also be expressed graphically using the "Abbott Firestone bearing curve." The slope of the Abbott Firestone bearing curve is helpful in analyzing how fast a surface will wear and the dimensional size change after wear-in. A typical bearing area curve is shown in Fig. 5-9.

SURFACE TEXTURE DESIGNATION

When surface control is not specified on a drawing, it is assumed that the surface produced by the operation will be satisfactory. If the surface texture is critical, the quality of the surface should be indicated by means of a surface-designating symbol. This symbol is a multipurpose one within which roughness, waviness, and lay ratings or values may be inserted to specify the desired surface. Only those values required to control the surface quality should be inserted in the symbol to prevent confusion and extra cost in part production. Unless otherwise specified, surface-designating symbols apply to the completed surface. Drawings or specifications for plated or coated parts should indicate whether the symbols apply before plating, after plating, or both before and after plating. When specifying surface texture parameters, it is important to specify the cutoff, particularly on short surfaces, and when there is a need for correlation between plants or with vendors.

The standard symbol used to designate surface roughness is the check mark as shown in Fig. 5-10, view a. This symbol indicates that the surface may be produced by any method. The roughness specification is placed to the left of the long leg. Specifications may be given as only one value or as a range. If two values are specified, the maximum value is usually critical for the function or performance of the surface; the minimum value would prevent costly overmachining of the surface. When only one value is given, the value indicates the maximum value that is acceptable for roughness. Implied in the single value specification is the understanding that a value less than the maximum is also acceptable. The roughness specification is given in either microinches or micrometers depending on the units used for the drawing.

On occasion, the surface texture symbol is modified to indicate whether material removal is required or prohibited and if other surface characteristics must be controlled. When the surface must be produced by machining, the symbol shown in Fig. 5-10, view b, is used. The horizontal bar indicates that machining is required and that material must be provided for that purpose. The number to the left of the symbol indicates the amount of stock to be removed (see Fig. 5-10, view c). Tolerances may be added to the basic value or given in a note.

The circle in the vee indicates that the surface must be produced by forming processes such as casting, forging, hot finishing, cold finishing, die casting, powder metallurgy, or injection molding without subsequent removal of material (see Fig. 5-10, view d). When surface texture characteristics other than roughness are specified, the symbol is drawn with a horizontal extension as shown in Fig. 5-10, view e.

For parts requiring extensive and uniform roughness control, a general note may be added to the drawing (see Fig. 5-11). The surface texture value in the note applies to each surface texture symbol specified without values. When surface roughness control of several operations is required within a given area or on a given surface, surface qualities may be designated as shown in Fig. 5-12.

As was previously mentioned, the surface texture symbol is also used to specify waviness and lay. Waviness specifications are indicated above the horizontal extension of the surface texture symbol. The first value given is the maximum waviness height rating, and the second value is the maximum waviness spacing. These values are given either in inches or millimeters. A measured value less than the specified maximum is acceptable. The lay symbol is placed to the right of the surface texture symbol. Refer to Fig. 5-5 for commonly used lay symbols and their meanings.

Figure 5-13 illustrates examples of roughness, waviness, and lay designation by inserting values in appropriate positions relative to the symbol. If the symbol of Fig. 5-14 was applied to the surface of a given part, its surface quality would have to conform to the following specification:

Roughness average, as measured across the lay by an electronic instrument set for a roughness-width cutoff of 0.030", may be either 63 or 32 μin. deviation from the meanline or any value between 63 and 32. The roughness-width rating must not be greater than 0.015". The waviness height, measured peak-to-

	Symbol	Meaning
(a) 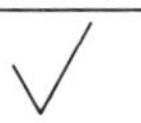		Basic surface texture symbol. Surface may be produced by any method except when the bar or circle (view b or d), is specified
(b) 		Material removal by machining is required. The horizontal bar indicates that material removal by machining is required to produce the surface and that material must be provided for that purpose
(c)	3.5 	Material removal allowance. The number indicates the amount of stock to be removed by machining in inches or millimeters. Tolerances may be added to the basic value shown or in a general note
(d) 		Material removal prohibited. The circle in the vee indicates that the surface must be produced by processes such as casting, forging, hot finishing, cold finishing, die casting, powder metallurgy, or injection molding without subsequent removal of material
(e) 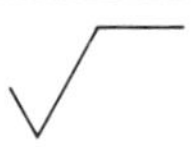		Surface texture symbol. To be used when any surface characteristics are specified above the horizontal line or to the right of the symbol. Surface may be produced by any method except when the bar or circle (view b and d), is specified

Fig. 5-10 Surface texture symbols. (*Based on ANSI Y14.36-1978; used with permission of the American Society of Mechanical Engineers*)

valley, should not exceed 0.002″. The waviness width between adjacent waves (peak-to-peak or valley-to-valley) should not exceed 2.000″.

MEASUREMENT OF SURFACE TEXTURE

Surfaces and their measurement provide a vital link between the manufacturing of engineering components and their suita-

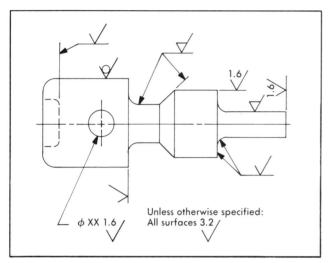

Fig. 5-11 Application of surface texture symbols. (*Based on ANSI Y14.36-1978; used with permission of the American Society of Mechanical Engineers*)

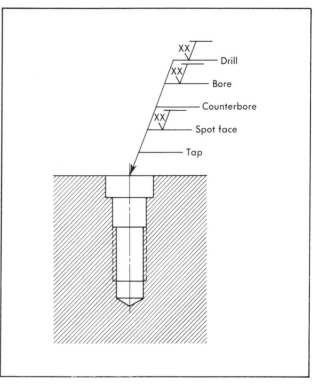

Fig. 5-12 Method of indicating surface texture symbols for several related operations within a given area.

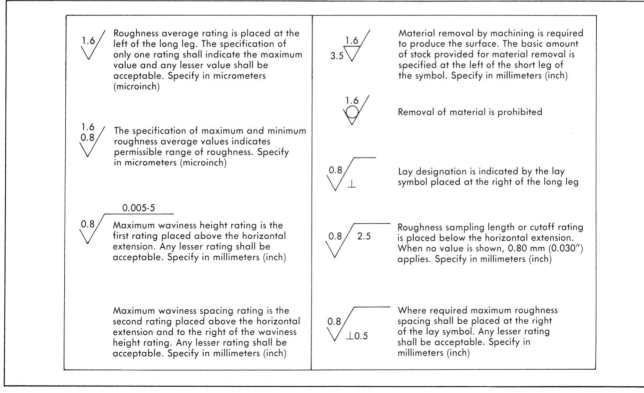

Fig. 5-13 Application of surface texture values to symbol. (*Based on ANSI Y14.36; used with permission of the American Society of Mechanical Engineers*)

SURFACE TEXTURE DESIGNATION

bility for an intended performance. The measurement of surface texture is not purely a means of quality control, but forms an essential part of the manufacturing process. When it is used correctly, it facilitates control of performance, process, material, and machine.

The use of the wrong instrument or methods for surface texture measurement can lead to failure of a product in its end use, even though the apparent surface texture exceeds specifications. Conversely, it may be that the finishing steps taken to prepare a metal surface raise the end cost of the product out of proportion to its practical value.

Surface characteristics of castings should never be considered on the same basis as those of machined surfaces. Castings are characterized by random distribution of nondirectional deviations from the nominal surface. Because of this, area methods are generally used to measure and control surface texture requirements on castings and other nondirectional lay surfaces.

Engineers should recognize that different areas of the same castings may have different surface textures. It is recommended that specifications of the surface be limited to defined areas of the casting. Practicality of and methods of determining whether a casting's surface texture meets the specification should be coordinated with the producer. The Society of Automotive Engineers Standard J435C, "Automotive Steel Castings," describes methods of evaluating steel casting surface texture used in the automotive and related industries.[7]

Three methods of surface texture measurement are currently used throughout industry. The most widely used method is the profile method. In the profile method, the topographic information is derived from a point-by-point scan of surface height as a function of a distance along a straight line on the surface.

The resulting profile must be analyzed by either analog or digital methods to derive parameters. The second method is referred to as the area method. Area methods directly produce a measurable parameter that represents some property of the surface topography averaged over the illuminated area. The third method compares sample parts to the other parts produced.

No general method of surface texture measurement may be considered superior to all others. The choice as to which method is employed should be based on the characteristics and parameters to be measured. In addition, considerations should be made regarding the functional purpose of the part as well as technical feasibility of the measurements.

Profile Methods

The profile method of surface texture measurement defines a single line that represents the entire surface. The two types of instruments widely used for this method are stylus and optical.

Stylus instruments. Stylus instrumentation for surface texture measurement is generally classified based on whether it operates with or without skids. Another classification is based on the type of transducer used for the instrument.

Stylus instruments that use skids are the simpler of the two and are usually only capable of measuring roughness average. For this reason, they are commonly referred to as roughness or roughness average meters. Roughness average meters may incorporate either a piezoelectric or inductive linear variable differential transducer, depending on the instrument manufacturer. The roughness average values are continuously updated and displayed on an analog meter or a digital display (see Fig. 5-15, view *a*). Roughness average meters find their widest use for receiving, in-process, or postprocess inspection.

Stylus instruments that do not use skids, referred to as skidless, always use inductive linear variable differential transducers and are generally capable of measuring several parameters. These instruments also require traversing drive units and an accurate datum reference to permit the measurement of waviness and surface profile (see Fig. 5-15, view *b*). An analog or microprocessor-based amplifier, as well as a graphic recorder/printer, are generally used with skidless instruments, thus permitting surface texture analyses and documentation.

The main components of a typical stylus instrument are the stylus, transducer, skids and shoes, traversing drive, and the amplifier.[8] When setting up a stylus-type instrument for use, it is

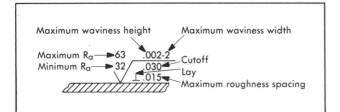

Fig. 5-14 Placement of various surface texture components on the symbol.

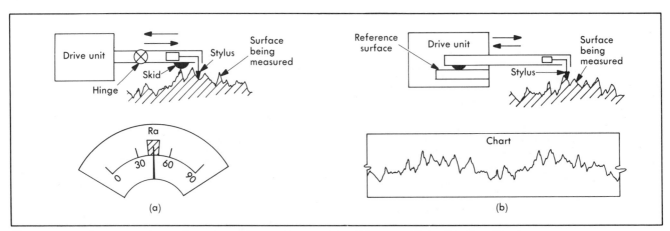

Fig. 5-15 Two primary types of stylus instruments exist (a) skid type and (b) skidless type. (*Federal Products Corp.*)

necessary to adjust the traversing length and cutoff. It is also necessary to periodically check the calibration of the instrument and the condition of the stylus.

To ensure that the stylus follows the contour of the surface being measured, a force is needed to hold it against the surface. If this force is too great, the stylus will plow through the surface irregularities instead of following them. When a soft surface must be inspected, an instrument with low stylus force should be used. Every instrument is designed to have a designated amount of stylus force; the operator cannot adjust this force. Values of stylus force are specified in ANSI Standard B46.1.

Principles of operation.[9] On the surface to be inspected, an element is selected in a location and orientation that is considered to be representative of the surface texture. A needle-type instrument member, referred to as the stylus, is moved over the selected surface element. The stylus is connected with a pickup that is maintained at a controlled level, yet permits the stylus to follow the surface of the part. Variations of the surface in relation to the level of the pickup translation cause the stylus to deflect from a reference position. The mechanical deflections of the stylus during its scanning movement along the part's surface are translated into electrical signals. The signals may reflect the velocity of the stylus deflections (roughness meters) or, more frequently, produce a voltage or current proportional to the amplitude of those deflections.

Stylus. The stylus is the element through which the instrument senses the departures of the traced surface element from a reference line. The stylus must have a fine point, permitting it to follow the textural variations of the surface, yet have a small measuring force and be of a form and dimension that will avoid marring the surface being traced. The point of the stylus is generally made of diamond with the basic form of a cone, having a 90° included angle and a spherical vertex. The radius of the stylus tip depends on the instrument type. Because the stylus is subject to wear and mechanical damage, it is advisable to check the stylus frequently to ensure that the tip radius does not exceed the specified value.

Transducer. The transducer or pickup converts the vertical displacement of the stylus into an electrical signal. The type of transducer used is largely determined by the manufacturer of the instrument. In addition, the type of transducer used is often based on whether the instrument is a skid-type stylus instrument or a skidless-type stylus instrument. Skid-type instruments generally use a velocity or piezoelectric transducer, while skidless-type instruments use an inductive linear variable differential transducer.

Skids and shoes. When the measurement of surface roughness is the only objective, it is a convenient and general practice to traverse the pickup along an envelope element of the surface. The imaginary envelope element is established as the path of a supporting member mounted on the pickup head and in continued contact with the object surface along which it is sliding (refer to Fig. 5-15, view *a*). The contact member is referred to as the skid and has a radius much larger than the stylus. When the contact member has a long, flat form, it is sometimes referred to as a shoe. The skid does not penetrate into the closely spaced valleys of the profile, but rests on the most protruding components of the surface.

Variations in the form and location of the skid can affect the result of the surface texture measurement. Most instrument manufacturers make different types of skids, with each type designed to accommodate different part configurations, materials, and dimensions.

Traversing drive. To accomplish the scanning of the surface being inspected along a specific element, the pickup must be traversed in a plane parallel with the surface. The traverse movement must be carried out at a speed that is set by the measuring characteristics of the instrument.

It is possible to approximate the requirements of controlled rate and uniform speed by manual traversing, when carried out by a skillful operator. A few types of surface roughness measuring instruments are available for shop applications with hand-held pickup heads. However, the majority of stylus-type measurements are made using an automatic mechanical traverse drive.

Mechanical traversing devices must satisfy several requirements. The following are some of these requirements:

- Uniform traversing speed.
- Controlled rate of advance, usually 0.100 or 0.300 ips (2.5 or 8.0 mm/s) for general use.
- Adjustable stroke length, usually in the range of 1/16 to 1″ (1.6 to 25 mm) or more.
- Adjustment means for height setting to accommodate work surfaces at different levels relative to the base of the instrument.

Amplifier. The amplifier is the general designation for the entire electronic instrumentation, except for the remotely located pickup. The amplifier is connected with the pickup through an electric cable and is operated by electric current, either from the shop power line (115/220 V) or from rechargeable nickel-cadmium or alkaline batteries.

Most amplifiers are equipped with several multiple-position switches for selecting the suitable factors of surface texture assessment. The two major selection categories are the cutoff selection and the roughness range selection. In addition, some amplifiers are capable of measuring several different surface texture parameters.

Microprocessors. The more recently developed microprocessor-based surface instrumentation allows the multiparameter approach to surface texture metrology. This multiparameter approach permits a more complete control of surface quality for better product performance, appearance, and uniformity.

The range of microcomputer systems offered provides carefully balanced combinations of measuring instrument, processor, and program, from which a system can be selected to suit individual requirements. Fast, accurate, and extensive measurement and analysis of surface characteristics can be obtained on applications ranging from industrial quality control to scientific research. Capabilities previously reserved for high-cost specialty and research equipment are now included in metrology systems for the workshop.

Microprocessor-based instruments not only provide assistance in alignment, faster setup, multiparameter readings, and additional accuracy, but also can do multitrace assessments to look at surface characterization over an area. Multiple readings of the many parameters can be averaged and presented with minimum and maximum readings. These systems are also capable of statistical analyses. By studying the standard deviation of a surface parameter, it is possible to determine the consistency of the machining process.

Traversing length. The traversing length is the length of profile that is traversed by the stylus to establish a representative measurement. To provide full readings with the response times specified for continuously averaging-type instruments, the traversing length used for any measurement should be com-

SURFACE TEXTURE DESIGNATION

patible with the selected cutoff. In general, the traversing length for continuously averaging instruments is at least five times the selected cutoff. For surfaces that are not long enough to permit a traversing length of five times the cutoff, the measurements are suitable for comparative purposes only. Under these conditions, profile traces may be more informative.

Cutoff. The cutoff is the electrical response characteristic of the roughness average measuring instrument that is selected to limit the spacing of the surface irregularities included in the assessment of roughness average. The cutoff selected for roughness measurements must be large enough to provide an adequate amount of information, yet small enough so that it does not include waviness deviations, which would distort a roughness assessment.

In specifying the cutoff or roughness sampling length, the value chosen should be based on considerations such as the manufacturing process, the characteristic dimension of the measured parts, and the observed or anticipated spacing of profile irregularities. As a general rule the cutoff should be between 5 and 40 times the maximum irregularity spacing.

Six different cutoff lengths can be specified ranging from 0.003 to 1.000″ (0.08 to 25 mm). If the roughness average of a surface is between 10 and 120 μin. (0.25 and 3.0 μm), a cutoff of 0.030″ (0.80 mm) is usually used. For a finer surface, a cutoff of 0.010″ (0.25 mm) is suitable and, for a roughness average below 2 or 3 μin. (0.50 or 0.75 μm), a 0.003″ (0.08 mm) cutoff should be specified.[10]

The effect of variation in cutoff can be understood better by referring to Fig. 5-16. The profile at the top is a trace of the true movement of a stylus over a surface, and the profiles below are interpretations of the same surface with cutoff value settings of 0.030, 0.010, and 0.003″ (0.80, 0.25, and 0.08 mm), respectively. It can be seen that the trace based on a 0.030″ cutoff includes most of the coarse irregularities and all the fine irregularities of the surface. The trace based on a 0.010″ cutoff excludes the coarser irregularities, but includes the fine and medium-fine. The trace based on 0.003″ cutoff includes only the very fine irregularities. In this example, the effect of reducing the cutoff has been to reduce the roughness height indication. However, had the surface been made up of irregularities no greater than those of the bottom trace, the roughness height indications would have been the same for all three cutoff settings.

Calibration. To ensure compliance of the instrument's indications with the concepts and dimensional relationships of the standard, the stylus instrument must be verified periodically. Verification or calibration is performed with precision reference specimens or step-height specimens. The precision reference specimen is a flat block that has one, two, or three fields of consecutive parallel grooves, which have specific shape and size, on one side of the block. Depending on the manufacturer, these blocks can have fields representing a roughness average of 233 μin. (5.8 μm), 125 μin. (3.2 μm), 35 μin. (0.9 μm), 20 μin. (0.5 μm), and down to 1-2 μin. (0.025-0.050 μm). Special fields are also available. Some of the fields are intended for calibration verification, while others serve as a check of the instrument stylus. Precision reference specimens are not intended to have the appearance of characteristics of commonly produced surfaces, nor are they intended for use in visual or tactile comparisons. The characteristics of reference specimens are specified by ANSI Standard B46.1.

When verifying the instrument, the stylus of the instrument is traced across the field at a standard speed and in a direction normal to the lay. The average roughness indications of the instrument should agree with the value specified for the reference specimen.

On blocks having 125 μin. (3.2 μm) and 20 μin. (0.5 μm) fields, the 20 μin. field is never used for calibration. It is only used to monitor diamond wear on the stylus. Instrument calibration is performed on the 125 μin. field, and then the 20 μin. field is measured. The difference in percent from the readings on the 125 μin. field represents the percent change in value due to diamond wear. Calibrating the stylus instrument with the 20 μin. field could cause as much as a 50% error in actual reading.

Microprocessor-based instruments use a single field of a given depth for calibration. As inductance change is measured for a known depth, the instrument can be calibrated over its total measuring range.

Optical instruments. The optical instruments used commonly in profiling methods of surface texture measurement are based on interferometry. Interferometry is an important technique for determining the roughness and figure of high-quality optical surfaces. The schematic of a two-beam interferometer is shown in Fig. 5-17.

A collimated optical wavefront is split into two coherent beams by a partially transmitting mirror. One beam is reflected from a smooth flat reference surface, while the other is reflected from the surface being tested; the reflected beams are then recombined at the mirror. An image of the surface is produced by the lens at 0. Under conditions of perfect alignment, a circular pattern of parallel light and dark fringes is observed.

When the reflected beams are not aligned properly, variations in the fringe patterns occur. Waviness and roughness features can be determined by counting the number of fringes and measuring any deflections within a fringe. The accuracy of this technique depends on the type of light source used.

Another type of optical profiling instrument is based on the Mirau interferometer (see Fig. 5-18). In this design, a beam splitter and reference surface are placed close to the surface to be scanned. Instead of moving either the workpiece or the instrument to develop the surface profile, the surface image is detected by a linear photodiode detector array. The phase information on each element of the array is developed by vibrating the reference mirror piezoelectrically and then processing the reference modulated signals in the photodiode elements.

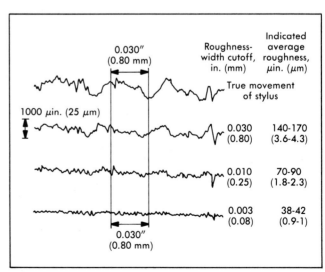

Fig. 5-16 Effect of various roughness width cutoff values.

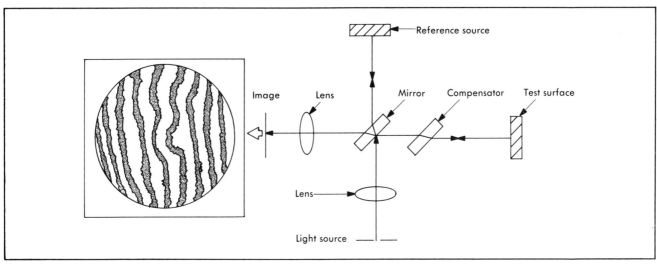

Fig. 5-17 Schematic of a two-beam interferometer.

The accuracy of the output surface profiles does not depend on the straightness of travel or velocity stability of any moving stage, but does depend on the quality of the reference mirror. Scanning length is limited by the magnifications of the available objective lenses.

Area Methods

The term *area methods* is used to denote those techniques that measure a representative area of a surface and produce quantitative results that depend on area averaged properties of the surface texture. Some of the more common techniques used include capacitance, optical, and pneumatic. When carefully used in conjunction with calibrated roughness comparison specimens or pilot specimens, these techniques may be used as comparators to distinguish the surface texture of parts manufactured by a similar process and to produce useful results in repetitive surface roughness measurements of components from a production run.

Capacitance techniques. The capacitance technique uses a probe containing a sensor of predetermined area (typically circular or rectangular) to establish capacitance with an identical area on a surface. An insulator covers the sensor to electrically isolate it from the workpiece surface and prevent a short circuit from occurring (see Fig. 5-19).

During measurement, the sensor rests on the surface peaks and provides a measure of the roughness voids between the two surfaces. The sensor's shape is designed to conform with the surface being measured. For example, a concave or convex sensor would be used to measure circular surfaces. When the probe is pressed against the workpiece, capacitance is established, and a signal is transmitted to the system's electronic circuitry. A readout device displays a roughness average of the

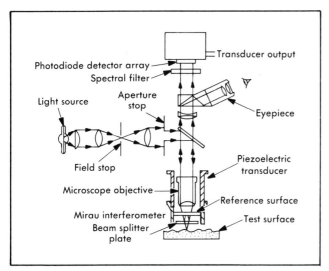

Fig. 5-18 Schematic diagram of optical profiling instrument developed by Wyant, et al.[11, 12]

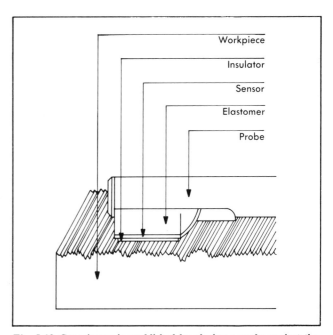

Fig. 5-19 Capacitance is established by placing a probe against the workpiece surface. (*Extrude Hone Corp.*)

SURFACE TEXTURE DESIGNATION

area that can be compared to R_a values obtained by stylus instruments.

Capacitance instruments are relatively insensitive to surface lay because an area is measured. Because of this, these instruments can be used for measuring workpieces produced by electrical discharge machining and casting. Generally, these instruments are calibrated to the type of surface texture being measured. The surface to be assessed and the sensor should be clean before measuring. Because insulated and nonconductive surfaces cannot establish capacitance, this technique is limited to conductive or semiconductive workpieces.

Operating principle. Capacitance-type surface measuring instruments are based on the parallel-plate capacitor principle. This principle states that the capacitance between two conducting elements is directly proportional to their area and the dielectric constant of the medium between them and inversely proportional to their separation. This principle is represented by the following equation:

$$C = KA/d \qquad (1)$$

where:

C = capacitance, F
K = dielectric constant of the medium between the plates, F/in. (F/m)
A = area of the capacitor plates, in.^{2} (m^2)
d = average distance between plates, in. (m)

The surface of the workpiece represents one plate of the capacitor, and the other plate is represented by the instrument sensor. When the sensor is placed on the workpiece, the peaks and valleys of the surface create an airspace between the plates. The airspace is generally referred to as a dielectric. As the plate separation distance increases, the airspace increases. Because the electrical capacitance changes as the airspace between the two plates changes, the surface roughness of the workpiece is proportional to the capacitance.

Calibration. To obtain a surface roughness value, the average thickness of the airspace is converted into a standard surface roughness parameter. This conversion is accomplished by comparing the capacitance of the surface in question with the capacitance and corresponding roughness value of a reference surface that was previously entered into the instrument. For example, if the measured capacitance indicates that the airspace of the measured surface has twice the airspace of the reference surface, then the measured surface would have a surface roughness value twice that of the reference surface. Reference surfaces must be machined by the same process as the surfaces being measured.

Optical techniques. According to the laws of physical optics, the radiation from a collimated beam of laser light reflected by a rough surface is scattered into an angular distribution. The resulting specular intensity, angular scattering pattern, speckle pattern, and polarization state depend on the roughness heights, the spatial wavelengths, and the wavelength of light. Because of this, a class of techniques has been developed to monitor the roughness condition of the surface optically. This class of techniques does not include the optical profiling techniques discussed previously.

This discussion will be limited to the light-scattering method. For information on the other methods, refer to articles listed in the bibliography.

The light-scattering method makes use of the scattering property of rough surfaces to determine a characteristic quantity for roughness. In practice, the surface to be tested is illuminated by an infrared light. Some of the radiation is scattered back to the diode array, which determines its distribution and intensity, by means of the measuring lens (see Fig. 5-20). The optical roughness value S_N, defined as the variance of the intensity distribution, is calculated from the measured values by a microcomputer.

Measurements using these instruments take less than 50 ms and can be performed on moving surfaces. A compressed air cleaning or simple wiping is recommended for parts coated with a thick oil film. The light-scattering method can be used to measure roughness of parts made from metals, semiconductors, ceramics, and plastics.

Pneumatic techniques. When an air jet is held in close proximity and perpendicular to a rough surface, the resultant flow of air out of the orifice is a function of the roughness of the surface against which it impinges. Instruments based on this phenomenon have been used to assess surface roughness. Many different orifice shapes have been used, including circular, oval, square, and long slit.

Comparison Methods

When the roughness average, R_a, requirements exceed 63 μin. (1.6 μm), most companies use a visual check rather than a measurement of the roughness profile.[12] Often the visual check is aided through the use of sample parts (pilot specimens) that have proper surface finish and are known to perform satisfactorily. These parts are set aside from production and referred to by machine operators so the finishes may be duplicated. To ensure reasonable accuracy, pilot specimens should be rated by properly calibrated measuring instruments.

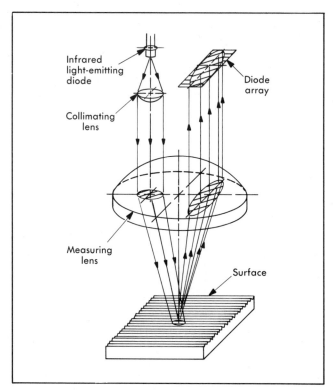

Fig. 5-20 Schematic of scattered-light sensor used in light-scattering method. (*Rodenstock Precision Optics, Inc.*)

Because pilot specimens are of the same size, shape, material, and physical characteristics as all production parts from the same machine setup, it is often possible to determine by sight or feel when production parts begin to deviate significantly from the established norm indicated by the pilot specimen. If control is required at more than one station, pilot specimens may be cut into the required number of pieces. Electroformed or plastic replicas of the pilot specimens may also be used.

Visual aids and types of comparator instruments, other than the stylus type, are sometimes useful when comparing the work with pilot specimens. However, when using replicas of pilot specimens for visual inspection, suitable precautions should be taken to ensure the accuracy of observation. Visual appearance is not necessarily a reliable index of roughness because it is dependent on such factors as the specular properties of the material, the lighting conditions, viewing angle, roughness width and color, as well as roughness height.

SURFACE INTEGRITY

In components subject to contact fatigue, surface integrity is critically related to performance. Surface integrity is a relatively new term covering the nature of the surface condition that is developed in hardware by controlled manufacturing processes. It is achieved by the selection and control of manufacturing processes according to the evaluation of the process effects on specific engineering properties of the work materials.

Nearly all components are manufactured using some type of metal removal process. These processes might consist of chip removal, such as turning, milling, or drilling, or the removal of material by an abrasive, such as grinding, sanding, honing, or polishing. In addition, metal is being widely removed by nontraditional material removal processes. Each metal removal process may produce a characteristic surface alteration or differences in the extent of the alteration. This surface alteration makes the subsurface quite different from the interior of the material. The surface and subsurface alterations may be extensive and deep or may be very superficial and quite shallow.

The quality of a machined surface is becoming increasingly more critical for satisfying the demands for superior component performance, longevity, and reliability. Structures for commercial and military aerospace, automotive, and capital goods industries are being subjected to more severe conditions of stress, temperature, and hostile environments. In addition, section size is being reduced in response to the goal of reduced weight. Thus the surface condition of a component has an ever-increasing influence on its performance.

Surface integrity must be considered in the manufacture of highly stressed components used in applications involving human safety, high cost, and predictable component life. Because the control of surface integrity generally adds cost to the manufacturing process, it is important to determine whether a surface integrity problem exists. Portions of this subchapter are abstracted or reprinted by permission from the *Machining Data Handbook*.[14] Some of the problems for which the application of surface integrity principles can be helpful are as follows:

- Overheating or burning when grinding high-strength alloys.
- Microcracks and surface irregularities.
- Distortion and loss of dimensional quality, particularly in thin components.
- Residual tensile stresses lowering fatigue endurance strength.
- Residual stresses combined with severe environments leading to early stress-corrosion failures.
- Reduction in fatigue strength from metallurgically altered surfaces produced by thermal processes.

- Metallurgical or mechanical alterations produced as a result of excessively high removal rates or process energy.
- Thin sections of components operating at high stress levels.
- Applications where life or safety reliability concerns are particularly stringent.
- Holes with high depth-to-diameter ratios when maintaining drill sharpness may be difficult.

A practical balance must be found between overcontrolling the manufacturing process with its attendant costs and unneeded benefits. Undercontrolling the process can lead to possible decreases in quality, increases in scrapped components, or losses of reliability. Proper application of surface integrity practices can result in cost improvement and quality enhancement by insisting on greater quality only on surface areas where needed and relaxing specifications for the remaining component surfaces.

SURFACE ALTERATIONS

Surface integrity is concerned primarily with the host of effects a manufacturing process produces below the visible surface of a component. The subsurface characteristics occur in various layers or zones.[15] The altered material zones (AMZ) can be as simple as a stress condition different from that in the bulk of the material or as complex as a microstructure change interlaced with intergranular attack. Changes can be caused by chemical, thermal, electrical, or mechanical energy and may affect both the physical and the mechanical properties of the material. The principal causes of alterations to a surface during material removal operations are as follows:

- High temperatures and high-temperature gradients.
- Chemical reactions or absorption on recently machined surfaces.
- Excessive electrical currents.
- Excessive energy densities during processing.
- Mechanical deformation by cutting tool edge.

The subsurface material zones can be grouped by the principal energy modes that produce them, as shown in Table 5-2. Table 5-3 lists alterations that have been observed in several classes of materials as a result of various machining processes.

Processes are usually operated over a range of conditions.[18] The roughing and finishing modes are one reflection of these differing intensities or energy densities. From a surface integrity and quality assurance standpoint, it is necessary to consider the change in surface effects over the full range of energy levels expected to be used. These data can then be used to establish reasonable quality control limits. This range of process intensity levels is often implied in the machining terminology that indicates increasingly intense processing, such as the following:

- Low-stress surface.
- Finish machining (or "gentle").
- Conventional (or "standard").
- Roughing (or "off-standard").
- Abusive (or accidental conditions).

The surface integrity of components produced with roughing or off-standard operating conditions is frequently less than that produced under standard conditions. The standard surface integrity evaluations should include at least two levels of process intensity. It should be emphasized that abusive and gentle processing can be differentiated ultimately only by mechanical testing (fatigue or stress-corrosion) and/or service performance.

Nomenclature[19]

cracks Narrow ruptures or separations that alter the continuity of a surface. Cracks are usually tight and characterized by sharp edges or sharp changes in direction with a depth-to-width ratio of 1:4 or greater. They are discernible with the naked eye or with 10X or less magnification.

craters Surface depressions with rough edges, approximately round or oval and shallow, usually with a depth-to-width ratio of less than 4:1. The term *crater* is frequently applied to the impressions left by the individual spark discharges in electrical discharge machining (see Fig. 5-21). It is also used to describe massive depressions resulting from short circuits in electrical discharge or electrochemical machining.

fold See laps.

TABLE 5-2
Altered Material Zones by Principal Energy Mode[16]

MECHANICAL:
- Plastic deformations (as result of hot or cold working)
- Tears and laps and crevice-like defects (associated with "built-up edge" produced in machining)
- Hardness alterations
- Cracks (macroscopic and microscopic)
- Residual stress distribution in surface layer
- Processing inclusions introduced
- Plastically deformed debris as a result of grinding
- Voids, pits, burrs, or foreign material inclusions in surface

METALLURGICAL:
- Transformation of phases
- Grain size and distribution
- Precipitate size and distribution
- Foreign inclusions in material
- Twinning
- Recrystallization
- Untempered martensite (UTM) or overtempered martensite (OTM)
- Resolutioning or austenite reversion

CHEMICAL:
- Intergranular attack (IGA)
- Intergranular corrosion (IGC)
- Intergranular oxidation (IGO)
- Preferential dissolution of microconstituents
- Contamination
- Embrittlement—by chemical absorption of elements such as hydrogen, chlorine, etc.
- Pits or selective etch
- Corrosion
- Stress corrosion

THERMAL:
- Heat-affected zone (HAZ)
- Recast or redeposited material
- Resolidified material
- Splattered particles or remelted metal deposited on surface

ELECTRICAL:
- Conductivity change
- Magnetic change
- Resistive heating or overheating

SURFACE ALTERATIONS

TABLE 5-3
Summary of Possible Surface Alterations Resulting from Various Metal Removal Processes[17]

Material	Conventional Metal Removal Methods		Nontraditional Removal Methods		
	Milling, Drilling, or Turning	Grinding	EDM	ECM	CHM
Steels: Nonhardenable 1018	R, PD, L & T	R, PD	R, MCK, RC	R, SE, IGA	R, SE, IGA
Hardenable 4340 D6ac	R, PD, L & T, MCK, UTM, OTM	R, PD, MCK, UTM, OTM	R, MCK, RC, UTM, OTM	R, SE, IGA	R, SE, IGA
Tool steel D2	R, PD, L & T, MCK, UTM, OTM	R, PD, MCK, UTM, OTM	R, MCK, RC, UTM, OTM	R, SE, IGA	R, SE, IGA
Stainless (martensitic) 410	R, PD, L & T, MCK, UTM, OTM	R, PD, MCK, UTM, OTM	R, MCK, RC, UTM, OTM	R, SE, IGA	R, SE, IGA
Stainless (austenitic) 302	R, PD, L & T	R, PD	R, MCK, RC	R, SE, IGA	R, SE, IGA
Precipitation hardening 17-4 PH	R, PD, L & T, OA	R, PD, OA	R, MCK, RC, OA	R, SE, IGA	R, SE, IGA
Maraging (18% Ni) 250 Grade	R, PD, L & T, RS, OA	R, PD, RS, OA	R, RC, RS, OA	R, SE, IGA	R, SE, IGA
Nickel and cobalt base alloys: Inconel alloy 718 René 41 HS 31 IN-100	R, PD, L & T, MCK	R, PD, MCK	R, MCK, RC	R, SE, IGA	R, SE, IGA
Titanium alloy: Ti-6Al-4V	R, PD, L & T	R, PD, MCK	R, MCK, RC	R, SE, IGA	R, SE
Refractory alloys: TZM	R, L & T, MCK	R, MCK	R, MCK	R, SE, IGA	R, SE
Tungsten (pressed and sintered)	R, L & T, MCK	R, MCK	R, MCK	R, SE, MCK, IGA	R, SE, MCK, IGA

Key: R—Roughness of surface
 PD—Plastic deformation and plastically deformed debris
 L & T—Laps and tears and crevice-like defects
 MCK—Microcracks
 SE—Selective etch
 IGA—Intergranular attack

UTM—Untempered martensite
OTM—Overtempered martensite
OA—Overaging
RS—Resolution or austenite reversion
RC—Recast, respattered metal, or vapor-deposited metal

CHAPTER 5

SURFACE ALTERATIONS

hardness alterations Changes in the hardness of a surface layer as a result of heat, mechanical deformation, or chemical change during processing. Alterations of less than ±2 points Rockwell C or equivalent from the hardness of the bulk of the material are not considered significant.

heat-affected zones (HAZ) Those portions of a material not melted, yet subjected to sufficient thermal energy to produce microstructural alterations or microhardness alterations (see Fig. 5-22).

intergranular attack (IGA) A form of corrosion or attack in which preferential reactions are concentrated at the surface grain boundaries, usually in the form of sharp notches or discontinuities (see Fig. 5-23). These effects are sometimes supplemented by intergranular oxidation derived from exposure to elevated temperatures or intergranular corrosion derived from exposure to active chemical reagents.

laps Defects in a surface from continued plastic working of overlapping surfaces (see Fig. 5-24).

low-stress surface A surface containing a residual stress less than 20 ksi (138 MPa) or 10% of tensile strength, whichever

is greater, at depths below the surface greater than 0.001″ (0.025 mm). It is sometimes called a stress-free surface.

metallurgical transformations Microstructural changes resulting from external influences. These changes include phase transformation, recrystallization, alloy depletion, chemical reactions, and resolidified, redeposited, or recast layers (see Fig. 5-25).

microcracks Cracks requiring greater than 10X magnification for discernment (see Fig. 5-26).

pits Shallow depressions resembling a small crater with rounded edges and less than a 4:1 depth-to-width ratio. It also describes a specialized form of localized or selective etching or corrosion that results in holes or pockets left by the mechanical removal of small particles or inclusions from the surface. Pits are also the result of dents from the impingement of foreign particles against the surface. Pits are sometimes associated from electrochemical action into regions slightly removed from the high current density regions (see Fig. 5-27).

plastic deformation A microstructural change as a result of exceeding the yield point of the material and generally includes elongation of the grain structure and increased hardness (see Fig. 5-28).

recast material A general term applied to surfaces that have at some point in the processing become molten and then reso-

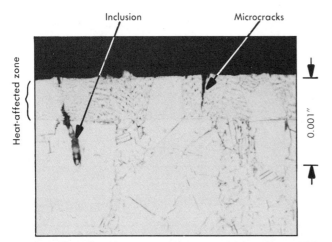

Fig. 5-21 Craters produced in Inconel 718 (solution-treated and aged) from electrical discharge machining. The scanning electron microscope was set at 90° and had a magnification of 215X.[20]

Fig. 5-22 Heat-affected zone caused by laser machining of Inconel 718 (solution-treated and aged). Magnification is at 1000X. Note epitaxial growth of grains nucleating from base-metal grains. Microcracks and an inclusion are also shown.[21]

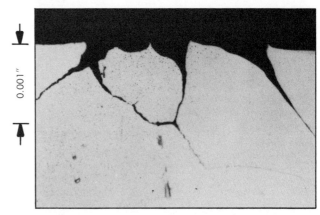

Fig. 5-23 Intergranular attack of Waspaloy (aged and hardened to R$_C$40) caused by electrochemical milling. Magnification is 1000X.[22]

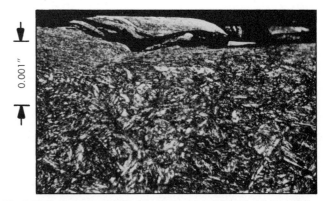

Fig. 5-24 Laps, folds, and tears in 4340 steel (quenched and tempered, R$_C$50) caused by drilling. Magnification is 1000X with orientation perpendicular to the lay. (*Used with permission of the Machinability Data Center*)

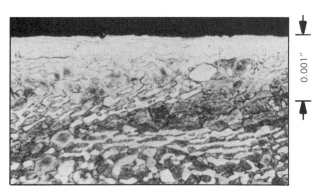

Fig. 5-25 Metallurgical transformation (reformed alpha case crystals) of titanium, Ti-6Al-4V, during grinding; plastic deformation has also occurred. Magnification is 1000X. (*Used with permission of the Machinability Data Center*)

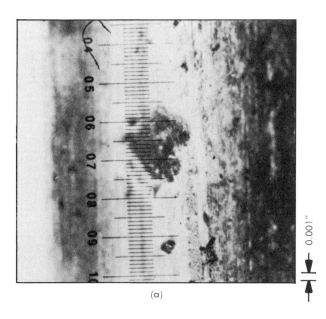

(a)

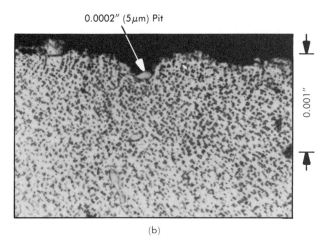

(b)

Fig. 5-27 Pit in René 80 (solution-treated) as a result of grinding: (a) surface view of pit magnified 40X and (b) section of pit magnified 1000X.[24]

lidified. Frequently includes a conglomerate mixture of redeposited or remelted material (see Fig. 5-30).

recrystallization The formation of a new, strain-free grain or crystal structure from that existing in the material prior to processing, usually as a result of plastic deformation and subsequent heating or from a phase change during heating (see Fig. 5-29).

redeposited material Material that, in the material removal process, is removed from the surface and then, prior to

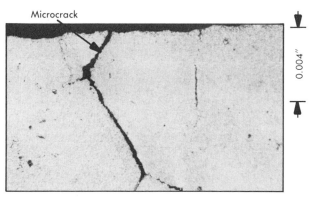

Fig. 5-26 Microcrack in Udimet 700C as a result of grinding. Magnification is 250X.[23]

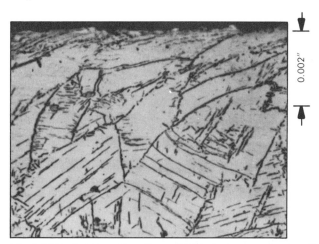

Fig. 5-28 Plastic deformation of Inconel 718 (solution-treated and aged) as a result of turning with a dull tool; deformation is approximately 0.0036″ (0.091 mm) deep. Magnification is 500X.[25]

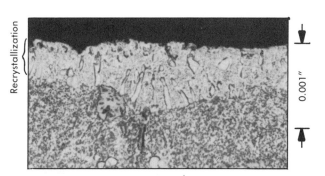

Fig. 5-29 Recrystallized layer in René 80 from age heat treatment following grinding. Magnification is 1000X.[26]

CHAPTER 5

SURFACE ALTERATIONS

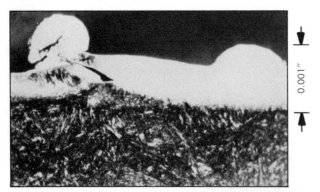

Fig. 5-30 Recast, redeposited, and splattered 4340 steel (quenched and tempered, R_C50) as a result of electrical discharge machining. Untempered martensite exists in the 0.002″ (0.05 mm) deep heat-affected zone. Magnification is 1000X.[27]

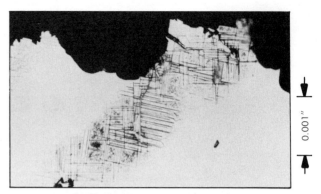

Fig. 5-31 Selective etching of Inconel 718C (solution-treated and aged, R_C40). Magnification is 1000X.[28]

solidification, is reattached to the surface. It is sometimes called splattered metal (see Fig. 5-30).

remelted material The portion of the surface that becomes molten during the metal removal process but is not removed from the surface prior to resolidification (see Fig. 5-30).

residual stresses Stresses that are present in a material after all external influences (forces, thermal gradients, or external energy) have been removed.

resolidified material See remelted material.

seams See laps.

selective etch A form of in-process corrosion or attack in which preferential reactions are concentrated within and through the grains or concentrated on certain constituents in the base material (see Fig. 5-31).

splattered metal See redeposited material.

Machining Processes

In machining processes such as milling or drilling, the gentle operations are those employing machining conditions that provide long tool life and use a sharp tool (the tool is removed before it gets too dull). Abusive machining operations are those in which a tool is used even after it has become dull. It is also promoted by employing improper tools, speeds, feeds, and cutting fluids. In general, abusive machining conditions tend to promote higher temperature and/or excessive plastic deformation.

Many of the adverse effects of abusive machining are readily evaluated by examination of the surface layer microstructure. Because the microstructural alterations are usually quite shallow, in many cases less than 0.001″ (0.02 mm), it is necessary to employ special procedures for sectioning and mounting specimens. These special procedures maintain edge retention of the critical surface that is to be examined.[29]

Figure 5-32 is a typical data sheet illustrating the metallurgical and microhardness changes that occur in drilling 4340 steel, quenched and tempered to R_C52. The gently drilled hole has essentially the same structure at the surface as in the base metal (view a). The abusively drilled hole has an untempered martensitic layer, R_C61, about 0.001″ (0.025 mm) deep (view b). An overtempered martensitic layer with a hardness as low as R_C43 is found below the untempered martensite (UTM). The total altered layer is 0.010″ (0.25 mm) deep. Microhardness traverses are shown for both gentle and abusive drilling conditions in view c.

The surface alterations and microhardness changes that occur when milling are similar to those previously described for drilling. Abusive milling of 4340 steel often produces streaks of untempered martensite (see Fig. 5-33). These streaks are pro-

(b)

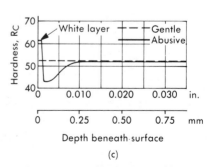

(c)

Fig. 5-32 Surface characteristics of AISI 4340 (quenched and tempered, R_C52) produced by drilling; magnification is 250X: (a) gentle conditions, no noticeable microstructural surface alterations; (b) abusive conditions, rehardened primary martensite layer R_C61 approaching 0.001″ (0.025 mm) deep and subsurface overtempered zone having hardness as low as R_C43. Total depth of effect is 0.010″ (0.25 mm); and (c) microhardness traverse for both gentle and abusive drilling conditions.[30]

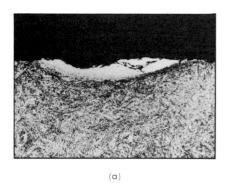
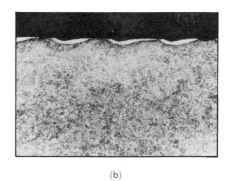
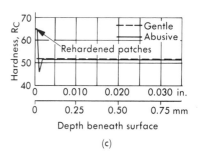

(a)   (b)   (c)

Fig. 5-33 Surface characteristics of AISI 4340 (quenched and tempered, R_C 52) produced by face milling: (a) photomicrographs of abusive conditions magnified 250X showing white rehardened patches of martensite; (b) photomicrographs of abusive conditions magnified 500X; and (c) microhardness traverse for both gentle and abusive conditions. Thin zones of overtempered martensite 0.001″ (0.025 mm) deep, with hardness as low as R_C 46 are found beneath each patch.[31]

duced by a dull tooth. The interval of the patches of untempered martensite correspond to the feed per tooth.

When drilling is permitted to continue with an especially dull drill, microcracking has been found sometimes to accompany the formation of UTM (see Fig. 5-34). Drilling of steels as well as other alloys with a high-speed steel drill that "burns out" during the drilling operation can actually result in a portion of the drill bit becoming friction welded to the bottom of the hole (see Fig. 5-35). The hardness of the friction-welded layer is almost R_C 70.

Abusive drilling, milling, or grinding of aged R_C 52 18% nickel maraging steel tends to produce a soft (R_C 30) layer on the surface. This soft layer is caused by resolution of the aged maraging steel due to the high temperature produced by machining (see Fig. 5-36). This phenomenon has been given the name austenite reversion.

Grinding Processes

In surface grinding, gentle conditions are those that keep the grinding wheel sharp, while abusive conditions are those that promote wheel dulling. The important operating parameters that influence whether a grinding operation is gentle or abusive include grain size, wheel grade, wheel speed, depth of cut, grinding fluid, and the wheel dressing procedure. Figure 5-37 shows surfaces produced by gentle, conventional, and abusive grinding of 4340 steel hardened to R_C 50. Gentle grinding produced no visible surface alterations, whereas conventional grinding showed evidence of spotty surface rehardening and underlying overtempering or softening. Abusive grinding pro-

duced a rehardened surface layer averaging 0.001″ (0.025 mm) deep and an underlying overtempered zone approximately 0.004″ (0.01 mm) deep.

Nontraditional Machining Processes

Electrical discharge machining (EDM) tends to produce a surface that contains a layer of recast splattered metal. This recast layer is hard, frequently porous, and, in many cases, contains cracks. Below the splattered and recast metal it is possible to have the same surface alterations and microstructure that occur in abusive machining. The effects are more pronounced when using roughing EDM conditions such as high power input.

Figure 5-38 shows a surface of 4340 steel hardened to R_C 50 using both finishing and roughing conditions. The surface produced under roughing conditions contains particles of recast metal that are splattered onto a white layer of rehardened martensite totaling 0.003″ (0.08 mm) deep and having a hardness of R_C 62. An overtempered zone as soft as R_C 46 is found beneath the surface. The total depth of the layer affected under roughing conditions approaches 0.010″ (0.25 mm). The surface

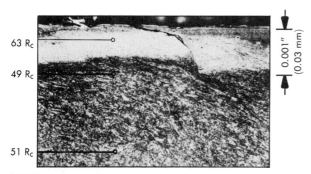

63 R_C

49 R_C

51 R_C

0.001″ (0.03 mm)

Fig. 5-34 Cross section of hole, perpendicular to hole axis, drilled with a dull drill in 4340 steel hardened to R_C 48.[32]

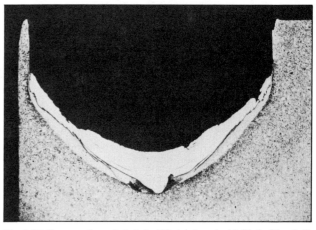

Fig. 5-35 Cross section of a hole in 410 stainless steel drilled with a dull drill; wearland was 0.060″ (1.52 mm). The drill broke down at the corner during test, and friction welded a portion of the high-speed steel drill bit to the workpiece. The base metal exhibits a rehardened and subsequent overtempered zone as a result of the high localized heating. Magnification is approximately 10X.[33]

SURFACE ALTERATIONS

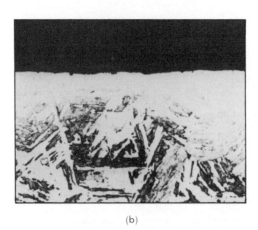
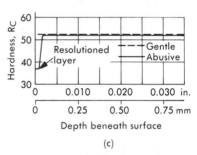

(a)   (b)   (c)

Fig. 5-36 Surface characteristics of 18% nickel maraging steel (grade 250, aged R_C 52) produced by drilling: (a) gentle conditions—thin trace of cold work can be seen on surface with magnification at 250X; (b) abusive conditions—an averaged or resolutioned layer 0.001″ (0.025 mm) deep at R_C 37 is found on the surface with magnification at 250X, total affected depth is approximately 0.002″ (0.05 mm); and (c) microhardness traverse for gentle and abusive drilling conditions.[34]

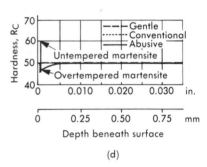

(a)   (b)   (c)   (d)

Fig. 5-37 Surface characteristics of AISI 4340 (quenched and tempered, R_C 50) produced by grinding: (a) gentle conditions, surface texture is R_a 40; (b) conventional conditions, surface texture is R_a 40; (c) abusive conditions, surface texture is R_a 50; and (d) microhardness traverse for gentle, conventional, and abusive grinding conditions.[35]

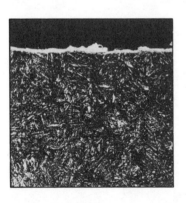

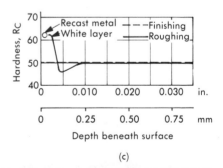

(a)   (b)   (c)

Fig. 5-38 Surface characteristics of AISI 4340 steel (quenched and tempered R_C 50) produced by electrical discharge machining with magnification at 500X: (a) finishing conditions—discontinuous patches of recast metal plus a thin layer of rehardened martensite, no hardness change detected; (b) roughing conditions—particles of recast metal (R_C 62) splattered on a white layer of rehardened martensite; and (c) microhardness traverse for finishing and roughing conditions for EDM.[36]

produced under finishing conditions contains discontinuous patches of recast metal plus a thin layer of rehardened martensite 0.0001″ (0.0025 mm) deep.

On a cast Inconel 718 alloy, roughing EDM conditions produced a hard recast layer and a soft zone (average depth)

0.005″ (0.13 mm) below the surface. The recast layer contained extensive cracking that extends into the base material.

Other thermal processes such as electron beam machining (EBM) and laser beam machining (LBM) tend to produce similar types of surface alterations as EDM. Figure 5-39 illustrates the heat-affected zone produced on Inconel 718 by laser beam machining. The intense, localized heat produced by the laser beam resulted in a minor recast surface layer at the entrance and exit of the hole produced.

Electrochemical machining (ECM) is capable of producing a surface that is essentially free of metallurgical surface-layer alterations.[38] However, when the ECM process goes out of control or when ECM action occurs in regions adjacent to the main electrode face, selective etching or intergranular attack can occur. Abusive (out-of-control) ECM conditions also tend to promote greater surface roughness than gentle conditions (see Fig. 5-40).

Accidents in ECM can also lead to dangerous surface alterations. A short circuit between the electrode and the work can cause extreme overheating and microcracking. A poor connection between the anode and the workpiece can also produce a "spot-weld-type" overheated zone.

Electrochemical machining also has a tendency to produce a soft layer on the surface. This surface-softening effect is produced on many high-strength and thermal-resistant materials by ECM, chemical milling (CHM), and electropolishing. It may be sufficiently severe and deep enough to affect the fatigue strength and other mechanical properties of metals.

Residual Stress and Distortion

Conventional machining processes develop a residual stress in the surface layer. This residual stress has been found to be a major cause of workpiece distortion.

In grinding, the residual stress tends to be tensile when abusive conditions are used. Figure 5-41 shows that the stress may be zero or even compressive at the surface, but becomes tensile below the surface. By using gentle grinding conditions, the stress can be reduced in magnitude and can even become compressive. The greater the area under the residual stress curve, the greater the distortion of the workpiece (see Figs. 5-41 and 5-42).

In milling, the residual stress tends to be compressive. For example, when face milling 4340 steel hardened to $R_C 52$, the stresses are tensile at the surface, but go into compression below the surface (see Fig. 5-43). The duller the tool, the deeper the compressively stressed layer and the greater the distortion (see Fig. 5-44). In contrast to this, the nontraditional processes such as ECM, CHM, and ECG produce essentially stress-free surfaces.

Mechanical Properties

The characteristics of the surface alterations produced in machining are known to affect fatigue and stress-corrosion

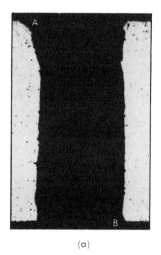 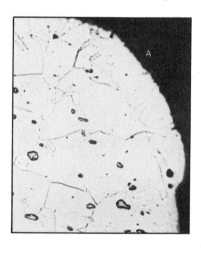 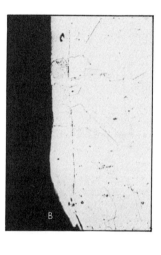

(a)   (b)

Fig. 5-39 Heat-affected zones produced by laser beam machining on Inconel 718: (a) two pulses, 0.050″ (1.27 mm) thick; magnification is 50X; (b) enlargement of entrance and exit showing continuous grain structure through heat-affected zone; magnification is 250X.[37]

 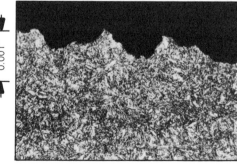 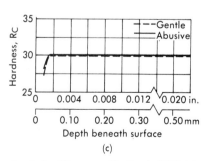

(a)   (c)

Fig. 5-40 Surface characterstics of AISI 4340 steel (quenched and tempered, $R_C 30$) produced by electrochemical milling; magnification is 500X: (a) gentle conditions—slight surface pitting and hardness loss, but without other visible changes; surface texture is $R_a 10$; (b) abusive conditions—pronounced surface roughening plus hardness loss, but without visible effect on microstructure; surface texture is 140 R_a; and (c) microhardness traverse for gentle and abusive conditions during ECM.[39]

SURFACE ALTERATIONS

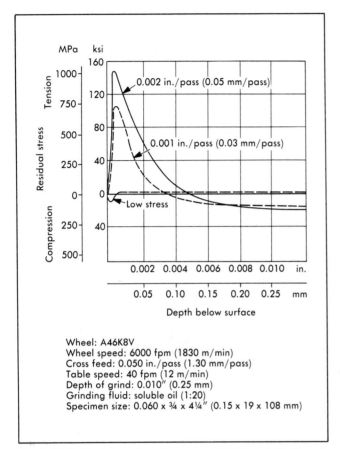

Fig. 5-41 Residual stress in surface-ground D6AC steel, R_C56, and effect of downfeed.[40]

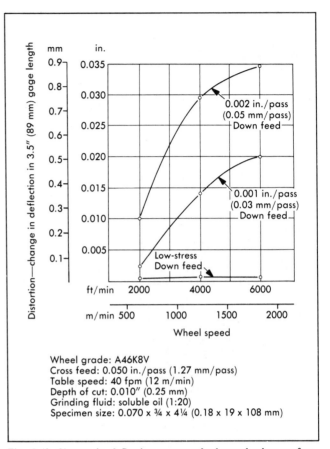

Fig. 5-42 Change in deflection versus wheel speed when surface grinding D6AC steel, R_C56, and the effect of downfeed.[41]

properties of many materials. From investigations on high-strength steels, it has been found that abusive grinding of 4340 steel at R_C50 can reduce the endurance limit by 35% with respect to low-stress gentle grinding. During abusive grinding, there is a tendency to form patches or streaks of untempered martensite or overtempered martensite on the surface. When either of these two microconstituents are present, the fatigue strength drops significantly. For example, it has been found that the presence of a depth of untempered martensite from 0.0005 to 0.0035" (0.013 to 0.089 mm) produces a drop in endurance limit from 110 ksi (758 MPa) to 70 or 75 ksi (482 or 517 MPa).

Retempering of the workpiece containing untempered martensite does not restore the fatigue strength because it merely reduces the hardness of the untempered martensite to that of the base material. Retempering does not affect the soft over-tempered martensite that is formed under the untempered martensite in hardened steel. The residual stress produced by low-stress grinding is generally compressive. Retempering of the low-stress surface produces little effect on the residual stress pattern.

Abusive grinding, which produces untempered and overtempered martensite, tends to produce a tensile stress in the surface layer. In this case, the deeper the untempered martensitic layer, the deeper the residual stress layer. However, the maximum tensile residual stress does not appear to be affected by the depth of the untempered martensite.

The effects of various types of grinding processes on fatigue characteristics of 4340 steel, quenched and tempered to R_C50, are illustrated in Fig. 5-45. The range of the endurance limit varies from 102 ksi (700 MPa) for gentle surface grinding to 62 ksi (427 MPa) for abusive grinding. The endurance limit produced by electropolishing and hand grinding is also shown. The endurance limit of surfaces can be improved by a postoperative treatment, such as shot peening. Improvements in the endurance limits of the previously cited operations due to shot peening are shown in Fig. 5-46. For example, the endurance limit of 98 ksi (675 MPa) after abusive grinding was increased to 118 ksi (814 MPa) by shot peening.

Fatigue characteristics of beta-rolled Ti-6Al-4V vary from 13 ksi (90 MPa) for abusive grinding to 62 ksi (427 MPa) for gentle grinding. Fatigue strength of Inconel 718, when subjected to EDM, ECH, ELP, and surface grinding, are indicated in Fig. 5-47. Gentle surface grinding produced an endurance limit of 60 ksi (414 MPa). There was a reduction in the endurance limit for ELP, ECM, and EDM, which had values of 42, 39, and 22 ksi (290, 269, and 152 MPa), respectively. In addition, variations in the machining practices (gentle versus abusive conditions) of ECM and EDM did not improve the endurance limit of the material. Various postmachining treatments are useful in improving the endurance limit. Stress relief and heat treatment produced either insignificant or minor improvements in fatigue strength. However, worthwhile improvements were achieved by shot peening.

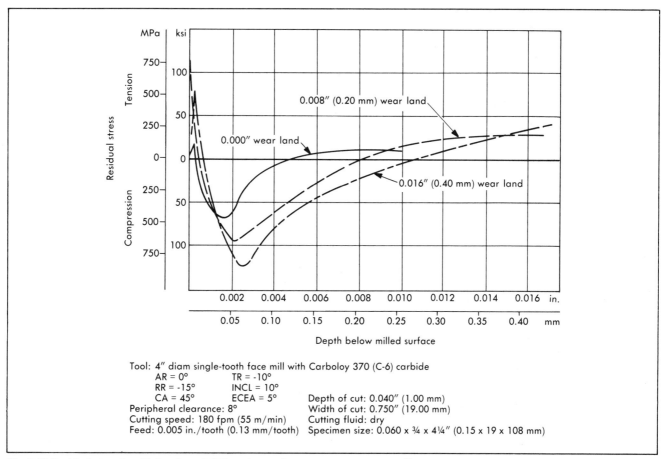

Fig. 5-43 Residual stress in milled surface of 4340 steel, quenched and tempered to R$_C$52.[42]

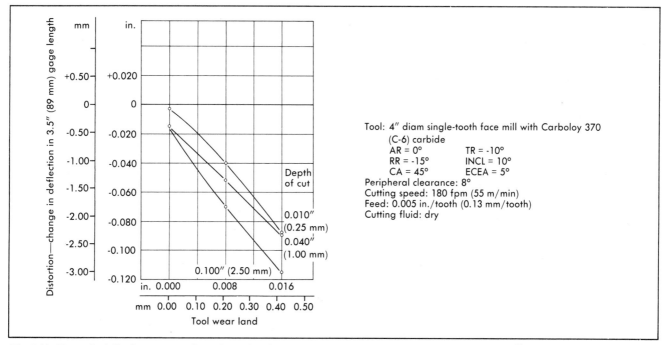

Fig. 5-44 Change in deflection versus tool wearland when face milling 4340 steel, quenched and tempered to R$_C$52.[43]

SURFACE ALTERATIONS

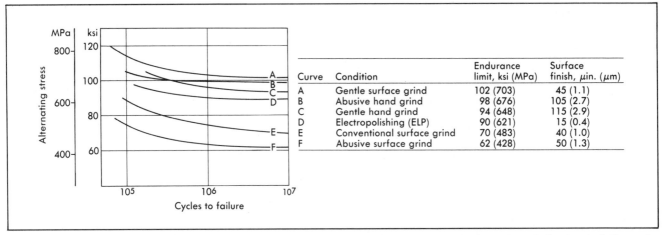

Curve	Condition	Endurance limit, ksi (MPa)	Surface finish, μin. (μm)
A	Gentle surface grind	102 (703)	45 (1.1)
B	Abusive hand grind	98 (676)	105 (2.7)
C	Gentle hand grind	94 (648)	115 (2.9)
D	Electropolishing (ELP)	90 (621)	15 (0.4)
E	Conventional surface grind	70 (483)	40 (1.0)
F	Abusive surface grind	62 (428)	50 (1.3)

Fig. 5-45 Fatigue characteristics of AISI 4340 steel (quenched and tempered, R_C 50). Metal removal conditions: surface grinding, hand grinding, and electropolishing. Mode: cantilever bending, zero mean stress. Temperature: 75°F (24°C).[44]

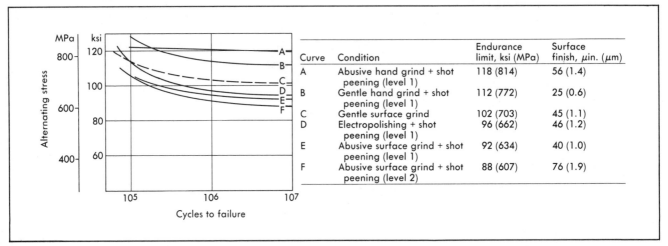

Curve	Condition	Endurance limit, ksi (MPa)	Surface finish, μin. (μm)
A	Abusive hand grind + shot peening (level 1)	118 (814)	56 (1.4)
B	Gentle hand grind + shot peening (level 1)	112 (772)	25 (0.6)
C	Gentle surface grind	102 (703)	45 (1.1)
D	Electropolishing + shot peening (level 1)	96 (662)	46 (1.2)
E	Abusive surface grind + shot peening (level 1)	92 (634)	40 (1.0)
F	Abusive surface grind + shot peening (level 2)	88 (607)	76 (1.9)

Fig. 5-46 Fatigue characteristics of AISI 4340 steel (quenched and tempered, R_C 50). Metal removal conditions: machining and shot peening. Mode: cantilever bending, zero mean stress. Temperature: 75°F (24°C).[45]

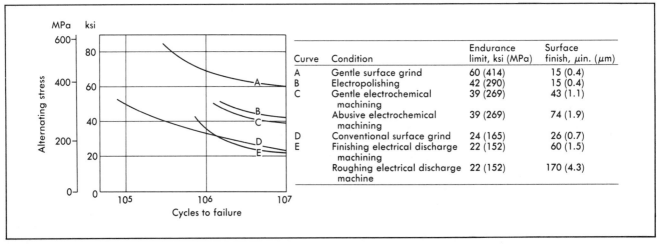

Curve	Condition	Endurance limit, ksi (MPa)	Surface finish, μin. (μm)
A	Gentle surface grind	60 (414)	15 (0.4)
B	Electropolishing	42 (290)	15 (0.4)
C	Gentle electrochemical machining	39 (269)	43 (1.1)
	Abusive electrochemical machining	39 (269)	74 (1.9)
D	Conventional surface grind	24 (165)	26 (0.7)
E	Finishing electrical discharge machining	22 (152)	60 (1.5)
	Roughing electrical discharge machine	22 (152)	170 (4.3)

Fig. 5-47 Fatigue characteristics of Inconel 718 machined in the solution-treated and aged condition, R_C 44. Metal removal conditions: surface grinding, electrical discharge machining, electrochemical machining, and electropolishing. Mode: cantilever bending, zero mean stress. Temperature: 75°F (24°C).[46]

EVALUATION PROCEDURES

A summary of the fatigue strength of a variety of steels, titanium, and nickel-based alloys is shown in Fig. 5-48 for grinding, in Fig. 5-49 for end milling, and in Fig. 5-50 for nontraditional machining methods. From these charts, it can be seen that the fatigue strength of these alloys is closely associated with the material removal process used as well as the operating parameters of each individual process.

EVALUATION PROCEDURES

Experimental procedures have been developed to provide three increasingly deeper levels of surface integrity evaluation. The procedures differ in the extent of data that they provide and must be tailored to meet a plant's specific needs.

The minimum data set is the least expensive approach to surface integrity evaluation and should be considered only as a screening test for the analysis of surface effects. It is essentially metallographic information supplemented with microhardness measurements and surface texture measurements. Components of the minimum data set are given in Table 5-4.

The standard data set provides more in-depth data than the minimum data set for critical applications. It includes results from the minimum data set along with residual-stress profiles and high cycle fatigue screening tests (see Table 5-5). Generally, the standard data set has information at two or more diverse levels of process intensity to represent finishing and roughing machining conditions.

The extended data set provides data gathered from statistically designed fatigue programs and yields data for detailed designing. It consists of the standard data set, fatigue tests, stress-corrosion tests, and mechanical tests (see Table 5-6).

To ensure a high degree of surface integrity, it is necessary to employ process control. It is also important to provide quality control by inspection processes on machined components. At the present time, however, only a limited number of practical nondestructive test (NDT) methods are available for inspection

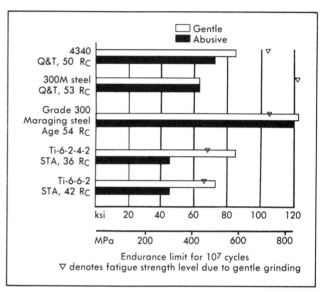

Fig. 5-49 Summary of fatigue strengths for end-milled surfaces having cantilever bending and zero mean stress and being at room temperature.[48]

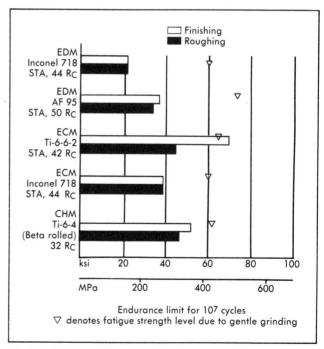

Fig. 5-50 Summary of fatigue strengths for nontraditionally machined surfaces having cantilever bending and zero mean stress and being at room temperature.[49]

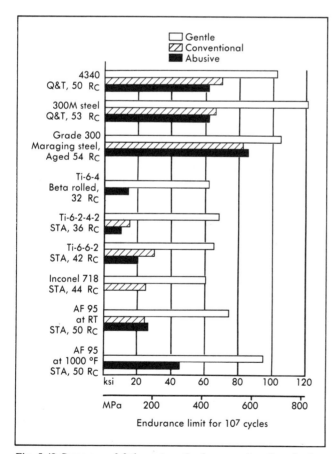

Fig. 5-48 Summary of fatigue strengths for ground surfaces having cantilever bending and zero mean stress and being at room temperature.[47]

EVALUATION PROCEDURES

(see Table 5-7). For example, untempered and overtempered martensite can be determined by a macroetching technique, but this technique is applicable only to steels. Penetrant inspection procedures are available for inspection of relatively large

TABLE 5-4
Minimum Surface Integrity Data Set[50]

1. Surface texture
   a. roughness measurement or microtopographic map
   b. lay designation or photo

2. Macrostructure (10X or less)
   a. macrocracks or surface imperfections
   b. scanning electron microscopes
   c. macroetch indications (fluorescent penetrant or magnetic flux)

3. Microstructure
   a. microcracks
   b. plastic deformation
   c. phase transformations
   d. intergranular attack
   e. microdefects
   f. built-up edge or deposits of debris
   g. recast layers
   h. selective etching
   i. metallurgical transformations

4. Microhardness alterations
   a. heat-affected zones

TABLE 5-5
Standard Surface Integrity Data Set[51]

1. Minimum data set

2. Residual stress profile or distortion measurements

3. Fatigue tests (screening only)

TABLE 5-6
Extended Surface Integrity Data Set[52]

1. Standard data set

2. Fatigue tests

3. Stress-corrosion tests

4. Additional mechanical testing
   a. tensile
   b. stress rupture
   c. creep
   d. friction, wear, sealing, bearing performance
   e. fracture toughness
   f. low cycle fatigue
   g. elevated or cryogenic temperature
   h. crack propagation
   i. surface chemistry

cracks. Development in ultrasonic and eddy current devices for detection of the surface alterations holds some promise, but there is a need for more reliable NDT equipment to ensure positive identification of surface alterations. Additional information on NDT can be found in Chapter 6, "Nondestructive Testing," of this volume.

Metallographic Sectioning and Special Preparation Techniques

Microscopic examination is an important and inexpensive means for rapid initial surface integrity evaluation. However, special metallographic techniques are necessary for studying surface phenomena. Surface microstructure alterations are generally very shallow, usually on the order of 0.001-0.003" (0.02-0.08 mm). Under very abusive conditions, alterations as deep as 0.005-0.015" (0.13-0.38 mm) have been noted. Often, significant microstructural alterations, microcracks, or flaws as shallow as 0.0001" (0.0025 mm) in depth are developed during material removal processing. Thus, it is necessary to employ sectioning, coating with a thin layer of electroless nickel mounting, and other metallographic techniques that do not alter or destroy the pertinent surface and that maintain a high degree of edge retention.

Various types of microscopes are available for the evaluation of surface metallurgy, including optical microscopes, scanning electron microscopes (SEM), and transmission electron microscopes (TEM). Optical microscopes are the least expensive and the most widely applicable method. It is advisable to examine metallurgical mounts first in the unetched condition, thereby accentuating the profile, microcracks, inclusions, voids, and crevice-like defects. After etching, specimens are re-examined for microstructural identification and grain boundary conditions.

Microhardness Determinations

Microhardness determinations can be made on the previously described metallurgical mounts using a microhardness tester with either a Knoop or a Vickers indenter. Microhardness studies are important for identifying the possible overall effects of heat-affected zones caused by specific material removal operations. Examples of surface effects revealed by microhardness variations include the following:

- Softening from resolutioned austenite.
- Chemical softening (sometimes associated with chemical machining or electrochemical machining).
- Heat-affected zones.
- Plastic deformation or work-hardened zones.

Additional information on hardness testing can be found in Chapter 7, "Mechanical Testing and Balancing," of this volume.

Residual Stress Determination

Distortion may occur in the manufacture of components as a result of heat-treating or material removal processes that can leave substantial residual stresses in the surface layers. Most of the machining-induced residual stress occurs in the first 0.0005-0.010" (0.013-0.25 mm) below the surface. Some of the descriptors used in residual stress are shown in Fig. 5-51. Because single surface residual stress measurements can be quite misleading, a profile for the first few thousandths of an inch below the surface is essential. The peak value and its depth below the surface are related to high cycle fatigue strength and magnitude of distortion.

EVALUATION PROCEDURES

TABLE 5-7
Testing Techniques Used to Detect and Locate Surface Inhomogeneities in Metals[53]

Metallurgical Inhomogeneity	Nondestructive Techniques			Destructive Techniques
	Commonly Employed	Specialized	Possible with Further Developments	
Macrocracks	Visual inspection Binocular inspection Magnetic particle Penetrant Eddy current Acid macroetch	Ultrasonic pulse echo Automatic optical scanning	Acoustic impact	Optical metallography
Microcracks	Binocular inspection High-sensitivity fluorescent penetrant Magnetic particle	Ultrasonic pulse echo, surface waves, and lamb waves	Radioactive gas penetrant High-frequency ultrasonic Acoustic impact Surface electrical resistance	Optical metallography Scanning electron microscopy Transmission electron microscopy
Tears, laps, and pits	Visual with etch Magnetic particle Eddy current Penetrant	Automatic optical scanning	Radioactive gas penetrant	Optical metallography Scanning electron microscopy
IGA and selective etch		High-sensitivity fluorescent penetrant		Macroetch Optical electron microscopy Transmission electron microscopy
Surface phase transformation (OTM, UTM, resolutioning, etc.)	Macroetch	X-ray diffraction Magnetic particle	Ultrasonic velocity Surface electrical resistance Eddy current	Optical metallography
Composition changes (oxidation, decarb, etc.)			Laser probe Mass spectrometry X-ray spectroscopy	Wet chemical analysis Electron microprobe
Surface hardness changes	Superficial hardness testing Ultrasonic hardness testing	Eddy current X-ray diffraction	Beta backscatter	Microhardness traverse
Redeposited and resolidified metal	Macroetch Visual inspection			Optical metallography
Recrystallization and grain growth		Ultrasonic attenuation	Radioactive gas penetrant	Optical metallography
Plastic deformation (cold work, hot work)	Superficial hardness testing	Eddy current Magnetic particle	Beta backscatter Radioactive gas penetrant Ultrasonic velocity	Optical metallography Microhardness traverse
Inclusions and voids	Ultrasonic pulse echo shear wave, surface wave, and lamb wave Penetrant X-ray radiography Eddy current Magnetic particle	Gamma radiography Neutron radiography	Radioactive gas penetrant	Optical metallography

(continued)

PROCESS GUIDELINES

TABLE 5-7—*Continued*

| Metallurgical Inhomogeneity | Nondestructive Techniques | | | Destructive Techniques |
	Commonly Employed	Specialized	Possible with Further Developments	
Residual stresses	X-ray diffraction	Ultrasonic velocity	Eddy current Electrochemical potential Ultrasonic attentuation Magneto-absorption	Parting-out Layer removal X-ray diffraction
Distortion	Visual inspection	Metrology		

Source: M. Field, J.F. Kahles, and J.T. Cammett.[12]

There are several methods of determining the residual stress profile. The two most common are layer removal deflection and X-ray diffraction techniques. In the layer removal deflection technique, the change in curvature of a strip specimen after a test cut is determined using a fixture such as that shown in Fig. 5-52. The distortion or change in deflection in a 3.5″ (88.9 mm) gage length can be plotted against various machining parameters and can be used as a measure of the relative effect of various parameters or various metal removal operations.

The use of X-ray diffraction for measuring residual stress has generally superseded the deflection test strip method. Much smaller areas can be measured with greater accuracy; accuracy of ±5% can be obtained.

PROCESS GUIDELINES

Well-developed methods for evaluating surface integrity exist today, but data from which guidelines can be drawn and trends or patterns can be uncovered are only slowly accumulating. Because of this, established guidelines must be considered only as general or starting recommendations. Each material-process combination is unique and can have variable effects, depending on the metallurgical state of the material and the energy intensity level used during processing. The designer should assess the critical areas on the workpiece and apply surface integrity specifications to these areas only; otherwise,

component costs may be excessive. The manufacturing engineer, in turn, should realize that maintaining the proper sequence of operations is as important to surface integrity as the selection and precise maintenance of the correct process operating parameters.

Currently, most of the surface integrity investigations and data collections have involved material removal processes. This does not indicate that forming, coating, or other processes are exempt from surface integrity considerations, only that insufficient data are available for these processes.

Some general guidelines for all material removal processes are as follows:

1. Thorough component or product testing is one of the best assurances/checks of surface integrity. The tests should be run with surfaces produced by the complete and exact sequence of production operations.
2. Surface integrity requirements should only apply to the critical or highly stressed zones of the component part. The requirements should not be applied "all over."
3. Highly stressed areas of critical components should be evaluated carefully to assess the impact of the full sequence of processes that generate the "as shipped" surface. The control of the sequence of processes is as important to surface integrity as is the selection and maintenance of operating parameters.
4. Control of the metallurgical state of the material is as important as control of the process parameters.

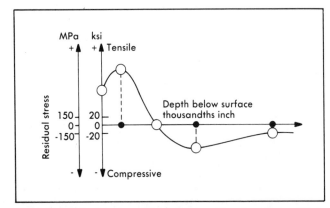

Fig. 5-51 Residual stress profile descriptors. Key: 1, surface residual stress—value at zero depth; 2, peak stress (tensile)—value at defined depth; 3, crossover—depth in thousandths of an inch (hundredths of a millimeter); 4, peak stress (compressive)—value at defined depth; 5, depth of residual stress—depth below the surface where stress declines to and remains less than 20 ksi (138 MPa), an inconsequential value, or less than 10% of tensile strength.[54]

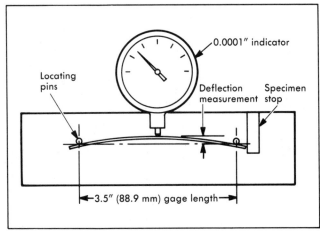

Fig. 5-52 Deflection measurement fixture.[55]

5. Material inhomogeneities or anomalies (sometimes even those within specification limits) can have component integrity effects as serious as the surface integrity effects from manufacturing processes.

6. Designers, shop supervisors, and quality control and process engineers must be educated and trained to increase their appreciation of the magnitude of surface integrity effects from manufacturing processes.

7. The surface integrity from processes other than material removal or machining processes should also be evaluated.

8. The surface integrity effects from conventional machining are of the same magnitude as those from nontraditional machining.

9. Metallographic sections at high magnification taken parallel and perpendicular to the lay pattern provide an effective early alert to potential surface integrity problems.

10. Postprocessing treatments such as heat treatment, shot peening, roller burnishing, and low-stress grinding may offset some, but not necessarily all, of the otherwise detrimental surface integrity effects.

11. Hand-controlled operations have a tendency to produce variability in surface effects and should be considered suspect.

12. Low process energy intensities and low material removal rates are characteristic of most, but not all, material removal processes that provide acceptable surface integrity.

13. Rigid, high-quality machine tools and fixtures are desirable.

14. Cutting fluids should be fresh or well controlled and carefully, completely, and quickly removed from the workpiece when the operation is complete.

15. Deburring of all machined edges is desirable.

16. Parts stored for extended periods should be covered with a protective coating to prevent corrosion.

Chip Cutting Process Guidelines

Because conventional machining processes have been used so long, it is easy to forget that they are characterized by mechanical plastic deformation, regular lay patterns, and sometimes substantial heat effects from too forceful a passage of the cutting edge over the surface. The degree of dullness of the tool is a major factor in determining the surface effects. At the end of the tool life, extensive roughness, tears, laps, or deposited built-up edges can result in abused surfaces.

Conventional mechanical machining surface integrity guidelines have been developed principally from data generated by single or multiple-point tools operated in the turning, milling, or drilling mode. Surface integrity data for the mechanical nontraditional processes are not extensive and should be investigated in critical applications using techniques described under general guidelines. Generally, the low energy levels and gentle material removal rates result in a minimum of altered material zones.

Guidelines that promote good surface integrity results in chip cutting processes are as follows:

1. Sharp tools are essential for establishing surface integrity in turning, milling, and similar single-point tool cutting processes. Plastic flow is frequently present, and dull tools can produce laps, tears, and roughness that can be initiating sites for fatigue failure.

2. Maximum flank wearlands should be limited to 0.010-0.015" (0.25-0.38 mm). This is the point at which the wearland becomes visible to the naked eye.

3. Cutting parameters should be selected that assist in keeping tools sharp.

4. Form cutters tend to produce surface damage more readily in roughing than finishing tools that generate a form.

5. The heat from the passage of a cutting tool, especially a dull one, can produce metallurgical transformations.

6. Evidence of burning on the surface should initiate a check of depth of disturbance, which can extend to 0.010" (0.25 mm).

7. Residual stresses from dull cutting tools are frequently compressive below the surface.

8. Sharp drills should be used to help avoid serious surface-layer alterations.

9. Dwelling during drilling should be avoided; galling, torn, or discolored surfaces should be cause for rejection or correction.

10. Drill fixturing rigidity is desirable as long as chip ejection is not restricted.

11. Deburring is imperative on both entrance and exit of holes.

12. Drilled and reamed holes should be chamfered on both exit and entrance.

13. Reaming stock allowances should be controlled.

14. A maximum number of holes per reamer should be specified and maintained despite visual appearance of reamer.

15. Hand feeding of straight reamed holes should be avoided.

16. Alignment, tool geometry, and tool condition are important controls in hand reaming.

17. Finish-boring operations should maintain roughness limits and avoid laps and tears. Only very small wearlands can be tolerated, with about 0.005" (0.13 mm) as a limit. One finish pass per cutting edge is a frequently set limit.

18. Honing is an excellent finishing operation for developing surface integrity.

19. Corrosion potential of some cutting fluids should be checked. Old fluids should be checked because they often corrode workpieces more rapidly.

20. Finish roughness values should not serve as the only criteria for development of fatigue strength.

Abrasive Material Removal Process Guidelines

The heat in the workpiece generated by abrasive machining is the principal ingredient affecting surface integrity. The amount of heat is proportional to the intensity with which the process is applied. Thermal properties of the material and its metallurgical response to the heating level control the degree of surface effects.

Grinding produces the greatest range of fatigue endurance sensitivity among the several material removal processes and alloys studied to date. Guidelines that promote good surface integrity results in abrasive material removal processes are as follows:

1. Low-stress grinding techniques can reduce distortion and surface damage. Frequent coarse dressings of softer grade wheels, lower infeed, and reduced grinding wheel speeds with lubricating-type cutting fluids are the prin-

cipal elements of low-stress grinding. A shallow depth of low-value tensile or compressive residual stress can be attained.

2. Higher work material speeds can aid both productivity and surface integrity. Lower wheel surface speeds aid surface integrity without sacrificing productivity.

3. Frequent coarse dressings of grinding wheels can reduce surface damage by keeping the wheels open and sharp, thus helping to reduce temperatures at the wheel-workpiece interface.

4. Modifications to established low-stress grinding procedures should not be attempted unless testing confirms that they can be tolerated.

5. If low-stress grinding is specified for finishing operations, conventional grinding can be used to within 0.010" (0.25 mm) of the finished size, provided that the work materials are not sensitive to cracking.

6. Lubricating-type fluids and coolants should have a strong and positively directed flow and should be checked for their chemical action on the specific material being ground.

7. Conventional grinding conditions should not be used for finish grinding of highly sensitive alloys such as high-strength alloys, high-temperature nickel and cobalt-based alloys, and titanium or molybdenum alloys.

8. The heat-affected zones from rough grinding can be much deeper than the surface discolorations might indicate. Microhardness traverses can generally detect the depth of surface alterations.

9. High-stress grinding of martensitic steels can create untempered martensitic zones with overtempered martensitic zones below them. Both of these zones limit fatigue strength.

10. Crack detection tests should be made after rough grinding of materials. Existing surface cracks can propagate ahead of grinding when finishing some thermally sensitive materials. Low-stress grinding should be used to remove more than the altered material zones from any prior conventional grinding operation.

11. Hand grinding of sensitive materials should only be done under careful control.

12. Strict instructions and controls over power hand sanders should be maintained.

13. Abrasive cutoff frequently has a harsh and deep surface effect, and these altered layers should be removed by more gentle processes.

14. Surface X-ray residual stress measurements can be misleading. A full profile is best, or enough checks should be made below the surface to correct for penetration of the X-rays and the slope of the profile.

15. Good dressing action on the grinding wheel is promoted by cleanliness and sharpness of the dressing tool. Pauses or dwells in the dressing tool action can dull the wheel surface, particularly with the roll-form, crush-roll, or form-block dressing tools.

Electrical Material Removal Process Guidelines

The molecule-by-molecule dissolution of the electrically conductive workpiece in electrochemical machining (ECM) is a forceless material removal that does not introduce any residual stresses in the workpiece. Surface texture is smooth, does not have any lay pattern, and can approach a metallograph-polish caliber even to revealing individual grain patterns. The absence of beneficial residual stress and/or cold working in the surface frequently results in high cycle fatigue strengths less than those produced with conventionally prepared surfaces.

The key to good ECM surfaces is a careful match of the electrolyte composition with the metallurgical state of the workpiece material plus careful control of the operating parameters, especially current density. The common electrical material removal processes are electrochemical deburring (ECD), electrochemical grinding (ECG), electrochemical honing (ECH), electrochemical machining (ECM), electrochemical polishing (ECP), electrochemical turning (ECT), electrostream milling (ESM), and shaped-tube electrolytic machining. Guidelines that promote good surface integrity results in electrical material removal processes are as follows:

1. Surface roughness standards should be reassessed when applying ECM because it produces unusual surface textures with no lay pattern.

2. Well-controlled ECM does not induce any stresses into the surface.

3. High current densities are desirable in the cutting gap for good finishes and rapid metal removal.

4. The current density in the workpiece should be carefully planned to prevent overheating in the material.

5. Relentless process controls should be supplemented with periodic metallographic checks from representative surfaces.

6. The work material heat-treated state should be precisely known and controlled to ensure the best repeatability of ECM surfaces.

7. Contact between the electrolyte and workpiece without current flow should be minimized.

8. Localized overheating of the workpiece as a result of poor connections or short circuits should be carefully examined for the extent of any damage. Removal of the surface discoloration is insufficient.

9. Careful and complete rinsing of the electrolyte from the workpiece is essential. Ultrasonic agitation of the cleaning bath is helpful.

10. Selective etching, excessive roughness, intergranular attack, or pitting are evidences of less-than-optimum operating conditions or tooling practices. These conditions can occur on surfaces subjected to low current density in the presence of the electrolyte or in areas adjacent to the main electrode cutting face.

11. Room-temperature fatigue endurance strength is generally lower as compared to that of low-stress conventionally ground specimens and represents the unblemished or unaffected material properties state. The lack of any residual stress in electrochemically machined surfaces can account for the differences observed in fatigue strength.

12. The use of a post-ECM shot peening or rolling treatment may be desirable to enhance component fatigue strength.

13. Anomalies in the workpiece surface or microvariations in material composition can influence the surface quality and may be exposed by ECM.

14. Some surface softening will occur in many, but not all, materials.

15. An increase in roughness of the ECM surface can be a

significant alert to the departure from optimum or preplanned operating conditions.

16. Hydrogen embrittlement is not attributable to ECM.

Thermal Material Removal Process Guidelines

Thermal material removal processes utilize a variety of heat sources to melt, vaporize, or sublime the workpiece surface. Because of the techniques employed for material removal, these processes always result in a heat-affected area on the surface. The magnitude depends primarily on the energy density impinging on the surface and the thermal characteristics of the workpiece material. The texture is random and can exhibit splattered, recast, cracked, or spalled material. Finishing or gentle operating parameters, when carefully controlled, can minimize these effects. Thermal stresses, generally tensile, are present as microhardness variations.

Some of the common thermal material removal processes currently being used are electron beam machining (EBM), electrical discharge grinding (EDG), electrical discharge machining (EDM), electrical discharge sawing (EDS), electrical discharge wire cutting (EDWC), laser beam machining (LBM), and plasma arc machining (PAM). Guidelines that promote good surface integrity results using thermal material removal processes are as follows:

1. The surface texture is composed of a random array of overlapping craters or cusps, sometimes with macrocracks at the roughing level of processing.
2. Surface roughness standards should be reassessed when using these processes because they produce unusual surface textures with no lay patterns and require different methods of checking.
3. The prior metallurgical condition of the workpiece is as important in generating surface quality as is the selection of operating parameters.
4. Careful monitoring of the preselected operating parameters is necessary. Some older types of equipment do not maintain their initial settings throughout a long day or run.
5. The depth of the heat-affected zone (HAZ) or recast structure on the surface is approximately proportional to the magnitude of the energy impinging on that surface. It is always present to some degree.
6. The HAZ can induce hardness variations and a substantial tensile residual stress in the surface layers.
7. The depth of the HAZ below the recast layers is approximately equal to the depth of the maximum recast. The recast layer in EDM can be controlled precisely and is usually only a few ten-thousandths of an inch thick.
8. Fatigue strength is frequently severely reduced by the HAZ(s).
9. Highly stressed or critical surfaces should have the HAZ produced by thermal material removal processes removed or modified by a postprocessing treatment.
10. Removal of the altered material zones (AMZ) may not be necessary if component or laboratory tests show that design requirements are being satisfied.
11. Microholes (those less than one millimeter in diameter) produced by thermal processes may not be detrimental to fatigue endurance strength. A check by facture mechanics of the critical hole size for a specific material is desirable.
12. On thin components, high current densities may over-

heat the workpiece because the bulk material of the workpiece serves as a heatsink.
13. Thorough cleaning to remove dielectric fluids, beads, and vapor residue is desirable.
14. The microcracks per inch of cross section can be a valuable clue to the relative thermal sensitivity of materials.

Chemical Material Removal Process Guidelines

The chemical family of material removal processes is characterized by an absence of stress introduced into the workpiece as a result of the process. The gentle chemical action of dissolution, molecule by molecule or grain face by grain face, is typically smooth. However, smooth surfaces [less than 32 μin. (0.8 μm) R_a] are slightly roughened, while rough surfaces [125 μin. (3.2 μm) R_a] or more are usually smoothed.

Common chemical material removal processes are chemical machining (CHM), electropolishing, photochemical machining, and the thermochemical machining. Guidelines to promote good surface integrity results in these processes are as follows:

1. Chemical machining does not induce any significant stress in the machined surfaces.
2. Surface roughness standards should be reassessed when applying CHM because it produces surfaces with unusual textures and no lay pattern.
3. The chemical reagents must be matched to the expected metallurgical state of the work material.
4. Surface roughness variations during processing can be a good indicator of changes in the processing conditions or a change in the metallurgical state of the work material.
5. Careful rinsing of the solutions from the finished workpiece is essential.
6. The control of the metallurgical and heat-treat state of the work material is as essential as the control of the process parameters.
7. Selective etching, intergranular attack, and pitting can result from off-standard conditions such as high etchant temperatures, incomplete stirring, depleted or unbalanced solutions or contaminated solutions, and variations in the metallurgical state of the work material.
8. Weld areas usually show a different rate of cutting than the base material and an increase in surface roughness.
9. Steel, titanium, and nickel-based alloys that are susceptible to hydrogen embrittlement should have a post heat treatment of a few hours at a temperature of about 375 to 400°F (191 to 204°C). Treatment should be applied immediately after chemical processing.
10. Room-temperature high cycle fatigue strength generally is lower when compared to conventionally prepared low-stress ground specimens. This is probably caused by the absence of residual surface stresses.
11. The use of posttreatments to add a compressively stressed surface layer may be desirable for enhancing a component's fatigue strength.
12. A test coupon for metallurgical evaluation should be made at least at 90-180 day intervals or whenever the chemical solution is changed.
13. For quality assurance, a deviation of one operating parameter by more than 10% from the preplanned value should be cause for alarm and checking. If more than

one parameter has deviated by more than 10%, the operation should be shut down until corrections have returned the process to a controlled state.

Posttreatment Process Guidelines

Finishing operations or posttreatment processing have been widely used to improve surface roughness or appearance, to remove undesirable surface layers, or to enhance the beneficial compressive layers. The surface integrity produced by these finishing processes, or sequence of processes, should be assessed with the same diligence as that used for the prime fabricating process. While shot peening has been the most extensively used posttreatment, consideration should be given to other techniques to achieve the desired effects. Often, other treatments may be used that result in less cost or greater productivity or better quality assurance.

Some of the effective posttreatment processes are listed in Table 5-8. Guidelines that promote good surface integrity results from posttreatment processes are as follows:

1. Careful washing should be employed to remove all traces of fluids used during machining that could contribute to stress corrosion.
2. Low-temperature heat treatment will remove any hydrogen picked up during processing.
3. Heat treatments following material removal are of limited usefulness.
4. Abrasive tumbling can be effective for improving surface texture and for adding a modest compressive residual stress to aid fatigue strength.

TABLE 5-8
Posttreatment Processes

Abrasive flow machining

Roller burnishing

Belt sanding

Hand grinding

Chemical machining

Honing

Peening—shot, sand, and glass bead

Buffing

Abrasive barrel tumbling

Chemical vapor deposition

Electrochemical deburring

Electrochemical polishing

Electropolishing

Heat treatment

Low-stress grinding

Laser shock treatment

Ultrasonic cleaning

Ultrasonic peening

Vibration stress relief

5. Peening with steel shot or sand or glass beads can be useful to add substantial beneficial compressive residual stress, improve surface cleanliness, and enhance fatigue strength.
6. Mechanically gentle processing can be effective with specific evaluation of each situation.
7. The benefits of shot peening can be nullified or severely decreased by exposure to high local stresses or temperatures or by vibration that allows the surface stress to relax by plastic deformation either from creep or yielding during "postpeen" processing or during operation.
8. The possibility that peening, burnishing, lapping, and similar processes can cover up, but not overcome, the existing microcracks should be assessed.
9. Human variability means that hand finishing should be avoided if possible or controlled rigorously.
10. It is possible to overpeen surfaces and create excessive core stresses, microcracks, untempered martensite, laps, or similar abuses.
11. The junction between peened and unpeened surfaces should be "feathered" to avoid stress concentrations.

References

1. *Machining Data Handbook*, vol. 2, 3rd ed. (Cincinnati: Metcut Research Associates Inc., Machinability Data Center, 1980), p. 18-3.
2. W. P. Koster and J. F. Kahles, "Surface Finish—Not a Definitive Measure of Part Quality," *Machining Briefs*, No. 2, 1985.
3. *Machining Data Handbook*, op. cit., p. 18-6.
4. "Surface Texture," ANSI B46.1 (New York: American Society of Mechanical Engineers, 1985).
5. Howard E. Boyer and Timothy L. Gall, eds., *Metals Handbook, Desk Edition* (Metals Park, OH: American Society for Metals, 1985), p. 27-23.
6. *Ibid.*
7. Alex N. Tabenkin, "The Growing Importance of Surface-Finish Specs," *Machine Design* (September 20, 1984), pp. 99-102.
8. *1983 SAE Handbook*, vol. 1 (Warrendale, PA: Society of Automotive Engineers, 1983), p. 6.12.
9. Francis T. Farago, *Handbook of Dimensional Measurement*, 2nd ed. (New York: Industrial Press, Inc., 1982), pp. 377-382.
10. Tabenkin, *loc. cit.*
11. J. C. Wyant, et al., "An Optical Profilometer for Surface Characterization of Magnetic Media," *ASLE Trans 27* (Park Ridge, IL: American Society of Lubrication Engineers, 1984), pp. 101-113.
12. B. Bhushan, J. C. Wyant, and C. L. Koliopoulos, "Measurement of Surface Topography of Magnetic Tapes by Mirau Interferometry," *Applied Optics*, vol. 24, 1985, pp. 1489-1497.
13. *Machining Data Handbook*, op. cit., p. 18-5.
14. *Machining Data Handbook*, op. cit., pp. 18-39 to 18-134.
15. *Ibid.*, p. 18-40.
16. G. Bellows and D. N. Tishler, *Introduction to Surface Integrity*, Report TM70-974 (Cincinnati: General Electric Co., 1970).
17. M. Field, J. F. Kahles, and J. T. Cammett, "A Review of Measuring Methods for Surface Integrity," *Annals of the CIRP*, 21(2) (Paris: International Institute for Production Engineering Research), pp. 219-238.
18. *Machining Data Handbook*, op. cit., p. 18-47.
19. *Ibid.*, pp. 18-42 to 18-43.
20. *Surface Integrity Encyclopedia* (Special unpublished collection of data and effects from specific material process combinations.) Maintained for reference by the Machinability Data Center, Cincinnati.
21. *Ibid.*
22. W. P. Koster, et al., *Surface Integrity of Machined Structural Components*, U.S. Air Force Technical Report AFML-TR-70-11 (Cincinnati: Metcut Research Associates Inc., 1972).

REFERENCES

23. *Surface Integrity Encyclopedia, op. cit.*
24. *Ibid.*
25. *Ibid.*
26. *Ibid.*
27. W. P. Koster, et al., *loc. cit.*
28. *Ibid.*
29. L. R. Gatto and T. D. DiLullo, *Metallographic Techniques for Determining Surface Alterations in Machining*, SME Technical Paper IQ71-225 (Dearborn, MI: Society of Manufacturing Engineers, 1971).
30. M. Field, "Surface Integrity in Conventional and Nonconventional Machining," *Seminar on Advancements in Machine Tools and Production Trends* (State College, PA: Pennsylvania State University, July 1969).
31. M. Field, W. P. Koster, and J. B. Kohls, *Machining of High Strength Steels with Emphasis on Surface Integrity*, AFMDC 70-1 (Cincinnati, OH: Air Force Machinability Center, 1970).
32. M. Field, *op. cit.*
33. *Ibid.*
34. M. Field, W. P. Koster, and J. B. Kohls, *op. cit.*
35. M. Field, *op. cit.*
36. *Ibid.*
37. G. Bellows, "Surface Integrity of Thermal Removal Processes," *Seminar on Laser Applications in Machining and Welding* (State College, PA: Pennsylvania State University, July 1970).
38. _____ , *Surface Integrity of Electrochemical Machining*, G. E. Report R60AEG172 (Cincinnati: General Electric Co., July 1969).
39. M. Field and J. F. Kahles, "Review of Surface Integrity of Machined Components," *Annals of the CIRP*, 20(2) (Paris: International Institute for Production Engineering Research, 1971), pp. 153-163.
40. M. Field and J. F. Kahles, *The Surface Integrity of Machined and Ground High Strength Steels*, DMIC Report 210, October 1964, pp. 54-77.
41. *Ibid.*
42. *Ibid.*
43. *Ibid.*
44. W. P. Koster and J. B. Kohls, *Relation of Surface Integrity to Cost and Reliability of Structural Components*, SME Technical Paper IQ72-207 (Dearborn, MI: Society of Manufacturing Engineers, 1972).
45. *Ibid.*
46. *Ibid.*
47. *Ibid.*
48. *Ibid.*
49. *Ibid.*
50. G. Bellows and D.N. Tishler, *Introduction to Surface Integrity*, Report TM70-974 (Cincinnati: General Electric Co., 1970).
51. *Ibid.*
52. *Ibid.*
53. M. Field, J. F. Kahles, and J. T. Cammett, *op. cit.*
54. G. Bellows, *Low Stress Grinding: For Quality Production*, MDC 78-103 (Cincinnati: Metcut Research Associates Inc., Machinability Data Center, 1978).
55. M. Field, J. F. Kahles, and J. T. Cammett, *op. cit.*

Bibliography

Brodmann, R., et al. "Surface Quality Inspection in Rocker Arm Manufacturing Using an Optical Roughness Measuring Device." *Industrial & Production Engineering*, 1983/3, pp. 126-129.

_____ , and Thurn, Gerd. "Optical Roughness Measuring Instrument for Fine-Machined Surfaces." *Optical Engineering* (May/June 1985), pp. 408-413.

Fromson, J. E.; Brecker, J. N.; and Shum, L. Y. "A Universal Surface Texture Measuring System." *SME NAMRC V Proceedings*. Dearborn, MI: Society of Manufacturing Engineers, 1977, p. 23.

"Instrument Tracer Surface Roughness." MIL-I-45177A. Philadelphia: Naval Publications and Form Center, 1981.

Jansson, D. G.; Rourke, J. M.; and Bell, A. C. "High-Speed Surface Roughness Measurement." *Journal of Engineering for Industry* (February 1984), pp. 34-39.

Peters, J.; Vanherck, P.; and Sastrodinoto, M. "Assessment of Surface Typology Analysis Techniques." *Annals of the CIRP*, vol. 28/2/1979. Paris: International Institute for Production Engineering Research, 1979.

Risko, D. G. "Quick Non-Destructive Method for Measuring Surface Finish Using Capacitance." *The Carbide and Tool Journal* (January 1981), p. 26.

Sherwood, K. F., and Crookall, J. R. "Surface Finish Assessment by an Electrical Capacitance Technique." *Proceedings*. London: Institution of Mechanical Engineers, 1967-1968, pp.344-349.

"Surface Roughness." ISO R468. Geneva, Switzerland: International Organization for Standardization, 1966.

Vorburger, T. V., and Hembree, G. G. *Characterization of Surface Topography*. Gaithersburg, MD: National Bureau of Standards.

_____ , and Teague, E. C. "Optical Techniques for On-Line Measurement of Surface Topography." *Precision Engineering*, vol. 3, 1981.

NONDESTRUCTIVE TESTING

Nondestructive testing is the examination of an object or material in a manner that will not impair its future usefulness. The purpose of the actual test may be to detect internal or surface flaws, measure thickness, determine material structure or composition, or measure or detect any of the object's or material's properties. Whatever the actual test may be used for, the three primary reasons for nondestructive testing are (1) to prevent accidents and save human lives, (2) to ensure product reliability, and (3) to make a profit for the user.[1]

Nondestructive testing is also referred to as nondestructive evaluation (NDE), nondestructive inspection (NDI), and nondestructive testing and inspection (NDTI). In this chapter, the term *nondestructive testing* (NDT) will be used because it is generally the most commonly accepted term.

All nondestructive tests include the following five basic elements:[2]

1. A source that supplies a suitable form and distribution of probing medium to appropriate regions of the test objects.
2. A modification of the probing medium or its distribution within test objects as a result of discontinuities or variations in material properties.
3. A sensitive detector responsive to changes in distribution or character of the probing medium.
4. A means of indicating or recording signals from the detector in forms useful for interpretation.
5. An observer or device capable of interpreting the indications or records in terms of test material properties or discontinuities.

In selecting the NDT method for the evaluation of a specific discontinuity, it is necessary to keep in mind that NDT methods may supplement each other. In addition, several methods may be capable of detecting the same defect. The selection of one method over another is based on variables such as type and origin of discontinuity, material manufacturing process, accessibility of the part, level of acceptability desired, equipment available, and cost. A planned analysis of the task must be made for each part requiring this type of testing.

Because the inspector is the most important aspect of any NDT method, inspectors must be certified to ensure competency. Each company is responsible for developing their own certification program. In developing this program, most companies follow the recommended practice proposed by the American Society for Nondestructive Testing (ASNT). However, work is being done to have ASNT act as a central certification administrator.

An inspector becomes certified after successfully completing a written, practical, and vision test. Certification is for a specific NDT method as well as for the industry in which the inspector will be working. Certification for one method does not imply that the inspector is certified for other methods.

Three levels of certification exist in NDT: Level I, Level II, and Level III. Level I inspectors have theory in the particular NDT method along with some hands-on testing practice. They are considered trainees and always work under a Level II inspector. Level II inspectors are qualified to perform the test without supervision, buy or reject parts, and test equipment for calibration. Level III inspectors have the final authority over any decisions and are qualified to evaluate parts, design testing procedures to meet customer requirements, and interpret codes and specifications. Before advancing to the next higher level, the inspector must spend a certain amount of time at the lower level as well as pass the test for the next level. To maintain certification, the inspector must pass an eye exam every year for near-vision acuity, for vision acuity, and for color vision and pass a written test every three years.

The purpose of this chapter is to provide manufacturing engineers with an overview of the various nondestructive test methods that are commonly used in industry, along with their potential applications. It is not intended to provide step-by-step guidelines for how a test should be conducted for a particular application. Table 6-1 summarizes the principal features of the test methods discussed in this chapter.[3] Additional information on the various methods can be found in the references and bibliography listed at the end of the chapter.

Contributors of sections of this chapter are: Harold Berger, President, Industrial Quality, Inc.; *Sam Currie*, General Manager, Ardrox, Inc.; *Donald C. Gates*, President, Reliance Industries; *Allen T. Green*, Technical Director, Acoustic Emission Technology Corp.; *John Johnston*, Engineering Manager, Staveley NDT Technologies, Inc., Sonic Systems Div.; *William J. Lang*, Sales Manager, Lenox Instrument Co., Inc.; *William E. Mooz*, President, Met-L-Chek Co.; *James Pellicer*, Sensors Engineer, Staveley NDT Technologies, Inc., Nortec Div.; *Robert T. Pitlak*, Director Technical Consulting, Pitlak Corp.; *Michael David Stebel*, Technical Assistant to the President, Manager, Technical Communications, UPA Technology, Inc.; *Fred Wiesinger*, Applications Engineering Manager, Uson Corporation.
   Reviewers of sections of this chapter are: J. Dennis Allison, NDT Specialist, Nuclear Products Dept., Westinghouse Canada, Inc.; *William H. Bailey*, Quality Methods Engineer-NDT, Quality Engineering, Cleveland Pneumatic Co.; *Jerry Ball*, Radiographer, Conam Inspection, A Unit of Qualcorp; *Frank G. Becher*, Vice President, Industrial Fiberoptics Dept., Olympus Corp.; *Kenneth N. Becker*, President, NDX Corp.; *Scott Benson*, Sales Manager, Accutron, Inc.; *Harold Berger*, President, Industrial Quality, Inc.; *Grant D. Bolwell*, General Manager, Elektro-Physik, Inc.; *J. S. Borucki*, Vice President Marketing, Ardrox, Inc.; *William V. Bowles*, Industrial Imaging Specialist, Health Sciences Div., Eastman Kodak Co.; *B. J. Brunty*, Brunty & Associates; *Briant Brush*, Technical Supervisor, Industrial X-ray Laboratory, AGFA-GEVAERT, Inc.;

NONDESTRUCTIVE TESTING

TABLE 6-1
General Description of Common NDT Methods

Method	Principle	Material
Visual inspection	Illuminate the test specimen with light and then examine the specimen with the eye. May include the use of optical aids	Most materials
Liquid penetrant	A liquid penetrant is drawn into surface flaws by capillary action, then revealed by developer material to aid in visual inspection	Nonporous materials, metals, plastics, and glazed ceramics
Magnetic particle	Magnetic particles, attracted by leakage flux at surface flaws of magnetic object, aid visual inspection	Magnetic materials
Ultrasonic	Sound vibration waves are introduced into a test object. This energy is reflected and scattered by inhomogeneities or becomes resonant. Information is interpreted from cathode ray tube or read from a meter	Metals, plastics, ceramics, glass, rubber, graphite, and concrete
Radiographic	General—penetrating radiation is differentially absorbed by materials, depending on thickness and type of material	Most materials
Eddy-current	Alternating-current coil induces eddy currents in test object. Flaws and material properties affect flow of current. Information derived from meter or cathode ray tube indications	Metals
Leak testing	Material flows across an interface at a leak site. Rate of flow is pressure, time, and leak size dependent. Detection of the trans-interface migration is done using one of several techniques	Totally independent of materials
Infrared	Electromagnetic radiation from test object above a temperature of absolute zero is detected and correlated to quality. Information is displayed by meter, recorder, photograph, or cathode ray tube	Most materials

Reviewers, cont.: **Bill Buschur**, *National Sales Manager/Industrial*, *Welch Allyn, Inc., Video Div.*; **Donald A. Carignan**, *President*, *Instrument Technology, Inc.*; **Paul H. Christensen**, *Supervisor, Eddy Current Dept., Conam Inspection, A Unit of Qualcorp*; **Paul O. Crombie, Jr.**, *Engineer, Quality Assurance Labs and Nondestructive Testing, McDonnell Douglas Corp.*; **Sam Currie**, *General Manager*, *Ardrox, Inc.*; **Dr. W. E. Dance**, *Manager, Neutron Radiography, Vought Missiles and Advanced Programs Div., LTV Aerospace and Defense Co.*; **Andrew J. Dancisin**, *Applications Development Manager, Industrial X-ray Laboratory, Philips Electronics Instruments, Inc.*; **Bryan M. DiVeto**, *Sales Coordinator, K. J. Law Engineers, Inc.*; **Donald D. Dodge**, *Principal Engineer, Manufacturing Development Center, Ford Motor Co.*; **CMS John F. Dorgan**, *Field Liaison Manager, Nondestructive Inspection Program Office, U.S. Air Force*; **Dr. David Dornfeld**, *Associate Professor, Mechanical Engineering Dept., University of California-Berkeley*; **H. L. Dunegan**, *President, Dunegan Corp.*; **James E. Engel**, *NDT/Quality Engineer, General Dynamics, Convair Div.*; **Timothy P. Flaherty**, *General Manager, Hocking NDT, Inc.*; **Gene Foley**, *President, Gene Foley, Inc.*; **Donald C. Gates**, *President, Reliance Industries*;

TABLE 6-1—*Continued*

Applications	Advantages	Limitations
Inspecting accessible surfaces. Internal surfaces may be inspected using a rigid or flexible borescope	Simple, easy to perform, low in cost	Dependent on inspector; can only detect surface flaws
Detect surface flaws such as cracks, porosity, pits, seams, and laps	Simple to perform, applicable to complex shapes, and inspection can be made on site	Can only detect surface flaws. Surfaces must be clean. The penetrant washes out of large defects. Standards are difficult to establish
Detect surface flaws such as cracks, laps, and seams. Capable of detecting some subsurface flaws	Easy to interpret, fast, and simple to perform	Material must be ferromagnetic. Parts must be relatively clean. Usually requires high current source. Parts must be demagnetized. Standards are difficult to establish
Detect inclusions, cracks, porosity, bursts, laminations, structure, lack of bond, thickness measurement, and weld defects	Variety of inspection elements and circuitry permits selective high sensitivity. High-speed test. Can be automated and recorded. Penetrates up to 60′ (18 m) in steel. Indicates flaw location. Access to only one surface usually needed	Difficult to use with complex shapes. Surface may affect test. Defect orientation affects test. Comparative standards only. Requires couplant
Can detect internal defects such as inclusions, porosity, shrink, hot tears, cracks, cold shuts, and coarse structure in cast metals; lack of fusion and penetration in welds. Detection of missing parts in an assembly	More standards established than for other methods. Internal defects detected. Permanent film record. Automatic thickness gaging	Health precautions necessary. Defect must be at least 2% of total section thickness. Film processing requires time, facilities, and care. Difficult to use on complex shapes. Most costly NDT method
Material composition, structure, hardness changes, cracks, case depth, voids, large inclusions, tubing weld defects, laminations, coating thickness, porosity	Intimate contact between coil and material not required. Versatile. Special coils can be easily made. Operation can be automated. Electric circuit design variations permit selective sensitivity and function. Sensitive to surface and near-surface inhomogeneities	Sensitive to many variables. Sensitivity varies with depth. Reference standards needed. Response often comparative
Any vessel containing a product at a pressure different from ambient or a vessel in which a pressure different from ambient can be created for evaluation	Provides assurance that the vessel will contain contents as designed. Advantages vary for the technique used	Varies from technique to technique
Discontinuities that interrupt heat flow such as flaws, voids, inclusions, lack of bond. Higher or lower than normal resistances in circuitry	High sensitivity. One-sided inspection possible. Applicable to complex shapes and assemblies of dissimilar components. Active or passive specimens	Emissivity variations in materials, coatings, and colors must be considered. In multilayer assemblies, hot spots can be hidden behind cool surface component. Relatively slow

(continued)

Reviewers, cont.: Sidney W. Gill, *Engineering Specialist-Quality*, *General Dynamics*, *Convair Div.;* **MSgt. Gary E. Grankey***, Assistant Field Liaison Manager*, *Nondestructive Inspection Program Office*, *U.S. Air Force;* **Allen T. Green***, Technical Director*, *Acoustic Emission Technology Corp.;* **Nand K. Gupta, Ph.D.***, Senior Laboratory Director*, *Bio Imaging Research*, *Inc.;* **Kenneth P. Hacke***, Technical Specialist*, *Nondestructive Testing*, *McDonnell Aircraft Co.;* **Orv Hammer***, Materials Engineer*, *Ardvoc*, *Inc.;* **Charles L. Harpster***, General Manager*, *Advance Test Equipment Co.;* **Jim Higgins***, Director Industrial Marketing*, *Lumonics*, *Inc.;* **Hiroyuki Imai***, Vice President*, *Research and Development*, *Diaguide*, *Inc.;* **Dr. R. G. Hurley***, Principal Research Engineer*, *Scientific Research Laboratories*, *Ford Motor Co.;* **John Johnston***, Engineering Manager*, *Staveley NDT Technologies*, *Inc.*, *Sonic Systems Div.;* **Paul Kearney***, Product Manager Video/Industrial*, *Welch Allyn*, *Inc.;* **William J. Lang***, Sales Manager*, *Lenox Instrument Co.*, *Inc.;* **Grant C. McClellan***, Manager*, *Experiment Coordination and Control*, *Hot Fuel Examination Facility*, *Argonne National Laboratory;* **James R. Mitchell***, Director of Sales and Field Applications*, *Physical Acoustics Corp.;* **Raymond Momsen***, Radiographic Supervisor*, *Conam Inspection*, *A Unit of Qualcorp;*

TABLE 6-1—*Continued*

Method	Principle	Material
Acoustic emission	Acoustic emission is a transient elastic wave generated by the rapid release of energy from a localized source within a solid material. Rate and amplitude of high-frequency acoustic emissions are noted and correlated to structure or object characteristics	Solid materials as well as liquids and fluids
Neutron radiography	Neutron beam is attenuated by test object; attenuation pattern of test object is recorded at image plane after conversion of transmitted neutron beam and subsequent detection by film or other imaging device	Neutrons are especially sensitive to hydrogenous materials (adhesives, explosives, and moisture), lithium, boron, cadmium, and several rare-earth materials
Holographic	An optical means of capturing and recording the wavefronts resulting from a distorted object and then comparing them with the image of an undistorted object	Bonded and composite structures. Automotive or aircraft tires. Three-dimensional imaging

VISUAL INSPECTION

Visual inspection is probably the most widely used of all the nondestructive tests.[4] It is simple, easy to apply, quickly carried out, and usually low in cost. The basic principle used in visual inspection is to illuminate the test specimen with light and then examine the specimen with the eye. In many instances, optical aids are used to assist in the examination.

The effectiveness of visual inspection is influenced by the quality of lighting. The inspector is responsible for ensuring that adequate lighting is available. The type of examination being performed determines how much illumination is necessary. Adequate illumination levels for different types of examinations have been defined and are referenced in some standards and specifications.

The information obtained from visual inspection can be permanently recorded in hard copy form with photographs, videotapes, or motion picture films. The hard copy permits comparison of the inspected specimen to a known normal or abnormal standard. In addition, several experts can study the record to obtain a more objective interpretation and evaluation. Comparisons can also be made with prior inspections to determine whether there has been crack growth or progressive changes. However, most evaluations are made immediately based solely on what is seen. Any comparisons made are done from memory. With this approach, a valid inspection is based on the inspector's visual acuity and competence.

Some of the optical aids used in visual inspection are mirrors, magnifiers, borescopes, video devices, microscopes, and optical comparators. The discussion in this section is limited to mirrors and magnifiers, borescopes, and video devices. Microscopes and optical comparators are discussed in Chapter 3, "Inspection Equipment and Techniques," of this volume.

MIRRORS AND MAGNIFIERS

Mirrors are invaluable to the inspector because they permit visual inspection inside pipes, threaded and bored holes, and castings, as well as around corners when necessary. The two main types of mirrors commonly used are the dental mirror and the movable end mirror. The dental mirror is usually a small circular mirror set on a 6″ (150 mm) long handle and positioned at a 45° angle. It permits the inspector to view areas not available for direct viewing. The movable end mirror has a pivoting mirror on a control arm. The pivot allows the inspector to view

Reviewers, cont.: William E. Mooz, President, Met-L-Chek; Tom Nelligan, Applications Engineer, Panemetrics, Inc.; Richard L. Newacheck, President, Aerotest Operations, Inc.; George Nygard, Sales Manager, Inspectech; Kanji Ono, Professor of Engineering, Material Science and Engineering Dept., University of California-Los Angeles; James Pellicer, Sensors Engineer, Staveley NDT Technologies, Inc., Nortec Div.; Harry Pikaar, Technical Director, Sherwin Inc.; Robert T. Pitlak, Director Technical Consulting, Pitlak Corp.; Peter Raffelsberger, Director of Research and Development, Fischer Technology, Inc.; John M. Raney, Technical Director, Nondestructive Evaluation Systems, Systems Research Laboratories, Inc.; Terry Reed, Holographic Div., Newport Corp.; Larry Rentz, Section Manager, McDonnell Aircraft Co.; Allen D. Reynolds, Engineer/Director of Training, Mean Free Path Corp.; Richard A. Roberts, Nondestructive Testing Engineer-Quality Laboratories, McDonnell Aircraft Co.; Robert F. Roller, Chief Engineer, Sensotec, Inc.; Fred J. Schlieper, Product Manager, Industrial Radiography Systems, Radiation Div., Varian Associates; J. Thomas Schmidt, Manager, Chemical Laboratory, Magnaflux Corp.; Brad Sharp, Holographic Div., Newport Corporation;

TABLE 6-1—*Continued*

Applications	Advantages	Limitations
Determine or monitor integrity of structures such as weldments or castings	Remote and continuous real-time surveillance of structures is possible. Inaccessible flaws can be determined. Permanent record can be made	Part must be stressed. Nonpropagating flaws cannot be detected. Nonrelevant noise must be filtered out. Transducers must be placed on the object being tested
Detects cracks, voids, and density changes. Presence, absence, or mislocation of internal components of suitable composition	Good penetration of most structural metals. High sensitivity to favorable materials. Permanent record. Complementary to X-ray information	Cost. Not readily portable. Potential health hazard for operators
Detects strain, plastic deformation, cracks, debonded areas, voids, and inclusions. Measures vibration	Contact or special surface preparations are not required. Applicable to complex shapes	Vibration-free environment is required. Difficult to identify type of flaw detected.

the inside of an object, see around corners, or move the mirror to scan an area of interest.

Magnifiers can be used as an aid to almost every type of inspection because they bring out small details and defects. The four main types of magnifiers are single-lens magnifiers, headband magnifiers, measuring magnifiers, and eyepiece loupes.

A single-lens magnifier consists of a single biconvex lens in a holder with a handle. It is usually 1-3″ (25-75 mm) in diameter. Single-lens magnifiers are lightweight, portable, and durable in construction. They are generally used when a specimen magnification of 1.5-10X is required.

Headband magnifiers consist of a pair of rectangular lenses with a holder attached to a headband. Because the magnifier is fixed to a headband, both hands are free to measure and manipulate the part being inspected. The headband magnifier is normally used for fine, detailed inspection of small parts.

The measuring magnifier is a small two-lens handheld magnifier. A measuring scale is etched on the front surface of the lenses. Measuring magnifiers are available in magnifications of 7-20X. In use, the measuring magnifier is placed against the part so the transparent sides can permit light to reach the surface being examined. Several scales are available for measurement in inches, millimeters, or degrees, as well as diameters.

The eyepiece loupe is constructed much like the measuring magnifier, but does not have a scale etched on the lens. The loupe is also attached to a headband. It is commonly used by jewelers because it provides good magnification, from 5-30X, and allows both hands to be free. It is best used for detailed inspection of small items such as threads and electronic components and circuits.

BORESCOPES

The two primary types of industrial borescopes are rigid borescopes and flexible borescopes or fiberscopes. The type used depends on the application. In addition to the rigid and flexible borescope, other types of borescopes are made for specialized applications. Another borescope option that has been recently developed is the video device, described subsequently. Like industrial borescopes, it can be either rigid or flexible in design.

Most borescopes are designed to operate on 110 V, but they can be designed for other voltages. Light sources for borescopes using fiber-optics are often capable of operating from a variety of voltages, cycles, and even a-c or d-c input power. They can also be designed to operate on batteries for full portability. Generally, the illumination of borescopes is by visible light, but black light or a combination of both visible and black light illumination is available. Borescopes can also be supplied with fittings for use with still, motion, or television cameras, permitting documentation of the inspected part. A special adapter allows two operators to view the same part simultaneously.

Reviewers, cont.: **Donald E. Sharpe**, *Manager, Technical Services, Automation/Sperry, A Unit of Qualcorp;* **Amos Sherwin**, *Manager, Sherwin Inc.;* **Richard J. Shuford**, *Supervisory Materials Research Engineer, Composites Development Div., Army Materials Technology Laboratory;* **Kermit Skeie**, *Consultant, Ardrox, Inc.;* **Philip H. Smith**, *President, AGEMA Infrared Systems;* **Michael David Stebel**, *Technical Assistant to the President, Manager, Technical Communications, UPA Technology, Inc.;* **Robert A. Sweig**, *Engineering Specialist in Quality, General Dynamics, Convair Div.;* **Alan Thomas**, *Sales Manager, Ardrox, Inc.;* **Phil M. Townsend**, *Sales Manager, Walker Scientific, Inc.;* **Keith J. Tupper**, *Product Sales Manager, Inficon Leybold-Heraeus, Inc.;* **Bruce Tyler**, *President, Triad Manufacturing Corp.;* **John J. Veno**, *Specialist, Nondestructive Test, Aircraft Engine Business Group, General Electric Co.;* **Angelo A. Vitale**, *Engineering Supervisor of NDT Systems, K. J. Law Engineers, Inc.;* **Fred Wiesinger**, *Applications Engineering Manager, Uson Corporation;* **Michael J. Wrysch**, *Senior Reliability Engineer, Detroit Diesel Allison, General Motors Corp.;* **William C. Worthington**, *Product Manager, Inficon Leybold-Heraeus, Inc.*

VISUAL INSPECTION

Applications

Borescopes are used in a variety of industries to ensure product quality without having to destroy the part in periodic testing. They are also widely used in equipment maintenance programs, eliminating the need for costly teardowns when checking for in-service defects.

A manufacturer of hydraulic cylinders uses a borescope to inspect the interior of the bores for pitting, scoring, tool marks, or other flaws that could cause failure in service. The borescope can also ensure that burrs have been successfully removed from blind or intersecting holes. Another manufacturer uses borescopes to check for manufacturing defects in assembled diesel engines. The borescope is inserted in the combustion chamber through the injector nozzle, permitting inspection of valves, cylinder sleeves, and piston crowns for defects that could cause premature engine failure. A manufacturer of cast intake manifolds uses borescopes to check the internal water and air passages for core sand, flash, and blockage. In the aircraft and aerospace industry, borescopes are used to verify bond integrity of difficult-to-reach components joined together with adhesives. They are also used in assembly areas to ensure the proper placement and fit of seals, gaskets, and subassemblies.

Selection Considerations

Although there are only two main types of borescopes, there are a variety of ways that the borescope can be manufactured. The two primary considerations of borescope selection are the workpiece inspected and the environment in which the borescope will be used.

Workpiece. The workpiece or the object to be inspected determines the specifications for the borescope and the illumination required. Some of the factors to be considered are objective distance, size of defect, entry port size, size of object, reflectivity, depth of object, and location of area to be examined.

The distance that the area being inspected is from the objective lens helps determine the illumination source required, the objective focal distance for maximum sharpness, the resolving power, and the magnification of the borescope. Defect size influences the magnification and resolution requirements of the borescope; small defects such as hairline cracks require high magnification. The maximum borescope diameter is determined by the size of the entry port.

When the size of the object being inspected is combined with the objective distance, the lens angle or field of view required to inspect the entire surface can be determined. The viewing angle is also important when the surface is not aligned with the borescope end. Rigid borescopes are designed with various fixed viewing angles.

Light-absorbing or dark surfaces such as those coated with carbon black deposits require higher levels of illumination than light surfaces. In addition, it is important to take into consideration the amount of heat generated by the light source. Rubber or plastic materials could be deformed from the heat of the light. Fiber-optic guided illumination may be used for applications that cannot tolerate heat because a filter removes the heat frequencies (infrared) of light.

If portions of the object are at different planes, then the borescope must have sufficient focus adjustment or depth of field to visualize the different planes sharply. The location of the area being inspected in relation to the entry port determines the type or orientation of the viewing head as well as the length of the borescope required.

Environment. Borescopes can be manufactured to withstand a variety of environments. Although most borescopes are capable of operating in temperatures from -30 to 150° F (-34 to 66° C), a specially designed borescope can be used at temperatures to 3500° F (1925° C). Borescopes can also be made for use in a liquid medium.

Special borescopes are required for use in pressures above ambient as well as atmospheres exposed to radiation. Radiation can cause the multicomponent lenses and image bundles to become brown. When borescopes are used in atmospheres exposed to radiation, quartz fiberscopes are generally used. Borescopes used in a gaseous environment should be made explosionproof to minimize damage caused by an accidental explosion.

Rigid Borescopes

The rigid borescope is generally selected for applications in which a straight line path exists between the viewer and the object to be inspected. It is similar in design to a telescope, but while a telescope narrows the field of view for observation at a distance, the borescope spreads the view for closeup work.

The main components of a rigid borescope are a tubular shell, eyepiece, optical lenses, viewing head, and a light source (Fig. 6-1). The shell can be made in one piece or in modular sections, depending on the length of the borescope. Typical borescopes are available in lengths from 4″ to 150′ (100 mm-45 m) and in diameters from 0.067 to 2.75″ (1.7 to 70 mm). The shell is generally made from aluminum or stainless steel, depending on the environment in which it will be used.

The image is brought to the eyepiece by an optical train consisting of an objective lens or prism, relay lenses, and an eyepiece lens. The relay lenses preserve the image resolution

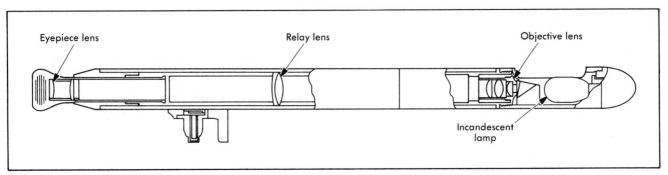

Fig. 6-1 Typical components in a rigid borescope with incandescent illumination. (*Lenox Instrument Co.*)

throughout the entire length of the borescope. Because the object image is formed between the lenses, only one adjustment is required for both diopter correction and object focusing on those scopes designed with focus capability. Many scopes are of the fixed focus design. Object magnification is usually from 3 to 4X, but powers up to 50X are available.

The viewing head determines the direction of view and the field of view. Common viewing head designs are right-angle, circumference, bottoming, forward oblique, and retrospective (Fig. 6-2).

Right-angle heads bend the cone of view at right angles to the borescope's axis, providing a lateral view. This type of head is generally used for applications requiring critical inspection or when certain areas must be inspected.

Circumference or panoramic heads are designed for inspection of tubing or other cylindrical structures. A centrally located mirror permits right-angle viewing of an area just scanned by the panoramic view.

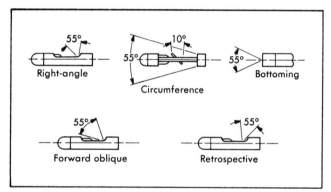

Fig. 6-2 Viewing head designs for both rigid and flexible borescopes. (*Lenox Instrument Co.*)

The bottoming head permits the inspection of the area directly ahead of the viewing head. It is commonly used when examining facing walls or the bottom of blind holes and cavities.

Forward oblique heads bend the viewing direction at an angle to the borescope axis, permitting the inspection of corners at the end of a bored hole. The retrospective viewing head bends the cone of view at a retrospective angle to the borescope axis, providing a view of the area just passed by the advancing borescope. It is especially suited for inspecting the inside neck of cylinders and bottles.

Illumination of the area to be inspected is achieved with either an incandescent lamp or fiber-optics. Lamps give a broader general illumination of the area to be inspected, while fiber-optics give a bright beam of light. Because scopes with incandescent lamps at the top generate heat, the amount of heat given off must be taken into consideration for certain applications. Scopes with fiber-optic illumination generally provide cool light except when special high-intensity mercury arc or xenon light sources are used without proper infrared infiltration.

Flexible Borescopes

Flexible borescopes or fiberscopes are primarily used in applications that do not have a straight passageway to the point of observation. A typical fiberscope consists of an image guide fiber bundle, an objective lens, protective sheath, eyepiece lens, focus and diopter rings, and remote controls for the top articulation (Fig. 6-3). These components are then connected to any one of a variety of light sources.

The optical bundles carry up to 40,000 glass fibers. Each individual fiber consists of a central core of high-quality optical glass coated with a thin layer or cladding of another glass having a different reflective index. The cladding prevents the light entering the end of the fiber from escaping or passing through the sides to an adjacent fiber in the bundle. The number

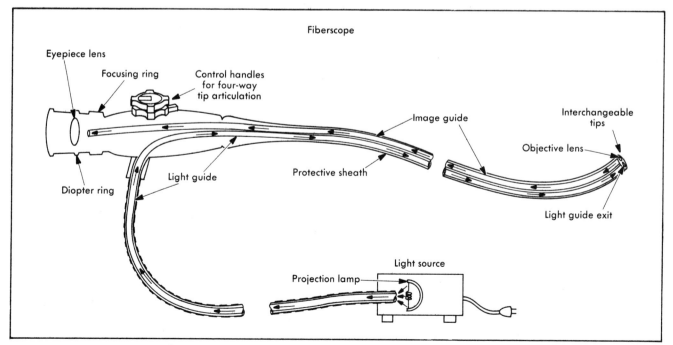

Fig. 6-3 Typical components in a flexible borescope. (*Olympus Corp.*)

VISUAL INSPECTION

of fibers used is determined by the diameter of the image guide. Fiberscopes are available in diameters from 0.071 to 0.512″ (1.8 to 13 mm) and in lengths up to 30′ (9 m). Special quartz fiberscopes come in lengths up to 300′ (100 m).

The optical bundle used to carry the light from the light source to illuminate the object is called the light guide bundle. Fibers used in the light guide bundle are generally 30 μm (0.001″) in diameter. The second optical bundle, called the image guide, is used to carry the image formed by the objective lens back to the eyepiece. Fibers in the image guide must be precisely aligned so that they are in an identical relative position to each other at their terminations for proper image resolution. Image guide fibers are from 0.0002 to 0.0007″ (6.5 to 17 μm) in diameter; the actual diameter is another factor in obtaining correct image resolution.

The fiber-optic bundles are protected by a sealed housing of flexible stainless steel conduit, which allows the fibers to bend around corners or sharp elbows. Fiberscopes usually have a controllable bending section near the tip to direct the scope during insertion and to scan an area once it is in position. Different viewing heads as discussed under rigid borescopes are also available on fiberscopes.

The objective lens at the scope tip can be moved in and out by remote control to focus the fiberscope for different viewing distances. Some fiberscope manufacturers also have a separate diopter adjustment to compensate for differences in eyesight. The diopter adjustment permits the fiberscope to be used without corrective lenses.

Specialized Borescopes

Other types of borescopes with custom configurations are also available for specialized applications. Some of the types and their use are as follows:

- Rigid chamberscopes are specifically designed for internal inspection of engines and tanks. They have higher illumination and greater magnification than rigid borescopes.
- 360° radial view scopes for inspecting piping with internal diameters from 0.118 to 48″ (3 to 1220 mm).

- Environmentally protected housings that allow immersion, exposure to radiation, and operation under high temperatures.
- Hybrid optical/mechanical devices for measuring and for surface evaluation procedures.
- Rigid scopes with flexible tips for remote scanning.
- Periscopes for easy, safe checking of remote viewing ports and hazardous processes.
- Borescope eyes for industrial robots.
- Closed-circuit TV systems.
- Measuring fiberscopes to determine defect size.

VIDEO DEVICES

Video devices used for visual inspection incorporate a probe, video processor, and a color display monitor. The probe can be flexible or rigid and is available in sizes from 3/8 to 9/16″ (9.5 to 14 mm) diam and in lengths from 4.9 to 100′ (1.5 to 30 m). An electronic sensor, located in the tip of the probe, transfers the object image electronically to the processor. The probe also houses a fiber-optic bundle for illuminating the area being inspected.

In operation, the probe is inserted through small-diameter tubing, ports, and passages to the location requiring inspection. The electronic sensor gathers the reflected light and converts it to analog information. The processor digitizes, assembles, and relays this information to the monitor for display. When necessary, the display can be frozen for detailed examination. A record of the electronic image can also be made for review or permanent documentation. The high-quality electronic image allows for treatment of the image with modern electronic image enhancement techniques, defect measurement through electronic means, transmission of the image through a telephone modem, and the interface to electronic-based automatic inspection equipment.

Like borescopes, video devices can be used for quality control, preventive maintenance, and problem diagnosis. Typical applications include checking welds, coatings, or seals; inspecting voids, blockages, or deterioration; locating loose or vibrating parts; and monitoring the flow of solids and liquids.

LIQUID PENETRANT INSPECTION

The liquid penetrant inspection process is a simple method of locating defects on the surface of metals or other nonporous materials. It is based on the oil and whiting process used by the railroad industry until the mid-1930s. In practice, a dyed liquid penetrant is applied to the surface of the prepared workpiece (Fig. 6-4). After a period of time, the excess penetrant is removed and an absorbent developer is applied. The developer causes the penetrant to be drawn out of any cracks or discontinuities, indicating the locations of defects.

Liquid penetrant inspection can be used to inspect all types of surface cracks, porosity, laminations, and bond joints. In addition, it can be used to inspect for leaks in tubing, pipes, tanks, and welds. Liquid penetrant inspection is effective on any relatively hard, nonporous material.[5] Its widest usefulness is in finding flaws in nonmagnetic metals such as aluminum, magnesium, stainless steels, copper, brass, and various other metals

and alloys, including titanium, beryllium, and zirconium. It is also applicable on magnetic metals, vitrified ceramics, powdered metals, glass, and some plastics.

ADVANTAGES AND LIMITATIONS

The versatility of the liquid penetrant process is responsible for its many advantages. For example, portable penetrant kits consisting of aerosol spray cans of penetrant materials can be used in the field to detect small flaws. In field applications, electricity or special equipment may not be required, and the inspection is reliable, inexpensive, and rapid. Liquid penetrant inspection can also be used in a production line setting. High-sensitivity fluorescent penetrants are capable of identifying extremely small flaws.

Because of the way the process works, liquid penetrant inspection only finds flaws that are open to the surface of the

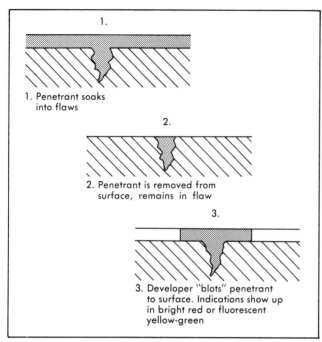

Fig. 6-4 Picture diagram of liquid penetrant inspection: (a) penetrant soaks into flaws, (b) penetrant is removed from surface but remains in flaws, and (c) developer blots penetrant to surface. Indications show up in bright red or fluorescent yellow-green.

part being tested. Flaws beneath the surface require a different detection method. The part must also be clean and dry because the penetrant cannot enter surface defects that are already filled with dirt, oil, grease, paint, water, or other contamination.

Proper training is required to correctly prepare and process the workpiece for inspection. The surface condition of the part also affects whether or not it can be inspected with liquid penetrants. For example, rough or porous surfaces produce heavy background indications as the penetrant locates the small cavities responsible for the roughness or porosity. When this occurs, it is difficult to locate small defects. Mechanical surface treatments such as wire brushing, shot peening, and sanding also create problems for liquid penetrant inspection techniques. These surface treatments tend to smear the metal surface and cover the cracks, thus preventing the penetrant from entering the cracks.

PENETRANTS

A penetrant is a liquid material that, when applied to the surface being inspected, has the ability to wet the entire surface and get into fine openings. In addition to these characteristics, a penetrant should have stability when exposed to heat and cold, it should have a distinctive color, it should not evaporate, and it should be nontoxic. Most penetrant formulations contain penetrating oils, a dye, and other ingredients to improve performance. For most applications, penetrants are formulated to be used around 70° F (21° C), but special penetrants are formulated for use at temperatures as low as -20° F (-29° C) or as high as 350° F (175° C).

Types of Penetrants

Penetrants can be classified according to the type of dye used as a tracer, the method required for removing excess penetrant,

and the sensitivity level. Two types of dyes are commonly used, the yellow-green fluorescent dye and the visible, deep-red or reddish-purple dyes. Penetrants with fluorescent dyes are only visible under black light, while the visible dyes are easily seen under white light.

With respect to the method required for removing penetrant, penetrants can be classified as water-washable, postemulsifiable, or solvent-removable. Water-washable penetrants have a high emulsifier content, permitting the excess penetrant on the part surface to be removed in a water wash. Postemulsifiable penetrants do not contain an emulsifier; instead, an emulsifier is applied to the surface of the part in a separate operation. The emulsified penetrant can then be removed in a water wash. The exact penetrant removal technique employed depends on whether the penetrant is removed by a lipophilic or hydrophilic emulsifier. Solvents are used to remove solvent-removable penetrants from the part surface by wiping the surface of the part that has been penetrated.

The four sensitivity levels of liquid penetrants are low, medium, high, and ultrahigh. Sensitivity depends on such factors as the visibility of the penetrant, capillary action, and resistance to overwash. In general, water-washable penetrants have low to medium sensitivity whereas postemulsified penetrants have medium sensitivity when used with a lipophilic emulsifier and high to ultrahigh sensitivity when used with a hydrophilic remover.

Selection of Penetrants

Penetrants are usually selected for a given application based on the size, shape, and weight of the parts; the number of parts to be inspected; the cost; and the degree of sensitivity required. On a practical basis, penetrants are divided into the following six systems or variations of systems:[6]

1. Postemulsifiable fluorescent penetrants.
2. Solvent-removable fluorescent penetrants.
3. Water-washable fluorescent penetrants.
4. Postemulsifiable visible-dye penetrants.
5. Solvent-removable visible-dye penetrants.
6. Water-washable visible-dye penetrants.

Postemulsifiable fluorescent penetrants are the most sensitive of all penetrants and are capable of locating wide, shallow flaws as well as tight cracks. They are commonly used for high-production work because only a short penetration time is required.

Solvent-removable fluorescent penetrants are used for spot inspection or when water cannot be conveniently used. They can be more sensitive than water-washable penetrants when properly used, but the caution and additional time required for solvent application often precludes their use for high-production inspection.

The use of water-washable fluorescent penetrants requires less time than the other fluorescent penetrants. These penetrants can be used for both small and large parts and are good on rough surfaces and in hard-to-reach areas such as threads and keyways. Water-washable fluorescent penetrants often cannot reliably reveal open, shallow flaws, and in some instances, they cannot locate tight cracks. Care must be exercised when using these penetrants to keep from removing the penetrant from the flaws.

Postemulsifiable visible-dye penetrants should be used whenever a higher sensitivity than water-washable visible-dye pene-

LIQUID PENETRANT INSPECTION

trants is required. Solvent-removable visible-dye penetrants are portable and can be used both in the shop and in the field.

Water-washable visible-dye penetrants are fast acting and simple to use. However, they are the least sensitive of all penetrants because the penetrant is often removed from wide, shallow flaws. This type of penetrant is not generally used for locating tight cracks.

DEVELOPERS

Developers are materials designed to draw the penetrant from flaws or cracks in the surface of the part being inspected. The drawing or blotting action of the developer spreads the penetrant available at the defect, thus increasing the amount of light emitted or increasing the amount of contrast.

Types of Developers

The two primary types of developers used are dry and wet. Wet-type developers are further classified as water-suspendible, water-soluble, and nonaqueous or solvent-suspendible. Dry developers consist of fine powder that is generally white in color. They are almost exclusively used with fluorescent penetrants.

Water-suspendible developers are furnished as dry powders, which are mixed with water by the user. This type of developer was the most widely used wet developer. Water-suspendible developers are normally used in conjunction with fluorescent penetrants and automated inspection of small to medium-sized lots. Because these devclopers have a tendency to mask off small indications, they are generally not used for inspection on critical parts.

Water-soluble developers use materials that are soluble in water. This type of developer eliminates the problems inherent in water-suspendible developers and is becoming the most widely used type of wet developer. As a general rule, water-soluble developers are more conducive to high-sensitivity inspection.

Nonaqueous developers are almost universally used with visible-dye penetrants. Because of their sensitivity, they are also used for spot inspections with fluorescent penetrants. These developers are generally premixed by the manufacturer to the proper concentration. To prevent the solvent from evaporating, nonaqueous developers must be kept in containers that are tightly closed. They are also applied from small aerosol spray cans. Caution is required when using solvents, and they are not recommended for high-production use.

Developer Selection

Because developers play such an important role in liquid penetrant inspection, it is important that the right one be used for a given job.[7] Some of the guidelines for developer selection are as follows:

- Use wet developers in preference to dry developers on smooth surfaces in production runs.
- Use dry developers in preference to wet developers on rough surfaces for large parts and/or production runs.
- Water-suspendible developers cannot be used reliably where sharp fillets or blind cavities may mask indications of flaws because of developer accumulation.
- Solvent developers are effective for revealing fine, deep cracks and are satisfactory for finding wide, shallow flaws when applied as a spray.

- Cleaning and reinspecting a rough surface is difficult if a wet suspension-type developer was used for a prior inspection.

PROCESS DESCRIPTION

The procedure followed when performing a liquid penetrant test is generally the same even though several different types of penetrants and developers are used. The basic steps include substrate preparation, penetrant application, penetrant removal, developer application, and inspection and interpretation. Figure 6-5 is a process flowchart comparison of the commonly used penetrants.

Substrate Preparation

The surface of the part being inspected must be clean and dry to achieve maximum penetrant penetration. Dirt, lint, wax, paint, grease, scale, moisture, or any other material can fill and clog the surface openings, preventing the penetrant from entering the suspected defects. Dirt or other material on the surface can also hold the penetrant, resulting in false defect indications.

In general, the type of soil on the surface dictates the type of cleaning method to use. One of the best methods of part cleaning is vapor degreasing. Because the parts are hot when they come from the degreasing tank, all solvent and water is driven off by the heat. Commercial penetrant suppliers also provide a suitable cleaning solvent.

Scale is best removed by vapor blasting because it will not close up small surface openings. Shot blasting, sandblasting, wire brushing, or metal scraping are not recommended for scale removal because these methods tend to cover up the defects by peening or wiping over the surface. Additional information on cleaning methods can be found in Volume III, *Materials, Finishing and Coating*, of this Handbook series.

Penetrant Application

When the penetrant is allowed to remain on the surface of the part, penetrant is drawn into small surface openings by capillary action. The rate of penetration can sometimes be increased by warming the parts, vibrating the parts, or by applying the penetrant to the part under a vacuum.

The penetrant is allowed to remain on the surface of the part for a period of time depending on the material of the part, the type and size of defect, and the type of penetrant used. Penetration times vary from a fraction of a minute to many minutes and even hours. Most penetrant manufacturers give a suggested penetration time as well as application temperature for the various types that they produce.

Penetrants can be applied to the surface of the part being inspected by dipping, spraying, or brushing. The method selected is determined by the size, shape, and number of parts to be inspected.

When a large quantity of parts are inspected, the penetrant should be applied by dipping. Using a hoist, large parts are dipped in a tank containing the penetrant; small parts should be arranged in racks or baskets before dipping to prevent the formation of air bubbles or pockets, which prevent the penetrant from reaching the entire surface area. If air bubbles or pockets do form, the parts should be rotated to ensure complete wetting. The parts should then be raised from the tank and allowed to drain.

Penetrants are usually applied by spraying when only a few parts are being inspected or when certain areas of a part are to

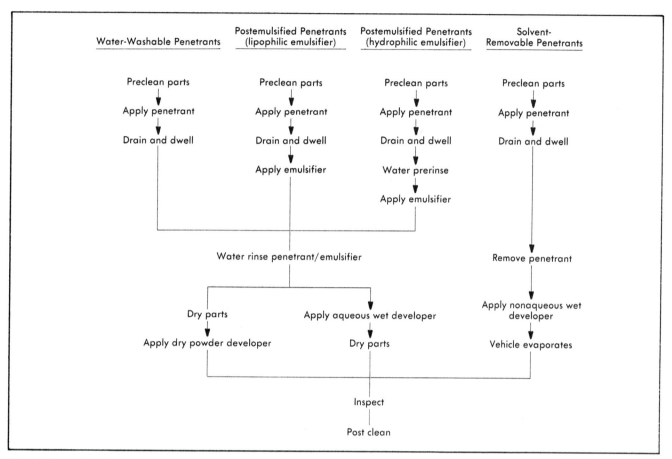

Fig. 6-5 Process flowchart of commonly used penetrants.

be inspected. Spraying may be performed with conventional spray equipment, electrostatic spray equipment, and with small aerosol cans containing the penetrant.

Penetrant Removal

The penetrant removal step removes the excess penetrant from the unflawed surface, but not from the surface cracks or flaws. Proper removal of the penetrant from the part surface is essential to satisfactory inspection.

As was previously mentioned, three basic types of penetrants are commonly used: (1) water-washable, (2) postemulsifiable, and (3) solvent-removable. The type of penetrant used generally determines the techniques used for penetrant removal.

Water-washable. Although water-washable penetrants are formulated to be removed by water, it is important to use the proper washing methods. The most common method of washing parts is water spraying.[8] Spraying can be done by hand or with fixed spray nozzles in an automatic production line.

The water should be broken up into a spray of coarse droplets rather than a solid stream, and the pressure should be maintained at 30-40 psi (205-275 kPa); higher water pressures may remove the penetrant from the surface flaws or cracks. Water temperature should be maintained at 55-95°F (13-35°C). When fluorescent-type penetrants are used, the washing should be done under a black light to avoid overcleaning but at the same time to ensure complete cleaning.

Other washing methods that are used include dipping and hand washing. In dipping, the part(s) is immersed in the bath of water and then moved about while submerged. When dipping is used, the penetrant must emulsify on contact with water and disperse readily into the water bath. Hand washing can be used to remove the penetrant from limited areas. It is usually performed using a wet cloth or sponge.

Postemulsifiable. The procedures used for removing postemulsifiable penetrants are based on whether the emulsifier is either lipophilic or hydrophilic. In general, the process involves applying the emulsifier to the part surface and then removing the emulsified layer. When fluorescent-type penetrants are being removed, it is necessary to do the cleaning under a black light to ensure complete cleaning.

Lipophilic emulsifiers. After the specified penetrant dwell time has elapsed, an emulsifier is applied to the surface of the part. The preferred method of applying the emulsifier is dipping because the whole surface of the part becomes covered with emulsifier at practically the same time, permitting a more accurate control of emulsification time.[9] When the part surface has been coated, the part should be removed from the tank and allowed to drain.

The emulsifier dwell time is crucial because too little time results in an excessive fluorescent background that can obscure a flaw; too much time can remove penetrant entrapped in a flaw, greatly reducing sensitivity. Dwell-time tables have not been established because of the number of factors influencing

LIQUID PENETRANT INSPECTION

dwell time. Optimum times must be established by trial for each of the different types of parts being inspected.

Spraying or flowing the emulsifier on simple contoured parts is also acceptable, providing no appreciable time is required to coat the entire part surface. The emulsifier should not be applied by brushing or hand wiping because the action of the applicator mixes the emulsifier into the penetrant prematurely and irregularly, making it impossible to accurately control the emulsification time.

The emulsified layer is generally removed by water spraying. As is the case with water-washable penetrants, the water should be broken up into a spray of coarse droplets, and the pressure should be between 30 and 45 psi (205 and 310 kPa). The temperature of the water should also be maintained at 55-95° F (13-35° C).

Hydrophilic emulsifiers. After the specified dwell time, the part is generally subjected to a plain water prerinse, which removes up to 90% of the surface penetrant. The water spray should consist of coarse water droplets at a pressure of 10-30 psi (70-205 kPa) and a temperature of 60-90° F (28-32° C). A typical spraying cycle is from 30 to 120 seconds.

The remaining surface penetrant can be removed by applying a mixture of emulsifier and water to the surface of the part. The emulsifier is generally applied by air-agitated immersion or spraying. Each application method offers certain advantages and limitations.

In dipping, the part is immersed in an emulsifier bath of varying concentrations; concentrations vary from 5 to 35% emulsifier with the remaining percentage being water. Low-concentration baths require longer contact time than high-concentration baths. The part should be moved around while immersed to provide a continual supply of fresh solution to the part surface. Agitation can also be achieved with an air manifold. The primary advantage of dipping is its effectiveness on hollow or complex part geometries. A limitation of this method is the emulsifier's poor tolerance to penetrant contamination.

In spraying, the emulsifier concentration varies from 0.1 to 0.5%. The recommended water spray pressure range is from 10 to 35 psi (70 to 240 kPa). Some of the advantages of this method are that it does not require a separate tank, it works well on simple contoured parts, and it can be easily automated.

Following the penetrant removal, the part is subjected to a plain water spray rinse. The purpose of this rinse is to remove any residues that could contaminate the developer or hinder the development process. The recommended cycle is a plain water spray of 30-90 seconds duration. The water pressure is approximately 10-30 psi (70-200 kPa), and water temperature is 60-100° F (28-38° C).

Solvent-removable. Another way that the excess penetrant can be removed from the part surface is by wiping the surface with a solvent-wetted cloth. This method produces a clean surface, but can easily remove the penetrant from the flaws or defects if solvent application is too liberal. Penetrant removal by solvent wiping is generally limited to field inspections.

Drying

Although drying was not listed separately as one of the basic steps of the liquid penetrant process, it is an essential step that can affect the inspection results. For the penetrant to come back out of surface openings and give clear indications with the help of developers, the surface around the discontinuity must be clean and dry. Drying also aids the formation of indications in many instances.

The parts are dried right after the water washing operation if a dry developer is being used. When an aqueous developer is used, the developer is applied to the part surface after the water washing, and then the part is dried.

Several methods are used for drying the parts. The most popular method is the recirculating hot air drying method. In this method, the parts are allowed to soak in an enclosed space that recirculates heated air. For parts with sections 1/4″ (6 mm) thick or greater, the air temperature is maintained at approximately 225° F (105° C). For parts with sections thinner than 1/4″ thick, the air temperature is from 150 to 160° F (65 to 70° C). The objective in drying is to dry the surface in the shortest time possible without raising the temperature of the part above 150° F. Warming the part slightly helps bring the penetrant out of the cracks or flaws, resulting in stronger and sharper indications.

Other drying methods that can be used are wiping the part surface with a cloth or paper towels, blowing the water off with an air blast, and drying at room temperature. Wiping the surface with a cloth or paper towel is simple and quite satisfactory when a local area of a large part is being examined. However, the surface of the part should be allowed to air dry before applying the dry developer powder. This method cannot be used for wet developers.

Blowing the water off with a low pressure blast of air is sometimes used. If the pressure is too high, the blast of air could remove the penetrant out of the cracks. The air should also be filtered to prevent the surface from being contaminated. Room temperature drying is an extremely slow process, although it is the only method for certain applications. Because of the time that elapses for drying, the penetrant from large cracks can bleed out causing the indication to spread and lose definition.

Developer Application

Two basic types of developers are generally used in liquid penetrant inspection, a dry developer and a wet developer. Wet developers are further classified as water-suspendible, water-soluble, and nonaqueous. Although the application methods vary for the different types of developers, only a light coating is required.

Dry developers. The parts must be clean and dry before applying the dry developer powder. Any damp areas will catch and hold excessive amounts of powder.

The powder is applied to the surface by dipping, spraying, or dusting techniques. Any excess powder can be removed by shaking or tapping the parts. A current of air can also be used to blow off excess powder as long as the pressure is low.

Because the powder draws the penetrant out of the cracks and flaws, a development time is required so that the indications achieve their maximum intensity. The development time varies from a few minutes to more than an hour and depends on the type of material and defect being inspected. As a general guide, the development time should be based on the development of indications being observed. Heavy bleed-out areas of penetrant should receive additional developer to prevent the surface spread of the penetrant.

Aqueous developers. Aqueous developers (water-suspendible and water-soluble) are applied to the parts being inspected right after water washing and before drying. The simplest method of developer application is dipping the parts in a bath containing the developer. Small parts are usually placed in a basket and dipped. The parts should be removed from the developer bath as soon as their surfaces are evenly coated because the wetting agents in the bath tend to remove some penetrant from flaws or cracks. The excess developer should be allowed to drain off the parts before putting them in the dryer. A recirculating hot air dryer is recommended for drying the parts. In general, the parts should be removed from the dryer as soon as the developer has dried to a smooth white film. When the parts are cool enough to handle, inspection can proceed.

Other methods used for applying aqueous developers are flow coating and spraying. For field applications, the developer can be applied from an aerosol can.

To obtain a uniform coating on the part surface, the developer concentration must be maintained. It is also important to keep the bath agitated to prevent particles of suspension-type developers from settling. Most aqueous developer baths are formulated to operate at 70-90°F (21-32°C).

Nonaqueous developers. Nonaqueous developers are usually applied by spraying from a pressurized spray can or a paint spray gun. When used in bulk form, it is to keep the powder thoroughly mixed in the solvent. The surface of the part should be dry and at ambient temperature when the developer is applied.

Inspection and Interpretation

Before inspecting the parts it is important that the proper development time has elapsed to obtain the maximum indication intensity. The proper development time for a given part with a certain type of defect can only be determined by experiment. However, the manufacturer of the penetrant and developer can provide the user with approximate times.

Parts should not be handled more than necessary before inspection to prevent the defect indications from smearing. Inspection is carried out by examining the part for color contrast between the penetrant drawn out and the background surface.[10] Parts being inspected with visible-dye penetrants are examined under white light. Parts being inspected with fluorescent-dye penetrants are examined in a dark area under black or ultraviolet light. It is advisable to wait for at least 30 seconds before inspecting under black light after being in a white light environment. This waiting period or eye adaptation time allows the inspector's eyes to become acclimated to the darkness. The adaptation period varies for each inspector. The maximum waiting period should be 5 minutes.

The interpretation of the characteristic patterns indicating the types of defects is important.[11] A crack or cold shut is indicated by a line of penetrant. Dots of penetrant indicate pits or porosity in the material. A series of dots may indicate a tight crack, cold shut, or partially welded lap. Figure 6-6 shows some typical defect indications.

A rough estimate of the opening size may be estimated by the width of the indication or spreading of the penetrant on the developer. This estimate applies when the same parts are routinely inspected. The width of the indication changes constantly and is always a magnitude larger than the actual void. Interpretation can only be learned by experience and consequently should only be done by experienced inspectors.

On occasion, it is necessary to reinspect the parts on which indications are found. To do so, the parts should first be thoroughly cleaned. The developer can be removed by washing, scrubbing, or wiping. Vapor degreasing or solvent soaking is then used to remove the penetrant. The same type of penetrant must then be applied to the surface of the part. For example, if fluorescent-dye penetrants were used initially, they should be used again rather than visible-dye penetrants. In no case may

fluorescent-dye penetrants destroy the fluorescence of fluorescent-dye penetrants.

After inspection, subsequent processes may require that the parts be clean, necessitating removal of all traces of developer and penetrant.[12] All the penetrant should have been removed except that retained in defects before applying the developer. The best way to remove the developer is a detergent wash in an automatic washer. A power wash gun can also be used if part quantities are limited.

EQUIPMENT

The type of equipment selected for liquid penetrant inspection determines whether or not the inspection method will be an economical and productive operation or a costly and wasteful means of discarding parts that may not be defective.[13] In general, liquid penetrant inspection equipment can be classified in one of the three following categories:

1. Simple, hand-operated, portable equipment that can be moved about easily as needed.
2. Stationary equipment that is somewhat universal in the variety of parts it can accommodate.
3. Specialized high-volume units built to accommodate one or a very few specific parts. The equipment is generally designed to function as an integral part of a production line.

The components that are included in a complete system depend on the number of processing steps required for the penetrant. Typical components in a given system would include:[14]

- Precleaning station; this is usually separated from the penetrant equipment line.
- Penetrant application station, including drain rack.
- Emulsifier station, used only for postemulsifiable penetrants.

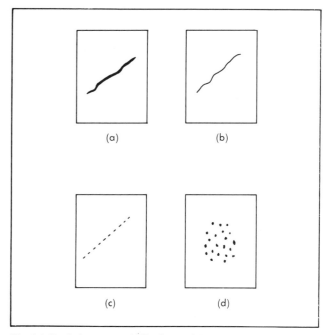

Fig. 6-6 Typical penetrant indications: (a) large crack or opening, (b) tight crack or cold shut, (c) partially welded lap, and (d) pits or porosity.

LIQUID PENETRANT INSPECTION

- Solvent-remover station, used only with visible-dye penetrants.
- Washing station, used with water-washable and post-emulsifiable penetrants.
- Wet-developer station.
- Dryer.
- Dry-developer station.
- Inspection station.
- Postcleaning station.

Portable Equipment

In its simplest application, liquid penetrant inspection can be performed with a minimum of equipment. Generally the cleaner, penetrant, solvent/emulsifier, and developer are supplied in small aerosol cans. These materials can be taken directly to the machine or part to be tested. The actual inspection of visible-dye penetrants can be carried out under normal shop illumination. When fluorescent penetrants are used, a portable black light and a screen or hood are also required.

General-Purpose Equipment

General-purpose equipment includes small units capable of handling only a few parts per hour as well as large combinations of units through which production quantities of parts can be processed. The equipment, regardless of size or capacity, is generally characterized by the following attributes:

- All functions of the inspection technique are provided in a single piece of equipment or a combination of small units.
- Processing is primarily carried out manually or with the aid of simple handling devices such as roller conveyors and hoists.
- The number of shapes or type of parts that can be inspected is almost unlimited, within the dimensional limitations of a particular unit.

Multiple-Component Stationary Units

When higher production rates than possible with general-purpose equipment are required, multiple-component equipment should be used. In this type of installation, individual units are purchased for a single phase of the process, and then all the units are combined together. This type of approach provides flexibility and permits an installation to be tailored to meet specific needs or plant layouts.

Specialized High-Volume Units

In manufacturing operations where parts are made in high volume on conveyorized production lines, inspection of parts at production line speed may be desirable. In such cases, it is generally necessary to design special equipment so that its operation will be coordinated with the overall production system. The equipment is generally designed with moving conveyors provided with holding fixtures. With most systems, an operator is only required for loading and unloading the parts onto the carriers. For some applications, robots can be used for loading and unloading. The parts then proceed unattended through the entire operation and are finally presented for examination by an inspector in a suitable booth.

Special production-type equipment is generally designed to handle only one or a few similar types of parts. If properly designed and built, it is capable of yielding the least expensive and most uniform penetrant inspection available. The speed of inspection is determined by the requirements of the production line. Inspection booth size is determined by the number of inspectors needed.

SAFETY AND SPECIFICATIONS

Penetrant materials must pass rigorous scrutiny to be approved by the various governing bodies. Although this ensures that most penetrant materials are formulated from chemicals that can be safely handled, there are a number of safety precautions that should be observed.

Protective clothing such as rubber aprons and gloves should be worn to keep the penetrant liquids from contacting the skin. The emulsifiers and removers are strong detergents and can dry the skin because they remove the natural oils. Repeated contact with penetrant materials should be avoided. Adequate ventilation should also be provided when using dry powder and non-aqueous developers.

It is advisable that the worker be acquainted with the safety recommendations supplied with each penetrant material. If excessive contact with the liquid penetrant occurs, the worker should be treated in accordance with the material data safety sheet. Usually this means flushing the area exposed with large quantities of water and calling a physician.

There are a large number of specifications and standards relevant to liquid penetrant inspection and penetrant materials. Table 6-2 lists the various standards in current use.

TABLE 6-2
Liquid Penetrant Testing Standards

Specifying Body	Standard Number	Standard Title
American Society for Testing and Materials	E165	Standard Recommended Practice for Liquid Penetrant Inspection
	E270	Definition of Terms Relating to Liquid Penetrant Inspection
	E433	Reference Photographs for Liquid Penetrant Inspection
U.S. Department of Defense	MIL-F-38762	Fluorescent Penetrant Inspection Units
	MIL-I-6866	Penetrant Method of Inspection
	MIL-I-6870	Nondestructive Inspection Requirements for Aircraft and Missile Materials and Parts
	MIL-STD-410	Qualification and Certification of Inspection Personnel

(continued)

TABLE 6-2—*Continued*

Specifying Body	Standard Number	Standard Title
Naval Sea Systems Command	MIL-STD-271	Nondestructive Testing Requirements for Metals
	MIL-STD-2132	Nondestructive Examination Requirement for Special Applications
Society of Automotive Engineers	AMS 2645G	Fluorescent Penetrant Inspection
	AMS 2646B	Contrast Dye Penetrant Inspection
	AMS 3155B	Oil, Fluorescent Penetrant, Water Soluble
	AMS 3156B	Oil, Fluorescent Penetrant, Solvent Soluble
	AMS 3157A	Oil, Fluorescent Penetrant, High Fluorescence Solvent Soluble
	AMS 3158	Solution, Fluorescent Penetrant, Water Base
U.S. Air Force	MIL-I-25135	Penetrant Inspection Materials (This is the basic specification document for both visible dye and fluorescent penetrant materials for the U.S. Air Force, Navy, and industrial contractor specifications)

MAGNETIC PARTICLE TESTING

Magnetic particle testing (MT) is one of the oldest and most widely used nondestructive test methods. It is used for locating surface and subsurface flaws in ferromagnetic materials such as iron, steel, and nickel and cobalt alloys.

Typically, the part being tested is magnetized, and then finely divided magnetic particles are applied to its surface either during or immediately following magnetization. Any discontinuities that generally lie in a direction perpendicular to the magnetic field cause a leakage field to be formed at and above the surface of the part (see Fig. 6-7). The leakage field gathers and holds the magnetic particles at the location of the discontinuity so that it can be visually evaluated. The gathered particles not only indicate the location of the discontinuity, but also provide some indication of its size, shape, and extent.

The principal industrial uses of MT are in-process and final product inspection, maintenance and overhaul of equipment, and machinery maintenance. Although in-process magnetic particle testing is used to detect discontinuities and imperfections in material and parts as early as possible in the sequence of operations, final inspection is needed to ensure that rejectable discontinuities or imperfections detrimental to the use or function of the part have not developed during processing.

Portions of this subchapter are abstracted with permission from *Classroom Training Handbook, Magnetic Particle Testing.*[15]

ADVANTAGES AND LIMITATIONS

The magnetic particle method is a sensitive means of locating surface and near-surface cracks in ferromagnetic materials. Indications may be produced by very small cracks as well as those large enough to be seen by the naked eye. Exceedingly wide cracks will produce a particle pattern at the corner of the surface and crack even if the surface opening is too wide for the particles to bridge.

Discontinuities that do not actually break through the surface also are indicated in many instances by this method, although certain limitations must be recognized and understood. If a discontinuity has reasonable depth and is close to the

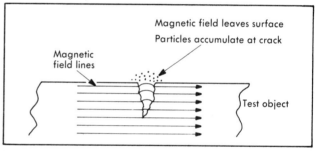

Fig. 6-7 Cross section of a part undergoing magnetic particle testing.

surface, a sharp indication can be produced. If the discontinuity lies deeper, the indication is less distinct.

The size and shape of the parts inspected by this method are almost unlimited. However, abrupt changes in dimension can cause problems with indication interpretation. In general, elaborate precleaning is not necessary, and cracks filled with nonmagnetic foreign materials can also be detected.

Magnetic particle testing has certain limitations that must be taken into consideration. For example, thin coatings of paint and other nonmagnetic coverings, such as plating, can adversely affect the sensitivity of MT. Other limitations are the following:

- Magnetic particle testing will only work on ferromagnetic materials. Nonmagnetic materials such as aluminum, magnesium, copper, lead, tin, titanium, and their alloys, as well as austenitic stainless steels, cannot be inspected by this method.
- For best results, the magnetic field must be in a direction that will intercept the principal plane of the discontinuity at right angles. This may require two or more sequential inspections with different magnetizations.
- Demagnetization after inspection is often necessary. On aircraft parts, demagnetization is required 100% of the time.

MAGNETIC PARTICLE TESTING

- Postcleaning to remove remnants of the magnetic particles or carrying solutions clinging to the surface may sometimes be required after inspection and demagnetization. On aircraft parts, postcleaning is required 100% of the time.
- High currents are sometimes required.
- Care is necessary to avoid local heating and burning of finished parts or surfaces at the points of electrical contact.
- Although magnetic particle indications are easily seen, experience and skill are required to interpret their significance.

OPERATING PRINCIPLES

To ensure reliable inspection, it is important to understand the fundamental principles of magnetic particle testing and to use the proper techniques. If improper techniques are used, some discontinuities may be missed, and defective parts may be accepted. For maximum sensitivity, the part being tested should be magnetized with the direction of the magnetic field perpendicular to the anticipated direction of the defects.

Surface leakage of the magnetic fields used in MT disclose and define the presence, outline, and location of discontinuities. A magnetic field exists within and around a permanent magnet or within and around a conductor carrying an electric current. The magnetic field surrounding a permanent bar magnet has polarity, but the magnetic field surrounding a conductor does not.

The concept of lines of force is useful for describing a magnetic field. As illustrated in Fig. 6-8, a bar magnet is covered with a sheet of paper, and iron filings are scattered over the paper. The iron filings arrange themselves in characteristic patterns paralleling the lines of force. All the lines of force as a group are referred to as magnetic flux. The lines of force never cross; they seek the path of least magnetic resistance; they are most densely packed at the poles of the magnet; they flow from north to south poles outside the magnet. A cross-sectional view of the existing lines of force reveals the flux density within the magnet. The more lines of force per unit area results in a stronger magnetic field both within and without of the magnet.

A permanent bar magnet is the best known example of longitudinal magnetization. The direction of the magnetic flux in a bar magnet is parallel to the long axis of the bar. Therefore, it has two magnetic poles, one north and one south. Longitudinal magnetization is said to exist in an object when the flux lines travel in a direction essentially parallel to one of its axes and may be identified by the existence of a magnetic pole at each end of the selected axis.

If a bar magnet is bent, it becomes a horseshoe magnet (see Fig. 6-9, view a). When the magnet is bent further to make a complete loop and the ends fused together, the poles disappear and a closed magnetic circuit is formed (view b). The circular field is the closest approach to a leakage-free magnetic field. If the circle is cut, either partially or all the way through, poles reappear as shown in view c.

Although it is normal to conceive of magnetic fields as being either circular or longitudinal, in many cases the actual field is a combination of the two. This is known as a distorted field. Distorted fields may be produced intentionally or they may be unavoidable. When produced intentionally, distorted fields are of great value in accomplishing the desired result, which is to produce a magnetic field at an angle perpendicular to the direction of a possible discontinuity. Distorted fields are often helpful, and in some instances essential, to the success of certain magnetic particle test procedures.

If a bar magnet is broken in two, each piece immediately becomes a bar magnet with a north and a south pole. If the two bars are again fused together, with opposite magnetic poles adjacent, the poles in this area disappear. If the bar is cut only partially through, two opposite poles will appear, and a leakage field will exist in the area of the cut. From Fig. 6-10 it can be seen that leakage fields are actually magnetic lines of force that leave the bar and pass through the air from one pole to another of opposite polarity. Because the new poles were created by the interruption of the normal paths of the lines of force within the magnet, it follows that nonmetallic inclusions in a magnetized article, or changes in the material of the article, will also cause the creation of two opposite poles and a resultant leakage field. The changes can be caused by variations in alloying, hardness, geometry, or homogeneity.

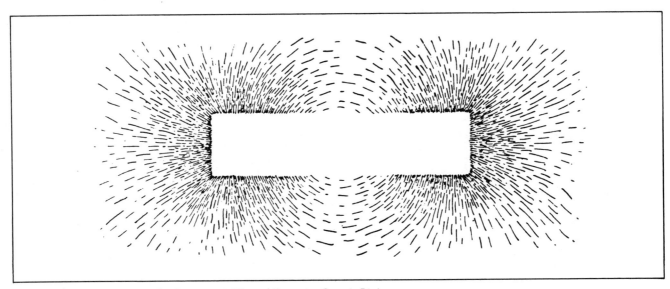

Fig. 6-8 Magnetic field surrounding bar magnet. (*General Dynamics, Convair Div.*)

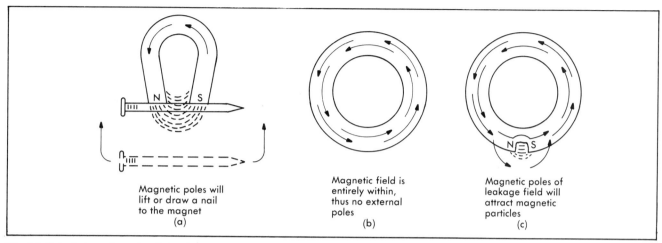

Fig. 6-9 Poles in horseshoe, closed-circuit, and notched closed-circuit magnets. (*General Dynamics, Convair Div.*)

When an electric current passes through a conductor, a magnetic field is formed in and around the conductor. If the conductor has a uniform shape, the density at the external field is uniform at any point along the length of the conductor. At any point on the conductor, the magnetic field is strongest at the surface of the conductor and uniformly decreases as the distance from the conductor increases. The direction of the magnetic field (lines of force) is at a 90° angle to that of the current in the conductor.

An easy method for determining the direction of an electrically induced magnetic field is to imagine grasping the conductor in the right hand with the thumb pointing in the direction of current flow. The fingers will then point in the direction of the magnetic field (see Fig. 6-11). This method is known as the right-hand rule. It is important to recognize that the field actually surrounds and is uniform the entire length of the conductor.

When a current-carrying conductor is formed into a loop, the lines of force circling the conductor form a magnetic field inside and outside the loop (see Fig. 6-12). Inside the loop the field is similar to that of a bar magnet and is said to be a longitudinal magnetic field. The strength of the magnetic field is proportional to the number of loops made by the conductor and the amount of current flowing through the conductor. Two or more loops connected together are considered a coil.

MAGNETIC PARTICLES

The actual medium used for magnetic particle inspection consists of finely divided ferromagnetic particles of low magnetic retentivity. These particles, or powder, are applied to the workpiece either dry or in a liquid suspension. The particles composing the medium in both the wet and dry method should:

- Be nontoxic.
- Be finely divided and within correct size range.
- Be ferromagnetic.
- Be free of contaminants.
- Possess high permeability.
- Possess low retentivity.
- Provide high color contrast (visibility).

Properties

A knowledge of available detecting mediums and their effect on the indications obtained is essential to successful testing.

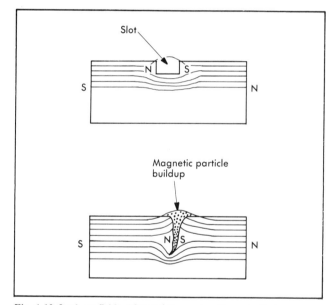

Fig. 6-10 Leakage fields. (*General Dynamics, Convair Div.*)

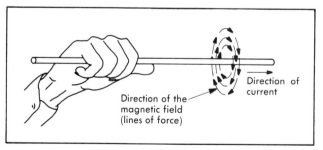

Fig. 6-11 Right-hand rule.

Four properties enter into the selection of a satisfactory medium: magnetic, geometric, mobility, and visibility.

Magnetic properties. The particles of the testing medium must possess two important magnetic properties: high permeability and low retentivity. Permeability is defined as the degree

MAGNETIC PARTICLE TESTING

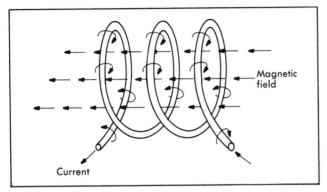

Fig. 6-12 Longitudinal field inside coil. (*General Dynamics, Convair Div.*)

of ease with which a particle is magnetized; retentivity is that property that causes particles to retain, to a greater or lesser degree, a certain amount of residual magnetism. Particles incorporating high permeability and low retentivity are strongly attracted to leakage fields, but do not remain magnetized when removed from the influence of the magnetic field.

Geometric properties. The spherical-shaped particle offers a high degree of mobility, but is not as strongly attracted to leakage fields because of its shape. On the other hand, the long, slender, jagged particle is strongly attracted to leakage fields but has low mobility. A multifacet, semiround particle is a good compromise in that it reasonably combines the optimum qualities of the other two shapes for general-purpose inspection. Particle size is an important consideration. Small particles are required to detect weak leakage fields. Larger sizes are used only when specifications allow their use because a weak leakage field is unable to hold a large particle, but is able to retain one of smaller size. Based on these requirements, dry powder magnetic particles are made up in a wide range of sizes—though most general-purpose powders will pass through a 100-mesh screen.

In the wet method, iron oxides as well as iron powders are used as magnetic particles. Oxides are of lower permeability than the metallic particles and have neither the most desirable shape nor variety of sizes. They are extremely fine in size so that they will remain in suspension to maintain mobility as long as possible before settling out. Even so, the bath must be continually agitated to maintain the particles in suspension. It is important to have a variety of particles with sizes ranging from 2 to 40 μm (80 to 1600 μin.). The smaller size particles are used to detect threshold indications.

Mobility. When the particles are applied to a part either during or after magnetization, they must be applied in such a way that they are free to form a pattern or indication in the presence of leakage fields. In the dry method, mobility is obtained by dusting or blowing the particles over the surface of the article. The ideal procedure, from the point of mobility, is to float a cloud of particles with very low velocity up to the surface being tested. This condition is obtainable only with special equipment. The floating action permits the leakage field at the discontinuity to catch and hold some particles as they move by. Mobility is also obtained by vibrating the part after the particles have been applied. Because the influence of an alternating field causes the particles to "dance," alternating current is used advantageously to provide mobility. One of the advantages of the wet method is the excellent mobility of the suspended particles. A low-viscosity petroleum distillate or water is used so that the mobility of the suspended particles is not impeded by the liquid.

Visibility. An indication must be readily visible. A good light source is essential. The choice of particle color is entirely dependent on visibility. With various types of surfaces, from highly polished articles to rough castings, no one color is always satisfactory. The most widely used particles are colored gray, red, and black. The gray powder has excellent contrast against practically all surfaces, with the exception of certain silver-gray sandblasted surfaces. The fluorescent types of particles are coated with a material that fluoresces brilliantly under an ultraviolet or black light, thereby increasing visibility.

Wet Suspension Bath

Dry magnetic particles are used directly as supplied from the manufacturer. However, wet magnetic particles are used in a bath that must be continuously maintained. The bath used with the wet method of magnetic particle testing consists of a liquid vehicle in which the particles are suspended. The liquid vehicles used are usually a light distillate meeting OSHA requirements for open tank usage. Water, suitably treated with anticorrosion, antifoam agents, may also be used. The vehicle must be non-fluorescent and, for safety purposes, nontoxic and nonvolatile, with a flashpoint above 200°F (93°C). Gloves should be used when handling the vehicle because skin irritation may result from direct contact with the solvent.

The particles used are obtainable in a dry form or in a highly concentrated liquid form and may be either fluorescent or nonfluorescent. To achieve the required test sensitivity, the degree of particle concentration in the bath must be correct—too light a concentration leads to very light indications of discontinuities; too heavy a concentration results in too much overall surface background, which may mask or cause incorrect interpretation of discontinuity indications. It is necessary to check the manufacturers' specifications for allowable concentrations. The amount of particles available at the point of inspection must be closely controlled for repetitive results. Some automatic equipment monitors particle concentration continually and shuts down the equipment if the correct level is not maintained.

Agitation. While the bath is in use, it must be constantly agitated to maintain the particles in suspension. A short period of agitation prior to use is generally required because particles settle out when the unit is turned off. The sides of the tank should also be brushed to remove any of the adhering particles.

Agitation is usually accomplished by electrically driven pumps or by compressed air. Compressed air agitation, although effective, is less desirable because moisture and foreign matter carried by the air may contaminate the bath and shorten its useful life. Compressed air agitation also causes rapid evaporation of a water-based suspension. It will also cause flammable vapors to be present over a petroleum bath. The particle concentration should be checked periodically because the vehicle evaporates, and particles are lost as they are removed from the bath on the test specimens.

Settling test. The suspension is agitated for 30 minutes to ensure an even distribution of the particles in the vehicle. After allowing a volume of suspension to flow through the hose, 100 cc (ml) of the bath is pumped through the hose nozzle into a pear-shaped centrifuge tube and allowed to settle for 30 minutes or more after passing the sample through a demagnetizing coil. The amount of particles (measured in cc or ml) settling in the bottom of the centrifuge tube indicates the concentration of

MAGNETIC PARTICLE TESTING

solid matter (particles) in the bath. In measuring the solid matter in the centrifuge tube, foreign material such as lint and dirt, which settles on top of the particles, should not be considered. If the particle reading is high, liquid (vehicle) is added; if low, particles are added.

Bath maintenance. The strength of the bath is maintained by adding particles or oil as indicated by results of the settling test. The procedure for adding particles is identical to the procedure used in the initial preparation of the bath. Particles are added to the bath directly over the pump intake to achieve proper dispersion.

When in use, the bath eventually becomes contaminated by dirt, lint, and chips to a degree that efficient formation of discontinuity indications is hindered. The degree of contamination is determined by the amount of foreign matter settling with the paste in the bottom of the centrifuge tube during the settling test. The bath should be checked on a regular schedule depending on the inspection volume—daily or even hourly if the volume is high, weekly if the volume is low. When the bath is contaminated beyond usefulness, it is discarded, the bath tank and the liquid system are thoroughly cleaned, and a new bath is mixed. Contamination can be minimized by keeping the bath covered when not in use. A principal problem is either contamination from fluorescent culling oils or a high degree of dye solubility in the selected vehicle. An excessive fluorescent background will seriously reduce contrast and materially affect the reliability of the test.

PROCESS DESCRIPTION

In general, magnetic particle testing consists of three primary steps: (1) magnetization, (2) particle application, and (3) pattern interpretation. Because MT checks for many types of discontinuities in many types of ferromagnetic materials, many variations in the actual procedures employed exist. The procedures used when performing the test affect the results produced. Three other steps also required for most applications of MT are: (1) substrate preparation, (2) demagnetization, and (3) final cleaning. Commonly used standards for MT are listed in Table 6-3.

TABLE 6-3
Magnetic Particle Testing Standards

Specifying Body	Standard Number	Standard Title
American Society for Testing and Materials	A275	Magnetic Particle Examination of Steel Forgings
	A456	Magnetic Particle Inspection of Large Crankshaft Forgings
	E45	Standard Practice for Determining the Inclusion Content of Steel
	E125	Standard Reference Photographs for Magnetic Particle Indications on Ferrous Castings
	E269	Definition of Terms Relating to Magnetic Particle Inspection
	E709	Standard Recommended Practice for Magnetic Particle Examination
U.S. Department of Defense	MIL-STD-271, ACN-1	Nondestructive Testing Requirements for Metals
	MIL-STD-1949	Magnetic Particle Inspection
	MIL-I-6867	Magnetic Inspection Units
	MIL-M-23527	Magnetic Particle Inspection Unit, Lightweight
	MIL-I-83387	Magnetic Rubber, Inspection Process
Society of Automotive Engineers	AMS 2300F	Premium Aircraft-Quality Steel Cleanliness, Magnetic Particle Inspection Procedure (also MAM 2300)
	AMS 2301G	Aircraft Quality Steel Cleanliness, Magnetic Particle Inspection Procedure
	AMS 2303A	Aircraft Quality Steel Cleanliness, Martensitic Corrosion Resistant Steels, Magnetic Particle Inspection Procedure
	AMS 2640J	Magnetic Particle Inspection
	AMS 3040	Magnetic Particle Inspection, Material Dry Method
	AMS 3041A	Magnetic Particles, Wet Method, Oil Vehicle
	AMS 3042A	Magnetic Particles, Wet Method, Dry Powder
	AMS 3043A	Magnetic Particles, Wet Method, Oil Vehicle, Aerosol Canned
	AMS 3044B	Magnetic Particles, Fluorescent Wet Method, Dry Powder
	AMS 3045B	Magnetic Particles, Fluorescent Wet Method, Oil Vehicle, Ready to Use
	AMS 3046B	Magnetic Particles, Fluorescent Wet Method, Oil Vehicle, Aerosol Packaged

MAGNETIC PARTICLE TESTING

Surface Preparation

Prior to magnetic particle testing, the test specimen is thoroughly cleaned. Cleaning may involve removal of loose flake, slag, rust, grease, heavy buildup of paint, or other organic materials that interfere with the final test results. Sandblasting equipment, wire brushes, files, and chipping hammers are suitable for removal of interfering substances. Approved chemical cleaning methods are also acceptable. The smoother the surface, and the more uniform its color, the more favorable are the conditions for formation and examination of the particle pattern. Mechanical surface preparation methods such as shot peening and vapor blasting are not recommended because they may reduce the definition of indications. Additional information on cleaning methods can be found in Volume III of this Handbook series.

When it is necessary to perform magnetic particle testing on specimens that have been covered with anticorrosive protective coatings such as primers, paints, or cadmium, chromium, nickel, or zinc plating, the coatings do not necessarily have to be removed, because discontinuity indications are not usually affected. The acceptable thickness limit of such coatings is up to and including 0.005″ (0.13 mm). Parts coated by ion vapor deposition (IVD) should be tested by MT before being coated. The high amperage used during magnetization may melt local contact areas.

All holes and openings are plugged leading to internal areas where complete removal of magnetic substances or other matter cannot be readily accomplished. Any material that can be completely removed and is not detrimental to the part may be used for plugging. When necessary, all surfaces or component parts that can be damaged by the particles are masked.

Magnetization

The way in which a part is magnetized can be classified in several different ways. The first classification is based on whether or not the magnetizing force is maintained during particle application. The two methods, residual and continu-ous, will be discussed under particle application. The second classification is based on the character of the field, and the third is based on the type of current used. Of increasing importance are special magnetizing methods used to obtain stronger magnetic fields and better field distribution than conventional methods within the part being tested. These special methods also result in showing more of the discontinuities at one time.

Magnetizing field. Either circular or longitudinal magnetization can be used with MT. For maximum sensitivity, the part should be magnetized with the direction of the magnetic field perpendicular to the direction of the anticipated defect(s).

Circular magnetization. A circular magnetic field is induced into a part either by passing current directly through the article (direct magnetization), by passing current through a conductor encircled by the article (indirect magnetization), or by the use of prods. In direct magnetization, the magnetic field will be uniform throughout the length of the article if the article is uniform over its length. Care should be exercised to ensure good, positive contact to prevent arcing.

One way of directly inducing a circular field is accomplished by passing a current through the part as shown in Fig. 6-13, view *a*. This method is called a "head shot." Another direct method of inducing a circular field is by the use of prods. Prod magnetization is used when the size or location of the part does not permit the use of a head shot or central conductor. Current flow and field distribution are shown in view *b* of Fig. 6-13. The field between the prods is distorted somewhat by the interaction of the two fields produced. Prod magnetization is most effective when the prods are spaced 6-8″ (150-200 mm) apart.

In the indirect method of inducing a circular field, the part to be magnetized is placed so that a current-carrying conductor induces a magnetic field into the part. This method is known as the "central conductor technique" and is illustrated in view *c* of Fig. 6-13. The use of a central conductor also minimizes the possibility of a part being burned by the flow of excess current if poor contact is made with the heads. An insulated central conductor should be used to minimize any arcing between the part and conductor.

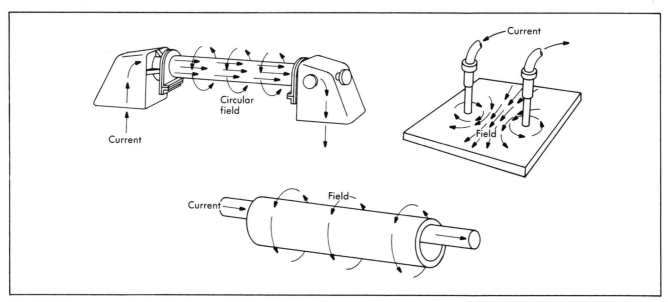

Fig. 6-13 Circular magnetization by direct and indirect methods. Direct methods include (a) the head shot and (b) prods; indirect circular magnetization is done with a central conductor. (*General Dynamics, Convair Div.*)

MAGNETIC PARTICLE TESTING

When it is necessary to pass current through the test part, care is exercised to prevent arcing or overheating at the contact areas. All contact areas are clean, and the part is mounted horizontally between the contact plates. Suitable head pressure is exerted to ensure good electrical contact. Large, heavy parts are mounted in suitable fixtures to ensure proper orientation. The bath solution should be flowed over the contact areas in an effort to maintain a cool contact before applying the current. The duration of the current flow should be as short as possible.

When it is necessary to pass current through large, cylindrically shaped parts, contact balls are recommended. Because protective coatings generally interfere with the flow of current, they are removed at the area of contact. A central conductor must be used when testing internal surfaces of enclosed or cylindrically shaped parts for longitudinal discontinuities. A central conductor is also used for circular magnetization of other shapes when applicable. The central conductor should have an insulating coating to prevent arcing. The diameter of the conductor is as near the size of the openings as practicable, yet allowing for inspection of inside diameter. Multiple test parts on a single conductor may be tested, provided they are separated to avoid contact with each other during magnetization.

Longitudinal magnetization. Longitudinal magnetization is accomplished by the use of longitudinal fields set up by a coil or solenoid. When the length of a part is at least two times its diameter, the part may be successfully magnetized by placing it lengthwise in the field of a coil or solenoid. This is referred to as a "coil shot" and is shown in view *a* of Fig. 6-14. In a coil, the field strength is approximately proportional to the current (in amperes) times the number of turns of the coil. Thus, field strength in a coil is usually indicated in units of ampere-turns. In general, the maximum length covered in a single shot is 18″ (460 mm); longer parts are done in increments of 18″.

When a coil is used for magnetization, it should be 10 times the diameter of the part. Because the flux density is strongest at the inner surface of the coil, the part is held against this surface. If the part is not placed on the surface, it will be attracted with considerable force.

A yoke may also be used to magnetize a part longitudinally. Essentially, it is a temporary horseshoe magnet made of soft, low-retentivity iron that is magnetized by a small coil wound around its horizontal bar. When the energized yoke is placed on a part, the flux flowing from the yoke's north pole through the part to the south pole induces a local longitudinal field in the part (see Fig. 6-14, view *b*). However, the magnetic field produced by the yoke does not lie entirely within the part. An external field is present that is a deterrent to locating subsurface discontinuities. If magnetic particles are applied sparingly at the area between the poles, indications of surface discontinuities are easily seen.

Magnetizing current. Direct current (d-c), full-wave rectified current (FWDC), alternating current (a-c), and half-wave rectified current (HWDC) are used as magnetizing currents in MT. Only one type of current is required for a given test. The type of current used for magnetization affects the strength, direction, and distribution of magnetic fields. It is generally accepted that the best types of magnetizing currents are alternating and full-wave rectified currents. A comparison of the sensitivity of various types of currents and methods is shown in Fig. 6-15.

Alternating current is most often available from utility services at voltages ranging from 110 through 440 V. Commonly used single-phase alternating current usually alternates direction of current flow at 60 Hz. Alternating current is best suited for locating surface discontinuities because it tends to flow near the surface of the conductor. This phenomenon is known as "skin effect."

Full-wave direct current is achieved using alternating current, rectifiers, and transformers to attain the proper magnetization level. Either single or three-phase a-c can be rectified to provide a moderately rippled or almost battery discharge type of direct-current flow. Both surface and subsurface discontinuities can be detected with FWDC; it is especially useful for detecting subsurface flaws by the wet method because of the certainty of complete coverage as well as the ease and speed with which the bath can be applied.

The basic half-wave rectified circuit utilizes a rectifier connected in series between the a-c voltage source and the load resistance. The rectifier permits current to flow only during the positive half-cycles of the applied a-c voltage. Half-wave rectified current is generally used on portable equipment. It is best

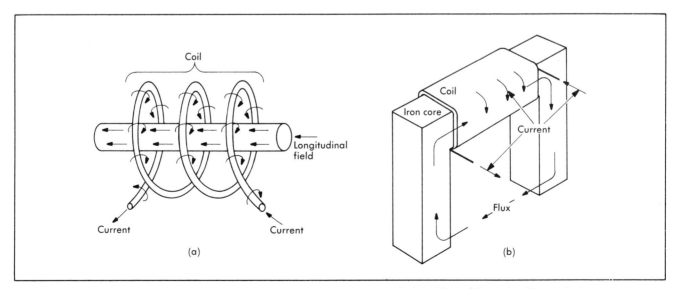

Fig. 6-14 Longitudinal magnetization: (a) magnetization in a coil and (b) yoke magnetization. (*General Dynamics, Convair Div.***)**

MAGNETIC PARTICLE TESTING

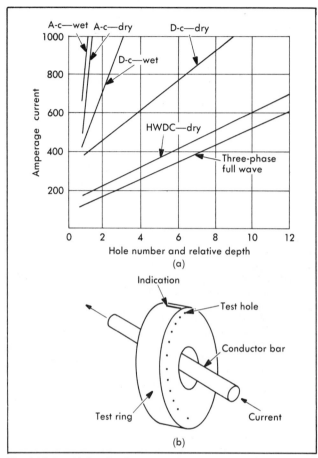

Fig. 6-15 Sensitivity of various types of currents and test methods. The graph in view *a* is based on the magnetization of the test ring in view *b*. The holes in the test ring are in 0.070″ (1.80 mm) increments beneath the surface.

suited for locating below-the-surface discontinuities with dry powders. In most instances, other NDT methods are preferred for detecting subsurface discontinuities.

Special methods. Several special methods are also employed for magnetizing the part being tested. In the induced current technique, there is no electrical contact with the part and no possibility of burning. The part being tested is placed within a magnetic field, and the field is caused to collapse quickly. The current induced through the part is at right angles to the collapsing field, and the flux surrounding the induced current is used to disclose discontinuities. Current strength depends on the strength of the original field and the speed with which it collapses. The induced current technique is generally used on ring-shaped parts to detect discontinuities paralleling the parts circumference. An example of a part for which this technique is used is a bearing race. Bearing balls are also sometimes magnetized using this technique.

Multidirectional magnetization is, in effect, the overall magnetization of the part in one operation. The multidirection is achieved by processing the part using at least two and sometimes three different magnetizing circuits. Rapidly alternating or sequentially energizing the circuits swings the field up to 90° in the part and discloses discontinuities lying in varied directions. Some of the ways of developing multidirectional magnetization are out-of-phase half-wave circuits, sequenced d-c

shots, and d-c overlayed with a-c. No matter which way magnetization is achieved, the part is left with only one residual field. When using this technique, the bath should not be applied once current flow has stopped.

Current requirements. The required amount of magnetizing current is affected by the permeability of the material, the shape and thickness of the part, and the type of discontinuity sought. When a part is not uniform in section, it is necessary to use one value of current for the thinner sections and a second, third, or more values of current for heavier sections. In circular magnetization, the length of the part being tested does not affect the current requirement. The electrical resistance will, however, increase with length and so will require more electrical energy to develop the required amperage. In longitudinal magnetization, specimen length is a factor to be considered. It is always proper to use the smaller current value first to test the thinner section and then proceed with successively higher currents to test the increasingly larger sections. This avoids overmagnetization of the thinner sections so that a heavy background of particles is not attracted and held, thereby obscuring any indications. Whenever a higher field has been imposed than is required for a subsequent test, it is necessary to demagnetize the specimen before applying the lower amperage.

Circular magnetization. The recommended current values for circular magnetization vary because of the different factors involved. An acceptable rule is to use from 700 to 1200 A/in. (280 to 480 A/cm) diam or the greatest diagonal width of cross section. The amperages given in Table 6-4 are suggested aver-

TABLE 6-4
Average Magnetizing Current for Circular Magnetization of Solid and Tubular Parts

Greatest Width or Diameter,* in. (cm)	Approximate Magnetizing Current, A
0.40 (1.0)	280-480
0.50 (1.3)	350-600
0.75 (1.9)	525-900
0.80 (2.0)	560-960
1.00 (2.5)	700-1200
1.20 (3.0)	840-1440
1.50 (3.8)	1050-1800
1.60 (4.0)	1120-1920
2.00 (5.0)	1400-2400
2.40 (6.0)	1680-2880
2.50 (6.3)	1750-3000
2.80 (7.0)	1960-3360
3.00 (7.6)	2100-3600
3.20 (8.0)	2240-3840
3.50 (8.9)	2450-4200
3.60 (9.0)	2520-4320
4.00 (10.0)	2800-4800

* On tubular parts, the measurement must be made based on the actual cross-sectional areas of the tube and then compared to a solid tube of equal area.

ages for various diameters and widths. For this reason, the values may be incorrect for certain alloys and shapes.

The best way to determine the magnetizing current strength is by referring to test specimens having similar indications. In addition, the operator should refer to the test specification for the test being performed for actual current values. Levels of current density can be experimentally established using either a calibrated shim or a Hall-effect meter.

Longitudinal magnetization. For reliable coil magnetization (longitudinal), the part to be magnetized must be at least twice as long as its diameter or width. This relationship is known as the length-diameter (L/D) ratio. When parts have a L/D ratio less than 2, extension keepers may be used. The L/D ratio and the number of turns in a coil determines the required amperage for coil shots, providing the following conditions are met:

- The part has a length to diameter ratio (L/D) of between 2 and 15.
- The part, or section thereof, to be magnetized is not greater than 18″ (460 mm) long.
- The cross-sectional area of the part is not greater than 1/10 the area of the coil opening.
- The part is held against the inside wall of the coil and not positioned in the center of the coil.

If the foregoing conditions are met, the equation for determining a correct amperage is:

$$I = \frac{45,000}{(N) \cdot (L/D)} \qquad (1)$$

where:

I = amperage
N = number of turns in coil
L = length, in. (mm)
D = diameter or cross-sectional width, in. (mm)

Particle Application

The technique used to apply the magnetic particles to the part being tested depends on when the particles are applied and the type of particles being used. Magnetic particles are applied to the part after the part has been magnetized and the magnetizing force removed (residual method), and when the current is flowing through the part (continuous method).

The residual method depends entirely on the retentivity of the part. This method may be used on hardened steels and other highly retentive materials because they will retain a sufficient amount of magnetism after the magnetizing force has been removed. The residual magnetic fields produce leakage fields at discontinuities that are strong enough to hold the particles. If a-c is used, care must be exercised to prevent the part from being demagnetized when the current is broken. This method is generally limited to detecting surface cracks. The residual method is sometimes used after the continuous method to verify questionable indications. The continuous method is more sensitive than the residual method and is suitable for all magnetic steels. This method is used to check for surface and subsurface (when using d-c) discontinuities. It is the only method that can be used in multidirectional magnetization.

As was previously discussed, magnetic particles are available in the form of a dry powder (dry technique) or in a liquid suspension (wet technique). The selection of the type of particle used depends on the type of flaw sought and the size, shape, and portability of the part being tested. Dry particles and HWDC

are most effective for subsurface flaws and are generally used in conjunction with portable equipment; inspection is normally performed in the field. Wet suspensions are usually superior to dry particles for finding fine and shallow flaws. They are generally used for production line inspection, where the inspector examines many components of similar dimension.

Dry magnetic particles are commonly applied from shaker cans or bulbs. This method is the simplest, but not necessarily the best. Electrically powered particle-blowing equipment is usually economical in its use of particles and, in most instances, is the most satisfactory way of floating the dry particles to the test surface with minimum velocity. The excess particles are removed with a gentle air stream. Reclamation and reuse of the particles is not recommended.

The nonfluorescent wet suspension is used in both the wet residual and wet continuous methods. The suspension is applied either by flowing, spraying, brushing (continuous method only), or submersing the part in the bath. Contrast colors of particles are black for light machined surfaces and red for articles that have been heat discolored or have received black oxide surface treatment.

The fluorescent wet suspension is used with both the wet residual and wet continuous methods and is applied to the part by flowing, spraying, or immersion of the part into the bath. The particles are coated with a fluorescent material that, when inspected under a black light, fluoresces brilliantly. For proper viewing, the intensity of the black light at the surface of the part being inspected must be a minimum of 1000 $\mu W/cm^2$.

Pattern Interpretation

Every magnetic particle pattern produced is due to some disturbance set up in a magnetic field resulting in a flux leakage. However, the pattern cannot, in itself, reveal what the discontinuity is. The inspector must therefore be able to determine whether the pattern results from a serious discontinuity warranting rejection of the part, an insignificant discontinuity, or some nonrelevant magnetic disturbance. It is vitally important to locate all discontinuities because any discontinuity may constitute a stress riser, which may lead to failure of a part that is highly and repeatedly stressed. A discontinuity is considered a defect when its presence interferes, or is likely to interfere, with the use for which the part is designed.

The greatest aid in interpretation of the various patterns is the knowledge of discontinuities that are likely to be present in any given instance. An understanding of the characteristics of different discontinuities along with the locations where they commonly occur assist the inspector in knowing what to look for, when, and where to look for them. It is also important to know the history of the part being tested, its composition, and especially what processes it has been through.

Discontinuity indications. Three types of indications are commonly produced on parts inspected by MT. The largest and most important type of discontinuities consists of those that are exposed to the surface. Surface discontinuities produce distinct, clean-cut, and tightly held indication patterns. Subsurface discontinuities tend to produce indications that are less distinct, diffused, or fuzzy rather than sharp-outlined indications observed by surface discontinuities. A discontinuity open to the surface is likely to be more harmful to a part than a subsurface discontinuity.

A third type of indication produced results from nonrelevant magnetic disturbances and is not due to discontinuities in the material. These indications are similar to those of discontinui-

MAGNETIC PARTICLE TESTING

ties, but closer examination reveals that they are nonrelevant. The causes of these indications are numerous. The most common cause is overmagnetization. Because a material with a given permeability can only contain a certain magnetic field, the excessive flux is forced out of the part. These flux lines attract particles like any other leakage field. Other causes of nonrelevant indications are abrupt variations in the article shape and rough surfaces that hold the particles mechanically rather than magnetically. Contact with magnetized parts can also cause nonrelevant indications.

Discontinuity formation. When considering the entire list of discontinuities that can be located by MT, it is logical to consider the life history of the metal from solidification to part failure. The formation of discontinuities can be grouped into three stages: (1) inherent, (2) processing, and (3) in-service.

Inherent discontinuities. Inherent discontinuities are related to the melting and original solidification of the metal in the ingot. As the metal is poured, gas bubbles and slag are entrapped in the ingot. The ingot is then cropped, removing most of the impurities gathered in the top. However, some of the entrapped discontinuities find their way into the finished product. Some of the more common inherent discontinuities that occur are inclusions, porosity, pipe, and segregation.

Processing discontinuities. Processing discontinuities are those produced by forming or fabrication operations. These discontinuities are subdivided into primary processing discontinuities and finish processing discontinuities. Table 6-5 lists those discontinuities that are sometimes formed during the primary processing of metals. It also gives possible causes of the discontinuity along with the likely location. Table 6-6 lists those discontinuities that are sometimes formed by the process required to complete the manufacture of a part. Any discontinuities that were present in the parent metal will also be present in the finished item. At times, a subsurface discontinuity will become a surface discontinuity as metal is removed.

Service discontinuities. Service or fatigue discontinuities are important discontinuities to be considered. Parts that are in service and may develop defects due to metal fatigue are considered extremely critical and demand the close attention of nondestructive testing personnel. Fatigue cracks normally develop in, or adjacent to, areas of stress concentration such as holes, fillets, keyways, splines, and threads.

Preserving indications. A number of methods exist for the preservation of magnetic particle indications for future reference.

Lacquer transfer technique. A transparent lacquer can be applied over the indication if it is desired to retain the indication in place on the test specimen. Spraying or dipping are more effective than brushing because brushing tends to disturb and mar the pattern. Stock lacquers are thinned at least 3:1 before application. When the magnetic particles are applied in wet suspensions, the surface should be allowed to dry before applying the lacquer.

Another technique uses a colored lacquer mixed together with magnetic particles of a different color. After the lacquer-particle mixture is applied, the magnetic field is induced before the lacquer sets. The pattern becomes permanently fixed after the lacquer dries.

Photographic technique. Photographic techniques can be used to make an excellent record of both nonfluorescent and fluorescent powder patterns. When photographing fluorescent indications, a special lens filter must be used to filter out the black light. Test specimens require thorough cleaning of random fluorescent smears. Proper lighting is also required.

Transfer technique. In the transfer tape method, a strip of transparent tape is carefully laid over the indication and gently pressed down with the fingers or a rounded stick. If the dry particle method is used, the excess particles must be carefully blown away or removed before the tape is laid over the indication. If the wet particle method is used, sufficient time should be allowed for the suspension to evaporate before the tape is laid over the indication.

When the tape is peeled off, it brings the indication with it. The strip is then laid on white paper for photographing, on tracing paper for blueprinting, or on a page of a permanent record book.

Magnetic rubber. Magnetic rubber is a liquid silicone-based material containing magnetic particles in suspension. When using the material, the catalized liquid is poured onto the inspection surface; clay dams may be used to hold the liquid in specific areas. While the liquid begins to set, the part is magnetized. This attracts the magnetic particles to the leakage fields. The process takes several minutes to complete, and a dimensional and surface replica results with the magnetic particles frozen in position of the indications caused by the anomolies. When dry, the rubber impression may be removed for evaluation. This is an excellent method to inspect bolt holes, internal surfaces, and keyways that are not readily accessible.

Demagnetization

Ferrous materials usually retain some residual magnetism after the magnetizing current is shut off. The strength of the residual field depends on the retentivity of the material and the strength of the magnetizing force. Complete demagnetization is difficult, if not impossible, to obtain; thus, the demagnetization process is limited to reducing the residual field to an acceptable level. One method of demagnetization subjects the magnetized part to the influence of a continuously reversing magnetic field that gradually reduces in strength. This causes a corresponding reversal and reduction of the field in the part. Although some residual magnetization will remain, this method quickly reduces the field to insignificant proportions. Two other methods used for demagnetizing a part include placing the part in an alternating electrical field and then moving it away from the field, and heating the part beyond its Curie temperature.

For practical purposes, it is always correct to utilize a field indicator after performing demagnetization (assuming magnetization was last performed longitudinally) to determine that residual field strength has been reduced to a desired level. The field indicator is a small, pocket-sized device that measures the strength of the leakage field against a set of small enclosed permanent magnets that restricts the needle movement on a relative scale. A satisfactory residual field for most applications is ±3 oersteds. An oersted is a unit of the external magnetic field on a specific part. If the part has been subject to circular magnetization, the residual field cannot be indicated; it must be first converted to a longitudinal field.

A common error in magnetic particle testing is to assume that demagnetization is required for every application. Whether or not to demagnetize a part depends on a number of factors. Demagnetization is usually required if:

1. A strong residual field might interfere with subsequent operations, such as welding or machining. Strong fields can "flow" the weld metal as it is deposited, or magnetic chips may cling to the cutting tool and interfere with machining.

TABLE 6-5
Primary Processing Discontinuities

Process	Discontinuity	Caused By	Location
Casting	Cold shut	Lack of fusion between two intercepting surfaces of metal as it flows into the cast	Surface
	Hot tear	Difference in cooling rates between thin sections and thick sections	Surface
	Shrinkage cavity	Lack of enough molten metal to fill the space created by shrinkage	Subsurface
	Microshrinkage	Improperly designed mold causing premature blockage at mold gate	Subsurface
	Blowholes	Inability of external gases to escape from the mold	Surface
	Porosity	Entrapped internal gases	Surface or subsurface
	Inclusions—metallic and nonmetallic	Impurities in parent metal	Surface and subsurface
	Segregation—metallic and nonmetallic	Material not homogenized	Surface and subsurface
Forging	Lap	Folding of metal in a thin plate on the surface of the forging	Surface
	Burst	Forging at improper temperature	Surface or subsurface
	Inclusions—metallic and nonmetallic	Impurities in parent metal	Surface and subsurface
	Segregation—metallic and nonmetallic	Material not homogenized	Surface and subsurface
Rolling	Laminations (flat plate)	Flattening and lengthening of discontinuities in parent metal	Subsurface
	Stringers (bar stock)	Flattening and lengthening of discontinuities in parent metal	Subsurface
	Seams (bar stock)	Lengthening of surface cracks in parent metal	Surface
Welded pipe	Lack of fusion	Incomplete weld	Surface (inner or outer)
	Laminations	Present in the parent metal (sheet or plate material)	Subsurface
Seamless pipes and tubes	Seams	Present in the parent metal (round bar stock)	Outer surface
	Slugs	Metal buildup on piercing mandrel	Inner surface
	Gouges	Sizing mandrel dragging	Inner surface
Extrusions	Seams	Present in parent metal	Surface
	Porosity	Present in parent metal	Surface or subsurface
	Galling (cracks)	Improper metal flow through the die	Surface

MAGNETIC PARTICLE TESTING

TABLE 6-6
Finish Processing Discontinuities

Process	Discontinuity	Caused By	Location
Grinding	Cracks	Excess localized heat created between grinding wheel and material	Surface
Heat treating	Stress cracks	Stresses built up by improper processing—unequal heating or cooling	Surface
Explosive forming	Cracks and tears	Extreme deformation overstresses the material	Surface
Welding	Crater cracks (star, transverse, longitudinal)	Improper use of heat source	Surface or subsurface
	Stress cracks	Stresses built up by weld contraction (if material is restrained)	Surface
	Porosity	Entrapped gases	Surface or subsurface
	Slag inclusions	Incomplete cleaning of slag from the weld between passes	Surface or subsurface
	Tungsten inclusions	Excessive current used during tungsten arc welding	Subsurface
	Lack of penetration	Improper welding technique	Surface or subsurface
	Lack of fusion	Improper welding technique	Subsurface
	Undercut	Improper welding technique	Surface
	Overlapping	Weld overlaps parent metal—not fused	Surface
Bending	Cracks	Overstress of material	Surface
Machining	Tears	Working with dull tools or cutting too deep	Surface
Pickling and etching	Cracks	Relief of internal stresses	Surface
Electroplating	Cracks	Relief of internal stresses	Surface

2. The part is a moving part of an assembly and a deposit of accumulated magnetized particles might cause wear.
3. Leakage fields might interfere with nearby instruments that work on magnetic principles; for example, compasses or indicators of various types.
4. Residual fields might interfere with proper cleaning of the part.
5. The part is to be magnetized at a lower magnetizing force in a different direction than the original or previous test.
6. Specified by procedural standards.

Demagnetization is usually not required or necessary:

1. On parts of soft steel or iron where retentivity is low.
2. If, after the magnetic particle test, the part is to be heat treated.
3. On large castings, weldments, or vessels where residual fields will have no material effect.
4. If the part is to be magnetized again in another direction at the same or higher amperage.

5. If the part is likely to become remagnetized during handling by being placed on a magnetic chuck or being lifted with an electromagnetic lifting fixture.

Two methods are generally used for demagnetization: alternating-current demagnetization and direct-current demagnetization.

Alternating-current demagnetization. The most convenient method of demagnetization uses a specially built demagnetization coil. When such a coil is energized by passing the current through its windings, it induces a magnetic field in the part placed in the coil. Because current direction reverses itself, the polarity of the induced magnetic field also reverses with each reversal of the current. As the part is withdrawn from the coil, the magnetic field becomes weaker the further the part is withdrawn from the coil. Demagnetization is accomplished only if the part is removed from the influence of the demagnetizing coil while the current is flowing; if the current is stopped while the part is still in the influence of the magnetic field, the part may still retain some magnetism. In another method, alternating current flows through a central conductor, the part, or an encircling coil. The current is gradually reduced to zero.

Direct-current demagnetization. Because the magnetic field produced by alternating current does not penetrate very deeply below the surface of the material, some parts may be difficult to demagnetize completely. This is particularly true with large, heavy, or unusual-shaped parts. Direct current can be used to demagnetize if provisions for controlling the amount of current and for reversing the direction of the current are made. Direct-current demagnetization is usually more complete and effective than alternating-current demagnetization. Some magnetic particle testing equipment is provided with facilities for d-c demagnetization. Without such equipment, d-c demagnetization is a slow operation. Demagnetization is preferably done on individual parts rather than on groups of parts.

To demagnetize with direct current, the part is placed in a coil, clamped or put on a central conductor, and connected to a source of direct current. The current is adjusted to a value at least as great (but usually greater) than that initially used for magnetization. A magnetizing shot is given at this initial value. The direction of the current is then reversed, the current value reduced, and a magnetizing shot is given at the new value. This process of reversing and reducing the current is accomplished by the unit and is continued until the lowest value is reached.

For best results in demagnetization when using a coil, the diameter of the demagnetization coil is just large enough to accommodate the part. If demagnetization of a small part is performed in a large coil the part is placed close to the inside wall or corner of the coil because the demagnetization force is strongest in that area.

Final Cleaning

Magnetic particles should be completely removed from all articles after test and demagnetization. Cleaning is accomplished by use of air, solvents, washes, and wiping equipment suitable to the size and complexity of the task. After cleaning, the part is returned to its original state by the removal of all plugs used to seal holes and cavities during the testing process. When water is used as a part of postcleaning, a rust prevention step may be required.

EQUIPMENT

The equipment used to process articles for magnetic particle testing ranges from heavy, complex, and automated systems weighing several tons to small, lightweight, portable units. The following are requirements to be considered when selecting equipment for magnetic particle testing:

- Wet or dry method.
- Magnetization method (a-c, d-c, or both).
- Degree of automation.
- Incorporated or separate demagnetization capability.
- Amperage required.
- Tank capacity for wet horizontal equipment.
- Air supply requirements.
- Line voltage requirements.
- Accessories required.

Wet Horizontal Equipment

Wet magnetic particle equipment is available or can be built to handle parts of almost any length. The type of equipment illustrated in Fig. 6-16 enables magnetization of parts ranging

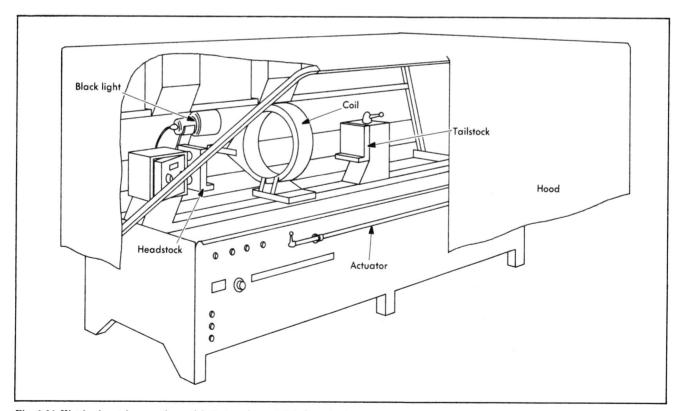

Fig. 6-16 Wet horizontal magnetic particle test equipment. (*Ardrox, Inc.*)

MAGNETIC PARTICLE TESTING

from a few inches (centimeters) to approximately 12′ (3.6 m) in length. Head openings of 54-144″ (1370-3660 mm) are commonly available.

During tests, the part is clamped between the head and tail stock for circular magnetization. For longitudinal magnetization, the coil is moved so that the area to be tested is encircled by the coil. The magnetizing current cycle is energized by means of either a pushbutton or a bar. The bar usually extends across the front of the equipment and can be made inactive by disengaging the switch actuator. An air-operated contact, controlled by a foot pedal, clamps the part securely in place between the heads. The equipment also incorporates an automatic shot-duration timer, usually factory set for one-half second. When using an accessory, a manually controlled shot timer bypasses the automatic timer, and an overload relay protects the equipment if the designed duty cycle is exceeded.

The amperage and duty cycle of the equipment varies between models and manufacturer's types. Maximum output ratings of such equipment usually range from approximately 3000 to 10,000 A. Equipment with considerably lower or higher range is available. Some "wet" equipment of this type also incorporates provisions for both alternating and direct magnetizing currents and a step switch demagnetizing system. Most equipment has a thermal circuit breaker that interrupts the operation if an overload occurs and, after sufficient cooling time, restores it again.

Mobile Equipment

It is often necessary to bring the test equipment to a part located in another area. The type of equipment used is mobile and sturdy and is able to provide various types and methods of required tests.

A typical mobile piece of magnetic particle equipment is illustrated in Fig. 6-17. This type of equipment operates on 220 or 440 V a-c and provides both a-c and half-wave d-c variable up to approximately 6000 A. Selection of a-c or half-wave d-c is accomplished by switching cables on output lugs located on the front of the unit. Cables ranging in length from 15 to 30′ (4.5 to 9 m) may be further extended to as long as 100′ (30 m) by additional lengths.

Prods are usually used with mobile equipment; however, clamps and magnetic leeches serve the same purpose. Yokes or the wrapping of a cable into a coil can also be used. In addition, a central conductor may be hooked up between the two cables if needed. While the dry magnetic particle powder is most frequently used with this type of equipment, the wet method can also be employed by the use of an external tank or expendable one-time materials.

Portable Equipment

Figure 6-18 shows a typical portable magnetic particle testing unit. Portable equipment is available in a variety of sizes, shapes, and weights, with a variety of input voltages and amperage outputs. Portable equipment makes testing possible in formerly inaccessible areas. Portable equipment operates on the same principles as stationary equipment; however, the compactness and ample amperage output makes portable equipment a prime tool for testing a variety of articles. Portable equipment is usually operated on 110/220 V a-c and is rated between 500 and 1000 A output depending on model and type. Some models provide only a-c output, others provide only d-c output, and others have the capability of providing both a-c and d-c.

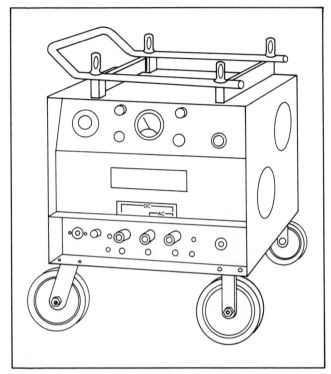

Fig. 6-17 Mobile magnetic particle test equipment. (*Ardrox, Inc.*)

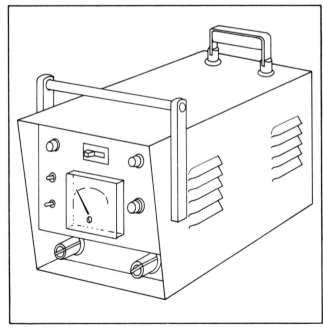

Fig. 6-18 Portable magnetic particle test equipment. (*Ardrox, Inc.*)

The main difference between stationary equipment and portable equipment, besides the lower amperage rating, is the omission of the reversing stepdown feature used for demagnetization. This does not limit the use of the equipment because demagnetization can usually be accomplished by pulling the part through an alternating-current coil field.

Demagnetizing Equipment

Most common types of demagnetization equipment consist of an open, tunnel-like coil utilizing a-c at the incoming frequency, usually 60 Hz. The larger equipment incorporates a track or carriage to facilitate moving large and heavy articles. Smaller demagnetization equipment such as tabletop units, yokes, or plug-in cable coils may be feasible for demagnetization of small articles. The large stationary equipment, however, is preferable when multidimensional articles are involved.

Accessories

An extensive number of accessories are available for use in magnetic particle testing. Some are available from the manufacturers of magnetic particle equipment; others are made up for specific purposes. The need for accessories usually depends on the type and method or application of the test selected. An accessory may speed up a procedure, but if its use in any way impairs the quality of the test, the accessory defeats its purpose. Table 6-7 illustrates some frequently used accessories and their application.

Lighting

When nonfluorescent particles are being used, an illumination level of at least 50 ft-c (538 lm/m^2) of visible light is required at the surface of the test specimen. The illumination level must be checked periodically to ensure that the proper illumination level is being maintained.

Black light equipment is standard when performing fluorescent inspections. In some instances, more than one black light may facilitate the test. A portable black light may be used with mobile or portable equipment when fluorescent testing is performed. The black light equipment usually consists of a current-regulating transformer, a mercury arc bulb, and a filter. The bulb used should emit light in the 320-380 nm wavelength frequency. The bulb and filter are contained in a reflector lamp unit, and the transformer is housed separately.

Care must be exercised not to look directly into the bulb or filter. Any light escaping from around the edges of the filter may cause eye damage similar to that caused by a welder's arc. The latest equipment has incorporated the filter into the glass envelope of the bulb to prevent light from escaping around a separate filter.

For correct test results the lamp should produce an intensity of 1000 μW/cm^2 in a 3″ (75 mm) circle. Most lamps will produce this intensity at a distance of 15″ (380 mm) from the surface of the part. The deep red-purple filter is designed to pass only those wavelengths of light that will activate the fluorescent material. Because dust, dirt, and oil greatly reduce the intensity

TABLE 6-7
Accessories and Their Uses

Cables	Used with mobile or portable magnetic particle equipment to carry the current to prod or solenoid
Centrifuge tube	Used in measuring concentration and strength of the liquid testing medium
Clamps	Used instead of prods to facilitate good contact with article or when one-person operation is required
Contact blocks	Used to facilitate cable connection from stationary equipment for external use of prods or coils
Demagnetizing unit	Used to demagnetize ferrous metals containing residual magnetism
Field indicator	Used in measuring residual magnetism in an article
Leeches	Used as prods or clamps
Liquid applicator	Used in applying fluorescent or nonfluorescent test medium—can be either manual, electric, or air operated
Mesh	Used between contact points and article tested to avoid sparking and burns
Pie gage	Used to determine proper field direction and field strength on a part
Powder applicator	Used to apply magnetic particle powder to the test area—can be a powder puff or powder blower, hand operated, electric, or air
Prods	Used for magnetizing of welds, sheet, or plate

of the emitted light, the filter and lamp must be cleaned frequently. The full intensity of the lamp is not attained until the mercury arc is sufficiently heated. At least 5 minutes warmup time is required to reach the required arc temperature; for mercury arc bulbs with separate filters, up to 20 minutes may be required. Once turned on, the lamp is usually left on during the entire test or working period because switching on and off shortens the life of the bulb.

ULTRASONIC TESTING

Ultrasonic testing (UT) is a widely used nondestructive method of testing materials. It involves the use of beams of high-frequency sound waves introduced into the material being inspected to detect flaws, measure thickness, or evaluate material properties. The sound waves travel through the material and are reflected back by a material discontinuity to the source of the sound. The reflected beam is then detected and analyzed to define the presence and location of flaws.

Portions of this subchapter are abstracted with permission from *Classroom Training Handbook, Ultrasonic Testing.*[16] Table 6-8 lists various standards associated with UT.

APPLICATIONS

Materials capable of being tested by ultrasonic energy are those that transmit vibrational energy. Metals can be tested by UT in thicknesses up to 30′ (9 m). Noncellular plastics, ceram-

ULTRASONIC TESTING

TABLE 6-8
Ultrasonic Testing Standards

Specifying Body	Standard Number	Standard Title
American Society for Testing and Materials	A388	Ultrasonic Examination of Heavy Steel Forgings
	A418	Ultrasonic Inspection of Turbine and Generator Steel Rotor Forgings
	A503	Ultrasonic Examination of Large Forged Crankshafts
	A745	Ultrasonic Examination of Austenitic Steel Forgings
	B548	Specification for Standard Method for Ultrasonic Inspection of Aluminum Alloy Plate for Pressure Vessels
	B594	Ultrasonic Inspection of Aluminum-Alloy Products for Aerospace Applications
	E114	Recommended Practice for Ultrasonic Pulse-Echo Straight-Beam Testing by the Contact Method
	E164	Ultrasonic Contact Inspection of Weldments
	E213	Ultrasonic Inspection of Metal Pipe and Tubing for Longitudinal Discontinuities
	E214	Immersed Ultrasonic Testing by the Reflection Method Using Pulsed Longitudinal Waves
	E273	Ultrasonic Inspection of Longitudinal and Spiral Welds of Welded Pipe and Tubing
	E317	Evaluating Performance Characteristics of Ultrasonic Pulse-Echo Testing Systems Without the Use of Electronic Measurement Instruments
	E494	Measuring Ultrasonic Velocity in Materials
	E500	Standard Definitions of Terms Relating to Ultrasonic Testing
	E587	Ultrasonic Angle Beam Examination by the Contact Method
	E588	Detection of Large Inclusions in Bearing Quality Steel by the Ultrasonic Method
	E664	Measurement of the Apparent Attenuation of Longitudinal Ultrasonic Waves by Immersion Method
	E797	Measuring Thickness by Manual Ultrasonic Pulse-Echo Contact Method
U.S. Department of Defense	MIL-STD-271	Nondestructive Testing Requirements for Metals
	MIL-STD-410	Qualification and Certification of Inspection Personnel
	MIL-STD-770	Ultrasonic Inspection of Lead
	MIL-STD-1263	Qualification and Certification of Inspection Personnel (Ultrasonic)
Society of Automotive Engineers	AMS 2630	Ultrasonic Inspection
	AMS 2631	Ultrasonic Inspection of Titanium Alloys
	AMS 2632	Ultrasonic Inspection of Thin Materials—0.5" (13 mm) and Thinner

ics, glass, new concrete, organic materials, and rubber can also be tested.

The three main areas in which UT is currently being used are (1) determination of structural integrity, (2) thickness measurement, and (3) evaluation of material properties.

Determining Structural Integrity

When checking parts for structural integrity, the inspector is looking for discontinuities or flaws in the part. Some of the flaws that can be detected by UT include cracks, gross porosity, lack of fusion, laminations, inclusions, segregates, stringers, and bonding faults. Subsurface flaws are usually of primary importance, but UT can also be used to detect surface-breaking discontinuities such as cracks in tubing.

Some of the major types of components that are ultrasonically inspected for the presence of flaws are the following:[17]

- Mill components—rolls, shafts, drives, and press columns.
- Power equipment—turbine forgings, generator rotors, pressure piping, weldments, pressure vessels, nuclear fuel elements, and other reactor components.
- Jet engine parts—turbine and compressor forgings and gear blanks.
- Aircraft components—forging stock, frame sections, and honeycomb sandwich assemblies.

- Machinery materials—die blocks, tool steels, and drill pipe.
- Railroad parts—axles, wheels, and bolted and welded rail.
- Automotive parts—forgings, ductile iron castings, and brazed and/or welded components.

Thickness Measurement

The thickness of a part can be determined from transit time measurements or resonance techniques. When measuring thickness, either the material velocity must be known or appropriate reference standards must be used. Access to only one surface is required, but opposite surfaces must be nearly parallel with the entry surface.

Ultrasonic thickness gaging is widely used in the plastics industry to nondestructively check the wall thickness of molded containers, in the foundry industry to check casting thickness, and in the metal fabrication industry to measure thickness of rolled or machined parts.

Material Property Evaluation

Evaluation of material properties is generally applicable to those elastic or structural properties that affect the propagation of acoustic waves such as hardness, elasticity, density, grain structure, and crystal orientation. Applications range from laboratory investigations, such as the measurement of dynamic elastic moduli, to in-process monitoring of nodular iron castings.

ADVANTAGES AND LIMITATIONS

The principal advantages of ultrasonic testing in comparison with other methods of nondestructive testing are the following:[18]

- Superior penetrating power, permitting detection of flaws deep in the part.
- Ability to detect extremely small flaws.
- Greater accuracy than other nondestructive methods in determining the position of internal flaws, estimating their sizes, and characterizing them in terms of nature, orientation, and shape.
- Only one surface need be accessible.
- Operation is electronic, providing almost instantaneous indications of flaws. This makes the method suitable for immediate interpretation, automation, rapid scanning, in-line production monitoring, and process control.
- With most systems, a permanent record of inspection results can be made.
- Volumetric scanning ability, permitting inspection of a volume of material extending from the front surface to the back surface of a part.
- Presents no radiation hazard to operations or nearby personnel and has no effect on nearby equipment and materials.
- Portability.

Disadvantages of UT include the following:[19]

- Operation requires careful attention by experienced technicians.
- Technical knowledge is required for development of inspection procedures.
- Parts that are rough, irregular in shape, very small or thin, or not homogeneous are difficult to inspect.

- Discontinuities that are present in a shallow layer immediately beneath the surface may not be detectable.
- Couplant is needed to provide effective transfer of the ultrasonic beam between the transducer and part being tested.
- Reference standards are required, both for calibrating the equipment and for characterizing flaws.

OPERATING PRINCIPLES

Sound is the mechanical vibration of particles in a medium (material). When a sound wave travels in a material, the particles in the material vibrate about a fixed point at the same frequency as the sound wave. The particles do not travel with the wave, but only react to the energy of the wave; it is the energy of the wave that moves through the material.

Ultrasonics is the name given to the study and application of sound waves having frequencies higher than those that the human ear can hear. People with normal hearing can hear frequencies up to 16 or 20 kHz; frequencies for UT range from 100 kHz to 100 MHz.

In UT, sound waves are generated by applying electrical pulse to a piezoelectric element (transducer). The transducer transforms the electrical energy into mechanical vibrations and transmits the vibrations through a coupling medium (usually a liquid) into the material being tested. These pulsed vibrations propagate through the part with a velocity that depends on the density and elasticity of the material. When sound waves strike an interrupting object, some of the energy is reflected. The reflected waves are picked up by a second or the same transducer. Waves that are reflected before reaching the back surface of the part indicate the presence and location of discontinuities in the part.

Sound Waves

Several types of sound waves travel through solid material. The two waves most commonly used for UT are longitudinal or compression and shear or transverse. With longitudinal waves, the particles vibrate back and forth in the same direction as the motion of the sound (see Fig. 6-19). The particles vibrate back and forth in a direction that is at right angles to the motion of sound with shear waves.

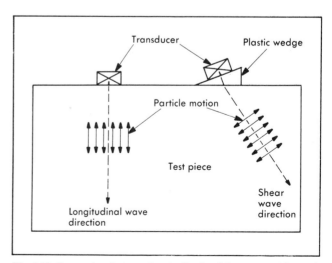

Fig. 6-19 Comparison between longitudinal and shear waves. (*General Dynamics, Convair Div.*)

ULTRASONIC TESTING

It is also possible, within certain limits, to produce waves that travel along the free boundary or surface of a solid. These surface waves, referred to as Rayleigh waves, penetrate the material to a depth of only a few wavelengths. Another type of surface wave occurs when a surface wave is introduced into a material that has a thickness equal to three wavelengths or less. This type of surface wave is referred to as a Lamb wave.

Ultrasonic vibrations in liquids or gases are only propagated as longitudinal waves because of the absence of shear rigidity in liquids and gases. Longitudinal, shear, and surface waves can be propagated in solid materials.

The high-frequency particle vibrations of sound waves are propagated in homogeneous solid parts in the same manner as directed light waves. Because of this, sound waves can be reflected, focused, and refracted.

Sound Wave Frequencies

Most ultrasonic testing is conducted in the range from 100 kHz to 100 MHz. These frequencies, which are far beyond the audible range, propagate in the test material as waves of particle vibrations. Sound waves of all frequencies can penetrate fine-grained material without difficulty. However, when using high frequencies in coarse-grained material, interference in the form of scattering may be expected. Greater depth of penetration may be achieved by using lower frequencies.

Selection of the test frequency is governed by the nature of the test application. Low frequencies, up to about 1 MHz, readily penetrate through the test material because of the small amount of attenuation of low frequencies. They are also scattered less by coarse structure and can be used when the surface is rough. However, the divergence of low-frequency beams is large, making it difficult to resolve small flaws. High-frequency transducers emit a more concentrated beam with better resolving power. As the frequency increases, resolution increases, but penetration decreases. A disadvantage in the use of the high frequencies is that they are scattered more by coarse-grained material.

All available frequencies may be used in immersion testing. Frequencies above 20 MHz are not generally used in contact testing because of the fragility of the thinner high-frequency transducers. As the test frequency is increased, the wavelength correspondingly decreases and approaches the dimensions of the molecular or atomic structure.

Sound Wave Velocities

Ultrasonic waves travel through solids and liquids at relatively high speeds. The velocity of a specific mode of sound is a constant through a given homogeneous material. The acoustic velocities of various materials related to ultrasonic testing are often given in centimeters per second x 100,000 (cm/s x 10^5) or inches per second x 100,000 (ips x 10^5). Table 6-9 lists the velocities of a longitudinal wave through several different types of material to illustrate the wide range of velocities. These differences in velocity are due to differences in the density and elastic properties of each material, among other factors. Density alone cannot account for the extremely high velocity of sound in beryllium, which is less dense than aluminum. The acoustic velocity of water and mercury are almost identical, yet mercury is 13 times as dense as water.

Acoustic Impedance

When ultrasonic waves traveling through one medium impinge on the boundary of a second medium, a portion of the

TABLE 6-9
Ultrasonic Velocity in Different Materials

Material	Density, lb/in.^{3} (g/cm^3)	Longitudinal Velocity, ips x 10^{-5} (cm/s x 10^{-5})
Air	0.00004 (0.001)	0.130 (0.33)
Water	0.036 (1.000)	0.587 (1.49)
Plastic (acrylic)	0.043 (1.180)	1.050 (2.67)
Aluminum	0.101 (2.800)	2.460 (6.25)
Beryllium	0.066 (1.820)	5.040 (12.80)
Mercury	0.469 (13.000)	0.560 (1.42)

incident acoustic energy is reflected back from the boundary while the remaining energy is transmitted into the second medium. The characteristic that determines the amount of reflection is the acoustic impedance of the two materials on either side of the boundary. If the impedances of the two materials are equal, there will be no reflection; if the impedances differ greatly (as between a metal and air, for instance), there will be virtually complete reflection.

Acoustic impedance is used in ultrasonic inspection of materials to calculate the amounts of energy reflected and transmitted at impedance discontinuities and to aid in the selection of suitable materials for effective transfer of acoustic energy between components in ultrasonic inspection systems.

The acoustic impedance of metals and alloys is influenced by variations in structure and metallurgical condition. For longitudinal waves, the acoustic impedance can be calculated by the equation:

$$Z_l = \rho V_l \qquad (2)$$

where:

Z_l = acoustic impedance of longitudinal wave, g/cm^2·s
ρ = density of material, g/cm^3
V_l = longitudinal wave velocity, cm/s

Angle of Incidence

When an ultrasonic wave is incident at right angles to an interface between two materials, transmission and reflection of the sound wave occur at the interface without any change in beam direction. At any other angle of incidence, the phenomena of mode conversion (a change in the nature of the wave motion) and refraction (a change in direction of wave propagation) must be considered. These phenomena may affect the entire beam or only a portion of the beam. The sum total of the changes that occur at the interface depends on the angle of incidence of the initial beam, the velocities of the waveforms in both materials, and the ability of a waveform to exist in a given material.

Critical Angles

Sound beams passing through a medium are refracted when entering a second medium of different sound velocity at an incident angle other than normal. For small incident beam angles, sound beams are refracted and subjected to mode conversion, resulting in a combination of shear and longitudinal waves. As the angle of incidence is increased, the first critical angle is reached when the refracted longitudinal beam angle reaches 90°. At this point, only shear waves exist in the second medium. The region between normal incidence and the first critical angle is not as useful for ultrasonic testing as is the region beyond the first critical angle, where only shear waves are produced. The presence of two beams results in confusing signals.

When selecting a contact shear wave angle beam transducer, or when adjusting an immersed transducer at an incident angle to produce shear waves, two conditions are considered. First, and of prime importance, is that the refracted longitudinal wave must be totally reflected (its angle of refraction must be 90° or greater) so that the penetrating beam is composed of shear waves only. Second, within the limits of the first condition, the refracted shear wave must propagate through the test piece in accordance with the requirements of the test.

As the incident angle is increased further, the second critical angle is reached when the refracted shear beam angle reaches 90°. At this point, all shear waves are reflected, and in the case of contact testing, surface waves are produced. In immersion testing, the liquid medium dampens the production of surface waves to a large degree. Surface waves have been produced in experimental tests on immersed articles.

Absorption

Absorption of ultrasonic energy occurs mainly by conversion of mechanical energy into heat. Elastic motion within a substance as a sound wave propagates though it alternately heats the substance during compression and cools it during rarefaction. Because heat flows so much more slowly than an ultrasonic wave, thermal losses are incurred, which progressively reduce energy in the propagating wave. A related thermal loss occurs in polycrystalline materials; a thermoelastic loss arises from heat flow away from grains that have received more compression or expansion in the course of wave motion than did adjacent grains. For most polycrystalline materials, this effect is most pronounced at the low end of the ultrasonic frequency spectrum.

Scattering

Scattering of an ultrasonic wave occurs because most materials are not truly homogeneous. Crystal discontinuities such as grain boundaries, twin boundaries, and minute nonmetallic inclusions tend to redirect small amounts of ultrasonic energy out of the main ultrasonic beam. Also, especially in mixed microstructures or anisotropic materials, mode conversion at crystallite boundaries tends to occur because of slight differences in acoustic velocity across the boundaries.

Scattering is highly dependent on the relation of crystallite size (mainly grain size) to ultrasonic wavelength. When grain size is less than 0.01 times the wavelength, scatter is negligible. When the grain size is 0.1 times the wavelength or larger, excessive scattering may make it impossible to do valid ultrasonic inspections.

Diffraction

Diffraction is the bending of a wavefront as it interacts with a boundary. To understand the importance of diffraction in UT, the transducer could be viewed as an opening through which an ultrasonic beam passes. At the boundary of the opening (represented by the circumference of the transducer), the beam cannot pass straight through, but is bent outward or away from

the centerline of the beam because of diffraction. The result is a reduction in the useful on-axis intensity of the sound beam directly in front of the transducer.

The amount of energy lost, or bent away, from the central axis of the second beam depends on the relationship between the circumference of the transducer and ultrasonic wavelength. If the transducer circumference is many wavelengths across, there is little diffraction loss. When the transducer circumference is one wavelength or less in size, energy is radiated in all directions. This reduces the amount of useful energy available directly in front of the transducer.

Large-diameter, high-frequency transducers lose only a small amount of energy to diffraction. Small-diameter, low-frequency transducers exhibit the greatest diffraction loss.

Near-Field and Far-Field Effects

The face of the transducer element vibrates in a complex manner that can be most easily described as a mosaic of tiny individual crystals, each vibrating in the same direction but slightly out of phase with its neighbors. Each element in the mosaic acts like a point source and radiates a spherical wave outward from the plane of the transducer face.

Along the central axis of the composite ultrasonic beam, the series of acoustic pressure maxima and minima become broader and more widely spaced as the distance from the transducer face, d, increases. When d becomes equal to the length of the near field, the acoustic pressure reaches a final maximum and decreases approximately exponentially with increasing distance.

In the far field of an ultrasonic beam, the wavefront expands with distance from a transducer. The angle of divergence from the central axis of the beam from a circular transducer is determined from ultrasonic wavelength and transducer size.

PROCESS DESCRIPTION

Ultrasonic testing, like other NDT techniques, follows a set pattern of events that are designed to give consistent test results. Ultrasonic testing consists of the following basic steps:

- Calibration of the test system.
- Standardization of the test system.
- Performance of the test.
- Interpretation of results.

The type of test required for a particular component is usually specified in a test specification that tells the operator the type of discontinuities to look for and the type of test required to locate the discontinuities. The test specification also defines the limits of acceptability and gives other basic facts pertinent to the test. It is up to the operator to follow the specification.

The first step in any ultrasonic test is to be sure that the test instrument is calibrated. Calibration of the instrument ensures the proper performance of the test instrument and the linearity of the response of the instrument to discontinuities of different sizes and depths. The response of the instrument must be proportional to the size and depth of the reflecting area of the discontinuity.

The next step in the test procedure is to standardize the testing system to be used in the test. Standardizing the testing system is the adjustment of the equipment controls so that the operator can be sure that the instrument will detect the discontinuities being sought. It consists of setting up the instrument system exactly as it is to be used in the test and adjusting the controls to give an adequate response to discontinuities of

ULTRASONIC TESTING

known size and depth in reference standards. The size and depth of the discontinuities are specified in the test specification.

Once the testing system is standardized, the actual testing can begin. The test instrument controls are not to be adjusted during actual testing because adjusting the controls negates the standardization and requires restandardization of the instrument. After the ultrasonic test has been performed, the results must be interpreted. In interpreting the results of an ultrasonic test, many factors must be taken into consideration.

Preliminary Preparation

Ultrasonic testing begins with an examination of the test specimen to determine the appropriate technique. After the technique has been chosen, components are selected from available equipment to perform the test. Many variables affect the choice of technique; for example, the test specimen may be too large to fit in an immersion tank. In the case of large fixed structures, the testing unit is moved to the test site. This may require portable testing equipment. Other factors are the number of parts to be tested; the nature of the test material; test surface roughness; methods of joining such as welding, bonding, or riveting; and the shape of the specimen. If the testing program covers a large number of identical parts and a permanent test record is desirable, an immersion technique with automatic scanning and recording may be suitable. One-of-a-kind or odd-lot jobs may be tested with portable contact testing units. Each application requires some study as to the most practical, efficient technique.

When setting up any test, an operating frequency is selected, a transducer is chosen, and a reference standard is established. The test specimen is carefully studied to determine its most common or probable discontinuities; for example, in forgings, laminar discontinuities are found parallel to the forging flow-lines. Discontinuities in plate are usually parallel to the plate surface and elongated in the rolling direction; surface cracking may also occur. Defects in pipe depend on the method of manufacture. If possible, a sample specimen is sectioned and subjected to metallurgical analysis.

Frequency selection. The ability to use high test frequencies is an advantage of immersion testing. In contact testing, 20 MHz is usually the maximum frequency. Low frequencies permit penetration of ultrasonic waves to a greater depth in the material, but may cause a loss of near-surface resolution and defect detectability. A sample test specimen is used to evaluate sound beam penetration with a high-frequency transducer (10-100 MHz for immersion and 1-10 MHz for contact) and to observe the total number of back reflections. If there is no back-surface echo, a lower frequency is required. Successively lower frequencies are tried until several back-surface reflections are obtained. If near-surface resolution is required, it may be necessary to turn the part over and retest from the opposite side or to use a high-frequency unit temporarily, following the low-frequency scan. If the second surface is not accessible, then angle beam (shear wave) testing may be required.

Transducer selection. Transducer selection is largely governed by the optimum frequency, as was discussed previously. In immersion testing, other considerations include the possibility of using a paintbrush transducer for high-speed scanning to detect gross discontinuities or the possibility of using a focused transducer for improved detectability of small discontinuities in near-surface areas. It should be noted that with a given transducer diameter, beam spreading decreases as the frequency is raised. For example, of two 3/8" (9.5 mm) diam transducers,

one 10 MHz and the other 15 MHz frequency, the 15 MHz unit is more directive. In contact testing, angle beam units are generally used for testing welds.

Reference standards. Commercial ultrasonic reference standards are adequate for many test situations, provided the acoustic properties of the test specimen and the reference standard are matched or nearly matched. In some cases, responses from discontinuities in the test specimen differ from the indications received from the defect in the reference standard. For this reason, a sample test specimen may be sectioned, subjected to metallurgical analysis, and studied to determine the nature of the material and its probable discontinuities. In some cases, artificial discontinuities in the form of holes or notches are introduced into the sample to serve as a basis for comparison with discontinuities found in other specimens. From these studies, an acceptance level is determined that establishes the number and magnitude of discontinuities allowed in the test specimen. In all cases, the true nature of the test material is determined by careful study of the sample specimen, and a sensible testing program is established by an intelligent application of basic theory.

Testing Techniques

Ultrasonic testing is accomplished with one of two basic methods: immersion or contact testing. In immersion testing, a waterproof transducer is placed at some distance from the test specimen, and the ultrasonic beam is transmitted into the material through a water path or column. The water distance appears on the display as a fairly wide space between the initial pulse and the front-surface reflection because of the low velocity of sound in water.

In contact testing, the transducer is placed in direct contact with the test specimen, with a thin liquid film used as a couplant. On some contact units, plastic wedges, wear plates, rigid delay lines, or flexible membranes are mounted over the face of the crystal.

Immersion testing. Any one of three techniques may be used in the immersion method: (1) the water immersion technique, (2) the bubbler or squirter technique, and (3) the wheel transducer technique (see Fig. 6-20). In all three of these techniques, a further refinement is the use of focused transducers that concentrate the sound beam (much like light beams are concentrated when passed through a magnifying glass).

Water immersion technique. In the water immersion technique, both the transducer and the test specimen are immersed in water (see Fig. 6-20, view a). The sound beam is directed through the water into the material, using either a straight beam technique for generating longitudinal waves or one of the many angle beam techniques for generating shear waves. In many automatic scanning operations, focused beams are used to detect near-surface discontinuities or to define minute discontinuities with the concentrated sound beam.

The transducers generally used in immersion testing are straight beam units that accomplish both straight and angle beam testing through manipulation and control of the sound beam direction. The water path distance must be considered in immersion testing. This is the distance between the face of the transducer and the surface of the test specimen. This distance is usually adjusted so that the time required to send the sound beam through the water is greater than the time required for the sound to travel through the test specimen. When done properly, the second front-surface reflection will not appear on the oscillo-

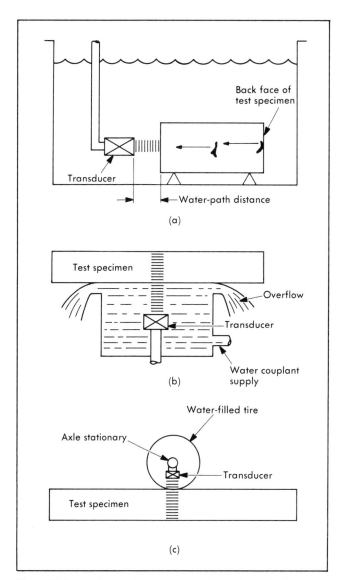

Fig. 6-20 Immersion testing: (a) water immersion technique, (b) bubbler technique, and (c) wheel transducer technique. (*General Dynamics, Convair Div.*)

scope screen between the first front and first back-surface reflections.

In water, sound velocity is about one quarter that of aluminum or steel; therefore, a 1″ (25 mm) depth of water path will appear on the oscilloscope screen as equal to 4″ (100 mm) of metal path in steel. As a rule of thumb, the transducer is positioned so that the water distance is equal to one-quarter the thickness of the part, plus 1/4″ (6 mm). The correct water-path distance is particularly important when the test area shown on the oscilloscope screen is gated for automatic signaling and recording operations. The water-path distance is carefully set to clear the test area of unwanted signals that cause confusion and possible misinterpretation.

Bubbler technique. The bubbler technique is a variation of the immersion method. In the bubbler technique, the sound beam is projected through a water column into the test specimen (see Fig. 6-20, view *b*). It is used with an automated system for high-speed scanning of plate, sheet, strip, cylindrical forms, and other regularly shaped parts. The sound beam is projected into the material through a column of flowing water and is directed perpendicular to the test surface to produce longitudinal waves or is adjusted at an angle to the surface to produce shear waves.

Wheel transducer technique. The wheel transducer technique is related to the immersion method in that the sound beam is projected through a water-filled tire into the test specimen (see Fig. 6-20, view *c*). The transducer, mounted in the wheel axle, is held in a fixed position, while the wheel and tire rotate freely. The wheel may also be mounted on a stationary fixture and the material moved past it. The position and angle of the transducer mounting on the wheel axle may be constructed to project straight beams or to project straight or angle beams.

An adaptation of the wheel transducer technique is a unit with the transducer mounted in the top of a water-filled tube. A flexible membrane on the lower end of the tube couples the unit to the test surface.

Contact testing. Contact testing is divided into three techniques, which are determined by the sound beam wave mode desired: the straight beam technique for transmitting longitudinal waves in the test specimen, the angle beam technique for generating shear waves, and the surface wave technique for producing Rayleigh or Lamb waves. Transducers used in these techniques are held in direct contact with the material using a thin liquid film for a couplant. The couplant selected is high enough in viscosity to remain on the test surface during the test. For most contact testing, the couplant is relatively thin.

Straight beam technique. The straight beam technique is accomplished by projecting a sound beam perpendicularly to the test surface of the test specimen to obtain pulse-echo reflections from the back surface or from discontinuities that lie between the two surfaces. This technique is also used in the through-transmission technique using two transducers where the internal discontinuities interrupt the sound beam, causing a reduction in the received signal.

Pulse-echo techniques may use either single or double straight beam transducers. Figure 6-21, view *a*, shows the single-unit straight beam transducer in use. With the single unit, the transducer acts as both transmitter and receiver projecting a pulsed beam of longitudinal waves into the specimen and receiving echoes reflected from the back surface and from any discontinuity lying in the beam path.

The double or dual-transducer unit is useful when the test surface is rough or when the specimen shape is irregular and the back surface is not parallel with the front surface. It is also useful for accomplishing good near-surface resolution. One transducer transmits and the other receives. Both transducers are usually combined in one unit.

Two transducers are used in the through-transmission technique, one on each side of the test specimen as shown in Fig. 6-21, view *b*. One unit acts as a transmitter and the other as a receiver. The transmitter unit projects a sound beam into the material, the beam travels through the material to the opposite surface, and the sound is picked up at the opposite surface by the receiving unit. Any discontinuities in the path of the sound beam cause a reduction in the amount of sound energy reaching the receiving unit. For best results with this technique, the transmitter unit selected must be an effective generator of acoustic energy, and the receiver unit must be an effective receiver of acoustic energy.

ULTRASONIC TESTING

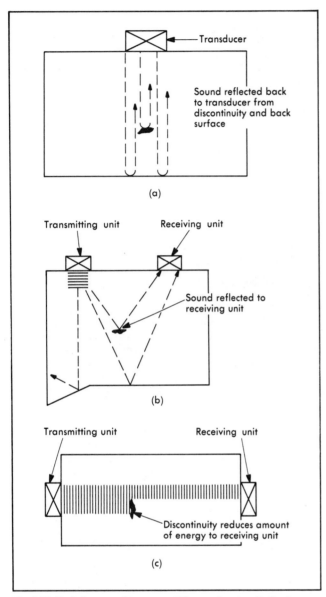

Fig. 6-21 Techniques used in contact UT to produce longitudinal waves in the part being tested: (a) single transducer, pulse-echo technique and (b) through-transmission technique. (*General Dynamics, Convair Div.*)

Angle beam technique. The angle beam technique is used to transmit sound waves into the test material at a predetermined angle to the test surface. According to the angle selected, the wave modes produced in the test material may be mixed longitudinal and shear, shear only, or surface modes. Usually, the shear wave mode is used in angle beam testing. Figure 6-22 shows an angle beam unit scanning plate and pipe material. In the angle beam technique, the sound beam enters the test material at an angle and propagates by successive zigzag reflections from the specimen boundaries until it is interrupted by a discontinuity or boundary where the beam reverses direction and is reflected back to the transducer.

Angle beam techniques are used for testing welds, pipe or tubing, sheet and plate material, and for specimens of irregular shape where straight beam units are unable to contact all of the

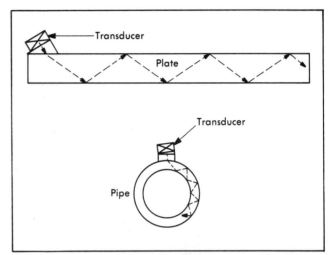

Fig. 6-22 Angle beam technique used in contact UT. (*General Dynamics, Convair Div.*)

surface. Angle beam transducers are identified by case markings that show the sound beam exit point and indicate the angle of refraction in steel for shear waves.

Surface wave technique. The surface wave technique requires special angle beam transducers that project the sound beam into the test specimen at a grazing angle where almost all of the beam is reflected. For test specimens where near-surface discontinuities are encountered, surface wave transducers are used to generate Rayleigh surface waves in the test material.

Interpretation

Ultrasonic test indications from subsurface discontinuities within the test specimen are usually related, or compared, to indications from holes, slots, or notches of varying depths or sizes in standard test blocks. These comparisons are a fairly accurate means of evaluating the size, shape, and position of discontinuities. Test conditions, and the discontinuities themselves, are sometimes the cause of indications that are difficult to interpret. This type of difficulty can only be resolved by relating the ultrasonic indications to the probable type of discontinuity with reference to the test conditions.

Impedance of the material, surface roughness, surface contour, attenuation, and angle of incidence are all to be considered when evaluating the size and location of an unknown discontinuity by the amplitude of the indication received. The simplest method is to compare the indication of the discontinuity with indications from a test block similar to the test specimen in alloy, shape, and back-surface reflections. The experienced operator also learns to discriminate between the indications of actual defects and false or nonrelevant indications.

Immersion test indications. Immersion test indications, generally displayed on A-scan pulse-echo units, are interpreted by analysis of three factors: the amplitude of the reflection from a discontinuity, the loss of back-surface reflection, and the distance of the discontinuity from the surfaces of the article (see Fig. 6-23). Individual discontinuities that are small, compared with the transducer element diameter, are usually evaluated by comparing the amplitude of the test specimen echoes with the test block echoes. Because the surface of the test specimen and the surface of a discontinuity within it may not be as smooth as the surface of the test block and the flat-bottomed hole in the test block, the estimated size of the discontinuity may be smaller than its actual size.

Discontinuities that are larger than the element diameter are evaluated by noting the distance the transducer is moved over the test specimen while an indication is still maintained. In this case, the amplitude has no quantitative meaning; the length of time the amplitude is maintained does indicate the extent of the discontinuity in one plane. A loss or absence of back-surface reflection is evidence that the transmitted sound has been absorbed, refracted, or reflected so that the energy has not returned to the transducer. Evaluating this loss does not determine the size of the discontinuity as precisely as the comparison method used on small discontinuities. When relatively large discontinuities are encountered, the back-surface reflection may be eliminated because the sound beam is not transmitted through the discontinuity.

Contact test indications. Contact test indications, in many instances, are similar or identical to immersion test indications. Interference from the initial pulse at the front surface of the test specimen and variations in efficiency of coupling produce nonrelevant effects that are sometimes difficult to recognize in contact testing. As in immersion testing, signal amplitude, loss

of back reflection, and distance of the discontinuity from the surfaces of the article are all major factors used in evaluation of the display. Typical indications encountered in UT include those from discontinuities such as nonmetallic inclusions, seams, forging bursts, cracks, and flaking found in forgings, as shown in Fig. 6-24.

EQUIPMENT

Ultrasonic test equipment consists of the transducer, which converts electrical pulses into sound waves; related transmission cables; and the ultrasonic test instrument, which generates the initial electric pulse to the transducer and also electronically processes and interprets the received pulses from the transducer. The great majority of ultrasonic testing is accomplished with the pulse-echo method. In this method, individual pulses of sound with high frequency and short duration are sent into the test material. A small amount of testing is also done by the resonance method. In the resonance method, continuous, rather than pulsed, ultrasound is used.

In recent years, improvement in the performance of pulse-echo equipment, along with the versatility of the pulse-echo method, has made the resonance method obsolete in all but very specialized applications. For this reason, only the equipment used for the pulse-echo method is described.

In addition to the transducer and test instrument, other components are also necessary for UT. Couplants are used in contact ultrasonic testing to ensure sound transmission between the transducer and test surface. Tanks and bridge/manipulators are required in immersion scanning applications. Standard reference blocks are used to calibrate or standardize the test instrument.

Transducers

In ultrasonic testing, the ear of the system is the transducer. It consists of a specially prepared piezoelectric element that transforms electrical pulses into high-frequency sound and vice versa. The resonant frequency of the transducer may be between 100 kHz and 100 MHz; the most commonly used frequencies are 1, 2.25, 5, 10, and 15 MHz.

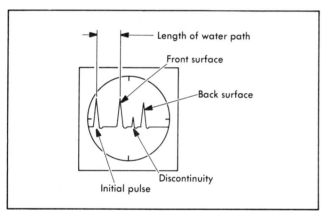

Fig. 6-23 Typical indication of a small discontinuity in immersion UT. (*General Dynamics, Convair Div.*)

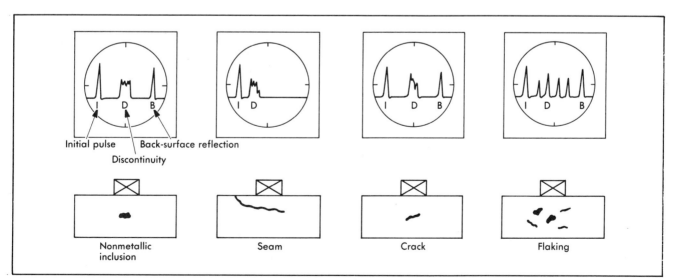

Fig. 6-24 Typical contact test discontinuity indications. (*General Dynamics, Convair Div.*)

ULTRASONIC TESTING

The shape of the transducer crystal or element may be circular, square, or rectangular. Common circular sizes are 1/8, 1/4, 3/8, 1/2, 3/4, and 1″ (3, 6, 9, 12, 18, and 25 mm). Square or rectangular transducers range in size from 1/4 x 1/4 to 1 x 1 (6 x 6 mm to 25 x 25 mm) in 1/4″ (6 mm) increments. Construction of a typical transducer is shown in Fig. 6-25.

In addition to the size and frequency, the damping of a transducer is critical to its performance. In general, transducers have either a low damping factor (narrow-band transducers) or a high damping factor (broad-band transducers). Narrow-band transducers are designed to have as much efficiency as possible, but with only moderate depth resolution. Broad-band transducers, on the other hand, have optimum depth resolution, but with a decrease in efficiency. The efficiency of a transducer refers to its ability to convert electrical energy to mechanical energy and back.

The depth resolution of a transducer refers to its ability to separate the echoes from two reflectors close together in depth. A measure of a transducer's depth resolution is the time required for the transducer to stop ringing or vibrating after having been supplied with a large voltage.

The lateral resolution of a transducer refers to its ability to separate the echoes from two reflectors located side by side at the same depth. Lateral resolution is determined by the beam diameter of the transducer, which in turn depends on its construction and operating frequency. An unfocused transducer, which produces a wide beam, has poorer lateral resolution than a comparable focused transducer.

Sensitivity is the term commonly used to describe a transducer parameter that combines efficiency and lateral resolution. It is defined as the ability of a transducer to detect echoes from small discontinuities. If two transducers generate the identical beam diameter, the transducer with the greater efficiency will have the greater sensitivity. Similarly, a transducer with a smaller beam diameter will have greater sensitivity than a transducer of identical efficiency but with a larger beam diameter.

The important distinction between sensitivity and the other transducer parameters (efficiency, depth resolution, and lateral resolution) is that sensitivity cannot be experimentally determined without a suitable test block. Consequently, transducer manufacturers rarely use sensitivity as a measure of transducer performance.

Materials. The three most common piezoelectric materials that have been used in ultrasonic transducers are quartz, lithium sulfate, and polarized ceramics. Virtually all modern transducers are made from polarized ceramics. With the replacement of crystalline quartz and lithium sulfate with polarized ceramics, it is no longer proper to refer to the transducer element as the crystal.

Quartz. In the past, quartz transducers were used almost exclusively, but with the development of new materials they are now rarely used. Quartz has excellent chemical, electrical, and thermal stability. It is insoluble in most liquids and is very hard and wear resistant. Quartz also has good uniformity and resists aging. Unfortunately, it is the least efficient generator of acoustic energy of the commonly used materials. It also suffers from mode conversion interference and requires high voltage to drive it at low frequencies.

Lithium sulfate. Lithium sulfate transducers are the most efficient receivers of ultrasonic energy and are intermediate as generators of ultrasonic energy. They do not age and are affected very little by mode conversion interference. Lithium sulfate is very fragile, soluble in water, and limited to use at temperatures below 165° F (74° C). Like quartz, lithium sulfate has been replaced by polarized ceramics in most modern transducers.

Ceramic. The polarized ceramic transducers are the most efficient generators of ultrasonic energy. They operate well on low voltage, are practically unaffected by moisture, and are usable up to about 570° F (300° C).

Two generic classes of polarized ceramics are in common use today: lead metaniobate and lead zirconate titanate. Lead metaniobate ceramics are generally used in broad-band transducers because of their high damping factor and almost complete freedom from mode conversion interference. Transducers that formerly were made from lithium sulfate are now made from lead metaniobate ceramics.

Lead zirconate titanate ceramics are generally used in the fabrication of high-efficiency narrow-band transducers. However, transducers made from this material suffer from fairly strong radial mode conversion interference and require suppression with a tuning indicator.

Both of these materials are somewhat brittle, but are chemically stable and resistant to aging. Barium titanate, the first polarized ceramic, is no longer used because of its tendency to age.

Types of transducers. Several different types of transducers are currently being used. The type of transducer selected depends on the specific application.

Contact transducers. Contact transducers are placed directly on the part to be tested and introduce sound into the part at 90° to the surface. The elements are protected from the surface by a durable wear plate, and the shape of the element is generally circular.

Either broad-band or narrow-band transducers may be used for flaw testing, while broad-band transducers are chosen for thickness gaging because of superior resolution. Low-frequency (about 1 MHz) narrow-band transducers can penetrate more than 10′ (3 m) in most metallic substances. High-frequency (up

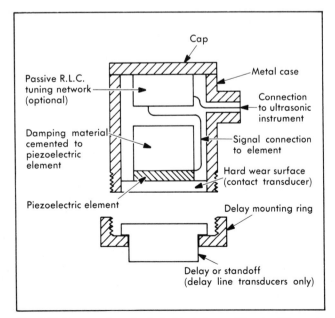

Fig. 6-25 Cross section of a typical transducer. (*Staveley Ultrasonic NDT Technologies, Inc., Sonic Div.*)

Cap

Metal case

Connection to ultrasonic instrument

Passive R.L.C. tuning network (optional)

Damping material cemented to piezoelectric element

Signal connection to element

Hard wear surface (contact transducer)

Piezoelectric element

Delay mounting ring

Delay or standoff (delay line transducers only)

to 20 MHz) broad-band transducers can perform precise thickness gaging on thin materials or detect close proximity flaws because of the short pulse duration.

Delay-line transducers. Delay-line transducers are also used in direct contact with the surface. The piezoelectric element is separated from the surface by a delay line of plastic or metal to either protect the element from high-temperature surfaces or to improve the resolution on thin materials by separating the returned sound from the large initial pulse produced by the transducer and ultrasonic test instrument. Delay-line transducers can be used to accurately gage the thickness of materials as thin as 0.005″ (0.13 mm).

Dual transducers. Dual transducers have one element to transmit the initial pulse and a separate element to receive the ultrasonic pulses reflected from internal flaws or from the other side of the test specimen. Dual transducers often have the sending and receiving elements angled slightly toward each other so that the ultrasound can focus on flaws in the test specimen that are just below the surface. The focusing effect also allows dual transducers to effectively measure pitting and corrosion on the inside surface of pipes.

Angle beam transducers. The angle beam transducer is constructed with an integral or removable wedge that causes the sound to be introduced at an angle other than 90° to the surface of the test specimen. These transducers generally have square or rectangular elements. The commonly used angles are 45, 60, and 70° away from normal to the surface.

When angle beam transducers are used, mode conversion occurs when the sound enters the test specimen; thus the ultrasonic wave is no longer a longitudinal sound wave, but is a shear sound wave. The velocity and wavelength of shear waves are approximately one half that of corresponding longitudinal waves.

Angle beam transducers are used for testing welded materials when the weld bead prevents use of contact transducers being placed on top of the weld or when angular sound waves provide a better beam orientation for flaw testing.

A special type of angle beam transducer is a surface wave transducer. With these transducers, mode conversion causes the ultrasound to travel along the surface of the test specimen and detect surface or near-subsurface discontinuities. The surface wave can also travel around radiused areas of the surface as long as the sound wavelength is smaller than the radius of curvature.

Immersion transducers. Immersion transducers are not held in direct contact with the test specimen, but are separated by a liquid transmitting medium such as water or oil. The use of immersion transducers offers a number of advantages over the contact transducer, although the associated equipment necessary to perform the scanning and immerse the test specimen increases the initial cost. Among the advantages and features of immersion transducer testing are the following:

- Mechanical scanning of the transducer is possible because the liquid in which the specimen is immersed reliably couples the ultrasonic waves to the tested part, regardless of the surface condition of the test specimen.
- The direction of the sound beam can be easily altered as required by the geometry of the part being tested.
- Through-transmission techniques can be used. With these techniques, separate transmitting and receiving transducers are on opposite sides of the test part.
- The ultrasonic beam can be easily focused with immer-

sion transducers. With available focusing techniques, the sound beam can have a cross section as small as 0.005″ (0.13 mm), and the detectability of minute flaws [0.001″ (0.03 mm) or smaller] is possible. In focusing, however, the depth of field of the sound beam is restricted, and the transducer will lose penetrating capability for thick sections. In addition, the smaller beam size requires more scanning time if 100% inspection is required. In some cases, the sound beam is focused into an elongated rectangular area known as a line focus so that small-flaw detectability is optimized while the scanning speed is maintained because of the width of the sound beam.

Multielement transducers. A multielement or array transducer consists of a number of elements individually pulsed in an appropriate pattern. With appropriate synchronization of the pulses to each individual element, these transducers can either improve scanning speed while maintaining small-flaw detectability or dynamically focus or angulate the sound beam because of the acoustic interaction of the separate elements. Multielement transducers, however, require additional expense and complexity in the associated ultrasonic test instrument.

Couplants

One of the practical problems in ultrasonic testing is the transmission of the ultrasonic energy from the source into the test specimen. If a transducer is placed in contact with the surface of a dry part, very little energy is transmitted through the interface into the material because of the presence of air between the transducer and the test material. The air causes a great difference in acoustic impedance (impedance mismatch) at the interface.

A couplant is used between the transducer face and the test surface to ensure efficient sound transmission from transducer to test surface. The couplant, as the name implies, couples the transducer ultrasonically to the surface of the test specimen by smoothing out the irregularities of the test surface and by excluding all air from between the transducer and the test surface. The couplant can be any of a vast variety of liquids, semiliquids, pastes, and even some solids, that will satisfy the following requirements:

- A couplant wets (fully contacts) both the surface of the test specimen and the face of the transducer and excludes all air from between them.
- A couplant is easy to apply.
- A couplant is homogeneous and free of air bubbles or of solid particles, in the case of a nonsolid.
- A couplant is harmless to the test specimen, transducer, and operator.
- A couplant has a tendency to stay on the test surface, but is easy to remove.
- A couplant has an acoustic impedance value between the impedance value of the transducer face and the impedance value of the test specimen, preferably approaching that of the test surface.

In most immersion test applications, clean, de-aerated tap water, with an added wetting agent, is used for a couplant. For certain applications, corrosion inhibitors are also added. The water temperature is usually maintained at 70°F (21°C) by automatic controls for operator comfort. Wetting agents are added to the water to ensure that the surface is thoroughly wet, thereby eliminating air bubbles.

ULTRASONIC TESTING

In contact testing, the choice of couplant depends primarily on the condition of the test surface (rough or smooth), the temperature of the test surface, and the position of the test surface (horizontal, slanted, or vertical). One part glycerine with two parts water, and a wetting agent, is often used on relatively smooth horizontal surfaces. For slightly rough surfaces, light oils (such as SAE 20 motor oil), with a wetting agent added, are used. Rough surfaces, hot surfaces, and vertical surfaces require the use of a heavier oil, or grease, as a couplant. In all cases, the couplant selected must be as thin as possible to be consistent with effective results.

Test Instrument

The ultrasonic test instrument must be capable of producing the individual pulses to the transducer and electronically processing the returned pulses from the transducer. A block diagram of a typical instrument is shown in Fig. 6-26.

The main components of the test instrument are the clock, pulser, receiver, gate, and CRT display.

Clock. The clock determines the number of times per second that the pulser is triggered. For testing in thick specimens, the pulse repetition rate, as determined by the clock, must be low so that all the relevant returning pulses are received from the transducer before the next initial pulse is triggered. For high-throughput testing, however, the clock frequency may be set at 10,000 pulses per second or higher so that the test specimen receives 100% coverage. On instruments with a cathode ray tube (CRT), the clock also starts the horizontal sweep on the CRT, so that time of flight (depth) for returned echoes is proportional to the horizontal position of the indication on the CRT.

Pulser. The pulser sends short-duration, high-energy electrical pulses to the transducer, which transforms them into sound waves. The pulser may have a voltage output of 100-600 V or more and may be variable from broad-band (half-cycle) to narrow-band (multicycle) response. In addition, the pulser may produce either a spike pulse or a square-wave pulse. Pulse-width controls are used to match the pulser to the transducer's resonant frequency. A damping control further improves the pulse shape and amplitude to optimize a particular test.

Receiver. The receiver is generally a wide band (up to 30 MHz), high-sensitivity (80 dB or more) radio-frequency receiver. Additional tuning networks may be added to match the receiver impedance with the capacitive reactance of the transducer. In addition, the receiver must have linear gain response to allow the amplitude of the received sound waves to be accurately measured.

Most instruments allow the receiver to be either directly linked with pulser output (for use with single-element transducers) or disconnected from the pulser (for use with a dual-element transducer or two separate transducers, one sending sound and one receiving). Some instruments also have distance-echo correction (DEC) capability. This capability enables the gain of the receiver to be varied in time according to a user-settable pattern with each pulse repetition so that inherent variations in received-echo amplitudes, caused by test specimen attenuation or transducer beam spread, can be corrected.

Gate. A time-domain gate is used on many instruments so that the operator may have outputs (visual, audible, or electronic signals) that indicate the presence of a flaw larger than the alarm level at a particular depth of interest in the test specimen. Some instruments are designed to output both the flaw amplitude and the flaw depth, while other instruments may have two separate gates to monitor both the interior flaws and the reflection from the back surface of the test specimen.

CRT display. In many portable instruments, the operator interprets the integrity of the test specimen directly from the

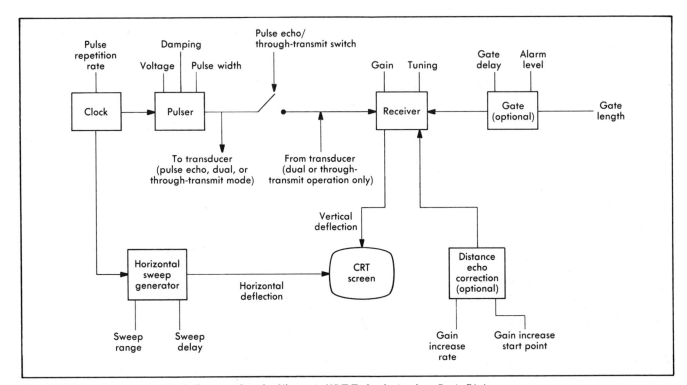

Fig. 6-26 Ultrasonic instrument block diagram. (*Staveley Ultrasonic NDT Technologies, Inc., Sonic Div.*)

CRT or oscilloscope. Horizontal position is proportional to the depth of a discontinuity, and vertical displacement is proportional to the size of the discontinuity. The CRT may be adjusted by means of delay and range controls to best view the area of interest in the test specimen. On instruments with automatic gates, the CRT is still necessary to assist in the initial setup of the instrument, although it need not be constantly viewed during the test procedure.

Thickness gaging equipment. When thickness gaging, rather than flaw evaluation, is of primary importance, special adapters may be incorporated in the test instrument to digitally display the thickness of the test specimen. Such equipment may also be configured as a dedicated thickness instrument, which would have automatic gain control (AGC) receiver but no CRT display. The AGC receiver ensures that the returned ultrasound from the back surface of the material is amplified sufficiently to trigger the time-of-flight circuitry. For critical thickness gaging or unusual test specimen geometry, however, it may be necessary to have manual control over the receiver gain. When manual control is required, it is advisable to use a CRT display to optimize the instrument settings

Data presentation. Test instruments may represent the data using one of three methods: (1) A-scan system, (2) B-scan system, or (3) C-scan system. The A-scan system produces a quantitative display on a CRT or an oscilloscope screen of the echo amplitude and elapsed time obtained at a single point on the surface of the part being tested. The horizontal position indicates elapsed time (from left to right) and the vertical deflection shows amplitudes. The height of the indications represent the intensities of the reflected sound beams and may be used to determine the size of the discontinuity.

The B-scan system produces a quantitative cross-sectional display on a CRT of elapsed time data obtained along a plane perpendicular to the surface of the part being tested. Echoes are indicated by bright spots on the screen rather than by deflections of the time trace. The position of the bright spot along the axis perpendicular to the transducer position axis, usually measured from top to bottom on the screen, indicates the depth of the echo within the part being tested. In high-speed scanning, the cross section image is retained long enough to evaluate the entire sample and to photograph the image for a permanent record.

The C-scan system records echoes from internal portions of the part being tested as a function of the position of each reflecting interface within an area. Flaw size and position are shown on a readout that is superimposed on a plan view of the part being tested. Flaw depth is not shown, but it may be determined semiquantitatively by restricting the range of depths covered in a scan. Some recorders produce a shaded scan line to indicate the flaw outline, while other recorders indicate the flaw outline by an absence of scan lines. Gray-scale C-scan systems provide print intensity proportional to echo amplitude.

Data acquisition. The ultrasonic method of NDT allows varying degrees of automation for data acquisition methods. Many applications require portable instrumentation for on-site testing, with test personnel manually scanning the test specimen with a handheld transducer and either visually monitoring the CRT or using audible or visual indications for flaws. Digital readouts are generally used in the case of thickness gaging.

On-line production ultrasonic testing utilizes electronic outputs that mark defective pieces or activate sorting equipment. In addition, hard copy of the data is generally in the form of strip chart recorder output or a plan view of the test specimen generated by a flatbed or polar drum recorder (known as a C-scan recording).

Computerized Ultrasonic Testing

In recent years the reduction in cost for micro and minicomputers has made computer-controlled ultrasonic testing economically viable. A computerized system may involve either digital acquisition and storage of ultrasonic data or additional computerized automation to control the setting of the ultrasonic instrument, control the scan pattern of the transducer (typically an immersion test), and digitize, process, and store the resulting data. A block diagram of a computerized ultrasonic testing system is shown in Fig. 6-27. Test time may be greatly reduced and operator error minimized with the use of automated systems.

High-Speed Scanning Equipment

Ultrasonic tanks and bridge/manipulators are necessary equipment for high-speed scanning of immersed test specimens. Modern units consist of a bridge and manipulator, mounted over a fairly large water tank, to support a pulse-echo testing unit and a recorder. Drive power units move the bridge along the tank side rails, while traversing power units move the manipulator from side to side along the bridge. Most of these units are automated, although some early units are manually operated. On most automatic units, a C-scan recorder is also mounted on the bridge.

Ultrasonic tank. The ultrasonic tank may be of any size or shape required to accommodate the test specimen. Coverage of the specimen by a foot or more of water is usually sufficient. Adjustable brackets and variable-speed turntables are provided on the tank bottom for support of the test specimen. The water couplant in the tank is clean, de-aerated water containing a wetting agent. For operator comfort, the water temperature is usually maintained at 70° F (21°C) by automatic controls.

Bridge/manipulator. The bridge/manipulator unit is primarily intended to provide a means of scanning the test specimen with an immersed transducer. The version shown in Fig. 6-28 has a bridge with a carriage unit at each end so the bridge

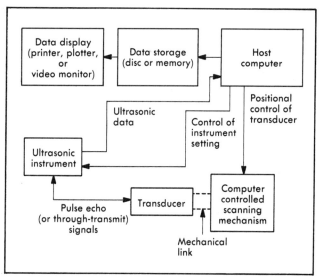

Fig. 6-27 Computerized ultrasonic testing system. (*Staveley Ultrasonic NDT Technologies, Inc., Sonic Div.*)

ULTRASONIC TESTING

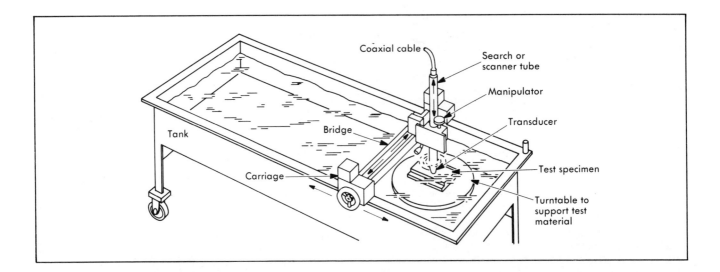

may be easily moved along the tank side rails. The manipulator is mounted on a traversing mechanism that allows movement of the manipulator from side to side. The traversing mechanism is an integral component of the bridge assembly. The search tube is usually held rigid, as shown, at right angles to the surface of the test specimen. Locking knobs are provided on the manipulator to allow positioning of the search tube in two planes for angle beam testing.

When the equipment is automated, electric motors are added to power the bridge carriage, the traversing mechanism, and the up-down movement of the search tube. The pulse-echo unit and the recording unit are also mounted on the bridge, with all power cords secured overhead to allow movement of the bridge along the full length of the tank.

Standard Reference Blocks

In ultrasonic testing, all discontinuity indications are compared to indications received from testing a reference standard. The reference standard may be any one of many reference blocks, or sets of blocks, specified for a given test. Ultrasonic standard reference blocks, often called test blocks, are used in ultrasonic testing to standardize the ultrasonic equipment and to evaluate the discontinuity indication received from the test part. Standardizing does two things: (1) it verifies that the instrument/transducer combination is performing as required, and (2) it establishes a sensitivity, or gain, setting at which all discontinuities of the size specified, or larger, will be detected. Evaluation of discontinuities within the test specimen is accomplished by comparing their indications with the indication received from an artificial discontinuity of known size and at the same depth in a standard reference block of the same material.

Standard test blocks are made from carefully selected ultrasonically inspected stock that meets a predetermined standard of sound attenuation, grain size, and heat treatment. Discontinuities are represented by carefully drilled flat-bottomed holes. Test blocks are carefully made and tested so that the only discontinuity present is the one that was added intentionally. The three most familiar sets of amplitude reference blocks are: the Alcoa-Series A area/amplitude blocks; the Alcoa-Series B, or Hitt, distance/amplitude blocks; and the ASTM basic set of blocks that combine area/amplitude and distance/amplitude blocks in one set.

RADIOGRAPHIC TESTING

Radiographic testing (RT) is a versatile nondestructive test method for use in modern industry. A radiograph is similar to a photographic record produced by the passage of X-rays or gamma rays through an object onto a film. When film is exposed to X-rays, gamma rays, or light, an invisible change, called a latent image, is produced in the film emulsion. The areas exposed darken when the film is immersed in a developing solution; the degree of darkening depends on the amount of exposure and the amount of developing. After development, the film is rinsed, preferably in a special bath, to stop development. The film is next put into a fixing bath, which dissolves the undarkened portions of the sensitive salt and hardens the emul-sion. It is then washed to remove the fixer and dried so that it may be handled, interpreted, and filed.

Portions of this subchapter are abstracted with permission from *Classroom Training Handbook, Radiographic Testing*[20] and *Radiography in Modern Industry*.[21] Standards and specifications associated with radiographic testing are given in Table 6-10.

APPLICATIONS

The ability of X-ray and gamma ray radiation to penetrate all engineering materials and the differential rates of absorption for different materials is responsible for the extensive use of this nondestructive inspection technique throughout industry.[22]

TABLE 6-10
Standards and Specifications for Radiographic Testing

Specifying Body	Standard Number	Standard Title
American Society for Testing and Materials	E94	Standard Recommended Practice for Radiographic Testing
	E142	Standard Method for Controlling Quality of Radiographic Testing
	E155	Standard Reference Radiographs for Inspection of Aluminum & Magnesium Castings
	E186	Standard Reference Radiographs for Heavy Walled (2 to 4.5"/51 to 114 mm) Steel Castings
	E192	Standard Reference Radiographs of Investment Steel Castings for Aerospace Applications
	E272	Standard Reference Radiographs for High-Strength Copper Base and Nickel Copper Alloy Castings
	E280	Standard Reference Radiographs for Heavy Walled (4.5 to 12"/114 to 305 mm) Steel Castings
	E310	Standard Reference Radiographs for Tin Bronze Castings
	E390	Standard Reference Radiographs for Steel Fusion Welds
	E431	Interpretation of Radiographs of Semiconductors and Related Devices
	E446	Standard Reference Radiographs for Steel Castings Up to 2" (51 mm) in Thickness
	E505	Standard Reference Radiographs for Inspection of Aluminum and Magnesium Die Castings
	E586	Standard Definitions of Terms Relating to Gamma and X-Radiography
	E592	Standard Guide to Obtainable ASTM Equivalent Penetrameter Sensitivity for Radiography of Steel Plates 0.25 to 2" (6 to 51 mm) Thick with X-Rays and 1 to 6" (25 to 152 mm) Thick with Cobalt 60 Method of Test for Hermeticity of Electronic Devices by Dye Penetration
	E689	Reference Radiographs for Ductile Iron Castings
	E746	Determining the Relative Image Quality Response of Industrial Radiographic Film
	E747	Controlling Quality of Radiographic Testing Using Wire Penetrameters
	E801	Controlling Quality of Radiographic Testing of Electronic Devices
	E802	Reference Radiographs of Gray Iron Castings up to 4.5"
	E803	Determining the L/D Ratio of Neutron Radiographic Beams
	G46	Recommended Practice for Examination and Evaluation of Pitting Corrosion
U.S. Department of Defense	MIL-STD-139	Radiographic Inspection: Soundness Requirements for Aluminum and Magnesium Castings (for Small Arms Parts)
	MIL-STD-248	Welding and Brazing Procedure and Performance Qualifications
	MIL-STD-271	Nondestructive Testing Requirements for Metals
	MIL-STD-278	Fabrication, Welding, Inspection, and Repair for Machinery, Piping, and Pressure Vessels in Ships of the U.S. Navy
Society of Automotive Engineers	AMS 2635	Radiographic Inspection

Accordingly, radiographic inspection methods are extensively used for flaw detection in castings, weldments, solid propellants, missile hardware, and finished assemblies as well as some other applications. The parts inspected by radiographic testing range in size from microminiature electronic parts to large missile rocket motors.

Castings

The increasingly wide use that radiographic testing methods have in the castings field results from the fact that most of the flaws and discontinuities inherent in ferrous and nonferrous castings can be readily detected by this inspection medium. Shrinkage, gas porosity, inclusions, hot tears, cold cracks and

RADIOGRAPHIC TESTING

shuts, core shifts, and major surface irregularities may be detectable by radiographic, electronic imaging, or fluoroscopic inspection techniques. In addition, the following discontinuities that are peculiar to light metal (aluminum and magnesium) castings are detectable: gas holes, dross, inclusions, segregation, microshrinkage, hydrogen porosity, microporosity, shrinkage, sponge, cold shuts, and other discontinuities common to light metal castings.

Weldments

Radiographic inspection of weldments is an accepted procedure for the detection of internal discontinuities. It is used in the establishment of welding procedures to qualify welders and especially to control quality of welded joints in finished products. The following imperfections or discontinuities are detectable by radiography: porosity, cracks, lack of or inadequate penetration and fusion, undercut, inclusions, and other discontinuities common in welded joints.

Solid Propellant

Solid propellant rocket motors are inspected radiographically to detect cracks, voids, unbonded surfaces, foreign material inclusion, and other anomalies.

Missile Hardware

Items such as nozzles are inspected for cracks, unbonded surfaces, and internal conformance to specifications.

Finished Assemblies

Radiographic testing is applicable to the inspection of fabricated assemblies relative to placement of internal components, such as electronic devices, mufflers, fuel tanks, bonded honeycomb, and tires. Electrical connections as well as the position of bolts and nuts in finished enclosures are frequently checked by radiography. Neutron radiography (discussed in a separate section of this chapter) of assemblies provides a capability to verify proper placement of hydrogen-containing materials in metal assemblies. By this method, rubber O-rings, plastic parts, propellants, fluid levels, and similar materials can be detected even when these objects are inside metallic containers.

Miscellaneous Applications

Radiography in the inspection of forgings, powder metal parts, and nonmetallic materials such as plastic, rubber, and ceramics require specialized application techniques. In the past, radiographic techniques have been less frequently applied to these items; however, more modern equipment and a better understanding of inspection procedures have made radiography a useful tool in inspection of these items.

ADVANTAGES AND LIMITATIONS

Some of the advantages of radiographic testing as a quality assurance procedure are the following:

- Can be used with most materials.
- Provides a permanent visual-image record of the test specimen on film when desired.
- Reveals most discontinuities of a material.
- Discloses fabrication errors and often indicates necessary corrective action.
- Reveals assembly errors.

There are both physical and economic limitations to the use of radiographic testing. Geometric exposure requirements make it difficult to use radiographic testing on specimens of complex geometry. When proper orientation of radiation source, specimen, and film cannot be obtained, radiographic testing is of little use. Similarly, any specimen that does not lend itself readily to two-side accessibility cannot be inspected by this method. Because radiographs are patterned by material density differences in the specimen, they are of little value in detecting small discontinuities not parallel to the lines of radiation. Laminar-type discontinuities are therefore often undetected by radiographic testing. If laminar-type discontinuities are suspected in a specimen, the radiation source, the specimen, and the film must be oriented to present the greatest possible discontinuity density difference to the rays. The greatest dimension of the suspected discontinuity must be parallel to the radiation beam and equal to about 2% of the material thickness.

Safety considerations imposed by the use of X-rays and gamma rays must also be considered as a limitation. Compliance with safety regulations, mandatory in radiographic testing, is time consuming and requires costly space utilization and construction practices. Radiographic testing is a relatively expensive means of nondestructive testing. It is most economical when it is used to inspect easily handled material of simple geometry with high rates of test. It becomes expensive when it is used to examine thick specimens that require high energy potential equipment.

PRINCIPLES

Both X-rays and gamma rays are forms of electromagnetic radiation, differing from radio frequency and visible light by their wavelengths. The portion of the electromagnetic spectrum to which these radiations are conventionally assigned is shown in Fig. 6-29. X-rays and gamma rays having the same wavelength are physically identical.

Radiographic nondestructive testing is based on the following characteristics of X-rays and gamma rays:

- They are electromagnetic with energy inversely proportional to their wavelength.
- They have no electrical charge and no rest mass.
- In free space they travel in straight lines at the velocity of light.
- They can penetrate matter, the depth of penetration being dependent on the wavelength of the radiation and the nature of the matter being penetrated.
- They are absorbed by matter, the percentage of absorption being a function of the matter density and thickness, and the wavelength of the radiation.
- They are scattered by matter, the amount of scatter being a function of the matter density and the wavelength of the radiation.
- They can ionize matter.
- They can expose film by ionization.
- They can produce fluorescence in certain materials.
- They are invisible and incapable of detection by any of the body senses.
- They can impair or destroy living cells.

X-Rays

X-rays and electromagnetic waves of lower energy are generated when rapidly moving electrons interact with matter. When an electron of sufficient energy interacts with an orbital electron of an atom, a characteristic X-ray may be generated. It is called characteristic because its energy is determined by the

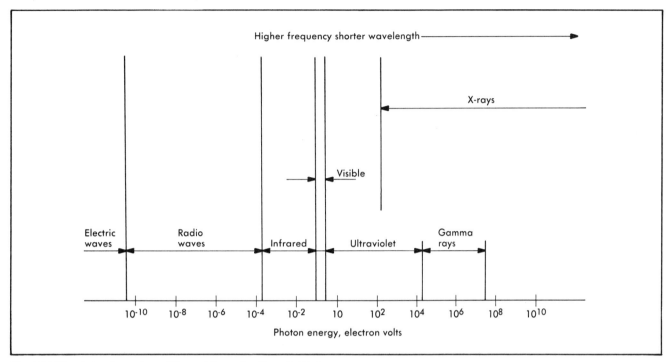

Fig. 6-29 The electronic spectrum. (*General Dynamics, Convair Div.*)

characteristic composition of the disturbed atom. When electrons of sufficient energy interact with the nuclei of atoms, bremsstrahlung (continuous X-rays) are generated. They are called continuous because their energy spectrum is continuous and is not entirely dependent on the disturbed atoms' characteristics. To create the conditions required for the generation of X-rays, there must be a source of electrons, a target for the electrons to strike, and a means of accelerating the electrons in the desired direction.

Gamma Rays

Gamma rays are distinguished from X-rays only by their source, rather than by their nature. They are emitted from the disintegrating nuclei of radioactive substances, and the quality (wavelength or penetration) of the radiation cannot be controlled by the user. Some gamma-ray-emitting radioactive isotopes, such as radium, occur naturally. Others, such as cobalt 60, are artificially produced. In industrial radiography the artificial radioactive isotopes are used almost exclusively as sources of gamma radiation.

The strength of a gamma ray source is measured in terms of the number of nuclei that decay (emit one or more gamma rays) each second. A 1 curie source undergoes 3.7×10^7 disintegrations per second. The strength of the source declines exponentially with time; the time required to drop to one half its initial value is called its half-life.

FILM

Radiographic film consists of a thin, transparent plastic sheet coated with an emulsion of gelatin containing a radiation-sensitive silver compound. On the average, the gelatin emulsion is usually applied to both sides of the plastic sheet in layers about 0.0005″ (0.013 mm) thick. For certain applications the gelatin emulsion is only applied to one side of the sheet. Coating the sheet on both sides doubles the amount of radiation-sensitive silver compound on the sheet, thus increasing the film speed and contrast. It also eliminates parallax problems when looking at very small discontinuities under magnification.

When X-rays, gamma rays, or light strike the grains of the sensitive silver compound in the emulsion, a change takes place in the physical structure of the grains. This change is of such a nature that it cannot be detected by ordinary physical methods; however when the exposed film is treated with a chemical solution, a reaction takes place, causing the formation of black metallic silver. It is this silver, suspended in the gelatin on both sides of the base, that constitutes the image.

Because the radiation source, the specimen, and the conditions of exposure determine the amount of radiation reaching the film at any given point, the radiographer is primarily concerned with those film characteristics that determine the density and sharpness of the processed film image in the finished radiograph. The usefulness of any radiograph is measured by its impact on the human eye. Areas of high density (areas exposed to relatively large amounts of radiation) will appear dark gray; areas of light density (areas exposed to less radiation) will appear light gray. The density difference between any two film areas is known as contrast. The sharpness of the film image is known as definition. Successful interpretation of any radiograph relies on contrast and definition detectable by the eye.

Radiographic contrast is a combination of subject contrast and film contrast. For any particular specimen, radiographic contrast depends on radiation energy applied (penetrating quality), film contrast characteristics, exposure (the product of radiation intensity and time), use of screens, film processing, and scattered radiation.

Subject contrast is the ratio of radiation intensities passing through any two selected portions of a specimen. Homogeneous specimens of little thickness variation have low subject

RADIOGRAPHIC TESTING

contrast. Those of large thickness variation usually have high subject contrast. Subject contrast is determined by specimen density and thickness and the radiation energy applied. Normally, as the energy of the applied radiation is lowered, the subject contrast is increased. High subject contrast is desirable except when detail is lost in the extremely dark and light areas of the radiograph.

The ability of film to detect and record different radiation exposures as differences in density is called film contrast. Radiographic film is fabricated with a variety of emulsions that give different film contrasts and other properties, such as speed and graininess. The film contrast values of any particular film are usually expressed as a relationship between film exposure and the resulting film density. The relationship is expressed in the form of film characteristic curves.

Radiographic films are available in a number of different types of packages, each ideally suited for particular classes of radiography. The most popular form is to have the film packaged as individual sheets; the sheets may also be enclosed in an individual paper folder (interleaved). Other forms in which radiographic film is packaged are light-tight envelopes, envelopes with either lead oxide or lead screens, and long rolls.

The selection of a film for the radiograph of any particular part depends on the thickness and material of the specimen and on the voltage range of the available X-ray machine. In addition, the choice is also affected by the relative importance of high radiographic quality or short exposure time. Film contrast, speed, and graininess are interrelated; fast films usually have large grains and poor resolution, whereas slow films have fine grain and good resolution. Therefore, though it is economically advantageous to make exposures as short as possible, the use of fast film is limited by the graininess that can be tolerated in the radiograph. Film manufacturers have created films of various characteristics, each designed for a specific purpose.

PROCESS DESCRIPTION

Radiographic testing, like other NDT techniques, follows a set pattern of events to give consistent test results. The three primary steps in RT are exposing the specimen to X-rays or gamma rays, processing the exposed film (radiograph), and viewing and interpreting the radiograph.

Exposure

The diagram in Fig. 6-30 shows the essential features in the exposure of a radiograph. The focal spot is a small area in the X-ray tube from which the radiation emanates. In gamma radiography, it is the size of the radioactive material that is the source of radiation. In either case the radiation proceeds in straight lines to the object; some of the X-rays pass through and others are absorbed, the amount transmitted depending on the nature of the material and its thickness. For example, if the object is a steel casting having a void formed by a gas bubble, the void results in a reduction of the total thickness of steel to be penetrated. Hence, more radiation will pass through the section containing the void than through the surrounding metal. A dark spot, corresponding to the projected position of the void, will appear on the film when it is developed; thus a radiograph is a kind of shadow picture, the darker regions on the film representing the more penetrable parts of the object and the lighter regions representing those more opaque to X-radiation or gamma radiation.

In general, the density of any radiographic image depends on the amount of radiation absorbed by the sensitive emulsion of

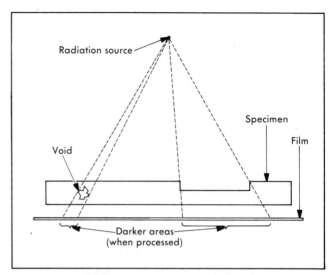

Fig. 6-30 Basic radiographic process. (*General Dynamics, Convair Div.*)

the film. This amount of radiation in turn depends on the total amount of radiation emitted by the X-ray tube or gamma ray source, the amount of radiation reaching the specimen, the proportion of the radiation that passes through the specimen, and the intensifying action of screens, if they are used.

Emitted radiation. The total amount of radiation emitted by an X-ray tube depends on tube current (milliamperage), kilovoltage, inherent filtration of the X-ray window, and the time the tube is energized. When the other operating conditions are constant, a change in milliamperage causes a corresponding change in the intensity of the radiation emitted. The kilovoltage applied to the X-ray tube primarily affects the energy (wavelength) of the beam and also the intensity of the beam to a lesser degree. As the kilovoltage is raised, X-rays of shorter wavelength, and hence of more penetrating power, are produced. As would be expected, the total amount of radiation emitted at a certain kilovoltage and milliamperage is directly proportional to the time the tube is energized.

The product of the milliamperage and time is often referred to as the exposure factor or rate. Algebraically, this is expressed by the equation:

$$E = Mt \tag{3}$$

where:

E = exposure factor, mA/min or mA/s
M = tube current, mA
t = exposure time, min or s

Therefore the amount of radiation from a given source remains constant if the exposure remains constant.

The total amount of radiation emitted from a gamma ray source during exposure depends on the activity of the source (stated in curies) and the time of exposure. The intensity is approximately proportional to the activity of the source. Because gamma ray energy is fixed by the nature of the isotope, there is no variable to correspond to the kilovoltage factor in X-radiography. Penetrating power can only be changed by changing the gamma ray source.

Radiation reaching the specimen. The radiation intensity reaching the specimen varies inversely with the square of the distance between the X-ray tube or source and the detector (film). This relationship is known as the inverse square law. Mathematically, the inverse square law is expressed as:

$$\frac{I_1}{I_2} = \frac{D_2^{\,2}}{D_1^{\,2}} \qquad (4)$$

where I_1 and I_2 are the intensities at distances D_1 and D_2, respectively. The inverse square law is used when computing radiographic exposures and safety procedures.

Radiation absorption. When X-rays or gamma rays strike an absorber, some of the radiation is absorbed, and another portion passes through the specimen. It is the intensity variation of the transmitted radiation from area to area in the specimen that forms the useful image in a radiograph. However, not all the radiation is either completely removed from the beam or transmitted. Some is deviated within the specimen from its original direction—that is, it is scattered and is non-image-forming. This scattered radiation, if not carefully controlled, will expose the film and tend to obscure the useful radiographic image.

The X-ray absorption of a specimen depends on its thickness, on its density, and most important of all, on the atomic nature of the material. The thicker or the more dense of two specimens having similar composition will absorb the most radiation, necessitating an increase in kilovoltage or exposure rate, or both, to produce the same photographic result. However, the atomic elements in a specimen usually exert a far greater effect on X-ray absorption than either the thickness or the density. Like X-ray absorption, gamma ray absorption also depends on specimen thickness, density, and composition.

Source-to-film distance. Because source size (focal spot) is usually within acceptable dimensions on most equipment, the selection of the correct source-to-film distance (SFD) permits good radiography. In general, the term *source-to-film distance* is used with gamma ray equipment, and the term *target-to-film distance* is used with X-ray equipment. For this discussion, the two terms are considered synonymous.

Three factors must be considered when selecting the source-to-film distance: (1) source size, (2) source side of specimen to film distance (essentially the specimen thickness if the specimen is in contact with the film), and (3) the maximum allowable geometric unsharpness (Ug) specified in the radiographic procedure. If a maximum geometric unsharpness value is not available, 0.020″ (0.5 mm) would be an acceptable value to use for a specimen thickness under 2″ (50 mm).

Geometric unsharpness is the fuzziness or "shadow" around a radiographic image. This area of unsharpness, also called the penumbra, results from the geometry relationship between the source size, the source-to-specimen distance, and the source side of the specimen to film distance. This relationship is illustrated in Fig. 6-31 and expressed in the equation:

$$Ug = \frac{ft}{d} \qquad (5)$$

where:

Ug = geometric unsharpness, in. (mm)
 f = diameter of source (focal spot), in. (mm)
 t = distance from the source side of the specimen to the film (specimen thickness if in contact with the film), in. (mm)
 d = distance from source to specimen, in. (mm)

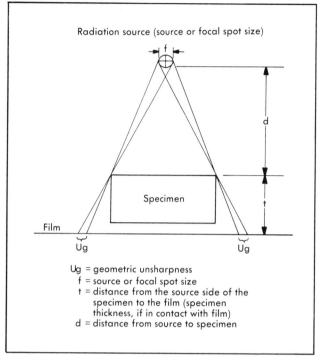

Fig. 6-31 Geometric construction for determining geometric unsharpness.

To obtain minimum geometric unsharpness, the radiation source must be small, the distance from the specimen to the film must be as small as possible, and the distance from the source to the specimen must be relatively great. In addition, it is essential that the radiation beam be normal to the plane of the film to minimize unsharpness. If there is too much geometric unsharpness, the radiograph will be uninterpretable, and the image densities on the radiograph will not be in agreement with the full specimen thickness.

Source-to-film distance can also be estimated with a rule of thumb. The SFD should not be less than 7-10 times the specimen thickness. These two methods of determining SFD are acceptable for most applications of radiography except when thin specimens are radiographed. Commonly used distances for thin specimens are from 18″ (900 mm) and up.

Exposure charts. Exposure charts exist for both X-rays and gamma rays. X-ray exposure charts show the relationship between material thickness, kilovoltage, and exposure time (see Fig. 6-32). Exposure charts are accurate for determining exposures in the radiography of material with uniform thickness, but they serve only as rough guides for objects, such as complicated castings, having wide variations of thickness.

Exposure charts are usually available from manufacturers of X-ray equipment. Because these charts cannot be used for different X-ray machines unless suitable correction factors are applied, individual laboratories sometimes prepare their own. Any given exposure chart applies to a set of specific conditions. These fixed conditions are the following:

- The X-ray machine used.
- The X-ray energies used. A family of curves are usually drawn on a single chart.
- A certain source-film distance.

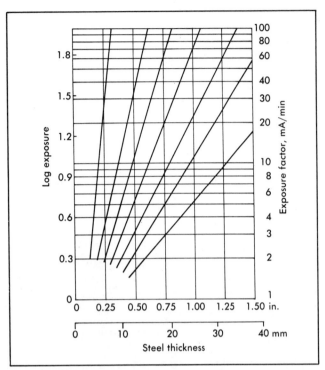

Fig. 6-32 Typical X-ray exposure chart for steel. This chart has been designed for a certain type of film, for use with lead screens, and at a film density of 1.5. Source-to-film distance is 40″ (1000 mm). (*Eastman Kodak Co.*)

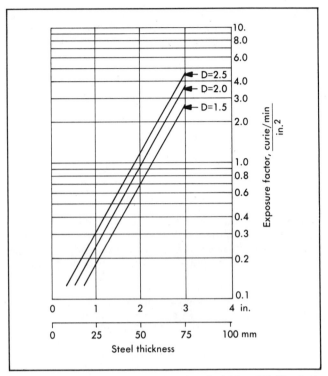

Fig. 6-33 Typical gamma ray exposure chart for iridium 192. The chart is designed for a certain type of film. (*Eastman Kodak Co.*)

- A particular film type.
- Processing conditions used.
- The film density on which the chart is based.
- The type of screens (if any) that are used.

A typical gamma ray exposure chart is similar to X-ray exposure charts. However, with gamma rays, there is no variable factor corresponding to the kilovoltage. Therefore, a gamma ray exposure chart contains one line, or several parallel lines, each of which corresponds to a particular film type, film density, or source-film distance (see Fig. 6-33). Gamma ray exposure guides are also available in the form of linear or circular slide rules. These contain scales on which can be set the various factors of specimen thickness, source strength, amount of radiation needed to expose film to desired density, and source-film distance and from which exposure time can be read.

Processing

Once a radiographic exposure has been made, the film must be processed so that the latent image produced by the radiation becomes visible. All of the procedures involved in making a radiograph are important because processing errors can make an otherwise worthwhile radiograph useless. Each step in film processing is dependent on the step preceding it and, in turn, affects those following. Processing techniques can be divided into manual processing and automated processing.

To obtain consistently good results, the following general precautions must be observed in processing radiographic film:

- Maintain chemical concentrations, solution temperatures, and processing times within prescribed limits.
- Use equipment, tanks, trays, and holders that withstand the chemical action of the processing solutions without contaminating the solutions.
- Equip the darkroom with suitable safeguards and lighting controls to avoid fogging film.
- Maintain thorough cleanliness.

Manual processing. If the volume of work is small or if time is of little importance, radiographs may be developed by hand. The most common method of manual processing is known as the tank method.

In the tank method, the processing solutions and wash water are in tanks deep enough for the film to be suspended vertically. Prior to processing, the film is removed from the film holder used during exposure. This removal is accomplished under darkroom conditions to avoid film fog. The film is grasped by its edges or corners to avoid bending, wrinkling, or crimping while handling. The film is then placed in a processing holder that holds the film firmly by each of its four corners and is designed to fit the dimensions of the processing tanks. Once placed in the processing holder, the film is ready for processing. The five separate steps in the tank method are development, arresting development, fixing, washing, and drying.

Development. In development, the silver bromide particles in the exposed portion of the film emulsion are reduced to metallic silver. This process commences when film is placed in the developer solution. The amount of silver bromide changed is a function of time and the chemical strength and temperature of the solution. Assuming that the chemical strength remains constant, the density of the radiographic image created through the developing process is proportional to the length of time the film remains in the solution and inversely proportional to the solution temperature. To obtain consistent results, the temperature is kept within narrow limits, and the development time is determined by the type of film being processed. In practical applications, the contrast and density desired in industrial radiographs is obtained with a solution temperature of 68° F (20° C) and a development time between 5 and 8 minutes.

Arresting development. When film is removed from the developing solution, a quantity of the solution remains within the emulsion, and the developing action will continue until the solution is removed. Excess developing solution is removed from the film by lightly dipping it in water before the stop bath. The stop bath, a solution of acetic acid and water, serves to remove this residual developer solution from the film and prevents uneven development and film streaking. The stop bath also neutralizes the alkaline remnants of the developer, permitting the acid in the fixer solution to function in the desired manner.

Fixing. If the unexposed silver bromide remaining in the film emulsion after completion of the developer and stop bath processes is not removed, it will darken on exposure to light and ruin the radiograph. The fixer, a mildly acid solution, dissolves and removes the silver bromide from the unexposed portions of the film without affecting the exposed portion. It also hardens the emulsion gelatin, permitting warm air drying.

When first placed in the fixer solution, the film becomes clouded from the dissolution of the silver bromide. In time, dependent on the strength of the fixer solution, the film clears, but the dissolution and hardening processes are still going on. The total time required for fixing is two to three times the amount of time necessary to clear the film. It should not exceed 15 minutes. Longer fixing time, indicative of a weak solution, can cause abnormal swelling of the film emulsion, improper hardening, overly long drying times, and loss of lesser film densities.

Washing. After fixing, films undergo a washing process to remove the fixer from the emulsion. The film is thoroughly immersed in running water so that all of the emulsion surface is in contact with constantly changing water. Best results are obtained with a water temperature of 65-70° F (18-24° C). The wash tank should be large enough to handle the number of films going through the developing and fixing processes without crowding, and the hourly flow of water should be between four and eight times the volume of the tank. Each film is washed for a period of time equal to twice the fixing time. When a number of films are proceeding through the processing cycle, each film is first placed in the drain end of the tank and then progressively moved toward the intake. This procedure ensures that the last wash any film receives is with fresh water.

After the film is washed, it is dipped in a tank containing a solution of water and a wetting agent. This solution breaks up bubbles on the film surface and prevents streaks from forming on the dried film.

Drying. The final step of film processing is drying, usually accomplished by hanging the film in a drying cabinet. Drying cabinets are designed to permit flow of heated and filtered air to reach both sides of the film. If no drying cabinet is available, the film may be air dried by hanging it in a position where air circulates freely.

Automatic processing. Automatic film processing machines are a processing system built around film, chemicals, and mechanics. They are used whenever the volume of work makes them economical. The machines accomplish all required processing; the only manual operation necessary is loading and unloading the film. Though the processing steps used in an automatic unit are the same as those for tank processing, the entire processing cycle is completed in less than 15 minutes. This high-speed processing is made possible by the use of special chemicals, continuous agitation of the film, maintenance of all solutions at relatively high temperatures, and drying with jets of heated air.

Radiograph Interpretation

A radiograph is useless unless properly interpreted. To properly interpret a radiograph, it is necessary to have a thorough knowledge of the entire procedure that has produced the radiograph: setup parameters, exposure parameters, film type, intensifying screens used, film development parameters, and the characteristics of the part radiographed. In addition, the interpreter must be thoroughly experienced and have access to suitable reference radiographs. A description of the various flaw indications that can be detected by RT is given in Table 6-11.[23]

The two basic overall parameters that the interpreter must know in regard to a given radiograph are the radiographic sensitivity and the definition. Radiographic sensitivity is measured in terms of the minimum percentage of the thickness of the subject item that corresponds to the least discernible change in photographic density of the final radiograph. Definition refers to the smallest discernible size (in lateral dimension) due to a change of given (equivalent) thickness. Both sensitivity and definition are established by the use of penetrameters.

The examination of the finished radiograph should be made under conditions that favor the best visibility of detail combined with a maximum of comfort and a minimum of fatigue for the interpreter. To be satisfactory for use in viewing radiographs, an illuminator must fulfill two basic requirements. First, it must provide light of an intensity that will illuminate the areas of interest in the radiograph to their best advantage, free from glare. Second, it must diffuse the light evenly over the entire viewing area. The color of the light is of no optical consequence, but most interpreters prefer bluish white. An illuminator incorporating several fluorescent tubes meets this requirement and is often used for viewing industrial radiographs of moderate density.

For routine viewing of high densities, one of the commercially available high-intensity illuminators should be used. These provide an adjustable light source, the maximum intensity of which allows viewing of densities of 4.0 or even higher. Such a high-intensity illuminator is especially useful for the examination of radiographs having a wide range of densities corresponding to a wide range of thicknesses in the object and when viewing double films.

The contrast sensitivity of the human eye (that is, the ability to distinguish small brightness differences) is greatest when the surroundings are of about the same brightness as the area of interest. Thus, to see the finest detail in a radiograph, the illuminator must be masked to avoid glare from bright light at the edges of the radiograph or transmitted by areas of low density. Subdued lighting, rather than total darkness, is preferable in the viewing room. The room illumination must be such that there are no troublesome reflections from the surface of the film under examination.

Special Techniques

Fluoroscopy. Fluoroscopy is the process in which an X-ray-produced image is observed visually on a fluorescent screen (see Fig. 6-34). It is a relatively low-cost, high-speed process and is

RADIOGRAPHIC TESTING

TABLE 6-11
Characteristics of Typical Flaws Detected by
Radiographic Testing

Flaw	Description
Gas holes	Appear on the radiograph as dark, smoothly outlined surfaces. When these holes are filled with dross, they appear less dark, and their outline is oftentimes less regular than that of a gas hole
Gas porosity	Appears on the radiograph as minute dark, round spots. Depending on the degree of severity, the minute round spots may be so small as to give radiographic indications varying from a fine granular appearance to those in which discrete round spots are clearly visible
Elongated voids	This condition is similar to that of round gas porosity except that the elongated shape of the voids gives it a more mottled appearance
Shrink porosity	Appears as a dark image on the radiograph similar to gas porosity, except that the voids are raggedly outlined structures
Shrinkage cavities	Appear as dark, irregularly outlined cavities. They may vary from small isolated cavities to relatively large ones. These cavities occur most often in the fillets and heavier parts of a casting
Inclusions	Appear on the radiograph as dark or light spots or areas. When inclusions are heavier or denser than the metal in which they occur, inclusions have lower image density than does the surrounding metal
Misruns	Appear on the radiograph as dark and mostly well-defined outlines
Segregation	Segregation of metal appears in light and dark blotches on the radiograph as an almost snowflake-like pattern
Cold shuts	Appear on the radiograph as well-defined intermittent or continuous dark lines
Cracks	Appear on radiographs as dark intermittent or continuous lines

easily adapted to production line requirements. Its disadvantages are the following:

- Cannot be used with specimens that are thick or of dense material because the intensity of the radiation passing through the specimen would be too low to sufficiently brighten the screen.

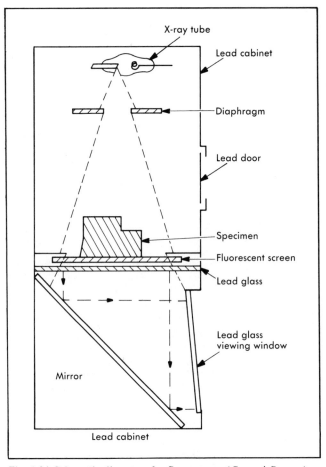

Fig. 6-34 Schematic diagram of a fluoroscope. (*General Dynamics, Convair Div.*)

- Relatively poor sensitivity because of the short source-to-screen distance required to obtain sufficient brightness and the low contrast and coarse grain of the screen.
- Subjects the operator to greater amounts of radiation than other radiographic methods.
- Is dependent on the human eye.
- Does not produce a permanent record.

Despite the foregoing disadvantages, fluoroscopy is widely used in applications where rapid scanning of articles for gross internal discontinuities or abnormal conditions is desirable. By use of fluoroscopy, a number of articles can be screened prior to submitting the lot to radiographic test; those with gross defects can be immediately rejected, with resultant cost savings.

Image intensifier. An extension of fluoroscopy involves the use of image intensifiers. An image intensifier is designed to overcome the disadvantages of fluoroscopy caused by the relatively low brightness of the image. It also serves to protect the operator from radiation. The image intensifier consists of an image tube and an optical system (see Fig. 6-35). The image tube converts the X-ray image on the fluorescent screen to electrons and accelerates and electrostatically focuses the electrons to produce the image on the smaller fluorescent screen. The optical system magnifies the image on the small screen causing it to appear as if the viewer were looking directly at a normal-sized screen.

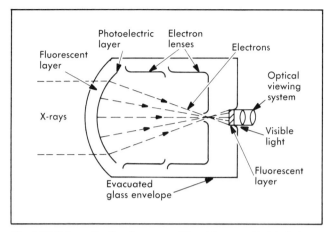

Fig. 6-35 Schematic of an image amplifier. (*Eastman Kodak Co.*)

The brightness amplification factor is the product of the reduction in screen area and the energy of electron acceleration. Dependent on image tube design and construction, this factor ranges from 100 to 1000. By use of a suitable camera and a closed-circuit television system, the X-ray image produced by the image amplifier may be viewed on a monitor screen; if desired, the image may be photographed to produce a permanent record.

Electronic imaging radioscopy (real-time imaging). Electronic imaging radioscopy is a relatively new technology that became available in the 1970s. It is basically a form of fluoroscopic inspection with extensive use of computers as a means of enhancing the images. Two system designs are commonly used with this technique: (1) closed system and (2) open system. The closed system consists of a tube-type image intensifier, a lens-coupled video camera, an optional image processor, and a video display terminal. It is similar in operation to the image intensifier described previously, but with image processing capabilities.

The open system consists of a camera enclosure that contains a fluorescent screen mounted in the opening port, a front reflective mirror, a lens, a very low light-level camera, and associated hardware necessary for mounting the items in the enclosure. Coupled to this enclosure is an image processor, a control computer, computer keyboard and terminal, and a video display terminal.

In an open system, X-rays are passed through the part being inspected and strike the fluorescent screen, causing an image to be formed in visible light. This light is reflected from the mirror and is gathered by a lens and then viewed by the camera. The camera signal is sent to the image processor, where it is digitized and processed. The resultant image is displayed on the video terminal for interpretation. For recording purposes, these images can be stored on videotapes or on hard or floppy disks.

Xeroradiography. Xeroradiography is a "dry" radiographic process that uses electrostatically charged plates to record an X-ray image. The basis of the process is the peculiar characteristic of selenium that causes it to become a relatively good electrical conductor when exposed to X-rays. The plate used to record the X-ray image consists of a thin layer of selenium bonded to a backing plate of aluminum. Under darkroom conditions, an electrostatic charge is placed on the selenium by passing a high-potential charging bar across the surface of the plate at a uniform velocity. The selenium, having good insulation properties, will retain the charge. The sensitized (charged) plate is then

placed in a light-tight cassette, or holder, and used in X-ray exposures in the same way as film.

If a permanent record is desired of a xeroradiograph, the image may be photographed or transferred to a special adhesive white paper. The transfer process uses paper coated with a plastic adhesive. When the paper is pressed on the xeroradiograph, it lifts the powder image from the selenium plate. The image is permanently affixed to the paper by applying sufficient heat to soften the plastic coating and then permitting it to cool.

Stereoradiography and double exposure (parallax). A single radiographic image has length and width, but does not have perspective. When it is necessary to know the depth of a flaw in a thick specimen, two radiographic methods are available, stereoradiography and double exposure (parallax).

Stereoradiography. Stereoradiography gives the viewer a three-dimensional effect by use of two radiographs of the specimen and a stereoscope. The two radiographs are made with two different positions of the X-ray tube in relation to the specimen. The two positions are displaced from each other by a distance equal to the separation of a human's eyes. The stereoscope, through optical means, permits the viewer to view the two radiographs simultaneously while allowing each eye of the viewer to see only one of the radiographs. The right eye sees the image of the right shift position of the X-ray tube, and the left eye sees the image of the left shift position. The brain combines and merges the two images into one in which true perspective and spatial relationships are apparent. Stereography is little used in industrial radiography, but is of value in flaw location or structural visualization (see Fig. 6-36).

Double exposure. Double exposure (parallax) methods of determining flaw depth in a specimen are more positive than stereoradiography because they are based on physical measurements of the radiographic image and do not depend on human depth perception. One such method is illustrated in Fig. 6-37. Lead markers M_1 and M_2 are respectively attached to the front and back surfaces of the specimen. Two exposures, each one approximately one half the time required for a normal exposure, are made. The distance between F_1 and F_2 is predetermined, and the tube is located at F_1 for one exposure and at F_2 for the other. The position of the film image of the flaw and of M_1 will perceptibly change as a result of the tube shift, while the M_2 image shift will be small if not imperceptible.

Flash radiography. Flash radiography permits the observation of high-speed events in opaque materials. It is used primarily for observation of explosive or rupture processes. Analogous to flash photography, flash radiography freezes the motion of projectiles and high-speed machinery by use of high voltage, high current, and extremely short time duration exposures. The tube and the high-voltage circuits of flash radiography equipment differ in design from conventional X-ray equipment. The tube has a cold cathode, and electron emission is initiated by a third electrode located near the cathode. The high-voltage circuit contains capacitors that are charged to peak voltage and then discharged in a high-voltage pulse. Tube current reaches as high as 2000 A, but because of the fractional microsecond duration of the exposure, the tube is not damaged.

In-motion radiography. In-motion radiography is any radiographic method wherein the source of radiation, the specimen, or the film is moving during the exposure. Many special in-motion radiographic techniques are in use, each of them designed to serve a specific purpose and application. These techniques use mechanical arrangements to move the X-ray machine, the specimen, or in many cases, motion picture

RADIOGRAPHIC TESTING

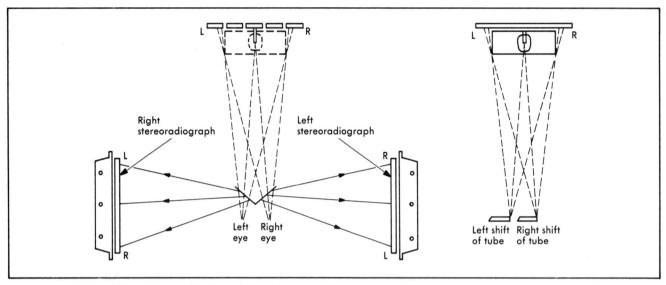

Fig. 6-36 Stereoscopic radiography. (*Eastman Kodak Co.*)

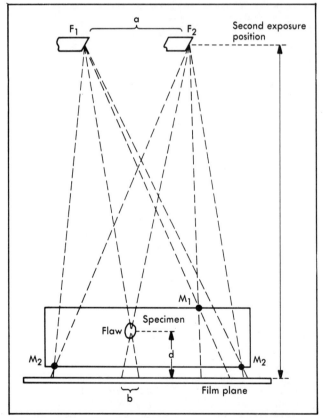

Fig. 6-37 Diagram of parallax technique. (*Eastman Kodak Co.*)

cameras loaded with X-ray film. The one requirement for in-motion radiography is that during exposure the position of the film and the specimen relative to each other must remain fixed. This requirement is met by synchronizing the movement of the specimen and the film or by fixing the specimen and film in position and moving only the source of radiation.

EQUIPMENT

Before selecting any equipment for radiographic testing, an analysis of the specimen for inspection should be performed. This analysis would involve determining the types of material being tested and the maximum and minimum thicknesses. The types of material and specimen thicknesses being tested dictate the X-ray potential or gamma ray energy required to achieve sufficient penetration. Consideration must also be given to the size and weight of the specimen, the steps in the production process where inspection is best suited, and the quantity to be inspected in a given time. The type of manufacturing facility and the size, weight, and quantity of products to be inspected establish equipment requirements.

Selection

Because of its flexibility and fewer radiation hazards, X-radiography is preferred to gamma radiography. Gamma radiography is usually selected for industrial applications that involve the following:

- High radiation energy requirements when high-energy X-ray machines are not available.
- Low testing rates.
- Simultaneous exposure of many specimens.
- Confined areas where X-ray cannot be used.
- Field inspections in areas where electrical power is difficult to obtain.

Selection of equipment for a particular test consists of the following related decisions:

- Selection of RT as a test method.
- Selection of X-radiography or gamma radiography.
- Selection of specific X-ray or gamma ray equipment.

Additional factors to consider are available equipment, the time allotted for the test, and the number or frequency of similar specimen tests.

Ideally, there is a best equipment selection for any radiographic test. Practically, most radiography is accomplished by using the equipment available. The equipment lends itself to numerous adaptations, and by knowledgeable choice of film and exposure, any particular equipment can be used for a variety of tasks. For this reason, the capabilities of individual X-ray machines and isotope cameras overlap in many areas of test. Except in large production installations or in a test laboratory, it is impractical to have multiple radiographic equipment. Therefore, it is the responsibility of radiographic test and quality assurance personnel to ensure that the equipment and techniques selected are capable of performing the required task.

X-Ray Equipment

The generation of X-rays requires a source of free electrons, a means of moving the electrons in the right direction, and a suitable material for the electrons to strike. The two primary elements in any X-ray machine are the X-ray tube and the power supply. Other components such as shielding, tubeheads, control panels, and coolers are designed to support the function of the tube or to meet safety requirements.

Factors to consider when selecting X-ray equipment are radiation energy, radiation output, source size, and range of operation. It is usually best to obtain a unit that emits a spectrum containing a large portion of the short wavelengths. Longer wavelength X-rays that improve radiographic contrast can be obtained by operating the equipment at low energies. With the designs being equal, an X-ray machine that has the highest output in roentgens per minute at a given distance is the best selection. Machines with the smallest target area, yet capable of providing a useful quantity of radiation, have the best sensitivity. A tradeoff must be made regarding the operating range of the machine and its cost; machines with large ranges are the most expensive.

X-ray tube. The productive portion of X-ray equipment is the tube. It consists of two electrodes, the cathode and the anode, enclosed in a tube envelope (see Fig. 6-38). When current is applied, the filament portion of the cathode functions as a source of free electrons and the anode as the target on which the electrons strike. X-ray tubes that are equipped to produce two size focal spots have two filaments; one of the filaments is larger than the other.

Tube envelope. The tube envelope is constructed of glass or ceramics that have a high melting point to withstand the extreme heat generated at the anode. Structurally, the envelope

has sufficient strength to resist the implosive force of the high-vacuum interior. A high-vacuum environment for the tube element is necessary to:

- Prevent oxidation of the electrode materials.
- Permit ready passage of the electron beam without ionization of gas within the tube.
- Provide electrical insulation between the electrodes.

The shape of the envelope is determined by the electrical circuitry used with the tube and the desired tube use. Electrical connections through the envelope to the tube's electrodes are made through insulation material able to withstand the temperature, pressure, and electrical forces of the X-ray generating process, or by connection to the envelope itself. Electrical connections to the envelope are accomplished by the use of metal alloys that have a coefficient of thermal expansion similar to that of the glass or ceramic. The alloy is fused with, and becomes part of, the envelope.

Cathode. The cathode of the X-ray tube incorporates a focusing cup and the filament or filaments. Usually constructed of very pure iron and nickel, the focusing cup functions as an electrostatic lens whose purpose is to direct the electrons in a beam toward the anode. The electron-emitting portion of the cathode is the filament, which is brought to the required high temperature by the flow of electrical current through it. The filament is usually a coil of tungsten wire, which has the desired electrical and thermal characteristics. The placement of the filament or filaments within the focusing cup and the shape of the cup determine the dimensions of the electron beam and the resultant area of X-ray emission at the target.

Because of the electrical characteristics of tungsten, a small flow of current through the filament suffices to heat it to temperatures that cause electron emission. Any change in the voltage applied to the filament varies the filament current and the number of electrons emitted. On most X-ray machines, control of tube current is obtained by regulating the voltage applied across the filament through transformer action.

Anode. The anode of the X-ray tube is a metallic electrode of high electrical and thermal conductivity. Usually, it is made of copper with the portion directly facing the cathode being tungsten, gold, or platinum. It is these latter materials that function as the target.

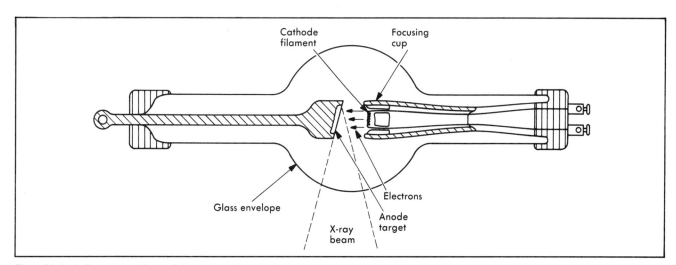

Fig. 6-38 Basic X-ray tube. (*General Dynamics, Convair Div.*)

CHAPTER 6

RADIOGRAPHIC TESTING

Copper and tungsten are the most common anode materials because copper has the necessary electrical and thermal characteristics and tungsten is an economically feasible, dense material with a high melting point. A dense target material is required to ensure a maximum number of collisions when the electron beam strikes the target. Material with a high melting point is necessary to withstand the heat of X-ray generation.

The sharpness of a radiographic film image is partly determined by the size of the radiation source (focal spot). The electron beam in most X-ray tubes is focused so that a rectangular area of the target is bombarded by the beam. Usually the anode target is set at an angle, and the projected size of the bombarded area, as viewed from the specimen, is smaller than the actual focal spot. This projected area of the electron beam is the effective focal spot. In theory, the optimum tube would contain a pinpoint focal spot. In practice, the size to which the focal spot can be reduced is limited by the heat generated in target bombardment. If the focal spot is reduced beyond certain limits, the heat at the point of impact destroys the target.

X-rays are radiated in all directions from the tube target and, once created, cannot be focused or otherwise directed. The direction of useful X-radiation is determined by the target positioning at the tube anode and the placement of lead shielding about the tube. With selected positioning of the target and variations in shielding placement, almost any beam configuration desired can be obtained.

Power supply. The operating voltage (difference in electrical potential between the cathode and anode) applied to an X-ray tube determines the penetrating effect of X-radiation. In short, the higher the voltage, the greater the electron velocity and the shorter the wavelengths of the generated X-rays. The high voltage necessary to generate short waves of great penetrating power is obtained from transformers, electrostatic generators, or accelerators.

Iron-core transformers. The majority of X-ray equipment used in industrial radiography uses iron-core transformers to produce required high voltages. The basic limiting factors to iron-core transformer use are their size and weight. Iron-core transformers are used to produce voltages up to 420 kV, usually in self-rectified circuits; however, they are often used with half and full-wave rectifiers, voltage doublers, and constant-potential circuits. Iron-core transformers in modern X-ray equipment are either mounted in tubehead tank units with the tube or are separately housed.

Resonant transformers. In the 250-4000 kV range, the resonant transformer is effectively employed. Similar to iron-core transformers, resonant transformers produce high voltage from a low-voltage input, but the use of a resonant secondary lends itself to a compact lightweight design. The X-ray tube is mounted in the central axis of the transformer.

Electrostatic generators. Electrostatic generator X-ray equipment is designed to operate in the 500-6000 kV range. Two motor-driven pulleys drive a nonconducting charging belt. Electrons from the charging point pass to the belt and are transferred to the corona cap at the corona point. The accumulated high voltage at the corona cap serves to accelerate the beam of electrons emitted by the filament. The equipotential plates distribute the high voltage evenly along the length of the tube. To minimize high voltage leakage, the generator is enclosed in a pressurized gastight chamber.

Linear accelerators. Linear accelerators utilize radio frequency energy in a tuned waveguide to produce an induced field, which is directly related to the length of the waveguide sections and the radio frequency. By selection of waveguide lengths and use of a known frequency, electrons injected into the guide are accelerated toward the target by the action of the constantly changing induced field. Theoretically, electrons may be accelerated to velocities approaching the speed of light by this means with resultant generation of extremely short wavelength and high-energy X-rays. In practice, the length of linear accelerator required to obtain electron velocities equivalent to those used in industrial radiography is about 6' (1.8 m).

Betatron accelerators. The betatron accelerates electrons in a circular path by magnetic induction. Its operation is based on transformer principles, because an alternating current applied to the primary (excitation) coil produces a strong variation in the magnetic field in the core of the doughnut-shaped secondary. The magnets strengthen this magnetic field. As the magnetic field starts to increase in strength, electrons are injected from a hot-cathode injection gun into the "doughnut." The voltage induced by the increasing field causes the electrons to accelerate. The electrons will circle within the doughnut thousands of times in one cycle of applied voltage, increasing their energy with each rotation. At the moment the magnetic field is at its peak and is about to decrease, a pulse of current is applied to an auxiliary coil that distorts the magnetic field and ejects the electrons from their circular path. The high-energy electrons strike the target and produce X-rays of extremely short wavelength and great penetration power.

Gamma Ray Equipment

Gamma rays are produced by the nuclei of isotopes undergoing disintegration because of their instability. Radiation from these materials cannot be shut off. Therefore, gamma ray equipment is designed to provide radiation-safe storage and remote handling of the radioisotope source. Most equipment used in the production of gamma rays consists of the radioactive source and the gamma ray projector.

Sources. The three most commonly used sources are cobalt 60, iridium 192, and thulium 170. Cobalt 60 is supplied in the form of a capsuled pellet and may be obtained in different sizes. It is used for radiography of steel, copper, brass, and other medium weight metals of thicknesses ranging from 1 to 10" (25-250 mm).

Iridium 192 is used for radiography of steel and similar metals of thicknesses between 1/4 and 3" (6 and 75 mm). Its relatively low-energy radiation and its high specific activity combine to make it an easily shielded, strong radiation source of small physical size. Like cobalt 60, iridium 192 is also available in capsuled pellet.

Thulium 170 is the best isotope known for the radiography of thin metals. Because it has soft-wave radiation, thulium 170 can be contained in small cameras. It is usually supplied in capsules containing thulium oxide (Tm_2O_3) powder.

Because all the radioisotope material is producing gamma rays, the focal spot in gamma radiography is the surface area of the material as viewed from the specimen. For this reason, it is desirable that the gamma ray source be as small as possible. Most isotopes in gamma radiography are cylinders whose diameter and length are approximately equal. When the isotope source is not a right cylinder, it is necessary to place the smallest area of the source parallel to the plane of the specimen for maximum sharpness of film image.

Gamma ray projector. Gamma ray projectors store the radioactive source when not in use and provide a means of exposing the specimen and film to radiation. Most projectors are made from a mass of heavy metal, such as lead or uranium, and contain a passage leading to its geometric center. The amount of metal used is predetermined to reduce the radiation at the surface to a safe level.

Two styles of projectors are commonly used in gamma radiography. The first style stores the radioactive source in a shield case assembly when it is not being used. When exposure is required, the source is moved to the tip of the guide tube with a reel assembly (see Fig. 6-39).

The second style of projector does not require the source to be moved from the shield case assembly for exposure. Instead, a cone section of the case is designed to swing away, permitting the unobstructed escape of radiation (see Fig. 6-40). Both styles of projectors are also referred to as a radioisotope camera.

Accessory Equipment

To produce high-quality radiographs, accessory equipment is required.

Diaphragms, collimators, and cones. Diaphragms, collimators, and cones are thicknesses of lead fitted to the tubehead of X-ray equipment or built to contain a gamma ray source and designed to limit the area of radiation. They decrease the amount of scatter radiation by limiting the beam to the desired specimen area. Many X-ray machines have built-in adjustable diaphragms designed so that the beam at a fixed distance covers a standard film size area.

Filters. Filters are sheets of high atomic number metal, usually brass, beryllium, copper, steel, or lead, placed in the X-ray beam at the tubehead. By absorbing the "soft" radiation of the beam, filters reduce subject contrast, permitting a wide range of specimen thicknesses to be recorded with one exposure, and eliminate scatter caused by soft radiation. Filters are particularly useful in radiography of specimens with adjacent thick and thin sections.

Another device similar to filters is a beam flattener. Beam flatteners are made with predetermined varying thicknesses and are designed to preferentially absorb portions of the X-ray beam.

Screens. In general, less than 1% of the available radiation energy is absorbed by the film to produce an image. Screens are used to convert the unused energy into a form that can be absorbed by the film. The two types of screens commonly used are fluorescent and lead. Fluorescent screens emit light that lessens the exposure necessary to produce a given density. Lead screens emit electrons under the action of X-rays and gamma rays, thus permitting a shorter exposure than would be required without lead screens.

Masking material. Masking is the practice of covering, or surrounding, portions of the specimen with highly absorbent material during exposure. Masking reduces the specimen exposure in the masked areas, eliminating much scatter. Commonly used masking materials are lead, barium clay, and metallic shot.

Masking materials should be thick enough so that radiation absorption of the material is appreciably greater than that of the specimen; otherwise, it will become a source of scatter. In any circumstance, the sole purpose of masking is to limit scattered radiation by reducing the area of or about the specimen exposed to the primary beam.

Penetrameters. The penetrameter is a device whose image on a radiograph is used to determine radiographic quality level (sensitivity). It is not intended for use in judging the size or in establishing acceptance limits of discontinuities.

The standard ASTM penetrameter is a rectangle of metal with three drilled holes of set diameter. It is composed of

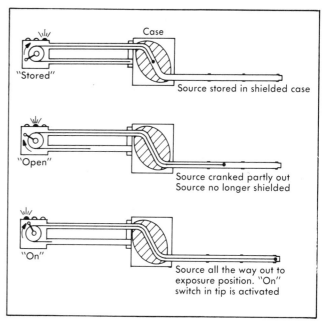

Fig. 6-39 Operation of a typical gamma ray emitter. (*General Dynamics, Convair Div.*)

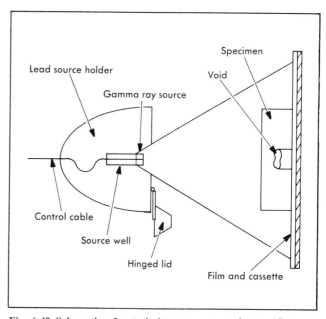

Fig. 6-40 Schematic of a typical gamma ray projector. (*Eastman Kodak Co.*)

material identical or radiographically similar to the material being radiographed. Each penetrameter is identified by an identification number that gives the maximum thickness of material for which the penetrameter is normally used or the thickness of the penetrameter in thousandths of an inch.

A number of other penetrameter designs are also in use. The German DIN (Deutsche Industrie-Norm) penetrameter is one that is widely used. It consists of a number of wires of various diameters sealed in a plastic envelope that carries the necessary identification symbols. The image quality is indicated by the thinnest wire visible on the radiograph. The system is such that only three penetrameters, each containing seven wires, can cover a very wide range of specimen thicknesses. Sets of DIN penetrameters are available in aluminum, copper, and steel. Thus a total of nine penetrameters is sufficient for the radiography of a wide range of materials and thicknesses.

Linear and angular measuring devices. Correct source-to-film distance and knowledge of specimen thicknesses are required for any radiographic setup. For these measurements, a 6″ machinist's scale and a tape measure are tools of the radiographer. When a task requires radiography at an angle other than that normal to the plane of the specimen, a plumb bob and protractor may be used to determine the correct angular setup.

Positioning devices. Except for special techniques such as in-motion radiography or the position of the source (either X-ray or gamma ray), the specimen and the film should remain fixed during exposure. With X-ray equipment, the floor, a table, or any stable surface may suffice to support the specimen. With gamma ray equipment, support of the specimen is identical with that of X-ray, and specially designed holders (usually tripods) are used to position the cable containing the source. Any positioning arrangement complying with safety considerations and that does not cause excess scatter radiation is acceptable.

Identification and orientation markers. To permit correct interpretation of the finished radiograph, the specimen and the radiograph must be marked so that the specimen and its orientation can be identified with the radiograph. This is accomplished by affixing lead numbers or letters to or adjacent to the specimen during exposure and marking the specimen in identical fashion with a marking pen or by scribing. The lead numbers or letters that are attached with masking tape appear on the radiograph. Comparison of the radiograph with the marked specimen eliminates any possibility of wrong identification.

Area shielding equipment. The control of scatter radiation is effected only by proper use of shielding techniques. Areas in which radiography takes place must be adequately protected against both side and back scatter. In permanent installations, this is accomplished by use of lead-shielded rooms or compartments. When permanent installations are not available, the radiographer uses lead screens and places them so that areas reached by the primary radiation are shielded. The area immediately beneath or behind the film should always be covered with lead.

Darkroom Equipment

The loading bench, film storage cabinets and bins, processing tanks, and film dryers are standard darkroom equipment. The "dry" and "wet" areas of the darkroom are separated to prevent inadvertent water or chemical damage to film.

The relative sizes of the tanks fixes the amount of work that can be done. A 5 gal (20 L) developer tank, at normal development times, can handle approximately 40 films per hour. Developer and stop bath tanks should be the same size, fixer tanks twice as large, and wash tanks at least four times as large.

Film drying cabinets should have a filtered air intake, film racks, exhaust fan, and a heating element. Because drying is the last processing step, the dryer may be conveniently located for ease in film handling.

SAFETY

One of the most important considerations in the X-ray or gamma ray laboratory is the provision and exercise of adequate safeguards for the personnel. Because radiation cannot be detected by any of the human senses and its damaging effects do not become immediately apparent, personnel protection is dependent on detection devices and adequate shielding.

Any of the body tissues may be injured by excessive exposure to X-rays or gamma rays, the blood, the lens of the eye, and some internal organs being particularly sensitive. Unless exposure to X-rays or gamma rays is kept at a minimum, the cumulative effect may cause injury to the body. It is, therefore, essential that workers in the radiographic department be adequately protected against radiation at all times. Furthermore, protective measures should be so arranged that persons in nearby areas are also safe. Precautions should be particularly observed when radiography is done in the work areas of the shop rather than in a specially constructed department.

This section is designed to present some of the basic radiographic safety procedures, protection devices, and detection equipment. It is not an interpretation of government regulations, nor is it to be considered as a complete safety guide.

The United States Nuclear Regulatory Commission (USNRC) enforces safety regulations covering the handling and use of radioisotopes. The Interstate Commerce Commission, the Civil Aeronautics Board, and the United States Coast Guard enforce safety regulations covering the transportation of radioactive material. States also have similar regulations covering use, handling, and transportation of radioactive material and the use of X-ray devices. All of these regulations are designed to limit radiation exposure to safe levels and to afford protection for the general public. This government emphasis on safety practices indicates the mandatory nature of sure and certain safety practices in all radiation areas. The radiographer who is a licensee of the USNRC or who is employed by a licensee must have knowledge of and comply with all pertinent regulations. Radiography is safe, but it is only as safe as those working with it permit it to be.

Radiation Dose Measurement

For radiation safety purposes, the cumulative effect on the human body of radiation exposure is of primary concern. Because the damaging effects of radiation to living cells are dependent on both the type and the energy of the radiation to which they are exposed, it is impractical only to measure radiation quantitatively. For this reason, exposure is first measured in physical terms, and then a factor allowing for the relative biological effectiveness of different types and energies of radiation is applied.

The units used to measure radiation exposure are roentgen, rad, rbe, and rem.

Roentgen. The roentgen (r) is the unit measure of X-radiation or gamma radiation in air. It is defined as the quantity of radiation that will produce one electrostatic unit (esu) of charge in one cubic centimeter of air at standard pressure and temperature. One roentgen of radiation represents the absorption by ionization of approximately 83 ergs of radiation energy per gram of air. In practical application, the milliroentgen (mr), one thousandth of a roentgen, is often used. The roentgen is a physical measurement of X-radiation and gamma radiation quantity.

Rad. The rad (radiation absorbed dose) is the unit of measurement of radiation absorption by humans or other matter. It is defined as a measure of energy imparted to matter by ionizing radiation per unit mass of irradiated material at the place of interest and is equal to 100 ergs per gram. The roentgen applies only to X-rays and gamma rays; the rad applies to any type of radiation.

Rbe. The value assigned to various types of radiation, determined by the radiation's effect on the human body, is called rbe (relative biological effectiveness). Rbe values have been calculated by the National Committee on Radiation Protection.

Rem. The rem (roentgen equivalent man) is the unit used to define the biological effect of radiation on an individual. It represents the absorbed dose in rads multiplied by the relative biological effectiveness of the radiation absorbed.

Detection and Measurement Instruments

Various techniques, based on the characteristic effects of radiant energy on matter, are employed in detection and measurement devices. Chemical and photographic detection methods are used, as well as methods that measure the excitation effect of radiation on certain materials. In radiography, however, the instruments most commonly used for radiation detection and measurement rely on the ionization produced in a gas by radiation. Because the hazard of radiation is calculated in terms of total dose and dose rate, the instruments used for detection and measurement logically fall into two categories: (1) instruments that measure total dose exposure and (2) instruments that measure dose rate (radiation intensity).

Dose exposure instruments. Common instruments that measure the total amount of radiation received are pocket dosimeters, pocket chambers, and film badges. During radiographic operations, radiographers and their assistants should wear film badges and either pocket dosimeters or pocket chambers. If a pocket dosimeter or pocket chamber is discharged beyond its range, the individual's film badge should be processed immediately.

Dose rate instruments. Because of the number of instruments that would be required and the excessive amount of time necessary for their use, dosimeters and pocket chambers cannot be readily used for radiation area surveys. Such surveys require an instrument capable of obtaining and presenting an instantaneous measurement of radiation intensity. Two instruments in common use are the ionization chamber instrument and the Geiger counter.

Radiation Protection

Exposure to radiation may be caused by the direct beam from the X-ray tube or by scattered radiation arising from objects in the direct beam. The three primary means of controlling body exposure to radiation are time, distance, and shielding. In addition, it is important to clearly designate containers of radioactive materials, areas housing those containers, and areas exposed to radiation.

The USNRC requires a sign with the symbol shown in Fig. 6-41 to be placed in conspicuous locations in all exposure areas and on all containers in which radioactive materials are transported, stored, or used. On each sign, the word "Caution" or the word "Danger" must appear. Other wording required is determined by specific sign use. Area signs bear the phrases "Radiation Area," "High-Radiation Area," or "Airborne Radioactivity Area" as appropriate. Containers of radioactive materials and areas housing such containers must be marked with signs or labels bearing the radiation symbol and the words "Radioactive Material(s)." Special tags bearing the radiation symbol and the phrase "Danger—Radioactive Material—Do Not Handle.

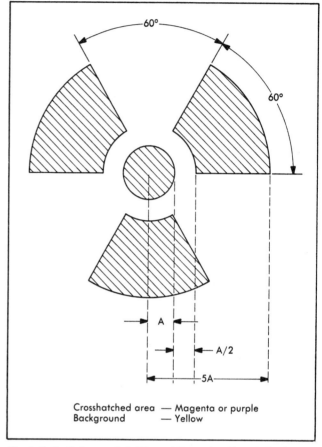

Fig. 6-41 Radiation symbol. (*General Dynamics, Convair Div.*)

Notify Civil Authorities If Found" must be attached to sealed sources not fastened to or contained in an exposure device.

Allowable working time. The amount of radiation absorbed by the human body is directly proportional to the time the body is exposed to the radiation. A person receiving 2 mr in 1 minute at a given point in a radiation field would receive 10 mr in 5 minutes. Allowable working time can be calculated by the following equation:

$$W_A = E_P/E_R \qquad (6)$$

where:

W_A = allowable working time, hr/wk
E_P = permissible exposure, mr/wk
E_R = exposure rate, mr/hr

The exposure rate is determined by measuring radiation intensity with an ionization chamber instrument. The value for permissible exposure is different for monitored radiation workers than for unmonitored nonradiation workers.

Working distance. The greater the distance from a radiation source, the lower the exposure received. The inverse square law is used to calculate radiation intensities at various distances from a source.

Shielding. The most common material used to protect against radiation is lead. It is easily available and comparatively low in cost. Shielding protective measurements are usually expressed in terms of lead thickness. Particular care must be exercised to ensure leakproof shielding. Adjacent sheets of lead must be overlapped, and nails or screws that pass through the lead must also be covered with lead. Pipes, conduits, and air ducts passing through the walls of the shielded area must be completely shielded.

The thickness of lead shield employed is dependent on the energy of the radiation requiring shielding and the use (occupancy) of the surrounding areas. If the spaces above, below, and about the exposure area are all occupied, then all of the exposure area—wall, ceiling, and floor—must be shielded. If the room is on the top floor of the building, it is not necessary to shield all of the ceiling; similarly, if the room is on the bottom floor not all of the floor need be shielded.

Although lead is the most efficient of the easily available shielding materials, other structural materials such as concrete and brick are often used. At voltages greater than 400 kV, the thickness of lead shielding would be so great as to make it difficult to fasten the lead to the walls. At these higher potentials, concrete is used as shielding because of its relative effectiveness and its construction simplicity.

Because all of the energy of X-radiation or gamma radiation cannot be stopped by shielding, it is practical to measure shielding efficiency in terms of half-value layers. The half-value layer is the amount of shielding that will stop half of the radiation of a given intensity. Shielding efficiency is also measured in tenth-value layers. A tenth-value layer is the amount of shielding that will stop nine-tenths of the radiation of a given intensity. Half and tenth-value layers are listed in various handbooks and should be used for original safety calculations. Final safety verification should be made by actual radiation measurements.

Gamma ray requirements. Gamma radiation cannot be shut off, and protection must be provided at all times. The penetrating capability of gamma radiation makes it impractical to rely on shielding for protection during gamma radiography; a combination of distance and shielding is usually employed. The radiation danger zone is roped off and clearly marked with conspicuous signs; only those persons making the radiograph are permitted in the zone. The extent of the danger zone is based on calculations of safe distance as determined by the source strength. In calculating the area of the danger zone, the possible effects of scatter radiation are considered, and the calculations are confirmed by intensity measurements.

The continuous gamma radiation from radioisotopes necessitates strict accountability of radioactive sources. When not in use, they are stored in conspicuously labeled lead vaults and/or depleted uranium 238 storage containers. After every use, intensity measurements are taken to insure that the source is safely housed, and the storage pig is not permitting leakage radiation.

Electrical Safety

The radiographer must comply with safe electrical procedures when working with X-ray equipment because modern X-ray machines use high-voltage circuits. Permanently installed X-ray facilities are designed so that personnel trained in safe practices will encounter little electrical hazard; however, portable X-ray equipment requires certain electrical precautions.

EDDY-CURRENT TESTING

Electromagnetic testing is a term that describes the broad spectrum of electronic test methods involving the interaction of magnetic fields and circulating currents. A widely applied technique within this category is eddy-current testing.

Eddy-current testing (ET) involves the use of a varying magnetic field produced by a test coil to induce small, circulating currents called eddy currents into electrically conductive materials. Certain properties within the material have an effect on the eddy currents thus induced. The eddy currents themselves set up a magnetic field that interacts with the magnetic field of the coil in such a way that the electrical signal of the test coil is changed. Any change in the eddy currents is reflected by a change in the test coil electrical signal. Because the electrical signal of the test coil can be monitored by instruments, any factor existing in the material under test that affects the eddy currents can be detected.

This subchapter discusses the basic principles of ET, its application in industry, the operating techniques, and the equipment used. Portions of this subchapter are abstracted with permission from *Classroom Training Handbook, Eddy Current Testing.*[24] Standards associated with eddy-current testing are given in Table 6-12. When referring to these standards, it is important to refer to the most recent revision.

APPLICATIONS

In ET, the word *flaw* has a much wider meaning than it does for other forms of nondestructive testing. Applications of eddy-current testing fall into one of four general categories: (1) metal sorting, (2) surface or subsurface discontinuity detection, (3) thickness measurement, and (4) inside diameter tube inspection. Because a continuous indication is a part of the basic testing system, automatic production testing is feasible. Depending on the equipment and test conditions, ET has been used to:[25]

- Detect discontinuities such as seams, laps, slivers, scabs, pits, cracks, voids, inclusions, and cold shuts.
- Sort for chemical composition on a qualitative basis.
- Sort for physical properties such as hardness, case depth, and heat damage.
- Measure conductivity and related properties.
- Measure dimensions such as the thickness of metallic coatings, plating, cladding, wall thickness, inside or outside diameter of tubing, corrosion depth, and wear.
- Measure the thickness of nonmetals when a metallic backing sheet can be employed.

ADVANTAGES AND LIMITATIONS

Some of the advantages of eddy-current testing include the following:

- The signal indicating the status of the material is obtained almost instantaneously. There is no requirement for allowing time for the indication to develop.

TABLE 6-12
Eddy-Current Testing Standards

Specifying Body	Standard Number	Standard Title
American National Standards Institute	ANSI/ASTM B499	Measurement of Coating Thickness by the Magnetic Method: Nonmagnetic Coatings on Magnetic Basis Metals
	ASNI/ASTM B529	Measurement of Coating Thickness by the Eddy Current Test Method: Nonconductive Coatings on Nonmagnetic Basis Metal
American Petroleum Institute	API 5A	Specification for Casing, Tubing, and Drill Pipe
	API 5AC	Specification for Restricted Yield Strength Casing and Tubing
	API 5AX	Specification for High Strength Casing, Tubing, and Drill Pipe
	API 5L	Specification for Line Pipe
	API 5LU	Specification for Ultra High-test Heat Treated Line Pipe
	API RP 5A5	Recommended Practice for the Field Inspection of New Casing, Tubing, and Plain End Drill Pipe
American Society for Testing and Materials	B244	Method for Measurement of Thickness of Anodic Coatings of Aluminum and of Other Nonconductive Coatings on Nonmagnetic Base Metals with Eddy Current Instruments
	B342	Test Method for Electrical Conductivity by Use of Eddy Currents
	B554	Recommended Practice for Measurement of Thickness of Metallic Coatings on Nonmetallic Substrates
	E215	Standardizing Equipment for Electromagnetic Testing of Seamless Aluminum Alloy Tube
	E243	Electromagnetic (Eddy Current) Testing of Seamless Copper and Copper Alloy Tubes
	E268	Definition of Terms Relating to Electromagnetic Testing
	E309	Eddy Current Examination of Steel Tubular Products Using Magnetic Saturation
	E376	Measuring Coating Thickness by Magnetic Field or Eddy Current (Electromagnetic) Test Methods
	E426	Electromagnetic (Eddy Current) Testing of Seamless and Welded Tubular Products, Austenitic Stainless Steel and Similar Alloys
	E566	Electromagnetic (Eddy Current) Sorting of Ferrous Metals
	E570	Flux Leakage Examination of Ferromagnetic Steel Tubular Products
	E571	Electromagnetic (Eddy Current) Examination of Nickel and Nickel Alloy Tubular Products
	E690	In-situ Electromagnetic (Eddy Current) Examination of Nonmagnetic Heat Exchanger Tubes
	E703	Electromagnetic (Eddy Current) Sorting of Nonferrous Metals
	E1004	Electromagnetic (Eddy Current) Measurements of Electrical Conductivity
	E1033	Electromagnetic (Eddy Current) Examination of Type F-Continuously Welded (CW) Ferromagnetic Pipe and Tubing Above the Curie Temperature
	G46	Recommended Practice for Examination and Evaluation of Pitting Corrosion
U.S. Department of Defense	MIL-STD-271	Nondestructive Testing Requirements for Metals
	MIL-STD-288	Inspection Procedure for Determining the Magnetic Permeability of Wrought Austenitic Steel
	MIL-STD-1537	Electrical Conductivity Test for Measurement of Heat Treatment of Aluminum Alloy, Eddy Current Method
Society of Automotive Engineers	SAE G-3	Determination of Aluminum Alloy Tempers Through Electrical Conductivity Measurement

EDDY-CURRENT TESTING

- The testing procedures are readily adaptable to GO/ NOT-GO situations.
- The method is sensitive to many physical and metallurgical variables.
- The only link between the test equipment and the item under test is a magnetic field.
- The equipment for the most part can be self-powered and therefore portable.
- Automatic production testing is feasible.
- On-site, in-service inspection capability.

Some of the limitations include the following:

- Success of the testing procedure is directly related to suppressing variables not of interest.
- Variations in test procedures may be required to determine which variable is being indicated.
- The procedures are applicable to conductive materials only.
- The depth of penetration is restricted—approximately 1/2″ (13 mm) in aluminum with standard probes.
- Testing of ferromagnetic metals is sometimes difficult.

PRINCIPLES

Eddy-current testing is based on the same principles of electricity and magnetism that are used to generate electric power. In 1820, Hans Christian Oerstead discovered that the flow of electricity through a wire created a field of magnetic force around the wire. With this understanding, electricity was used to produce electromagnets capable of lifting heavy weights. Because of the relationship between electricity and magnetism, many people studied to see if magnetism could produce electricity. In 1832, Michael Faraday discovered that the movement of the invisible magnetic field past the conductor caused electricity to flow in the conductor.

In eddy-current testing, the alternating current flowing through a test coil produces an alternating magnetic field in the coil. When the test coil is brought near to or placed on a material that is capable of conducting electrical current, the magnetic field passes into (cuts) the material, and circular (eddy) currents are induced in the material (see Fig. 6-42). As

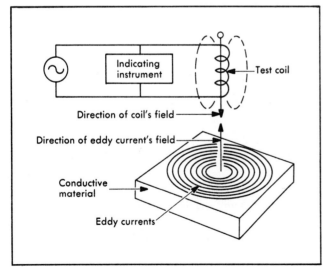

Fig. 6-42 Basic eddy-current test system. (*General Dynamics, Convair Div.*)

the coil's magnetic field alternates, eddy currents flow in one direction and then the other. The flow of eddy currents in the material causes a fluctuating magnetic field of its own. This magnetic field is always in opposition to the coil's magnetic field; thus when the test coil is placed on conductive material, the strength of the coil's magnetic field is lessened. This change in the magnetic field causes a change in the impedance of the coil that in turn causes a change in the current flowing through the coil. This change can be detected by a meter placed in the test circuit. It then follows that anything that affects the eddy currents will affect the impedance of the coil and thus be detectable by the test circuit.

Properties affecting eddy currents. The material properties that affect the eddy currents induced in the test material are conductivity, dimensions, and permeability. Variations in these properties cause changes in the impedance of the test circuit.

Conductivity. Conductivity of a material is defined as the ability of the material to carry electrical current. It is generally specified as the number of amperes of current that will flow through a given size (cross-sectional area) of the material when a given voltage is applied to the material. Because this definition is cumbersome to use in ET, the International Annealed Copper Standard (IACS) is usually used instead.

In the IACS system, the conductivity of unalloyed (pure) annealed copper is selected as the standard. The conductivity of all other materials are then expressed as a percentage of this standard. Each type of material has an inherent conductivity that is different from every other type of material.

Although the inherent conductivity of a material is always the same, there are internal factors that can cause what appears to be a change in the inherent conductivity. These are: (1) changes in the hardness of the material, (2) temperature of and residual stresses in the material, and (3) the presence of a coating or cladding of another material.

Alloys. Alloys are combinations of other metals and/or chemical elements with a base metal. Each metal or chemical element has an individual effect on the conductivity of the base metal. The conductivity of the base metal is changed to a value relatable to the composition of the alloy; thus it is possible to identify basic metals and their alloys by measuring their conductivities.

Hardness. When a metal or alloy is subjected to heat treatment (or to excessive heat during normal operation) the metal will become harder or softer, depending on the material. This change in hardness is brought about by an internal change in the material, which also affects the conductivity of the material. This change in conductivity can also be detected by eddy-current test methods. An improper heat treatment can be detected in this manner.

Temperature and residual stresses. The ambient temperature and internal residual stresses of a material under test also have an effect on the conductivity of the material. These changes can also be detected by eddy-current testing. An increase in the temperature of the material normally results in a decrease in the conductivity of the material. Residual stresses cause an unpredictable, but detectable, change in conductivity.

Conductive coatings. The presence of a conductive coating on a conductive material changes the inherent conductivity of the base metal just as an alloy would; however, if the thickness of the cladding varies, the conductivity will vary. This change in thickness can be detected by eddy-current testing methods.

Dimensional factors. Dimensional factors of the material that are of concern in ET fall under two types: (1) the dimension and shape of the material under test and (2) the presence of discontinuities in the material.

Material thickness. Eddy currents do not penetrate throughout a thick material, but tend to be concentrated near the surface; thus there is a finite or limited depth of penetration. For mathematical reasons, it has become useful to define the standard depth of penetration as the distance from the surface of the article to the point where the current density is approximately 37% of the current density at the surface.

The depth of penetration of eddy currents in a material depends on the inherent conductivity of the material (the greater the conductivity, the less the penetration) and the frequency of the alternating current used to energize the test coil (the lower the frequency, the greater the penetration). Figure 6-43 shows the standard depth of penetration for several materials at various operating frequencies.

When the material is thin enough, so that all of the coil's magnetic field is not utilized in creating eddy currents, the strength of the eddy current is reduced. This appears to the test circuit as an apparent difference in conductivity from that of the thicker piece of the material.

Discontinuities. The flow of eddy current within the material is affected by the presence of discontinuities such as cracks, porosity, or inclusions. Discontinuities cause an apparent decrease in the flow of electricity in the material by increasing the length of the path along which the current must flow. This results in a reduction of current flow that causes a change in the electrical signal of the test circuit.

The magnitude of the indication caused by a discontinuity is primarily dependent on the amount of current disrupted by the discontinuity. In other words, the depth, width, and length of the discontinuity determines the change in indication.

Permeability. When an energized test coil is placed on nonmagnetized ferromagnetic material, the field is greatly intensified by the magnetic properties of the material so that a large change in the impedance of the test coil occurs. If the magnetic field strength at various locations varies even slightly, these small variations have a large effect on the electrical signal of the coil. These changes in the electrical signal of the coil are often so large (in comparison to the changes caused by changes in conductivity or dimension) that they mask all other changes. When specimen geometry permits, this effect may be overcome by magnetizing the material to saturation using a separate coil powered by direct current. Magnetic saturation effectively eliminates any variations in the residual magnetic field due to magnetic variables and thus allows other variations to be measured. After testing is completed, the part must be demagnetized.

Spacing

Liftoff and fill factor are the terms used to describe any space that occurs between the part being tested and the test coil. Liftoff and fill factor are essentially the same thing—one is applied to surface coils and the other is applied to encircling and internal coils.

When a surface coil is energized and held in air above a conductor, the impedance of the coil has a certain value. As the coil is moved closer to the conductor, the initial value will change when the field of the coil begins to intercept the conductor. Because the field of the coil is strongest close to the coil, the electrical signal will continue to change until the coil is directly on the conductor. Conversely, once the coil is on the conductor any small variation in the separation of coil and conductor will change the electrical signal of the coil. The liftoff effect is so

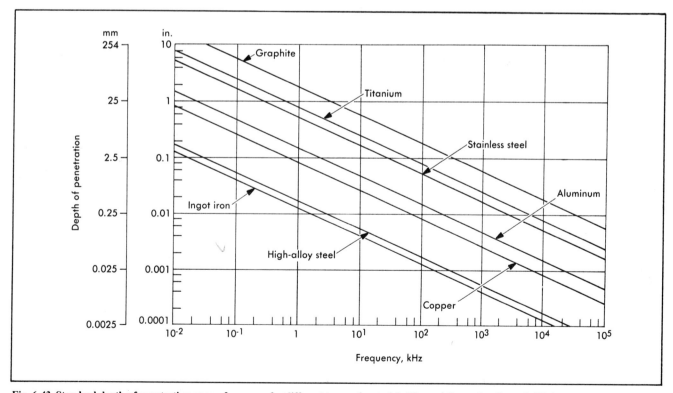

Fig. 6-43 Standard depth of penetration versus frequency for different types of material. (*General Dynamics, Convair Div.*)

EDDY-CURRENT TESTING

pronounced that small variations in spacing can mask many indications.

In an encircling coil or an internal coil fill factor is a measure of how well the conductor (test specimen) fits the coil. It is necessary to maintain a constant relationship between the diameter of the coil and the diameter of the conductor. Again, small changes in the diameter of the conductor can cause changes in the electrical signal of the coil. This can be useful in detecting changes in the diameter of the conductor, but it can also mask other indications.

Test Frequencies

The frequencies used in eddy-current testing range from about 5 Hz to 6 MHz or more.[26] In general, the lower frequencies are used for testing magnetic materials; however, the actual frequency used in any specific eddy-current inspection will depend on the thickness of the material being tested, the desired depth of penetration, the degree of sensitivity or resolution required, and the purpose of the test.

Selection of testing frequency is normally a compromise. For instance, penetration should be sufficient to reach any subsurface flaws that must be detected or to determine material parameters (such as case hardness). Although penetration is greater at lower frequencies, it does not follow that the lowest possible frequency should be used. Unfortunately, as the frequency is lowered, the sensitivity to flaws decreases somewhat, and the speed of testing may also decrease. Normally, therefore, the highest possible frequency that is still compatible with the penetration depth required is selected. The choice is relatively simple when only surface flaws must be detected, in which case frequencies up to several megahertz may be used. When flaws at some considerable depth below the surface must be detected or when flaw depth or flaw size are to be determined, low frequencies must be used and sensitivity may be sacrificed.

When testing ferromagnetic materials, relatively low frequencies are normally used because of the low penetration in these materials. Higher frequencies can be used when it is necessary to test surface conditions only. Even the higher frequencies used in these applications are still considerably lower than those used to test nonmagnetic materials for similar conditions.

EQUIPMENT

Eddy-current test equipment ranges from simple portable units to complex automatic or console-type apparatus.[27]

Regardless of the complexity, each system must have at least the following elements:

- A source of magnetic field capable of inducing eddy currents in conductive materials.
- A sensor or probe that is capable of sensing minute changes in the magnetic fields caused by eddy currents.
- A means of interpreting the measured changes in magnetic field.

Instruments

Many different types of eddy-current instruments are currently available; they are all similar in principle, but vary in function and accessories. Every test instrument contains a source of alternating current. In some instruments the source is at a fixed frequency, but in others the frequency can be varied. Multifrequency instruments can be employed to achieve high resolution in more than one area of interest. The test instrument also contains a means of interpreting the signal received from the test coil. Interpretation of the change may be achieved by impedance analysis, phase analysis, or modulation analysis. The procedure used depends on the manufacturer of the instrument and the intended application.

Test Coils

The test coil is an essential part of every eddy-current test system. The test coil induces eddy currents in the material being tested in such a way as to produce a signal indicating the presence of a discontinuity and possible information about the nature of the discontinuity. With most commercial equipment, various sizes and shapes of test coils are supplied and are expressly designed for use with that equipment. From these coils, the operator must choose the one that is most closely suited to the geometry of the part being tested and is capable of establishing an eddy-current pattern of a size sufficiently small to be consistent with the dimensions of the smallest flaw of interest.

The characteristics of the test coil are affected by the part's conductivity, permeability, mass, and homogeneity. The electrical characteristics of the test coil are also affected by the test system's frequency, coil size, current, and spacing.

Coil types. Three basic types of test coils are used in ET: (1) surface coil, (2) encircling coil, and (3) internal or bobbin-type coil (see Fig. 6-44). Special coil configurations are also available from equipment manufacturers for specialized applications.

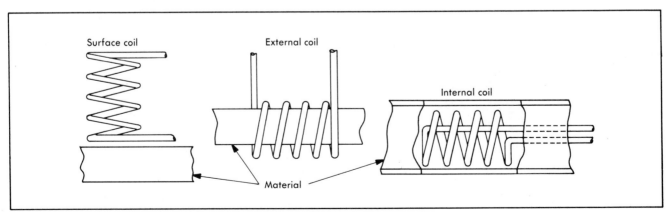

Fig. 6-44 Basic test coil types for eddy-current testing. (*General Dynamics, Convair Div.*)

Surface coils are generally placed on the surface of the part so that they are perpendicular to the part surface. Encircling coils are particularly adapted to testing tubing (or bars) because the coil can be passed over the tube (or the tube passed through the coil) at a fairly rapid pace. The magnetic field induces eddy currents in the bar that encircles the entire circumference of the tube or rod so that the entire section under the coil is inspected at any one instant.

As with the encircling coil, the internal coil induces currents that encircle the entire circumference of the tube so that the entire section surrounding the coil is inspected. Because the currents induced in the material are strongest near the coil, the internal coil is more sensitive to defects lying on or near the inner surface of tubing, and encircling coils are more sensitive to defects lying on or near the outer surface.

Coil arrangements. Several different coil arrangements are commonly used in ET. The specific arrangement depends on the test situation.

Single coil. In the single-coil arrangement, the same coil is used to induce eddy currents in the part and to sense the part's reaction on the eddy currents. This arrangement can be used for all three types of test coils.

The single coil will only test the area under the coil and does not compare itself with a reference standard (external reference). Because it tests the part without comparison, it is called absolute.

Double coil. In the double-coil arrangement, the primary coil establishes the magnetic field and induces eddy currents in the part being tested, and the secondary coil detects changes in eddy-current flow (see Fig. 6-45). The secondary coil has the indicating device connected across the coil and is not connected to an a-c source. Normally, the secondary coil is located inside the primary coil. This coil arrangement can also be used with all three types of test coils.

Differential coil. The differential-coil arrangement provides a means to balance out effects that are the same (see Fig. 6-46). The two coils are wound and connected so that the output of one coil cancels the output of the other coil when the material properties are the same under both coils. A slight difference in material properties causes an imbalanced output indication. Comparison of the material properties can come from the actual part being tested or from an external reference standard.

Through transmission. In a through-transmission system, eddy currents are induced into thin material by a transmitting coil placed on one side of the material. The presence of eddy currents are sensed by a receiving coil placed on the opposite side of the material (see Fig. 6-47).

In the through-transmission system, the field of the receiving coil is affected only by those electromagnetic fields that have passed through the material; thus the receiving coil is affected by discontinuities lying anywhere between the inner and outer surfaces of the material.

Reflection. Another arrangement utilizing two separate coils is the reflection method. In the reflection method, the transmitting coil (driver) and the receiving coil (pickup) are placed on the same side of the material. The receiving coil is affected by the eddy currents induced in the material by the transmitting coil. This arrangement is generally best suited for deep penetration applications.

Reflection with dual pickups. Another type of coil system utilizes three coils mounted in one probe. The three coils consist of two detector coils (pickups) located atop each other and inside a transmitter coil (driver). The detector coils are exactly alike except that they are wound in opposition. When the transmitter coil is energized, the field is intercepted by the detector coils, and a voltage is induced. Because the coils are exactly alike, the induced voltages are identical, but because the detector coils are wound in opposite directions, the two voltages cancel each other, and there is no signal output. If one end of the probe is placed near a conductive material, the magnetic field at that end of the probe is changed. The detector coil nearest the material detects this change, but the other detector coil, being further removed from the surface of the material, does not; thus an imbalance occurs, and a signal is produced. Variations in the material will also cause a change in the electrical signal of the near-surface coil and not affect the other coil.

Indicating Devices

An important part of the eddy-current test system is the part of the instrument that gives the technician the indication of the change in electrical charge. Several different types of devices are commonly used. The device may be an integral part of the test set, it may be a module that is plugged into the test set, or it may be a separate unit connected to the test set with a cable. The indicating device used should be of adequate speed, accuracy, and range to meet the requirements of the test system.

Two types of meters are commonly used as indicating devices: (1) analog meters and (2) digital meters. The visual output of an analog meter varies as a continuous function of the input to the meter. Response is immediate and the scales can usually be calibrated to read specific values directly. The output of a digital meter is shown in discrete steps in time; input is measured at a given moment and the value is numerically displayed. Because the output of a digital meter is in numbers, possible reading error is less likely than with an analog meter, but the output is relatively slow. Digital meters are used mainly with conductivity measurements.

Another type of indicating device used to display the output of a test circuit is an oscilloscope. Oscilloscopes give an instantaneous, continuous presentation, are highly accurate, provide calibration capabilities so that values may be read directly, have a broad range, and the presentation is adjustable so that parameters of particular interest may be studied more closely.

Strip-chart recorders provide an analog recording of values at reasonably high speeds. The strip-chart recorder is one method that produces a permanent, fairly accurate record. Several channels can be recorded at the same time.

For most inspection systems, a visible or audio alarm can be used to indicate when the specified values have not been attained. Cathode ray tubes with a storage capability are also available and allow visual comparison of indications.

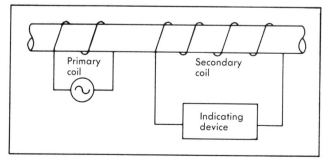

Fig. 6-45 Double coil arrangement. (*General Dynamics, Convair Div.*)

EDDY-CURRENT TESTING

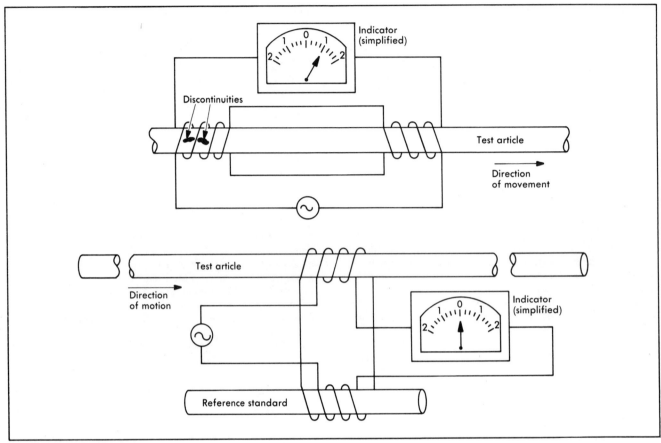

Fig. 6-46 Double coil differential arrangements. (*General Dynamics, Convair Div.*)

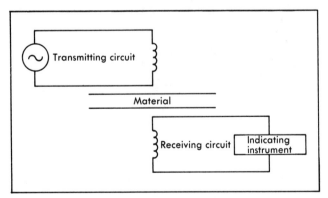

Fig. 6-47 Through-transmission eddy-current coil arrangement. (*General Dynamics, Convair Div.*)

Standards

As in other types of nondestructive testing, the most useful data is obtained by comparing the data from an item under test with data from a reference standard. Standards furnish an exact value that has been established by authority, custom, or agreement as the norm by which other like parts may be judged. Standards also help in the design of procedures developed to measure those quantities that are represented by the standard. Standards often define the limits of acceptability of an item and serve to ascertain that the equipment being used is capable of

measuring that quantity to the required degree of accuracy. A standard is also used to make sure that the equipment provides consistent sensitivity each time the equipment is used.

In eddy-current testing, standards are most often manufactured to fit a particular test situation; however, commercially prepared standards for use in checking the conductivity of a material are available and are usually supplied with conductivity measuring instruments. Discontinuity standards should duplicate the test situation for material type and geometry. In addition, they should include discontinuities that establish the maximum discontinuity that is acceptable and also establish the sensitivity of the system. The two types of discontinuity standards used are natural discontinuity standards and artificial discontinuity standards. When external comparison techniques are used, the reference standard must be free of discontinuities.

TESTING TECHNIQUES

As was mentioned previously, ET can be used in a variety of applications. Each specific application, in turn, has specific techniques that must be followed to ensure accurate results. The success of an eddy-current test depends on the following:[28]

- Proper coil design and arrangement.
- Selection of the proper test frequency or frequencies.
- Selection of the proper instrument.
- Use of proper technique procedures.
- Optimization and maintenance of electromagnetic coupling (liftoff) between the coil and the test piece.

- Selection of the most suitable stage in the manufacturing process for the test procedure.

Because ET involves the use of magnetic fields and conductive materials, the operator must make sure that the tests are performed in areas that are free of any magnetic or electrical disturbances; for example, any conductive material, including all parts other than the part being tested, should be kept at least 12″ (300 mm) away from the test coil. Tabletops that are made of a conductive material are a common source of error. Test coils must also be kept away from the magnetic fields produced by large motors and transformers.

Discontinuity Detection

When the test coil of an eddy-current test system is placed on an electrically conductive material, a certain impedance value is established in the test circuit that results from the presence of the eddy currents in the material. If the coil is then moved over an area that has a discontinuity, the eddy-current flow will be impeded by the presence of the discontinuity. This change in eddy-current flow causes a change in the test coil as it moves across the discontinuity. Care must be taken to ensure that the coil is always in contact with or consistently spaced from the material at all times because any change in the space between the coil and the material will also cause a change. Readings are calibrated with standards having known defects, either natural or manufactured, in the same kind of material.

Material Sorting

When the test coil is placed on a particular kind of conductive material, a specific electrical signal is established in the test circuit. Any other specimens of the same kind of conductive material will cause the same signal in the test circuit provided that the thickness of all the specimens of the material exceeds the depth of penetration of the eddy currents. Readings should be taken at different locations on a particular piece of material to be certain that the reading is not affected by a discontinuity. Liftoff is a factor to be avoided. Signal values are established on a sample of known material, and then the readings obtained from test samples are compared with the reading obtained from the known sample.

Nonconductive Coating Thickness Measurement

To obtain measurements of the thickness of a nonconductive coating on conductive material, the test coil is placed on a sample of the same material that has a known thickness of nonconductive coating. When the test coil is placed on this standard, an electrical signal is established in the test circuit that represents that specific coating thickness. Any variation in the thickness of the nonconductive coating on the test samples will be indicated as a change in this signal. Maximum and minimum coating thickness limits may be established in the same manner.

Conductive Coating Thickness Measurement

The procedure for measuring the thickness of conductive coatings, or cladding, over conductive material is similar to the procedure for measuring the thickness of nonconductive coatings. The test coil is first placed on standards that have a coating of the correct thickness (or that represent the maximum and minimum allowable thicknesses of the coating); thus the electrical signals for these standards are established. When the test coil is placed on the samples to be tested, variations in the thickness of the cladding are shown by variations in this signal. Any readings obtained that fall outside the established limits indicate that the conductive coating is not within allowable tolerances. Liftoff is a factor to be avoided, and the operator should be aware of the effect of discontinuities on the readings obtained.

Material Thickness Measurement

To measure the thickness of thin materials, standards of the same material are carefully machined to known thicknesses. Meter readings obtained from these standards establish the reference points for those thicknesses of that material. Variations in thickness of the test material are then reflected by changes in the meter reading. The meter scales may be calibrated so that a particular reading indicates a particular thickness, but the operator must be continually aware of the possibility of the existence of other factors that would also affect the reading on the meter.

Hardness Measurement

During age hardening of aluminum or titanium alloys, the hardness and conductivity of the material change simultaneously so that the degree of hardening may be obtained by measuring the conductivity of the test specimen and comparing it with a standard of that material with a known hardness. The operator must be aware of the effects of discontinuities and liftoff on the meter readings.

LEAK TESTING

Leak testing is a form of nondestructive testing capable of determining the existence of leak sites and, under proper conditions, measuring the quantity of material passing through these sites.[29] The term *leak* refers to a hole or passage through which a fluid passes in either a pressurized or evacuated system. Two types of leaks exist: real leaks and virtual leaks. A real leak is a discrete hole or passage through which a fluid may flow. Virtual leaks are sources of gradual desorption of gases from surfaces or components within a vacuum system.

Leakage refers to the mass flow of fluid regardless of the size of the leak. Leakage rate is the quantity of fluid per unit of time that flows through the leak at a given temperature as a result of a specified pressure difference across the leak.

Leakage rate is usually expressed as the product of some measure of pressure and volume per unit of time. The unit of leakage rate most commonly used is standard cubic centimeters per second (std·cm³/s). It is also frequently referred to as atmosphere cubic centimeters per second (atm·cm³/s). The preferred leakage rate unit as adopted by the International System (SI) is pascal cubic meters per second (Pa·m³/s). One Pa·m³/s is approximately equal to 10 std·cm³/s. The National Bureau of Standards uses the units moles/s when referring to

CHAPTER 6

LEAK TESTING

leakage rate because the other units only define a specific gas flow if the temperature at which the gas occupies the volume is explicitly stated.

Leak tightness is a relative term. Too often specifications are given in unrealistic terms such as "leaktight," "no leaks," or "no leakage." However, nothing manufactured can ever be completely free of leakage, and in most cases, it is uneconomical to even try. Consequently, a balance must be made between the increasing costs of finding smaller leaks and their importance to the functioning of the unit over its useful life. Leak tightness therefore has no meaning except in relation to the substance that is to be contained, its normal operating conditions, and the objectives with respect to safety, contamination, and reliability. Leak tightness is the practical leakage that is acceptable under normal operating circumstances.

Gas flow is an integral part of leak testing. A knowledge of the various gas flow modes is important for comparing flows of liquids and gases as well as for determining the best test conditions for a leak test. The three gas flow modes encountered in leak testing are viscous, transition, and molecular; viscous flow is further divided into turbulent and laminar flow. Turbulent flow occurs at leakage rates more than 10^{-3} std·cm³/s (10^{-4} Pa·m³/s), laminar flow in the range of 10^{-2} to 10^{-7} std·cm³/s (10^{-3} to 10^{-8} Pa·m³/s), transition flow in the range of 10^{-6} to 10^{-8} std·cm³/s (10^{-7} to 10^{-9} Pa·m³/s), and molecular flow at leakage rates less than 10^{-7} std·cm³/s (10^{-8} Pa·m³/s).

Laminar flow is generally the type of flow mode that is of greatest concern in leak testing. The two most important features of laminar flow leaks are the following:

1. An increase in the pressure difference across the leaks causes the flow rate through the leak to increase proportionately to the square of the pressure difference; therefore the easiest way of increasing detection sensitivity is to supply increased pressure.
2. The leakage rate is inversely proportional to the test gas viscosity; therefore the less viscous the tracer gas, the more sensitive the test.

Many standards and specifications exist for leak test procedures. Some of these are listed in Table 6-13. In addition to these standards, a major publication for large vessels is the *Boiler and Pressure Vessel Code* published by the American Society of Mechanical Engineers. When referring to this publication, it is recommended that the user refer to the latest addenda because the standard is revised on a regular basis.

Several leak testing methods are commonly being used in industry. The major methods and techniques are briefly described in Table 6-14. As the table indicates, each method/technique has its own advantages, limitations, and optimum sensitivity range. Because of this, not all methods are useful for every application. The sensitivities of the more popular test methods are shown in Fig. 6-48.

The correct choice of the leak test method/technique should optimize cost, sensitivity, and reliability of the test. By applying a number of selection criteria, the choice can often be narrowed to two or three methods, with the final choices being determined by special circumstances or cost effectiveness. Some of the general factors that should be considered when selecting a leak test method are the following:

- The design and specification requirements.
- The nature and accuracy of test information needed.
- The type or size of the leak to be inspected.
- The size and accessibility of the system.

Figure 6-49 is a flow diagram that can be used when selecting a leak test method for a particular application. The methods are categorized based on whether they can be used to find a leak location, monitor leakage, or measure system leakage. The methods are then categorized based on the size of the parts being tested and whether the test is performed under pressure or in a vacuum.

BUBBLE EMISSION TESTING

Bubble emission testing is the oldest documented method used to detect leaks. In recent years, this method often has been displaced by more modern methods; however, bubble emission testing will continue to be used by industry, especially when the permissible leakage is large, the production rate is low, and operator subjectivity is allowable.

There are two basic techniques in bubble emission testing. In the first technique, the part being tested is completely immersed in water. In the second technique, a low surface tension liquid film is applied to the surface of the part being tested.

Bubble emission testing operates on the basis of a differential pressure at a leak creating a flow of gas.[30] The escaping gas in turn produces one or more bubbles in the testing environment. These bubbles indicate the leak location; the frequency and size of the bubbles can be used to estimate the leakage rate.

Advantages and Limitations

The major advantages of bubble emission leak testing are the following:

- The cost of the equipment is usually less than that of other methods for detecting a leak.
- The location of a leak or leaks can usually be found.
- Relatively small leaks can be detected if sufficient time is allowed or special film solutions are used.

The major limitations of this method are the following:

- An operator is always required, with inherent subjectivity. Some work has been done with automatic bubble detection by means of collection and optical sensing, but the method has not come into general use.
- Immersion test time for small leaks is often longer than for other test methods; a leak rate of 1×10^{-5} std·cm³/s (1×10^{-6} Pa·m³/s) requires about 150 seconds per bubble in untreated water.
- A number of undetected small leaks, such as occur with porosity, can have a cumulative leak rate greater than the limit. This is primarily of concern when testing parts that must retain compressed air or gas.
- The part is wetted, which could cause corrosion and plugging of small leaks.
- In most instances the work environment is wet, with attendant operator discomfort.
- Liquid in immersion tanks (usually water) must be filtered or replaced for clarity and sometimes must be treated to prevent organic growth.
- Pressurized air must be clean and dry.
- Bubbles emitted from the bottom of submerged parts may not be apparent within an allotted test time.
- The liquid film technique is time consuming.

TABLE 6-13
Leak Testing Standards

Specifying Body	Standard Number	Standard Title
American Society for Testing and Materials	E425	Definitions of Terms Relating to Leak Testing
	E427	Practice for Testing for Leaks Using the Halogen Leak Detector (Alkali-Ion Diode)
	E432	Guide for the Selection of a Leak Testing Method
	E479	Guide for Preparation of a Leak Testing Specification
	E493	Test Methods for Leaks Using the Mass Spectrometer Leak Detector in the Inside-Out Testing Mode
	E498	Methods of Testing for Leaks Using the Mass Spectrometer Leak Detector or Residual Gas Analyzer in the Tracer Probe Mode
	E499	Methods of Testing for Leaks Using the Mass Spectrometer Leak Detector in the Detector Probe Mode
	E515	Methods of Testing for Leaks Using Bubble Emission Techniques
	E677	Method of Testing for Leaks of Spherical Ground Joints
	E741	Practice for Testing for Air Leakage in Buildings by Tracer Dilution Method
	E779	Testing for Air Leakage in Buildings by Fan Pressurization Method
	E1002	Method of Testing for Leaks Using Ultrasonics
	E1003	Method for Hydrostatic Leak Testing
	E1006	Method for Ammonia Colorimetric Leak Testing
	F78	Specification for Calibration of Helium Leak Detectors by Use of Secondary Standards
	F97	Recommended Practice for Determining Hermeticity of Electronic Devices by Dye Penetration
	F98	Recommended Practice for Determining Hermeticity of Electronic Devices by Bubble Test
	F134	Recommended Practices for Determining Hermeticity of Electronic Devices with a Helium Mass Spectrometer Leak Detector
	F730	Determining Hermeticity of Electronic Devices by Weight Gain Test
	F785	Determining Hermeticity of (Sealed) Electronic Devices by Radioisotope Test
	F816	Test Method for Fine/Gross Leak Testing of Electronic Devices (for Large Package Microcircuits)
U.S. Department of Defense	MIL-I-2556C	Leak Detection Compound, Oxygen Systems
	MIL-I-3516C	Leak Detector, Refrigerant Gas: Acetylene Burning with Search Hose
	MIL-L-83774	Leak Detector, Full System
	MIL-STD-1441	Equipment, Leak Detection, Helium, for Chemical Munitions
U.S. Government	Federal Test Method Std. #151 b-Method 441	Leak Testing (Helium Mass Spectrometer)
	Federal Test Method Std. #151 b-Method 442	Leak Testing (Pressurized Gas)
	Federal Test Method Std. #151 b-Method 443	Leak Testing (Vacuum)

LEAK TESTING

TABLE 6-14
Leak Testing Methods

Method	Technique Description	Advantages	Limitations
Bubble emission leak testing (BLT)	In *liquid film solution* testing, a uniform film of solution is applied to part and then inspected for leakage by looking for small bubble formation	Accurate leak location. Easy to learn and do. Inexpensive. Good sensitivity to 10^{-5} std·cm³/s (10^{-6} Pa·m³/s)	Requires pre and postcleaning. Operator dependent. Slow and time consuming. Nonquantitative, therefore, difficult to estimate a leakage rate. Large leaks can be missed, and small leaks can be plugged
	In *immersion* testing, the part is pressurized and then dunked into a special liquid bath. Leaks are indicated by small bubbles	Similar to liquid film solution testing. Sensitivity is approximately 10^{-4} std·cm³/s (10^{-5} Pa·m³/s)	Similar to liquid film solution leak testing except not as time consuming and large leaks should not be missed
	In the *vacuum box* test, a specially designed box (open one side and window other side) fits over an area of applied film solution, and a partial vacuum is created. The part is then inspected for bubble formation	Similar to liquid film solution testing except sensitivity is 10^{-3} std·cm³/s (10^{-4} Pa·m³/s). Access to only one side is needed. Does not require presssurization	Similar to liquid film testing except requires special design boxes that can be difficult to apply and evaluate. Bubble indications are difficult to evaluate
Mass spectrometer leak testing (MSLT)	In a *detector (sniffer) probe* test, the part is pressurized with a tracer gas (helium) and the operator probes (sniffs) outside of part for escaping tracer gas from leaks	Leak/area location with approximate semiquantitative leakage rate. Sensitivity to 10^{-5} std·cm³/s (10^{-6} Pa·m³/s). Helium is readily available, reasonable in cost, and nontoxic	Initial cost high. Operator dependent. Time consuming. Requires training and experience. Difficult to scan large part or surface. Testing is more complex than most leak testing methods
	In *tracer (spray) probe* testing, a part is evacuated to a very low vacuum with the leak detector connected directly or tied into part system. The outside of the part is then sprayed with tracer gas (helium) over suspect areas	Similar to detector probe test except more accurate with increased sensitivity to 10^{-7} std·cm³/s (10^{-8} Pa·m³/s)	Similar to detector probe test except scanning is not as difficult. Requires special internal cleaning of part
	In a *hood accumulation* test, a part is evacuated and directly connected as in the tracer probe test. The tracer gas is then encased around the part or areas to be tested by a special enclosure, hood, or plastic bag	Accurate overall total leakage rate measurement. Sensitive to 10^{-10} std·cm³/s (10^{-11} Pa·m³/s) and reliable. Widely used, available, and can be automated. Usually no clean-up after testing	Similar to detector probe test except no scanning. Requires special internal cleaning. Special materials should be used to minimize "outgassing" on internal surfaces. Large leaks may be difficult to evaluate in higher tracer gas background. No leak location
	In a *bell jar accumulation* test, a part is pressurized with a tracer gas. It is then completely enclosed using a special encloser. This enclosure, or bell jar, is designed to be evacuated to low vacuum. Any leaks in the part are accumulated in annulus of bell jar	Similar to hood accumulation test, but can be even more accurate and reliable. Also much more automated for production line use. Highly developed test system with associated equipment is easily available from a variety of companies	Similar to hood accumulation test except outside surface and enclosure must be clean. Requires extremely leaktight enclosure with low outgassing materials

(continued)

TABLE 6-14—*Continued*

Method	Technique Description	Advantages	Limitations
	In a *helium bombing* test, sealed parts are put into a chamber and pressurized or bombed with helium. Parts are then removed and given a bell jar accumulation test	Similar to detector probe test, but with an inaccurate leakage measurement and no leak location. Systems can be automated for GO and NOT-GO testing of very small parts	Similar to bell jar accumulation test
Halogen detector leak testing (HDLT)	In a *detector (sniffer) probe* test, the part is pressurized with a halogen tracer gas (R-12, R-11, and SF6), and the operator scans or probes for escaping tracer gas. This technique can be reversed as in tracer probe test under MSLT, but it is not usually done	Good area/leak location with semiquantitative leakage rates. Sensitivity to 10^{-6} std·cm^3/s (10^{-7} Pa·m^3/s) or better. Detector units are relatively simple and compact, ranging from handheld devices to sensor production units. Calibrated standard leaks are available	Operator dependent. Requires training and experience. Time consuming and difficult to test large surfaces. Frequent calibration and checking of halogen background. Some sensor units are at high temperature so care must be exercised in combustible atmospheres. Halogen gases can cause toxic gases and corrosion within part at high temperature. Short life on sensor unit
	In an *accumulation (shroud/hood/enclosure)* test, the part is pressurized with halogen tracer gas and then encased in an enclosure (shroud or hood) that can accumulate any leaking tracer gas from the part	Detectors are similar to those used in detector probe test, but sensor unit is connected or tied into enclosed area for direct and accurate leakage measurement or monitoring. Quantitative measurement with sensitivity to 10^{-8} std·cm^3/s (10^{-9} Pa·m^3/s). High production and automation can be programmed or designed into test system. 100% tracer gas not required. Easily available standard leaks for calibration	Similar to detector probe test except scanning is not required. Therefore, no leak location provided. Requires leaktight fixtures for enclosure. Can be quite expensive
Pressure change/measurement leak testing (PCMT)	In *pressure decay* testing, the part being tested is pressurized with air or a safe gas and then monitored for leakage by special pressure devices or transducers	Fast, repeatable, accurate, and easy to do. No postcleaning needed. Can be used for high production and automation. Programmed to accept or reject. Low cost and safe gases (air) are used	No leak location. Poor sensitivity. Not accurate on large parts. Safety concern when using high pressures and hazardous gases
	In *absolute pressure change* testing, the part is pressurized as in pressure decay testing, but special instruments are used to correct for changes in atmospheric conditions such as temperature, dew point, and barometric pressure. All corrections are done relative to absolute gas laws and relationships	Good leakage measurement. Low-cost safe gases can be used. Can be used on large system. Special instruments and devices used are usually part of final system anyway. Data processing and programs can be added	Similar to pressure decay testing except more accurate on large parts or systems. Requires experience and training on ideal gas laws. Halogen and hazardous gases not recommended. Can be expensive

(continued)

TABLE 6-14—Continued

Method	Technique Description	Advantages	Limitations
	In *reference vessel* testing, a special vessel is made similar in design to the part/system being tested. A setup similar to absolute pressure change testing is also used	Similar to absolute pressure change test, except no correction is required for atmospheric changes	Similar to absolute pressure change test except it can be more expensive
	In a *pressure increase* test, the part being tested is pressurized and then encased in an enclosure or shroud. Any leaks into annulus area of enclosure is accumulated and measured	Similar to pressure decay test, but not quite as accurate or as sensitive	Similar to pressure decay test, but may contain more elaborate instruments and/or equipment
	In a *pressure rate-of-rise (ROR)* test the part/system is evacuated to a low vacuum and measured for leakage using thermal or ionization gages. Part may be heated for outgassing reasons	Similar to absolute pressure change test, but used for vacuum systems. Special devices are the thermocouple or ionization gage used. Also can be used to verify cleanliness of a vacuum system (outgassing)	Similar to absolute pressure change test except no gases are used. Is more expensive than absolute pressure change test
	In a *flow measurement (dynamic flow)* test, special flow measuring devices are used to measure air/gas leakage from air into a part or interannulus area	Similar to pressure increase test, but not as accurate or sensitive	Similar to pressure increase test
Ultrasonic leak testing (ULT)	In a *turbulent/sonic flow* test, a special ultrasound detector receives ultrasound energy emanating from a gas leak	Leak location. Fast and convenient. Simple to do and learn. No pre or postcleanup. Any gas can be used. Can detect from a distance	Gross leak only (of the turbulent/sonic flow) to 10^{-1} std·cm^3/s (10^{-2} Pa·m^3/s). Operator dependent. Nonquantitative. Other ultrasonic noises may interfere
	In a *sound generator* test, detector as above except using a separate sound generator on one side and receiving generated sound through leak on other side	Similar to the turbulent/sonic flow test except a gas is not required. Can be automated	Similar to the turblent/sonic flow test except requires access to both sides
Pressure leak testing (PLT)	In the *hydrostatic (hydraulic)* test, a part is pressurized with a liquid (usually water or oil), and operator looks for liquid leakage. Also can observe for pressure loss. (This test is frequently combined with a proof test that is done first.)	Good leak location. Easy to learn and do. Relatively inexpensive. Reasonably safe, especially when compared to pneumatic test. Sensitivity can be increased with special enhancer (see chemical dye penetrant test)	Requires cleanup before and after. Nonquantitative. Liquid plugs small leaks. Sensitivity to only 10^{-2} std·cm^3/s (10^{-3} Pa·m^3/s)

(continued)

TABLE 6-14—*Continued*

Method	Technique Description	Advantages	Limitations
	In *pneumatic (pressure loss)* testing, the part is pressurized with a gas (usually dry air or nitrogen), and the operator observes for pressure drop on a pressure gage or device (again can be combined with a preproof test). This technique can be considered a variation of the pressure decay technique of the pressure change/measurement test method	Fast, easy to do and learn; no cleanup after. Sensitivity is increased when film solution is used	No leak location unless film solution is used. Safety concern with overpressure. Poor sensitivity
	In *hydropneumatic* leak testing, a large component is given a hydrostatic test at the bottom and a pneumatic test at the top	As stated for hydrostatic and pneumatic testing	As stated for the hydrostatic and pneumatic techniques. Safety concern because large volumes and low pressures can present a greater hazard potential than small volumes and high pressures
Chemical-based leak testing (CBLT)	In *chemical dye penetrant* testing, a color dye penetrant is applied to one side of the part being tested. After a certain dwell time, a visual inspection is made for dye on other side. Usually a contrast developer is used	Good leak location. Easy to do, learn and evaluate. Relatively inexpensive. Requires no external pressurization or enclosure	Application of penetrant and developer very messy, thus requires cleaning after and before. Test is time consuming. Nonquantitative. May plug leaks
	Fluorescent dye penetrant testing is similar to chemical dye penetrant testing except an ultraviolet black light is used with or without a developer	Same as chemical dye penetrant testing. Sensitivity can be increased with black light, low-viscosity fluids, and even pressurization. This technique is sensitive to leak rates up to 10^{-4} std·cm^3/s (10^{-5} Pa·m^3/s)	Same as chemical dye penetrant testing
	Colormetric leak testing uses a tracer gas (ammonia) that reacts with a color or smoke developer	Similar to chemical penetrant dye testing, but the part is enclosed and usually pressurized. Fast response for large leaks. Sensitivity to 10^{-7} std·cm^3/s (10^{-8} Pa·m^3/s) using color developer and high pressure and tracer concentration. Cost is reasonable for sensitivity attained	Similar to chemical penetrant dye testing exept a big safety concern in use of usual tracer gas. Ammonia also reacts with copper, copper alloys, and wood. Smoke developer is time consuming
	A *chemical pH sensor* is a strip or badge that reacts and changes color when a certain acidic or alkaline tracer gas is present	Similar to chemical penetrant dye testing. Provides good monitoring ability of specified gases	Similar to chemical penetrant dye testing, but not too messy. Also could be a safety concern
Voltage discharge leak testing (VDLT)	In a *white spark* test, a special electrical probe scans an area. A bright white spark indicates a leak	Leak location. Fast, easy to do and learn. No cleanup after	Used on nonconductive materials only. Low sensitivity. Nonquantitative. Safety concern when high voltages are used

(continued)

TABLE 6-14—*Continued*

Method	Technique Description	Advantages	Limitations
	Color change test has voltage applied through part, and gas leakage into part is indicated by a gaseous color change	Similar to the white spark test except may not give leak location	Can only be used on vacuum system of glass or ceramics. Low sensitivity. Non-quantitative
Conductivity leak testing (CLT)	In a *thermal conductivity detector* test, leaks or leakage are detected by electronically measuring leaking tracer gas's thermal conductivity from that of ambient air using a wheat-stone bridge circuit. The detector probe mode is usually used, but equipment can be designed for accumulation or other modes	Good leak/area location. Sensitivity to 10^{-5} std$\cdot$cm/s (10^{-6} Pa$\cdot$m^3/s) when used with helium tracer. Can be semi-quantitative. Calibration leak standards are available	Requires operator training and experience. Tracer gas contamination in ambient air decreases sensitivity. Requires frequent background and calibration checks. Probing is time consuming.
	The *thermocouple gage* test is similar to the thermal conductivity detector test, but a thermocouple gage is used directly into the system of the part tested	Similar to pressure rate-of-rise technique except higher pressure may be used (still usually below atmospheric pressure) and an ionization gage is not required	Similar to pressure rate-of-rise technique, but not as expensive or sensitive
	A *catalytic combustible detector* test detects the amount of tracer gases by burning them and measuring temperature and conductivity changes within a wheatstone bridge circuit. The detector probe mode is usually used, but other modes can be used	Good leak location, but best for area monitoring for combustible gases, such as methane or propane. Easy to use and compact, from hand-held units to larger production units. Sensitivity to 10^{-5} std$\cdot$cm^3/s (10^{-6} Pa$\cdot$m^3/s), but usually instrument is designed to measure in percent concentration	Similar to thermal conductivity detector test. Safety is also a concern unless a good back-flash arrester is used
	Solid-state semiconductor unit is similar to a catalytic combustible except a sensor bead or thermistor semiconductor measures amount of a tracer gas	Similar to catalytic combustible detector test above except units can be also designed for a wider variety of hazardous gases. Can measure in percent or parts per million. Are smaller than above units	Similar to catalytic combustible detector test, but safer
	Photo-ionization unit uses an ultraviolet light field that ionizes organic compounds in tracer gases. This results in a conductivity change in the circuit. The accumulation mode without enclosure is usually used	Good area monitoring for benzene and other hydro-carbons. Safe in combustible gas atmospheres unless UV light breaks by dropping unit. Can be automated with alarms	Similar to thermal conductivity test except probing is usually not done

(continued)

TABLE 6-14—*Continued*

Method	Technique Description	Advantages	Limitations
	A *flame-ionization unit* uses a hydrogen gas flame (zero or baseline setting). When organic tracer compounds are burned in a flame, they are ionized, thus measuring a conductivity change in circuit. The accumulation made without any special enclosure is usually used	Similar to photo-ionization unit, but more widely used. Does not use UV light. Not affected by moisture in air	Similar to catalytic combustible detector test except probing is usually not used
Gas absorption leak testing (GALT)	An *infrared (IR) absorption detector* measures leakage of a specific tracer gas that has a characteristic absorption for infrared radiation. The accumulation made without any special enclosure is usually used	Good accuracy and sensitivity when NH_3, CO_2, CO, and other hydrocarbons are used as tracer gas. Good area and in-line flow monitoring	Requires operator training and experience. Expensive when tied into a monitoring and a computer system. Requires background and calibration checks
	An *ultraviolet (UV) absorption unit* is similar to the infrared absorption detector, but measures the characteristic absorption for ultraviolet radiation. The accumulation made without special enclosure is usually used	Similar to infrared absorption detector. Better on chlorinated and aromatic hydrocarbons	Similar to infrared absorption detector
	Gas chromatographs units are designed to scan, compare, and monitor a carrier gas versus a sampled gas and then fractionate it into its constituents. Accumulation mode is usually used	Good accuracy and sensitivity to compared gas. Can identify many compounds	Similar to infrared absorption detector, but *can* be very expensive and complicated
Radioisotope leak testing (RLT)	In a *radioflo-accumulation* test, the part is pressurized with tracer gas and then enclosed. A special scintillation (Geiger) counter is used to determine amount of tracer gas leakage (usually Kryton 85). In special cases, the part may not be enclosed, but scanned	Leak test method with sensitivity to 10^{-12} std $\cdot$ cm^3/s (10^{-13} Pa $\cdot$ m^3/s) under normal operation. Very fast, accurate, and reliable. Good for small high-production parts. Automated system can be used	Uses a radioactive gas, thus requiring a radiation safety program and officer. Extensive training and experience. Complex to use. Requires special cleanup during and after testing. Leaking parts must be cleaned or disposed of properly. Expensive. Cannot evaluate gross/large leaks
	A *radioflo-bombing* test is similar to a helium bombing test, but a special counter is used	Similar to radioflo-accumulator test except not as accurate, reliable, or sensitive	Similar to radioflo-accumulation test except some large leaks can be completely missed

LEAK TESTING

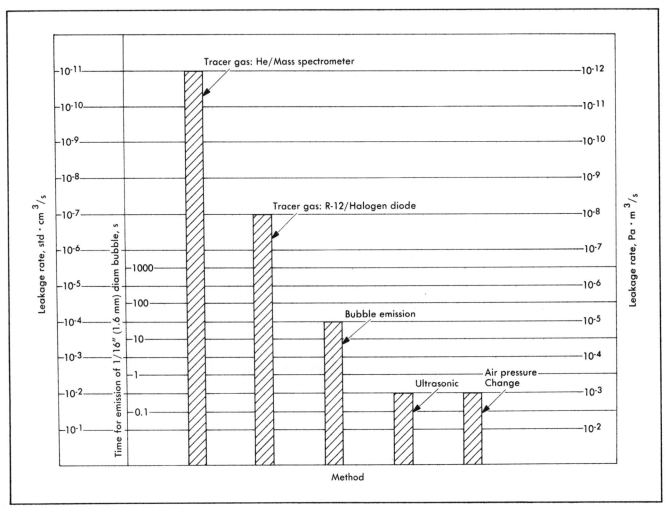

Fig. 6-48 Sensitivities of leak testing methods. (*Reliance Industries*)

Applications

Bubble emission leak testing is generally applicable when:

1. Operator subjectivity can be tolerated.
2. The production rate is low or the allowable leak is large, such as 10^{-2} std·cm³/s (10^{-3} Pa·m³/s).
3. The production run is short.
4. The exact leak location must be identified.
5. The part cannot be reliably sealed.
6. Economic considerations do not allow other test methods.

Some specific applications are:

1. Hydraulic and pneumatic tanks.
2. Tubing and pipe assemblies.
3. Engine blocks.
4. Castings.
5. Valves and valve seats.

Testing Techniques

As was mentioned earlier, two basic techniques are used in bubble emission leak testing: (1) immersion leak testing and (2) film solution leak testing. In immersion leak testing, the part being tested is pressurized and then immersed in the indicating medium. The part is allowed to remain in the medium for a period of time, and an examination is made for bubbles. Visual inspection of the part for bubbles should be made at distances less than 2′ (0.6 m) for best results. Dry compressed air is most commonly used for pressurization, but other gases are used in special circumstances. Water is generally used as the testing medium, although other liquids are also used for specific applications.

In film solution leak testing, the entire part is internally pressurized using air or some other safe gas. The part surface is then covered with a liquid film solution that permits visible bubble formation. On some occasions, the liquid film is common household liquid soap mixed with water. However, such soaps may contain certain chemicals that may be inadvisable to use on some materials. Chemically neutral commercial solutions are available. These solutions also have a longer operating life than the soap solutions and give more precise indications of leakage.

For applications where both sides of the part are not accessible and/or only a specific area of the part needs to be tested, specially designed vacuum boxes can be used. These boxes are open along the surface that is placed over the part, and the opposite side is transparent. Special elastomeric seals are placed

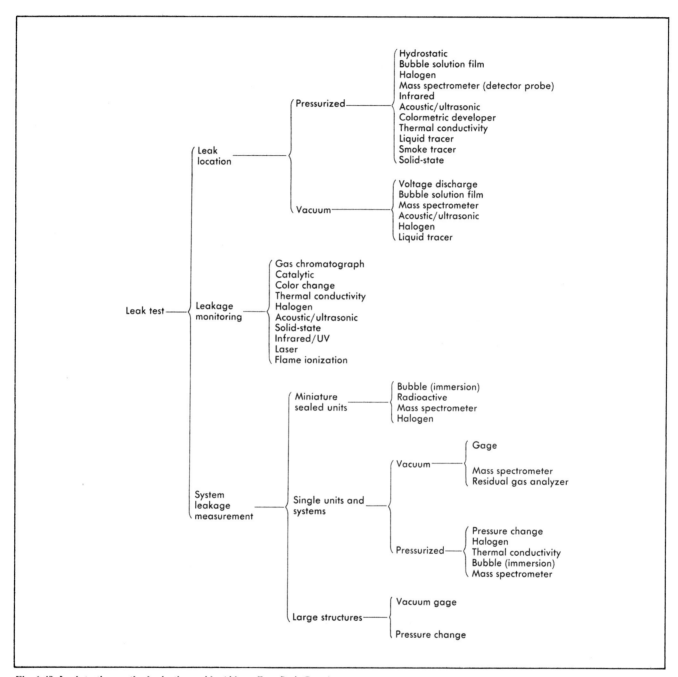

Fig. 6-49 Leak testing method selection guide. (*Mean Free Path Corp.*)

on the open side of the box to conform to uneven surfaces and to ensure proper sealing. During testing, the area being tested is coated with the liquid film solution and is then covered with the box. A vacuum pump evacuates the air inside the box. The atmospheric pressure on the outside forces the box against the test surface. Bubble formation on the test surface can be viewed through the transparent top. The main advantages of the vacuum box technique are that seal force is automatically obtained and only one surface need be accessible. A major problem encountered with this technique is sealing on a rough surface, such as those with a weld or an overlap.

A variation of the vacuum box technique involves holding a pressurized box against the surface being tested. The film solution is applied to the opposite side of the surface. The primary limitation to this technique is the high retaining force required to hold the pressurized box against the test surface.

General Principles

It is sometimes erroneously assumed that if no bubbles appear to be floating upward from a submerged part in some time, such as 15 seconds, then no leakage exists. This is, of course, not true. A standard production test time of 15 seconds without a free bubble in reality permits a leakage rate of about 1×10^{-4} std·cm^3/s (1×10^{-5} Pa·m^3/s) if an eventual bubble of 0.06" (1.5 mm) diam is assumed. This is due to the possibility of a free bubble occurring at slightly more than 15 seconds. Figure 6-50 shows bubble frequency versus time for various bubble sizes in immersion testing.

Immersion test times typically run from 5 to 60 seconds, with a requirement that no leak-caused bubbles appear. The type of flow occurring within a leak when a single bubble appears within this time is laminar. A characteristic of laminar flow leaks is that the leak rate varies as the difference of the squares of the absolute pressures across the leak. For example, if a test gage pressure is increased six times, from 10 to 60 psi (70 to 420 kPa), the leak flow will increase about 10 times. Increasing the test pressure can thus provide a large gain in sensitivity or a reduction in test time.

Bubble volumes can vary up to 25 times for some submerged parts, due only to leak geometry and point of emission. Because bubble size cannot be practically measured with either the immersion or liquid film test, no great accuracy can be placed on the methods in typical production conditions.

Surface tension reducing additives added to immersion test water can appreciably improve the test sensitivity per unit of time. Free bubble size is reduced, and the tendency for bubbles to remain attached to the test part is reduced. An addition of less than 3% by volume of additive can reduce the time for free bubble formation by 50-90%. Additives generally require deionized water, and the exact improvement in emission time depends on total test conditions. Tripling the rate of bubble emission reduces the bubble diameter by 42%, but the greater frequency of bubble emission more than compensates for the reduction in visibility.

Small leaks are easily plugged with water, grease, or oil. It is therefore important that a part be clean and dry before a test; this is a requirement for any type of leak test. With bubble testing, the test pressure should always be applied before the part is immersed or the film solution applied to prevent the water or solution from blocking a small leak.

Equipment

If water is used, the tank should be of a nonrusting material. Stainless steel is often used for larger parts, especially when internal fixturing must be supported. Illumination through portholes is highly recommended. Two methods of viewing are used: downward toward the liquid surface and through transparent sides or portholes in the tank. While side viewing pro-

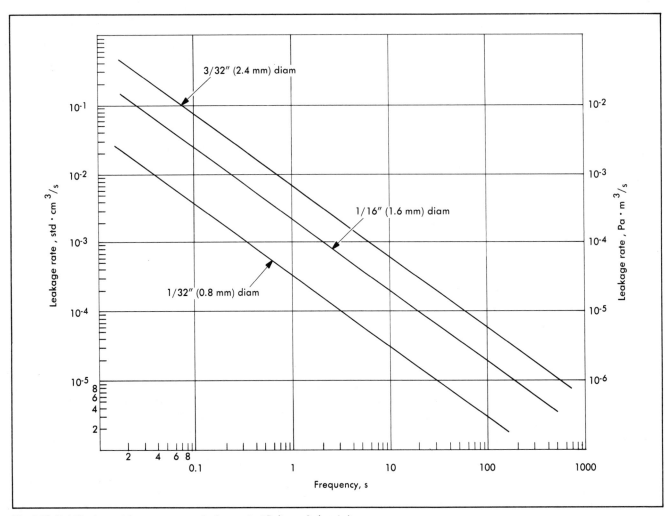

Fig. 6-50 Bubble size and frequency versus leakage rate. (*Reliance Industries*)

vides a much better test, the operator usually must walk around the tank or the part must revolve to check for bubbles.

When a part is submerged, there is a tendency for air to be trapped in crevices as well as underneath the part. As the air detaches and rises in bubbles it can be mistaken for leaks, which can be detrimental when the production cycle time is short and/or the part is large. To minimize this problem, the part can be moved after immersion, either linearly or in a circular path. Another method used is draining the liquid after each test and then refilling the tank after the next part is in place; however, part movement is difficult to implement, and a fast tank fill causes vision-reducing turbulence and bubbles for a period of time after filling.

A regulator is used to reduce line pressure, and a manual or solenoid-operated valve is used for filling and exhausting. It is advisable to include a safety valve or safety pressure switch if higher than specified test pressure can pose a hazard to the operator.

Parts requiring internal pressurization must be sealed at one or more points, and the means of sealing must allow entry and exit of the air or gas. Seals may be standard items such as O-rings, square-cut rings, or lip seals. The seal is usually made from one of the elastomer-type materials. The type of elastomer is dependent on application, with urethane often favored for special seals because of its durability in production usage.

Seals may be manually installed prior to testing or may be applied in a part holding fixture, either manually such as with an overcenter lever arrangement or by a pneumatic or hydraulic cylinder. Few commercially available complete sealing mechanisms exist because most parts have unique requirements. One exception is the availability of manual sealing devices for small tube and pipe inside diameters.

Automatic seal application can range from the simple case of a seal held at the end of an air cylinder rod to assemblies that can accommodate lateral and angular misalignment of the sealed port. In some cases, seal force must be held within close limits, requiring an adjustable cylinder rod stop, with the seal application force transmitted through a spring.

Safety

A major problem with immersion testing on a production line where an open tank of water is used is the difficulty in keeping the operator dry. This may be a health and a morale problem, especially in cold work areas, because the floor is often wet. A raised drain platform and, if necessary, boots should be provided. Rubber gloves and rubber aprons are also helpful.

Flammable liquids such as alcohol are sometimes used in bubble emission testing when water will affect the part and when rapid evaporation is desired. This test method is done inside closed chambers having transparent sides and sometimes with conveyor equipment. The safest method of operation is to eliminate any oxygen above the liquid or in the drying area by flooding with nitrogen. A less safe method is to maintain a rich vapor-air mixture to prevent burning. Vapors should be exhausted with a sufficient quantity of air to prevent any possibility of burning. In addition, all electrical equipment should be properly grounded and any sources of static or sparks eliminated.

When immersion testing, and sometimes liquid film testing, cause a wet working environment, it is important to eliminate any possibility of electric shock. All electrical equipment must

be securely grounded, and ground fault lights should be installed in all applicable situations. Electrical components such as motors and solenoid valves are usually found on production line equipment.

Water contamination is easily avoided through frequent or continuous liquid changing and, if required, addition of bacteria-killing chemicals. Service companies can test and treat water in large test installations.

TRACER GAS LEAK TESTING

Tracer gas leak testing is one of the many ways that have been devised to test products for leakage. A typical tracer gas leak test consists of the following three basic steps:

1. A tracer gas in a detectable amount is introduced to one side of the surface to be tested.
2. A differential pressure is produced across the surface with the higher pressure at the tracer gas side.
3. A suitable instrument is used to detect the presence of tracer gas on the lower pressure side.

When performing a tracer gas leak test, it is advisable to use the highest test pressure possible within the design safety factor. This is because a leak rate in the laminar flow range varies with the difference of the squares of the absolute pressures across the leak. If the pressure of tracer gas is not changed, an increase of backup pressure with air or a neutral gas dilutes the tracer gas linearly, but increases the total flow rate by nearly the square of the pressure. Thus, by using a high test pressure, it is possible to either reduce the amount of tracer gas used per test or, if the concentration of tracer gas is maintained, increase the test sensitivity. The test part must be dry because small leaks are easily plugged by any liquid. Dryness is also important because some tracer gas detectors are adversely affected by high amounts of water or hydrocarbon vapors.

A variety of gases have been and are used as tracer gases. Commonly used safe gases include helium, the refrigerant halides (R-12, R-22), and to a lesser extent sulfur hexafluoride. The reasons for the use of these gases are availability, cost, safety, gas characteristics, and the development of equipment that is sensitive to minute amounts of these gases.

The use of helium tracer gas and the mass spectrometer for leak detection was developed during the 1940s to maintain the leaktight integrity of large gaseous diffusion systems. Since that time the use of helium mass spectrometer leak detectors has accelerated, and the system has entered every industry where leaks must be detected.

Halogen tracer gas leak testing originated in the refrigeration industry when halide gas came into use. Leak detection was first done using an open flame color-change type of detector until the modern high-sensitivity compact electronic detector was developed. From its initial application in the refrigeration industry, the use of halogen gases for leak testing has spread into many other industries. Sulfur hexafluoride is used in leak testing large electrical power transformers as well as other applications.

In addition to products containing a detectable gas, tracer gas leak testing can be used for a variety of other applications. A few of the potential applications are listed in Table 6-15. When production rates warrant the cost, automatic systems with dedicated fixturing may be used. Loading and unloading may be manual or fully automatic, and automatic checking of the detector calibration at preset intervals may be included.

LEAK TESTING

TABLE 6-15
Potential Applications of Tracer Gas Leak Testing

Pneumatic and hydraulic valves, compressors, pumps and fittings

Heat exchangers and radiators

Engine fuel system pumps, valves, connectors, and injectors

Brake system master and wheel cylinders and proportioning valves

Shock absorbers

Wheels

Pneumatic and hydraulic reservoirs and tanks

Fuel tanks

Beverage cans

Electronic circuit packages, switches, relays, and crystals

Electronic sensors

Fire extinguishers

Body implants

(Reliance Industries, Inc.)

Advantages and Limitations

The major advantages of tracer gas leak testing in general are the following:

- Lower leak rates can be detected than with any other method.
- Leak sensing times can be short, often ranging from 1 to 8 seconds for production systems.
- Production systems can be automated.
- Test time does not increase greatly with part volume.
- Part temperature does not affect testing, although in some instances the leak path may be affected.

The major limitations of tracer gas leak testing are the following:

- Equipment is more expensive than that of other methods. Cost of gas varies with fill volume, partial pressure requirement (percentage used with a neutral or safe gas), fill pressure, and required leak rate sensitivity.
- The exact location of a leak can be determined with manually operated probes, but cannot be found in automatic production machines. Some parts, however, permit automatic location of a leak "zone."
- Periodic calibration is required; for some equipment this is performed automatically.

Mass spectrometer leak testing. Specific advantages of leak testing with the mass spectrometer are the following:

- Leak test sensitivity is unsurpassed except by the radio-isotope method. Under ideal conditions, leakage equivalent to a single underwater bubble emission in 7 years can be detected.
- Can detect molecular flow leaks as well as laminar flow leaks.
- Calibrated leak standards are readily available from a variety of manufacturers with NBS calibration or traceability.
- Highly developed systems and associated machine components are readily available from a variety of manufacturers.
- Helium, which is generally used as the tracer gas, is widely available at reasonable cost and is nontoxic. The sensitivity of the mass spectrometer often permits a low percentage of helium in a mixture with a gas such as nitrogen.
- The mass spectrometer can be employed in fully automated production leak test systems.
- In a small or uncomplicated system, response time is typically under 10 seconds.
- In some modes of testing, such as leakage accumulation, a reasonably accurate measurement of total leakage is possible.

Limitations of finding leaks with the mass spectrometer method are the following:

- Initial cost of equipment is higher than that of other common leak test methods.
- The system is relatively complex in comparison to other systems.
- The system must be calibrated with a known leak.
- The system is adversely affected by small leaks to the atmosphere.
- The test is adversely affected by material outgassing and helium permeation of mechanical joints such as O-rings.
- Components and/or the system usually requires special cleaning.
- The atmosphere contains about five parts helium per million, which is detrimental to high-sensitivity probing, especially the detector probe technique.

Halogen detector leak testing. Specific advantages of leak testing with R-12, R-22, or other refrigerant gases are the following:

- Commercially available electronic detectors have high sensitivity to very small leaks. The ultimate leak sensitivity is 10^{-7} std·cm^3/s (10^{-8} Pa·m^3/s), with 10^{-6} std·cm^3/s (10^{-7} Pa·m^3/s) generally obtainable in the larger units. Only helium mass spectrometer systems offer higher sensitivity. In some cases, the detector probe technique using halogen is more sensitive than with helium because halogens do not diffuse in air as quickly as helium.
- Detectors are relatively simple, low in cost, and range from handheld, portable devices to units designed for production use.
- In most instances when the gas is used specifically for leak testing, only a small percentage of tracer gas is required. The tracer gas is generally mixed with pure air or a safe neutral gas such as nitrogen.
- Production type detectors may be used in manual or fully automated test systems.
- Typical leak detection time runs from 2 to 10 seconds in automated production equipment. Handheld probe response time is 1/2 to 2 seconds.
- Calibrated leak standards are commercially available, with NBS calibration or traceability.

Some of the specific limitations of halogen detector leak testing are the following:

- Gas cost per test varies with part volume and the partial pressure percentage mix required. It may be insignificant for a part having only a few cubic inches of volume, but may become a factor for a part of a few cubic feet or more.

- The detector must be calibrated to a known leakage rate.
- The small sensor element used in production detectors has a short life of about 1000-2000 operating hours, depending on usage and clean air supply between tests. Replacement cost of the sensor element in production-type detectors exceeds $100; replacement cost is less for sensors used in small handheld units.
- The halogen diode responds to most halogen-containing vapors and is therefore subject to interference.
- Care must be taken that there are no open flames, welding, or other sources of high temperature present with high concentrations of test gas. Toxic gases can be generated. Normal dispersion of the test gas in air when used in unconfined areas or design of equipment for exhausting outside will avoid this problem.

Testing Techniques

A number of techniques exist for tracer gas leak testing. The technique used generally depends on the application.

Detector (sniffer) probing. The detector probing technique (inside-out, manual probing) is done with several gases, but primarily helium or a halogen gas. It consists of moving a small probe having a low flow suction inlet tube over the test area (see Fig. 6-51, view *a*). The speed (as determined by calibration) at which the probe is moved over the test surface is from 1/2 to 2 ips (13 to 50 mm/s). The distance from the probe tip to the leak site will affect the response of the instrument; operators must maintain constant spacing as well as constant speed. A line connecting the probe to the main instrument can be several feet long.

Probing cannot provide an accurate measurement of leakage because gas exiting from a leak will accumulate in some amount depending on air movement, diffusion of tracer gas, part geometry, and, when applicable, time from gas fill to leak test. However, in many instances it is desired to have no detectable leakage, so the lack of exact measurement is not detrimental. A probe should be calibrated to a leak standard using a high safety factor.

Leak response time for either helium or halogen probe systems is from 1/2 to 2 seconds, depending on length of probe line. The amount of tracer gas used in the test mixture may vary from 1 to 100%, the latter being the case in charged refrigeration systems.

Tracer (spray) probing. The tracer probe (outside-in, atmospheric pressure) technique is usually done with helium gas and a mass spectrometer. The test part must be capable of being connected to the leak detector and being evacuated to a high vacuum (see Fig. 6-51, view *b*). The tracer gas spray, usually in high concentration, may be applied manually or automatically. Automatic spraying may allow the use of a partial enclosure.

Leak detection time is generally under 10 seconds. Gas usage is relatively high for manual spraying, and leak size measurement is poor; however, for some products, such as large complex pipe assemblies, the tracer probe technique may be the only practical leak testing technique. This technique is useful in finding leaks in industrial vacuum equipment used for melting, brazing, or metallizing.

Bell jar accumulation. In the bell jar accumulation technique (inside-out, vacuum chamber), the part is pressurized with a tracer gas and then completely enclosed in a special enclosure (see Fig. 6-51, view *c*). This enclosure or bell jar is evacuated

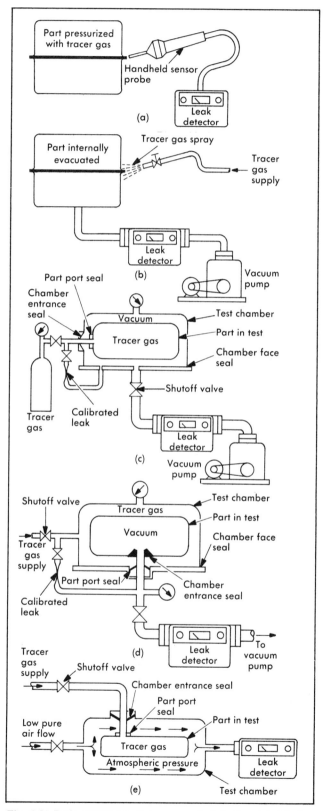

Fig. 6-51 Basic techniques of tracer gas leak testing: (a) detector probing, (b) tracer probing, (c) bell jar accumulation, (d) hood accumulation, and (e) accumulation flow. (*Reliance Industries*)

to a low vacuum. Any leaks are accumulated in the annulus of the bell jar.

Helium, halogen, or sulfur hexafluoride gas may be used in the bell jar accumulation technique; however, helium is generally used for leakage rate limits smaller than 10^{-5} std·cm^3/s (10^{-6} Pa·m^3/s).

An indication of the total leakage rate may be obtained with a mass spectrometer by measuring the rate of tracer gas accumulation. The general method requires that the part must either be capable of being sealed, with tracer gas introduction through a leaktight seal, or must contain trapped pressurized tracer gas. When the part allows a connection, it is sometimes evacuated before introduction of the tracer gas, allowing a very fast internal dispersal. The vacuum chamber must withstand the atmospheric crushing force.

Hood accumulation. Helium is generally used for the hood accumulation (outside-in, vacuum chamber) technique, and the tracer gas mix can be applied under pressure (see Fig. 6-51, view *d*). The part must be capable of leaktight connection and must withstand a high internal vacuum. An advantage of this technique is that the tracer gas usage is minimized when the chamber is capable of being closely fitted to the part.

In production line systems, the mass spectrometer system pumping speed is a major cycle time consideration for larger parts. An indication of the total part leakage rate may be obtained by measuring the rate of tracer gas accumulation.

Accumulation flow. When the leak rate limit is relatively large, such as 10^{-4} std·cm^3/s (10^{-5} Pa·m^3/s), the accumulation flow (inside-out, atmospheric pressure) technique has several advantages for production line use (see Fig. 6-51, view *e*). Any of the tested tracer gases may be used. Test cycle time for smaller parts can be from 5 to 10 seconds. The chamber does not have to withstand internal or external pressure, and the method lends itself to automation. The part also must be capable of leaktight connection or must contain trapped pressurized tracer gas.

Other techniques. Helium mass spectrometer leak testing is often used to test hermetically sealed electronic devices such as integrated circuit (IC) packages. Sealed parts may be placed in a chamber, and after chamber evacuation, they are subjected to helium under pressure; this process is called the helium bombing technique. Alternatively, gas may be introduced prior to or during the part sealing process. Test variables of tracer gas concentration, pressure, bombing time, and time from bombing to test are closely controlled. The sensitivity attainable with this technique depends on the volume within the part.

Another technique for testing small hermetically sealed parts uses radioactive kryton 85 radioactive gas. Parts are bombed with a mix of the tracer gas and nitrogen and cleaned externally with a neutral gas flow. A scintillation counter is then used to determine the amount of gas remaining in the part compared to the original amount, the opposite of any other tracer gas method. A reasonably accurate quantitative leak rate measurement is possible with this technique. Because the parts are often tested in batches, the throughput is high.

The use of a radioactive gas requires strict control of the entire procedure with elaborate radiation safety control and precautions as required by various governmental agencies. Operators must be thoroughly trained. When all precautions are taken, the danger is minimal.

Equipment

Helium mass spectrometer. Helium mass spectrometer equipment is all based on the principle of sorting charged particles under vacuum. Depending on the manufacturer, the design, function, and operation of the various components may vary. Figure 6-52 shows the basic components of one type of automatic mass spectrometer leak detector.

The diagram in Fig. 6-53 shows the general arrangement of one mass spectrometer design. Entering gas molecules are positively ionized by electrons from a heated filament and are accelerated toward an exit slit in the extractor plate. The narrow beam of molecules enters a magnetic field that, because of its imparting a curved path to the molecules, sorts them by mass. The path of a molecule is determined by its speed, mass/charge ratio, and the geometry and strength of the magnetic field. Ions with a specific mass/charge ratio will pass

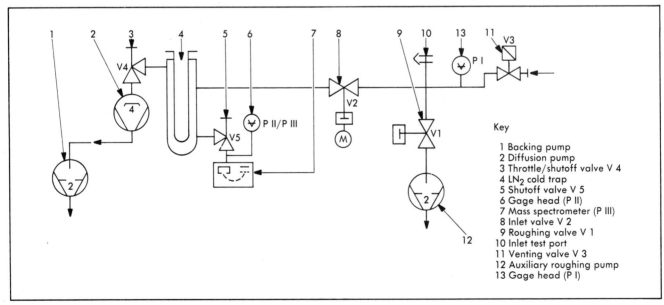

Key

1 Backing pump
2 Diffusion pump
3 Throttle/shutoff valve V 4
4 LN$_2$ cold trap
5 Shutoff valve V 5
6 Gage head (P II)
7 Mass spectrometer (P III)
8 Inlet valve V 2
9 Roughing valve V 1
10 Inlet test port
11 Venting valve V 3
12 Auxiliary roughing pump
13 Gage head (P I)

Fig. 6-52 Schematic of mass spectrometer leak test system. (*Inficon, Leybold-Heraeus, Inc.*)

through a slit in the intermediate target plate and then through a final slit to enter the 90° electrostatic field. Ions passing through the electrostatic field strike the collector plate, causing a small current to flow, which is amplified. The resultant is a measurement of helium presence.

Mass spectrometer systems have more manual and automatic controls than are found in other types of leak test equipment; however, setup is not difficult, and correct operation and calibration are easily verified. The stability of most modern equipment allows operation on fully automated production lines.

Some of the general sizes and categories of helium mass spectrometer leak detectors available are the following:

1. Portable: about 60 to 120 lb (27 to 54 kg) weight and 3 ft³ (0.08 m³) volume, with probe or vacuum connection. Hand carried or on cart; power connection required.
2. Small console or desk: 500 to 1000 lb (225 to 450 kg) weight, with a vacuum connection for external testing.
3. Small console or desk: 500 to 1000 lb (225 to 450 kg) weight, with a small test chamber built into the top.
4. Large industrial NEMA-12 cabinet: 1500 to 2500 lb (680 to 1130 kg) weight, with some large components such as roughing pumps and liquid nitrogen tanks mounted externally.

Several manufacturers offer high-vacuum accessories such as manual and power-operated valves, particulate traps and tubing flanges, nipples, tees, crosses, elbows, adapters, and weld fittings. These are usually made of stainless steel.

Halogen diode detector. The heart of the halogen detector instrument is the sensor (sometimes called a halogen diode), which is a small device of typically less than 1 in.³ (16.4 cm³) in size and structurally simple. The three major elements of the sensor are a platinum wire heater, positive ion emitting material at a positive voltage, and a grounded collector (see Fig. 6-54). These elements are contained within a cylinder having electrical connector pins at one end and small ports at each end for inlet and outlet airflow. An airflow of approximately 5 std·cm³/s (0.5 Pa·m³) at atmospheric pressure is drawn through the sensor. The presence of less than one part halide gas per million parts of air will cause a marked increase in ion emission. The resultant increase in current is amplified for meter reading and

audiovisual signal actuation. The halogen sensor is nonlinear when the sensed gas exceeds more than a few parts per million in air. Exposure to a high gas concentration will affect sensitivity temporarily; when the detector is used in a system, this effect can be reduced or eliminated.

Production instruments have a cable several feet long from the instrument cabinet to a probe. The sensor may be located in the probe handle or in the cabinet, depending on the manufacturer. A small bellows-type pump within the cabinet provides airflow through a line within the cable to obtain suction at the probe. The cable houses wires for a leak indicating light in the probe handle and also for the sensor when it is mounted within in the handle.

Calibration. Calibration is important because all electronic tracer gas detectors change in sensitivity over time. Calibration of both mass spectrometer and halogen diode leak testers is accomplished with reference leaks using the same gas that is used in testing. Standard leaks are available from several different sources.

Safety

The safety aspects of tracer gas leak testing are the following:

1. Toxicity of gases.
2. Flammability or combustibility of gases.
3. Atmospheric oxygen deficiency.
4. Explosion or implosion.
5. Mechanical machinery hazards.
6. Electrical hazards.
7. Cleaning hazards.
8. Temperature hazards.

Tracer gases used in special situations may be quite toxic. Examples of some of these toxic trace gases are sulfur dioxide, acetone, ammonia, and hydrogen chloride. Radioactive kryton 85 also poses special problems in system leakage avoidance and in detection of leakage. Nitrous oxide, which has been used in general-purpose tracer gas leak testing, is moderately toxic.

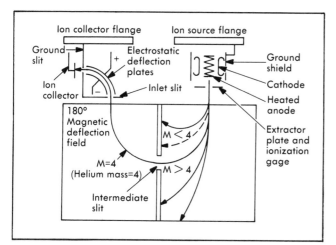

Fig. 6-53 Diagram of a modern mass spectrometer sensor. (*Inficon, Leybold-Heraeus, Inc.*)

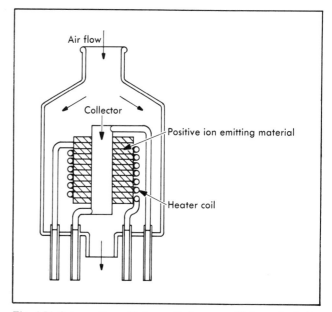

Fig. 6-54 Cross section of halogen diode sensor. (*Inficon, Leybold-Heraeus, Inc.*)

CHAPTER 6

LEAK TESTING

Limits have been set by the Occupational Safety and Health Administration (OSHA) for exposure to toxic gases; exposure warning badges and automatic warning detectors are usually available for the more toxic gases. Helium is nontoxic, and the refrigerant R-12 (dichlorodifluoromethane) is essentially nontoxic. A limit of 8 hours exposure to 1000 parts per million of R-12 has been set. High concentrations of R-12 generate toxic gases when brought into contact with flames, red-hot surfaces, cigarettes, and matches.

Neither helium nor R-12 are combustible or flammable. Gases that are combustible are rarely used for leak testing. The occasional industrial practice of detecting these hazardous gas leaks with an open flame is not recommended. Sensitive detectors (gas absorption and conductivity leak test methods) are available for the detection of combustible and toxic gases.

Oxygen is present in the atmosphere at about 21%. With a reduction to about 18%, there is a marked effect on heartbeat, and dizziness may occur. Further depletion of oxygen will cause unconsciousness and death. Any gas that is otherwise nontoxic can cause oxygen depletion in confined areas. Factory leak testing will rarely provide confined areas large enough for a person to enter. One exception is testing of large pressure vessels. Confined areas or vessels that could present a hazard under any possible normal or abnormal situation, such as an equipment failure, should be provided with automatic oxygen alarm detectors and should, if possible, be thoroughly blown out with air after each test occurrence. It is also important to remember that light gases (such as helium) rise and heavy gases (refrigerants) fall over a period of time. This means that heavy gases, such as R-12, stratify and settle at the bottom, thus depleting areas of needed oxygen.

Many leak tests involve high pressure, high vacuum, and sometimes large surface areas. An explosion or implosion would be extremely hazardous because of the energy stored in any compressed gas. A loose hose exhausting high pressure can whip and cause severe injury. Pressurized tanks, chambers, and lines should be designed or selected with high safety factors. The ASME code for pressure vessels should be followed. Safety valves or rupture disks, safety pressure switches, and other devices that can be included to provide a fail-safe operation should be incorporated in the system. Gas cylinders must be handled with great care because they are highly pressurized. Cylinders should never be moved without the cap in place; OSHA requires that cylinders be secured against tip-over with safety chains. A considerable body of codes, regulations, and plant standards have been developed to promote operator safety. All potential injury-causing situations must be guarded against if possible. Unfortunately, safety devices can be and often are rendered inoperative. Machines must always be regarded as potential product liability problems.

Electrical equipment used in commercial tracer gas leak detectors often operates at a high voltage. As long as the detector and any associated equipment are properly grounded, there is little hazard unless cover panels are removed. Many leak detectors have internal parts that operate at high temperatures; again, these present no hazard in operation unless a cover panel is removed. Only experienced personnel should be allowed to work on leak detection equipment.

AIR LEAK TESTING

In air leak testing, the test part, whether it is an engine block, artificial kidney, water faucet, or simple casting, can be simplified to represent a sealed pressure vessel (see Fig. 6-55). During the test, regulated air pressure or vacuum is applied to the part through a manual or automatic operating valve. Leakage within the part is detected by loss of pressure or vacuum (pressure/vacuum decay) or by the need to continually add air to make up for air escaping from the test part.

Devices used for detecting pressure loss can be as simple as a pressure gage or a pressure switch or as complex as electronic pressure transducers with feedback of small pressure changes to electronic instrumentation. The electronic instrumentation amplifies the signal received from the transducer and provides a visual readout of the pressure changes to aid decision-making. Devices used for detecting flow (added makeup air) can be as simple as a water manometer, variable area flowmeter, or bubble jar or as complex as electronic transducers with feedback of small flow changes to electronic instrumentation.

In all types of flowmeters, some pressure loss will occur across the measuring element. Some meters require extended time to allow a stable measurement to be made. The most popular airflow system is the differential type.

Applications

When deciding whether a part is a candidate for air leak testing, it is necessary to consider the type of liquid or gas used in service as well as the operating pressure of this liquid or gas. Components that operate with liquid are excellent candidates for air leak testing. The primary advantage of using air over liquid is the speed at which the test can be performed; however, it is necessary to keep in mind that air will pass through some leaks that will not pass liquid. Because of this, a maximum allowable air leakage rate should be specified.

Components and assemblies that operate with gas or vacuum are also applicable for air leak testing; however stringent air leak test specifications are required. For some applications, such as air conditioning and refrigeration components, air leak testing is used as a pretest to identify units that have large leaks.

Table 6-16 lists some automotive components that are tested in various phases of manufacturing and assembly by pressure decay leak testing. The components are categorized by the type of medium used and the functional area.

Testing Techniques

Manual and automatic methods are used for air leak testing. The majority of the leak testing instruments operate automatically. Many of these instruments have electronic memories and incorporate a compensation network. All air leak systems require precise regulation of air supply pressure, such as obtained from a bleedoff-type pressure regulator.

Manual method. Four manual techniques are used in air leak testing. Three are based on leakage flow indication and one

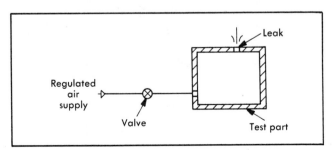

Fig. 6-55 Typical air leak testing diagram. (*Uson Corporation*)

TABLE 6-16
Automotive Components Tested by
Pressure Decay Leak Testing

Liquid-Containing Components

Engine cooling and oil systems

Break components: wheel cylinders, master cylinders, and calipers

Fuel systems: carburetors, fuel pumps, and injectors

Power train: transmissions, transaxles, and internal components of transmissions and axles

Cooling components: radiator, heater core, and hoses

Power steering: power steering pump and steering gear

Gas-Containing Components

Exhaust gas: exhaust manifolds, mufflers, emission control components, catalytic converter, exhaust piping, and oxygen sensors

Refrigerant:* air conditioning compressor, condensers, condensing valve, accumulator, and hoses

Vacuum Components

Actuators: brake booster, climate control vacuum motors, intake manifolds

Emission control devices: EGR valve, thermal vacuum switches, filters, canisters, purge valves, and restrictors

(*Uson Corporation*)
* Not normally tested by air leak testing.

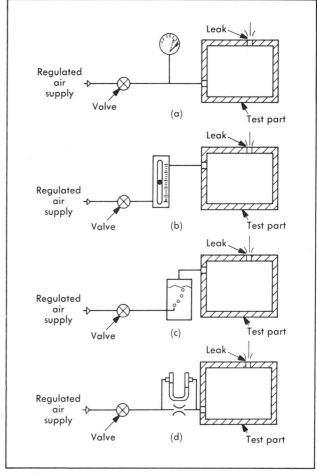

Fig. 6-56 Air leak test arrangements: (a) pressure decay, (b) variable airflow meter, (c) bubble jar flow indicator, and (d) manometer flow measurement. (*Uson Corporation***)**

is based on pressure decay. In their simplest form, these techniques usually are not suitable for production leak testing. Basic manual techniques are used in experimental work when establishing the maximum allowable air leak rate for a new product.

The four techniques are illustrated in Fig. 6-56. All of these techniques are effected by adiabatic heating of the air as it is compressed into the test part. For good sensitivity, it is therefore necessary to allow time for pressure to stabilize as the heat dissipates.

Pressure decay. Leak testing with a pressure gage or water/mercury manometer is leak testing in its most simple form (see Fig. 6-56, view *a*). A pressure gage or manometer is connected to the pneumatic piping or test part to continually monitor the test pressure. The gage is monitored at the beginning of the leak test and monitored again for pressure loss after a time period (seconds to hours). The accuracy of this technique depends on the seals and gage selection.

Variable area flowmeter. The variable area flow meter is a simple form of flow testing. The flowmeter is placed in series with the pneumatic piping and test part (see Fig. 6-56, view *b*). A leaking part will require continuous makeup air to maintain pressure. The makeup air is supplied to the test part through the flowmeter. The internal ball of the flowmeter may experience unusual wear from the up-and-down hammering from pressurization, leakage, and depressurization, depending on system

piping. The flowmeter technique is operator dependent and creates difficulty in reading minimum and maximum leakage.

Bubble jar flow indication. The bubble jar technique is similar to the variable area flowmeter. The jar is placed in series with the pneumatic piping and test part (see Fig. 6-56, view *c*). A leaking test part will require makeup air, which is supplied through the bubble jar. Following pressurization, a stream of bubbles will be seen initially because of adiabatic heating. A leak will create a flow of bubbles after stabilization.

Manometer flow measurement. The water manometer is placed in parallel with a flow restrictor or orifice plate (see Fig. 6-56, view *d*). Air flowing through the orifice plate into the test part creates a pressure differential at the manometer.

Because the flow orifice becomes extremely small for measuring small leakage rates, this flow testing technique is normally not used on leakage rates lower than 1.6 std·cm³/s (0.16 Pa·m³/s). The small orifice must be carefully maintained because of possible plugging and coating from the continuous flow of air.

Automatic method. Currently there are four basic techniques used for automatic air leak testing (see Fig. 6-57). Two techniques involve pressure decay and two involve leakage flow measurement.

LEAK TESTING

Differential pressure decay. The differential pressure decay technique compares the pressure in a reference chamber to the pressure in the test item following a stabilization period (see Fig. 6-57, view *a*).

In this technique, the volume of the reference chamber is equal to that of the test item, to balance the adiabatic effect and thus reduce stabilization time.

Pressure decay. The pressure decay technique with electronic memory is the most commonly used technique because of the fast leak test cycle. This technique eliminates the reference chamber and additional valves required for differential pressure

decay testing (see Fig. 6-57, view *b*). The test part pressure curve is memorized, and the pressure loss is measured before actual stabilization.

Differential pressure flow. With the differential pressure flow technique, the differential pressure across a restriction element measures leakage flow to the test part after stabilization (see Fig. 6-57, view *c*). This is the slowest technique and is not normally used for testing parts having leakage rates below 1.6 std·cm³/s (0.16 Pa·m³/s).

Thermal flow. In the thermal flow leak technique, the leakage flow is determined electronically by measuring heat loss of

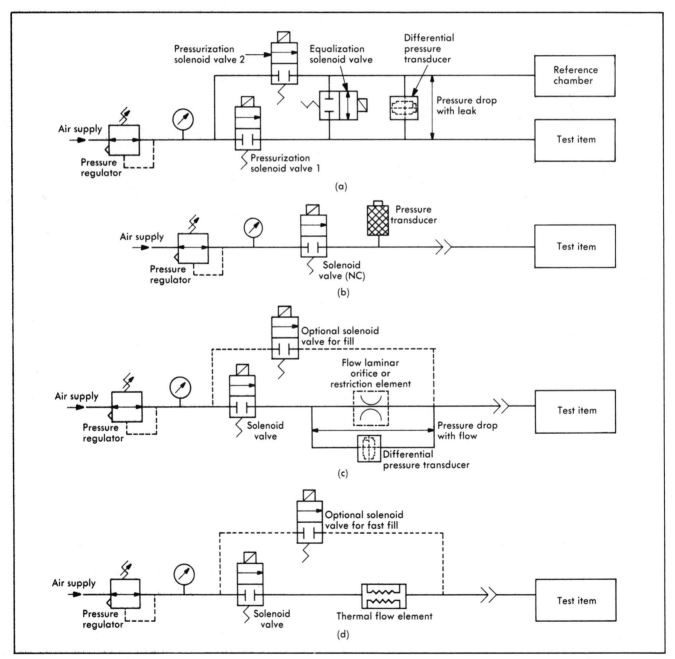

Fig. 6-57 Air pressure automatic leak tests: (a) differential pressure decay, (b) pressure decay, (c) differential pressure flow, and (d) thermal flow. (*Uson Corporation*)

air passing the heated (thermal) element (see Fig. 6-57, view *d*). Because of the long time requirement for a stable flow measurement, this technique is normally used for laboratory-type applications.

Automatic Leak Testers

Advanced-design testers are capable of performing air leak flow testing using all of the common automatic leak testing techniques previously described. The versatility of these microprocessor-based leak testers allows testing with various pressure, flow, or vacuum sensors. These testers can manually or automatically select multiple testing routines, such as sequential or simultaneous testing of leak, flow, and pressure.

Advantages. The advantage of automatic leak testing equipment is that no judgment decision for the amount of leakage or the accept/reject decision is required of the operator. Additionally, air pressure is relatively inexpensive, easy to apply, easy to remove, noncontaminating, and normally available in most manufacturing facilities. Air leak testing is also clean and dry, eliminating messy and dangerous workstations, part cleanup, and drying associated with water immersion stands and hydrostatic testing.

Limitations. Automatic air leak testing is only as good as the mechanical structure and seals of the automatic test fixture. Minute movements of seals and structures during the leak test cycle can change the pressure inside the test part in excess of the leakage (pressure loss) being measured. Properly designed test fixtures can eliminate this problem. Improperly designed fixtures can go unnoticed because of the lack of understanding of their importance.

Automatic air leak testing does not show the leak location. Normally, rejected parts go to a repair station where leak location (for repair) is revealed by the use of bubble emission.

Another limitation to air leak testing may be an undesirable combination of the test parameters. All leak testing cannot be performed using automatic air leak testers. A test part with a small maximum allowable air leak rate specification, high test pressure, and large test volume is normally not a good candidate for pressure decay leak testing.

Test cycle time. A typical cycle in an automatic leak test consists of pressurization, stabilization, decay period, and venting time. Other factors to take into consideration in the overall cycle evaluation are production rate, clamp/unclamp time, and part transfer.

Pressurization for most parts requires from 0.5 to 4.0 seconds, depending on part volume and test pressure. To allow the system to stabilize, a stabilization time equal to the decay period is generally used. The amount of time allowed for decay (leakage rate sensitivity) is based on part volume, maximum allowable leak rate, and test pressure. A stabilization period is required to allow transients caused by the closing of the pressurization solenoid to die out and to allow the adiabatic heating to complete itself.

Manufacturers of air leak testing equipment generally provide a chart that can be used to determine the decay period (see Fig. 6-58). These charts are normally designed for a specific transducer and test pressure. To determine the decay period for a specific application, the horizontal line of the leak rate would be intersected with the vertical line of the part volume.

The decay period for components tested at a different pressure or volume can also be determined, however, because the test times are directly proportional to the increase or decrease in pressure or volume. For example, if the test pressure of the part

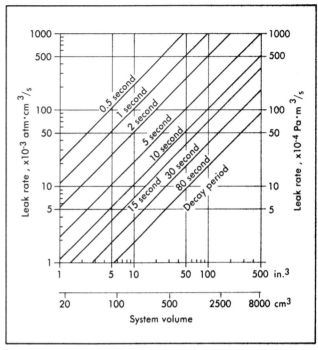

Fig. 6-58 Leak rate sensitivity chart for a 20 psig (138 kPa) pressure transducer and a test pressure of 20 psig. (*Uson Corporation*)

being tested is twice the pressure of the chart (all other variables the same), the decay period would be twice as long.

When using the flow or differential pressure decay technique, the time for pressurization, stabilization, and decay period may change; however, the total test cycle time will always require at least the total time established from the electronic memory pressure decay method. In most applications, the flow or differential pressure method requires longer total cycle times than the electronic memory pressure decay method.

Safety

In general, air leak testing is considered safe for workers and the environment; however, hazards in leak testing do exist.

Because typical shop air compressors normally maintain an air supply of approximately 80-100 psig (550-690 kPa), most air leak testing is performed at pressures between 0-80 psig (0-550 kPa). When testing above 30 psig (200 kPa), automatic exhausting of the test pressure prior to opening the test fixture should be considered. The exhausted air should be diverted to a safe area. The exhaust function prevents the possibility of injury that may occur when the test fixture opens and allows a large quantity of air and chips to escape suddenly. When testing in higher pressures such as 500-2000 psig (3.5-14 MPa), safety shields should cover the station prior to the pressurization. Vessels containing large volumes that require leak testing near their yield strength should not be tested with air.

Automatic testing and clamping fixtures should have safety shields that prevent people from placing their hands into an unsafe area. On manual load/unload fixtures, the use of a two-hand safety start system should be utilized. This system requires that both of the operator's hands push individual start buttons and maintain the pushed position until the fixture is completely closed.

THERMAL NONDESTRUCTIVE TESTING

THERMAL NONDESTRUCTIVE TESTING

Thermal nondestructive testing is a general term for the various methods used to detect flaws and an undesirable distribution of heat during service.[31,32,33] The methods used normally can be classified as either noncontact or contact. Noncontact methods depend on thermally generated electromagnetic energy radiated from the part being tested. At moderate temperatures this is predominantly the infrared region. Because of this, infrared testing is the most important branch of noncontact thermal testing. Direct contact methods place a thermally sensitive device or material in physical and thermal contact with the test part.

The noncontact and contact methods can be further classified as either thermographic or thermometric methods. Thermographic methods depend on the thermal gradients that occur on the surface of the part. When these methods are used, a map of the equal temperature contours is obtained. With thermometric methods, a precise value of the temperature is obtained. Figure 6-59 shows the various devices or materials that are used for these methods.

A frequent use of infrared detection in NDT is the examination of microcircuits and small electronic components. Printed circuit boards must be coated before inspection because the components in the board have different emissivity values. If the boards are not coated, the data obtained by scanning is of little value. Infrared techniques are also useful for detecting defects/delaminations in composite materials and for in-process quality control during plastic processing and composite manufacturing.[34] In the automotive industry, these techniques have been used to detect blocked water tubes and fin-to-tube disbonds in aluminum radiators.[35] They are also used to quantitatively examine temperatures on die surfaces of semipermanent mold die castings for improved casting quality.[36]

INFRARED THEORY

Infrared radiation, like visible-light radiation, occupies a specific region of the electromagnetic spectrum (see Fig. 6-60). The wavelengths of the visible portion extend from 0.4 to 0.75 μm, and the infrared portion extends from about 0.75 to 1000 μm. Although wavelengths are normally given in micrometers (μm), other units such as microns (μ), nanometers (nm), and angstroms (Å) have also been used. The relationship between these different wavelength measurements is:

$$1\ \mu m = 1\ \mu = 1000\ nm = 10,000\ \text{Å}$$

Thermography occupies the region in the mid-IR range, from 2 to approximately 10.5 μm. Figure 6-61 shows the visible absorption band and the infrared absorption band for thermographic equipment using an indium antimonide (InSb) detector. Although other detectors are available for infrared detection, they do not have adequate sensitivity for some of the elevated temperatures encountered in manufacturing operations. Thermal radiation emitted from objects such as people, plants, and buildings falls within this region. As the temperature of an object is increased, energy is radiated at a higher rate and at shorter wavelengths. As the temperature is increased further, emission of red light occurs, which is joined by yellow, green, blue, and violet components in the visible band. For example, an ingot of iron heated to 1800° F (982° C) would have a bright orange appearance; however only approximately 65 millionths of the energy radiated by the ingot would fall within the visible band.

Energy is lost from an object in three different modes: (1) conduction, (2) convection, and (3) radiation. When an object is surrounded by air, conduction losses can be treated as part of the convection losses. Thermography measures only the infrared radiative component of the energy loss and expresses that amount in isotherm units that can be converted to Btu/ft²-hr (W/m²), provided a standard temperature is known. The amount of energy radiated from an object is expressed by the Stefan-Boltzmann law:

$$E = \epsilon\, \sigma\, T^4 \tag{7}$$

where:

E = total energy radiated, Btu/ft²-hr (W/m²)
ϵ = emission coefficient (emissivity)
σ = Stefan-Boltzmann constant
T = absolute object temperature, °R (K)

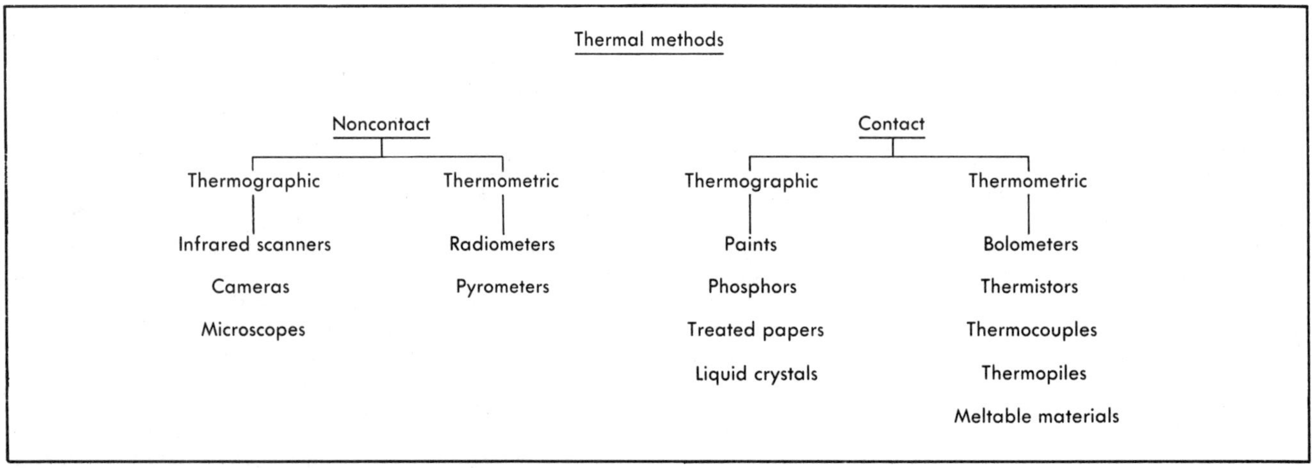

Fig. 6-59 Devices or materials used for thermal nondestructive testing.

THERMAL NONDESTRUCTIVE TESTING

The emissivity of an object is defined as the ratio of the spectral radiant power from that object to that from a black body at the same temperature. The total emissive power of a black body is proportional to the fourth power of its absolute temperature. Emissivity is usually a function of wavelength, λ. The emissivity value of a black body material is one; the value for any other material is less than one. The emissivity factor for a given object must be obtained to calculate the absolute temperature of that object from the measured radiation. The values for emissivity obtained by using thermography are the average of the values occurring over the middle infrared wavelength interval utilized by the thermal detector.

Unoxidized metals represent a case of almost perfect opacity and high spectral reflectivity that does not vary greatly with the wavelength. Consequently, the emissivity of metals is low, only slowly increasing with temperature. For nonmetals, emissivity tends to be high and decreases with temperature.

Typical emissivities for a variety of common materials are listed in Table 6-17; however, the values are meant to be used only as a guide because they depend on the spectral response of the instrument used to obtain them. Extensive emissivities for materials have been documented in the literature.

The large variation in emissivity is one of the major limitations in the use of thermography, particularly for quantitative measurements. The apparent temperature of objects at the same actual temperature can vary by a factor of 20 if corrections for emissivity are not made. Thus, an accurate knowledge of the emissivities of the object being viewed is essential to proper interpretation of the thermal images.

NONCONTACT METHODS

Any object at a temperature above absolute zero radiates energy in the infrared bandwidth. Several devices are available that detect this radiation and then convert it to a proportional electric signal for display. The display may be a numerical readout, a line graph of temperature versus position, or a thermal picture.

The greatest advantage of using noncontact methods is that the output can be detected without disturbing the thermal pattern; measurements can also be made rapidly and accurately. The major limitation is that the surface emissivity of the part

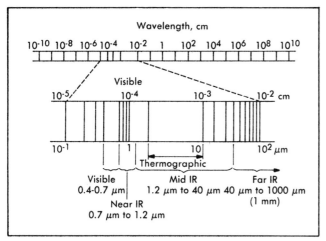

Fig. 6-60 Electromagnetic spectrum showing region of infrared active thermography.

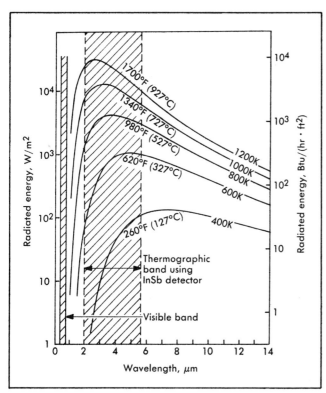

Fig. 6-61 Energy distribution for a black body at various temperatures.

TABLE 6-17
Emissivity Values for Various Materials

Material	Temperature, °F (°C)	Emissivity (ϵ) (Good emitters)
Human skin	90 (32)	0.98
Matte black lacquer	212 (100)	0.97
Distilled water	68 (20)	0.96
Common red brick	86 (30)	0.93
White bond paper	68 (20)	0.93
Planed oak wood	68 (20)	0.90
Stainless steel, oxidized	140 (60)	0.85
Copper, heavily oxidized	68 (20)	0.78
Aluminum anodized sheet	212 (100)	0.55
Cast iron, polished	104 (40)	0.21
Stainless steel, buffed	68 (20)	0.16
Steel, polished	212 (100)	0.07
Copper, polished	212 (100)	0.05 (poor emitters)

THERMAL NONDESTRUCTIVE TESTING

being tested must be known because the amount of radiation is a direct function of emissivity.

Thermographic

Noncontact thermographic methods are probably the most universally applied technique, and in addition to presenting a thermal contour map of the surface being inspected, these methods also provide detailed thermometric information. Two basic types of infrared detectors are commonly being used in thermography: (1) photon detectors and (2) thermal detectors. Most modern thermal imaging systems use either photon detectors or pyroelectrics, a type of thermal detector, as the infrared sensor. The sensor receives the radiation from the scene or target and converts it into an electrical signal for processing and display.

Photon detectors use solid-state materials that produce voltage, current, or resistance changes when irradiated by photons. These semiconductor materials are wavelength dependent and are generally classified as either photoconductive or photovoltaic detectors. Photoconductive devices are semiconductors whose conductivity changes when irradiated by photons. Photons of sufficient energy will cause bound electrons to jump into the conduction band and hence to become available as charge carriers. The response time of photoconductor materials is fast; times shorter than 1 +s have been reported. Photovoltaic cells are composed of p-n junction semiconductor materials. These cells produce a voltage when irradiated by photons. These devices also are characterized by a rapid response time. For maximum sensitivity, and to reduce extraneous thermal noise, it is usually necessary to cool the semiconductor material to low temperatures. Many commercially available thermographic detector systems require that liquid nitrogen be used for this purpose.

Thermal detectors respond to total radiant energy and are thus wavelength independent. In addition, these detectors do not require cooling as do photon detectors. Therefore the size, weight, cost, and complexity can be reduced.

Pyroelectrics are a special class of thermal detector. Unlike the others, they respond only to a change in temperature, rather than to the temperature itself.

Although the heart of a thermal-imaging system is its infrared detector, the detector is but one of several interacting subsystems. The other subsystems incorporated in a thermal-imaging system are: optical system for collecting the radiance from the target, spectrally filtering, and focusing it onto the detector; scanning system for dissecting the target or a chopper for modulating the radiance; detector system including any preamplifiers and ancillary circuits; signal processor system for receiving the low-level signal from the detector(s), amplifying it, limiting the bandwidth, extracting the information contained in the signal, and delivering this information to the display system; and a display system, which is generally a video monitor. A schematic diagram of a thermal-imaging system using photon detectors is shown in Fig. 6-62.

Thermometric

Noncontact thermometric measuring devices depend on the response of a thermal detector to infrared radiation. These devices are particularly useful when monitoring or measuring surface temperatures remotely. Thermometric devices are used in applications where a single component is under evaluation or when the cost limitation precludes the use of thermographic

devices. The two most commonly used devices are radiometers and pyrometers.

Radiometers. Radiometers measure incident radiation. A typical radiometer consists of some type of hollow cavity with an aperture in one end and a thermal detector mounted internally. The thermal detector is located in such a position that radiation is focused on it. Because thermal detectors have a uniform response without regard to infrared wavelength, the radiometer is often used to measure total radiation. If the radiometer has a lens system, it will be restricted to the infrared transmission characteristics of the lenses. Current-imaging radiometers operate in the 3-5 μm or 8-12 μm spectral range and have temperature sensitivities of 0.9° F (0.1° C). They can measure temperatures up to 1800° F (1000° C) and are TV compatible.

Pyrometers. Pyrometers are used in nondestructive testing in much the same way as the noncontact thermographic devices. These instruments are not as accurate as other scanning devices, but they are simpler, more rugged, more portable, and less expensive.

Pyrometers are available in the form of infrared microscopes, medium focusing range thermometers, and long-distance focusing thermometers. Depending on the instrument, temperature can be measured from below -32° F (0° C) to 212° F (100° C).

CONTACT METHODS

As was the case with noncontact methods, contact methods can be further divided into those devices and materials that detect the temperature thermographically or thermometrically. The primary advantage of using contact-type materials or devices is the low initial investment, particularly if small areas are being inspected; however, this cost advantage disappears as the area or number of pieces examined increases. The operator skill required and the effectiveness of contact and noncontact methods in detecting flaws are about equivalent.

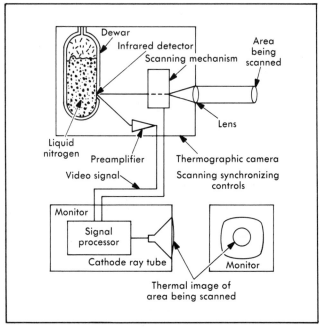

Fig. 6-62 Schematic of thermal-imaging system using a photon detector.

THERMAL NONDESTRUCTIVE TESTING

The major limitation of contact materials is that they alter the heat flow in the surface being tested. Another limitation is that their use is not readily automated.

Thermographic

Contact thermographic methods require the surface being tested to be coated with a temperature-sensitive material. These materials react to thermal change by changing color or appearance. The type of coating material selected for a particular application depends on its characteristics as well as the characteristics of the part being tested. The coating materials commonly used are paints, thermal phosphors, treated papers, liquid crystals, and other temperature-sensitive coatings.

Paints. Temperature-sensitive paints are available to cover a temperature range of 100-2900° F (40-1600° C). As the temperature of the part increases, the coating undergoes several color transitions. Under favorable circumstances, the temperature of the part can be estimated with an accuracy of ±9° F (5° C).

These coatings can be applied by brushing, spraying, or dipping. In general, only a thin film is required. Temperature-sensitive paints have been used to observe the isotherms in the vicinity of a welding operation, for determining the preheat temperature of weldments, and for the inspection of porosity in castings.

Thermal phosphors. Thermal phosphors are organic compounds that emit visible light when excited by ultraviolet radiation. The amount of light emitted is inversely proportional to the temperature of the phosphor. The sensitivity of the phosphor varies according to the intensity of illumination. Sensitivity is also affected by flaw size, location, and test material characteristics. Thermal phosphors can be applied as a paint, in a tape, in a strippable coating, or as a phosphor powder.

Treated papers. Several different types of thermally sensitive papers can be used for thermographic inspection. They are usually bonded to the test surface with an adhesive or with a vacuum hold-down arrangement.

One type of treated paper has an organic coating on it that melts once a certain temperature is achieved. The paper is black and the coating is white. When the melting temperature is reached, the coating is absorbed into the paper, causing it to change colors.

Another type of paper is coated with a plastic film containing a large number of air bubbles. The paper is black and the plastic film has the appearance of being white. Like the organic coating, the plastic film melts when a certain temperature is reached, revealing the black paper beneath it.

Liquid crystals. Liquid crystals exhibit the properties of both a liquid and a crystal at certain temperatures. As these crystals undergo a temperature change, they appear to change in color. When the crystals are heated to their melting point, they become a liquid and are essentially colorless. Any additional heat causes the crystals to undergo a "color play," which is a certain color change sequence. For most nondestructive tests, this color play occurs at a point slightly above room temperature. Under typical conditions, liquid crystals can detect a temperature difference of approximately 0.4° F (0.2° C).

Liquid crystals may be applied by brushing, spraying, or dipping. The applied film is usually between 0.010 and 0.020" (0.25 and 0.50 mm) thick. Because liquid crystals function by reflecting light, they are more easily seen against a dark background.

The primary advantages of liquid crystals are their initial low cost in comparison to infrared detectors and the low operator skill required. However, liquid crystals are normally not used on large structures because their cost would be prohibitive.

Thermometric

Several different types of contact devices are used to measure surface temperatures. For certain applications, these devices may be used in direct contact with the part being tested or as a radiation detector.

Bolometers. Bolometers are thermal detectors that are based on the principle that the resistance of a material changes as it is heated. The bolometer allows the radiation to impinge on a very fine wire or a thin metallic film, blackened to increase absorption. The resistance change is then a direct function of the radiation absorbed. The temperature coefficient of a bolometer is from 0.15 to 2%/° F (0.3 to 0.5%/° C).

Thermistors. Thermistors, or thermally sensitive resistors, are semiconductors that undergo a reduction in resistance as their temperature rises. Their temperature coefficient is approximately 2%/° F (4%/° C). The limiting factor of the thermistor is thermal noise.

Thermocouples and thermopiles. Thermocouples consist of a junction of two dissimilar metals. As the junction temperature is raised, a thermoelectric electromotive force (emf) is produced. Thermocouples are always used in pairs in a bridge circuit so that the measured temperature is a direct function of the emf produced by the sensing thermocouple as subtracted from the emf produced by a reference thermocouple that is held at a known temperature. As with all thermal detectors, thermocouples may be used as a contact sensor or they can be used in noncontact applications to sense infrared radiation only.

Thermopiles are merely a series of thermocouple junctions; they produce an increase in electromotive force as a direct function of the number of junctions. Although thermopiles do have a higher output signal, the response time is reduced because of the increased mass that must be heated.

Meltable materials. Wax-like crayons rated to melt at various temperature increments between 100 and 3200° F (38 and 1760° C) are commercially available. These crayons have a melting point within a nominal tolerance of ±1% of the rated temperature value. They are normally used by making a mark with one or more of them on a surface before it is heated. The true temperature indication occurs only when the mark melts. Color or color intensity of the crayon may change during heating, but this is not an indication of temperature. By using an appropriate range of these crayons arranged in a suitable pattern, general observations can be made regarding the isothermal pattern (or thermograph) of a heated area.

TESTING CONSIDERATIONS

When performing thermal testing, several precautions should be observed to obtain accurate results. First of all, the surface being tested should be uniformly clean. Oily surfaces may reduce or prevent the adherence of contact materials. Some contact materials, such as liquid crystals, are very sensitive to contamination. Any contamination on the surface may reduce the overall response or cause a shift in color. Contamination will also change the surface emissivity and result in spurious infrared responses.

All contact materials and infrared detectors should be periodically calibrated or checked for sensitivity. Although most contact materials have a rather long shelf life, contamination,

ACOUSTIC EMISSION TESTING

exposure to strong light, or high humidity, for example, can sharply reduce shelf life. Infrared instruments are subject to drift over time and therefore should be calibrated against known temperature standards.

When testing passive devices, heating and/or cooling should be as uniform as possible and identical on each piece. Reversible coatings (those which may be cycled back and forth through their response temperature) should neither be held for extended

periods above their response temperature nor severely overheated; loss in sensitivity will result.

The radiation from a device usually represents only a fraction of the total heat dissipated. Convection and conduction may be responsible for much larger heat losses than radiation; hence they should be held constant during the test. Active devices should be allowed to warm up and stabilize prior to making temperature measurements.

ACOUSTIC EMISSION TESTING

Almost all materials produce an acoustic emission (AE) when they are stressed. Other terms used to describe this phenomenon are stress-wave emission and microseismic emission. An acoustic emission is a sound wave or, more properly, a stress wave that travels through a material. An acoustic emission may be generated by the following:

- Cracking or delaminations in composite structures such as aircraft parts, industrial storage tanks, pipes, and circuit boards.
- Fracture and crack propagation in metallic structures such as piping, pressure vessels, and weldments.
- Deformation of materials during testing or manufacturing.
- Nugget formation or overwelding during spot welding.
- Leaking gases and fluids in steam traps or valves.
- Bearing failure and lack of lubrication.

Acoustic emission testing is a recent nondestructive test method that has application in a variety of industries. During a typical test, a sensor is mounted on the test piece, which is subsequently subjected to a load. If a defect grows in the test piece, distinct acoustic emission signals are generated by the resulting fracture or deformation. The sensor converts the acoustic emission signals into electrical signals, which are then amplified, filtered, and processed to obtain predetermined types of information. A cathode ray tube, video display tube, or another type of device is used to display the processed data as a function of test duration, applied load, or signal location.

Acoustic emission testing is related in many ways to ultrasonic testing because both methods measure sound waves to detect defects. The main difference between the two methods is the source of the sound waves. In ultrasonic testing, the sound waves are transmitted into the test piece through the sensor. Defects are then detected and located based on the interaction between the sound wave and defect. In AE testing, the sound waves are generated from within the test piece in the course of the relaxation of the stored strain energy.

APPLICATIONS

Although the first industrial application of AE testing took place in 1964, the phenomenon of acoustic emission was observed hundreds of years ago. The most common example is in the production of pottery vases. After the vases were fired in a kiln, the potter listened to the sounds given off by the vases as they cooled. If an improper production technique was used, the glaze gave off cracking noises, indicating that the vases were defective and would fail under service.

Another example is the noise that is heard when certain metals are bent, even though no cracks are produced. This

sound was first heard with tin and was referred to as tin cry; magnesium and zinc also show this effect. The emission from these metals is due to a deformation process called twinning.

With the continual improvement in electronic detection equipment, the use of AE testing has increased. Perhaps the greatest attribute to the technology is its ability to be utilized in an extremely broad range of applications. The types of materials for which AE testing can be used are virtually unlimited. Industries currently using this technique include aerospace, nuclear, medical, and transportation. Acoustic emission testing can also be used to help understand and evaluate fabrication methods such as welding, spot welding, bonding, machining, drilling, cutting, and sawing. Table 6-18 lists the areas in which AE testing is currently being used. The applications are divided into four categories: (1) during production, (2) preservice, (3) in-service, and (4) research. Acoustic emission testing is performed for research in all these areas.

ADVANTAGES AND LIMITATIONS

Like the other test methods, AE testing is not a panacea for all applications. It does, however, provide certain advantages over some of the other methods such as radiographic and ultrasonic testing. Some of the advantages of acoustic emission testing are the following:

- The ability to monitor a complete structure in real time.
- The sensitivity to the presence of active flaws, although it requires other methods to characterize the exact size of flaws.
- The ability to detect discontinuities that may be inaccessible to other NDT methods.
- The ability to be used in harsh environments.
- The applicability for use during proof testing of structures that will be stressed sufficiently to produce defect extension or gross plastic deformation.

The main limitation of AE testing as a nondestructive test method is that it can only detect flaws that are growing; the mere presence of defects, however large, is not detected. Either an external or internal force must act on the flaw, causing it to grow. The type and amount of acoustic emission generated is dependent on the behavior of the material. Other limitations of this method are the following:

- Spurious signals may be difficult to separate.
- Limited quantitative information is provided.
- Experience required for proper usage and data interpretation.

TABLE 6-18
Applications of Acoustic Emission Testing

Area of Use	Category	Area of Use	Category
Adhesive bond	1,2,3	Machining	1
Aerial manlift devices	2,3	Maintenance	2,3
Aircraft structures	2,3	Nondestructive testing	2,3
Anodized coatings	2,3	Nuclear reactors	2,3
Autoclaves	2,3	Offshore platforms	2,3
Beam lead bonding	1,2	Oil storage tanks	2,3
Bearings	2,3	Oxide formation/cracking	1,2,3
Biological	3	Pavements	3
Boiling/bubble cavitation	1,2,3	Phase changes (liquid-solid)	1,2,3
Bridges	2,3	Plating	1,2
Burning efficiency	2,3	Porcelain enamel	
Cable, wire rope, and synthetic rope	2,3	Pressure vessel testing	2,3
Ceramics and glass	1,2,3	Quality control	1,2,3
Composites	1,2,3	Railroad	1,2,3
Concrete	2,3	Residual stress	2,3
Corona	1,2,3	Rocket motor cases	2,3
Corrosion	3	Rotating machinery	2,3
Crack detection	2,3	Seismology	3
Creep	3	Source location	1,2,3
Dams	2,3	Stamping	1
Defects	2,3	Stoneware	1,2,3
Dielectric liquids	2,3	Submarine	2,3
Earthquakes	3	Vibration	2,3
Electric breakdown	1,2,3	Welds	1,2,3
Electroplating	1	Wood products	1,2,3
Failure analysis	2,3		
Fatigue	3		
Fracture mechanics	2,3		
Friction	2,3		
Geotechnical (soil, earth, and rock)	2,3		
Heat treatment	1		
Hydrogen embrittlement	1,2,3		
Hydrostatic testing	2		
In-flight monitoring	3		
Ice	2,3		
Leak detection	1,2,3		
Loose parts monitoring	1,2,3		

Category code: 1 = during production
2 = pre-service
3 = in-service

CHAPTER 6

ACOUSTIC EMISSION TESTING

PRINCIPLES

Acoustic emission is defined as the transient elastic waves generated by the rapid release of energy from a localized source or sources within a material.[37] This rapid release of energy is generally induced by stress. While the stress cannot be heard, the results of the stress can be heard.

Two types of acoustic emission exist: (1) burst and (2) continuous. A single burst of emission occurs as the result of a particular energy release process or event. Burst-type emissions are generated by twinning, microyielding, and the development of microcracks and macrocracks. Individual bursts last from a few microseconds to several milliseconds. When these bursts are frequency shifted to the audible range, they would sound like a series of clicking sounds.

Continuous emission refers to the emission coming from rapidly occurring events. In metals and alloys, continuous-type emission is associated with dislocation movements. In the audible range, they sound like a continuous hissing. If burst emissions occur so rapidly that the bursts overlap, the result is continuous emission. Burst-type emissions generally have larger amplitudes than continuous-type emissions.

Emission Signal Strength

The acoustic emission signals that are usually encountered in nondestructive testing are so weak that they need to be amplified by 60 dB or more to be detected. An example of a weak AE signal is the signal produced by lightly touching the tip of a feather to a metal rod. Acoustic emission techniques are actually so sensitive that they can detect displacements in metal as small as 10^{-12} in./in. (mm/mm), if they occur in microseconds duration. The loudest signals that can be detected come from brittle crack growth, delamination and fiber failure in composites, and cavitation.

Frequency Range

The frequencies encountered in acoustic emission range from the low end of the audible spectrum up into the megahertz range. The theoretical upper limit of acoustic emission frequencies is not known. It depends on how rapidly the emission process starts or stops and on the duration of the process. In a practical case, the measured frequency spectrum depends on the characteristics of the material through which the emission has traveled and on the equipment that is used to measure it. The specific material characteristics that are of importance are the size and shape of the material and its frequency-dependent attenuation effects. The transducer and the electronic filters in the instrumentation are the principal equipment components that affect the frequency spectrum.

In actual practice, frequencies below some arbitrary limit, such as 30 kHz, are filtered out to avoid interference from unwanted sources of noise such as machinery, impact sounds, or electrical equipment. High frequencies (greater than a few megahertz) are lost because of attenuation or because they are removed by the instrumentation.

The frequencies that are commonly used for AE testing lie between 50 kHz and 1 MHz. It should be kept in mind, however, that there are frequencies above and below this range that may be useful in some applications.

Stress Waves

The types of stress waves given off by an acoustic emission source depend on the nature of the source and its location within the material. A source below or at the surface of a solid can produce longitudinal, shear, and surface waves. Waves produced from below the surface radiate in all directions from the source. When they reach the surface, they are reflected, and a part of their energy is converted to other types of waves, including surface waves. If the source of the emission is in a plate, most of the energy will be propagated as shear waves, plate waves, and surface waves. The signal that is detected by a typical sensor is usually a surface wave because they are attenuated less.

Attenuation of AE Signals

The intensity of an acoustic emission signal decreases as the distance from the source increases. The reasons for this decrease are geometrical factors, mode conversion, and energy absorption and scattering.

The principal effect that the geometry (size and shape) of a test specimen has on the acoustic emission is in determining the type of wave that carries the energy from the source to the sensor. Size and shape also determine the relative strengths of the acoustic emission frequencies that reach the sensor. The effect of geometrical factors depends on the size of the acoustic emission source, the wavelength of the acoustic emission signal, and the presence or absence of nearby reflecting surfaces.

Energy loss due to mode conversion can occur if an acoustic emission signal is reflected one or more times from a surface before reaching the sensor. A fraction of the energy reaching the surface will be converted to a surface wave. The rest is reflected and partially converted to another wave type. The waves that undergo reflection also undergo a decrease in amplitude due to the spherical spreading that occurs more rapidly than in the case of surface waves. Surface waves and plate waves spread out only in two directions; thus for an acoustic emission source in a plate, it is these waves that are usually detected at large distances from the source.

The loss mechanisms due to scattering and absorption in solids are complex. They increase with increasing frequency and, in polycrystalline materials, can be attributed to such processes as thermoelastic relaxation effects within individual grains, scattering at grain boundaries due to an abrupt change in elastic properties upon crossing the boundary, absorption due to induced movements of lattice imperfections such as impurity atoms or dislocations, hysteresis losses of ferromagnetic and ferroelectric origin, and scattering from inclusions, dispersed phases, or voids.

Kaiser Effect

Some form of stress must be applied to the test piece to cause it to give off acoustic emission. Emission is only given off while the specimen is deforming; when the specimen stops deforming, the emission stops. The test piece will continue to be quiet while the stress is being removed unless sufficient energy has been stored to cause deformation to continue. When the stress is reapplied, it must exceed the previous level before any AE is produced. This irreversibility is known as the Kaiser effect (see Fig. 6-63).

The Kaiser effect in metals can be used to obtain information as to whether crack growth occurs during fatigue testing or structural qualification of such products as pressure vessels or piping systems. If there has been no crack growth, applying a static load slightly larger than that previously applied should generate very little, if any, acoustic emission. If a crack is growing under load, there will be acoustic emission.

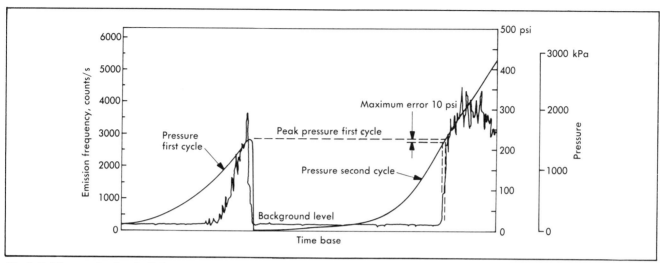

Fig. 6-63 Diagram showing the Kaiser effect on a 6061-T6 aluminum diaphragm.[38]

For composite materials, the lack of the Kaiser effect is referred to as the Felicity effect. Because the phenomena of the Kaiser effect is less absolute in composite materials, a ratio of the applied load at which acoustic emission resumes to the previously applied maximum load has been named the Felicity ratio. A clear indication of strength degradation is evident as this ratio decreases. Another indication of strength degradation is detection of acoustic emission during load-holding periods.

INSTRUMENTATION AND SIGNAL PROCESSING

Acoustic emission signals coming from a sensor are first prepared for processing by suitable amplification and filtering. The signals are then processed to extract the data that they contain. Once the data are processed, they are displayed for evaluation or they are recorded, permitting analysis at a later date. A diagram of a typical acoustic emission system is shown in Fig. 6-64.

Sensors

An acoustic emission sensor works on the same principle as a contact microphone on a guitar or other musical instrument. The essential parts of an acoustic emission sensor are a piezoelectric element, wear plate or shoe, and a metal case. The case supports and protects the transducer as well as provides shielding from unwanted electrical interference.

The active part of the sensor is a piezoelectric transducer element. The piezoelectric element converts the stress wave received into an electrical signal that is picked up by the electrodes (see Fig. 6-65). The electrical signal is then amplified and fed into suitable instrumentation.

The most common piezoelectric transducer material is lead zirconate titanate.[39] Some types of this ceramic are more efficient for receiving sound waves than others. Another type of material used for transducers is lead metaniobate. This material is less sensitive than lead zirconate titanate, but can be used at temperatures as high as 650° F (340° C). In contrast, PZT-5 (a certain type of lead zirconate titanate) can only be used up to 350° F (175° C). Lithium niobate ($LiNbO_3$) can also be used as a high-temperature sensor up to 1200° F (650° C).

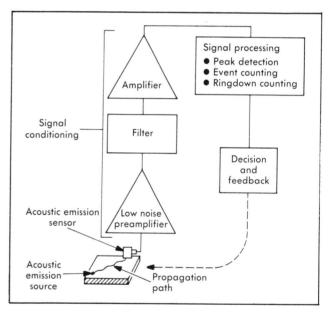

Fig. 6-64 Typical acoustic emission detection system. (*Acoustic Emission Technology Corp.*)

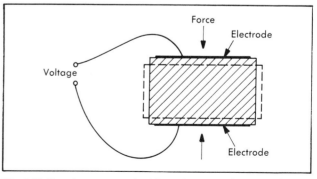

Fig. 6-65 Sound pressure received from the test specimen is picked up by the electrodes on the sensor and then converted into an electrical signal. (*Acoustic Emission Technology Corp.*)

ACOUSTIC EMISSION TESTING

The dimensions of the piezoelectric element and the mounting technique determine the resonant frequency of the sensors, which are typically between 50 kHz and 1 MHz. The mounting technique also determines the amount of transducer damping. Extra damping material in the transducer is sometimes coupled behind the element to obtain a more uniform frequency response.

Signal Conditioning

The signal from a sensor must be amplified and unnecessary frequencies filtered out prior to processing. Commonly, it is necessary to amplify the signal to approximately 1 V. Amplification is usually done with a low noise level preamplifier located next to the sensor or sometimes contained in the sensor housing, especially when:

- The spurious electrical noise is high.
- The distance between the sensor and the instrumentation must be more than a few feet.

The incoming signal is filtered to reject low and high frequencies. The band of frequencies that is passed by the filter is determined for each application to eliminate unwanted noise. The cutoff frequencies depend on the background noise levels, the frequency spectrum of the sensor, the dimensions of the workpiece, and the source of the signal. Frequencies below 50 kHz are usually noise and vibration from the environment and might be so strong that they would overload the amplifiers. High frequencies above 1.0 MHz are eliminated because they might contain stray electrical signals from sources such as a nearby radio station. The attenuation at each end of the filter passband is typically 48 dB per octave.

Signal Processing

The amplified and filtered acoustic emission signals are processed to do one or more of the following:

- Specify the amount of acoustic emission activity by a number.
- Accept acoustic emission signals and reject all other acoustic signals.
- Identify some waveform characteristic of the signal that will help to determine the type of acoustic emission source.
- Obtain a number that is proportional to the energy in the acoustic emission.
- Locate the source of the acoustic emission.

Acoustic emission activity can be interpreted either by measuring the characteristics of the waveform, including ringdown counts, or by measuring the root-mean-square (rms) voltage of the continuous-type signal. Both techniques are relatively simple. The advantage of the counting technique is that it is possible to record a limited number of acoustic emission events in test specimens that show only a small amount of activity over a long period of time.

Counting. The counting of acoustic emission signals is usually performed by event counting or ringdown counting. A typical oscillating AE signal is shown in Fig. 6-66, view *a*. An event count is registered every time the pulse drops below a preset threshold voltage (see view *b*). In ringdown counting, each of the oscillations in the event is counted until an oscillation drops below the threshold voltage (see view *c*). Thus, there are many ringdown counts for each event. The symbols N_e and N are used to represent event count and ringdown count,

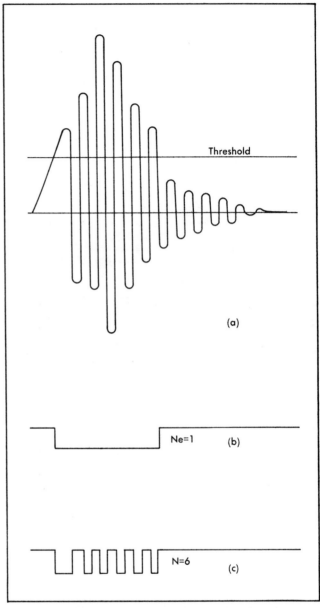

Fig. 6-66 Amplified and filtered acoustic emission signals are processed: (a) typical emission signal, (b) event counting, and (c) ringdown counting. (*Acoustic Emission Technology Corp.*)

respectively. Ringdown counting gives a relative measure of the amplitude of the signal because the larger the signal, the greater the number of oscillations before the signal falls below the threshold level.

Acoustic emission count data can vary widely depending on the experimental conditions. Factors that influence acoustic emission counting are the following:

- The preset threshold voltage level.
- Resonances in the test structure.
- Sensor resonances and damping.
- Type of coupling between the sensor and the test structure.
- The rate at which the structure is loaded.

Because of the influence of these factors, it may be difficult to compare results obtained by different observers. Comparisons can only be made by carefully calibrating the complete system, including the sensor.

The total number of counts received by a sensor can be displayed on a digital counter or chart recorder. When the limit of the counter is reached, the instrument recycles and starts over again, or the operator can set the instrument to zero and start a new count.

Counts can also be displayed as count rate, which is determined by counting the pulses or oscillations that occur per unit of time. The symbols N_e and N are used for event count rate and ringdown count rate, respectively.

Counting techniques are generally not suitable for continuous-type emission if comparisons are to be made with the results of other tests. This is because the AE count depends so strongly on the setting of the threshold voltage, and this can easily be different from one test to another. A measurement of the rms voltage produced by the total acoustic emission signal is more satisfactory in this instance.

Root-mean-square voltage. A simple way to measure acoustic emission intensity is to use an rms voltmeter. The rms voltmeter gives a number related to count rate and includes the effect of low-level signals below a preset threshold voltage.

Changes in the rms voltage are hardly recognized when only a few acoustic emission events are occurring per second. Sensitivity is poor because an rms voltmeter reading is usually an average over a period of about one second.

Discrimination techniques. An ideal acoustic emission test should measure only the signals of interest and reject all others. The rejected signals might be irrelevant acoustic emission sources, loose parts hitting each other, frictional noises, flow noise, cavitation in pumps and piping, or other unidentified background noises.

Several techniques are used to separate the wanted signals from the unwanted signals. The techniques used are as follows:

- Adjustment of the threshold level.
- Spatial filtering. Rejection of signals coming from outside the area of interest.
- Spatial discrimination. Rejection of signals based on time arrival measurements.
- Waveform discrimination. Rejection of signals that have waveform characteristics outside of a preset range.
- Pulse rise-time discrimination.
- Discrimination by gating the AE signal with external parametric values.
- Frequency discrimination.

Locating AE sources. Common source location methods in use are "first-sensor-hit," "order-of-arrival," and "time difference." First-sensor-hit and order-of-arrival methods rely on the information as to which sensor receives an acoustic emission signal first, second, and so on, and give the knowledge on source location. These two methods are also known as zone location methods. Time difference measurements provide source location through triangulation techniques. These techniques are based on the constant velocity of acoustic signal propagation in a material.

In the zone location methods, the length, surface area, or volume of material covered by the sensors is called a zone. Further subdivision of the zone into sectors is based on the order-of-arrival information.

Exact, approximate, or empirical solutions are capable of source location to a much finer resolution than zone location methods. They are also frequently used to define where other nondestructive tests should be more thoroughly conducted.

NEUTRON RADIOGRAPHY

Neutron radiography is a form of nondestructive testing that uses a neutron beam to form a radiographic image of a test piece. Neutrons are subatomic particles that are characterized by relatively large mass and a neutral electric charge. They are constituents of all atomic nuclei except ordinary hydrogen. The pertinent difference between X-rays or gamma rays and neutrons is that the neutron does not interact with the electrons in matter. Instead, it interacts directly with the atomic nucleus, either by scattering or by being absorbed by the nucleus.[40] For example, in radiography (X-ray or gamma ray) the attenuation of the rays increases as the atomic number of the test specimen increases. In neutron radiography, however, some low atomic number elements attenuate a beam of neutrons more strongly than some high atomic number elements. Also, elements having adjacent atomic numbers can have widely different attenuations. Figure 6-67 demonstrates the increasing attenuation of X-rays for elements with increasing atomic numbers while showing that the attenuation of neutrons is significantly different. Because the attenuation pattern for neutrons and X-rays are often quite different, the two techniques can frequently provide information that is complementary.

Neutrons, like X-rays, come in different energies; their characteristics vary with energy. Table 6-19 summarizes the neutron energy classes of interest in neutron radiography. Most work has been done with thermal neutrons because of the excellent discrimination capability for various materials. Interest in cold-neutron radiography is increasing because cold neutrons provide improved sensitivity to materials such as hydrogen and improved transparency for materials such as iron. Epithermal neutrons are used extensively for nuclear fuel radiography. Fast neutrons are seldom used because detection is relatively difficult.

APPLICATIONS

Neutron radiography has been used for nondestructive testing since the 1960s.[41] Although the applications were initially in the nuclear and aerospace industries, the use of neutron radiography is now also being realized in other industries.[42,43] The four general categories in which neutron radiography is currently being used are: (1) detection of high neutron attenuation material in a matrix or assembly of materials that are transparent to neutrons, (2) inspection of radioactive material, (3) detection of isotopic content, and (4) inspection of relatively thick neutron-transparent material. Categories two and three are primarily limited to the nuclear industries.

With the increasing use of composite materials and honeycomb structures in the aircraft and aerospace industries, neu-

NEUTRON RADIOGRAPHY

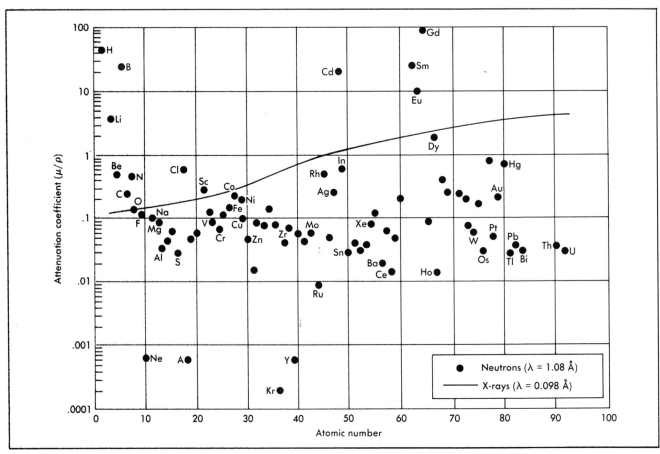

Fig. 6-67 Relative attenuation characteristics of the elements for X-rays (solid line) and thermal neutrons (dots). (*Industrial Quality, Inc.*)

TABLE 6-19
Neutron Energies and Characteristics for Radiography

Term	Comments	Energy Range
Cold	Cold neutrons provide decreased transparency for most materials, but also increased efficiency of detection. A particular advantage is the reduced scatter in materials at energies below the Bragg cutoff	Less than 0.01 eV
Thermal	Thermal neutrons provide good discriminatory capability between different materials	0.01 eV to 0.5 eV
Epithermal	These are characterized by energies somewhat greater than thermal. Epithermal neutrons show greater transmission for most materials	0.5 eV to 10^4 eV
Resonance	Certain nuclei exhibit strong absorption characteristics at well-defined energies called resonance absorptions. Neutrons in these specific energy ranges are referred to as resonance neutrons and provide excellent discrimination for particular materials at energies of resonance. Greater transmission and less scatter occur in samples containing materials such as hydrogen and enriched reactor fuel materials	1 eV to 10^2 eV
Fast	Fast neutrons provide good penetration. Good point sources of fast neutrons are available. At the lower energy end of the spectrum, fast neutron radiography may be able to perform many inspections performed with thermal neutrons, but with a panoramic technique. Poor material discrimination occurs, however, because the cross sections tend to be small and similar. Detection with good resolution is difficult	10^3 eV to 20 MeV

tron radiography can offer advantages because of the excellent sensitivity to adhesives and resins. In some cases, combinations of materials are well suited for neutron inspection. For example, the high strength of a boron aluminum composite metal depends on the distribution and continuity of the boron fibers. Because the neutron beam is absorbed more readily by the boron fibers than the aluminum, a neutron radiograph will show the position of the boron in the aluminum matrix.

In honeycomb structures, neutron radiography is able to detect uneven distribution of bonding material, absence of bonding material on one or both skins, meniscus rings or bubbles, and movement of bonding material along cell walls. These defects can be detected because the epoxy adhesives used in these structures have high neutron attenuation. When a neutron radiograph is made, the metal honeycomb structure is relatively transparent while the adhesive shows up clearly.

Neutron radiography is used extensively for the inspection of small explosive components such as explosive bolts, shaped charges, and explosive lines. The explosive charge can be visualized readily through metal walls with neutrons, providing a unique inspection result.

Detection of corrosion in aircraft structure is an active application area for neutron radiography. Because corrosion products are typically hydroxides, the buildup of the corrosion product can often be detected before an appreciable loss of metal occurs. Other nondestructive methods for corrosion detection depend on observation of metal loss.[44]

Another area of application for neutron radiography is checking for residual core material in cast turbine blades. The blades are made by molding metal around a ceramic core, which is later removed by leaching to leave internal cooling passages open. Small amounts of residual core material can be detected by neutron radiography if the core material contains certain rare-earth materials found in ceramics. Normally the sensitivity is enhanced by adding gadolinium to the ceramic core material; gadolinium acts as a contrast agent. Alternately, the untagged residual core material can be "tagged" by a process using a vacuum followed by soaking in gadolinium nitrate solution.

Neutron time-lapse radiographs and dynamic detectors, such as neutron image intensifiers, have been used to obtain information about changing events. In many of the applications, observation of fluid flow in metallic assemblies has been the goal. Heat pipes have been tested to optimize the fluid flow and heat transfer of the system. Extensive motion studies of lubricants and fuels have also been conducted in engines and engine components to learn more about the dynamics.[45,46,47,48] Many of these studies have been done with cold neutrons because they have better sensitivity to the hydrogenous fluid than thermal neutrons. In addition, they have better penetration through the surrounding metal.

ADVANTAGES AND LIMITATIONS

Neutron radiography can provide image information that is difficult or impossible to obtain by other methods. Although the technique tends to be relatively expensive compared to other nondestructive testing methods, the unique capability of the method for imaging items such as corrosion, adhesives, explosives, fluids, and ceramics in metallic assemblies makes neutron radiography a valuable technique. It can be used to outline the extent of cracks or delaminations open to the surface if a contrast agent, such as a liquid penetrant, is applied. The method also offers isotopic sensitivity and capability to inspect highly radioactive materials.

A user should be aware that neutron irradiation of objects usually leads to some level of radioactivity. Therefore the objects inspected may become radioactive; however, this has not been a serious problem because the neutron levels and exposure times are relatively low. Irradiated objects may sometimes be retained for an hour or so until they have decayed to safe levels. One of the main deterrents to using neutron radiography is the need to transport the test pieces to a nuclear reactor when high-quality radiographs are required. Portable sources described later produce lower quality radiographs than nuclear reactor sources or require long exposures (hours to days) to obtain the equivalent high grade.

NEUTRON SOURCES

Sources for neutron radiography include nuclear reactors, radioactive isotopes, accelerators, and subcritical assemblies. Nuclear reactors provide relatively high-intensity neutron beams for radiography. Radioactive isotopes such as californium 252, which emits neutrons by spontaneous fission, have been used for neutron radiography. This manmade isotope decays to half intensity (half-life) in a period of 2.65 years. It is a prolific source of neutrons, emitting 10^{12} neutrons per second per gram. Other radioactive sources emit neutrons by alpha particle or gamma ray interactions with targets such as beryllium.

Accelerators can produce neutrons by accelerating charged particles at targets such as deuterium, tritium, lithium, and beryllium. The accelerators that have been used in the mega electron volt energy range are the Van de Graaff and cyclotron. Typical reactions include acceleration of protons on lithium or deuterons on beryllium. High-energy X-rays can also be used to produce neutrons from targets such as beryllium or uranium. Low-energy accelerators of the Cockroft-Walton type have also been used to produce neutrons by accelerating deuterons on a tritium target. Typical acceleration voltages are in the few hundred thousand volt range. Sealed tube systems are also available; these accelerators operate very much like an X-ray machine.

In a subcritical assembly, nuclear reactor fuel is added to the moderator surrounding a fast-neutron source to multiply the number of neutrons available. The systems are typically designed so that they are easier to license and operate than a reactor. Typical multiplication factor for the neutron beam intensity is in the order of 30 times.[49]

Because fast-neutron sources must be moderated and collimated to make them most useful for neutron radiography, many of the neutrons emitted from the source do not end up in a useful direction. Typically, there is a reduction of about 10^6 times in going from the fast-neutron yield from the source to the thermal neutron intensity in a collimated beam. Table 6-20 summarizes approximate characteristics of the various types of neutron sources for radiography.

DETECTION METHODS

A neutron radiograph is made by passing a beam of neutrons through a test object. If the neutrons react with any of the material's atomic nuclei, they are absorbed or scattered, attenuating the beam. The beam emerges from the test sample with information about the object's internal structure in the form of differences in attenuation. The principles that govern exposure and processing of neutron radiographs are similar to those for X-ray or gamma ray radiographs.

NEUTRON RADIOGRAPHY

TABLE 6-20
Average Characteristics of Thermal Neutron Radiographic Sources

Type of Source	Typical Radiographic Intensity*	Equivalent Quality Exposure Time	Characteristics
Radioisotope	10^1 to 10^4	Hours to days	Stable operation, medium investment cost, possibly portable
Accelerator	10^3 to 10^6	Minutes to hours	On-off operation, medium cost, possibly mobile
Subcritical assembly	10^4 to 10^6	Minutes to hours	Stable operation, medium to high investment cost, mobility difficult
Nuclear reactor	10^5 to 10^8	Seconds to minutes	Stable operation, high investment cost, not mobile

* Neutrons per square centimeter per second at the image detector.

Neutron radiographs are usually detected on X-ray film. Because neutrons interact very little with the emulsion of photographic film, an intermediate converter screen must be used. This screen converts the neutron image to a form of radiation that is photographically detectable.

Depending on the application, two primary exposure techniques are used in neutron radiography: (1) direct exposure and (2) transfer exposure. In the direct exposure technique, the film and conversion screen are placed in the neutron beam together (see Fig. 6-68, view *a*). When the neutron is captured, the screen-secondary radiation is given off to expose the film. Conversion screens for this technique are commonly made from thin sheets of gadolinium metal or gadolinium oxysulfide. When using screens made from gadolinium metal, the X-ray film is exposed by low-energy electrons. Normally, one gadolinium screen is used with single-emulsion film. When using gadolinium oxysulfide screens, the X-ray film may be sandwiched between two screens, and the film is then exposed by visible light.

In the transfer exposure technique, used primarily to inspect radioactive objects, the film is not directly exposed to the neutron beam because the gamma radiation from the object would fog the film. Instead, only a special conversion screen is exposed to the neutron beam, and this screen becomes temporarily radioactive. After the exposure is terminated, the conversion screen is placed in intimate contact with the film, and the pattern of radioactivity on the screen produces an imaging exposure on the film (see Fig. 6-68, view *b*). Common conversion screen materials for this technique are indium and dysprosium.

The direct exposure technique is faster than the transfer exposure technique because the film exposure occurs during the initial exposure step; however, the transfer exposure technique is well adapted to the radiography of highly radioactive materials such as irradiated nuclear fuel elements.

Other detection methods are also used for neutron radiography. Track-etch methods make use of plastic films in which radiation damage etch-pits can reveal the neutron image. This technique, like the transfer exposure technique, is insensitive to gamma radiation; therefore the major use has been to detect neutron images in the presence of intense radiation fields.

A relatively new technique called digital neutron radiography makes use of lithium 6, boron 10, and helium 3 isotope

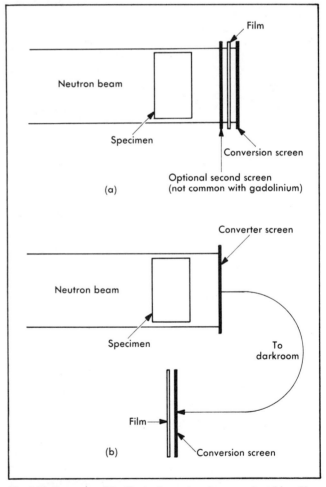

Fig. 6-68 Exposure of the film to the neutron beam can be achieved by one of two primary techniques: (a) direct exposure and (b) transfer exposure. (*Eastman Kodak Co.*)

detectors in a linear array. The linear array of detectors is translated to form a two-dimensional image of the neutron signal. Because of the low noise characteristics of individual detectors, this method has potential of improving the contrast resolution; however, this type of imaging system is relatively expensive.

Real-time neutron radiographic methods are also in use. The light emitted from phosphor screens can be used to provide prompt response systems to investigate dynamic events. The light can be picked up directly by low light-level television cameras or can first be enhanced by an image-intensifier tube.

SPECIFICATIONS AND STANDARDS

Standards are available to address the important parameters of a neutron radiography system. Three standards are available from the American Society for Testing and Materials (ASTM). Document E748 is a tutorial document that describes the general method and provides guidance when performing the test.[50] Image quality measurements for thermal neutron radiography are outlined in ASTM E545.[51] This approach makes use of test pieces whose images on a neutron radiograph can be analyzed to determine an image quality measure. The geometry of the imaging beam, particularly in terms of the unsharpness related to the image of an object somewhat removed from the detector, is covered in E803.[52] Geometric unsharpness for X-radiographs relates to the radiation source focal spot size and the distances for the object and detector. Similar measurements are involved in neutron radiography.

Other documents are also available. A glossary of more than 150 neutron radiographic terms has been published as a military standard.[53] A book of reference neutron radiographs, specifically related to the inspection of nuclear fuel, is widely used in the nuclear community.[54]

As with other nondestructive testing procedures, neutron radiographic testing requires trained, qualified operators. The industry guide for the training and certification of neutron radiographic operators is SNT-TC-1A as published by the American Society for Nondestructive Testing.[55] This document outlines the training and practical experience needed to qualify for various levels of responsibility.

HOLOGRAPHIC NONDESTRUCTIVE TESTING

Holographic nondestructive testing (HNDT) or holographic interferometry combines holography with interferometry, permitting the detection of material defects and impending fatigue failure, the measurement of residual stress, and vibration mode analysis. Holography is a two-step process that permits the reconstruction of three-dimensional images. A hologram of an object is formed in the first step of the process. In the second step, the original image is recreated, thus permitting the observer to see an exact replica of the image in size and position. The recreated image also displays depth of field and parallax.

When producing a hologram, light emitted by a laser source is split into an object beam and a reference beam (see Fig. 6-69). The object beam is expanded and directed toward the object, where part of it is reflected toward the recording medium, which is usually a high-resolution photographic film. In recent years, thermoplastic emulsions have become available. Although the reference beam travels directly to the film, it is diverted so that the optical paths of both beams are approximately equal. Because the two beams are from the same coherent source, they interfere with each other as they pass through each other. The film emulsion receives exposure wherever constructive interference occurs and virtually no exposure where destructive interference occurs. The varying exposure results in a very fine pattern in the emulsion of the film. This fine pattern diffracts the beam to form a reconstruction of the object beam when the film is illuminated after development by a replica of the reference beam. The replica of the object can be viewed or photographed.

Two holograms can also be made of the same object in a single photographic emulsion before and after a certain deformation. When the hologram is reconstructed, the two wavefronts are simultaneously recreated. This results in a set of fringes superimposed over the image of the object; the spatial frequency of these fringes provides information regarding the deformation of the object. Because each fringe relates to the deformation of the surface, variation in the geometry of a fringe is directly relatable to the topology or three-dimensional shape of the surface. The variation in the shape of the surface depends on the manner in which the object is deformed. Deformation is commonly achieved by acoustic, thermal, or mechanical stresses. The type of stress used is determined by the part, its accessibility, and the type of flaw.

APPLICATIONS

Holographic nondestructive testing has made the precision of interferometric measurements—previously restricted to regular, specularly reflecting surfaces under laboratory conditions—applicable to generalized objects in industrial environments. As a result, the technique has been utilized in a wide range of nondestructive testing applications. For example, in the area of structural analysis, HNDT has been used for nondestructive testing of aircraft panels and honeycomb structures; aircraft wing assemblies and fins; detection of cracks,

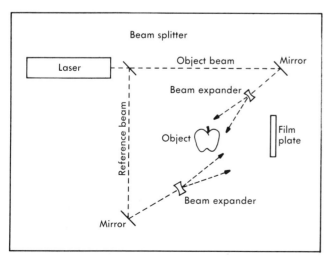

Fig. 6-69 Recording a hologram. (*Apollo Lasers*)

HOLOGRAPHIC NONDESTRUCTIVE TESTING

delaminations, and disbonds; and rotating structures such as turbine blades and naval propellers, small arms barrels, vibrating vehicle components, rock mechanics, and computer components. Holographic techniques have been used to record flowfields associated with turbine blades, projectiles, wind tunnels, rocket engines, and plasmas, as well as to analyze particle fields associated with aerosols, liquid droplets, pollutants, and spacecraft waste tanks. Finally, in the life sciences, HNDT has been applied to studies in dentistry, chest motions, hearing mechanisms, and pelvic movements. References to a variety of specific applications may be found in several review articles,[56,57] and fundamental treatments of holography are available in several books.[58,59,60]

ADVANTAGES AND LIMITATIONS

The advantages of HNDT are many. It is, first of all, a noncontact technique; thus objects may be studied without disturbing their motions by adding accelerometers or strain gages. Furthermore, sharply curved surfaces or other areas where the addition of such devices is awkward may be readily studied. It is a full-field technique; thus displacements may be studied across an entire surface rather than at discrete points. It offers interferometric precision; therefore, although a variety of techniques can be used to study much larger motions, HNDT can resolve displacements of less than one micrometer.

Pulsed lasers can provide sufficient energy to record double-pulse holographic interferograms of large objects. Furthermore, extremely short exposure times (approximately 30 nanoseconds) and pulse separations (approximately 1 microsecond) permit studies of fast transient events in the presence of relatively large general motions.

The limitations of HNDT fall into three general areas. First, the technology is different and relatively new. The equipment required is expensive, and while a high skill level is not required to operate a holographic laser, some training is required. Secondly, the technique measures only displacements. Strain must be calculated from displacement data and material properties. Finally, the holographic interferogram does not give quantitative data directly. While a number of applications such as crack detection can be conducted with only visual inspection of a hologram, a variety of others rely on quantitative evaluation of the fringes in the hologram. Great progress has been made in development of techniques that produce quantitative results.

TEST METHODS

Depending on the application, three types of test methods are used in HNDT: (1) double exposure, (2) real-time, and (3) time-average. A recent method employing similar principles is referred to as shearography.

Double Exposure

In the double exposure method, a hologram exposure is made of the part being evaluated in its undeformed state. Before removal or processing of the photographic plate, a second exposure is made of the part while it is deformed due to heat or stress. The plate is then processed and replaced approximately in the reference beam. Two wavefronts individually reconstruct from the hologram the undeformed part and the deformed part. The two wavefronts interfere with each other to give representative fringes of the deformation.

An advantage of this technique is that it does not require the hologram to be precisely placed in the reference beam; however it does not permit the observation of a continuously changing deformation. It is also difficult to quantitatively determine the deformation pattern from the fringes for a complex three-dimensional part. But it can provide qualitative information about locations of stress concentrations or deformations.

Double exposure holographic interferometry has also been applied to the field of fluid dynamics and aerodynamics; however the mechanism of the holographic process is usually different than what has previously been described. Another area of application of this method is to provide contour maps of non-specular three-dimensional parts.

An extension of the double exposure method is multiple exposure holographic interferometry. In this technique, several exposures are made of the part with precisely equal increments of distortion between each exposure.

Real-Time

In the real-time method, a hologram is made of the undeformed part. The photographic plate is processed and then repositioned so that the image coincides with the test part. When the part is deformed, two wavefronts are formed. The first wavefront, which is diffracted by the hologram, is the reconstruction of the original part, and the second is the actual wavefront scattered by the deformed part and transmitted through the hologram. These two wavefronts are coherent with respect to each other and interfere to give a fringe pattern that represents the amount of deformation incurred by the part being tested.

Real-time HNDT is used primarily for analyzing that which changes with time, such as with vibrating objects. It can also be used to examine gas and airflow patterns.

Time-Average

The time-average method is primarily used for the study of vibrating objects. In this method, a hologram is made of a part vibrating at some natural frequency; the exposure is much longer than the period of vibration. During reconstruction, an infinite number of wavefronts are reconstructed from this time-averaged hologram. Each one of these wavefronts are from the part at a different point in its cycle. At some places on the part, the vibration amplitude is such that the average is zero so that a dark fringe is seen. When the average is maximum, bright fringes are readily visible.

Shearography

Both HNDT and shearography are noncontacting optical methods. Shearography differs from HNDT in that it measures displacement gradients directly instead of displacements.[61] It is also an imaging process, thereby requiring a lens. Consequently, the field of view as well as the tolerance to depth of field are limited.

In shearography, the part being tested is illuminated by an expanded laser beam, and its image is taken with an image-shearing camera (see Fig. 6-70).[62] Like the double exposure method, two images are taken. One image is made of the part in the undeformed state, and a second image is made after deformation. The processed film produces a fringe pattern that depicts the gradients of the surface displacements due to the deformation. Defects and internal flaws produce anomalies in the fringe pattern; fringe anomalies usually appear as localized areas of high fringe density. Shearography is commonly used in the inspection of tires. It can also be used in testing composite laminates and sandwich honeycomb structures.

HOLOGRAPHIC NONDESTRUCTIVE TESTING

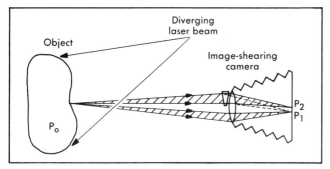

Fig. 6-70 Schematic diagram for shearographic nondestructive testing.

EQUIPMENT

Basic equipment required for holographic nondestructive testing consists of a laser with sufficient output and coherence length, an assortment of mirrors, beamsplitters and simple lenses, and a film plate. The optical elements should be housed in mounts that provide sufficient fine adjustment to accurately align the system. If continuous-wave lasers are to be used, the system must be mounted on a rigid platform that isolates the system from ambient vibrations. Pulsed lasers, because of their very short exposure times, need only be isolated enough to ensure long-term alignment.

In practice, the film should be located behind a shutter to minimize the amount of time during which ambient lighting must be turned off. With pulsed lasers, the combination of a shutter and appropriate optical filter over the film often permits recording a hologram without turning off general lighting.

Lasers for continuous-wave holography (such as time-average) are generally of the helium-neon or argon variety. These lasers deliver outputs from a few milliwatts to about 10 W. Pulsed lasers are generally ruby or frequency-doubled neodymium yttrium-aluminum-garnet (Nd:YAG) lasers. Ruby lasers can deliver holographic pulses containing tens of joules, required for holography of large objects, but are limited to pulse repetition rates of about 1 Hz. To be useful for holography, the YAG laser must possess uniphase wavefront, narrow line width, and second harmonic wavelength. Either laser can be double or multiple pulsed with pulse separations as short as 1 microsecond.

A diagram of a modular holographic camera system is shown in Fig. 6-71. The camera contains a HeNe polarized laser, electronic laser beam shutter, spatial filter, and test part mounting stage. During exposure, an electromagnetic shutter

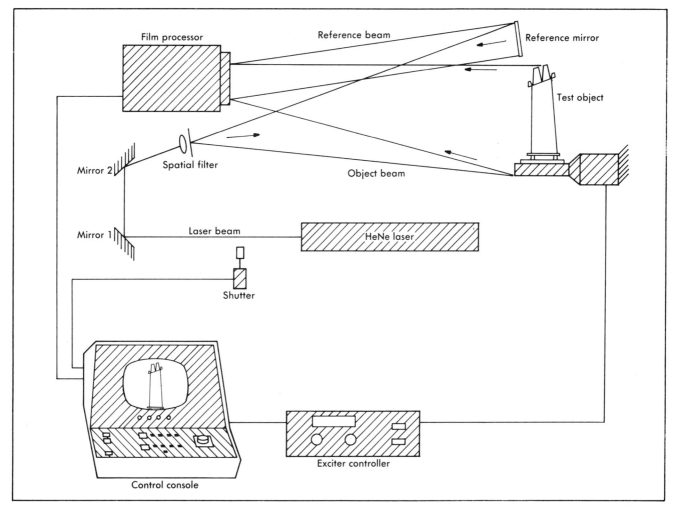

Fig. 6-71 Diagram of a modular holographic camera system. (*Laser Technology, Inc.*)

PLATING AND COATING MEASUREMENT

passes the beam to a series of mirrors and through the spatial filter. At the filter, the beam is expanded and optically filtered to remove any "noise" caused by dust on the lens and mirrors. The expanded beam illuminates the test part being inspected; a portion of the beam strikes the mirror/polarizer assembly, thus generating the reference beam. Beam ratio can be adjusted by rotating the polarizer. A microprocessor-based photodetector determines and displays the set beam ratio. The exposure and processing of the hologram is completely automatic; the hologram can also be displayed on the video monitor. With this system, holograms can be made using double exposure, real-time, and time-average methods.

SAFETY

The laser exhibits a number of characteristics, some of which are rather unique, that must be understood to ensure safe use. First of all, it must be recognized that most lasers utilize power supplies that usually develop high voltages. Although virtually all high-power lasers are designed with electrical interlocks that turn off the voltage if the cabinet is opened, normal precautions associated with similar electronic equipment should be observed. In addition, only well-trained personnel should be allowed to attempt to service the laser.

A unique characteristic of the holographic laser is its high degree of coherence. Because of this, very high optical intensities can be obtained, and beams can travel great distances with very little change in intensity; thus the potential for ocular damage exists not only from the direct output of the laser but from reflections off distant objects as well. A comprehensive review of laser safety considerations has been prepared by Sliney and Wolbarsht.[63]

Lasers sold in the United States comply with rigorous federal safety regulations requiring appropriate interlocks, controls, and warning labels; thus the use of appropriate filtered laser goggles and familiarity with basic laser safety guidelines, such as those detailed in the Laser Institute of America's *Laser Safety Guide* and the American National Standard for the Safe Use of Lasers (ANSI Z136.1-1980), should ensure safe use.

PLATING AND COATING THICKNESS MEASUREMENT

Several methods are currently being used for the nondestructive measurement of plating and coating thickness. The most widely used methods are X-ray fluorescence (XRF), beta ray backscatter (BBS), eddy current, electromagnetic induction, electrical resistance, and Hall effect. The instruments that employ these methods are essentially comparators and must be calibrated with reference standards having known coating thicknesses.

In each of these methods, the plating/coating thickness is indirectly measured by exploiting the differences between the physical properties of the coating and the base material. This indirect measurement involves probing the sample being tested with radiation (X-ray or beta), electric current (d-c or a-c), magnetic flux, or an electric field and detecting the sample's response. The response of the sample to the probing varies at a predictable rate in proportion to the thickness of the deposit.

Because each coating/base application exhibits specific physical property differences between the substrate and coating, not every test method is suitable for every coating/substrate application. For example, when gold is plated on a nickel substrate, a substantial difference in atomic numbers exists—gold is 79 and nickel is 28; therefore a test method that is sensitive to atomic number differences, such as BBS and XRF, would be most suitable for this application. However, when nickel is plated on a copper substrate, the difference between atomic numbers is very small and is not suitable for use with the BBS method. Because nickel is magnetic and copper is nonmagnetic, a test method that is sensitive to magnetic permeability should be selected; the XRF and Hall-effect methods could be used in this application. Table 6-21 lists the various methods that can be used for different coatings on various substrate materials.

X-RAY FLUORESCENCE

The X-ray fluorescence (XRF) method is widely used in the measurement of plating and coating thickness because of its versatility, accuracy, and precision and its capability to rapidly measure small surface areas. Initially, XRF instrumentation was exclusively used in a laboratory environment because it was only capable of measuring bulk samples and required highly trained operators. As a result of recent instrument advances, the XRF method is now used to measure surface areas as small as 0.003″ (0.08 mm) with high precision and accuracy. The size of the part that can be measured by XRF is limited to the size of the X-ray test chamber.

X-ray fluorescence coating thickness measuring instruments employ an X-ray tube to generate the primary beam and detectors that discriminate the energies of the X-rays emitted by the sample base and coating as well as any interlayers. The X-ray tube provides an extremely stable and high-intensity beam that is collimated to a small cross section by collimators. When the X-rays strike the sample, each component material in the sample will emit characteristic X-rays. The emitted radiation is then processed by the XRF instrument, resulting in an X-ray spectrum of the sample. Specialized algorithms in the instrument's software analyze the spectrum and determine the coating thickness based on calibration with known thickness standards.

X-ray fluorescence instruments are completely shielded, and the X-rays are blocked by a shutter until the actual measurement begins. The measurement can only take place after the X-ray chamber door is closed. The new XRF instruments are safer than the older radioisotope-based XRF instruments because the X-ray tube can be turned off at any time.

X-ray fluorescence instruments are used predominantly in the electronic field to measure the coating/plating thickness on parts such as electrical connectors, silicon wafers, integrated circuit leadframes, hybrid circuits, printed wiring boards, computer memory discs, wire, contacts, relays, and chip carriers. Typical coatings measured by XRF instruments are gold, silver, nickel, palladium, rhodium, tin-lead, cobalt, iron oxide, and tin plated over substrates such as copper alloys, nickel alloys, silicon, and aluminum. The most significant application capabilities of XRF are the simultaneous measurement of gold and nickel on gold-nickel-copper or iron-alloy plated parts and the measurement of tin-lead plating composition and thickness.

PLATING AND COATING MEASUREMENT

BETA RAY BACKSCATTER

The beta ray backscatter (BBS) method has been used for more than 20 years to measure the plating thickness of gold, silver, tin, tin-lead, copper, and photoresist coatings on printed wiring boards and small electronic parts. For a given coating to be measurable with BBS instruments, there must be at least a 20% difference in atomic number between the coating and base materials. The thickness of nickel on copper, copper on zinc, chrome on steel, and nickel on Kovar cannot be measured with BBS instruments because the atomic numbers of these combinations are too close. Although the BBS method is not as versatile as the XRF method and cannot measure small surface areas, the BBS method does have certain advantages over the XRF method.

One advantage is that BBS instruments generally cost much less than an equivalent XRF instrument. Beta ray backscatter instruments are also capable of measuring the thickness of materials with low atomic numbers, such as photoresist and organic membranes, but XRF instruments cannot measure these materials. In addition, BBS instruments can often measure thicker deposits than XRF instruments. For example, the maximum gold-plating thickness that can be measured by XRF is approximately 8 μm (300 μin.), and BBS can measure thicknesses more than 25 μm (1000 μin.).

The plating thickness measurement of beta ray backscatter instruments is based on the principle that the beta backscatter count rate increases with the atomic number of a material. The backscatter of beta particles (electrons) results from collisions with atomic nuclei within the sample. Nickel backscatters beta rays at a significantly lower rate than gold. If a thin coating of gold is deposited on a substrate of nickel or copper for example (nickel and copper having a significantly lower atomic number than gold), then more beta rays will be backscattered from the coated sample than from the bare nickel or copper base. Because gold has a higher atomic number than the base in this case, the count rate continues to increase nonlinearly with the thickness of the coating until a saturation thickness is reached. The saturation thickness is the coating thickness that is sufficient to keep the beta rays from penetrating through to the substrate. By means of a calibration curve stored in the instrument's memory, the instrument computes the thickness of the unknown samples.

A BBS system contains a basic unit, a probe, probe guide, and thickness standards. Most of the modern BBS units on the market are microprocessor based and are easy to use. They feature calibration memory permitting thickness measurements to be made without having to recalibrate, even after the instrument has been turned off.

Beta ray backscatter probes consist of a sealed radioisotope source of beta rays, a detector, and a mask or aperture. Typical sources are promethium (Pm) 147, thallium (Tl) 204, and strontium (Sr) 90. A source is selected for a given application based on its energy level and the coating thickness that must be measured. For example, Pm 147 can measure a gold coating up to 2 μm (80 μin.) thick, and Tl 204 can measure a gold coating more than 10 μm (400 μin.) thick. The source should be replaced after it reaches its first half-life. Half-life is the time required for the source to drop to one half its initial energy level. In addition, the Nuclear Regulatory Commission (NRC) requires that the source be leak tested every six months by the manufacturer or other licensed facility.

The aperture at the end of the probe serves to define the measuring area and comes in a variety of sizes in both circular and rectangular geometries. Because the part to be tested must cover the opening completely, BBS is a contacting method as contrasted with the noncontacting nature of XRF. This makes XRF highly preferable for complex-shaped test specimens.

Probe guides come in many types to facilitate precise probe positioning on large or small parts. In the case of the latter, the parts are usually placed onto the probe aperture, which points upward, and are held in position with a pressure pin.

EDDY-CURRENT METHOD

Instruments operating on the eddy-current principle are commonly used to measure nonconductive coatings on nonmagnetic metals. Examples of these applications are anodized coatings on aluminum and coatings of paint, epoxy, or Teflon on aluminum, copper, or brass substrates. The eddy-current technique may also be used for measuring plated metals on conductive or nonconductive substrates as long as there is a significant difference in electrical conductivity between the coating and base materials. Examples of these applications are zinc, cadmium, tin, copper, and nickel on steel as well as copper on plastics and aluminum on silicon.

In eddy-current coating thickness measuring instruments, a probe containing a small coil is supplied with a high-frequency alternating current. Eddy-current probes are available to measure the coating thickness on surfaces as small as 0.1" (2.5 mm). The frequency selected is from 100 kHz to 6 MHz depending on the coating material and the coating thickness to be measured. The probe is applied to the surface of the sample being tested, and a flow of eddy current is induced in the sample. Eddy currents flow in closed circular paths, and their depth of penetration is inversely proportional to the square root of the probe frequency and inversely proportional to the conductivity of the sample. The flow of eddy currents in the sample results in a magnetic field that causes a change in the probe signal's amplitude and phase.

In the measurement of nonconductive films on nonmagnetic metals, the increasing coating thickness is seen as an increasing liftoff or separation from the conductive base. The separation from the conductive base decreases the magnitude of the eddy currents induced in the sample, and the instrument interprets this as an increase in the coating thickness.

For the measurement of highly conductive coatings on less-conductive bases, the thickness of the plating increases proportionately to the magnitude of the eddy-current flow. Because the coating has a higher electrical conductivity than the base, this increases the eddy-current reaction and allows small changes in thickness to be sensed.

ELECTROMAGNETIC INDUCTION METHOD

The electromagnetic induction method is a very simple method and is used in measuring the thickness of any nonmagnetic coating on magnetic steel, iron, or Kovar. Electromagnetic induction measures the liftoff distance of the probe from the magnetic substrate. The technique is relatively insensitive to electrical conductivity and total insensitive to other properties of nonmagnetic platings and coatings; therefore any coating may be measured as long as it is completely nonmagnetic.

In the electromagnetic induction method, the probe is essentially a transformer (see Fig. 6-72). The primary winding of the probe is supplied by the basic unit with an alternating current, typically between 70 and 300 Hz. When the probe is held at a significant distance from a magnetic material, the probe operates as an extremely inefficient transformer and very little volt-

PLATING AND COATING MEASUREMENT

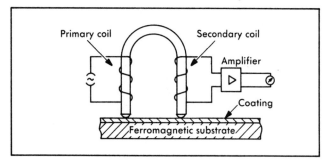

Fig. 6-72 Electromagnetic induction probe. (*UPA Technology, Inc.*)

age is induced in the secondary winding. As the probe is brought closer to a magnetic material, the efficiency steadily increases, and more voltage is induced in the secondary winding; thus the output voltage of the probe increases.

As the introduction of a nonmagnetic coating onto the magnetic base will effectively increase the distance between the probe and the magnetic substrate, the output of the probe will decrease. As the coating gets thicker—in other words, as the probe liftoff distance increases—the output of the probe will steadily decrease. It is this principle that enables instruments utilizing the electromagnetic induction principle to measure small differences in coating thicknesses.

The basic unit translates the probe's output signals into thickness readings by a pre-established calibration using a bare sample of the actual base material used in the part to be tested along with thickness standards. In this case, the standards are usually gaging sheets made of plastic or metal foils.

Some modern microprocessor-based instruments combine the eddy-current and electromagnetic induction principles in one unit. Because each of these techniques has advantages and disadvantages, putting both into one unit has a very practical and synergistic effect.

For example, zinc on steel may be measured with eddy currents or electromagnetic induction; however, eddy currents are extremely sensitive to differences in zinc-plating baths (the conductivity of the deposit is different for cyanide and noncya-

TABLE 6-21
Selection of Coating Thickness Measurement Methods

Substrate Material	Coating material							
	Aluminum	Lead	Chromium	Anodized films	Enamel, paint, rubber, varnish, plastics	Gold	Cadmium	Copper
Aluminum and Al alloys	—	B,X	B,E,X	B	B,E	B,X	B,X	B,X
Gold	X	X	X	X	X	—	X	X
Kovar	B,M	B,M,X	M,X	—	B,M	B,M,X	B,M,X	M,X
Titanium	B,X	B,X	X	X	B,E,X	B,X	B,X	B,X
Copper and Cu alloys	X	B,X	B,X,E	X	B,E,X	B,X	B,X	—
Magnesium and Mg alloys	—	B,X	B,E,X	—	B,E	B,X	B,X	B,X
Nickel	X	B,X	B,X	X	B,X	B,X	B,X	X,Q
Glass, ceramic, and plastic materials	B	B,X	B,X	—	B	B,X	B,X	B,E,X
Silver	X	B,X	B,X	X	B,E,X	B,X	X	B,X
Steel, magnetic	B,M,X	B,M,X	M,X	—	B,M,X	B,X,M	B,M,Q, X	M,X
Steel, nonmagnetic	B,X	B,X	X	X	B,E,X	B,X	B,X	X
Zinc	X	B,X	X,B	X	B,E,X	B,X	B,X	X

Code:
B = beta ray backscatter
X = X-ray fluorescence
E = eddy current
M = magnetic
N = modified magnetic

PLATING AND COATING MEASUREMENT

nide baths, for example). The conductivity variations can affect the accuracy unless the difference between the actual plating and the thickness standards is taken into account and corrected for. Electromagnetic induction, by contrast, is quite insensitive to these differences.

HALL EFFECT

The measurement of nickel coatings over copper substrates poses some peculiar problems that make measurement by eddy currents or electromagnetic induction undesirable. Electromagnetic induction instruments utilizing reverse-mode probes can measure nickel over copper in many cases; however in practice the primary windings waveform does include higher order harmonics of the fundamental frequency that actually set up eddy-current flow in the copper as well as the nickel. This eddy-current effect results in large uncertainties in the nickel readings. For measurements of nickel over copper on printed circuit boards, variations in copper thickness can affect accuracy, and measuring the nickel under the gold is difficult.

Eddy-current instruments are also less than ideal for measuring the thickness of nickel on copper substrate for the previously stated reasons. In addition, the electrical conductivity of nickel deposits can vary not only from bath to bath but from day to day using the same bath. The variances in conductivity results in large measurement uncertainties.

The Hall-effect method uses direct current that is applied through a semiconductor. A magnet provides a source of magnetic flux through the semiconductor at right angles to the current flow. This results in a d-c voltage at right angles to both the current flow and magnetic lines of force.

As the magnetic flux becomes concentrated because of the presence of a magnetic layer, the Hall voltage increases. Thus, instruments utilizing the Hall-effect principle are well suited to measuring nickel over copper. As mentioned earlier, XRF can accurately measure nickel coatings over copper substrates, but it is more expensive.

Because the Hall effect does not "see" any nonmagnetic material at all, nickel may be measured on printed circuit boards even through gold or other thin (less than 1 mil or 25

TABLE 6-21—*Continued*

				Coating material						
Solder	Brass	Nickel	Nickel, electroless	Palladium	Platinum	Rhodium	Silver	Zinc	Tin
B,X	B,X	B,N,X	B,X	B,X	B,X	B,X	B,X	B,Q,X	B,X
X	X	X	X	X	—	B,X	B,X	X	X
B,M,X	X,M	N,X	X	B,X,M	B,X,M	B,X,M	B,X,M	M,X	B,M,X
B,X	B,X	N,B,X	X	B,X	B,X	B,X	B,X	B,X	B,X
B,X	X	N,X	X	B,X	B,X	B,X	B,X	X	B,X
B,X	B,X	B,N,X	B,X	B,X	B,X	B,X	B,X	B,X	B,X
B,X	X	—		B,X	B,X	B,X	B,X	X	B,X
B,X	B,X	B,N,X	B,X	B,X	B,X	B,X	B,X	B,X	B,X
B,X	B,X	B,X,N	B,X	X	B,X	X	—	B,X	X
B,M,X	X,M	X,N	M,N X	B,X,M	B,X,M	B,X,M	B,X,M	M,B,X	B,M,X
B,X	X	N,X	X	B,X	B,X	B,X	B,X	B,X	B,X
B,X	X	N,X	X	B,X	B,X	B,X	B,X	—	B,X

(Fisher Technology, Inc.)

micrometers) platings. For measuring on very small parts, or where it is also necessary to measure the gold (as is usually the case for incoming inspection), one should use XRF rather than Hall effect.

MICRORESISTANCE METHOD

The microresistance method is used for measuring the thickness and quality of copper plating in printed circuit board through-holes (see Fig. 6-73). The method depends on the precise measurement of the true resistance of the cylinder of copper lining the hole. The resistances involved are on the order of a few hundred microhms.

A good microresistance instrument must be capable of injecting d-c current uniformly through the hole and then picking up the resulting voltage drop. Advanced instruments use pulsed direct current to eliminate the effects of electromagnetic interference. The current is also uniformly introduced by means of conical contacts that cover as much of the circumference of the hole as possible, leaving a small gap for the voltage pickup contacts.

With the current known (by internal reference and self-calibration), the voltage drop is converted to resistance by Ohm's Law. The resistance is converted to thickness by the formula:

$$R = \frac{K \rho T}{\pi t (D+t)} \qquad (8)$$

where:

R = measured resistance, microhms ($\mu \Omega$)
K = conversion constant (394 British, 10 metric)
ρ = resistivity of copper (1.69 $\mu \Omega$-cm)
T = thickness of laminate material (dielectric only)
t = copper thickness
D = hole internal diameter

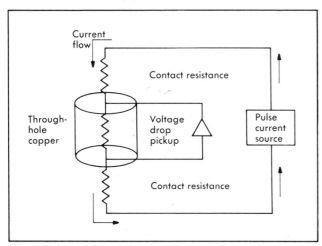

Fig. 6-73 Microresistance testing of printed circuit board through-holes. (*UPA Technology, Inc.*)

References

1. Robert C. McMaster, ed., *Nondestructive Testing Handbook*, Vol. I (New York: The Ronald Press Co., 1959), p. 1.1.
2. *Ibid.*, p. 4.8.
3. "Nondestructive Tests," SAE J358, *SAE Handbook* (Warrendale, PA: Society of Automotive Engineers, 1983), p. 3.46.
4. Warren J. McGonnagle, *Nondestructive Testing* (New York: McGraw-Hill Book Co., 1961), p. 16.
5. Carl E. Betz, *Principles of Penetrants* (Chicago, IL: Magnaflux Corp., 1963), p. 23.
6. Howard E. Boyer, ed., *Metals Handbook*, 8th ed., Vol. II (Metals Park, OH: American Society for Metals, 1976), p. 30.
7. *Ibid.*, p. 28.
8. Betz, *op. cit.*, p. 149.
9. Bernard W. Boisvert, et al., "The Fluorescent Penetrant Hydrophilic Remover Process (Part 1)," *Materials Evaluation* (January 1983), pp. 34-42.
10. McMaster, *op. cit.*, p. 6.5.
11. McGonnagle, *op. cit.*, p. 62.
12. Betz, *op. cit.*, p. 175.
13. McMaster, *op. cit.*, pp. 7.1 to 7.8.
14. Betz, *op. cit.*, p. 242.
15. *Classroom Training Handbook, Magnetic Particle Testing*, CT-6-3 (San Diego: General Dynamics, Convair Div., 1977).
16. *Classroom Training Handbook, Ultrasonic Testing*, CT-6-4 (San Diego: General Dynamics, Convair Div., 1981).
17. Howard E. Boyer and Timothy L. Gall, eds., *Metals Handbook, Desk Edition* (Metals Park, OH: American Society for Metals, 1985), p. 33-40.
18. *Ibid.*
19. *Ibid.*
20. *Classroom Training Handbook, Radiographic Testing*, CT-6-6 (San Diego: General Dynamics, Convair Div., 1983).
21. Richard A. Quinn and Claire C. Sigl, eds., *Radiography in Modern Industry*, 4th ed. (Rochester, NY: Eastman Kodak Co., 1980).
22. "Penetrating Radiation Inspection," SAE J427b, *SAE Handbook*, vol. 1 (Warrendale, PA: Society of Automotive Engineers, 1983), p. 3.53.
23. McMaster, *op. cit.*, pp. 24.4 to 24.12.
24. *Classroom Training Handbook, Eddy Current Testing*, CT-6-5 (San Diego: General Dynamics, Convair Div., 1979).
25. "Eddy Current Testing by Electromagnetic Methods," SAE J425, *SAE Handbook*, vol. 1 (Warrendale, PA: Society of Automotive Engineers, 1983), p. 3.49.
26. Howard E. Boyer and Timothy L. Gall, eds., *Metals Handbook, Desk Edition* (Metals Park, OH: American Society for Metals, 1985), p. 33-16.
27. Richard L. Pasley and James A. Birdwell, "Eddy Current Testing," *Nondestructive Testing, A Survey*, NASA SP-5113 (Washington, DC: National Aeronautics and Space Administration, 1973), p. 108.
28. "Eddy Current Testing by Electromagnetic Methods," *loc. cit.*
29. "Leakage Testing," SAE J1267, *SAE Handbook*, vol. 1 (Warrendale, PA: Society of Automotive Engineers, 1983), p. 3.50.
30. *Ibid.*
31. Robert E. Englehardt and William A. Hewgley, "Thermal and Infrared Testing," *Nondestructive Testing, A Survey*, NASA SP-5113 (Washington, DC: National Aeronautics and Space Administration, 1973), pp. 119-140.
32. E. G. Henneke and K. L. Reifsnider, *Quality Control and Nondestructive Evaluation Techniques for Composites - Part VII: Thermography—A State-of-the-Art Review*, AVRADCOM Report No. TR 82-F-5 (Watertown, MA: Army Materials Technology Laboratory, 1982).
33. J. Cohen, *Elements of Thermography for Nondestructive Testing*, NBS Technical Note 1177 (Washington, DC: National Bureau of Standards, 1983).
34. "Infrared Heat Measurement Finds New Uses in Plastics," *Plastics Technology* (August 1983), pp. 13-15.
35. E. P. Papadakis, H.L. Chesney, and R.G. Hurley, "Quality Assurance of Aluminum Radiators by Infrared Thermography," *Materials Evaluation* (March 1984), pp. 333-336.
36. Ronald G. Hurley, "Temperature Measurements on Semipermanent Mold Surfaces Using Infrared Thermography," *Thermosense V Conference Proceedings*, held October 25, 1982, Detroit, MI (Bellingham, WA: Society of Photo-Optical Instrumentation Engineers), pp. 89-91.
37. "Definition of Terms Relating to Acoustic Emission Testing," ASTM E 610 (Philadelphia: American Society for Testing and Materials, 1977).
38. H.L. Dunegan and C.L. Tatro, "Passive Pressure Transducer Utilizing Acoustic Emission," *Review of Scientific Instruments*, vol. 38, no. 8 (1967), pp. 1145-1147.

39. "Definition of Terms Relating to Acoustic Emission Testing," *loc. cit.*

40. C. Gerald Gardner, "Radiography," *Nondestructive Testing, A Survey*, NASA SP-5113 (Washington, DC: National Aeronautics and Space Administration, 1973), p. 89.

41. H. Berger and W.N. Beck, "Neutron Radiographic Inspection of Radioactive Irradiated Reactor Fuel Specimens," *Nuclear Science and Engineering*, vol. 15 (1963), pp. 411-414.

42. H. Berger, ed., "Practical Applications of Neutron Radiography and Gaging," *ASTM Special Technical Publication 586* (Philadelphia: American Society for Testing and Materials, 1976).

43. J.P. Barton and P. von der Hardt, eds., *Proceedings of the First World Conference on Neutron Radiography* (Dordrecht, Holland: D. Rerdel Publishing Co., 1983).

44. H. Berger, "Neutron Radiographic Detection of Corrosion," *ASTM Symposium on Nondestructive Testing and Electrochemical Methods of Monitoring Corrosion in Industrial Plants*, held May 1984, Montreal, Ontario (Philadelphia: American Society for Testing and Materials, 1985).

45. P.A.E. Stewart, "Cold Neutron Imaging for Gas Turbine Inspections," *Real-Time Radiologic Imaging: Medical and Industrial Applications*, ASTM STP 716 (Philadelphia: American Society for Testing and Materials, 1980), pp. 180-198.

46. D.A.W. Pullen, "Radiographic Photogrammetry Yields Valuable Data in Studies of Running Gas Turbines," *Mechanical Engineering Technology* (July 1981), pp. 27-31.

47. P.A.E. Stewart and J. Heritage, "Cold Neutron Fluoroscopy of Operating Automotive Engines," *Proceedings of the First World Conference on Neutron Radiography* (Dordrecht, Holland: D. Reidel Publishing Co., 1983), pp. 635-642.

48. John D. Jones, et al., *Real Time Neutron Imaging Applied to Internal Combustion Engine Behavior*, SAE Technical Paper Series No. 850-560 (Warrendale, PA: Society of Automotive Engineers, 1985).

49. K.L. Crosbie, et al., "Californium Multiplier Part I: Design for Neutron Radiography," *Materials Evaluation*, vol. 40, No. 5 (1982), pp. 579-583.

50. "Standard Practices for Thermal Neutron Radiography of Materials," ASTM E 748-85 (Philadelphia: American Society for Testing and Materials, 1985).

51. "Standard Method for Determining Image Quality in Thermal Neutron Radiographic Testing," ASTM E 545 (Philadelphia: American Society for Testing and Materials, 1981).

52. "Standard Method for Determining the L/D Ratio of Neutron Radiographic Beams, ASTM E 803 (Philadelphia: American Society for Testing and Materials, 1981).

53. "Glossary of Terms and Definitions for Neutron Radiographic Testing," MIL-STD-1948 (1985).

54. J.C. Domanus, ed., *Reference Neutron Radiographs of Neutron Reactor Fuel* (Dordrecht, Holland: D. Reidel Publishing Co., 1984).

55. "Personnel Qualification and Certification in Nondestructive Testing," SNT-TC-1A (Columbus: American Society for Nondestructive Testing, 1980).

56. D. Dudley, *Holography*, NASA Special Publication 5118 (Washington, DC: National Aeronautics and Space Administration, 1973).

57. R.T. Pitlak and R. Page, "Pulsed Lasers for Holographic Interferometry," *Optical Engineering* (July/August 1985), pp. 639-644.

58. R. J. Collier, C. B. Burckhardt, and L. H. Lin, *Optical Holography* (New York: Academic Press, 1971).

59. C. M. Vest, *Holographic Interferometry* (New York: John Wiley and Sons, 1979).

60. R. K. Erf, *Holographic Nondestructive Testing* (New York: Academic Press, 1974).

61. Y. Y. Hung, "Shearography versus Holography in Nondestructive Evaluation," *SPIE Proceedings*, vol. 604 (Bellingham, WA: The International Society for Optical Engineering, 1986).

62. _____ , "Shearography: A New Optical Method for Strain Measurement and Nondestructive Testing," *Optical Engineering*, vol. 21, no. 3 (1982), pp. 391-395.

63. David Sliney and Myron Wolbarsht, *Safety with Lasers and Other Optical Sources* (New York: Plenum, 1980).

Bibliography

Caulfield, H.J., ed. *Handbook of Optical Holography*. New York: Academic Press, 1979.

Dunegan, H.L.; Harris, D.O.; and Tetelman, A.S. "Detection of Fatigue Crack Growth by Acoustic Emission Techniques." *Materials Evaluation* (October 1970), pp. 221-227.

Ebbeni, J., ed. "Industrial Applications of Holographic Nondestructive Testing." *SPIE Proceedings*, vol. 349. Bellingham, WA: The International Society for Optical Engineering, 1982.

Erf, R.K., ed. *Speckle Metrology*. New York: Academic Press, 1978.

Graphical Solution for the Helium Leak Detector and Radioisotope Methods of Hermetic Test. Special Publication 400-73. Washington, DC: National Bureau of Standards, 1982.

Guthrie, A. *Vacuum Technology*. Somerset, NJ: John Wiley and Sons, 1963.

Halogen Leak Detector Manual. Lynn, MA: General Electric Co. Instrument Products Operation.

Halogen Leak Detector Manual. #ID-4816. Shenandoah, GA: General Electric/YEW of America.

Helium Leak Detection Manual. #4820-48000. Wilmington, DE: DuPont, 1982.

Hottel, H.C. *Heat Transmission*, 3rd ed. New York: McGraw-Hill Book Co., Inc., 1954.

Hudson, R.D. *Infrared System Engineering*. New York: John Wiley and Sons, 1969.

Hurley, C.W. and Kreider, K.G. *Application of Thermography for Energy Conservation in Industry*. NBS TN-923. Washington, DC: National Bureau of Standards, Oct. 1976, pp. 24-27.

Introduction to Helium Mass Spectrometer Leak Detection. Palo Alto, CA: Varian Associates, Inc., 1980.

Introduction to Vacuum and Leak Detection. Plainview, NY: Veeco Instruments, Inc., 1980.

Kraus, R.W. *Introduction to Mass Spectrometry and Its Applications*. Englewood Cliffs, NJ: Prentice-Hall, 1965.

"Leakage Testing Handbook." NASA-GE Contract NA5 7-396. Report #IST-295. Springfield, VA: National Technical Information Service, 1969.

Lewin, G. *Fundamentals of Vacuum Science and Technology*. New York: McGraw-Hill Book Co., 1965.

McMaster, Robert C., ed. *Leak Testing*, Vol. I. Nondestructive Testing Handbook, 2nd ed. Columbus: American Society for Nondestructive Testing, 1982.

Metals Handbook, 8th ed., vol. 11. Metals Park, OH: American Society for Metals, 1976.

O'Hanlon, John F. *User's Guide to Vacuum Technology*. Somerset, NJ: John Wiley and Sons, 1980.

"Practice for Acoustic Emission Monitoring During Continuous Welding." ASTM E 749. Philadelphia: American Society for Testing and Materials.

"Practice for Acoustic Emission Monitoring During Resistance Spot-Welding." ASTM E 751. Philadelphia: American Society for Testing and Materials.

"Recommended Practice for Acoustic Emission Monitoring of Structures During Controlled Simulation." ASTM E 569. Philadelphia: American Society for Testing and Materials.

"Recommended Practice for Mounting Piezoelectric Acoustic Emission Contact Sensors." ASTM E 650. Philadelphia: American Society for Testing and Materials.

"Recommended Practice for the Qualification and Certification of Personnel." SNT-TC-1A (all supplements). Columbus, OH: American Society for Nondestructive Testing.

Streeter, V.L., and Wylie, E.B. *Fluid Mechanics*, 8th ed. New York: McGraw-Hill Book Co., 1985.

Vacuum Technology: Its Foundations, Formulae and Tables. San Jose, CA: Leybold-Heraeus, Inc., 1985.

Warren, C., and Blockman, G. *Energy Conservation Guidebook*. Secaucus, NJ: AGEMA Infrared Systems, 1977.

Wilson, N.G., and Beavis, L.C. *Handbook of Vacuum Leak Detection*. New York: American Vacuum Society, 1976.

MECHANICAL TESTING AND BALANCING

MECHANICAL TESTING

Material testing is needed to learn about existing material properties and to develop new materials. Various tests are performed to explain why something works or does not work, or to meet a need not satisfied by existing materials. Material selection implies a choice to be made from several different materials. Testing is necessary to properly evaluate a material's potential for meeting the desired properties, as well as to identify any inherent shortcomings that may affect its performance. Quality control testing is done by the producer to control composition and uniformity of a specific material and by the manufacturer to confirm the specified properties and compare competing materials or sources of a given material.

Table 7-1 outlines the mechanical tests discussed in this chapter and the properties determined by them. Sheet metal formability is discussed in Volume II, *Forming*, and material properties are discussed in Volume III, *Materials, Finishing and Coating*, of this Handbook series. Following the discussion of the various tests, the pertinent American Society for Testing and Materials (ASTM) test methods are identified for metals, plastics, rubber, and wood. It is significant to point out that the same property can be determined by more than one test, with differing resulting values. For example, yield strength is determined by tension, compression, and torsion tests. Its value by the tension test may differ from that determined by the other two tests. It is important, therefore, that the service and test stresses be of the same type. Frequently, experience shows that for a given metal the values obtained from different tests are the same; once this fact is established, it is acceptable to perform the easier test.

It is usually necessary to machine or otherwise prepare a specimen of the material to be tested. The shape and size of specimens vary with the test to be made and the size of the material available. For example, there are various dimensions for standard tension specimens depending on the thickness of the stock available.

Mechanical testing can benefit from automated data acquisition and analysis systems. Computer-aided systems have been developed and used for many types of tests, tension and fatigue tests in particular. A suitable computer-aided testing system can perform one or all of the following functions: (1) calibrate and control the equipment that excites the specimen or structure, (2) monitor and record the data generated during the test, and (3) manipulate the data for analysis and automatically summarize the information in suitable tables, graphs, or frequency distributions.

TEST METHODS

The ASTM specifications and test methods appear in annual volumes of the Book of Standards published by ASTM. These specifications and test methods are classified as either "tentative" or "standard" and are prepared by committees of specialists. Initially, all the specifications and test methods are classified as tentative. Tentative methods are revised over a period of time until they are adopted as standards; adopted standards are also revised from time to time.

Three methods that are applicable to the testing of many materials are designated ASTM E 4, E 6, and E 83; these cover the load verification of testing machines, the definition of terms relating to methods of testing, and the method of verification and classification of extensometers, respectively. The primary mechanical test methods for metals are given in Table 7-2, for plastics in Table 7-3, for wood in Table 7-4, and for rubber in Table 7-5. Many of the testing procedures have been adopted as standards by the American National Standards Institute (ANSI).

Contributor for this chapter is: Ray Achterberg, Sales Engineer, Gisholt Balancers, Gilman Engrg. & Mfg. Co., A Unit of AMCA.

Reviewers of sections of this chapter are: Ray Achterberg, Sales Engineer, Gisholt Balancers, Gilman Engrg. & Mfg. Co., A Unit of AMCA; **J. E. Blair III**, Advertising Manager, Newage Industries, Inc.; **David H. Borrup**, Supervisor, Process Planning, United Technologies, Pratt & Whitney; **Thomas M. Broughton**, Sales Manager, Tinius Olsen Testing Machine Co.; **Steven Bucher**, Technical Quotations Manager, Micro-Poise Div., Ransburg Corp.; **Ronald Felix Buck**, Manager of Engineering, Balance Engineering, General Motors Technical Center; **Andrew R. Fee**, Technical Director, Page-Wilson Corp.; **James E. Rainey**, Head, Metallurgical and Mechanical Testing Dept., National Testing and Research Laboratory, Inc.; **Norbert H. Scott, Sr.**, Senior Manufacturing Engineer, Electric Motor Division—C.M.E., Emerson Electric Co.; **Louis Small**, President, Service Physical Testers; **D. G. Stadelbauer**, Executive Vice President, Schenck Trebel Corp.; **Peter St. Clair**, Analyst—Evaluation Engineer, Aircraft Engine Business Group, General Electric Co.; **Wayne Utterback**, Sales Manager, Gilman Engrg. & Mfg. Co., A Unit of AMCA; **Robert Zenk**, Manager of Research & Development, Gilman Engrg. & Mfg. Co., A Unit of AMCA.

MECHANICAL TESTING

TABLE 7-1
Mechanical Tests and Determined Properties

Tension	Compression	Flexure	Direct Shear	Torsion
Elongation	Compressive strength	Modulus of rupture	Shear strength	Angle of twist
Reduction in area	Yield strength	Transverse strength		Modulus of rupture
Tensile strength	Drop-of-the-beam	Flexural strength		Shear strength
Yield strength	"Dividers" method	Proportional limit		Yield strength
Drop-of-the-beam	Stated offset	Tangent		Stated offset
"Dividers" method	Proportional limit	Modulus of elasticity		Proportional limit
Stated offset	Tangent	Initial modulus		Tangent
Proportional limit	Stated offset			Modulus of elasticity
Tangent	Elastic limit			Modulus of rigidity
Stated offset	Modulus of elasticity			Initial modulus
Elastic limit	Initial modulus			
Modulus of elasticity	Tangent modulus			
Initial modulus	Secant modulus			
Tangent modulus				
Secant modulus				

Notched-Bar Impact	Hardness	Fatigue	Creep	Stress-Rupture*
Notch sensitivity	Hardness number	Fatigue strength	Rate of elongation	Time to fracture
Charpy	Brinell	Endurance strength	Minimum creep rate	Total elongation
Izod	Rockwell	Endurance limit	Total elongation	Reduction in area
Notch temperature	Rockwell (super-	Endurance ratio		
sensitivity	ficial)	Notch sensitivity		
Charpy	Vickers	ratio		
% Shear	Knoop			
Ductility	Scleroscope			
	Microcharacter			
	and others			

* If time-elongation measurements also are made, the properties listed under Creep also may be determined.

TABLE 7-2
Methods Related to Mechanical Tests on Metals

Subject	Title	ASTM Designation
Bend ductility	Free Bend Test for Ductility of Welds	E 16
	Guided Bend Test for Ductility of Welds	E 190
	Semi-guided Bend Test for Ductility of Metallic Materials	E 290
Calibration	Verification of Testing Machines	E 4
	Verification and Classification of Extensometers	E 83
Compression	Compression Testing of Metallic Materials at Room Temperature	E 9
	Compression Testing of Metallic Materials at Elevated Temperature with Conventional or Rapid Heating Rates and Strain Rates	E 290
	Compression Testing of Cast Iron	E 256
Creep	Recommended Practices for Conducting Creep, Creep-Rupture, and Stress Rupture Tests of Metallic Materials	E 139
	Recommended Practices for Conducting Creep and Creep-Rupture Tension Tests of Metallic Materials under Conditions of Rapid Heating and Short Times	E 150
Definitions	Definitions of Terms Relating to Mechanical Testing	E 6
	Methods and Definitions for Mechanical Testing of Steel Products	

(continued)

TABLE 7-2—*Continued*

Subject	Title	ASTM Designation
Definitions, cont.	Definitions of Terms Related to Heat Treatment of Metals	E 44
	Definitions of Terms Relating to Metallography	E 7
Drop weight	Conducting Drop Weight Test to Determine Nil-Ductility Transition Temperature of Ferritic Steels	E 208
	Drop Weight Tear Tests of Ferritic Steels	E 436
Fracture tests	Test for Plane-Strain Fracture Toughness of Metallic Materials	E 399
	Test for Sharp-Notch Tension Testing of High-Strength Sheet Materials	E 338
Hardness	Test for Brinell Hardness of Metallic Materials	E 10
	Test for Rockwell and Rockwell Superficial Hardness of Metallic Materials	E 18
	Test for Vickers Hardness of Metallic Materials	E 92
	Test for Microhardness of Materials	E 384
	Standard Hardness Conversion Tables for Metals	E 140 and A 370
	Test for Indentation Hardness of Metallic Materials by Portable Hardness Testers	E 110
Impact	Notched-Bar Impact Testing of Metallic Materials	E 23
	Impact Testing of Cast Iron	E 327
Stress relaxation	Recommended Practice for Stress-Relaxation Tests for Materials and Structures	E 328
Tension	Tension Testing of Metallic Materials	E 8
	Recommended Practice for Elevated Temperature Tension Tests of Metallic Materials	E 21
	Recommended Practice for Tension Tests of Metallic Materials at Elevated Temperatures with Rapid Heating and Conventional or Rapid Strain Rates	E 151
	Recommended Practice for Conducting Time-for-Rupture Notch Tension Test of Materials	E 292
	Tension Testing of Metallic Foil	E 345
Torsion	Test for Shear Modulus at Room Temperature	E 143
Transverse test	Transverse Testing of Gray Cast Iron	A 438

TABLE 7-3
Methods Related to Mechanical Tests on Plastics

Subject	Title	ASTM Designation
Bearing strength	Method of Test for Bearing Strength of Plastics	D 953
Compressive tests	Method of Test for Compressive Properties of Rigid Plastics	D 695
	Method of Test for Deformation of Plastics under Load	D 621
Creep tests	Recommended Practices for Testing Long-Time Creep and Stress-Relaxation of Plastics under Tension or Compression Loads at Various Temperatures	D 2990, D 2991
	Test for Tensile Creep and Creep-Rupture of Plastics	D 2990
Fatigue test	Test for Flexural Fatigue of Plastics by Constant-Amplitude-of-Force	D 671
Flexure test	Test for Flexural Properties of Plastics	D 790

(continued)

MECHANICAL TESTING

TABLE 7-3—*Continued*

Subject	Title	ASTM Designation
Hardness tests	Test for Rockwell Hardness of Plastics and Electrical Insulating Materials	D 785
	Test for Indentation Hardness of Rubber and Plastics by Means of a Durometer	D 2240
Impact tests	Tests for Impact Resistance of Plastics and Electrical Insulating Materials	D 256
	Test for Brittleness Temperature of Plastics and Elastomers by Impact	D 746
	Test for Impact Resistance of Polyethylene Film by Free-Falling Dart Method	D 1709
Impact tests	Test for Brittleness Temperature of Plastic Film by Impact	D 1790
	Test for Impact Resistance of Thermoplastic Pipe and Fittings by Means of a Tup (Falling Weight)	D 2444
Shear test	Test for Shear Strength of Plastics	D 732
	Test for Apparent Horizontal Shear Strength of Reinforced Plastics by Short Beam Method	D 2344
Stiffness	Test for Stiffness of Plastics by Means of a Cantilever Beam	D 747
	Stiffness Properties of Plastics as a Function of Temperature by Means of a Torsion Test	D 1043
Stress rupture	Test for Environmental Stress Rupture of Type III Polyethylenes Under Constant Tensile Load	D 2552
Tensile test	For Tensile Properties of Plastics	D 638
	For Tensile Properties of Thin Plastic Sheeting	D 882
	For Tensile Properties of Rigid Cellular Plastics	D 1623
	For Tensile Properties of Plastics by Use of Microtensile Specimens	D 1708
	Tensile Strength of Molded Electrical Insulating Materials	D 651
	Tensile Properties of Plastics at High Speeds	D 2289
Torsion	Tests for Dynamic Mechanical Properties of Plastics by Means of a Torsional Pendulum	D 2236

TABLE 7-4
Methods Related to Mechanical Tests on Wood

Subject	Title	ASTM Designation
Shear	Plywood in Shear Through-the-Thickness	D 2719
Shear	Shear Modulus of Plywood	D 3044
Tensile	Testing Small Clear Specimens of Timber	D 143
Tensile	Static Tests of Timbers in Structural Sizes	D 198
Tensile	Testing Veneer, Plywood, and Other Glued Veneer Constructions	D 3499, D 3500, D 3501, D 3502, D 3503
Tensile	Evaluating the Properties of Wood-Base Fiber and Particle Panel Materials	D 1037
Hardness	Standard Specification for Modified Wood	D 1324

TABLE 7-5
Methods Related to Mechanical Tests on Rubber

Subject	Title	ASTM Designation
Compressive tests	Tests for Compressive-Deflection Characteristics of Vulcanized Rubber	D 575
	Tests for Compression Set for Vulcanized Rubber	D 395
Fatigue tests	Tests for Compression Fatigue of Vulcanized Rubber	D 623
	Dynamic Testing for Ply Separation and Cracking of Rubber Products	D 430
Flexure tests	Test for Young's Modulus in Flexure of Elastomers at Normal and Subnormal Temperatures	D 797
	Test for Crack Growth of Rubber	D 813
Hardness tests	Test for International Hardness of Vulcanized Rubber	D 1415
	Test for Indentation Hardness of Rubber and Plastics by Means of a Durometer	D 2240
Impact tests	Tests for Impact Resistance of Plastics and Electrical Insulating Materials	D 256
Tensile tests	Tension Testing of Vulcanized Rubber	D 412
	Tension Testing of Hard Rubber	D 2707

HARDNESS TESTS

Most hardness tests yield numerical values that are based on a material's resistance to indentation under the conditions imposed by the particular test. Resistance to scratching is another measure of hardness, as is the measurement of the energy absorbed by a material when struck by a falling object. Hardness numbers alone, because they indicate characteristics more than properties of materials, have practical significance only when correlated with service experience or a particular material property.

Perhaps the most common use of hardness tests is in quality control, where they are used to check material uniformity or processing treatment. Hardness numbers also provide a quick indication of the numerical value of a particular property of a material; before a hardness number can be used in this way, a relationship to the property must be established, and a comparison range must be defined. By correlating a series of hardness numbers with the corresponding service experience of a material in a particular use, it is possible to evaluate similar materials for use in the same application.

In most applications, the hardness of the material as a whole—the general hardness—can be used for comparison with service experience or a particular property; applicable methods are the Brinell, Rockwell, scleroscope, and Vickers hardness tests, which are carried out on a macroscale. In some applications, such as the testing of metals for bearings, the hardness of the constituents or grains of the metal provides the most useful information for correlation with other data. Hardness tests must then be carried out on a microscale and might be considered measurements of particle hardness; the Knoop and microcharacter hardness tests are particularly applicable to, although not limited to, these measurements. Other methods have also been developed to permit testing on special applications such as aircraft skins (ASTM B 7). These methods generally yield results that correlate to a common scale such as Rockwell C.

In selecting a hardness test, consideration must be given to the thickness of the specimen to be tested. The thickness must be such that the backing material or anvil on which the specimen rests has no effect on the indentation of the penetrator in the specimen. An imprint on the undersurface of a specimen after a test is a definite indication that the specimen was too thin for the particular hardness test used. Satisfactory hardness tests for various minimum thicknesses of uniformly hardened steel can be determined from the curves in Fig. 7-1. If a certain specimen is too thin, a test using a lighter load or a larger indentor should be selected.

Booklets supplied by testing machine makers contain many general statements about the particular hardness test for which the machine is designed. A few such statements are:

1. Make sure the surface and size of specimen are compatible with the type of test to be made. For example, do not use the Brinell test for very small or thin specimens, and a metallographic finish may be necessary on specimens for microhardness tests.
2. Make sure that the testing machine is correctly set up for the desired type of hardness test, such as the correct load on the correct indentor in the Rockwell test.
3. Use the proper supporting means for the shape of specimen being tested. In the Rockwell test, use a flat anvil for large, flat specimens; a spot anvil for small specimens; and V-anvils for rounds.
4. In all cases where static loading is used, apply the load gently and without shock. In a Brinell or Rockwell test, bring the specimen gently into contact with the indentor and apply the total load with the same care. (Of the systems specified in ASTM E 103 for rapid indentation,

HARDNESS TESTS

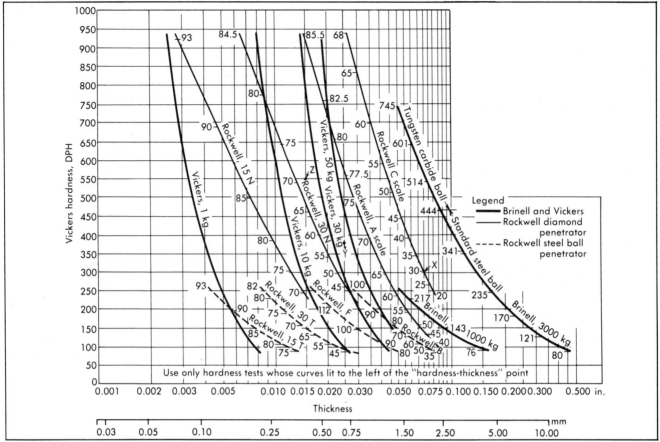

Fig. 7-1 Selector chart for hardness tests for steel.

the counterbalanced-spring, top-loaded type requires less care in loading than the deadweight type does.)

5. Make proper use of the observations of the test in obtaining the hardness numbers. For example, in a Vickers test, be sure to use the particular table corresponding to the load used.

The Brinell test finds wide use on large parts such as castings and forgings of low to medium hardness; the Rockwell and Vickers tests on small parts and those of low, medium, or high hardness; and the scleroscope test for quick, routine inspection and for shop tests. The Vickers test is particularly versatile because it has a wide uniform scale and permits the use of an extensive range of loads. Durometers are widely used for quick checks on rubber and plastics. Shore scales are generally used for plastics testing and the international rubber hardness degrees (IRHD) are used for rubber.

Some types of hardness testers are available in both hand-operated and motorized models. The motorized models are particularly advantageous for production testing of simply shaped small pieces that can be fed or placed into the tester quickly. For heavier and more complicated pieces, the chief advantage of the motorized model is less fatigue of the operator. Portable equipment is also marketed.

Brinell Hardness Test

In the Brinell hardness test, a known load is applied for a given length of time to the surface of the specimen through a hardened-steel or carbide ball of known diameter. The diameter of the resulting permanent indentation is measured and is usually converted to a Brinell hardness number by the use of standard tables. The Brinell hardness number may be calculated from the equation:

$$Bhn = \frac{P}{(\pi D / 2)(D - \sqrt{D^2 - d^2})} \qquad (1)$$

where:

Bhn = Brinell hardness number
P = applied load, kg
D = diameter of steel ball, mm
d = diameter of impression, mm

There are two types of Brinell hardness testing machines in general use: hydraulic and deadweight lever-loading. Proving rings are generally used for calibrating the loads of the testers. Test blocks in any Brinell range also measure the load in an indirect manner.

A microscope especially designed for measuring Brinell indentations is generally used for diameter measurements. It contains a scale having 0.1 mm (0.004″) graduations and permits an estimation of 0.02 mm (0.0008″) to be made. A separate graduated scale is usually supplied for calibrating the microscope.

Automatic Brinell machines generally use hydraulics to produce a standard Brinell indentation, but do not make an optical width measurement. An automatic machine makes a depth-of-penetration measurement that correlates to the optical width-of-penetration measurement as per ASTM E 103. The depth measurement is much faster and easier to machine mechanically, which allows the system to be used for in-line and process control applications.

The standard ball diameter is 10.000 mm (0.3937") with a permissible variation in this diameter of 0.005 mm (0.000197"). The ball should have a Vickers hardness number of 850 using a 10 kg load, and it may be used on materials having a Brinell hardness number less than 442; a carbide ball can be used on material having a Brinell hardness number not more than 630. The ball should not show a permanent change in diameter greater than 0.005 mm (0.0002") when pressed with the test load against a specimen.

The type of ball—generally tungsten carbide—should be reported for Brinell hardness numbers greater than 442.

The required thickness of uniformly hardened steel specimens can be determined from Fig. 7-1. In general, the thickness of the specimen should be at least 10 times the depth of the impression. The nominal dimensions of the specimens in the plane of the surface being tested should be such that there is no flow of the material at the edges of the specimen during the test. The top and bottom surfaces of the specimen should be finished with about No. 0 emery paper to provide good seating of the specimen on the anvil and to remove surface variations that might interfere with the measurement of the indentation. In general, the finish should be such that the edge of the indentation is clear enough to permit the diameter measurement to 0.1 mm (0.004") and the estimation of the diameter to 0.02 mm (0.008").

Rockwell and Rockwell Superficial Hardness Tests

The Rockwell and the Rockwell superficial hardness tests are both based on the same principle. The tests yield an arbitrary number that is related to the difference in the depth of penetration of a penetrator subjected to a minor (initial) and a major (final) load under specified conditions. The Rockwell superficial hardness test is designed particularly for measuring the hardness of thin materials or case-hardened metals. The primary differences between the Rockwell and the Rockwell superficial hardness tests are lighter minor and major loads and a tester of higher sensitivity in the Rockwell superficial hardness test. The depth of penetration for the Rockwell superficial hardness test is approximately 0.00004" (0.001 mm) for each scale division. For the Rockwell hardness test, the penetration is approximately 0.00008" (0.0002 mm) for each scale division.

Rockwell hardness tests. The minor load in a Rockwell hardness test is always 10 kg. The major load varies and may be 60, 100, or 150 kg. The penetrators most commonly used are a 1/16" diam steel ball and a spheroconical diamond. The latter has a spherical apex of 0.2 mm radius and an included angle of 120°. The spheroconical diamond penetrator is generally called a Rockwell scale penetrator. Steel ball penetrators 1/8, 1/4, and 1/2" in diameter are used occasionally for plastics and soft metals. The penetrators and the major loads for a number of the Rockwell hardness scales are given in Table 7-6. The suggested use for the scales also is indicated in the table. Various loads and penetrators are listed; a decision as to the best combination to use should be based on testing requirements, parameters, and experience.

A Rockwell hardness testing system is used to perform the Rockwell hardness test. The load can be applied to the specimen at the bottom or the top, depending on the machine design. Both loading systems operate in conformance to ASTM E 18, but they offer different advantages for different applications. Bottom-loading machines allow more operator control during test procedures than do top-loading machines, but top-loading machines are more frequently used in an automated system than are bottom-loading machines. A check on the system's accuracy is carried out with the use of standard Rockwell test blocks obtained from the manufacturer of the testing machine. Test blocks in the range of the hardness being measured should be used in accordance with ASTM E 18 specifications.

The thickness of the material tested should be at least such that no imprint shows on the undersurface after the test is completed. The required thickness for uniformly hardened steel specimens can be determined from Fig. 7-1. The surface of the test material must be clean and smooth. All but very large diameter rounds should have a small flat finished on them and the hardness taken on this area. If this is not done, the hardness reading will be offset and a correction should be made. The correction for various diameters and for the different scales is listed in ASTM E 18. For control tests on rounds of the same size, the correction is not necessary, and the indicated hardness may be used for reference.

Rockwell superficial hardness test. The Rockwell superficial hardness scales are given in Table 7-7. As indicated there, the Rockwell superficial hardness number read from the measuring device of the testing machine is suffixed with the scale designation. For example, 81 HR 30N represents a Rockwell superficial hardness number of 81 on a Rockwell 30N scale. The procedure for performing a Rockwell superficial hardness test is the same as that followed for a regular Rockwell hardness test.

Vickers Hardness Test

The Vickers hardness test consists of applying a known load for a specified time to the surface of a material through a square-base-pyramid diamond having 136° between opposite faces. The Vickers hardness number, also known as the diamond pyramid hardness, is the applied load in kilograms divided by the area of the permanent indentation in square millimeters. The test is very similar to the Brinell test except for the indentor used.

The two diagonals of the resulting square permanent indentation are measured with a micrometer microscope and then averaged. The average diagonal is usually converted to a Vickers hardness number by the use of tables supplied with the testing machine. The Vickers hardness number may be calculated by the use of the equation:

$$DPH = \frac{1.854L}{D^2} \qquad (2)$$

where:

DPH = Vickers hardness number or diamond pyramid hardness
L = the applied load, kg
D = length of average diagonal, mm

The Vickers hardness number is, for all practical purposes, independent of the load used in making the test. The depth of the indentation is approximately one-seventh of the measured diagonal.

HARDNESS TESTS

TABLE 7-6
Rockwell Hardness Scales

Scale Symbol	Penetrator	Major Load, kg	Color of Dial Figures	Suggested Use
A	Brale	60	Black	For extremely hard material that might chip the diamond under higher load. For thin hard sheets where light loading is desirable.
B	1/16″ ball	100	Red	For medium-hard metals such as low and medium-carbon steels in the annealed condition. Useful range B 0 to 100.
C	Brale	150	Black	Most commonly used for metals harder than B 100. Useful range C 20 upward. Should not be used below C 20.
D	Brale	100	Black	Used when a lighter load than the 150 kg load of the C scale is desirable.
E	1/8″ ball	100	Red	For testing very soft metals.
F	1/16″ ball	60	Red	Covers same range in hardness as E scale but uses 1/16″ ball.
G	1/16″ ball	150	Red	For metals a little too hard for the B scale.
L	1/4″ ball	60	Red	Used when a lighter load than the 100 kg load of M scale is desirable for plastics and wood.
M	1/4″ ball	100	Red	For testing plastics and wood.
R	1/2″ ball	60	Red	Used for soft plastics.

TABLE 7-7
Rockwell Superficial Hardness Scales*

Major Load, kg	Prefix Symbol	
	N-Scale Brale Penetrator	T-Scale 1/16″ Ball Penetrator
15	15-N	15-T
30	30-N	30-T
45	45-N	45-T

* In addition to the N and T scales, special scales are designated W, X, and Y. As with the N and T scales, the Rockwell superficial hardness number should be prefixed with the major load used while the letter indicates the penetrator used; that is, W scale, 1/8″ diam steel ball; X scale, 1/4″ diam steel ball; and Y scale, 1/2″ diam steel ball.

A load ranging from 50 g to 120 kg is usually available on a Vickers hardness tester. For general hardness measurements, a load of 30 kg is suggested; for soft, thin, or surface-hardened metals, a load of 10 kg or less is suggested. Practically the full range of hardnesses encountered in metals may be covered by the proper selection of the load.

The thickness of the specimen should be at least such that no imprint appears on its undersurface after the test. The required thickness for uniformly hardened steel specimens can be determined from Fig. 7-1. The surface of the specimen should be flat and of sufficient finish so that any remaining scratches do not cause difficulty in locating the corners of the indentation when the diagonals are measured. Polishing the surface with No. 3/0 emery paper is usually satisfactory.

Scleroscope Hardness Tests

Scleroscope hardness is based on the height of rebound of a steel "hammer" falling on a specimen from a fixed height.

The hammer is approximately 1/4″ (6 mm) in diameter and 3/4″ (19 mm) long with a rounded striking tip on its normally downward end. The hammer falls freely in a glass tube that has a scale graduated into 140 divisions. The height of the first rebound, which is the scleroscope hardness, is determined by visual observation or a dial indicating device. Repeat tests should not be made in the same location.

A scleroscope is a portable hardness tester. For this reason, it finds wide application in hardness measurements on large sections of metals, particularly when it is not convenient to take the piece into a testing laboratory. The approximate minimum thickness of metal that can be tested with a scleroscope is 0.01″ (0.3 mm). Another advantage of a scleroscope hardness test is that the hammer does not leave an impression in the surface of the material being tested. Highly polished and close tolerance surfaces can be checked without damage or introduction of notches that might contribute to a premature fatigue failure in service.

Small or thin specimens must be clamped firmly to the anvil of the scleroscope or to a large piece of metal to avoid inertia effects. As the size of specimen increases, clamping becomes unnecessary, and the test piece is merely placed on a very large piece of metal. Extremely large pieces are tested without any auxiliary backing metal. The surface to be tested must be located in a horizontal plane.

Other Tests

Other methods employing machines, but secondary in importance for the manufacturing engineer, are the Knoop hardness, microcharacter hardness, and durometer tests.

Knoop hardness test. The Knoop hardness test may be classed as a microhardness test because the impressions are usually extremely small. It is particularly suited for making hardness surveys and measuring the hardness of very small parts, thin sections, thin cases, and individual grains or particles. The test consists of applying a known load for a specified time to the surface of the material through a diamond having unequal longitudinal and transverse included angles. The Knoop hardness number is the applied load divided by the unrecovered projected area. Often a tester will be used for both Knoop and light-load Vickers testing merely by switching penetrators.

Microcharacter hardness test. The microcharacter hardness test is particularly suited for microscopic hardness surveys and hardness measurements on extremely thin metal parts and constituents of alloys. The standard load ranges from only 3 g up to 9 g for extremely hard materials. The combination of lenses used with the microscope should permit reading to 1 μm (0.00004") with reasonable accuracy.

Durometer test. The durometer measures hardness in a number of scales in terms of the amount of indentation of a spring-loaded indentor beyond the hardness tester's presser foot or stop ring while the latter is firmly pressed against a specimen. The hardness number is read from a scale graduated from 0 to 100. Different types of hardness numbers are obtained by the use of different indentors and loads. The durometer is a portable hardness tester used extensively for hardness measurements on rubber, plastics, and, in a number of instances, soft metals.

Hot Hardness Tests

The hardness of metals at elevated temperatures can be determined by a number of different methods. In some cases, conventional room temperature hardness testers have been modified so that the specimen and the penetrator are both at the test temperature. Zmeskal described the use of the Rockwell hardness tester using a Brale penetrator in which both specimen and penetrator are heated and mentioned that a series H Brale is particularly suited for tests at elevated temperatures.[1] The hardness numbers are reported in the conventional Rockwell scales (Fig. 7-1) for a Brale penetrator.

The Brinell hardness tester also has been modified to perform hardness tests with a heated specimen and penetrator.[2] A sintered carbide ball penetrator is used for this type of hardness test at elevated temperatures. In each case the specimen and the penetrator were surrounded by an electrically heated furnace.

Another method of measuring hot hardness makes use of the mutual indentation produced on two cylinders of the same metal under a known load.[3] In this method, two cylinders of the same metal are placed in an electrically heated furnace and mounted one above the other with their longitudinal axes parallel. A known load is applied to the cylinders at test temperature through hardened-steel backing blocks using a modified Brinell hardness testing machine. The area of indentation is determined after the cylinders are removed from the furnace and cooled. The cylinder hardness number is the applied load in kilograms divided by the area of the indentation in square millimeters. The cylinder hardness number multiplied by 1.52 gives a converted Brinell hardness number.

Traverse Tests

Often a series of hardness tests at regularly specified intervals along an axis of hardness variation is called a traverse test. This test may be performed to determine the rate of quenching or the case-hardening depth of a specimen. Generally, a case-hardness traverse test is performed of a sectional sample and a measurement made for the depth of hardness to R_C50, which is the effective case depth, or the total depth of the case.

Hardness Conversions

Hardness tests are made under arbitrary conditions; hence there is no basic correlation for converting hardness numbers from one scale to another. The best that can be done is to calibrate one scale in terms of another, but the hardness conversion relation for one type of material or metal does not usually apply to another type of material or metal. Hardness conversion tables for steel, cartridge brass, nickel, and high-nickel alloys are given in ASTM E 140. A hardness conversion table for steel having uniform chemical composition and heat treatment is given in Volume III, *Materials, Finishing and Coating*, of this Handbook series.

TENSION TEST

The tension test, as the name implies, is used to determine the properties of a material under tension. The properties determined are applicable when an applied load is in the direction perpendicular to the cross-sectional area carrying the load.

In this test, a suitable specimen is loaded to failure in tension between self-aligning grips of a tensile testing machine. Extensometers are generally attached to the specimen until the loading reaches a point that is just above the value of the yield stress. The extensometers are then removed from the test specimen. Observations of the applied load and the corresponding elongations, which are converted to stress and strain, respectively, provide the data for plotting a stress-strain diagram. Values for the various tensile properties are determined from the diagram by prescribed methods and from direct load and dimensional measurements. The properties most commonly determined are yield strength, tensile or ultimate strength, elongation, and reduction in area. The proportional limit, elastic limit, and modulus of elasticity are determined less frequently, because the other properties usually suffice, and they require less care and accuracy in their determination.

Elevated and low-temperature tensile properties are determined by essentially the same methods as those used at normal temperatures. The chief differences are the provisions for maintaining specimen temperature and the necessary modifications for measuring strains. An electrically heated furnace, mounted on the testing machine in a manner to enclose the specimen, provides elevated temperatures. An insulated container of coolant, mounted on the testing machine so that the specimen is in the coolant, provides low temperatures. Dry ice (solid carbon dioxide), acetone mixtures, and low-temperature boiling liquids, such as liquid nitrogen, are used as coolants. In all cases, means are taken to ensure uniform specimen temperature.

Strain measurements usually are made with an autographic-type extensometer having extension arms that transmit the strain to the autographic extensometer, which is outside the temperature-controlled chamber. These modifications permit the measurement of the tensile properties, elongation, reduction in area, ultimate strength, and yield strength without too much difficulty.

Tensile Strength

The *tensile or ultimate strength* is the maximum load applied during a test divided by the original cross-sectional area of the specimen. It is generally reported in pounds per square inch (psi) or megapascals (MPa).

TENSION TESTS

Percent Elongation

The *percent elongation* is the percentage increase in the original gage length as determined from the assembled fractured specimen. The two pieces of a fractured round tensile specimen are generally clamped together between mounted centers for measuring the final distance between the points marking the gage length. Sometimes specimens are held together as closely as possible by manual means. It is customary to report the gage length actually used.

Reduction in Area

The *reduction in area* is the percentage decrease in cross-sectional area at the fracture area of the specimen. The final dimension is measured with the fractured specimen clamped or held together in the same manner described for elongation measurements.

Yield Strength

Yield strength is the stress at which a material exhibits a specified limiting permanent set. There are three methods for determining this value: (1) Under a constant rate of loading, some materials exhibit a sudden arrest in the load being applied. The load at the time of arrest is converted to stress and is termed the yield strength by the "drop-of-the-beam" method. (2) Another method is to use a pair of dividers set at the initial gage length and watch for a visible elongation between two gage marks. The load at the instant any elongation is observed is converted to stress and is termed the yield strength by the "dividers" method. The yield strength determined by either of these two methods is sometimes called the "yield point." (3) The third method of determining the yield strength is known as the "offset" method. The yield strength is determined from the stress-strain diagram (curves starting at zero stress, zero strain) by drawing a line parallel to the straight or elastic portion of the curve starting at zero stress and the prescribed strain, usually 0.2%. The yield strength for the prescribed offset is taken as the stress corresponding to the intersection of this straight line and the stress-strain curve. Figure 7-2 illustrates this method of obtaining the yield strength. In the figure, the stress corresponding to R is the yield strength for the offset Om.

All three methods are applicable to materials having sharp-kneed stress-strain curves in the range of yield. The last, or offset, method is particularly adapted to materials having smooth and gradually curving stress-strain curves. In reporting yield strength data, the method used and the offset should be stated. The yield strength is generally reported in psi or MPa.

Elastic Limit

The *elastic limit* is the greatest stress that a material is capable of withstanding without a permanent deformation remaining upon complete release of the stress. It is seldom determined for metals as a routine test because the values do not differ widely from values found for the proportional limit.

Proportional Limit

The *proportional limit* is the greatest stress that a material is capable of withstanding without deviating from the law of proportionality of stress to strain. The "tangent proportional limit" is determined by visual examination as the stress at the tangent point of the straight-line section of the stress-strain diagram to the remainder of the curve. The proportional limit is also determined by the offset method used for determining yield strength. The offset used for the proportional limit is generally 0.01%. The proportional limit is sometimes called the "proportional elastic limit" and is reported in psi or MPa.

Modulus of Elasticity

The *modulus of elasticity* is the ratio, within the elastic limit of a material, of stress to corresponding strain. It is the slope (stress divided by strain) of the initial straight portion of the stress-strain curve and is designated by the line OA in Fig. 7-3. The tangent modulus of elasticity is the slope of a straight line drawn tangent at B to the stress-strain curve at a stated stress. Up to the proportional limit of a material, the tangent modulus and the modulus of elasticity are equal; therefore, the former is used only above the elastic limit. The secant modulus of elasticity is the slope of the line OC drawn from the origin of the stress-strain diagram (zero stress, zero strain) to some stated stress on the curve above the elastic limit.

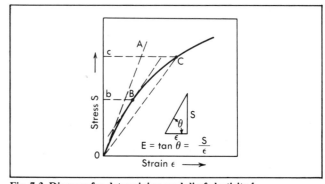

Fig. 7-3 **Diagram for determining moduli of elasticity.**[5]

COMPRESSION TESTS

Compressive strength is generally defined as the maximum stress in compression that a metal will withstand before rupture. However, when a metal fails in this manner, it is usually accompanied by shearing stress in a diagonal direction. In the case of a material that does not fail by fracture, the compressive stress is usually regarded as an arbitrary value that produces sufficient permanent distortion to make the material unusable. The values of yield point and elastic limit in compression are usually about 110-115% of their values in tension.

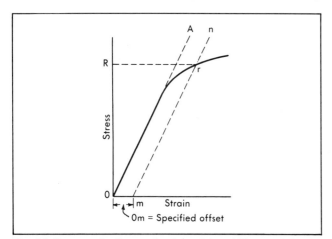

Fig. 7-2 **Stress-strain diagram for determining yield strength by the offset method.**[4]

TRANSVERSE BENDING TESTS

The compression test is used to determine the properties of materials under compression. The properties determined are applicable when the load is in a direction normal to the cross-sectional area carrying the load and tends to compress the material. In the test, a suitable specimen is loaded in compression between the platens of a universal testing machine. In most cases, the loading is generally not carried to complete failure of the specimen, owing to the ductility of most metals. Strain gages are attached to the specimen until the loading reaches a point just above the load that corresponds to the yield stress. The strain gages are then removed, and the loading is discontinued unless it is desired to load the specimen to failure. Observations of the applied load and the corresponding deformations converted to stress and strain, respectively, provide the necessary data to plot a stress-strain diagram. Values for the different compressive properties are then determined by prescribed methods from the stress-strain diagram. The properties most commonly determined are yield strength, proportional limit, and modulus of elasticity; compressive strength and elastic limit are seldom determined.

Although it would appear that compressive properties are no more difficult to determine than tensile properties, this is far from the fact. Parallelism of the testing machine platens and of specimen ends is a factor of great importance and is frequently overlooked or underestimated. If special care is not exercised to ensure a high degree of parallelism of the platens and specimen ends, uniform axial loading will not be obtained. The latter is necessary for reliable results. Self-aligning hemispherical or ball-mounted platens are desirable for such work.

TRANSVERSE BENDING TESTS

A beam supported at both ends and carrying a transverse load at the center is referred to as being in bending. Similarly, a column carrying an eccentric load parallel to its longitudinal axis is in bending. In each case, one part of the cross section of the material is under tension, and the other part is under compression. Tests involving bending usually are made on materials under the type of loading for a beam. Bending tests are classified into two groups, the distinguishing feature being the type of information obtained from each. Tests to identify the strength properties of the material in bending are generally called flexural tests. Tests to determine the relative response of the material to bending are called bend tests.

Flexural Tests

Flexural tests, to determine the strength properties of metals in bending, are most widely used for the more brittle metals such as cast iron. For cast iron, these tests are more commonly referred to as transverse tests. The general setup for a transverse test is quite similar to that of a beam supported at both ends and loaded transversely at the center with means provided for measuring the deflection at the beam's midpoint. The beam or specimen is loaded to failure in the transverse direction. After the applied load exceeds that corresponding to the proportional limit of the metal under test, the deflection measuring device is removed. Observations of the applied loads and the corresponding deflections provide data for a load-deflection diagram. A coordinate plot of simultaneous load and deflection observations gives a curve similar to a stress-strain curve for a tension or compression test. Load is generally plotted as the ordinate. Values for the various properties are determined by prescribed methods from the diagram and direct load observations.

The *maximum or outer fiber stress* for a specimen of rectangular cross section may be calculated from the equation:

$$S = \frac{3PL}{2bd^2} \qquad (3)$$

where:

S = maximum fiber stress, psi (MPa)
P = load, lb (N)
L = span length, in. (mm)
b = specimen width, in. (mm)
d = specimen depth, in. (mm)

For a round specimen, the maximum or outer fiber stress can be calculated from the equation:

$$S = \frac{8PL}{\pi D^3} \qquad (4)$$

where D is the specimen diameter in inches (millimeters). These equations assume proportionality between stress and strain; therefore, correct calculations of the stress can be made only up to the proportional limit.

The *flexural strength* is the maximum observed load converted to stress by Eq. (3) or Eq. (4). This value is also referred to as the transverse modulus of rupture or the transverse strength. The flexural strength is the value that has come into common use for determining the strength of cemented-carbide tool materials and similar low-ductility products.

The *proportional limit in bending* is the stress corresponding to the load at the point of tangency of the straight-line portion of the load-deflection curve to the remainder of the curve. The load from the curve is converted to maximum fiber stress by Eq. (3) or Eq. (4).

The *modulus of elasticity* in bending for a specimen of rectangular cross section is calculated from the equation:

$$E = \frac{KL^3}{4bd^3} \qquad (5)$$

where:

E = modulus of elasticity, psi (MPa)
K = slope of the straight-line portion of the load-deflection curve, lb/in. (N/mm)

For a round specimen, the modulus can be calculated using the equation:

$$E = \frac{4KL^3}{3\pi D^4} \qquad (6)$$

where D is the specimen diameter in inches (millimeters).

Bend Tests

Bend tests yield no property useful in design calculations. They are instead a control test to determine the relative abilities of materials to withstand bending. A measure of ductility is usually associated with them. In brief, the tests generally consist of bending a specimen about a radius or upon itself and making observations to determine if it was sufficiently ductile in bending to withstand the conditions imposed by the test.

A standard bend test method for the ductility of metals is described in ASTM E 290. Free and guided bend tests for evaluating the soundness of welded specimens are covered by ASTM E 190, ASME Section 9, AWS 1.1, and API 1104. Toughness evaluations are made by bending notched specimens

DIRECT SHEAR TESTS

slowly in universal testing machines and measuring load, deflection, and energy absorption. A particular material may exhibit brittle or ductile behavior depending on the specimen dimensions and testing temperature. Slow-bend tests are commonly made on specimens prepared with weld beads on the tension face.

Two other bend tests are worthy of mention. One consists of determining the number of degrees a specimen will bend around a given radius before failure occurs by cracking. The other consists of determining by trial the minimum radius over which the specimen may be bent by 180° without cracking. The bending operation in these tests may be carried out by any available means as long as the specimen is made to conform to the radius about which it is being bent.

DIRECT SHEAR TESTS

Shear stresses result from the application of a load in the plane or line of the cross section bearing the load. Direct shear is present when one layer of a material is made to move on the adjacent layer in a linear direction. Transverse loading of a rivet or bolt in a plate produces shearing stresses in it. When the load is carried by one plane or cross section of the rivet, as in a single-lap riveted joint, it is called single shear. When the load is carried by two cross sections as in a double-lap riveted joint, it is called double shear. If the opposing forces producing shear do not act in the same plane or line, bending stresses are set up. Therefore, in a direct shear test it is important to have the opposing forces at the cross section, which transmits the load, act in the same plane or line, at least with reasonable precision.

A jig with a specimen in place is mounted between the platens of a universal testing machine and loaded to failure of the specimen in shear. The tensile loading features of the testing machine, including self-aligning drawbars, are used with the jig shown in Fig. 7-4. The compressive loading features are used with the jigs shown in Fig. 7-5. With the latter jigs, it is important that the specimens are firmly clamped and that the load is distributed uniformly over the specimen in the direction normal to the cross section under shear. The maximum load at failure is observed.

The shear strength is the maximum observed load divided by the cross-sectional area that is sheared. For example, the shear strength of a cylindrical specimen sheared in the jig shown in Fig. 7-4 is the maximum observed load up to failure divided by twice the cross-sectional area of the cylinder.

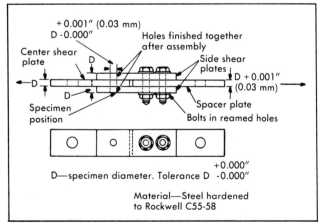

Fig. 7-4 Shear jig for tensile loading in self-aligning fixtures.

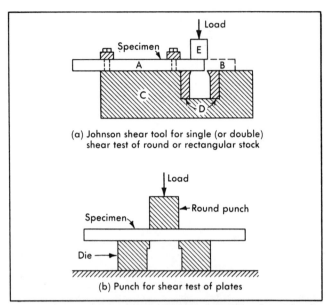

(a) Johnson shear tool for single (or double) shear test of round or rectangular stock

(b) Punch for shear test of plates

Fig. 7-5 Shear jigs for compressive loading. In the field of plasticity, the term "shear strength" refers to the stress acting on the plane under consideration. (*Davis, Troxell, and Wiscocil*)

TORSION TESTS

Torsion shear is produced by rotation or by torque. In this type of shear, one layer of a material is made to rotate on an adjacent layer. This type of shear is present in rotating shafts, such as crankshafts or driveshafts, when power is being transmitted.

In a torsion test, equal and opposing moments are applied at opposite ends of a suitable specimen in planes perpendicular to the specimen's longitudinal axis. When placing the specimen in the testing machine, it is important that the longitudinal axis of the specimen coincides with the common axis about which the heads of the testing machine rotate. The applied torque is generally increased until the specimen fractures. A device known as a troptometer is usually attached to the specimen to measure the amount of twist during the application of torque. Observations of the applied torque and corresponding twist of rotation, which are converted to stress in the outer fiber and strain in the outer fiber, respectively, provide the data for plotting a stress-strain diagram. The properties commonly determined are shear strength or modulus of rupture, yield strength, proportional limit, modulus of elasticity or modulus of rigidity, and angle of twist.

The *stress in the outer fiber* of a solid round test section is calculated by the equation:

$$S = \frac{16M}{\pi D^3} \qquad (7)$$

where:

S = shearing stress in outer fiber, psi (Pa)
M = applied torque, in.-lb (N·m)
D = diameter of test section, in. (m)

For tubular specimens,

$$S = \frac{16DM}{\pi(D^4 - d^4)} \qquad (8)$$

where D is the outside diameter of the tubing, and d is the inside diameter. Stresses calculated by these equations are true only up to the proportional limit.

The *strain in the outer fiber* for either round or tubular specimens is calculated by the equation:

$$s = \frac{DZ}{2gr} \qquad (9)$$

where:

   s = unit shear strain in outer fiber, in./in. (mm/mm)
   D = outside diameter of specimen, in. (mm)
   Z = troptometer reading, in. (mm)
   g = gage length, in. (mm)
   r = radius of troptometer, measured from axis of specimen, in. (mm)

The *shear strength* is the maximum observed torque applied up to fracture of the specimen and converted to stress in the outer fiber by Eq. (7) for stress. This value is often referred to as the modulus of rupture.

The observed applied torque and corresponding troptometer readings are converted by Eqs. (7), (8), and (9) to stress and strain in the outer fiber. The values so obtained are then plotted as a stress-strain diagram.

The *yield strength* is determined from the stress-strain diagram by the offset method described previously in the discussion of tension tests. It is a good practice to report the offset used in obtaining yield strength values.

The *proportional limit* is the stress at the point of tangency of the straight-line portion of the stress-strain curve to the remainder of the curve.

The *modulus of elasticity* is the slope (stress-strain) of the straight-line portion of the stress-strain curve. This value is quite often referred to as modulus of rigidity. It is generally expressed in psi or GPa.

The permanent angle of twist is determined on the assembled fractured specimen in degrees per inch (millimeter) of length. For this value, the angular twist, in degrees, over the gage length of the line originally drawn parallel to the longitudinal axis of the specimen is measured, and the observed value is divided by the gage length in inches (millimeters).

The hot-twist test is a modified torsion test conducted at a number of temperatures within the possible range of useful forming temperatures to evaluate the hot-working characteristics of metals. The number of twists before the specimen fractures and the torque required to maintain the twisting at some definite rate are determined. The temperature at which the number of twists is greatest, if a maximum exists, is the one that should not be exceeded during hot working. The hot-twist test is particularly suitable for evaluating hot workability because it can reproduce the strain rates of specific operations and because the predominant stresses are in shear, as they are in most deformation operations.

NOTCHED-BAR IMPACT TESTS

Notched-bar impact tests are commonly called impact tests, implying that the test results are applicable to problems involving shock loading or impact. Unfortunately, this is not the case because practically all specimens used in impact tests are notched. The type of specimen and the method of breaking it were originally designed and used to show a variation in notch sensitivity for steels that exhibit a ductile fracture in the tensile test. Impact tests are, in reality, notched-bar tests. There are true impact tests, such as ballistics tests, but these are performed infrequently.

Impact tests, such as the Charpy and Izod tests with notched specimens, measure the amount of energy absorbed in fracturing the specimen. The true worth of these values is to determine the relative notch toughness of two or more materials under the particular test conditions. Values determined under one set of test conditions are not convertible to values for other test conditions.

In the case of steels, the results of impact tests at various temperatures frequently show a relatively sudden drop in impact value accompanied by a change from a ductile to a brittle fracture. For many steels, this change occurs in the region not far above or below room temperature. Therefore, it is important to know the temperature sensitivity for many applications that involve atmospheric and subatmospheric temperatures. Standard tests show only the sensitivity that is developed by the particular bar and notch used in the test, and larger parts and structures with more severe notch conditions will show low-temperature brittleness at higher temperatures. In general, ductile nonferrous metals and alloys and austenitic steels retain notch toughness down to very low temperatures.

Most metals are sensitive to the velocity with which they are struck; this sensitivity is not usually taken into account in tests made with conventional impact machines, whose striking velocities nearly all fall in the range 11-18 fps (3.4-5.5 m/s). The effect of velocity can be measured, but seems to be significant in causing brittle failures only when the notch and temperature conditions are critical.

Charpy Impact Test

In the Charpy impact test, a notched specimen is supported as a simple beam and is fractured by a single blow. The single blow is delivered to the specimen midway between the supporting anvils and on the side opposite the notch. The specimens in general use have either a keyhole or a V-notch of standard dimensions. A V-notch is preferred by many testers because it has been more widely correlated with service and because it gives a wider range of values. However, tougher materials give false values when the bar does not break fully because they absorb energy when the bar is forced through the anvil.

In the test, the specimen is placed on the anvils horizontally. The line of impact is on the face of the specimen opposite the notch and in the plane bisecting it. The specimen is broken with a single blow delivered by a pendulum from a raised position, and the energy absorbed is read directly from a scale (Fig. 7-6).

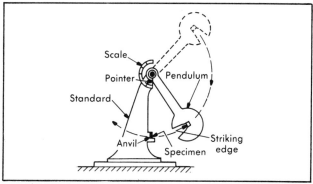

Fig. 7-6 Charpy impact testing machine.

NOTCHED-BAR IMPACT TESTS

Charpy impact values are generally reported in foot-pounds (newton-meters). When reporting the impact value, it is necessary to include the type of notch used and the test temperature.

The Charpy impact machine is the most convenient means of making impact tests at low and elevated temperatures. The specimen is brought to the desired temperature, quickly transferred to the testing machine, and broken in the usual manner in a matter of five seconds. For low temperatures, the specimen is immersed in a coolant, such as a mixture of solid CO_2 and acetone, that is at the desired test temperature. For elevated temperatures, electrically heated muffle furnaces controlled at the desired test temperatures are satisfactory. In each case, sufficient time must be allowed for the specimen to come to the desired temperature before it is tested; 20 minutes at the temperature is usually sufficient for soaking.

Modern methods of evaluating toughness by Charpy tests are based on the transition zone or temperature range in which the energy values and the percentage of shear fracture change markedly, as shown in Fig. 7-7. For a particular type of test, lower transition temperatures indicate better fracture toughness. When a series of notched specimens of ferritic steel are tested at various temperatures, the change in fracture characteristics is sometimes abrupt. The rate of change in energy values, volume of the deformation zone, or percentage of shear texture on the fracture surface depends on the loading rate and specimen geometry characterizing the test, and on metallurgical characteristics of the test piece. Therefore, the significance to be attached to the particular definition of ductile-brittle transition temperature should be based on a known correlation between that criterion and service performance.

Although transition temperature curves provide more data about the fracture characteristics of a steel, many specifications require only tests at specific temperatures. This appears to be a satisfactory expedient as long as comparisons are restricted to steels of the same general type. In such instances, the number of specimens and the minimum or average test values, or both, are usually mentioned. The sensitivity of notched-bar tests and the significance of apparent differences in test performance are directly related to the number of specimens tested. Statistical methods of analyzing notched-bar data are generally used because they permit attaching confidence limits to transition temperatures.

A wide variety of criteria have been used by various investigators to define transition temperatures in Charpy impact tests. Some are based on the average temperature giving a particular energy value, and others are based on the amount of deformation occurring at a particular location on the specimen. A common practice is to measure the fraction of shear texture on the fractured surfaces of Charpy bars. When such information is available, particular levels of percent shear area can be used to define a Charpy transition temperature. The definitions for transition temperatures used by different investigators in evaluating results of Charpy V-notch tests include the following:

1. Energy-level transitions
   a. Average temperature for a particular energy level, such as the 15 ft-lb (20 N·m) transition temperature (V_{15} TT). Other specific energy levels, such as 10, 20, and 30 ft-lb (13.5, 27, and 40 N·m), are also used.
   b. Average temperature for a particular percentage of maximum energy required for rupture at the highest temperature investigated; for example, 50% of maximum energy (50% METT).
2. Deformation-level transitions
   a. Temperature where the average lateral expansion on the compression side of the specimen is a fixed amount, such as 0.015″ (0.38 mm) (LE 15-mils TT).
   b. Temperature where the lateral contraction is a fixed amount, such as 3%.
3. Shear-texture transitions
   The temperature corresponding to a particular percentage of shear or fibrous texture on the fractured surface, such as the 80% shear texture transition temperature (80% SATT).

Izod Impact Test

In the Izod impact test, a notched specimen of square or round cross section is used, having the V-notch with a fixed radius at the bottom. It is supported as a cantilever with the root of the notch in line with the edge of the vise in which the specimen is clamped. It is broken with a single blow, which is delivered to the notched face of the specimen at a specified distance above the vise.

The standard pendulum type of Izod impact testing machine is used. The general features of this type of machine are the same as those for the Charpy impact testing machine shown in Fig. 7-6. The chief differences are: (1) a vise is used to hold the specimen in the vertical position, and (2) the hammer of the pendulum is shaped to clear the vise and strike the specimen a specified distance above it.

A template is used for aligning the root of the notch with the top of the vise. Izod impact values are generally reported in foot-pounds or newton-meters. It is necessary to report the type of specimen and the test temperature used.

Drop-Weight Test

The drop-weight test has been used extensively to investigate factors affecting the initiation of brittle fractures in structural steels. The test determines the nil ductility transition (NDT) temperature under standardized conditions. The techniques were devised for measuring the fracture initiation of ferritic

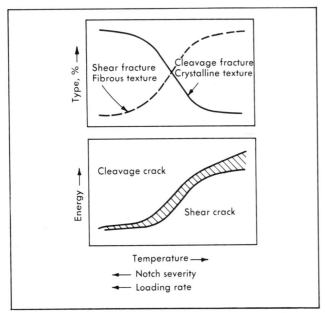

Fig. 7-7 Concepts involved in evaluating fracture toughness of steel.

plates in thicknesses of 5/8″ (16 mm) or more. The test has seldom been used for thin plates and is not recommended for steel sections less than 1/2″ (12 mm) thick. Procedures for conducting the test are described in ASTM E 208.

The drop-weight test employs a small weld bead on the specimen surface as a crack starter. The weld deposit develops a small cleavage-crack flaw in a weld notch during testing. The method of testing is illustrated in Fig. 7-8. Nil ductility transition temperatures determined for a particular steel with any of the standard specimens are expected to agree within ±10° F (5.6° C).

The weld bead of a particular type of hard-facing alloy (Murex Hardex N) is centrally located on the surface of the specimen. The bead, approximately 2 1/2″ (64 mm) long and 1/2″ (12 mm) wide, is notched [0.1″ (2.5 mm) maximum width] a distance of 0.075 ± 0.005″ (1.91 ± 0.13 mm) from the original surface of the specimen before testing. By a falling weight, the specimen is broken as a simple beam with the weld notch on the tension side by a falling weight. A cleavage crack forms in the weld bead when the deflection is about 3° and then propagates into the rest of the specimen; the stop is used to prevent appreciable plastic deformation.

The NDT temperature is determined by testing specimens over an appropriate range of temperatures. The NDT temperature is defined as the highest temperature at which a specimen fractures to one or both edges of the tensile surface, and similar specimens do not break when tested at a temperature higher by 10° F (5.6° C). If a visible crack in the weld bead does not propagate to either edge of the tensile surface of the specimens, it is classified as showing no break. A test is considered invalid if the weld-deposit notch does not develop a visible crack in the parent metal, or if the specimen is not deflected enough to contact the anvil stop. Although the preferred procedure is to test several specimens in a range of temperatures, some specifications require testing only two specimens at a particular temperature. The test specimens must exhibit a no-break behavior to provide some assurance that the NDT temperature is below that used for testing.

Geometrical effects resulting from relatively small variations in specimen thickness and stop distances influence the measured NDT temperatures. For that reason, some NDT values reported prior to 1965 are not comparable with those determined later. Current practice is to use specimens with standardized dimensions, sometimes necessitating machining.

Drop-Weight Tear Test

Section thickness is known to affect the resistance to fracture propagation in the cleavage mode and to influence the microstructure of as-rolled ferritic steels. Thus there are both advantages and disadvantages in choosing tests that employ either full-thickness or standard-dimension specimens. Standardized specimens simplify judgments on the effects of metallurgical variables, but the geometrical effects of size on toughness must be considered when judging the suitability of materials for specific applications.

In addition, many structures are made from steel sections too thin to permit preparation of standard specimens. For these reasons, laboratory tests on full-thickness test specimens are often desirable.

The drop-weight tear test employs full-thickness plate specimens with the dimensions shown in Fig. 7-9 and has been used successfully in recent years by several laboratories in studies on pipeline steels and some other materials. A sharp-pointed tool-steel chisel is pressed into the specimen with a hydraulic ram to produce a notch 0.200″ (5.08 mm) deep with a root radius of 0.0003-0.001″ (0.008-0.03 mm). The small radius combined with cold work ensures that a cleavage fracture will be initiated during testing. The specimens are stood on edge and broken rapidly, as simple beams such as large Charpy bars are broken. The energy can be provided by a dropping weight or by a large pendulum. The latter method permits measurement of breaking energies. The usual practice is to judge the performance of a specimen on the basis of the average percentage of shear texture on the fractured surface. The regions within one specimen thickness of the notch and of the opposite edge of the specimen are neglected in estimating the shear area. Those regions are omitted from consideration because of initiation and cold-working effects. The transition temperature zone, which is unusually narrow in this test, is determined from a plot of shear area against temperature. The procedure for conducting drop-weight tests is described in ASTM E 436.

Tensile Impact Tests

Tensile impact tests generally are made with a Charpy-type impact machine, modified to satisfy the conditions of the test. A round specimen with a central reduced section approximately 0.25″ (6 mm) in diameter is most commonly used. One end of the specimen is attached to the pendulum of the testing machine. A "dog," attached to the other end of the specimen in a horizontal position, contacts a pair of anvils at the time of impact. Care must be taken to adjust the dog to the specimen so that the impact occurs when the pendulum is in the position of "zero" energy and that all parts of the dog contact the anvils at the same time. The specimen is broken with a single blow delivered in the direction of its longitudinal axis, and the energy

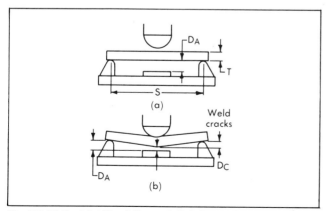

Fig. 7-8 Method for Naval Research Lab drop-weight test: (a) setup and (b) in presence of small crack during test, yield-point loading is terminated by contact with a stop.[6]

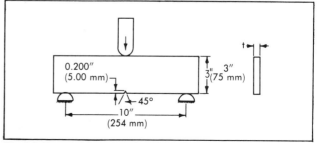

Fig. 7-9 Drop-weight tear test specimen.[7]

FATIGUE TESTS

absorbed is reported in foot-pounds or newton-meters. Sometimes gage marks are placed on the reduced section, and the elongation of the assembled fractured specimen is determined. It is good practice to give all the details of the test when reporting tensile impact data.

FRACTURE TOUGHNESS TESTS

The linear elastic fracture mechanics approach to judging fracture toughness has been studied intensively for many years. It is appropriate for quantifying fracture and crack growth resistance of materials. Fracture mechanics leads to parametric values that can be used in design if careful consideration is given to differences between testing and service conditions.

Toughness tests based on fracture mechanics characterize strong materials on the basis of their tolerance for cracks and resistance to brittle fracture. It is based on the assumption and experience that cracks or flaws exist in materials and grow when the intensity of the stress field near the edge of the crack reaches a critical value. It is also assumed that the stress intensity is proportional to the square root of the crack parameter. The crack parameter is usually taken as half the crack length because the calculations are usually concerned with disc-like flaws growing to a free surface, such as through-thickness failures in plates. The fracture toughness value for quasi-plane strain, termed K_{IC}, is reported in units of kpsi $\sqrt{inch}$; higher values indicate better toughness.

The fracture toughness value is also known as the critical stress intensity factor for the opening mode of cracking in the stress state of quasi-plane-strain. The critical stress intensity factor characterizes the resistance of a material to fracture in the presence of a sharp crack under severe tensile constraint when the plastic region at the tip of the crack is small compared with the size of the crack and the specimen. The K_{IC} value is believed to represent a lower limiting value of fracture toughness; it varies with testing temperature and speed.

Conducting fracture toughness studies requires special equipment and careful measurements and techniques. The methods and precautions to use in determining K_{IC} values on specimens 0.25″ (6.4 mm) thick or thicker are described in ASTM Standard E 399. The specimens are notched and fatigue-cracked prior to testing. One type of specimen is single-edge-notched and loaded as a beam in three-point bending. The compact tension specimen is single-edge-notched and pin-loaded in tension. A variety of specimens are permitted by the standard because the appropriate dimensions increase with the square of the ratio of toughness to the yield strength of a material. If the stock available for testing is not of appropriate size, valid K_{IC} values cannot be determined by the standard method. Thinner materials can be tested by other types of specimens, if the materials are sufficiently brittle.

The stress intensity factor not only describes the instability of a crack in a material under load, but it also appears to describe the stable extension of a crack under cyclic loadings at stress intensity levels below those characteristic of conditions critical for fracture. Because fracture toughness evaluations are becoming increasingly important and experimental techniques and methods of data interpretation are changing rapidly, the reader is urged to consult current publications.

FATIGUE TESTS

Fatigue tests are concerned with the progressive failure of materials under repeated loading. Fatigue properties of a material are usually determined from a series of tests on a number of similar specimens. In one kind of test, a specimen is subjected to cycles of fully reversed (tension to equal compression) nominal stress and the number of cycles withstood to rupture is recorded. Then other specimens are subjected to cycles of other different stress ranges. A plot known as an *S-N* curve, is then made of stress, *S*, against number of cycles, *N*, to failure (Fig. 7-10).

Usually *S* is plotted as the ordinate on either a Cartesian or a logarithmic scale and *N* as the abscissa on a logarithmic scale. Some materials (particularly steels) show curves that flatten out at large values of *N*. The stress level at which this occurs, and below which fatigue lifetime would presumably be infinite, is called a fatigue limit. Some materials may not exhibit well-defined fatigue limits; hence, the stress level at an arbitrary long lifetime (say, more than 10^7 cycles) is used as a design fatigue limit for such a material. It should be kept in mind that, in the presence of other deteriorating factors (such as corrosion and elevated temperature), a material may not have a fatigue limit.

Fatigue tests may, of course, be run under various kinds of loading such as rotating bending, plane bending, axial loading, and repeated torsion. In many of these (axial loading, for example), another parameter emerges. Tests may be run at a fixed value of mean load and an *S-N* curve obtained by plotting the maximum stress (or the stress amplitude) against *N*; other curves may be obtained at other values of mean stress. Thus a material may be characterized, not by a single fatigue value, but by many values.

Experience has shown that notches, sharp changes in section, and other stress intensifiers seriously effect the lifetime of a metal part under repeated stressing. These effects, which have resulted in many failures, are not necessarily predictable from fatigue test data on unnotched specimens. Hence, evaluation of a material for a specific use often includes tests of notched as well as unnotched specimens and some kind of specification of "fatigue notch sensitivity."

Moreover, since a great deal of discrepancy is found in results of fatigue tests, it is important that allowance for this be made in design. An *S-N* curve, such as that illustrated in Fig. 7-10, determined by testing a few (six to eight) specimens may not adequately characterize a material.

Nevertheless, the information obtained from fatigue tests is useful in evaluating metals for applications involving a large number of stress repetitions during the expected service life of the metal. Rapidly moving machines and parts in which stress fluctuations occur many times during their service life are most subject to failure by fatigue. The failure starts, after a number of stress repetitions, with a small crack. It progresses during

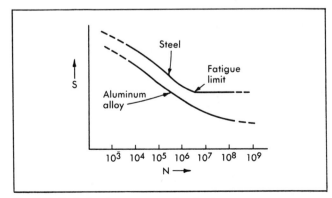

Fig. 7-10 Typical endurance curves for aluminum.

additional repetitions of stress until the remaining cross section is not sufficient to carry the load, and failure occurs rather suddenly and without significant elongation. The fracture appears brittle and generally gives an indication of the location at which the failure started.

The effect of a notch on the endurance properties of a particular part or piece of metal depends on the stress concentration imposed by the notch. To evaluate the inherent endurance properties of metals, it is necessary, therefore, to use specimens as free of notches as possible.

In the rotating-beam flexural-loading fatigue test, the specimen is a part of a rotating beam supported at both ends and loaded symmetrically at two points (the ends of the specimen) between the supports. The bending moment over the length of the specimen is constant. One side of the specimen is under tension, and the other side is under compression. As the specimen rotates, the outer fibers of the specimen are repeatedly stressed through a cycle of completely reversed stress.

With the specimen mounted properly in the testing machine and the machine started, the load to produce an outer fiber stress equal to approximately 75% of the tensile strength of the material under test is immediately but gently applied. The number of cycles to failure and the outer fiber stress are recorded. If the fracture occurs outside the cross section of minimum diameter, the diameter at the fractured section should be measured and used for calculating the stress in the outer fiber. This procedure is repeated for outer fiber stresses decreasing in increments of 5-10% until approximately 10,000,000 cycles are required to fracture a specimen of steel. This practice is satisfactory for steel because it is observed that a stress that fails to fracture steel in 10,000,000 cycles can be withstood indefinitely. Most other materials do not have such a well-defined endurance limit, and they must generally be tested for a considerably larger number of cycles, the actual number depending on the interest in the material and the service conditions.

A plot is made, as previously described, of stress against the number of cycles to produce failure using log-log or semilog paper. Stress is generally plotted as the ordinate and the number of cycles as the abscissa. Figure 7-10 shows typical S-N curves for steel and aluminum.

The *fatigue or endurance strength* is taken from the S-N curve by reading the stress corresponding to a stated number of cycles. The *endurance limit*, when such is present, is the limiting stress below which the material will withstand an indefinitely large number of stress cycles without failure. In general, steels have true endurance limits while most other materials do not. The above-mentioned fatigue strength is generally used for materials other than steel, and the number of stress cycles for which it holds must be stated.

The *endurance ratio* is the endurance limit divided by the tensile strength of the material. If the material does not have an endurance limit, the ratio is the fatigue strength divided by the tensile strength. In the latter case, the number of cycles corresponding to the fatigue strength used should be stated.

The *notch sensitivity ratio in fatigue* is the endurance limit for polished unnotched specimens divided by the endurance limit for notched specimens. If the material has no true endurance limit, fatigue strengths are used in this ratio, and the number of cycles corresponding to the stresses used should be stated. Partially or totally reversed flexure tests are used for sheet materials which cannot be tested by means of the rotating-beam method.

CREEP TESTS

Creep is the continuing change in dimension with time of a material under stress. Materials exhibit creep, particularly at elevated temperatures, even at stresses below their short-time proportional limits.

Creep tests are usually made under a constant tensile load. A selected constant tensile load is applied to a specimen at a selected elevated temperature, and the resulting elongation is observed at sufficient intervals of time to define the relationship between elongation and time. When the observed data are plotted, elongation is usually made the ordinate and time the abscissa. Because the load is not applied until the specimen has reached temperature, there is an initial elastic elongation. If the load is above the proportional limit, the initial elongation will also include some plastic deformation. Some plots of creep-time-elongation data include the initial elongation that occurs on application of the load and some do not.

Figure 7-11 shows two typical creep curves in which the initial elastic elongations are included. The lower curve in the figure illustrates the type of creep curve obtained when the combination of stress and temperature used in the test does not cause failure of the specimen during the test. The first stage of creep is evidenced by a high but decreasing rate of elongation. The second stage is characterized by an approximately constant rate of elongation. Usually a total test time in excess of 1000 hr is required to establish the approximately constant rate of elongation. The minimum creep rate is observed during the second stage. The upper curve of Fig. 7-11 illustrates the type of creep curve obtained when the combination of stress and temperature used in the test produces failure of the specimen. This curve shows the third, or final, stage of creep, which is characterized by an increased rate of elongation. The time and elongation at which second-stage creep changes to the third stage of increasing creep rate is called the transition point.

Creep-Rupture Tests

Creep-rupture tests are similar to creep tests. They differ only in being intentionally continued until the test specimen ruptures. In addition to the conventional creep data, rupture time, elongation, and reduction in area are also obtained from creep-rupture tests.

Stress-Rupture Tests

Stress-rupture tests are made by loading a test specimen to failure as in a creep test, but without the use of an extensometer. No strain data are obtained, only time to rupture, elongation, and reduction in area values. Stress-rupture tests are often made using circumferential V-notches in the specimen to determine notch sensitivity under the testing conditions.

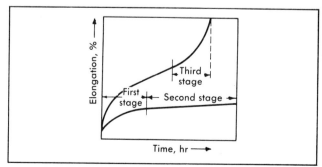

Fig. 7-11 Typical creep curves.

STRESS ANALYSIS

RAPID METAL IDENTIFICATION TESTS

Various tests, when applicable, are used as a rapid means of identifying a metal without resorting to methods of quantitative chemical analysis. They are often used to sort unidentified or mixed materials. Such a test does not determine the chemical composition, but determines whether or not a selected property of an unknown metal is the same as that of a known metal. Judgment must be exercised in identification testing because of the possibility that more than one material may have a particular value of a given property.

Rapid identification tests depend on different approaches: chemical behavior, visual observation of the color and luster of the material or the appearance of its chips or sparks, or instrumented measurements. The most useful tests are those that can be conducted in place without sampling in plant environments. Rapid identification tests should be reliable, portable, and inexpensive.

Magnetic Tests

Magnetic tests generally involve the comparison of a magnetic property of a known metal with that of an unknown metal. A permanent magnet is used to differentiate between magnetic and nonmagnetic metals. When both metals are magnetic, the comparison is made with special techniques and equipment.

Spark Tests

Spark testing consists of holding a piece of metal against a rotating grinding wheel and observing the characteristics of the sparks produced. Various grades of steel give sparks with typical patterns that serve as means of identification. Even small added quantities of some elements, such as aluminum and titanium, can be detected by experienced practitioners. With care and practice, spark testing can be a reliable and inexpensive method of rapid metal identification. Over the years, the industrial use of spark testing has declined, but the art is still being practiced.

Hardness-After-Quenching Test

The carbon content of a steel can be estimated by determining the R_C hardness of a small sample that has been water-quenched from its hardening temperature. Curves are available that show the relationship between maximum hardness and carbon content and may be used for converting the observed R_C hardness to approximate carbon content.

Thermoelectric Test

When the junction formed by two dissimilar metals in contact with each other is heated, an electromotive force is set up. If the two metals forming the junction are identical, the electromotive force is zero. A galvanometer connected across the ends of the two metals opposite the junction may be used to indicate the presence or absence of an electromotive force and hence the dissimilarity or identity, respectively, of the two metals forming the junction. Routine checking with this test method is generally done with special equipment.

Chemical Spot Tests

There are a number of chemical spot tests, each of which will indicate the presence or absence of an element in a metal. A chemical test generally consists of applying a few drops of one or more chemical reagents to a spot on the unknown metal and watching for some characteristic result, such as a particular color.

STRESS ANALYSIS

Experimental stress analysis is the term applied to the determination of the location, direction, and approximate intensity of stress in a part; no mechanical properties are determined. In practice, strains are measured and the corresponding stresses are obtained by multiplying the known modulus of elasticity of the material under test by the observed strains.

Practical stress analysis methods include photoelasticity, brittle coatings, resin-based coatings, ceramic-based coatings, and strain gages. These methods are generally applicable to parts of any size, shape, or material.

Photoelasticity

In the photoelastic method of stress analysis, a model of the part is made from a transparent plastic material and is loaded as in service. Polarized light is transmitted through the model and the stresses are calculated from the fringe pattern that is observed.

Brittle Coatings

Brittle coatings are applied to the entire surface of the structure. The coatings crack in response to strains within the material produced by external loads. When the strain has reached a certain value, fractures occur in the coating at right angles to the principal tension strains, so peak and localized stresses can be evaluated. These are the points of greatest tension stress; therefore, a direct correlation exists between the crack patterns in the coating and possible fatigue failure. Used quantitatively, the brittle coatings also measure the strain level within ±10% accuracy. Another use of brittle coatings is to survey stresses over an entire structure. This overall stress picture shows how loads are carried by the parts and indicates how to obtain a proper and efficient distribution of material.

Resin-Based Coatings

Resin-based coatings are applicable to most stress problems and are supplied graded for threshold strain, temperature, and humidity. The strain range is from 0.0005 to 0.0030 in./in. (mm/mm); temperature range is from 10 to 120° F (-12 to 50° C); and the humidity range is from 0 to 100%. Before the coating is applied, the part surfaces must be degreased and sprayed with an aluminum undercoat. The part under test and the calibration bars are sprayed with a coating selected to meet the test conditions expected. Coatings are normally dried for about 16 hours, but drying can be done in 6 hours at slightly elevated temperatures.

Ceramic-Based Coatings

Ceramic-based coatings extend the temperature range of rapid metal tests and are graded for threshold strain and for the coefficient of thermal expansion of the metal involved. Normal range of strain is about 0.0003-0.0015 in./in. (mm/mm) and coatings are usable on metals with the coefficient of expansion ranging from 5×10^{-6} to about 9×10^{-6} in./in./° F (2.8×10^{-6} to 5×10^{-6} mm/mm/° C). Surfaces are prepared by sandblasting, and coatings are sprayed, air-dried, and fired at approximately 1000° F (540° C) for a certain length of time, depending on the size of the part. Ceramic-based coatings are calibrated similarly to resin-based coatings, but the calibration bars must be made of the same material as the test structure.

Bonded Strain Gages

The bonded, resistance strain gage is the most widely used strain measurement tool for experimental stress analysis. It consists of a grid of very fine wire or a thin metallic foil bonded to an insulating backing called a carrier matrix. The electrical resistance of this grid material varies linearly with strain. Strain gages are small and light, will operate over a wide temperature range, and can respond to both static and dynamic strains.

There are many types, shapes, and sizes of commercially made strain gages having gage lengths from 0.008 to 4.0″ (0.20 to 102 mm). Strain gage selection is based on the operating temperature, state of strain, and the stability requirements for the gage installation. It is recommended that the tester refer to the strain gage manufacturer for assistance in selecting the proper strain gages, adhesives, and protective coatings for a specific application. Adhesives are available for bonding these gages to surfaces for use at temperatures ranging from -320 to 1100° F (-196 to 595° C).

In use, the carrier matrix is attached with an adhesive to the part being tested. When the part is loaded, the strain on the surface is transmitted to the grid material by the adhesive and carrier matrix. The strain in the part is found by measuring the change in electrical resistance of the grid material.

Strain gages are generally attached to the part being tested in arrangements of two or four gages, following one of the three installation patterns shown in Fig. 7-12. The two strain gages, A and B, are installed to measure the moment, M, in the beam. Gages C and D (with C^1 and D^1 on the opposite side of the beam) will measure the force, L. Gages E and F (with E^1 and F^1 on the opposite side) will measure torque, T. Each set of gages is connected in a Wheatstone-bridge circuit.

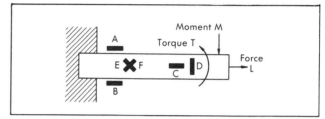

Fig. 7-12 Beam gaged to measure force, moment, and torque components.

BALANCING

Balancing is an operation whereby the mass distribution of a rotating body or rotor is altered to minimize first-order vibrations at the support bearings. Portions of this subchapter are abstracted with permission from the publications *Balancing Made Simple*,[8] *Fundamentals of Balancing*,[9] and *Balance Engineering Manual #31*.[10]

The word rotor is used throughout this discussion to describe any rotating body requiring balancing. Balancing is normally performed by placing the rotor into a machine specifically designed for that purpose. However, a rotor can also be balanced in its own bearings and supporting structure.

An unbalanced rotor will cause vibrations and stress in the rotor itself and in its supporting structure. Rotors are balanced to achieve one or more of the following purposes:

- Increase bearing life.
- Minimize vibration.
- Minimize audible and signal noises.
- Minimize operating stresses.
- Minimize operator annoyance and fatigue.
- Minimize power losses.
- Increase product quality.
- Satisfy customers.

BALANCING NOMENCLATURE

The following definitions are abstracted with permission from "American National Standard Balancing Terminology," ANSI S2.7-1982, published by the Acoustical Society of America.[11]

amount of unbalance The quantitative measure of unbalance in a rotor, without reference to its angular location. It is obtained by taking the product of the unbalance mass and the distance of its center of gravity from the shaft axis.

angle of unbalance The polar angle at which an unbalance mass is located with reference to the given coordinate system.

axis of rotation The line about which a body rotates.

balancing A procedure for checking the mass distribution of a rotor and then adjusting it to ensure that the vibration of the journals and/or forces on the bearings at a frequency corresponding to service speed are within specified limits.

center of gravity The point in a body through which passes the resultant of the weights of its component particles for all orientations of the body with respect to a uniform gravitational field.

centrifugal balancing machine A balancing machine that provides for the support and rotation of a rotor and for the measurement of vibratory forces or motions due to unbalance.

correction mass A mass attached to a rotor in a given correction plane for the purpose of reducing the unbalance to the desired level.

correction plane A plane perpendicular to the shaft axis of a rotor in which correction for unbalance is made.

counterweight A weight added to a body so as to reduce a calculated unbalance at a desired place.

couple unbalance The condition of unbalance in which the central principal axis intersects the shaft axis at the center of gravity.

critical speed A characteristic speed such that the predominant response of the system or rotor occurs at a resonance.

dynamic unbalance That condition of unbalance in which the central principal axis is neither parallel to nor intersects with the shaft axis.

field balancing The process of balancing a rotor in its own bearings and supporting structure rather than in a balancing machine.

gravitational balancing machine A balancing machine that provides for the support of a rigid rotor under nonrotating conditions and provides information on the amount and angle of the static unbalance.

hard bearing balancing machine A balancing machine having a balancing speed range below the natural frequency of the suspension and rotor system.

UNBALANCE

index balancing A procedure whereby a component is repetitively balanced and then indexed by 180° on an arbor or rotor shaft. After each index, one half of the residual unbalance is corrected in the component. The other half of the unbalance is corrected in the arbor or rotor shaft until both are in balance.

initial unbalance Unbalance of any kind that exists in a rotor before balancing.

mass centering The process of determining the principal mass axis of a rotor and then machining journals, centers, or other reference surfaces to bring the axis of rotation defined by these surfaces into close proximity with the mass axis.

multiplane balancing A balancing procedure that requires unbalance correction in more than two planes. Used for flexible rotors.

principal inertia axis The term used to designate the one central principal axis (of the three such axes) most nearly coincident with the shaft axis of the rotor. It is sometimes referred to as the balance axis or the mass axis.

rotor A body, capable of rotation, generally with journals that are supported by bearings.

single-plane balancing A procedure used for adjusting the mass distribution of a rigid rotor to ensure that the residual static unbalance is within specified limits.

soft bearing balancing machine A balancing machine having a balancing speed above the natural frequency of the suspension and rotor system.

specific unbalance The amount of static unbalance divided by the mass of the rotor.

static unbalance The condition of unbalance in which the central principal axis is displaced only parallel to the shaft axis.

two-plane balancing A procedure used for adjusting the mass distribution of a rigid rotor to ensure that the residual dynamic unbalance is within specified limits.

unbalance reduction ratio The ratio of reduction in the unbalance by a single correction to the initial unbalance.

unbalance tolerance The maximum amount of unbalance permissible in a rigid rotor with respect to a radial plane.

UNBALANCE

A rotating element having an uneven mass distribution or unbalance will vibrate because of the excess centrifugal forces exerted during rotation by the heavier side of the rotor. Unbalance causes centrifugal force, which in turn causes vibration. Common units used for expressing unbalance are oz.in., g.in., and g.mm. Each of these units expresses a mass multiplied by its distance from the shaft axis.

Centrifugal force increases proportionately to the square of the increase in speed. For example, if the rotor's speed is doubled, the centrifugal force quadruples. The magnitude of this force for 1 oz·in. of unbalance can be found from Fig. 7-13. The centrifugal force developed by a known unbalance in a rotor rotating at a known speed can be determined by:

$$F = KUN^2 \qquad (10)$$

where:

F = centrifugal force, lb
K = constant (1.7759 x 10^{-6})
U = amount of unbalance, oz·in.
N = speed of rotation, rpm

To obtain the centrifugal force in newtons, multiply the force in pounds by 4.448.

Types of Unbalance

The two most frequently encountered types of unbalance are static unbalance and dynamic unbalance. Two other types of unbalance found in rotating parts are couple unbalance and quasi-static unbalance.

Static unbalance. Static unbalance, at one time referred to as force unbalance, exists when the principal axis of inertia is displaced parallel to the shaft axis. Figure 7-14 shows an eccentric rotor on knife-edges. If the knife-edges are level, the rotor will turn until the heavy or unbalanced spot reaches the lowest position.

Static unbalance can be corrected by a single mass correction placed opposite the center of gravity in a plane perpendicular to the shaft axis and intersecting the center of gravity. If the unbalance is large enough, it can be detected with conventional gravity-type balancing machines. This type of unbalance is found primarily in narrow, disc-shaped parts such as flywheels and turbine wheels.

Dynamic unbalance. Dynamic unbalance is the most common type of unbalance and exists when the central principal axis of inertia is neither parallel to nor coincident with

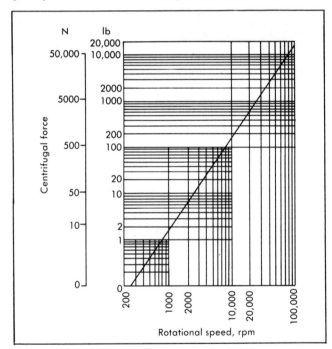

Fig. 7-13 Centrifugal force produced by 1 oz.in. (720 g.mm) unbalance at various speeds.

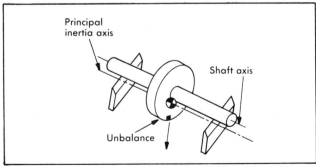

Fig. 7-14 Concentric disc with static unbalance. (*Schenck Trebel Corp.*)

the shaft axis (Fig. 7-15). It can only be corrected by mass correction in at least two planes perpendicular to the shaft axis.

Couple unbalance. Couple unbalance, at one time called moment unbalance, occurs when two equal unbalance masses are positioned at opposite ends of a rotor and spaced 180° from each other (Fig. 7-16). Unlike dynamic unbalance, the principal axis of inertia intersects the shaft axis at the center of gravity in couple unbalance.

Common units for expressing couple unbalance are g·in.^{2} (gram·inch·inch) or oz·in.^{2}; the second inch dimension refers to the distance between the two planes of unbalance. This type of unbalance cannot be corrected by a single mass in a single correction plane. At least two masses are required, each mass in a different transverse plane and 180° opposite to each other.

Quasi-static unbalance. Quasi-static unbalance is a special case of dynamic unbalance. It exists when the central principal axis of inertia intersects the shaft axis at a point other than the center of gravity (Fig. 7-17). Quasi-static unbalance represents the specific combination of static and couple unbalance when the angular position of one couple component coincides with the angular position of the static unbalance.

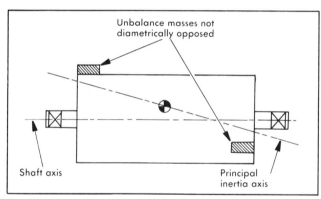

Fig. 7-15 Dynamic unbalance. (*Schenck Trebel Corp.*)

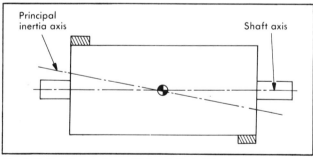

Fig. 7-16 Couple unbalance. (*Schenck Trebel Corp.*)

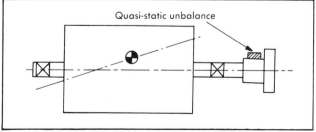

Fig. 7-17 Unbalance in coupling causes quasi-static unbalance in rotor assembly. (*Schenck Trebel Corp.*)

Causes of Unbalance

Unbalance in rotating parts and assemblies can be caused by one or more of many factors, some of which are not readily apparent. If proper consideration is given to balance requirements in the design, processing, and manufacturing stages, the unbalance in the finished part can be kept to a minimum and the cost of balancing operations reduced. Some of the causes of unbalance in manufactured parts are:

- Tolerances in fabrication, including casting, machining, forging, and assembly.
- Variation within the material such as voids, porosity, inclusions, grain size, density, and finishes.
- Nonsymmetrical part design.
- Nonsymmetry in use, including distortion, dimensional changes, and shifting of parts due to rotational stress, aerodynamic forces, and temperature changes.

Manufacturing processes are the major source of unbalance. Unmachined portions of castings or forgings that cannot be made symmetrical with respect to the shaft rotational axis introduce substantial unbalance. Manufacturing tolerances and processes that permit any eccentricity or lack of squareness with respect to the shaft axis are also sources of unbalance. The tolerances necessary for economical assembly of a rotor permit radial displacement of the parts in the assembly and thereby introduce unbalance.

Limitations imposed by design often introduce unbalance effects that cannot be adequately corrected by design refinements. For example, electrical designs impose a requirement that one coil be at a greater radius than the other coils in a certain type of universal motor armature. It is impractical to design a compensating unbalance into the armature.

Fabricated parts such as fans often distort nonsymmetrically under service conditions. Designs and economic considerations prevent the adaptation of methods that might eliminate this distortion and thereby reduce the resulting unbalance.

Ideally, rotating parts should always be designed for inherent balance, whether a balancing operation is to be performed or not. When low service speeds are involved and the effects of a reasonable amount of unbalance can be tolerated, this practice may eliminate the need for balancing. In parts that require unbalanced masses for functional reasons, these masses can often be counterbalanced by designing for symmetry about the shaft axis.

Effects of Unbalance

Unbalance in just one rotating component of an assembly may cause the entire assembly to vibrate. This induced vibration in turn may cause excessive wear in bearings, bushings, shafts, spindles, and gears, resulting in a reduction of their service life. Vibrations set up highly undesirable alternating stresses in structural supports and frames that may eventually lead to their complete failure. Performance is decreased because the unbalance force is absorbed by the supporting structure. Vibrations may also be transmitted to adjacent machinery and seriously impair their accuracy or proper functioning.

BALANCING PROCESS

The balancing process usually consists of three general operations. In the first operation, the unbalance is measured to determine the amount and angle of unbalance in the correction plane or planes. The part is then corrected using a variety of methods. The correction can be made on the balancing machine or on a separate machine. Finally a second measurement is made of the residual unbalance in the part.

Prior to processing a part for the balancing operation, the level to which a part is to be balanced and the maximum unbalance to be corrected for should be considered. These considerations help define the type of equipment required for the part to be balanced. Because many balancing processes follow the normal distribution, there is a probability that some of the parts are already within the balance tolerance and do not require any balancing. Refer to Chapter 2, "Statistical Methods For Quality And Productivity Design And Improvement," of this volume for additional information on the normal distribution and probability.

To evaluate the balancing process, the specific unbalance and the ratio of maximum initial unbalance to specified tolerance should be calculated. The specific unbalance, e, is the balance tolerance divided by the part weight. It represents the approximate displacement of the center of gravity from the centerline of rotation and is in units of length (μin. or μm).

When the specific unbalance is greater than 1000 μin. (25 μm), normal machining tolerances for tooling and conventional balancing machines are usually adequate. When the specific unbalance is less than 1000 μin. (25 μm), special care must be taken in the tooling design and the selection of the balancing machine. Extreme care must be taken in tool design, and high-quality balancing machines must be used if the specific unbalance is below 10 μin. (0.25 μm).

The maximum initial unbalance to tolerance ratio, R, represents the worst part to be balanced. It is calculated by dividing the initial unbalance by the tolerance unbalance. For many balancing processes, a value of R equal to or less than 10 indicates a simple, easy-to-control balancing operation. When R is between 10 and 15, precision tooling, exact balancing machine measurements, and precise control of the correction process are required. High precision in all areas is required when R is greater than 15.

Another way of looking at the maximum initial unbalance to tolerance ratio, or the worst part to be balanced, is by determining the number of runs necessary to reduce the initial unbalance to the desired residual unbalance. The balancing machine to be used has an unbalance reduction ratio (URR) that can be determined by testing. This ratio indicates the accuracy of the balance machine reduction capability and can be used to determine the approximate machine run time and labor time required to balance the worst part. This ratio is usually given in percentage.

If a machine has a 90% unbalance reduction ratio, it will reduce the initial unbalance by 90%. If the remaining unbalance (remaining 10% of the initial unbalance) exceeds the residual unbalance requirement, subsequent run(s) and correction(s) will be required. The subsequent runs will each have a reduction capability of 90%. The relationship of R versus URR is shown in Table 7-8.

Measurement of Unbalance

Several methods are used to obtain a reference signal by which the phase angle of the amount-of-unbalance indication signal may be correlated with the rotor. On end-drive machines (where the rotor is driven by a universal-joint driver or similarly flexible coupling shaft) a phase reference generator, directly coupled to the balancing machine drive spindle, is used. On belt-drive machines (where the rotor is driven by a belt over the

TABLE 7-8
Ratio of Maximum Initial Unbalance to Tolerance (R)
Compared to the Unbalance Reduction Ratio (URR)

R	URR	R	URR
2	50.00	18	94.44
3	66.67	20	95.00
4	75.00	22	95.45
5	80.00	24	95.83
6	83.33	26	96.15
7	85.71	28	96.43
8	87.50	30	96.67
9	88.89	32	96.88
10	90.00	34	97.06
12	91.67	36	97.22
14	92.86	38	97.37
16	93.75	40	97.50

rotor periphery) or on self-driven machines, a stroboscopic lamp flashing once per rotor revolution or a scanning head (photoelectric cell with light source) is employed to obtain the phase reference.

The scanning head requires a single reference mark on the rotor to obtain the angular position of unbalance, but the stroboscopic light necessitates attachment of an angle reference disc to the rotor or placing an adhesive numbered band around it. Under the once-per-revolution flash of the strobe light the rotor appears to stand still so that an angle reading can be taken opposite a stationary mark.

With the scanning head, an additional angle indicating circuit and instrument must be employed. The output from the phase reference sensor (scanning head) and the pickups at the rotor-bearing supports are processed and result in an indication representing the amount of unbalance and its angular position.

Figure 7-18, view a, illustrates an indicating system that uses switching between correction planes. This is generally employed on balancing machines with stroboscopic angle indication and belt drive. In Fig. 7-18, view b, an indicating system is shown with two-channel instrumentation. Combined indication of amount of unbalance and its angular position is provided simultaneously for both correction planes on two vectormeters having illuminated targets projected on the back of translucent overlay scales. Displacement of a target from the central zero point provides a direct visual representation of the displacement of the principal inertia axis from the shaft axis. Concentric circles on the overlay scale indicate the amount of unbalance, and radial lines indicate its angular position. Some manufacturers use digital meters or CRT screens to display the amount and angle of unbalance.

Instead of using a phase reference generator, a stroboscopic lamp, or a scanning head, one manufacturer uses a dual-channel angle marking device to mark the correction angle on the part while it is rotating. The device consists of an ink supply, an air pressure system, twin marking guns, and an electronics package that is interfaced with the balancer controls (Fig. 7-19). In operation, an automatic signal triggers the air guns for firing at the proper angle.

Correcting Unbalance

Unbalanced conditions in a rotor can be corrected by material removal, material addition, or by moving the centerline of rotation (mass centering). The selected correction

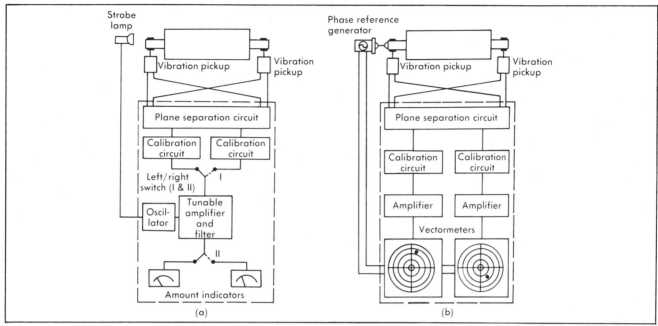

Fig. 7-18 Block diagrams of typical balancing machine instrumentation: (a) the amount of unbalance is indicated on analog meters and the angle location is indicated by a strobe light and (b) combined amount and angle of unbalance is indicated on vectormeters. (*Schenck Trebel Corp.*)

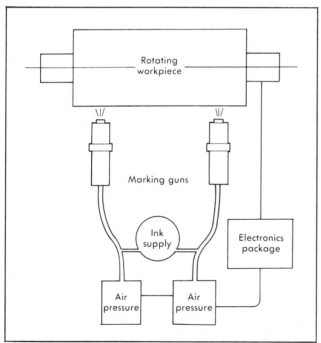

Fig. 7-19 Diagram of two-channel marking device to mark angle location. (*Gilman Engineering and Manufacturing Co.*)

method should ensure that there is sufficient capacity to allow correction of the maximum unbalance that may occur. In many cases, the design of the part or the material itself will determine the method of correction, but in other cases there will be a choice of methods. The residual unbalance and the cost of the correction method should also be considered when selecting a particular method.

The ideal method permits reduction of the maximum initial unbalance to less than the specified balance tolerance in a single correction step. If the correction method selected is not capable of reducing the initial unbalance to less than balance tolerance in a single step, a preliminary correction should be made. A second step, using the same or another method, is then made to reduce the remaining unbalance to its permissible value.

Material removal. If the design of the part permits, unbalance correction by removal of material is generally preferred over addition of material. To facilitate balancing, an extra volume of material should be incorporated in the part's design. Conventional machining methods are generally used to remove any material, with drilling, milling, and grinding being the most common. When balancing jet engine components, it is preferable to use hand-operated tools because of the cost of sophisticated rotors.

Drilling. Drilling is the most widely used method of unbalance correction. In manual operations, the cost of drilling equipment is relatively low and maintenance is simple. Drilling is a fast operation, and the amount of material removed during drilling can be accurately controlled. Depending on the application, a hole with varying depths or a varying number of standardized holes may be preferable.

Milling. Milling permits accurate removal of mass when the rotor surfaces, from which the depth of cut is measured, are machined surfaces and when means are provided for accurate measurement of cut with respect to those surfaces. Milling is sometimes used for balancing parts with thin walls and when material can only be removed to a shallow depth. It is often preferable on aluminum parts where the alternative is drilling a large number of small holes.

Grinding. Grinding is generally used as a trial-and-error method of unbalance correction. It is difficult to evaluate the actual mass of the material removed during grinding. This method is used only when the rotor design does not permit a more economical type of correction.

BALANCING PROCESS

Other material removal methods. In addition to drilling, milling, and grinding, other metal removal methods are used for correcting unbalance. Lasers have been used for correcting unbalance conditions in small parts while they are rotating, but removal rates are low. Punching is often used on sheet metal parts instead of drilling, which would require special drills. Shearing is also performed for limited applications.

Material addition. As stated previously, unbalance correction by removal of material is preferable if at all possible, but in many cases this method cannot be used. Some of the disadvantages of correcting unbalance conditions by material addition are: (1) the cost of providing the necessary material; (2) the material must be supplied in increments, which limits the accuracy; (3) the added material may come off unless securely fastened; and (4) the cost of purchasing some material addition equipment is greater than material removal equipment. However, in the case of balancing jet engine rotors, balancing by material addition is preferred because individual components are commonly replaced during maintenance.

Welding on weights. Unbalance correction by welding on weights is the most widely used material addition method. It is fast and can be easily adapted to perform the balance operation on the balancing machine. When welding is performed on the balancing machine, the welding current should be properly isolated to prevent damage to support and spindle bearings and other machine components.

Automotive driveshafts are almost exclusively balanced by welding on weights. Other applications are sheet metal parts used in automatic transmissions, torque converter assemblies, large-sized fans and blowers, and brake drums.

Adding solder. Small parts that have low initial unbalance can be successfully corrected by adding solder. If the lengths of solder are marked off in suitable increments, accurate amounts can be added. The limiting factor in using solder is that the production rate depends to a large extent on operator dexterity.

Adding weights to predrilled holes. Some parts and assemblies do not readily lend themselves to the more common methods of unbalance correction. An application of such an assembly is an automobile engine. If a series of predrilled holes is provided in the periphery of the flywheel and harmonic balancer, drive pins can be inserted into these holes for correction purposes. A variation of this would be to place screws in tapped holes. Rivets could also be used if the part is too thin for either pins or screws. The amount of correction possible by this method is rather limited, and the angular accuracy is limited by the number of holes provided.

Other methods. In addition to the previously described methods, other less common methods have been used for specialized applications. Spring clips can be snapped on to the vanes of blower assemblies to correct dynamic unbalance. Jet engine components can be balanced by inserting washers under bolt heads or by adding different-sized washers, bolts, nuts, or slugs at designated positions.

Mass centering. Mass centering is a process whereby a rough forging or casting is rotated in a specially designed balancing machine prior to any machining. Provision is made in the mass centering machine to move the workpiece in relation to its axis of rotation until balance is obtained. The workpiece is then centered in this position and all subsequent machining is performed from these centers.

Because material removal is uneven at different parts of the shaft, the machining operation will introduce some new unbalance. A final balancing operation is therefore still required. In general, the more machining or material that must be removed after the initial centering, the less effective the mass centering operation becomes. Although the main application of mass centering has been in the fabrication of crankshafts, the process can be applied to a variety of parts.

Selecting correction points. The three factors that need to be taken into consideration when selecting the point or plane of correction are:

- The proposed correction must not interfere with the function of the part.
- The correction must not weaken or distort the part.
- The correction should not distract from the appearance of the part.

For static unbalance corrections, the correction plane should generally be as close as possible to the part's center of gravity to minimize the introduction of couple unbalance. If there are large unmachined areas on the part, it is better to make the correction at or near the center of gravity of the unmachined areas. It is usually better to correct one half of the unbalance on each side of a narrow part than to make the correction only on one side of the part.

Correction planes for dynamic unbalance should be as close as possible to the ends of the part. By doing so, the amounts of correction required will be reduced. The effect of unbalance correction at one end on the unbalance at the other end is also reduced by separating the correction planes as far as the part allows.

BALANCE TOLERANCES AND SPECIFICATIONS

Theoretically, zero unbalance is an obtainable goal for a rotor being balanced; however, this is not obtainable in practice because of balancing cost considerations and various rotor limitations. Therefore, a tolerance must be set to allow a certain amount of residual unbalance, just as tolerances are set for other machine shop operations. When establishing this tolerance, it is necessary to determine how much residual unbalance can be permitted while still holding detrimental effects to an insignificant or acceptable level.

The tolerances given in ISO 1940 usually produce satisfactory results. In this standard, various types of rigid rotors are grouped according to quality grades as shown in Table 7-9.

To determine a reasonable balance tolerance, the quality grade required for the rotor is determined from Table 7-9. The permissible residual unbalance, U_{per}, per unit of rotor weight can then be determined by locating the applicable quality grade at the rotor's maximum service speed in Fig. 7-20.

Every quality grade listed in Fig. 7-20 incorporates four bands except at the upper and lower extremes of the graph. The bands can be considered (from top to bottom in each grade) substandard, fair, good, and precision. For critical applications, it is possible to select the tolerance in the next better grade.

It is important to understand that these tolerances apply only to rigid rotors. Recommendations for flexible rotor tolerances are given in ISO 5343.

The product designer must not only select the balance tolerances, but must indicate the planes in which the measurement for and the correction of unbalance are required. However, for a new product it is difficult to determine the maximum initial unbalance. A rough estimate of the unbalance can be obtained from prototype parts, even though they are generally not manufactured in the same manner as the final product. A

TABLE 7-9
Balance Quality Grades for Various Groups of Representative Rigid Rotors
in Accordance with ISO 1940 and ANSI S2.19

Balance Quality Grade G*	Rotor Types—General Examples	Balance Quality Grade G*	Rotor Types—General Examples
G 4000	Crankshaft drives** of rigidly mounted slow marine diesel engines with uneven number of cylinders.†	G 6.3	Parts of process plant machines. Marine main turbine gears (merchant service). Centrifuge drums. Fans. Assembled aircraft gas turbine rotors. Flywheels. Pump impellers. Machine tool and general machinery parts. Medium and large electric armatures (of electric motors having at least 80 mm shaft height) without special requirements. Small electric armatures, often mass-produced, in vibration insensitive applications and/or with vibration damping mountings. Individual components of engines under special requirements.
G 1600	Crankshaft drives of rigidly mounted large two-cycle engines.		
G 630	Crankshaft drives of rigidly mounted large four-cycle engines. Crankshaft drives of elastically mounted marine diesel engines.		
G 250	Crankshaft drives of rigidly mounted fast four-cylinder diesel engines.†		
G 100	Crankshaft drives of fast diesel engines with six or more cylinders.† Complete engines (gasoline or diesel) for cars, trucks, and locomotives.‡	G 2.5	Gas and steam turbines, including marine main turbines (merchant service). Rigid turbogenerator rotors. Rotors. Turbocompressors. Machine tool drives. Medium and large electric armatures with special requirements. Small electric armatures not qualifying for one or both of the conditions stated in G 6.3 for such. Turbine-driven pumps.
G 40	Car wheel,§ wheel rims, wheel sets, and driveshafts. Crankshaft drives of elastically mounted fast four-cycle engines (gasoline or diesel) with six or more cylinders.† Crankshaft drives for engines of cars, trucks, and locomotives.		
		G 1	Tape recorder and phonograph drives. Grinding machine drives. Small electric armatures with special requirements.
G 16	Driveshafts (propeller shafts, cardan shafts) with special requirements. Parts of crushing machinery. Parts of agricultural machinery. Individual components of engines (gasoline or diesel) for cars, trucks, and locomotives. Crankshaft drives of engines with six or more cylinders under special requirements.	G 0.4	Spindles, discs, and armatures of precision grinders. Gyroscopes.

* The quality grade number represents the maximum permissible circular velocity of the center of gravity in mm/sec.
** A crankshaft drive is an assembly that includes the crankshaft, a flywheel, clutch, pulley, vibration damper, rotating portion of connecting rod, etc.
† For the purposes of this recommendation, slow diesel engines are those with a piston velocity of less than 30 fps (9 m/sec); fast diesel engines are those with a piston velocity of greater than 30 fps (9 m/sec).
‡ In complete engines, the rotor mass comprises the sum of all masses belonging to the crankshaft drive.
§ G 16 is advisable for off-the-car balancing due to clearance or runout in central pilots or bolthole circles.

realistic value of the maximum initial unbalance can only be obtained after the actual production is achieved.

The following data should be included on drawings, specification sheets, or other documents that are intended to specify a required balance tolerance:

- Maximum permissible residual unbalance in each correction plane or statement of rotor mass, service speed, and balance quality grade.
- Location of correction planes.
- Location where corrections can be made. The type of correction method and the maximum amount that can safely be added or removed should be stated, taking into account required rotor strength or other considerations.
- Type of bearings and their locations in the balancing machine.

- Drive arrangements.
- Balancing speed.
- In certain cases, it is necessary to include the status of manufacture or degree of assembly of the rotor when ready for balancing.

BALANCING SPEED

The primary factor in determining the rotational speed at which a rotor is balanced is the type of rotor being balanced. The two main types of rotors are rigid rotors and flexible rotors. A rotor is considered rigid when it can be corrected in any two planes, and, after that correction, its unbalance does not significantly change up to the maximum service speed and when running under conditions that approximate those of the final supporting system. A rotor is considered flexible when, because

BALANCING SPEED

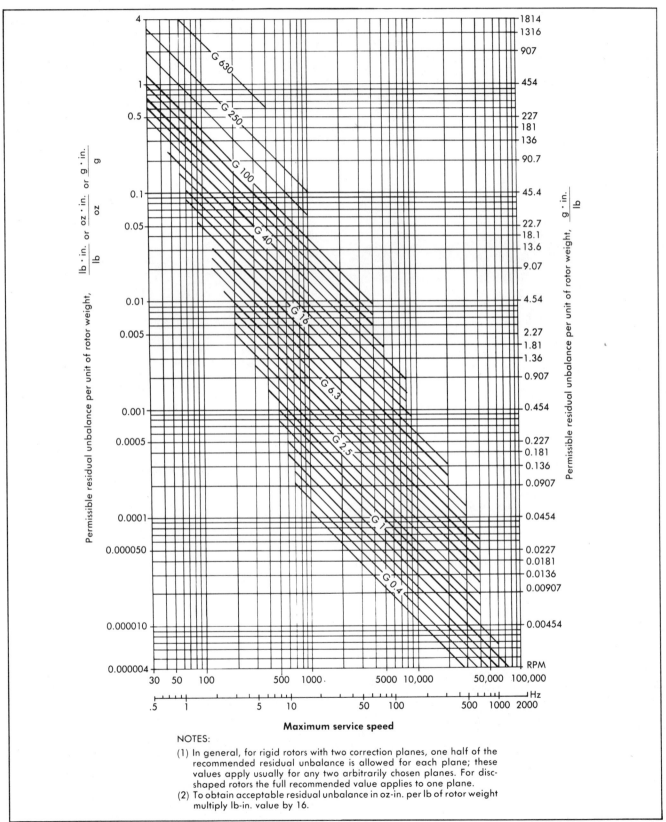

Fig. 7-20 Maximum residual specific unbalance corresponding to various balancing quality grades G in accordance with ISO 1940. (*International Organization for Standardization*)

NOTES:

(1) In general, for rigid rotors with two correction planes, one half of the recommended residual unbalance is allowed for each plane; these values apply usually for any two arbitrarily chosen planes. For disc-shaped rotors the full recommended value applies to one plane.

(2) To obtain acceptable residual unbalance in oz-in. per lb of rotor weight multiply lb-in. value by 16.

of elastic deflection, it does not comply with the definition of a rigid rotor.

Rigid rotors can be balanced at speeds lower than their service speeds whereas flexible rotors must be balanced at or near their service speed. When determining the balancing speed for rigid rotors, the following requirements should be considered:

- The balancing speed should be as low as possible to decrease cycle time, the horsepower requirement, wind, noise, and danger to the operator.
- The balancing speed should be high enough so that the balancing machine has sufficient sensitivity to achieve the required balance tolerance.

BALANCING MACHINES AND EQUIPMENT

Balancing machines are devices that measure both the magnitude of unbalance and its angular position in each of one, two, or more selected correction planes. The equipment should give complete and specific information in regard to the correction necessary to balance the part. The information should also be presented in a manner directly related to the correction method so that no interpretations are required of the operator. For example, if drilling is the correction method, the machine should read in increments of drill depth or in the number of holes at a specified depth. The type of equipment used depends on the type of unbalance being measured, the accuracy required, and the desired production rate.

External vibrations, electrical noise, and poor maintenance can easily destroy the balancing machine's accuracy. Therefore, a step-by-step procedure recommended by the machine manufacturer should be followed periodically to test for machine stability, repeatability, sensitivity, accuracy, and linearity. When tooling is used, it must also be tested periodically for accuracy and repeatability.

Balancing machines and equipment are divided into two general categories, gravity (nonrotating) and centrifugal (rotating), as shown in Table 7-10. These two general categories can be further subdivided based on the type of unbalance the machine can measure, the attitude of the rotor axis with respect to the machine, the design of the machine, and the class of the machine. Balancing machines can also be categorized based on their intended application.

Gravity Balancing Machines

Gravity balancing machines, also called nonrotating or static balancing machines, measure the unbalance in a rotor by means of gravity. As indicated in Table 7-10, these machines are only capable of measuring static unbalance. The three basic designs are knife-edges, roller stand, and pendulum.

Static balancing is satisfactory for rotors having relatively low service speeds and axial lengths that are small in comparison with the rotor diameter. A preliminary static unbalance correction may be required on rotors having a combined unbalance so large that it is impossible in a dynamic, soft suspension balancing machine to bring the rotor up to its proper balancing speed without damaging the machine. If the rotor is first balanced statically, it is usually possible to decrease the initial unbalance to a level where the rotor may be brought up to balancing speed and the residual unbalance measured. Such preliminary static correction may not be required on hard suspension balancing machines. For some applications, static balancing is also performed on narrow, high-speed rotors that are subsequently assembled to a shaft and balanced again dynamically.

Knife-edges. The simplest type of static balancing equipment consists of two horizontal, parallel bars or knife-edges. Some equipment has a built-in level and leveling screws for adjusting the knife-edges (Fig. 7-21). When the rotor is placed on the knife-edges, the heavy or unbalanced side of the workpiece will seek a position directly below its axis. When using these devices, it is important to keep the knife-edges level and free from nicks, scratches, or burrs.

Roller stands. In roller stands, a set of balanced rollers or wheels is used in place of the knife-edges (Fig. 7-22). Rollers have the advantage of not requiring as precise an alignment or leveling as knife-edges. Rollers also permit runout readings to be taken. The amount and angular position of unbalance are determined in the same manner as with knife-edges. The

TABLE 7-10
Classification of Balancing Machines

Principle Employed	Unbalance Indicated	Attitude of Shaft Axis	Type of Machine	Available Classes
Gravity (nonrotating)	Static (single-plane)	Vertical	Pendulum	
		Horizontal	Knife-edges	
			Roller sets	
Centrifugal (rotating)	Static (single-plane)	Vertical	Soft suspension	Not classified
			Hard suspension	
		Horizontal	Not commercially available	
	Dynamic (two-plane); also suitable for static (single-plane)	Vertical	Soft suspension	II, III
			Hard suspension	III, IV
		Horizontal	Soft suspension	I, II, III
			Hard suspension	IV

BALANCING MACHINES

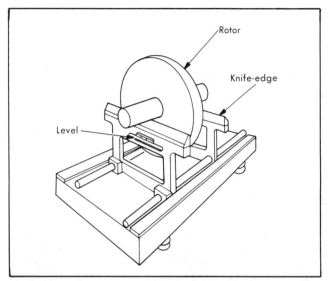

Fig. 7-21 Static balancing machine with knife-edges and built-in level. (*Balance Engineering, General Motors Corp.*)

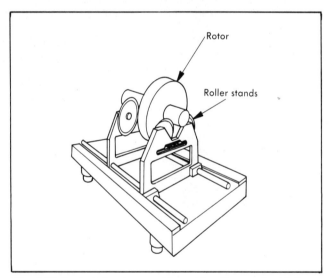

Fig. 7-22 Static balancing machine with roller stands. (*Balance Engineering, General Motors Corp.*)

quality to which parts can be balanced on these rollers is limited to the amount of friction that must be overcome in the roller bearings.

Pendulums. In pendulum or pivot-type balancing devices, the disc to be balanced is supported by a flexible cable. The cable is fastened to a point on the disc that coincides with the center of the shaft axis, slightly above the transverse plane containing the center of gravity. The heavy side of the disc will tend to seek a lower level than the light side, thereby indicating the angular position of the unbalance. Balancing is achieved by adding mass to the diametrically opposed side of the disc until it hangs level.

In modified versions of this type of balancing device, the cable is replaced by a hardened ball-and-socket or by a spherical air bearing, which supports the part to be balanced from underneath. The hardened ball-and-socket configuration is commonly used for automobile wheel balancers, and the air bearing is used for industrial and aerospace balancers.

Centrifugal Balancing Machines

The two types of centrifugal balancing machines in use today are soft and hard bearing machines. These two types are also divided into classes based on the method of calibrating the machine for various parts.

Soft bearing machines. Soft bearing balancing machines are the oldest type of balancers. They derive their name from the soft or flexible vibratory suspension system used in the work-support structures of the machine.

The flexible suspension system permits the rotor to vibrate freely in one direction, which is horizontal and perpendicular to the rotor shaft axis under certain conditions. The flexible suspension may also provide immunity from floor vibrations. The resonance of the rotor and bearing system occurs at one half, or less, of the lowest balancing speed. By the time the balancing speed is reached, the angle of lag and the vibration amplitude have stabilized and can be measured with reasonable certainty.

Because displacement of the principal axis of inertia in the balancing machine bearings is dependent on rotor mass, bearing and suspension mass, rotor moments of inertia, and the distance between bearings, calibration varies between parts of different mass and configuration. The method of calibration is dependent on the class of machine.

Hard bearing machines. Hard bearing balancing machines are essentially of the same construction as soft balancing machines, except that their supports are significantly stiffer in the transverse horizontal direction. As a result of the stiffer supports, the horizontal frequency for these machines occurs at a frequency several orders of magnitude higher than that for a comparable soft suspension machine. The hard suspension machine is designed to operate at speeds well below this resonance. Because of the extreme stiffness of the supports, these machines may require more elaborate foundations.

Hard bearing balancing machines measure rotor unbalance forces independent of the rotor weight or configuration. Because unbalance forces are measured in hard bearing machines rather than vibratory excursions, these machines can be permanently calibrated for the entire range of workpieces to be encountered. Calibration is a built-in function of the machine and is independent of the operator. The inputs to the balancer control are rotor dimensions and desired balancing speed range.

Classes. Centrifugal balancing machines may be categorized by the type of unbalance they can measure (static or dynamic), the attitude of the journal axis of the workpiece (vertical or horizontal), or the type of rotor support system employed (soft or hard suspension). In each category, one or more classes of machines are commercially built (refer to Table 7-10).

Class I. Machines in the Class I category are of the soft suspension type. They do not indicate unbalance directly in weight units (such as ounces or grams in the actual correction planes), but indicate only displacement and/or velocity of vibration at the bearings. The instrumentation does not indicate the amount of weight that must be added or removed in each of the correction planes.

Balancing with this type of machine involves a lengthy trial-and-error procedure for each rotor, even if it is one of an identical series. The unbalance indication cannot be calibrated for specified correction planes because these machines do not have the feature of plane separation. Field balancing equipment usually falls into this class.

Class II. Machines in the Class II category are of the soft bearing type using instrumentation that permits plane separation and calibration for a given rotor type, if a balanced master or prototype rotor with calibration masses is available. However, the same trial-and-error procedure as for Class I machines is required for the first of a series of identical rotors.

Class III. Machines in the Class III category are of the soft suspension type using instrumentation that includes an integral electronic unbalance compensator. Any unbalanced rotor may be used in place of a balanced master rotor without the need for trial-and-error correction. Plane separation and calibration can be achieved in one or more runs with the help of calibration masses. This class also includes soft suspension machines with electrically driven shakers fitted to the vibratory part of their rotor supports. New digital electronics allow storage of the initial calibration values, permitting simple, one-number recall if an identical rotor is to be balanced.

Class IV. Machines in the Class IV are of the hard bearing type. They are permanently calibrated by the manufacturer for all rotors falling within the weight and speed range of a given machine size. Unlike the machines in other classes, these machines indicate unbalance in the first run without individual rotor calibration. This is accomplished by the incorporation of an analog or digital computer into the instrumentation associated with the machine. The instrumentation then indicates the magnitude and angular position of the required correction mass for each of the two selected planes.

Applications

The three main areas in which balancing machines are used are universal, semiautomatic, and automatic operations. Machines for each of these operations are available in both nonrotating and rotating types, the latter for correction in either one or two planes.

Universal balancing machines. Universal balancing machines are adaptable for balancing a considerable variety of sizes and types of rotors. These machines commonly have a capacity for balancing rotors whose weight varies as much as 100 to 1 from maximum to minimum. The elements of these machines are adapted easily to new sizes and types of rotors. Amount and location of unbalance are observed on suitable instrumentation by the machine operator as the machine performs its measuring functions. This category of machine is suitable for maintenance or job-shop balancing as well as for many small and medium lot-size production applications.

Semiautomatic balancing machines. Semiautomatic balancing machines are of many types. They vary from an almost universal machine to an almost fully automatic machine. Machines in this category may perform automatically any one or all of the following functions in sequence or simultaneously:

- Retain the amount of unbalance indication for further reference.
- Retain the angular location of unbalance indication for further reference.
- Measure amount and position of unbalance.
- Couple the balancing machine drive to the rotor.
- Initiate and stop rotation.
- Set the depth of a correction tool depending on indication of amount of unbalance.

- Index the rotor to a desired position depending on indication of unbalance location.
- Apply correction of the proper magnitude at the indicated location.
- Inspect the residual unbalance after correction.
- Uncouple the balancing machine drive.

The most complete semiautomatic balancing machine performs the entire balancing process and leaves only loading, unloading, and cycle initiation to the operator. Other semiautomatic balancing machines provide the means for retaining measurements to reduce operator fatigue and error. The features that are economically justifiable on a semiautomatic balancing machine may be determined only from a study of the rotors to be balanced and the production requirements.

Automatic balancing machines. Fully automatic balancing machines with automatic transfer of the rotor are also available. These machines may be either single or multiple-station machines. In either case, the parts to be balanced are brought to the balancing machine by conveyor, and balanced parts are taken away from the balancing machine by conveyor. All the steps of the balancing process and the required handling of the rotor are performed without an operator. These machines also may include means for inspecting the residual unbalance as well as monitoring means to ensure that the balance inspection operation is performed satisfactorily.

In single-station automatic balancing machines, all functions of the balancing process (unbalance measurement, location, and correction) as well as inspection of the complete process are performed sequentially in a single station. In a multiple-station machine, the individual steps of the balancing process may be performed concurrently at two or more stations (Fig. 7-23). Automatic transfer is provided between stations at which the amount and location of unbalance are determined; then the correction for unbalance is applied; finally, the rotor is inspected for residual unbalance. Such machines generally have shorter cycle times than single-station machines.

Field (Portable) Balancing Equipment

A third general category of balancing machines is field balancing equipment, also called portable balancing equipment. This type of equipment provides sensing and measuring instruments only. The necessary measurements for balancing a rotor are taken while the rotor runs in its own bearings and under its own power.

Basically, field balancing equipment consists of a combination of transducer and meter that provides an indication proportional to the vibration magnitude. The vibration magnitude may be displacement velocity or acceleration, depending on the transducer and readout system used. The transducer can be handheld, attached to the machine housing by a magnet or clamp, or permanently mounted.

Computerization

In recent years, the practice of balancing has entered into a new stage—computerization. While analog computers have been in use on electronic balancing machines ever since such machines came on the market, it is the application of digital computers to balancing that is relatively new. At first, desktop digital computers were used in large, high-speed balancing and overspeed spin test facilities for multiplane balancing of flexible rotors. As computer hardware prices dropped, their application to more common balancing tasks became feasible. The constant

BALANCING MACHINES

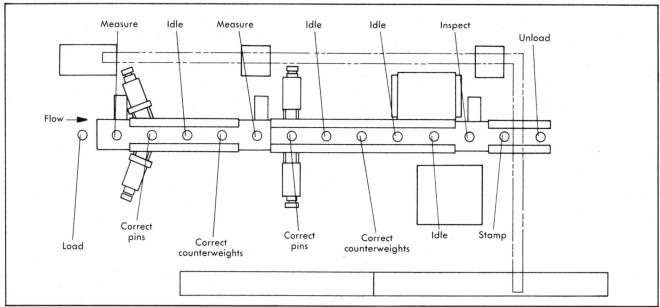

Fig. 7-23 Multiple-station automatic crankshaft balancer. (*Gilman Engineering and Manufacturing Co.*)

demand by industry for a simpler balancing operation performed under precisely controlled conditions with complete documentation led to the combination of the small, dedicated, table-top computer with the hard-bearing balancing machine. The advantages that a computerized balancing system provides versus the customary manual system are the many standard and not-so-standard functions a computer performs and records with the greatest of ease.

Different computers may be used depending on the application. The computer may be mounted in the balancing machine's instrumentation console or in a central electronic data processing room. A single computer may control one balancing machine or a series of machines.

Basic computer programs are available for single and two-plane balancing, field balancing, and flexible rotor balancing. Software libraries for optional subroutines are also growing.

Safety

The design of balancing machines aims to minimize hazards from the use of the machine itself. Rising demand for still greater safety in the work environment calls for additional protection, especially with respect to the rotor to be balanced. Special-purpose balancing machines, such as those used in the mass production automotive industry, normally provide all the necessary measures of safety because the workpiece as well as the operating conditions of the machine can be taken into account by the machine manufacturer. However, when multi-purpose balancing machines are used, the workpieces to be balanced are generally unknown and beyond the control of the machine manufacturer; safety measures are limited to covering the end-drive coupling and/or the drive belt.

National and local safety codes generally cover the hazards from machine components. Hazards associated with the spinning rotor in a balancing machine may be separated into several different categories and resolved by a variety of measures. Some of the recognized hazards and countermeasures are listed in Table 7-11.

TOOLING

During the balancing operation, the part to be balanced must be accurately located with respect to its axis of rotation in final assembly. The part must also be located accurately with respect to the balancing machine axis. For location accuracy, the same surfaces that will locate the part in use or assembly should be specified for location on the balancing machine.

The simplest type of locator used on vertical machines is a solid pin or plug that fits into the bore of the part being balanced. The minimum residual unbalance achievable with this type of tooling depends on the bore tolerance plus the clearance required for loading and unloading the part. If these balance errors are unacceptable, some type of expanding arbor will be required. A manual or air-operated collet arbor will take up the bore clearance and enable the unbalance readings to be accurate within the limitations of the indicating system.

Locating parts on an outside diameter presents more of a problem than locating parts on an inside diameter. The simplest method is to locate the part in a pilot diameter, providing the balance tolerance will permit the necessary clearance. If a more accurate location is required, then either a spring finger type of collet or diaphragm chuck can be used.

For horizontal machines, the tooling must run in roller or half bearing supports. Ground concentric journals of hardened steel are typical design features.

For belt-drive machines, a driven diameter or pulley having a smooth, concentric, flat steel surface without serrations should be used. Adding serrations to the pulley usually induces a large amount of noise that may interfere with the unbalance measurement. Provisions should also be made for photocell and/or angle reference mark to transfer the indicated angle of unbalance from the balancing machine instrument to the part. A means for correction of unbalance on the tooling should also be provided.

Tooling should be made as precisely as possible. Concentric ground diameters are required to prevent eccentricity and out-of-squareness of the parts to be balanced.

TABLE 7-11
Potential Hazards When Using Balancing Machines

Hazard	Safety Countermeasures
Disengagement or failure of the end-drive coupling. One end of the universal-joint drive may remain coupled to the balancing machine or rotor with the free end whipping around.	The common device for protection in such a case is an enclosure around the universal-joint shaft.
Operator becoming entangled in the belt drive.	The usual protective devices are belt covers over the motor and tensioning pulleys. More complete protection is offered by machine enclosures.
Axial rotor movement off the machine support due to excessive axial thrust from skewed support rollers or from windage.	This hazard usually does not occur on machines with end drives as long as the end-drive coupling prevents axial motion. On belt-drive machines, axial motion is prevented by axial thrust stops.
The rotor lifting out of the machine's open bearings due to excessive initial unbalance, or shifting or separation of large masses during rotation.	This condition may be prevented by use of closed bearings or, in case of support rollers, by safety hold-downs.
The operator coming in contact with any part of the spinning rotor such as blades or other protruding components.	This hazard may be prevented by awareness barriers, fences, or enclosures.
A small rotor particle such as welding bead, bolt, key, or correction mass separating from the rotor during rotation.	On small rotors, this hazard may be resolved by using safety glasses or shields. Large rotors require enclosures.
A rotor component such as a blade separating from the rotor during rotation.	See preceding countermeasures.
The rotor or major components failing during high-speed balancing or overspeed testing.	Burstproof enclosures such as pits or bunkers are required to contain these hazards. Under certain conditions, other safety measures such as vacating the surrounding workshop area may be acceptable.

References

1. O. Zmeskal, "Hot Hardness Testing," *Metal Progress*, vol. 51, no. 1 (1947).
2. P. Rabbe and G. Pomme, "La Durete' a Chaud," *Revue de Metallurgie*, vol. 63 (1966), pp. 719-725.
3. O. E. Harder and H. A. Grove, "Hot Hardness of High Speed Steel and Related Alloys," *Transactions of American Institute of Mining and Metallurgical Engineers*, I and S Division, vol. 105 (1933).
4. "Definition of Terms Relating to Methods of Mechanical Testing," ASTM E 6 (Philadelphia: American Society for Testing and Materials).
5. H. E. Davis, G. E. Troxell, and G. T. Wiscocil, *The Testing and Inspection of Engineering Materials*, 2nd ed. (New York: McGraw-Hill Book Co., 1955).
6. P. P. Puzak and W. S. Pellini, *U.S. Naval Research Laboratory Report 5831* (Washington, DC: 1962).
7. G. M. McClure, A. R. Duffy, and R. D. Eiber, "Fracture Resistance in Line Pipe," *ASME Transactions Series B*, vol. 87, no. 3 (August 1965), pp. 265-278.
8. *Balancing Made Simple* (Janesville, WI: Gilman Manufacturing and Engineering Co., 1980).
9. *Fundamentals of Balancing*, 2nd ed. (New York: Schenck Trebel Corp., 1983).
10. *Balance Engineering Manual No. 31*, 3rd ed. (Warren, MI: Balance Engineering, General Motors Corp., 1962).
11. Acoustical Society of America, *American National Standards Institute Balancing Terminology*, ANSI S2.7-1982 (New York: 1982).

Bibliography

Achterberg, R. C. *Computerized Balancing*. SME Technical Paper MS82-247. Dearborn, MI: Society of Manufacturing Engineers, 1982.
"Balancing Equipment for Jet Engine Components—One or More Planes." ARP 587A. Warrendale, PA: Society of Automotive Engineers, 1972.
"Balancing Machines—Description and Evaluation." ISO 2953. Geneva, Switzerland: International Organization for Standardization, 1975.
"Balancing Quality of Rotating Rigid Bodies." ISO 1940. Geneva, Switzerland: International Organization for Standardization, 1973.
"Design Criteria for Balancing Machine Tooling." ARP 1382. Warrendale, PA: Society of Automotive Engineers, 1977.
Lysaght, Vincent E. *Indentation Hardness Testing*. Bridgeport, CT: Wilson Instrument Div., American Chain and Cable Co., 1949.
Lysaght, V. E., and DeBellis, A. *Hardness Testing Handbook*. Bridgeport, CT: American Chain and Cable Co., 1969.
Mechanical Testing, vol. 8, 9th ed. Metals Park, OH: American Society for Metals, 1985.
Meinhold, Ted F. "Measuring and Analyzing Vibration." *Plant Engineering* (October 4, 1979).
Muster, Douglas, and Stadelbauer, Douglas G. "Balancing of Rotating Machinery." *Shock and Vibration Handbook*, 2nd ed. New York: McGraw-Hill Book Co., 1976.
"Procedures for Balancing Flexible Rotors." (ANSI S2.42). New York: Acoustical Society of America, 1982.
Rieger, Neville F., and Crofoot, James F. *Vibrations of Rotating Machinery*. Clarendon Hills, IL: The Vibration Institute, 1977.

CHAPTER 7

BIBLIOGRAPHY

Small, L. *Hardness: Theory and Practice*. Ann Arbor, MI: Cushing Malloy, 1960.

"Standard Test Method for Brinell Hardness of Metallic Materials." *E 10 Annual Book of ASTM Standards*, vol. 03.01. Philadelphia: American Society for Testing and Materials, 1984.

"Standard Test Methods for Microhardness of Materials." *E 384 Annual Book of ASTM Standards*. Philadelphia: American Society for Testing and Materials, 1984.

"Standard Test Methods for Rockwell Hardness and Rockwell Superficial Hardness of Metallic Materials." *E 18 Annual Book of ASTM Standards*, vol. 03-01. Philadelphia: American Society for Testing and Materials, 1984.

"Standard Test Methods for Vickers Hardness of Metallic Materials." *E 92 Annual Book of ASTM Standards*. Philadelphia: American Society for Testing and Materials, 1984.

"Static Balancing Equipment for Jet Engine Components." ARP 588A. Warrendale, PA: Society of Automotive Engineers, 1972.

ASSEMBLY

MECHANICAL FASTENING

Assembly in manufacturing often involves some type of mechanical fastening of a part to itself, or two or more parts or subassemblies together, to form a functional product or a higher level subassembly. Mechanical fasteners are available in a wide variety of types and sizes to suit the individual requirements for different joint and assembly designs. Types discussed in this chapter include integral, threaded, nonthreaded, and special-purpose fasteners. Other methods of mechanical fastening also discussed in this chapter are stitching and stapling, shrink and expansion fitting, and injected metal assembly.

The numerous mechanical fasteners available have resulted in inconsistent nomenclature and made identification difficult. While it would be desirable to have all fastener names based on their shapes and/or features, many are named for their application or the product on which they are used, the materials from which they are made, or their size. A comprehensive glossary of terms for mechanical fasteners is presented in ANSI Standard B18.12. The terms used for many different fasteners are presented in subsequent sections.

Most mechanical fasteners are now being produced by cold forming (extruding and upsetting), as discussed in Volume II, *Forming*, of this Handbook series, but some are made by warm or hot forging. Advantages of the cold forming process include fast and economical production, design versatility, high quality, increased strength, and material savings.

While standard mechanical fasteners are available in many types and sizes, there are numerous requirements and an increasing demand for special fasteners. For some applications, fastener manufacturers can meet special requirements with only slight alterations to existing fasteners, thus reducing costs compared to designing an entirely new special fastener.

Metrication of mechanical fasteners has progressed further than for most other products, particularly in the automotive industry. General Motors Corp. started metrication for its 1977 line of large cars, and today about 95% of the attachments on all its cars are made with metric fasteners. One major advantage of metrication has been the reduced number of standard fasteners with respect to thread diameter-pitch combinations. Metric and inch standards are discussed in subsequent sections devoted to individual types of fasteners.

Selection of a specific mechanical fastener or fastening method depends primarily on the materials to be joined, the function of the joint, strength and reliability requirements, weight limitations, dimensions of the components, and environmental conditions. Other important factors that must be carefully considered include costs, available installation equipment, appearance, and whether the assembly has to be dismantled. Value analysis in the product design stage can often make assembly easier and more economical by reducing the number of components in the assembly or by modifying the design or processing to facilitate assembly.

When dismantling of assemblies is required, threaded or other types of fasteners that can be removed quickly and easily should generally be used. However, such fasteners should not have a tendency to loosen after installation. When disassembly is not necessary, permanent fasteners such as rivets or threaded fasteners locked with adhesives are often used. Permanent joints are also often made by other processes, such as welding, brazing and soldering, and adhesive bonding, which are discussed in Chapters 9, 10, and 11, respectively, of this volume.

Required shear and tensile strengths must be known before a mechanical fastener or fastening process can be selected. Applications subject to vibration and/or cyclic stresses often require the use of self-locking fasteners, locknuts, rivets, or processes such as welding or adhesive bonding. The weight of the fastener is also a critical consideration for some applications; assemblies requiring a large number of fasteners can suffer a significant weight penalty.

Fasteners exposed to corrosive environments, high or low temperatures, or other severe conditions must be made from or coated with materials that will withstand the conditions. A variety of

Contributors of sections of this chapter are: Frank Arsenault, Product/Project Engineer, Bostitch Div., Textron Inc.; Richard C. Baubles, Vice President, Research and Development, Jacobson Mfg. Co., Inc.; Wallace Berliner, Chief Product Engineer, Truarc Retaining Rings Div., Waldes Kohinoor, Inc.; Joseph J. Braychak, Product Development Manager, POP Fasteners Div., Emhart Fastener Group; Lawrence B. Curtis, Manager, Sales and Application Engrg., Equipment Div., Fisher Gauge Ltd.; Richard L. Davis, Manager, Applications Engrg. and Service, Heli-Coil Products, Div. of Mite Corp.; W. E. Duffey, President, Driv-Lok, Inc.; Robert S. Eckles, Vice President and General Manager, Brainard Rivet Co.; Richard B. Ernest, Vice President—Engrg., Penn Engrg. & Mfg. Corp.; Dr. John L. Frater, Associate Professor, Cleveland State University; Donald Johnston, Sales/Marketing Specialist, GEMCOR Drivmatic Div.; Michael M. Joseph, Application Engineer, Southern Screw, Div. Farley Metals, Inc.; Kenneth E. McCullough, Manager, Technical Services, SPS Technologies; John Nasiatka, Sales Engineer, Duo-Fast Corp.; Michael M. Plum, Manager, Magneform Business Dev., Maxwell Laboratories, Inc.; James F. Sullivan, Sales Engineer, Stitching Products, Acme Packaging, Div. of Interlake, Inc.; Dr. H. E. Trucks, Consultant; Paul W. Wallace, Vice President, Engrg., Aerospace Div., SPS Technologies; Stephen M. Ward, Spiralox Design Engineer, Ramsey Piston Ring Div., TRW Automotive Products Inc.

Reviewers of sections of this chapter are: Wayne F. Allgaier, Mech. Engrg. & Fabrication, Advanced Products and Mfg. Engrg. Staff, General Motors Corp., General Motors Technical Center; Frank Arsenault, Product/Project Engineer, Bostitch Div., Textron Inc.; George C. Bartholomay, Sales Manager, Industrial Retaining Ring Co.; Richard C. Baubles, Vice President, Research and Development, Jacobson Mfg. Co., Inc.;

INTEGRAL FASTENERS

materials and coatings are used to suit different requirements. Zinc-coated carbon steel fasteners are resistant to normal atmospheric corrosion, and stainless steel fasteners are used extensively for applications in corrosive industrial applications. Materials, finishes, and coatings for specific fasteners are discussed later in this chapter.

INTEGRAL FASTENERS

Integral fasteners are formed areas of the component part or parts that function by interfering or interlocking with other areas of the assembly. This type of fastening is most commonly applied to formed sheet metal products and is generally performed by lanced or shear-formed tabs, extruded hole flanges, embossed protrusions, edge seams, and crimps. In all these methods, the joint is made by some method of metal shearing and/or forming.

Details of the various shearing and forming operations are presented in Volume II, *Forming*, of this Handbook series. Other processes used for fastening and assembling that are also discussed in Volume II include beading, hemming, bulging, swaging, expanding, shrinking, roll forming, and electromagnetic forming.

LANCED OR SHEAR-FORMED TABS

Tabs, also called ears, flaps, lugs, and prongs, are a versatile construction element for lightweight products made from sheet metal components. The economic advantages of tabs for assembly are reduced material use, lower labor costs, reduced weight, and reduced tooling costs. Lanced tabs are used most widely for permanent assembly but rarely for temporary or even semipermanent assembly.

A common use of a tab bent or curved around a shaft, wire, or cable to locate and hold the parts firmly is shown in Fig. 8-1, view *a*. A similar design is the lanced bridge, view *b*, in which both ends of the lanced area remain attached.

Tabs that are shear formed in one part may be introduced into matching slots or holes in a second part and then folded over, as shown in Fig. 8-2. According to the best bending techniques, the tab should always be bent so that its burred edge is located on the inside of the bend. The finish bend of the tab should always be in the same direction as the primary bend. In some cases, auxiliary parts are included in the tab fastening design, as shown in Fig. 8-3.

The best shapes for tab ends are round or half round (see Fig. 8-4, view *a*), tapered (view *b*), square with chamfered corners (view *c*), or triangular. These shapes are easier to introduce into slots than the square tab (view *d*), which should never be used for folded fastenings. The matching slots should be made with dimensions somewhat larger than the tab thickness. However, the punches used to form the slots may be weak, so the shapes of

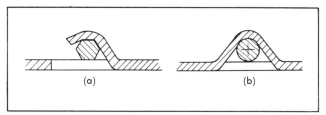

Fig. 8-1 Methods of fastening shafts, wires, or cables to metal plates: (a) lanced tab and (b) lanced bridge.

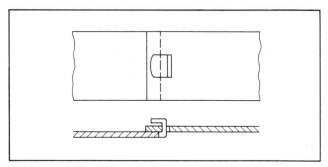

Fig. 8-2 Shear-formed tab folded through a slot for fastening.

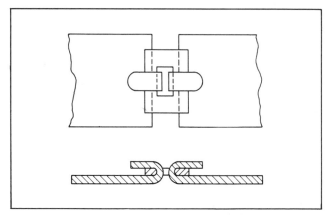

Fig. 8-3 Auxiliary part included in a tab fastening design.

Reviewers, cont.: Daniel P. Baumann, President, Bracker Corp.; *Robert L. Beers*, Marketing Manager, Specialty Fastener Div., Rexnord; *Wallace Berliner*, Chief Product Engineer, Truarc Retaining Rings Div., Waldes Kohinoor, Inc.; *John H. Bickford*, Vice President, Manager of Power-Dyne Div., Raymond Engrg., Inc.; *Paul R. Bonenberger*, Fastening Systems, W3-C Structural Analysis, Engrg. Building, General Motors Technical Center; *James L. Bowman*, Corporate Vice President Engrg., Long-Lok Fasteners Corp.; *Robert E. Branshaw*, Marketing Manager, Ind. Fastening Systems Group, Microdot; *Joseph J. Braychak*, Product Development Manager, POP Fasteners Div., Emhart Fastener Group; *Paul L. Cady*, Supervisor—Sales Engrg., Chicago Rivet & Machine Co.; *Vito Cardone*, Vice President/ Manufacturing, Anderton-United Products; *Donald H. Chadwick*, Vice President—Engrg., Rockford Products Corp.; *W. S. Clement*, Advertising Manager, Southco, Inc.; *Richard G. Cooper*, Technical Sales Dept., Avdel Engineered Assembly Systems; *George Davis*, General Manager, Dzus Fastener Co., Inc.; *Richard L. Davis*, Manager, Applications Engrg. and Service, Heli-Coil Products, Div. of Mite Corp.;

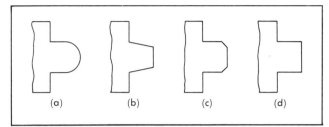

Fig. 8-4 Shapes for fastening tabs: (a) desirable round or half round, (b) desirable tapered, (c) desirable chamfered square, and (d) undesirable sharp-cornered square.

the slots should be revised whenever possible to allow use of reinforced punches; Fig. 8-5 illustrates a satisfactory solution with triangular slots. To reduce tool costs and tool maintenance, simple round holes instead of elongated slots may be applicable.

One folded tab alone has little strength, and, in the case of thin, large stampings, it is better to use two or more tabs if possible. For strength in the greatest number of directions, the tab should be bent alternately unless the stamping is U-shaped. The joint is strongest if the tabs are stressed for shear (see Fig. 8-6) instead of for tension, as is usually the case. If there is not enough space for more than one tab, the tab may be split longitudinally, with the two halves bent in opposite directions for additional joint strength. The designer should remember that the tabs should be bent at least 45° across the grain direction of the metal to prevent cracking and tearing.

Metal stampings employed as inserts in moldings, castings, and rubber parts must be properly anchored. A simple 90° lanced tab performs this task (see Fig. 8-7, view *a*), and two tabs provide greater strength. If the stamping is not totally embedded in the molding but forms one of the surfaces of the assembly, the tabs must be inclined to resist both transverse and longitudinal loads (views *b* and *c*).

For greater efficiency and flexibility, lanced tabs may be shaped or even tapped for use with discrete fasteners. Two of the most characteristic of these types of tabs are the speed nut, which is formed by shaping two opposite arched prongs in the lanced part to accept a threaded screw, and the speed clip, which is usually a separate part formed by lancing to accept and clamp smooth, unthreaded studs, rivets, and tubes.

Temporary bayonet-lock joints for parts such as small light bulbs and their holders are often formed by projections created by lancing (see Fig. 8-8, view *a*). The same design is often found in caps for small containers (view *b*).

EXTRUDED HOLES

A simple, inexpensive method of increasing the length of a hole in sheet metal is to form an integral, extended collar

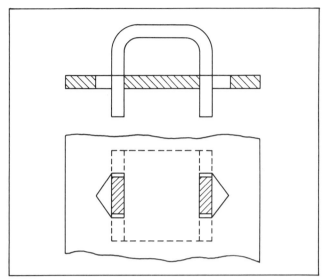

Fig. 8-5 Use of triangular fastening slots to allow slot-punch reinforcement.

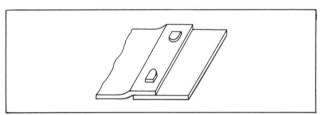

Fig. 8-6 Folded tabs stressed for shear rather than tension.

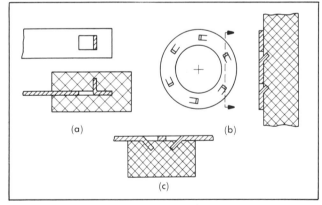

Fig. 8-7 Methods of fastening metal stampings to castings and moldings.

Reviewers, cont.: **Lon DeHaitre**, *Abbott Interfast Corp.;* **J. DeHaven**, *President, Yardley Products Corp.;* **Anthony DeMaio**, *Vice President, Mfg. and Engrg., Gesipa Fasteners USA, Inc.;* **Thomas S. Doppke**, *Senior Fastener Engineer, Truck and Bus Group, General Motors Corp.;* **Max F. Dorflinger**, *President, Nylok Fastener Corp.;* **W. E. Duffey**, *President, Driv-Lok, Inc.;* **Robert S. Eckles**, *Vice President and General Manager, Brainard Rivet Co.;* **Richard B. Ernest**, *Vice President—Engrg., Penn Engrg. & Mfg. Corp.;* **Stephen Feldman**, *Chief Engineer, Industrial Fasteners Corp.;* **Robert J. Finkelston**, *Manager, Systems Engrg., Aerospace Div., SPS Technologies;* **William H. Gibbons**, *Consultant—Marketing, Communications, Engineered Fasteners Div., Eaton Corp.;* **Loren Godfrey**, *Director—Technical Services, Associated Spring Barnes Group Inc.;* **Harland S. Graime**, *Plant Manager, Acme Rivet & Machine Corp.;* **Frederick E. Graves**, *F. E. Graves Associates, Consulting Engineers;* **Joseph P. Guy**, *Marketing Manager, Engineered Fasteners, The BFGoodrich Co.;* **Fred A. Hammerle**, *Manager of Product Engrg., Fasteners Div., TRW Assemblies and Fasteners Group;*

INTEGRAL FASTENERS

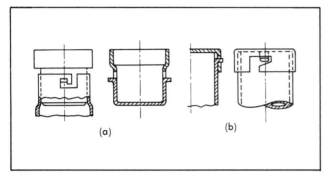

Fig. 8-8 Tabbed bayonet locks for temporary joints.

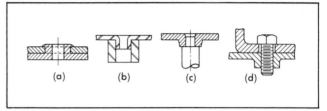

Fig. 8-9 Uses of an extruded hole for joining: (a) as a rivet with end flared or swaged, (b) as an interference fitting, (c) with a riveted shaft, and (d) with a bolt fastener.

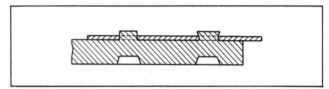

Fig. 8-10 Embossed protrusions before and after flattening to form an integral rivet.

around the hole. The hole is then called an extruded, flanged, collared, embossed, or drifted hole. Extruded holes are widely used as integral fasteners, not only on flat surfaces but also on curved, bent, or drawn surfaces.

In the majority of cases, extruded holes are used for joining two components, one of which is the sheet metal part with the hole. The extruded collar is often used as an integral hollow rivet for joining two thin sheet metal components. The free end of the flange is simply flared or swaged out, creating a head that forms a firm joint (see Fig. 8-9, view a). Common eyelets belong to this type of fastening method. If the length of the flange with respect to the thickness of the second part is favorable, the end of the flange may be curled to form the head.

Tubing may be joined with an extruded hole by means of a bead in the tubing, which acts as a stop, and by flaring or half curling the end of the tube. Tubing may also be fastened by interference fitting of its inner diameter to the flange (see Fig. 8-9, view b). A proper guide for shaft riveting may be provided by an extruded hole (view c); but often, for limited-strength joints, the shaft may simply be press fit in the flange, with knurling for increased joint strength and torsional resistance. The shaft may also be fastened by beading the flange.

Perhaps the most common use of extruded holes for fastening is in conjunction with discrete fasteners. As shown in Fig. 8-9, view d, the flange is tapped and acts as an integral nut with a separate screw or bolt. The nut is twice or more the sheet metal thickness, and the strength of the joint is considerably increased.

EMBOSSED PROTRUSIONS

Embossed protrusions, also referred to as partial extrusions, lugs, and extruded dowels, are bosses forced out from the surface of a metal sheet or part on one side of the material. Such protrusions may be used as integral rivets to form permanent joints, as shown in Fig. 8-10. However, this fastening method

has limitations. The bosses must be formed on comparatively thick stock, not less than 0.10" (2.5 mm) thick, and the part to be fastened must never be more than half the thickness of the embossed part because the length of the boss is generally limited to a fraction of stock thickness and is not sufficient to make a regular rivet head. For this same reason, joint strength is usually low.

To perform the riveting operation, a proper anvil, as illustrated in Fig. 8-11, must be used to support the boss and prevent it from being depressed back into the parent part. For economic reasons, such riveting should be used only in mass production when the building of the dies needed for the operation is justified.

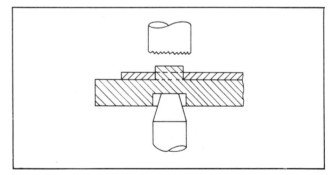

Fig. 8-11 Tools for integral rivet-boss flattening.

Reviewers, cont.: Richard I. Hatch, Director—Technical Marketing, Johnson Steel & Wire Co., Inc.; Girard S. Haviland, Manager, Engrg. Center, Loctite Corp.; James F. Hester, Jr., American Rivet Co.; Robert E. Keeler, Townsend Div., Textron Inc.; David J. Koetsier, Sales Manager, Groov-Pin Corp.; George M. Loucas, Manager, Process Engrg., Fasteners Div., TRW Assemblies and Fasteners Group; Robert A. Main, Jr., Plant Manager, John M. Dean, Inc.; Vincent J. Manobianco, President, Groov-Pin Corp.; George E. Marshall, Customer Service Manager, Chicago Steel & Wire Div., Keycon Industries, Inc.; Bill McClelland, Production Engineer, Smalley Steel Ring Co.; Kenneth E. McCullough, Manager, Technical Services, SPS Technologies; John C. McMurray, Technical Director, Russell, Burdsall & Ward Corp.; John C. Moodey, Chief Engineer, Specialty Fastener Div., Rexnord; Ray Okolischan, Vice President—Engrg., Carr Lane Mfg. Co.; W. Richard Pamer, Product Engineering Supervisor, Russell, Burdsall & Ward Corp.; Ralph E. Rau, Jr., Vice President, Stimpson Co., Inc.; B. F. Reiland, Director of Research, Camcar Div., Textron Inc.; Glen N. Rohn, Sales/Marketing Manager, VSI Automation Assembly; Thomas Russo, Chief Engineer, Acme Rivet & Machine Corp.; Charles H. Saurer, Supervisor—AFM Program, Fairchild Republic Co.;

SEAMS

Seaming is often used to interlock the edges of two separate sheet metal parts or the opposite edges of a given curved or bent part. While the chief purpose of seaming is assembly, seams also reinforce the assembly and eliminate sharp edges. Seams are used when other mechanical assembly methods would be impractical or uneconomical and when welding would cause excessive distortion. Seaming also often provides greater strength and tightness under high temperature conditions than do other joining methods. Seams are normally used on metal sheets 0.011-0.050″ (0.28-1.27 mm) thick; heavier gage sheets require too much force for the seaming operation.

Seams may be classified as follows according to the shape of the workpiece to be joined:

- *Jacket or longitudinal seams.* Straight seams for the bodies of tubular workpieces or simple formed parts.
- *Circumferential seams.* Closed seams such as those used for joining a top or a bottom to the tubular body of a can or for joining two tubular parts.

The most common seam for light-gage sheets is the simple or single-lock seam, also known as the standard seam or folded-pipe seam. The edges to be seamed are first bent to acute angles; then they are fitted together, and the seam is flattened closed. In most cases the two joined areas must be flush, as shown in Fig. 8-12. The seam may be located inside or outside the workpiece.

For higher strength, a double-lock seam is formed in the following steps: the two edges are bent square, with one edge bent longer than the other; the longer leg is bent over the shorter one; a standing seam is formed; and the seam is bent down and flattened against the joined parts (see Fig. 8-13).

The seams just described are direct seams; that is, they are formed directly on the parts. In special cases, an indirect seam using an intermediate connector strap or plate may be formed to fasten parts; such as a seam is shown in Fig. 8-14.

The width of a seam cannot be chosen arbitrarily. Seams that are too small are weak, not tight enough, and difficult to form. Seams that are too large demand too much plastic flow, and they overstress the sheet metal; they also increase stock usage unnecessarily. Correct seam size depends on the size of the components, stock thickness, shape, whether the seam is

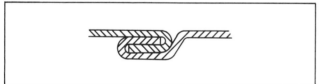

Fig. 8-12 Simple or single-lock seam flattened flush with joined areas.

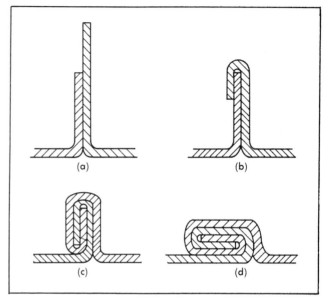

Fig. 8-13 Steps in forming a double-lock seam.

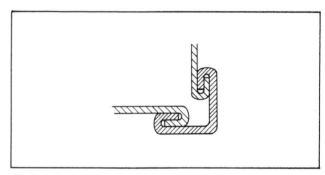

Fig. 8-14 Indirect seam with an intermediate connector plate.

straight or circumferential, and whether the seaming is performed manually or mechanically. For sheet metal up to 1/32″ (0.08 mm) thick, the seam should be between 3/16 and 1/2″ (4.8 and 12.7 mm) wide and should be proportionately wider for heavier material.

CRIMPS

Crimps are permanent interlocking joints in sheet metal assemblies created by deforming the thin wall of one or both of the fitted components. Crimped fastening methods may be classified roughly into the following five groups:

Reviewers, cont.: **Jerry Sessa**, Cherry Aerospace Fasteners, Cherry Div., Textron Inc.; **Jay Stafford**, Project Engineer, Specialty Fastener Div., Rexnord; **David P. Stanger**, Weber Automatic Screwdrivers & Assembly Systems, Inc.; **Werner R. Stutz**, Vice President, Taumel Assembly Systems; **James F. Sullivan**, Sales Engineer, Stitching Products, Acme Packaging, Div. of Interlake, Inc.; **Frank R. Thomas**, Vice President, International Eyelets, Inc.; **Robert A. Thomson**, National Sales Manager, H. K. Metalcraft Mfg. Corp.; **John A. Trilling**, Director of Engineering, Holo-Krome Co.; **Ward E. Walker**, Manager—Product Development, C.E.M. Co., Inc.; **Paul W. Wallace**, Vice President, Engrg., Aerospace Div., SPS Technologies; **Stephen M. Ward**, Spiralox Design Engineer, Ramsey Piston Ring Div., TRW Automotive Products Inc.; **Brian Waterhouse**, Engineering Manager, Anderton International; **Jim Weston**, Product Manager, Specialty Fasteners Div., Rexnord; **L. T. Whyte**, Machine Sales Manager, Acme Rivet & Machine Corp.; **Charles J. Wilson**, Industrial Fasteners Institute; **James G. Youness**, Marketing Specialist, Eaton Corp.; **James A. Zils**, Manager, Product Development and Product Engrg., Russell, Burdsall & Ward Corp.; **Bill Zoller**, Product Specialist, Specialty Fastener Div., Rexnord.

INTEGRAL FASTENERS

1. Matching beads (formed inward or outward).
2. Matching dimples (formed inward or outward).
3. Formed ribs or flanged unions.
4. Holding beads.
5. Special shapes.

Crimping cannot be employed without limitations. The sheet metal of the deformed components should be thin, preferably less than 0.030″ (0.76 mm). The stock must also be naturally ductile or softened by an annealing process. Copper, tin, brass, aluminum, and low-carbon steel have the proper yield characteristics and are often fastened by crimping.

Beading

Matching beads are used for crimping pipe and tubing together when the outer diameter of one component matches the inner diameter of the other, as shown in Fig. 8-15. The two beads are formed together in light-walled ductile tubing; but to avoid overstress in heavier gages and harder metals, it is customary to form the inner bead first, with the outer bead formed against the inner one after assembly. If two tubes have the same diameters, one of them may be expanded or necked down for a short length before beading to allow them to be fitted together.

Tubing may be joined to a round bar by turning a groove in the bar and forming a matching bead in the tube against the groove. Solid shafts may also be fastened to extruded hole flanges by crimping the flange into a groove machined in the shaft (see Fig. 8-16); two shafts are sometimes coupled by flanges in this way.

Dimpling

Matching dimples often serve well for fastening when joint tightness requirements are not too severe. The holding strength of dimples is usually low. The simplest dimples are round, although dimples may be formed rather deeply and assume the shape of double-slit bridges. For increased strength, several dimples may be formed (see Fig. 8-17, view *a*), although only a single dimple is required for very simple cases. As in beading, thin, soft materials allow both inner and outer dimples to be formed simultaneously; but in harder, thicker materials, the internal component must be spot drilled or grooved before assembly (view *b*).

Dimple crimping is used not only on tubular parts but also on flat or prismatic components. For example, in the assembly of a sheet metal stamping to a machined workpiece, the stamping, into which a properly located round hole has been previously punched, is introduced into a milled slot in the machined part; the machined workpiece is slightly deformed by a stubnosed punch so that part of it interlocks with the hole in the stamping (see Fig. 8-18). When parts with cross-sectional shapes other than cylindrical are crimped, generous corner radii must be provided to facilitate assembly.

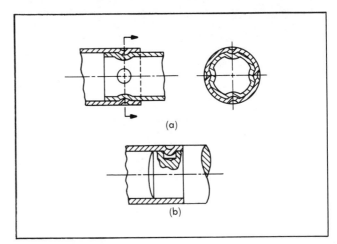

Fig. 8-17 Crimped dimple fastening of tubular parts: (a) with several dimples for increased strength and (b) with internal component spot drilled before assembly.

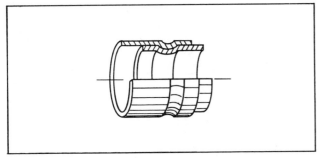

Fig. 8-15 Use of matching beads for crimp fastening of pipe or tubing.

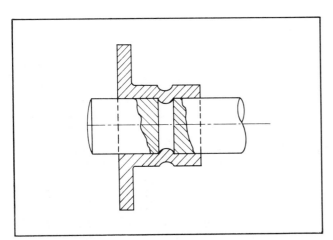

Fig. 8-16 Crimped bead fastening of a solid shaft to a flange.

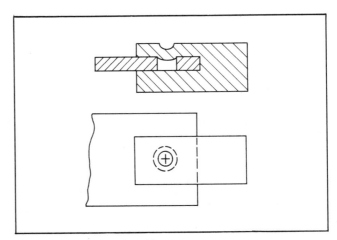

Fig. 8-18 Dimple crimping of flat components.

THREADED FASTENERS

Threaded fasteners are separate components having internal or external threads for mechanically joining parts. The most common types of threaded fasteners include bolts, studs, nuts, and screws, all discussed subsequently in this section.

A primary application of threaded fasteners is for joining and holding parts together for load-carrying requirements, especially when disassembly and reassembly may be required. Typical assemblies for several types of threaded fasteners are illustrated in Fig. 8-19. Threaded fasteners are also used extensively for assemblies subject to environmental conditions such as elevated temperatures and corrosion.

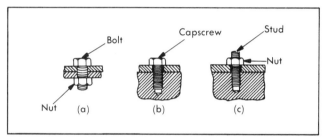

Fig. 8-19 Typical assemblies using threaded fasteners: (a) bolt and nut, (b) capscrew, and (c) stud.

Advantages of threaded fasteners include their commercial availability in a wide range of standard and special types, sizes, materials, and strengths. Extensive standardization efforts have made most threaded fasteners interchangeable. Most of these fasteners are easy to install, remove, and replace, thus providing a low-cost method of assembly. They are capable of joining identical or different materials and workpieces of various configurations.

TYPES OF THREADED FASTENERS

Details about many of the different types of threaded fasteners are presented individually later in this section. This discussion is limited to the distinction between bolts and screws, the different heads available on threaded fasteners, how the dimensions of these fasteners are identified, threads used on the fasteners, and the development of standards.

Bolt or Screw?

Bolts are cylindrical, externally threaded fasteners available with various shaped heads. They are generally assembled through holes in parts and tightened with internally threaded nuts. Screws are also cylindrical, externally threaded fasteners, but they are generally assembled by inserting into blind holes in assembled parts, by mating with preformed internal threads, or by forming their own threads. Tightening is usually accomplished by applying torque to the screwheads.

Confusion with respect to nomenclature exists, however, because some bolts and screws are capable of being assembled with nuts or into threaded holes. End use is one method of distinguishing between bolts and screws. Recess-drive, externally threaded fasteners are generally called screws; hex-head, externally threaded fasteners are sometimes called bolts, and other times, screws. One simplified classification is that externally threaded fasteners having nominal diameters over 1/4″ are generally called bolts and below 1/4″ are called screws, but this is not a rigid rule because of overlapping of some fastener sizes. Means of distinguishing between screws and bolts are discussed in ANSI Standard B18.2.1, "Square and Hexagonal Bolts and Screws, Inch Series." ISO terminology identifies screws as having threads extending to their heads, while bolts have unthreaded portions under their heads.

Heads and Recesses Available

Threaded fasteners are available with many different head styles and recessed drives (see Fig. 8-20). Other styles not illustrated include ball, button, square, and T-heads. Headless fasteners have either enlarged or preformed ends. The body of a threaded fastener is the unthreaded portion of its shank.

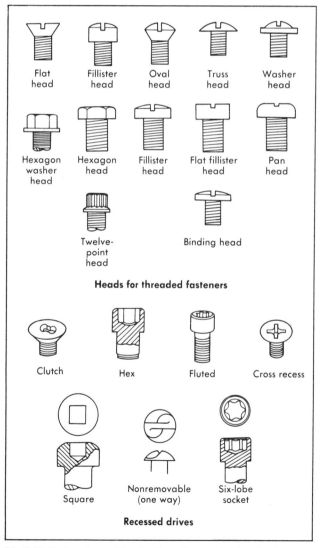

Fig. 8-20 Various types of head styles and recessed drives for threaded fasteners.

THREADED FASTENERS

Various recesses available, some of which are shown in Fig. 8-20, include the following:

- Slotted—a straight recess, either formed or cut, is produced laterally across the head, perpendicular to the body.
- Cross recess—a formed recess that produces a tapered cross indent in the head, axially to the body.
- Hex socket—a formed recess in the shape of a hexagon with either a flat or tapered bottom.
- Fluted socket—a formed recess with flutes at the corners of the indentation.
- Clutch—a formed recess for use with a clutch driver.
- Security recess—recesses of various designs formed for nonremoval or removal only with special drivers.

Dimension Identification

Terms commonly used in designating the size and dimensions of threaded fasteners are presented in ANSI Standard B18.12. Some typical examples are illustrated in Fig. 8-21.

Threads Used

Threaded fasteners are made with either inch or metric threads. Details with respect to thread form, pitches, tolerances, and classes for Unified Standard threads are presented in Volume I, *Machining*, of this Handbook series and ANSI Standard B1.1, "Unified Inch Screw Threads." Metric screw threads are also discussed in Volume I, as well as in the following ANSI Standards:

B1.13M, "Metric Screw Threads—M Profile"
B1.21M, "Metric Screw Threads—MJ Profile"
B1.18M, "Metric Screw Threads for Commercial Industrial Fasteners"

Coarse threads are stronger than fine threads for fasteners of 1″ (25 mm) size and larger. The coarse threads permit easier assembly, are less effected by burrs during assembly, and are more desirable where corrosion or thread damage is possible. Coarse threads are generally recommended for fastener materials having lower tensile strengths.

Fine threads are used extensively for fasteners in the aircraft, aerospace, and automotive industries, where wall thicknesses necessitate fine-pitch threads. Because fine threads are not as deep as coarse threads, their tensile stress areas are larger and the clamping forces that can be developed are greater.

Standardization

Threaded fasteners have undergone and are undergoing extensive standardization. Fasteners in the inch series have been completely standardized, based on the Unified Standard screw-thread system, agreed on in 1948 by the United States, the United Kingdom, and Canada. In the early 1970s, the Industrial Fasteners Institute (IFI) started an Optimum Metric Fastener System (OMFS) program. The purpose of this program was to examine current metric practices and develop technical improvements, cost-saving benefits, and simplification.

Working with the International Organization for Standardization (ISO), a single system of international engineering standards for metric fasteners is now completed. The ISO is a federation of national standards-writing bodies from all major manufacturing countries of the world. The American National Standards Institute (ANSI) is the U.S. member.

Many of the ANSI standards agree with ISO standards; some differences for technical reasons exist but do not interfere with functional interchangeability. Many applicable standards are cited subsequently in sections on individual fasteners. The development of ANSI and ISO metric standards offered the advantage of reducing the number of individual configurations in existence, thus reducing costs. Fastener standards are published in the U.S. by ANSI, the American Society of Mechanical Engineers (ASME), the American Society for Testing and Materials (ASTM), the Society of Automotive Engineers (SAE), and IFI. Standards published by ISO are available from ANSI.

Inspection and quality assurance procedures for general-purpose metric fasteners are presented in ANSI Standard B18.18.1M and IFI Standards J-23 through J-26. Allowable limits for surface discontinuities on metric bolts, studs, and screws are covered in ASTM Standard F 788 and on metric nuts in IFI Standard 533. The testing of mechanical properties of external and internal-threaded fasteners, washers, and rivets is presented in ASTM Standard F 606.

MATERIALS, FINISHES AND COATINGS

Mechanical fasteners are made from a variety of materials, with steels being the most common. Selection of a material for a specific fastener depends primarily on application requirements. Well-manufactured bolts, studs, and screws develop strengths equivalent to the strength of the base material.

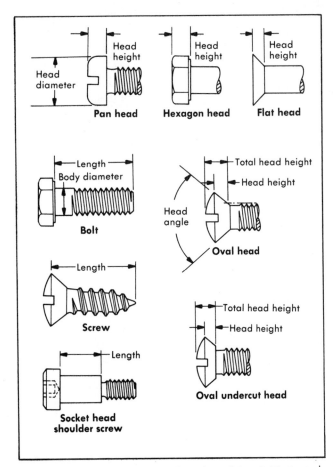

Fig. 8-21 Terms used to designate dimensions of threaded fasteners.[1]

THREADED FASTENERS

TABLE 8-1
Typical Tensile Strengths and Relative Corrosion
Resistance of General Material Categories

General Material Categories*	Typical Tensile Strengths, ksi (MPa)	Relative Corrosion Resistance**
Low-carbon steels	60-74 (414-510)	1
Low-carbon martensitic (boron) steels	120-150 (827-1034)	1
Medium-carbon steels	120 (827)	1
Alloy steels	150-180 (1034-1241)	1
Aluminum alloys	55 (379)	3
Copper alloys	50-80 (345-552)	3
Chromium steels	170 (1172)	2
Chromium-nickel steels	75-160 (517-1103)	4
Tool steels	260 (1793)	1
Titanium alloys	60-165 (414-1138)	5
Nickel alloys	80-200 (552-1379)	5
Cobalt alloys	85-260 (586-1793)	5

(*SPS Technologies*)

* Listed in approximate order of increasing cost.
** Relative corrosion resistance: 1—lowest, 5—highest.

General material categories presented in Table 8-1 are listed in order of increasing cost. Not all materials in each category are suitable for manufacturing fasteners, nor are all fastener materials listed. This table shows typical tensile strengths of the various material categories and their relative corrosion resistance, with 1 being the lowest. However, both strength and corrosion resistance vary with the specific environment encountered in service. Detailed information about the different materials and their mechanical properties is presented in Volume III, *Materials, Finishing and Coating*, of this Handbook series.

Material Selection

Factors that must be considered in selecting a fastener material include the loads to be encountered, the materials to be joined, and the service environment. Data with respect to joint function that should be known include loads (both static and dynamic) to be applied, design life, reliability, strength-to-weight ratio, and resistance to creep, environmental corrosion, and temperatures. Formability and/or machinability of the materials are also important considerations as they affect the cost of the fasteners.

Steels for Fasteners

Low-carbon steels, generally unhardened or cold worked, are used for some fasteners. Fasteners made from low-carbon, SAE 1018 steel, not heat treated, have an ultimate tensile strength to about 74 ksi (510 MPa); those made from medium-carbon, SAE 1038 steel, also not heat treated, have an ultimate tensile strength to about 120 ksi (827 MPa). Most bolts and screws are made from medium-carbon steels and are heat treated. Alloy steels, such as SAE 4037, 4137, and 8740, generally heat treated, are used for higher strength requirements. such as an ultimate tensile strength of 150 ksi (1034 MPa). Most

nuts are made from low-carbon steels that are cold worked in the forming process and generally not heat treated.

Chemical, mechanical, and strength requirements for metric bolts, studs, and screws made from carbon and alloy steels are presented in ASTM Standard F 568. This standard includes 13 property classes having various treatments such as partial or full annealing, cold working, and quenching and tempering. Requirements for metric nuts made from carbon and alloy steels are given in ASTM Standard A 563 M, having eight property classes; the inch series is covered in ASTM Standard A 563.

Mechanical and material requirements for externally threaded fasteners in the inch series are presented in SAE Standard J429, for machine screws in J82, and for nuts in J995. Test methods for determining the mechanical properties of externally and internally threaded fasteners are specified in ANSI/ASTM Standard F 606-79a.

Requirements for metric bolts, studs, and screws made from stainless steels are presented in ASTM Standard F 738. This standard includes eight groups of stainless steels: three austenitic, such as AISI/SAE grades 304, 305, 316, 321, and 347; one ferritic, AISI/SAE grade 430; three martensitic, AISI grades 410, 416, and 431; and one precipitation-hardening grade. Metric nuts made from the same eight groups of stainless steels are included in IFI Specification 517. Inch series, stainless steel screws and bolts are presented in ASTM Standard F 593; nuts are presented in F 594.

Other Alloys Used

The iron-based superalloy A-286 is used for some fastener applications having operating temperatures to about 1200° F (650° C). Tool steels are being used for high-strength, high-temperature applications to temperatures of about 1000° F (540° C), with AISI Type H11, chromium-type, hot-work tool steel being a common choice. Some superalloys, such as René 41 and Waspaloy, are usable at temperatures to 1400° F (760° C). There are also special materials with limited use potential to a temperature of 2000° F (1095° C), and some tungsten alloys are used at even higher temperatures.

Nonferrous Metals

Aluminum-based alloys, copper and copper-based alloys, nickel and nickel-based alloys, and titanium and titanium-based alloys are nonferrous metals used for fasteners. Chemical, mechanical, and strength requirements for metric bolts, studs, and screws made from these metals are presented in ASTM Standard F 468 M. Metric nuts made from the same nonferrous metals are specified in ASTM Standard F 467 M.

Nonmetallic Materials

Where fasteners are subjected to certain corrosive, magnetic, or electrical environments, they are sometimes made from plastics. Fasteners are being made from nylon, vinyl, polycarbonates, acetals, polyethylenes, polystyrenes, fluorocarbons, and other plastics. The use of fasteners made from plastics requires consideration of design strength and temperature requirements, and the economics of assembly should be favorable. Advantages of nonmetallic fasteners include excellent corrosion resistance, light weight, nonmagnetic properties, good thermal and electrical insulation, elimination of the need for special finishes or coatings, and easy coloring. However, fasteners made from plastics will creep or relax under loads and are generally suitable only for light-load applications.

THREADED FASTENERS

Platings and Coatings

Environmental conditions and temperatures encountered in service are critical considerations in selecting a material for a specific fastener. Platings and coatings are often applied to fasteners for improved corrosion resistance or appearance and, in some cases, to provide lubricity. The term "finish" is commonly applied to a chemical or organic treatment of a fastener surface after machining or forming, but it is also used to indicate the resulting surface condition from manufacturing operations or the degree of dimensional precision of the fastener.

Plating can protect fasteners by providing barriers to the environment and/or by sacrificially and chemically inhibiting corrosion. The amount of protection provided by most plating is directly related to the thickness of the plate. However, plating thickness is limited by the dimensional fit tolerances of the fastener threads and wrenching surfaces, which are usually, respectively, four and two times the nominal plating thickness. Selection of a specific plating material requires consideration of the joint design, materials in the joint and the fastener, the service environment, and maintenance and life requirements. The effects of platings on the tightening characteristics of fasteners must also be considered.

When possible corrosion in service is not a critical problem, unplated fasteners are often supplied with a corrosion-retardant oil-dip finish, a black oxide coating, or a phosphate and oil coating. When additional corrosion resistance is required for carbon or alloy steel fasteners, it is common practice to apply cadmium or zinc coatings. Tin, nickel, copper, and chromium are other metals also used for coating. Coating is accomplished by electroplating, mechanical plating, or, in the case of zinc, sometimes by batch galvanizing (hot dipping).

Caution is required to prevent hydrogen embrittlement of fastener materials, which generally occurs in high-hardness steels and alloys, generally $R_C 36$ and above. Embrittlement results from the absorption of atomic hydrogen, usually during electroplating, chemical treatments prior to plating, or acid cleaning. The possibility of embrittlement can be minimized by mechanically cleaning, electroplating in special baths, and then baking the fasteners immediately or as soon as possible after plating. Embrittlement can also be minimized by mechanical plating or vacuum deposition. A phenomenon similar to hydrogen embrittlement can occur in fasteners made from high-hardness steels (generally higher than $R_C 40$) under certain stress and corrosion conditions. This delayed "hydrogen embrittlement" is referred to as hydrogen-assisted cracking.

The corrosion resistance of stainless steel fasteners is sometimes improved by passivating. This chemical treating process, generally consisting of a nitric acid dip, dissolves ferrous particles and surface impurities and produces an invisible, passive oxide film on the surfaces of the fasteners. Aluminum alloy fasteners, as well as some fasteners made of titanium alloys, are sometimes anodized, forming an anodic or oxide film on the surfaces. Zinc alloys are chromated for extra protection.

Chromate-phosphate bonded, aluminum coatings are being applied to titanium fasteners used in aluminum aircraft-wing skins.[2] Although titanium has excellent corrosion resistance, the aluminum coating is used to prevent the wing skin from corroding sacrificially to the titanium fasteners. A centrifugal, dip-and-spin process is used to apply these coatings to small parts such as fasteners.

Detailed information on conversion (phosphate, chromate, and oxide) coatings, anodizing, electroplating, mechanical plating, hot dipping (zinc galvanizing and aluminizing), and the vapor deposition processes is presented in Volume III.

STRENGTH OF BOLTED JOINTS

Bolted joints are used for a wide variety of assembly applications. Designs include lap, flanged, and butt joints, as well as variations and combinations of these designs. All joint members of an assembly, including the fasteners (see Fig. 8-22), may be subjected to tension, torsion, shear, bending, or compressive stresses, or a combination of these forces. Tensile strength of the fastener is generally the mechanical property of primary interest, but shear strength, hardness, and fatigue strength can also affect the performance. If the external tension load exceeds the bolt load, the bolt will experience stress variations and, finally, fatigue failure. For elevated temperature applications, creep and strength at the elevated temperature must also be considered.

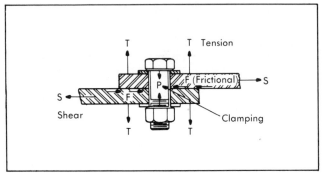

Fig. 8-22 Typical forces acting on a bolted connection.

Preloading

Design of a reliable bolted joint requires knowledge of the joint loading, the joint materials, selection of the proper fastener, and determining the correct amount of preload to be applied during assembly. While it is necessary to have a bolt strong enough to carry the required loads, it is the proper preload (clamping load) that ensures joint integrity or rigidity. The initial tension must be greater than any external tensile loads applied to the joint and/or must create frictional forces between the joint members that exceed any external shear loads applied to the joint.

A fastener made from ductile material should be tightened to develop as high a preload as is compatible with the expected service loading. Bolt preload in some instances for rigid joints may extend beyond yield and into the plastic range. When a nut is tightened on a bolt, the nut is compressed and the bolt stretches elastically. The approximate amount of elongation of a fully threaded steel bolt is about 0.001 in./in. (mm/mm) of grip per 30 ksi (207 MPa) of stress, within the elastic limit of the bolt material. This is true for all steel bolts regardless of the diameter and heat treatment of the bolts.

The maximum preload that should be applied to any bolted joint depends on the loads to be encountered in service, as well as the types of fasteners being used. In general, the higher the strength of the fastener, the smaller the range between tensile and yield loads.

During tightening, frictional resistance introduces torsional shear stresses that reduce the amount of preload. Also, as soon as a bolt is tightened, load relaxation begins. From 2 to 5% of the preload can be lost during the first few minutes after tightening and another 5% during a few days to a month. Poor surface finishes, burrs, coatings, and foreign matter on the fasteners can also further reduce the preload. Additional long-term relaxation in metallic joints is generally only significant at elevated temperatures, above 480° F (250° C).

Tensile and Proof Stresses

The strength of fasteners is generally specified by tensile and proof stress values. The proof stress of an externally threaded fastener is the maximum tensile stress at which no permanent deformation occurs in the fastener. Proof load is a specified test load that a fastener must withstand without any indication of permanent elongation. Tests for determining the ability of fasteners to pass the proof load include the yield strength test and the uniform hardness test specified in ASTM Standard F 606.

Proof and tensile stresses for certain SAE grades of steel bolts, studs, and screws in the inch series are presented in Table 8-2. Caution must be exercised in the use of various steels. Steels with similar tensile strengths may be processed differently, including various tempering temperatures, and may behave differently at elevated or reduced temperatures. The SAE steel grades are designated by numbers, with increasing numbers representing increasing tensile stresses. Proof and tensile loads for various sizes of the same grade fasteners are given in Table 8-3.

Tensile stresses are determined from the following equation:

$$S = \frac{P}{A} \tag{1}$$

where:

S = tensile stress of material, psi (MPa)

P = tensile load of fastener, lb (N)
A = tensile stress area, of the critical section of the fastener (generally the threaded section), in.^{2} (mm^2)

The tensile load, P, to break the threaded portion of a bolt, stud, or screw (assuming there are no shearing or torsional stresses) is calculated from the following equation:

$$P = S \times A \tag{2}$$

For inch threads, the tensile stress area, A (the effective cross-sectional area), of the external thread is determined by the following equation:

$$A = 0.7854 \left(D - \frac{0.9743}{n} \right)^2 \tag{3}$$

where:

A = tensile stress area, in.^{2}
D = basic major diameter of thread, in.
n = number of threads per inch

For metric threads, A is calculated as follows:

$$A = 0.7854 (D - 0.9382P)^2 \tag{4}$$

where:

A = tensile stress area, mm^2
D = nominal thread diameter, mm
P = thread pitch, mm

Mechanical and material requirements for metric, externally threaded, steel fasteners are presented in SAE Standard J1199.

TABLE 8-2
Materials, Proof Stresses, and Tensile Stresses for
Certain SAE Grades of Steel Bolts, Studs, and Screws*

SAE Grade Designation	Steel	Treatment	Nominal Diameter, in.	Proof Stress, ksi (MPa)	Tensile Stress, ksi (MPa)
1	Low or medium-carbon	---	1/4 through 1 1/2	33 (228)**	60 (414)
2	Low or medium-carbon	---	1/4 through 3/4†	55 (379)**	74 (510)
			Over 3/4 to 1 1/2	33 (228)	60 (414)
5	Medium-carbon or low-carbon martensitic	Quenched and tempered	1/4 through 1	85 (586)	120 (827)
			Over 1 to 1 1/2	74 (510)	105 (724)
8	Medium-carbon alloy, or low or medium-carbon martensitic‡	Quenched and tempered	1/4 through 1 1/2	120 (827)	150 (1034)

* Abstracted with permission from SAE Standard J429, "Mechanical and Material Requirements for Externally Threaded Fasteners."

** Rarely stress-relieved, except for carriage bolts.

† Grade 2 requirements for 1/4 through 3/4" diam apply only to bolts 6" and shorter in length and to studs of all lengths. For bolts and screws longer than 6", Grade 1 requirements apply.

‡ Fine-grain steel with hardenability that will produce a minimum hardness of R_C47 at the center of a transverse section one diameter from the threaded end of the bolt, stud, or screw after oil quenching (see SAE Standard J407).

THREADED FASTENERS

TABLE 8-3
Tensile Stress Areas, Proof Loads, and Tensile Strengths for Certain Sizes
and SAE Grades of Steel Bolts, Studs, and Screws*

Nominal Product Diameter and Threads/in.	Tensile Stress, Area, in.² (mm²)	SAE Grade Designation							
		1		2		5		8	
		Proof Load, lb (kN)	Tensile Strength, min, lb (kN)	Proof Load, lb (kN)	Tensile Strength, min, lb (kN)	Proof Load, lb (kN)	Tensile Strength, min, lb (kN)	Proof Load, lb (kN)	Tensile Strength, min, lb (kN)
Coarse-thread series (UNC):									
1/4-20	0.0318 (20.52)	1050 (4.67)	1900 (8.45)	1750 (7.78)	2350 (10.45)	2700 (12.01)	3800 (16.90)	3800 (16.90)	4750 (21.13)
3/8-16	0.0775 (50.00)	2550 (11.34)	4650 (20.68)	4250 (18.93)	5750 (25.58)	6600 (29.36)	9300 (41.37)	9300 (41.37)	11,600 (51.60)
1/2-13	0.1419 (91.55)	4700 (20.91)	8500 (37.81)	7800 (34.69)	10,500 (46.70)	12,100 (53.82)	17,000 (75.62)	17,000 (75.62)	21,300 (94.74)
3/4-10	0.334 (215.48)	11,000 (48.93)	20,000 (88.96)	18,400 (81.84)	24,700 (109.87)	28,400 (126.32)	40,100 (178.36)	40,100 (178.36)	50,100 (222.84)
1-8	0.606 (390.97)	20,000 (88.96)	36,400 (161.91)	20,000 (88.96)	36,400 (161.91)	51,500 (229.07)	72,700 (323.37)	72,700 (323.37)	90,900 (404.32)
1 1/4-7	0.969 (625.16)	32,000 (142.34)	58,100 (258.43)	32,000 (142.34)	58,100 (258.43)	71,700 (318.92)	101,700 (452.36)	116,300 (517.30)	145,400 (646.74)
1 1/2-6	1.405 (906.45)	46,400 (206.39)	84,300 (374.97)	46,400 (206.39)	84,300 (374.97)	104,000 (462.59)	147,500 (656.08)	168,600 (749.93)	210,800 (937.64)
Fine-thread series (UNF):									
1/4-28	0.0364 (23.48)	1200 (5.34)	2200 (9.79)	2000 (8.90)	2700 (12.01)	3100 (13.79)	4350 (19.35)	4350 (19.35)	5450 (24.24)
3/8-24	0.0878 (56.65)	2900 (12.90)	5250 (23.35)	4800 (21.35)	6500 (28.91)	7450 (33.14)	10,500 (46.70)	10,500 (46.70)	13,200 (58.71)
1/2-20	0.1599 (103.16)	5300 (23.57)	9600 (42.70)	8800 (39.14)	11,800 (52.49)	13,600 (60.49)	19,200 (85.40)	19,200 (85.40)	24,000 (106.75)
3/4-16	0.373 (240.64)	12,300 (54.71)	22,400 (99.64)	20,500 (91.18)	27,600 (122.76)	31,700 (141.00)	44,800 (199.27)	44,800 (199.27)	56,000 (249.09)
1-12	0.663 (427.74)	21,900 (97.41)	39,800 (177.03)	21,900 (97.41)	39,800 (177.03)	56,400 (250.87)	79,600 (354.06)	79,600 (354.06)	99,400 (442.13)
1 1/4-12	1.073 (692.26)	35,400 (157.46)	64,400 (286.45)	35,400 (157.46)	64,400 (286.45)	79,400 (353.17)	112,700 (501.29)	128,800 (572.90)	161,000 (716.13)
1 1/2-12	1.581 (1020.00)	52,200 (232.19)	94,900 (422.12)	52,200 (232.19)	94,900 (422.12)	117,000 (520.42)	166,000 (738.37)	189,700 (843.79)	237,200 (1055.07)

* Abstracted with permission from SAE Standard J429, "Mechanical and Material Requirements for Externally Threaded Fasteners."

Shear and Fatigue Strengths

While joints are often subjected to shear loads, the shear strengths of threaded fasteners are seldom specified, except in the case of aircraft, aerospace, and other critical applications. An increase in the number of shear planes, experienced when more than two components are bolted together, generally increases the shear loads that a joint can safely endure. Single shear strengths of the fasteners are often estimated to equal 55-65% of the tensile strengths. By providing the proper level of clamp load, the force exerted on the components of a joint should be large enough to keep them from sliding, thus preventing the introduction of shear.

Fatigue strengths are important for structural, aircraft, aerospace, and other critical applications. The fatigue strength is only important when an assembly is exposed to repetitive cyclic loads. The use of cold-rolled threads, thread roots, and fillets, rolled after heat treatment, increases the fatigue strength of bolts and studs because of the residual compressive stresses, work hardening, and improved grain flow resulting from the cold rolling. An important factor with respect to the fatigue life of an externally threaded fastener is that the preload must exceed the external cyclic load.

Assembly Tools

The function of tools used in assembling threaded fasteners (see Fig. 8-23) is to apply the required torque and rotation. The

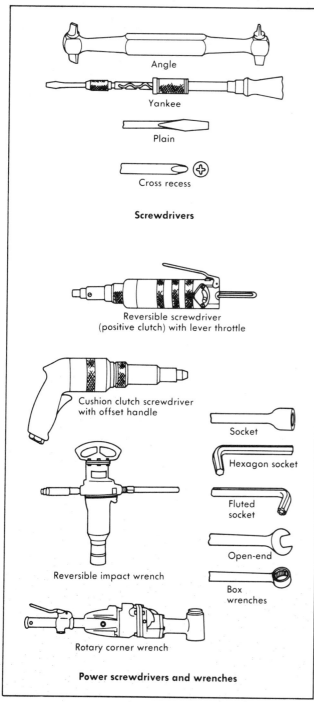

Screwdrivers

Power screwdrivers and wrenches

Fig. 8-23 Hand and power-operated screwdrivers and wrenches.

tools require appropriate wrenching surfaces and the power necessary for the assembly operation. Both hand and power-operated wrenches, nutrunners, and screwdrivers are used for tightening the threaded fasteners, the choice of tools depending primarily on production requirements. Tools are available with or without detachable sockets and bits. It is essential that openings in or points on the tools fit the bolt heads, nuts, or screw slots properly to prevent damage.

Power tools are commonly operated by compressed air, but hydraulic and electric tools are increasing in popularity. Multispindle nutrunners are used extensively in high-production industries such as automotive. Torque tools, both screwdrivers and wrenches (see Fig. 8-24), are also in common use, with torque adjustment often provided by slip clutches.

Power tools generally consist of a motor and reduction gearbox that reduces the motor speed from a 5000-10,000 rpm range to output speeds in the 30-300 rpm range. Impact tools do not have gearboxes. Instead, torque is developed through a hammer impacting mechanism. Power ratchet tools generate torque by a hydraulic cylinder applying force to a lever arm.

Automatic drilling and riveting machines, as well as industrial robots, are also being used for the installation of threaded fasteners. These machines are discussed in a subsequent section of this chapter.

Methods of Preloading

Accurate preloading is essential for reliable bolted joints. Torque has been used for many years to determine the amount of preload in assembling with threaded fasteners. An approximation of the desired torque for required bolt tension can be obtained by using the following equation:

$$T = CDF \qquad (5)$$

where:

T = torque, lb-in. (N·m)
C = torque coefficient
D = bolt diameter, in. (m)
F = bolt tension required, lb (N)

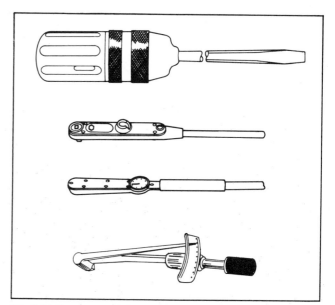

Fig. 8-24 Torque screwdrivers and wrenches.

THREADED FASTENERS

Arbitrary values for the torque coefficient, C (for noncritical applications), are 0.22 for steel fasteners with a dry zinc plate and 0.15 for fasteners with a dry cadmium plate. Values differ for other materials and change with the use of different lubricants.

Determining the amount of preload by torque alone is not accurate because only rotational forces are measured, not clamping forces. Also, there are many variables that influence torque, including the hardness and surface finish of the fastener, thread fit, friction and lubrication, and the presence of burrs, contaminants, and rust. Various methods for measuring torque and newer methods of controlling preload more accurately are discussed briefly in the remainder of this section.

Operator feel. Using the operator's judgment to feel the proper amount of preload with a hand wrench is the oldest and a low-cost method of assembly. However, it is an inaccurate method of tightening and varies from operator to operator. Estimates indicate there is a torque variation of ±35% with this method of preload measurement.

Torque wrenches. The use of torque wrenches is a popular method of preload measurement because of its simplicity and low cost. Accuracy is estimated to be ±15-25% or more of desired preload, but these tools are still being used extensively, especially for noncritical assembly applications. Torque-tension tests duplicating the assembly process are possible and provide more accurate information for setting torque specifications than do calculations.

Impact wrench nutrunners. These tools rely on repetitive torque impulses to tighten fasteners, with desired torque values being preset at the tools. Repetitive accuracy of these tools is poor because of variations in torque-action dynamics and operator dependence. Also, impact tools are noisy in operation. While impact wrenches are still used, they are generally limited to noncritical applications.

Stall motors. Stall-type tightening devices are superior to impact wrenches with respect to repetitive accuracy. A variety of air-powered tools are available that deliver good preload repeatability, providing the tool is properly lubricated and maintained; also, the air supply pressure must not fluctuate appreciably. A limiting factor is reliance on torque alone as a measure of fastener tension, but the tools are satisfactory for many applications.

Improved reliability is obtained with torque-monitored stall motors, consisting of a transducer and electronic units added to a stall-type tightening device. Torque is monitored throughout the rundown of the fastener, and torque output signals can be used for various purposes, such as automatic acceptance or rejection of the assemblies, a control warning system, or workpiece marking.

A further advancement of stall-motor devices is to feed the torque monitoring signal back to the motor to automatically stop fastener tightening when a predetermined torque has been achieved. As shown in Fig. 8-25, the signal from a reaction-type torque transducer is amplified and fed into a torque set-point comparator module. When the preset torque level is reached, the output from the comparator energizes a fast-acting air shutoff valve mounted on the low-inertia air motor. In addition to stopping the motor, the transducer torque signal can also be used for monitoring and actuating quality assurance devices.

Torque-turn (turn-of-the-nut) tightening. In the torque-turn technique, often called turn-of-the-nut tightening in the automotive industry, the fastener is first tightened to a low threshold level, using only torque as the starting parameter. The threshold

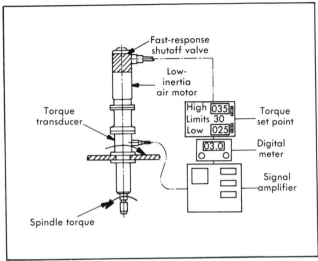

Fig. 8-25 Feedback-controlled, stall-type tightening device.

level has a torque value just sufficient to seat the fastener against the mating parts. When the predetermined threshold torque has been reached, the fastener is rotated an additional number of degrees for tightening.

The specific amount of angular rotation performed after the threshold torque has been reached is usually determined experimentally, either by measuring bolt elongation or using strain gages. A limitation of the torque-turn method is possible improper seating during tightening because of rough or warped surfaces. In such cases, subsequent rotation will be used for seating rather than stretching of the fastener for required tension. This tightening system is usually limited to fasteners that have a large range between tensile and yield strengths.

Bolt extension tightening. In the so-called bolt extension method of tightening, the elongation of the bolt is monitored during the tightening process until a predetermined axial extension has been achieved. The relationship between bolt elongation and load, determined by analysis or test, is a function of bolt geometry and material elasticity.

In practice, the measurement of bolt elongation is usually accomplished by accurately measuring the distance between two precision ground surfaces, one on top of the bolt head and the other on the end of the threaded portion of the bolt. Sometimes a long, small-diameter hole is drilled axially along the centerline of the bolt, the hole stopping just short of breaking through the opposite end of the bolt. Extension of the bolt can then be measured from one end using a precision depth gage.

Use of washers and flanges. The use of special deforming washers offers a relatively inexpensive and convenient means of indicating the amount of preload from tightening. When used properly, the washers are said to be capable of determining preload within ±10%. Bolts and nuts are available with resilient wave-shaped flanges (see Fig. 8-26). When the bolts or nuts are tightened, the wavy flanges flatten to indicate tightness by means of feeler gages. However, the use of such washers or flanges do not accurately inspect the amount of torque applied or indicate excessive loading.

Electronic systems. There have been many recent advances in electronic control systems, which are being increasingly used especially for critical applications to ensure more reliable assemblies. Many of these systems use signals from both torque transducers and rotational angle encoders (see Fig. 8-27) to monitor and/or control fastener tightening. Microprocessors are used in many systems to instantaneously monitor the relationship between torque rate and angle of rotation and to stop the motor at the proper moment.

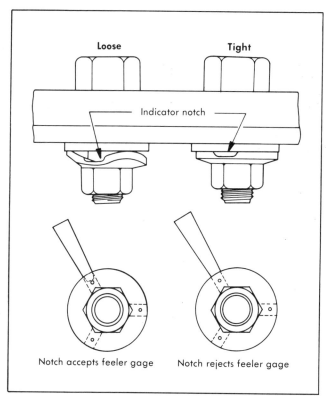

Fig. 8-26 Wavy flange on bolt flattens to indicate tightness. (*Russell, Burdsall & Ward Corp.*)

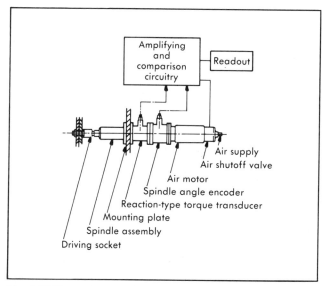

Fig. 8-27 Electronic control system monitors signals from both a torque transducer and a rotational angle encoder.

Ultrasonic monitoring. With this system, a single, high-frequency sound wave is emitted from a transducer held against one end of a bolt. The sound wave traverses the length of the bolt and is reflected back to the transducer. The change in time from emission to return indicates an increase in bolt length resulting from tightening. A microprocessor is used to indicate the amount of elongation or the stress level in the threads.

Fastener Loosening and Failure

Major causes of failure of threaded fasteners include improper tightening (clamp load), mismatch of the bolt-nut combination (causing thread stripping), hydrogen embrittlement, and stress corrosion. Loosening is not often a problem under static loading conditions, but can be a critical factor with cyclic loading. The best protection against loosening and failure is selecting an optimum fastener and applying the proper preload.

Loosening of threaded fasteners is generally caused by transverse vibration or possibly by axial vibration, or both. Transverse vibration causes slippage between mating surfaces, thus reducing the friction created by the preload, and results in shear loading. Axial vibration causes a radial sliding motion between the thread flanks, reducing friction. Loosening can sometimes be minimized or eliminated by using fasteners that are designed to resist loosening, including various types of nuts, bolts, screws, and flanged products, all discussed later in this chapter.

Fastener Marking

Manufacturers marks are required on fasteners by many specifications. Any bolt or screw 5 mm (0.2″) or larger that does not carry an appropriate engineering capability mark in conformance with various standards may have questionable strength and performance.

BOLTS AND STUDS

Bolts are externally threaded fasteners generally assembled with nuts (refer to Fig. 8-19, view *a*). While most bolts are headed, some are not. The means of distinguishing between bolts and screws are discussed in ANSI Standard B18.2.1, "Square and Hexagonal Bolts and Screws, Inch Series," and in the introduction to this section on threaded fasteners. Studs are cylindrical rods threaded on one or both ends or throughout their lengths (refer to Fig. 8-19, view *c*).

Bolts are available in a wide variety of types and sizes, a few of which are shown in Fig. 8-28. Some of the head styles and drives (refer to Fig. 8-20) are the same as used for screws, discussed later in this chapter, but most bolts have round, square, or hexagonal heads.

Hex-Head Bolts

Bolts with hexagonal heads (commonly called hex heads, the term that will be used throughout this section) are the most commonly used. These heads have a flat or indented top surface, six flat sides, and a flat bearing surface. The flat sides facilitate tightening the bolts with wrenches. Hex heads are often used on high-strength bolts and are easier to tighten than bolts with square heads. They are generally available in standard strength grades as specified by ASTM, SAE, and other organizations and to special strength requirements for specific applications.

General data and dimensional specifications for hex-head bolts in the inch series are presented in ANSI Standard B18.2.1. Similar information for metric size bolts is presented in the

BOLTS AND STUDS

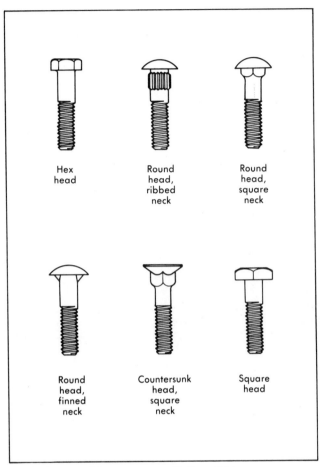

Hex head

Round head, ribbed neck

Round head, square neck

Round head, finned neck

Countersunk head, square neck

Square head

Fig. 8-28 A few of the many types of bolts available.

following ANSI Standards: B18.2.3.5M for hex-head, B18.2.3.6M for heavy hex-head, and B18.2.3.7M for heavy hex-head, structural bolts. Structural bolts are also specified in ASTM Standards A 325 and A 490.

Round-Head Bolts

Round-head bolts have thin circular heads with rounded or flat top surfaces and flat bearing surfaces. When provided with an underhead configuration that locks into the joint material, round-head bolts resist rotation and are tightened by turning their mating nuts. Included in this classification, even though the configurations differ, are countersunk and T-head bolts.

Variations of round-head bolts include those with square, ribbed, or finned necks on the shanks below the heads to prevent the fasteners from rotating in their holes. Specifications for round-head and countersunk bolts are included in ANSI Standard B18.5. Data for metric sized, round-head, square-neck bolts are presented in ANSI/ASME Standard B18.5.2.2M, and short, square-neck bolts are covered in Standard B18.5.2.1M.

Round-head, square-neck bolts. These bolts have integral, square necks on the shanks under their heads. They are also available with short square necks for use in sheet metal. Step bolts are round-head, square-neck bolts with extra large head diameters and thin heads. They are used in fastening step treads, flooring, and similar assemblies.

Round-head, ribbed-neck bolts. These bolts, formerly designated ribbed-head carriage bolts, have ribbed, serrated, or splined necks on the shanks under their heads. These ribs, serrations, or splines engage the ID of the bolthole to provide rotation resistance.

Round-head, finned-neck bolts. These bolts have two integral, diametrically opposed fins at the junction of their heads and shanks.

Countersunk bolts. These bolts have circular heads, flat top surfaces, and conical bearing surfaces with an included angle of about 80°. They are available with or without driving slots in their heads. Bolts without driving slots in their heads require some other feature for wrenching. Countersunk bolts having a 114° included angle and square necks on the shanks under their heads were formerly designated countersunk carriage bolts. Flat, countersunk head, elevator bolts have large-diameter circular heads with flat top surfaces, shallow conical bearing surfaces, and integral square necks under their heads. They provide large bearing areas with nearly flush surfaces and are used extensively for softer metals.

T-head bolts. These bolts have rectangular heads with rounded top surfaces and flat bearing surfaces.

Square-Head Bolts

These bolts have square-shaped, external wrenching heads. Dimensional specifications are presented in ANSI Standard B18.2.1, and they are available in two strength grades. Lag bolts, sometimes called lag screws, usually have square or hex heads, gimlet or cone points, and thin, sharp, coarse-pitch threads. They produce mating threads in wood or other resilient materials and are used in masonry with expanding anchors.

Battery bolts have square heads and are generally stainless steel or lead or tin coated for clamping onto battery terminals. Fitting-up bolts have square heads and coarse-pitch, 60° stub threads. They are used for the preliminary assembly of structural steel components. T-bolts are square-head bolts used in the T-slots of machine tools.

Bent Bolts

Bent bolts are cylindrical rods having one end threaded and the other end bent to various configurations. These include eyebolts, hook bolts, and J-bolts. Other bent bolts, such as U-bolts, have both ends threaded. The ends of bent bolts are usually square (as sheared).

Hook bolts. These bolts have their unthreaded ends bent to form acute or right angle, round (semicircular), square (two right-angle bends), or J-shaped hooks. The bent portions of these bolts are available flattened.

U-bolts. These bolts, having threads at both ends, are available with round bends (bent at the middle to a semicircular shape) or square bends (bent at the middle to form two right angles).

Eyebolts. These bolts have their forged ends in the form of closed anchor rings. Specifications for eyebolts made from carbon steel are presented in ASTM Standard A 489. These high-strength fasteners are used extensively as mountings for rigging and moving heavy machinery.

Forged eyebolts have flattened and pierced rings, with or without collars or shoulders under their rings. These forgings are called aircraft, bossed, collared, shouldered, or drop bolts. Collars or shoulders on such bolts limit the distance that the bolts can be inserted into mating parts. Specifications for forged eyebolts are presented in ANSI Standard B18.15.

Other Bolt Types

There are many other types of bolts available for various applications. Only a few of the more common types are discussed in this section.

Flanged washer-head bolts. These bolts are made with circular underhead collars to provide increased bearing areas and to protect material finishes. The integral collars often eliminate the need for separate washers.

Machine bolts. These are general-purpose fasteners, generally supplied with nuts, having cylindrical bodies below various heads (hex, square, or round). Joint bolts are machine bolts having conical points.

Internal wrenching fasteners. These fasteners, normally screws rather than bolts, have large cylindrical heads, and flat top and bearing surfaces. Recessed hexagonal sockets are common for driving. High-strength and 12-point heads are used for high-temperature applications. Fasteners of this type with heads having tapered sides are used by the aircraft industry.

Plow bolts. These bolts have countersunk heads, coarse threads, and means provided in their heads or shanks to prevent rotation. Methods of preventing rotation include square necks under the heads, triangular or rectangular keys in the heads, or square, pyramidal-shaped heads. Dimensional specifications for plow bolts are presented in ANSI Standard B18.9.

Stove bolts. These bolts, formerly a commercial standard, are now supplied as equivalent size machine screws with nuts, discussed later in this chapter.

Stripper bolts. These bolts, used extensively in the tool and die industry, are now called shoulder capscrews, discussed later in this chapter.

Track bolts. These bolts, originally designed for use with square nuts in joining railroad track rails, have circular heads with oval or mushroom-shaped tops and oval or elliptical-shaped necks below their heads to prevent rotation. Dimensional specifications for track bolts and nuts are presented in ANSI/ASME Standard B18.10.

Expanding bolts. Fasteners that expand radially when axial loads are applied are available in various designs. One expanding-type headed bolt is described later in this chapter under the subject "Special-Purpose Fasteners."

Self-locking bolts. Free-spinning, prevailing-torque, and chemical locking methods of providing self-locking action for bolts are discussed later in this chapter under the subject "Self-Locking Threaded Fasteners."

Studs

Studs are unheaded, externally threaded fasteners. They are available with threads on one or both ends or continuously threaded. Studs with collars and threaded on one or both ends are also available (see Fig. 8-29). Heat-treated and/or plated studs are available to suit specific requirements. They are also made with chamfered or dog-point ends.

An advantage of studs for some applications, such as the assembly of large and heavy components, is that they can serve as pilots to facilitate mating of the components. These fasteners also facilitate the automatic assembly of various components. For many applications, studs provide fixed external threads and nuts are the only components that have to be assembled.

Double-end studs. These studs are made with conventional, free-running threads at both ends or with a conventional thread at one end and an interference-fit thread at the other end; an unthreaded body is between the ends. Clamping-type studs with

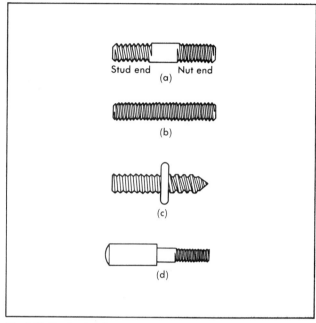

Fig. 8-29 Studs of various types: (a) double-end stud of interference-thread type, (b) continuous-thread stud, (c) collared stud with machine screw thread on left end and thread for plastics on right end, and (d) shouldered stud. (*Tri-West Products Inc.*)

free-running threads at both ends are sometimes called stud bolts or bolt studs. They are used to clamp two components together with nuts on both ends of the studs.

Studs with free-running threads on one end and interference-fit threads on the other end are sometimes called tap-end studs. The end with the free-running thread is known as the nut end and the other is the stud end. A finer pitch thread is commonly used on the stud end. Variations in the amount of interference fit for specific applications are obtained by changing the pitch diameter of the thread on the stud end.

Double-end studs are available with coarse, fine, or spaced threads. They are also made with special locking threads, discussed later in this chapter under the subject "Self-Locking Threaded Fasteners." Double-end locking studs are also available with external serrations that broach soft parent material or that are installed in prebroached holes to minimize the possibility of stud rotation. Stud bodies between the threaded ends are supplied unfinished or finished (full or undersize), depending on requirements.

Continuous-thread studs. These studs, threaded their entire lengths with conventional, free-running threads for the assembly of nuts on both ends, are sometimes called bolt studs or threaded rods. Dimensional specifications for continuous-thread studs are presented in ANSI Standard B16.5.

Collared studs. These studs are available with threads on only one end and a collar near the opposite end, or with a collar between threads at both ends. The collars are larger in diameter than the threads. Studs with collars near one end or the centers of the studs and threads at the opposite end are frequently used to carry gears, pulleys, levers, or other components and are often provided with holes for cotter pins or grooves for retaining rings or washers. Shoulder screws are similar to collared studs except that all or part of their unthreaded portions are of a uniform diameter larger than the threads.

NUTS

Some studs with collars near their centers have machine screw threads at one end and tapping screw threads at the other end, or machine screw threads at both ends. Others have machine screw threads at one end and threads for plastics at the opposite ends, facilitating the assembly of plastics to metal.

Other studs. Welded studs are discussed in a subsequent section of this chapter under the subject "Captive Threaded Fasteners." Spring-clip stud receivers are described in the following section, "Special-Purpose Fasteners." Hangar bolts are stud-type rods having a lag-bolt or wood screw thread and gimlet point at one end and a machine screw thread at the other.

NUTS

Nuts are internally threaded fasteners that fit on bolts, studs, screws, or other externally threaded fasteners for mechanically joining parts. They also serve for adjusting, transmitting motion, or transmitting power in some applications, but generally require special thread forms. Nuts are available in a wide range of standard and special types (see Fig. 8-30), sizes, materials, and strengths to suit specific requirements.

Hex and square nuts, sometimes referred to as full nuts, are the most common. Hex nuts are used for most general-purpose applications. Square machine screw nuts are usually limited to light-duty and special assemblies. Regular and heavy square nuts are often used for bolted flange connections.

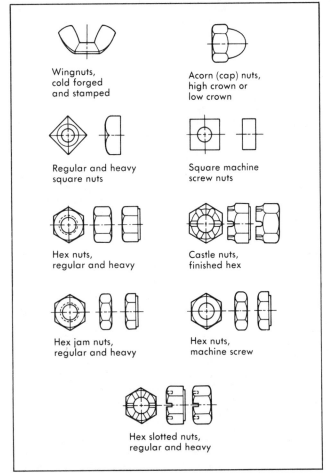

Fig. 8-30 Various types of nuts. (*Tri-West Products Inc.*)

Wingnuts, cold forged and stamped

Acorn (cap) nuts, high crown or low crown

Regular and heavy square nuts

Square machine screw nuts

Hex nuts, regular and heavy

Castle nuts, finished hex

Hex jam nuts, regular and heavy

Hex nuts, machine screw

Hex slotted nuts, regular and heavy

Nuts are available in regular and heavy types. Regular nuts are used for average load conditions, and heavy nuts, generally being thicker and having heavier walls, are generally used for high loading conditions. Nuts in sizes of 5/8" or smaller are generally double chamfered. Larger nuts may be double chamfered or have a washer-face bearing surface and chamfered top. Threaded holes in the nuts are generally countersunk on the bearing surfaces, with included angles of 90-120°.

Materials for Nuts

Carbon steels are the most common metals for nuts. They are also available made from alloy steels, corrosion-resistant steels, aluminum alloys, brass, bronze, and plastics. Material selection depends on application requirements and service conditions. Some nuts are heat treated, but most are not. Nut strength is a combination of material strength, thread type, and nut thickness. Various platings and coatings are also available. For heavy coatings, overtapping, as specified in ASTM Standard A 563, may be applicable.

Minimizing Loosening

Self-loosening of assemblies using threaded fasteners can be minimized in several ways. Mechanical means include the use of jam, castle, and slotted nuts, discussed in this section. Other methods include using self-locking nuts of the free-spinning, captive lockwasher, prevailing-torque, and chemical locking types, discussed subsequently in this chapter under the subject "Self-Locking Threaded Fasteners."

Hex Nuts

Hex nuts have hexagonal bases, with or without washer faces, and six flat sides that serve as wrenching surfaces. They are available in various dimensional series, including heavy and regular. The nuts are also made in different thicknesses, such as standard, jam (thin), and thick. Castle and slotted types are also available.

Dimensional specifications for hex nuts in the inch series, including thick, heavy, jam, slotted, and castle types, are presented in ANSI Standard B18.2.2. The data for metric Style 1 hex nuts is included in ANSI Standard B18.2.4.1M and for Style 2 in ANSI Standard B18.2.4.2M. Style 2 nuts are about 10% thicker than Style 1 nuts. Metric heavy hex nuts are the subject of ANSI Standard B18.2.4.6M.

Flanged nuts. These nuts have an integral flange to provide increased bearing areas to distribute the loads. The top surface of the flange is conical or slightly rounded (convex). Dimensional specifications for metric hex flange nuts are presented in ANSI Standard B18.2.4.4M. Inch nuts are covered in IFI Standard 107.

Hex jam nuts. These are thin nuts generally used on shear joints or to obtain locking action. For some applications, after a jam nut has been seated, the full nut is tightened to the required preload while the jam nut is held stationary. This procedure provides good locking, but the joint may not be well preloaded. It may be preferable to load the joint with the full nut and then jam the thin nut on top of the assembly. Specifications for metric hex jam nuts are presented in ANSI Standard B18.2.4.5M.

Slotted nuts. These nuts have slots for cotter pins or wires to lock the nuts in place when used with mating fasteners having holes in their shanks. Slotted nuts, formerly known as castellated nuts, have cylindrical portions at their slotted ends equal in length to the slot depths and slightly smaller in diameter than the hexagon widths.

Slotted nuts have opposed slots through the centers of their flats, with the slots on the ends opposite the bearing surfaces and perpendicular to the axes of the nuts. Microslotted nuts are the same, but have more slots than standard slotted nuts. Tri-slotted nuts have three large slots. Specifications for metric slotted hex nuts are included in ANSI Standard B18.2.4.3M.

Prevailing-torque nuts. These nuts, mentioned previously in this section, are discussed in detail in a subsequent section of this chapter under the subject "Self-Locking Threaded Fasteners." Dimensional specifications for prevailing-torque type, steel hex locknuts are presented in IFI Standard 100; flange locknuts are covered in IFI Standard 107. Metric nut dimensions are included in ANSI Standard B18.16.3M, and performance specifications are covered in B18.16.1M.

Square Nuts

Square nuts have square bases, generally without washer faces, and four flat sides for wrenching purposes. They are available in regular and heavy series with varying proportions. General data and dimensional specifications for square nuts in the inch series are presented in ANSI Standard B18.8.2.

Machine Screw Nuts

Machine screw nuts are hex or square nuts of proportions suitable for use with machine screws. They are almost always used for light-duty applications, such as for joining sheet metal assemblies, where strength requirements are minimal. Specifications for machine screw nuts are included in ANSI Standard B18.6.3.

Wingnuts

Wingnuts, sometimes called thumb nuts, have so-called "wings," generally two per nut, designed for manual tightening without wrenches or drivers. Four types of wingnuts in the inch series are specified in ANSI Standard B18.17. Type A is cold formed or forged, Type B is hot forged, Type C is die cast, and Type D is stamped from sheet metal. Types C and D have three wing styles with different wing heights. Types A, B, and D are generally made from carbon steel, corrosion-resistant steel, or brass. Type C wingnuts are cast from a zinc alloy.

Single-Thread Nuts

Single-thread nuts, sometimes called spring nuts, are formed by stamping a thread-engaging impression (arched prongs) in a flat piece of metal (see Fig. 8-31). These nuts are generally made from high-carbon spring steel (SAE 1050-1064), but are also available in corrosion-resistant steel, beryllium copper, and other metals.

Single-thread nuts are made in many shapes and styles, but all depend on spring action for their holding power and resistance to vibration. Flat, circular, and round types are common, and some have spanner holes for driving. They are also available in J and U-types that snap over the edges of panels or into hole locations, holding themselves in place for blind assemblies. Angle nuts having a single thread impression on each leg are used to join perpendicular components.

As an alternative to full nuts, single-thread nuts permit faster assembly and reduced weight with lower costs. Other advantages include minimum torque requirements, easy disassembly, and elimination of the need for lockwashers. Single-thread nuts

are specifically limited to light-duty applications, but are available with other type threads for some heavier duty applications.

Stamped Nuts

Stamped nuts are hex fasteners stamped from spring steel or other metals, with prongs formed to engage mating threads. They are similar to single-thread nuts in that they rely on spring action for clamping and resistance to loosening, but they have more prongs to engage the threads on the mating fastener. Applications include replacements for full nuts in low-stress uses and as retaining nuts against full nuts (see Fig. 8-32). Stamped nuts are made with integral washers, in closed top or bottom styles, and as wingnuts.

Captive Nuts

Captive (self-retained) nuts are often used on thin materials and for blind locations. They include plate or anchor nuts, caged nuts, clinch and self-clinching nuts, and self-piercing nuts, all discussed in a subsequent section of this chapter under the subject "Captive (Self-Retained) Threaded Fasteners."

Other Types of Nuts

There are many other types of nuts available, most designed for the requirements of specific applications. A few of the more common types are described in this section.

Crown nuts. These nuts, also called acorn or cap nuts, are hex fasteners having an acorn-shaped top and a blind threaded hole. They are available with high or low crowns. Their closed tops protect the projecting ends of mating, externally threaded fasteners and provide a pleasing appearance. They are commonly used when the projecting ends of externally threaded fasteners may be hazardous, as in toys.

Track-bolt nuts. These square nuts were originally designed for use with track bolts in joining railroad track rails. They are available with 45 or 60° chamfers. Dimensional specifications

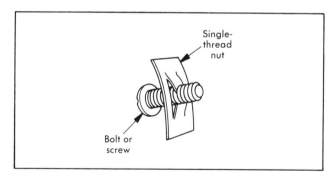

Fig. 8-31 Single-thread nut.

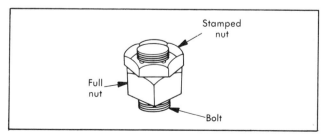

Fig. 8-32 Stamped nut applied and tightened after full nut is in place.

CHAPTER 8

NUTS

for track-bolt nuts are presented in ANSI Standard B18.10.

Coupling and conduit nuts. Coupling nuts, generally thin and round, are used to connect pipes or tubes. They are generally stamped and are available in square, hexagonal, or octagonal shapes. Conduit nuts are used to connect electrical pipe or fittings to boxes. Most conduit nuts are round and have ears that provide wrenching surfaces, locking action, and electrical grounding. These nuts normally have one to two threads that are either tapped or formed. Most conduit nuts are made from steel, but they are also available as zinc die castings.

Panel nuts. These thin nuts, normally hexagonal, are similar to conduit nuts but are used to assemble externally threaded fasteners to panels. They typically have fine or extrafine threads and are available made from steel, brass, or zinc alloy.

T-nuts. These square nuts having T-shapes are designed to fit into the T-slots on machine tools.

Barrel and sleeve nuts. These nuts are made in two types. Type 1 is a blind, internally threaded fastener having an external shape like a machine screw (see Fig. 8-33). Type 2 is a cylindrical nut having its internal thread at a right angle to the axis of the cylinder. Sleeve nuts are essentially the same as Type 1 barrel nuts except that their threads extend throughout their entire lengths.

Aircraft nuts. These nuts, usually of high strength and light weight, conform to material and dimensional standards promulgated by the aerospace industry and other organizations.

Round nuts. These nuts have plain cylindrical peripheries with no provisions for wrenching onto mating threads. They are usually applied by hand tightening. Round nuts having part(s) of their cylindrical peripheries knurled to facilitate hand tightening are called knurled nuts.

Spline nuts. These internally threaded cylindrical fasteners have external splines or serrations that hold them in place when the nuts are forced into holes that are slightly smaller in diameter. They are also cast in place in plastics and low-strength, die cast alloys.

Internal wrenching nuts. These cylindrical nuts have sockets in their ends for wrenching (see Fig. 8-34).

Captive nuts. Plate, anchor, and weld nuts; push and snap-in nuts; clinched and self-clinching (press) nuts; and self-piercing nuts are discussed later in this section under the subject "Captive (Self-Retained) Threaded Fasteners."

Self-locking nuts. Nut-washer assemblies, nuts with elements made of plastics, locknuts, and other free-spinning and prevailing-torque fasteners are discussed subsequently under the subject "Self-Locking Threaded Fasteners."

SCREWS

Screws are externally threaded fasteners capable of being inserted into holes in assembled parts, of mating with preformed internal threads, or of cutting or forming their own threads. They are generally tightened or released by rotating the screwheads. Because of their basic design, it is possible to use some screws, which are sometimes called bolts, in combination with nuts. Criteria for distinguishing between such screws and bolts are delineated in ANSI Standard B18.2.1, "Square and Hexagonal Bolts and Screws, Inch Series." ISO terminology identifies screws as having threads extending to their heads, with bolts having unthreaded portions under their heads.

Screws are available in a wide variety of types and sizes to suit specific requirements for different applications. Major types discussed in this section include machine screws, capscrews, setscrews, sems (screw and washer assemblies), and tapping screws. Other types of screws not discussed in this section include lag, miniature, wood, and thumb or wing designs. Self-locking screws and other fasteners of the free-spinning, prevailing-torque, and chemical locking types are discussed in a succeeding section of this chapter.

Head Styles

Screws are available with many different head styles and drives, some of which are illustrated earlier in this chapter (refer to Fig. 8-20). Selection depends primarily on the joint material, type of assembly equipment to be used, joint loading, and appearance requirements. Means provided integral with the heads for driving the screws include slots, recesses, and wrenching surfaces.

Round heads. These commonly used heads have flat bearing surfaces and spherical-sector top surfaces, with slots or recesses for driving.

Flat heads. These heads have flat top surfaces and conical bearing surfaces for flush mounting with work surfaces when the mounting holes are countersunk. Screws are made with the conical bearing surfaces at various angles. Included angles of 82 and 100° are most common for inch series screws, but 90° is standard for metric series screws. Heads with a 100° included angle are thinner and larger in diameter than those with an 82° angle and are generally preferred for use with soft metals or nonmetallic materials. There is some usage of flat heads that have an included angle of 130° for aircraft composite structures. Flathead screws are available with slots or recesses for driving, and they should seat flush in the mounting holes. Hole clearance must be provided to allow for head eccentricity.

Flat trim heads. These heads have a smaller diameter and shorter height than standard flathead screws. Screws with these heads are sometimes called "shear head" fasteners because they are often used where shear is the principle concern; however, tensile strength is poor. Recessed drives are generally used for screws with this type of head.

Flat undercut heads. These heads are essentially the same as 82° flat heads except that they are undercut to make them about one-third thinner, thus slightly increasing the thread length.

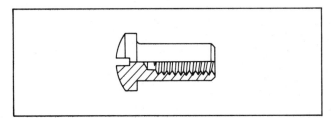

Fig. 8-33 Type 1 barrel nut with a fillister head.

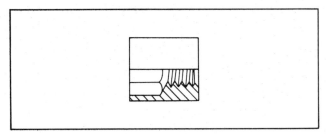

Fig. 8-34 Internal wrenching nut.

They are commonly used for joining thin materials and are generally the standard for short-length screws.

Fillister heads. These heads have rounded top surfaces, cylindrical side surfaces, flat bearing surfaces, and small diameters. High side surfaces and deep slots or recesses permit applying high torque loads. They are commonly used in counterbored holes. Flat fillister heads are similar to fillister heads except that their top surfaces are flat, permitting driving flush with work surfaces in counterbored holes.

Pan heads. These heads have flat bearing surfaces and, for slotted designs, flat top surfaces that are rounded into cylindrical side surfaces. This design provides an optimum combination of head thickness and bearing surface, as well as good driving characteristics, and is therefore often the preferred design. Recessed pan heads, having semielliptical top surfaces rounded into the cylindrical side surfaces, provide thicker heads to accommodate recessed drives.

Binding heads. These heads have rounded top surfaces, tapered side surfaces, and flat bearing surfaces that are generally undercut adjacent to the threaded shanks. The undercut permits binding wire without fraying and tends to captivate solid or stranded wires when tightened. However, undercuts are only provided at the option of the screw manufacturer unless specifically ordered.

Button and truss heads. Button heads have low, rounded top surfaces and large, flat bearing surfaces. Truss heads, sometimes called oven heads or stove heads, are similar to button heads except that their heads are larger in diameter for a given screw size. The thin truss heads are used extensively for covering large holes in sheet metal, to provide extra holding power, or for soft materials.

Washer heads. These heads, sometimes called flanged heads, have circular collars that provide large, flat surfaces for increased bearing areas and to protect material finishes during assembly. This design eliminates the need for separate assembly of washers. Various head styles, such as round or hex heads, are provided on top of the collars. Corrugated patterns are sometimes formed on the bearing surfaces to prevent rotation, but there are no industry standards for such heads.

Hex heads. These heads have flat or indented top surfaces, six flat sides, and flat bearing surfaces. The flat sides facilitate driving with wrenches. Some hex heads have their flat sides cross drilled to accept safety wires or pins.

Oval heads. These heads have rounded top surfaces and conical bearing surfaces, with the included angle between the conical surfaces generally being 82° for inch series screws and 90° for metric series. The oval tops are sometimes desirable for their neat appearance.

Oval undercut heads. These heads are essentially the same as standard oval heads except that they are undercut, thus making them about one-third thinner and increasing their thread lengths slightly. They are often used for short-length screws.

Oval trim heads. These heads are of smaller diameter and shorter height than standard oval heads and controlled radii at the junctions of their top and bearing surfaces. Recessed drives are generally used for screws with this type of head.

Ball heads. These heads are approximately spherical in shape. Special screws with such heads are frequently used for ball-and-socket swivel applications.

Headless. Special screws of this type have no heads and are provided with slots, recesses, or sockets in one end.

Square heads. These heads have flat top surfaces, four flat sides, and flat bearing surfaces. When used on setscrews, which are discussed later in this section, these heads have rounded top surfaces and may be tapered or radiused into their bodies under the heads.

Socket heads. These heads have flat, chamfered top surfaces; smooth or knurled cylindrical side surfaces; and flat bearing surfaces. A hexagonal or splined (sometimes called fluted) recessed drive socket is formed in the center of the top surface. These heads are also available in flat and button head styles.

T-heads. These heads are oblong shaped and have rounded top surfaces, flat sides, and flat bearing surfaces. The heads are generally not used to drive the screws.

Twelve-point heads. These heads, sometimes called double-hex heads, have flat or indented top surfaces; 24 short, flat sides; circular collars at the bottoms of their heads; and flat bearing surfaces. Screws with these heads are used extensively for fastening aircraft components because they ensure good wrench engagement and permit high tightening forces.

Screw Points

Various configurations are used on the ends of screw shanks to suit specific requirements. The points used on setscrews and tapping screws are discussed subsequently in this section.

Chamfered points. Truncated conical points facilitate the insertion of screws into holes at assembly. The ends of chamfered points are flat and perpendicular to the axes of the screws, and the included angles of the chamfers vary from 45 to 90°. When cold formed, these points are called header points. The minimum diameter of the point is generally equal to or slightly less than the minor diameter of the screw thread. Chamfered points are mandatory for capscrews.

Plain points. The screw ends are cut or sheared flat, perpendicular to the screw axes, but may be slightly concave when the threads are rolled.

Cone and needle points. Sharp conical points are used for perforating or aligning requirements. Needle points are longer cone points used for piercing operations.

Pinch points. These short, sharp, conical points generally have an included angle of 45°, but the included angle can vary from 30 to 90°. They are used on small tapping screws. The points can be rolled when threading.

Oval points. Screws with oval points have radiused ends.

Spherical points. These are oval points in which the point radii are equal to half the shank diameters.

Pilot points. These cylindrical points have diameters smaller than the shank diameters of the screws. They facilitate the alignment and starting of screws and other fasteners and are commonly called dog points, semidog points, or cone points.

Gimlet points. These are threaded conical points generally having an included angle of 40-50°. They are used on some thread-forming and wood screws.

Cup points. These points are discussed subsequently in this section under the subject "Setscrews."

Machine Screws

Machine screws are usually inserted into tapped holes, but are sometimes used with nuts. They are generally supplied with plain (as sheared) points, but for some special applications they are made with various types of points. Machine screws have slotted, recessed, or wrenching heads in a variety of styles and are usually made from steel, stainless steel, brass, or aluminum. Many machine screws are made from unhardened materials, but hardened screws are available. Grade 5 screws have a minimum tensile strength of 120 ksi (827 MPa) and Grade 8

SCREWS

screws, 150 ksi (1034) MPa). They have replaced the formerly commercial standard stove bolts.

Complete general and dimensional data for slotted and recessed-head machine screws and machine screw nuts is presented in ANSI Standard B18.6.3. Specifications for metric machine screws are included in IFI Standard 513, which will be withdrawn when the planned ANSI Standard B18.6.7M is published.

Capscrews

Capscrews are manufactured to close dimensional tolerances and are designed for applications requiring high tensile strengths. Heat-treated, alloy steel capscrews have tensile strengths to 180 ksi (1240 MPa). Metric socket-head capscrews have tensile strengths varying from 830 to 1220 MPa. They are available in standard sizes from 1/4 to 3" diam.

The shanks of capscrews are generally not fully threaded to their heads, but some are, and the ends are as specified in ANSI Standard B18.2.1. They are made with hex, socket, or fillister slotted heads (see Fig. 8-35). Low-head capscrews are available for applications having head clearance problems. Most capscrews are made from steels, stainless steels, brasses, bronzes, and aluminum alloys. Standard nomenclature for hex-head capscrews is illustrated in Fig. 8-36.

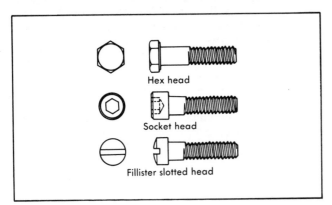

Fig. 8-35 Capscrews with various heads.

Shoulder capscrews have cylindrical shoulders (larger in diameter than the threads, but smaller in diameter than the heads) under their heads to serve as bearings or spacers and necked portions between the threads and the shoulders. These shoulder screws, formerly called stripper bolts, are used extensively in the tool and die industry.

General data and dimensional specifications for hex-head capscrews in the inch series are presented in ANSI Standard B18.2.1. Hex-head capscrews in the metric series are specified in ANSI Standard B18.2.3.1M. Dimensional differences of these metric capscrews from those in ISO Standard 4014 are very few and relatively minor and do not affect their functional interchangeability. Formed, hex-head capscrews in the metric series, which are cold formed with fully upset (untrimmed) heads, are covered in ANSI Standard B18.2.3.2M, conforming essentially with ISO Standard 4015. Heavy, hex-head capscrews in the metric series are the subject of ANSI Standard B18.2.3.3M.

Dimensional data for socket-head and shoulder capscrews in the inch series is presented in ANSI/ASME Standard B18.3. Metric series, socket-head capscrews are the subject of ANSI Standard B18.3.1M. Other standards for socket-head capscrews include ANSI B18.3.4M for buttonhead screws and ANSI/ASME Standard B18.3.5M for flat countersunk-head screws.

Data and dimensions for slotted-head capscrews in the inch series are presented in ANSI Standard B18.6.2. Metric, socket-head shoulder screws are the subject of ANSI Standard B18.3.3M. Hex-head, flanged (washer) capscrews in the metric series are specified in ANSI Standard B18.2.3.4M and ANSI/ASME Standard B18.2.3.9M.

Setscrews

Setscrews (see Fig. 8-37) are hardened fasteners generally used to hold pulleys, gears, and other components on shafts. Hardness of the shaft is an important consideration in selecting a proper setscrew. They are available in various styles, with square-head, headless-slotted, hex-socket, and splined (fluted) socket styles being the most common. Holding power is provided by compressive forces, with some setscrews providing additional resistance to rotation by penetration of their points into the shaft material.

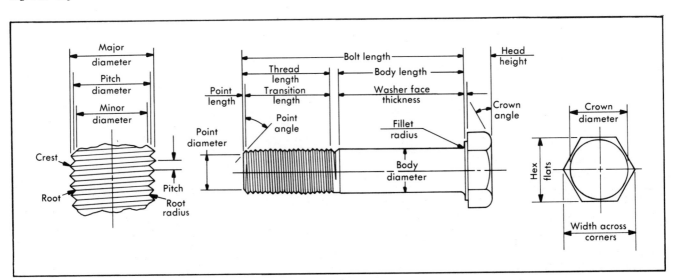

Fig. 8-36 Standard nomenclature for hex-head capscrews. (*Tri-West Products Inc.*)

Drive types. The drive configuration determines how much torque can be transmitted for clamping. For example, less torque can be transmitted through slotted-head setscrews than can be transmitted through hex or splined socket-head setscrews, resulting in less holding power. The torque that can be applied to square-head setscrews is about twice that of socket-recess setscrews.

Point styles. Setscrews are available with various point styles (see Fig. 8-37) to suit specific requirements. Cup and cone points are used without spotting holes in the shafts and penetrate deeper than oval or flatpoint setscrews.

Flat points. These are designed for holding with minimum penetration. They are used for frequent relocation of parts on shafts, especially on hardened steel shafts, with minimum deformation to the shaft surfaces. Flats are sometimes ground on the shafts for better contact. Flatpoint setscrews are also desirable where the walls of the assembly components are thin or as a backing for soft metal plugs.

Cup points. These are the most commonly used points on setscrews. They provide good holding power with slight penetration. Cup-point setscrews are used on shafts having hardnesses to within R_C 10-15 points of the screw hardnesses and where digging-in of the points is not undesirable. They are available with knurled cups, knurled outer cones, hexagonal recesses, and other designs to provide more secure self-locking.

Oval points. Oval-point setscrews are used where frequent adjustments are required or where excessive indentation of the shafts or mating parts is undesirable. They are also used where the points contact angular surfaces. Sometimes, spots or grooves of oval section are provided on the assembly components for better seating.

Cone points. Setscrews with this type of point are used for permanent locations of components. Spotting holes are frequently provided on the components, especially hardened shafts, to accommodate the points, with the points usually entering the holes to half the point lengths.

Dog points. Setscrews with cylindrical dog points are generally used for the permanent location of components. The flat-end points are spotted in holes or slots having the same diameters as the dog points. Half dog points are the most

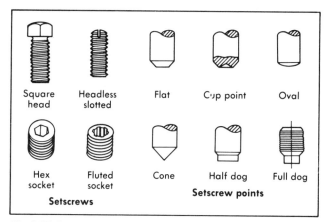

Fig. 8-37 Common types of setscrews and setscrew points.

commonly used; full dog points are for applications requiring longer points.

Standards. General data and dimensional specifications for socket-head setscrews in the inch series are presented in ANSI Standard B18.3. Similar information for square-head and slotted headless setscrews in the inch series is contained in ANSI Standard B18.6.2. Metric, socket-head setscrews are covered in ANSI Standard B18.3.6M. These metric setscrews are functionally interchangeable with those specified in ISO Standards 4026, 4027, 4028, and 4029.

Sems—Screw and Washer Assemblies

Sems is a generic word for a preassembled screw and washer fastener. The washer is placed on the screw blank prior to roll threading and becomes a permanent part of the assembly after roll threading, but is free to rotate. Sems are available in various combinations of head styles and washer types (see Fig. 8-38 and Table 8-4). Washers commonly used include flat (plain), conical, spring, and toothed lockwashers, discussed later in this chapter. Some manufacturers produce sems with as many as four washers per assembly.

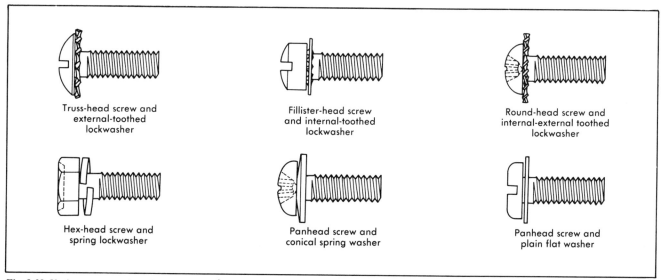

Truss-head screw and external-toothed lockwasher

Fillister-head screw and internal-toothed lockwasher

Round-head screw and internal-external toothed lockwasher

Hex-head screw and spring lockwasher

Panhead screw and conical spring washer

Panhead screw and plain flat washer

Fig. 8-38 Various screw and washer assemblies.[3]

SCREWS

TABLE 8-4
Screw and Washer Assembly Combinations[4]

Screw Head Style	Toothed Lockwasher			Spring Lockwasher	Conical Spring Washer	Plain Washer
	External	Internal	Internal-External			
Fillister		X	X	X	X	X
Flat	X					
Hex	X	X	X	X	X	X
Hex washer	X	X	X	X	X	
Oval	X					
Pan	X	X	X	X	X	X
Round	X	X	X	X	X	X
Truss	X	X	X	X	X	X
Hex socket	X	X	X	X		X

Sems are used extensively in mass production industries, such as automotive and appliance, and are suitable for automatic assembly operations. These fasteners permit more convenient and rapid assembly by eliminating the need for a separate washer assembly operation, ensure the presence of the proper washer in each assembly, and prevent the loss of washers during maintenance.

General data and dimensional specifications for sems in the inch series are presented in ANSI Standard B18.13. Similar information on metric sems is contained in IFI Standard 531.

Tapping Screws

Tapping screws (see Fig. 8-39) cut or form mating threads when driven into holes. Self-drilling, self-piercing, and special tapping screws are also available. They are made with slotted, recessed, or wrenching heads in various head styles and with spaced (coarse) inch or metric threads. Tapping screws are generally used in thin materials, but some can be driven through materials to 1/2" (12.7 mm) thick. Additional information on thread forming and cutting screws for plastics is presented in a subsequent section of this chapter under the subject "Special-Purpose Fasteners."

Advantages of tapping screws include rapid installation because nuts are not needed and access is required from only one side. Mating threads fit the screw threads closely, with no clearances necessary. Underhead serrations or nibs on some screws increase locking action and minimize thread stripout.

Thread-forming screws. When these screws are driven, material adjacent to the holes is displaced and flows around the screw threads. Applications are typically in materials where large internal stresses are permissible or desirable to increase resistance to loosening. There are five types: AB, B, BP, A, and C (see Fig. 8-40), as well as high-performance, thread-rolling screws, and special thread-forming screws for plastics.

Type AB. These tapping screws have spaced threads and gimlet points and are generally used in thin metals, resin-impregnated plywood, asbestos compositions, and soft woods.

Type B. These tapping screws have spaced threads and blunt points with incomplete entering threads. They are used in thin to medium-thickness metals, nonferrous castings, and some plastics, 0.050-0.200" (1.27-5.08 mm) thick.

Type BP. These tapping screws have spaced threads the same as Type B, but have conical points extending beyond the incomplete entering threads. They are used in assemblies where

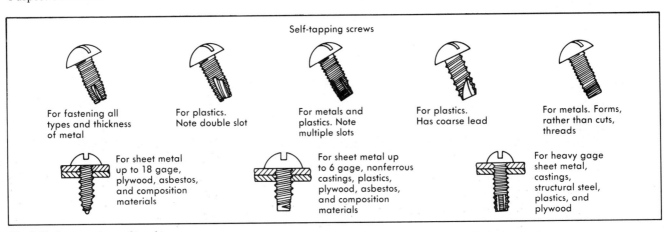

Fig. 8-39 Common types of tapping screws.

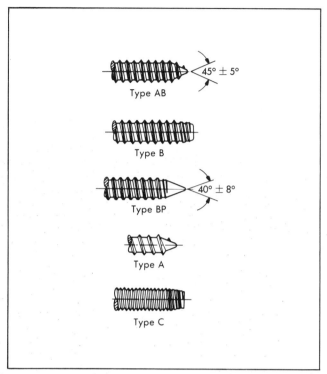

Fig. 8-40 Types of thread-forming tapping screws. (*Southern Screw*)

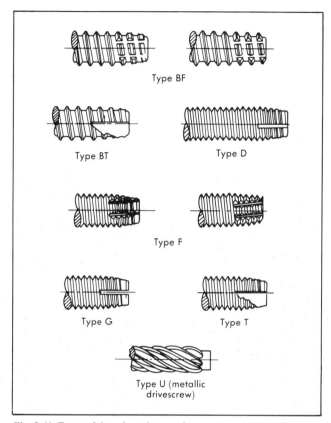

Fig. 8-41 Types of thread-cutting tapping screws and a metallic drivescrew. (*Southern Screw*)

holes are misaligned and for piercing fabrics to tap thin metals, nonferrous castings, and some plastics.

Type A. These tapping screws have coarse-spaced threads and gimlet points. They are not recommended for new product designs and are being supplanted by Type AB screws.

Type C. These tapping screws have threads of machine screw diameter-pitch combinations, blunt points, and tapered, incomplete entering threads. They are used where machine screw threads are preferred to the spaced threads on other thread-forming screws. However, their use is declining, primarily because of the high driving torques required, and they are not recommended for new product designs.

High-performance, thread-rolling screws. Tapping screws of various designs having performance capabilities beyond those normally expected of other standard thread-forming screws are available for roll forming the threads. Tightening requirements are generally low, depending on hole size, material thickness, and other factors, and they can be used in thicker materials. General data and dimensional specifications for these types of screws in the inch series are presented in IFI Standard 112.

Screws for plastics. There are several designs of thread-forming screws for plastics. One, Type BHL, has dual-lead, spaced threads consisting of alternate high and low thread profiles. These screws are suitable for forming threads in softer plastics and are available with cutter slots for cutting threads in harder plastics.

Thread-cutting screws. These screws have cutting edges and chip cavities that create mating threads by removing material from the assembly component. They are used in materials where internal stresses are undesirable or where excessive driving torques are required with thread-forming screws. Thread-cutting screws are made in the following types: BF, BT, D, F, G, and T (see Fig. 8-41).

Type BF. These thread-cutting screws have spaced threads, blunt ends, and tapered entering threads, complete or incomplete. Serrations on the points cut the mating threads, and some chips may fall into the product being assembled. These screws are used in thin metal and some light-duty plastic bosses.

Type BT. Thread-cutting screws of this type, also known by manufacturers designation 25, have wide shank slots to cut the mating threads. They are used in sheet metal of medium thickness and plastics.

Types D, F, G, and T. These thread-cutting screws have threads of machine screw diameter-pitch combinations, blunt points, and tapered entering threads having one or more cutting edges and chip cavities. The tapered threads on Type F screws may be complete or incomplete; all other types have incomplete tapered threads.

Types D and T, also known by manufacturers designations 1 and 23, respectively, as well as Type F screws are used in aluminum and zinc die castings, steel sheets and shapes, cast irons, and some plastics. Type G screws are also used to cut threads in thin materials, but are used more extensively in tapped holes as adjustment screws.

Metallic drivescrews. These screws, designated Type U (see Fig. 8-41), have multiple-start threads of large helix angle and flat pilot points. When forced under pressure into workpieces made of metals or plastics, they make permanent fastenings.

Self-drilling and piercing screws. Starting holes are not required with these screws. Self-drilling tapping screws have self-contained drills, the points of which produce holes when the screws are driven. Portions of the screws behind the drilling

SCREW THREAD INSERTS

tips cut or form the mating threads. There are two basic types of self-drilling screws: one with spaced threads and the other with machine screw type threads. Basic point types are milled, die point (cold-forged), and combination cold-forged points with milled slots. Self-piercing screws have pointed tips to produce pilot holes.

Special tapping screws. Tapping screws with preassembled captive washers are called sems, discussed previously in this section. Tapping screws coated with sealing materials are also available. Other special tapping screws include self-captive and double-lead thread types.

These types of special tapping screws combine coarse-pitch starting threads with finer-pitch threads further along the screw shanks. The coarse threads produce pilot threads, and then the fine threads change the pitch of the mating threads produced. Because of the pitch change, the screws cannot be removed easily.

Standards. Dimensional specifications and general data for tapping and metallic drivescrews in the inch series are presented in ANSI Standard B18.6.4. Metric sizes are specified in IFI Standard 502, which will be withdrawn when the planned ANSI Standard B18.6.5M is published. Thread-rolling tapping screws in the inch series are covered in IFI Standard 112 and SAE Standard J81 and in the metric series in SAE Standard J1237. Metric size, self-drilling tapping screws are specified in IFI Standard 504, and inch sizes are specified in SAE Standard J78.

Captive Screws

Captive screws remain attached to panels or assembly components after they have been disengaged from their mating parts. Advantages include fast assembly and disassembly and elimination of the possibility of the screws coming loose and damaging other assembly components or becoming lost. Other types of captive (self-retained) threaded fasteners are discussed in a subsequent section of this chapter.

Various methods are used to attach the screws. Figure 8-42 illustrates a snap-in captive screw assembly. Retaining rings and nut retainers are used in some designs to captivate the screws, and split washers can be added after the screws have been inserted. Other designs use a ferrule or sleeve that is pressed, swaged, or flared to the assembly component. Captive screws are available with various head styles and drives, single or multiple-lead threads, and spring loading for partial or full retraction.

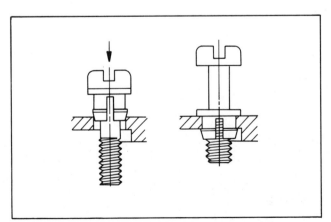

Fig. 8-42 Snap-in captive screw assembly. (*Specialty Fastener Div., Rexnord*)

SCREW THREAD INSERTS

Screw thread inserts are threaded plugs or spiral coils that serve as tapped holes for bolts, studs, and screws. They provide strong threads, allowing frequent assembly and disassembly of externally threaded fasteners.

Applications

The major application for screw thread inserts is to provide strong threads in lightweight materials, such as plastics, aluminum, magnesium, and wood. Such lightweight materials are weaker and less resistant to wear than iron or steel, and the disadvantages of having to tap them can be avoided by using threaded inserts. Inserts are also used sometimes in hard materials to provide wear-resistant threads, thread-locking features, and to permit the repair of damaged assemblies by replacing the inserts. Certain floating types of inserts can be used to allow nuts to align themselves radially.

Selection Factors

Selecting an optimum insert for a specific application requires consideration of several factors. Assembly strength, thread size, length, weight, and unit and installed costs are the major criteria. Additional consideration must be given to the insert and fastener materials, plating and coatings used for corrosion protection or lubrication, and the provision for internal thread-locking features. The many types of inserts available are designed to meet almost every need.

Assembly Design

It is important to design threaded assemblies to ensure the correct loading of mating parts. When designing clearance diameters of component parts, the insert and not the parent material should carry the load (see Fig. 8-43). The correct

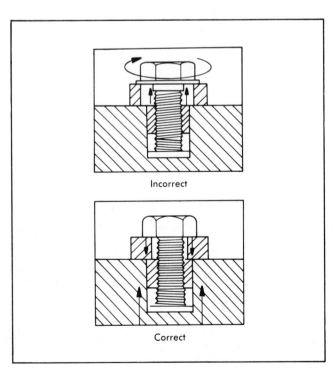

Incorrect

Correct

Fig. 8-43 Incorrect and correct methods of designing assemblies with screw thread inserts.

assembly is referred to as a "clamping condition" and the incorrect assembly as a "jackout" (torque tension) condition. However, with externally threaded inserts, the external thread transmits load to the parent material.

The insert length and external thread (on externally threaded inserts) allow selection so that the tensile strength of the assembly exceeds the tensile strength of the bolt or screw. The length of thread engagement required depends on the shear strength of the parent material. From a repairability standpoint, if the assembly is overloaded, the bolt should fail, not the insert assembly.

Testing Assemblies

Insert assemblies are tested using four different procedures: measuring tensile strength, rotational torque, jackout torque (see Fig. 8-44), and backout torque. The minimum, ultimate tensile strength is the axial force required to pull the insert out of the parent material a predetermined amount, generally at least 0.020″ (0.51 mm). Rotational torque is the torque required to turn the insert in the parent material. Jackout torque (torque tension) is the torque, applied to a mating screw, that pulls the

insert out of the parent material through a spacer having adequate clearance for the outside diameter of the insert. Backout torque is the amount of rotational torque applied in a counterclockwise direction to start the insert backing out of the parent material.

Types of Inserts

A wide selection of screw thread inserts, some of which are illustrated in Fig. 8-45, is available to suit various applications. Some, such as wire thread, solid bushing, thread-cutting, and thread-forming inserts, have both external threads (to hold the

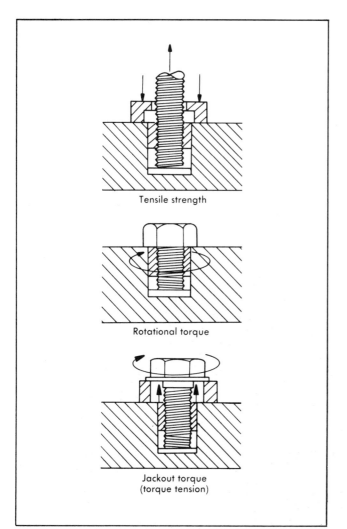

Fig. 8-44 Three methods used to test assemblies containing screw thread inserts.

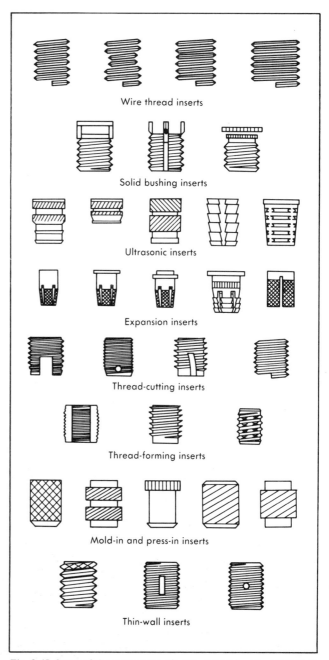

Wire thread inserts

Solid bushing inserts

Ultrasonic inserts

Expansion inserts

Thread-cutting inserts

Thread-forming inserts

Mold-in and press-in inserts

Thin-wall inserts

Fig. 8-45 Some of the many types of screw thread inserts. (*Heli-Coil Products, Div. of Mite Corp.*)

SCREW THREAD INSERTS

inserts in place) and internal threads (to accommodate the fasteners). Others, such as ultrasonic, expansion, mold-in, cast-in, potted-in, and press-in inserts, have only internal threads and are used in drilled or cored holes and solid or sandwich-panel or honeycomb materials.

Wire thread inserts. Helically coiled wire thread inserts are precision-formed screw thread coils, generally made of 18-8 (AMS 7245) stainless steel wire having a diamond-shaped cross section. They are manufactured from round wire that is cold rolled into a diamond shape to a tensile strength above 200 ksi (1380 MPa) and a hardness of R_C43-50. The resultant surface finish is 8-16 μin. (0.20-0.41 μm). This wire is wound into a helical coil that, when installed into holes tapped for specific screw thread inserts, forms conventional 60° internal screw threads. These inserts are also frequently used to repair damaged threads.

Standards. Wire thread inserts and tooling comply with the following military and federal standards and specifications:

MS122076 through MS122275	Insert, Corrosion Resistant, Helical Coil, Coarse Thread.
MS124651 through MS124850	Insert, Corrosion Resistant, Helical Coil, Fine Thread.
MS21208	Insert, Screw Thread, Free Running.
MS21209	Insert, Screw Thread-Screw Locking.
MS33537	Insert-Standard Dimensions, Assembly.
MIL-T-21309	Tools for Inserting and Extracting Helical Coil Inserts.
FED-STD-H28	Screw Thread Standards for Federal Services.

Insert designs. There are two designs of wire thread inserts: standard, which provides a smooth, free-running thread, and screw-locking. The screw-locking design provides self-locking (prevailing) torque on the externally threaded member by a series of chords formed on one or more of the insert coils (see Fig. 8-46). Both designs have a driving tang for installation, which is notched for easy removal after installation.

Insert sizes. Wire thread inserts are larger in diameter, before installation, than the receiving tapped hole. During installation, the inserting tool reduces the diameter of the insert. After installation, the insert coils expand outward with a spring-like action, permanently anchoring the insert in the tapped hole.

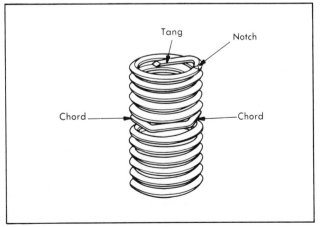

Fig. 8-46 Series of chords on one or more coils of wire thread inserts provides self-locking (prevailing) torque on fastener. Driving tang is used for installation, and notch facilitates removal of tang.

Inserts are available in UNC sizes No. 1 through 1 1/2" and UNF sizes No. 2 through 1 1/2". They are also available in UNEF, UNS, UN, metric, spark plug, and pipe thread sizes. The metric sizes available are M2 through M39 coarse and M8 through M39 fine.

Insert materials. Wire thread inserts are available in stainless steel (AMS 7245) for normal applications up to 800° F (425° C). Some manufacturers recommend Inconel X-750 (AMS 7246) for applications from 800 to 1000° F (425 to 540° C) or where low magnetic permeability is required. Phosphor bronze (AMS 7247) is recommended for low-permeability, salt water applications or for electrical conductivity requirements.

Advantages. The advantages of using wire thread inserts include the following:

- Minimum thread wear. Erosion of the threads from repeated assembly and disassembly is virtually eliminated because of the insert hardness and smooth surface finish.
- Design flexibility. Five insert lengths are available in each thread size.
- Corrosion resistance. The stainless steel used provides superior corrosion resistance and minimizes galvanic action in normal applications.
- Minimum space and weight. Helically coiled inserts are smaller in diameter and lighter (in some sizes) than other type inserts. They can generally be incorporated in existing designs having minimum wall thicknesses where no provision has been made for inserts. Space, weight, and cost savings include the elimination of lock washers, nuts, lock wires, locking compounds, plastic pellets/patches, and other locking mechanisms.

Applications. Typical uses for helically coiled, screw thread inserts include original equipment applications on aerospace, industrial, military, nuclear, automotive, communications, commercial, and other products. In addition, the products are supplied in repair-kit form, which includes drills, taps, inserts, and installation tools for repairing tapped holes that have been stripped or damaged because of overtightening, corrosion, or other reasons.

Installation and removal. Special taps are used to prepare holes for helically coiled inserts. Conventional drilling and tapping methods are employed. The class of fit of the final assembly is determined by the tapped hole; tap and gage are selected for the class of fit required.

Various designs of hand tools are available for inserting wire thread inserts. Finer pitch inserts generally have to be prewound to a smaller diameter for installation. Prewinding consists of threading the insert through a special tool to elastically compress the insert for easy entry into the hole. Large coarse pitch inserts need only a threaded mandrel tool for installation.

For high-volume production, power tooling is available to speed installation rates. Such tooling consists of a radial arm-mounted or handheld air motor driver. The inserts can be bulk loaded or coiled into plastic strip and supplied on reels for easier and faster loading into the tool.

Insert driving tangs must be removed to eliminate interference with the assembled bolt. Automatic tang-breakoff tools consist of a spring-loaded punch that strikes the tang, breaking it off at the notch. Such tools are also available in pneumatic models for higher production rates. For insert sizes more than 1/2", long-nose pliers are sometimes used to remove the tangs. With some insert sizes, it is difficult to remove the tangs.

For removing inserts, extracting tools, consisting of a two-sided blade on a T-handle, are available. The tool is applied to the insert and struck a light blow with a hammer. It is then turned counterclockwise while maintaining a steady downward pressure.

Solid bushing inserts. For applications requiring maximum structural reliability, positive-locked solid bushing inserts are available in several thread combinations, styles, and materials, and in a wide variety of standard sizes. They are used for many different applications, including structural and component parts of aircraft, electronic units, and gas turbine engines, where high reliability and strength are essential. They offer most of the advantages previously discussed for wire thread inserts.

Solid bushing inserts consist basically of a solid bushing that is threaded internally and externally. Terms such as lightweight, standard-wall, heavy-duty, and extra-heavy-duty are used to describe the thread combinations available. For example, a 1/4"-20 internal thread, lightweight insert could have a 3/8"-16 external thread. The heavy-duty insert with the same internal thread could have a 7/16"-14 external thread. The extra-heavy-duty insert with the same internal thread could have a 1/2"-13 external thread.

Pullout strength of a solid bushing insert is calculated by multiplying the minimum shear engagement area of the insert by the minimum ultimate shear strength of the parent material. Solid bushing inserts provide strong, permanent, reliable, and wear-resistant threads in virtually any material that can be tapped. Depending on the design and manufacturer, there are three basic methods of insert retention: keyring-locked, key-locked, and ring-locked. All three of these methods provide a positive mechanical lock that prevents insert rotation due to vibration or the insert coming out with the bolt, stud, or screw.

Keyring-locked. A hardened ring with two prongs is prepositioned on the insert (see Fig. 8-47, view *a*) and acts as a depth stop for locating the insert. The ring is driven downward, self-broaching into the parent material along axial slots on the outside diameter of the insert.

Key-locked. The two or four prepositioned keys (called kees by one insert manufacturer), the number depending on insert thread size, are driven downward into the parent material along axial slots on the outside diameter of the insert (see Fig. 8-47, view *b*). The prepositioned keys automatically set the insert at the proper depth below the surface of the parent material. Inserts are available with keys made from materials and having configurations that permit self-broaching parent materials with hardnesses in excess of $R_C 40$, thus eliminating the need for prebroaching.

Ring-locked. An internally and externally serrated lock ring is driven downward, broaching the external serrations into the parent material. The internal serrations mate with those on the insert flange.

Internal thread lock. Solid bushing inserts are also available with an internal thread-locking feature. The purpose is to provide a locking torque to secure the bolt or screw. The locking device is designed to maintain sufficient locking torque even after as many as 15 installations and removals of the fastener. Methods of obtaining the locking action vary depending on the insert size, style, manufacturer, and application. Typical locking methods include the following:

- Dimpling the outside diameter of the insert to provide a deflected internal thread.
- Slotting and crimping the insert on its bottom end.
- An integral plastic ring crimped into the insert on its bottom end.
- The use of nylon pellets.

Standards. Military standards covering solid bushing inserts include NAS 1838 through 1854, MIL-I-45914, MS51830 through 51834, NAS 1394 and 1395, and MS51990 through 51998.

Insert materials. Solid bushing inserts are made from several different materials, with selection of the material depending on the requirements for a specific application. Corrosion-resistant AISI Type 303 stainless steel and A-286 superalloy are used extensively. Type 303 is recommended for industrial and aerospace applications where high corrosion resistance is required. Alloy A-286 is recommended where the heat-treatable characteristics and high strength of this material are desirable and can be used in place of cadmium-plated SAE 4140 or carbon steel for other industrial and aerospace applications.

For applications requiring high-strength alloy steels, SAE 4140 chromium-molybdenum steel is sometimes used. Precipitation-hardening A-286 stainless steel is recommended where the characteristics of high strength and temperature resistance to 1200° F (650° C) are required.

Installation and removal. Solid bushing inserts are installed in standard-drilled, counterbored or countersunk, and tapped holes. Keyring-locked inserts are rotated to the correct position and then driven into the parent metal (see Fig. 8-48). Key-locked inserts are installed similarly (see Fig. 8-49). Installation

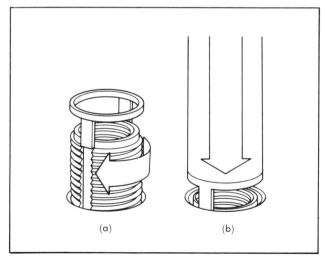

Fig. 8-48 Method of installing solid bushing inserts: (a) rotating to correct depth position and (b) driving lock ring (or keys) into the parent metal. (*Heli-Coil Products, Div. of Mite Corp.*)

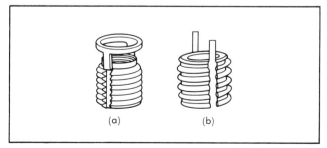

Fig. 8-47 Methods of retaining solid bushing inserts: (a) keyring-locked and (b) key-locked.

SCREW THREAD INSERTS

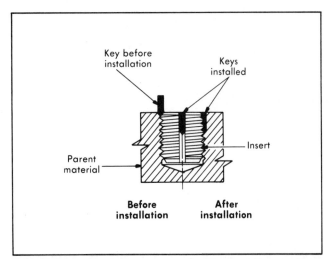

Fig. 8-49 Installation of key-locked solid bushing insert. (*Specialty Fastener Div., Rexnord*)

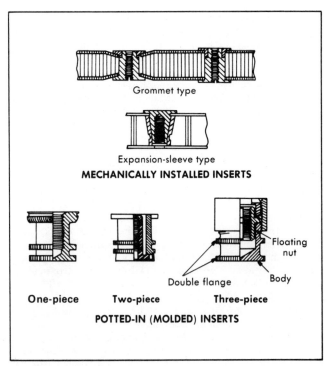

Fig. 8-50 Inserts for honeycomb and sandwich-panel materials. (*Specialty Fastener Div., Rexnord*)

tooling used varies from handheld tools, which can be used with a hammer or chucked in an arbor press, to pneumatic, impact, and other type tools. Most high-volume installation is being done with pneumatic tools that can install an insert in less than 5 seconds. When necessary, the inserts can be removed by drilling out the lock ring or keys and using a screw-type extractor. Identical inserts can be installed in the original holes without any reworking of the holes being necessary.

Honeycomb and sandwich-panel inserts. These inserts are designed to provide strong metal threads in honeycomb and sandwich-panel materials for aircraft, electronics, and similar applications. There are two basic types: those that are mechanically installed and those that are potted-in or molded (see Fig. 8-50).

Mechanically installed inserts. These inserts come in two configurations: grommet and expansion sleeve types. Both types are designed for applications where moderately heavy structural loads are a factor. The high column strength of these two-piece inserts eliminates the crushing of panels under high compression loads. The fasteners are lightweight and require no potting material, thus minimizing overall panel weight, a key consideration in sandwich-panel construction. Optional thread self-locking features eliminate the need for locknuts and nut plates, reducing costs and providing versatility. Installation is simple: a through hole is made in the parent material, and the insert is installed using pneumatic or hand-operated tools.

Potted-in inserts. These inserts are used for blind applications having access to only one side of the panel. They come preassembled, with one, two, or three-piece configurations, and provide moderately high tension pullout and shear load capabilities. Installation requires a cored hole in one side of the panel; the insert is set in place, and potting material is injected into the surrounding area. Vent holes are provided for injection and to show when the potting material has filled in around the insert. Military standards covering potted or molded-in inserts include NAS 1832 through 1836.

Self-threading inserts. There are two types of self-threading inserts: thread-cutting and thread-forming. These inserts are used primarily in aluminum, magnesium, plastic, and wood products. Thread-forming inserts are generally used in softer materials; thread-cutting inserts are used in stronger or more

brittle materials. A major advantage of self-threading inserts is the elimination of the need for tapping operations.

Self-threading inserts are installed into drilled, cored, or molded holes. The thread-cutting or thread-forming action retains the insert in place by friction. Because of the large outside diameter (shear area) of the insert, the pullout strength will usually exceed the breaking strength of the threaded fastener, except in very weak materials.

Self-threading inserts are available in a wide variety of designs and in inch and metric thread sizes. They are typically available in brass, stainless steel, and case-hardened steel. Other design variations include the use of plastic patches or pellets, or distorted external threads for added rotation resistance and internal thread-locking features. Several insert types have a symmetrical design, which is advantageous for automatic feeding systems used in high-production applications. In addition to the solid bushing type, helically coiled, self-tapping inserts are available for wood and fiberboard materials.

Self-threading inserts provide high assembly strengths and lower insert costs. Installation costs are also less because they are used in drilled or cored holes, thus eliminating hole preparation and tapping costs. Also, no tangs have to be removed after installation.

Slotted-type inserts for plastics. This type of insert can be used in either thermoplastic or thermoset plastic materials. The insert has two slots that provide cutting edges, much the same as a tap. When driven into a cored or drilled hole, the insert cuts its own thread. Friction between the insert and plastic holds the insert in place after installation. Slotted-type inserts are also available for soft materials, such as zinc die castings and aluminum sand castings.

Hole-type inserts. This type of insert is designed for tough-to-thread materials, such as wrought aluminum, magnesium, mild steel, and tough aluminum-alloy castings. A cross hole in the insert acts as a thread-cutting device when the insert is driven into the receiving hole.

Fluted self-tapping inserts. This type of insert utilizes three external flutes for cutting action and chip retention. They are used in plastics, soft metals, and wood. Such inserts are made in brass, steel, and stainless steel. Symmetrical inserts permit simplified adaptation to automated feeding systems. Nonsymmetrical versions are also available with a lead-in pilot and special external-thread forms having a flat, upper thread flank for reduced radial stresses and high pullout resistance.

Waveform, external-thread inserts. This type of insert has external threads extending almost the entire length for maximum thread engagement. It is a thread-forming insert and is symmetrical in design to allow for automated installation. The external threads have wave crests with depressions that serve to secure the insert in place while minimizing stress on the parent material. The inserts are available in short, medium, and long lengths; made from brass or stainless steel; and of locking or nonlocking design.

Thin-wall inserts. Thin-wall inserts are solid bushing inserts with an internal and external thread. They are installed in drilled and tapped holes. These inserts have a thinner wall between the internal and external threads than standard and heavy-duty solid bushing inserts. Their smaller outside diameter provides a space and weight savings advantage over other solid bushing inserts. They are supplied with or without an internal thread-locking feature. Typical materials include stainless steels and plated steels.

One type of thin-wall insert features an external serrated area at the top that is swaged outward into the base material to lock the insert in place. Another type of thin-wall insert consists of an internally threaded solid bushing with a nylon locking element in the external thread. The locking element, either a pellet or patch, retains the insert in place when the insert is screwed into the drilled and tapped receiving hole.

Ultrasonic inserts. Ultrasonic inserts are designed to provide strong metal threads in thermoplastics at an economical cost. The inserts are installed into plastics using ultrasonic welders or thermal equipment that generates heat at the insert-plastic interface. A narrow zone of plastic is remelted around the annular and longitudinal grooves in the insert (see Fig. 8-51) that, when resolidified, provides the high strength of a molded-in insert. Advantages of installation after molding include increased productivity due to reduced open mold time and elimination of scrapped parts and damaged molds.

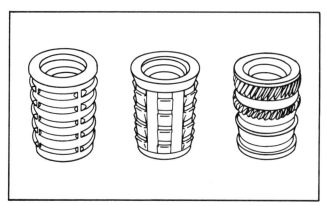

Fig. 8-51 Ultrasonic inserts provide strong metal threads in parts molded from thermoplastics.

Design features of ultrasonic inserts permit automated feeding, rapid installation, and optimum transfer of frictional energy from the insert to the plastic. Most insert designs feature knurls and undercuts or ribs for torque and pullout resistance. Some designs use axial flutes instead of knurls. The knurls and undercuts are filled with molten plastic during installation from the downward compressive force. The difference in cooling rates of the metal insert and plastic produces a microscopic relief zone that prevents the compressive radial stresses normally associated with molded-in inserts.

Ultrasonic inserts are supplied primarily in brass, but are also available in aluminum, plated steel, and stainless steel. The inserts are available in a variety of shapes and sizes. To obtain maximum assembly strength, the wall thickness of the plastic part should be one-half to one times the outside diameter of the insert. If the insert application is in a circular boss, the boss diameter should be two to three times the insert diameter. Thinner walls and bosses may be used, but this may affect the assembly strength.

Molded-in inserts. Molded-in inserts are used where application and production factors make it practical to have the inserts cast or molded into place while the part is being formed. This type is frequently used in thermoset plastics, rubber, and ceramics. They are especially advantageous in thermoset plastics in which ultrasonic insertion is not possible or where self-threading inserts induce severe stresses.

One drawback with respect to molded-in inserts is the overall installed cost, which is generally higher than other inserts. The open mold time required to load the inserts increases the molding cycle. Another factor is the difference in cooling rates of the metal insert and the plastic material; the difference can induce stresses that can cause cracking or crazing of the plastic.

Molded-in inserts are typically available in brass, aluminum, and stainless steel. They are supplied in either blind-end or open-end designs and normally incorporate external knurls and undercuts to secure the insert in the parent material. Accuracy of the internal thread is important to ensure snug fits on mold core pins. Also, flat ends are required to prevent flash on the top surface of the parts.

Expansion inserts. Expansion (pressed-in) inserts are used to provide strong metal threads in thermoplastic or thermoset plastic materials after molding. They are supplied primarily in brass, but are available in other materials. While expansion inserts are generally more expensive than other types of inserts, simple assembly without the need for costly installation equipment is a cost advantage. The inserts are installed in a drilled or molded hole either manually or with automated equipment. High pullout and rotational strength is provided without subjecting the walls of the receiving holes to any significant axial forces during installation.

Expansion inserts are locked in place by radial expansion of the knurled or finned portions on the outside of the insert. One type of insert incorporates a two-piece configuration, consisting of a threaded insert and a captive spreader plate. When the spreader plate is depressed, the knurled portion expands and anchors the insert in the hole. Tooling as simple as a punch and hammer, as well as an arbor press, can be used for installation. For high volume, the inserts are suitable for automated feeding equipment.

Another type of expansion insert uses the mating threaded fastener to expand the insert. As the assembly fastener enters the insert, it expands the knurled or finned portion, anchoring

CAPTIVE THREADED FASTENERS

the insert in the hole. Full pullout and rotational strength is achieved only when the screw engages the full thread length of the insert.

Inserts for special applications. There are many other types of inserts available, most of them designed for special applications. Some of the more common include cast-in, floating, blind-end, solid, and hydraulic inserts. Miniature inserts and high-strength aluminum inserts are also available for aerospace and electronic applications where space and weight are critical requirements.

Cast-in inserts. These inserts are similar to the molded-in inserts discussed previously, but are designed for use in nonferrous metal die castings as well as plastic molded parts.

Floating inserts. These inserts are designed to permit radial movement to compensate for misalignment of mating fasteners. They are used frequently for the assembly of curved surface parts or for use with recessed or flush screws.

Blind-end inserts. These inserts have their bottom ends closed to isolate the assemblies. This design protects the fastener threads from contaminants and prevents the fastener or foreign objects from contacting critical areas of the assembly.

Hydraulic inserts. These inserts have built-in seals to protect hydraulic or fuel system ports and to prevent fluid from leaking through the inserts.

Solid inserts. These inserts are used for relocating holes that have been drilled and tapped in wrong locations. Other applications include plugging holes, salvaging castings, and providing hard, wear-resistant pads on soft materials.

Replaceable sleeves. These components consist of separate, internally threaded cores used to replace damaged threads in cast-in inserts.

CAPTIVE (SELF-RETAINED) THREADED FASTENERS

Captive threaded fasteners are preassembled to and become an integral part of assembly components (panels, brackets, and chassis). They are captivated fasteners used for the subsequent acceptance of mating fasteners, such as bolts, studs, nuts, or screws. The fasteners are captivated by various means, including riveting, welding, pressing, caging, clinching, and swaging.

Captive fasteners are available in many types designed to meet almost every need. The types of captive fasteners discussed in this section include plate, anchor, and caged nuts; push and snap-in fasteners; clinch and self-clinching nuts; and self-piercing fasteners. Sems (screw and washer assemblies), which are not self-retained fasteners; captive screws; and screw thread inserts are discussed in preceding sections of this chapter. Rivets of the internally threaded and compression types are discussed in the "Blind Rivets/Fasteners" section of this chapter.

Advantages of Captive Fasteners

Captive fasteners can provide strong threads in thin materials, permitting repeated assembly and disassembly of their mating fasteners. For some applications, they permit the use of thinner materials in assemblies. Captive fasteners permit fastening from one side of assemblies in blind locations, resist loosening, ensure the positive positioning of mating fasteners, and minimize the possible loss of fasteners. Versatility is another advantage of captive fasteners: they can be installed during fabrication of a product, many can be installed after components have been coated or painted, or they can be finished as part of the assembly.

Typical Applications

Captive fasteners are used in many different consumer, industrial, and military products. They are commonly used in sheet metal, die castings, or molded plastics where the materials are too soft or thin to permit tapping threads or where additional thread strength is required. They are also often necessary for inaccessible or blind locations. As inserts for thin components or printed circuit boards, they can provide features of prevailing torque, floating action, or a means of standing off a secondary panel or component.

Selection Criteria

There are four basic criteria to be considered when specifying captive fasteners: functional requirements, reliability, tooling and equipment requirements, and installed cost. Many times, manufacturing engineers do not have the prerogative of making the best selection for their purposes. They must satisfactorily install the fastener that has been designed into the product being manufactured. However, the considerations of proper fastener selection are still important for manufacturing engineers, because they may be able to obtain a design change if they can prove that a different fastener is more reliable and/or more cost effective. As a result, these selection considerations are as important to the manufacturing engineer as they are to the design engineer.

Functional requirements. Loads to be applied and environmental conditions in service must be known for proper fastener selection. Product size, clearances available, and whether frequent removal and/or replacement are necessary must also be considered.

Reliability in service. Reliability depends on many factors, including proper size and condition of the insertion holes, the thickness and hardness of the assembly component, proper installation, and the design of the fastener and the assembly. Performance specifications for the fastener that should be tested include resistance to torque out (rotation), torque through, and pushout. For some applications, shear strength is also an important consideration. Specifying any fastener that has been developed by a specific manufacturer by adding "or equivalent" to the drawing or purchase order can be a dangerous practice. The "equivalent" fastener may be lower in cost, but it may also be of different material, poor quality, or improperly heat treated. Testing for adherence to standard specifications is essential.

Tooling requirements. Tooling and equipment needed for the preparation of the mounting holes and also for the installation of the fasteners must be considered. Size, shape, and tolerances for the holes, and adaptability of the installation equipment to automation, when necessary for production requirements, are important factors.

Installed cost. The installed cost, including the cost of equipment and tools, should be the primary consideration, rather than just the cost of the fasteners. Some low-cost fasteners may require high-cost installation and/or low production rates. Also, rejects due to the failure of poorly designed, manufactured, or installed fasteners contribute to high production costs. More expensive fasteners often have lower installed costs.

Plate, Anchor, and Weld Nuts

Plate nuts, also called anchor nuts, have one or more mounting lugs projecting from the bases of their threaded bodies or a flange (see Fig. 8-52) for permanent attachment by riveting or welding to the surface of the part to be assembled. When multiple nuts are required, channel assemblies consisting of a number of nuts in a long mounting carrier are used. Some forms of plate nuts are called T-nuts. Mounting lugs on the baseplate and flanges are available in various shapes and sizes to suit requirements. Prong-type nuts have straight or twisted projections that grip soft materials such as wood.

The nuts are made in nonfloating (fixed), radial floating (two-piece construction), and self-aligning designs. Floating types are available in permanently assembled styles and with removable/replaceable nut elements. Internally threaded portions of these fasteners can be equipped with nylon inserts, elliptical offsets, or segments that bend inward for self-locking purposes. Capped nuts are available to cover the ends of mating fasteners, and the holes can be countersunk in riveted types for flush mounting.

These types of captive fasteners provide good resistance to torque out, torque through, and pushout when properly riveted or welded. However, installation costs are generally high. Also, weld nuts must be installed prior to finishing the assemblies unless removable-type nuts are used.

Riveted nuts. Riveting of plate or anchor fasteners is common. However, this method of attachment requires the production of holes in the part to be assembled and the use of rivets and riveting equipment, thus adding to installation costs. Three or more holes are needed—two or more for rivets and one for the mating fastener.

Welded nuts. These types of captive fasteners are attached by resistance welding (projection or spot). Welding eliminates the need for producing rivet holes in the assembly component, but installation costs are often higher than with other types of captive fasteners because of the need for welding equipment and operations. Weld nuts are available with piloted ends for greater alignment accuracy. Locking features for torque control are sometimes provided.

Spot welding equipment is generally less costly than that for projection welding. However, projection welding permits more flexibility in design and often provides higher quality and/or more reliable assemblies. The nuts used for projection welding have embossed or coined projections on their flanges.

Other weld nuts. Solid nuts without flanges are also used. These nuts have lugs, embossments, or annular rings to facilitate attachment by resistance welding. Close control of amperage, force, and cycle time is required in projection welding such nuts. Capacitor-discharge welding and automatic feeding of the nuts are being used for some applications.

Caged Nuts

In caged nuts, a standard nut, usually square, is retained in a spring-steel box or cage (see Fig. 8-53). The nuts can be staked to the retainers or assembled loosely to provide float for possible misalignment. Lugs on the retainers can be snapped into square holes, slipped over panel edges, or locked behind panels. On some designs, the lugs engage and lock the threads of the mating fastener. Advantages of caged nuts include eliminating the need for riveting, welding, clinching, or staking, but they are usually hand installed. These nuts also permit easy replacement in case of thread damage during assembly or while in service.

Other Push or Snap-In Fasteners

Nuts similar to plate or anchor nuts, having internally threaded bushings and baseplates, are available for pushing or snapping into assembly components. These fasteners, sometimes called clip nuts, eliminate the need for riveting or welding, but are generally limited to lighter duty applications.

A push-in type, panel-retained fastener is illustrated in Fig. 8-54. Two spring-resilient loop legs extend from a flat plate in which there is a single helical thread for accepting a tapping

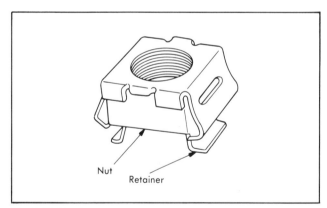

Fig. 8-53 Caged nut.

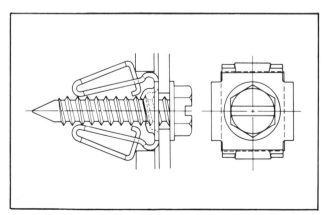

Fig. 8-54 Push-in type, panel-retained fastener. (*Fasteners Div., TRW Assemblies & Fasteners Group*)

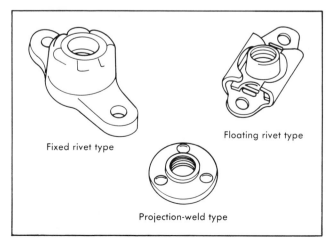

Fig. 8-52 Several types of plate, anchor, and weld nuts.

CAPTIVE THREADED FASTENERS

screw. When the fastener is pushed into a hole in a panel, the two loops compress together and then snap back, with the shoulder tops pressing firmly against the back of the panel for retention. When the screw is applied, it experiences prevailing-torque resistance from the helical-form thread. Removal is prevented by the blocking of the shoulder sections of the loops, thus keeping them from deflecting inward. The fastener can be used in both sheet metal and plastics.

Clinched Nuts

These captive fasteners are solid nuts having pilot collars projecting from one end. The collar is inserted into a hole in the assembly component and spread, flared, or rolled over to produce a "clinch" (see Fig. 8-55). Possible limitations are that special tooling is required for clinching, and the nut collars must be soft enough to permit plastic flow. Also, hole diameters must be held to close tolerances, generally a total of 0.003-0.004″ (0.08-0.10 mm).

Self-Clinching Fasteners

Self-clinching nuts, sometimes called press nuts, have a pilot shank containing knurls or ribs and an undercut, recess, or groove (see Fig. 8-56). They are installed simply by pressing into holes in the sheet materials. All self-clinching fasteners must be harder than the materials into which they are inserted to effect cold flow of the materials instead of distortion of the fasteners. For this reason, most are heat treated.

Various designs of self-clinching fasteners (see Fig. 8-57) include blind, floating, self-locking, floating self-locking, prevailing-torque, and removable nut features. Broaching-type self-clinching fasteners are used extensively in printed circuit boards made of plastics. Specially formed axial grooves around the fastener shank broach (cut) into the boards, creating a firm interference fit. In addition to nuts, self-clinching fasteners are available as inserts (flush on both sides), studs, nonthreaded pins (used as guides), and spacers and standoffs to hold assembly components apart from each other.

Installation of self-clinching fasteners can be done manually or with a press. Forces required for insertion generally vary from 1000 to 12,000 lb (4.45 to 53.4 kN), depending on fastener type and size. Generally, only simple shapes are needed for the punches and anvils.

When production quantity and consistent quality requirements dictate, automatic equipment is available for installing self-clinching fasteners. Some automated presses are specifically designed to feed these fasteners into punched or drilled holes and to seat them correctly with parallel squeezing forces. Feeding rates are three to six times faster than manual insertions. Also, the squeezing action is adjustable to compensate for variations in thickness and hardness of the assembly component and height of the fasteners. Depending on the complexity of configuration of the assembly component and how much handling is necessary, an operator can install up to 20 self-clinching fasteners per minute.

Self-Piercing Fasteners

Self-piercing and clinching nuts for thin sheet materials generally have a piloted body, an undercut or back tapered pilot, and a shoulder or embossment feature (see Fig. 8-58, view *a*). When pressed into an assembly component, they pierce their own mounting holes, and material from the component flows into the undercuts or around the back tapered pilots for secure

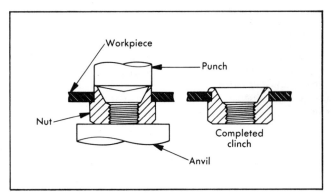

Fig. 8-55 Installation of clinch nut.

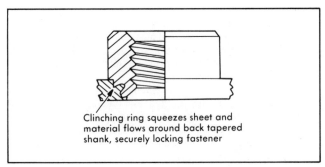

Fig. 8-56 Self-clinching nut. (*Penn Engineering & Mfg. Corp.*)

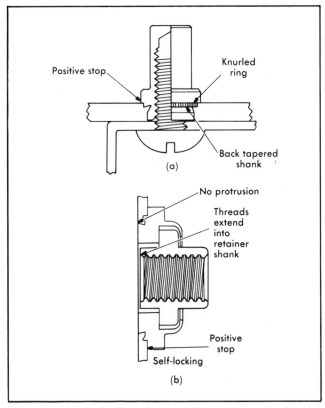

Fig. 8-57 Self-clinching fasteners: (a) blind and (b) floating. (*Penn Engineering & Mfg. Corp.*)

fastening. They are available in strip form for feeding under a press ram or in loose bulk form for hopper feeding. The assembly components must be fixtured or automatically located to ensure proper fastener location.

Another category of self-piercing and clinching nuts (see Fig. 8-58, view *b*) for higher strength applications is specifically designed for use in structural bracket components formed from thicker sheet and plate materials. These nuts are manufactured from medium-carbon steels and heat treated to develop the full strength available from SAE Grade 8 or property class 10 bolts. These nuts are available for plate thicknesses ranging to 0.354″ (8.99 mm).

Nut Retainers

Nut retainers (see Fig. 8-59) are clinched in position by the controlled collapse of the portions that extend through the attachment holes. They are used extensively for blind-side installations and are available made from steel, aluminum, and various other metals, and in different styles. Flush mounting

with countersunk heads and closed ends for watertight installations are two of the more common types, in addition to the flanged-head style shown. For additional antirotation protection, keyed or hex styles are available.

Studs

Studs and other externally threaded fasteners are available in self-clinching designs (see Fig. 8-60, view *a*). Weld studs and screws (view *b*) are also available. For capacitor-discharge welding, weld studs and screws are made with a single, small projection in the center of their heads. Projection welding by capacitor discharge permits attaching studs to thin metal with minimum distortion or discoloration. However, some large studs must be arc welded in place.

Self-clinching studs are supplied for flush head mounting, with thin heads for mounting to thin sheet, and as structural studs, with heads stronger in tension than the threads. All are simply pressed into thin sheet metal and become self-retained with a simple punch and anvil. Broaching studs can be used for pressing into brittle materials, such as printed circuit boards.

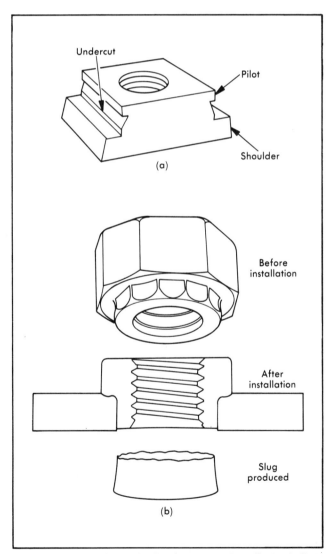

Fig. 8-58 Self-piercing and clinching nuts. (*Russell, Burdsall & Ward Corp.*)

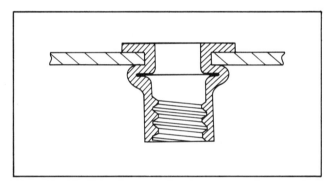

Fig. 8-59 Nut retainer.

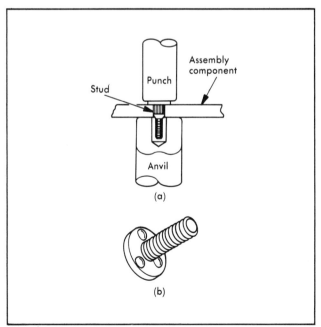

Fig. 8-60 Captive fasteners: (a) stud with knurled shank and (b) weld screw with projection-weld projections under head.

CHAPTER 8

CAPTIVE THREADED FASTENERS

Bolt-Nut Combination

A self-retaining, positive-locking bolt-nut combination is shown in Fig. 8-61. The fastener consists of a retained receptacle assembly attached to the blind surface (inside) of a structure and a sleevebolt that passes through and is retained in the attachment or panel. Self-locking is provided by the configuration of the internal threads in the sleevebolt.

Installation of Captive Fasteners

As a general rule, it is recommended that most self-retained fasteners be installed after the sheet metal has been finished by methods such as plating, anodizing, and painting. However, sometimes this cannot be easily done because panels, chassis, and other assembly components are often fabricated by welding, and fasteners must be installed in difficult places prior to welded assembly of the unit.

If a steel assembly with steel fasteners is to be plated, the fasteners should be unplated when installed. These could be projection welded fasteners or heat-treated, self-clinching fasteners. Expensive problems and spoiled products can result if, for instance, cadmium-plated fasteners are installed in base steel sheet and the assembly is subsequently prepared for zinc plating. The cleaning and stripping of the cadmium is not compatible with the zinc process; thus, blackened fasteners, streaked plating on the sheet, and/or severely etched fasteners may result if the proper procedure is not followed. Care must

also be exercised to prevent hydrogen embrittlement, especially with fasteners having a hardness of more than $R_C 35$.

The preparation of assemblies of heat-treated steel fasteners, with the exception of those made from stainless steel, in steel sheet must also be done with care because acid cleaners will etch the high-carbon surface of the fastener before the low-carbon sheet material. Once the fastener has been severely etched, exposing the carbon, it is virtually unplatable. Always advise plating suppliers of the material from which the installed fasteners are made and whether they are heat treated. Plating of heat-treated fasteners requires extreme care and may change the torque ranges of self-locking fasteners.

The anodizing process will destroy either steel or stainless steel fasteners if they are installed in aluminum before anodizing. If fasteners must be installed in aluminum before anodizing, then the fasteners must be made of aluminum alloy.

Painting can be done after the fastener installation, but if the threads are to freely accept their mating fastener they must be masked. With any fastener having a nylon locking element, care must be taken to protect the nylon if the paint is baked.

Following are 10 simple rules for correctly installing captive fasteners. Some of these rules apply particularly to specific types of fasteners, such as clinched (press) nuts, but most are generally applicable to all fasteners. Specific information on installation techniques and special tooling requirements can be obtained from the fastener manufacturer or supplier.

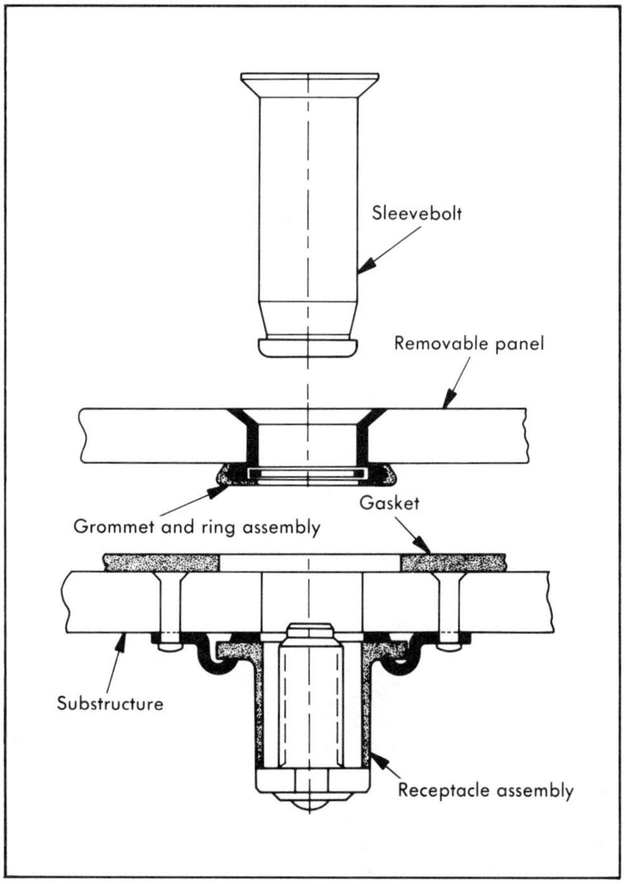

Fig. 8-61 Self-retaining, positive-locking bolt-nut combination. (*SPS Technologies*)

1. Provide a mounting hole of proper size for each fastener.
2. Be sure the fastener shank or pilot is within the hole before force is applied to complete the installation.
3. Apply a squeezing force between parallel surfaces. Sometimes the parallel surface may need to have a relief hole or shoulder to match the specific fastener design.
4. Use sufficient force to embed the clinching ring around its entire circumference, or to spread or flare the shank of the clinch nut, or to provide the proper weld contact for a projection-weld nut. Most fastener designs provide a physical or visual stop feature to determine when the fastener is completely and properly installed.
5. Do not install steel or stainless steel fasteners in aluminum before the aluminum panels have been anodized. The cleaning and anodizing process will destroy the fastener.
6. Do not deburr or countersink the mounting holes for self-clinching fasteners because the sharp corner is necessary to provide sufficient cold flow of sheet material into the undercut of the fastener. Do provide a countersink for clinched (press) nuts that have their shanks spread and for rivets when required.
7. Do not install the fastener closer to the edge of the sheet than specified by the manufacturer. Minimum edge distances are specified to keep the sheet from bulging or to keep the head of the fastener from overhanging the edge of the sheet. When these limitations are violated, the performance of the fastener may suffer, and the hole position of the thread will become out of tolerance.
8. Do not oversqueeze, as this may flatten the fastener head, distort the threads, and/or buckle the panel into which it is installed. Any distortion to the top of a locking fastener will destroy its prevailing-torque characteristics.

SELF-LOCKING THREADED FASTENERS

9. Do not install clinched (press) nuts with a hammer blow. Doing so does not allow sufficient time for the sheet material to cold flow and may distort the shape of the fastener and the gageability of its threads. A squeezing force is required for optimum performance of most captive fasteners.

10. Except for nut retainers, do not install a screw in the head side of a fastener; install from the opposite side. This type of installation directs the load toward the sheet. Except for standoff-type fasteners, the joint assembly should always have the screw mated with the nut so that the self-clinching portion of the assembly is being clamped to the sheet material. The joint assembly should always pull a self-retained fastener in its direction of installation.

SELF-LOCKING THREADED FASTENERS

Self-loosening of assemblies using threaded fasteners can be minimized in several ways. Mechanical means include the use of toothed-type washers, discussed subsequently in this chapter. Jam nuts and castle (slotted hex) nuts, for use with cotter pins or locking wires, discussed previously in this chapter, are also employed. Problems with and deficiencies of these means of minimizing loosening, especially under cyclic loading conditions, have resulted in the increased use of self-locking fasteners.

There are many different types of self-locking fasteners available, each having some advantages and disadvantages. Most of these fasteners are satisfactory for some applications, but no one type is suitable for all applications. The three basic types of self-locking fasteners are: free-spinning, prevailing-torque, and chemical locking. Locknuts are more common than locking bolts or screws. Self-locking types of screw thread inserts are discussed previously in this chapter.

Selecting a locking system that will give the best performance at the lowest cost for a given application requires careful consideration of many factors. Critical considerations include reliability, the fastener material, cost, ease of assembly, reusability, and operating requirements and conditions. Performance and dimensional specifications provide only a limited amount of help in choosing the optimum self-locking fastener for a specific assembly. There is no cross-referencing between specifications because performance characteristics often differ.

For example, two widely used specifications for self-locking nuts are Military Specification MIL-N-25027 and IFI Standard 100. The military specification requires 15 reuses from a locknut, but does not require the nut to be seated. In contrast, the IFI standard requires a relatively high seating load. Depending on the application, more reuses may or may not be better. For critical applications, no self-locking nut can be reused reliably without further treatment or testing.

Free-Spinning Fasteners

Captive toothed washers. Free-spinning devices for self-locking are provided on bolts, nuts, or screws, usually in the form of toothed captive washers that facilitate assembly but increase cost. However, while fastener costs are higher, assembled costs are generally lower. Screw and washer assemblies (known generically as sems) are discussed previously in this chapter. Such free-spinning fasteners can be rotated easily and seated against the work surface before any significant torque is

required. This can be an advantage where long travel (run-ons) is required for seating. Additional tightening causes digging into the bearing surface, which results in the locking action. Preloading of free-spinning fasteners is essential to develop proper locking action. If digging in of the teeth can cause failures of clamped parts, this type fastener should not be used.

Integral teeth. Self-locking fasteners having integral teeth or serrations (see Fig. 8-62) use the preloaded tension of the fasteners for part of the locking action, but add mechanical engagement between bolt or screwhead, or nut, and the bearing surface. This provides an additional amount that the pretension must relax before fastener disengagement. However, if the bearing surface on the work is harder than the teeth or serrations, there will be no additional locking action. Both the bolt and the nut should be toothed to prevent relative rotation.

Spring washers. Spring washers, of cylindrically curved, waveform, conical, Belleville, or helical design (all discussed later in this chapter), add some slight additional tension to the amount applied in preloading. While there are many different designs of these so-called self-locking fasteners with spring washers, most should be tightened sufficiently to flatten the washers. Performance varies with different designs.

As long as pretension is maintained to keep the bearing surfaces engaged, no locking is necessary. However, if the assembly relaxes and the clamp load is lost, a common occurrence under shock and cyclic loading, the fasteners will disengage.

Self-locking threads. Special or modified taps are also used to produce self-locking threads in locknuts (see Fig. 8-63). At the bottom of the nut thread, the thread is angled to form a wedge ramp. Wider clearances thus provided permit easy rotation of the nut for assembly, making it a free-spinning

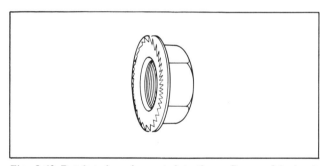

Fig. 8-62 Ratchet-shaped serrated teeth on flange of locknut embed into bearing surface for locking action.

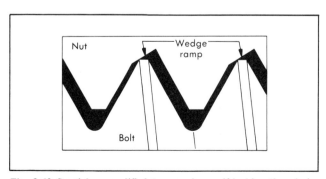

Fig. 8-63 Special or modified taps produce self-locking threads in locknuts. Wedge ramps force bolt threads into locking position. (*Spiralock Nut, Microdot*)

SELF-LOCKING THREADED FASTENERS

fastener. However, when the nut is seated, tightening pulls the bolt threads along the wedge ramps for metal-to-metal thread mating and self-locking. A clamp load is essential for optimum performance of this type of self-locking thread.

Prevailing-Torque Fasteners

Prevailing-torque fasteners are based on an interference fit between the mating threads. Unlike free-spinning fasteners, they require continuous tightening during installation. However, prevailing-torque fasteners do not require contact with seating surfaces; they stay in whatever position where tightening stops as the result of their built-in self-locking action. The locking torque is generally retained independent of the clamping load. The two major kinds of prevailing-torque fasteners are the plastic additive types and all-metal fasteners with distorted or deflected thread types.

Plastic additive types. Nuts and bolts are available with elements made of plastics to provide an interference fit with mating threads. Advantages are that the elements are non-damaging to mating threads, and the nuts or bolts are reusable after disassembly. A possible limitation is that the plastics are limited with respect to maximum service temperatures.

Various types of nuts and bolts with elements made of plastics are available. Patches of the material are bonded to the threads in some types (see Fig. 8-64), and plugs or rods are embedded in the threads in other types. The patches are made in different thicknesses and lengths and the plugs and rods in different diameters and lengths to suit application requirements. In another type of locknut (see Fig. 8-65), a plastic collar is held by crimping metal over the collar or fusing the collar into a groove. All plastic additive, self-locking fasteners are especially suitable for applications involving considerable vibration because the plastics act as vibration dampers.

Distorted or deflected threads. Various designs of all-metal locknuts, some of which are shown in Fig. 8-66, use distorted or deflected threads or nut shapes to provide an interference fit. One type, called center-lock nuts, has depressions made in the outer faces of standard nuts (see view *a*) to cause thread deformation. This type of locknut is generally satisfactory to be reused only a few times because of the limited number of deformed threads.

Additional locking action is obtained by providing spring action. Circumferential spring action is provided by using an out-of-round nut or an out-of-round crown on the nut (see Fig. 8-66, view *b*). Elliptical-type locknuts (view *c*) are available as true ellipses, where the nut is distorted across one axis, and trilobular ellipses, where the nut is distorted inward at every other hexagon flat. True ellipses have more spring action, but trilobular ellipses have less distortion of the wrenching surfaces on the nuts. For many applications, the nuts are heat treated to improve the wear resistance of the contact surfaces and to provide a more resilient spring action. The effectiveness of these nuts depends on rigid adherence to all thread tolerances.

Slotted locknuts (see Fig. 8-66, view *c*), sometimes called spring nuts, are another means of providing self-locking action with deflected threads. The ID of the slotted sections is slightly less than the OD of the bolt to provide a spring frictional grip on the bolt threads.

Separate locking means. Pins, wires, or springs, fitted to locknuts, are also being used for self-locking action. The locknut shown in Fig. 8-67 has a hardened projecting pin that impinges against the bolt to provide a ratchet-like locking action. The reuse of such nuts is limited by wear of the pin tips.

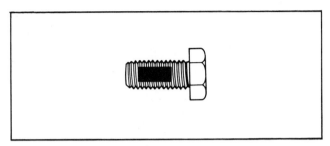

Fig. 8-64 Bolt with nylon patch.

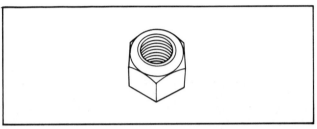

Fig. 8-65 Nylon collar grips bolt threads with this prevailing-torque locknut.

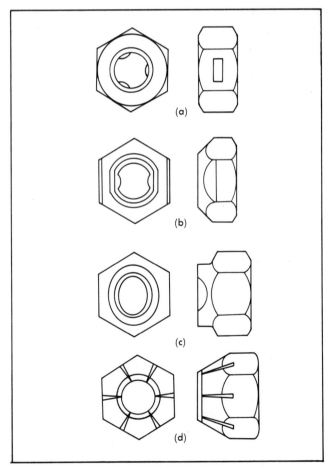

Fig. 8-66 Four types of prevailing-torque locknuts: (a) depressions in outer faces of nut deform threads, (b) distorted crown on nut provides spring grip on bolt threads, (c) elliptical type locknut, and (d) slotted sections deflect inward to grip threads.

SPECIAL-PURPOSE FASTENERS

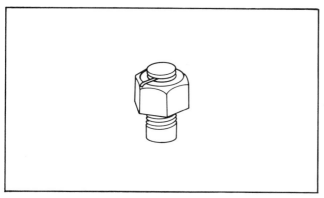

Fig. 8-67 Nut has a projecting pin that provides a locking action.

Chemical Locking

Chemical locking as a method of minimizing the loosening of threaded fasteners is accomplished by coating the fasteners with an adhesive. Adhesives commonly used and methods of applying include using strips of two-component epoxies, applying a single-component anaerobic at assembly, and preapplying microencapsulated epoxies or anaerobics. Certain types of cyanoacrylate adhesives are also being used. All of the adhesives are available in different strengths to suit application requirements.

Advantages of using adhesives for locking include simple and easy application and curing, and good performance under severe service conditions. Adhesives provide a fluid seal and prevent corrosion of the threads. Anaerobic adhesives remain liquid while exposed to air, but when oxygen is excluded by the mating threads, they cure rapidly. Curing produces a thermoset bond, providing a solid plastic, zero-clearance fit between the mating threads, regardless of the thread tolerances.

Limitations of using adhesives for locking are that the shelf life of most adhesives is about one to four years, not all metals or plastics can be bonded with equal strength, and their use is restricted by temperature and other environmental conditions. However, most adhesives retain about 50% of their full strength at temperatures to 300° F (150° C) and some to 425° F (220° C). Another limitation is that adhesives lose their effectiveness when the fasteners are disassembled. Reuse of the fasteners without the reapplication of adhesive is questionable.

Preapplication of adhesive by the microencapsulation method is generally limited to high-volume requirements because of the cost of coating. The microcapsules, with liquid adhesive centers, form a dry inert coating on the threads. The shearing action of thread engagement crushes the capsules and allows the adhesive to be distributed over the threads and cure. In most cases, not all the capsules are broken in initial assembly. This allows the fastener to be reused, generally not more than one time, without recoating, but with a progressive loss of locking efficiency.

SPECIAL-PURPOSE FASTENERS

Despite the many types and sizes of standard mechanical fasteners available, there is an increasing demand for special fasteners to meet specific requirements. Special fasteners include modified standard fasteners and fasteners designed to perform one or more special functions for specific applications.

Special fasteners, including threaded and nonthreaded types, sometimes perform several functions and often reduce assembly costs or the number of parts required for an assembly. In some cases, they permit the use of thinner and less expensive panel materials by using the strength of the fasteners to meet requirements. Some special fasteners may cost more than standard fasteners, and their use should therefore be based on reduced assembly costs and/or improved product quality.

It is beyond the scope of this section to cover the many different types of special-purpose fasteners available, and only some of the more commonly used fasteners will be discussed. Other special-purpose fasteners, such as push and snap-in types, are discussed in a preceding section of this chapter, "Captive (Self-Retained) Threaded Fasteners."

QUICK-OPERATING FASTENERS

Many quick-operating fasteners, also called quick-release fasteners, are now being used so extensively that they are no longer considered to be special-purpose fasteners. They are used most commonly when repetitive access to components is required. Major types of quick-operating fasteners include turn-operated, lever-actuated, lift-and-turn (a combination of turn-operated and lever-actuated), slide-action, push or pull,

magnetic-action, and various designs of hose clamps. The types include turn-operated, stud-receptacle fasteners with fast-lead threads; fasteners that operate with push-action draw latches that pull edge-mating panels together; slide latches that retain edge-mating panels perpendicular to their surface planes; and detent latches using magnetic attraction or a specially shaped stud that expands spring-loaded receptacle blades.

Turn-operated fasteners are generally of the stud or pawl type, with quarter-turn panel fasteners being one of the most commonly used. Many turn-operated fasteners operate against spring pressure that clamps the fastened part against its support. Some can be released by finger pressure, but tools are often required for unlocking.

One design of turn-operated fasteners consists of a stud assembly, a grommet, and a receptacle (see Fig. 8-68, view *a*). The grommet is secured to a removable panel by dimpling or countersinking the panel and then pushing the dimple back with a special closing tool (view *b*) or using a snap ring (view *c*). The receptacle can be fastened to the underside of the base component with two rivets (view *d*), and the fastener is locked or unlocked with a quarter turn of the stud. Studs are also available with winged or cross-recessed heads (view *e*), as well as other head styles.

With the high-strength, quick-operating fastener shown in Fig. 8-69, the stud is held to the panel by a retaining ring. The base is drilled and countersunk for two rivets to hold the receptacle. Locking or unlocking of the fastener is accomplished with a quarter turn of the stud. Receptacles are available for a

SPECIAL-PURPOSE FASTENERS

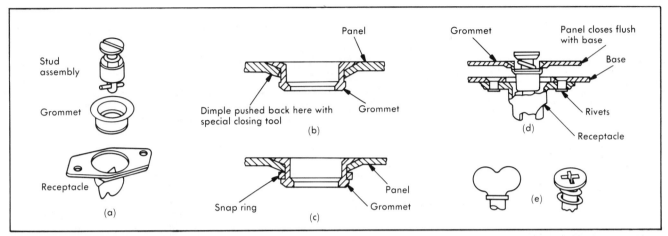

Fig. 8-68 Quick-operating fastener of the quarter-turn type.

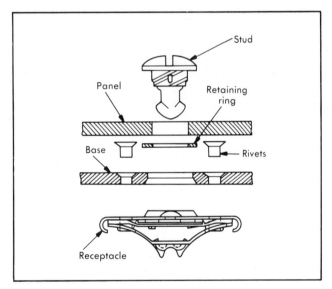

Fig. 8-69 High-strength, quick-operating fastener.

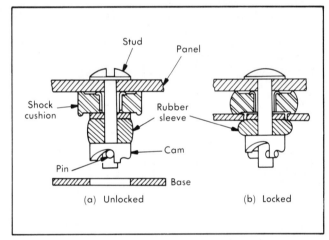

Fig. 8-70 Shock-mounted, quick-operating fastener.

variety of application methods. In addition to being riveted to the inner panel, they can be clipped in place, pressed into holes, or welded. Shock-mounted receptacles are often used.

Shock-mounted, quick-operating fasteners (see Fig. 8-70) reduce shock vibration and noise between the panel and the fixed base. Such fasteners are permanently attached to the panels by assembling the components and inserting pins with special pliers (view *a*). A half turn of the stud locks the panel to the base by compressing a rubber sleeve against the base (view *b*). The quick-operating fastener shown in Fig. 8-71 has a nylon ring (held captive in a groove on the underside of the stud head) for moisture and pressure sealing. A grooved pin is driven into the stud of this fastener during installation.

Most turn-operated, quick-operating fasteners are made of steel, but they are also available in other materials, including plastics. Receptacles are made in many types, such as slip-on (side-mount), snap-on, and press-in styles, and are clipped, riveted, or welded to the base. Studs may be removable or retained by snap rings and various types of grommets, including tool-deformed and push-on designs.

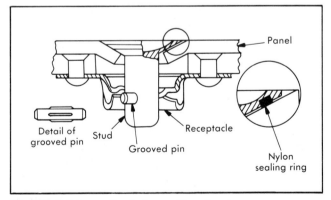

Fig. 8-71 Quick-operating fastener with sealing ring.

SPRING CLIPS

Spring clips are one-piece stamped fasteners or simple assemblies, generally self-retaining, that slip into holes or onto panel edges. They are held by spring tension and do not require secondary fasteners, such as bolts, screws, or rivets. Spring clips are usually made from hardened, high-carbon steel, but are available in other metals and plastics. Various coatings can be applied to suit application requirements. Dart-type spring clips have dart-shaped retainers to engage the holes or panels. Spring clips are made in many different shapes to hold various assembly components.

Stud receivers are spring clips designed for attaching to unthreaded rods, pins, or rivets. They are available in push-on, tubular, and self-threading types. Push-on receivers have two or more prongs that lock the fasteners in place when forced onto studs. So-called "Christmas-tree" clips or ratchet fasteners have multiple flexible ribs on their shanks and are available with various head and point styles. The ribs bend when the fastener is pressed into a hole and then snap back for retaining. Tubular spring clips have a split tubular sleeve for securing the unthreaded component of the assembly. Self-threading types have flutes or teeth that form threads as they are turned onto studs made of soft metals or plastics.

TAMPER-RESISTANT FASTENERS

Tamper-resistant fasteners, such as screws, bolts, quick-operating types, and other fasteners, are designed to be difficult to disassemble, thus minimizing unauthorized entry, vandalism, or theft. This is often accomplished by providing the fasteners with unusual heads, such as special sockets or recesses, standard sockets with integral pins or inserts, heads with one-way slots or nonstandard shapes, and breakoff (breakaway) heads. Such fasteners generally require the use of special tools for disassembly. Fasteners can be made permanent by riveting, welding, or adhesive bonding.

EXPANDING FASTENERS

Fasteners that expand radially when an axial load is applied remove clearances between the holes and the fasteners, thus ensuring rigid joints. Typical applications include linkage and structural joints, and as rod-end bearing pins. Assemblies with expanding fasteners permit periodic adjustments to compensate for wear or to vary the fit as desired.

The design of one type of expanding fastener is illustrated in Fig. 8-72. Radial expansion is accomplished by a series of alternately tapered segments that have free axial movement on the supporting bolt body (unthreaded portion of the bolt shank). When an axial load is applied by the nut, the outer tapered segments expand into the bore of a hole; the inner tapered sections contract against the bolt body, thus removing any clearances. Similar designs are available for blind bolts and pins.

SELF-SEALING FASTENERS

When required to retain gases or liquids, fasteners are available with preassembled or built-in seals. The choice of sealing material, such as rubber, neoprene, silicone, nylon, or polyethylene, depends on the pressure and temperature to which the seal will be exposed, possible reaction of the material to the gas or liquid, environmental factors such as corrosion, and cost. Some thread-locking materials and interference fits, discussed previously in this chapter, serve as seals for some applications.

FASTENERS MADE OF PLASTICS

The increasing use of fasteners made of plastics makes them no longer special-purpose assembly components. Threaded

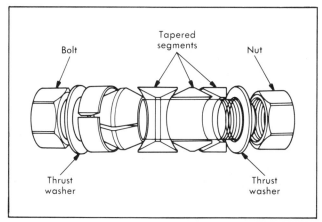

Fig. 8-72 Expanding type of headed bolt. (*Adjustable Bushing Corp.*)

fasteners being made of plastics include bolts, studs, nuts, and screws; nonthreaded fasteners include rivets, washers, retaining rings, and pins.

Advantages of plastic fasteners include low cost, light weight, corrosion and chemical resistance, and electric insulation. Versatility is another advantage; fasteners can be produced in various colors, with molded-in inserts, and in special shapes. Dimensional standards for fasteners made of plastics are the same as for metal fasteners. A possible limitation is lower load-carrying capacity than metal fasteners.

Nylons, acetals, polypropylenes, polyvinyl chlorides, and polyethylenes are among the plastics being used most commonly for fasteners. A discussion of the various plastics and their properties is presented in Volume III, *Materials, Finishing and Coating*, of this Handbook series. Some fasteners are made with glass or metallic fibers in the plastics for improved properties; others are made from two or more different plastics for the same reason. Nylon screws are available with reinforcing metal cores.

MECHANICAL FASTENERS FOR PLASTICS

The more extensive use of plastics in various products and the many types of plastics available have increased the demand for special fasteners. Advantages of such fasteners over standard types often include lower torque requirements for driving the fasteners into assemblies, higher shear strengths because of the special threads used, and the capability of withstanding higher torque loads before the fastener threads begin to strip the plastics. Screw thread inserts, discussed previously in this chapter, are used extensively to hold fasteners in plastics.

Many types of special fasteners are available because requirements vary with the plastics used in the assemblies. The plastics must be sufficiently strong to withstand the strain of fastener insertion, and the fasteners must distribute the loads and stresses properly. General requirements for special fasteners used in plastics include large flank areas on their threads, wide thread spacing, and sharp threads.

Special fasteners of the thread-forming type, which eliminate the need for tapping and inserts, thus resulting in lower costs, are used most extensively for softer plastics. Thread-cutting fasteners are more common for harder plastics. Metal inserts are sometimes provided in the plastics components, especially if the fasteners must be removed periodically. Most fasteners are available with a variety of head and point styles.

SPECIAL-PURPOSE FASTENERS

Thread-forming types of special fasteners for plastics are generally made of low-carbon steels, SAE 1018 to 1022, and are case hardened to about R_C45. The fasteners are commonly zinc plated, but other finishes are also available. One fastener design has a single-lead, spaced (high pitch) thread with a sharp 40° profile and large root diameter. This design provides ample material between the threads formed.

Another type of special fastener has a trilobular-shaped, single-lead, coarse thread with a one to two-thread tapered point. It roll forms threads in plastics without cutting and minimizes radial stresses. A fastener developed specifically for use with heat-sensitive thermoplastics has a twin-lead thread. The number of threads is the same as a single-lead fastener, but each of the two leads has only half as many threads. This design permits faster insertion with less frictional heat generated.

Another special fastener for plastics has a double-lead thread of dual-height design. The lower thread on this fastener varies in height from one-third to one-half that of the higher thread. This design provides high strength and resistance to pullout forces. Push-in or push-on fasteners that require no rotation during assembly are also available. These fasteners have flexible barbs, rings, ribs, or threads on their shanks and are pressed into thermoplastic assemblies. The pressure flanks of the barbs, rings, ribs, or threads grip the material.

FASTENERS FOR COMPOSITE MATERIALS

The advent of advanced composite materials, which are finding increased use in the aircraft and aerospace industries because of their strength and light weight, has posed some fastening problems. Many metallic fasteners are fairly incompatible with composite materials because of corrosion. Stainless steel and titanium fasteners work relatively well for composites, but stainless steel introduces some weight penalties, and titanium results in increased costs.

The Vought Corp., through both in-house funding and an Air Force Materials Laboratory contract, has been working on the development of composite fasteners. Fasteners made of glass or graphite-reinforced plastics do not corrode galvanically, are lightweight, and reduce costs because corrosion-resistant coatings and sealants are not required.

One design for a sleeve-and-pin type fastener made of glass-reinforced epoxy is illustrated in Fig. 8-73. When these fasteners are made from thermosetting plastics, they are installed with an adhesive. When made from thermoplastic materials, they swell on installation, thus eliminating the need for close hole tolerances.

BOLT-NUT COMBINATION

A self-retaining, positive-locking bolt-nut combination is shown in Fig. 8-74. The locking feature of this special-purpose fastener consists of a spring-loaded plunger pin loaded and two hardened steel balls positioned within the shank of the bolt. Spring force maintains the plunger in an extended position, securely maintaining the balls in an expanded position. This expansion provides a mechanical lock with mating axial grooves or splines in the nut. To unlock the fastener, it is necessary to depress the plunger pin, which allows the balls to retract and permits the nut to rotate freely on the bolt. Because of the hollow design of the bolt, tension applications should be avoided. Shear applications, such as clevis joints, where the bolt-nut is free to turn with the joint, are the primary uses for this type of fastener.

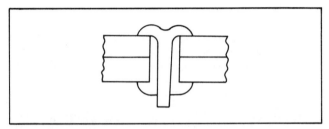

Fig. 8-73 Glass-reinforced epoxy fastener for use with composite materials.

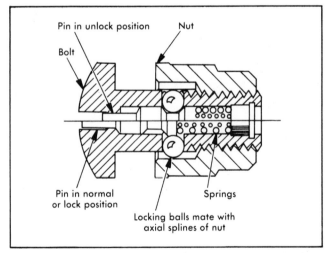

Fig. 8-74 Self-retaining, positive-locking bolt-nut combination. (*Specialty Fastener Div., Rexnord*)

RIVETS

A rivet is a one-piece, unthreaded, permanent fastener consisting of a head and a body. It is used for fastening two or more pieces together by passing the body through a hole in each piece and then clinching or forming a second head on the body end. Once set in place, a rivet cannot be removed except by chipping off the head or clinched end. The terminology for a rivet and a riveted joint is illustrated in Fig. 8-75.

A major advantage of rivets is that they can be installed economically and rapidly and are suitable for automatic assembly operations. Other advantages include low cost and the fact that rivets are good for joining dissimilar materials of different hardnesses or thicknesses. A possible limitation is that the impact required for clinching can deform thin sheets. Rivets with large heads or washers can be used to spread the stresses.

Rivets are usually less expensive than threaded fasteners, but their strength in shear or tension may be lower, especially when compared with heat-treated bolts.

Riveting is the primary fastening method used by the aircraft and aerospace industries for joining together members such as skins, channels, spars, and other structural components and subassemblies. The process is also used in many other industries for a wide variety of assemblies. In addition to their use as fasteners, rivets also serve as electrical contacts, inserts, spacers, and pivot shafts.

RIVET TYPES

There are six basic types of small rivets: solid, semitubular, tubular, bifurcated (split), compression, and special solid types as shown in Fig. 8-76. Structural rivets are large-diameter solid rivets (1/2″ diam and over). Blind rivets and eyelets are discussed in subsequent sections of this chapter.

Solid Rivets

Solid rivets are one of the most commonly used rivets. They perform a good job of hole filling, resulting in high shear and compressive strengths. Solid rivets under 1/2″ diam are classified as small and those more than 1/2″ diam as large. The major distinction between the two types is that small rivets are always annealed and large rivets are never annealed unless specified by the user.

Semitubular Rivets

Semitubular rivets are another widely used type. They have a straight or tapered hole in one end, with a hole depth normally not exceeding the shank diameter of the rivet.

Tubular Rivets

Deep-drilled, full-tubular rivets have cavities extending practically the full lengths of their shanks. Some companies consider a tubular rivet to be any small rivet whose cavity depth exceeds 1 1/2 times the shank diameter. Full-tubular rivets are used for assembling leather, plastic sheets, wood, fabric, or similar materials. With such materials, these rivets can pierce their own holes, and the slugs of material are compressed inside the rivet cavities. The shear strengths of these rivets are less than for semitubular rivets of comparable size.

Compression Rivets

Compression rivets are formed by two members: one solid and the other a deep-drilled or extruded tubular member. The diameters of the solid shank and the drilled or extruded hole produce a compression or pressed fit when the parts are assembled. Because most rivets of this type are made with special tooling, close concentricity tolerances can be held between the head and the shank, and both heads have the same appearance when assembled.

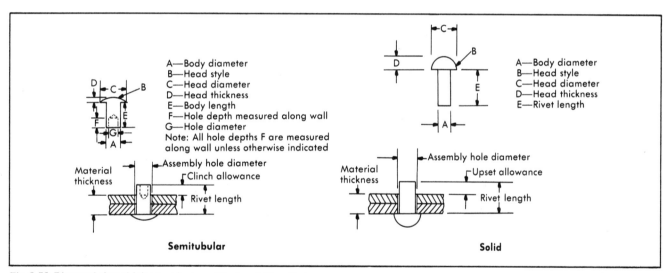

Fig. 8-75 Rivet and riveted joint terminology. (*Brainard Rivet Co.*)

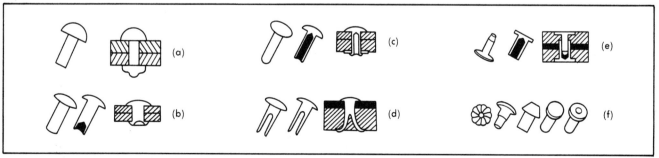

Fig. 8-76 Types of small rivets: (a) solid, (b) semitubular, (c) tubular, (d) bifurcated (split), (e) compression, and (f) special rivets with decorative heads and various shoulders.

RIVETS

Split (Bifurcated) Rivets

Split (bifurcated) rivets, as the name implies, are solid rivets whose bodies are split by either sawing or punching to form two legs or prongs. The sawed rivet provides a greater taper and stronger legs to fasten light-gage metals or heavier sections of fiber, wood, or plastics. The punched type is more suitable for lighter piercing of nonmetallic materials. Normally these rivets are furnished with an inside bevel at the end of the legs to control the direction in which the legs are to spread. If desired, an outside bevel may be specified to aid in driving.

Rivet Caps

Caps are often used in combination with full-tubular and split rivets to conceal the clinch. Functioning as a washer, the cap prevents the clinch from tearing through the material, adds strength, and gives the appearance of a second head.

Special Solid Rivets

Various types of solid rivets include those: (1) with a straight tenon, (2) with a shoulder to use as a pivot, (3) with fluted or knurled shanks to facilitate use as an insert in a molding or casting or as a hinge pin, (4) with ornamental heads for cosmetic hardware or such products as fountain pens or pocket lighters, or (5) with special heads such as balls, cams, or hex configurations to perform other functions besides that of fastening. Gage pointers for television channel selectors, electrical contacts, and bearing pivots for gages and instruments are typical applications. It is difficult to classify some of these designs as belonging to the rivet or special-product category. For example, the fastener shown in Fig. 8-77 combines the permanence of a rivet with the disassembling feature of a nut.

Structural Rivets

Large rivets, 1/2″ diam and larger, commonly called structural rivets, are cold squeezed or compressed, depending on the application. For structural steel work, rivet diameters range from 1.2 to 1.4 times the square root of the thickness of the thickest of the riveted plates. Smaller sizes are usually preferred for multiple-riveted joints. For aluminum, the rivet diameter usually ranges from one to three times the thickness of the thickest plate that it holds, depending on the anticipated stresses.

Metal Piercing Rivets

Thin metals can be pierced by semitubular, tubular, split, and pointed rivets. With semitubular and tubular rivets, piercing is done by the tubular walls of the rivets; with split rivets, piercing is accomplished with the legs or prongs of the rivets. The walls and legs are sometimes hardened to facilitate piercing. Metals pierced with such rivets include low-carbon steels and aluminum alloys, generally having a hardness less than $R_B 50$.

Pointed rivets do not pass through both parts to be joined and do not require clinching. They generally have a groove behind their pointed end into which material from the assembly component flows for locking purposes. Pointed rivets are generally limited to light-duty applications such as attaching nameplates.

Rivet Head Styles

Rivets are made with various head styles, some of which are shown in Fig. 8-78. Rivets in the semitubular and full-tubular

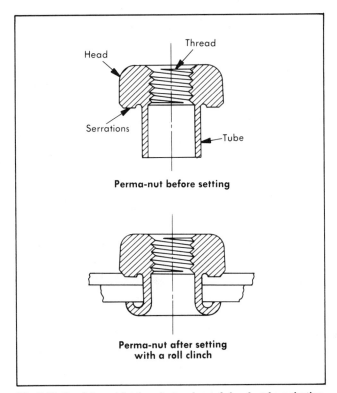

Perma-nut before setting

Perma-nut after setting with a roll clinch

Fig. 8-77 Special combination rivet and nut, fed and set by a riveting machine.

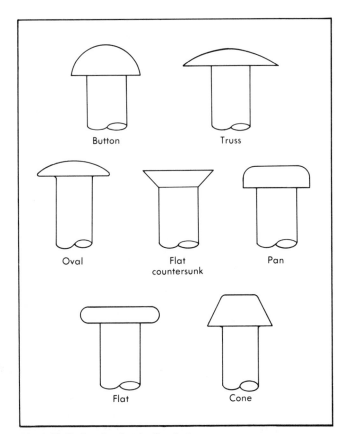

Button   Truss

Oval   Flat countersunk   Pan

Flat   Cone

Fig. 8-78 Various head styles for rivets.

classifications are generally made in oval, truss, or countersunk head styles. Split rivets are also available in these three general head styles, although oval head designs are more common. Dimensional and specification data for some representative standard rivets are presented in Tables 8-5, 8-6, and 8-7.

Selection of a specific type and head style depends primarily on the job to be done, the joint location, strength requirements, and the appearance of the joint. When shear is the only considerable stress applied, appearance requirements may be the governing factor. If the rivet is to be subjected largely to tension, it should have a relatively high head, such as the button, cone, or pan head, and is generally of the solid rivet type. When a flush surface is desired, the countersunk-head rivet may be used. Buttonhead rivets are generally used in structural steel applications. Because tubular and split rivets can be automatically fed and set with greater speed and less power than are needed for solid rivets, they are especially desirable for requirements of smaller diameters.

Rivet Materials

Any metal that can be cold worked is suitable for making rivets. The metals most commonly used for rivets include

TABLE 8-5
Data for Some Solid Rivets*

Solid Rivet Work Holes											
Fractional Body Diameter Designation	1/8	5/32	3/16	1/4	5/16	3/8	7/16	1/2	5/8	3/4	7/8
Body diameter range	0.121-0.127	0.152-0.158	0.182-0.191	0.244-0.253	0.304-0.316	0.365-0.380	0.428-0.443	0.478-0.523	0.600-0.655	0.725-0.780	0.850-0.905
Work hole diameter, reference only (5-7% larger than rivet diameter)	0.128	0.159	0.191	0.257	0.323	0.391	0.453	0.531	0.656	0.781	0.906

Solid Rivet Lengths for Various Grips										
		Rivet Diameters								
Grips	1/4	3/8	1/2	5/8	3/4	7/8	1	1 1/8	1 1/4
1/2	1 1/8	1 1/4	1 1/2	1 5/8	1 3/4	2	2 1/4	---	---
5/8	1 1/4	1 3/8	1 5/8	1 3/4	1 7/8	2 1/8	2 3/8	---	---
3/4	1 3/8	1 1/2	1 3/4	1 7/8	2 1/8	2 1/4	2 1/2	---	---
7/8	1 1/2	1 5/8	1 7/8	2	2 1/4	2 3/8	2 5/8	---	---
1	1 5/8	1 3/4	2	2 1/8	2 3/8	2 1/2	2 3/4	2 7/8	---
1/8	1 3/4	1 7/8	2 1/8	2 1/4	2 1/2	2 5/8	2 7/8	3	---
1/4	1 7/8	2	2 1/4	2 3/8	2 5/8	2 7/8	3	3 1/8	---
3/8	2	2 1/8	2 3/8	2 1/2	2 3/4	3	3 1/8	3 1/4	---
1/2	2 1/8	2 1/4	2 1/2	2 3/4	3	3 1/8	3 3/8	3 1/2	3 3/4
5/8	2 1/4	2 3/8	2 5/8	2 7/8	3 1/8	3 1/4	3 1/2	3 5/8	3 7/8
3/4	2 3/8	2 1/2	2 3/4	3	3 1/4	3 3/8	3 5/8	3 3/4	4
7/8	2 1/2	2 5/8	2 7/8	3 1/8	3 3/8	3 1/2	3 3/4	3 7/8	4 1/8
2	2 5/8	2 3/4	3 1/8	3 1/4	3 1/2	3 3/4	3 7/8	4	4 1/4
1/8	2 3/4	2 7/8	3 1/4	3 3/8	3 5/8	3 7/8	4	4 1/8	4 3/8
1/4	2 7/8	3	3 3/8	3 1/2	3 3/4	4	4 1/4	4 1/4	4 1/2
3/8	3	3 1/8	3 1/2	3 5/8	3 7/8	4 1/8	4 3/8	4 3/8	4 5/8
1/2	3 1/8	3 1/4	3 5/8	3 7/8	4	4 1/4	4 1/2	4 5/8	4 3/4
5/8	3 1/4	3 3/8	3 3/4	4	4 1/8	4 3/8	4 5/8	4 3/4	4 7/8
3/4	3 3/8	3 1/2	3 7/8	4 1/8	4 3/8	4 1/2	4 7/8	4 7/8	5 1/8
7/8	3 1/2	3 5/8	4	4 1/4	4 1/2	4 5/8	5	5	5 1/4
3	3 5/8	3 3/4	4 1/4	4 3/8	4 5/8	4 3/4	5 1/8	5 1/8	5 3/8
1/8	---	---	4 3/8	4 1/2	4 3/4	4 7/8	5 1/4	5 1/4	5 1/2
1/4	---	---	4 1/2	4 5/8	4 7/8	5	5 1/2	5 1/2	5 5/8
3/8	---	---	4 5/8	4 3/4	5	5 1/8	5 5/8	5 5/8	5 3/4
1/2	---	---	4 3/4	5	5 1/8	5 1/4	5 3/4	5 3/4	5 7/8
5/8	---	---	4 7/8	5 1/8	5 1/4	5 3/8	5 7/8	5 7/8	6
3/4	---	---	5	5 1/4	5 3/8	5 1/2	6 1/8	6 1/8	6 1/4
7/8	---	---	5 1/8	5 3/8	5 1/2	5 5/8	6 1/4	6 1/4	6 3/8

(continued)

RIVETS

TABLE 8-5—*Continued*

Grips	Solid Rivet Lengths for Various Grips								
	Rivet Diameters								
	1/4	3/8	1/2	5/8	3/4	7/8	1	1 1/8	1 1/4
4	---	5 3/8	5 1/2	5 5/8	5 3/4	6 3/8	6 3/8	6 1/2	
1/8	---	---	5 1/2	5 5/8	5 3/4	5 7/8	6 1/2	6 1/2	6 5/8
1/4	---	---	5 5/8	5 3/4	5 7/8	6 1/8	6 5/8	6 5/8	6 3/4
3/8	---	---	5 3/4	5 7/8	6	6 1/4	6 3/4	6 3/4	6 7/8
1/2	---	---	5 7/8	6	6 1/4	6 3/8	6 7/8	6 7/8	7
5/8	---	---	6	6 1/8	6 3/8	6 1/2	7	7	7 1/8
3/4	---	---	6 1/8	6 1/4	6 1/2	6 5/8	7 1/8	7 1/8	7 1/4
7/8	---	---	6 1/4	6 3/8	6 5/8	6 3/4	7 3/8	7 3/8	7 3/8
5	---	---	6 1/2	6 5/8	6 3/4	6 7/8	7 1/2	7 1/2	7 5/8
1/8	---	---	6 5/8	6 3/4	6 7/8	7	7 5/8	7 5/8	7 3/4
1/4	---	---	6 3/4	6 7/8	7	7 1/8	7 3/4	7 3/4	7 7/8
3/8	---	---	6 7/8	7	7 1/8	7 1/4	7 7/8	7 7/8	8
1/2	---	---	7	7 1/8	7 3/8	7 1/2	8 1/8	8 1/8	8 1/8
5/8	---	---	7 1/8	7 1/4	7 1/2	7 5/8	8 1/4	8 1/4	8 1/4
3/4	---	---	7 1/4	7 3/8	7 5/8	7 3/4	8 3/8	8 3/8	8 3/8
7/8	---	---	7 3/8	7 1/2	7 3/4	7 7/8	8 1/2	8 1/2	8 1/2
6	---	---	7 5/8	7 3/4	7 7/8	8	8 5/8	8 5/8	8 3/4
For countersunk deduct	1/4	1/4	3/8	1/2	5/8	3/4	7/8	7/8	1 1/16

(*Brainard Rivet Co.*)

* All dimensions in inches.

TABLE 8-6
Data for Some Full-Tubular and Split Rivets*

	Full-tubular rivets			Split rivets		
Fractional body diameter designation	9/64	3/16	3/32	1/8	9/64	3/16
Body diameter range	0.141-0.146	0.182-0.188	0.086-0.090	0.113-0.117	0.144-0.149	0.187-0.192
Work hole:						
Recommended min	0.154	0.199	0.093	0.128	0.154	0.199
Corresponding drill size	23	8	42	30	23	8
Clinch allowance:**						
Nominal	1/8	3/16	5/64	3/32	1/8	9/64
Max	5/32	1/4	7/64	1/8	5/32	11/64
Rivet length:						
Min	3/16	3/16	3/16	3/16	3/16	3/16
Increments	1/32	1/32	1/32	1/32	1/16	1/16

 * All dimensions in inches.
** For star or corrugated clinch.

aluminum alloys; brass, bronze, and other copper alloys; low, medium, and high-carbon steels; alloy steels; and corrosion-resistant steels. Rivets are also available made from plastics.

Rivets are often supplied with a natural (as-processed) finish, with no plating or other coating. However, they can be provided with various plated finishes, including zinc, cadmium, nickel, tin, copper, and brass.

Standards for Rivets

General and dimensional data for small solid rivets, 7/16" nominal diameter and smaller, are presented in ANSI Standard B18.1.1. Similar data for metric sizes of small solid rivets, 12 mm diam and smaller, is given in ANSI Standard B18.1.3M. Large solid rivets, 1/2" diam and larger, are covered in ANSI Standard B18.1.2.

TABLE 8-7
Data for Some Semitubular Rivets*

Fractional body diameter designation	1/16	3/32	0.099	1/8	9/64	3/16	7/32	1/4
Body diameter range	0.058-0.061	0.085-0.089	0.095-0.099	0.118-0.123	0.141-0.146	0.182-0.188	0.210-0.217	0.244-0.252
Work hole:								
Recommended min	0.064	0.093	0.104	0.128	0.154	0.199	0.234	0.265
Corresponding drill size	52	42	37	30	23	8	15/64	17/64
Clinch allowance:								
Nominal	0.032	0.046	0.051	0.064	0.076	0.098	0.102	0.130
Max	0.038	0.055	0.061	0.077	0.092	0.118	0.141	0.159
Rivet length:								
Min	1/16	5/64	5/64	3/32	1/8	5/32	3/16	7/32
Increments	1/64	1/64	1/64	1/64	1/32	1/32	1/16	1/16
Dimensional tolerances:**								
Body diameter	±0.0015	±0.002	±0.002	±0.0025	±0.0025	±0.003	±0.0035	±0.004
Head diameter	±0.005	±0.005	±0.005	±0.005	±0.005	±0.006	±0.007	±0.007
Head thickness	±0.002	±0.003	±0.003	±0.005	±0.005	±0.005	±0.007	±0.007
Length up to 3/8	±0.005	±0.005	±0.005	±0.010	±0.010	±0.010	±0.010	±0.010
Length more than 3/8	±0.007	±0.007	±0.007	±0.010	±0.010	±0.010	±0.015	±0.015

 * All dimensions in inches.
** Also applicable to full-tubular and split rivets (Table 8-6).

Dimensional specifications for general-purpose, semitubular, full tubular, and split rivets and rivet caps are presented in ANSI Standard B18.7. Data on general-purpose, semitubular, metric rivets is included in ANSI Standard B18.7.1M.

DESIGN OF RIVETED JOINTS

When specifying the rivet, the relationship between the diameters of the rivet body and the work hole must be determined to realize maximum shear strength. Excess work-hole diameter will prevent the rivet from filling the hole to form a solid assembly and will result in improper fastening. On the other hand, an undersized work-hole diameter slows up automatic feeding and clinching of the rivet.

Hole Sizes

Recommended hole sizes for various types and sizes of rivets are given in Tables 8-5, 8-6, and 8-7. If the hole is not clean and straight, these recommendations should be increased. When two or more rivets are to be set in the same assembly, tolerances between centers should be taken into account when establishing hole dimensions. If molded or cast parts are to be joined, the tolerances of pieces produced in different molds or dies should be taken into account, because variations can prevent high-production assembly.

Upset and/or Clinch Allowances

Upset and clinch allowances, no less important than hole clearances, are also given in Tables 8-5, 8-6, and 8-7. Three rules of thumb have been developed for sizes not listed in the tables:

1. For solid rivets, the upset material should be about 1.5 times the diameter of the body, plus 1/16″ for large rivets. Spin setting usually requires less volume of material, and 1.0 times the diameter of the body is a good starting reference.

2. Maximum length of clinch for full-tubular and bifurcated rivets should be figured at 100% of shank diameter.

3. Maximum length of clinch for semitubular rivets should be 50-70% of shank diameter to prevent buckling and ensure a tight set. If a semitubular rivet has been properly selected, its clinch allowance will force the tubular portion of the rivet to disappear in the clinch and a solid shank will remain, providing maximum strength.

To establish proper rivet length for a roll clinch, add the total compressed thickness of the workpieces to be assembled to the nominal clinch allowance recommended for the rivet body diameter to be used. In the case of a flat countersunk-head rivet, follow this procedure and then subtract the thickness of the rivet head. If the rivet length so determined does not conform to the fractional length listed in the increments shown in Table 8-5, use the next longer increment and check against the maximum clinch allowance shown. If this gives a greater-than-maximum clinch allowance, specify the next shorter length. If the rivet to be used is of an intermediate body diameter not listed in the table, the nominal clinch allowance may be figured at 50-55% of the maximum body diameter and the maximum at 65% thereof.

When roll clinches are desired on full-tubular rivets driven through work without prepunched holes, use semitubular clinch allowances in Table 8-5 as a guide. However, for best results, it is suggested that samples of work be submitted to the rivet manufacturer for recommendation of rivet applications.

Types of Joints

In rivet joint design, either lap or butt joints are generally used. In chain-rivet joints, the rivets are in even rows; in stagger-rivet joints, the rows are staggered diagonally. When rivets are used to join metal parts together, they must be selected to match the materials (type and thickness) to be joined and spaced to

RIVETS

meet the load requirements of the joint. Rivet joints should always be designed so that the rivets are subjected only to shear loads. The centerline through a row of rivets drawn parallel to the joint edge is known as the gage line. The distance from the edge of the joint to the first gage line is edge distance. Spacing or pitch is the distance between rivets. Because of the infinite number of possible joint configurations and load conditions, only the most general guidelines can be given.

Rivet Spacing

In general, pitch or spacing of rivets should be as large as practicable without impairing the efficiency of the joint. It depends, to a great extent, on the proportions of the members being joined. Minimum spacing, about three times the rivet diameter, is that which permits driving without interference; maximum spacing is generally limited to about eight times the thickness of the heaviest plate. In tension members, too small a spacing may reduce the effective area of the members carrying the stresses. In compression members, too great a spacing may allow buckling of the members between the rivets. Equations for determining the pitch of rivets are listed in Table 8-8.

RIVET AND JOINT STRENGTHS

There are many applications in which rivets under tensile stress are satisfactory; however, specifications strictly prohibiting the use of rivets in tension are usually justified. If a beam is attached to a column with an angle riveted to the web, the top rivets holding the angle to the column are in tension. The same care should be exercised in the use of rivets in tension that is used in selecting a safety factor for a structure. Attention should be paid to proper driving of rivets, because a marked change in cross section between the head and the shank will cause incipient weakness. A properly driven rivet, having a head of adequate size, will not loosen or fail until the tensile stress is well in excess of the tensile yield because the tensile load is counteracted by the tensile stress in the rivet.

Under repeated loading or reversal of stresses, a structure may fail at a stress below its ultimate tensile strength when under static load. Such failures are due to fatigue and are caused by such discontinuities or stress raisers as holes in the plate (and especially by cracks at the periphery of the hole), which are more critical and generally larger than inconsistencies in the rivet. Fatigue failures of riveted joints usually occur in the plate and rarely in the rivet.

TABLE 8-8
Pitch of Rivets for Various Types of Joints

Rows of rivets	Shear	Pitch P*
1	Single	$0.644 d^2/t + d$
1	Double	$0.13 d^2/t + d$
2	Single	$1.288 d^2/t + d$
2	Double	$2.26 d^2/t + d$
3	Single	$1.93 d^2/t + d$
3	Double	$3.30 d^2/t + d$

Note: Distance between rows in staggered riveting of multiple-riveted joints = $P/2 + d/4$, approximately. Edge distance (distance from the centerline of the hole to the edge of the plate) should be not less than 1 1/2 times the hole diameter.

* P = the center-to-center distance between adjacent rivets in one row; d = the rivet diameter; t = the thickness of the plate.

Experience has shown that a plate containing a hole will have an endurance limit of about one-third its tensile strength, but the amount will vary in actual practice. For example, a punched hole will have a lower endurance limit than a well-drilled hole, and a punched or drilled hole that is reamed will have a higher limit than a drilled hole. The one-third endurance limit applies only to an open hole and is improved by filling the hole with the rivet. The following six general conclusions have been drawn from tests of various riveted joints:

1. Riveted joints in double shear have better fatigue strength than those in single shear.
2. Fatigue strength tends to increase with rows of rivets.
3. Cold-driven steel rivets are better in fatigue than hot-driven rivets, but the variation between hot and cold-driven aluminum rivets is negligible.
4. Fatigue strength increases with rivet size.
5. Fatigue strength of joints varying in alloy have the same relation as strength of the basic alloy.
6. Butt-riveted joints have greater fatigue strength than lap joints. Similarly, a butt-joint, double-spliced plate has greater fatigue strength than a single-spliced plate.

The efficiency of a riveted joint is the ratio of the strength of the joint to the strength of the thinnest plate being joined. The strength of the joint is that at which failure can be expected in bearing, shear, or tension and is determined by the following equations:

For shear strength:

$$P_s = S_s A N \qquad (6)$$

where:

P_s = joint shear strength, lb (N)
S_s = specified shear strength of rivet, psi (MPa)
A = cross-sectional area of rivet, in.^{2} (mm^2)
N = number of shear planes

For tensile strength:

$$P_u = S_u (p - d)t \qquad (7)$$

where:

P_u = joint tensile strength, lb (N)
S_u = specified ultimate shear strength of the plate, psi (MPa)
p = pitch (spacing) of rivets, in. (mm)
d = rivet hole diameter, in. (mm)
t = plate thickness, in. (mm)

For bearing strength:

$$P_b = S_b A_c \qquad (8)$$

where:

P_b = joint bearing strength, lb (N)
S_b = specified ultimate bearing strength of plate, psi (MPa)
A_c = projected bearing area of rivet, in.^{2} (mm^2)

In each of the above equations, it is assumed that the rivet is in pure shear. Rocking of a riveted frame and other secondary effects produce bending and tensile stresses in the rivets. The calculated load should be divided by a suitable safety factor to compensate for these stresses. Generally, the factor of safety should approximate those used for the compressive and tensile loads in the other structural members. Tensile failure in the plate of a riveted joint is resisted by the metal between the rivets. If the pitch is too small, the plate will tear along the gage line when the joint is stressed.

CLINCHING (SETTING) OF RIVETS

Clinching, setting, or driving of rivets, commonly called riveting, is done in several ways with a variety of equipment. Riveting is done both hot and cold. However, because of the speed and efficiency of modern tools and machines, as well as the introduction of new rivet materials, the cold method has replaced hot riveting for most industrial applications.

Quality of Clinch

For solid rivets, there are a variety of conditions that should be considered. Too thick a workpiece for the diameter of the rivet causes buckling. Use of the correct length of rivet shank is important to form the desired upset head. If too long a length is used, buckling occurs; if too short a length is used, an incomplete head will be formed.

Hole diameter must also be correct. Too large a hole can cause buckling and/or underfilled holes, resulting in loose joints. In staking joints (the same as for upsetting or spinning), it is preferable to use the preformed head on the side of the thinner material of the joint; clinching then takes place against the thicker material. Punched holes generally improve the quality of the joint because the holes are perpendicular to the surface and have no heavy burrs.

There are no universal quality standards for clinched rivet assemblies because requirements vary with different applications. Acceptability is often determined simply by visual inspection and testing the tightness of the joint. Using a rivet having the proper shank length is necessary to obtain a full uniform roll in the crimp. Other factors that can result in poor clinching include improper hole diameters; inadequate rivet support; worn, misaligned, or improperly designed tools; improper rivet material or size; and flaws in the rivets.

Methods of Clinching

Methods of clinching rivets can be divided into the following three broad classifications:

1. *Impact*. A succession of blows, including hand and pneumatic hammer riveting.
2. *Compression*. Squeeze riveting tools are available for either hand or power operation and in both portable and stationary models.
3. *Combination*. Compression combined with rolling or spinning.

Impact riveting. This method, often called peening, is a common way of producing heads on solid rivets. The method is used frequently when the thickness or hardness of different parts in an assembly vary.

Compression (squeeze) riveting. Compression riveting is commonly used to fasten two or more parts where the rivet holes are slightly mismatched. The compression tends to distort the rivet body and fill the holes.

Combination riveting. Spin riveting is often used where a better bearing surface for the rivet head is required. This method has less tendency to distort the rivet body, which is an advantage for assemblies where one or more of the parts must be free to rotate. Possible limitations to the use of spin riveting include much slower production and higher tooling costs than other riveting methods.

Aircraft practices. When fabricating aircraft, aluminum rivets are often driven by placing the driving tool against the manufactured head and a bucking bar against the shank end of the rivet. This system can be reversed as in structural riveting, and the driving tool then consists of a hammer that is fitted with a rivet set.

For flathead or flat countersunk-head rivets, a flat set is used. For brazier, round, or buttonhead rivets, a cupped set having the approximate curvature of the rivet head is used. In an emergency, a flat set can be used for other than flathead rivets and will flatten the rivet head but will not weaken the head provided no cracking occurs.

The cupped set should be slightly wider and shallower than the head. If the set is not wide enough, the shank of the rivet will be forced up into the head because the initial impact is not directly on the center of the head. This will result in damage to the sheet or ringing of the head. A short, straight set is the most efficient, but in many cases it is impossible to get the hammer close to the work because of interference from the part or other members. Curved or offset rivet sets may be used in such cases, but they have a tendency to shear off the rivet head because the impact is struck at an angle. As a result, curved or offset rivet sets should be used only when necessary.

Because the shape and size of the bucking bar for a particular job vary with the size of the rivet, the thickness of the material, and the conditions under which driving is to take place, there are many designs and sizes of bucking bars. If no interference exists, a square, cold-rolled steel bar of the proper weight is employed. When riveting is not simple, bucks are designed to overcome the interference and still provide the inertia for proper upsetting. The right bucking bar for a specific application can be chosen only by experience and examination of the application or by actual tests. If the rivet is bent or the sheet is dimpled during the riveting process, the buck is too heavy.

Because a flat or squash upset helps simplify design of the buck and does not require a special bucking bar for each rivet diameter, this type of driven head is normally specified. However, the flat driven head requires more driving pressure and longer rivets than the cone-point head. When high driving pressure and long rivets are not desirable, and the shape of the bucking bar is not too complicated, the cone-point head should be used. The recommended shape and dimensions of the cone-point head are shown in Fig. 8-79, view *a*. The degree of upset for this type of head is easily checked by measuring the diameter of the upset, which should be maintained as close as possible to 1.5 times the nominal shank diameter. If the proper shank length is used and the above limitation maintained, the other head dimensions will be controlled automatically. If the dimensions are followed, several rivet sizes can be driven with the same buck. To help center the buck on the rivet shank, the skirt can be flared out slightly, but this limits it to use on only one size rivet.

When a more rounded head is desired, a buttonhead upset can be used. The dimensions of the driven buttonhead for rivets less than 1/2" diam are shown in Fig. 8-79, view *b*. For rivets 1/2" and larger, a smaller buttonhead should be used (view *c*). The pressures required to drive the buttonhead are about double that of the conehead.

Hole Preparation

While some rivets, previously discussed, can pierce their own holes, most rivet holes are either punched, drilled, or reamed

RIVETS

prior to riveting. Punched and drilled holes are made to finished size in one operation. Reamed holes are punched or drilled undersize and then reamed to finished size. Rivet holes are often drilled undersize to be used as pilot holes when locating the part in an assembly jig. After the part is located and clamped in position, the pilot hole is drilled to the finished size.

Hole size. The diameter of a rivet hole is critical and contributes much to the strength of the riveted joint. The rivet hole should be just large enough to afford easy insertion of the rivet. If the hole is too large, bulging and separation of the assembly components, bent rivets, or eccentric upsets and loose rivets will result. Rivet hole clearances vary from 0.003″ (0.08 mm) for thin-gage stock to 0.032″ (0.81 mm) for a 1″ (25 mm) plate. Burrs or chips must be removed from the rivet hole or from the immediate vicinity of the joint to ensure a tight joint.

Holding sheets. If an operator works from one end of a line of rivets to the other, the aluminum sheets will creep and spread so the holes at the opposite end of the sheet will be out of alignment. To prevent this creep, aluminum sheets are held tightly together at intervals with bolts, rivets, screws, or sheet holders, as shown in Fig. 8-80. The sheet holders are then removed as the riveting progresses along the line of rivets. When rivets are used as sheet holders, the sheets are first riveted at intervals and the intermediate holes are then riveted.

Dimpling/countersinking. Flush rivets, as shown in Fig. 8-81, view *a*, are specified for riveting aircraft skin panels to eliminate the drag created by other types of rivet heads. A flat-headed rivet is used and driven so the top of the head is flush with the skin surface after it is driven. The area around the rivet hole is dimpled or countersunk to allow the rivet head to be located below the skin panel surface. The dimpling or countersinking may be accomplished by any of the following methods:

1. Predimpling or press countersinking with dies.
2. Predimpling or press countersinking with a die and the rivet.
3. Machine countersinking.
4. Combination machine countersinking and predimpling.
5. Combination machine countersinking and dimpling.

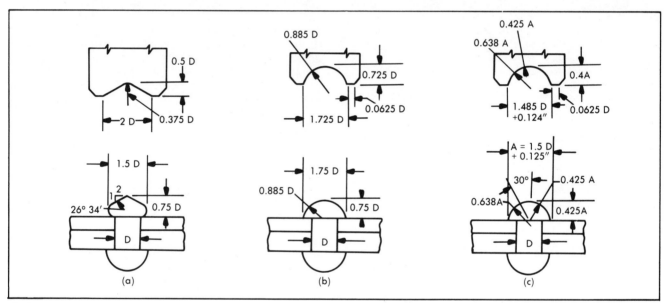

Fig. 8-79 Recommended proportions of rivet heads: (a) cone point, (b) button head for less than 1/2″ diam rivets, and (c) button head for 1/2″ diam rivets and larger.

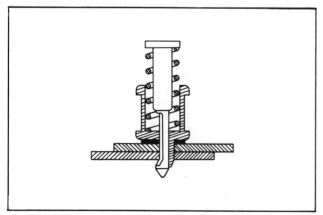

Fig. 8-80 Holder for aligning holes in aluminum sheets during riveting.

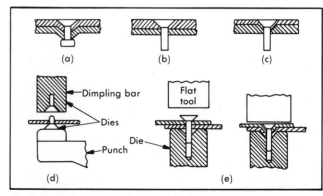

Fig. 8-81 Flush riveting: (a) typical joint; (b) countersunk joint in heavy stock; (c) same as (b), but with dimpling; (d) predimpling; and (e) combined dimpling and riveting.

The method used depends on the thickness of the sheet, the accessibility of the rivet holes, and the speed at which the operation can be done.

Dimpling and predimpling are essentially the same in that both require a dimpling bar and employ either a pneumatic hammer (one-shot type) or squeezer. The pneumatic hammer is usually employed as a portable tool if the part or assembly may be difficult to manipulate. The pneumatic hammer usually makes one dimple at a time, whereas the squeezer may be set to produce 8-10 dimples simultaneously. The difference between these methods is that the predimple method uses a punch, as shown in Fig. 8-81, view *d*, while the dimple method employs the rivet itself to form the sheet, as shown in view *e*.

These two methods are limited by the gage of the sheets being riveted. The limit is about 0.064 to 0.091" (1.63 to 2.31 mm), depending on the diameter of the rivet and the alloy and temper of the material. For thick sheet not easily formed, the material may be machine-countersunk as shown in Fig. 8-81, view *b*. When material of a gage too heavy to be dimpled is to be joined to thin-gage material, machine countersinking may be combined with dimpling or predimpling of thin stock, as shown in view *c*.

Portable Riveting Tools

It is important that the correct shape and size of riveting tool be used and that excessive driving pressures be avoided. Excessive pressure in driving may result in bulging of the edge of the piece being riveted; buckling or other distortion, particularly if thin material is used; and weakening or fracturing of metal adjacent to the hole. Several types of portable riveting tools are shown in Fig. 8-82.

Rivet holes tend to get out of coincidence during the driving operation because of slippage, swelling of the metal, or warping

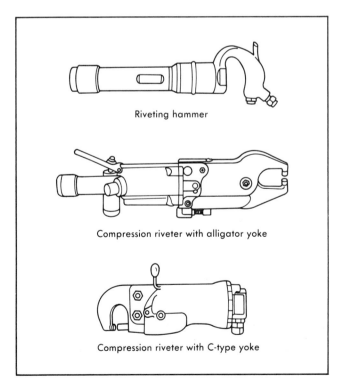

Riveting hammer

Compression riveter with alligator yoke

Compression riveter with C-type yoke

Fig. 8-82 Portable riveting tools.

caused by heat. For this reason, the work should be tight to prevent slippage and to prevent the rivets from squeezing out between the parts of the joint.

Pneumatic hammers. Portable pneumatic hammers are used extensively for riveting. These tools operate with compressed air that accelerates a mass and transfers force through a rivet, the force stopping on impact with a bucking bar and forming a head on the rivet. They may be of the one-shot, slow-hitting, or fast-hitting type. One-shot pneumatic hammers are the easiest to control because the rivet is driven with a single blow. However, one-shot hammers cannot be used to rivet thin sheets because of the danger of damaging the sheet, and they are limited as to size and alloy of rivet that can be driven. A one-shot hammer can be operated by hand or mounted on a pedestal and operated mechanically. The slow-hitting hammer, which strikes from 900 to 2500 blows per minute, is most popular. With a little practice, it can be easily controlled to produce a sound rivet. The fast-hitting hammer is harder to control and is used only to a limited extent. It strikes from 3000 to 5000 blows per minute.

Squeeze riveters. The best control in riveting is obtained by using a squeeze (compression-type) riveter. A squeeze riveter differs from a pneumatic hammer in that the set and the buck (called dollies) are integral parts, and the upset is produced by a slow squeezing action. After this type of riveter is set up, it is relatively easy to produce properly upset shanks with well-centered heads. However, squeeze riveters are slower than hammers and their use is limited by the structural design of the assembly. Because of the latter factor, squeeze riveters are used primarily for subassembly work.

Squeeze riveters are either portable, semiportable, or mounted and can be mechanically or pneumatically operated. Mounted squeezer tools can be set up in multiples (or gangs), thus making it possible to set more than one rivet at a time. Multiple squeeze-riveting is fast and efficient and produces uniform upsets while holding work to a minimum. The only limitation of multiple squeeze-riveting is the nature of the assembly being riveted. The dolly sets, which are comparable with the set and bucking bar used with the hammer, are made of steel, and the same cupping dimensions are used.

Riveting Machines

Manual or automatic riveting machines, bench or floor-mounted (see Fig. 8-83), use the same principle of operation as portable riveting tools. The rivet is fed from the hopper to a track that deposits it, shank down, in the center of the upper jaws (see Fig. 8-84). As the cycle proceeds, a driver descends and contacts the rivet head, forcing it downward past the point where the jaws come to a stop. This action pushes the rivet through the jaws and onto a spring-mounted plunger on the lower arm of the machine. With continued downward motion, the plunger pin retracts and guides the rivet through the work until it bottoms against the lower die and is clinched. When the driver and the jaws retract, the plunger pushes the rivet and work off the die.

The anvils used to form the clinch are expendable tools. They vary in design with the type of rivet and the service required of the assembly. To design an anvil to perform as required, the following design criteria must be considered: (1) diameter of rivet body; (2) type, diameter, and depth of hole in the rivet; (3) thickness of the materials being assembled; (4) type of clinch required; and (5) clearance of workpiece. Because each

RIVETS

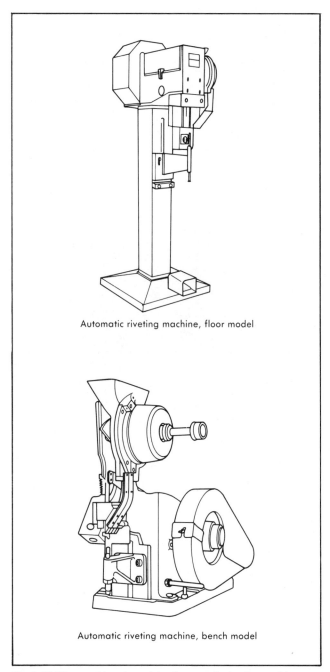

Automatic riveting machine, floor model

Automatic riveting machine, bench model

Fig. 8-83 Floor and bench models of automatic riveting machines.

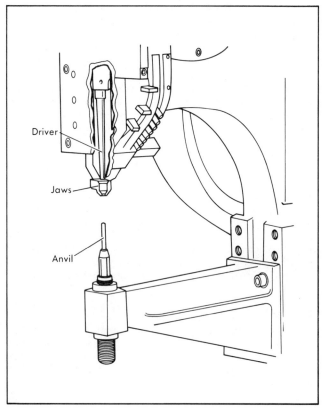

Fig. 8-84 Driver, jaws, and anvil mounted on a riveting machine.

different rivet style requires a particular anvil form to give the desired clinch, it is recommended that the riveting machine manufacturer specify the proper anvil.

Generally, semitubular rivets are roll set; full-tubular rivets are star set. Roll setting forms the rivet into a smooth roll clinch, either against the work, against a washer, or in space in the case of a pivot pin or small shaft. Star setting splits the end of the rivet into six or eight equal segments as the clinch is formed. Star setting is often specified for clinching against soft materials, such as leather, wood, and fabric, when a larger diameter clinch is desired.

Bifurcated (split) rivets are usually set against a solid form that bends back the prongs and presses them into the work to provide a smooth clinch. If a washer or cap is employed, it is held in a solid tip, and the tubular or bifurcated fastener is driven through the work and the hole in the cap and clinched against this member. Compression rivets are not set, but are pressed together to form a tight fit. This is accomplished by feeding the male half from the top arm of the riveting machine while holding the bottom half against a flat anvil.

Safety requirements for the construction, care, and use of rivet setting equipment are presented in ANSI Standard B154.1.

Automatic Drilling and Riveting Machines

The high cost, low production rates, and inconsistent results associated with manual riveting, especially for joining aluminum components in the aircraft industry, has led to the extensive use of automation in fastening. Machines are available that automatically position and clamp the assembly, drill and/or countersink the required holes, feed and insert the proper rivets, head the rivets by upsetting, and unclamp the assembly (see Fig. 8-85). Industrial robots, some with computer vision as a sensory feedback, are also being used for automated fastening.

Advantages. The automatic drilling and riveting process permits faster production at lower cost. In many applications, improvements in production rates of up to 10 times have been realized. Another important advantage is the improved quality of the joints produced. Hole diameters can be held to 0.001″ (0.03 mm) and countersunk depths maintained to a tolerance of 0.0005″ (0.013 mm). Close control of the countersunk depths often eliminates the need for shaving the rivet heads, and rigid

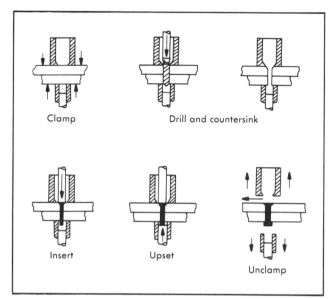

Fig. 8-85 Sequence of operations for automatic riveting. (*GEMCOR Drivmatic Div.***)**

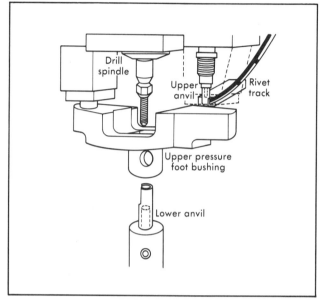

Fig. 8-86 Tooling components for automatic drilling and riveting.

clamping during drilling makes deburring unnecessary. These machines, with proper upper and lower tooling, will handle all standard type rivets and all materials capable of being squeezed. Controlled parameters of machine operation contribute to high-order repeatability, with a rivet reject rate of less than 1%.

Applications. In addition to extensive use by the commercial aircraft industry, automatic fastening is being applied in a growing number of other industries. Materials joined include aluminum, titanium, and other metal alloys, as well as composite materials. The automatic machines are also being used for the application of threaded fasteners, nut plates, and blind fasteners, in addition to rivets.

Applications include the assembly of helicopter tail sections, cargo-bay doors for the space shuttle, dish-shaped antennas, and components for military vehicles. The technology is also being used in the primary assembly line for the all-aluminum Hummer vehicle, which is now being produced to replace the U.S. Army jeep.

Automatic drilling and riveting machines are also being used for the application of slug rivets—low-cost, headless slugs of aluminum alloy. The slugs are hydraulically squeezed from both ends, forming leakproof interference fits. This technique has eliminated the need for fuel tanks previously built into the wings of large aircraft. By making fuel storage integral with the wings (called wet wings), fuel-carrying capacity has been increased and weight and complexity of the wings decreased.

Drilling and riveting machines. Hydraulically powered machines for automatic drilling and riveting consist essentially of a C-frame carrying the tooling and a positioning system for moving the assemblies to be fastened. Because of the wide variations in the size, shape, and weight of assemblies, as well as the types of fasteners, there are no standard or universal machines. Instead, a family of machines have been built, with throat depths ranging from 6 to 168″ (152 to 4267 mm) and throat heights to 111″ (2819 mm).

Tooling. The basic tooling for a machine is illustrated in Fig. 8-86. With the workpieces to be joined firmly clamped in the machine, a drilling unit moves into place to produce the hole.

The drilling unit is then moved aside and, with the clamping force still applied, a riveting unit is moved into position. A rivet is automatically fed from one or more hoppers, down a track, and into feed fingers that insert it into the hole. In this position, the rivet is hydraulically squeezed against the upper anvil to form the required head. Clamping pressure is then released, and the assembly is removed or repositioned for additional fastening.

The machines exert as much as 6000 lb (27 kN) of clamping force and up to 50,000 lb (222 kN) of force for heading the rivets. Average cycle time is 3 1/2 seconds, and production rates of more than 24 rivets per minute are attained. When required, the formed rivet heads are shaved flush on the same automatic machine. For hot dimpling, a three-position tooling head is used. Tooling at the first position has a built-in cartridge heater and produces a male dimple profile. Drilling is performed at the second position and upsetting at the third.

Positioning systems. Methods of moving assemblies for automatic drilling and riveting vary from simple manual means to sophisticated electronic controls. Manual positioning is used extensively for smaller and lighter assemblies, as well as those with access problems. These systems are generally equipped with bearings and/or rollers to minimize friction, and chains or straps and a sling arrangement are often used for vertical movements.

Semiautomatic positioning systems are generally equipped with hydraulic and/or pneumatic cylinders, and electric motors to jog the assemblies into position. In positioning with computer numerical control (CNC), a preprogrammed microprocessor automatically energizes servomotors to accurately control positioning. A six-axis CNC positioning system is shown schematically in Fig. 8-87. The CNC units can also be used to control cycling of the machine.

Hole-location methods. Several methods are used to locate the holes for automatic drilling and riveting. In one method, a masking template containing the desired rivet hole pattern is placed on the assembly, sprayed, and then removed, leaving dots on the assembly. One of the dots is then positioned in alignment with a fiber-optic or laser light system and the machine cycle is initiated. Then the procedure is repeated. Another method of hole location is to provide a pilot pin in the lower anvil that enters predrilled pilot holes in the assembly.

Accessory equipment. Various accessories are available for use with automatic drilling and riveting machines. One is a closed-loop servosystem for controlling drilling speed and feed. Speeds are variable from 100 to 6000 rpm and feed rates from 1 to 96 ipm (25 to 2438 mm/min). Another accessory is a system to automatically select the proper length rivet. With this system, the thickness of the assembly stack is measured, and encoders send signals to a programmable controller that selects a proper rivet from a number of vibratory feeder bowls.

Orbital Riveting

Orbital riveting (see Fig. 8-88) is a low-pressure, line-of-contact (T), cold forming process. The riveting tool, mounted in a rotating spindle, is inclined at a slight angle (3-6°) so that the tool axis intersects the centerline, P, of the spindle at the working end of the tool. As the orbiting tool is fed toward the work, material at the end of the rivet shank is incrementally displaced to form the required head. Machines are available for pneumatic or hydraulic operation and in bench, floor, and opposed-head models. Modular heads that fit most machines are also available with one or more spindles. Multispindle systems with center distances ranging from 3/16 to 20" (5 to 508 mm) and multilevel assembly systems are being used.

An important advantage of orbital riveting is the consistently high-quality results attained, with close tolerances and smooth finishes. Because there is no impact between the tooling and the workpiece, the process is quiet. Versatility is another advantage; a wide range of metals and plastics can be formed in this way, and many other forming operations, in addition to riveting, can be done on these machines. The process requires less power and force than most other riveting methods. Typical head shapes and forming peens are illustrated in Fig. 8-89.

Radial Riveting

Radial riveting is similar to orbital riveting except that the tools move in a planetary or rosette motion instead of being mounted in rotating spindles. In the rosette forming pattern, R, shown in Fig. 8-90, each loop of the rosette path is guided through center Z. The longitudinal axis of the riveting tool always overlaps the center of rivet point N. A cycloidal movement guides the tool through the rosette pattern. The rivet material is spread radially outward and inward, with some tangential overlapping, to form the required head.

Advantages of radial riveting are the same as those just discussed for orbital riveting. However, radial riveting is said to impart improved conductivity to the materials because of the kneading action. As a result, it is used extensively in the production of electrical contact points.

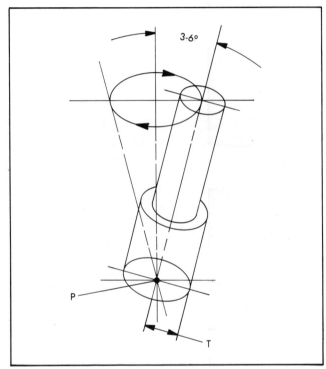

Fig. 8-88 Orbital riveting. (*VSI Automation Assembly*)

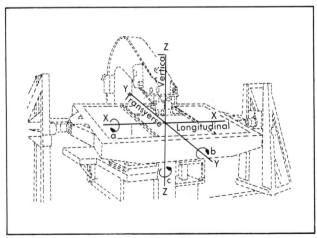

Fig. 8-87 Six-axis CNC positioning system. (*GEMCOR Drivmatic Div.*)

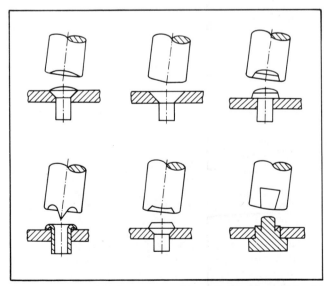

Fig. 8-89 Typical forming peens used in orbital riveting and heads produced. (*Weber Automatic Screwdrivers & Assembly Systems*)

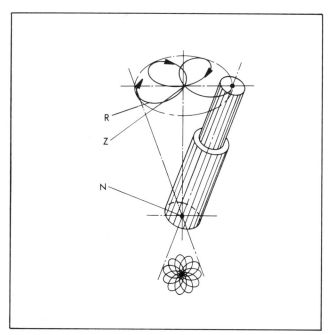

Fig. 8-90 Radial riveting. (*Bracker Corp.*)

Electromagnetic Riveting

Electromagnetic riveting (EMR) allows fast semi to fully automatic, single-impact riveting with the advantages of built-in repeatability and quality assurance. Systems used for electromagnetic riveting are capable of installing up to 20 rivets per minute. They can also install rivets made from various materials up to 3/4″ diam and allow rapid changes of conventional rivet dies to easily adapt to varying end uses. With EMR, rivets can be installed to precision interference profiles for fluidtight and fatigue-critical applications.

Quality characteristics of EMR include high fatigue ratings, low reject rates, good and uniform finished-rivet cosmetics, and low structural distortion and damage probability. Rivet installation with manual EMR tools requires little operator training and creates comparatively low noise and minimal operator fatigue. Electromagnetic riveting systems are relatively low in cost and require a minimum of floor space and maintenance.

Manual EMR equipment consists of a power pack connected to two semiportable, handheld rivet guns (see Fig. 8-91) by special power transmission cables. The power pack contains the capacitor bank and each rivet gun contains a coil abutting against a copper-faced driving ram. The work cycle consists of charging the capacitor bank to a preset voltage level, followed by a rapid discharge through the series-connected coils. Synchronized by the current, the guns produce electromagnetic forces on the rams, rapidly forming a rivet with equal and opposite forces (see Fig. 8-92).

Because of the dynamic impact principle in the EMR process, rather than the static force application in hydraulic machines, EMR guns can be held by hand or incorporated in fully automated truss-frame type structures with practically unlimited throat depths. Computer-controlled sensing devices prohibit firing unless the guns are precisely aligned.

Deformation energy applied in the process is 400 ft-lbf (542 J), with a deformation time of 5×10^{-4} second. The maximum charge voltage for the power pack is 6000 V, and the pack has a

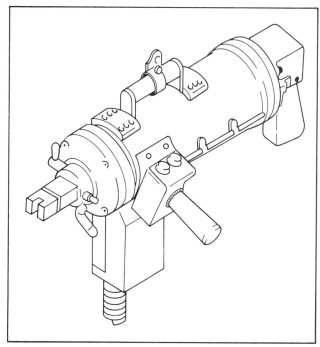

Fig. 8-91 Handheld gun for electromagnetic riveting. (*Maxwell Laboratories Inc.*)

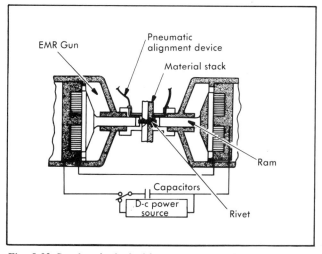

Fig. 8-92 Synchronized, dual-impact method of electromagnetic riveting. (*Maxwell Laboratories, Inc.*)

maximum stored-energy rating of 6500 J. The energy requirement for clinching a 3/8″ diam aluminum rivet is 2600 J. Handheld guns used are about 6 1/2″ (165 mm) diam by 23 1/2″ (597 mm) long. Because each gun weighs 75 lb (34 kg), they are used with counterbalances for manual operation.

BLIND RIVETS/FASTENERS

Blind rivets are mechanical fasteners having self-contained mechanical, chemical, or other features that form upsets on their blind ends and expand their shanks to join parts of assemblies. This design permits the fasteners to be installed in the holes of joints that are accessible from only one side.

BLIND RIVETS

Advantages and Limitations

In addition to their use in joints that are accessible from only one side, blind rivets are increasingly being applied where both sides of joints are accessible. The reasons include lower installed costs, faster and easier assembly, and/or improved appearance. Another important advantage of blind rivets is that the operators have no negative effect on the consistently uniform and reliable tightening of the joint.

Blind rivets are suitable for fastening many materials, including plastics, and they are resistant to vibration and tampering. These rivets are suitable for semiautomatic and automatic assembly, with feed rates to 3000 per hour. In addition to fastening, the rivets can serve as pivot shafts, spacers, electrical contacts, nut plates, and stops. Some blind rivets have a mechanical lock between the mandrel and the stem, providing high fatigue resistance.

A possible limitation is that some blind rivets require special installation tools. Also, ample clearance is required for the pulling heads and setting tools used with some types of blind rivets.

Nomenclature

The following glossary consists of selected terms commonly used with respect to blind rivets.

body The component of a blind rivet that does the fastening. The starting rivet has a primary head and, when set, has a secondary head. The cross section of the rivet body is usually round, and its outside diameter establishes the rivet size.

    primary head The original head on the rivet body. After setting, it is always located on the access side of the joint.

    secondary head (blind head) The head formed on the blind side of the joint as the result of pulling the mandrel or driving the pin into the rivet body—a process known as upsetting.

breaker groove/notch A notched area on the shanks of some mandrels defining the location at which the mandrel breaks under a predetermined tensile load.

core The axially located hole in the rivet body. It may or may not extend the full length of the rivet body, depending on style.

end The part of the rivet body located at the extremity of the shank opposite the primary (starting) head. It may be closed, open, or split.

grip range The minimum to maximum thickness of materials that can be joined properly with a blind rivet of a given length.

mandrel or pin The portion of a blind rivet that is preassembled in the rivet body. During rivet setting, pulling or driving the mandrel or pin forms the secondary (blind) head. The mandrels can be smooth, serrated, or threaded.

shank The part of the rivet body extending from the underside of the head to the extreme end.

soft set A rivet that requires a mandrel tensile break load less than standard.

standoff A type of setting in which the primary head of the rivet does not come in contact with the joint surface.

Classification of Blind Rivets

Blind rivets can be made from any material that can be cold formed. The metals most commonly used include steels, stainless steels, aluminum alloys, brasses, bronzes, other copper alloys, and titanium. Blind rivets are also available made from plastics. The rivets are generally available with shank diameters from 3/32 to 1/4″ and 2.4 to 6.3 mm, but special rivets have been made with shank diameters to 3/4″. The major types of blind rivets are pull-mandrel, drive-pin, threaded, and chemically expanded.

Pull-mandrel. Blind rivets of this type generally consist of a rivet body and a mandrel or, sometimes, a locking collar. In setting, the rivet is inserted into holes in the parts to be joined, the mandrel is gripped and pulled axially, and its head upsets the rivet body to form a blind head. These rivets are further classified into pull-through mandrel, break-mandrel, non-break-mandrel, and flush-break, self-plugging multigrip types.

Pull-through mandrel. In setting these rivets, the mandrel is pulled completely through the rivet body, resulting in a hollow rivet. Plugs can be inserted to seal the holes. Dimensional, mechanical, and performance requirements for inch sizes of pull-through mandrel blind rivets are presented in IFI Standard 117; metric sizes are covered in IFI Standard 520.

Break-mandrel. As shown in Fig. 8-93, a rivet of this type is inserted into holes in the workpieces to be assembled, and the setting tool is placed over the mandrel of the rivet. When the tool is actuated, the tool jaws grip the mandrel and pull it into the rivet body, thus forming a secondary head. The mandrel then breaks at a predetermined point, leaving part of the mandrel locked in the rivet body; the remainder of the mandrel is discarded. Specifications for break-mandrel blind rivets are presented in IFI Standards 114 (inch sizes) and 505 (metric sizes). National Aerospace Standards (NAS) 1400 and 1740, and Military Specification MIL-R-7885 cover locked stem, flush-break versions.

Nonbreak-mandrel. During setting of this type rivet, the mandrel is pulled into or against the rivet body, but does not break. Such rivets require that the mandrels be dressed in a subsequent operation.

Flush-break, self-plugging multigrip. These positive-locking, pull-mandrel blind rivets are suitable for use in joining the component parts of assemblies having varying grip ranges and where structural integrity is a design requirement. Specifications for these rivets are presented in IFI Standard 134.

Drive-pin. A drive-pin blind rivet has a pin within the rivet body, the pin projecting above the rivet head (see Fig. 8-94, view *a*). In setting (view *b*), the rivet is inserted into holes in the parts to be joined, and the pin is forced into the rivet body until the pin end is flush with the top of the primary head of the rivet. This action flares or spreads the end of the rivet body, thus forming the secondary (blind) head. Requirements for inch sizes of drive-pin blind rivets are presented in IFI Standard 123.

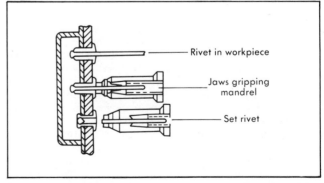

Fig. 8-93 Setting a blind rivet that has a break-type pull-mandrel. (*POP Fasteners Div., Emhart Fastener Group*)

Rivet in workpiece

Jaws gripping mandrel

Set rivet

Threaded. Threaded blind rivets have internally threaded rivet bodies. A rivet is threaded onto the mandrel of an installation tool and inserted into holes in the assembly components (see Fig. 8-95, view *a*). When the tool mandrel is pulled or rotated, the walls of the rivet body are bulged outward to form a blind head (view *b*). If upset by rotating, the mandrel may be left in the rivet body or replaced to provide sealing or increased shear and tensile properties.

Figure 8-96 illustrates a compression-type blind fastener consisting of a threaded machine screw, made from carbon or stainless steel, which is mechanically joined to a slotted aluminum rivet sleeve. A neoprene composition washer provides a positive seal. The fastener is inserted into a hole and installed with a power driver equipped with a holding sleeve. As the screw turns, the sleeve is pulled into four clamping tines that provide the holding power. These fasteners are available with clamping sleeves made from plastics to provide increased corrosion resistance.

Chemically expanded. Chemically expanded blind rivets, often called explosive rivets, have hollowed ends filled with an explosive chemical. In setting, the rivet is inserted into holes in the assembly components and either heat or an electrical current is applied to the rivet head.

Body Styles

Blind rivets are available with various body styles. These styles include open, closed, and split ends; slotted shanks; and special designs, such as soft-set rivets.

Open-end rivets. After setting, open-end blind rivets resemble conventional tubular rivets, discussed previously in this section. However, unlike the tubular rivet, the mandrel head is retained within the blind head of the rivet (see Fig. 8-97). The dimensions of some open-end blind rivets are presented in Table 8-9. Various combinations of different body and mandrel materials are available (see Table 8-10).

Closed-end rivets. These rivets are made with cup-shaped closed ends that remain closed on the blind sides of the assemblies after setting. This design provides sealing, preventing the passage of gases or liquids through or around the set rivets. Closed-end blind rivets provide 100% mandrel head retention, which can be important for electronic applications. Dimensional, mechanical, and performance requirements for break-mandrel, closed-end blind rivets are presented in IFI Standards 126 (inch sizes) and 509 (metric sizes).

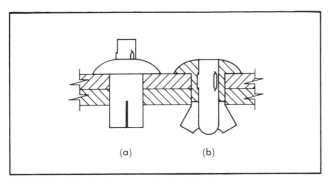

Fig. 8-94 Drive-pin blind rivet: (a) before setting and (b) after setting. (*Southco, Inc.*)

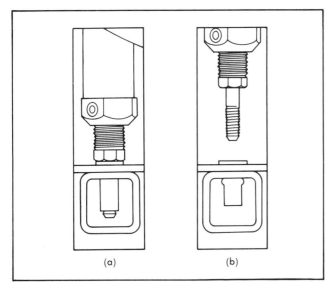

Fig. 8-95 Threaded blind rivet: (a) before setting and (b) after setting. (*Aerospace and Defense Div., The BFGoodrich Co.*)

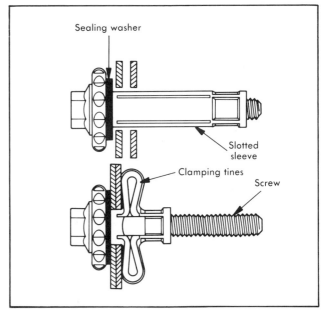

Fig. 8-96 Compression-type blind fastener before (top view) and after installation. (*Fabco Fastening Systems, Townsend Div., Textron Inc.*)

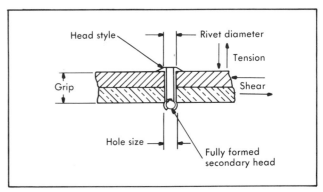

Fig. 8-97 Terminology for open-end blind rivets.

BLIND RIVETS

T-rivets. The so-called T-rivet (see Fig. 8-98) is one example of a split-end rivet. In setting a T-rivet, a hardened steel mandrel cuts the end of the aluminum body into a trifurcated shape.

Slotted-shank rivets. The shanks of these rivets have one or more axial slots that extend from the undersides of the heads and terminate short of the open ends. The remaining portions of the shanks are hollow cylinders, similar to open-end rivets. They are available in types having strength characteristics ranging from those of self-plugging structural types to soft-set, semifilled types. All slotted-shank rivets feature a large blind side bearing surface and extended grip ranges (see Fig. 8-99).

Soft-set rivets. These rivets are identical in appearance to open-end rivets. However, they have a body made from a softer-than-standard aluminum alloy and a mandrel that breaks at a lower tensile strength than standard mandrels. Soft-set rivets require only moderate setting pressures, which are essential in fastening some of the more brittle plastics or similar materials, as well as thin parts.

TABLE 8-9
Dimensions of Open-End Blind Rivets*

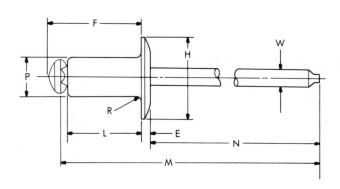

Nominal Diameter	D	H	E ±0.004	R max	W, + 0.002, -0.001	Rivet No.	L ±0.015	M, Nominal	N min	F max = L max plus:	Recommended Grip Range
3/32	0.092 + 0.004	0.188 ± 0.010	0.028	0.015	0.057	32	0.225	1 7/16	1.00	0.100	0.032-0.125
						34	0.350	1 7/16			0.126-0.250
						36	0.475	1 7/16			0.251-0.375
1/8	0.124 + 0.004	0.350 ± 0.012	0.036	0.015	0.076	41	0.188	1 3/8	1.00	0.120	0.032-0.062
						42	0.250	1 3/8			0.063-0.125
						43	0.313	1 7/16			0.126-0.187
						44	0.375	1 1/2			0.188-0.250
						45	0.438	1 9/16			0.251-0.312
						46	0.500	1 5/8			0.313-0.375
						48	0.625	1 3/4			0.376-0.500
						410	0.750	1 7/8			0.501-0.625
5/32	0.155 + 0.004	0.312 ± 0.016	0.043	0.018	0.095	52	0.275	1 1/2	1.06	0.140	0.063-0.125
						53	0.338	1 9/16			0.126-0.187
						54	0.400	1 5/8			0.188-0.250
						56	0.525	1 11/16			0.251-0.375
						58	0.650	1 13/16			0.376-0.500
3/16	0.186 + 0.005	0.375 ± 0.018	0.051	0.020	0.114	62	0.300	1 9/16	1.06	0.160	0.063-0.125
						64	0.425	1 11/16			0.126-0.250
						66	0.550	1 13/16			0.251-0.375
						68	0.675	1 15/16			0.376-0.500
						610	0.800	2 1/16			0.501-0.625
						612	0.925	2 3/16			0.626-0.750
						614	1.050	2 5/16			0.751-0.875
						616	1.175	2 7/16			0.876-1.000
1/4	0.249 + 0.006	0.500 ± 0.025	0.069	0.022	0.151	84	0.475	1 7/8	1.25	0.180	0.063-0.250
						86	0.600	2			0.251-0.375
						88	0.725	2 1/8			0.376-0.500
						810	0.850	2 1/4			0.501-0.625
						812	0.975	2 3/8			0.626-0.750
						814	1.100	2 1/2			0.751-0.875
						816	1.225	2 5/8			0.876-1.000

(POP Fasteners Div., Emhart Fastener Group)

* All dimensions in inches.

Head Styles

A variety of heads, both protruding and flush, are provided on blind rivets. Common protruding heads are the dome and large-flanged types. Countersunk heads are the most common flush type.

Dome heads. These heads have a flange diameter equal to twice the body diameter. This design generally provides sufficient bearing surface to retain all but parts made from extremely soft or brittle materials.

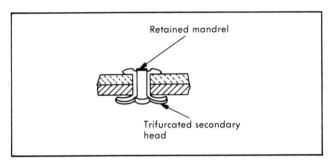

Fig. 8-98 T-rivet has a split end that is spread by a mandrel. (*POP Fasteners Div., Emhart Fastener Group*)

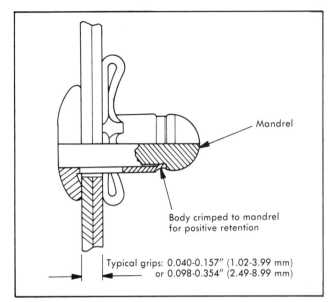

Fig. 8-99 Slotted-shank, semifilled core, multigrip rivet for assembling soft or brittle materials. (*Avdel Engineered Assembly Systems*)

TABLE 8-10
Typical Strengths of Various Sizes of Open-End Blind Rivets
Having Bodies and Mandrels of Different Materials

Material		Rivet Diameter, in.	Typical Ultimate Strengths, lb (N)	
Body	Mandrel		Shear	Tensile
Aluminum	Aluminum	3/32	85 (378)	135 (600)
		1/8	155 (689)	235 (1045)
		5/32	225 (1001)	350 (1557)
		3/16	315 (1401)	500 (2224)
		1/4	460 (2046)	750 (3336)
Aluminum	Steel	3/32	125 (556)	175 (778)
		1/8	210 (934)	325 (1446)
		5/32	340 (1512)	490 (2180)
		3/16	445 (1979)	720 (3203)
		1/4	890 (3959)	1200 (5338)
Copper	Steel	3/32	N.A.	N.A.
		1/8	215 (956)	300 (1334)
		5/32	N.A.	N.A.
		3/16	N.A.	N.A.
		1/4	N.A.	N.A.
Steel	Steel	3/32	150 (667)	250 (1112)
		1/8	295 (1312)	425 (1890)
		5/32	410 (1824)	570 (2535)
		3/16	590 (2624)	815 (3625)
		1/4	1245 (5538)	1505 (6694)
Stainless steel	Steel	3/32	230 (1023)	280 (1245)*
Stainless steel	Stainless steel	1/8	550 (2446)	700 (3114)
		5/32	900 (4003)	1130 (5026)
		3/16	1100 (4893)	1375 (6116)
		1/4	1700 (7562)	2100 (9341)*

(*POP Fasteners Div., Emhart Fastener Group*)

* IFI minimum values.
N.A.—not available.

BLIND RIVETS

Large-flanged heads. These heads (see Fig. 8-100, view *a*) have twice the under-the-head bearing surface of comparable rivets with dome heads. They are designed for fastening parts made from soft or brittle materials.

Countersunk heads. Whenever flush surfaces are required, countersunk-head blind rivets (see Fig. 8-100, view *b*) are often specified. These heads usually have a 120° included angle.

Blind Rivet Selection

Many factors must be considered for the selection of a proper blind rivet for a specific application. The most important factors include joint strength and thickness, rivet and workpiece materials, and hole size.

Joint strength. The tensile and shear values required for the application should be determined first. These values will vary with the rivet diameter and material.

Joint thickness. The total thickness of the workpiece materials to be joined determines the length of rivet required. Insufficient rivet length will not allow the formation of a full secondary head on the blind side of the assembly, thus affecting joint strength and mandrel head retention of the set rivet.

Materials. In general, the material from which the rivet is made should have the same physical and mechanical properties as the materials to be fastened. Marked differences in the materials may result in joint failure because of fatigue or galvanic corrosion. However, as previously mentioned, various combinations of different rivet body and mandrel materials are often used (refer to Table 8-10). Blind rivets are also available with a wide variety of finishes.

Hole size. The diameter of the hole in relation to rivet diameter is an important factor with respect to the success of blind riveting. Too small a hole can cause difficulty in insertion and can hinder rivet expansion in the materials to be fastened. Too large a hole will reduce shear and tensile strengths of the joint, causing bulging or separation of the joint. It can also cause pull-through, a condition in which the mandrel break point occurs above the primary head of the rivet, leaving a jagged protrusion.

Other considerations. Head styles on the blind rivets, previously discussed, can also be an important consideration in selection. Low-profile dome heads are appropriate for most applications, large-flanged heads for increased bearing surfaces, and countersunk heads for flush surface requirements. Closed-end sealing or self-plugging, locked-mandrel rivets are used extensively for water or vapor tightness needs and whenever positive mandrel retention is required. Soft-set, controlled-expansion, pull-through or semifilled, slotted-shank rivets are desirable to prevent damage to workpiece materials. T-rivets and self-plugging, slotted-shank, multigrip rivets are often used for high-strength fastening applications.

Design Practices

Careful design is essential for successful fastening with blind rivets. Variables that must be considered include the configuration and thickness of the joint, materials used, access for the tooling, rivet size and spacing, hole size, and the tightness attained in clinching. Care is necessary to avoid interferences that prevent the tooling from placing the primary head flush against the workpiece (see Fig. 8-101).

When narrow channels must be assembled, ample tool clearance is essential (see Fig. 8-102). If this is impossible, blind rivets should be set from the reverse side. Special nosepiece extensions are available for setting tools to accommodate designs where the rivets must be set inside narrow channels or counterbores. However, the use of such nosepiece extensions frequently requires special rivets with longer mandrels. When drive rivets are used, a piece of bar stock can be placed against the pin to allow the driving force to be transmitted through a narrow channel.

When assembling a soft material to a hard material, a backup washer is sometimes used, forming the secondary head against the backup washer. A better practice is to use a rivet having a large-flanged head and set the secondary head against the hard material. This same practice also applies when fastening thick materials to thin materials.

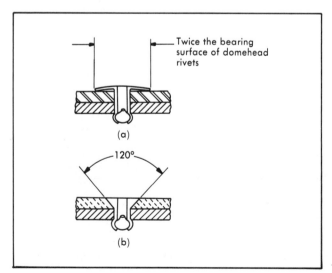

Fig. 8-100 Blind rivets with: (a) large-flanged head and (b) countersunk head.

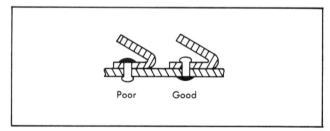

Fig. 8-101 Design to permit tooling to be placed flush against workpiece.

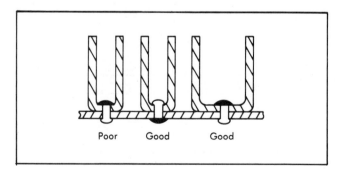

Fig. 8-102 In assembling narrow channels, blind rivets should be set from the reverse side or a wider channel used.

Pivoting joints can be produced by providing a small clearance between the primary head of the rivet and the surface of the workpiece. This is easily accomplished by modifying the nosepiece of the setting tool. Blind rivets can be set in blind holes or slots (see Fig. 8-103) because of the expansion of the rivet body during clinching. For maximum joint strength, the distance from the centerline of the rivet to the edge of the workpiece material should not be less than twice the diameter of the rivet (see Fig. 8-104).

Blind Rivet Tooling

Tools for setting blind rivets generally consist of two basic components: a pulling head and gripping jaws. The rivet is placed into the workpiece or in some cases, into the tool. The tool is then actuated, causing the pulling head to retract. Retraction of the head causes the gripping jaws, housed in a jaw case that is based on the inclined plane principle, to move forward. This action causes the teeth on the jaws to firmly grip the mandrel. The mandrel, jaws, and pulling head then retract as a unit, while the rivet body is held in position by pressure applied by a nosepiece. The mandrel enters the body of the rivet, forms the secondary head, and breaks at a predetermined point with a predetermined tensile load. Portable tools are available for magazine loading of the rivets.

Most setting tools for blind rivets fall into three basic categories: hand, pneumatic, and pneumatic-hydraulic or electric tools.

Hand tools. These tools are manually operated and usually rely on a fulcrum principle or linkage to develop the required mechanical advantage. Plier-type tools are limited in the size rivets they can set—up to a 3/16″ diam steel-steel combination rivet. Scissor-type hand tools can set the entire range of rivet

sizes. Hand tools are useful for low-volume applications or where air is not readily available. Drive-pin blind rivets are quickly installed with an ordinary hammer.

Pneumatic tools. These tools are operated solely by air, in combination with a linkage or some other mechanical converting device.

Pneumatic-hydraulic tools. These tools are usually air operated. The air enters a pressure chamber at a given pressure, forcing the hydraulic fluid into a pulling chamber, which retracts and sets the rivet. Hydraulic tools have the highest rivet-setting capacity and are suitable for most blind rivets.

Electric tools. These tools are generally used where threaded mandrels or center screws are set by tightening.

Problems in Blind Riveting

Problems that sometimes occur when blind riveting include the following:

- Mandrel protrusion—a condition in which the mandrel shank projects above the primary head after the rivet is set. This can be caused by oversized holes in the workpieces.
- Partial pull-through—a condition in which the mandrel head is pulled into the material being fastened, instead of breaking off as it contacts the back of the workpiece. This may be caused by the workpiece being too soft for the rivet used.
- Premature break—refers to a mandrel that breaks prior to setting the secondary head. The probable cause is the mandrel being too weak for the tensile load applied.
- Pull-through—a condition in which the mandrel head is pulled entirely through the inside of the rivet body. The mandrel head may be pulled entirely out of the rivet, may protrude slightly, or may even slide freely through the full length of the rivet body. Oversized holes in the workpieces can cause this condition.
- Head popper—a term used to describe a mandrel head falling out of a rivet body after placing. This is caused by the rivet being too short in relation to the work thickness.
- Hi-break—a mandrel that breaks above the intended break point. This can generally be avoided if the tool is held in accurate alignment with respect to the centerline of the hole into which the rivet is set.

EYELETS

Eyelets are thin-walled tubular fasteners having a flange or formed head on one end. Most are formed from metal strip, but some are machined, and are set during assembly by forcing their small diameter ends against dies that curl or funnel the edges and clinch the eyelets against the workpieces. The assembly of eyelets, called setting or eyeleting, requires access to both sides of the parts to be assembled.

Eyelets differ from rivets in that their bores extend completely through the fasteners. Grommets, not discussed in this section, are large eyelet-type fasteners designed for securing by curling their tubular ends over formed washers to provide strength in holes through resilient materials.

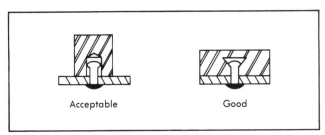

Fig. 8-103 Designs for setting blind rivets in blind holes or slots.

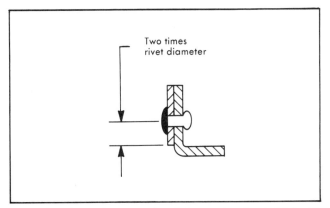

Fig. 8-104 Distance from centerline of rivet to edge of material should be at least twice the rivet diameter.

Applications

Eyeleting is used extensively in the metalworking industry as a fastening method for the assembly of many different types of light-gage parts. Typical applications include the assembly of

EYELETS

automotive components, electrical and electronic components (including use as terminals), hardware, toys, paper products, shoes, textiles, and garments.

Advantages

Eyelets can be inserted at high rates of production, and the process is easily adaptable to automatic assembly. From an economic standpoint, eyelets are one of the lowest cost fasteners available. They can be obtained in a wide variety of materials, sizes, and styles. Also, they can be set by relatively unskilled labor.

Types of Eyelets

Eyelets are available in many different sizes, materials, finishes, and styles.

Sizes. Standard eyelets are usually available in barrel (tubular body section) diameters from 1/16 to 1/4" and in lengths from 1/16 to 7/16". Both the diameters and the lengths are made in 1/32" increments. Nonstandard eyelets are made in a wide range of sizes.

Materials. Eyelets can be made from any formable metal. The metals most commonly used include low-carbon steels, such as SAE 1006 or 1008; aluminum alloys, including 5050 and 5052; zinc alloys; and brasses, bronzes, and other copper alloys, as well as pure copper. Stainless steels, such as AISI Type 305, are also used for making eyelets.

Finishes. Eyelets are supplied with a wide range of finishes. Plated finishes that are common include zinc, cadmium, nickel, tin, solder, copper, brass, and even silver and gold. The fasteners can also be painted, and most eyelet manufacturers have the capability of color matching to samples.

Head styles. Three basic head styles for eyelets are: rolled, flat, and funnel-flanged (see Fig. 8-105). A rolled flange offers the maximum bearing surface for a tightly set eyelet and provides a neat appearance. Flat-flange eyelets offer a low head profile to ensure clearance for parts in close proximity to assemblies, but the metal is subject to splitting in flat setting. However, the flat flange is advantageous for use with soft materials in which rolled flanges may cut the materials when set. Funnel-flange eyelets have been specially designed to meet the needs of the electronics industry. They are made with a funnel flange having an included angle of 90°, or in some few cases 60°, which affords a good solder fillet between the underside of the flange and the board.

Eyelets are also available with many other standard and special heads and configurations to suit specific application requirements. Closed-end eyelets provide a blind hole to exclude dirt and can also be used as spindles. Square-flanged eyelets are used in square, recessed holes or between tabs to prevent rotation. Other styles include bell-flanged, square-barrel, oval and oblong, and shoulder eyelets, as well as telescoping eyelets and neck washers.

Assembly Design

In designing an assembly for fastening with eyelets, a fundamental consideration is whether the assembly can be inserted into the eyeleting machine. Stroke length and throat depth of the machine determine the maximum size of the parts that can be inserted. Also, the eyelets must be accessible from both sides of the assembly.

When using eyelets as fasteners, consideration must be given to eyelet length, hole clearance, and eyelet spacing in designing the assemblies.

Eyelet length. When selecting the proper eyelet length, there is considerable variation in the allowance that should be made for setting the eyelet. This allowance varies with the eyelet material, the material against which the eyelet is to be set, and the type of set to be used. If the eyelet is too long, it will tend to buckle when set; if too short, the strength of the grip will be reduced. For many applications, a safe clinch allowance is 0.046-0.062" (1.17-1.57 mm); for electronics work, ±0.030" (0.76 mm) is often used. The best procedure is to contact the eyelet manufacturer for a recommendation.

Hole clearance. The amount of clearance provided in holes in which eyelets are to be inserted depends on several factors, including eyelet size and the type of assembly. In general, the minimum hole size should be about 0.003 to 0.004" (0.08 to 0.10 mm) larger than the barrel diameter of the eyelet. Too small a hole will create positioning problems during setting and will reduce the strength of the assembly.

Eyelet spacing. The spacing between eyelets is not critical for most applications. With a single-spindle machine used to set several eyelets separately, the eyelets can be spaced close enough so that the flanges almost contact each other.

Eyelet Setting

Setting (clinching) of eyelets is done by tooling that upsets or curls the barrel ends of the eyelets (see Fig. 8-106). Hardness of material from which the assembly component is made is a critical consideration in eyelet setting. When setting an eyelet in an assembly consisting of both a hard and a soft material, the

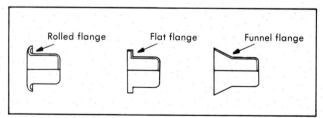

Fig. 8-105 Three basic head styles for eyelets. (*POP Fasteners Div., Emhart Fastener Group*)

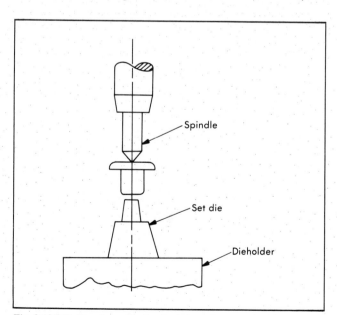

Fig. 8-106 Tooling for setting eyelets.

clinch should be made on the harder material whenever possible. Figure 8-107 illustrates the following setting dies for producing various clinch configurations:

- Roll form die (view *a*). A medium-roll setting die is most common and is considered a standard. The anvil form of this die is designed to provide a maximum roll diameter without splitting the eyelet. Close-roll dies provide rolls of smaller diameter and are used when space is a limiting factor. Wide-roll dies produce wider rolls but there is a greater tendency for the eyelets to split.
- Corrugated die (view *b*). This type of setting die has serrations machined into the anvil. The result is a scored setting with the eyelet barrel cut into equal segments. Corrugated setting provides greater holding power in some types of fabrics.
- Bifurcating die (view *c*). This setting die segments the eyelet barrel to provide one or two posts for wire wrapping.
- Spear-point die (view *d*). This setting die has three sharp cutting edges to pierce materials such as closely woven fabrics, plastics, and rubber-like materials.
- Hood die (view *e*). This setting die acts in conjunction with the eyelet to punch through plastics, paper, and other thin materials.
- Receding-pilot die (view *f*). A spring-loaded pilot in this die has a portion of the setting form machined into it. It is used to align holes and lead eyelets through the holes.
- Prepunch die (view *g*). This type die is used on double-stroke setting machines. On the first stroke, the die punches a hole in soft materials, and on the second stroke it receives and sets an eyelet.

- Needle-point die (view *h*). This setting die has a sharp point that is used to separate loosely woven fabrics.

Eyeleting Machines

The basic operation of eyeleting machines is similar to that of riveting machines. Hand-fed machines are available in bench and floor models, with hand, foot, electric, or pneumatic power. Setting tools used on the machines are made specifically for the particular eyelets to be used. Semiautomatic and automatic machines are available with special positioning and feeding devices for single or multiple settings. Automatic clamping devices eliminate the need for punching material from the workpieces.

On a typical semiautomatic machine, eyelets are placed in a hopper that contains a rotating hopper brush for orienting the eyelets to be fed into a raceway. Feeding is done through a slot in the hopper, specially designed to allow each eyelet to enter the raceway in one position. The eyelet then sits at the bottom of the raceway, held in position by spring-loaded fingers. The raceway is held in an outboard position by a cam affixed to the main driveshaft. When the machine is actuated, the main shaft rotates. This causes the raceway, by virtue of the cam design, to position the eyelet at the centerline of the spindle. At the same time, the spindle has begun to move downward, picking the eyelet from the raceway and completing the clinching action. Many machines use a vibrating bowl to achieve orientation before the eyelets enter the raceway.

Programmable and microprocessor controls and mechanical positioners are used to locate assemblies for setting. Several eyelets, as well as different length eyelets, can be set on a single machine, and different style eyelets can be set with a change of the tooling.

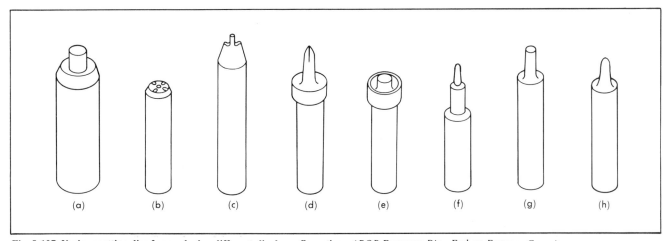

Fig. 8-107 Various setting dies for producing different clinch configurations. (*POP Fasteners Div., Emhart Fastener Group*)

RETAINING RINGS

Retaining rings, sometimes called snap rings, are fastening devices that provide shoulders and/or bearing surfaces for locating or limiting the movement of parts on shafts or in bores or housings. They are designed to exert a radial clamping force. For most applications, the rings provide a removable means of fastening. Some are designed to take up end play caused by accumulated tolerances or wear of the parts being retained. Retaining rings are usually made from spring steel or other materials having good spring properties to allow deformation during assembly and a return to original ring shape for use.

RETAINING RINGS

ADVANTAGES

Retaining rings provide a number of advantages over other fastening systems, including the following:

- *Product simplification.* With retaining rings, it is often possible to reduce the number and complexity of components in an assembly. A single ring, used in conjunction with a flat cover or face plate, for example, can replace an expensive custom-designed cover plate and four or more screws, bolts, or other threaded fasteners.
- *Savings on parts and materials.* Retaining rings can be used to eliminate machined shoulders, set collars, cotter pins and washers, threaded sleeves, and many other bulkier and more expensive fastening devices.
- *Reductions in size and weight.* In addition to being smaller and lighter than the fasteners they replace, retaining rings often can be used with shorter shafts and thinner housings, with substantial savings on materials as well as size and weight.
- *Elimination of expensive machining.* Retaining rings often eliminate the need for drilling, tapping, threading, facing, turning, and other costly machining operations. Ring grooves can usually be cut simultaneously, at no extra cost, during shaft cutoff and chamfering or bore drilling operations.
- *Faster assembly.* Retaining rings can be assembled quickly and economically, even by unskilled labor, with pliers, applicators, dispensers, and other hand tools, or with semiautomatic or automatic assembly equipment for high-volume mass production.

TYPICAL APPLICATIONS

Retaining rings are specified for a wide variety of consumer, industrial, and military products. In one application for garden hose reels (see Fig. 8-108), retaining rings have replaced formed and welded stops for positioning the hose connector sleeves, resulting in a reduction in assembly costs of 50% per unit. For tapping attachments (see Fig. 8-109), retaining rings have been found to be 10 times more cost efficient than threaded fasteners to lock collet assemblies and other components in housings and to position and secure clutch bearings and sleeves.

For industrial pumps, self-locking retaining rings are used to hold plastic rollers on shafts; the rings are pushed over the ends of the shafts and no grooves or other machining operations are needed. In the original design, the shafts were drilled and tapped, and the rollers secured by washers and screws. Savings with retaining rings amount to 74 cents per assembly.

TYPES OF RETAINING RINGS

The three major types of retaining rings are:

1. Stamped, tapered-section retaining rings. These rings have a tapered radial width that decreases symmetrically from their center sections to their free ends.
2. Spiral-wound retaining rings. These rings have one or more turns of rectangular, rounded-edge material that is wound on edge to provide a continuous coil. Rings with a single turn have a gap; those with two or more turns are of gapless design.
3. Wire-formed (wire-wound or bent-wire) retaining rings. These rings have a uniform cross-sectional area.

TAPERED-SECTION RETAINING RINGS

There are more than 50 functionally different types of tapered-section retaining rings manufactured. They are available in about 1200 standard inch and metric sizes for shafts and bores from 0.040 to 10″ (1 to 250 mm) diam. Rings as large as 40″ (1000 mm) in diameter have been produced for special applications.

Selection Factors

Engineers considering the use of retaining rings, either in original product design or as replacements for other fastening devices, should consider the following factors:

- *Product and ring size.* Size becomes a reference point for starting the selection process, but not every ring is suitable for every product.

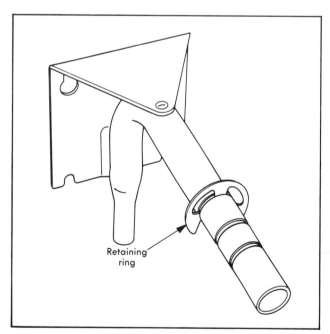

Fig. 8-108 Retaining ring replaces formed and welded stop for positioning the connector sleeve on a garden hose reel. (*Waldes Kohinoor, Inc.*)

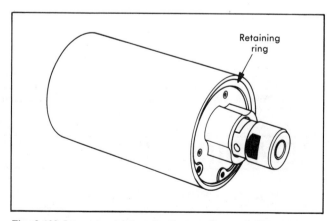

Fig. 8-109 Internal retaining ring locks collet assembly and other components in housing of tapping attachment. (*Waldes Kohinoor, Inc.*)

- *Clearance dimensions.* Clearance will affect the manner in which rings can be assembled, either in an axial or radial direction. It will also affect installation and removal of rings for field service or product maintenance.
- *Thrust load capacity.* If the ring will be required to withstand substantial thrust loads or impacts, certain types can be considered while others must be eliminated.
- *Feasibility of machining ring grooves.* Most rings designed to withstand high thrust loads are seated in grooves. If the grooving cannot be done economically or if grooves are impractical for any reason, then self-locking rings should be considered.
- *End play take-up.* This capability is a critical factor when an assembly includes parts with large tolerances or where components will be subject to wear that will cause objectionable looseness or wobble. Bowed and beveled rings, discussed subsequently in this section, should be considered. Precision-ground, graded-thickness rings are also available.
- *Environmental conditions.* If the ring will be subjected to extreme temperatures or corrosive conditions, extra protection should be considered—either in the form of special materials or finishes.
- *Assembly volume.* The quantity of rings to be assembled per unit of time will determine the kind of assembly tools that can be used and also the ring types suitable for each. For the assembly of most rings, the manufacturing engineer will have a choice of hand tools, semiautomatic tools, or high-speed automatic equipment, all discussed later in this section.

Materials Used

Most stamped, tapered-section retaining rings are made of carbon spring steel (SAE 1060-1090). Certain small sizes are fabricated only of beryllium copper (Alloy No. 25, CDA No. 172). Beryllium copper is also available for product applications in which the retaining rings must resist galvanic corrosion and provide good stress-corrosion resistance.

Stainless steel (PH 15-7 Mo or equivalent) rings are also available and provide good corrosion resistance and temperature resistance to 900° F (480° C). For lower temperature applications, rings of AISI Type 420 stainless steel may be used to 650° F (345° C).

Aluminum (Alclad 7075-T6) is another alternative material often specified for corrosion resistance, light weight, and resistance to many acidic chemicals.

Heat Treatment

Austempering is used by most manufacturers to harden retaining rings. This heat-treating process provides a number of advantages over conventional quench-and-temper processes, including increased toughness and impact strength and better fatigue resistance in cyclic loading—both at given levels of hardness or ultimate tensile strengths. The austempering process, monitored by automatic instrumentation, requires reliable process timing to ensure complete transformation to the desired bainite structure, thus avoiding brittleness caused by incomplete transformation and residual untempered martensite. Proper furnace atmospheres, carefully controlled, are required to prevent decarburization.

Austempering provides an average increase in tensile strength of 4.34% and an increase in yield strength of 2.74%. Because of the bainite structure, elongation is increased an average of 27.4%. This increased ductility permits the rings to deform instead of breaking under certain unexpected use conditions where operational problems cause very high stresses on localized areas of the ring when loads suddenly exceed rated values. The ability to elongate under load also is related to the rings' ability to absorb shock loads and to maintain longer life under many cyclic loading conditions. This is especially important because of the relatively high levels of hardness specified for the rings.

Finishes

Unplated spring steel rings are generally supplied with an oil dip finish or a black, corrosion-retardant phosphate coating. Zinc plating with an optional dichromate passivation treatment is available as a special finish when extra corrosion resistance is needed. Beryllium copper and aluminum rings are usually supplied without additional finish; stainless steel rings are generally passivated.

Mechanical plating is used by some ring manufacturers to replace conventional electroplating for depositing zinc and other corrosion-resistant finishes. The mechanical plating process prevents hydrogen embrittlement that can lead to ring failure. Mechanical plating also provides greater resistance to stress corrosion, again with the objective of avoiding ring failure in extreme environmental operating conditions. Various coating and plating processes, including mechanical plating, are discussed in Volume III of this Handbook series.

Ring Types

Stamped, tapered-section retaining rings are classified in several ways. *Internal rings* are used to position and secure components in bores and housings; *external rings* hold parts on shafts, pins, studs, and bosses. There are also rings for *axial assembly*, *radial assembly* and *end play take-up*. While most rings are seated in accurately located grooves, *self-locking rings* are available that do not require any groove or other preparatory machining.

Several types of internal and external tapered-section retaining rings are illustrated in Fig. 8-110. Other types not shown include beveled, double-beveled, interlocking, reinforced, heavy-duty, high-strength, and triangular. In addition, there are many other special rings that have been developed for unusual fastening requirements.

Axially assembled retaining rings. These rings are characterized by a tapered radial width that increases symmetrically from the free ends to the center section. In contrast to uniform-section rings, which undergo oval deformation when they are compressed for assembly in a bore or expanded for installation over a shaft, tapered-section rings remain circular during assembly. The tapered-section rings also remain circular after release, which provides the maximum contact surface with the bottom of the groove and is important for achieving high static and dynamic thrust load capacities. The lug design is another characteristic of axial rings; holes in the lugs permit pliers to grasp the rings securely during assembly or disassembly.

Lugs on inverted retaining rings form uniform circular shoulders, concentric with bores or shafts, making them ideal for parts having large corner radii or chamfers. Heavy-duty rings resist high thrust and impact loads and eliminate the need for spacer washers in bearing assemblies. Permanent-shoulder rings are available for small diameter shafts; when compressed

RETAINING RINGS

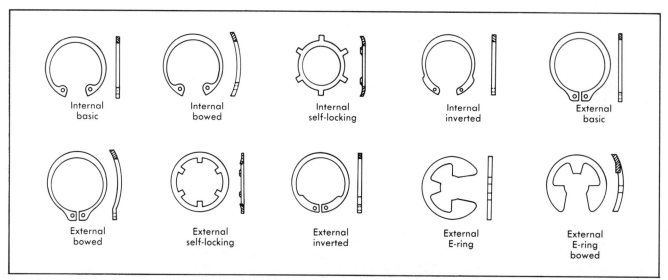

Fig. 8-110 Types of internal and external tapered-section retaining rings. (*Industrial Retaining Ring Co.*)

into grooves, their notches deform to close gaps, thus providing shoulders that cannot be dislodged.

Radially assembled retaining rings. In many product applications, it is not feasible to assemble retaining rings in an axial direction. Clearance dimensions or the need for easy access to parts during field service or maintenance dictate the use of radially assembled rings that are installed at a 90° angle to the shaft—either directly in the plane of the groove or, in the case of self-locking types, onto the shaft.

Radial rings do not have lugs for the use of pliers. Instead, they have a large gap between the free ends that permits the fasteners to be pushed over a shaft. Because they do not provide as much contact with the shaft as the axial external rings, most radial rings offer somewhat lower thrust load capacity. Rings are available, however, that provide substantially greater gripping strength and load capacity than conventional E-rings and other radial types. These rings are thicker and have tapered-section bending arms that exert strong spring force when the ring is installed.

Crescent-shaped rings form narrow, uniformly concentric shoulders and are used extensively for assemblies where clearance is limited. E-rings provide large shoulders on small diameter shafts and are often installed in deep grooves for added thrust capacity. Two-part, interlocking rings are balanced to withstand high rotary speeds, heavy thrust loads, and relative motion between parts.

End play take-up. In many assemblies, tolerances or wear in the retained parts can cause objectionable end play. Several axially and radially installed rings have been developed to solve this problem in different ways.

Bowed internal and external rings. These rings resemble the basic axially assembled types, but are bowed around an axis normal to the diameter bisecting the gap. The design enables the rings to function as springs as well as fasteners, taking up end play resiliently and dampening vibrations and oscillations. Bowed E-rings and locking-prong rings are assembled radially and provide the same resilient take-up.

Beveled rings. These rings, available in both internal and external axial types, have a 15° bevel on the groove-engaging edge (on the outer edge of internal rings and the inner edge of

external rings). Internal-beveled rings are available in two types: one having a single beveled edge and the other with a double-beveled construction. The double-beveled rings eliminate the need to orient the fasteners prior to assembly, thus ensuring correct installation during field service; however, these rings do not have the load-bearing capability of conventional rings.

Beveled rings are installed in grooves having a corresponding 15° bevel on the load-bearing wall. When the ring is seated in the groove, it functions as a wedge between the retained part and the outer groove wall. If there is end play between the ring and the abutting part, the fastener's spring action causes the ring to seat more deeply in the groove, taking up the end play.

Self-locking retaining rings. As their name suggests, self-locking retaining rings do not require a groove or other preparatory machining. They exert a frictional hold against axial displacement from either direction and are ideal for products in which the rings will be used merely as positioning and locking devices that are not subjected to substantial thrust loads. In addition to eliminating the need for grooves, self-locking rings provide another advantage: because they may be positioned at any point inside a bore or on a shaft, they automatically compensate for accumulated tolerances in the retained parts.

Self-locking rings are available in both circular push-on types with prongs, which must be destroyed for removal, and in axially and radially assembled versions that can be reused following disassembly. One type is installed in a radial direction on a shaft or pin and, during the initial assembly, cuts shallow indentations on the shaft; the grooves increase the ring's holding power against axial displacement from both directions.

Load Capacities

The maximum allowable thrust load capacity of a retaining ring assembled in a groove on a shaft or inside a bore is usually specified by the ring manufacturer for each type and size of ring. In the case of one ring manufacturer, the values are given for rings installed on hardened shafts or in hardened bores (P_r), rings assembled on soft shafts or in soft bores (P_g), and rings abutted by parts having the maximum specified corner radii or chamfers (P^l_g).

Standards

Metric dimensional specifications for many tapered-section retaining rings are presented in two ANSI standards. Standard B27.7M includes basic internal, basic external, and E-rings. Standard B27.8M includes heavy-duty external rings, reinforced E-rings, and C-type rings.

Many inch sizes of tapered-section retaining rings also conform to the U.S. Department of Defense Military Specification MIL-R-21248B and Military Standards MS16624 through MS16634, MS90707 and 90708, MS3215 through MS3217, and MIL-STD 1515-A.

Ring Assembly

A variety of tools can be used for fast and economical assembly and disassembly of retaining rings. These tools include pliers, applicators and dispensers, and semiautomatic and automatic tools.

Pliers. These tools (see Fig. 8-111) are among the most popular for axially assembled rings. They are designed to grasp the rings securely by their lugs, compress internal types for insertion into bores or housings, or expand external types so they can be slipped over the ends of shafts or similar parts. Many pliers have adjustable stops that limit the travel of the tips. On internal ring pliers, the stops can be set for automatic alignment with the lug holes for faster assembly; on pliers for external rings, the tips can be set to avoid accidental overspreading of the rings. Most pliers are made with straight tips, but they are also available with 45 or 90° angle tips for assembly where clearances are limited.

Ratchet pliers. These tools facilitate assembly and disassembly of large rings that require substantial force to be compressed or expanded. The ratchet locks the pliers at different stages of compression or expansion without the operator having to maintain constant pressure on the handles. The ratchet also serves as a safety device to prevent the ring from springing loose accidentally.

Applicators and dispensers. These devices are designed for use with radially assembled rings supplied in convenient tape-wrapped cartridges, which are slipped over the spring rail of a dispenser so the tape can be removed. An applicator is then used to grasp the bottom ring in the stack and assemble it on a shaft, pin, or similar part (see Fig. 8-112). Offset applicators are ideal for assemblies having limited clearances. Because the ring's gripping power on the shaft is greater than the holding power of

the applicator jaws, when the ring is seated in a groove it remains in position when the applicator is withdrawn.

Semiautomatic tools. These portable tools combine an applicator and dispenser in a single tool. They, too, are loaded with tape-wrapped cartridges and dispensed singly when the trigger is activated.

Automatic tools. These tools are intended for high-volume, mass-production ring installations where the cost of the tools will be amortized quickly by savings in assembly time. Such tools make possible savings of 30-50% compared to costs for ring assembly with pliers. One automatic air-driven tool is loaded with tape-wrapped ring cartridges and suspended over the work. To install a ring, the operator places the workpiece in a nest, positions the tool over the workpiece, and squeezes the trigger. An air-driven sleeve pushes the ring down over a tapered mandrel, spreading the fastener so that it can clear the shaft and seat it in the groove (see Fig. 8-113). When the ring reaches the groove and snaps into position, the operator releases the trigger. The sleeve is retracted automatically and the next ring in the stack is positioned for assembly. Custom-designed automatic tools are available for a variety of ring types and product applications.

SPIRAL-WOUND RETAINING RINGS

Spiral-wound retaining rings having two or more turns offer the advantage of providing a 360° retaining shoulder because they are of gapless design. These rings are also available with single turns; with this design they have gaps. Spiral-wound retaining rings can be made without incurring tooling costs for applications requiring special sizes. Another advantage of spiral-wound retaining rings is that they can be easily installed and removed without the need for special tooling. These attributes provide greater flexibility for the designers of assemblies incorporating retaining rings.

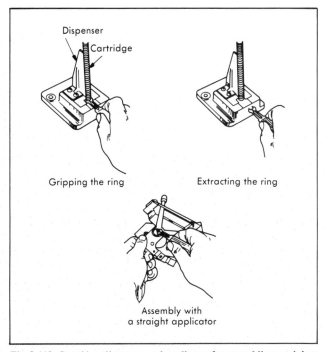

Fig. 8-112 Cartridge, dispenser, and applicator for assembling retaining rings. (*Waldes Kohinoor, Inc.*)

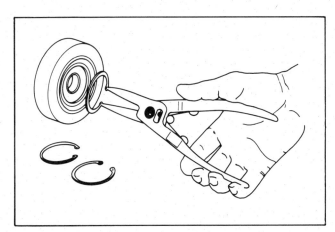

Fig. 8-111 Retaining ring pliers. (*Waldes Kohinoor, Inc.*)

RETAINING RINGS

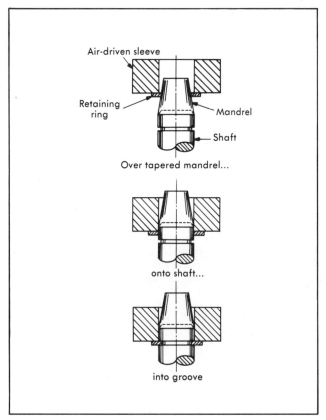

Fig. 8-113 Assembly of retaining rings with automatic tool. (*Waldes Kohinoor, Inc.*)

Air-driven sleeve

Retaining ring

Mandrel

Shaft

Over tapered mandrel...

onto shaft...

into groove

Applications

The use of spiral-wound retaining rings is widespread in industries making everything from small electrical appliances to the space shuttle. While most applications are for the retention of components of assemblies, there are many other uses, including the following:

- *Vibration dampers.* Spiral-wound, statically balanced rings function well as dampening devices when balance of the assembly is critical.
- *Oil dams.* Spiral-wound rings are used to form an oil reservoir for spline gears in mechanical couplings and other applications.
- *Backup rings.* Spiral-wound rings are used as backup rings for packings in cylinders because of the 360° shoulders they provide.
- *Oil or grease slingers.* Spiral-wound rings have been employed successfully as slinger rings in many applications; however, if high rotary speeds are involved, it might be necessary to use a self-locking ring.
- *Spacer or shim stock.* Spiral-wound rings are used as spacers or shims for positive tolerance take-up.
- *Location stops.* Spiral-wound rings are used successfully as location stops in a number of applications, but if impact loads are involved, care must be taken to use a properly designed ring.
- *Spring-loading components.* Dished spiral-wound rings can function as spring components in assemblies to exert a controlled load on other components.

Ring Selection

Selecting the proper retaining ring for a specific application requires careful evaluation of the following six factors:

1. Overall function of and requirements for the ring.
2. Type of thrust load (static or dynamic) and thrust capacity of the ring and groove.
3. Centrifugal forces and balance requirements.
4. Tolerance take-up requirements.
5. Method of assembly and disassembly.
6. Environment—maximum temperature and corrosive conditions.

Ring Materials and Finishes

Consideration of the selection factors will normally dictate the type of material that should be used to make the ring. The standard materials for spiral-wound retaining rings are SAE 1070 to 1090 carbon spring steels and AISI Type 302 stainless steel; however, there are optional materials available such as AISI Type 316 stainless steel, austenitic superalloy A286, beryllium copper, and phosphor bronze.

Each type of material offers special benefits, depending on the specific application. The 1070 to 1090 carbon spring steels provide high strength at low cost. Type 302 stainless steel withstands ordinary rusting; Type 316 is commonly used in the food industry. Superalloy A-286 and Inconel X-750 are used where high temperatures, to 900° F (480° C) for A-286 and 1200° F (650° C) for Inconel X-750, are encountered. Beryllium copper is nonmagnetic; resists rusting and corrosion from seawater, sea air, and most alkaline solutions; and has the lowest resistivity of the materials used. Phosphor bronze is also nonmagnetic and is used for applications where this characteristic is a major consideration. Some specifications for these materials are presented in Table 8-11.

Some of the materials used for spiral-wound retaining rings are provided with special finishes. For example, the carbon spring steels are available with phosphate coating or black oxide coating. The stainless steels are available with an optional passivation cleaning process.

Rings of Standard Design

Standard, spiral-wound retaining rings, available in both internal and external designs (see Fig. 8-114), have one or more turns of rectangular, rounded-edge material. Those with two or more turns have no gaps and provide a 360° shoulder. Their flexible cross sections allow easy assembly and disassembly without special tools. The laminated construction with two or more turns permits high axial deflections under thrust loads without overstressing the rings. Uniform wall thickness is an advantage when radial clearances are critical.

Special Designs

The spiral-wound design of the rings lends itself to custom fitting for special applications. For example, overall ring thickness can be varied by changing the material thickness or by increasing the number of turns. Different ring diameters, from 7/16 to 54″ (11 to 1372 mm) and larger, are easily manufactured to suit requirements. When the rings are made from a thin material, tabs, prongs, and other devices can be formed for special assembly and disassembly needs. Reverse-wound rings (wound in the opposite direction) are used for special applications. For example, with a rotating assembly having a tendency

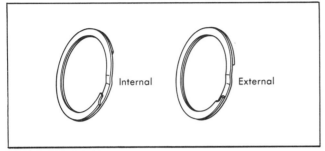

Fig. 8-114 Internal and external designs of standard, spiral-wound retaining rings.

to unwind a ring out of its groove, the ring is wound so that the direction of rotation tightens the ring to the groove bottom.

Ring Configurations

Spiral-wound retaining rings are offered in varying configurations to meet particular design needs. For instance, standard, catalog-series rings differ from each other by the number of laminations or turns of material, in addition to the various material cross sections. Light-duty applications often use rings having a one-turn design. Heavy-duty rings have an increased material cross section and a higher number of turns.

Special design configurations (see Fig. 8-115) include the following:

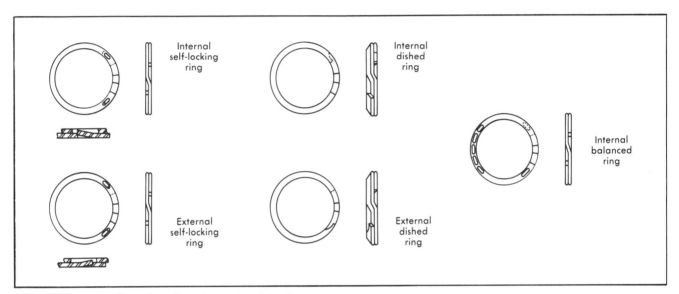

Fig. 8-115 Various configurations of spiral-wound retaining rings.

TABLE 8-11
Specifications of Materials Used for Spiral-Wound Retaining Rings

Material	Thickness, in. (mm)	Min Tensile Strength (Max Work Stress During Installation), ksi (MPa)	Shear Strength, ksi (MPa)	Allowable Working Stress Under Load, ksi (MPa)	Modulus of Elasticity, psi (GPa)	Recommended Max Service Temp, °F (°C)
Carbon spring steels, SAE 1070 to 1090	0.0067-0.0148 (0.170-0.376)	269 (1855)	153 (1055)	242 (1669)	30 x 10^6 (207)	250 (120)
	0.0150-0.0213 (0.381-0.541)	255 (1758)	138 (951)	218 (1503)		400 (205)
	0.0215-0.0433 (0.546-1.100)	221 (1524)	126 (869)	199 (1372)		400 (205)
	0.0435 plus (1.105)	211 (1455)	120 (827)	190 (1310)		400 (205)
Stainless steel, AISI Type 302	0.0080-0.0160 (0.203-0.406)	210 (1448)	119 (820)	178 (1227)	28 x 10^6 (193)	400 (205)
	0.0162-0.0230 (0.411-0.584)	210 (1448)	119 (820)	178 (1227)		
	0.0232-0.0480 (0.589-1.219)	200 (1379)	114 (786)	170 (1172)		
	0.0482-0.0610 (1.224-1.549)	185 (1276)	105.5 (727)	157 (1082)		
	0.0612 plus (1.554)	175 (1207)	100 (689)	157 (1082)		
Beryllium copper	All thicknesses	175 (1207)	100 (689)	149 (1027)	17.9 x 10^6 (123)	225 (105)
Phosphor bronze	0.0100-0.0250 (0.254-0.635)	106 (731)	60.5 (417)	90 (621)	14.5 x 10^6 (100)	225 (105)
	0.0252-0.0500 (0.640-1.270)	95 (655)	54 (372)	80.6 (556)		
	0.0502 plus (1.275)	90 (621)	51.3 (354)	76.5 (527)		
A-286 superalloy	All thicknesses	200 (1379)	114 (786)	170 (1172)	31 x 10^6 (214)	900 (480)

(Ramsey Piston Ring Div., TRW Automotive Products, Inc.)

RETAINING RINGS

1. *Self-locking rings.* This ring design has a precision tab-and-slot locking arrangement at each end of the ring. It is typically used to withstand the high centrifugal forces found in high-speed shaft applications and the effects of vibration and shock or impact loads.
2. *Dished, resilient take-up rings.* This type of ring overcomes objectionable end play created by the buildup of tolerances in ring thickness, groove locations, and retained part tolerances. The dish in the ring may also be used to exert a controlled axial force or to function simply as a spring member.
3. *Balanced rings.* These rings are statically balanced for high-speed applications by incorporating a series of slots opposite the ring gap. If a balanced ring is to be used on a shaft, it will normally have self-locking features.

End Conditions and Crimping

Standard and special end conditions (see Fig. 8-116) are available for spiral-wound retaining rings; however, the purpose of all end conditions is the same: to provide a method of removing the rings from the grooves. Material cross sections sufficiently flexible to offset themselves naturally while in the grooves are not crimped, but thicker material section rings are offset by crimping (see Fig. 8-117) when necessary.

Thrust Load Capacity

The most important criterion in determining which ring is best suited for a specific application is thrust load capacity. The retaining ring and groove must both be considered when analyzing the thrust load capacity, because the capability of the assembly is only as strong as its weakest link. In designing a ring for an application, it must be determined whether the groove or the retaining ring is likely to fail first.

Types of thrust loads. A static, uniformly applied load is usually assumed. Dynamic and eccentric loads, however, are frequently encountered. The success of retaining rings in applications where shock or impact loads are encountered depends, in addition to the factors that affect the static-thrust capacity, on mass and velocity of the retained part as it strikes the ring. Applications involving impact loads require testing.

Eccentric loading occurs many times in practice but is not often anticipated. Eccentric loading can be caused by the following:

1. Face of the retained part not being machined parallel to the retaining ring.
2. Cocking of the retained part by an external force applied to it at a distance from the retaining ring. Such a case is commonly encountered when a retaining ring is used to hold a large gear or hub on a splined shaft.
3. Axial misalignment of mating parts, as is often the case with mechanical couplings. If eccentric loads are anticipated, the thickest possible ring in the deepest groove should be used.

Vibration. Vibration introduced by impact loading must also be considered. If the frequency of the system coincides with the resonant frequency of the retaining ring, the ring can fail. If such vibration causes concern, the critical resonant frequency of the retaining ring in the radial direction should be determined.

Centrifugal capacity. Proper functioning of a retaining ring depends on the ring remaining seated on the groove bottom. However, centrifugal loading can overcome initial cling built into an external ring and cause it to lose its grip on the groove bottom. To avoid this, the allowable steady-state speed of a retaining ring should be determined.

Rotation between parts. The use of spiral-wound rings to retain a rotating part should be limited to applications with low thrust loads and with rotation in only one direction. External rings should be wound in the direction of rotation of the rotating part; internal rings should be wound against the direction of rotation of the rotating part. Failure to observe these criteria will cause the ring to wind out of the groove. Spiral-wound retaining rings are available with right-hand windings as standard and left-hand windings as an option.

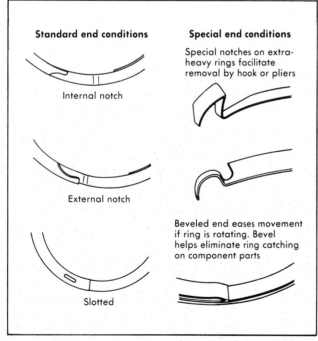

Fig. 8-116 Standard and special end conditions for spiral-wound retaining rings. (*Ramsey Piston Ring Div., TRW Automotive Products Inc.*)

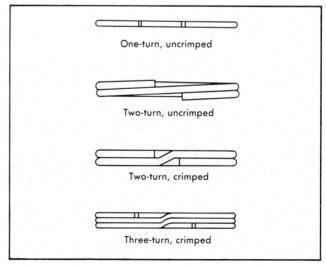

Fig. 8-117 Uncrimped and crimped, spiral-wound retaining rings.

Retaining Ring Failure

When considering the retaining ring alone, the mode of failure could result from shearing of the ring. Shear failure occurs when:

1. The ring is installed in a groove and loaded with a retained part with both the ring and the part having compressive yield strength greater than 45 ksi (310 MPa).
2. The load is applied through a retained part and groove, both having sharp corners and line-to-line contact.
3. The ring is too thin in section compared to the ring diameter.

Groove Failure

The most common type of groove failure is the yielding of the groove material. This occurs when the thrust load, which applies its force through the retaining ring and onto the corner of the groove, exceeds the compressive yield strength of the groove (see Fig. 8-118). This yielding allows the ring to tilt and come out of the groove without the ring overstressing (if the cross section of the ring is flexible enough), or tilt, take a permanent set, and work its way out of the groove. Either way, it is the result of the low compressive yield strength of the groove with respect to the thrust load that causes the failure.

When dishing of the ring occurs due to the yielding of the groove material, it is a bending moment that occurs across the cross section of the ring that generates a maximum stress at the ID of the ring. This stress is in the form of a tensile stress. If exceeded beyond the yield point, the ring ID will grow in diameter and become permanently dished in shape. To determine the thrust load capacity of a ring based on groove deformation, the allowable angle of ring deflection must first be calculated; the thrust load, based on groove yield, can then be determined.

Groove design and machining. A properly designed and machined groove is just as important to the overall capability of the assembly as is the retaining ring. The walls of the grooves should be perpendicular to the shaft or bore diameter; the grooves should have square corners on the top edge and radii at the bottom, within the tolerances specified by the manufacturer. Test data indicates that ultimate thrust capacity is greatly affected when these conditions do not exist, for both static and dynamic-type loading.

Groove location. In most applications, grooves are located near the end of a shaft or housing bore to facilitate installation and removal of the rings. If the groove is located too close to the end of the shaft or bore, it may shear.

Groove material. There are a number of ways to increase the thrust load capacity of a particular retaining ring application. Changing the workpiece material into which the grooves are cut is one method. The effect of groove yield strength on thrust capacity for a typical application is illustrated in Fig. 8-119.

Safety Factors

A safety factor of two is generally used for thrust load calculations where the load is applied through a retained part and groove with both having sharp corners and where minimum side clearance between the retained part and the shaft or bore exists. In applications where the summation of the maximum chamfer (or radius) on the retained part, the maximum chamfer (or radius) on the groove, and the maximum side clearance of the retained part (see Fig. 8-120) are within the values recommended by the ring manufacturer, a safety factor of four should

be applied. Recommended maximum total radius or chamfer specifications are intended to be used as guidelines by the designer. They ensure the validity of published or calculated values of static thrust loads.

Retaining rings that are used where specific recommended limits are exceeded will show a marked decrease in thrust load capacity unless the groove depth, ring width, or compressive

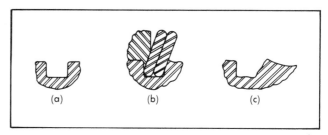

Fig. 8-118 Localized yielding under axial thrust load: (a) groove profile before loading, (b) yielding of both retained part and groove under load, and (c) groove profile after loading beyond thrust capacity.

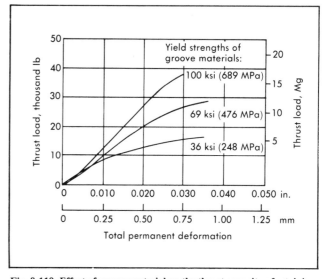

Fig. 8-119 Effect of groove material on the thrust capacity of retaining rings. (*Ramsey Piston Ring Div., TRW Automotive Products Inc.*)

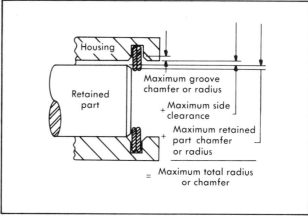

Fig. 8-120 Maximum total radius or chamfer.

RETAINING RINGS

yield strength of the groove material is increased. Figure 8-121 shows how the thrust load capacity is directly proportional to the groove depth. The effect of various chamfers on the thrust capacity is illustrated in Fig. 8-122. Effects of excessively large chamfers or radii can be minimized by inserting a spacer between the retained parts and the retaining rings, however, the spacers must be strong enough not to dish under load.

Applicable Standards

Dimensional specifications for many general purpose, uniform cross section, spiral retaining rings are presented in ANSI Standard B27.6. Military Specification MIL-R-27426 covers the procurement requirements for uniform cross-sectional, spiral-wound retaining rings. This specification has been approved by the U.S. Department of Defense and is for use by the departments of the Army, Navy, and Air Force. The specification lists two types, with two classes under each type, as follows:

Type I—External
Medium-duty external series, identified as Class 1
Heavy-duty external series, identified as Class 2
Type II—Internal
Medium-duty internal series, identified as Class 1
Heavy-duty internal series, identified as Class 2

Ring Installation

Because of the cross-sectional flexibility of spiral-wound rings, they may be installed manually by spreading the turns, inserting one end in the groove, and spiraling the remainder of the ring until the last turn snaps into the groove. When normal care is exercised and the recommended dimensions for the housing bore or shaft are maintained, this manual method is satisfactory for low to medium assembly rates and can also be acceptable for some high-volume applications.

For higher production requirements, the most commonly used method for installing rings is the semiautomatic method. This procedure requires a sleeve with a tapered bore or a tapered plug and mating plungers. Variations of the tapered sleeve or plug are sometimes necessary to overcome special installation problems. For example, a modified tool form is necessary when a retaining ring must be installed over or through splines, threads, or polished surfaces. This modification is usually in the form of a thimble extension (see Fig. 8-123) that covers and protects the critical area while the ring passes over it. These installation fixtures must be designed within limitations to avoid excessive stress when expanding or collapsing the ring during installation. Overstressed rings, unless adequate compensation has been made, will not grip the groove bottom and a decrease in thrust capacity will result. For applications where there are extremely high volumes involved, the use of completely automatic installation tooling may be warranted.

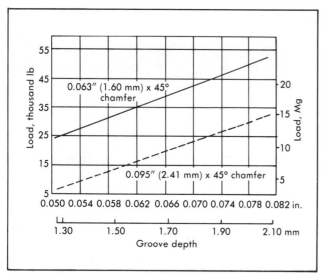

Fig. 8-121 Relationship of groove depth to thrust load at which ring failed when loaded through retained parts having chamfers shown. Yield strength of groove material is 69 ksi (476 MPa); yield strength of retained part material is 100 ksi (689 MPa). (*Ramsey Piston Ring Div., TRW Automotive Products Inc.*)

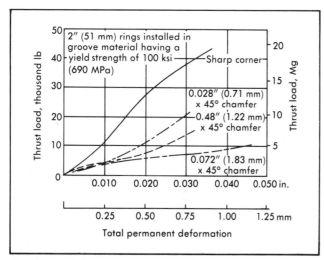

Fig. 8-122 Effect of chamfer size on thrust capacity of spiral-wound retaining rings. (*Ramsey Piston Ring Div., TRW Automotive Products Inc.*)

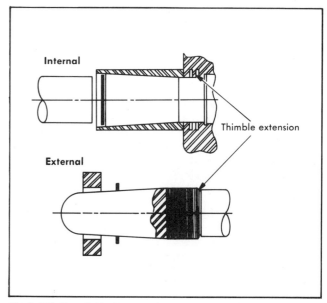

Fig. 8-123 Use of thimble extension to protect finished surfaces and threads during assembly of retaining rings with sleeve and plunger.

Inspecting the Installation

Once installed, the ring should be inspected for proper seating against the groove bottom. Foreign matter in the groove, overstressing during installation, or improper machining of the grooves can prevent the ring from functioning properly. Sometimes, visual inspection is sufficient; however, in more critical assemblies, gaging is recommended. Figure 8-124 shows typical go and not-go gages used for inspecting internal and external ring assemblies.

Ring Disassembly

A ring can be removed by simply inserting a screwdriver to lift one end of the ring from the groove and then spiraling out

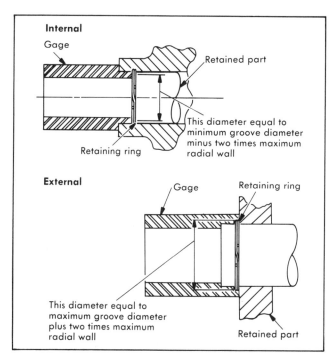

Fig. 8-124 Typical go and not-go gages used to inspect internal and external ring assemblies.

the remainder of the ring. Some of the special end configurations available on rings are designed to permit easy removal with pliers.

WIRE-FORMED RETAINING RINGS

Wire-formed retaining rings, also called wire-wound or bent-wire rings, are split rings formed and cut from spring wire of uniform cross-sectional size and shape. The grain flow follows the contours of these rings for equalized distribution of stresses. The rings can be formed to ensure full peripheral contact on shafts or in housings.

Materials and Finishes

Spring steel, SAE 1060, is the most common material used for making wire-formed retaining rings, but steels ranging from SAE 1010 to 1095 are employed for some rings. Hardnesses range from R_C42 to 53, and tensile strengths range from 192 to 280 ksi (1324 to 1931 MPa). Wire-formed rings are also available made from stainless steel, bronze, brass, beryllium copper, and aluminum alloys.

Corrosion inhibition is achieved several ways, the standard being an oil-based rust preventive for carbon steel rings. Cadmium and zinc plating and other finishes are also available. Some ring manufacturers offer mechanically applied finishes.

Ring Sizes and Types

Standard, wire-formed retaining rings are made in sizes ranging from 1/8 to 30″ (3.2 to 762 mm) diam, with larger sizes available by special order. The rings are made in a variety of cross-sectional shapes (see Fig. 8-125), with rectangular, square, or round being the most popular, depending on the ring function and requirements. Round-section rings, used in rounded grooves, have less load-bearing capacity than rectangular or square-section rings. Tapered-section rings help to take up end play caused by tolerances on ring thicknesses, groove locations, and the retained components.

Rectangular-section rings generally have thicknesses ranging from 2 to 5% of their diameters and widths that are 2-3 times their thicknesses. The grooves for accommodating rectangular-section rings must have minimum widths of 1.15 times the ring thicknesses. Some standard gap profiles made by one ring manufacturer are illustrated in Fig. 8-126.

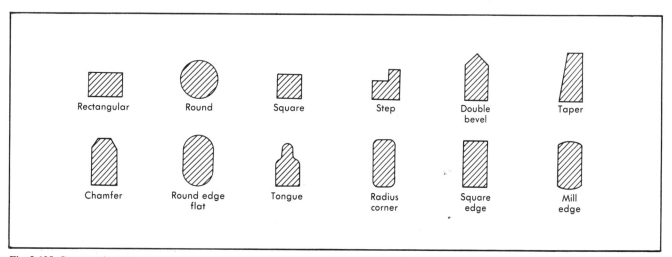

Fig. 8-125 Cross-sectional shapes of wire-formed retaining rings. (*Engineered Fasteners Div., Eaton Corp.*)

RETAINING RINGS

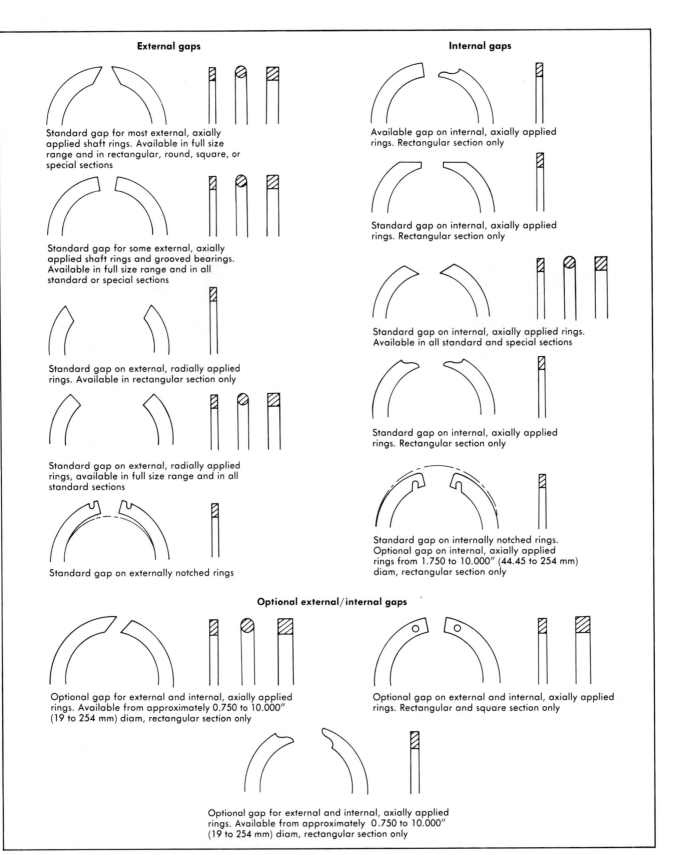

External gaps

Standard gap for most external, axially applied shaft rings. Available in full size range and in rectangular, round, square, or special sections

Standard gap for some external, axially applied shaft rings and grooved bearings. Available in full size range and in all standard or special sections

Standard gap on external, radially applied rings. Available in rectangular section only

Standard gap on external, radially applied rings, available in full size range and in all standard sections

Standard gap on externally notched rings

Internal gaps

Available gap on internal, axially applied rings. Rectangular section only

Standard gap on internal, axially applied rings. Rectangular section only

Standard gap on internal, axially applied rings. Available in all standard and special sections

Standard gap on internal, axially applied rings. Rectangular section only

Standard gap on internally notched rings. Optional gap on internal, axially applied rings from 1.750 to 10.000" (44.45 to 254 mm) diam, rectangular section only

Optional external/internal gaps

Optional gap for external and internal, axially applied rings. Available from approximately 0.750 to 10.000" (19 to 254 mm) diam, rectangular section only

Optional gap on external and internal, axially applied rings. Rectangular and square section only

Optional gap for external and internal, axially applied rings. Available from approximately 0.750 to 10.000" (19 to 254 mm) diam, rectangular section only

Fig. 8-126 Standard gap profiles for wire-formed retaining rings. (*Engineered Fasteners Div., Eaton Corp.*)

External rings. These rings are designed to go over shafts, outer races of bearings, and similar parts and to snap into grooves, exerting radial tension toward the ring centers. They are generally assembled axially to hold parts on shafts. External clip rings are open-style rings for radial assembly to shafts, which is easier than axial assembly. External closed rings are full-diameter rings having gaps smaller than the wire thicknesses. Closed rings are assembled axially over the ends of shafts; radii or chamfers on the shaft ends facilitate assembly.

Internal rings. These rings are designed to enter housings or bores and snap into grooves, exerting radial tension outward from the ring centers. Internal rings are assembled axially to retain parts; they are available to snap into the outer races of bearings to overcome thrust loads in either direction.

Thrust Capabilities

Failure of retaining ring assemblies is generally the result of groove deformation, the most common cause, or ring shear. Continued overstressing causes rings to enlarge in diameter, become dished, and extrude out of their grooves. Ring shear can result from the retained components and the grooves having excessively high compressive yield strengths; sharp, unradiused corners of the retained components and the grooves being in line-to-line contact; and the thickness-to-diameter ratio of the ring being too high (ring material too thin). The amounts of thrust loads that various rings will absorb are specified by the ring manufacturers.

Ring Assembly and Disassembly

For reduced costs, and easiest assembly and disassembly, rings having the smallest cross-sectional area that meets thrust requirements should be used. Internally notched rings allow the use of standard, round-point, contracting pliers for assembling and removing. Also, the segments of internally notched rings adjacent to the gap ends have preformed radii that permit the rings to be assembled more easily and reduce the possibility of scoring the housing or bore.

External rings. The use of a tapered plug and bushing provides a fast method of forcing external rings axially into grooves and can be adapted to mechanized assembly. When shaft ends are rounded or chamfered, hollow-sleeve plungers can be used in place of the tapered plug and bushing.

Plier-type hand tools are often desirable for assembling or removing external rings when the grooves are not near the ends of the shafts or to keep the shafts from being scored by the rings. Where the ring sections are thick compared to their diameters, stop-action pliers are available to prevent the possibility of ring overexpansion. Pliers with offset bases are made for applications where the grooves are concealed by the parts that are to be retained.

Internal rings. Some of the same basic tools used for the assembly and disassembly of external rings can also be used for internal rings. To use a tapered bushing and plunger, the bushing is tapered to the ID of the housing and made with a locating shoulder that centers over the housing (see Fig. 8-127). A slight chamfer on the housing bore helps guide the ring and compensates for slight hole misalignment. As the ring is pressed into the tapered bushing, it compresses to the bore diameter and then snaps into the groove. The plunger can be operated by hand or mechanically.

Contracting-type pliers are also used for the assembly and removal of internal rings. A spiral assembly method can be used with rings having certain gap profiles. One end of the ring is inserted in the groove and installation is completed by spirally prying the remainder of the ring into place. Removal is accomplished by disengaging one end of the ring with a pointed tool and then prying out the remainder of the ring.

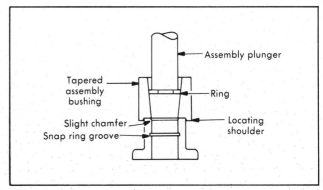

Fig. 8-127 Tapered bushing and plunger method of assembling internal rings. (*Engineered Fasteners Div., Eaton Corp.*)

PINS

Pins provide a simple and low-cost method of mechanical fastening. They are available in straight-cylindrical or tapered designs, with or without heads, and generally rely on elastic compression for their gripping power. Applications of pins are common in industrial machines and in commercial products.

Pins are used as locking devices, locating elements, pivots, and bearing faces. They often secure the positions of two or more parts relative to each other. Applications are primarily for shear loading where there is not a high amount of end loading. Most pins are hardened for maximum strength and permanent assembly, but some are used soft so that they will shear before the assembly or mechanism is damaged.

An advantage of pins, in addition to their low cost and effectiveness, is that many of them can be inserted in simple drilled or cored holes. However, some press-fit pins require varying degrees of hole preparation for proper insertion. Application methods vary from the simple use of hammers to automated assembly machines for high-volume requirements.

A wide variety of standard types and sizes of pins are available, and special designs are made for specific applications. Major classifications of pin types are:

- Machine pins, including straight-cylindrical, dowel, tapered, clevis, cotter, and wire pins.
- Radial locking pins, including grooved, knurled, and spring pins.
- Quick-release pins, such as push-pull and positive locking types.

CHAPTER 8

PINS

STRAIGHT PINS

Solid, straight-cylindrical pins are usually cut from wire or bar stock and have unground surfaces. They are available in chamfered or square-end designs. Square-end straight pins can have the corners on both ends broken with small radii.

Straight pins are generally made from cold-drawn, low or high-carbon steel wire, rod, or bar. High-carbon steels are generally heat treated. Pins are also available made from stainless steels, brasses, and other metals. Standard straight pins have nominal diameters ranging from 1/16 to 1″. Dimensional and general data for inch-size straight pins is presented in ANSI Standard B18.8.2. Metric-size pins are also available.

DOWEL PINS

Dowel pins are precision, straight-cylindrical pins available in hardened and ground types and in unhardened and ground types. They are used extensively in the production of machines, tools, dies, jigs, and fixtures to retain parts in fixed positions or to preserve alignments. Dimensional and general data for dowel pins is presented in ANSI Standard B18.8.2. Military Standards MS-16555 and MS-16556 also pertain to dowel pins.

Hardened and Ground Machine Dowel Pins

These pins are available in standard and oversize series, ranging from 1/16 to 1″ diam and 3/16 to 6″ long, as well as in metric sizes. Standard inch-size pins, intended for initial installations, have basic diameters 0.0002″ more than their nominal diameters. Oversize pins, intended for replacement use, have basic diameters 0.001″ more than nominal diameters. Both series are made from carbon or alloy steels.

The pins are ground or ground and lapped to within ±0.0001″ of the required basic diameters and to produce a roundness within 0.0001″ about their longitudinal axes. One end of each pin is chamfered (4-16°), and the other end is crowned for press fitting into a drilled and reamed hole.

Hardened and Ground Production Dowel Pins

These pins are similar to the standard-size series of hardened and ground machine dowel pins. Differences include that standard inch sizes only range from 1/16 to 3/8″ diam, with lengths from 3/16 to 3″; the corners at both ends of the pins are rounded; and the pins are made from a carbon steel that is case hardened to produce a minimum surface hardness of R_C58. These pins are generally employed for volume production applications, using automated installation equipment.

Unhardened Ground Dowel Pins

These pins are often used where strength, shock, and wear resistance requirements do not warrant the additional cost of hardened pins. Standard inch sizes range from 1/16 to 1″ diam, with lengths from 1/4 to 4″. They are generally produced by grinding the OD of commercial wire or rod to size. Corners at both ends of the pins are chamfered. The pins are usually made from carbon steel or brass.

TAPERED (TAPER) PINS

Tapered pins, commonly called taper pins, inserted by a drive fit, are often used to position parts or to transmit low torque forces. They have a taper of 1/4″ per foot, measured on the diameter, and both ends are crowned with a spherical radius. Tapered pins are available in commercial and precision classes, with the precision pins having closer tolerances. The pins are generally made from AISI 1211 steel or cold-drawn AISI 1212 or 1213 steel.

The basic diameter of a tapered pin is the diameter at its large end. The diameter at the small end equals the basic diameter minus 0.02083 times the pin length. A series of numbered pin sizes have been standardized. The sizes range from No. 7/0 (0.0625″ diam at the large end) to No. 14 (1.5210″ diam at the large end). Lengths vary from 1/4 to 13″. Dimensional and general data for the pins is presented in ANSI Standard B18.8.2.

Threaded tapered pins are available for use with tapered sleeves. They can align oversized holes and are used extensively for pressworking dies. The threaded portions allow the pins to be removed from the sleeves, and pullers are then used to remove the sleeves.

CLEVIS PINS

Clevis pins are solid pins having cylindrical heads at one end and a drilled hole for a cotter pin at the other end (see Fig. 8-128). They are commonly used as pivots in many mechanisms and for use with clevices and rod-end eyes in industrial applications.

Basic diameters of standard clevis pins range from 3/16 to 1″. The pins are generally made from AISI 1010 to 1020 or 1211 steel, left soft or case hardened. Dimensional specifications for standard clevis pins are presented in ANSI Standard B18.8.1.

COTTER PINS

Cotter (split) pins are double-bodied pins formed from half-round wire. A loop at one end of each pin provides a head and various point styles are available (see Fig. 8-129). They are used in clevis pins and other pinned assemblies. The pins are driven

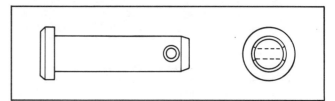

Fig. 8-128 Clevis pin.[5]

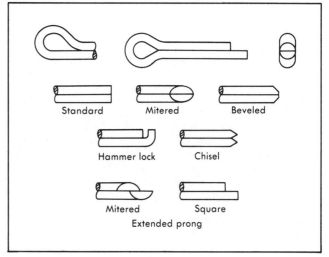

Standard   Mitered   Beveled

Hammer lock   Chisel

Mitered   Square

Extended prong

Fig. 8-129 Cotter pins and various point styles.[6]

into holes, the loop heads limiting travel, and their legs are split for locking. Cotter pins have been standardized into 18 sizes with nominal sizes (basic pin diameters) ranging from 1/32 to 3/4″. They are generally made from AISI 1015 steel but are also available in brass, bronze, stainless steel, and aluminum. Dimensional and general data for cotter pins is presented in ANSI Standard B18.8.1.

WIRE PINS

Formed spring-wire pins or clips are of two-legged design, similar to cotter pins. However, unlike a cotter pin, only one leg of a wire pin is inserted in the hole, and the pin holds itself in place by elastic compression.

GROOVED PINS

Grooved pins are solid, unground, straight-cylindrical pins having three longitudinal grooves equally spaced around their peripheries. No metal is removed during manufacture of the pins. Instead, the grooves are formed by a swaging operation in which three tools penetrate the nominal diameter of the pin to a predetermined depth. Metal displaced by the tools forms a raised portion or flute along each side of each groove.

The crests of the formed flutes produce an expanded diameter, shown as D_x in Fig. 8-130. Amount of expansion varies with the size of the pin and the material from which it is made, but the expanded diameter can be precisely controlled. Holes into which grooved pins are to be inserted are drilled slightly larger than the nominal diameters of the pins, but never smaller. When the expanded portions of a pin are compressed in a hole, the displaced metal is forced back into the grooves, thus developing radial holding forces. The locking action is a function of the expanded diameter and the effective length of engagement.

Various configurations of grooved pins are illustrated in Fig. 8-131. Standard inch sizes cover the range from 1/16 to 1/2″ diam, with lengths from 1/8 to 4 1/2″. The pins are generally made from cold-drawn, low-carbon steel wire or rod that can be surface hardened if required. Pins are also available made from alloy steels, stainless steels, and copper alloys. Alloy steel pins are sometimes through hardened to increase their shear strengths. Dimensional specifications for grooved pins are presented in ANSI Standard B18.8.2. The pins are also

manufactured to the following military specifications: MS-35671 through MS-35679, MS-51605, MS-51606, and DOD-P-63464. Grooved drive studs having various head styles (see Fig. 8-132) are also available.

KNURLED PINS

Knurled pins are similar to grooved pins in that there are serrations around the nominal diameter of the pin that, when compressed, result in radial holding forces that retain the fastener in place. However, whereas a grooved pin has only six raised portions, knurled pins have many smaller raised sections around the nominal diameter. A knurled section may either be a straight, helical, or diamond configuration. Examples of these different types of knurls are shown in Fig. 8-133.

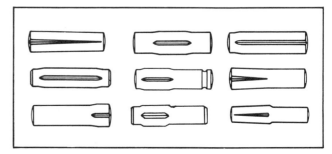

Fig. 8-131 Various configurations of grooved pins.

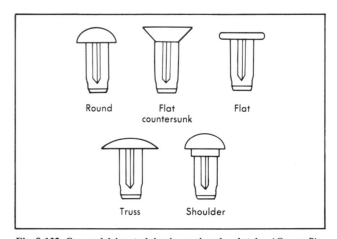

Fig. 8-132 Grooved drive studs having various head styles. (*Groov-Pin Corp.*)

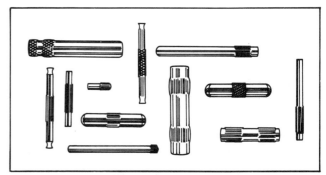

Fig. 8-133 A few of the many knurled pins available.

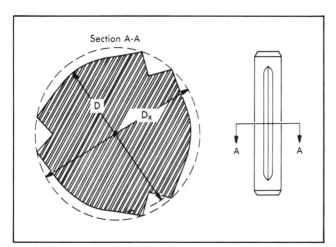

Fig. 8-130 Grooved pin having a nominal diameter, D, and an expanded diameter, D_x. (*Driv-Lok, Inc.*)

PINS

There are no standard diameters and lengths for knurled pins. Most are manufactured to customer design specifications that give the length of the knurl, the number of teeth around the body of the pin, the amount of expansion required for the specific application, and the type of lead-in configuration desired. The pins are made from a variety of materials, hard or soft, with hardened, high-carbon steel being common. Knurled pins are used extensively for setting in die castings and plastic moldings and for securing relatively thin cross sections.

KNURLED DRIVE STUDS

Knurled (ribbed), hardened studs (see Fig. 8-134) are designed for applications in materials subject to plastic deformation. Such materials include cold and hot-rolled steels, zinc die castings, and sand or die castings made from aluminum or magnesium alloys. They are recommended to ensure secure fastening in applications subject to vibration.

The two sets of longitudinal ribs on these studs are offset one from the other by one-half pitch. The lower set of ribs, first engaged during insertion, forces the hole wall material into the valleys between ribs. The flow of displaced material is then deflected to follow the offset path when the upper ribbed section engages and the stud is securely locked in the work material.

BARBED PINS

Barbed pins and studs (see Fig. 8-135) provide positive fastening for plastics, wood, and other soft materials. Standard pins are available in diameters of 3/16, 1/4, 5/16, and 3/8″, with lengths from 1 to 2″ in 1/4″ increments. Pins with barbs at both ends provide holding power in both directions. The pins and studs are made from low-carbon steel, aluminum, and brass. Sets of three barbs are located at 120° positions around the peripheries of the pins and studs. The impressed barbs displace a predetermined amount of material, with the crests of the barbs creating an expanded diameter for locking.

SPRING PINS

Spring pins are made in slotted (split) tubular and coiled (spirally wrapped) designs. Pins of both designs have smaller cross-sectional areas than solid pins of the same diameter, sometimes resulting in lower shear strengths. However, some heat-treated spring pins have higher shear strengths than low-carbon solid pins. Also, spring pins provide good shock and vibration absorption, and stresses are distributed equally. Also, their inherent springiness makes insertion in holes easier.

When manufactured, spring pins are made oversized with respect to the diameters of the holes in which they will be inserted. When inserted, the pins are compressed, resulting in radial forces against the hole walls to retain the pins in the desired positions. Standard slotted pins are available in basic diameters (nominal sizes) ranging from 1/16 through 1/2″, with lengths from 1/8 to 6″. The outer peripheries of spring pins deviate somewhat from true roundness in their free states because of the way they are made.

Standard slotted pins are made from either an AISI 1070 to 1095 carbon steel or an AISI Type 420 corrosion-resistant steel. Special metals include AISI 6150H alloy steel, AISI Types 302 and 410 corrosion-resistant steels, and beryllium copper. For high-carbon steels, the hardness range is usually R_C46-53, and for corrosion-resistant steels, R_C43-52. Both ends of all pins are chamfered to facilitate installation.

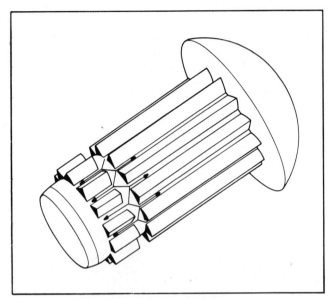

Fig. 8-134 Knurled drive stud. Arrows indicate flow of workpiece material. (*Groov-Pin Corp.*)

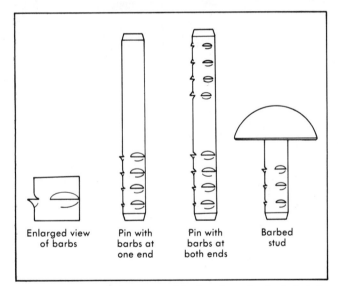

Enlarged view of barbs   Pin with barbs at one end   Pin with barbs at both ends   Barbed stud

Fig. 8-135 Pins barbed at one and both ends, and a barbed stud. (*Driv-Lok, Inc.*)

Standard finishes for spring pins consist of application of a light oil, phosphate coating, or cadmium or zinc plating. Dimensional and general data for spring pins is presented in ANSI Standard B18.8.2. The pins are also made according to Military Specifications MS-16562, MS-171401, and MS-9047.

Slotted Tubular Pins

Slotted tubular types of spring pins (see Fig. 8-136) are generally manufactured from flat strips of metal by a progressive roll forming technique. The strip metal is first run through a coining operation that forms the chamfers, and then a series of rolls form the pins into cylindrical configurations. After forming, the pins are broken off (not cut), deburred, and then heat treated to a spring temper.

Coiled Pins

With spirally coiled or wrapped pins, sometimes called spiral-wrapped pins, compression during insertion starts at the outer edges and moves through the coils to the centers of the pins. This action provides continued flexibility after insertion and eliminates possible damage to the holes. When pressure on the pin is relieved, as happens in shock and vibration loading, the pin action reverses.

Coiled pins are made in three classes (see Fig. 8-137) to suit various requirements. Heavy-duty pins provide the highest shear strengths, but with some reduction in shock-absorbing capability. Standard-duty pins provide an optimum combination of shear strength and shock absorption. Light-duty pins are designed specifically for applications requiring minimum radial forces to prevent cracking brittle materials or those with thin cross sections.

QUICK-RELEASE PINS

Special-purpose, quick-release pins are used where rapid assembly and disassembly are required. Two major types of quick-release pins are push-pull and positive locking.

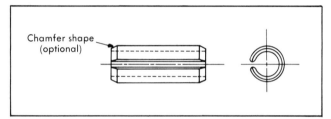

Fig. 8-136 Slotted tubular type of spring pin.

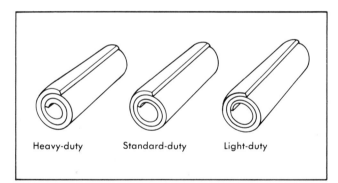

Fig. 8-137 Three classes of spirally coiled spring pins. (*Spirol International*)

Push-Pull Pins

The shanks of these pins contain detents consisting of buttons or balls backed by resilient plugs or springs (see Fig. 8-138). When the pins are inserted into holes, the buttons or balls exert a locking action. In pin withdrawal, the buttons or balls are automatically depressed.

Positive-Locking Pins

Several designs of positive-locking pins are available. One design uses a plunger-actuated mechanism. When the plunger is moved in one direction, a locking element projects from the pin; movement in the other direction retracts the locking element. A double-acting, ball-lock, positive-acting pin is illustrated in Fig. 8-139. Release is achieved by pulling or pushing the handle. Another design uses a cammed core in the pin to expand a ramped sleeve against the hole bore.

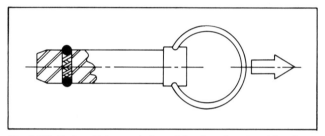

Fig. 8-138 Push-pull detent pin for quick-release locating. (*Carr Lane Mfg. Co.*)

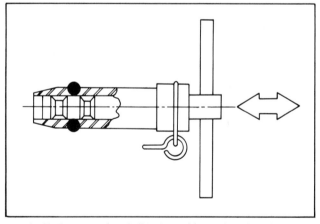

Fig. 8-139 Double-acting, ball-lock, positive-acting pin. (*Carr Lane Mfg. Co.*)

WASHERS

Washers are simple fastener components, often consisting of cylindrical slugs of metal with holes in their centers. They are available in numerous types and sizes, and proper selection can be critical to the successful and economical operation of many assemblies.

Washers serve many functions, depending on the specific application. A primary use is to serve as seats under bolt heads and nuts to distribute stresses and loads. In such applications they also provide surfaces for uniform torque control in tightening bolt-nut assemblies. Other uses for washers include compensating for oversize bolt holes, adjusting for proper grip length, providing spring tension, protecting assembly surfaces, sealing the assembly, and providing electrical connections. In some cases, washers serve as insulators or corrosion barriers.

Major types of washers include flat (plain), spring, and special-purpose. They are available in many sizes and are made from a variety of materials, including steel, stainless steel, brass, copper, bronze, aluminum, lead, zinc, and nonmetallics such as plastics and paper. For some applications, washers are plated or coated to help resist corrosion.

FLAT (PLAIN) WASHERS

Flat (plain) washers are circular or square, relatively thin components having central holes that fit around bolts or screws and under heads or nuts (see Fig. 8-140) to provide bearing surfaces. These washers are made from steel, brass, copper, silicon bronze, stainless steel, and nonmetallic materials.

Dimensional specifications for flat (plain) washers are presented in ANSI Standard B18.22 for inch sizes and Standard B18.22M for metric sizes. Two types of washers are covered in the B18.22.1 standard; Type A washers have more liberal tolerances and are suitable for most assemblies, and Type B washers have closer tolerances and are available in narrow, regular, and wide series. Metric washers (ANSI Standard B18.22M) are available in soft or hardened steel, with ODs from 4 to 110 mm and thicknesses from 0.70 to 8.50 mm.

Beveled Washers

Beveled washers are flat, square, or circular components having a taper between opposite bearing surfaces. Dimensional specifications for these washers are presented in ANSI Standard B18.23.1 for inch sizes and Standard B.18.23.2M for metric sizes.

Open Washers

Open washers, also called horseshoe or C-washers, are flat, circular components having slots with widths equal to the hole diameters that extend from the holes to the peripheries of the washers (see Fig. 8-141). This design permits installation or removal of the washer from the shank of a fastener without removing the fastener from the assembly.

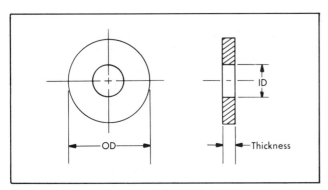

Fig. 8-140 Flat (plain) washer having an ID that fits around a bolt or screw.

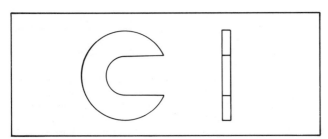

Fig. 8-141 Open-type flat washer, also called a horseshoe or C-washer.

SPRING WASHERS

A spring washer is a single fastener component that replaces a separate spring and washer, thus reducing costs and space requirements and decreasing assembly weight. Applications include minimizing vibration in mechanically fastened joints, compensating for wear or expansion, and helping to keep mating parts together. Various spring washers can withstand a wide range of pressures, but they have limited deflections; larger deflections can be obtained by stacking them. The possibility of hydrogen embrittlement in hardened spring washers can be minimized by proper plating and baking after plating. Major types of spring washers include cylindrically curved, waveform, conical design, Belleville, toothed lockwashers, and helical spring lockwashers.

Cylindrically Curved

Cylindrically curved spring washers (see Fig. 8-142) are used extensively for applications involving light loads and repetitive motion cycles and for those requiring flexibility. These washers have an almost linear spring rate throughout their deflection ranges, but both maximum height and maximum deflection are generally limited to less than half their ODs. Also, because the washers expand, sufficient space must be provided for the expansion.

Waveform

Waveform spring washers (see Fig. 8-143) are used as cushion springs, spacers between parts mounted on shafts, and to compensate for end play. They are efficient for static loads, small working ranges, and where axial space is limited. Spring

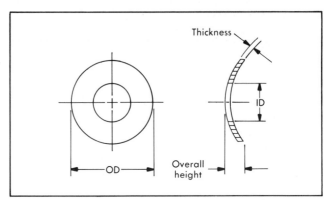

Fig. 8-142 Cylindrically curved spring washer.

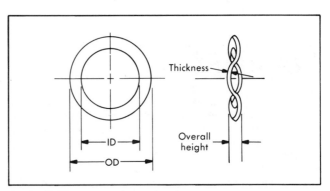

Fig. 8-143 Wave-type spring washer.

rates are approximately linear until the washers are almost flattened. Maximum deflection is about one-fourth of the washer OD.

Waveform washers generally have three, four, or six waves, and wave height is usually twice the amount of deflection. Washers with more waves allow a reduction in thickness for a given load, but decrease the allowable deflection. Space must be provided to compensate for some radial expansion when these washers are compressed; however, they expand less than cylindrically curved washers.

Conical Design

Standard conical-shaped washers (see Fig. 8-144) are formed with a slight dish, and their edges are sheared parallel to their centerlines. They provide stronger spring action than other types of washers, but give less deflection. As a result, they are used extensively as compression springs for high loads in limited spaces. Both the material thickness to rim width ratio and the cone height to rim width ratio should not exceed 1:10.

Belleville Washers

Belleville spring washers are similar in shape to conical washers, but they are made to more precise dimensional tolerances. In 1867, Julien Belleville of Paris obtained a United States patent on this type of washer; they provide greater spring action with load-bearing strengths comparable to conical washers of the same size. The load-deflection curve of Belleville washers can be linear or nonlinear, depending on the height-to-thickness ratio.

Toothed Lockwashers

Toothed lockwashers, available with external, internal, and external and internal teeth (see Fig. 8-145), are popular types of spring washers. They combine high holding capacity with small overall thicknesses. Such washers are used extensively to lock fasteners, such as bolts and nuts, to the component parts of assemblies or to increase the friction between fasteners and assemblies.

Dimensional specifications for toothed lockwashers are presented in ANSI Standard B18.21.1 for inch sizes and Standard B18.21.2M for metric sizes. Two styles of washers are included in the standards, Types A and B, with both styles providing a substantial amount of spring action. Their teeth (actually twisted or bent prongs or projections) bite into the fastener and work surfaces being secured to provide a locking action.

Helical Spring Lockwashers

Helical spring lockwashers (see Fig. 8-146) are used for one or more of the following purposes:

1. To provide increased bolt tension per unit of applied torque, thus ensuring tighter assemblies.
2. To provide hardened bearing surfaces for more uniform torque control.
3. To provide uniform load distribution.
4. To provide protection against looseness resulting from vibration and corrosion.

Dimensional specifications for helical spring lockwashers are presented in ANSI Standard B18.21.1 for inch sizes and Standard B18.21.2M for metric sizes. Most washer sections are slightly trapezoidal in shape with the thickness at the inner periphery greater than the thickness at the outer periphery.

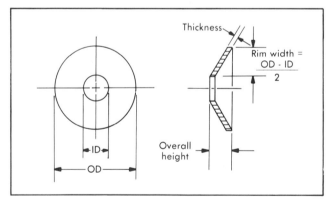

Fig. 8-144 Conical-type of spring washer.

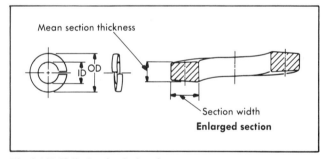

Fig. 8-146 Helical spring lockwasher.

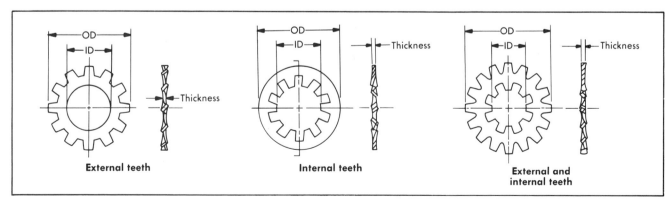

Fig. 8-145 Types of toothed lockwashers.

WASHERS

However, some washers are stamped from sheet metal, resulting in either rectangular or square cross sections; the washers are coiled so their free height is about equal to twice the thickness of the washer sections.

Many special helical spring lockwashers are available, some of which are shown in Fig. 8-147. View *a* shows a lockwasher designed for use with fasteners on soft materials such as wood, rubber, plastics, fiber compositions, or soft sheet metal. The free end of this washer imbeds itself in the bearing surface to prevent rotation during tightening. The other end is turned upward to engage with the bearing face of the fastener to prevent loosening. View *b* shows a positive nontangling type designed to resist backoff. Double-coil washers (view *c*) provide a greater reactive range.

Hi-collar helical spring lockwashers (Fig. 8-147, view *d*) are designed for use with socket-head capscrew applications. They are advantageous in areas where space is limited and the screwheads are hidden or recessed. Wide bearing washers (view *e*), sometimes used in place of flat washers, are designed for spring tension, load distribution, and for use on castings with uneven surfaces and large clearance holes. With ribbed-type lockwashers (view *f*), the rib on the inner periphery, when under compression, wedges itself into the adjacent nut thread. This increases thread friction between the nut and bolt and brings about a locking effect, while the compression of the helical washer develops bolt tension.

OTHER WASHER TYPES

Many other washers are available to suit specific requirements. Typical examples are slotted Belleville, cup, and flanged cup washers illustrated in Fig. 8-148. Some washers are specially designed to provide more or less deflection, unusual locking arrangements, increased surface contact, or for other reasons. Some spring washers are spherically curved to provide an extra stiffening effect, resulting in slightly higher spring rates than comparable conical washers.

Other modifications of spring washers include providing two flat contact areas to eliminate surface scoring and scalloping

of their peripheries for greater spring movement and more uniform pressure distribution. Finishing washers, available in raised and flush types, are designed to accommodate the heads of flat or oval-head screws and provide additional bearing area on the material being fastened. Fairing washers provide flush surfaces when used with flathead screws on aluminum aircraft skins to spread pressures over a large area and eliminate localized strains. Sealing washers are made of soft materials that are sometimes bonded to metallic washers. Other types include countersunk, formed bevel, spherical lug, recess spindle, and bearing retainer washers.

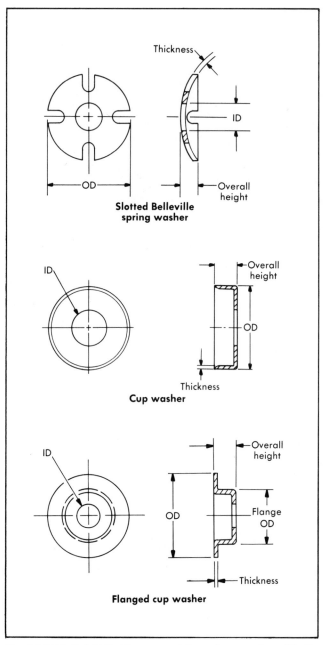

Slotted Belleville spring washer

Cup washer

Flanged cup washer

Fig. 8-148 Slotted Belleville, cup, and flanged cup washers. (*H. K. Metalcraft Mfg. Corp.*)

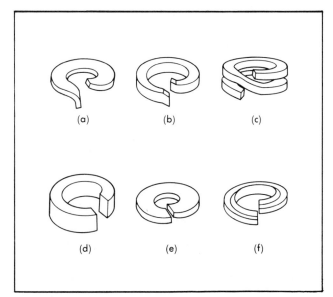

Fig. 8-147 Special helical spring lockwashers.

INDUSTRIAL STITCHING AND STAPLING

Stitching and stapling are similar processes in that they both use U-shaped fasteners for product assembly. They differ, however, in how the fasteners are made and applied. Stitches are formed on machines that also apply them, while staples are individually preformed and applied from strips, generally with portable pneumatic tools.

WIRE STITCHING

Wire stitching is a fastening method in which U-shaped stitches are formed from a coil of steel wire by a machine that also applies the stitch to the materials being joined together. When the method is used to fasten together two or more pieces of metal, or to fasten one or more pieces of metal to nonmetallic materials, it is referred to as metal stitching.

The use of wire stitching (or metal stitching) is especially indicated when one or more of the following prevail:

1. When it is necessary to join together dissimilar metals or nonmetallic materials to metals.
2. When high-speed fastening is required.
3. When elimination of predrilled or prepunched holes is desired.
4. When an encircling fastener is required.
5. When it is desirable to fasten together coated materials, such as those that have been galvanized, with a minimum amount of disturbance to the coating.

Applications

Stitching is used for a wide variety of applications in many different industries. The process is used extensively in the graphic arts field for binding pamphlets, magazines, and books. Another major use is in the production of corrugated boxes. In the electronics industry, stitches are used to form soldering terminals, jumpers, or other type connections.

There are many applications of stitching for joining two or more metals, or metals to nonmetallic materials. Typical applications include joining door hinges to frames, assembling washer and dryer drums, applying metal hinges to plastic housings, mounting rubber gaskets onto plastic or metal surfaces, and joining lining material to metal for brake assemblies.

Several applications of stitching are shown in Fig. 8-149. View *a* illustrates the use of stitches to attach the bottoms and tops of steel springs to pieces of fiberboard to form mattress frameworks. In view *b*, stitches are used to secure steel belting to an eyebolt of a mounting assembly for TV antennas.

Metal stitching facilitated the redesign of a line of industrial floor sweepers (see Fig. 8-149, view *c*). Rows of bristles are placed on top of a steel strip and then a second steel strip is added and held in place with a hand clamp. Eight or nine stitches are then placed along the outer edge of the assembly. Rubber feet are attached to aluminum ladder legs (see view *d*) on metal stitching machines. The wire stitches are driven through three layers of material: rubber, aluminum, and rubber.

Materials Fastened

The most frequently stitched metals are flat-rolled and extruded aluminum, hot and cold-rolled steel, stainless steel, soft sheet brass, and sheet copper. Among the most frequently stitched nonmetallic materials are sheet cork, leather, sheet asbestos, fiberboard, standard and tempered pressed wood, sponge and solid rubber, phenolics and other plastics, solid wood, and plywood.

The thickness of materials that can be stitched depends on several factors, the most important of which is the kind of

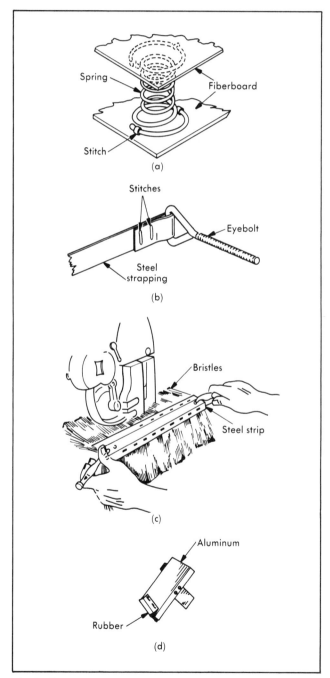

Fig. 8-149 Typical applications of wire stitching.

STITCHING AND STAPLING

material. Metals and nonmetallic materials that are commonly stitched together, along with their recommended maximum stitchable thicknesses, are shown in Table 8-12. It should be noted that while these thicknesses occasionally can be surpassed, there are times when it is impossible to stitch the maximum thickness because of work hardening in the metal after a forming operation. The condition of the stitching machine, the type of wire used, and the shape of the part are also determining factors.

For example, if 3003 aluminum is to be stitched with a loop-type clinch to cold-rolled steel, the designer must check to see that the total thickness of the aluminum does not exceed the 0.093″ (2.36 mm) dimension for soft aluminum, as listed in the metal-to-metal column (left side) of Table 8-12. The total thickness of the cold-rolled steel should not exceed 0.050″ (1.27 mm), as shown in the metal-to-metal column (right side).

Likewise, if half-hard aluminum is to be stitched to sponge rubber, the designer must check to see that the total thickness of the half-hard aluminum does not exceed the 0.080″ (2.03 mm)

dimension listed in the metal-to-nonmetal column (left side) of the table; the total thickness should not exceed the 1/2″ (13 mm) dimension for the sponge rubber, as shown in the metal-to-nonmetal column (right side).

Types of Stitches

A stitch consists of a crown and two legs as shown in Fig. 8-150, view a. While the leg length, L, can be varied within the capacity of the stitching machine, the C dimension remains constant and can be changed only by replacement of a number of parts. With the exception of the unclinched stitch, the stitches become a distinctive type only after they are clinched. The standard loop clinch is used to fasten both metallic and nonmetallic materials to sheet-metal combinations; the bypass loop is especially adapted for attaching rods, small tubes, and springs to flat sections. The outside loop is used when it is desirable to bury the stitch ends in nonmetallic materials.

The various types of stitches are the result of five basic loop-type clincher profiles (see Fig. 8-151) that are available on

TABLE 8-12
Recommended Maximum Thicknesses for Assembly by Metal Stitching

Metals	Metal-to-Metal Thickness		Metal-to-Nonmetal Thickness	
	Thickness of one metal piece, in. (mm)	Can be stitched to one metal piece of this thickness, in. (mm)	Thickness of one metal piece, in. (mm)	Can be stitched to any of these thicknesses, in. (mm)
Aluminum:				
Soft: 3003, 5052, 6061, Alclad 2024-0, 2014-T, and 7075-T	0.093 (2.36)	0.093 (2.36)	0.125 (3.18)	
Half-hard: 3003 and 5052	0.064 (1.63)	0.064 (1.63)	0.080 (2.03)	
Hard: 6061-T, Alclad 2014-T, and 7075-T	0.040 (1.02)	0.040 (1.02)	0.064 (1.63)	1/2 (13) sheet cork
Extrusions	0.062 (1.57)	0.062 (1.57)	0.093 (2.36)	3/8 (9.5) leather 1/4 (6.4) sheet asbestos
Steel:				1/2 (13) fiber
Cold-rolled (1010)	0.050 (1.27)	0.050 (1.27)*	0.078 (1.98)	1/2 (13) sponge rubber 1/4 (6.4) solid rubber
Hot-rolled	0.050 (1.27)	0.037 (0.94)*	0.062 (1.57)	1/8 (3.2) phenolics**
Galvanized sheet	0.037 (0.94)	0.037 (0.94)*	0.050 (1.27)	3/16 (4.8) plastics 3/8 (9.5) standard Masonite
Stainless steel, Type 302:				1/4 (6.4) tempered Masonite
Full-hard	0.010 (0.25)	0.010 (0.25)	0.020 (0.51)	3/8 (9.5) wood†
Half-hard	0.012 (0.30)	0.012 (0.30)	0.025 (0.64)	
Quarter-hard	0.015 (0.38)	0.015 (0.38)	0.030 (0.76)	
Annealed	0.020 (0.51)	0.020 (0.51)	0.040 (1.02)	
Sheet brass, soft	0.030 (0.76)	0.030 (0.76)	0.050 (1.27)	
Sheet copper	0.035 (0.89)	0.035 (0.89)	0.064 (1.63)	

(Acme Packaging, Div. of Interlake, Inc.)

* $R_B 50$ or softer.
** Must be able to penetrate without cracking.
† Grain structure may cause legs to wander in greater thicknesses.

standard stitching machines. When it is desired to clinch on the metal side, both the teardrop profile (view *a*) and the two-groove profile with one end closed (view *b*) are used. The latter profile is available in depths of 0.062 and 0.094″ (1.57 and 2.39 mm). Both the two-groove open profile (view *c*) and the four-groove open profile (view *d*) are used in metal and nonmetal combinations when it is desired to embed the standard-loop

clinch in nonmetallic materials. The bypass profile (view *d*) is used primarily to obtain the narrow 1/4″ (6.4 mm) crown cross section and is also used for bypass stitching in which the legs are wrapped around bars and tubing up to 1/4″ diam.

Of particular importance to the designer are the shapes and sizes of the clincher blocks in which the clincher profiles are located, as well as the shapes and sizes of the clincher arms or holders on which the blocks are mounted. Because of the many types and sizes available, it is recommended that machine manufacturers be contacted for specific information.

Stitch Strength

Stitch strength varies with the tensile strength of the wire used, the type of material in which it is located, the placement of the stitch in relation to the direction of shear, and the thickness of the material. Stitches can be applied to the workpieces either perpendicular, parallel, or diagonal to the line of pull. Perpendicular and diagonal stitches have higher shear strength than do parallel stitches.

Stitch Spacing

The stitch placements illustrated in Fig. 8-152 are in general accordance with the limitations of standard stitching machines due to the space required by the stitch-forming and clincher mechanisms. However, the maximum number of stitches are rarely required, and the placements shown can be altered for special applications. Usually the number of stitches used is the same as the number of fasteners they are intended to replace.

Stitching Wire Sizes

Stitching wire most commonly used in metal stitching applications is high-carbon steel. Many sizes of low-carbon steel wire are also used for industrial stitching applications.

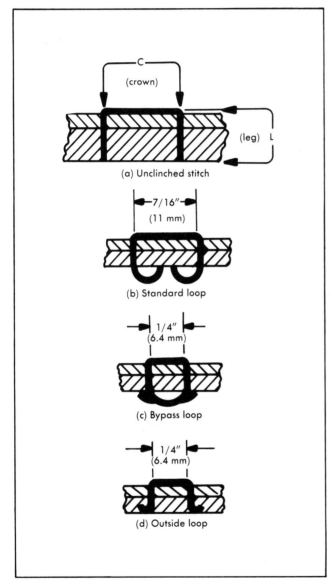

Fig. 8-150 Nomenclature and types of wire stitches.

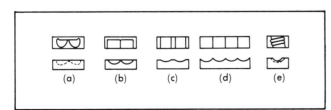

Fig. 8-151 Wire-stitch clincher profiles.

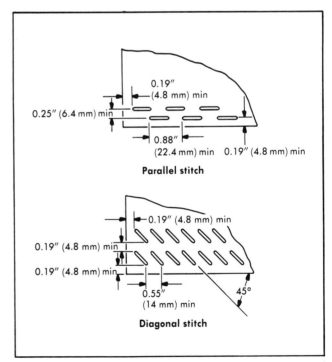

Fig. 8-152 Recommended minimum stitch spacing based on maximum holding capacity.

STITCHING AND STAPLING

Tables 8-13 and 8-14 give the wire sizes and properties of low and high-carbon steel wires, respectively. Metal stitching wire is available in different grades having various tensile strengths to penetrate materials of different hardness and thickness. The more difficult the material is to penetrate, the higher the tensile strength required.

TABLE 8-13
Sizes and Properties of Low-Carbon Steel Stitching Wire

Gage No.*	Diameter, in. (mm)	Tolerance, in. (mm)
17	0.0540 (1.372)	±0.0015 (0.038)
18	0.0475 (1.206)	
19	0.0410 (1.041)	
20	0.0348 (0.884)	±0.0010 (0.025)
21	0.0317 (0.805)	
22	0.0286 (0.726)	
23	0.0258 (0.655)	
24	0.0230 (0.584)	
25	0.0204 (0.518)	
26	0.0181 (0.460)	±0.0007 (0.018)
27	0.0173 (0.439)	
28	0.0162 (0.411)	
29	0.0150 (0.381)	
30	0.0140 (0.356)	

(American Wire Products Assn.)
Specifications: Tensile strengths—120-150 ksi (827-1034 MPa). Ductility—The wire shall withstand a kink test in which a length of wire is formed into a loop and the loop tightened until the resultant opening is no larger than the diameter of the wire. The loop is then opened until the ends are at right angles without fracturing. Finishes—Galvanized, tinned, liquor, or bright finishes.
* Washburn and Moen, which is the same as the U.S. Steel Wire Gage system.

TABLE 8-14
Sizes and Properties of High-Carbon Steel Stitching Wire

Gage No.*	Wire Diameter, in. (mm), ±0.0010″ (0.025 mm)
17	0.0540 (1.372)
18	0.0475 (1.206)
19	0.0410 (1.041)
20	0.0348 (0.884)

Grade	Tensile Strength, ksi (MPa)
230	220-249 (1517-1717)
260	250-289 (1724-1993)
290	290-319 (1999-2199)
330	320-360 (2206-2482)

(American Wire Products Assn.)
Specifications: Ductility—The finished wire shall withstand a kink test in which a length of wire is formed into a loop and the loop tightened until the resultant opening is no larger than the diameter of the wire. The loop is then opened until the ends are at right angles without fracturing. Finishes—Tinned, galvanized, liquor, or bright.
* Washburn and Moen, which is the same as the U.S. Steel Wire Gage system.

Stitching Machines

There are many models of stitching machines available, two of which are shown in Fig. 8-153. View *a* is a machine with a straight, solid arm; the machine in view *b* has a deep throat (distance from the stitching point to the vertical frame of the machine). Machines are made with different throat depths and have straight, overhung, gooseneck, or other style arms to suit specific requirements. Compact stitching machines for bench or portable operation are also available.

All stitching machines feed accurate lengths of wire directly from a coil, cut and form the wire into U-shaped stitches, and then drive the stitches through the materials to be joined. The operating speeds range up to 300 stitches per minute.

Stitching machines are self-contained units consisting of a motor, clutch-brake, driveshaft, and stitching head. The head is mounted on the machine frame and a switching device, such as a foot treadle, is provided to control the clutch-brake unit. Wire drawn from a coil is passed through straightening rollers and fed to a cutoff die and knife. The adjustable cutoff unit shears the wire to required lengths.

A mandrel or anvil having a spring-actuated gripper holds the wire during cutoff and positions the cutoff lengths under formers. The formers bend each wire length over the mandrel to produce a U-shaped stitch and guide and support the stitch as it is driven into the work material. A driver, mounted between the formers, exerts pressure on the crown of the stitch to force it through the work material. Air jets are generally provided to eject slugs of material pushed out by the legs of the stitch.

Assembly components to be joined are placed over a clincher, mounted on an arm or bracket under the formers. The clincher turns the legs of the stitch back against the assembly after they have penetrated the work material. Different types of clinchers commonly used are illustrated in Fig. 8-151.

INDUSTRIAL STAPLING

Conventional U-shaped staples, cohered into convenient, easy-to-handle strips, are becoming increasingly popular for industry to use in product fastening applications. Staples are available made from wire ranging from 0.026 to 0.072″ (0.66 to 1.83 mm) diam and 1/8 to 2 1/2″ (3.2 to 63.5 mm) long. Staples are normally available made from aluminum, bronze, Monel, stainless steel, and low, medium, and high-carbon steel wire, with a galvanized, tin, or liquor protective finish. They are also available with their crowns painted to blend with the materials with which they are to be used.

Staples are also available in many different crown sizes and types, and with various leg lengths and types of points. For example, one manufacturer offers staples with 20 different crown sizes and wire cross sections. Each size is made for optimum performance for different fastening applications.

Staple Points

Some of the more common staple points used for industrial fastening are illustrated in Fig. 8-154.

Chisel point. The points on the legs of these staples have an equal chisel-type cut from both sides, resulting in a straight-in action when the staples are driven. Although the chisel point does not provide as much holding power in soft wood as does the divergent point, it is a good all-purpose point and is recommended for many applications. The chisel point staple is the correct one to use when a clinching anvil is employed to form and clinch over the staple.

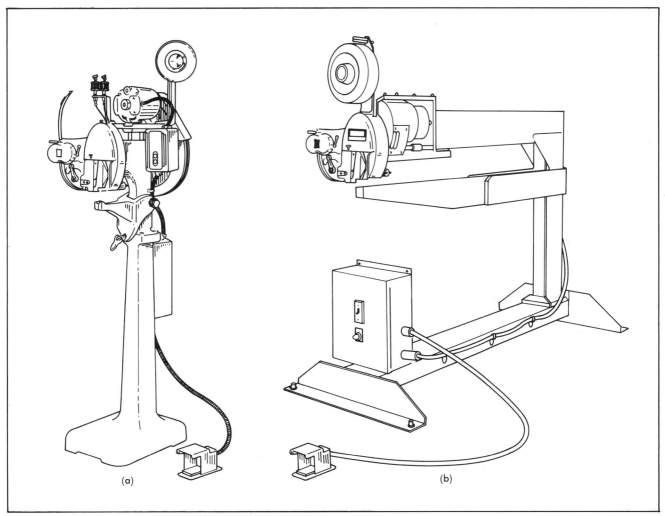

Fig. 8-153 Two types of stitching machines: (a) with straight, solid arm and (b) with deep throat.

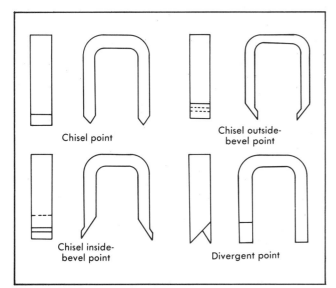

Fig. 8-154 Common types of staple points.

Chisel inside-bevel point. The points on the legs have a chisel edge cut from the inside out. Staples with these points are used for going through soft materials against a steel plate, so that legs automatically outside-clinch when striking the steel plate.

Chisel outside-bevel point. The points on the legs have a chisel edge cut from the outside in. Staples with these points are also used for going through soft materials against a steel plate, so that the legs automatically inside-clinch when striking the steel plate.

Divergent point. This is a sawtooth cut, with the direction of the cut on each leg being in opposite directions. When the staple is driven into wood, each leg follows the cut of its point, resulting in a twisting or diverging action. This is a good point for shorter staples driven into soft wood; it drives well and holds well. This point is not recommended for long staples or for driving into hard wood because the diverging action of the legs becomes too extreme.

Tooling Used

Staples used by industry for fastening applications are normally applied with pneumatic portable tools. The size of the tool is proportional to the size of the staple to be driven.

STITCHING AND STAPLING

Because stapling tools are relatively small in size, they are easy to work with and easy to mount side by side in a fixtured arrangement.

Most pneumatic stapling tools are made for conventional single-fire operation; each time the trigger is pulled, a staple is driven. When the trigger is released, the next staple in the strip is advanced into position to be driven on the next trigger pull.

Tools are also available for auto-fire operation. With an auto-fire tool, when the trigger is pulled, the tool will continue to automatically drive staples until the trigger is released. The tool has a speed control adjustment to regulate the rate at which staples are being driven. The tool also has an auto-fire lockout to permit conventional single-fire operation.

Auto-fire tools are frequently used in applications where many staples have to be driven close together in any easy-to-follow pattern, such as in upholstering work. Auto-fire tools with operating speeds of up to 600 staples per minute are quite common.

Using mounted stapling tools with a remote control firing system, such as a foot switch, parts can be assembled at high production rates. These tools permit a complex staple fastening pattern to be completed in one split-second operation.

Small stapling tools that drive staples up to 9/16" (14.3 mm) long can be nested together to provide staples on 1 5/8" (41.3 mm) centers. Larger tools that drive staples up to 1 1/2" (38 mm) long require a spacing of 2 1/2" (63.5 mm) centers.

When tools are to be used in mounted applications, the tool staple capacity per loading and the time required to load staples become important factors to consider. Tools can be made with extended magazines for increased staple capacity. Some automatic tools hold up to 4000 staples at one loading.

Stapling Applications

There are many applications for joining materials together where staples are the lowest cost fastener to use. However, there are two situations where staples should not be used: (1) when repetitive, fast, and easy removal of the fastener is required, and (2) when the shear and tension force requirements of the assembly exceeds the strength of the wire.

Selection factors. Staple crown size, type of wire, style of point, and leg length are all critical factors to be considered in selecting the correct staple for a given application. Staples are typically used in a clinched configuration going through two or more thicknesses of materials.

When piercing through metals or hard materials, such as plastics or wood, material thickness and hardness are critical factors to consider. A general rule is that a steel staple will effectively pierce through two thicknesses of mild cold-rolled steel equal to the diameter of the wire used to make the staple. For example, a staple made from 0.062" (1.57 mm) diam steel wire will pierce through two thicknesses of 0.032" (0.81 mm) cold-rolled steel.

Buckling problems. When the total thickness or hardness of the materials to be stapled together exceeds the column strength of the staple, the staple will buckle. Staple buckling, however, can easily be overcome. This is accomplished by providing two clearance holes in the part made from the thicker or harder material, thus allowing the staple legs to pass freely through the part. The only resistance remaining for the staple is as it pierces and passes through the second part. A pilot hole must also be provided in the part with the clearance holes for registering a locating pin on the tool. This will ensure that the staple legs will line up with the two clearance holes.

Automotive applications. Stapling is used extensively in the automotive industry. Most applications involve joining parts made from dissimilar metals or metal parts to nonmetal parts. Figure 8-155 illustrates two typical applications: View *a* is the attachment of 0.020" (0.51 mm) thick aluminum door trim to a plastic door panel; view *b* is the attachment of carpet to a 0.032" (0.81 mm) thick steel rear seat support.

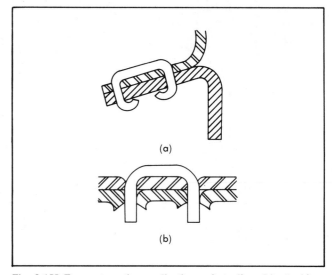

Fig. 8-155 Two automotive applications of stapling: (a) attaching aluminum door trim to plastic panel and (b) attaching carpet to steel seat support. (*Duo-Fast Corp.***)**

SHRINK AND EXPANSION FITS

A shrink fit is composed of two normally interfering parts in which the interference has been eliminated during assembly by dimensional change in one or both of the parts by heating one part only or by heating one part and cooling the other. An expansion fit is one that is achieved by cooling only the male or internal member of an assembly. This discussion embraces both concepts under the term *shrink fits*.

Because of its high joint strength, the shrink fit is useful in heavy construction where high holding power is required. It is effective in assembling parts whose materials have different properties or corrosion resistance, such as a steel shell over an aluminum or copper liner. It can sometimes permit a rather weak, low-cost material to be used in a prestressed condition and thus replace a more costly high-strength material.

ADVANTAGES

The advantages of expansion fits over ordinary press fitting are the greater allowances possible with nitrogen cooling and freedom from longitudinal scratches on the work by press fitting. Subzero temperatures can facilitate removal of some assembled parts. In the case of large bushings, a tight-fitting, cup-type container filled with a subzero convection fluid can be inserted, and the bushing will be able to be fairly easily removed after shrinking.

Cooling of an internal member of an assembly provides, in the case of liquid nitrogen, a 390° F (215° C) differential from room temperature. Such a differential obtained by heating the external member would bring its temperature to 460° F (240° C). This can be disadvantageous for most aluminum alloys and certain steels, particularly where the parts are massive, whereas subzero refrigeration does not distort, warp, or otherwise have an effect on the parts.

Cooling below the dew point, however, causes condensation and moisture trapped in the joint may cause subsequent corrosion. Also, cooling below 32° F (0° C) may cause icing, which can cause a dimensional change, a different fit, and a bad joint. If these problems are significant, as with precision bearing fits, a low-humidity environment should be used.

METHODS OF CHANGING DIMENSIONS

Dimensional change can be obtained by heating the hub or cooling the shaft, or by combining the two methods. The optimum method is dependent on a large number of factors, some of which are:

1. Dimensional change required to ensure success in assembly.
2. Effect of shrinking process on physical properties of parts.
3. Effect of shrinking process on surface condition of parts.
4. Susceptibility of the parts to be damaged in any other way by the method being considered.
5. Size and shape of parts.
6. Quantity of assemblies.
7. Available equipment.
8. Availability of materials required.
9. Relative cost.

Sources of Heat

The sources of heat that may be used in heating the hub include:

1. Hot water, brine, oil, or molten metal baths.
2. Steam.
3. Air-gas or oxygen-gas hand torches.
4. Oil, gas, or electric furnaces (controlled atmosphere may be utilized to protect parts).
5. Electric resistance heaters.
6. Electric induction heaters.

Heat guns, similar to hair dryers, are often used to quickly heat small parts such as bearing races. The parts should be placed on insulated surfaces that do not conduct heat.

Cooling Methods

The methods that may be used in cooling the shaft are:

1. Immersion in liquids cooled by ice, dry ice (solid carbon dioxide), or refrigeration.
2. Cooling in refrigerator.
3. Packing in dry ice.
4. Immersion in liquid air or liquid nitrogen.

REQUIREMENTS FOR SHRINK FITTING

Basic requirements for making successful shrink fittings include the following:

1. Parts should be properly designed:
   a. Adequate interference should be used to ensure satisfactory strength of finished assembly.
   b. Allowable working stresses must not be exceeded (shrinkage stresses are usually additive to the working stresses).
   c. A check must be made by calculation to see that the parts can be readily assembled in the shrunken or expanded state with the selected interference.
   d. In general, a surface finish of high quality should be specified.
   e. Corners or edges should be chamfered, and generous fillets should be specified.
2. Parts must be machined accurately and carefully inspected visually and dimensionally. Variations in interference can occur due to noncylindricality of the contacting surfaces.
3. All parts should be cleaned and thoroughly dried prior to heating or cooling and assembly.
4. After parts have been removed from the heating or cooling medium, assembly should proceed rapidly.
5. The operator must prevent sticking due to misalignment of parts.
6. Careful planning of each step of the process is necessary to ensure success in making the final assembly. It is suggested that the assembly procedure be rehearsed prior to actual assembly.

Uneven temperature changes after bringing two parts together often causes uneven initial contact. This may result in relative motion between the parts, uneven stress distribution, and unacceptable stress concentrations. Rings that have to be seated against shoulders on shafts may become unseated because of these problems; contact pressure should be used to seat the rings against the shaft shoulders, but care must be taken because of the heat-sink effect of the pressing tool.

PRESSURES AND STRESSES IN SHRINKAGE FITS

When two members have been assembled, radial pressure set up at their adjacent surfaces causes the two parts to be held firmly together. The radial pressure thus created is proportional to the amount of interference utilized and to the modulus of elasticity of the material of each member. It is also dependent on the size of the outer member with respect to the inner member and whether the inner member is hollow or solid.

If the hub and hollow shaft are fabricated from the same material, the radial pressure, P, exerted between the hub and the shaft (see Fig. 8-156) can be calculated by the equation:

$$P = E\Delta \, \frac{(b^2 - a^2)(c^2 - b^2)}{2b^3(c^2 - a^2)} \qquad (9)$$

where:

P = radial pressure, psi (Pa)
E = modulus of elasticity, psi (Pa)
Δ = interference = outside radius minus the inside radius at ambient temperature, in. (mm)
a = inside radius of shaft or inner cylinder, in. (mm)

SHRINK AND EXPANSION FITS

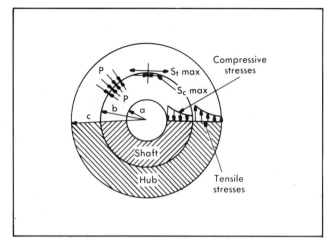

Fig. 8-156 Stresses in shrink and expansion fits.

b = nominal outside radius of shaft or inner cylinder, in. (mm)
c = outside radius of hub, in. (mm)

If the inner member is solid, such as in the case of shrinking a gear onto a shaft or pressing a pin into a cylindrical member, the inside shaft radius or inner cylinder (a) is set to zero and Eq. (9) becomes:

$$P = E\Delta \left(\frac{c^2 - b^2}{2bc^2} \right) \quad (10)$$

If the hollow shaft and hub are fabricated from different materials, the radial pressure can be calculated as follows:

$$P = \frac{\Delta}{\dfrac{b}{E_o} \left(\dfrac{c^2 + b^2}{c^2 - b^2} + \mu_o \right) + \dfrac{b}{E_i} \left(\dfrac{b^2 + a^2}{b^2 - a^2} - \mu_i \right)} \quad (11)$$

where:

E_o = modulus of elasticity for outer member, psi (Pa)
E_i = modulus of elasticity for inner member, psi (Pa)
μ_o = Poisson's ratio for outer member
μ_i = Poisson's ratio for inner member

On occasion, a large plate may be shrunk on a hollow shaft. A plate is considered large when the smallest dimension from the centerline to an edge of the plate, c, divided by the outside diameter of the shaft, b, is greater than 7 ($c/b > 7$). When this operation is performed, c is assumed to approach infinity. If both members are fabricated from the same material, Eq. (9) becomes:

$$P = E\Delta \left(\frac{b^2 - a^2}{2b^3} \right) \quad (12)$$

If both members are fabricated from different materials, the radial pressure can be calculated by the equation:

$$P = \frac{\Delta}{\dfrac{b}{E_o}(1 + \mu_o) + \dfrac{b}{E_i} \left(\dfrac{b^2 + a^2}{b^2 - a^2} - \mu_i \right)} \quad (13)$$

As a result of the radial pressure, circumferential tensile stresses and radial compressive stresses are set up in the hub.

The maximum tensile stress, $S_t\ max$, occurs at the bore of the hub and is calculated by the equation:

$$S_t\ max = \frac{P(c^2 + b^2)}{c^2 - b^2} \quad (14)$$

The maximum radial stress, $S_r\ max$, in the hub occurs at this same location and can be calculated by the equation:

$$S_r\ max = -P \quad (15)$$

The effective stress, $S_e\ max$, at this point using the Tresca criteria (maximum shear stress) is calculated by the equation:

$$S_e\ max = \frac{2Pc^2}{c^2 - b^2} \quad (16)$$

The maximum compressive stress, $S_c\ max$, occurs at the bore of the cylinder because of the restrictive effort of the hub. For thick cylinders, the compressive stress at the bore of the inner cylinder is calculated by the equation:

$$S_c\ max = \frac{2Pb^2}{b^2 - a^2} \quad (17)$$

For example, if a steel hub 10" (254 mm) long, 16" (406.4 mm) OD, and 12" (304.8 mm) ID is to be shrunk on a hollow steel cylinder or shaft 12.010" (305.05 mm) OD and 8" (203.2 mm) ID, the radial pressure exerted between the two members, the maximum tangential tensile stress, $S_t\ max$, occurring in the hub, and the maximum tangential compressive stress, $S_c\ max$, occurring in the hollow shaft can be calculated from the following:

a = 4" (101.6 mm)
b = 6" (152.4 mm)
c = 8" (203.2 mm)
Δ = 6.005"-6.000" = 0.005" (0.13 mm)

Therefore, from Eq. (9):

$$P = \frac{29,000,000 \times 0.005(36 - 16)(64 - 36)}{2 \times 216 \times (64 - 16)} = 3916\ psi\ (27\ MPa),\ \text{radial pressure}$$

from Eq. (14):

$$S_t\ max = \frac{3916\ (64 + 36)}{64 - 36} = 13,986\ psi\ (96\ MPa),\ \text{maximum tensile stress in hub}$$

from Eq. (16):

$$S_e\ max = \frac{2 \times 3916 \times 64}{64 - 36} = 17,902\ psi\ (123\ MPa),\ \text{maximum effective stress in hub}$$

and from Eq. (17):

$$S_c\ max = \frac{2 \times 3916 \times 36}{36 - 16} = 14,098\ psi\ (97\ MPa),\ \text{maximum compressive stress in hollow shaft}$$

The allowable stress is normally the yield strength of the material divided by a factor of safety. For ductile materials such as most steels and aluminum, the effective stress is:

$$S_e\ max \leq \frac{S_y}{N} \quad (18)$$

where:

S_y = yield strength, psi (Pa)
N = factor of safety

For brittle materials such as cast iron, the maximum stress theory is normally used and the tangential stress can be approximated by:

$$S_t \, max \leq \frac{S_y}{N} \tag{19}$$

In the case of a shaft, the maximum tangential stress occurs at the inside diameter. At this point, the radial stress is zero and the tangential stress and the effective stress have the same magnitude. For this case, the tangential stress can be calculated by:

$$S_t \, max = -\frac{2Pa^2}{b^2 - a^2} \tag{20}$$

The effective stress is:

$$S_e \, max = \left| S_t \, max \right| = \frac{2Pa^2}{b^2 - a^2} \tag{21}$$

For nonsymmetrical geometries, the stress analysis methods previously discussed cannot be used. In those cases, the finite element method is a powerful computer tool for analyzing the stresses. When using the finite element method, a statically equivalent loading is applied using thermal strains. Because the thermal loading of the finite element model is equivalent to the shrink-fit model, stresses and deformations predicted by the finite element model converge to the actual shrink-fit values.

Analyzing the stresses using finite element methods can be performed using any of the commercially available finite element computer programs. In areas where high stress gradients occur, eight-node quadrilateral elements are recommended.

DIMENSIONAL CHANGES DUE TO TEMPERATURE CHANGES

The approximate size change, per unit of length or diameter, occurring when parts are heated or cooled may be determined from the curves in Fig. 8-157. When using these curves to determine size change for a given material on heating or cooling, simply start at the temperature specified, follow across horizontally to the material in question, then follow the vertical lines to read the size change. The size change per inch or

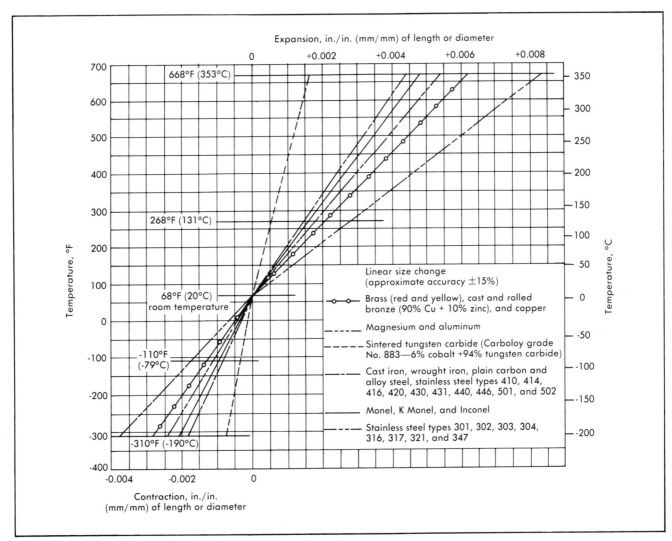

Fig. 8-157 Dimensional changes due to temperature changes.

SHRINK AND EXPANSION FITS

millimeter, multiplied by the length or diameter of the part, gives the actual size change of the part.

For those materials not covered by the curves in Fig. 8-157 and for those engineers desiring to make their own calculations, Eqs. (22) through (24) may be used. The following symbols are used in those equations:

£ = coefficient of linear thermal expansion, in./in./°F (m/m/°C). The coefficients for some materials are given in Table 8-15.

T_1 = ambient temperature, °F (°C)

T_2 = temperature to which parts are to be heated or cooled, °F (°C)

d_1 = diameter at temperature T_1, in. (mm)

d_2 = diameter at temperature T_2, in. (mm)

K = required size change due to temperature change, in. (mm). When part is cooled: $K = d_1 - d_2$; when part is heated: $K = d_2 - d_1$.

T = temperature change required or affected ($T = T_1 - T_2$). Note that when the parts are cooled from room

TABLE 8-15
Physical Properties of Some Common Materials for Shrink Fitting

Material	Tensile Strength, ksi (MPa)	Yield Strength, ksi (MPa)	Modulus of Elasticity, in Tension or Compression psi x 10⁶ (GPa)	Poisson's Ratio	Coefficient of Thermal Expansion μin./in./°F (μm/m/°C)
Aluminum, forged:					
2014-T6	70 (483)	30 (207)	10.3 (710)	0.33	11.5-13.6 (20.7-24.5)
2017-T6 and 2025-T6	55 (379)	30 (207)	10.3 (710)	0.33	11.5-13.6 (20.7-24.5)
Brass, red:					
cast	40 (276)	15 (103)	14 (965)		10.4 (18.7)
hard	69 (476)	55 (379)	14 (965)		
Brass, yellow, hard	65 (448)	50 (345)	14 (965)		11.3 (20.3)
Bronze (90% Cu-10% Zn):					
hard	52 (359)	47.5 (328)	17 (1172)		
annealed	37.5 (259)	11.5 (79)	17 (1172)		
Copper (99.9%):					
annealed	31.5 (217)	10 (69)	16 (1103)		9.3 (16.7)
hard	43.5 (300)	40 (276)	16 (1103)		9.3 (16.7)
Inconel, cold drawn and annealed	90 (621)	35 (241)	31 (2137)	0.29	6.7 (12)
Invar, forged	65-85 (448-586)	40-60 (276-414)	21.4 (1475)	0.31	
Iron:					
cast	30 (207)	---	17.7-20.4 (1220-1407)		6.7-7.5 (12-13.5)
wrought	47 (324)	30 (207)	29 (1999)		
Magnesium:					
AM-C575	46 (317)	26 (179)	6.5 (448)	0.34	14 (25.2)
AM-C585	48 (331)	38 (262)	6.5 (448)	0.34	14 (25.2)
Monel, cold drawn and annealed	80 (552)	25 (172)	25.5 (1758)	0.32	
Monel K, cold drawn and annealed	100 (689)	50 (345)	26 (1793)	0.32	7.4 (13.3)
Sintered tungsten carbide, 6% cobalt (Carboloy grade 44A)	---	---	95 (6550)*	0.26	
Stainless steel, AISI Type:					
310	80 (552)	35 (241)	29 (1999)		9.7 (17.5)
410	65 (448)	35 (241)	28 (1931)		6.5 (11.7)
Steel, SAE:					
1020, cold drawn and annealed	63 (434)	38 (262)	29 (1999)	0.29	6.7 (12)
1050, hot rolled and annealed	98 (676)	47 (324)	29 (1999)	0.29	6.7 (12)
1095	84 (579)	33 (228)	29 (1999)	0.29	6.7 (12)

* Composite value shown; individual values for Young's modulus in compression and tension differ.

temperature, T_2 becomes a minus quantity. Therefore, $T = T_1 - (-T_2) = T_1 + T_2$

For heating,

$$d_2 = d_1 + \pounds(T_2 - T_1)d_1 \qquad (22)$$

For cooling,

$$d_2 = d_1 - \pounds(T_1 - T_2)d_1 \qquad (23)$$

For example, assume a ring 10″ (254 mm) ID of a material having linear coefficient of expansion equal to 0.000007 in./in./°F (4 μm/m/°C). It is required to heat this ring from room temperature, 68°F (20°C), to 500°F (260°C) to make a shrink assembly. By Eq. (13), the inside diameter, d_2, of this ring, when heated, is:

$$d_2 = 10 + 0.000007 (500 - 68) 10 = 10.03024″ (254.7681 \text{ mm})$$

It is required to make a 10″ (254 mm) diam shaft of the same material as in the preceding problem. To assemble this shaft, it was decided to cool the shaft to -300°F (-184°C). By Eq. (14), the outside diameter, d_2, of this shaft, when cooled, is:

$$d_2 = 10 - 0.000007 [68 - (-300)] 10 = 9.974″ (253.34 \text{ mm})$$

The temperature change to effect a given size change is given by the following equation:

$$T = \frac{K}{\pounds d_1} \qquad (24)$$

For example, assume a 10″ (254 mm) diam piece is to be heated or cooled to effect a size change of 0.010″ (0.25 mm). Using the same material as in the examples for Eqs. (13) and (14), where:

$$\pounds = 0.000007 \text{ in./in./°F}$$

$$T = \frac{0.010}{0.000007 \times 10} = 143 \text{ °F (62°C)}$$

Table 8-15 lists physical properties of some common materials that may be encountered in making shrink fits.

STRENGTH OF SHRINK-FIT ASSEMBLIES

According to Faupel,[7] the forces that a shrink-fit assembly can withstand without relative movement or separation of the parts are:

For axial holding power:

$$F = 2Lbp_f f \qquad (25)$$

For torsional holding power:

$$T = 2Lb^2 p_f f' \qquad (26)$$

where:

F = axial force, lb (N)
L = length of fit, in. (mm)
b = interface radius or outside radius of inner component of two-shell shrink-fit assembly, in. (mm)
p_f = shrink-fit pressure, psi (Pa)
f = coefficient of friction between shell and liner
f' = torsional coefficient of friction
T = torque, in.-lb (N·m)

Average values for coefficients of friction, f, for use in Eqs. (16) and (17), are listed in Table 8-16. Torsional coefficients of friction, f', must usually be determined by experiment.

It has also been shown that the holding power of shrink fits is related not only to radial pressures, but also to the surface finish of mating parts and, in some cases, to the age of the shrink fit. Comparative tests were made with ground shafts and bores vs. ground shafts and machined bores. Ground surfaces were 10-12 μin. (0.25-0.30 μm), machined surfaces were 60-125 μin. (1.52-3.18 μm). Two general observations were:

1. With interferences above 0.003 in./in. (mm/mm), the added holding power per unit increase in interference was greatly reduced. This could suggest an optimum interference value that would provide maximum holding power.
2. The finer the finish on the mating surfaces, the greater the holding power for a given interference. This increase was on the order of 15-25%.

SAFETY PRECAUTIONS

To avoid the hazards that accompany the use of heat or cold, the operator or engineer should understand the nature of materials frequently used in making shrinkage fits. Some important safety precautions are:

1. When employing methods utilizing heat, the operator should be protected by heat-resistant gloves, shields, and protective clothing.
2. When cooling with inflammable solutions, such as alcohol cooled by dry ice, the following precautions should be taken:
   a. Alcohol is not to be ignited.
   b. Smoking should not be permitted.
   c. Fire extinguishers should be provided.
   d. Operator should not inhale gas rising from the surface of alcohol.
   e. Operator should be fully clothed and wear goggles and heat-resistant gloves.
3. When liquid air or liquid nitrogen (98%) is used for cooling, the remaining liquid becomes increasingly rich in liquid oxygen. The latter promotes combustion and explosions when in contact with combustible materials. These facts impose the following safety precautions:
   a. Containers for liquid air or liquid nitrogen must be made of noncombustible materials and must be as free as possible from dust, dirt, grease, oil, and other impurities.
   b. Parts must be thoroughly clean prior to cooling.
   c. Operators should be completely clothed, shirt collar must be buttoned, shirt sleeves should overlap cuffs or gloves, and trouser legs should cover the tops of shoes to prevent liquid from coming in contact with the body or being caught in clothing.
   d. Smoking should not be permitted.
   e. Combustible materials should not be permitted in the vicinity.
   f. Unevaporated residue of liquid should be disposed of properly.
   g. Liquid air or liquid nitrogen containers must not be stoppered. Evaporating gases must be permitted to escape without restriction.
   h. Liquid nitrogen used for cooling may boil violently when parts are immersed; escaping gases and splashing liquids could burn the skin. Also, breathing the gases should be avoided.

INJECTED METAL ASSEMBLY

TABLE 8-16
Average Coefficients of Friction for Shrink-Fit Assemblies

Materials	Assembled with						
	Al Alloys	Mg Alloys	Cu Alloys	Cr-Ni Alloys (18-8 to 18-12)	SAE Steels	Cr Steels (5-27%)	Cast Iron (pure)
Aluminum alloys	0.9	0.8	0.7	0.6	0.6	0.6	0.2
Magnesium alloys	---	0.8	0.6	0.5	0.5	0.5	0.2
Copper alloys	---	---	0.6	0.5	0.5	0.5	0.3
Cr-Ni alloys (18-8 to 18-12)	---	---	---	0.4	0.4	0.4	0.2
SAE steels	---	---	---	---	0.4	0.4	0.2
Cr steels (5-27% Cr)	---	---	---	---	---	0.4	0.2
Cast iron (pure)	---	---	---	---	---	---	0.3

(*Linde Div., Union Carbide Corp.*)

INJECTED METAL ASSEMBLY

Injected metal assembly (IMA) is a parts assembly process created by injecting molten metal into a die cavity to form a hub or other shaped joint. Surface contact is 100% between the components forming the assembly and the joint. The joint is achieved by the injection under pressure of the molten metal. During the rapid solidification and cooling of the molten metal, it shrinks minutely, permanently locking the components together. The joint, if properly designed, is stronger than the parts being joined.

THE PROCESS

The molten metal injection process is basically simple. Once the components to be assembled are located within the assembly tool, the operating head containing the tool is advanced by a moving mechanism onto an injection nozzle. Molten metal injection occurs through the actuation of an injection unit by means of an external pneumatic cylinder that pumps the metal through the nozzle into the tool. The tool contains the cavity that forms the hub or joint and the components being assembled.

Injecting molten metal into a die cavity holding premanufactured parts, to assemble such parts accurately and securely, is not a new process. It originated in the United States more than a century ago with a nationally known clockmaker. Little used until the mid-1940s, the concept has since grown in development and application.

ADVANTAGES AND LIMITATIONS

Primary advantages of assembly by injecting molten metal are cost savings, improved product quality, and the versatility of the process. Up to 80% savings in assembly costs have been reported by users of the process.

Cost Savings

Reduced part requirements. Parts of an assembly can often be eliminated by combining several components—injecting and forming them as an integral part of the hub or joint. Cams, ratchets, pinions, keys, spacers, shims, and other parts are not required for many injected metal assemblies. Cost savings result by eliminating the need to manufacture, stock, and handle such parts. Reductions in the diameters and types of stock required, as well as the amount of machining needed, for shafts also reduces costs.

Relaxed tolerances. More liberal tolerances can be specified for the locations and diameters of holes in the parts to be assembled, thus reducing the cost to manufacture them, without affecting the accuracy and repeatability of the assemblies. This is permissible because the pressurized molten metal fills all voids and compensates for inaccuracies.

Reduced preprocessing costs. Preassembly cleaning or chemical preparation of the metal surfaces is not required. This is possible because the joints are mechanically locked rather than joined by adhesion between the metal surfaces.

Low cost of the process. Except for the molten metal injection machine and tooling, no other special equipment, such as ovens, jigs, and presses, is required. Also, alloys injected in the process are low in cost. Machines needed for the process can be incorporated into production lines, thus reducing material handling costs. While the components to be assembled are usually loaded and unloaded manually, the process can be completely automated, eliminating the need for any manual operations. Operators can be quickly trained to achieve high production rates.

Reduced inspection costs. Assembly tools in the injection machines are often used as checking fixtures, thus minimizing or eliminating the need for postprocess inspection. This is possible because the assembly tool locates and holds the parts by their functional surfaces.

Reduced postprocessing costs. Because injected metal assembly leaves no sprues, gates, runners, or flash, subsequent trimming and cleaning operations are not required. Other secondary operations are rarely needed.

Improved Product Quality

Overall consistency and repeatability of assemblies made with the injected metal process are excellent. Rejects and the need for rework are minimal. The process is clean and odorless, and assemblies are ready for any subsequent processing required or installation into end products.

Versatility

Flexibility permitted in the design of assemblies is a major advantage of the injected metal process. Dissimilar materials can be easily joined, mainly because of the rapid dissipation of heat through the water-cooled tooling. Materials joined by the process include most metals, plastics, elastomers, ceramics, glass, and even paper products.

Limitations

One possible limitation to use of the injected metal process is that the joints are permanent. Disassembly cannot be accomplished without destroying the injected metal hubs. Another limitation to the process is the production of assemblies for high-load applications where locking configurations must be designed into the parts.

DESIGNING PARTS FOR INJECTED METAL ASSEMBLY

The proper design of a shaft for injected metal assembly generally requires the provision of a knurl on the shaft where it meets the other part or parts to be assembled to it. If the other part or parts have a hole into which a shaft or similar item is to be assembled, the hole should incorporate undercuts, ridges, grooves, keys, or lugs into which the molten metal shrinks when solidified, thus forming a permanent mechanical lock (see Fig. 8-158). The shrinkage is directed toward the theoretical center of the injected hub and is at 90° to the load lines of force developed by the assembly.

With press-fit and most other assembly processes, the strength of the joint is dependent on component precision, such as interference for press fits or the proper clearance for silver soldering or brazing. With IMA, the injected molten metal flows into the void between the components, completely filling it and the cavity. This permits and compensates for inaccuracies in hole diameters and alignments.

METALS INJECTED

The metals that can be injected by IMA are restricted to those used in hot-chamber die casting operations, discussed in Volume II, *Forming*, of this Handbook series. Zinc and lead alloys are most commonly used for injected metal assembly operations. These alloys are inexpensive and easily obtainable from most metal suppliers. Zinc alloys No. 3 and No. 5 are recommended and receive alloy certification from the supplier. Lead alloy, or type metal as it is commonly called, is also

certified as to the percentage of various metals forming the alloy. There is a strong possibility that one of the new zinc-aluminum alloys will soon be a media candidate for use with the injected metal process.

STRENGTH OF ASSEMBLIES

Zinc has an undeserved reputation of being one of the weaker metals. This is a common misconception that has been disproved in a number of applications. Many engineers seem somewhat surprised at the strength of zinc joints produced by IMA.

Injected metal joints are solid metal, usually zinc, but occasionally lead alloy. The cost difference between these two metals is within a few cents per pound. Zinc, being the stronger, is used for the majority of applications. Molten zinc has excellent fluidity, making it easy to inject into thin cross sections and intricate shapes. This property permits freedom of design combined with a tensile strength of up to 41 ksi (283 MPa), which in most cases gives a joint that is stronger than the original parts. In torque tests conducted on the shaft-gear assembly shown in Fig. 8-158, with diameters of the steel shafts ranging from 0.062 to 0.625″ (1.57 to 15.88 mm), knurl lengths of 0.062-0.250″ (1.57-6.35 mm), and zinc hub lengths of 0.120-0.250″ (3.05-6.35 mm), the shafts fractured before the breaking torques of the joints could be measured.

A hub and clutch plate to be assembled by IMA was required to withstand a torque of 108 ft-lbf (146 N·m). In torque tests using a steel shaft, the injected metal hub showed no sign of failure when the shaft sheared at 160 ft-lbf (214 N·m).

Test data on the strength of injected metal joints is difficult to compile because of the variety of material combinations to be joined, as well as the many joint sizes and shapes. However, many destructive tests have confirmed that zinc alloy joints can be designed to be stronger than the components being assembled.

TYPICAL APPLICATIONS

The modern use of this assembly method was started in Canada by a small toolmaking company. This company was asked by an electrical equipment manufacturer to investigate the possibility of providing an improved and faster method of assembling the disc and shaft of a watt-hour meter used in the majority of houses in North America. The first injected metal assembly machine was the solution to this production requirement. High accuracy in concentricity, perpendicularity, and assembly balance eliminated several time-consuming operations, such as shaft straightening and dimensional checking. Some time later, a standard gear and shaft were used to produce several different gear and shaft assemblies in the meter's gear train (see Fig. 8-159), with substantial cost savings.

Cable Terminations

Zinc alloy terminations are being injected onto the ends of wires and cables. Because of the rapid heat conduction from molded zinc, plastic-covered wires and cables can be safely terminated without damage to the plastic. The terminations are as strong as those produced by swaging and provide substantial savings in both time and cost.

Virtually any shape of termination can be die cast in zinc alloy. When a higher load-bearing cable is required, the end is upset or "birdcaged" (see Fig. 8-160) so that the molten metal can flow between the strands of the cable, filling the voids and crevices. The shrinkage of the injected alloy contracts onto the wire forming a positive lock. Pull tests show that a birdcaged

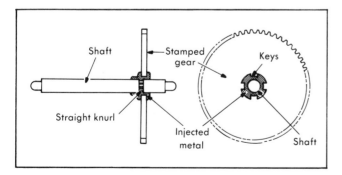

Fig. 8-158 Assembly of a gear to a shaft by injecting molten metal between the components. As the metal cools, it shrinks onto the knurl in the shaft and into the keys in the bore of the gear. (*Fisher Gauge Ltd.*)

INJECTED METAL ASSEMBLY

cable will fail before the termination pulls off the cable or is damaged.

Abrasive Points

When assembling abrasive points (small grinding wheels), the abrasive material and the steel mandrel are held in the required relationship in the assembly tooling during injection. The molten zinc alloy enters the voids between the abrasive material and the knurled mandrel ends. The zinc alloy penetrates the grains and solidifies, thus securing the abrasive to the

mandrel. Assemblies can be handled immediately after ejection from the tool. Assembly costs have been greatly reduced due to high production rates, the low cost of the zinc alloy, and elimination of the curing time involved in the previous cementing method.

Riveting

Another useful variation of injected metal assembly is its use to "rivet" similar or dissimilar materials by injecting molten zinc alloy into what would normally be rivet holes. The rivet heads are formed by a cavity within the tooling that holds the parts in their correct relationship. An advantage over conventional riveting is that the rivet holes do not need to be accurate or even in alignment. Compensation for misaligned holes can be made even if they vary in size or shape (see Fig. 8-161).

Holes can be accommodated that are offset, oversize, or undersize up to one quarter of their maximum cross section. Virtually all materials that can be conventionally riveted can be joined by this method. Very brittle or soft materials are good applications. No secondary operations or repositioning after assembly is required; parts are held in the tooling by their functional surfaces rather than by having their end positioning dictated by the accuracy of hole location and size.

Electric Motor Rotors

Injected metal assembly is particularly efficient when two or more components need to be assembled into one complete subassembly, as is the case with the rotors of small induction or stepper motors. One nominal size of center hole can accommodate several shaft diameters. An annular gap between the rotor and shaft of 0.030″ (0.76 mm) or more is filled by the injected molten metal. This eliminates the stocking or manufacture of different rotors for each size shaft.

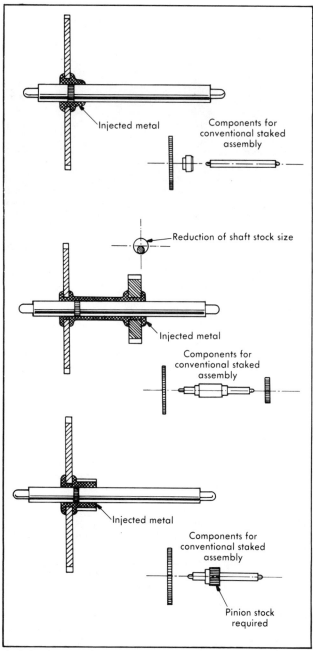

Fig. 8-159 A standard gear and shaft are used to produce several different assemblies, resulting in substantial cost savings. (*Fisher Gauge Ltd.*)

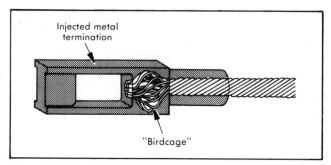

Fig. 8-160 Cable will fail before the termination separates from the cable. (*Fisher Gauge Ltd.*)

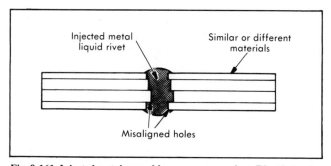

Fig. 8-161 Injected metal assembly can serve as a rivet. Rivet holes do not require accurate size, shape, or alignment. (*Fisher Gauge Ltd.*)

Different rotor versions can be assembled in the same tooling by using easily interchanged inserts. Shrink fitting, pressing, and cementing are no longer necessary. Almost any shape hub can be formed during injection. Variations in rotor heights pose no problem and previously required shims or spacers are no longer needed. A spring or air-loaded bushing in the mold contacts the end of the rotor to compensate for any height variance.

Locking Tubes to Plates

A conventional method of securing a tube to a plate normally requires a bushing with precise diameters and tight tolerances on the diameter of the hole in the plate. With the IMA method, close tolerances are not necessary because the injected molten metal forms a ring. As the ring cools, it shrinks into premade grooves in the tube and into peripheral holes in the plate (see Fig. 8-162). This permanently locks the two components together, and no secondary operations are necessary.

EQUIPMENT USED

A typical machine used for injected metal assembly is shown in Fig. 8-163. Assembly tooling is mounted at the front of an operating head that rocks forward onto an injection nozzle. Molten metal in the holding pot is injected under pressure through the nozzle and into the tooling, which holds the parts to be assembled. Machines are usually air operated, but on rare occasions hydraulic power is used. Equipment is available for completely manual, semiautomatic, or fully automatic operation.

Manual Operation

On manually operated machines, the components to be assembled are usually loaded manually, and the completed assemblies are also removed by hand. Manual operation is common when joining delicate and accurate assemblies. However, partial automation, in which difficult-to-feed components are manually loaded and easy-to-feed parts are automatically loaded, is ideal for some applications.

Depending on the specific application, manually operated machines have production rates of up to 600 assemblies per hour. Production rates vary with the complexity of the assembly, the number of components in the assembly, the need for orientation of functional surfaces in the tooling, and the degree of automation utilized.

Semiautomatic Operation

On semiautomatic machines for injected metal assembly, the timing of each machine function is precisely controlled by electronic programmer units. With these machines, the operating heads incorporating the assembly tooling can be changed in about 10 minutes, while an appropriate electronic control panel is plugged in for programming.

Automatic Operation

Fully automatic machines are equipped with programmable logic controllers. Parts feeders, pick-and-place units, industrial robots, or other automated equipment are used to load components into the tooling, unload the completed assemblies, and transfer them to a conveyor. Also, spherical replenishment ingots of the alloy used are automatically fed into the melting pot when the level in the pot reaches a preset depth.

Fully automatic equipment is generally used to produce a specific assembly because changeover to produce a different assembly can be expensive both in capital cost and lost production time. Also, parts feeding units can only handle limited variations of assembly components. However, there is a trend toward the increased use of fully automated equipment. Production rates of up to 1200 assemblies per hour are possible with automatic operation.

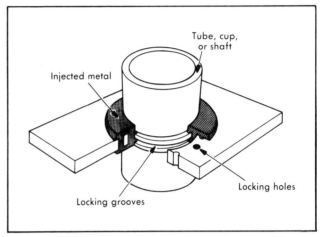

Fig. 8-162 In assembling a tube to a plate, the injected metal forms a ring, thus eliminating the need for close tolerance components. (*Fisher Gauge Ltd.*)

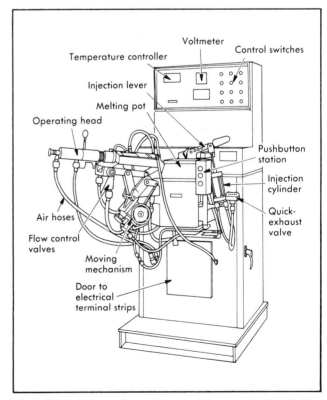

Fig. 8-163 Typical machine used for injected metal assembly. Tooling is mounted on the front of an operating head that rocks forward onto an injection nozzle. (*Fisher Gauge Ltd.*)

CHAPTER 8

INJECTED METAL ASSEMBLY

TYPICAL TOOLING

Tooling for injected metal assembly is made from AISI Type M2 high-speed steel to close tolerances. The tooling consists essentially of a die made in two parts: a fixed die and a movable die (see Fig. 8-164). A hemispherical nozzle seat is lapped into the fixed die, and a tapered sprue hole leads from the seat to the cavity. Provision for water cooling is furnished in tooling used with zinc alloy as the assembly medium; no water cooling is needed when lead is used.

Die cavities are lapped longitudinally to a smooth finish of 8 μin. (0.20 μm) and the diameters of sealing surfaces are maintained to tolerances within 0.0005" (0.013 mm). Provision is generally made for the tool to be rotated to shear the sprue, and the die cavity must be circular to accommodate this rotation. If this is not possible, the fixed die plate must be designed to rotate.

Die halves are located by means of rings. The tooling is provided with a "parts-in-place" safety switch to prevent the injection of molten metal if the parts to be assembled are not correctly located in the die.

When zinc is used as the assembly medium, a fine spray of lubricant may be applied as a parting agent after each assembly has been ejected from the tooling. High-quality spindle oil is used to lubricate moving parts of the tooling. Wear in the die cavity is almost nonexistent, but components such as core and ejection pins do wear and must be replaced periodically by oversized pins. The pin sleeves must also be resized and honed.

OPERATING PARAMETERS

Melting or metal holding pots on injected metal assembly machines are heated by replaceable electrical elements, the wattage of the elements depending on the capacities of the machines. Temperature controllers monitor the operation of the heating elements. The optimum operating temperature for zinc alloys is 825° F (440° C) and for lead alloys, 700° F (370° C).

The IMA machines are usually pneumatically operated and clean, dry air is required. On a standard semiautomatic machine, the air pressure required is between 80 and 100 psi (550 and 690 kPa). The maximum air requirement is 2 cfm (57 L/min). This results in an injection pressure at the nozzle of about 4000 psi (27.6 MPa).

If a mounted point is being assembled (a small grinding wheel on a mandrel), the pressure needed at the nozzle is about half that normally required. Reducing valves control the pressure required for each machine function, which varies with different assembly applications. Recommended pressure and timing charts are supplied by the machine manufacturer for different assemblies.

For machines using zinc alloy as the assembly medium, a gas torch is required to maintain thermal equilibrium as the nozzle contacts the cold tooling at each injection cycle. Cooling water at the rate of 0.5 gpm (2 L/min) is also needed on these machines, and drains are required to dispose of the warmed water.

SAFETY CONSIDERATIONS

Operators of IMA machines should wear protective clothing such as safety shoes or boots, safety glasses, and a smock or apron. Every effort has been made by the manufacturer of these machines to provide protection for the operator and other personnel in the vicinity of the machine against injury from accidental contact with molten metal or from the machine's moving parts. Covers for the metal holding pot not only protect personnel, but prevent such materials as lead from contaminating a zinc-charged pot and especially serve to keep out water, which could cause a severe metal eruption. Guards and shields protect personnel against pinch points on the machine.

A number of electrical interlocks are incorporated into the assembly machines. These include the following:

- A parts-in-place switch that prevents the machine from cycling should the parts to be assembled not be in the correct attitude in the tooling or even not be present.
- A die-lock switch that prevents the machine from cycling if the die is not correctly closed and locked.
- An operating-head advance switch that prevents metal injection should the injection nozzle tip not be in correct engagement with the hemispherical seat in the assembly tooling.

References

1. "Glossary of Terms for Mechanical Fasteners," ANSI B18.12 (New York: American Society of Mechanical Engineers).
2. A. E. Simmons, Jr., *High Technology Coatings Made Practical for Fastener Applications*, SME Technical Paper AD83-865 (Dearborn, MI: Society of Manufacturing Engineers, 1983).
3. "Glossary of Terms for Mechanical Fasteners," *loc. cit.*
4. *Ibid.*
5. *Ibid.*
6. *Ibid.*
7. H. J. Faupel, "Designing for Shrink Fits," *Machine Design* (January 1954).

Bibliography

Bohm, Rudolf. "Selecting Spring Washers." *Machine Design* (July 12, 1973).
Dallas, Daniel B. "The Evolution of Torque Control." *Manufacturing Engineering* (September 1976), pp. 32-33.
Dorflinger, Max F. "Guidelines for Selecting Locknuts." *Fastener Technology* (December 1982), pp. 32-33.

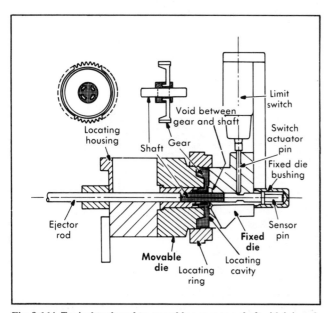

Fig. 8-164 Typical tool used to assemble a gear to a shaft with injected metal. (*Fisher Gauge Ltd.*)

Finkelston, R. J., and Wallace, P. W. *Advances in High-Performance Mechanical Fastening*. SAE Technical Paper 800451. Warrendale, PA: Society of Automotive Engineers, 1980.

FitzPatrick, Peter R., and Barto, John J., Jr. "The Anatomy of a Robotic Drilling and Riveting System." *Robotics Today* (June 1984), pp. 75-79.

H. K. Metalcraft Manufacturing Corp. *The Design of Spring Washers*. Lodi, NJ: 1983.

Johnston, Donald L. *Past, Present, Future Production Riveting*. SME Technical Paper MF84-474. Dearborn, MI: Society of Manufacturing Engineers, 1984.

Long-Lok Fasteners Corp. *What Every Engineer Should Know About Self-Locking Fasteners*. Lancaster, TX.

Movich, Richard C. *Robotic Drilling and Riveting Using Computer Vision*. SME Technical Paper MS80-712. Dearborn, MI: Society of Manufacturing Engineers, 1980.

Neu, Horst W. *Successful Automatic Riveting Program Management*. SME Technical Paper AD83-869. Dearborn, MI: Society of Manufacturing Engineers, 1983.

Parmley, Robert O. *Standard Handbook of Fastening and Joining*. New York: McGraw-Hill Book Co., 1977.

Saurer, Charles H. *Automatic Fastening—Aerospace Style*. SME Technical Paper AD83-866. Dearborn, MI: Society of Manufacturing Engineers, 1983.

Treer, Kenneth R. *Automated Assembly*. Dearborn, MI: Society of Manufacturing Engineers, 1979.

Vasilash, Gary. "Fasteners: Finding the Right Fit and Keeping It." *Manufacturing Engineering* (October 1979), pp. 59-64.

WELDING AND CUTTING

Welding is a materials joining process in which localized coalescence (joining) is produced along the faying surfaces of the workpieces. Coalescence is produced either by heating the materials to suitable temperatures, with or without the application of pressure, or it is produced by the application of pressure alone.

With some welding processes, filler material is added during welding.

Some of the thermal cutting processes are also discussed in this chapter. Related processes of brazing and soldering are discussed in Chapter 10 of this volume. Thermal spraying and hard-facing processes are discussed in Volume III.

OVERVIEW OF WELDING PROCESSES

There are more than 50 different welding processes, some of which are listed in Table 9-1. Most of these are discussed in detail in this chapter. The processes can be classified as either fusion or solid-state (nonfusion) methods.

Fusion welding processes, in which the workpieces are melted together at their faying surfaces, are the most commonly used processes. Arc, resistance, and oxyfuel gas welding are the predominant fusion processes. Filler metals often used with the arc and oxyfuel gas welding methods have melting points about the same as or just below those of the metals being joined.

In solid-state welding, the workpieces are joined by the application of heat and usually pressure, or by the application of pressure only. However, with these processes, the welding temperature is essentially below the melting point of the materials being joined or if any liquid metal is present it is squeezed out of the joint. No filler metal is added during welding.

DEFINITIONS OF SELECTED TERMS

The following glossary consists of terms commonly used in the welding industry. It is adapted with permission from the AWS publication A3.0, "Welding Terms and Definitions," published by the American Welding Society (AWS). Other definitions pertinent to a specific welding process are presented in the subsequent section of this chapter that discusses the process.

autogenous weld A fusion weld made without the addition of filler metal.

backhand welding A welding technique in which the welding torch or gun is directed opposite to the progress of welding. Sometimes referred to as the "pull gun technique" in the gas metal arc welding (GMAW) and the flux-cored arc welding (FCAW) processes.

backing A consumable or nonconsumable material (base metal, weld metal, carbon, or granular material) placed at the root of a weld joint for the purpose of supporting molten weld metal. Nonconsumable metal backing may be water-cooled to prevent sticking.

braze welding A welding process variation in which a filler metal, having a liquidus above 450°C (840°F) and below the solidus of the base metal, is used. Unlike brazing, in braze welding the filler metal is not distributed in the joint by capillary action.

coalescence The growing together or growth into one body (joining) of the materials being welded.

complete fusion Fusion that has occurred over the entire base material surfaces intended for welding and between all layers and weld beads.

complete joint penetration Joint penetration in which the welding energy has completely fused the base metal adjacent to the weld joint surfaces throughout its total thickness. If filler metal is added, it must also be fused and completely fill the joint groove if one exists.

composite joint A joint produced by welding used in conjunction with a nonwelding process. See weldbonding.

continuous weld A weld that extends continuously from one end of a joint to the other. When the

Contributors of sections of this chapter are: Professor William Baeslack, Dept. of Welding Engineering, Ohio State University; Joseph A. Bagley, Owner, Beamo Welding; Stephen R. Baron, Director of Technical Services, MG Industries; Howard B. Cary, Vice President, Advanced Welding Systems Div., Hobart Brothers Co.; Janet Devine, Vice President-Technical Director, Sonobond Ultrasonics; David E. Ferguson, President, Duffers Scientific, Inc.; Hans D. Fricke, President, Orgo-Thermit Inc.; Richard D. Green, Marketing Manager, MAPP Products; Gregory Hall, Unimation Inc.; Roy Hardwick, Assistant Vice President - Technology, Explosive Fabricators, Inc.; Gene Meyer, Production Manager, Victor Equipment Co.; Charles C. Pease, Chief Metallurgist, KSM Fastening Systems; Michael M. Plum, Manager, Magneform Business Development, Maxwell Laboratories, Inc.; Andrew Pocalyko, Technical Superintendent (retired), Detaclad Operations, E. I. duPont deNemours & Co.; Donald E. Powers, Assistant to President, Leybold-Heraeus Vacuum Systems Inc.; Jim Powers, Application Engineer, Sciaky Bros., Allegheny International; Terry N. Raymond, Plasma Welding Product Specialist, Thermal Dynamics Corp.; Frederic D. Seaman, Engineering Advisor, Materials and Manufacturing Technology, IIT Research Institute; Richard D. Smith, The Lincoln Electric Co.; Dietmar E. Spindler, General Manager, Manufacturing Technology, Inc.; Richard E. Trillwood, President, E. B. Engineering, Inc.; Terry L. VanderWert, Marketing Manager, Laserdyne Div., Data Card Corp.; Cecil C. Wristen, Manager, Applications Laboratory, Advanced Robotics Corp.

CHAPTER 9

WELDING PROCESSES

TABLE 9-1
Welding Processes

Fusion Methods

Arc welding (AW):
    shielded metal arc welding (SMAW)
    submerged arc welding (SAW)
    gas metal arc welding (GMAW)
    flux-cored arc welding (FCAW)
    gas tungsten arc welding (GTAW)
    plasma arc welding (PAW)
    electrogas welding (EGW)
    carbon arc welding (CAW)
        gas carbon arc welding (CAW-G)*
        shielded carbon arc welding (CAW-S)
    bare metal arc welding (BMAW)*
    atomic hydrogen welding (AHW)*
    stud arc welding (SW)

Oxyfuel gas welding (OFW):
    oxyacetylene welding (OAW)
    oxyhydrogen welding (OHW)
    air-acetylene welding (AAW)*
    pressure gas welding (PGW)

Resistance welding (RW):
    resistance spot welding (RSW)
    resistance projection welding (RPW)
    resistance seam welding (RSEW)
    upset welding (UW)
    flash welding (FW)
    percussion welding (PEW)
    high-frequency resistance welding (HFRW)

Electroslag welding (ESW)

Electron beam welding (EBW)

Laser beam welding (LBW)

Thermit welding (TW)

Solid-State Methods

Diffusion welding (DFW)	Cold welding (CW)
Friction welding (FRW)	Forge welding (FOW)
Ultrasonic welding (USW)	Coextrusion welding (CEW)
Explosion welding (EXW)	Hot pressure welding (HPW)

* Obsolete or seldom used processes.

joint is essentially circular, it extends completely around the joint.

corrosive flux A flux with a residue that chemically attacks the base metal. It may be composed of inorganic salts and acids, organic salts and acids, or activated rosins or resins.

depth of fusion The distance that fusion penetrates into the base metal or into the previous pass from the surface melted during welding.

dilution The change in chemical composition of a welding filler metal caused by the admixture of the base metal or previously deposited weld metal in the deposited weld bead. It is normally measured by the percentage of base metal or previously deposited weld metal in the weld bead.

electrode A component of the welding circuit through which current is conducted to the arc, molten slag, or base metal. It may or may not be consumable, depending on the particular welding process.

filler metal The metal to be added in making a welded, brazed, or soldered joint.

fillet weld A weld of approximately triangular cross section using filler metal to join intersecting surfaces, such as a lap joint, T-joint, corner joint, or intersecting pipes or tubes. A fillet weld does not normally use a specially prepared groove. Filler metal is used to fill the flat or curved surface intersections.

flange weld A weld made on the edges of two or more members to be joined, usually light gage metal, at least one of the members being flanged.

flare-bevel groove weld A weld in a groove formed by a member with a curved surface in contact with a planar

Reviewers of sections of this chapter are: Thomas E. Alves, Head, Manufacturing Engineering Section, Code 20431, Naval Ordnance Station; **Professor William Baeslack**, Dept. of Welding Engineering, Ohio State University; **Joseph A. Bagley**, Owner, Beamo Welding; **Steve Barhorst**, Manager - Process Research & Development, Advanced Welding Systems Div., Hobart Brothers Co.; **Kenneth M. Barrette**, Director of Engineering, Quantum Laser Corp.; **Jack W. Barton**, National Sales Manager, Hypertherm, Inc.; **David M. Beneteau**, Plant Engineer, Centerline (Windsor) Ltd.; **Omer Blodgett**, Design Consultant, The Lincoln Electric Co.; **Al E. Burnell**, Engineer, Technical Services, Harris Calorific Div., Emerson Electric Co.; **Dr. Fred Burns**, President, Apollo Lasers; **Susan N. Burns**, Technical Writer, Coherent General; **Laura E. Cahill**, Operations Coordinator, Center for Metals Fabrication, Battelle Columbus Laboratories; **Diego Calvo**, Sales Engineer, Advanced Technologies, Inc.; **Howard B. Cary**, Vice President, Advanced Welding Systems Div., Hobart Brothers Co.; **William Chiasson**, Hobart Brothers Co.; **Anthony R. Comer**, National Sales Manager, Teledyne Peer;

member. This is actually a fillet weld because no weld preparation such as beveling is required.

flux Material used to prevent, dissolve, or facilitate removal of oxides and other undesirable surface substances. It is completely removable after welding.

forehand welding A welding technique in which the welding torch, gun, or coated electrode is directed toward the progress of welding. With this method, the weld puddle is kept in front of the torch, gun, or coated electrode.

full fillet weld A fillet weld whose size is equal to the thickness of the thinner member joined.

fusion The melting together of filler metal and base metal (substrate), or of base metal only, which results in coalescence (joining) when the molten metal solidifies during cooling.

fusion welding Any welding process or method that uses fusion to complete the weld.

groove weld A weld made using filler metal in the groove between two members to be joined. A true groove weld requires mechanical preparation, such as gouging, machining, or grinding prior to welding.

heat-affected zone (HAZ) That portion of the base metal that has not been melted, but whose mechanical properties or microstructure have been altered by the heat of welding, brazing, soldering, or cutting.

keyhole A technique of welding in which a concentrated heat source penetrates completely through a workpiece forming a hole at the leading edge of the molten weld metal. As the heat source progresses, the molten metal fills in behind the hole to form the weld bead. Keyhole welding cannot be accomplished with welding processes using exposed electrodes.

spatter The metal particles expelled during welding and that do not form a part of the weld.

tack weld A weld made to hold parts of a weldment in proper alignment until the final welds are made.

undercut A groove melted into the base metal adjacent to the toe or root of a weld and left unfilled by weld metal. Undercut is actually a washout effect usually caused by motion of the weld puddle when improper welding techniques are used.

weld A localized coalescence (joining) of metals or nonmetals produced either by heating the materials to suitable temperatures, with or without the application of pressure or by the application of pressure alone and with or without the use of filler material.

weldability The capacity of a material or dissimilar materials to be welded under the fabrication conditions imposed into a specific suitably designed structure and to perform satisfactorily in the intended service.

weld bead A metal deposit resulting from a weld pass.

weldbonding A joining method that combines resistance spot welding or resistance seam welding with adhesive bonding. The adhesive may be applied to a faying surface before

welding or may be applied to the areas of sheet separation after welding.

weld brazing A joining method that combines resistance welding with brazing.

welding rod A form of filler metal used for welding or brazing that does not conduct the electrical current. A welding rod can be either coated with flux or uncoated and is melted by an external energy source such as the burning of gases, carbon arc, or plasma jet.

PROCESS SELECTION

Each welding process has advantages for certain applications, but several different processes can often be used for a specific application. Factors that should be considered in selecting the optimum process include the following:

- The materials to be joined.
- The joint design, including location and orientation, as well as the thickness and configuration of the parts that are being joined.
- Access to the joint from one or both sides.
- Production requirements (rate and total).
- Available equipment.
- Tooling requirements.
- Edge preparation necessary.
- Welder or machine operator skills.
- Environmental condition requirements.
- Effects of the process on the properties of the weldment.
- Weld quality.
- Service conditions to be satisfied, including loading and operating temperature for the finished product or structure.
- Cost—the economics of the process, including labor and overhead rates, and the cost of power and consumable materials.
- Safety considerations.

Some guidelines for selecting certain fusion welding processes are presented in Table 9-2. Specific advantages and limitations of these and other methods are discussed in subsequent sections of this chapter devoted to the various welding processes.

DESIGNING FOR WELDING

To realize the potential cost savings possible with welding, assemblies or structures should be designed as weldments, rather than duplicating the designs of existing castings or forgings. While most metals can be joined by welding, specifying an easily weldable material when possible reduces costs. The suitability of different welding processes for joining various materials is discussed in subsequent sections of this chapter.

Reviewers, cont.: Janet Devine, Vice President-Technical Director, Sonobond Ultrasonics; *Michael Donaty*, Director, Advertising-Sales Promotion, Sonics & Materials; *J. J. Douglass*, Marketing Manager, Detaclad Operations, E. I. duPont deNemours & Co.; *Dana Elza*, Director, Laser Applications Test Lab, Coherent General; *John Fitzgerald*, Director of Marketing, Control Laser Corp.; *T. J. Geiermann*, Director of Product Development, Newcor Bay City, Div. of Newcor, Inc.; *Daniel L. Gherasim*, Applications Manager, Raytheon Co.; *Richard D. Green*, Marketing Manager, MAPP Products; *Edward A. Green*, Product Manager, Resistance Welder Sales, The Taylor-Winfield Corp.; *Professor William L. Green*, Dept. of Welding Engineering, Ohio State University; *Brian Grinsell*, Thompson Welding Systems; *Ben Grzegorek*, President, Technitron, Inc.; *Ronald C. Hanson*, Manager, Electron Beam Systems, Sciaky Bros., Inc.; *Rod Hawkins*, Vice President Marketing, American Technology, Inc.; *Roger A. Holmes*, Director of Engineering, Sciaky Bros., Inc.; *Al Jacobs*, Senior Welding Engineer, EBTEC Corp.; *W. H. Kearns*, Editor, Welding Handbook, American Welding Society;

WELDING PROCESSES

TABLE 9-2
Guidelines to Select a Fusion Welding Process

Selection Criteria	Arc Welding						Other Welding Processes		
	SMAW	FCAW	GMAW	SAW	GTAW	PAW	OFW	EBW	LBW
Design application									
Primary structural	B	B	B	B	A	A	C	A	A
Secondary structural	A	A	A	B	B	B	B	B	B
Noncritical	A	A	A	B	C	C	B	B	B
Dissimilar metal	B	B	B	C	A	A	C	A	A
Joint configuration									
Butt	A	A	A	A	A	A	A	A	A
Tee	A	A	A	B	B	B	B	B	B
Edge	B	B	B	C	A	A	B	A	A
Corner	B	B	B	C	B	B	B	C	C
Welding positions	A	A	A	C	A	A	B	C	B
Equipment portability	3	3	3	3	3	3	4	1	1
Capital cost	1	2	2	3	2	2	1	4	4
Operator factor	1	3	3	4	2	2	2	4	4
Deposition rate	2	3	3	4	1	1	1	1	1
Filler metal utilization	1	2	3	4	4	4	3	4	4
Thickness of parts									
0.001-0.02″ (0.03-0.5 mm)	D	D	D	D	B	B	D	A	A
0.02-0.05″ (0.5-1.3 mm)	C	C	B	D	A	A	B	A	A
0.05-0.10″ (1.3-2.5 mm)	B	C	B	D	A	A	B	A	A
0.10-0.25″ (2.5-6.4 mm)	B	B	A	C	A	A	B	A	A
0.25-0.50″ (6.4-12.7 mm)	A	A	A	B	B	B	B	A	B
0.50-1.0″ (12.7-25 mm)	A	A	A	B	C	C	B	A	C
1.0-2.5″ (25-64 mm)	A	A	A	A	C	C	C	A	C
2.5″ (64 mm) and over	A	A	A	A	C	C	C	A	D
Thick to thin	B	B	B	C	A	A	B	A	A
Alloy class									
Plain, low-carbon steel	A	A	A	A	B	B	B	C	B
Low-alloy steel	B	B	B	B	B	B	C	B	B
High-strength steel	B	B	B	B	B	B	D	B	C
300 stainless steel	B	B	B	B	A	A	C	A	A
Aluminum	D	B	B	D	A	A	C	A	C

(*Center for Metals Fabrication, Battelle Columbus Laboratories, and* Metal Progress, *Vol. 102, No. 5, pp. 62-65*)
A—most satisfactory, B—satisfactory, C—restricted usage, D—not recommended.
1—lowest, 4—highest.

Reviewers, cont.: *Thomas Kugler, Applications Engineer, Photon Sources, Inc.;* **John K. Lawson***, Manufacturing Research Specialist, Dept. 11-22, Lockheed California Co.;* **Richard B. Leachy***, Chief Executive Officer, Coatings, Inc.;* **Sylvio Mainolfi***, Manager of Technical Marketing, Branson Sonic Power Co.;* **Ted R. Marshall***, Mechanical Engineering Technician, Code 20431, Naval Ordnance Station;* **J. Mazumder***, Associate Professor of Mechanical Engineering, College of Engineering, University of Illinois at Urbana-Champaign;* **Gene Meyer***, Production Manager, Victor Equipment Co.;* **Carl B. Miller, Jr.***, Vice President, U. S. Laser Corp.;* **Dr. Daryle W. Morgan***, Dept. of Engineering Technology, Texas A & M University;* **G. J. Mulder***, President, Orgo-Thermit Inc.;* **Richard F. Pall***, Manager-Marketing Communications, Nelson Stud Welding Div., TRW Assemblies & Fasteners Group;* **Gregory Pawlowski***, Marketing Communications, Photon Sources, Inc.;* **Charles C. Pease***, Chief Metallurgist, KSM Fastening Systems;* **George D. Pfaffman***, Director of Marketing, TOCCO Div., Park-Ohio Industries;* **Michael M. Plum***, Manager, Magneform Business Development, Maxwell Laboratories, Inc.;*

Performance Requirements

A comprehensive stress analysis is necessary for the optimum design of a welded joint. Such an analysis requires knowledge of properties of the materials to be joined, the filler metal, the joint design, the factor of safety to be used, and the performance requirements. Performance requirements that must be considered include static, dynamic, and impact loads; corrosion and abrasion resistance; and service temperatures to be encountered.

Joint Selection

Most common fusion welds (except in resistance welds) can be designed for either complete or partial joint penetration. The selection of the type of joint and weld to use in a particular application depends on many factors, including the following:

1. The load and its characteristics—whether the load induces tension, compression, bending, or shear in the weld.
2. The manner in which the load is applied—whether the load application is steady, variable (possible fatigue), or sudden (impact).
3. The cost of the joint preparation, welding, and inspection.
4. Distribution of the load or stresses in the weld joint.

The joint to select is the one that meets the load and service requirements at the least cost. Types of joints, welds, and grooves used for different welding processes are discussed in subsequent sections of this chapter.

Location of Welds

In many cases, the location of the welds in relation to the parts joined has an effect on the strength of the welded joint. For example, repeated tests show that when other factors are equal, welds having their linear dimension transverse to the lines of stress are approximately 30% stronger per average unit length than welds with their linear dimension parallel to lines of stress. This is due to the stress distribution along the bead, but also depends on the relative strength characteristics of the parent weld metal.

If the load on the weld is to be properly distributed, the welds should be located to take advantage of the shape of the sections joined. Resistance to a rotating effect of one member at a joint is best obtained by welds further apart rather than by a single weld or welds close together. If possible, welded joints should be designed so that bending or prying action is minimized. Symmetrical joints are most desirable because they are stronger than nonsymmetrical joints, the stress in symmetrical joints being more evenly distributed.

Stress distribution. In some designs, it may be desirable to analyze the distribution of stress through the welds in a joint. Any abrupt change in the surface, such as a notch or saw cut in a square bar under tension, increases the local stress or causes stress concentration if the stress is applied transversely to the notch or cut. As an illustration of this principle, the weld shown in Fig. 9-1, view *a*, will have considerably more concentration of stress than the weld shown in view *b*. The weld in view *c* allows a much more uniform transfer of stress with a resulting minimum stress concentration. In many cases such concentration of stress might be small and of minor consequence. However, for heavy or repeated loadings, the designer should carefully consider this matter as well as possible fatigue failure. High stress conditions also occur during welding, as well as in service, and must be considered separately.

Stress in a weld having its linear dimension approximately parallel to the line of force is not as evenly distributed. Under many load conditions, which are not at all unusual, the stress is greater at the ends of the weld than in the middle. It is therefore advisable in certain conditions to continue the bead around the corner of the joint, called "boxing," and not end at a point of stress concentration. When this is done, far greater resistance to a tearing action on the weld is obtained.

Joint placement. Good accessibility to the joints is essential for optimum welding. Placing welds in locations that are practically inaccessible and designing joints that require overhead welding when a slight modification would allow flat (downhand) welding are basic errors that can be made by designers unfamiliar with the welding process.

If an angle is to be joined to a plate primarily for stiffening and the edge of the plate serves as the locating surface, then the location of the angle is not of vital importance. Method *a* in Fig. 9-2 uses the edge of the plate, while method *b* uses the angle to the locating surface. Both of these are relatively easy to fabricate and are considerably stronger than the method shown in view *c*. Also, the method shown in view *c* is more expensive because both the angle and plate are locating surfaces, and it is

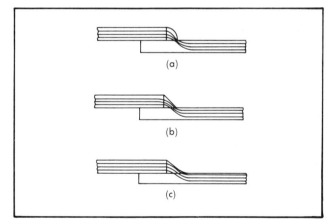

Fig. 9-1 Stress distribution through welded joints.

Reviewers, cont.: Andrew Pocalyko, Technical Superintendent (retired), Detaclad Operations, E. I. duPont deNemours & Co.; Donald E. Powers, Assistant to President, Leybold-Heraeus Vacuum Systems Inc.; Terry N. Raymond, Plasma Welding Product Specialist, Thermal Dynamics Corp.; William F. Ridgway, Director Technical Services, Eutectic Corp.; George R. Salter, Technical Director, Edison Welding Institute; C. R. Schroder, Weldaloy Products Co.; Frederic D. Seaman, Engineering Advisor, Materials and Manufacturing Technology, IIT Research Institute; Mark Siehling, Electrical Engineer, Goodrich Div., Conrac Corp.; R. A. Sommer, Vice President, Research & Development Dept., Ajax Magnethermic Corp.; Dietmar E. Spindler, General Manager, Manufacturing Technology, Inc.; Richard E. Trillwood, President, E. B. Engineering, Inc.; H. N. Udall, Director of R & D, Thermatool Corp., An Inductotherm Co.; Gerald D. Uttrachi, Director, Industry Marketing, L-TEC Welding & Cutting Systems; Terry L. VanderWert, Marketing Manager, Laserdyne Div., Data Card Corp.

WELDING PROCESSES

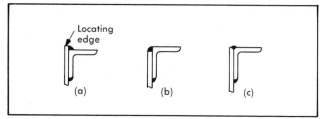

Fig. 9-2 Positioning of parts for welded joints.

necessary to scarf these or machine the weld, which removes much of the weld metal and reduces strength.

WELD QUALITY

To make a good, reliable weld requires not only a knowledge of the proper procedures but also a knowledge of how to recognize a good weld, how to recognize faults in a weld, and how to correct those faults. Failure at this point can be harmful to the quality of welding and can substantially increase its cost.

Some discontinuities resulting from welding have no effect on weld integrity, but others may be unacceptable defects.

Discontinuities commonly associated with welding include spatter, undercut, incomplete fusion, cracks, porosity, slag inclusions, inadequate joint penetration, and overlap. Some of these that frequently occur with various welding processes are indicated in Table 9-3.

Inspection and Testing

If standard welding procedures are used as specified, the end result can be virtually guaranteed by in-process inspection. To get the best results, therefore, the best time to inspect a weld is while it is being made. A check of edge preparation, weld position, electrode type and size, current, and travel speed used, as well as surface appearance of the completed weld, can indicate to a qualified inspector the quality of the weld. An experienced inspector can often predict poor or good quality welds by listening to the sound of the welding operation. Also, excessive sparks or spatter indicate poor welding techniques.

A good surface does not have cracks or serious undercut, overlap, surface holes, or slag inclusions. The ripples and width of bead should be uniform, and, with butt joints, the welds should be flush or slightly above the plate surface, but without excessive reinforcement. If there is more than a slight variation

TABLE 9-3
Some Discontinuities Commonly Associated with Various Welding Processes[1]

Welding Process	Type of Discontinuity						
	Porosity	Slag Inclusions	Incomplete Fusion	Inadequate Joint Penetration	Undercut	Overlap	Cracks
Stud welding			X				X
Plasma arc welding	X		X	X			X
Submerged arc welding	X	X	X	X	X	X	X
Gas tungsten arc welding	X		X	X			X
Gas metal arc welding	X	X	X	X	X	X	X
Flux-cored arc welding	X	X	X	X	X	X	X
Shielded metal arc welding	X	X	X	X	X	X	X
Carbon arc welding	X	X	X	X	X	X	X
Resistance spot welding			X				X
Resistance seam welding			X				X
Projection welding			X				X
Flash welding			X				X
Upset welding			X				X
Percussion welding			X				X
Oxyacetylene welding	X		X	X			X
Oxyhydrogen welding	X		X	X			X
Pressure gas welding	X		X				X
Cold welding			X				X
Diffusion welding			X				X
Explosion welding			X				
Forge welding			X				X
Friction welding			X				
Ultrasonic welding			X				
Electron beam welding	X		X	X			X
Laser beam welding	X		X				X
Electroslag welding	X	X	X	X	X	X	X
Induction welding			X				X
Thermit welding	X	X	X				X

from these standards, a check should be made on plate preparation, root openings, polarity, current, speed, electrode angle, distance from workpiece, and other techniques.

There are many different codes, standards, and specifications that apply to welded products or structures that bear stresses. Products and structures that are subject to such regulations include aircraft, ships, railroad cars, boiler and pressure vessels, construction equipment, buildings, pressure piping, and nuclear reactors. These products usually require visual and nondestructive testing, as well as some destructive testing, to ensure quality.

Organizations issuing standards related to welding include the American Petroleum Institute (API), the American Society of Mechanical Engineers (ASME), the American Society for Testing and Materials (ASTM), and the American Welding Society (AWS). Typical standards include the API standard for welding pipelines and related facilities, the ASME Boiler and Pressure Vessel Code, and the AWS structural welding code, D1.1. Such standards and codes are used primarily to guide inspection procedures, but they are sometimes adopted by local, state, or federal governments for enforcement.

For critical applications, sample weldments or specimens are given destructive tests to determine the expected performance from welded joints. Such tests may include chemical analysis and mechanical tests to determine tensile strength, yield strength, ductility, hardness, rupture strength, bending, fracture toughness, and fatigue life. Mechanical testing is discussed in Chapter 7 of this Handbook volume. The methods for mechanical testing of welds are presented in ANSI/AWS Standard B4.0.

Nondestructive testing of welds is done by various methods, some of which are shown in Table 9-4. More detailed information on nondestructive testing methods is presented in Chapter 6 of this volume. A guide for the nondestructive inspection of welds is presented in ANSI/AWS Standard B1.0.

Distortion Control

The stresses in a piece of steel resulting from rolling the steel in the mill; from cutting, forming, and shaping in manufacturing prior to welding; or from the heat cycle of the welding process are many and varied. For the majority of welding applications, the stresses do not create any problem. The forces tending to cause distortion are present in every weld made, and, unless proper techniques are used, the weldment may distort enough that considerable time and money must be spent to correct the distortion.

Simple rules can be followed that will aid materially in the prevention and control of distortion. In many cases the application of a single rule will be sufficient. In others a combination of the following rules may be required:

1. Change the workpiece design.
2. Use the most suitable welding process.
3. Reduce the effective shrinkage force.
4. Make shrinkage forces work to reduce distortion.
5. Balance shrinkage forces with other forces.

Reducing the effective shrinkage force. Do not make weld beads of excessive size. Bead size is generally specified to meet service requirements of the joint, and using more weld metal is a waste of time and money. Fillet welds are generally made slightly convex (see Fig. 9-3, view *a*). During cooling, the shrink forces tend to reduce tension on the outer surfaces of the weld, thus reducing distortion and the possibility of cracking. With concave welds (view *b*), the shrink forces during cooling tend to

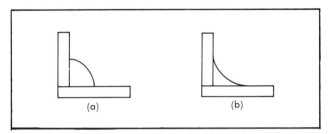

Fig. 9-3 Fillet welds: (a) convex and (b) concave.

increase the surface tension, increasing distortion and the possibility of cracking.

It is possible to reduce the effective shrinkage force through proper edge preparation. To obtain the proper fusion at the root of the weld with a minimum of weld metal, the bevel should not exceed 30° on each side. Proper fitup is also important; the plates to be welded should be spaced at the minimum dimension necessary to provide the required joint preparation. While restrained, heat is passed along the weld joint for localized stress relieving. When cooled, this initial pass provides reinforcement for additional passes. To control severe distortion, the workpiece can be preheated before securing the fixture. A minimum amount of weld metal will then be needed to produce a strong joint, while allowing space for better penetration.

Use few passes; this is another way to make an intelligent use of weld metal. Angular distortion is often a major problem. In general, angular distortion is approximately 1° per pass if welding is done with improper techniques and no restraint. A small initial pass can be easily restrained with proper fixturing.

In some cases, distortion in the longitudinal direction is a problem. In such cases, the number of passes should be increased rather than decreased because of the greater ability of a small bead to stretch longitudinally compared with a large bead. This apparently paradoxical relationship is a function of the thickness of the plate and its natural resistance to distortion. There is inherent rigidity against the longitudinal bending of a plate, provided that the plate is thick enough.

Light gage sheets have little rigidity in this direction and will therefore buckle easily unless the sheets are fixtured in a curved manner. Unless the two plates to be welded are restrained and curved, there is no lateral rigidity whatsoever because each of the two plates is free to move angularly with relation to another. As a result, lateral distortion is more common if the sheet is welded flat without proper fixtures.

Another means of reducing the effective shrinkage force is to place the weld as close as possible to the neutral axis so that it does not have sufficient leverage to pull the plates out of alignment. This is why double V-groove welds made with small, fast passes minimize distortion. To reduce the effective shrinkage force further by minimizing the amount of weld metal, use several small, fast passes and cool between passes. Intermittent welds may in many cases be used instead of continuous welds, allowing time to cool between welds. Intermittent welds also distribute heat more widely throughout the structure.

Making shrinkage forces work to minimize distortion. Figure 9-4, view *a*, shows a T-joint being welded with the vertical plate out of alignment before the fillet is deposited. When the weld shrinks, it will pull the vertical plate to its correct 90° position. Another method is to space parts before welding. Experience indicates how much space should be allowed for any given job so the parts will be in correct alignment after welding

WELDING PROCESSES

TABLE 9-4
Reference Guide to Major Methods for the Nondestructive Testing of Welds

Method	Equipment	Detects	Advantages	Limitations	Remarks
Visual	Magnifying glass Weld-size gage Pocket rule Straightedge Workmanship standards	Surface flaws—cracks, porosity, unfilled craters, slag inclusions Warpage, under-welding, over-welding, poorly formed beads, misalignments, improper fitup	Low cost Can be applied while work is in process, permitting correction of faults Gives indication of incorrect procedures	Applicable to surface defects only Provides no permanent record	Should always be the primary method of inspection, no matter what other techniques are required Is the only "productive" type of inspection. Is the necessary function of everyone who contributes to the making of the weld
Radiographic	Commercial X-ray or gamma units, made especially for inspecting welds, castings, and forgings Film and processing facilities Fluoroscopic equipment	Interior macroscopic flaws—cracks, porosity, blowholes, nonmetallic inclusions, incomplete root penetration, undercutting, icicles, and burnthrough	When the indications are recorded on film, gives a permanent record When viewed on a fluoroscopic screen, a low-cost method of internal inspection	Requires skill in choosing angles of exposure, operating equipment, and interpreting indications Requires safety precautions. Not generally suitable for fillet-weld inspection	X-ray inspection is required by many codes and specifications Useful in qualification of welders and welding processes Because of cost, use only where other methods will not provide assurance required
Magnetic-particle	Special commercial equipment Magnetic powders—dry or wet form; may be fluorescent for viewing under ultraviolet light	Excellent for detecting surface discontinuities—especially surface cracks	Simpler to use than radiographic inspection Permits controlled sensitivity Relatively low-cost method	Use on ferromagnetic materials only Requires skill in interpretation of indications and recognition of irrelevant patterns Difficult to use on rough surfaces	Elongated defects parallel to the magnetic field may not give pattern; for this reason the field should be applied from two directions at or near right angles to each other
Liquid penetrant	Commercial kits, containing fluorescent or dye penetrants and developers Application equipment for the developer A source of ultraviolet light—if fluorescent method is used	Surface cracks not readily visible to the unaided eye Excellent for locating leaks in weldments	Applicable to magnetic, nonmagnetic materials Easy to use Low cost	Only surface defects are detectable Cannot be used effectively on hot assemblies	In thin-walled vessels, will reveal leaks not ordinarily located by usual air tests Irrelevant surface conditions (smoke, slag) may give misleading indications
Ultrasonic	Special commercial equipment, either of the pulse-echo or transmission type Standard reference patterns for interpretation of RF or video patterns	Surface and subsurface flaws, including those too small to be detected by other methods Especially for detecting subsurface lamination-like defects	Very sensitive Permits probing of joints inaccessible to radiography	Requires high degree of skill in interpreting pulse-echo patterns Permanent record is not readily obtained	Pulse-echo equipment is highly developed for weld inspection purposes The transmission-type equipment simplifies pattern interpretation where it is applicable

(Lincoln Electric Co.)

is completed. The distance between the two segments of Fig. 9-4, view *b*, was to be accurately controlled. Correct spacing of the parts prior to welding allowed them to be pulled into the correct position by the shrinkage forces of the welding.

Shrinkage force can be put to work in many cases by prebending or prespringing the parts to be welded. For example, when the plates in Fig. 9-5 are sprung away from the weld side, the counterforce exerted by the clamps overcomes most of the shrinkage tendency of the weld metal, causing it to yield. But when the clamps are removed, there is still a slight tendency for the weld to contract, and this contraction or shrinkage force pulls the plates into exact alignment.

Balance shrinkage forces with other forces. Often the structural nature of parts to be welded provides sufficiently rigid balancing forces to offset welding shrinkage forces. This is particularly true in heavy sections where there is inherent rigidity because of the arrangement of the parts. If, however, these natural balancing forces are not present, it is necessary to balance the shrinkage forces in the weld metal to prevent distortion. This balancing can be accomplished by the use of a proper welding sequence that places weld metal at different points about the structure so that as one section of weld metal shrinks it will counteract the shrinkage forces in the welds already made.

A simple example of a proper welding sequence is presented in Fig. 9-6. Welds 3 and 4 do not join the weldment sections and, as a result, do not apply shrinkage forces. These two welds simply replace metal removed for access in making welds 1 and 2, which are near the neutral axis and are easily restrained. Welds 5 and 6 join the sections, but are narrow in width. As a result, total lateral shrinkage is small. Welds 7 and 8 complete the weldment and serve both structural and cosmetic purposes.

Peening the bead compresses the metal and relieves tensile stresses, thus helping to reduce distortion. Peening should be used with great care, however, for too much peening may damage the weld metal.

The most important method of avoiding distortion is the use of clamps, jigs, or fixtures to hold the work in a rigid position during welding. In this way the shrinkage stresses in the weld are balanced with sufficient counterforces to minimize distortion. What actually happens is that the balancing forces of the jig or fixture cause the weld metal itself to stretch, thus preventing most of the distortion. Changing the polarity of the welding current used can often affect distortion.

PREHEATING AND STRESS RELIEVING

In some welding operations, especially when arc welding hardenable steels, it is necessary to apply heat to the assembly before starting the welding. In other welding operations, postheating (the application of heat after welding) is needed to relieve the internal stresses that have been developed or to make metallurgical changes by softening the structure. With certain weldments, heat may also be applied between welding passes to maintain a required temperature. Each of these applications of heat has a bearing on the quality of weld or the integrity of the finished weldment. In code work, control of temperature before, during, and after welding may be rigidly specified.

Preheating—When and Why

Preheating is used for one of the following reasons:

1. To reduce shrinkage stresses in the weld and adjacent base metal—especially with highly restrained joints.
2. To provide a slower rate of cooling through the critical temperature range (about 1600 to 1330°F (870 to 720°C). This reduces hardness or susceptibility to cracking of both the weld and heat-affected area of the base plate.
3. To provide a slower rate of cooling through the temperature area of about 400°F (205°C), allowing more time for any hydrogen to diffuse away from the weld and adjacent plate to avoid underbead cracking.

Slowing the cooling rate. The amount of heat in the weld area and the temperature are both important factors in slowing the cooling rate. A thick plate could be preheated to a specified temperature in a localized area, and the heating could be ineffective because of rapid heat transfer (the reduction of heat in the welding area) and thus have no marked effect on slowing the cooling rate. Having a thin surface area at a preheat temperature is not enough if there is a mass of cold metal beneath it into which the heat can rapidly transfer.

Welding at low ambient temperatures or on steel brought in from outside storage on cold winter days greatly increases the need for preheat. Although preheating removes moisture from the joint, it is usually not specified for that purpose.

Amount of preheat required. The amount of preheat required for any application depends on such factors as base metal chemistry, plate thickness, restraint and rigidity of the

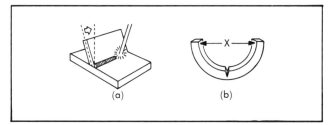

Fig. 9-4 Using shrinkage forces to advantage: (a) by inclining a plate before welding and (b) by spacing parts.

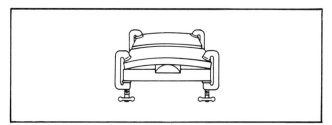

Fig. 9-5 Prebending parts before welding to utilize shrinkage forces.

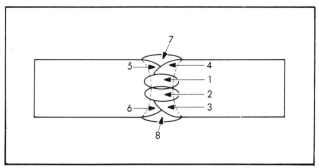

Fig. 9-6 Welding sequence to balance shrinkage forces.

WELDING PROCESSES

members, and heat input of the process. Unfortunately, there is no method for metering the amount of heat put into an assembly by a preheat torch. The best shop approach for estimating the preheat input is to measure the temperature at the welding area by temperature-indicating crayon marks or pellets. These give approximate measures of temperature at the spots where they are placed; the temperature measurements are taken as indexes to the heat input and are correlated with thickness of metal and chemistry of metal in tables specifying minimum preheat temperatures. Portable pyrometers are also used for measuring surface temperatures. Temperature is the gage to preheat inputs, and preheating to specified temperatures is the practical method of obtaining the amount of preheat needed to control the cooling rate after welding.

There are various guides for use in estimating preheat temperatures, including the recommendation of the suppliers of special steels. No guide, however, can be completely and universally applicable because of the varying factors of rigidity and restraint in assemblies. Recommendations are thus presented as "minimum preheat recommendations," and they should be accepted as such.

Methods of preheating. The method of preheating depends on the thickness of the plate, the size of the weldment, and the heating equipment available. In the production welding of small assemblies, preheating in a furnace is the most satisfactory method. Another satisfactory method is torch heating. This produces a hot flame and burns clean. Torches can be connected to convenient gas and compressed air outlets around the shop. Acetylene, propane, and oil torches can also be used. On large weldments, banks of heating torches may be used to bring the material up to temperature quickly and uniformly.

Electrical strip heaters are used on longitudinal and girth seams on plate up to 2″ (51 mm) thick. The heaters are clamped to the plate parallel to the joint and about 6″ (152 mm) from the seam. After the plate reaches the proper preheat temperature, the heaters may remain in place to add heat if necessary to maintain the proper interpass temperature. Other means of preheating are induction heating, often used on piping, and radiant heating.

High accuracy is not required in preheating carbon steels. Although it is important that the work be heated to a minimum temperature, no harm is done if this temperature is exceeded by 100°F (55°C). This is not true, however, for quenched and tempered steels, because welding on an overheated plate may cause damage in the heat-affected zone. For this reason the temperature should be measured as accurately as possible with such steels.

Interpass temperatures. Usually a steel that requires preheating to a specified temperature also must be kept at this temperature between weld passes and until welding is completed. With many weldments, the heat input during welding is adequate to maintain the interpass temperature. On a massive weldment, however, it is not likely that the heat input of the welding process will be sufficient to maintain the required interpass temperature. If this is the case, torch heating between passes may be required.

Once an assembly has been preheated and the welding begun, it is desirable to finish the welding as soon as possible to avoid the need for interpass heating. Because the purpose of preheating is to reduce the quench rate, it logically follows that the same slow cooling should be accorded all passes. This can only be accomplished by maintaining an interpass temperature that is at least equal to the preheat temperature. If this is not done, each individual bead will be subjected to the same high quench rate as the first bead of a nonpreheated assembly.

Preheating pointers. The following rules and considerations can reduce the cost and increase the efficiency of preheating:

- A cardinal rule when welding materials that require preheat is "keep it hot." It is costly to reheat to maintain assembly temperature.
- Preheat requirements can be reduced when running two automatic welding heads a few inches from each other—such as on each side of a web that is being fillet welded to a flange. The heat input into the flange will be essentially double that resulting from a single head.
- Do not overlook the value of a preheat to prevent weld cracking in weldments with highly restrained joints, even though steel chemistry does not call for a preheat.
- Heat flow from a T-joint is faster than for a butt joint. Heat has three avenues for escape from a conventional T-joint, while only two from a conventional butt joint.
- Even though adequately preheating a thick section increases the fabrication cost, experience with field repairs usually shows that preheating is worth the cost.
- Consider the use of a different alloy to minimize the need for preheating.

Stress Relieving

Stress relieving is defined as heating to a suitable temperature (for steel, below the critical), holding long enough to reduce residual stresses, and then cooling slowly enough to minimize the development of new residual stresses. Stress relieving should not be confused with normalizing or annealing, which are done at higher temperatures. Details of various heat treating processes are presented in Volume III, *Materials, Finishing and Coating*, of this Handbook series.

The ASME Code requires certain pressure vessels and power piping to be stress-relieved. This is to reduce internal stress. Other weldments such as machine tool bases are stress-relieved to attain dimensional stability after machining.

Heating and cooling must be done slowly and uniformly; uneven cooling could nullify much of the value of the heat treatment or even cause additional stresses in the weldment. In general, the greater the difference between maximum and minimum thickness of the component parts, the slower should be the rate of temperature change. If the ratio of maximum to minimum thickness of the component parts is less than four to one, heating and cooling rates should not exceed 400°F (220°C) per hour divided by the thickness in inches of the thickest section. If the ratio of the thicknesses of the component parts vary more, rates should be reduced accordingly. For example, with complex structures containing members of widely varying thicknesses, heating and cooling rates should be such that the maximum temperature difference of sections of the same weldment should not exceed 75°F (42°C). Temperatures of critical sections can be monitored using thermocouples mounted on the weldment.

The stress-relief range for most carbon steels is 1100-1200°F (595-650°C), and the soaking time is usually one hour per inch (25 mm) of thickness. For the low-alloy chrome-molybdenum steels, with the chromium in the range of 1/2 to 2 1/4% and the molybdenum up to 1%, the stress-relief range is 1250-1300°F (675-705°C) for one hour. Some of the higher alloy steels require more soaking time.

Local stress relieving can be done on girth joints of pipe and pressure vessels when required by codes. The same precautions are necessary as for furnace heating: slow heating, time at temperature, and slow cooling.

THE COST OF WELDING

As with all other manufacturing processes, costs include the expenses for capital equipment, expendable materials, labor, and overhead. Related costs for welding are the possible needs for edge preparation, preheating and postweld treatments, slag removal, finishing, and inspection and testing. Welding costs depend on many factors, including the type of joint and weld, the materials to be joined, weld size, the process used, deposition efficiency, and operator skill.

Overhead costs are generally prorated as a percentage of labor costs. Labor costs are usually based on time per weld or increment of weld length. They are, of course, high for manual welding and much less for semiautomatic, automatic, and robotic welding. Capital equipment costs, however, are much higher for the latter methods. The cost of expendable materials varies with the welding process used and can include the expenses for electrical power, filler metals and fluxes (electrodes, rods, or wire), and shielding gases, if used.

Specific methods of determining the cost of arc welding, based on the amount of weld metal deposited and time requirements, are discussed later in this chapter. Some cost factors involved with other welding processes are also discussed in subsequent sections. When the cost of a specific method has been determined accurately, it should be compared with the costs of other welding processes that can be used, as well as the alternatives of casting, forging, mechanical fastening, or adhesive bonding.

SAFETY CONSIDERATIONS

As with any manufacturing process, there are hazards associated with welding and cutting. Detailed recommendations with respect to safety in welding and cutting are presented in ANSI/AWS Standard Z49.1. Fire prevention in the use of these processes is the subject of the National Fire Protection Asso-

ciation (NFPA) Standard 51B. Some specific precautions for various welding and cutting processes are presented later in this chapter with the discussions of the different processes.

General Requirements

Properly trained personnel are critical to safety in welding and cutting. Machines and equipment used must be well maintained, and working areas should be kept clean, dry, and free of hazards. Warning signs should be posted to designate welding and cutting areas and the need for protective devices. Screens are often provided as protection for surrounding areas.

Machines and Equipment

Machines and equipment used for welding and cutting should meet all industry standards such as those issued by the National Electrical Manufacturers Association (NEMA). The frames of electrical machines should be grounded, and the machines should not be operated above their rated capacity. All cables and connections should be of high quality and well maintained by keeping them dry and free from oil or grease. Electrode holders should be well insulated and of proper design to prevent overheating.

Operator Protection

The operators of welding and cutting equipment must be protected from hazards such as burns, glare, electrical shock, and harmful fumes. Handshields, helmets, or goggles equipped with filter glass for eye protection are necessary with electric arc welding or cutting. Specifications for welding helmets, handshields, face shields, goggles, and spectacles are presented in ANSI Standard Z87.1.

Nonflammable clothing, including aprons and gloves, are generally required. Adequate ventilation by means of smoke and fume exhaust systems are often necessary, especially in confined spaces. Excessive noise levels require ear protection. Regulations issued by the Occupational Safety and Health Administration (OSHA), as well as local codes, specify requirements with respect to ventilation and noise.

OXYFUEL GAS WELDING AND CUTTING

Oxyfuel gas welding (OFW) is a group of welding processes that produces coalescence by heating materials with an oxyfuel gas flame or flames, with or without the application of pressure, and with or without the use of filler metal. In these processes, the base metal, as well as filler metal, if used, is melted by the flame from the tip of a welding torch.

Oxyfuel gas cutting is a group of cutting processes used to sever or remove metals by means of the chemical reaction of oxygen with the base metal at elevated temperatures. In the case of oxidation-resistant metals, the reaction is facilitated by the use of a chemical flux or metal powder.

OXYFUEL GAS WELDING

The three most commonly used oxyfuel gas welding processes are:

- Oxyacetylene welding (OAW). In this process, heating is done with a gas flame or flames obtained from the

combustion of acetylene with oxygen. The process may be used with or without the application of pressure and with or without the use of filler metal.
- Oxyhydrogen welding (OHW). In this process, heating is done with a gas flame or flames obtained from the combustion of hydrogen with oxygen. The process is used without the application of pressure and with or without the use of filler metal.
- Pressure gas welding (PGW). In this process, coalescence is produced simultaneously over the entire area of abutting surfaces by heating them with flames obtained from the combustion of a fuel gas with oxygen. The process entails the application of pressure, but without the use of filler metal.

A fourth oxyfuel gas welding process, air-acetylene welding (AAW), uses heating obtained from the combustion of acetylene with air, without the application of pressure and with or

OXYFUEL GAS WELDING AND CUTTING

without the use of filler metal. However, by using air instead of oxygen, the resulting available heat is lower. As a result, the AAW process is obsolete or seldom used.

In a few cases, methylacetylene-propadiene stabilized (MPS), butane, ethylene, natural gas, propane, or other petroleum derivatives or mixtures are used as fuel gases. These gases, however, are generally limited to welding some metals having lower melting temperatures because of the lower flame temperatures and are used more extensively for oxyfuel gas cutting discussed later in this section. Because acetylene in combination with oxygen produces a flame with the highest temperature, acetylene is the fuel gas used most extensively for welding.

Advantages and Applications

Oxyfuel gas welding offers considerable flexibility because the operator can control the rate of heat input, the temperature in the weld zone, the rate of filler metal deposition, and speed, making it suitable for joining most metals. Other advantages are that no power source is required, and the equipment can also be used for related operations such as bending and straightening, preheating and postheating, and torch brazing. A limitation is that the process is slower than most other welding methods on thicker metals.

The equipment required for oxyfuel gas welding is comparatively simple, compact, usually portable, and inexpensive, making it especially useful for maintenance and repairs, odd job-shop work, and certain types of tube and pipe welding. It is the preferred process for welding of lead, and it is also preferred in many cases for cast iron when a joint defect of any considerable magnitude is to be repaired. Oxyhydrogen welding is generally restricted to aluminum or lead alloys. Pressure gas welding has been used for uniting links of rail and pipe, for making rings, and for similar applications where bar or pipe sections of essentially similar cross sections are to be joined. Although it has some highly specialized favorable applications, its use is generally on the decline.

Joint Designs

The correct joint design for oxyfuel gas welding is one of the more important considerations contributing to successful welding. In general, joint types suitable for metal arc welding may be used. Butt joints (square, single-V, double-V, and double-U), square-T and double-bevel T, single and double-fillet lap, half-open corner, and edge joints are suitable for oxyfuel gas

welding. Joint designs requiring separate backing welds are rarely used. Although other joint designs for arc welding may also be used for gas welding, they are not in common use. Oxyfuel gas welding differs from arc welding in one other fundamental—the use of backing structures on joints welded from one side. Backing structures, or backup strips, are frequently used in arc welding but *should not be used* in gas welding. Their presence in a gas weld renders complete fusion at the root virtually impossible.

Generally, metal thicknesses up to 5/32″ (4 mm) are welded with the square butt joint. For heavier metal from 3/16″ (4.8 mm) up to about 1/2″ (12.7 mm), the single-V butt joint is frequently used. When access to both sides of the joint is possible, the double-V butt joint offers economies in materials and consequently greater welding speeds; it is usable on thicknesses from about 1/2″ upward. Butt joints are suitable for connections in which the members lie in the same plane and for parts intersecting at right angles, such as corners and T's. For lapped members, it is necessary to use corner joints, T-joints, or lap joints. In each of these cases, the welds joining such assemblies are fillet welds. Therefore, although there are relatively large numbers of joint types, there are but two fundamental weld types: the butt and the fillet.

Methods of Welding

Oxyfuel gas welding may be performed by one of two methods: forehand welding or backhand welding. These designations are derived from the direction of welding.

Forehand welding. In this technique (see Fig. 9-7, view *a*), the torch and the welding rod are disposed in the joint so that the torch points ahead in the direction of welding, and the rod precedes the torch. Distribution of the heat and molten metal is secured by imparting to the torch and rod opposite oscillating motions in semicircular paths on large weldments. With sections 1/4″ (6.4 mm) thick or more, care must be taken to prevent these motions from alternately exposing first one and then the other side of the weld puddle to the air. Exposure of the molten puddle to air can cause oxidation of the weld metal and consequent lowering of weld quality.

In backhand welding (see Fig. 9-7, view *b*), the torch and the welding rod are disposed in the joint so that the torch points back at the completed weld, and the rod is interposed between the torch and the weld puddle. This arrangement permits a simpler distribution of the heat and molten metal. It has the further advantage that the flame playing back on the molten

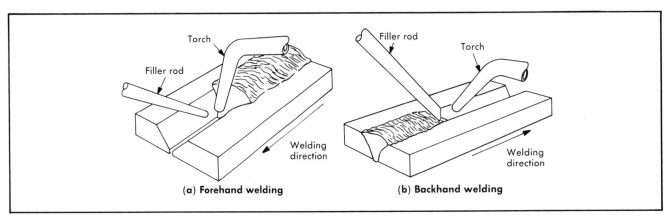

(a) Forehand welding   (b) Backhand welding

Fig. 9-7 Fundamental methods of oxyfuel gas welding.

puddle, and the completed weld protects them from the atmosphere. Backhand welding commonly progresses at faster speeds than forehand welding. In addition, backhand welds are of higher quality. Moderately faster speeds can be achieved with a slightly reducing flame, which can increase the carbon content and thus reduce the melting point.

Braze welding. Braze welding is a method whereby a groove, fillet, or slot weld is made with a nonferrous filler metal having a melting point below that of the base metal, but above 800°F (425°C). The filler metal is not distributed in the joint by capillary attraction as in brazing. Braze welding, as generally practiced, employs a brass filler rod composed of 60% copper and 40% zinc, with small additions of tin, manganese, iron, or silicon. Such welding rods are covered by "Specifications for Copper and Copper Alloy Bare Welding Rods and Electrodes," AWS A5.7.

The term *braze weld* is particularly appropriate because the juncture between the brass and the steel, cast iron, or other base metal is the same as that encountered in capillary brazing (discussed in Chapter 10). It consists of diffusion of the brass filler material into the base metal. However, once the thin film of brass is "tinned" on the metal surface, subsequent additions of brass to the joint are made by welding brass on brass. The brass may be applied to most ferrous and nonferrous metals that melt above 1000°F (540°C) except aluminum, magnesium, and other such alloys that do not use copper-based filler metal. It is particularly useful on sheet metal, because its low temperature of application minimizes distortion. It is also satisfactory on galvanized iron, where it may be applied without destroying the galvanizing, provided appropriate fluxes are employed.

Hard facing (surfacing). Hard facing is a process by means of which hard, wear-resistant alloys are applied to the surfaces of softer metals, thereby prolonging their service life. Standard oxyfuel gas welding techniques are employed except that melting of the base metal is avoided, and a strongly reducing or carburizing flame is used. Melting the base metal tends to dilute the alloying ingredients in the deposit with resultant loss of hardness. Consequently, only surface fusion (sometimes called "sweating") is used. Varying degrees of hardness and toughness are obtainable, thus providing wear-resistant metal to suit a variety of conditions. Additional details on hard facing are presented in Volume III of this Handbook series.

Welding Various Metals

The welding of steels with the oxyfuel gas process may be accomplished with either the forehand or the backhand technique. Forehand welding requires the use of 45° bevels and 90° V's to provide room for manipulation of torch and rod. Backhand welding, requiring only 30° bevels and 60° V's, uses less welding rod and gas, and consequently progresses at faster speeds and at lower cost. Also, because there is less "working" of the molten metal, the weld quality is higher. A strictly neutral flame should be used except when welding with low-alloy steel rods, in which case a slight excess of acetylene for a reducing or carburizing flame should be used.

Welding rods of classification RG 60 will yield the best quality and most economical welds on mild steels (SAE 1010-1025). Rods of classifications RG 45 and RG 65 may also be used; the former yields lower strengths but satisfactory ductilities, while the latter is higher in strength with lower ductility. For the welding of wrought iron, classification RG 60 rods are recommended. For steels of the low-alloy, high-strength types, rods conforming to classification RG 65 should be used.

Preheating of steel assemblies for welding is generally not necessary unless the mass is very great or temperatures are lower than 32°F (0°C). The oxyacetylene flame normally provides sufficient preheating in operation.

Braze welding may be employed on steel, particularly in those cases for which it is desired to reduce distortion to a minimum, such as sheet metal assembly or the attachment of a boss to the center of a large plate. Braze welding is also used on galvanized iron, because this procedure disturbs the galvanizing the least. Flux for braze welding is applied by dipping the heated rod end into the powdered flux. Paste fluxes are painted on the work and the rod. Factory flux-coated brass rods are frequently used.

Cast iron. Cast iron may be welded readily, the only difficulty being in avoidance of cracking and hard zones. Preheating to 900-1100°F (480-595°C), coupled with slow cooling, will generally avoid both these troubles. Preheating may be accomplished with torches on small and medium-sized castings, but furnaces should be used for large units. The preheat temperature should be maintained during welding. After welding, the casting should be brought up to 1100°F again and covered with a heat-resistant material to retard cooling; furnace-heated castings should be cooled slowly in the furnace. Thicknesses up to 1/4 or 3/8" (6.4 or 9.5 mm) can be welded in a single layer; heavier sections require multiple layers, one layer for each 1/4" thickness.

Welding should be performed with a neutral or slightly excess acetylene flame. Welding rods should match casting analysis; for example, a gray cast iron rod high in silicon for gray iron castings (classification RCI) and alloy analyses for alloy castings (classification RCI-A). Flux is essential for successful welding. The amount used depends on the condition of the casting; low-grade castings need more flux than good-quality cast iron. The flux is sprinkled on V'd surfaces before tacking and welding; the heated rod end is also dipped in flux as the welding progresses. Castings must be V'd along the line of weld by chipping or machining. Oxygen cutting is not readily adaptable to cast iron, and several other gas arc processes work better. If these processes are used, the cut surfaces are chipped or sandblasted.

Cast iron may also be braze welded when the presence of a dissimilar metal and color is not objectionable. Less preheating, generally 400-600°F (205-315°C), is necessary, localized application frequently being sufficient. Brass deposits made with rods of classifications RCuZn-A, RCuZn-B, RCuZn-C, and RCuZn-D have greater strength and ductility than cast iron, hence they give very satisfactory service. Flux is necessary to secure tinning of brass to cast iron and to control the molten brass.

Copper. For welded copper assemblies, only deoxidized or oxygen-free copper should be used. If electrolytic copper is used, the welded joint will be weak adjacent to the weld because of the segregation of copper oxide in a zone parallel to the weld. Welding rods for deoxidized copper should conform to classification RCu of AWS A5.27. Because copper has high heat conductivity, larger tip sizes will be needed than for equivalent sections of steel. A neutral or slightly oxidizing flame is used. Flux is necessary and is applied by dipping the heated rod end into the flux container. Heavy sections, 1/2" (12.7 mm) and greater, are sometimes welded in a vertical position, with two operators welding simultaneously from opposite sides.

Copper alloys are commonly welded with rods of the same analysis; however, any copper alloy containing lead in excess of 0.5% must be considered unweldable because such alloys will

OXYFUEL GAS WELDING AND CUTTING

generally crack upon the application of heat. Special welding fluxes compounded for the alloy involved are usually necessary. Braze welding may also be employed on most copper alloys but must be of the deoxidized variety. Standard braze welding flux is employed in the conventional manner.

Aluminum and aluminum alloys. Of all the aluminum compositions available, alloys best suited for oxyfuel gas welding are 1100, 3003, 3004, 5050, 5056, 6061, and 6063. Gas welding is not recommended for 2011, 2014, 2024, and 7075 alloys. Compositions of 1100 and 3003 alloys are substantially pure aluminum; the others contain appreciable quantities of alloying ingredients. Commercially pure and higher purity aluminum are generally welded with the same grade of filler metal as the base metal. The 1100 alloy is used when maximum resistance to corrosion and high ductility are of prime importance and high strength is not needed. A 95% aluminum-5% silicon alloy (4043) is recommended for the other alloys. This filler metal has greater strength and minimizes the tendency toward cracking. For welding ordinary aluminum castings, 4043 filler metal or one containing 4% copper and 3% silicon is frequently used. However, if the casting is to be subsequently heat treated, filler metal of the same analysis as the base metal should be used.

The edges of aluminum are prepared for gas welding in the same manner as similar thicknesses of steel. On thin material up to about 1/16" (1.6 mm) thick, a 90° flange of a height equal to the material thickness should be formed on all edges to be welded (see Fig. 9-8, view *a*). The flanges will prevent excessive warping and buckling and serve as filler metal when they are melted down, thus making a filler rod unnecessary. Unbeveled butt welds may be made on metal thicknesses from 1/16 to 3/16" (1.6 to 4.8 mm), but it is necessary to notch the edges (view *b*). These notches facilitate full weld penetration, prevent local distortion, and minimize burning of holes through the joint. Single-V welds (view *c*) may be used on aluminum up to about 7/16" (11 mm) thick, with notches to supplement the beveled edges.

Thorough cleaning of aluminum by degreasing and caustic dips is necessary for successful welding. Special aluminum welding fluxes are required, and these are mixed with water or alcohol and painted on the edges, top, and bottom of the joint and the welding rod. Flux residue after welding should be removed by scrubbing with hot water or by dipping in chemical rinses to eliminate attack on the weld and adjacent metal.

Nickel and nickel alloys. Nickel and the alloys Monel and Inconel are all weldable by the oxyacetylene process. The welding rods should match the base metal in analysis. Flux, designed for use with the metal, is necessary for the welding of Monel and Inconel; no flux is required for nickel. In general, the same joint designs and techniques as used for steel welding may be employed with these metals. Braze welding, while a possible application, is rarely used, silver brazing being preferred.

Other metals and alloys. The chrome-nickel and straight chrome steels may be welded by the oxyacetylene process. Experience indicates, however, that this process is best on thinner sections, with arc welding yielding better results on heavier thicknesses. Welding rods should match the base metal in analysis, and flux specifically for stainless steels must be used. Braze welding is rarely used because it can produce deleterious grain-boundary cracking; silver brazing is preferred.

Magnesium and its alloys may be oxyacetylene welded with some difficulty; flux is necessary, and its complete removal after welding is a problem. Inert gas shielded arc welding eliminates the necessity for flux, hence it is preferred. Welding rods should match base metal analysis.

Lead and its alloys can be welded by gas welding using oxyacetylene, oxyhydrogen, oxypropane, or oxygen-natural gas flames. The lower temperature flames are commonly used for thinner sections. As no flux has been developed for lead, it is necessary to scrape the edges and surfaces to be welded just before welding. Welding rod should match base metal analysis. Multilayer welds are used on thicknesses greater than 1/4 or 3/8" (6.4 or 9.5 mm).

Joining dissimilar metals. Success in the joining of dissimilar metals by welding or braze welding depends on the melting points and the reactions of the metals when molten. Carbon steels may be joined to copper, brass, nickel, nickel alloys, and cast iron by braze welding or brazing. Fluxes are necessary; in some cases special fluxes will be needed for the nonferrous metals. In general, aluminum and its alloys cannot be joined to other base metals by any of the oxyacetylene welding processes, and magnesium and its alloys are subject to the same limitation. Chrome-nickel stainless steels and straight chrome steels may be welded to carbon steel. The welding rod should normally match the analysis of the material having the higher alloy content to prevent severe hardening of the weld metal. Flux should be used with an alloy-based metal and filler rods. Direct gas welding of dissimilar metals is usually not possible unless they contain the same elements and have fairly close melting temperatures.

Equipment Used

Equipment for oxyacetylene welding is specially designed and manufactured not only to meet service requirements but also to provide safe operation. Details on the use and installation of oxyacetylene welding and cutting equipment are contained in the literature supplied by the manufacturer. This literature usually contains important safety and operating instructions that should be followed closely. For the performance of oxyacetylene welding, the minimum necessary equipment consists of gas supplies, regulators, hoses, and torches.

Gas supply. Most oxygen used for oxyfuel gas welding is produced commercially from the air by a liquefaction and rectification process at a usual purity of 99.5% minimum. It is compressed in seamless steel cylinders at a normal pressure of 2200 psi (15 MPa) or more. Sizes of cylinders commercially available range from 122 ft³ (3.4 m³) at 2200 psi to more than 300 ft³ (8.4 m³) at 2640 psi (18.2 MPa). High-pressure cylinders with pressures to 5000 psi (34.5 MPa) are now available. Oxygen is also supplied in portable liquid cylinders providing gas volumes to 4500 ft³ (126 m³). Stationary tanks of liquid oxygen containing more than 60,000 ft³ (1680 m³) are also used, with gas piped to various welding stations.

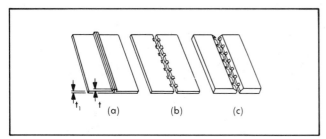

Fig. 9-8 Edge preparation of aluminum sheets for oxyfuel gas welding: (a) flanged thin sheets, (b) notched edges, and (c) beveled and notched edges.[2]

Acetylene is produced by the action of water on calcium carbide or by the distillation of petroleum products in chemical plants. In some parts of the United States, chemically distilled acetylene is most common and less expensive. The free gas, however, cannot be compressed in cylinders, because it would dissociate violently at certain pressures and temperatures. Therefore acetylene is dissolved in acetone under pressure. Furthermore, the acetylene cylinders are filled with a porous filler to avoid the creation of voids where the gas could collect freely under pressure. Consequently, acetylene is measured by weight, 1 lb (0.45 kg) being approximately equal to 14.5 ft³ (0.41 m³) at standard temperature and pressure. Cylinders of apparently equal volumes will show variation in pressures and gas content. However, the actual gas volume is indicated in both cubic feet and pounds or cubic meters and kilograms.

When these two gases are correctly combined in a properly designed torch, the resulting neutral flame produces a temperature of about 5586°F (3085°C). Thus it is possible to melt nearly all commercial metals and alloys locally and thereby effect the fusion necessary for welding. Three adjustments of an oxyacetylene flame are possible, and all have practical significance. The most commonly used flame adjustment is known as the neutral flame (see Fig. 9-9). It is secured when approximately equal volumes of oxygen and acetylene are burned. The highest temperature is at the tip of the inner cone of the flame; the outer envelope serves to provide a reducing atmosphere, which protects the molten metal.

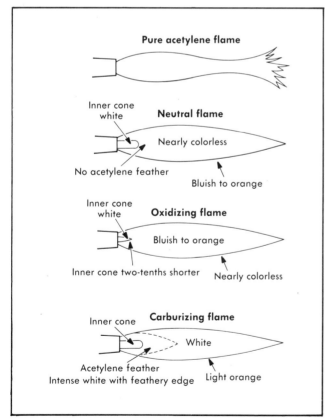

Fig. 9-9 Types of oxyacetylene flames. A neutral flame is used for almost all gas welding. An oxidizing flame is rarely used and a carburizing flame is occasionally helpful when flame hardening or brazing. (*Victor Equipment Co.*)

If slightly more acetylene is admitted to the flame, a reducing or oxidizing flame is obtained, as shown in Fig. 9-9. This flame is particularly useful in welding steel with low-alloy types of welding rods. If the amount of excess acetylene, as measured by the "feather," exceeds 1 1/2 times the length of the inner cone, the flame is of no practical use in most welding. Larger values of excess acetylene are employed in hard facing or surfacing, where the addition of carbon from the flame to the molten puddle will increase the hardness of the finished deposits.

When more oxygen is used, the "oxidizing flame," with a maximum temperature of 5720°F (3160°C), is created (refer to Fig. 9-9). This flame should be avoided in all cases except in the welding of copper and copper-based alloys.

For oxyhydrogen welding, compressed hydrogen at a purity of 99.5% is available in steel cylinders. The combination of oxygen and hydrogen to produce the oxyhydrogen flame is accomplished with the same torches as those used for oxyacetylene welding. In actual application, the theoretical proportions are varied by increasing the amount of hydrogen used, thus ensuring a reducing atmosphere in the flame.

Oxyacetylene welding operations, when performed on a small scale or in widely scattered locations, may secure the gases direct from cylinders. For somewhat larger production operations, the gas supplies may be centralized by means of manifolds. A separate manifold system must be used for each gas. The oxygen and acetylene are conducted from their respective manifolds through appropriate piping systems to the using points. When very large volumes of oxygen are needed, the pipeline is supplied from a bulk delivery station. Large volumes of acetylene are supplied from acetylene generators or special cylinder trailers feeding the pipeline. Oxygen fuel-gas systems for welding and cutting should be installed as specified in NFPA Standard 51.

Both oxygen and acetylene are supplied in cylinders that are manufactured, tested, and maintained in accordance with the regulations and specifications of the Department of Transportation. Therefore users must not tamper with, alter, or otherwise change these cylinders in any respect. If anything unusual develops with a compressed gas cylinder, it should be removed outdoors away from any source of ignition, and the supplier should be notified immediately. Their instructions on handling and disposal should be followed. Special requirements for the handling of acetylene are discussed subsequently in this section.

Regulators. The pressures in oxygen, acetylene, and hydrogen cylinders are high to compress a sufficient volume of gas into the cylinders to permit economical transportation. Because the pressures at the points of use are appreciably less, it is necessary to employ regulators to reduce cylinder pressures to satisfactory working values. Regulators for cylinders are available in single and two-stage designs, the latter being used when a more constant delivery pressure is required. Special types of regulators are used for pipeline applications. Selection of regulators is based on the gas to be controlled, the maximum delivery pressure, and the maximum flow. Regulators should be used only on gases for which they are designed and should never be interchanged. Some oxygen regulators are designed to contain the explosive forces that can occur if contaminants are allowed to enter the system.

Hoses. The hoses for conveying oxygen and acetylene must be specially constructed for this work. Hoses for oxygen, acetylene, and hydrogen should conform to the requirements of "Specifications for Welding Hose," issued by the Rubber Manufacturers Association. Acetylene hose is generally colored

OXYFUEL GAS WELDING AND CUTTING

red and oxygen hose, green. Twin hose should have two distinct and complete gas passages. Special fittings must be used for connecting hoses to equipment. Oxygen fittings employ right-hand threads, and acetylene and other fuel gas hoses use left-hand threads, designed to prevent interchange of hoses.

Torches (mixers, tips). The term *torch* commonly refers to the complete assembly of the handle (including the control valves), the mixing head, and the tip (see Fig. 9-10). Each of these elements is usually a separate piece, although the tip and mixer are sometimes provided as a unit.

Two types of torches are in common use today—the medium-pressure type and the low-pressure or injector type. In the medium-pressure torch, the gases are supplied under positive pressures, generally above 3 psi (20.7 kPa), increasing with each increase in tip size. The low-pressure or injector type of torch is generally used for natural gas at pressures usually less than 1 psi (6.9 kPa), with oxygen at higher pressures than with the medium-pressure torch. The injector, located in the head or handle of the torch, is constructed on the venturi principle.

Each tip has a specific pressure range requirement. Using slightly higher gas pressures in all tips generally causes no problems. Excessive pressure can increase the risk of reverse flow and backfire. Using lower gas pressures will cause overheating, extinguishing of the flame, or even flashbacks or backfire of burning gases.

Equipment for machine welding. The oxyacetylene flame is used for a number of machine welding operations, including tube welding and pressure welding. However, the heating requirements for such operations are so great that almost invariably the gases are supplied from bulk systems or gas manifolds. Jobs involving only a limited amount of welding may be accomplished with hand equipment, supplemented with suitable jigs for positioning the work.

Fundamentally, torches for machine welding or pressure welding are constructed in the same manner as hand equipment. Generally, however, they are provided with a large number of small flames to produce the required heat. In view of the larger gas flows needed, it is necessary to employ larger capacity regulators, hoses, and fittings.

Welding rods. Oxyfuel gas welding of metals may be accomplished without the addition of filler metal (welding rods)

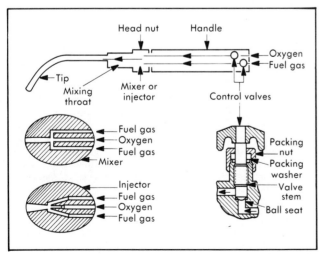

Fig. 9-10 Simplified sketch of a typical oxyacetylene welding torch. (*L-TEC Welding & Cutting Systems*)

if the flanged-edge joint is employed. However, this joint is suitable for sheet metal only, and its use is further limited by the cost of preparing the flanged edges. Therefore, welding rods must be considered in practically every gas welding application except pressure gas welding, which does not use filler metal. The chemical analysis of the weld deposit should approximate that of the base metals welded. Because it is impossible for commercial reasons to have welding rods to match all the various analyses of metals, rods should be selected that will deposit welds having mechanical properties matching those of the base metal. However, if corrosion resistance is the principal requirement of the welded assembly, the chemical analysis of the weld should match that of the base metal.

Steel welding rods. Welding rods for iron and steel are covered by AWS A5.2, "Specifications for Iron and Steel Oxyfuel Gas Welding Rods." This specification provides for three classification numbers, RG 45, RG 60, and RG 65, which are differentiated by tensile strength and ductility as measured on all-weld-metal test specimens. The two digits represent the stress-relieved tensile strength of the test specimens in thousands of pounds per square inch [1000 psi (1 ksi) equals 6.9 MPa]. Generally, classification RG 60 welding rods are used for welding requiring the highest quality on mild steel.

Cast iron welding rods. Welding rods for use on cast iron are discussed in "Specifications for Welding Rods and Covered Electrodes for Cast Iron Welding," AWS A5.15. Under this specification, the usual initial letter R indicates welding rods. Following this are the chemical symbols of the principal alloying elements in the rod composition. Because cast iron welding rods are an important classification in this specification, they are identified by the letters CI rather than chemical symbols. Thus classification RCI is the familiar gray cast iron welding rod and classification RCI-A and B are alloy cast iron rods.

Brass (bronze) welding rods. Brass rods, sometimes called bronze rods, are used for braze welding and for the welding of brass. These brass welding rods are covered by "Copper and Copper-Alloy Gas Welding Rods," AWS A5.27. All classifications under this specification start with the initial letter R, indicating welding rods, followed by the chemical symbols of the principal elements appearing in the alloys. The principal classifications of brass welding rods are RCuSi-A and RCuSi-B, which are welding rods used with oxyfuel welding. Classifications RCuZn-A, RCuZn-B, RCuZn-C, and RCuZn-D are the brass rods widely used for braze welding as well as the welding of brasses of the same composition.

In braze welding operations, a flux is necessary to clean the base metal surfaces and also control the oxidation of the elements in the rods. The same flux is also employed for welding copper with deoxidized-copper welding rods.

Aluminum welding rods. Welding rods for weldable grades of aluminum-based metals are covered by "Specifications for Aluminum and Aluminum-Alloy Welding Rods and Bare Electrodes," AWS A5.10. Under this specification, following the letter R is the ASTM designation for the alloy composition to identify the analysis of the welding filler metal.

Hard-surfacing rods. Filler metals for surfacing are covered by "Specifications for Surfacing Welding Rods and Electrodes," AWS A5.13. Under this specification, surfacing welding rods are identified by means of the letter R and the chemical symbols indicating the principal elements of the alloys involved. If, under an alloy combination, more than one analysis is employed, the classification number utilizes the letters A, B, and so on, for further differentiation. Finally, where further modifications of a composition are encountered, these letters may be supplemented by arabic numerals to give further classification. One example of surfacing filler-metal classification is RCoCr-A, the cobalt-chromium type of hard-facing filler metal. Because there are three ranges of chemistry for this group, there are also classifications RCoCr-B and RCoCr-C.

Welding rods for other metals. Welding rods are available for most commercial metals. The following AWS filler-metal specifications are available for gas welding rods: "Specifications for Corrosion-resisting Chromium and Chromium-nickel Steel Bare and Composite Metal Cored and Stranded Arc Welding Electrodes and Welding Rods," ANSI/AWS A5.9, and "Specifications for Nickel and Nickel Alloy Bare Welding Rods and Electrodes," ANSI/AWS A5.14.

Jigs and fixtures for oxyfuel gas welding. In welding, the functions performed by workholding devices do not parallel those of workholders for machining. As a result, either of the terms *jig* or *fixture* may be applied to equipment for holding, aligning, or positioning weldments.

The reasons for the use of welding jigs may be summarized as follows:

1. The heat of welding causes metal parts (particularly sheet metal) to warp, buckle, and distort. Therefore, the first function of a jig is to absorb and dissipate this heat in the jig structure. If this is not possible, it must control the distortion by physical restraint.
2. The jig must locate the component parts of an assembly so that all of the finished parts coming from the jig will be uniform.
3. The jig must hold the assemblies in the most convenient position for welding.

The first function listed is best performed by clamping, which may be accomplished in several ways. The most common and probably the oldest method in use is the stake type. Because the heat of the oxyacetylene flame plays over a wide area, the jig structure should be constructed of metal capable of withstanding this heat. Although cast iron is probably the best for this service, stainless steels may be applied to localized areas subject to heating. If necessary to abstract a large amount of heat, both the stakes and the anvil may be cored for circulation of water. The stakes are generally provided with hinges at one end for easy insertion of the work; the other end is equipped with quick-acting clamps for fast locking.

In designing for the restraint of metals during welding, three factors must be considered: (1) the coefficient of expansion, (2) the thermal conductivity, and (3) the reaction of the molten weld metal and heated base metal to the stresses that will be set up. For example, certain aluminum alloys, if restrained in a jig during welding, will crack adjacent to the weld. This difficulty is overcome by using the jigs only for aligning and tack welding, performing the final welding outside the jig. Another example is copper, which has such high heat conductivity that supplementary heating is usually necessary. If a jig structure were to be introduced, even more heat would be required and would perhaps make the welding impossible. This condition is overcome by welding copper without benefit of jigs, letting the distortion come where it may. Subsequently the assembly is reformed into the desired shape.

The location of parts of an assembly to secure product uniformity is accomplished by the use of bosses, dowels, stops, and toggle clamps, either separately or in conjunction with other elements. Alignments of sections may be secured with a V-block incorporated in the jig structure.

Welding in the flat position is both simplest and most conducive to fast welding speeds. Therefore, whenever possible, jigs for welding should be designed to position the parts so that welding may be performed in this position. This positioning may usually be effected by mounting the jig assembly on trunnions that will provide 360° rotation about one axis. When rotation about two axes is necessary, the jig may be mounted in a gimbal. Commercial weldment positioners usually are provided with a table, rotatable through 360° and capable of being tipped through an arc of 180°.

Operating Parameters

The rates of production with manual oxyacetylene welding depend to a large degree on the skill of the operator. The mass of the unit will also materially govern the amount of gases required and welding time. Therefore any data provided must be qualified as recorded on work performed by a reasonably competent operator under average conditions.

In oxyacetylene welding with the forehand technique, approximately 18-20 ft³ (0.5-0.56 m³) of acetylene is required to deposit 1 lb (0.45 kg) of steel welding rod. Under these conditions, the oxygen consumed will be about 10% greater than the acetylene consumption. With the backhand procedure, the values are about 16 to 18 ft³ (0.45 to 0.5 m³) of acetylene per pound of rod deposited, and, because the slight-excess acetylene flame is used, the oxygen consumption will be about 5% less than the acetylene volume. These figures are only approximations. For accurate data, tests should be made on production runs, and the cylinders should be weighed before and after each unit is welded. The difference in weight is the gas consumed.

Table 9-5 provides a further guide to manual oxyacetylene welding. It represents the composite experience of a large number of operators in daily contact with oxyacetylene welding. It should, however, be regarded as an average; the maximum values indicated can be exceeded. Note that welding-tip sizes are given in terms of acetylene flow rather than in tip numbers or drill sizes. Tip numbers are arbitrarily assigned by each manufacturer and have little relation to one another. Drill sizes are useless without an indication of the operating pressures. Manufacturers will supply, on request, charts showing the acetylene flows for their various tip sizes. Data on welding rods (sizes and quantities) will apply in general to all classification of rods. However, a reduction in quantity of rod used per foot or meter of weld may be expected if classification RG 60 rods are used.

The data given in Table 9-5 are for single-layer welds in the thicknesses shown. Single-layer welds would normally be used up to 5/16″ (7.9 mm) only; multilayer welds would be used in heavier metal. Generally, two layers are used up to 1/2″ (12.7 mm) and three layers above that size. Multilayer welding may be expected to show a reduction in gas consumption amounting to 5-10% and an increase in welding speed of 5-7%.

Safety Considerations

General requirements. The following factors are all critical to ensure safety in oxyfuel gas welding:

- Well-trained operators with skilled supervision.
- Proper operation and frequent maintenance of all equipment.
- Good housekeeping to provide a clean, dry area with

OXYFUEL GAS WELDING AND CUTTING

TABLE 9-5
Data for Manual Oxyacetylene Welding of Steel

Metal Thickness, in. (mm)	Joint Preparation	Welding Rod Size, in. (mm)	Welding Rod, lb/ft (kg/m)	Tip Size (acetylene consumption), ft³/hr (m³/hr)	Welding Speed, ft/hr (m/hr)
1/64 (0.4)	Square	---	---	0.2-0.7 (0.01-0.02)	26-30 (7.9-9.1)
1/32 (0.8)	Square	---	---	0.6-1.6 (0.02-0.04)	22-25 (6.7-7.6)
1/16 (1.6)	Square	1/16 (1.6)	0.013 (0.02)	1.04-4.0 (0.03-0.11)	18-21 (5.5-6.4)
3/32 (2.4)	Square	3/32 (2.4)	0.030 (0.04)	2.0-6.0 (0.06-0.17)	14-17 (4.3-5.2)
1/8 (3.2)	Square	1/8 (3.2)	0.053 (0.08)	3.0-10.0 (0.08-0.28)	11-13 (3.4-4.0)
3/16 (4.8)	90° V	3/16 (4.8)	0.15 (0.22)	6.0-17.0 (0.17-0.48)	7.5-8.5 (2.3-2.6)
1/4 (6.4)	90° V	3/16 (4.8)	0.27 (0.40)	11.0-30.0 (0.31-0.84)	6-7 (1.8-2.1)
5/16 (7.9)	90° V	1/4 (6.4)	0.42 (0.62)	19.0-36.0 (0.53-1.01)	4.5-5.5 (1.4-1.7)
3/8 (9.5)	90° V	1/4 (6.4)	0.60 (0.89)	30.0-50.0 (0.84-1.40)	4-5 (1.2-1.5)
1/2 (12.7)	60° V	1/4 (6.4)	0.60 (0.89)	37.0-60.0 (1.04-1.68)	4-5 (1.2-1.5)
5/8 (15.9)	60° V	5/16 (7.9)	0.87 (1.29)	49.0-75.0 (1.37-2.10)	3.5-4.5 (1.1-1.4)
3/4 (19.1)	60° V	5/16 (7.9)	1.31 (1.95)	62.0-103.0 (1.74-2.88)	2.5-3.5 (0.8-1.1)

proper ventilation and no flammable or combustible materials.

The operation and maintenance of equipment should conform to the provisions of ANSI Standard Z49.1, "Safety in Welding and Cutting." Equipment used for oxyfuel gas welding should not be lubricated because oil or grease is easily ignited and burns violently in the presence of oxygen. Care must be taken to ensure that all connections are tight, and no smoking should be permitted in the welding area.

Pertinent information with regard to safety in oxyfuel gas welding is contained in the following material available from the Compressed Gas Association (CGA):

Safety Bulletin SB.8, "Use of Oxyfuel Gas Welding and Cutting Apparatus"

Pamphlet E-1, "Standard Connections for Regulator Outlets"

Pamphlet P-1, "Safe Handling of Compressed Gases"

Standard V-1, "Compressed Cylinder Valve Inlet and Outlet Connections"

Valuable information with respect to fire prevention is contained in ANSI/NFPA Standard 51, "Oxygen-Fuel Gas Systems for Welding and Cutting."

Gas cylinders. Cylinders containing compressed gases should be handled and moved carefully and kept upright with caps over their valves. In use, the cylinders should be chained or otherwise secured to permanent fixtures to prevent their falling over. Valves should be opened slowly, and oxygen cylinders should not be emptied below a gage pressure of 25 psi (172 kPa). Oxygen and acetylene cylinders should be stored separately in a dry, well-ventilated room away from open flames. Never attempt to refill cylinders or mix gases in cylinders.

Gases. Explosive mixtures that can ignite result from gases being incorrectly mixed within regulators or hoses. Oxygen and fuel gases should be kept separated until they reach the torches.

Avoid any reverse flow of gases because of unequal pressures. Acetylene should not be used at gage pressures above 15 psi (103 kPa), and oxygen should not be used to blow off workpieces or clothing because of the danger of their being ignited by a spark.

Torches. Information on the proper operation and safety precautions for oxyfuel gas welding torches is presented in ANSI/AWS Standard C4.3, "Operators Manual for Oxyfuel Gas Heating Torch Operation," and ANSI/UL Standard 123, "Safety Standard for Oxyfuel Gas Torches." It is important to use the correct tip sizes and recommended gas pressures. Systems should be purged by bleeding each hose independently. The fuel gas should be lighted first, using a friction lighter, not matches or a cigarette lighter.

Protective attire. Goggles or eyeshields with filter lenses are necessary to protect the eyes. Gloves and other protective clothing are also essential for safety.

THERMAL CUTTING PROCESSES

There are several thermal processes used for severing and removing metal. Some of these that are difficult to regulate and not capable of producing good cuts include carbon arc cutting (CAC), shielded metal arc cutting (SMAC), oxygen arc cutting (AOC), gas tungsten arc cutting (GTAC), and oxygen lance cutting (LOC). These processes are not discussed in this Handbook series.

Other thermal processes that are being used for production applications include oxygen cutting (OC), plasma arc cutting (PAC), air-carbon arc cutting (AAC), and laser beam cutting (LBC). The latter three methods are discussed in subsequent sections of this chapter.

Oxygen cutting, sometimes called flame cutting, is a group of processes used to sever or remove metals by means of the chemical reaction of oxygen with the base metal at elevated temperatures. The most commonly used oxygen cutting process is oxyfuel gas cutting (OFC) in which the necessary temperatures for cutting are maintained by means of gas flames

OXYFUEL GAS WELDING AND CUTTING

obtained from the combustion that takes place between a specified fuel gas and oxygen.

Oxyfuel gas cutting is used most extensively to cut low and medium-carbon steels. Other readily oxidizable materials such as titanium can also be cut by this process. Oxidation-resistant materials such as stainless steel are cut by adding metal powder, such as iron, or chemical flux to the cutting oxygen stream. These processes are known respectively as metal powder cutting (POC) and chemical flux cutting (FOC).

OXYFUEL GAS CUTTING

Oxyfuel gas cutting is the most widely used thermal cutting process. It has been given many names, such as burning, flame cutting, oxygen cutting, and flame machining. The process can be performed with equipment ranging from lightweight, inexpensive, handheld cutting torches to costly, computer-controlled, multitorch cutting machines. Although the process has been used to cut steel up to 8' (2.4 m) thick, the majority of material cut is under 2" (51 mm) in thickness.

Advantages and Limitations

Oxyfuel gas cutting is a versatile process that can be used to cut straight lines or continual change of direction lines because the cutting oxygen stream acts as a tool with a 360° cutting edge. Cuts can be started at the edges of workpieces or piercing can be used to start a cut at any point on the work surface. With proper conditions, edge quality is good. Two or more pieces can be cut simultaneously by stack cutting, and edges can be bevel-cut for weld joint preparation. In addition, the process can operate in any axis with equal facility.

The process is fast compared to machining and slow compared to plasma arc cutting, but the speed can be increased by the use of multiple torches, cutting machines, and stack cutting. Heat-affected zones can be large with oxyfuel gas cutting, and workpieces can be distorted, especially if they are made from thin metals.

Cutting Fundamentals

Oxyfuel gas cutting is based on one fundamental process—the rapid burning or oxidation of iron in the presence of high-purity oxygen. A torch equipped with a cutting tip is used to control the operation. When iron is heated to a temperature of 1600-1700° F (870-925° C) and is then exposed to a stream of high-purity oxygen, the iron oxidizes (burns) rapidly and produces a stream of molten iron oxides and iron called slag. The space from which the iron has been removed is called the kerf (see Fig. 9-11).

Fuel gas and oxygen are mixed in the torch or tip to provide the desired volume and correct ratio to produce the preheat flames. First, they are used to preheat the metal to the ignition temperature so a cut can be started. In addition, the preheat flames clean the surface of the workpiece by burning, melting, or spalling action; protect the cutting oxygen stream from contamination by air; and transfer some heat into the oxygen stream. A smooth, properly sized oxygen orifice in the center of the tip provides a high-velocity, coherent stream of cutting oxygen. The oxygen jet provides the oxygen to burn the metal and also washes the molten slag out of the kerf.

In addition to molten slag, a large amount of heat is produced by the oxidation of iron. If this heat could all be induced to instantaneously transfer in the direction of the cut, preheat flames would not be necessary after the cut was started. However, this does not happen, so the preheat flames are

necessary to provide the heat to keep a cut going. One instance where preheat flames can be dispensed with after the operation is started is oxygen lancing (piercing of heavy sections).

Supplies and Equipment

In addition to oxygen and fuel gas, the oxyfuel gas cutting process requires pressure regulators, hoses, torches, cutting tips, spark lighters, tip cleaners, and protective clothing—essentially the same as for oxyfuel gas welding, discussed previously in this section.

Oxygen. High-purity oxygen is supplied as gaseous oxygen in high-pressure cylinders of various sizes and as a liquid in several sizes of portable cryogenic cylinders or large bulk cryogenic tanks, as discussed previously for oxyfuel gas welding. Cylinders may be used individually or manifolded to supply several workstations through a pipeline.

The oxygen used for cutting must have a minimum purity of 99.5%. If purity is less than that, cutting speed and quality will decrease, while oxygen consumption will increase. At oxygen purity below 95%, the operation becomes a melt and wash operation rather than a true cutting action.

Fuel gas. Several different fuel gases are used for preheat. They include acetylene, propane, natural gas, methylacetylene-propadiene stabilized (MPS), propylene, and some propane-base mixtures. High-quality cuts can be obtained with any of the fuel gases. However, the fuel gases vary in flame characteristics, and the effects of this should be considered when making a selection. The oxygen to fuel gas ratio needed for a neutral flame varies with the fuel gas used. For acetylene, the oxygen to fuel gas ratio is usually 1:1; for propane, about 4 1/2:1; for natural gas, 2:1; for MPS, 2 1/2:1; and for propylene, about 4:1.

Because the most expensive component of cost in cutting is labor, particular attention should be paid to cutting speed for straight line, shape, and bevel cutting; starting time for edge starts; and piercing time. Safety factors to be considered in fuel gas selection include resistance to backfire, ease of odor detection, and weight of cylinders. The cost and availability of the fuel in cylinder and bulk modes is also important, in addition to the cost of oxygen required. Thus, labor, fuel, and oxygen costs to perform some standard unit or work, such as 100' or 30 m of cut, should be determined for each gas of

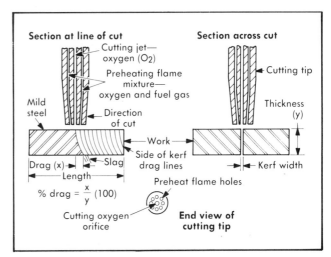

Fig. 9-11 Nomenclature for oxyfuel gas cutting. (*MAPP Products*)

OXYFUEL GAS WELDING AND CUTTING

interest. In some instances, cylinder handling can be quite costly and should be considered.

Natural gas is generally used from pipeline sources, while the other fuels are supplied in cylinders or, with the exception of acetylene, bulk storage tanks that are connected to a plant piping system. Plant piping systems should be installed in accordance with NFPA Standard 51, "Oxygen-Fuel Gas Systems for Welding and Cutting."

Pressure regulators. Regulators are used to reduce high source pressures to desired working pressures. They are available in single and two-stage constructions, as discussed previously in the section on oxyfuel gas welding. Regulators for attachment directly to cylinders usually have two gages (one to indicate cylinder pressure and the other, delivery pressure). Regulators for attachment to pipeline station drops are also available. They are usually of single-stage design and have one gage that indicates delivery pressure. Station regulators should never be attached directly to a high-pressure cylinder because they are not designed to withstand high inlet pressures. Always be sure that a regulator has an inlet pressure rating as high or higher than the pressure in the source to which it will be attached.

Regulators are designed and manufactured for use with specific gases. They should be used only with the gas for which they are designed. Manufacturers literature should be consulted to select proper equipment.

Hoses and fittings. Hoses, available in several sizes, are used to conduct the oxygen and fuel gas from the regulator to the torch. Oxygen hoses are usually colored green while fuel gas hoses are red. Oxygen fittings have right-hand threads and smooth outside surfaces. Fuel gas fittings have left-hand threads and are notched for easy identification. Fittings are designed to form gastight seals with the application of very little torque and can be damaged by overtightening.

Undersize hose or extensive lengths can result in pressure drops that may cause low flow rates at the torch. Low flow rates can cause poor performance or overheating of torches.

Torches. Cutting torches (see Fig. 9-12) are available in a wide variety of sizes and configurations for manual and machine cutting. They are classified by the manner in which the fuel gas and oxygen are mixed as tip mix or torch mix. In tip

mix torches, the fuel and oxygen are mixed in the cutting tip, while in torch mix torches the gases are mixed in the torch head or at some location before the torch head.

Torch mix torches can be further classified as positive pressure or injector type. Injector torches use a high-velocity oxygen stream exiting from a small orifice in a venturi to create a partial vacuum. This vacuum aspirates larger volumes of low-pressure fuel gas than could be obtained if only the fuel gas pressure were used. Injector torches usually operate with a fuel gas pressure of less than 2 psi (13.8 kPa).

Manual torches can be straight cutting torches or combination torches that consist of a cutting attachment fastened to a gas welding torch handle. Both have valves to control the fuel gas and preheat oxygen flows and a spring-loaded valve to control the cutting oxygen. Torches are available with 90, 75, or 180° heads. Most are of the two-hose type that have one inlet for fuel gas and another for the combined preheat and cutting oxygen.

Machine torches are most commonly of the three-hose type that utilize a separate hose to supply the cutting oxygen. They are usually equipped with a rack and mounted in torch carriers that allow the torch to be moved to a desired position.

Cutting tips. Cutting tips are available in a wide variety of sizes and types to cut many thicknesses of metal. The size of a cutting tip refers to the size of the cutting oxygen orifice. Although the cutting oxygen orifice is the same size regardless of what fuel gas is used, the flame ports vary in design for the various fuel gases. Different fuel gases burn at different velocities and temperatures, requiring different volumes of oxygen and fuel. Therefore, flame port size and quantity are varied to produce a stable flame that will provide sufficient heat.

All tips for acetylene are one piece, with drilled or swaged orifices. Tips for other fuel gases are sometimes one piece, but are often two-piece tips composed of shells and internal components with milled splines. Always use tips designed for the fuel gas that is being used.

The majority of tips for hand cutting are designated as standard pressure (or speed). They have a straight-bore oxygen orifice and usually employ cutting oxygen pressures in the range of 30 to 70 psi (207 to 483 kPa) gage. High-speed tips for machine cutting differ from standard tips in that the exit end of the cutting oxygen orifice is diverged. The divergence allows the use of higher oxygen pressure while still maintaining a coherent oxygen jet. High-speed tips provide speeds up to 20% faster than can be obtained with standard pressure tips.

Protective clothing and equipment. Oxyfuel gas cutting produces bright light, hot slag, and sparks. Appropriate protective clothing and equipment can minimize the hazards associated with these conditions. Safety considerations discussed previously for oxyfuel gas welding apply equally to oxyfuel gas cutting. Pertinent information is also contained in AWS Manual C4.2, "Operator's Manual for Oxyfuel Gas Cutting."

Cutting Procedures

Obtaining quality cuts with oxyfuel gas cutting requires the proper combination of preheat flame adjustment, oxygen pressure, tip size, coupling distance, and travel speed. Experienced operators can achieve these conditions with little difficulty.

Flame settings. Although neutral flame settings are used for most cutting operations, carburizing or oxidizing flames are used for some special applications. For example, slightly carburizing flames are used for stack cutting thin material or when a silvery cut surface is desired. Slightly oxidizing flames may be used in hand torches (to minimize secondary heat on

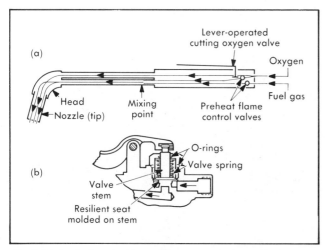

Fig. 9-12 Oxyfuel gas cutting equipment: (a) typical torch in which oxygen and fuel gas are mixed at a point between torch head and handle and (b) typical cutting oxygen valve. (*L-TEC Welding & Cutting Systems*)

operator's hand), for bevel cutting, and where fast starts are required for piercing or edge starts.

Oxygen pressure. Cutting oxygen pressure for each size and style of tip should be set as recommended by the manufacturer. If oxygen pressure is too low, speed will be reduced, slag formation can be excessive, drag lines may be more pronounced, and the kerf may be wide at the bottom of the cut. If cutting oxygen pressure is too high, concave cut surfaces can result. Too high an oxygen pressure can also cause notching.

Tip size. There is a tip size that will give the most economical cut for any thickness of steel. Any size tip can be used for a range of thicknesses, depending on cutting conditions. When machine cutting intricate shapes, it is sometimes desirable to use a slightly larger tip to produce a wider kerf that will allow cut pieces to fall free without hangup. Most manufacturers provide charts of recommended tip size and operating parameters for common plate thicknesses. These recommendations should be followed for best overall results.

Coupling distance. Coupling distance is the distance from the end of the primary flame cones to the plate surface (see Fig. 9-13). For most cutting operations this distance should be 1/16-1/8″ (1.6-3.2 mm). This distance becomes larger as plate thickness increases and may be 1″ (25 mm) or more for thicknesses more than 12″ (305 mm).

Faster preheat for starting a cut can be obtained if the ends of the primary flames are allowed to just impinge on the surface during the preheat operation. When bevel cutting, it is also desirable to allow the bottom flames to just touch the surface. Excessive preheat can result from too close a coupling distance or too large a flame. In either case, the top corner of a cut will be rounded instead of square, and excessive slag will be deposited on the bottom side of the workpiece.

Travel speed. There is an optimum travel speed for each set of cutting conditions. When everything is balanced, the correct speed for a quality cut will produce a steady ripping sound, and the spark stream under the plate will show about a 15° lead angle. A spark stream exiting opposite the direction of torch travel means that the speed is too high. Too high a speed will result in excessive rake in the drag lines, slag may adhere to the plate bottom, and there may be some concavity of the cut surface. Too slow a travel speed can cause a rough surface exhibiting pressure marks, and the top edge may be rounded.

Operating parameters. Some typical operating parameters for oxyfuel gas cutting with MPS as the fuel gas are shown in Table 9-6. Preheat gas flows, both oxygen and fuel gas, vary with the fuel gas used. Also, the recommendations are general and should be modified by experience in actual plant operation

and by the recommendations of equipment manufacturers. Cutting speeds are shown as a range. The lower numbers are for high-quality cuts that have square top edges, very smooth surface, and little, if any, drag or slag adherence. The higher numbers refer to production-quality cuts that are rougher and exhibit some drag and slag adherence. Higher speeds can be used if all that is desired is a severance cut.

The operating parameters will vary depending on the fuel gas and type of torch and tip being used. Operating data for the different fuel gases and equipment can be obtained from suppliers. When establishing the best speed for a particular operation, start the cut at a slower speed than anticipated. While observing results, increase the speed until cut quality is less than that desired. Then, reduce the speed slightly below that which produced desired results, bring it back up to operating speed, and continue to operate at that speed.

Torch, or lead, angle is the acute angle between the axis of the torch and the workpiece surface when the torch is pointed in the direction of the cut (see Fig. 9-14). When cutting light-gage steel, up to 1/4″ (6.4 mm) thick, a 40-50° torch angle allows much faster cutting speeds than if the torch were mounted perpendicular to the plate. On plate up to 1/2″ (12.7 mm) thick, travel speed can be increased with a torch lead angle, but the angle is larger, usually 60-70°. Little benefit is obtained from cutting plate more than 1/2″ thick with an acute lead angle. Plate more than this thickness should be cut with the torch perpendicular to the workpiece surface.

An angled torch cuts faster on thinner gage material. The intersection of the kerf and the surface presents a knife-edge that is easily ignited. Once the plate is burning, the cut is readily carried through to the other side of the work. When cutting heavy plate, the torch should be perpendicular to the workpiece surface and parallel to the starting edge of the work. This avoids problems of nondrop cuts, incomplete cutting on the opposite side of the thicker plate, gouging cuts in the center of the kerf, and similar problems.

Manual versus machine cutting. Whether cutting is performed manually or by machine, the same techniques and

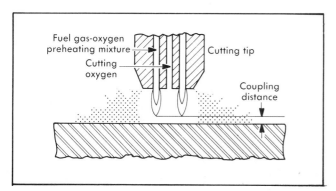

Fig. 9-13 Coupling distance in oxyfuel gas cutting. (*MAPP Products*)

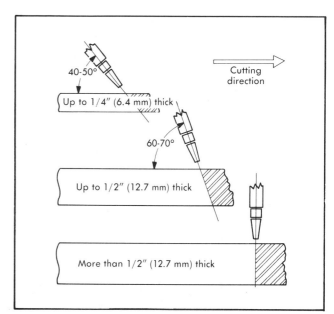

Fig. 9-14 Torch (lead) angle. (*MAPP Products*)

OXYFUEL GAS WELDING AND CUTTING

TABLE 9-6
Cutting Speeds, Gas Pressures and Flow Rates, and Kerf Widths for Cutting Various Plate Thicknesses with Different Tips*

Plate Thickness, in. (mm)	Tip Drill Size	Cutting Speed, ipm (mm/min)	Oxygen Cutting Pressure, Gage, psi (kPa)	Oxygen Cutting Flow Rate, ft³/hr (m³/hr)	Preheat Pressure, Gage, psi (kPa)	Preheat Flow Rate, ft³/hr (m³/hr)	Pressure, Gage, psi (kPa)	Flow Rate, ft³/hr (m³/hr)	Kerf Width, in. (mm)
One and two-piece general-purpose tips:									
3/16 (4.8)	72	22-26 (560-660)	20 (138)	45 (1.26)	2-10 (14-69)	8-20 (0.22-0.56)	2-6 (14-41)	4-8 (0.11-0.22)	0.05 (1.27)
1/4 (6.4)	68	22-26 (560-660)	35 (241)	60 (1.68)	2-10 (14-69)	6-20 (0.17-0.56)	2-6 (14-41)	4-8 (0.11-0.22)	0.06 (1.52)
3/8 (9.5)	68	20-26 (510-660)	40 (276)	60 (1.68)	5-10 (35-69)	8-20 (0.22-0.56)	2-8 (14-55)	5-10 (0.14-0.28)	0.06 (1.52)
1/2 (12.7)	62	20-26 (510-660)	45 (310)	85 (2.38)	5-10 (35-69)	8-20 (0.22-0.56)	2-8 (14-55)	5-10 (0.14-0.28)	0.07 (1.78)
5/8 (15.9)	62	18-24 (455-610)	50 (345)	90 (2.52)	5-10 (35-69)	8-20 (0.22-0.56)	2-8 (14-55)	5-10 (0.14-0.28)	0.07 (1.78)
3/4 (19.1)	56	16-21 (405-535)	45 (310)	115 (3.22)	5-10 (35-69)	10-20 (0.28-0.56)	2-10 (14-69)	6-10 (0.17-0.28)	0.09 (2.29)
1 (25.4)	56	14-19 (355-485)	50 (345)	120 (3.36)	5-10 (35-69)	10-20 (0.28-0.56)	2-10 (14-69)	10-15 (0.28-0.42)	0.09 (2.29)
1 1/4 (31.8)	54	13-18 (330-455)	45 (310)	160 (4.48)	10-20 (69-138)	10-20 (0.28-0.56)	2-10 (14-69)	10-15 (0.28-0.42)	0.11 (2.79)
1 1/2 (38.1)	54	12-16 (305-405)	50 (345)	170 (4.76)	10-20 (69-138)	20-40 (0.56-1.12)	2-10 (14-69)	10-15 (0.28-0.42)	0.11 (2.79)
2 (50.8)	52	10-14 (255-355)	50 (345)	220 (6.16)	10-20 (69-138)	20-40 (0.56-1.12)	2-10 (14-69)	12-20 (0.34-0.56)	0.12 (3.05)
2 1/2 (63.5)	52	9-13 (230-330)	55 (379)	235 (6.58)	10-20 (69-138)	20-40 (0.56-1.12)	6-10 (41-69)	12-20 (0.34-0.56)	0.12 (3.05)
3 (76.2)	49	8-11 (205-280)	50 (345)	290 (8.12)	10-30 (69-207)	20-40 (0.56-1.12)	6-10 (41-69)	12-20 (0.34-0.56)	0.14 (3.56)
4 (101.6)	49	7-10 (180-255)	55 (379)	310 (8.68)	10-30 (69-207)	30-40 (0.84-1.12)	6-10 (41-69)	12-20 (0.34-0.56)	0.14 (3.56)
6 (152.4)	39	5-8 (125-205)	60 (414)	675 (18.9)	10-30 (69-207)	30-40 (0.84-1.40)	8-15 (55-103)	12-20 (0.34-0.56)	0.20 (5.08)
8 (203.2)	39	4-6 (100-150)	65 (448)	720 (20.2)	20-40 (69-276)	30-50 (0.84-1.40)	10-15 (69-103)	12-20 (0.34-0.56)	0.20 (5.08)
10	30	3-5 (76-127)	60 (414)	940 (26.3)	20-40 (69-276)	36-60 (1.01-1.68)	10-15 (69-103)	15-25 (0.42-0.70)	0.26 (6.60)
12	30	3-5 (76-127)	65 (448)	990 (27.7)	20-40 (69-276)	36-60 (1.01-1.68)	10-15 (69-103)	15-25 (0.42-0.70)	0.26 (6.60)
14	18	2-4 (51-100)	65 (448)	1080 (30.2)	20-40 (69-276)	36-60 (1.01-1.68)	10-15 (69-103)	15-25 (0.42-0.70)	0.34 (8.64)
Two-piece high-speed tips:									
1/4 (6.4)	68	24-28 (610-710)	75 (517)	60 (1.68)	1-10 (7-69)	8-25 (0.22-0.70)	2-6 (14-41)	3-10 (0.08-0.28)	0.06 (1.52)
3/8 (9.5)	68	24-28 (610-710)	80 (552)	65 (1.82)	1-10 (7-69)	10-25 (0.28-0.70)	2-6 (14-41)	4-10 (0.11-0.28)	0.06 (1.52)
1/2 (12.7)	62	24-26 (610-660)	80 (552)	100 (2.80)	5-10 (35-69)	12-25 (0.34-0.70)	2-6 (14-41)	5-10 (0.14-0.28)	0.08 (2.03)
5/8 (15.9)	62	23-25 (585-635)	90 (621)	105 (2.94)	5-10 (35-69)	12-25 (0.34-0.70)	2-6 (14-41)	5-10 (0.14-0.28)	0.08 (2.03)
3/4 (19.1)	56	21-24 (535-610)	80 (552)	135 (3.78)	5-10 (35-69)	12-25 (0.34-0.70)	2-6 (14-41)	5-10 (0.14-0.28)	0.09 (2.29)
1 (25.4)	56	19-22 (485-560)	90 (621)	150 (4.20)	5-10 (35-69)	20-40 (0.56-1.12)	2-6 (14-41)	8-12 (0.22-0.34)	0.09 (2.29)
1 1/4 (31.8)	54	17-20 (430-510)	80 (552)	190 (5.32)	10-20 (69-138)	20-40 (0.56-1.12)	2-6 (14-41)	8-15 (0.22-0.42)	0.11 (2.79)
1 1/2 (38.1)	54	15-17 (380-430)	90 (621)	210 (5.88)	10-20 (69-138)	20-40 (0.56-1.12)	2-8 (14-55)	8-15 (0.22-0.42)	0.11 (2.79)
2 (50.8)	52	14-16 (355-405)	80 (552)	260 (7.28)	10-20 (69-138)	20-40 (0.56-1.12)	2-8 (14-55)	8-15 (0.22-0.42)	0.12 (3.05)
2 1/2 (63.5)	52	13-15 (330-380)	90 (621)	290 (8.12)	10-20 (69-138)	20-40 (0.56-1.12)	4-10 (28-69)	8-15 (0.22-0.42)	0.12 (3.05)
3 (76.2)	49	12-14 (305-355)	80 (552)	340 (9.52)	10-20 (69-138)	20-40 (0.56-1.12)	6-10 (41-69)	8-15 (0.22-0.42)	0.14 (3.56)
4 (101.6)	49	10-11 (255-280)	90 (621)	375 (10.50)	10-20 (69-138)	30-40 (0.84-1.12)	6-10 (41-69)	12-15 (0.34-0.42)	0.14 (3.56)

(MAPP Products)

* Based on the use of MPS as the fuel gas. Gas flow rates, both oxygen and fuel gas, will vary with different fuel gases.

principles are involved. Machine cutting has the advantages of higher speeds, smoother surfaces, improved dimensional tolerances, and reproducibility. In addition, multiple torch machines can produce several identical pieces simultaneously.

Edge starts. The most common method of cutting involves edge starts. Ideally, the top corner of the starting edge should be square. After the operating parameters have been set and the desired flame adjustment obtained, position the cutting tip about halfway over the edge, with the end of the preheat flames slightly above the surface. When the top corner becomes cherry-red, activate the cutting oxygen and start torch movement along the line of cut. Torch motion should be as smooth and steady as possible, while maintaining a constant torch-to-work distance. Speed of straight line cuts on material 1/2″ (12.7 mm) thick or less can be increased by tilting the torch to operate with a lead angle.

Pierce starts. When it is necessary to start a cut at some point other than the edge, pierce starts are used. With the exception of thin plate, piercing will usually require a heavier preheat flame than is needed for edge starts. If possible, pierces should be made in the scrap area.

In making pierces, the torch is held at the starting point, with the preheat flames just touching the surface. When ignition temperature is reached, rotate the tip slightly to ensure there is no cold spot in the center. Then, simultaneously, slowly turn on the cutting oxygen, lift the tip away from the plate, and start moving in the direction of cut. Until complete penetration is achieved, the slag will be blown upward. This technique will help prevent the slag from fouling or burning up the tip.

Beveling edges. Bevel cutting is often employed to prepare plate edges for subsequent welding. A single torch is used to produce an all-the-way-through bevel. Multiple torches in line can produce edges with a bevel-and-land double bevel or double bevel and land. When making multisurface edges, the lead torch will ordinarily be that which produces the lowermost surface.

The most common defect in bevel cutting is notching, which is usually a result of inadequate preheat. Tip size selection should be based on the length of the bevel cut, not just the vertical cut thickness. A larger than ordinary and slightly oxidizing flame should be used and the preheat flames allowed to almost touch the surface. Some of the cooler burning fuel gases will perform more satisfactorily if a preheating torch is placed plumb to the plate surface and slightly ahead of the beveling torch.

Quality of Cutting

The quality required from oxyfuel gas cutting depends on specific application requirements. Selection of the proper tip size, oxygen and fuel gas pressures, and speed for the section thickness to be cut can result in high quality. Modifications, however, are often required to compensate for the workpiece material, the condition of the work surface, quality requirements, and other factors.

With good equipment, skilled operators, and the proper parameters, tolerances of 1/32 to 1/16″ (0.8 to 1.6 mm) can be maintained on cuts through plate thicknesses to 2″ (51 mm). Closer control of tolerances and cut quality can generally be obtained with machine cutting, compared to manual cutting, because the parameters are not subject to operator decisions.

Figure 9-15 illustrates some cut surfaces produced with varying parameters. View a shows an optimum surface that can often be used for many applications without the need for subsequent machining. Drag lines, resulting from iron oxidizing

in the kerf, are inherent with oxyfuel gas cutting, but the light, regular, slightly sloping drag lines illustrated in this cut are not considered detrimental. In production cutting, the slope of the drag lines generally increases slightly, but the surfaces are reasonably smooth, giving a combination of quality and economy.

A cut surface resulting from an extremely fast speed is shown in Fig. 9-15, view b. The top edge is good, and the cut face is smooth, but slightly concave. Not enough time is allowed for the slag to blow out of the kerf, resulting in slag adhering to the bottom edge. View c shows the result of an extremely slow speed. Pressure marks on the cut face indicate too much oxygen for the cutting conditions. Either the tip is too big, the cutting oxygen pressure too high, or the speed too slow, resulting in a rounded or beaded top edge.

View d of Fig. 9-15 illustrates the result of excessive preheat, which causes a rounded top edge. Excessive preheat does not increase cutting speed, but rather wastes gases. When cutting tips are too close to the work surfaces, the cuts have grooves and deep drag lines resulting from unstable cutting action. When the tips are too far from the work surfaces, the top edges of the cuts

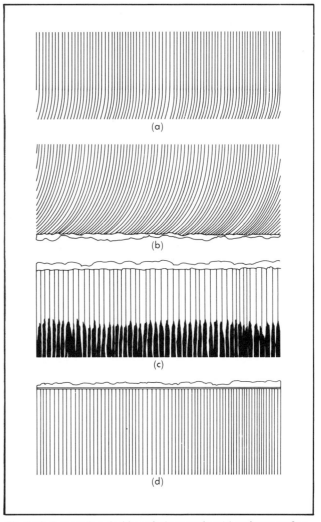

Fig. 9-15 Cuts produced with oxyfuel gas cutting: (a) optimum surface, (b) travel speed too fast, (c) speed too slow, and (d) preheat too hot. (*Harris Calorific Div., Emerson Electric Co.*)

are usually beaded or rounded, the cut faces are not smooth, and the faces are often beveled slightly. Dirt or scale in the tips can deflect the oxygen streams and may cause excessive slag, irregular cut surfaces, pitting, or undercutting.

Troubleshooting

Some possible troubles that may be encountered when cutting with oxyfuel gas, probable causes, and suggested remedies are presented in Table 9-7.

TABLE 9-7
Troubleshooting in Oxyfuel Gas Cutting

Possible Troubles	Probable Causes	Suggested Remedies
Cutting tip popping	Tip loose	Tighten tip nut
	Nicked seat	Replace tip
Torch difficult to light	Excessive gas pressure	Use recommended pressures
Flame not clearly defined, smooth, or even	Dirty tip	Clean or replace tip
Flame changes during cutting	Oxygen needle valve on torch handle partly closed	Open oxygen valve wide
	Oxygen cylinder almost empty	Replace cylinder with full one
Regulator not holding constant pressure	Defective seal	Replace regulator
Leak around needle valve	Packing nut loose	Tighten nut

(Harris Calorific Div., Emerson Electric Co.)

ARC WELDING AND CUTTING

Arc welding (AW) involves a group of fusion welding processes that produces coalescence (joining) of metals by heating them with an electric arc, with or without the application of pressure and with or without the use of filler metal. Most of these processes, listed in Table 9-1, are discussed in this chapter. Gas-shielded arc welding is a general term used to describe gas metal arc welding, gas tungsten arc welding, and flux-cored arc welding when gas shielding is used.

Arc cutting is a group of cutting processes that melts the metal to be cut with the heat of an electric arc between an electrode and the metal. The processes used extensively in industry are plasma arc cutting and air-carbon arc cutting, discussed subsequently. Other arc cutting processes that are not used extensively or are used only for special applications are described briefly at the end of this section.

DEFINITIONS OF SELECTED TERMS

The following glossary consists of terms commonly used in arc welding and cutting. It is adapted with permission from publication A3.0, "Welding Terms and Definitions," published by the American Welding Society (AWS).

arc blow The deflection of an electric arc from its normal path because of magnetic forces.

arc strike A discontinuity consisting of any localized remelted metal, heat-affected metal, or change in the surface profile of any part of a weld or base metal resulting from an arc.

arc welding electrode A component of the welding circuit through which current is conducted between the electrode holder and the arc.

arc welding gun A device used in semiautomatic, machine, and automatic arc welding to transfer current, guide the consumable electrode, and direct shielding gas when used.

bare electrode A filler metal electrode consisting of a single metal or alloy that has been produced into a wire, strip, or bar form and that has had no coating or covering applied to it other than that which was incidental to its manufacture or preservation.

carbon electrode A nonfiller material electrode used in arc welding or cutting consisting of a carbon or graphite rod that may be coated with copper or other coatings.

coated electrode See preferred term covered electrode.

composite electrode Any of a number of multicomponent filler metal electrodes in various physical forms such as stranded wires, tubes, and covered wire.

consumable insert Preplaced filler metal that is completely fused into the root of the joint and becomes part of the weld.

covered electrode A composite filler metal electrode consisting of a core of a bare electrode or metal-cored electrode to which a covering sufficient to provide a slag layer on the weld metal has been applied. The covering may contain materials providing such functions as shielding from the atmosphere, deoxidation, and arc stabilization and can serve as a source of metallic additions to the weld.

crater In arc welding, a depression at the termination of a weld bead or in the molten weld pool.

deposition efficiency (arc welding) The ratio of the weight of deposited metal to the net weight of filler metal consumed, exclusive of stubs.

deposition rate The weight of material deposited in a unit of time. It is usually expressed as kilograms per hour (kg/hr) or pounds per hour (lb/hr).

emissive electrode A filler metal electrode consisting of a core of a bare electrode or a composite electrode to which a very light coating has been applied to produce a stable arc.

globular transfer (arc welding) The transfer of molten metal from a consumable electrode across the arc in large droplets.

hot wire welding A variation of arc welding processes (GTAW, PAW, SAW) in which a filler metal wire is resistance-heated as it is fed into the molten weld pool.

pulsed power welding An arc welding process variation in which the power is cyclically programmed to pulse so that effective but short duration values of a parameter can be utilized. Such short duration values are significantly different from the average value of the parameter. Equivalent terms are pulsed voltage or pulsed current welding; see also pulsed spray welding.

pulsed spray welding An arc welding process variation in which the current is pulsed to utilize the advantages of the spray mode of metal transfer at average currents equal to or less than the globular-to-spray transition current.

short-circuiting transfer (arc welding) Metal transfer in which molten metal from a consumable electrode is deposited during repeated short circuits.

spray transfer (arc welding) Metal transfer in which molten metal from a consumable electrode is propelled axially across the arc in small droplets.

FUNDAMENTALS OF ARC WELDING

By the application of intense heat during arc welding, the base metals at the joint are melted and caused to intermix either directly or, more commonly, with a molten filler metal. Upon cooling and solidification, a metallurgical bond results. Because the joining takes place by melting together one part with the other part, with or without a filler metal of suitable composition, the welded joint may have strength properties similar to those of the base metals. This is in contrast to nonfusion processes of joining that use a separate filler, such as soldering, brazing, or adhesive bonding, in which the mechanical and physical properties of the base materials cannot be duplicated at the joint.

In arc welding, the intense heat needed to melt metals is produced by an electric arc. The arc is generally formed between the work to be welded and an electrode that is manually or mechanically moved along the joint, or the work may be moved under a stationary electrode. The electrode may be a carbon or tungsten rod that conducts the welding current to the electric arc between the hot electrode tip and the workpiece. Also, it may be a specially prepared rod or wire that not only conducts the welding current and sustains the arc, but also melts and provides filler metal to the joint.

If a carbon or tungsten electrode is used and the joint requires added filler metal, that metal is added from a separate filler metal rod or wire. Most welding in the manufacture of steel products where filler metal is required, however, is accomplished with consumable electrodes—those that supply filler metal as well as conduct the welding current.

Basic Welding Circuit

The basic circuit for shielded metal arc welding is illustrated in Fig. 9-16. An a-c or d-c power source, equipped with appropriate controls, is connected by a cable to the workpiece and by a cable to an electrode holder that makes electrical contact with the welding electrode. When the welding circuit is energized and the electrode tip is momentarily touched to the workpiece and then withdrawn a short distance, an arc is created between the electrode and the work. The arc produces a temperature at the tip of the electrode more than adequate for melting most metals.

The heat produced melts the base metal in the vicinity of the arc and any filler metal supplied by the electrode or by a separately introduced rod or wire. A pool of molten weld metal is produced. This weld pool solidifies behind the electrode as it is moved along the joint being welded. A crater forms as the welding is interrupted as the result of the shrinkage of the metal during solidification. The result is a fusion bond and the metallurgical unification of the workpieces.

Arc Shielding

Use of the heat of an electric arc to join metals, however, requires more than the moving of the electrode with respect to the weld joint. Metals at high temperatures react chemically with the main constituents of air, oxygen, and nitrogen to form oxides and nitrides. Upon solidification of the molten weld pool, the oxides and nitrides reduce the strength and ductility properties of the welded joint. For this reason, the various arc welding processes provide some means for covering the arc, electrode tip, the arc, and the molten weld pool with a protective shield of gas or slag. This is referred to as arc shielding.

Arc shielding is accomplished by various techniques, such as the use of (1) a vapor-generating covering on consumable electrodes, (2) an inert gas or a granular flux covering the arc and molten pool, and (3) fluxing materials within the core of tubular electrodes that generate shielding vapors. Whatever the shielding method, the intent is to provide a blanket of gas or slag, or both, that prevents or minimizes contact of hot weld metal with air.

The shielding method also affects the stability and the energy of the arc. When the shielding is produced by an electrode covering, by electrode core substances, or by separately applied granular flux, a fluxing or alloying function, or both, are usually provided. Thus, the core materials in a flux-cored electrode may supply deoxidizing and alloying functions as well as a shielding function. In submerged arc welding, the granular flux applied to the joint ahead of the arc has a similar effect.

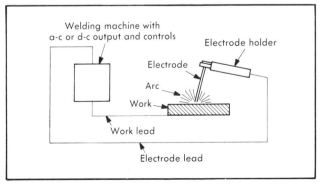

Fig. 9-16 Basic arc welding circuit.

ARC WELDING AND CUTTING

Figure 9-17 illustrates the shielding of the welding arc and molten weld pool with a covered electrode. The extruded covering on the filler metal rod, under the heat of the arc, generates a gaseous shield that displaces the surrounding air from the molten weld metal. It also supplies ingredients that react with deleterious substances on or in the metals, such as oxides and other compounds, and ties these substances up chemically in a slag. The slag, being lighter than the weld metal, rises to the surface of the molten weld pool and solidifies with the weld metal. This slag, after solidification, has a protective function; it protects the hot solidified metal from air.

While the main function of the arc is to supply heat, it has other functions that are important to the success of arc welding processes. It can be adjusted to (1) control the transfer of molten metal from the electrode to the work, (2) remove surface films, and (3) bring about complex gas-slag-metal reactions.

Nature of the Arc

An arc is an electric current flowing between two electrodes through an ionized column of gas called a plasma. The space between the two electrodes, between the electrode and the work in arc welding, can be divided into three areas of heat generation: the cathode, the anode, and the arc plasma.

A welding arc is characterized as a high-current, low-voltage conductor with a high concentration of electrons. Electrons are emitted from the negative cathode and flow to the positive anode; positive gas ions flow in the reverse direction.

Heat is generated in the cathode area mostly by the positive ions striking the surface of the cathode. Heat at the anode is generated mostly by the electrons. These have been accelerated as they pass through the plasma by the arc voltage, and they give up their energy as heat when striking the anode. The plasma, or arc column, is a mixture of neutral and excited gas atoms. In the central column of the plasma, electrons, atoms, and ions are in accelerated motion and constantly colliding. The hottest part of the plasma is the central column, where the motion is most intense. The outer portion of the arc flame is somewhat cooler and consists of recombining gas molecules that were dissociated in the central column. In general, the heat generated by the arc column is transferred by plasma flow to the weld pool.

The distribution of heat or voltage drop in the three heat zones can be changed. Changing the arc length has the greatest effect on the arc plasma. Changing the shielding gas can alter the heat balance between the anode and cathode. The addition of potassium salts to the arc reduces the arc voltage because of increased ionization.

In welding, the arc not only provides the heat needed to melt the electrode or the base metal, or both, but also, under certain conditions must supply the means to transport the molten filler metal from the tip of the electrode to the work. Several mechanisms for metal transfer exist. In one, molten drops of metal touch the molten weld pool in the joint and transfer is by surface tension. In another, the molten droplets are ejected at high speed from the electrode tip by an electromagnetic pinch, and they retain this speed unless slowed by gravitational forces. The droplets are accelerated by the arc plasma forces. These forces are the ones that transfer the molten filler metal in the overhead position in gas metal arc welding. In flat position welding, gravity is a significant force in filler metal transfer.

If the electrode is consumed during welding, the tip melts from the heat of the arc, and molten droplets of filler metal are detached and transported to the work through the arc column. If the electrode (carbon or tungsten) is not consumed during welding, filler metal is melted with the arc and deposited into the joint from a separate rod or wire.

More of the heat developed by the arc ends up in the molten weld pool with consumable electrodes than with nonconsumable electrodes, resulting in higher thermal efficiencies and narrower heat-affected zones. Typical thermal efficiencies with consumable electrodes range from 75 to 80% and for welding with nonconsumable electrodes from 50 to 60%.

Because there must be an ionized path to conduct electricity across a gap, the mere switching on of the welding circuit with a cold electrode poised over the work will not start the arc. The arc must first be ignited. This is accomplished either by supplying an initial voltage high enough to ionize the arc path or by momentarily touching the electrode to the work to form a high-resistance contact area of small cross section that becomes rapidly heated and "blows" like an electrical fuse to ignite the arc. High-frequency spark discharges are sometimes used for igniting gas tungsten arcs, but the most common method of striking an arc for all processes is the touch method.

Arc welding may be done with either a-c or d-c current. With d-c, the electrode may be either positive or negative. The choice of current and electrode polarity depends on the process, the type of electrode, the arc atmosphere, and the metal being welded. With both types of welding current, the variables, amperage and voltage, must be controlled to meet the requirements of the welding procedures.

Welding Current

The objective in commercial welding is to get the job done as fast as possible to minimize the time costs of skilled workers. One way to increase the speed of welding is to raise the welding current—use a higher amperage—because the faster electrical energy can be induced in the weld joint, the higher will be the metal deposition rate and the faster will be the welding rate.

With covered electrodes, there is a practical limit to the amount of current that can be used with an electrode of a particular diameter. Most covered electrodes are from 9 to 18" (230 to 455 mm) long. If the current density is raised too high, electrical resistance heating within the electrode will overheat the covering and decrease its effectiveness. In such cases, the covering ingredients react with each other or oxidize and fail to function properly. Also, the heating of the core wire increases the meltoff rate and changes the arc characteristics. Therefore,

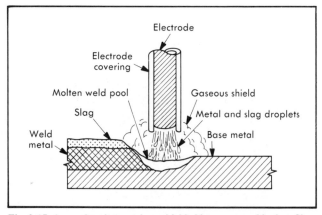

Fig. 9-17 Arc and molten pool are shielded by a gaseous blanket. Slag forms over hot solidified metal. (*Lincoln Electric Co.*)

electrode diameters must be chosen to be appropriate to the current requirements.

Essential Requirements

Essential requirements for optimum arc welding include use of the correct electrode type and size, welding current, arc length (arc voltage), travel speed, and electrode position.

Electrode size. Selecting the correct size of electrode requires careful consideration of many factors, including the following:

- The type, position, and preparation of the joint that is to be welded.
- The ability of the electrode to carry the required welding current without damage to the weld metal or loss of deposition efficiency.
- The base metal type, mass, and ability to maintain acceptable properties after welding.
- The characteristics of the assembly with reference to the effect of stresses set up by heat application.
- Specific weld quality requirements.
- Electrode cost.

In all cases, for shielded metal arc welds the largest size electrode possible should be used. Large covered electrodes cost less than smaller ones, and the welding speeds are higher. This is also generally true for wire electrodes. However, for resistive material, the advantage may be outweighed by the higher deposition rate achievable at the same current, using a smaller wire diameter and the resistive heating effect.

Current. If the current is too high, the electrode melts too fast, and the molten weld pool becomes too large and irregular. If too low, the heat is insufficient to properly melt the base metal, and the molten weld pool will be too small and irregular.

Arc length. If the arc length is excessive (the arc voltage too high), filler metal melts from the electrode in large globules that wobble from side to side as the arc wavers. This results in a wide, spattered, and irregular bead, with poor fusion between the base metal and deposited metals. A long arc is also more susceptible to air entrapment and possible porosity in the weld. If the arc is too short (the voltage too low), the heat is insufficient to melt the base metal properly. Also, the electrode often sticks to the work. High, uneven beads with irregular ripples and poor fusion often result. Maintaining the proper arc length concentrates the welding current in the joint and minimizes spatter.

Travel speed. When the welding speed is too fast, the pool does not remain molten for a sufficiently long time, the bead produced is narrow, penetration is reduced, and impurities and gases may be locked into the weld. When the speed is too slow, excessive filler metal is added to the joint, and the resultant weld bead is high and wide.

Electrode position. The electrode position is especially important in fillet welding and deep groove welding. In general, when making a fillet weld, the electrode should be held so that it bisects the angle between the plates and is perpendicular to the axis of the weld. If undercut occurs in the vertical member of a horizontal-vertical weld, lower the angle of the arc and direct the arc toward the vertical member.

WELDING VARIOUS METALS

While most metals and alloys can be arc welded satisfactorily, some are easier to weld than others. The degree of weldability varies primarily with the chemistry and properties of the

materials. Details with respect to classifications, typical properties, and applications of various engineering materials are presented in Volume III, *Materials, Finishing and Coating*, of this Handbook series. Properties of the shielding gases used for arc welding and contaminants from the atmosphere also affect the properties of the welds.

Cast Irons

Arc welding for the repair of iron castings uses steel or nickel electrodes. Some cast irons can be welded, but require considerable care; others are considered nonweldable. Most cast irons present the problem of having an extremely hard heat-affected zone when welded. Whether the free graphite is in the form of flake graphite (as in the case of gray irons), nodular graphite (ductile or malleable iron), or in solution (chilled iron), the cast material when melted by the welding arc will still contain 3-4% carbon, which is very susceptible to cracking.

Gray cast irons. These materials can be arc welded, but care is necessary to minimize dilution of the base metal to reduce the possibility of cracking and porosity. Gray irons with high phosphorus contents are most crack-sensitive. Nickel-based filler metals are normally recommended for the welding of gray cast irons.

Ductile (nodular) irons. These cast irons are more weldable than gray cast irons because of their reduced crack sensitivity. However, special procedures and filler materials are required, especially for ductile cast irons having high tensile strengths.

Malleable irons. These materials can be arc welded, but their ductilities are substantially reduced.

White irons. These cast irons are generally considered unweldable because the weld zones are too hard and brittle to withstand the thermal stresses of welding.

Processes used. Shielded metal arc welding is commonly used for repairing iron castings. Flux-cored arc welding is also being used, and gas metal arc welding has some limited application. Gas tungsten arc welding is sometimes used to repair small iron castings.

Carbon and Low-Alloy Steels

Steel chemistry. For economical, high-speed welding of carbon-steel plate, the composition of the steel should be within the preferred-analysis ranges indicated in Table 9-8. If one or more elements varies from the ranges shown, more costly procedures are usually required to produce acceptable welds.

TABLE 9-8
Preferred Analyses for Carbon Steels to be Arc Welded

Element	Composition, %	
	Preferred	High*
Carbon	0.06 to 0.25	0.35
Manganese	0.35 to 0.80	1.40
Silicon	0.10 or less	0.30
Sulfur	0.035 or less	0.05
Phosphorus	0.030 or less	0.04

(*Lincoln Electric Co.*)
* Additional care is required in welding of steels containing these amounts of the elements listed.

ARC WELDING AND CUTTING

Thus, steel compositions within the preferred ranges should be used whenever extensive welding is to be done.

As the carbon content of steel increases, weldability decreases. For steels having a carbon content more than 0.25%, rapid cooling from the welding temperature may produce a hard, brittle structure, particularly in the heat-affected zone adjacent to the weld. If sufficient hydrogen is absorbed from the arc, this area may be susceptible to cold cracking. Manganese content of less than 0.30% may produce internal porosity and cracking in the weld bead; cracking can also occur if the manganese content is more than 0.80%. For good weldability, the ratio of manganese to sulfur contents should be at least 10 to 1. Steels with low manganese to sulfur ratios may contain sulfur in the form of FeS, which can cause cracking in welds.

Sulfur reduces weldability. In any amount, sulfur promotes hot shortness in welds, and the tendency increases with increased sulfur. It can be tolerated up to about 0.035% (with sufficient Mn); more than 0.050% it can cause serious problems. For best welding conditions, the silicon content should not exceed 0.10%, but amounts up to 0.30% are not as serious as high sulfur or phosphorus contents. With respect to welding, phosphorus is considered an impurity and should be kept as low as possible. Steels with a phosphorus content more than 0.04% produce brittle welds, and the tendency to crack increases. Copper content up to about 1.50% has little or no effect on the weldability of a steel.

Low-carbon steels. In general, steels with carbon contents to 0.30% are readily joined by all common arc welding processes. Steels with very low carbon content, to 0.13%, are considered to be readily weldable, but they are not the best for high-speed production welding. Low carbon content and low manganese content (to 0.30%) tend to result in internal porosity. This condition can usually be corrected by modifying the welding procedure, usually by using a slower speed.

Steels with 0.15-0.20% carbon content have excellent weldability. They seldom require special welding procedures, and they can be welded with all types of mild steel electrodes. These steels should be used when possible for maximum production speed on assemblies or structures that require extensive welding.

Steels at the upper end of the low-carbon range, the 0.25-0.30% carbon grades, have very good weldability. However, when one or more of the elements is on the high side of permissible limits, hot cracking can result, particularly in fillet welds made at high speeds. With slightly lower welding speeds and currents, standard electrodes can be used for these steels. In thicknesses to 5/16" (8 mm), standard welding procedures apply.

Medium and high-carbon steels. These steels are more difficult and costly to weld than low-carbon steels. Medium-carbon steels can be welded successfully provided proper welding procedures, including appropriate preheat and interpass temperatures, are used. Preheat temperature should be maintained during the entire welding operation. Sometimes a postweld stress relief may be required.

High-carbon steels are almost always used in a hardened condition. Some farm equipment is built from rerolled rail stock (0.65% C), which is welded in the as-rolled condition using preheating and postweld stress relief.

It is advisable to make sample weld tests to determine the hydrogen cracking tendencies of steels containing 0.30% or more of carbon. If such tendencies are apparent, preheating of the steel may be necessary to retard cracking. The appropriate preheat temperature varies with steel composition, section size and shape, and the amount of heat input from the welding process. In general, the higher the carbon or alloy content and the thicker the plate, the higher the preheat temperature needed to prevent hardening.

Use of low-hydrogen welding processes can minimize the degree of preheating necessary. As a rule of thumb, preheat temperatures used with low-hydrogen electrodes can be 100-200° F (55-110° C) lower than those needed for electrodes other than low-hydrogen.

High-strength, low-alloy (HSLA) steels. Welding characteristics of most grades of HSLA steels do not differ markedly from those of low-carbon steels. To be weldable, however, high-strength steels must have sufficient ductility to avoid cracking from the rapid cooling inherent in welding processes. Weldable HSLA steels must be sufficiently low in carbon, manganese, and other deep-hardening elements to ensure that appreciable amounts of martensite are not formed in the heat-affected zone upon rapid cooling. Alternatively, high preheat temperatures as well as the use of low-hydrogen consumables may be necessary.

Quenched and tempered alloy steels. Most of these alloy steels can be welded with adequate control of welding procedures. If suppliers' recommendations are followed for controlling welding heat input, 100% joint efficiency can be expected in the as-welded condition for the 90,000 and 100,000 psi (620 and 690 MPa) yield strength grades.

If the heat-affected zone cools too slowly, the beneficial effects of the original heat treatment (particularly notch toughness) are destroyed. This can be caused by excessive preheat temperature, interpass temperature, or heat input. On the other hand, if the heat-affected zone cools too rapidly, it can become hard and brittle and may crack. This is caused by insufficient preheat and interpass temperature or by insufficient heat input during welding. Producers' recommendations should be followed closely.

Quenched and tempered steels can be welded by the shielded metal arc, submerged arc, and gas-shielded arc processes. Weld cooling rates for these processes are relatively rapid, and mechanical properties of the heat-affected zones approach those of the steel in the quenched condition. After welding, heat treatment such as quenching and tempering is not recommended.

Because of the desirability of relatively rapid cooling after welding, thin sections of these materials can usually be welded without preheating. When preheating is required, both maximum and minimum temperatures are important. Interpass temperature is just as important as preheat temperature and should be controlled with the same care.

Tool and Die Steels

Most arc welding processes can be used to make and repair tools and dies. The gas tungsten arc process is commonly used for thin sections, and the submerged arc, shielded metal arc, and flux-cored arc processes are used for thicker sections.

Surfaces of the tools and dies to be welded must be clean, dry, and smooth, with all cracks removed. All tool steels should be preheated prior to welding. Selection of the proper filler metal depends primarily on the composition and condition of the base metal and on service requirements.

Stainless Steels

Weldability of stainless steels takes into account not only the usual mechanical properties, but also the chemical characteristics that affect corrosion resistance. The choice of welding processes is limited because of possible reactions of chromium with carbon and oxygen at welding temperatures. More welding of stainless steel plate is done by manual shielded arc methods than by any other process, while the gas tungsten arc process is most commonly used for sheet stock. Electrodes for welding stainless steels are available in a wide variety of alloys.

Austenitic stainless steels. Most weldable of the AISI-type stainless steels are the austenitic grades, but even these alloys have limitations that require careful attention during processing. Austenitic steels have a high coefficient of thermal expansion, about 50% higher than that of carbon steel or of the 400-series stainless steels. This characteristic requires care to minimize distortion of welded parts. Some austenitic stainless steels are susceptible to the formation of sigma phase when exposed to certain high temperature ranges, which can cause cracking and corrosion under certain conditions. Welding can cause chromium carbide precipitation in the heat-affected zones in some stainless grades, which decreases corrosion resistance to some chemical media.

Carbide precipitation. Although mechanically satisfactory welds can be made on the chromium nickel (austenitic) stainless steels, heating these materials sometimes promotes intergranular corrosion. When the austenitic steels are heated in the sensitizing temperature range, 800-1400°F (425-760°C), or cooled slowly through that range, chromium carbide is precipitated from solid solution, mainly at grain boundaries. These chromium carbides may contain as much as 90% chromium from the metal immediately adjacent to the grain boundary. The reduced chromium content of the adjacent metal lowers corrosion resistance along the grain boundaries. This phenomenon is termed chromium carbide precipitation, and the type of corrosion it promotes is known as intergranular corrosion. Stainless steels having chromium contents of about 18% are very susceptible to chromium carbide precipitation. The thermal conditions that produce chromium carbide precipitation can occur during welding, particularly in multiple-pass welding, welding of heavy beads, or when two beads cross.

Thermal treatments. Various methods are used to reduce or prevent chromium carbide precipitation in austenitic stainless steels. One is to heat the weldment to the range 1850-2100°F (1010-1150°C) and rapidly cool it through the 1400-800°F (760-425°C) range. This thermal treatment dissolves the precipitated carbides (puts the carbon back into solution in the austenite and restores the chromium at the grain boundaries). Heat treatment has disadvantages, however. Exposure to high temperature may cause distortion in welded assemblies, and suitable heating furnaces may not be available for large welded structures.

Low-carbon stainless steels. Chromium carbide precipitation can be avoided by using stainless steels and electrodes having a low carbon content so that only limited carbides can precipitate at the grain boundaries. The 18-8 austenitic steels retain about 0.02% carbon in solid solution under all conditions. As the carbon content is increased to about 0.08%, the amount of carbide that can precipitate increases slowly. Above 0.08% carbon, precipitation can occur rapidly when the steel is exposed to the sensitizing temperature. Extra-low-carbon plate and welding electrodes cost slightly more than the standard grades, but results may be worth the higher cost, particularly when weldments are to be used in the as-welded condition.

Stabilized stainless steels. Stainless steels in which chromium carbide forms readily upon heating to the sensitizing temperature range are known as unstabilized grades. Examples of these are AISI Types 301, 302, 302B, 303, 304, and 308. Because chromium carbide precipitation increases with carbon content,

grades 304 and 308 are the best suited for welding. Maximum carbon content in these two grades is 0.08%; the others listed have a maximum limit of 0.15%.

If Types 304 and 308 stainless steels are welded with a single pass, the time in the sensitizing temperature range is so short that very little chromium carbide precipitation can take place. Thus, intergranular corrosion is not likely to occur in the heat-affected zones of single-pass welds, provided the service temperature of the weldment is not in the sensitizing range.

If the steel is thick enough to require multiple-pass welds or if the finished product will operate in the sensitizing temperature range, chromium carbide precipitation is likely to occur, even in grades 304 and 308. Intergranular corrosion will then occur if the weldment is subjected to a corrosive medium.

One way of preventing intergranular corrosion is to use stabilized grades of stainless steels that contain columbium or titanium. These elements have a greater affinity for carbon than chromium does; thus they form columbium or titanium carbide. The chromium remains in solution where it provides corrosion resistance.

Stainless steels that contain columbium or titanium are AISI Types 347 and 321. They can be subjected to the sensitizing temperature range with no effect on corrosion resistance.

Welding of stabilized stainless steels should be done with stabilized electrodes for best results. Because columbium transfers across an arc much more effectively than titanium, stabilization of electrodes is achieved with columbium additions.

Preheating and postheating. Austenitic stainless steels are best welded without preheat. No preheat, low interpass temperature, and a stringer-bead welding technique minimizes the time that the heat-affected zone is in the sensitizing temperature range, thereby reducing the amount of chromium carbide precipitation. Usually, postheating is not required for austenitic stainless steels, except when an anneal is needed to dissolve chromium carbides.

Martensitic stainless steels. The martensitic grades of stainless steels can be welded, although the weldability is not as good as that of austenitic grades. Typical grades are Types 403, 410, 420, and 440 A, B, and C. In the as-welded condition, there is a hard martensitic heat-affected zone, and usually a preheat is required to avoid cracking. Steels with up to 0.10% carbon content require no preheat or postheat. In the 0.10-0.20% carbon range, a 400-500°F (205-260°C) preheat is required, and the weld should be cooled slowly. Steels with more than 0.20% and up to 0.50% carbon content require a preheat of 500-600°F (260-315°C) and an anneal after welding. If a hardening and tempering operation follows the welding, this should be started immediately after the welding is finished. Some reduction in weld hardness can be obtained by heating to 1200-1400°F (650-760°C) and air cooling. For full annealing, the weldment is heated to 1500-1600°F (815-870°C), furnace cooled to 1100°F (595°C), and then air cooled.

Ferritic stainless steels. The welding quality of ferritic-type stainless steels is the poorest of the AISI types. The welding heats a zone in the base metal above a critical temperature and causes rapid grain growth of the ferrite. This coarse-grain zone lacks ductility and toughness. A small amount of martensite may also be present, which increases hardness. Postheating can reduce the hardness, but the objectionable properties of the coarse-grain heat-affected zone still remain.

Preheating is done only to reduce shrinkage stresses and avoid cracking on cooling. Thin sections should not be preheated. Thick sections, 1/4″ (6.4 mm) or more, should be

ARC WELDING AND CUTTING

preheated to 200-400°F (95-205°C), depending on the thickness and the amount of restraint. Postheating should be performed at 1450°F (790°C), followed by furnace cooling to 1100°F (595°C); the parts should then be cooled rapidly to room temperature.

Free-machining modifications of the three stainless categories (austenitic, martensitic, and ferritic) tend to lead toward porosity, segregation, and cracking during welding. This can often be avoided by proper electrode selection and taking precautions that the electrode covering is completely dry.

Titanium and Titanium Alloys

At elevated temperatures, titanium rapidly absorbs oxygen and nitrogen from the atmosphere, causing embrittlement in the weld. Additionally, heated surfaces can be severely contaminated. To ensure successful welding, air must be excluded from both the face and back sides of the weld area, including the cooling weld metal. In arc welding, this is accomplished by using a shielding gas. Commercially pure titanium and weldable titanium alloys can be welded successfully with all of the inert gas shielded arc welding processes and electron beam welding.

Aluminum and Aluminum Alloys

The introduction of new aluminum alloys and new welding processes has enhanced the use of aluminum in welded structures. Among these alloys are the heat-treatable 6000 and 7000 series and 2219 alloy. Heat-treatable alloys 6061 and 6063 also are widely used for welded structures; their as-welded yield strengths are good.

The aluminum-magnesium alloys, the 5000 series, are also widely used for welded structures, particularly where corrosion is a problem, as in marine applications. Weld ductility of these alloys is excellent, and they are well suited for applications subjected to impact and shock loading. Heat-treated 5000 series alloys generally soften when subjected to welding heat.

The two arc welding processes mostly used for aluminum are gas metal arc and gas tungsten arc. Generally, the gas tungsten arc process is used for thicknesses to 1/8" (3.2 mm), and the gas metal arc process is used for thicker sections.

Heat effects of welding. Welding heat adversely affects mechanical properties of welded joints in all aluminum alloys. The strength of the weld area is normally lower than that of the unaffected base metal. Although welds in sections that are in the annealed condition do not soften the base metal, the cast structure of the weld metal usually has lower strength than the base metal. However, welding with a suitable filler alloy, increasing the welding speed, and adding bead reinforcement usually strengthen the welded joint.

Some heat-treatable aluminum alloys in the T6 temper (solution heat treated, then artificially aged) are used in welded structural applications, where it is customary to proportion members on the basis of yield strength. The minimum tensile and compressive yield strength of 6061-T6 alloy sheet and plate in the weld heat zone adjacent to a butt joint is 20,000 psi (138 MPa) with Types 5356 or 5556 filler metals. This compares favorably with yield strengths of the heat-affected zones in other high-strength aluminum alloys.

Hot cracking of weld metal. Hot cracking is caused by stresses induced by contraction as the weld metal cools. Cracking of this type usually develops in the weld metal itself, but a similar type of cracking sometimes occurs in the heat-affected zone adjacent to the weld.

Cracking of welds during arc welding operations can also be caused by a hot-short characteristic of some resultant weld metal compositions. Hot-short compositions are weak at elevated temperatures. Hot cracking is a function of contraction stress and of the hot-shortness tendency of the alloy. Hot cracking can also be caused by excessive restraint on the weld bead during welding. Hot cracking does not normally occur in pure aluminum or in deposits of a eutectic composition.

Other factors that affect the amount of hot cracking that occurs in the weld include the solidification temperature range of the alloy, the coefficient of thermal expansion, the thermal gradients across the weld, the ratio of the volume of liquid remaining to the volume of solidified material, and the amount of restraint across the weld joint.

Hot cracking can be reduced by several methods, including the following:

- *Use higher welding speed.* As welding speed is increased, the heat input in the weld zone is decreased, and the weld cooling rate is increased. In turn, stresses created by temperature differentials between the hot weld metal and the cool base metal are less severe. Also, at high welding speeds, less weld metal is within the hot-short range at any one time. The same effect is also advantageous in welding aluminum alloys that are not hot-short. In addition, the faster cooling rate that occurs with higher welding speeds results in a finer dendritic grain structure in the weld, which is less susceptible to cracking.
- *Use preheat.* Preheating reduces the stress on the solidifying weld metal by reducing the temperature gradient across the weld zone and by permitting faster welding speeds. Preheating should not be used, however, unless the joint is unrestrained. The mechanical properties of the base metal are decreased by excessive preheating, except where the material is in the annealed condition. This is particularly true of heat-treatable alloys such as 6061.
- *Select a more compatible filler alloy.* A filler metal that will minimize hot-short cracking is one that, when dilution is considered, will give a metal weld composition that is not hot-short. A proper aluminum filler selection, using hot-short cracking tendency as a criterion, requires consideration of the relative cracking tendencies of various weld-metal compositions.
- *Change the joint design.* The chemical composition of an aluminum alloy affects its hot-short characteristics. The chemical composition of the weld metal is the result of dilution of the base metal with the filler metal, and the resultant weld metal may be highly susceptible to hot-short cracking. To reduce this susceptibility, the joint design can be changed to either increase or decrease the amount of dilution in the final weld metal. Selection of the proper joint design usually requires that sample weldments be prepared to evaluate crack susceptibility in cases where data on comparable welds are not available.

Filler metals. Correct choice of a filler metal should minimize the presence of intermetallic compounds and brittleness in aluminum fusion welds.

Strength. Some filler metals commonly used for inert gas welding, arranged in decreasing order of as-welded strength, are: 5039, 5556, 5183, 5356, 5654, 5554, 4043, and 1100. This order of strength generally holds true when these fillers are used to weld any alloy of the 5000, 3000, or 1100 series; the sequence does not necessarily apply to certain dissimilar alloy combinations or to assemblies that are heat treated.

Ductility. The arrangement of the same filler metals in decreasing order of as-welded ductility is: 1100, 4043, 5654, 5356, 5183, 5554, 5556, and 5039.

Elongation up to 50% can be expected with 1100 filler metal, while from 15 to 20% is normal for Types 5183 and 5356 filler metals. Ductility of the weld is often affected by dilution of the filler metal with the base material. For example, the elongation of 4043 weld metal can vary from 5 to 17%, depending on the type and quantity of base metal with which it is diluted. Table 9-9 lists recommended filler metals for various aluminum alloys for both maximum strength and maximum elongation.

Magnesium and Magnesium Alloys

Most magnesium alloys, except ZK60A, AZ63A, AZ92A, ZH62A, ZK51A, and ZK61A, are arc welded with the gas metal arc and gas tungsten arc processes in the same manner as aluminum alloys. Chemical or mechanical surface preparation is required prior to welding, and stress relieving may be necessary after welding.

Copper and Copper Alloys[3]

Coppers. Arc welding of oxygen-bearing coppers is difficult because the heat reduces the mechanical properties and corro-

TABLE 9-9
Recommended Filler Metals for Various Aluminum Alloys

Base Metal	Recommended Filler Metal*	
	For Maximum As-Welded Strength	For Maximum Elongation
1100	1100, 4043	1100, 4043
2219	2319	**
3003	5183, 5356	1100, 4043
3004	5554, 5356	5183, 4043
5005	5183, 4043, 5356	5183, 4043
5050	5356	5183, 4043
5052	5356, 5183	5183, 4043, 5356
5083	5183, 5356	5183, 5356
5086	5183, 5356	5183, 5356
5154	5356, 5183	5183, 5356, 5654
5357	5554, 5356	5356
5454	5356, 5554	5554, 5356
5456	5556	5183, 5356
6061	4043, 5183	5356†
6063	4043, 5183	5356†
7005	5039	5183, 5356
7039	5039	5183, 5356

(*Lincoln Electric Co.*)

* Recommendations are for plate of "0" temper.
** Ductility of weldments of these base metals is not appreciably affected by filler metal. Elongation of these base metals is generally lower than that of other alloys listed.
† For welded joints in 6061 and 6063 requiring maximum electrical conductivity, use 4043 filler metal. However, if both strength and conductivity are required, use 5356 filler metal and increase the weld reinforcement to compensate for the lower conductivity of 5356.

sion resistance. The use of inert gas shielding, however, minimizes embrittlement. For applications requiring good mechanical properties and corrosion resistance, oxygen-free or deoxidized copper should be used for arc welding. Clamping-type fixtures or tack welding, or both, are generally necessary to minimize distortion, and preheating is usually required.

Shielded metal arc welding is used for repair work on thin sections or dissimilar metals. Gas tungsten arc welding is effective for joining copper to 1/8″ (3.2 mm) thick or more. When welding with the gas metal arc process, deoxidized copper electrodes are required.

Copper-zinc alloys (brasses). Brass alloys require much less preheating for arc welding than unalloyed copper. Restraint during cooling after welding should be minimized to avoid cracking. The shielded metal arc, gas metal arc, and gas tungsten arc processes are commonly used for welding the low brasses (containing 80-95% copper) and the high brasses (containing 55-80% copper). Leaded alpha brasses are not suitable for welding.

Copper-tin alloys (phosphor bronzes). These alloys have a tendency to crack during cooling after welding if proper procedures are not followed. They should only be welded with the addition of filler metal having sufficient phosphorus to deoxidize the molten metal and prevent porosity. Gas metal arc welding is recommended for large weldments and thick sections. Preheating is not essential with this process, but the interpass temperature should not exceed 400°F (205°C). Gas tungsten arc welding is used primarily for minor repairs to castings. Shielded metal arc welding of heavy sections requires preheating to about 400°F.

Copper-aluminum alloys (aluminum bronzes). Alloys with low aluminum content (below 8%) are not generally used for welded fabrications because they are difficult to weld and have a tendency to crack. Alloys with higher aluminum content are being successfully joined by arc welding. The gas metal arc process is recommended for welding thick sections, and the gas tungsten arc process is used for thin sheets and for repairing castings. The shielded metal arc welding process is also used.

Copper-silicon alloys (silicon bronzes). These alloys are among the most weldable alloys of copper because the addition of silicon to copper reduces the thermal conductivity and the heat input requirements. Welding speeds can be high, and preheating is not necessary. Gas tungsten arc welding is generally the preferred process, but gas metal arc welding and shielded metal arc welding are also used.

Dissimilar Metals

Successful arc welding of dissimilar metals requires mutual solubility of the two metals being joined. For some applications, a filler metal that is soluble with the two base metals is used. In other cases, a composite insert is used between the two metals.

Similar coefficients of thermal expansion and melting points for the two base metals are also desirable. If not similar, the arc welding process providing the fastest heat input for rapid welding should be used. Intermetallic compounds formed by alloying of the two different base metals must be investigated to determine sensitivity of the weld to cracking, corrosion, embrittlement, and other detrimental characteristics.

JOINTS, WELDS AND GROOVES

The relationship between joint design and the production welding process is significant when arc welding is used. Much

ARC WELDING AND CUTTING

of the inherent cost advantage of welding can be lost through poor design, as well as through poor procedure control. Factors to be considered in designing for welding, including performance requirements, location of welds, stress distribution, and joint placement, are discussed in the introductory section of this chapter.

Types of joints are illustrated in Fig. 9-18. Groove and fillet welds (see Fig. 9-19) are the common types produced by arc welding. Major factors in the selection of the types of joints and welds are application requirements and costs. Combinations of fillet and groove welds are used for some joints, depending on the loading conditions.

Fillet Welds

Fillet welds are more economical than groove welds but they sometimes require more weld metal. Simple or no edge preparation is necessary, but some surface cleaning may be required. Fillet welds are generally preferred when stresses are low, when designs permit, and when required weld sizes are less than about 5/8″ (16 mm).

When feasible from the strength standpoint, intermittent fillet welding is used instead of continuous welding for greater economy and distortion control. Fillet weld size should be limited to that required; doubling the size of a fillet requires four times as much weld metal and increases the amount of distortion.

Single-fillet welds. These welds are generally limited to low loads. When the loading is not too severe, single-fillet welds are suitable for joining plates of all thicknesses. If fatigue or impact loads are to be encountered, however, stress distribution must be carefully studied. Loading on the joint must not place the root of the weld in tension because of the stress concentration.

Double-fillet welds. These welds are suitable for more severe load conditions than can be met by single-fillet joints. Smaller double-fillet welds are generally preferable to larger single-fillet welds. The two fillet welds are generally made the same size, but one fillet weld can be smaller than the other for some applications.

Groove Welds

Groove welds are of several types (see Fig. 9-20). A general classification is according to groove preparation: square, V, bevel, J, and U-shaped grooves. All groove welds should be designed for minimum cross-sectional area and most economical edge preparation. Shearing and flame cutting of the groove faces are common; machining of the faces is generally the most expensive method, but can result in the highest quality joints. Savings can often be realized by using simulated grooves. These consist of consumable backing materials, such as square or round rods, placed between the straight edges of the weldment components. The use of simulated grooves eliminates the need and cost for machining or cutting the component edges. For joining thick sections, double-groove welds require considerably less weld metal, but they require welding from both sides.

Square-groove welds. Edge preparation and welding costs are generally lower for these welds than other types of groove welds. Square-groove welds are suitable for all type loads, but joint strength depends on the amount of joint penetration. Complete fusion and complete joint penetration are generally

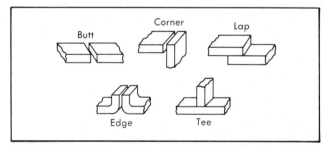

Fig. 9-18 Type of joints. (*Hobart Brothers Co.*)

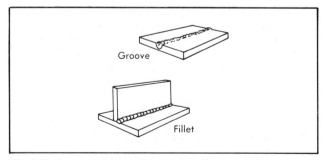

Fig. 9-19 Groove and fillet welds. (*Hobart Brothers Co.*)

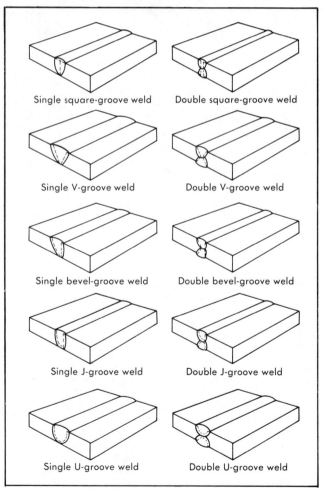

Single square-groove weld | Double square-groove weld

Single V-groove weld | Double V-groove weld

Single bevel-groove weld | Double bevel-groove weld

Single J-groove weld | Double J-groove weld

Single U-groove weld | Double U-groove weld

Fig. 9-20 Various types of groove welds. (*Reprinted from the AWS Welding Handbook with permission.*)

necessary for most welds, particularly when the load is cyclic or intermittent in nature. The base metal for this type of weld must have good weldability because a portion of the base metal in the joint area is melted during welding.

V-groove welds. Edge preparation costs are higher for these welds than for square-groove welds, and more filler metal is used in welding. Double V-groove welds require only about half as much filler metal as single V-groove welds, but edge preparation costs are higher, and the weldment may require manipulating to weld both sides. Cost of edge preparation should be weighed against the cost of welding when selecting the joint design.

Both single and double V-groove welds are suitable for all load conditions. Double V-groove welds are used to join plates of greater thickness where the work can be welded from both sides. Both types of V-groove welds are generally most economical when the depths of the grooves do not exceed 3/4″ (19 mm). As with square-groove welds, strength depends on the depth of penetration. Angular distortion of double V-groove welds can be reduced by alternating the beads—welding on one side and then the other to keep the joint aligned during welding.

Bevel-groove welds. Less joint preparation and filler metal are needed for these welds than for V-groove welds. Single bevel-groove welds are used, in most cases, for welding plates 1/2″ (13 mm) or thinner in work welded from only one side.

Double bevel-groove welds are suitable for longitudinal or transverse shear loads when welding can be done from both sides. The welds are generally most economical when the depths of the grooves do not exceed about 3/4″ (19 mm). Joint thickness should usually be 1 1/2″ (38 mm) or less for complete joint penetration.

J-groove welds. These welds have characteristics similar to bevel-groove welds. However, they are generally more economical for joining thick sections because less weld metal is required. Single J-groove welds are generally applied to plates 1″ (25 mm) and more in thickness. Double J-groove welds are often used for plates 1 1/2″ (38 mm) and more in thickness when welding can be done from both sides.

U-groove welds. These welds are used for applications similar to J-groove welds. Edge preparation costs are generally higher, but complete fusion is easier to obtain. Double J-groove welds require less weld metal than single U-groove welds, but edge preparation costs are higher, and the welds have to be made from both sides.

Other groove welds. Other types of groove welds used with the arc welding processes include V-groove welds with backing and flared V-groove and flared bevel-groove welds.

ARC WELDING DEFECTS

Defects commonly occurring as the result of arc welding include spatter, undercut, incomplete fusion, cracks, porosity, slag inclusions, inadequate joint penetration, and overlap. Distortion, common to other welding processes in addition to arc welding, is discussed in the introductory section of this chapter. Some of the discontinuities and corrective measures are summarized in Table 9-10.

Weld Spatter

Weld spatter may be objectionable from an appearance standpoint but of no consequence to the structural function of the weld; however, it may interfere with service if entrapped in an inaccessible cavity. Excessive spatter is not necessary, and its appearance on a weldment is an indication of improper welding. It may be caused by (1) excessive welding current, (2) wrong electrode, (3) wrong electrode polarity, (4) too large an electrode, (5) improper electrode position, (6) arc blow, discussed subsequently in this section, (7) too long an arc, (8) too little gas flow, or (9) dirty weld joint surfaces, or a combination of these factors.

To eliminate weld spatter: (1) select the proper current setting for the electrode size and the plate thickness, (2) be sure that the electrode does not have an inherent spatter-producing characteristic, (3) check to determine if the polarity is correct for the electrode, (4) use an electrode of the proper size for the plate thickness, (5) correct the electrode position for the procedure used, (6) see the discussion on arc blow for corrections, (7) decrease the arc length, (8) increase the gas flow (when the process uses gas), and (9) clean the surfaces to be joined. The application of antispatter compound to exposed surfaces adjacent to the weld joint can be helpful when sticking is encountered.

Undercut

Unless it is serious, undercut is more of an appearance discontinuity than a structural detriment. However, some inspection agencies will not accept undercut, particularly where cyclic loading is involved, and will demand that it be repaired by welding. For this reason, undercut should be avoided. It may be caused by the welding current and travel speed being too high, improper electrode position or manipulation, an excessive arc length, or too large an electrode. Undercut may be reduced by using the correct arc length, welding current, travel speed, and size of electrode. A uniform weave of the electrode will tend to prevent undercutting when making groove welds. Excessive weaving will cause undercut and slag inclusions and should be avoided.

Incomplete Fusion

Incomplete fusion is sometimes associated with inadequate joint penetration or cold laps and is a structural fault. Complete fusion is essential to full-strength welds. It should be the concern of both the welder and the inspector that correct procedures are used to obtain complete fusion. Incomplete fusion may be caused by improper current setting, welding technique, joint preparation, welding electrode size, electrode manipulation, or weldment positioning. All contact surfaces must be molten to achieve complete fusion by arc welding.

Thick plates require higher welding currents for a given electrode than thin plates do. Therefore, sufficient welding current should be used to ensure correct deposition of filler metal and a good depth of fusion in the base metal. In welding, the groove faces of the joint should be melted thoroughly. This is achieved by electrode manipulation and controlled by the weld current. In preparing the joint, the face of the groove should be clean and free of foreign material. The filler metal should be deposited using procedures that ensure good fusion between the joint faces. The electrode size for the first passes should be small enough to reach the root of the groove and yet permit good fusion.

Cracks

There are different kinds of cracks in welds, all of which are serious. All cracks should be examined to determine what corrective measures, if any, are needed. The most common cracks in a weld joint are crater cracks, underbead cracks, and

ARC WELDING DEFECTS

TABLE 9-10
Possible Causes and Suggested Solutions for Common Welding Problems

Problems	Possible Causes	Suggested Solutions
Excessive weld spatter	Too high a welding current	Use proper current setting
	Wrong, wet, unclean, or damaged electrode	Use proper electrode
	Wrong current polarity	Use correct polarity
	Arc blow	Reduce effect of arc blow
	Too long an arc	Use minimum arc length
Undercut	Too high a welding current	Use proper current setting
	Improper electrode manipulation	Correct welding procedure
	Travel speed too fast	Reduce speed
	Arc blow	Reduce effect of arc blow
Overlap	Too large an electrode	Reduce electrode size
	Travel speed too slow	Increase speed
	Improper electrode angle	Use correct angle
Poor fusion	Too low a welding current	Use proper current setting
	Improper welding technique	Correct welding procedure
	Improper joint preparation	Prepare joint correctly
	Improper electrode size	Use proper electrode
	Arc blow	Reduce effect of arc blow
Poor penetration	Too long an arc	Use minimum arc length
	Improper joint preparation	Prepare joint correctly
	Too low a welding current	Use proper current setting
	Improper size or type electrode	Use proper electrode
	Travel speed too fast	Reduce speed
Inclusions	Incomplete slag removal between passes	Completely remove slag
	Too large an electrode	Reduce size of electrode
	Travel speed erratic	Use uniform speed
	Improper welding technique	Correct welding procedure
Cracks	Base metal not weldable or clean	Use weldable metal and clean
	Improper joint preparation	Prepare joint correctly
	Improper welding technique	Correct welding procedure
	Joint restraint too rigid	Reduce restraint
	Welds too small or incorrect shape	Increase weld size; correct shape
	Cooling rate too rapid	Preheat before welding
	Defective electrode	Change electrode
Porosity	Improper or dirty base metal	Change base metal and clean
	Improper welding technique	Correct welding procedure
	Excessively long or short arc	Use proper arc length
	Welding current and travel speed too high	Reduce current and travel speed
	Wrong, wet, unclean, or damaged electrode	Use proper electrode
	Insufficient or improper shielding gas	Increase flow and check gas
Arc blow	Unbalanced magnetic field	Switch to a-c if possible and reduce welding current
	Excessive magnetism in parts or fixture	Reduce welding current and arc length. Move work connection as far from weld as possible. Weld toward a heavy tack weld or toward a completed weld
Distortion	Overwelding	Keep weld metal to a minimum
	Improper edge preparation	Keep bevel below 30°
	Improper tack welding	Tack-weld with allowance for distortion
	Excessive weld size	Make welds to specified size
	Improper setup and fixturing	Tack-weld or clamp parts securely

transverse and longitudinal cracks. Cracks in the heat-affected zone of metal along the edge of the weld are sometimes referred to as toe cracks.

Causes of cracks include: (1) base metal of poor weldability, (2) weld joints improperly prepared, (3) improper welding procedures, (4) excessive restraints on the joints (too rigid welds), (5) too small or poorly shaped welds, and (6) forces other than compression acting on the weld joint during cooling. Corrective measures to eliminate cracking include the following:

1. Avoid a high-sulfur, high-phosphorus steel. If it is necessary to weld this type of steel, use a low-hydrogen electrode. High-alloy and high-carbon steels, as well as thick low-carbon steels, should be preheated.

2. In preparing joints for welding, space the members so that the root opening is uniform. In some cases a root opening of 1/8" (3.2 mm) or more may be required in the welding groove; in other cases the parts may be butted closely together. The size of the weldment, the thickness of the base metal, and the welding process will determine the proper root opening.

3. Be sure that the welding procedure will provide sound welds with good fusion. Avoid welding with a stringer bead technique if cracking is a problem. Instead, use a weave-bead technique to deposit layers in the weld groove and complete sections 8-10" (203-254 mm) long. Too much heat input may result in hot cracking. Change to a less penetrating electrode. Weld uphill at 4° during the first pass to increase the weld bead cross section. Decrease the welding current and speed. Use a low-hydrogen electrode.

4. Be sure that both the structure to be welded and the welding sequence have been designed properly to minimize the restraint on the joints.

5. Always be sure that the weld metal has sufficient ductility to withstand the stresses that develop during welding. Do not use too small a weld bead between thick plates. Be sure to use welds of sufficient size on all joints.

6. Avoid crater cracks by filling the weld crater at the end of each weld bead or by reversing the direction of welding to end the weld on a finished bead instead of on base metal.

Porosity

Porosity in welds does not seriously affect weld strength unless the welds are extremely porous. Surface holes in the weld bead are undesirable from appearance and stress standpoints and can affect fatigue life. Another common form of porosity, aside from surface holes commonly referred to as blowholes, is gas pockets. One of the major causes of porosity is unsatisfactory base metal or incomplete cleaning prior to welding. Improper welding procedure also results in porosity. To reduce or avoid porosity:

1. Be sure that the base metal is clean and is a type that will not produce porosity in the weld. High sulfur, phosphorus, and silicon contents in steel sometimes produce gaseous reactions during welding that tend to cause blowholes and gas pockets. Nonferrous metals that are high in oxygen also tend to result in porous welds. Segregations and impurities in the base metal will contribute to porosity. The presence of hydrocarbons or moisture on the workpiece or electrode surface is also a source of porosity.

2. Change the welding procedure. Do not use excessive welding current, but be sure that each layer of weld metal is completely free of slag and flux before depositing the next layer. Decrease welding current and travel speed, reverse the polarity, and use a short arc. Most low-hydrogen electrodes will be helpful in eliminating porosity.

3. Ensure adequate gas shielding.

OTHER POTENTIAL PROBLEMS

Other problems sometimes encountered in arc welding include moisture pickup, arc blow, and burn-through.

Moisture Pickup

Covered electrodes exposed to humid conditions may pick up moisture in the covering. Excessive moisture may cause undercut, rough beads, porosity, and cracking. Moisture pickup is usually avoided by storing covered electrodes in a heated cabinet. If covered electrodes have become wet, they may be dried by baking them according to manufacturers' recommendations. Low-hydrogen electrodes that are not hermetically sealed in packages should be dried for at least two hours at a temperature between 450 and 500° F (230 and 260° C) before they are used. Some high tensile strength electrodes require baking at higher temperatures.

Arc Blow

Arc blow is a phenomenon encountered most frequently when welding with direct current. Current flowing through the electrode and the work sets up magnetic fields around the electrode that tend to deflect the arc from its intended path, particularly when the workpiece also has a high residual magnetic field. The arc may be deflected to the side, especially when welding longitudinal workpieces, but usually it is deflected either forward or backward from the direction of travel. Back blow is encountered when welding toward the ground connection, toward the end of a joint, or into a corner. Forward blow is encountered when welding away from the ground at the start of the joint. The conditions may become so severe that a satisfactory weld cannot be made, and incomplete fusion and excessive weld spatter are encountered. When welding with iron-powder electrodes or other heavily covered electrodes that produce thick slag covering, forward blow is especially troublesome because the forward fanning of the arc permits a heavy slag deposit on the crater to run forward under the arc.

The bending of the arc under these conditions, either forward or backward, is caused by the effects of an unbalanced magnetic field. When there is a greater concentration of magnetic flux on one side of the arc than the other, the arc always bends away from the greatest concentration.

During welding, magnetic flux is superimposed on the steel and across the joint to be welded. The flux in the plate does not cause difficulty, but an unequal concentration of flux across the unwelded joint or around the arc will cause the arc to bend away from the greater concentration. Because the flux passes through steel many times more readily than through air, the flux path tends to stay within the boundaries of the steel components. For this reason the magnetic flux around the electrode, when the electrode is near either end of the joint, must concentrate across the joint between the electrode and the end of the plate. This causes a high concentration of flux on one side of the arc at the start and finish of the weld, which tends to make the arc blow

ARC WELDING DEFECTS

away from the ends of the plates—a forward blow at the start end and a back blow at the finish.

The forward blow at the start of a weld is only momentary because the magnetic flux soon finds an easy path through the deposited weld metal behind the arc. Because the magnetic flux behind the arc is in the plate and weld, the arc is influenced mainly by the flux ahead of the arc, creating back blow as welding progresses along the joint. The flux ahead of the electrode becomes more concentrated as the arc approaches the end, with a corresponding increase in the back blow becoming very severe at the very end of the joint.

The welding current passing through the plates also causes the plates to act as a conductor with a flux field around it. The circles of flux are in planes perpendicular to the plates around the current path, between the electrode and the point at which the plates are grounded. This "ground effect" is most apparent on narrow plates, becoming less noticeable as the plates become wider.

Unless the arc blow is unusually severe, corrective steps will counteract the conditions causing the arc blow. All or only some of the following corrective steps may be necessary:

1. If the machine being used is of the type producing both alternating and direct current, switch to alternating current. Alternating the direction of the flow of current prevents the formation of strong magnetic fields. This method may be unacceptable for some qualified welding procedures.
2. Welding current may be reduced.
3. Weld toward a heavy tack weld or toward a weld already made.
4. Use a backstep sequence on long welds.
5. Connect additional copper leads to the existing ground lead and run them to different ground connection locations, making sure there are good ground contacts.
6. Place the work connection as far as possible from the joint to be welded.
7. If back blow is the problem, place the work connection at the start of the weld and weld toward a heavy tack weld.
8. If forward blow causes trouble, place the work connection at the end of the weld.
9. Wrap the work cable around the workpiece and pass current through it in such a direction that a magnetic field will be set up to neutralize the magnetic field causing the blow.
10. Hold as short an arc as possible to help the arc force counteract the arc blow.
11. Demagnetize the plate.

Burn-Through

The possibility of burn-through caused by a penetrating arc must be considered. Recommended designs to avoid burn-through are illustrated in Fig. 9-21.

PREHEATING AND STRESS RELIEVING

Preheating prior to arc welding, maintaining temperature during welding, and postheating after arc welding are often required, especially when welding hardenable steels. A detailed discussion of these heating processes is presented in the introductory section of this chapter.

Preheating and maintaining temperature during welding provide a slower cooling rate, reduce shrinkage stresses, and minimize the possibilities of cracking. Postheating relieves internal stresses, produces desired metallurgical (microstruc-

ture) changes affecting the properties of the base and weld metals, and provides dimensional stability.

METHODS OF APPLYING WELDING

For many years, arc welding has been applied by one of four methods: manual, semiautomatic, machine, and automatic welding. More recently, two new methods of application have been developed: automated and robotic arc welding.

Operator Factor

The operator factor is the ratio of arc time to total time. The operator factor for manual welding is usually in the 5 to 30% range due to the time needed to change electrodes and dependent on work organization. In semiautomatic welding, the operator factor increases to 10 to 50%, which greatly reduces the cost of depositing metal, but is still relatively low, again due to the fatigue factor of watching the arc, providing motion, and other requirements. Machine welding has an operator factor of from 40 to 75%, which greatly improves the productivity of welding. This is because the human fatigue factor is almost eliminated. However, the operator must still observe and supervise the welding equipment, and some time is required for equipment settings.

Automated and automatic welding have an operator factor of from 50 to 95% because the operator is not involved in making the weld, and the fatigue factor is greatly reduced. However, operators are still involved in loading and unloading equipment. The highest operator factor occurs when utilizing dual worktables or automatic feeding and unloading devices. A switch from manual or semiautomatic welding to machine, automatic, or automated welding will greatly reduce the cost of welding. This is true providing the volume requirements are

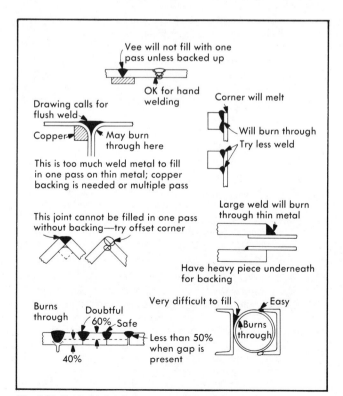

Fig. 9-21 Typical joint designs to avoid burn-through.

sufficiently high, in spite of the higher capital expense involved in automatic or automated equipment.

Method Selection

The decision as to which application method to use should be based on careful consideration of the following:

- Material, size, weight, and geometry of the components to be joined. It is generally difficult and costly to automate the welding of large, heavy, and complex-shaped parts.
- Design of the weld joint.
- Production requirements—batch size and frequency, including both present and anticipated future needs.
- Accuracy requirements for components to be assembled. Automation generally requires closer tolerances for parts to be assembled.
- Accuracy and quality requirements for the weldments that are produced.
- Initial, installation, and operating costs.
- Safety considerations.

Manual Welding

Manual welding, in which all functions are performed by hand, is used extensively for one-of-a-kind or low-production jobs; intricate welds that would otherwise require complicated and costly fixturing; large, heavy, and complex-shaped weldments; and many repair operations. A major disadvantage of manual welding is high cost because the process is so labor-intensive. Also, weld quality and productivity vary with the skill of the operator, and the working environment presents potential safety hazards.

Semiautomatic Welding

In semiautomatic welding, the maintenance of the arc and the feeding of the electrode are automatically controlled, but all the remaining functions, including the travel speed, are performed by the welder. This method is practical for medium-production requirements, long welds, or repetitive short welds.

Machine Welding

In machine welding, the machine performs the welding operation under the constant observation and control of an operator. For some applications, this method provides some of the desirable advantages of both semiautomatic and automatic welding. Carriages, tractors, or other devices are generally provided for travel motion, but the operator must observe the operation to make necessary corrections, such as proper arc placement in the joint. Major advantages include the capability for using high welding currents and multiple electrodes together with high welding speeds.

Automatic Welding

In automatic welding, the equipment performs the entire operation without the need for constant observation and adjustments by an operator. Such welding is generally warranted for high production volumes, when component fits and shapes allow, and the high cost of dedicated machines can be justified. Either the work or the gun, or both, are moved in automatic welding.

Possible benefits resulting from the use of automatic welding include improved and consistently uniform quality, increased productivity and reduced costs, and safer working conditions and improved environment for operators. Quality improvements result from more precise control of the welding parameters. Faster production often results from increased arc time. Cost savings ensue from reduced labor requirements, less material usage, and minimum scrap. Automatic welding can permit high welding currents, which provide high depths of penetration and fast deposition rates. More critical preparation of the workpieces, however, is generally required.

There are many types of standardized automatic equipment. For example, orbital pipe welding heads make circular welds on various diameters of pipe or tubing made from different materials and with various wall thicknesses. Self-propelled carriages are available for heavy-duty welding. A variety of other standardized welding tools provide arc motion or work motion; for example, seamers are used to produce longitudinal seams in small tanks made with thin shells.

Another type of standard automatic machine also used in making tanks is the welding lathe. In most applications, the tank heads fit inside the shells and fillet welds are made on the outside. Another specialized type of automatic machine often used in tank shops is known as a spud welder. These machines revolve the torches around vertical axes at the proper locations to weld spuds into the shells or heads of tanks.

Specialized or dedicated automatic welding machines are often employed in industries, such as automotive and appliance, where high production rates are required or lot sizes are large. While many dedicated machines are designed to weld a specific assembly, more complex machines are available that can be easily and quickly changed to accommodate a family of similar assemblies.

On many dedicated machines and fixtures, the workpieces normally move, and often the arc moves as well. Some machines are equipped with multiple arc welding guns and several workstations. Special cams or tracks are often used to provide guidance of the welding head(s). Control circuits for such machines are relatively simple and are based on time or position location for the start and stop of welding, with preset welding parameters.

Automated Arc Welding

Automated arc welding is welding with equipment that performs the entire operation without human observation or adjustment of controls. The process was developed to meet increasing demands for improved productivity and higher quality welds. It makes use of microprocessor memories, sensing devices, and programmable and adaptive controls. Sensing devices may continuously monitor the operation and feed back information to the control system, which modifies welding parameters or motion patterns to provide necessary changes. Quality welds are produced even when the weldment conditions are less than optimum, such as poorly fitted joints. Programs for automated welding can be recorded, stored, and reused when required.

The automated arc welding process produces more consistent, higher quality welds than automatic welding. While automatic welding can be programmed to produce quality welds, the results obtained depend on preparation of the components for welding. This preparation is usually not consistent. For example, springback can vary with different heats of metals to be joined, bend lines can differ and change joint fitup, flame-cut parts can vary because of torch tips,

ARC WELDING METHODS

cutting dies can also wear, and workpiece warpage during welding can affect results. All of these variations are accommodated with automated welding.

Robotic Arc Welding

Industrial robots are increasingly being applied to arc welding applications, primarily because of their versatility. High-volume production is not required for economical robotic arc welding. The versatility of robots makes them economically justifiable for low to medium production requirements. They are well suited for handling a variety of welding operations, small lot sizes, and parts having a variety of welds requiring different approach angles. Design changes are easily accommodated, and different parts are handled by changing the program and end-of-arm tooling.

Robots, however, are not applicable to all arc welding applications. Assemblies requiring welds that are difficult or awkward to reach and that necessitate long reaches are not generally suitable for robotic welding. Also, unlike a skilled operator, robots made with the present state of the art do not have the ability to sense what is happening during welding nor do they have the dexterity of an operator. Rapid advances in improved sensors and software capabilities, however, are narrowing the differences between robots and skilled welders.

Workcells or systems being used for robotic arc welding consist of five principal components: robot manipulator, controller, positioner, processing package, and tooling.

Robot manipulator. The most common arc welding robot manipulator is the articulated arm robot shown in Fig. 9-22. Other types, such as rectilinear or gantry robots, are less common. Robot manipulators are differentiated by their number of axes, work envelopes, repeatability, and types of drive.

Number of axes. An arc welding robot needs a minimum of five axes to perform effectively: three axes position the welding torch at the proper point in space, and two axes position the torch with the proper tilt and lead angles with respect to the weld joint. A sixth axis enables a robot to access difficult-to-reach joints and to follow the contour of a complex weld path.

Work envelopes. The work envelope is the space in which the robot manipulator can move the torch. In arc welding, the effective work envelope is smaller than the work envelope. A part may fit within the work envelope and at the same time not be able to be welded by the robot. In robotic arc welding, part of the robot's work envelope is used by the torch to gain access to the part and to position the torch at the proper tilt and lead angles with respect to the weld joint.

Repeatability. Repeatability is a measure of how close a robot can return the torch to a programmed point. When a robot is specified as having a repeatability of 0.008" (0.20 mm), it means that it can be taught a given point in space and return to that point within a radius of 0.008". The robot's total repeatability band is approximately 1/64" (0.4 mm) wide, and, under most circumstances, the width of the weld bead is not controlled to this accuracy. Because control of the weld bead width is normally less accurate than the control over the robot position, increasing robot repeatability to better than 0.008" does not improve the weld.

Types of drive. Arc welding robots are manufactured with both hydraulic and electric drives. Electric-drive robots are predominately used because, although robots with hydraulic drives have larger weight-handling capacity, the additional capacity is not required for moving a welding torch. A robot that can lift 20 lb (9 kg) is more than adequate for most arc

welding applications. A breakaway torch bracket provides an important feature to the welding robot by preventing damage to the robot during a collision with a part.

Robot controllers. The robot controller directs the workcell, exercising control over the manipulator, processing package, wire feeder, positioner, and tooling. The controller is generally instructed by the teach method of programming, which puts the controller through its cycle one step at a time. Recorded in the controller memory is the location of the three axes that locate the torch (X, Y, and Z coordinates) and the two axes that locate the torch tilt and lead angles.

If the arc is to be turned on, the controller is taught to turn the welding set on and to set the weld parameters. If a positioner is part of the workcell, the controller is instructed to move the positioner into the proper position. The controller may be taught to sense that the part is in position in the tooling through its external input signals.

The controller may also be instructed through its external output signals to activate air cylinders to clamp the part. The robot controller memorizes each step in the sequence of welding the part. Once the program is memorized, the controller plays back the sequence exactly as the program was taught.

Linear interpolation is an important feature of an arc welding robot controller. When a robot is programmed to make a weld on a straight line, the robot is taught one point at one end

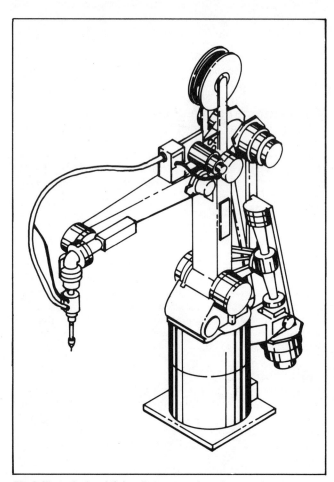

Fig. 9-22 Articulated (jointed) arm type of manipulator for robotic arc welding. (*Advanced Robotics Corp.*)

of the weld and a second point at the other end of the weld. Linear interpolation is the software feature of the robot controller that enables it to calculate the locations of the intermediate points. The linear interpolation feature also enables the controller to calculate the weld travel speed at the torch and to maintain constant torch tilt and lead angles with respect to the weld path.

When a robot controller is doing linear interpolation, it has to know the exact location of the end of the torch. Torch definition is the process of defining to the controller the exact location of the end of the torch. The location of the end of the torch, including its electrode stickout, must be measured and the values entered into the controller. After the torch definition is set and a program is taught, the torch definition cannot be changed without adversely affecting the program.

Circular interpolation is similar to linear interpolation, but three or more points are taught to the controller. The controller interpolates the intermediate points on a circular path through the points. A complete circle can be interpolated using four points spaced every 90 degrees.

A controller's ability to provide a wide range of welding travel speeds is important for a welding robot. A general-purpose welding robot needs to have a welding travel speed selection range varying from 2 to 200 ipm (50 to 5100 mm/min). This speed range will accommodate most arc welding processes. The speeds must be selectable in increments of 1 ipm (25 mm/min).

Robot controllers generally use two methods of selecting the welding process parameters. The older method has the controller select from among several independently preset, but not programmably set, combinations of weld process parameters. In this method, nation can be selected in the robot program.

Weld process parameters are not usually set using the familiar units of arc volts and rate of wire feed for gas metal arc welding. The robot programmer inputs so-called argument values into the robot controller, and the controller translates these values into the arc voltage and wire feed rate. This is somewhat inconvenient because the programmer must make a conversion from desired weld parameters to the argument values. This conversion is necessary because robots are generally designed to be interfaced with many different sizes and types of welding sets.

Means provided for editing the welding process parameters are important to optimizing the program. The important welding process parameters are arc voltage, wire feed rate, and travel speed. When a part is first programmed, these parameters will probably not be set at their optimum values. Adjusting the parameters will be necessary to arrive at the optimum values. The only way to accomplish this is to weld parts and observe the results.

Some controllers allow the arc voltage, wire feed rate, and travel speed to be adjusted while the robot is welding. This capability makes a robot easier to use. The programmer receives immediate feedback on the effects of parameter adjustments. As a result, the programmer can optimize the process using fewer parts and less time.

Other controllers allow the weld parameter adjustments to be made only while the controller is in an edit mode. With this type of controller, the programmer must weld a part, observe the result, edit the program, and then weld another part to observe the effect of the change in the weld parameter.

Program capacity is measured in terms of the number of points a controller can store in memory. Any robot with 1000 points of program capacity will probably exceed the require-

ments of most applications. Robots with 2000 points of program capacity are common. To put the size of programs in perspective, most programs have between 25 and 100 points. A 200-point program is a very large program that might commonly take 15 minutes to run. Often a tape recorder is connected to the controller to record the programs on tape.

Software diagnostics simplify robot programming, operation, and repair. The controller diagnostics can be evaluated based on the number of fault conditions identified and whether the fault condition is displayed as an error code or an English text description of the fault. A controller identifying 100 different fault conditions is common. The English text error messages are preferred to the coded error messages.

Positioners. Positioners used with welding robots can be distinguished by their number of axes, whether they have indexing or continuously variable positioning capability, and whether they can move in coordinated motion with the robot. Rotate and tilt are the two most common positioner axes; indexing positioners can only move between discrete positions.

In teaching a program using an index positioner, the programmer commands the controller to move the positioner to one of its index positions. Then, with the positioner stationary, the robot makes the welds that are accessible. A continuously variable positioner can be commanded to move to any position, and then, with the positioner stationary, the robot welds the part. Coordinated motion allows the programmer to specify torch speed and location relative to the weld joint.

Processing package (welding set). The processing package consists of the torch, wire feeder, water cooler, and welding power supply. Considerations in selecting this equipment do not differ significantly from other automated applications. The equipment must meet the capacity and duty cycle requirements of the application.

Tooling. Tooling (jigs, fixtures, clamps, and gages) is an important consideration in all welding operations and is discussed in a subsequent section of this chapter.

Sensors. Through-the-arc sensing is a common method of weld joint tracking available on arc welding robots that use the gas metal arc welding process. This contacting (tactile) seam-tracking method oscillates the torch across the joint and measures the changes in arc current as a result of changes in electrode stickout. The method is limited to joints with sidewalls that can be tracked. It cannot put a bead on a plate or a cover pass on a joint because the joints have no edges to track. Fillet welds are ideal for through-the-arc tracking.

Noncontacting, automatic seam-tracking systems are more versatile in handling various types of joints and workpieces and are able to obtain more data on the physical characteristics of the weld joint. Some noncontacting sensing methods use vision (including lasers), arc sensing, acoustics, magnetics, electro-magnetics (reluctance and eddy currents), and capacitive techniques. Visual and arc-sensing methods have been most successful with the present state of the art.

Robotic arc welding processes. Gas metal arc welding (GMAW) is the predominant welding process used in robotic arc welding. Occasionally, the gas tungsten arc welding (GTAW) or plasma arc welding (PAW) processes are also used with robots. Other welding processes are rarely used with welding robots. The high-frequency arc starter used with the GTAW and PAW processes can cause interference with the robot controller, which can make the controller unreliable. Robot controllers and high-frequency arc starters must be specially designed to overcome this problem.

ARC WELDING METHODS

Joint designs. Joint designs for robotic arc welding are most frequently single-pass fillets and partial-penetration welds. The reason for this is that parts that are small enough to be quickly moved in and out of a workcell do not require more weld metal than this to perform their intended function.

The ideal joint design for robotics consists of intermittent fillets in varying locations around the part. This type of weld joint takes advantage of the robot's best features. The robot can accurately locate the joint, make the weld, and then skip on to the next weld at high speed.

Robots can make multiple-pass fillet welds, partial-penetration groove welds, and full-penetration welds with backing strips. The oscillation and weaving functions that are common on many robots can easily be used to fill a groove weld in 1/2″ (12.7 mm) plate in one pass.

Safety considerations. Hazards exist with robotic arc welding because of possible malfunctions or operator carelessness. It is essential to ensure that nothing or no one is in the path of the robot movements. Protection can be provided by the use of proper warning and feedback devices. Interlocked barriers and presence-sensing devices are commonly used to surround the robot cell and prevent intrusion. The Robotic Industries Association (RIA) has introduced a Proposed American National Standard for Industrial Robots and Robot Systems containing guidelines for the construction, installation, care, and use of robots.

Tooling for Arc Welding

For either manual or automatic arc welding techniques, some tooling is usually necessary in the form of jigs, fixtures, clamps, dies, or gages. These tools frequently are inexpensive, and small-lot production lends itself to temporary tooling. The tooling itself is almost invariably of welded construction, which helps minimize cost and makes for versatility and flexibility.

The primary function of welding jigs and fixtures is to bring parts into accurate alignment and to present the assembled components in the best position for welding, which is downhand wherever possible, requiring joints to be in flat or near-flat position. In welding parlance, jigs are considered stationary while fixtures rotate, usually on trunnions, about a vertical or horizontal axis, either by hand operation or through motor and reduction-gear drive. Many standard types of welding positioners and tables can be purchased or built. They are readily adaptable to a wide variety of work, at lower cost than with more intricate and special single-purpose devices.

Fabrication of jigs and fixtures by arc welding is generally advisable. In most cases, standard steel shapes can be used, and the cost of patterns for castings avoided. Furthermore, welded construction permits easy modification. If a jig or fixture does not function exactly as anticipated the first time, economical alterations may be made by torch cutting and rewelding. Lightweight, high strength, portability, and easy storage are other advantages. If wear is involved, surfaces may be hard-faced with special high-alloy welding electrodes. As with any form of tooling, precision is needed in the construction of welding jigs, and stress relieving is seldom required.

Old or discarded machine equipment may sometimes be modified to serve as welding jigs, at a considerable savings over building an entirely new unit. A radial drill or perhaps an outmoded lathe might be adapted conveniently, with the addition of some air or toggle clamps to position the elements of a weldment.

For assembly of both large and small weldments, it is sometimes practical to provide two jigs, the first for assembly and positioning of the various components before they are manually tack welded. The tack-welded assembly is then transferred to a second jig, or simply to the floor, for completion of the welds either manually or automatically. In this way, distortion is held to a minimum, and accurate alignments are better assured.

For large weldments, especially when only two or three are being made, jigs and fixtures can be eliminated. Parts can be aligned for welding with the aid of a scale and square and then clamped for welding with C-clamps, wedges, or other holding devices such as magnetic clamps.

Many other expedients have been devised to minimize distortion and warpage. The problem of warpage is critical in welding thin material and can be overcome by using jigs or clamps of copper to which water-cooling tubes have been soldered. Another method of compensating for warpage is to shape jigs or fixtures with suitable curvature or camber so that when the weldment is completed it will allow for distortion to the desired final contour.

Costs can be materially reduced by exercising care in cutting, forming, and handling shapes to be welded to avoid a poor fitup in the jig. A gap of 1/64-1/32″ (0.4-0.8 mm) is preferable in most joints, helping to prevent angular distortion and weld cracking. However, such gaps should be uniform along the joint, particularly in automatic welding; the width of the gap affects welding speed significantly.

Basic principles governing the design of good jigs and fixtures for welded assemblies include the following:

1. Whenever possible, a fixture should be a positioner, enabling all welds to be brought to a convenient welding position.
2. A fixture should be strong and light, but sufficiently rigid to ensure accurate alignment.
3. A fixture should be easily and quickly positioned (by one hand, if possible); balancing may be necessary to enable this to be done. The use of light alloys will reduce the weight of moving parts. Air motors or electric motors are used for revolving fixtures, and air or hydraulic rams or racks are used for tilting fixtures.
4. The design should be as simple and inexpensive as possible; accuracy and elaboration should be no greater than required. Appearance should be disregarded. Welded construction is best, toolroom work should be avoided, and machining should be kept to a minimum.
5. A fixture should be built around the work and should locate and clamp components in position so that assembly, tacking, and welding may be carried out in one fixture. The fixture should ensure one-way correct assembly only.
6. Only essential dimensions should be controlled in a fixture.
7. Freedom of movement in one plane should be permitted to avoid locked-up stresses. Floating anchorage is recommended.
8. Joints must be readily accessible for welding. By slots or other means, the fixture should readily present seams on the reverse side of the object.
9. Parts should be prebent in the fixture, if necessary, for final accuracy.
10. Heat distortion should release rather than bind the

work in the fixture. Rams or bumpers may be used to dislodge heat-bound parts.

11. Fixtures should be kept cool to the touch by air, water, fins, or insulated handles.
12. Positioning of the operator by ladders, trestles, cradles, or trolleys is sometimes advisable.
13. If necessary, the fixture should be mounted on a separate positioner, form, or cradle. To facilitate shop flow, fixtures or positioners may be mounted on wheels or used in conjunction with floor-mounted or overhead conveyors.
14. Positioners with indexing arrangements may be used to give accurate, quick positioning.
15. Either integral or separate copper backing bars should be used in cases of poor fit or for light plate.
16. Clamps must operate quickly. Screws and moving parts should be protected against spatter. Avoid fusion to the fixture or clamps by slots or copper backing. Clamps and locating devices should not be separate from the fixture, but permanently part of it. Hinge them, if possible.
17. Loose nuts and bolts, wrenches, C-clamps, wedges and hammers, or hand screws should be avoided.
18. Quick-acting toggle clamps, eccentrics and cams, cranks, pinion and rack, air and hydraulic rams, solenoids, or magnetic clamps should be used.
19. Integral gas backing is highly important for some alloys and shapes of backup grooves.

Robotic arc welding. Unlike a skilled welder, a robot does not recognize and does not correct for deficiencies in the tooling. If the tool does not position the part correctly, the robot may weld the part in the wrong location. If the tool controls the part position by rigidly fixturing the part prior to welding, the distortion from welding can cause the part to bind in the fixture and be difficult to remove. For a tool to be successful, the stackup of tolerances must be controlled, the part must be accurately positioned, and the part must not bind in the fixture after welding. After meeting all these requirements, the fixture must be capable of being quickly loaded and unloaded so that operation of the fixture does not cause the robot to be idle an excessive amount of time.

Tooling may restrict accessibility to the part. The motion of the torch and the robot around the part must be investigated to ensure adequate accessibility. In some cases, part of the fixture can be removed by an air cylinder midway through the weld cycle to improve access. The operation of the air cylinder could be part of the controller program. In other cases, manually tacking the part in a fixture and then robotically welding the tacked part in a simple fixture is the best solution to the accessibility problem. Fixtures for robotic arc welding are generally custom designed for specific parts, the major requirement being to accurately locate the parts to be joined in their best positions.

Automatic and automated arc welding. Tooling problems in automatic arc welding are so dependent on the nature of the job to be done that few basic principles for guidance can be detailed. Each job must be studied and the solution worked out for it. Engineers employed by the manufacturers of automatic welding equipment are available for consultation and help in designing tooling.

Because arc blow, when using direct current, can be a problem common to different types of jobs, several basic principles apply to designing fixtures to minimize arc blow, including the following:

1. Make the clamping fingers and as much of the fixture as possible of nonmagnetic material.
2. Keep all steel parts far enough from the work and the arc so that very little detrimental magnetic-flux path will cross the gap to be welded or be in the way of the arc. A 1" (25 mm) minimum distance between steel parts and the work is recommended, with the top members 2" (50 mm) away from the arc.
3. Always ground at the start end. Try to have the actual point of contact between ground and work at the start end of the seam. Try the ground on the following locations before deciding which is best: (a) start end of top clamping fingers and (b) start end of work.
4. Weld toward the closed end of the fixture or close both ends so that there is a bridge for the magnetic flux at both ends; most of the flux will circulate in the frame rather than across the gap to be welded.
5. Eliminate tack welds, if possible, except at the very end of the seam. Tabs at the finish end are usually helpful. They provide an easy path for the flux that would otherwise crowd across the gap at the end of the weld.
6. If necessary, reduce travel speed.

In automated welding, the work is usually stationary and the welding head or arc moves. In these cases, the workholding devices may merely be a welding table with hold-down clamps. As the production rate increases, the complexity of various fixtures required to hold the individual pieces in specific locations generally increases. Such fixtures may involve tunnel clamps or even clamps powered with air or hydraulic cylinders.

For more complicated weldments, workholding fixtures may be mounted on universal positioners. Fixtures of this type have a tilt function from vertical to horizontal and may have a rotation function of 360°. This means that there are two axes of motion on the work motion device. The level of control determines whether they are coordinated or not.

The accuracy of motion devices is extremely important and, as the weldment becomes more complex or thinner materials or specific procedures are used, the accuracy must be improved. The highest degree of accuracy utilizes feedback sensing devices that monitor the location and provide signals to the controller of the exact location on a continuous basis.

Other work-motion devices can be rotating fixtures or rings, or headstock/tailstock units. Many special types of work-motion devices are available, and many of these are standardized and based on specific sizes and weight capacities. It is important to select devices having the weight capacity required. Weight capacity involves off-center loading, both from the vertical and rotational axes. As the off-center loading increases, the capacity of the machines must be reduced. It is also important to determine the accuracy required for the particular job because accuracy requirements increase the cost of this equipment.

The workholding device is usually custom-made for the particular weldment. Many such devices are used for tacking purposes only, while others may be used for the complete welding operation. Design of these fixtures is extremely important because torch accessibility must be provided for. Workholding fixtures must also be built sufficiently robust to counteract warpage forces involved in making the weldment; in addition, they must be easy to load and unload and must be protected against weld spatter and other possible abuses.

CHAPTER 9

ARC WELDING COSTS

ESTIMATING THE COST OF ARC WELDING

Determining arc welding costs is difficult because of the many variables involved. Most of the variables can be classified into labor, material, and overhead costs. Detailed welding procedure schedules can be helpful in cost estimating by specifying the following:

- Metals to be joined.
- Type of joint and weld, and weld size, all of which establish the amount of weld material required to complete the joint.
- The specific process to be used and the method of application (manual, semiautomatic, or automatic).
- Edge preparation requirements, which vary with material thickness and joint design.
- Material requirements: type and size of electrode or filler wire, flux, shielding gases, and any other consumables.
- Welding current, arc voltage, and polarity.
- Preheating and postheating, if required.
- Inspection requirements.
- Finishing requirements: straightening, machining, blasting, peening, grinding, or polishing.

Labor costs are based primarily on time: time per weld, time per increment of weld length, or time to weld an assembly. Such times depend on travel speed and deposition rates. Labor costs also include setup, fitup, and handling times, as well as arc time.

Manual Welding

Labor and overhead generally account for about 80 to 86% of the cost of making a joint. Electrode cost may be from 8 to 15% of the total cost. Power and equipment costs are usually as low as 2%. For most manual arc welding processes, it is only necessary to calculate electrode, labor, and overhead costs.

First, however, electrode consumption must be determined. Electrode requirements are estimated by the equation:

$$W = \frac{D}{1 - l} \qquad (1)$$

where:

W = weight of the electrodes required, lb (kg)
D = weight of the metal deposited, lb (kg)

l = percentage of electrode weight lost as stub ends, spatter, or flux coating

To find the weight of metal deposited, calculate the volume of deposited metal (the area of the weld multiplied by its length) and convert to weight by multiplying by the density of the weld metal in lb/in.^{3} (kg/mm^3). Tables 9-11 through 9-14 provide electrode weight requirements for welding steel, 0.283 lb/in.^{3} (0.008 kg/mm^3), in various joint configurations.

The divisor l in Eq. (1) is usually greater than 30% for any type of manual arc welding using coated electrodes. This percentage may be used as a first estimate, but the true percentage of electrode loss in operation should be found for each welding method and job production tests. After this percentage and the weight of the electrodes required are found, the electrode cost may be determined by multiplying the total weight by the electrode price per pound.

TABLE 9-11
Electrode Consumption Data for
Single Horizontal Fillet Weld in Steel

Fillet Size, in. (mm)	Electrodes Required, approx., lb/lin ft (kg/lin m) of weld*	Steel Deposited, lb/lin ft (kg/lin m) of weld
1/8 (3.2)	0.048 (0.07)	0.027 (0.04)
3/16 (4.8)	0.113 (0.17)	0.063 (0.09)
1/4 (6.4)	0.189 (0.28)	0.106 (0.16)
5/16 (7.9)	0.296 (0.44)	0.166 (0.25)
3/8 (9.5)	0.427 (0.64)	0.239 (0.36)
1/2 (12.7)	0.760 (1.13)	0.425 (0.63)
5/8 (15.9)	1.185 (1.76)	0.663 (0.99)
3/4 (19.1)	1.705 (2.54)	0.955 (1.42)
1 (25.4)	3.030 (4.51)	1.698 (2.53)

* Includes scrap ends and spatter.

TABLE 9-12
Electrode Consumption Data for Butt-Joint, Square-Groove Welds Welded on One Side in Steel

Base Metal Thickness, in. (mm)	Weld Width, in. (mm)	Gap Width, in. (mm)	Electrodes Required, approx., lb/lin ft (kg/lin m) of weld* Without Reinforcement	With Reinforcement**	Steel Deposited, lb/lin ft (kg/lin m) of weld Without Reinforcement	With Reinforcement**
3/16 (4.8)	3/8 (9.5)	0	---	0.16 (0.24)	---	0.088 (0.13)
		1/16 (1.6)	0.04 (0.06)	0.20 (0.30)	0.020 (0.03)	0.109 (0.16)
1/4 (6.4)	7/16 (11.1)	1/16 (1.6)	0.05 (0.07)	0.23 (0.34)	0.027 (0.04)	0.129 (0.19)
		3/32 (2.4)	0.07 (0.10)	0.26 (0.39)	0.039 (0.06)	0.143 (0.21)
5/16 (7.9)	1/2 (12.7)	1/16 (1.6)	0.06 (0.09)	0.27 (0.40)	0.033 (0.05)	0.153 (0.23)
		3/32 (2.4)	0.09 (0.13)	0.030 (0.45)	0.050 (0.07)	0.170 (0.25)

* Includes scrap ends and spatter.
** Reinforcement is the convex buildup of 0.07″ (1.8 mm) of weld metal on the weld face.

TABLE 9-13
Electrode Consumption Data for Butt-Joint, Square-Groove Welds Welded on Both Sides in Steel

Joint Dimensions, in. (mm)			Electrodes Required, approx., lb/lin ft (kg/lin m) of weld*		Steel Deposited, lb/lin ft (kg/lin m) of weld	
Base Metal Thickness, in. (mm)	Weld Width, in. (mm)	Gap Width, in. (mm)	Without Reinforcement	With Reinforcement**	Without Reinforcement	With Reinforcement**
1/8 (3.2)	1/4 (6.4)	0	---	0.21 (0.31)	---	0.119 (0.18)
		1/32 (0.8)	0.03 (0.04)	0.24 (0.36)	0.013 (0.02)	0.132 (0.20)
3/16 (4.8)	3/8 (9.5)	1/32 (0.8)	0.04 (0.06)	0.36 (0.54)	0.020 (0.03)	0.199 (0.30)
		1/16 (1.6)	0.07 (0.10)	0.39 (0.58)	0.040 (0.06)	0.218 (0.32)
1/4 (6.4)	7/16 (11.1)	1/16 (1.6)	0.10 (0.15)	0.147 (0.22)	0.053 (0.08)	0.261 (0.39)
		3/32 (2.4)	0.14 (0.21)	0.53 (0.79)	0.080 (0.12)	0.288 (0.43)

* Includes scrap ends and spatter.
** Reinforcement is the convex buildup of 0.07″ (1.8 mm) of weld metal on each weld face.

Total labor and overhead cost may be found by use of the following equation:

$$L = \frac{FH}{R} \qquad (2)$$

where:

L = total labor and overhead cost
F = length to be welded, ft (m)
H = labor and overhead rate per hour
R = rate of welding, ft/hr (m/hr)

The percentage of time that the welder is actually welding, the *operating factor*, must be divided into the total labor and overhead cost from this equation to determine the true cost of labor and overhead. The manual electrode welder is usually welding only 30% of the time or less; so the answer to this equation should be divided by 0.30 for a more accurate cost estimate.

Automatic Welding

Automatic welding with wire electrodes has a much higher deposition efficiency than manual welding. Whereas the deposition efficiency of manual welding is less than 70% because of flux coatings, stub ends, and spatter, the efficiency of automatic wire welding is 90% or higher. Therefore, a practical electrode cost equation for automatic wire welding is:

$$C = \frac{PE}{0.90} \qquad (3)$$

where:

C = electrode cost per foot (meter) of weld
P = weight of deposit per foot (meter) of weld, lb (kg)
E = price per pound of electrode wire

The electrode cost per foot (meter), C, is multiplied by the length of the weld for total electrode cost. For submerged arc

TABLE 9-14
Electrode Consumption Data for Butt-Joint, Single V-Groove Welds in Steel

Joint Dimensions, in. (mm)			Electrodes Required, approx., lb/lin ft (kg/lin m) of weld*		Steel Deposited, lb/lin ft (kg/lin m) of weld	
Base Metal Thickness, in. (mm)	Weld Face Width, in. (mm)	Gap Width, in. (mm)	Without Reinforcement	With Reinforcement**	Without Reinforcement	With Reinforcement**
1/4 (6.4)	0.207 (5.26)	1/16 (1.6)	0.15 (0.22)	0.25 (0.37)	0.085 (0.13)	0.143 (0.21)
5/16 (7.9)	0.311 (7.90)	3/32 (2.4)	0.31 (0.46)	0.46 (0.68)	0.173 (0.26)	0.258 (0.38)
3/8 (9.5)	0.414 (10.52)	1/8 (3.2)	0.50 (0.74)	0.70 (1.04)	0.282 (0.42)	0.394 (0.59)
1/2 (12.7)	0.558 (14.17)	1/8 (3.2)	0.87 (1.29)	1.15 (1.71)	0.489 (0.73)	0.641 (0.95)
5/8 (15.9)	0.702 (17.83)	1/8 (3.2)	1.35 (2.01)	1.68 (2.50)	0.753 (1.12)	0.942 (1.40)
3/4 (19.1)	0.847 (21.51)	1/8 (3.2)	1.94 (2.89)	2.35 (3.50)	1.088 (1.62)	1.320 (1.96)
1 (25.4)	1.138 (28.91)	1/8 (3.2)	3.45 (5.13)	4.00 (5.95)	1.930 (2.87)	2.240 (3.33)

* Includes scrap ends and spatter.
** Reinforcement is the convex buildup of 0.07″ (1.8 mm) on the weld face.

ARC WELDING COSTS

welding, the weight of the flux used is usually proportional to the weight of electrode used and can be accounted for by applying the appropriate factor to the electrode cost.

Labor and overhead costs for automatic welding are determined by the equation:

$$L = \frac{H}{T[(60 \text{ min/hr})/X]} \quad (4)$$

where:

L = total labor and overhead cost per foot (meter) of weld
H = labor and overhead cost per hour
T = travel speed, ipm (m/min)
X (English) = 12 in./ft
X (metric) = 1

Again, an operating factor must be applied to L to account for the percentage of time that the welder is actually welding. For automatic welding, this factor is usually greater than 60%.

If gas shielding is used in the automatic welding process, gas costs may be determined by the equation:

$$G = \frac{fc}{T[60 \text{ min/hr}]/X} \quad (5)$$

where:

G = gas cost per foot (meter) of weld
f = gas flow, ft^3/hr (m^3/hr)
c = gas price per cubic foot (cubic meter)
T = travel speed, ipm (m/min)
X (English) = 12 in./ft
X (metric) = 1

Cost savings may be obtained by automatic welding as a result of savings in metal finishing and cleaning costs, increases in work volume per work center, reductions in checking and straightening, decreases in area cleanup time, reductions in manufacturing cycle time, and many other factors. Each of these factors should be considered as part of the automatic welding cost estimate when automatic welding is being considered.

Reducing Welding Costs

In addition to the possibility of reducing costs by using semiautomatic or automatic arc welding, there are other cost-saving methods, both in weldment design and arc welding procedures.

Design. Major savings can be realized by specifying an easily weldable material that will not require costly electrodes or complex welding procedures. Proper joint design also provides cost savings. For thick metals, double-bevel and double-V welds reduce weld material requirements if welding can be done from both sides of the assembly. The cross-sectional area of all welds should be the minimum required for strength, and easy access should be provided to all joints to be welded. Intermittent fillet welds often provide sufficient strength with reduced costs.

In some cases, welded joints can be eliminated by using formed, bent, or rolled sections in the design, or bending the corners of plates. Overwelding and extra reinforcements should be avoided. Reinforcements and unequal-legged fillets waste weld metal and sometimes add little strength to the weldment.

Procedures. The availability of and adherence to detailed welding procedure schedules are essential for economy. Use of

the arc welding process that provides the highest deposition rate is generally the most economical. Positioning the workpieces to permit flat welding permits optimum efficiency, allows the use of larger electrodes, and is easier and more comfortable for the welder. Slight angles from absolutely flat, however, can sometimes result in significant increases in deposition rates.

Proper fitup requires accurately prepared components. Wide gaps between the pieces to be welded waste weld metal. Joint edges should be dry and clean of all foreign matter. The use of proper fixtures and welding sequences to minimize distortion reduces the need for subsequent straightening, machining, or other finishing. An efficient and proper size machine, the correct electrode and other consumables, and optimum operating parameters are all essential for minimum welding costs. Flux, if used, should be free from contamination by foreign matter.

PLANT LAYOUT FOR WELDING

Welding operations may be confined to a single department, with the product moved to and from it in the manufacturing sequence, or they may be integrated with the full production flow, along with presses, machine tools, assembly, and finishing equipment. Both arrangements have their merits. When straight-line material flow is dictated, it is frequently more advantageous to install welding equipment on-line. Even in the case of small assemblies, it is often possible to incorporate welding machines, particularly the automatic or semiautomatic types, directly into the production line. It may even prove expedient to have operators handle other processing equipment in addition to welding.

The total amount of space required for welding operations will naturally vary according to the scope of the operations and the size of the plant the operations are expected to service. In no case should operators be cramped into small booths. Awkward working conditions increase operator fatigue. Ventilating exhaust fans at the booths will also add to the efficiency and safety of the operators by removing irritating gases and fumes. Each welding station should be arranged to allow for free flow of material to and from the operation. It may also be desirable to provide storage space at the stations for some jigs and fixtures, if their frequency of use warrants. Providing for inspection during welding operations should also be taken into consideration when laying out the welding booths. It is prudent to provide for progressive expansion in allotting the area for welding operations.

SHIELDED METAL ARC WELDING

Shielded metal arc welding (SMAW) is an arc welding process that produces coalescence (joining) of metals by heating them with an arc between a covered (or coated) metal electrode and the work (see Fig. 9-23). Shielding is provided by decomposition of the electrode covering. Pressure is not used, and filler metal is obtained from the electrode. The SMAW process is commonly called stick-electrode or manual welding.

Applications

The shielded metal arc method is one of the oldest and the most widely used of the various arc welding processes. It is basically a manual process used by small welding shops, home mechanics, and farmers for the repair of equipment. The process also has extensive application in industrial fabrication, structural steel erection, weldment manufacture, and other commercial metals joining operations.

SHIELDED METAL ARC WELDING

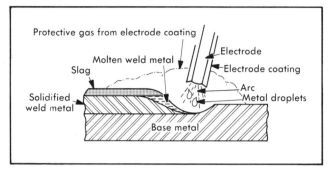

Fig. 9-23 Shielded metal arc welding. (*Hobart Brothers Co.*)

Advantages

Major advantages of shielded metal arc welding include application versatility and flexibility and the simplicity, portability, and low cost of the equipment required. The process is capable of welding thin and thick steels and some nonferrous metals in all positions. Table 9-15 lists some of the base metals and alloys welded with this method. Power-supply leads can be provided over long distances, and no hoses are required for shielding gas.

Limitations

Required periodic changing of the electrode is one of the major disadvantages of shielded metal arc welding for produc-

TABLE 9-15
Conditions for Joining Various Metals and Alloys by Shielded Metal Arc Welding

Base Metal or Alloy	Electrode Type	Electrode Classification	Welding Current and Polarity*
Aluminum and alloys**	Aluminum	Al-43	DCEP
Brass, navy	Not used		
Bronze:			
Aluminum**	Aluminum bronze	ECuAlA2	a-c or DCEP
Phosphor**	Phosphor bronze	ECuSnC	DCEP
Silicon**	Aluminum bronze	ECuAlA2	a-c or DCEP
Copper (deoxidized)**	Phosphor bronze	ECuSnC	DCEP
Copper nickel**	Copper nickel	ECuNi	DCEN or a-c
Inconel	Inconel	ENiCr1	DCEP
Iron:			
Cast	Nickel-based	ENi	DCEP
Wrought	Mild steel	E6010	DCEP
Lead	Not used		
Magnesium	Not used		
Monel	Monel	ENiCu1	DCEP
Nickel	Nickel	ENi1	DCEP
Nickel silver	Not used		
Steel:			
High-carbon	Low-hydrogen	†	‡
Low-alloy	Low-hydrogen	†	‡
Low-carbon	Mild steel	E60XX†	a-c or d-c
Manganese	Austenitic manganese	EFeMn-A	DCEP or a-c
Medium-carbon	Low-hydrogen	†	‡
Stainless (304)	Stainless steel	†	DCEP or a-c
Weathering	Low-alloy, low-hydrogen	E8018-C2	DCEP
Titanium	Not used		
Tungsten	Not used		

  * DCEP: d-c, electrode positive; DCEN: d-c, electrode negative.
  ** Shielded metal arc welding is not popular for these metals.
  † See text for electrode selection.
  ‡ Welding current depends on type of electrode selected.

SHIELDED METAL ARC WELDING

tion applications. This decreases the percentage of time actually spent in welding. Another disadvantage is the limitation placed on the current that can be used. High amperages, such as those used with semiautomatic guns or automatic welding heads, are impractical because of the long and varying length of electrode between the arc and the point of electrical contact in the jaws of the electrode holder.

Welding current is limited by the resistance heating of the electrode. The electrode temperature must not exceed the breakdown temperature of the covering. If the temperature is too high, the covering chemicals react with each other or with air and therefore do not function properly at the arc. As a result of limited temperatures, deposition rates and efficiency are low.

With the development of processes, such as semiautomatic, self-shielded, flux-cored arc welding, having similar or even superior versatility and flexibility, there is less justification for using shielded metal arc welding in applications requiring substantial amounts of weld metal.

Principles

With the shielded metal arc process, an electric arc is struck between the electrically grounded work and a 9-18″ (230-455 mm) length of covered metal rod—the consumable electrode. Covered electrodes generally range from 3/32 to 1/4″ (2.4 to 6.4 mm) diam. The electrode is clamped in an electrode holder, which is joined by a cable to the power source. The welder grips the insulated handle of the electrode holder and maneuvers the tip of the electrode with respect to the weld joint. When the tip of the electrode is touched against the work and then withdrawn to establish the arc, the welding circuit is completed.

Heat of the arc melts the base metal in the immediate area, the electrode's metal core, and any metal particles that may be in the electrode's covering. It also melts, vaporizes, or chemically breaks down the nonmetallic substances incorporated in the covering for arc shielding, metal protection, or metal conditioning purposes. The mixing of molten base metal and filler metal from the electrode provides the coalescence required to effect joining. As welding progresses, the covered rod becomes shorter. Finally, welding must be stopped to remove the stub and replace it with a new electrode.

Firecracker Welding

So-called "firecracker welding" is a variation of the shielded metal arc process in which a length of covered electrode is placed along the joint in contact with the parts to be welded. During welding, the stationary electrode is consumed as the arc travels the length of the electrode.

Current Used

Shielded metal arc welding is done with either alternating or direct current. Alternating current offers the advantage of eliminating arc blow, thus permitting the use of larger electrodes and higher currents. Also, the power source for a-c is lower in cost than for d-c.

Direct current provides a steadier arc and smoother metal transfer than a-c. Most covered electrodes operate better on electrode-positive polarity, which produces deeper penetration. Some covered electrodes are suitable for or designed for electrode-negative polarity, which produces a higher electrode melting rate. Direct current is generally preferred for welding thin sections, for vertical and overhead welding, and for welding with a short arc, but arc blow may be a problem.

GAS TUNGSTEN ARC WELDING

Gas tungsten arc welding (GTAW) is an arc welding process that produces coalescence (joining) of metals by heating them with an arc between a tungsten (nonconsumable) electrode and the work (see Fig. 9-24). Shielding is obtained by an envelope of an inert gas or gas mixture. Pressure and filler metal may or may not be used. The GTAW process is also known as TIG (tungsten inert gas), Heliarc, argon arc, and tungsten arc welding.

Applications

While a wide range of metal thicknesses can be welded, the gas tungsten arc method is especially adapted for welding thin metals where the requirements for quality and finish are exacting. It is one of the few arc welding processes that is satisfactory for welding such tiny and thin-walled objects as transistor cases, instrument diaphragms, and delicate expansion bellows. Gas tungsten arc welding is also used to join various combinations of dissimilar metals and for applying hard-facing and surfacing materials to steel. The process is performed manually, semiautomatically, or automatically.

Advantages

An important advantage of the gas tungsten arc process is that it is suitable for welding most metals, both ferrous and nonferrous, and producing high-quality joints. It is generally not used, however, for metals that melt at low temperatures, such as tin and lead. Materials weldable by the process include most grades of carbon, alloy, and stainless steels; aluminum and most of its alloys; magnesium and most of its alloys; copper and various brasses and bronzes; high-temperature alloys of various types; numerous hard-surfacing alloys; and such metals as titanium, zirconium, gold, and silver. The conditions for welding some of these materials are presented in Table 9-16.

Another advantage is that this process does not produce weld spatter because no filler metal crosses the arc. Also, because no fluxing agents are used, cleaning after welding is seldom required. Welding is possible in all positions.

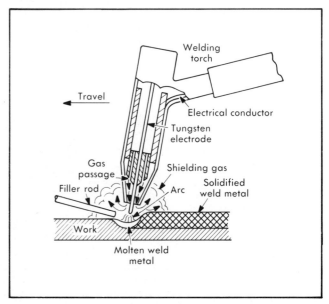

Fig. 9-24 Gas tungsten arc welding. When filler metal is required, it is fed into the pool from a separate rod. (*Lincoln Electric Co.*)

Limitations

A possible limitation to the use of the gas tungsten arc process is that it is slower than consumable-electrode arc welding processes. Also, this method requires an externally supplied inert shielding gas or a gas mixture, adding to the cost of welding. Any transfer of tungsten particles from the electrode to the weld causes hard, brittle contamination.

Principles

Essentially, the nonconsumable tungsten electrode is a torch—a heating device. Under the protective gas shield, metals to be joined may be heated above their melting points, without melting the electrode, so that material from one part coalesces with material from the other part. Upon solidification of the molten area, unification occurs. Pressure may be used when the edges to be joined are approaching the molten state to assist coalescence. Welding in this manner requires no filler metal.

If the work is too thick for the mere fusing of abutting edges and if groove joints or reinforcements, such as fillets, are required, filler metal must be added. This is supplied by a filler rod, manually or mechanically fed into the weld puddle. Both the tip of the nonconsumable tungsten electrode and the tip of the filler rod are kept under the protective gas shield as welding progresses. Compositions of the filler metals should match the base metals being joined.

In automatic welding, filler wire is fed mechanically through a guide into the weld puddle, generally at the leading edge of the weld puddle. When making thick joints manually, a variation in the mode of feeding is to lay or press a filler rod in or along the joint and melt it along with the joint edges. All of the standard types of joints can be welded with the gas tungsten arc process and filler metals.

Magnetic oscillation and control of the arc is being used with gas tungsten arc welding to eliminate or minimize arc blow.[4] A magnetic field is applied perpendicular to the electrode in the direction of the weld axis to deflect the welding arc across the joint. Oscillating the field oscillates the arc. This technique is used primarily for welding maraging steels and austenitic stainless steels. Arc oscillation has made it possible to increase the rate of welding while reducing total heat input and distortion. Weld surface appearance is also improved.

Tungsten is used as the nonconsumable electrode because of its high melting temperature. The material also generates a stable arc. The tungsten electrodes used may be pure tungsten, which is the least costly composition and is used for aluminum welding; 1-2% thoriated tungsten, which has long life and is used for steels; or zirconiated tungsten, which provides less contamination and is also used for aluminum.

The shielding gas may be argon, helium, or a mixture of both. Argon is used to provide better shielding at low flow rates. For flat and vertical welding, a gas flow of 15-30 ft³/hr (0.42-0.84 m³/hr) is usually sufficient, but overhead welding usually requires a slightly higher rate. Helium provides a hotter arc and is useful for welding thick sections. Detailed information about the gas tungsten arc welding process is presented in ANSI/AWS Standard C5.5.

The gas tungsten arc process is occasionally used with industrial robots, but gas metal arc welding (discussed next in this section) is the predominant process for robotic arc welding. The reason for the limited use is that the high-frequency arc starter generally used with the gas tungsten arc process can cause interference with the robot controller, making it unreliable. To overcome this problem, both the arc starter and the robot controller must be specially designed.

Current Used

Gas tungsten arc welding is done with either direct or alternating current. Direct current is used with either electrode-negative or electrode-positive polarity (see Fig. 9-25). Pulsed current is also used for some applications. A supply of high-frequency current is generally provided from a separate source.

DCEN. Electrode-negative polarity d-c is used most extensively for the gas tungsten arc process. It is satisfactory for

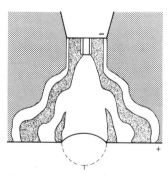 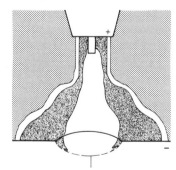 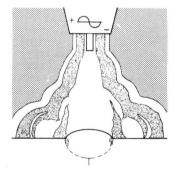

DCEN
Direct-current, electrode-negative
- for most metals except aluminum and magnesium
- narrow weld puddle
- deep penetration—faster welding on thicker workpieces
- fair surface oxide removal

DCEP
Direct-current, electrode-positive
- provides cleaning action needed for aluminum and magnesium
- wide weld puddle
- shallow penetration—ideal for thin workpieces
- excellent surface oxide removal
- range current very limited because of electrode overheating

AC
Alternating current
- for aluminum and magnesium welding
- combines characteristics of DCEN and DCEP for high electrode capacity and cleaning action
- narrower weld puddle than DCEP
- deeper penetration than DCEP
- excellent surface oxide removal

Fig. 9-25 Various current polarities used for gas tungsten arc welding. (*L-TEC Welding & Cutting Systems*)

GAS TUNGSTEN ARC WELDING

TABLE 9-16
Materials Welded and Typical Conditions for Gas Tungsten Arc Welding

Material	Welding Position	Tungsten Electrode Type[a]	Shielding Gas	Welding Current Type	Type of Weld
Aluminum	All	EWP, EWZr	Argon; 10-25% helium with argon (with increased gas flow) for increased penetration; 100% helium with gas flow increased about 100%	a-c high-frequency	Fillet
					Square groove
					V-groove
Copper and alloys[c]	Flat[d]	EWTh1, EWTh2	Helium; 75% helium, 25% argon; argon usually used for bronzes	d-c electrode negative; arc high-frequency for aluminum bronze	Fillet
					Square groove
					V-groove
Silicon bronze[e]	All	EWTh2, EWTh1	Argon; argon-helium mixture for higher heat	d-c electrode negative	Fillet and square groove
					Fillet and V-groove
Carbon and low-alloy steel	All	EWTh2, EWTh1	Argon; 75% helium, 25% argon sometimes used for heavier sections	d-c electrode negative	Fillet and square groove
Stainless steel	Flat[d]	EWTh2, EWTh1	Argon; 75% helium, 25% argon sometimes used for heavier sections	d-c electrode negative	Fillet
					Square groove

Material Thickness, in. (mm)	Electrode Diameter, in. (mm)	Filler-Rod Diameter, in. (mm)	Nozzle ID, in. (mm)	Shielding Gas Flow, ft³/hr (m³/hr)	Welding Current, A[b]	Travel Speed, ipm (mm/min)	No. of Passes
1/16 (1.6)	3/32 (2.4)	3/32 (2.4)	5/16 (7.9)	15 (0.42)	70-90	9 (229)	1
3/32 (2.4)	3/32 (2.4)	3/32 (2.4)	5/16 (7.9)	16 (0.45)	95-115	9 (229)	1
1/8 (3.2)	1/8 (3.2)	1/8 (3.2)	3/8 (9.5)	19 (0.53)	120-140	10 (254)	1
3/16 (4.8)	5/32 (4.0)	5/32 (4.0)	7/16 (11.1)	25 (0.70)	180-200	10 (254)	1
1/4 (6.4)	3/16 (4.8)	3/16 (4.8)	1/2 (12.7)	30 (0.84)	230-250	10 (254)	1
3/8 (9.5)	3/16 (4.8)	3/16 (4.8)	1/2 (12.7)	35 (0.98)	250-310	---	2-3
3/64 (1.2)	1/16 (1.6)	1/16 (1.6)	1/4 (6.4)	19 (0.53)	40-60	16 (406)	1
1/16 (1.6)	3/32 (2.4)	3/32 (2.4)	5/16 (7.9)	19 (0.53)	70-90	11 (279)	1
3/32 (2.4)	3/32 (2.4)	3/32 (2.4)	5/16 (7.9)	19 (0.53)	90-110	11 (279)	1
1/8 (3.2)	1/8 (3.2)	1/8 (3.2)	3/8 (9.5)	20 (0.56)	115-135	11 (279)	1
3/16 (4.8)	5/32 (4.0)	5/32 (4.0)	7/16 (11.1)	25 (0.70)	160-180	11 (279)	2
1/4 (6.4)	5/32 (4.0)	5/32 (4.0)	7/16 (11.1)	25 (0.70)	200-220	9 (229)	2
1/16 (1.6)	1/16 (1.6)	1/16 (1.6)	1/4 (6.4)	18 (0.50)	125-155	10 (254)	1
1/8 (3.2)	3/32 (2.4)	3/32 (2.4)	5/16 (7.9)	18 (0.50)	195-245	8 (203)	1
3/16 (4.8)	1/8 (3.2)	1/8 (3.2)	3/8 (9.5)	36 (1.01)	200-255	8 (203)	1
1/4 (6.4)	1/8 (3.2)	1/8 (3.2)	3/8 (9.5)	36 (1.01)	245-285	7 (178)	1
3/8 (9.5)	3/16 (4.8)	3/16 (4.8)	1/2 (12.7)	36 (1.01)	290-350	8 (203)	2
1/16 (1.6)	1/16 (1.6)	1/16 (1.6)	1/4 (6.4)	18 (0.50)	100-150	12 (305)	1
1/8 (3.2)	3/32 (2.4)	3/32 (2.4)	5/16 (7.9)	18 (0.50)	170-230	10 (254)	1
3/16 (4.8)	1/8 (3.2)	1/8 (3.2)	3/8 (9.5)	36 (1.01)	185-230	10 (254)	1
1/4 (6.4)	1/8 (3.2)	1/8 (3.2)	3/8 (9.5)	36 (1.01)	220-275	7 (178)	2
3/8 (9.5)	3/16 (4.8)	3/16 (4.8)	1/2 (12.7)	45 (1.26)	275-325	7 (178)	2
1/2 (12.7)	1/4 (6.4)	1/4 (6.4)	5/8 (15.9)	45 (1.26)	275-325	7 (178)	2
1/16 (1.6)	1/16 (1.6)	1/16 (1.6)	1/4 (6.4)	15 (0.42)	85-125	12 (305)	1
1/8 (3.2)	1/16 (1.6)	3/32 (2.4)	1/4 (6.4)	15 (0.42)	115-150	12 (305)	1
3/16 (4.8)	3/32 (2.4)	3/32 (2.4)	5/16 (7.9)	20 (0.56)	145-195	9 (229)	1
1/4 (6.4)	3/32 (2.4)	1/8 (3.2)	5/16 (7.9)	25 (0.70)	160-225	---	2
3/8 (9.5)	1/8 (3.2)	1/8 (3.2)	3/8 (9.5)	25 (0.70)	225-290	---	
1/2 (12.7)	1/8 (3.2)	1/8 (3.2)	3/8 (9.5)	25 (0.70)	245-295	---	
3/4 (19.1)	1/8 (3.2)	3/16 (4.8)	3/8 (9.5)	25 (0.70)	295-355	---	
1 (25.4)	5/32 (4.0)	1/4 (6.4)	7/16 (11.1)	25 (0.70)	295-360	---	
0.032 (0.81)	1/16 (1.6)	1/16 (1.6)	1/4 (6.4)	10 (0.28)	75-100	13 (330)	1
0.040 (1.02)	1/16 (1.6)	1/16 (1.6)	1/4 (6.4)	10 (0.28)	90-120	15 (381)	1
0.063 (1.60)	1/16 (1.6)	1/16 (1.6)	1/4 (6.4)	10 (0.28)	95-135	15 (381)	1
3/32 (2.4)	3/32 (2.4)	3/32 (2.4)	5/16 (7.9)	10 (0.28)	135-175	14 (356)	1
1/8 (3.2)	3/32 (2.4)	1/8 (3.2)	5/16 (7.9)	12 (0.34)	145-205	11 (279)	1
1/16 (1.6)	1/16 (1.6)	1/16 (1.6)	1/4 (6.4)	12 (0.34)	75-125	10 (254)	1
3/32 (2.4)	1/16 (1.6)	3/32 (2.4)	1/4 (6.4)	12 (0.34)	95-135	10 (254)	1
1/8 (3.2)	1/16 (1.6)	3/32 (2.4)	5/16 (7.9)	12 (0.34)	115-145	10 (254)	1
3/16 (4.8)	1/8 (3.2)	1/8 (3.2)	3/8 (9.5)	15 (0.42)	175-250	8 (203)	1
1/4 (6.4)	1/8 (3.2)	3/16 (4.8)	3/8 (9.5)	18 (0.50)	225-300	10 (254)	2
3/8 (9.5)	3/16 (4.8)	3/16 (4.8)	1/2 (12.7)	25 (0.70)	250-350	10 (254)	3
1/2 (12.7)	3/16 (4.8)	1/4 (6.4)	1/2 (12.7)	25 (0.70)	250-350	10 (254)	3
0.025 (0.64)	0.040 (1.02)	1/16 (1.6)	1/4 (6.4)	10 (0.28)	20-50	26 (660)	1
0.05 (1.3)	1/16 (1.6)	1/16 (1.6)	1/4 (6.4)	10 (0.28)	50-80	22 (559)	1
1/16 (1.6)	1/16 (1.6)	1/16 (1.6)	1/4 (6.4)	12 (0.34)	65-105	12 (305)	1
3/32 (2.4)	1/16 (1.6)	3/32 (2.4)	1/4 (6.4)	12 (0.34)	85-125	12 (305)	1
1/8 (3.2)	1/16 (1.6)	3/32 (2.4)	5/16 (7.9)	12 (0.34)	100-135	12 (305)	1
3/16 (4.8)	3/32 (2.4)	1/8 (3.2)	5/16 (7.9)	15 (0.42)	150-225	10 (254)	1

(continued)

TABLE 9-16—*Continued*

Material	Welding Position	Tungsten Electrode Type[a]	Shielding Gas	Welding Current Type	Type of Weld
					V-groove
Magnesium	Flat[d]	EWZr, EWP	Argon; 75% helium, 25% argon; 100% helium for thicknesses with gas flow increased 100%	a-c high-frequency	Fillet and square groove
					V-groove
Titanium[f]	All	EWTh2, EWTh1	Argon; argon-helium mixture for heavier thicknesses; backing gas and trailing gas recommended	d-c electrode negative	Fillet and square groove
					Fillet and V-groove

[a] Tungsten electrodes listed in order of choice for each material.
[b] Increase amperage when backup is used.
[c] Preheat 3/16″ (4.8 mm) copper 200° F (95° C); 1/4″ (6.4 mm) 300° F (150° C); 3/8″ (9.5 mm) 500° F (260° C); 1/2″ (12.7 mm) and thicker 900° F (480° C).
[d] Reduce welding current 10-20% for horizontal, vertical, or overhead position.
[e] Use AWS type RCuSiA filler rod. Use as small weld puddle and as high a travel speed as possible; inner base temperature should not exceed 200° F (95° C).
[f] Use filler metal one or two grades lower in strength than base metal.

welding most metals except aluminum and magnesium. Aluminum alloys, however, can be welded by using pure helium, a short arc, and removing surface oxides prior to welding. This current provides the hottest arc for a specific size electrode and produces deep, narrow welds with good penetration. Thick sections can be welded rapidly, but problems may occur in welding thin metals.

DCEP. Electrode-positive polarity d-c is the least used current for the gas tungsten arc process. However, its capability for removing surface oxides makes it useful for welding thin aluminum and magnesium parts. It produces a wide bead with shallow penetration and requires the use of large-sized electrodes with comparatively low currents to dissipate the heat produced.

Alternating current. The use of a-c combines the advantages of using a positive electrode without the associated current limitations of DCEP. The capabilities for removing surface oxides plus deep penetration often make a-c preferable for welding aluminum, magnesium, and beryllium copper.

Pulsed current. This type current offers the advantages of minimizing the heat-affected zone and increasing the depth-to-width ratios of weld beads. It is being used to join precision parts and for the automatic welding of pipe.

High-frequency current. A supply of high-frequency current is generally provided from a separate source for gas tungsten arc welding. When welding with d-c, the high-frequency current is used to initiate the arc (instead of touch or scratch starting) and is generally turned off after ignition. When welding with a-c, the high-frequency current is on continuously to initiate the arc and to ensure reignition at each half cycle during welding.

GAS METAL ARC WELDING

Gas metal arc welding (GMAW) is an arc welding process that produces coalescence (joining) of metals by heating them with an arc between a continuous, solid (consumable) electrode for filler metal and the work (see Fig. 9-26). Shielding is provided by an externally supplied gas or gas mixture. The GMAW process is also known as MIG (metal inert gas), MAG (metal active gas), CO_2, short-circuit arc, dip transfer, and wire welding.

Applications

Gas metal arc welding is performed using either a handheld gun or mechanical welding head or torch to which the electrode is fed automatically. The process is used extensively for high-production welding operations.

Advantages

The major features of gas metal arc welding are (1) the capability of obtaining high-quality welds in almost any metal, (2) the small amount of postweld cleaning it requires, (3) the

Material Thickness, in. (mm)	Electrode Diameter, in. (mm)	Filler-Rod Diameter, in. (mm)	Nozzle ID, in. (mm)	Shielding Gas Flow, ft³/hr (m³/hr)	Welding Current, A[b]	Travel Speed, ipm (mm/min)	No. of Passes
1/4 (6.4)	1/8 (3.2)	3/16 (4.8)	3/8 (9.5)	18 (0.50)	225-300	10 (254)	2
3/8 (9.5)	3/16 (4.8)	3/16 (4.8)	1/2 (12.7)	25 (0.70)	220-350	10 (254)	2-3
1/2 (12.7)	3/16 (4.8)	1/4 (6.4)	1/2 (12.7)	25 (0.70)	250-350	10 (254)	3
0.038 (0.97)	1/16 (1.6)	3/32 (2.4)	1/4 (6.4)	15 (0.42)	30-45	20 (508)	1
0.063 (1.60)	1/16 (1.6)	3/32 (2.4)	1/4 (6.4)	15 (0.42)	45-60	20 (508)	1
0.078 (1.98)	1/16 (1.6)	3/32 (2.4)	1/4 (6.4)	15 (0.42)	60-75	17 (432)	1
0.109 (2.77)	3/32 (2.4)	1/8 (3.2)	5/16 (7.9)	15 (0.42)	80-100	17 (432)	1
0.125 (3.18)	3/32 (2.4)	1/8 (3.2)	5/16 (7.9)	25 (0.70)	95-115	17 (432)	1
3/16 (4.8)	1/8 (3.2)	1/8 (3.2)	3/8 (9.5)	25 (0.70)	95-115	---	2
1/4 (6.4)	1/8 (3.2)	3/16 (4.8)	1/2 (12.7)	25 (0.70)	110-130	24 (610)	2
3/8 (9.5)	1/8 (3.2)	3/16 (4.8)	1/2 (12.7)	30 (0.84)	135-165	20 (508)	2
0.025 (0.64)	1/16 (1.6)	None	3/8 (9.5)	18 (0.50)	20-35	6 (152)	1
0.063 (1.60)	1/16 (1.6)	None	5/8 (15.9)	18 (0.50)	85-140	6 (152)	1
3/32 (2.4)	3/32 (2.4)	1/16 (1.6)	5/8 (15.9)	25 (0.70)	170-215	8 (203)	1
1/8 (3.2)	3/32 (2.4)	1/16 (1.6)	5/8 (15.9)	25 (0.70)	190-235	8 (203)	1
3/16 (4.8)	3/32 (2.4)	1/8 (3.2)	5/8 (15.9)	25 (0.70)	220-280	8 (203)	2
1/4 (6.4)	1/8 (3.2)	1/8 (3.2)	5/8 (15.9)	30 (0.84)	275-320	8 (203)	2
3/8 (9.5)	1/8 (3.2)	1/8 (3.2)	3/4 (19.1)	35 (0.98)	300-350	6 (152)	2
1/2 (12.7)	1/8 (3.2)	5/32 (4.0)	3/4 (19.1)	40 (1.12)	325-425	6 (152)	3

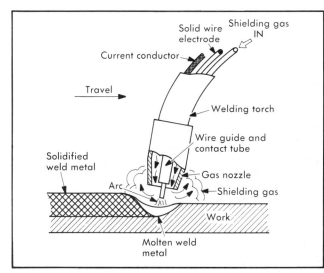

Fig. 9-26 Gas metal arc welding. (*Lincoln Electric Co.*)

visibility of its arc and weld pool to the welder, (4) its all-position capability, (5) its relatively high speed and economy, and (6) its elimination of slag entrapment in the weld. In addition, variations of the process have special advantages.

The gas metal arc process may be used to weld all of the major commercial metals, including carbon, alloy, and stainless steels, as well as aluminum, magnesium, copper, iron, titanium, and zirconium. It is a preferred process for the welding of aluminum, magnesium, copper, and many of the alloys of these reactive metals. Most of the irons and steels can be satisfactorily joined by this process, including the carbon-free irons; the low-carbon and low-alloy steels; the high-strength, quenched and tempered steels; the chromium irons and steels; the high-nickel steels; and some of the so-called superalloys.

Limitations

As with the gas tungsten arc process previously discussed, gas metal arc welding requires an externally supplied inert shielding gas or a gas mixture, adding to welding costs. Equipment required is complex and costly, and not readily portable. The welding gun must be kept close to the work to ensure adequate shielding, making it difficult for hard-to-reach joints.

Principles

The shielding gases used in the gas metal arc process—helium, argon, carbon dioxide, or mixtures thereof—protect the molten metal from reacting with constituents of the atmosphere. Although the gas shield is effective in shielding the molten metal from the air, deoxidizers are usually added as alloys in the solid electrode. Sometimes light coatings are applied to the electrode for arc stabilizing or other purposes. Lubricating films may also be applied to increase the electrode feeding efficiency in semiautomatic welding equipment. Reactive gases may be included in the gas mixture for arc conditioning functions.

When joining various materials, the welding techniques and procedures may vary widely. For example, carbon dioxide or argon-oxygen mixtures are suitable for arc shielding when welding the low-carbon and low-alloy steels. Pure inert gas, however, may be essential when welding highly alloyed steels. Types of gas and flow rates for welding various metals are listed with other welding conditions in Table 9-17. Recommended

GAS METAL ARC WELDING

TABLE 9-17
Typical Conditions and Shielding Gases for Joining Various Materials with Gas Metal Arc Welding

Material	Welding Process Variation	Welding Position	Type of Weld	Material Thickness,[a] in. (mm)	Electrode Diameter, in. (mm)
Aluminum and alloys	Metal-inert gas	All	Groove and fillet[b]	1/16 (1.6)	0.030 (0.76)[c]
				3/32 (2.4)	0.030 (0.76)[c]
				1/8 (3.2)	0.030 (0.76)[c]
				1/8 (3.2)	3/64 (1.2)
				3/16 (4.8)	3/64 (1.2)
				1/4 (6.4)	1/16 (1.6)
				3/8 (9.5)	1/16 (1.6)
				1/2 (12.7)[d]	3/32 (2.4)
				1/2 (12.7)	1/16 (1.6)
				3/4 (19.1)[d]	3/32 (2.4)
				3/4 (19.1)	1/16 (1.6)
				1 (25.4)[d]	3/32 (2.4)
				1 (25.4)	1/16 (1.6)
Copper and alloys	Metal-inert gas	Flat	Groove and fillet[e]	1/16 (1.6)	3/64 (1.2)
				5/64 (2.0)	3/64 (1.2)
				7/64 (2.8)	3/64 (1.2)
				1/8 (3.2)	3/64 (1.2)
				1/4 (6.4)	1/16 (1.6)
				1/4 (6.4)	1/16 (1.6)
				3/8 (9.5)	1/16 (1.6)
				1/2 (12.7)	1/16-3/32 (1.6-2.4)
				3/4 (19.1)	1/16-3/32 (1.6-2.4)
				1 (25.4)	1/16-3/32 (1.6-2.4)

Welding Current, A (d-c electrode positive)	Voltage	Wire Feed, ipm (mm/min)	Shielding Gas	Shielding Gas Flow, ft³/hr (m³/hr)	Travel Speed, ipm (mm/min)	No. of Passes
55-60	13-14	295-320 (7493-8128)	Thin and medium material—argon	15 (0.42)	14-24 (356-610)	1
90-100	16-18	330-370 (8382-9398)		30 (0.85)	24-36 (610-514)	1
110-125	20-22	410-460 (10 414-11 684)		30 (0.85)	30-33 (762-838)	1
110-125	19-21	175-190 (4445-4826)		35 (0.99)	22-26 (559-660)	1
150-190	19-21	215-225 (5461-5715)	Thick material— 50% argon, 50% helium	35 (0.99)	20-25 (508-635)	1
170-225	21-26	150-195 (3810-4953)		35 (0.99)	20-24 (508-610)	1
200-300	22-27	170-275 (4318-6985)		40 (1.13)	24-30 (610-762)	2-5
320-340	22-29	140-150 (3556-3810)		45 (1.27)	15-17 (381-432)	2-5
220-230	22-27	195-205 (4953-5207)		50 (1.42)	12-18 (305-457)	3-8
355-375	22-29	155-160 (3937-4064)		50 (1.42)	14-16 (356-406)	4
255-275	22-27	230-250 (5842-6350)	Increase gas flow rate 10% for overhead position	50 (1.42)	8-18 (203-457)	4-10
405-425	22-24	175-180 (4445-4572)		50 (1.42)	8-12 (203-305)	4
255-290	22-27	230-265 (5842-6731)		50 (1.42)	6-18 (152-457)	4-14
150-170	22-24	210-220 (5334-5588)	Addition of helium will help eliminate porosity and increase heat input	35 (0.99)	20-23 (508-584)	1
180-200	22-25	240-270 (6096-6858)		40 (1.13)	20-25 (508-635)	1
200-230	23-27	270-290 (6858-7366)		40 (1.13)	20-25 (508-635)	1
210-240	23-27	280-300 (7112-7620)		40 (1.13)	20-25 (508-635)	1
380-410	23-29	260-270 (6604-6858)		40 (1.13)	12-15 (305-381)	1
300-330	23-27	190-210 (4826-5334)		40 (1.13)	14-17 (356-432)	1
340-360	24-28	220-240 (5588-6096)		40 (1.13)	12-15 (305-381)	2
400-440	24-30	270-290 (6858-7366)		50 (1.42)	8-10 (203-254)	2
420-460	24-30	290-315 (7366-8001)		50 (1.42)	7-9 (178-229)	2-3
420-460	24-30	270-300 (6858-7620)		50 (1.42)	7-9 (178-229)	4

(continued)

GAS METAL ARC WELDING

TABLE 9-17—Continued

Material	Welding Process Variation	Welding Position	Type of Weld	Material Thickness,[a] in. (mm)	Electrode Diameter, in. (mm)
Carbon and low-alloy steel	Shorting arc	Flat; reduce welding current 10-15% for vertical and overhead	Groove and fillet[f]	0.025 (0.64)	0.030 (0.76)
				0.031 (0.79)	0.030 (0.76)
				0.038 (0.95)	0.035 (0.89)
				0.050 (1.27)	0.035 (0.89)
				1/16 (1.6)	0.035 (0.89)
				5/64 (2.0)	0.035 (0.89)
				1/8 (3.2)	0.035 (0.89)
				1/8 (3.2)	0.045 (1.14)
				3/16 (4.8)	0.035 (0.89)
				3/16 (4.8)	0.045 (1.14)
				1/4 (6.4)	0.035 (0.89)
				1/4 (6.4)	0.045 (1.14)
	Spray arc	Flat only	[g]	1/8 (3.2)	1/16 (1.6)
			[g]	3/16 (4.8)	1/16 (1.6)
			Butt	1/4 (6.4)	1/16 (1.6)
				1/4 (6.4)	3/32 (2.4)
				3/8 (9.5)	1/16 (1.6)
				3/8 (9.5)	3/32 (2.4)
				1/2 (12.7)	1/16 (1.6)
				1/2 (12.7)	3/32 (2.4)
				3/4 (19.1)	1/16 (1.6)
				3/4 (19.1)	3/32 (2.4)
			Fillet	1/4 (6.4)	1/16 (1.6)

Welding Current, A (d-c electrode positive)	Voltage	Wire Feed, ipm (mm/min)	Shielding Gas	Shielding Gas Flow, ft³/hr (m³/hr)	Travel Speed, ipm (mm/min)	No. of Passes
30-50	15-17	85-100 (2159-2540)	Welding grade CO₂ or 75% argon, 25% CO₂	15-20 (0.42-0.57)	12-20 (305-508)	1
40-60	15-17	90-130 (2286-3302)		15-20 (0.42-0.57)	15-22 (381-559)	1
55-85	15-18	70-120 (1778-3048)		15-20 (0.42-0.57)	35-40 (889-1016)	1
70-100	16-19	100-160 (2540-4064)		15-20 (0.42-0.57)	35-50 (889-1270)	1
80-110	17-20	120-180 (3048-4572)		20-25 (0.57-0.71)	30-35 (762-889)	1
100-130	18-20	160-220 (4064-5588)		20-25 (0.57-0.71)	25-30 (635-762)	1
120-160	19-22	210-290 (5334-7366)		20-25 (0.57-0.71)	15-25 (381-635)	1
180-200	20-24	210-240 (5334-6096)		20-25 (0.57-0.71)	27-45 (686-1143)	1
140-160	19-22	240-290 (6096-7366)		20-25 (0.57-0.71)	10-19 (254-483)	1
180-205	20-24	210-245 (5334-6223)		20-25 (0.57-0.71)	18-28 (457-711)	1
140-160	19-22	240-290 (6096-7366)		20-25 (0.57-0.71)	11-16 (279-406)	1
180-225	20-24	210-290 (5334-7366)		20-25 (0.57-0.71)	20-24 (508-610)	1
300	24	165 (4191)	Argon with 1-5% oxygen	40-50 (1.13-1.42)	35 (889)	1
350	25	230 (5842)			32 (813)	1
325-375	24-25	210-260 (5334-6604)			30 (762)	2
400-450	26-29	100-120 (2540-3048)			35 (889)	2
325-375	24-25	210-260 (5334-6604)			24 (610)	2
400-450	26-29	100-120 (2540-3048)			28 (711)	2
325-375	24-26	210-260 (5334-6604)			24 (610)	3
400-450	26-29	100-120 (2540-3048)			30 (762)	3
325-375	24-26	210-260 (5334-6604)			24 (610)	4
400-450	26-29	100-120 (2540-3048)			24 (610)	4
350	25	230 (5842)			32 (813)	1

(continued)

TABLE 9-17—*Continued*

Material	Welding Process Variation	Welding Position	Type of Weld	Material Thickness,[a] in. (mm)	Electrode Diameter, in. (mm)
Carbon and low-alloy steel	Spray arc	Flat only	Fillet	1/4 (6.4)	3/32 (2.4)
				3/8 (9.5)	1/16 (1.6)
				3/8 (9.5)	3/32 (2.4)
				1/2 (12.7)	1/16 (1.6)
				1/2 (12.7)	3/32 (2.4)
				3/4 (19.1)	1/16 (1.6)
				3/4 (19.1)	3/32 (2.4)
				1 (25.4)	1/16 (1.6)
				1 (25.4)	3/32 (2.4)
	CO_2 arc	Flat only	Fillet	0.050 (1.27)	0.045 (1.14)
				0.063 (1.59)	0.045 (1.14)
				0.078 (1.98)	0.045 (1.14)
				0.125 (3.18)	1/16 (1.6)
				3/16 (4.8)	1/16 (1.6)
				1/4 (6.4)	5/64 (2.0)
				3/8 (9.5)	3/32 (2.4)
				1/2 (12.7)	3/32 (2.4)
			Square groove[h]	0.050 (1.27)	0.045 (1.14)
				0.063 (1.59)	0.045 (1.14)
				0.078 (1.98)	0.045 (1.14)
				0.125 (3.18)	0.045 (1.14)
				3/16 (4.8)	1/16 (1.6)
				1/4 (6.4)	1/16 (1.6)

Welding Current, A (d-c electrode positive)	Voltage	Wire Feed, ipm (mm/min)	Shielding Gas	Shielding Gas Flow, ft³/hr (m³/hr)	Travel Speed, ipm (mm/min)	No. of Passes
400	26	100 (2540)			32 (813)	1
350	25	230 (5842)			20 (508)	2
425	27	110 (2794)			20 (508)	1
350	25	230 (5842)			24 (610)	3
425	27	105-110 (2667-2794)			26 (660)	3
350	25	230 (5842)			24 (610)	5
425	27	110 (2794)			26 (660)	4
350	25	230 (5842)			24 (610)	7
425	27	110 (2794)			26 (660)	6
280	26	350 (8890)	Welding grade CO_2	25 (0.71)	190 (4826)	
325	26	360 (9144)		35 (0.99)	150 (3810)	
325	27	360 (9144)		35 (0.99)	130 (3302)	
380	28	210 (5334)		35 (0.99)	85 (2159)	
425	31	260 (6604)		35 (0.99)	75 (1905)	
500	32	185 (4699)		35 (0.99)	40 (1016)	
550	34	200 (5080)		35 (0.99)	25 (635)	
625	36	160 (4064)		35 (0.99)	23 (584)	
270	25	340 (8636)		25 (0.71)	180 (4572)	
300	28	350 (8890)		35 (0.99)	140 (3556)	
325-330	29	350-360 (8890-9144)		35 (0.99)	105-110 (2667-2794)	
350	29	380 (9652)		35 (0.99)	100 (2540)	
375-425	30-31	260-320 (6604-8128)		35 (0.99)	70-75 (1778-1905)	
475	32	340 (8636)		35 (0.99)	55 (1397)	

(continued)

TABLE 9-17—*Continued*

Material	Welding Process Variation	Welding Position	Type of Weld	Material Thickness,[a] in. (mm)	Electrode Diameter, in. (mm)
Carbon and low-alloy steel	CO_2 arc	Flat only	Square groove[h]	3/8 (9.5)	3/32 (2.4)
				1/2 (12.7)	3/32 (2.4)
Stainless steel	All	Flat; reduce welding current 10-20% for other positions	Groove and fillet	1/16 (1.6)	0.035 (0.89)
				3/32 (2.4)	0.035 (0.89)
				1/8 (3.2)	0.035 (0.89)
				5/32 (4.0)	0.045 (1.14)
				1/4 (6.4)	0.045 (1.14)
Magnesium and alloys	Shorting arc	Flat	Square groove fillet	0.025 (0.64)	0.040 (1.02)
				0.040 (1.02)	0.040 (1.02)
				1/16 (1.6)	0.063 (1.60)
				3/32 (2.4)	0.063 (1.60)
				1/8 (3.2)	0.094 (2.39)
				5/32 (4.0)	0.094 (2.39)
				3/16 (4.8)	0.094 (2.39)
Magnesium	Spray arc	Flat	V-groove fillet	1/4 (6.4)	0.063 (1.60)
				3/8 (9.5)	0.094 (2.39)
				1/2 (12.7)	0.094 (2.39)
				1 (25.4)	0.094 (2.39)

[a] Material thickness also indicates fillet weld size.
[b] Use V-groove for 3/16″ (4.8 mm) thick and thicker.
[c] Use pull gun for 0.030″ (0.76 mm) wire.
[d] Flat-position value only; all others are all-position values.
[e] Use V-groove for 1/4″ (6.4 mm) thick and thicker.
[f] Root opening for square butt joints is one-half material thickness.
[g] Use V-groove for material 1/4 to 1/2″ (6.4 to 12.7 mm) thick; double V-groove for 1/2″ (12.7 mm) and thicker.
[h] Copper or steel backing required.

Welding Current, A (d-c electrode positive)	Voltage	Wire Feed, ipm (mm/min)	Shielding Gas	Shielding Gas Flow, ft³/hr (m³/hr)	Travel Speed, ipm (mm/min)	No. of Passes
575	34	160 (4064)		35 (0.99)	40 (1016)	
625	35	200 (5080)		35 (0.99)	33 (838)	
60-100	15-18	90-190 (2286-4826)	Flat and high-frequency only: argon with 1-5% O_2; 90% helium, 7.5% argon, 2.5% CO_2 for all CO_2 or 75% argon, 25% CO_2 when carbon pickup allowable	12-15 (0.34-0.42)	15-30 (381-762)	1
125-150	17-21	230-280 (5842-7112)		12-15 (0.34-0.42)	20-30 (508-762)	1
130-160	18-24	250-290 (6350-7366)		12-15 (0.34-0.42)	20-25 (508-635)	1
190-250	22-26	200-290 (5080-7366)		15-18 (0.42-0.51)	25-30 (635-762)	1
225-300	22-30	260-370 (6604-9398)		25-30 (0.71-0.85)	25-30 (635-762)	1
26-27	13-16	180 (4572)	Argon or helium—argon for heavier thicknesses	40-60 (1.13-1.70)		
35-50	13-16	250-340 (6350-8636)		40-60 (1.13-1.70)		
60-75	13-16	140-170 (3556-4318)		40-60 (1.13-1.70)		
95-125	13-16	110-130 (2794-3302)		40-60 (1.13-1.70)		
110-135	13-16	210-280 (5334-7112)		40-60 (1.13-1.70)		
135-140	13-16	130-140 (3302-3556)		40-60 (1.13-1.70)		
175-205	13-16	160-190 (4064-4826)		40-60 (1.13-1.70)		
240-290	24-30	550-660 (13 970-16 764)		50-80 (1.42-2.26)		
320-350	24-30	550-660 (13 970-16 764)		50-80 (1.42-2.26)		
350-420	24-30	385-415 (9779-10 541)		50-80 (1.42-2.26)		
350-420	24-30	385-415 (9779-10 541)		50-80 (1.42-2.26)		

practices for gas metal arc welding are presented in ANSI/AWS Standard C5.6.

Use of an argon-oxygen mixture as the shielding gas is sometimes referred to as the spray-transfer mode. Metal transfer tends to be in the form of a very fine spray of tiny metal droplets and vapor, and minimum cleanup is required after welding. Pulsed arc methods effect spray transfer with medium heat input, making these methods suitable for welding thin sections.

Another modification of the process, called short-circuit (short-arc) arc welding, uses repetitive short circuits through contact of the molten electrode with the weld puddle to cause metal transfer and permits joining thin sections of most steels. Welding with carbon dioxide shielding gas produces high-speed welds with minimum cost for shielding gas.

Characteristics of the process variations are listed in Table 9-18. Electrode wires used for joining mild and low-alloy steels by gas metal arc welding are listed in Table 9-19. All electrode

GAS TUNGSTEN ARC WELDING

wires are bare except for carbon steel wire, which is protectively coated, usually with a thin layer of copper.

Robotic Welding

Gas metal arc welding is the predominant process used in robotic arc welding. Frequently, a special interface is required to connect the power supply to the robot so that the weld parameters can be set under program control. Shielding gases used most frequently for robotic GMAW of steel are pure argon, argon with 2 or 5% oxygen, and argon with 10 or 25% carbon dioxide.

Joint designs for robotic arc welding are most frequently single-pass fillets, with partial-penetration welds. The reason for this is that parts small enough to be quickly moved in and out of a robotic workcell do not generally require more weld metal to perform their intended function. The ideal joint design for robotic arc welding consists of intermittent fillets in varying locations around the assembly.

Current Used

Gas metal arc welding is essentially a direct-current process, with alternating current rarely used. Electrode-positive polarity d-c (DCEP) is used most extensively because it produces a stable arc, smooth metal transfer, and deeper penetration than electrode-negative polarity d-c (DCEN). Electrode-negative polarity d-c tends to produce arc instability, poor transfer of

TABLE 9-18
Characteristics of Process Variations in Gas Metal Arc Welding

Process Variable	Inert Gas Shielding	Carbon Dioxide Shielding	Short-Circuiting Arc Welding Mode	Spray-Transfer Arc Welding Mode
Shielding gas	Inert gas	CO_2	CO_2 or CO_2 + argon	Argon + oxygen (1-5%)
Metal transfer	Various	Globular	Short-circuiting	Spray
Metals to be welded	Al and alloys, stainless steels, Ni and alloys, Cu alloys, Ti	Low and medium-carbon steels; low-alloy, high-strength steels; some stainless steels	Low and medium-carbon steels; low-alloy, high-strength steels; some stainless steels	Low and medium-carbon steels; low-alloy, high-strength steels; some stainless steels
Metal thickness	12 gage [0.109″ (2.77 mm) to 3/8″ (9.5 mm)] without bevel preparation; maximum thickness practically unlimited	10 gage [0.140″ (3.56 mm) to 1/2″ (12.7 mm)] without bevel preparation	20 gage [0.038″ (0.97 mm) to 1/4″ (6.4 mm)]; economical in heavier metals for vertical and overhead welding	1/4 to 1/2″ (6.4 to 12.7 mm) with no preparation; maximum thickness practically unlimited
Welding positions	All positions	Flat and horizontal	All positions (also for pipe welding)	Flat and horizontal
Major advantages	Welds most nonferrous metals, minimum cleanup	Low cost, high travel speed, deep penetration	Welds thin material, will bridge gaps, minimum cleanup	Smooth surface, deep penetration, high travel speed
Limitations	Cost of gases	Spatter removal sometimes required	Uneconomical in heavy thickness except out of position	Position, minimum thickness
Appearance of weld	Fairly smooth, convex surface	Relatively smooth, some spatter	Smooth surface, relatively minor spatter	Smooth surface, minimum spatter
Travel speeds	Up to 100 ipm (2540 mm/min)	Up to 250 ipm (6350 mm/min)	Maximum 50 ipm (1270 mm/min)— semiautomatic	Up to 150 ipm (3810 mm/min)
Range of wire diameters, in. (mm)	0.035 (0.89), 0.045 (1.14), 1/16 (1.6), 3/32 (2.4)	0.045 (1.14), 1/16 (1.6), 5/64 (2), 3/32 (2.4), 1/8 (3.2)	0.030 (0.76), 0.035 (0.89), 0.045 (1.14)	3/32 (2.4), 7/64 (2.8), 1/16 (1.6), 1/8 (3.2), 5/32 (4)
Electrode and shielding cost	Expensive electrode wires, relatively expensive gas	Least expensive gas	Reasonably priced electrode wires	More expensive gas
Overall welding costs	Least expensive for nonferrous metals	Least expensive for medium thickness	Least expensive on thin-gage steel and out of position	Least expensive on low-alloy steels

molten metal, and spatter, making it generally undesirable, but it is sometimes used when minimum penetration is desired.

Pulsed spray welding requires a special d-c power supply to provide two adjustable current levels. At one level, the pulse variables (pulse current and time, background current, time, and frequency) are automatically adjusted for an entire wire-feed speed range. These types of power sources can produce spray transfer at low average currents, in the range of 80-350 A, and produce practically no spatter, which reduces cleanup costs. Reduced heat input with this method results in minimum distortion and shrinkage. Also, large diameter wires can be used at lower average currents to improve feedability and reduce costs.

FLUX-CORED ARC WELDING

Flux-cored arc welding (FCAW) is an arc welding process that produces coalescence (joining) of metals by heating them with an arc between a continuous, consumable, tubular filler-metal electrode and the work. In self-shielded flux-cored welding, shielding is provided entirely by the constituents of the tubular electrode. In gas-shielded flux-cored welding, shielding is provided from an externally supplied gas or gas mixture.

Self-Shielded Flux-Cored Welding

The self-shielded flux-cored arc welding process is an outgrowth of shielded metal arc welding. The versatility and

TABLE 9-19
Electrode Wires Used for Joining Mild and Low-Alloy Steels by Gas Metal Arc Welding

AWS Classification	Typical Wire and Weld Deposit Composition, %				Tensile Strength, ksi (MPa)	Yield Strength, ksi (MPa)	Elongation in 2″ (51 mm), %	Reduction of Area, %	Charpy V-Notch, ft-lb (N · m)
	C	Mn	Si	Others					
E70S-1B:					100 (689)	85 (586)	22	55	
Wire	0.12	1.90	0.80	Mo 0.50					50 (68) at +70° F (20° C)
Deposit (CO_2)	0.10	1.40	0.55	Mo 0.50					20 (27) at -20° F (-29° C)
E70S-3:					75 (517)	63 (434)	24	50	
Wire	0.11	1.10	0.45						58 (79) at +70° F (20° C)
Deposit (CO_2)	0.09	0.62	0.26						18 (24) at -20° F (-29° C)
E70S-3:					78 (538)	65 (448)	26	58	
Wire	0.11	1.10	0.45						60 (81) at +70° F (20° C)
Deposit (CO_2)	0.09	0.70	0.20						20 (27) at -20° F (-29° C)
E70S-6:					88 (607)	68 (469)	28	60	
Wire	0.11	1.65	1.12						75 (102) at +70° F (20° C)
Deposit (CO_2)	0.10	1.20	0.60						25 (34) at -20° F (-29° C)
E70S-5:					78 (538)	65 (448)	28	60	
Wire	0.11	1.20	0.45	Al 0.70					50 (68) at +70° F (20° C)
Deposit (CO_2)	0.10	1.00	0.35	Al 0.05					20 (27) at -20° F (-29° C)
E4130:					150* (1034)	120* (827)	11*	35*	
Wire	0.30	0.50	0.31	Cr 0.90 Mo 0.21					
Deposit (argon)	0.25	0.40	0.25	Cr 0.75 Mn 0.20					
E8620:					100 (689)	90 (621)	20	55	
Wire	0.21	0.78	0.32	Cr 0.50 Ni 0.60 Mo 0.22					
Deposit	0.17	0.55	0.20	Cr 0.45 Ni 0.60 Mo 0.20					

* Oil quench 1600° F (870° C) and draw 925° F (495 °C)—all other values as welded.

FLUX-CORED ARC WELDING

maneuverability of stick electrodes in manual welding stimulated efforts to mechanize the shielded metal arc process. Developments consisted of making an electrode with self-shielding characteristics in coil form and feeding it mechanically to the arc (see Fig. 9-27), thus eliminating welding time lost in changing electrodes and the material lost as electrode stubs. The result of these efforts was the development of the semiautomatic and fully automatic processes for welding with continuous, flux-cored, tubular electrode "wires." Such fabricated wires contain in their cores the ingredients for fluxing and deoxidizing molten metal and for generating shielding gases and vapors and slag coverings.

Advantages. One of the advantages of the self-shielded flux-cored arc welding process is the high deposition rates possible with handheld semiautomatic guns. High deposition rates, automatic electrode feed, and elimination of lost time for changing electrodes have resulted in substantial production economies wherever the semiautomatic process has been used to replace stick-electrode welding. Decreases in welding costs as great as 50% have been common, and in some production welding, deposition rates have been increased as much as 400%. The process permits the use of long electrode extensions (the lengths of the unmelted electrodes extending beyond the ends of the contact tube during welding), which increase the deposition rate for a given voltage and current.

Another advantage of the process is its tolerance for poor fitup, which often reduces rework and repair without affecting final product quality. The tolerance of the semiautomatic process to poor fitup has expanded the use of tubular steel members in structures by making possible sound connections where perfect fitup would be too difficult or costly to achieve.

Operation. In essence, semiautomatic welding with flux-cored electrodes is manual shielded metal arc welding with a long electrode. By the press of the trigger, completing the welding circuit, the operator activates the mechanism that feeds the electrode to the arc. A gun is used instead of an electrode holder, but it is similarly light in weight and easy to maneuver. The only other major difference is that the weld metal of the

electrode surrounds the shielding and fluxing chemicals, rather than being surrounded by them.

Gas-Shielded Flux-Cored Welding

The gas-shielded flux-cored process is a hybrid of self-shielded flux-cored arc welding and gas metal arc welding. Tubular electrode wire is used, as in the self-shielded process (refer to Fig. 9-27), but the ingredients in its core are for fluxing, deoxidizing, scavenging, and, sometimes, alloying additions, rather than for these functions plus the generation of protective vapors. The process is similar to gas metal arc welding (refer to Fig. 9-26) in that a gas is separately applied to act as an arc shield.

Applications and advantages. The gas-shielded flux-cored process is used primarily for welding mild and low-alloy steels, as well as some stainless steels. It gives high deposition rates, high deposition efficiencies, and high operating factors. Radiographic-quality welds are easily produced, and the weld metal, with mild and low-alloy steels, has good ductility and toughness. The process is adaptable to a wide variety of joints and gives the capability for all-position welding.

Shielding gases. The supplementary external shielding gas normally used is carbon dioxide, although for stainless and certain alloy steels argon-carbon dioxide or argon-oxygen mixtures are used, depending on the base metal and the electrode type. Gas flow rate is dependent on the type of gas used, the base metal, the welding position, and the welding current.

Electrodes, Equipment, and Operating Parameters

The flux-cored electrode must be selected on the basis of base metal composition and strength and whether external shielding gas is to be used. Various diameters are available to allow welding in different positions, and they may be obtained in spools or coils. Tables 9-20 and 9-21 give recommendations for flux-cored arc welding under various conditions.

The self-shielding process is popular because equipment for supplying auxiliary shielding gas is not required. The electrode holder is also simpler and lower in cost.

Current Used

Electrode-positive polarity d-c (DCEP) is most commonly used for flux-cored arc welding; a-c is seldom used. Electrode-negative polarity d-c (DCEN) is also used, but only to a limited extent. Constant-current or drooping power supplies can be used, but the wire-feed unit must be designed to work with the power supply unit. Constant-voltage power supplies, the type most often used with FCAW, should only be used with continuous-feed electrode wire methods.

ELECTROGAS WELDING

Electrogas welding (EGW) is an arc welding process that produces coalescence (joining) of metals by heating them with an arc between a continuous filler-metal (consumable) electrode and the work. Molding shoes span the gap between parts being joined and confine the molten weld metal for vertical position welding. The electrodes may be either flux-cored or solid, and shielding may or may not be obtained from an externally supplied gas or gas mixture. There are two basic variations: one uses the solid consumable electrode wire and externally supplied shielding gas, normally CO_2 (see Fig. 9-28), and the second utilizes flux-cored electrode wire and does not ordinarily use an

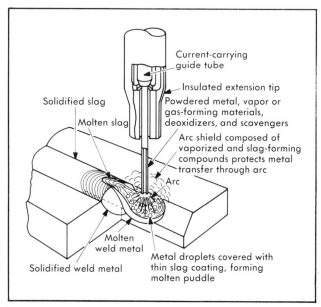

Fig. 9-27 Self-shielded, flux-cored arc welding. (*Lincoln Electric Co.*)

TABLE 9-20
Typical Conditions for Flux-Cored Arc Welding of Steel in the
Flat and Horizontal Positions Using 3/32″ (2.4 mm) Diam Electrode Wire

Material Thickness, in. (mm)*	Welding Current, A (d-c, electrode positive)	Arc Voltage, V	Wire Feed, ipm (mm/min)	Shielding Gas Flow, ft³/hr (m³/hr)**	Travel Speed, ipm (mm/min)	No. of Passes
1/8 (3.2)	300-350	24-26	100-120 (2540-3048)	35-40 (0.99-1.13)	25-30 (635-762)	1
3/16 (4.8)	350-400	24-28	120-150 (3048-3810)	35-40 (0.99-1.13)	25-35 (635-889)	1
1/4 (6.4)	350-400	24-28	120-150 (3048-3810)	35-40 (0.99-1.13)	20-30 (508-762)	1
3/8 (9.5)	475-500	28-30	180-210 (4572-5334)	35-40 (0.99-1.13)	15-20 (381-508)	1
1/2 (12.7)	400-450	25-28	150-170 (3810-4318)	35-40 (0.99-1.13)	18-20 (457-508)	2-3
5/8 (15.9)	400-450	25-28	150-170 (3810-4318)	35-40 (0.99-1.13)	14-18 (356-457)	2-3
3/4 (19.1)	400-450	25-28	150-170 (3810-4318)	35-40 (0.99-1.13)	14-18 (356-457)	5-6

These same settings can be used for self-shielded electrode welding.

 * For groove and fillet welds. Material thickness also indicates fillet-weld size. Use V-groove for 1/4″ (6.4 mm) and
   thicker; use double V-groove for 1/2″ (12.7 mm) and thicker.
** Welding grade CO_2.

external shielding gas because shielding gases are formed as the flux-cored electrode wire is consumed in the arc.

Applications and Advantages

Metals welded by the electrogas process include low-carbon steels, low-alloy high-strength steels, medium-carbon steels, and certain stainless steels. The process can also be used for welding quenched and tempered steels providing that the correct heat input is maintained for the type of steel being welded. The major use of electrogas welding has been for the field erection of storage tanks for oil, water, and other liquids. Another use is in the shipbuilding industry for joining shell plates.

Weld sizes. Under normal conditions, the minimum thickness of metal welded with electrogas is 3/8″ (9.5 mm). The maximum

TABLE 9-21
Typical Conditions for Flux-Cored Arc Welding with Various Size Electrodes

Electrode size, in. (mm)	Welding Position*					
	Flat		Horizontal		Vertical	
	Amperage†	Voltage‡	Amperage†	Voltage‡	Amperage†	Voltage‡
0.045 (1.2)	150-225	22-27	150-225	22-26	125-200	22-25
1/16 (1.6)	175-300	24-29	175-275	25-28	150-200	24-27
5/64 (2.0)	200-400	25-30	200-375	26-30	175-225	25-29
3/32 (2.4)	300-500	25-32	300-450	25-30		
7/64 (2.8)	400-525	26-33				
1/8 (3.2)	450-650	28-34				

Based on 2 1/2″ (63.5 mm) tip-to-work distance; shielding gas at 30-45 ft³/hr (0.85-1.27 m³/hr), depending on electrode size.
 * Applies to groove, bead, or fillet welds in position shown.
 † Amperage range can be expanded. Higher currents can be used, especially with automatic travel.
 ‡ Voltage range can be expanded. Voltage will increase when larger tip-to-work distance is used.

ELECTROGAS WELDING

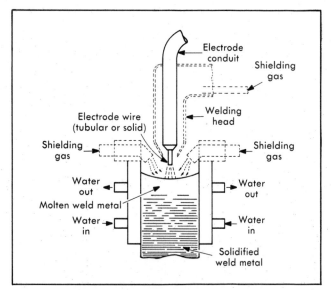

Fig. 9-28 Electrogas welding process. (*Hobart Brothers Co.*)

thickness, utilizing one electrode, is 3/4″ (19 mm). The height (or length) of the joint is practically unlimited. The process can be used for joints as short as 4″ (100 mm) and/or as long or high as 50′ (15 m).

Deposition rates and weld quality. The deposition rates for electrogas welding are relatively high. Deposition rates with flux-cored wires vary with wire types and manufacturer because the ratio of fill to metal varies.

Electrogas welding is considered a low-hydrogen type of process because hydrogen is not present in any of the materials involved in making a weld. The cooling rate of the deposit weld metal is somewhat slower than for gas metal arc or flux-cored arc welding and, hence, impurities are more likely to be removed.

Electrogas welds possess properties and characteristics surpassing welds made with the shielded metal arc process. The higher than normal heat input of electrogas welding reduces the cooling rate. This in turn allows larger grain growth of the weld metal and also in the heat-affected zone of the base metal. Large grain growth, however, can be detrimental because strength is reduced substantially, especially if proper weld procedures are not used. The lower cooling rate minimizes the risk of cracking and reduces the high hardness zones in the weld and heat-affected zone that are sometimes found with shielded metal arc welding. The hardness of the weld is normally uniform across the cross section of the weld and is very similar to the unaffected base metal.

Weld metal produced by electrogas welding will qualify under most codes and specifications. Ductility of the weld metal or electrogas weld is relatively high, in the range of 25% elongation. Impact requirements for electrogas welds will meet those required by the AWS Structural Welding Code. V-notch Charpy impact specimens producing 5-30 ft-lbf (6.8-40.7 N·m) at 0°F (-18°C) are normal and expected.

Limitations

The major limitation of the electrogas process is with respect to welding position, which is generally vertical. The process should not be used if the joint is at an angle in excess of 15° from the vertical. Also, the length (height) of the weld produced is limited by the length of the elevating mechanism for moving the weld head vertically.

Joint Design

Both fillet and groove welds can be produced by the electrogas process. For making fillet welds, a single molding shoe is required. This shoe fits on the face of the fillet and controls the fillet size. For groove welds, the square-groove design can be used up to the maximum possible with one electrode, usually 3/4″ (19 mm). V-groove welds can also be produced up to the maximum thickness or size of the V-groove.

If thicker metals need to be joined, double V-groove welds can be used. This offers the opportunity of making each half of the double V-groove weld independently. When this is done, the molding shoes must be designed specifically for the joint detail. The molding shoe for the root or narrow portion of the vee would fit in from the back side of the weld. The molding shoe for the face of the weld would be the same as for a square-groove weld. When making the second half of a double V-groove weld, a backing shoe is not required because the initial weld performs this function.

The ability to make both fillet and V-groove welds is one of the advantages of the electrogas welding process. Joint design for electrogas welding can be the same as for shielded metal arc, gas metal arc, or flux-cored arc welding.

Principles

The electrogas process shown in Fig. 9-28 is the solid electrode wire and externally supplied shielding gas variation. This process utilizes the heat of the arc between the continuously fed, consumable electrode wire and the work. Heat of the arc melts the surfaces of the base metal and the end of the electrode. Metal melted from the electrode, as well as metal melted on the surface of the abutting base metal of the weld joint, collect at the bottom of the cavity formed between the parts to be welded and the molding shoes. This is in the form of molten weld metal, which solidifies from the bottom of the joint and joins the parts to be welded.

Shielding of the molten metal from the atmosphere is provided by shielding gas that flows into the cavity and excludes atmospheric air. Electrogas welding is similar to electroslag welding (discussed later in this chapter) except that the arc is continuous from start to finish, and any slag present plays no part in heating the weld pool. Similarities are that electrogas welding is done in the vertical position, generally using molding shoes that may or may not be water cooled. The molding shoes are in contact with the joint to contain the molten weld metal in the cavity. The electrode is fed to the bottom of the joint by means of a wire-feeding system and contact tip. This mechanism will travel vertically along the joint to maintain the normal arc length between the electrode tip and the molten weld metal.

In many cases, one molding shoe is fixed and can be made of steel, thus becoming part of the joint, or the shoe can be made of copper so that it does not become part of the weld joint. On the side with the wire-feed mechanism, a sliding shoe is normally employed. This shoe rises with the wire-feed mechanism to maintain the weld metal within the cavity. Normally, only one electrode wire is used for making a weld.

A starting tab is necessary at the start of the weld because it takes a few moments for the process to stabilize and produce high-quality weld metal. Runoff tabs are normally required at the top of the joint so that the weld metal of the joint will extend above the parts being joined. Both the starting and runoff tabs are removed from the ends of the joint after the weld is completed.

Method of Application

The electrogas welding process is continuous; once the process has started it should be continued until the weld joint is completed. Although the process is automatic, the welding apparatus should be monitored by an operator, primarily to provide guidance or ensure that the electrode and arc are centered between the molding shoes and the parts being welded. It is also important to maintain shielding gas flow during the entire welding operation. The arc voltage is utilized to provide control of the vertical motion of the apparatus, the motion being controlled so that the arc length will remain constant from start to finish.

Molding shoes, particularly for the face of welds, should have sufficient relief to provide the normal reinforcement of a groove weld. For fillet welds, a smooth contour of the fillet can be obtained with the correct cross section of the molding shoe.

Equipment Requirements

Equipment for the electrogas welding process normally utilizes only one electrode, and oscillation of the electrode within the weld joint is not generally used. The welding head assembly is normally mounted on a carriage that is elevated as the weld progresses. For shipbuilding, the entire apparatus, which may also carry the welding operator, will move from the very bottom of the side of the ship to the top. This is done with a precision elevating system controlled by the arc voltage.

Smaller but similar equipment is utilized for welding large storage tanks. The control for the entire operation is mounted with the welding head and is conveniently available to the welding operator. This enables the operator to start the weld and have it run continuously until the joint is completed.

Electrode wire. The electrode wire must be matched to the material being welded and can be specified according to AWS Specification B5.26, "Consumables Used for Electrogas Welding of Carbon and High-Strength, Low-Alloy Steels." This specification covers both solid and flux-cored wires.

Shielding gas. The shielding gas, which is normally CO_2, should be specified as welding grade, with a minimum dew point of 0 to 40°F (-18 to 4.4°C). The shielding gas delivery system must provide efficient shielding of the molten metal to avoid atmospheric contamination. The start and stop of shielding gas flow is controlled by the system.

Wire feed. The wire-drive feed motor and control system is the same as used for other consumable electrode wire processes. Normally, the wire feed motor is mounted adjacent to the weld joint, with a contact tube delivery system bringing the electrode into the center of the joint and pointed downward within the cavity.

Molding shoes. The sliding molding shoes are normally water cooled and designed for the specific joint and application. They generally include a water-flow channel and are made of copper to avoid melting of the shoes. Water circulation should be of sufficient volume to avoid any surface melting of the retaining shoe. A water circulator that includes a heat exchanger is normally used. Size of the heat exchanger must be sufficient to remove the heat generated in the weld.

Current Used

The welding circuit used for the electrogas welding process is essentially the same as for the other continuous or consumable electrode processes. Electrode-positive polarity d-c (DCEP) is used. A constant-voltage system, with a constant and adjustable-speed wire feeder is used. The welding current may range from as low as 100 to as high as 400 A. The welding voltage ranges from 20 to 30 V. The power source must be rated at 100% duty cycle because some electrogas welds take more than an hour to complete. The current capacity of the machine must exceed the current required for the single electrode, according to the welding procedure schedule. Transformer-rectifier type machines are best suited for electrogas welding.

Welding Procedures

Even though the electrogas process is normally an automatic process, the operator must be continually alert to make adjustments as required during the welding operation. The operator must have a good knowledge of electrogas welding because of the different effects of changing various parameters. In some respects, the effects are opposite those expected when using the gas metal arc welding process. For example, increasing the wire-feed speed increases the welding current but does not increase the sidewall penetration of an electrogas weld. Increasing the welding voltage increases the gap between the end of the electrode and the molten metal, and this increases sidewall penetration.

If the electrode wire is not properly centered, the penetration on the opposite sides of the weld joint will be different and nonuniform. Also, the electrode should be centered between the molding shoes. However, if one molding shoe is steel rather than copper, the electrode should be directed more to the side of the joint with the copper retaining shoe.

If the retaining shoe does not fit tightly along the joint, the molten weld metal may run out of the cavity. If this happens, steps must be taken immediately to stop the leak. This is done by using a putty-like sealing preparation made of clay. Any leaks should be immediately sealed off to avoid loss of the weld.

The operator should make a rough calculation to determine the amount of electrode wire required for a specific joint. Sufficient wire should be available on the machine prior to starting the weld. Once the weld is started, it should run continuously until it is finished. If the operation stops for any reason, the machine should be turned off immediately, corrections made, and the weld restarted. At the point of stopping and restarting, there is normally an unfused area that must be gouged out and rewelded with an arc welding process capable of welding in the vertical position.

If the retaining shoes leak and water gets into the weld cavity, the operation must be stopped. This can create a safety hazard and will create gross porosity of the weld metal. With respect to water-cooled shoes, the operator must ensure that water flow is uninterrupted during the entire welding operation.

Welding procedure schedules for electrogas welding are presented in Table 9-22. These may not necessarily be the only conditions that can be used. It is possible that conditions can be adjusted to obtain optimum results, however, qualification tests should be made before utilizing published welding procedure schedules, especially when welding critical jobs. Recommended practices for electrogas welding are presented in ANSI/AWS Standard C5.7.

SUBMERGED ARC WELDING

Submerged arc welding (SAW) differs from other arc welding processes in that a blanket of fusible, granular mate-

SUBMERGED ARC WELDING

rial—commonly called flux—is used for shielding the arc and the molten metal (see Fig. 9-29). The arc is struck between the workpiece and a bare, consumable wire electrode, the tip of which is submerged in the flux. Because the arc is completely covered by the flux, it is not visible, and the weld is produced without the flash, spatter, and sparks that characterize open arc processes. Pressure is not used. The nature of the flux is such that very little smoke or visible fumes are developed.

The process is either semiautomatic or fully automatic, with the electrode(s) fed mechanically to the welding gun, head, or heads. In semiautomatic welding, the welder moves the gun, usually equipped with a flux-feeding device, along the joint. Flux feed may be by gravity flow through a nozzle concentric with the electrode, from a small hopper atop the gun, or it may be through a concentric nozzle tube connected to an air-pressurized flux tank.

Flux may also be applied in advance of the welding operation or ahead of the arc from a hopper run along the joint. In fully automatic submerged arc welding, flux is fed continuously to the joint ahead of or concentric to the arc. Fully

TABLE 9-22
Typical Procedure Schedule for Electrogas Welding

Two Electrodes—Nonoscillating					
Thickness T, in. (mm)	Maximum Height H, ft (m)	Root RO Opening, in. (mm)	Electrode Spacing ES, in. (mm)	Welding Voltage, V	d-c Current, A
3 (75)	20 (6)	1 (25)	2 1/2 (62)	41	850
4 (100)	20 (6)	1 (25)	2 1/2 (62)	44	850
5 (125)	20 (6)	1 (25)	2 1/2 (62)	47	850

Guide tube size—5/8" (15.9 mm) OD x 1/8" (3.2 mm) ID

Two Electrodes—with Oscillation*						
Thickness T, in. (mm)	Maximum Height H, ft (m)	Root RO Opening, in. (mm)	Oscillation Length, in. (mm)	Traverse Speed,** ipm (mm/min)	Welding Voltage, V	d-c Current, A
5 (125)	10 (3)	1 1/4 (31.4)	1 (25)	20 (500)	42	1500
6 (150)	10 (3)	1 1/4 (31.4)	2 (50)	40 (1000)	43	1500
8 (200)	10 (3)	1 1/4 (31.4)	4 (100)	80 (2000)	46	1500
10 (250)	10 (3)	1 1/4 (31.4)	6 (150)	120 (3000)	49	1500
12 (300)	10 (3)	1 1/4 (31.4)	8 (200)	120 (3000)	52	1500

Guide tube size—5/8" (15.9 mm) OD x 1/8" (3.2 mm) ID

Single Electrode—Nonoscillating				
Thickness T, in. (mm)	Maximum Height H, ft (m)	Root RO Opening, in. (mm)	Welding Voltage, V	d-c Current, A
3/4 (19)	20 (6)	1 (25)	36	500
1 (25)	20 (6)	1 (25)	39	600
2 (50)	20 (6)	1 (25)	40	700
3 (75)	20 (6)	1 (25)	43	700

Guide tube size—1/2" (12.7 mm) OD x 1/8" (3.2 mm) ID

Single Electrode—with Oscillation*						
Thickness T, in. (mm)	Maximum Height H, ft (m)	Root RO Opening, in. (mm)	Oscillation Length, in. (mm)	Traverse Speed,** ipm (mm/min)	Welding Voltage, V	d-c Current, A
2 (50)	5 (1.5)	1 1/4 (31.4)	1 1/4 (31.4)	25 (625)	40	700
3 (75)	5 (1.5)	1 1/4 (31.4)	1 1/4 (31.4)	45 (1125)	41	750
4 (100)	5 (1.5)	1 1/4 (31.4)	1 1/4 (31.4)	65 (1625)	44	750
5 (125)	5 (1.5)	1 1/4 (31.4)	1 1/4 (31.4)	85 (1925)	47	750

Guide tube size—5/8" (15.9 mm) OD x 1/8" (3.2 mm) ID

* Electrode diameter 3/32" (2.4 mm).
** Based on 10 second oscillation cycle. Water cooled shoes and slag flux used.

automatic installations are commonly equipped with vacuum systems to pick up the unfused flux left by the welding head or heads for cleaning and reuse.

Applications

With the proper selection of equipment, the submerged arc process is applicable to a wide variety of welding requirements by industry. It can be used with all types of joints and permits welding a full range of carbon and low-alloy steels, from 16-gage [0.063" (1.69 mm)] sheet to the thickest plate. It is also applicable to some high-alloy and heat-treated steels, as well as stainless steels, and is a favored process for rebuilding and hard-surfacing. Any degree of mechanization can be used, from handheld semiautomatic guns to boom or track-carried and fixture-held multiple welding heads. The submerged arc process is used extensively in ship and barge building, railroad car building, pipe manufacture, and in fabricating structural beams, girders, and columns where long welds are required. Automatic submerged arc installations are also key features of the welding areas of plants turning out mass-produced assemblies joined with repetitive short welds.

Advantages

The high quality of submerged arc welds, high deposition rates, deep penetration, adaptability of the process to full mechanization, and the comfort characteristics (no glare, sparks, spatter, smoke, or excessive heat radiation) make it a preferred process in steel fabrication. The high deposition rates attained by the use of high currents are chiefly responsible for the economies achieved with the process. Cost reductions when changing from the manual shielded metal arc process to submerged arc are frequently dramatic. For example, a hand-held submerged arc gun with mechanized travel may reduce welding costs more than 50%. With fully automatic multiarc equipment, it is not unusual for the costs to be only 10% of those with stick-electrode welding.

Welds made under the protective layer of flux have good ductility and impact resistance, and uniformity in bead appearance. Mechanical properties at least equal to those of the base metal are consistently obtained. In single-pass welds, the fused base metal may greatly influence the chemical and mechanical properties of the weld. For this reason, it is sometimes

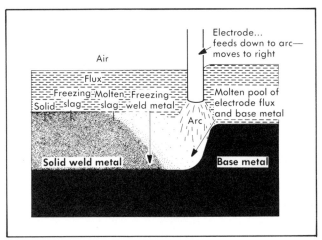

Fig. 9-29 Submerged arc process: enlarged cross-sectional view of arc welding under a blanket of flux. (*Lincoln Electric Co.*)

unnecessary to use electrodes of the same composition as the base metal for welding many of the low-alloy steels.

Limitations

Except for special applications, the submerged arc process is limited to welding in the flat and horizontal positions. As a result, workpieces must be flat or nearly flat. Flux, flux handling equipment, and workholding fixtures are required. Many joints also require the use of backing plates.

Because of its high penetration, the submerged arc process requires less deposited metal and, therefore, a change in joint design. Generally, for automatic welding, V-grooves should be wider than they are deep. The groove is used primarily to prevent buildup of the weld rather than to secure penetration. The vee should be made within 10% of expected bead width and only as deep as required to eliminate unnecessary buildup.

If a deep, narrow groove, such as that designed for hand welding, is used, internal bead cracking may result from internal shrinkage unless low currents are used. If the arc voltage used is too high with such a narrow groove, there will also be a possibility of slag inclusion and incomplete fusion at the bottom of the vee. With low voltage, an undercut may appear at the edge of the bead. The arc being deep in the groove, there may also be a tendency to wander to one side, resulting in a weld being off the seam. A good rule to follow is to have the weld 1 1/2 times as wide as it is deep, as shown in Fig. 9-30.

Edge preparation. Joint edges must be clean of all foreign matter such as moisture, rust, dirt, oil, grease, and paint primer. The abutting edges must be dry and free from foreign matter. Cleaning the top of the plates will not help very much.

Flux. The flux must also be free from contamination by foreign matter such as grease, water, mill scale, and iron oxide.

Fitup. For uniform results, the fitup must be accurately controlled. For sheet metal, seams should be tight where no gap is specified, and the maximum offset of the edges must be not more than 10% of the plate thickness and never more than 3/32" (2.4 mm). Drive fits are to be avoided, as they increase the tendency for cracking and porosity on heavy plate. A slight gap of 1/64 to 1/32" (0.39 to 0.8 mm) helps to minimize rigidity of the joint and reduce the tendency for cracking.

Gaps more than 1/32" (0.8 mm) should be sealed for satisfactory automatic welding. For square butt joints in plates to 3/8" (9.5 mm) thick, the sealing bead should be on the side of the first automatic pass. For plate thickness more than 3/8", seal on the second-pass side.

On butt welds with beveled edges, make the sealing bead on the automatic first-pass side. If work is held firmly against a platen, gaps can be allowed because the granular flux fills up the gap and supports the molten metal. If the molten flux runs out of the joint, the molten metal usually follows.

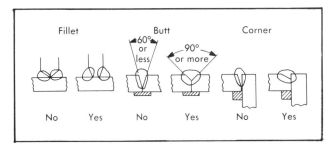

Fig. 9-30 V-grooves for submerged arc welds.

SUBMERGED ARC WELDING

Whenever plate edges, vee or square-butt, are open more than 1/32″ (0.8 mm), allowing flux to fall into the seam, precautions must be taken to eliminate trapped-slag porosity. This type of porosity consists of short, large-diameter holes, compared with the long, small-diameter holes found in the presence of moisture or rust.

The joint must be prepared so that the automatic weld completely remelts and eliminates all the flux in the groove or vee. This may require an increased cross section, manual-seal bead, or a change of joint design to a U-groove or wider vee (90°) so that the arc reaches the bottom of the vee. The other alternative is to allow a minimum of 5/32″ (4 mm) of unfused flux between a seal, whether a platen or a manual bead, and the deepest penetrated edge of the automatic weld. A good criterion to follow in the case of double-pass welding is to reduce the automatic welding current on the first pass to the point where only faint color can be seen on the bottom side of the seam.

Principles

During welding, the heat of the arc melts some of the flux along with the tip of the electrode. The tip of the electrode and the welding zone are always surrounded and shielded by molten flux, surmounted by a layer of unfused flux, with the electrode held a short distance above the workpiece. As the electrode progresses along the joint, the lighter molten flux rises above the molten metal in the form of a slag.

The weld metal, having a higher melting (freezing) point, solidifies while the slag above it is still molten. The slag then freezes over the newly solidified weld metal, continuing to protect the metal from contamination (while it is very hot and reactive) with atmospheric oxygen and nitrogen. Upon cooling and removal of any unmelted flux for reuse, the slag is readily peeled from the weld. In one variation, electric current passes between two electrodes that meet just above the surface of the work. In this so-called series submerged arc welding, the work is not part of the electrical circuit.

Fluxes

There are two general types of submerged arc fluxes, bonded and fused. In the bonded fluxes, the finely ground chemicals are mixed, treated with a bonding agent, and manufactured into a granular aggregate. The deoxidizers are incorporated in the flux. The fused fluxes are a form of glass resulting from fusing the various chemicals and then grinding the glass to a granular form. Fluxes are available that add alloying elements to the weld metal, enabling alloy weld metal to be made with a mild steel electrode.

The insulating blanket of flux above the arc prevents rapid escape of heat and concentrates it in the welding zone. Not only are the electrode and base metal melted rapidly, but the fusion is deep into the base metal. The deep penetration allows the use of small welding grooves, thus minimizing the amount of filler metal required and permitting fast welding speeds. Fast welding, in turn, minimizes the total heat input into the assembly, and thus, tends to prevent problems of heat distortion. Even relatively thick joints can be welded in one pass by the submerged arc process.

Current Used

Both a-c and d-c are used for submerged arc welding. Alternating current from a constant-current power supply is used primarily for automatic welding systems. A primary advantage of a-c is that it minimizes arc blow.

Direct current provides better control of bead shape, depth of penetration, and welding speed. Electrode-positive polarity d-c (DCEP) provides the best control of the bead shape. Electrode-negative polarity d-c (DCEN) provides the highest deposition rate, but penetration is lower.

With d-c, the power supply can be of the constant-voltage or constant-current type. Constant-voltage power supplies are more common for small-diameter electrodes and constant-current types for large-diameter electrodes. All power supply units should be rated at 100% duty cycle because most submerged arc welding operations are continuous.

High currents can be used in submerged arc welding, and extremely high heats are developed. Because the current is applied to the electrode a short distance above its tip, relatively high amperages can be used on small-diameter electrodes. This results in extremely high current densities on relatively small cross sections of electrode. Currents as high as 600 A can be carried in electrodes as small as 5/64″ (2 mm) diam, giving a density in the order of 100,000 A/in.^{2} (155 A/m^2)—6 to 10 times that carried in stick electrodes.

Because of the high current density, the meltoff rate is much higher for a given electrode diameter than with stick-electrode welding. The meltoff rate is affected by the electrode material, the flux, type of current, polarity, and length of wire beyond the point of electrical contact in the gun or head.

Operating Conditions

Proper wire sizes and other conditions for the submerged arc welding of mild steel are presented in Table 9-23. Variations from these conditions are permissible and often desirable, depending on the specific application.

Heat treatments are seldom required for welding low-carbon or structural steels, but are sometimes used to prevent warpage or ensure low hardness for subsequent machining. In the welding of high-carbon or alloy steels, however, preheating and postheating are common to keep the martensite content of the weld at a minimum.

STUD WELDING

Stud welding (SW) is an arc welding process that produces coalescence (joining) by heating with an arc between a metal stud or other fastener and base metal. When the abutting surfaces to be joined are heated to the proper temperature, they are brought together under pressure for solidification to take place. Shielding gas may or may not be used.

Applications

Studs are attached to only one side of workpieces, thus eliminating the need to have access to the reverse sides of assemblies. Stud-welded fasteners are used in place of rivets, drilled and tapped holes, and manually arc-welded fasteners.

Applications for stud welding include the attaching of insulation to ductwork, truck cabs, and bulkheads. Other applications include attachment of handles to cookware, heat transfer studs in boilers, heat radiation fins in motors, assembling electronic panels, securing electrical and hydraulic lines, and the attachment of panels in the automotive industry. Stud welding is being used extensively in shipbuilding, in the automotive industry, in both large and small appliance industries, and other industries where fasteners must be attached.

Stud and base materials are the same as those joined by other arc welding processes. Metals most frequently stud welded are

TABLE 9-23
Typical Conditions for the Submerged Arc Welding of Mild Steel

Material Thickness, in. (mm)	Type of Weld*	Electrode Diameter, in. (mm)	Welding Current, A (d-c, electrode positive)	Arc Voltage, V	Wire Feed, ipm (mm/min)	Travel Speed, ipm (mm/min)
0.063 (1.60)	Square groove	3/32 (2.4)	300	22	68 (1727)	100-140 (2540-3556)
		1/8 (3.2)	425	26	53 (1346)	95-120 (2413-3048)
	Bead	3/32 (2.4)	350	20	78 (1981)	120-160 (3048-4064)
0.078 (1.98)	Square groove	3/32 (2.4)	375	23	85 (2159)	100-140 (2540-3556)
		1/8 (3.2)	500	27	65 (1651)	75-85 (1905-2159)
	Bead	3/32 (2.4)	400	22	90 (2286)	120-160 (3048-4064)
0.109 (2.77)	Square groove	1/8 (3.2)	400	23	51 (1295)	70-90 (1778-2286)
		1/8 (3.2)	550	27	65 (1651)	50-60 (1270-1524)
	Bead	1/8 (3.2)	450	24	57 (1448)	70-90 (1778-2286)
	Fillet	1/8 (3.2)	400	25	51 (1295)	40-60 (1016-1524)
0.140 (3.56)	Square groove	1/8 (3.2)	425	26	53 (1346)	50-80 (1270-2032)
		5/32 (4.0)	650	27	55 (1397)	40-45 (1016-1143)
	Bead	1/8 (3.2)	600	30	77 (1956)	45-85 (1143-2159)
3/16 (4.8)	Square groove	5/32 (4.0)	600	26	50 (1270)	40-75 (1016-1905)
		3/16 (4.8)	875	31	55 (1397)	35-40 (889-1016)
	Fillet	1/8 (3.2)	525	26	67 (1702)	35-40 (889-1016)
1/4 (6.4)	Square groove	3/16 (4.8)	800	28	50 (1270)	30-35 (762-889)
		3/16 (4.8)	875	31	56 (1422)	22-25 (559-635)
	Fillet	5/32 (4.0)	650	28	56 (1422)	30-35 (762-889)
	V-groove	3/16 (4.8)	750	30	47 (1194)	25-40 (635-1016)
3/8 (9.5)	Square groove	3/16 (4.8)	950	32	61 (1549)	20-25 (508-635)
		3/16 (4.8)	First pass 500	32	27 (686)	30 (762)

(continued)

STUD WELDING

TABLE 9-23—*Continued*

Material Thickness, in. (mm)	Type of Weld*	Electrode Diameter, in. (mm)	Welding Current, A (d-c, electrode positive)	Arc Voltage, V	Wire Feed, ipm (mm/min)	Travel Speed, ipm (mm/min)
3/8 (9.5)			Second pass 750	33	47 (1194)	30 (762)
	V-groove	3/16 (4.8)	900	33	57 (1448)	23-25 (584-635)
	Fillet	3/16 (4.8)	950	31	61 (1549)	30-35 (762-889)
	Bead	5/32 (4.0)	650	31	56 (1422)	30-35 (762-889)
1/2 (12.7)	Square groove	3/16 (4.8)	975	33	63 (1600)	12-17 (305-432)
		3/16 (4.8)	First pass 650	34	40 (1016)	25 (635)
			Second pass 850	35	54 (1372)	23-27 (584-686)
	V-groove	3/16 (4.8)	950	35	61 (1549)	18-20 (457-508)
	Fillet	3/16 (4.8)	950	33	61 (1549)	14-17 (356-432)
	Bead	3/16 (4.8)	750	34	47 (1194)	23-27 (584-686)
3/4 (19.1)	Square groove	7/32 (5.6)	1000	35	49 (1245)	68 (1727)
		3/16 (4.8)	First pass 925	37	59 (1499)	12 (305)
			Second pass 1000	40	65 (1651)	11 (279)
	V-groove	7/32 (5.6)	950	36	46 (1168)	10-12 (254-305)
	Fillet	7/32 (5.6)	1000	35	49 (1245)	6-8 (152-203)
	Bead	7/32 (5.6)	950	36	46 (1168)	10-12 (254-305)

* Data are for the flat-horizontal fillet position. Backup required for groove welds may be either copper or steel (or flux).

low-carbon steels, ferritic and austenitic stainless steels, low-alloy steels, titanium, nickel alloys, aluminum, and copper alloys. In addition, zinc die castings, magnesium alloys, and zirconium alloys are stud welded.

Advantages

Stud welding is a rapid process. Up to 20 studs per minute can be welded by handheld equipment, while up to 50 studs or more can be welded utilizing automatic, capacitor-discharge stud welding equipment. Robotic systems with automatic feeds have been developed for stud welding.

Base plates can be as thin as 0.015″ (0.38 mm) when using the capacitor-discharge process, while the base plate thickness for arc stud welding should normally be no less than one-third of the stud diameter to achieve maximum strength.

Studs of various cross-sectional shapes, such as round, square, rectangular, and hexagonal shapes, are commonly welded. Stud welds are generally made to plane surfaces, but with appropriate accessories, studs can be welded to curved surfaces such as tubes and pipes.

Stud welding eliminates the need for drilling and tapping and provides a neat appearance. There is no need for cleaning or polishing after welding. Full fastener strength is developed—the weld is as strong as the fastener and parent metal. The fasteners cannot vibrate loose or drop off. The studs can be precisely positioned at any desired location. Recommended practices for stud welding are presented in ANSI/AWS Standard C5.4.

Limitations

Studs, fasteners, or other similar parts must be of a size and shape that permit chucking. Areas to be welded must be clean and free from rust, grease, oil, dirt, or plated materials. Studs or fasteners to be joined must be made of a weldable material, and one end must be designed for welding.

Types of Stud Welding

The two basic types of stud welding are arc stud welding and capacitor-discharge stud welding. In both methods, the stud serves as an electrode, and a gun is the electrode holder.

Method selection. In making the decision as to which of the two basic types of stud welding to use, several factors have to be considered. These factors include the stud or fastener size, stud base material strengths, and weld fillet clearance. In general, studs more than 1/2″ (12.7 mm) diam are arc stud welded, while studs less than 1/8″ (3.2 mm) diam are capacitor-discharge

welded. Studs from 1/8 to 1/2″ diam can be welded by either process, and the choice would depend on other factors.

Arc stud welding. Arc stud welding uses for its power a high-current d-c source, such as a welding generator, transformer-rectifier elding unit, or a bank of heavy-duty batteries. A welding gun with a chuck to hold the fastener, a controller with a timer, and interconnecting cables make up the rest of the necessary equipment. Figure 9-31 shows the electrical hookup for arc stud welding. Some equipment has the controller integrated directly into the power supply.

A weld timer in the controller can, depending on the stud diameter, range from 1/10 to 2 seconds. Current amplitude is controlled at the power source and, again depending on the stud diameter, can range from 200 to 2500 A or more.

A sectional view of a typical arc stud welding gun, along with pertinent accessories, is shown in Fig. 9-32. As shown in Fig. 9-33, view *a*, a ceramic arc shield completely surrounds the weld end of the stud during welding. This serves a twofold purpose in that it forms the molten metal into a fillet around the stud for added strength, and it also shields the operator from the arc. Arc welding studs range from 1/8 to 1 1/4″ (3.2 to 32 mm) diam.

Capacitor-discharge stud welding. This method uses a high-capacitance capacitor bank as a power source by charging the capacitors to a voltage generally between 100 and 200 V d-c.

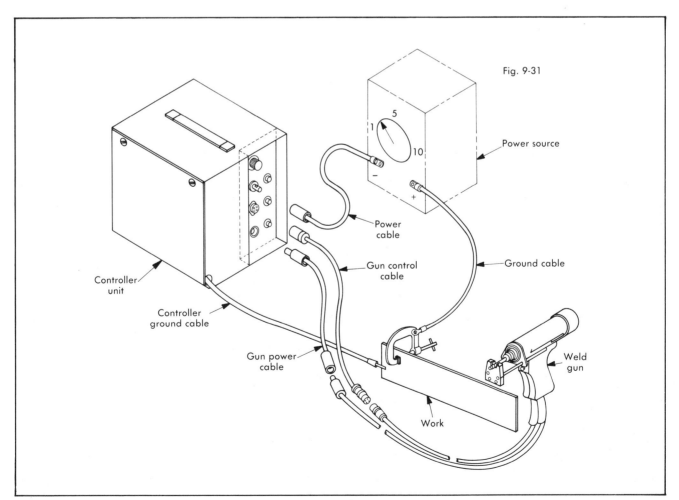

Fig. 9-31 Electrical arrangement for arc stud welding. (*KSM Fastening Systems*)

PLASMA ARC WELDING

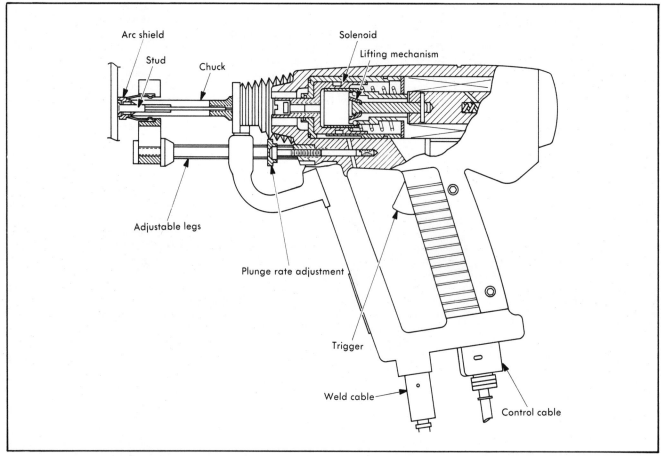

Fig. 9-32 Typical arc stud welding gun. (*KSM Fastening Systems*)

Capacitor discharge studs range in size from 0.020 to 1/2″ (0.51 to 12.7 mm) diam and generally have a small centrally located tip on the weld end. Figure 9-33, view *b*, shows the sequences occurring during a contact capacitor-discharge weld. Other versions of capacitor-discharge stud welding are available, such as gap capacitor-discharge stud welding and drawn-arc capacitor-discharge stud welding.

Gap welding. In gap welding, the stud is initially positioned away from the surface of the workpiece. Upon triggering the gun, the stud is forced toward the workpiece.

Drawn-arc welding. In this method of capacitor-discharge stud welding, the stud is initially in contact with the workpiece and then withdrawn through the use of a solenoid. After a precise, preselected time, the stud is forced into the base plate, similar to arc stud welding.

PLASMA ARC WELDING

Plasma arc welding (PAW) is an arc welding process that employs a high-temperature constricted or nonconstricted plasma column to obtain the melting and coalescence of most metals. The term *plasma* refers to a gas that has been sufficiently ionized to conduct an electrical current. The plasma is produced by forcing an inert gas and an electrical current from a tungsten electrode through a constricting orifice (nozzle). As a result, the plasma arc takes on a narrow columnar shape with properties that can enhance welding.

Applications

Plasma welding is not a new process, but only in the past few years has it gained significant acceptance. It has now proven its value in the area of repetitious automated welds and is being used most frequently as an alternative to the gas tungsten arc welding (GTAW) process.

Plasma welding is being used extensively in the automotive industry for the production of various subassemblies, such as alternator, transmission, drivetrain, and engine components. Other applications include formed sheet metal boxes, filing cabinets, computer cabinets, door and window frames, battery and capacitor canisters, and home appliances. The process is also being used in the production of pipe and tubing and for joining coils and other cylindrical components made from flat plate stock.

Advantages

For most applications, the plasma arc process offers increased electrode life, reliable arc starting, improved arc stability, better penetration control, and reduced current levels. In some cases, it permits increased travel speeds and improved weld quality. Also, the plasma arc process is less sensitive to operating variables.

Electrode protection. In the plasma arc process, the tungsten electrode, which is secured inside the plasma torch and behind the orifice, is protected from outside impurities that would normally attack a hot surface. With this protection, the electrode is not exposed to base material contaminants such as forming and stamping oils, degreasers, and surface oxides. These contaminants, under intense arc temperatures, can constantly attack a tungsten electrode, causing contamination and erosion. The tungsten electrode in plasma welding can operate many hours before requiring a change.

Reliable arc starting. Arc initiation for the plasma arc process is provided by a pilot arc (see Fig. 9-34, view *a*) that resides in the orifice area of the torch. The pilot arc is an arc that exists between the tungsten electrode and the orifice. It is started by imposing high frequency (from a small high-frequency generator inside the control console) on a low direct current for a short duration of time to start the ionization of the gas. Once the pilot arc has been established, the requirements for high frequency are no longer needed. The pilot arc now remains on to assist the starting of the main transferred welding arc (view *b*).

Limitations

Possible limitations of the plasma welding process include the high initial cost of the equipment, size of the torches, and the reduced accessibility to certain weld joint configurations. Plasma welding is also limited to metal thicknesses of approximately 3/8″ (9.5 mm) on stainless steel and 1/2″ (12.7 mm) on

titanium. The process is generally limited to flat, horizontal, or vertical-up welding when performing single-pass welds in the keyhole mode.

Principles of Operation

Plasma welding is commonly used in two modes of operation: melt-in fusion and keyhole fusion welding. An orifice (also called a nozzle or tip), which is inserted into the front end of the torch body, provides for the lamina flow of the plasma gas and constriction of the arc. The magnitude of this constriction is normally controlled by three variables—the orifice diameter, the plasma gas flow rate, and the electrode setback, which is the distance the electrode is recessed inside the torch (see Fig. 9-35). By operating any given size orifice at higher plasma gas flow rates and with the electrode placed at maximum setback, the most constricted arc will occur. This type of arc is typically used when making keyhole single-pass welds requiring increased penetration, narrower weld beads, minimized heat-affected zone, and reduced base material distortion. Keyhole welding is generally used on material thicknesses ranging from 0.090 to 0.254″ (2.29 to 6.45 mm).

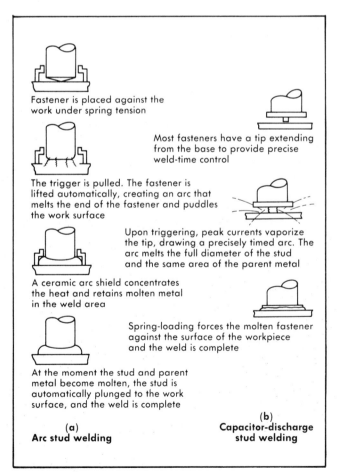

Fastener is placed against the work under spring tension

Most fasteners have a tip extending from the base to provide precise weld-time control

The trigger is pulled. The fastener is lifted automatically, creating an arc that melts the end of the fastener and puddles the work surface

Upon triggering, peak currents vaporize the tip, drawing a precisely timed arc. The arc melts the full diameter of the stud and the same area of the parent metal

A ceramic arc shield concentrates the heat and retains molten metal in the weld area

Spring-loading forces the molten fastener against the surface of the workpiece and the weld is complete

At the moment the stud and parent metal become molten, the stud is automatically plunged to the work surface, and the weld is complete

**(a)
Arc stud welding**

**(b)
Capacitor-discharge
stud welding**

Fig. 9-33 Basic types of stud welding: (a) arc stud welding and (b) capacitor-discharge welding. (*KSM Fastening Systems***)**

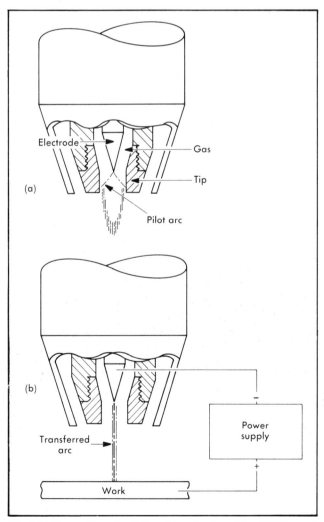

Electrode

Gas

Tip

(a)

Pilot arc

(b)

Transferred arc

Power supply

Work

Fig. 9-34 Current flows in pilot arc (view *a*) and arc (view *b*). (*Thermal Dynamics Corp.***)**

PLASMA ARC WELDING

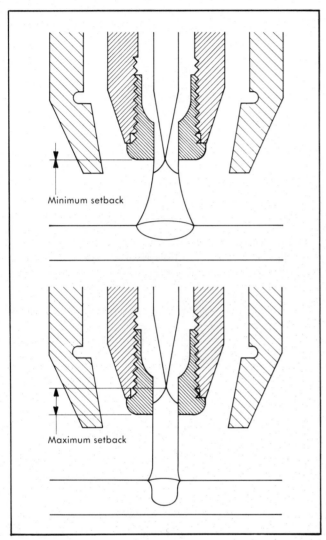

Fig. 9-35 Minimum and maximum electrode setback for plasma arc welding. (*Thermal Dynamics Corp.* **)**

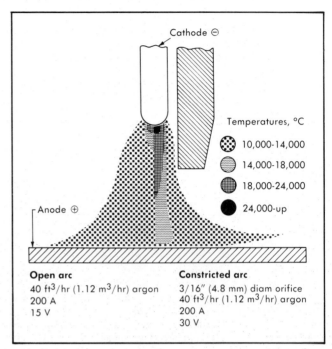

Fig. 9-36 Effect of arc constriction on voltage and plasma temperature.

By reducing the electrode setback and plasma gas flow rates, a softer, less constricted arc will occur. This type of arc is typically used for the melt-in fusion mode and allows for faster travel speeds on reduced base material thicknesses, 0.010 to 0.156″ (0.25 to 3.96 mm).

Typical electrical and thermal changes caused in an arc by constriction are shown in Fig. 9-36, wherein arc conditions are 200 A at 15 V with 40 ft^3/hr (1.12 m^3/hr) of argon. The left side of the figure shows the open gas tungsten arc form, and the right side shows the arc after it has been constricted by passing it through a 3/16″ (4.8 mm) diam orifice. With the same current and gas flow, arc voltage doubles to 30 V. The very high temperature zones of the arc have been projected downward. Constricting the arc tends to focus the arc energy on a smaller area of the workpiece because the constricted arc does not have the angle of divergence of the open arc.

Melt-In Fusion Welding

Generally, the melt-in mode is most often used with the plasma arc welding process. It is accomplished with a softer, less constricted arc, using lower plasma gas flow rates, a reduced electrode setback, and current levels in the range of approximately 1-200 A. This type of mode is similar to that of gas tungsten arc welding, with additional advantages in many applications. In addition to the advantages of plasma arc welding previously mentioned in this section, the melt-in mode offers easy adaptability to mechanized welding, reduced heat input for minimum distortion, a more directional arc (less arc wander), and improved penetration control.

Types of welds. The melt-in mode of the plasma process can be used for spot, corner and edge, flange, square butt, surface, and lap welds. Spot welding is typically used for tacking, joining, or sealing operations.

Plasma arc welding in the melt-in mode can be done in all positions. Typically, circumferential and longitudinal seam welds are made in the flat positions. Corner, edge, and surface (lamination) welds can be made at faster travel speeds with reduced heat input in the vertical-down position.

Operating parameters. Suggested starting parameters for plasma arc welding various steels (carbon, alloy, and stainless) of different thickness with the melt-in mode are presented in Fig. 9-37. Faster travel speeds may be required for corner, edge, and flanged welds.

Joint design and fixturing. Common practices in joint design and fixturing typically used with gas tungsten arc welding can also be used for plasma arc welding. The use of copper or aluminum heat sinks can enhance welding in many applications. When thin metals are welded, both joint edges must be in continuous contact and must melt simultaneously to fuse together into a single weld puddle. Separation between the joint edges before or during welding will allow the edges to melt separately and remain separate.

Much larger tolerances for joint fixturing can be obtained by flanging the edges. Turned-up edges act as preplaced filler wire to fill the gap and ensure melt contact of the sides of the joint.

They also stiffen the joint edges to minimize warpage from heat built up during welding. Flanging is recommended for all butt joints in foil thicknesses below 0.010″ (0.25 mm).

Keyhole Fusion Welding

Keyhole fusion welds are generally produced by using a stiff, more constricted arc. In the keyhole mode, penetration is obtained by the combination of plasma and gas momentum with thermal conduction. With increased plasma gas flow rates and electrode setback, a hole known as the *keyhole* is pierced through the entire metal thickness at the leading edge of the weld puddle, where the forces of the plasma jet (column) displace the molten metal. As the torch travel progresses constantly, the molten metal, supported by surface tension, flows behind the keyhole to form the weld bead.

Keyhole welding is almost exclusively performed in the automated mode. Manual keyhole welding is not generally recommended because of difficulties in maintaining consistent travel speeds, torch position, or filler material additions. The keyhole mode is typically used to produce square butt welds.

Advantages. Advantages of the keyhole mode of plasma arc welding include minimum preparation requirements for welding and the capabilities for producing single-pass welds with narrow beads at reduced current levels. Also, less filler metal is required, and visual proof is provided of 100% weld penetration.

Limitations. A possible limitation to use of the keyhole mode is that it should only be employed for automated operations. The process is also limited to the flat, horizontal, and vertical-up welding positions and is more sensitive to changes in operating variables.

Keyhole starting. In material thicknesses less than 0.090″ (2.29 mm), circumferential and longitudinal seam, keyhole welds can generally be started at full operating current, plasma gas flow rate, and travel speed. In this thickness range, the keyhole is developed with little disturbance in the weld puddle, and the weld surface and underbead are kept fairly smooth.

However, in material thicknesses greater than 0.090″, the operating parameters can produce a tunneling or gouging effect underneath the surface of the molten puddle, just prior to piercing the weld joint and starting the keyhole. Because this tunneling or gouging action may cause gas porosity or surface irregularities, starting tabs for longitudinal welds and programmed taper (up-slope) of plasma gas and current for circumferential welds is normally recommended.

Keyhole ending. If the welding current is turned off abruptly at the end of a keyhole weld, the keyhole may not close. This is not usually objectionable when stopping on ending tabs that are typically used on longitudinal welds. However, the requirement for plasma gas and weld current taper (down-slope) is recommended for the ending of the keyhole on circumferential welds. This allows lowering the arc force and heat input so that the molten metal can gradually flow into the keyhole and solidify.

Underbead gas backing. When keyhole welding requires the use of an underbead backing, it is recommended that a rectangular-shaped groove to support the weldment, provide underbead shielding gas, and allow for the venting of the plasma column be used. Groove dimensions of approximately 1 to 1 1/2 times the metal thickness wide and 2 to 2 1/2 times deep are recommended. Shallow-grooved backing bars will cause the weld to become inverted toward the surface. A typical backing bar is illustrated in Fig. 9-38.

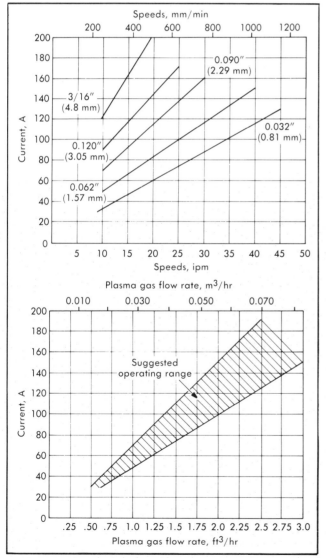

Fig. 9-37 Suggested starting parameters for plasma arc welding various steels of different thickness with the melt-in mode. (*Thermal Dynamics Corp.*)

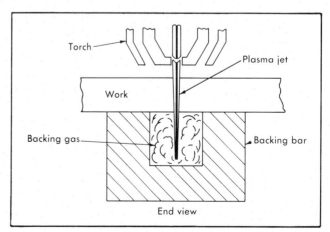

Fig. 9-38 Use of a backing bar in plasma arc welding.

Operating parameters. Suggested starting parameters for plasma arc welding various steels (carbon, alloy, and stainless) of different thickness with the keyhole mode are presented in Fig. 9-39. Electrode setback is at the maximum, and standoff from the work is between 1/8 and 1/4″ (3.2 and 6.4 mm) for this data.

Filler Metals

The exceptional penetrating power of the high-current plasma jet reduces the amount of filler wire, the number of passes, and the total arc time needed to join metal thicknesses requiring multipass welds. Grooves of vee or U shape for plasma arc welding may be much smaller than those for gas tungsten arc welding.

Filler wire can be added to the leading edge of a plasma arc weld puddle, exactly as in the gas tungsten arc process. Wire-height adjustments are not generally as critical with plasma arc welding because the wire can lift off the plate and melt into the plasma stream without contaminating the electrode. However, wire placement is still important because the wire can ball up when lifted from the plate, thus disrupting a keyhole weld.

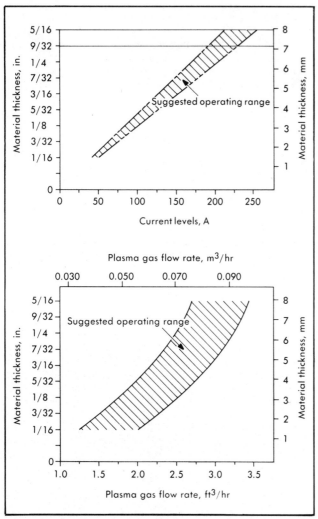

Fig. 9-39 Suggested starting parameters for plasma arc welding various steels of different thicknesses with the keyhole mode. (*Thermal Dynamics Corp.*)

Filler wire added to the leading edge of the puddle of a keyhole weld will flow around the keyhole to form a reinforced weld bead. This technique can be used on single-pass welds in materials up to about 1/4″ (6.4 mm) thick, generally with a square butt joint preparation. Filler wire is not generally added on the root pass of a multipass weld because the plasma jet melts the maximum amount of base metal that can be supported by surface tension. However, filler wire is sometimes added to improve metal flow.

Multipass Welding

In multipass welding, the root pass is usually a keyhole weld, followed by one or more nonkeyhole weld passes with filler metal. In the fill and cover passes, the force of the plasma jet is adjusted for suitable penetration by regulating the type and flow rate of plasma gas. Helium in the argon shielding gas is favored for some fill and cover passes because it provides a broader heat pattern and produces a flatter cover pass.

Gas Selection

The selection of the proper plasma and shielding gases for both the melt-in and keyhole modes of plasma arc welding is critical for optimum results. Because metals respond to impurities in both plasma and shielding gases, it is important that all gas supply lines be free from leaks and that all fittings are securely tightened.

Plasma gases. Argon and mixtures of argon and hydrogen are used as plasma gases for plasma arc welding.

Argon. Argon is the preferred plasma gas. It is totally inert, and its low ionization potential assures reliable arc starting and a dependable pilot arc. It also provides good arc stability and an excellent protective blanket for the tungsten electrode. Flow rates range from approximately 0.25 to 5.0 ft³/hr (0.007 to 0.014 m³/hr).

Argon-hydrogen mixtures. The addition of small amounts of hydrogen (about 5%) to argon is sometimes recommended. This increases the heat input to the weld puddle. Argon-hydrogen mixtures provide a hotter arc, assisting in both penetration and weld-puddle fluidity. However, the life of torch parts will be lower when using argon-hydrogen mixtures compared to argon alone. Flow rates range from approximately 0.25 to 5.0 ft³/hr (0.007 to 0.014 m³/hr), the same as for the use of argon alone.

Shielding gases. Argon and mixtures of argon and hydrogen are also used for shielding gases. Helium and mixtures of helium and argon are also used for shielding.

Argon. Argon may be used as a shielding gas for all metals. It provides good arc stability and effective cleaning at lower current levels (less than 20 A). It is also recommended for use in welding aluminum, copper alloys, titanium, and reactive metals. Flow rates range from approximately 10 to 20 ft³/hr (0.28 to 0.56 m³/hr).

In some cases, argon may not perform optimally because of the higher arc voltages that are used in plasma welding (18-32 V). Where the weld puddle is not fluid, slight undercutting occurs and/or surface oxidation of the weld is noticed. The use of argon-hydrogen mixtures, helium, or argon-helium mixtures may be necessary.

Argon-hydrogen mixtures. Argon-hydrogen mixtures are used as shielding gases to provide increased heat input to the weld. The addition of about 5% hydrogen to argon reduces surface tension of the molten pool, resulting in increased travel speeds. By reducing the surface tension of the molten metal, degassing of the weld pool is also facilitated so that the danger of gas inclusions in the form of porosity is lessened. At higher welding speeds, undercutting is also avoided, and a smoother weld surface is achieved.

In addition to providing increased arc heating efficiency, hydrogen has a fluxing effect that reduces the amount of oxides formed when joining stainless steels, nickel, and high-nickel alloys. When welding nickel or nickel alloys, the presence of hydrogen actually helps by preventing porosity. Nickel oxides formed by the entry of oxygen from the air are reduced by the presence of hydrogen. The hydrogen "attacks" any stray oxygen before it can form nickel oxides.

The permissible percentage of hydrogen varies from 1 to 15%. The percentage is indirectly related to the thickness of material being welded. With increased currents and reduced travel speeds on thicker materials, the hydrogen can become entrapped in the weld. This causes embrittlement of the weld.

In general, the thinner the workpiece, the higher the permissible percentage of hydrogen in a gas mixture that can be used. In automatic welding, a higher percentage of hydrogen can increase travel speeds on thinner materials, 0.062" (1.57 mm) thick or less. Flow rates range from approximately 10 to 20 ft³/hr (0.28 to 0.56 m³/hr).

Helium. The use of helium as opposed to argon for a shielding gas increases the weld heat by approximately 25%. This is due to the higher ionization potential of helium, which in turn increases the arc voltage. Helium is commonly used when welding aluminum alloys, copper alloys, and thicker sections of titanium. These materials will dissipate heat more rapidly and need the assistance of the helium. Flow rates for helium range from approximately 15 to 40 ft³/hr (0.42 to 1.12 m³/hr).

Helium-argon mixtures. The addition of helium to argon as a shielding gas produces a hotter arc for a given amount of welding current. A mixture must contain at least 40% helium before a significant change in heat can be detected. The argon has a tendency to stabilize the arc. Mixtures containing more than 75% helium will provide results very similar to pure helium. A mixture of 75% helium-25% argon is used for applications such as thicker segments of titanium or copper alloys. Flow rates range from approximately 15 to 40 ft³/hr (0.42 to 1.12 m³/hr).

Arc starting may become more difficult with the use of helium or helium mixtures. The addition of a trailing shield may be required when welding titanium or reactive metals to minimize any oxidation to the weld puddle.

Equipment Used

A typical plasma welding system consists of a pilot-arc control console, a d-c power supply with a suitable weld range, a plasma welding torch (manual or mechanized), and a closed-loop coolant recirculator.

Pilot-arc control console. The control is the "mixing box" into which power, gases, and coolant for the cooling of the torch are all supplied. It also contains a small d-c power supply for the pilot arc. Control of the plasma gas and the shield gas and the monitoring of the weld current are normally supplied. Some commercial consoles provide additional controls and meters to assist in weld parameter control.

Power supply. Plasma arc welding is done almost exclusively with the use of straight-polarity direct current. A typical d-c power supply with constant-current characteristics, remote contactor, current control, and suitable welding range should

be used for most operations. A solid-state power supply with a nonmechanical contactor is recommended when performing high duty cycle, short-duration welds. A sequence programmer consisting of current or gas slope (taper), pulse, and weld time is often required for many automated welding applications. Square-wave a-c or solid-state, silicon-controlled rectifier (SCR), variable-polarity power sources are used in the welding of aluminum.

Torches. A plasma welding torch suitable for the specific welding operation should be used. Torches are available with various head and size configurations. All plasma welding torches are liquid cooled, and the orifices of some torches are also liquid cooled, providing improved orifice life and higher current-carrying capacity. Most torches are designed with an orifice that is inserted into a water jacket. These types of torches cannot operate at the higher current levels (above 250 A), but do allow the changing of the orifice without disturbing a water seal.

Most orifices are of the single-port design, but a multiport tip design may provide improved weld characteristics in some thicker keyhole welding applications (see Fig. 9-40). The tungsten electrodes used are normally 2% thoriated, and their diameter varies as the current load changes. Lower current levels require smaller electrode diameters. Higher current or high duty cycles require larger electrodes to withstand the heat loads.

Coolant recirculator. A coolant recirculator of a nonferrous design is used for plasma arc welding. Deionized water to prevent the establishment of electrolysis in the torches is typically used.

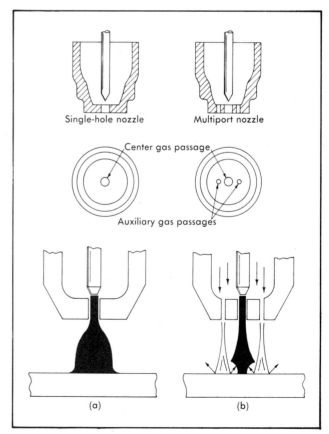

Fig. 9-40 Effects on plasma jet of (a) single-port and (b) multiport nozzles.

CHAPTER 9

PLASMA ARC WELDING

Welding Various Metals

All metals amenable to gas tungsten arc welding can be joined with the plasma arc process. Table 9-24 lists typical conditions for making butt welds in foils and thin gages of several metals with the melt-in mode of plasma arc welding.

Stainless steel. Typical plasma arc conditions for welding stainless steel are shown in Figs. 9-37 and 9-39. In each case the electrode setback distance is at a minimum of 1/8″ (3.2 mm), and the torch standoff distance is 1/8 to 3/16″ (3.2 to 4.8 mm). The equipment manufacturer's recommendations should be followed in selecting a particular torch nozzle for each set of welding conditions. The conditions for square butt joints presented in Table 9-24 are for undercut-free welds made without added filler metal. The addition of small amounts of filler metal will produce such welds at somewhat higher speeds.

Mild and high-strength steels. Recommended conditions for welding mild and high-strength steels are presented in Figs. 9-37 and 9-39. The metallurgy of some high-strength steels may necessitate preheating and postheating cycles to prevent cracking.

Titanium. Conditions for plasma arc welding titanium with the keyhole mode are shown in Table 9-25. Because this metal has a lower density than stainless and mild steels, keyhole welds can be made through thicker square butt joints in titanium. As with gas tungsten arc welding, plasma arc welding of reactive metals like titanium requires a trailing shield to prevent atmospheric contamination of the weld bead.

Aluminum alloys. The plasma arc welding of aluminum alloys using conventional d-c or a-c power sources has been severely limited because of problems with weld metal porosity and incomplete fusion. Recently, a variable-polarity power source has been developed that can provide high-quality keyhole welds in aluminum alloys. This power source generates a square-wave current output, with reverse and straight current amplitudes and durations that can be accurately and inde-

TABLE 9-24
Typical Operating Parameters for Plasma Arc Welding of Butt Joints in Foils and Thin Sheets, Melt-In Mode*

Material and Thickness, in. (mm)	Welding Current, A (d-c, electrode negative)	Travel Speed, ipm (mm/min)	Shielding Gas**
Inconel 718:			
0.012 (0.30)	6	15 (381)	Argon-1% H_2
0.016 (0.41)	3.5	6 (152)	Argon-1% H_2
Hastelloy X:			
0.005† (0.13)	4.8	10 (254)	Argon-1% H_2
0.010 (0.41)	5.8	8 (203)	Argon-1% H_2
0.020 (0.51)	10	10 (254)	Argon-1% H_2
Copper:			
0.003† (0.08)	10	6 (152)	Helium-25% A

* Orifice gas (argon) flow rate 0.5 ft³/hr (0.014 m³/hr) through a 0.030″ (0.76) diam orifice.
** Shielding gas flow 20 ft³/hr (0.56 m³/hr).
† Flanged butt joint.

TABLE 9-25
Typical Plasma Arc Welding Conditions for Titanium[a]

Thickness, in. (mm)	Travel Speed, ipm (mm/min)	Welding Current, A (d-c, electrode negative)	Arc Voltage, V	Nozzle Type[b]	Gas Flow[c] Plasma, ft³/hr (m³/hr)	Gas Flow[c] Shielding, ft³/hr (m³/hr)	Remarks
0.125 (3.18)	20 (508)	185	21	111M	8 (0.224)	60 (1.680)	Keyhole; square butt
0.187 (4.75)	13 (330)	175	25	136M	18 (0.504)	60 (1.680)	Keyhole; square butt
0.390 (9.91)	10 (254)	225	38	136M	32 (0.896)	60 (1.680)	Keyhole; square butt
0.500 (12.70)	10 (254)	270	36	136M	27 (0.756)	60 (1.680)	Keyhole; square butt
0.600 (15.24)	7 (178)	250	39	136M	30 (0.840)	60 (1.680)	Keyhole; 3/8″ (9.5 mm) nose; 30° included angle

[a] Torch standoff: 3/16″ (4.8 mm).

[b] Nozzle type: number designates orifice diameter in thousandths of an inch; M designates multiport design.

[c] Gas backup and trailing shield required for all welds.

[d] Argon used.

[e] Gas used: 75% He, 25% Ar.

[f] Gas used: 50% He, 50% Ar.

pendently controlled. Success of the variable-polarity process compared to conventional plasma arc welding results from the addition of up to 70 A of additional reverse polarity current to provide the required removal of the aluminum oxide on the plate surface.

Specific welding parameters, including the times and amperages for the straight and reverse polarities, have been determined for a variety of aluminum alloys. Although welding can be conducted in all positions, the vertical-up position offers the greatest flexibility and thickness capabilities, up to 3/4″ (19 mm). Table 9-26 provides typical variable-polarity plasma arc welding conditions for producing butt welds in 2219 and 5052 aluminum alloys.

Troubleshooting

Table 9-27 lists common problems encountered with plasma arc welding, possible causes and suggested remedies.

OTHER ARC WELDING PROCESSES

In addition to the methods already discussed, there are other arc welding processes, but most are obsolete or seldom used. The methods include carbon arc welding, bare metal arc welding, and atomic hydrogen welding.

Carbon Arc Welding

Carbon arc welding (CAW) is an arc welding process that produces coalescence (joining) of metals by heating them with an arc between a carbon (graphite) electrode and the work. No shielding is used, and pressure and filler metal may or may not be used. The process is the oldest form of arc welding and is seldom used now for joining because carbon can be introduced into the weld metal and make the joints brittle. When used, the process is normally performed manually with electrode-negative polarity d-c and is capable of welding thin metals. It is also used for brazing, discussed in Chapter 10.

Carbon arc welding is also used for cutting and gouging metals, as discussed subsequently in this section.

Gas carbon arc welding (CAW-G). This method is a variation of carbon arc welding in which shielding is obtained from a gas or gas mixture, resulting in higher quality welds. The process, however, has little or no commercial application.

Shielded carbon arc welding (CAW-S). This variation of carbon arc welding provides shielding from the combustion of a solid material fed into the arc or from a blanket of flux on the work, or both. Pressure and filler metal may or may not be used. This process is seldom used.

Twin carbon arc welding (CAW-T). In this variation of carbon arc welding, coalescence of metals is produced by heating them with an electric arc between two carbon electrodes. The work is not part of the electrical circuit. No shielding is used, and pressure and filler metal may or may not be used. This process is used primarily for maintenance operations, with small a-c arc welding machines generally employed as the power source. Copper-coated carbon electrodes are common.

Bare Metal Arc Welding

Bare metal arc welding (BMAW) is an arc welding process that produces coalescence (joining) of metals by heating them with an electric arc between a bare or lightly coated metal electrode and the work. Neither shielding nor pressure is used, and filler metal is obtained from the electrode.

A major disadvantage of welding with a bare electrode is that the molten weld metal and filler metal (if used) are exposed to the atmosphere. This can result in oxidation, improper fusion, porosity, high hardness, and poor ductility. Covered electrodes are now generally used for this process instead of bare or lightly covered electrodes.

Atomic Hydrogen Welding

Atomic hydrogen welding (AHW) is an arc welding process that produces coalescence (joining) of metals by heating them wit an electric arc aintained between two metal electrodes in an atmosphere of hydrogen. The arc is maintained entirely independent of the parts being welded. Shielding is provided by

TABLE 9-26
Typical Conditions for Plasma Arc Welding of Aluminum Alloys with Variable-Polarity Power Source

Aluminum Alloy and Thickness, in. (mm)	Position	Travel Speed, ipm (mm/min)	Welding Current, A	Additional Reverse-Polarity Current, A	Ratio of Straight to Reverse-Polarity Times, ms	Arc Voltage,* V	Gas Flow,** ft³/hr (m³/hr) Plasma	Shielding	Remarks†
2219, 0.25 (6.4)	Vertical	7 (178)	170	70	19/3	29	5.5 (0.154)	35 (0.980)	Keyhole, square-butt joint, 2319 filler
2219, 0.25 (6.4)	Flat	7 (178)	160	70	19/3	28	5.5 (0.154)	35 (0.980)	Keyhole, square-butt joint, 2319 filler
5052, 0.25 (6.4)	Vertical	8 (203)	180	70	19/4	30	5.5 (0.154)	35 (0.980)	Keyhole, square-butt joint, 5554 filler
5052, 0.25 (6.4)	Flat	5 (127)	140	70	19/4	27	5.5 (0.154)	35 (0.980)	Keyhole, square-butt joint, 5554 filler

* Torch standoff: 3/16″ (4.8 mm).
** Gas used: argon; no backup gas required.
† Orifice diameter: 0.125″ (3.2 mm).

OTHER ARC WELDING PROCESSES

TABLE 9-27
Troubleshooting Guide for Plasma Arc Welding

Trouble	Possible Causes	Remedies
Erratic or poor-appearing pilot arc	Worn torch parts	Check and replace required parts
	Improper electrode setting	Adjust setting
	Contaminated plasma gas	Check gas line for leaks
	Moisture in torch or leads	Plug tip and allow gas pressure to increase
	Contaminated coolant	Check coolant for contaminants
Welding arc will not transfer	Torch standoff too high	Reduce standoff distance
	Power supply not properly connected	Check work lead, negative lead, and contactor control cable
	Faulty electrode in torch	Check for sharp point and clean appearance of electrode
Welding tip damaged on startup	Improper installation of torch parts	Check installation procedure
	Improper electrode setback	Correct electrode setting
	Incorrect polarity	Check negative and positive leads for proper connections; check range switch of power supply
	Plasma gas flow rate too low	Increase flow rate
	Excessive current level	Reduce current or use tip with larger orifice
	Inadequate coolant flow	Check flow rate and pressure and the coolant filter
	Contaminated gas	Check gas line for leaks
	Moisture in torch	Check torch and hoses for leaks
	Contaminated coolant	Check coolant for contaminants
	Tip touching workpiece	Increase standoff distance
Tip damaged after a period of welding	Inadequate coolant flow	Check flow rate and pressure and the coolant filter
	Excessive current level	Reduce current or use tip with larger orifice
	Plasma gas flow rate too low	Increase flow rate
	Moisture in torch	Check torch and hoses for leaks
Not getting required penetration	Plasma gas flow rate too low	Increase flow rate
	Inadequate current level	Increase current
	Electrode setback at minimum	Increase setback distance
	Travel speed too high	Decrease travel speed
Porosity in welds	Contaminates on workpiece	Clean workpiece
	Plasma gas flow rate too high	Reduce flow rate
	Inadequate shielding gas coverage	Increase flow rate or use additional trailer shield
Slight undercutting in toe area of weld	Travel speed to high	Decrease travel speed
	Plasma gas flow rate too high	Decrease flow rate
	Orifice size in tip too small	Use tip with larger orifice
	Electrode setback at maximum	Decrease setback distance
	Inadequate current level	Increase current

(Thermal Dynamics Corp.)

the hydrogen. Pressure and filler metal may or may not be used, depending on the application.

The atomic hydrogen process of arc welding may be regarded as a forerunner of gas shielded and plasma arc welding. Although largely displaced by other processes that require less skill and are less costly, it is still preferred for some manual operations where close control of heat input is required. Heat input to the work is regulated by positioning the arc at various distances from the work.

In the atomic hydrogen process, the arc is established between the two tungsten electrodes in a stream of hydrogen gas, using alternating current. As the gas passes through the arc, molecular hydrogen is dissociated into atomic hydrogen under the intense heat. When the stream of hydrogen atoms strikes the workpiece, the environmental temperature is then at a level where recombining into molecules is possible. As a result of the recombining, the heat of dissociation absorbed in the arc is liberated, supplying the heat needed for fusing the base metal and any filler metal that may be introduced.

The atomic hydrogen process depends on an arc, but is really a heating torch. The arc supplies the heat through the intermediate of the molecular-dissociation, atom-recombination mechanism. The hydrogen gas, however, does more than provide the mechanism for heat transfer. Before entering the arc, it acts as a shield and a coolant to keep the tungsten electrodes from overheating. At the weld puddle, the gas acts as a shield. Because hydrogen is a powerful reducing agent, any rust in the weld area is reduced to iron, and no oxide can form or exist in the hydrogen atmosphere until it is removed.

Weld metal, however, can absorb hydrogen with unfavorable metallurgical effects. For this reason, the process gives difficulties with steels containing sulfur or selenium because hydrogen reacts with these elements to form hydrogen sulfide or hydrogen selenide gases. These are almost insoluble in molten metal and either bubble out of the weld pool vigorously or become entrapped in the solidifying metal, resulting in porosity.

ARC WELDING CONSUMABLES

Arc welding consumables are the materials used up during welding, such as electrodes, filler rods, fluxes, and externally applied shielding gases. With the exception of the gases, all of the commonly used consumables are covered by ANSI/AWS standards (see Table 9-28). This section briefly describes the electrode classification system and some of the factors to be considered in selecting the proper consumables. For detailed information, the applicable standard should be consulted.

Electrode Classifications

The AWS classifications of mild and low-alloy steel electrodes are based on an "E" prefix and a four or five-digit number (see Table 9-29). The first two digits (or three in a five-digit number) indicate the minimum required tensile strength in ksi (1 ksi = 6.89476 MPa). The next to the last digit indicates the position in which the electrode is capable of making satisfactory welds: 1 = all positions (flat, horizontal, vertical, and overhead), 2 = flat position and horizontal fillets, and 4 = flat, horizontal, overhead, and vertical-down. The last digit indicates the type of current to be used for welding and the type of covering on the electrode (see Table 9-30). Suffixes indicate the approximate alloy in the weld deposit (refer to Table 9-29).

Specifications for covered electrodes require that the classification number be imprinted on the covering. However, some

TABLE 9-28
Specifications for Arc Welding Rods, Electrodes, and Fluxes

ANSI/AWS Specification	Subject
A5.1	Carbon steel covered electrodes
A5.3	Aluminum and aluminum alloy electrodes
A5.4	Corrosion-resisting chromium and chromium-nickel steel electrodes
A5.5	Low-alloy steel covered electrodes
A5.6	Copper and copper alloy covered electrodes
A5.7	Copper and copper alloy bare rods and electrodes
A5.9	Corrosion-resisting chromium and chromium-nickel steel bare and composite metal cored and stranded electrodes and rods
A5.10	Aluminum and aluminum alloy rods and bare electrodes
A5.11	Nickel and nickel alloy covered electrodes
A5.12	Tungsten electrodes
A5.14	Nickel and nickel alloy bare rods and electrodes
A5.15	Rods and covered electrodes for welding cast iron
A5.17	Carbon steel electrodes and fluxes for submerged arc welding
A5.18	Carbon steel filler metal for gas-shielded arc welding
A5.19	Magnesium alloy rods and bare electrodes
A5.20	Carbon steel electrodes for flux-cored arc welding
A5.22	Flux-cored corrosion-resisting chromium and chromium-nickel steel electrodes
A5.23	Low-alloy steel electrodes and fluxes for submerged arc welding
A5.24	Zirconium and zirconium alloy bare rods and electrodes
A5.26	Consumables used for electrogas welding of carbon and high-strength, low-alloy steels
A5.28	Low-alloy steel filler metals for gas-shielded arc welding
A5.29	Low-alloy steel electrodes for flux-cored arc welding

ARC WELDING CONSUMABLES

TABLE 9-29
AWS Designations for Mild and Low-Alloy Steel Electrodes

A. The prefix "E" designates arc welding electrode.

B. The first two digits of four-digit numbers and the first three digits of five-digit numbers indicate minimum tensile strength:

E60XX	60,000 psi (414 MPa) minimum tensile strength
E70XX	70,000 psi (483 MPa) minimum tensile strength
E110XX	110,000 psi (758 MPa) minimum tensile strength

C. The next-to-last digit indicates position:

EXX1X	All positions
EXX2X	Flat position and horizontal fillets

D. The suffix (Example: EXXXX-A1) indicates the approximate alloy in the weld deposit:

— A1	0.5% Mo
— B1	0.5% Cr, 0.5% Mo
— B2	1.25% Cr, 0.5% Mo
— B3	2.25% Cr, 1% Mo
— B4	2% Cr, 0.5% Mo
— B5	0.5% Cr, 1% Mo
— C1	2.5% Ni
— C2	3.25% Ni
— C3	1% Ni, 0.35% Mo, 0.15% Cr
— D1 and D2	0.25-0.45% Mo, 1.75% Mn
— G	0.5% min Ni, 0.3% min Cr, 0.2% min Mo, 0.1% min V, 1% min Mn (only one element required)

electrodes can be manufactured faster than the imprinting equipment can mark them, and some sizes are too small to be legibly marked with an imprint. Although AWS specifies an imprint, color coding is accepted if imprinting is not practical.

Stainless steel electrodes are identified by the prefix E, the three-digit AISI analysis numbers, and a usability classification indicating the type of coating. Nonferrous electrodes are identified by the chemical symbols of their principal alloying elements, followed by group letters and subdividing numbers.

Selection Factors

Selection of the proper electrode for a specific application is one of the most important requirements in welding. This is because the type of electrode used and its covering influences the chemical and metallurgical properties of a weld joint, which must match or exceed the base metal in strength and ductility for optimum service.

Electrode selection is difficult because they are available in a wide variety of compositions, types, coverings, and sizes. In addition to bare and covered electrodes, they are available in composite, emissive, flux-cored, metal-cored, and stranded types. Standard stick electrodes generally range from 1/16 to 3/16" (1.6 to 4.8 mm) diam. Wire electrodes are usually available in five diameters: 0.030, 0.035, 0.045, 0.052, and 0.062" (0.76, 0.89, 1.14, 1.32, and 1.57 mm).

Some of the electrode types, classifications, and sizes for various metals are presented in the preceding tables for different arc welding methods:

Table	Process
9-15	Shielded metal arc welding
9-16	Gas tungsten arc welding
9-17 and 9-19	Gas metal arc welding
9-21	Flux-cored arc welding

TABLE 9-30
Welding Currents and Covering Types for Mild and Low-Alloy Steel Electrodes

Designation	Current	Covering Type
EXX10	d-c+ only	Organic
EXX11	a-c or d-c+	Organic
EXX12	a-c or d-c-	Rutile
EXX13	a-c or d-c±	Rutile
EXX14	a-c or d-c±	Rutile, iron powder (approximately 30%)
EXX15	d-c+ only	Low-hydrogen
EXX16	a-c or d-c+	Low-hydrogen
EXX18	a-c or d-c+	Low-hydrogen, iron powder (approximately 25%)
EXX20	a-c or d-c±	High iron oxide
EXX24	a-c or d-c±	Rutile, iron powder (approximately 50%)
EXX27	a-c or d-c±	Mineral, iron powder (approximately 50%)
EXX28	a-c or d-c+	Low-hydrogen, iron powder (approximately 50%)

Selection of the proper electrode requires consideration of many factors, including composition, strength, thickness, and shape of the parts to be joined; joint design and fitup; position of welding; welding current and production efficiency; cost; and service requirements.

Base metal composition. Composition of the base metal is a primary consideration, and electrode composition should in general match it as closely as possible. The base metal composition influences the need for preheating and/or postheating. Low-hydrogen electrodes are often used to avoid the need for preheating and postheating, especially for welding steels having carbon contents above 0.35%. For welding mild steels, any E60XX or E70XX is generally satisfactory.

Base metal strength. Mechanical properties of the base metal must be known and matched by the electrode material. Again, any E60XX electrode will generally be suitable for welding mild steel because its properties will be better than those of the base metal. For low-alloy steels, refer to the first two or three digits of the electrode classification number and select the one that most closely matches the base metal properties.

Thickness and shape of parts. To avoid weld cracking of thick and heavy metals with complicated designs, electrodes that provide maximum ductility should be selected. Low-hydrogen welding processes and electrodes (EXX15, 16, 18, or 28 types) are recommended.

Joint design and fitup. The last digit of the electrode number indicates whether the electrode has a deep, medium, or light-penetrating arc. Deep-penetrating arcs are used when complete joint penetration is required and welding is done from one side. Light penetration with a soft arc is necessary for welding thin material or wide root openings.

Welding position. The third (or fourth for five-digit classifications) digit of the classification number indicates the welding position for which the electrode can be used and should be matched with the application.

Welding current. Electrodes selected must match the power supply available. Some electrodes are designed for use with d-c; others, a-c; and some, either d-c or a-c (refer to Table 9-30). Correct polarity should also be observed.

Production efficiency. Some electrodes are designed for high deposition rates, but may be used only for certain welding positions. For high deposition rates and most efficient production with flat position welding, high iron powder (EXX24, 27, or 28) types or large diameter wires should be used. Other welding positions and conditions may require experimentation with various electrodes and sizes.

Service requirements. For severe service requirements, such as low or high temperatures and shock loading, the composition and properties of the electrode must closely match those of the base metal. Low-hydrogen processes and electrodes are generally preferable.

POWER SOURCE SELECTION

Many types of arc welding current sources are available, and the proper machine for the particular job must be chosen. There are two major categories of power sources: (1) the conventional *constant-current machine* with a drooping volt-ampere curve and (2) the *constant-voltage* or *modified constant-voltage machine* with a relatively flat curve. The constant-current machine can be used for manual welding and, under certain conditions, for automatic welding. The constant-voltage machine is used only for automatic or semiautomatic continuous electrode-wire arc welding processes. The volt-ampere output characteristic curves of these two types of machines, which best distinguish the types, are obtained by loading the machines with variable resistances and plotting the voltages across the electrodes and work terminals for each ampere of output. Specifi-

cations for electric arc welding apparatus are presented in ANSI/NEMA Standard EWI.

Constant-Current Machines

The conventional or constant-current (variable-voltage) arc welder is used for manual electrode welding (SMAW), GTAW, CAW, and SW processes. It can be used for automatic welding with larger diameter electrode wire, but only with a voltage-sensing wire feeder.

The constant-current machine produces a drooping volt-ampere output curve such as that shown in Fig. 9-41. Maximum output voltage is produced with no load (no current), and, as the load is increased, the output voltage decreases. Under normal conditions, the output voltage is between 20 and 40 V, and with the circuit open it is 60 to 80 V. Machines are available that produce either a-c or d-c power or both a-c and d-c power.

When covered electrodes are used, the actual arc voltage is controlled by the operator through variations in the arc length. If the arc length is decreased (a short arc), the arc voltage decreases, and the welding current remains relatively constant with constant-current power sources. A change in voltage changes the heat of the arc, although there is some current change. Thus, the welder has limited control over welding current and arc heat by lengthening or shortening the arc. Constant-current machines can be of the generator type, the transformer type, or the transformer-rectifier type.

Generator machines. Welding generators can be driven by three-phase electric motors or internal-combustion engines. The slope of the output curve of generator machines can be varied, thus giving the machines great flexibility. A range switch provides coarse welding-current adjustment, and a fine-adjustment control allows fine welding-current adjustment as well as control of the open-circuit voltage.

With a flatter curve and low open-circuit voltage, a change in arc voltage will produce a greater change in output current for such jobs as pipe welding. A steeper curve and a high open-circuit voltage will produce less change in output current for a change in arc voltage, producing the soft arc used in sheet metal welding.

Transformer machines. The transformer type of welding machine is the smallest, lightest, and least expensive. It produces only single-phase alternating current. The transformer takes power at line voltage, transforms it to power at the

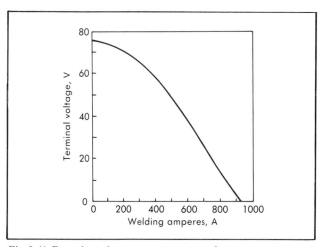

Fig. 9-41 Drooping volt-ampere output curve of a constant-current arc welding machine.

POWER SOURCE SELECTION

welding voltage, and gives it the proper voltage-amperage characteristics. The current output may be adjusted; the simplest method is by tapping the secondary transformer coil at different points to provide different output voltages. Plug or tap switches may be used to allow the variation in current, but in either case exact adjustment is not possible.

A continuous-output current control, either electrical or mechanical, is used on industrial-transformer welders. The mechanical type moves the core or the coils of the transformer, and a considerable amount of movement is required to effect a change in output current. The more advanced method of current adjustment is by use of electric circuits that saturate the transformer core to control the output current.

Transformer welding machines have lowest initial cost and are least expensive to operate. They also require less space than other types of welding machines and are normally quieter. In addition, the alternating current supplied by transformers reduces arc blow. However, transformers require single-phase power, which may create imbalance in power lines, and they have a low power-factor demand unless they are equipped with power-factor capacitors. Also, they do not have the flexibility of operation of the dual-controlled generator. Safety standards for transformer-type arc welding machines are presented in ANSI/UL Standard 551.

Transformer-rectifier machines. This type of machine is equipped with a rectifier that can change the alternating current supplied by the transformer to the direct current needed for operation with some electrodes. Transformer-rectifier welders can be made to use a three-phase input as well as the single-phase type. By means of a switch, the output of the machine can be changed from alternating to direct current of either polarity. The addition of a high-frequency oscillator and water and gas control valves makes this type of machine ideal for gas tungsten arc welding. The transformer-rectifier is more efficient than the generator welder and, it is quiet.

Converter machines.[5] These power supplies, also called rectifier-converters and inverters, take a-c line power, rectify it to d-c, convert it electronically to high-frequency a-c, transform it to welding voltage, and then convert it to d-c. Advantages include lighter and more compact units than conventional transformers-rectifiers, control of short-circuit metal transfer, and sensor monitoring of arc voltage.

Constant-Voltage Machines

A constant-voltage or modified constant-voltage welding machine provides a nominally constant voltage to the arc for any arc current. The characteristic output curve of this type of machine is shown in Fig. 9-42. This welder can be used only for automatic or semiautomatic arc welding with a continuously fed electrode wire and can produce only direct current.

The slight droop in the output curve of a constant-voltage machine can be increased or the slope can be made steeper by various means. Many machines have different taps or controls to vary the slope of the curve, and it is important that the proper slope be selected for the process and the type of work welded.

In continuous wire welding, the burnoff rate of a specific electrode type and size is proportional to the welding current. The constant-voltage machine produces the current required by the load, which is important for basic automatic welding control. The wire is fed by a constant-speed motor that can be adjusted to increase or decrease the feed rate, thus eliminating complicated circuitry and making the system self-regulating. As the feed is increased, the welding current increases, and, as the

feed is decreased, the current decreases. The voltage is regulated by a control on the power source.

Combination Machines

The most versatile welding machines are those in which constant-current and constant-voltage outputs are both available. Such machines can provide d-c welding power with either a drooping or a flat characteristic curve at the throw of a switch or by a change in terminals. This type of machine allows the use of any of the arc welding processes. It can be either a generator or a transformer-rectifier type.

Machine Specification

A welding machine is selected on the basis of:

1. The process or processes to be used.
2. The amount of current required.
3. The type of current needed (a-c or d-c).
4. The power available at the work site.
5. Convenience and economy.

Machines for different processes. The type of machine required for different arc welding processes is shown in Table 9-31. The welding current and duty cycle required determine the size of machine needed. Current, duty cycle, and voltage are determined by analysis of the job, consideration of weld joints and sizes, and consultation of the recommendations in the preceding tables. Power availability, the job site, personal preference, and economic considerations are all important to the final selection.

Duty cycle. Duty cycle is the ratio of arc time to total time in increments of 10 minutes. Percentage duty cycle is the ratio of the square of the rated current to the square of the load current multiplied by the rated duty cycle. Figure 9-43 is a graph that can be used to determine the percentage duty cycle of a welding machine. For example, the graph shows that a 400 A, 60% duty cycle machine could be used for a 300 A, 10 minute automatic welding job—that is, that the machine can be used at slightly more than 300 A at a 100% duty cycle. The graph also shows that a 200 A, 60% rated welder can be used at 250 A provided the duty cycle does not exceed 40% (4 minutes of each 10 minutes).

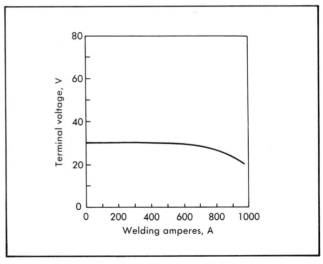

Fig. 9-42 Characteristic output curve of a constant-voltage arc welding machine.

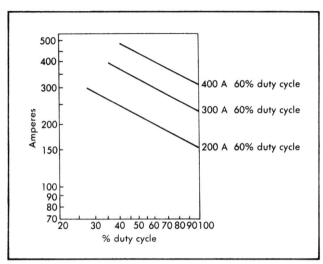

Fig. 9-43 Graph for determining percent duty cycle for an arc welding machine.

WIRE-FEEDER SELECTION

All automatic and semiautomatic arc welding systems use wire feeders to feed the electrode wire continuously into the arc. This maintains a stable arc at the desired welding current and arc voltage. The control circuit regulating the feeder may also regulate arc starting, gas and water flow, travel, and other auxiliary functions. Basically, wire feeders may be either the constant-speed type or the voltage-sensing type. They must match the power source, and they must feed the wire at the rate necessary to match the welding process used. The wire feeder must also have a motor capable of driving the wire through the conduit cable to the welding gun. The drive rolls should all be powered and grooved to avoid bending or flattening tubular electrode wire.

Voltage-Sensing Feeder

The voltage-sensing wire feeder senses the voltage across the arc and regulates wire feed to compensate for changes in that voltage. Voltage-sensing feeders are used with constant-current power sources and with either alternating or direct current. This device is generally used to feed large-diameter electrode wires and was originally developed for submerged arc welding. The feed system may include an automatic retracting device to initiate the arc automatically.

Constant-Speed Feeder

The constant-speed wire-feeder system operates by the fixed burnoff rate versus welding current relationship and must therefore be used only with a constant-voltage welding power source. The wire feed rate is preset by the speed control on the

TABLE 9-31
Machine Selection Guide for Various Arc Welding Processes

Welding Process	Current Type	Polarity, d-c	Welder Type	Amperage Range Required, A
Carbon arc welding*	d-c	Electrode positive or negative	Constant-current generator, transformer-rectifier, constant-voltage**	200-1300
Shielded metal arc welding	a-c, d-c	Electrode positive or negative	Constant-current generator, transformer, transformer-rectifier	75-500
Flux-cored arc welding	d-c	Electrode positive (negative for some electrodes)	Constant-voltage	200-1000
Gas metal arc welding	d-c	Electrode positive	Constant-voltage	150-1000
Gas tungsten arc welding	a-c, d-c†	Electrode positive or negative	Constant-current generator, transformer-rectifier	3-350
Submerged arc welding	a-c, d-c	Electrode positive	Constant-current, constant-voltage	200-1200‡
Stud welding	d-c	Electrode negative	Constant-current generator, transformer-rectifier	200-2300
Electroslag welding	d-c	Electrode positive	Constant-voltage	750-1000‡

  * Special machines available for heavy duty.
  ** Precautions must be taken to operate constant-voltage machines well within rated outputs.
  † High-frequency current capability also required.
  ‡ 100% duty cycle required.

WIRE-FEEDER SELECTION

feeder motor, and the constant-voltage welding machine supplies the amount of current needed to burn the wire at the proper rate to maintain the arc. This system is used for small-diameter electrode wires. It was originally developed for gas metal arc welding to eliminate stubbing and burnback. Wire-feed rates are adjustable over a wide range of speeds, which must include the speed for the conditions involved. The constant-speed wire feeder can be operated with a constant-current welder, but it will be difficult to adjust and control.

Microprocessor Control

Programmable microprocessors for the wire feeders of gas metal arc welding units permit control of arc voltage and wire-feed speed. One wire feeder has an optical tachometer that monitors wire-feed speed and sends digitized readings to the microprocessor for correcting any deviations that are noted from the preset voltage.

WELD QUALITY AND TROUBLESHOOTING

Weld quality requirements and inspection and testing procedures are discussed in the introductory section of this chapter under the subject "Overview of Welding Processes." Distortion and the means of preventing and controlling it, as well as preheating and stress relieving, are also covered.

Causes and cures for discontinuities—spatter, undercut, incomplete fusion, cracks, and porosity—commonly occurring as the result of arc welding are discussed previously in this section. Other problems sometimes encountered in arc welding, such as moisture pickup, arc blow, and burn-through, are also discussed earlier in this section, together with possible solutions. Table 9-32 summarizes possible problems in arc welding and presents suggested solutions; additional information is contained in the sections cited.

AIR-CARBON ARC CUTTING

Air-carbon arc cutting (AAC) is one of a group of arc cutting processes that melt the metals to be cut with the heat of an electric arc generated between an electrode and the base metals. This method and plasma arc cutting, discussed next in this section, are the ones used most extensively in industry. Other arc cutting processes that are not used extensively or used only for special applications are described briefly at the end of this section.

TABLE 9-32
Causes of and Solutions to Arc Welding Problems

Problem	Possible Causes	Suggested Solutions
Spatter	Welding current too high	Reduce amperage; increase voltage
	Improper, wet, unclean, or damaged electrode	Change electrode
	Arc length too long	Reduce arc length
	Arc blow	Reduce effect of arc blow (see discussion)
	Wrong electrode angle	Change angle
	Improper shielding gas	Change gas or mixture
Undercuts	Travel speed too high	Reduce speed
	Welding current too high	Reduce amperage; increase voltage
	Improper electrode manipulation	Change welding technique
	Electrode too large	Reduce electrode size
	Arc length too long	Reduce arc length
	Arc blow	Reduce effect of arc blow (see discussion)
Incomplete fusion	Welding current and/or voltage too high or too low	Use proper current, voltage, and polarity
	Improper travel speed	Use recommended speed
	Improper welding technique	Change procedure
	Faulty joint preparation	Change design and/or method of preparing joint
	Improper, wet, unclean, or damaged electrode	Change electrode
	Arc blow	Reduce effect of arc blow (see discussion)
Cracks	Base metal dirty or of grade with poor weldability	Clean workpiece, change material, or preheat
	Improper joint design and/or preparation	Change design and/or method of joint preparation

(continued)

TABLE 9-32—*Continued*

Problem	Possible Causes	Suggested Solutions
Cracks	Improper welding technique	Change procedure
	Weld bead too small	Increase bead size and make slightly convex
	Excessive restraint during welding	Reduce restraint
	Electrode and/or filler metal do not match base metal	Use proper electrode and filler, with increased ductility
	Cooling rate too rapid	Preheat
Porosity	Unsatisfactory or dirty base metal	Use base metal that will reduce porosity and keep clean
	Arc length too long or too short	Use recommended arc length
	Welding current too high	Reduce amperage; increase voltage
	Improper, wet, unclean, or damaged electrode	Change electrode; low-hydrogen electrodes help eliminate porosity
	Insufficient or improper gas shielding	Increase gas flow rate and check gas purity
	Travel speed too high	Reduce speed
	Improper joint design and/or preparation, or poor fitup	Change design and/or method of joint preparation
Arc blow	Unbalanced magnetic field during welding	Switch to a-c if acceptable
	Welding current too high	Reduce amperage; increase voltage
	Excessive magnetism in parts or fixture	Change location of connection on workpiece (see discussion)
	Arc length too long	Reduce arc length
Burn-through	Welding current too high	Reduce amperage; increase voltage
	Travel speed too low	Increase speed
	Improper shielding	Change gas or mixture
Distortion	Excessive shrinkage forces	Avoid overwelding, use proper edge preparation and fitup, and place weld close to neutral axis (see discussion)
	Absence of balancing forces (rigidity)	Balance shrinkage forces with proper welding sequence, clamps, jigs, and fixtures, and preheat and postheat when required
Inclusions	Incomplete slag removal between passes	Completely remove slag between passes
	Electrode too large	Use a smaller electrode
	Erratic travel speed	Use a uniform travel speed
	Improper welding technique	Change procedure
Insufficient penetration	Arc length too long	Reduce arc length
	Travel speed too high	Reduce speed
	Improper, wet, unclean, or damaged electrode	Change electrode
	Welding current too low	Increase amperage; reduce voltage
	Improper joint design and/or preparation, or poor fitup	Change design and/or method of joint preparation

AIR-CARBON ARC CUTTING

In air-carbon arc cutting, the metals to be cut are melted by the heat of a carbon arc, and the molten metal is removed by a blast of high-velocity compressed air (see Fig. 9-44), the air jet moving with the electrode. The process is generally performed manually, but can be operated semiautomatically or automatically. It can be used to cut steels and some nonferrous metals, and is also commonly used for gouging out defective welds, for repairing castings, and to prepare grooves for welding where precision cuts are not required.

The area cut with the air-carbon arc process is limited and, because the electrode is moved rapidly and metal is removed quickly, heating effects on surrounding areas are limited. Electrode speed and angle determine the depth of the groove, and electrode diameter determines width. Data for gouging carbon steel with this process is presented in Table 9-33. Recommended practices for air-carbon arc gouging and cutting are presented in ANSI/AWS Standard C5.3.

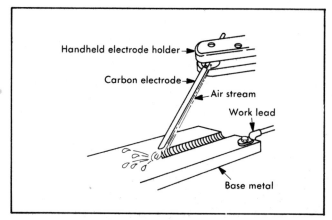

Fig. 9-44 Air-carbon arc cutting. (*Hobart Brothers Co.*)

TABLE 9-33
Typical Data for Gouging Carbon Steel with the Air-Carbon Arc Cutting Process

U Groove: Width, in. (mm)	U Groove: Depth, in. (mm)	Electrode Diameter, in. (mm)	Welding Current, A, (d-c, electrode positive)	Arc Voltage, V	Electrode Feed, ipm (mm/min)	Travel Speed, ipm (mm/min)	Length of Groove per Electrode, ft (m)	Length of Groove per min, ft (m)
1/4 (6.4)	1/16 (1.6)	3/16 (4.8)	200	43	6.2 (157)	82.0 (2083)	9.7 (2.96)	6.8 (2.07)
9/32 (7.1)	1/8 (3.2)		200	40	6.7 (170)	38.2 (970)	3.9 (1.19)	3.1 (0.94)
5/16 (7.9)	3/16 (4.8)		190	42	6.7 (170)	27.2 (691)	2.9 (0.88)	2.2 (0.67)
5/16 (7.9)	1/4 (6.4)	[To make 1/4″ (6.4 mm) deep groove, make two 1/8″ (3.2 mm) deep passes]						
5/16 (7.9)	3/32 (2.4)	1/4 (6.4)	270	40	4.0 (102)	54.0 (1372)	10.2 (3.11)	4.5 (1.37)
	1/8 (3.2)		300	42	4.0 (102)	51.0 (1295)	9.7 (2.96)	4.5 (1.37)
	3/16 (4.8)		300	40	6.7 (170)	38.2 (970)	4.0 (1.22)	3.1 (0.94)
	1/4 (6.4)		320	42	6.2 (157)	29.5 (749)	2.5 (0.76)	2.0 (0.61)
	3/8 (9.5)		320	46	3.6 (91)	15.0 (381)	3.0 (0.91)	1.2 (0.37)
3/8 (9.5)	1/8 (3.2)	5/16 (7.9)	320	40	3.0 (76)	65.5 (1664)	16.3 (4.97)	5.4 (1.65)
	3/16 (4.8)		400	46	4.3 (109)	46.0 (1168)	7.8 (2.38)	3.8 (1.16)
	1/4 (6.4)		420	42	3.8 (97)	31.2 (792)	6.0 (1.83)	2.6 (0.79)
	1/2 (12.7)		540	42	5.6 (142)	27.2 (691)	3.5 (1.07)	2.2 (0.67)

(continued)

TABLE 9-33—*Continued*

U Groove: Width, in. (mm)	U Groove: Depth, in. (mm)	Electrode Diameter, in. (mm)	Welding Current, A, (d-c, electrode positive)	Arc Voltage, V	Electrode Feed, ipm (mm/min)	Travel Speed, ipm (mm/min)	Length of Groove per Electrode, ft (m)	Length of Groove per min, ft (m)
7/16 (11.1)	1/8 (3.2)	3/8 (9.5)	560	42	4.2 (107)	82.0 (2083)	14.3 (4.36)	6.8 (2.07)
	1/8 (3.2)				3.3 (84)	65.0 (1651)	14.5 (4.42)	5.4 (1.65)
	3/16 (4.8)				2.6 (66)	41.0 (1041)	14.1 (4.30)	3.4 (1.04)
	1/4 (6.4)				3.0 (76)	29.5 (749)	7.3 (2.23)	2.4 (0.73)
	1/2 (12.7)				3.2 (81)	15.0 (381)	3.4 (1.04)	1.2 (0.37)
	11/16 (17.5)				3.5 (89)	12.2 (310)	4.2 (1.28)	1.0 (0.30)
9/16 (14.3)	1/8 (3.2)	1/2 (12.7)	1200	45	3.0 (76)	34.0 (864)	8.5 (2.59)	2.7 (0.82)
	1/4 (6.4)					22.0 (559)	6.3 (1.92)	1.8 (0.55)
	3/8 (9.5)					20.7 (526)	4.8 (1.46)	1.7 (0.52)
	1/2 (12.7)					18.5 (470)	4.5 (1.37)	1.5 (0.46)
	5/8 (15.9)					15.0 (381)	3.3 (1.01)	1.2 (0.37)
	3/4 (19.1)					12.5 (318)	2.5 (0.76)	1.0 (0.30)
13/16 (20.6)	1/8 (3.2)	5/8 (15.9)	1300	42	2.5 (64)	44.5 (1130)	19.7 (6.00)	3.6 (1.10)
	1/4 (6.4)					29.5 (749)	8.5 (2.59)	2.5 (0.76)
	3/8 (9.5)					20.0 (508)	5.6 (1.71)	1.8 (0.55)
	1/2 (12.7)					14.5 (368)	3.6 (1.10)	1.2 (0.37)
	5/8 (15.9)					13.0 (330)	3.5 (1.07)	1.0 (0.30)
	3/4 (19.1)					11.0 (279)	3.1 (0.94)	0.9 (0.27)
	1 (25.4)					10.0 (254)	2.1 (0.64)	0.8 (0.24)

Combination of settings and multiple passes may be used for grooves deeper than 3/4″ (19.1 mm).
All values are for d-c copper-coated electrodes, reverse polarity.
Air pressures throughout are 80-100 psi (552-689 kPa); 100 psi is recommended for 1/2 and 5/8″ (12.7 and 15.9 mm) electrodes.
A head angle of 45° is used for these settings, but when jointed electrodes are used, a head angle of 35° is often preferred.

PLASMA ARC CUTTING

Electrode holders for air-carbon arc cutting contain an airflow control valve, an air hose, and a cable. The air stream from orifices in the holder strike the molten metal directly behind the arc. Constant-voltage d-c is most common, but copper alloys cut better with a-c. Electrode-positive polarity removes metal faster than electrode-negative polarity, but the current carries carbon from the electrode to the base metal. The electrodes are generally a mixture of graphite and carbon with a coating of copper to increase their current-carrying capacity.

PLASMA ARC CUTTING

Plasma arc cutting (PAC) is an arc cutting process that severs metal by melting a localized area with the heat of a constricted arc. Molten metal is removed with a high-velocity jet of hot, ionized gas issuing from the orifice. The arc penetrates the workpiece as in keyhole welding with a plasma arc, previously discussed in this section. The voltage used for plasma arc cutting, however, is much higher, and the nozzle is designed to create a higher velocity arc to blow away the molten metal.

Applications

While originally developed for severing nonferrous metals, such as aluminum, and stainless steels, modifications of the plasma arc process and equipment now make it possible to cut any metal that conducts electricity. The method is being used extensively to cut carbon steel, generally from about 0.038 to 1 1/2″ (0.95 to 38 mm) thick. Operations performed include stack cutting, plate and pipe edge beveling, shape cutting, and piercing. Plasma cutting torches are being mounted integrally on CNC punch presses for making contours, slots, and large cutouts in sheet metal.

Advantages

A major advantage of the plasma arc process is the fast cutting speeds possible. Low-carbon steel, 1/2″ (12.7 mm) thick, can be cut at 100 ipm (2540 mm/min). Speed and cost advantages compared to oxyfuel cutting decrease, however, with increasing workpiece thicknesses.

The fast speeds possible with plasma arc cutting minimize thermal distortion and result in a narrow heat-affected zone. No preheating is required, and parts cut in this way can be handled immediately after the operation. More precise cuts can generally be made at lower costs than with air-carbon arc cutting.

Limitations

A possible limitation to the use of plasma arc cutting is that the top edges of the cuts are generally rounded, and the cuts are beveled (wider at the top than the bottom). Smoothness of the cut surfaces is generally satisfactory for most applications.

Another possible limitation is that capital equipment costs for plasma arc cutting are higher than for oxyfuel cutting. Also, power demands are high. Depending on the material and thickness to be cut, the power supply may have to provide up to 250 V at 1000 A.

Principles

In the basic plasma arc cutting process, a gas is forced under pressure through an orifice in a torch. The torch is connected to a d-c power source and straight polarity (electrode-negative) is used. In the torch, a portion of the gas is ionized by the discharge of a high-voltage arc between the electrode and the torch tip. A pilot arc created by a high-frequency generator forms a low-resistance path to ignite the main transferred arc between the negatively charged electrode and the positively charged workpiece.

The base metal is melted by a combination of the arc and the high-temperature plasma. Molten metal is blown out of the cut by the high-velocity plasma stream. Several modifications of the basic process have been developed to improve cutting speed and quality and to allow cutting of different materials. These modifications include gas-shielded, air cutting, oxygen injection, water-shielded, and water injection processes.

Gas-shielded plasma cutting. This method, also called dualflow, is similar to the basic process except that a secondary shielding gas is introduced around the torch nozzle (see Fig. 9-45, view *a*). An advantage of this method is that the nozzle can

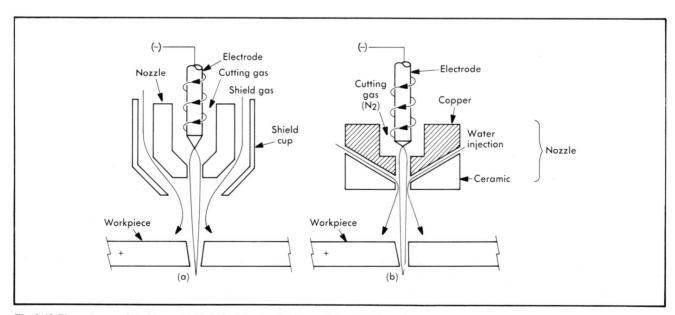

Fig. 9-45 Plasma arc cutting: (a) gas-shielded (dual flow) and (b) water-injected. (*Hypertherm, Inc.*)

be recessed within a ceramic shield cup to protect the nozzle from double arcing. Cutting of mild steel can be done slightly faster than with the basic process, but the cutting speeds for stainless steel and aluminum are essentially the same.

The cutting (orifice) gas is usually nitrogen, and the shielding gas varies with the metal to be cut. Oxygen or carbon dioxide are normally used as the shielding gases when cutting mild steel; carbon dioxide for stainless steel; and a mixture of argon and hydrogen for aluminum.

Air-plasma cutting. This modification was introduced for cutting mild steel. Oxygen in the air provides additional energy from the exothermic reaction with molten steel. Cutting speeds are increased about 25% compared to the basic process. While the process can be used to cut stainless steel and aluminum, the cut surfaces are heavily oxidized and unacceptable for many applications.

Special electrodes having zirconium or hafnium inserts must be used because tungsten will erode in seconds if the cutting gas contains oxygen. Even with these special electrodes, the service life is much less than what can be achieved with the conventional plasma cutting process.

Oxygen injection. This process refinement circumvented the electrode life problem associated with air cutting by using nitrogen as the cutting gas and introducing oxygen downstream in the nozzle bore. The process is used exclusively on mild steel and increases cutting speed by about 25% if the optimum gas mixture is used (80% N_2 - 20% O_2). The major disadvantages are lack of cut squareness, short nozzle life, and limited versatility (mild steel only).

Water shielding. Water-shielded plasma cutting is similar to the gas-shielded process except that water is substituted for the shielding gas. Cut appearance and nozzle life are improved because of the cooling effect provided by the water. Cut squareness, cutting speed, and dross tendency are not measurably improved because the water does not provide additional arc constriction.

Water injection. Use of a symmetrical, impinging water jet near the constricting nozzle (see Fig. 9-45, view b) further constricts the plasma flame. This results in faster cutting speeds, improved cut squareness with sharper corners, and increased nozzle life; however, usually only one side of the cut is improved. As a result, the direction of travel is important for optimum results. Another advantage of water injection is that good cut quality can be obtained on all metals with just one cutting gas, nitrogen. Water cooling of the top surface of the workpiece prevents the formation of oxides.

Operating Conditions

Recommended practices for plasma arc cutting are presented in ANSI/AWS Standard C5.2. Additional information on this process is also included in Volume I, *Machining*, and Volume II, *Forming*, of this Handbook series.

Typical conditions for cutting various materials and thicknesses with a plasma arc torch, water injection, and 100% nitrogen gas are presented in Table 9-34. The conditions listed are for optimum cut quality, not speed. If deviations from these conditions are necessary, they should be limited to changes in arc current, arc voltage, and travel speed, not gas and water flow rates. Thicker plates are cut with increased arc voltages, higher amperages (to 1000 A), increased torch to work distances, lower travel speeds, and no water injection.

Cutting speeds are inversely proportional to plate thicknesses. In beveling applications, the cutting speed is determined by the width of the cut face rather than the plate thickness.

TABLE 9-34
Typical Conditions for Cutting Various Materials and Thicknesses
with a Plasma Arc Torch, Water Injection, and 100% Nitrogen Gas

Material Thickness, in. (mm)	Torch to Work Distance, in. (mm)	Arc Voltage Setting, V	Arc Current Setting, A	Travel Speed, ipm (mm/min)
Mild steel:				
0.035 (1)	1/8 (3)	125	250	450 (11 430)
0.075 (2)	1/8 (3)	130	250	300 (7620)
1/8 (3)	3/16 (5)	135	260	200 (5080)
1/4 (6)	1/4 (6)	145	260	150 (3810)
1/8 (3)	1/4 (6)	140	300	200 (5080)
1/4 (6)	1/4 (6)	145	350	150 (3810)
3/8 (10)	1/4 (6)	150	380	125 (3175)
1/2 (13)	1/4 (6)	155	400	100 (2540)
1/2 (13)	3/8 (10)	160	500	115 (2920)
3/4 (19)	3/8 (10)	165	500	75 (1905)
1 (25)	3/8 (10)	165	600	60 (1525)
1 1/4 (32)	3/8 (10)	175	600	45 (1145)
1 1/4 (32)	1/2 (13)	185	700	50 (1270)
1 1/2 (38)	1/2 (13)	195	700	40 (1015)
1 3/4 (44)	1/2 (13)	200	725	35 (890)
2 (50)	1/2 (13)	205	725	30 (760)

(continued)

PLASMA ARC CUTTING

TABLE 9-34—*Continued*

Material Thickness, in. (mm)	Torch to Work Distance, in. (mm)	Arc Voltage Setting, V	Arc Current Setting, A	Travel Speed, ipm (mm/min)
Stainless steel:				
0.035 (1)	1/8 (3)	125	250	450 (11 430)
0.075 (2)	1/8 (3)	130	250	300 (7620)
1/8 (3)	3/16 (5)	135	260	200 (5080)
1/4 (6)	1/4 (6)	145	260	150 (3810)
1/8 (3)	1/4 (6)	140	300	200 (5080)
1/4 (6)	1/4 (6)	145	350	150 (3810)
3/8 (10)	1/4 (6)	150	380	125 (3175)
1/2 (13)	1/4 (6)	155	400	100 (2540)
3/4 (19)	5/16 (8)	160	400	50 (1270)
1 (25)	3/8 (10)	165	400	30 (760)
3/4 (19)	3/8 (10)	165	500	75 (1905)
1 (25)	3/8 (10)	165	550	60 (1525)
1 1/2 (38)	3/8 (10)	170	580	30 (760)
2 (50)	3/8 (10)	170	600	20 (510)
2 (50)	1/2 (13)	190	700	25 (635)
3 (75)	5/8 (16)	200	750	12 (305)
Aluminum:				
0.035 (1)	1/8 (3)	125	250	540 (13 715)
0.075 (2)	1/8 (3)	130	250	360 (9145)
1/8 (3)	3/16 (5)	135	260	240 (6095)
1/4 (6)	1/4 (6)	145	260	180 (4570)
1/8 (3)	1/4 (6)	140	300	240 (6095)
1/4 (6)	1/4 (6)	145	325	180 (4570)
3/8 (10)	1/4 (6)	150	350	150 (3810)
1/2 (13)	1/4 (6)	155	375	120 (3050)
3/4 (19)	5/16 (8)	160	400	60 (1525)
1 (25)	3/8 (10)	165	400	35 (915)
1 (25)	3/8 (10)	165	500	70 (1830)
1 1/2 (38)	3/8 (10)	170	550	35 (915)
2 (50)	3/8 (10)	170	600	25 (610)
2 (50)	1/2 (13)	190	700	30 (760)
3 (75)	5/8 (16)	200	750	15 (355)
Titanium:				
1/2 (13)	1/4 (6)	155	400	90 (2285)
1 (25)	3/8 (10)	165	550	50 (1270)
Brass:				
1/2 (13)	1/4 (6)	155	400	70 (1780)
Copper:				
1/2 (13)	1/4 (6)	155	400	60 (1525)
Cast iron:				
5/8 (16)	1/4 (6)	155	400	80 (2030)

(Hypertherm, Inc.)

Automation

While plasma arc cutting is done manually with handheld torches, semiautomatic or automatic machines are used for most applications. Common are machines having carriages that travel along tracks for straight-line cutting or along arcs for cutting curves. Pantograph shape-cutting machines for small simple shapes use scale models of the desired shapes that are traced by followers connected by arms to the cutting torch. Optical tracing is done with templates or drawings of the desired parts.

Industrial robots are being used for cutting pipe, pressure vessels, castings, and formed shapes. Plasma cutting torches are also being made an integral part of CNC punch presses to produce slots, contours, and cutouts in sheet metal. Shape-cutting machines equipped with CNC can be connected to computers to integrate design and material requirements. Computerized nesting of shapes for maximum material utilization is also possible with such equipment.

OTHER ARC CUTTING PROCESSES

In addition to air-carbon arc cutting and plasma arc cutting, discussed previously, there are several other arc cutting processes, but they are not used extensively or only for special applications. These include oxygen arc cutting, gas metal arc cutting, gas tungsten arc cutting, shielded metal arc cutting, and carbon arc cutting.

Oxygen Arc Cutting

In oxygen arc cutting, oxygen passes through a tubular electrode made from a ferrous metal and covered with a flux. An electric arc between the electrode and the workpiece provides the heat required for an oxidation reaction. Cuts produced in this way are not of high quality, but are satisfactory for some applications. The method is used primarily for underwater applications.

Gas Metal Arc Cutting

In gas metal arc cutting, an electric arc between a continuously fed wire electrode and the workpiece, with inert gas shielding, produces the required heat. Force from a pressure gradient in the gas ejects molten metal to form the kerf.

Gas Tungsten Arc Cutting

Gas tungsten arc cutting is similar to gas tungsten arc welding (GTAW) except that higher currents and shielding gas flows are used. Molten metal is blown away by the gas jet to form the kerf.

Shielded Metal Arc Cutting

In shielded metal arc cutting, standard covered electrodes are used without any compressed gas. Molten metal is removed by gravity.

Carbon Arc Cutting

In carbon arc cutting, heat is provided by an electric arc between a carbon electrode and the workpiece. Molten metal is removed by forces from the arc and by gravity.

SAFETY IN ARC WELDING AND CUTTING

Safety considerations with respect to general requirements, machines and equipment, and operator protection are discussed in the introductory section of this chapter under the subject "Overview of Welding Processes." These considerations are applicable to arc welding and cutting and should be reviewed. Detailed recommendations with respect to safety in welding and cutting are presented in ANSI/AWS Standard Z49.1. Fire prevention in the use of these processes is the subject of NFPA Standard 51B.

General Requirements

Good housekeeping is essential for safety in arc welding and cutting. All equipment should be kept in good, clean, and dry condition, with frequent inspections and maintenance. Welding areas should also be kept neat, clean, dry, and free of hazards. Flammable materials, liquids, or gases should be removed or stored in tightly sealed metal containers. Hot electrode stubs should be placed in metal containers.

Properly trained operators with skilled supervisors are critical to safety. Nonreflecting curtains or screens are advisable to protect others near the welding area. Warning signs should be posted to identify welding and cutting areas and the need for protective devices.

Eye Protection

Arc welding and cutting result in infrared radiation from the molten metal and ultraviolet radiation from the electric arc. Eye exposure to ultraviolet radiation causes irritation and repeated exposure may result in permanent eye injury. As a result, handheld shields, face shields, helmets, or goggles equipped with filter lenses are necessary.

Specifications for eye protection equipment are contained in ANSI Standard Z87.1, "Practice for Occupational and Educational Eye and Face Protection." Recommendations for filter lenses are presented in ANSI/AWS Standard Z49.1. Safety goggles should also be worn when chipping or grinding slag from welds.

Skin Protection

Burns can occur from contact with hot metal or sparks during arc welding or cutting. Overexposure to ultraviolet and infrared radiation from the electric arc can also cause severe skin burns. To prevent this, nonflammable protective clothing, including aprons and gloves, is generally required.

Respiratory Protection

Fumes, gases, and particulate matter in the air can cause respiratory problems. The hazard potential depends on the chemical composition of the materials used, the concentration of the chemicals in the breathing zone, and the duration of exposure. Air contaminants result from components of the electrodes, filler rods, and metals being joined, as well as shielding gases, when used. Ozone and oxides of nitrogen are the principal toxic gases produced by arc welding.

The best protection against respiratory problems is to provide adequate and effective, positive ventilation by means of exhaust systems. Supplied-air respirators may be required for welding in confined spaces. Regulations issued by OSHA, as well as local codes, specify requirements with respect to ventilation. Recommended practices for respiratory protection are contained in ANSI Standard Z88.1. Methods for sampling airborne particulates generated by welding and allied processes are presented in ANSI/AWS Standard F1.1.

ELECTROSLAG WELDING

Hearing Protection
Properly fitted ear plugs or other ear protection to prevent noise exposure may be needed, especially when cutting with the air-carbon arc and plasma arc processes, to meet OSHA regulations.

Electrical Shock
Electrical shocks experienced at welding voltages do not generally cause severe injury, but under certain conditions, they can be lethal. Even mild shocks can produce involuntary muscle contractions that may cause injuries. Wearing damp clothing or working in wet conditions reduces skin contact resistance and increases the risk of shock.

To minimize the possibility of electrical shocks, all machines used should meet national standards, such as those issued by NEMA, and the machines and equipment should be inspected and maintained on a regular schedule. All electrical equipment and the workpieces should be grounded, and cables of the correct size should be used. Electrode holders and connections should be fully insulated, and welding cables should be free of worn or frayed insulation. All connections should be kept tight, clean, dry, and in good condition. Operators and maintenance personnel should wear insulated gloves when making adjustments.

Safety with Various Processes
Shielded metal arc welding. Major requirements for this process are eye protection and protective clothing because of exposure to the electric arc and molten metal or slag spatter.

Gas tungsten arc welding. Safety precautions for this process are the same as for shielded metal arc welding except that a darker shade of lens is generally required for eye protection because the gas tungsten arc is more intensive.

Gas metal arc welding. Potential hazards with this process include fumes and gases, high-voltage electricity, ultraviolet radiation from the arc, and noise.

Flux-cored arc welding. Depending on the shielding used with this process (self or gas-shielded), safety precautions are similar to shielded metal arc welding or gas metal arc welding.

Electrogas welding. Safety considerations required for this process are much the same as for the other continuous-wire arc welding processes. Eye protection is required because the arc is continuous from start to finish of the operation. A consideration intrinsic to the process is the presence of larger than normal amounts of molten weld metal. If this metal escapes, it creates both a safety and a fire hazard. Workpieces to be welded must be securely braced to eliminate the possibility of their falling. Also, because heights are involved, precautions should be taken to prevent personnel from falling.

Submerged arc welding. There are few health and safety problems associated with this process. Fume and gas levels are generally negligible, radiation is usually nonexistent, and noise and heat levels are low. No eye protection is needed, but safety glasses and gloves are generally used. The safety glasses are often tinted to protect in case the arc is inadvertently exposed.

Plasma arc welding and cutting. With these processes, protection is required from the intense glare of the arc, spatter, fumes, and noise.

ELECTROSLAG WELDING

Electroslag welding (ESW) is a process in which coalescence of metals is produced by molten slag that melts the filler metal and the surfaces of the work to be welded. The molten weld pool is shielded by this slag, which moves along the full cross section of the joint as welding progresses.

Electroslag welding is not an arc welding process, but it is initiated by an arc that heats the slag. Also, it uses the same basic equipment as the other consumable-electrode arc welding processes and is most similar to electrogas welding, previously discussed in this chapter. When the arc is extinguished, the conductive slag is maintained molten by its resistance to electric current passing between the electrode and the work. In consumable-guide electroslag welding, the most commonly used variation of electroslag welding, filler metal is supplied by an electrode and its guiding member (see Fig. 9-46). Consumables used for electroslag welding of carbon and high-strength, low-alloy steels are specified in ANSI/AWS Standard A5.25.

APPLICATIONS
The major user of electroslag welding has been the heavy-plate fabrication industry, which includes manufacturers of frames, bases, and metalworking machinery. A frequent use of the process is the splicing of rolled steel plates to obtain a larger piece for a specific application.

Another major user of electroslag welding is the structural steel industry, for making subassemblies for steel buildings. It has also been used for field erection at building sites. A common application is the welding of continuity plates inside box columns. The continuity plate carries the load from one side of the column to the other side at the point of beam-to-column connections. Continuity plates must be welded with complete-penetration welds to the two sides of the box column. The electrical machinery industry also utilizes electroslag welding for producing electric motor housings.

PROCESS ADVANTAGES
The electroslag welding process is one of the most productive welding processes when it can be applied. Some of its advantages are:

1. Extremely high metal deposition rates. Electroslag has a deposition rate of 35-45 lb/hr (15.9-20.4 kg/hr) per electrode.
2. Ability to weld thick materials in one pass. Because there is only one pass, only one setup is required, and interpass cleaning is not necessary.
3. High-quality weld deposits. Weld metal stays molten longer, allowing gases to esape.
4. Minimized joint preparation and fitup requirements. Mill edges and square flame-cut edges are normally employed.
5. It is a mechanized process: once started, it continues to

completion. There is little operator fatigue because manipulative skill is not involved.

6. Minimized material handling. The equipment may be moved to the work, rather than the work moved to the equipment.
7. High filler-metal utilization. All of the welding electrode is melted into the joint. In addition, the amount of flux consumed is small.
8. Minimum distortion. There is no angular distortion in the horizontal plane. There is minimum distortion (shrinkage) in the vertical plane.
9. Minimal time. It is the fastest welding process for large, thick materials.
10. There is no weld spatter, and finishing of the weld is minimal.
11. There is no arc flash, so a welding helmet is not required.

LIMITATIONS

The major limitation of electroslag welding is that of welding position. The process can be used only when the axis of the weld is vertical. A tilt of up to 15° is permitted, but beyond this the process may not function correctly. A second limitation is that the process can be used only for welding steels. Also, the long thermal cycle of the process may result in low toughness of the weld metal and the heat-affected zone. High heat input and slow cooling can also produce coarse grain size.

A possible problem is lack of fusion at the sidewall on one surface if the electrode is incorrectly placed. Also, there may be lack of fusion if the weld stops and has to be restarted. These problems are rarely encountered, however, with the use of good welding practices.

STEELS WELDED

Steels welded by the consumable-guide electroslag process are low-carbon steels; low-alloy, high-strength steels; medium-carbon steels; and certain stainless steels. Quenched and tempered steels can be electroslag welded, but a post heat treatment may be necessary to compensate for the softened heat-affected zone.

Under normal conditions, the minimum thickness of steel welded with the consumable-guide method is 3/4" (19 mm). Maximum thickness that has been successfully welded with the electroslag process is 36" (914 mm). To weld this thickness, six individual guide tubes and electrodes are used.

A single electrode is used to weld steels ranging from 1 to 3" (25 to 76 mm) thick. From 2 to 5" (51 to 127 mm) thick, the electrode and guide tube are oscillated in the joint. From 5 to 12" (127 to 305 mm) thick, two electrodes and guide tubes are used and are oscillated in the joint. If oscillation is not employed, additional guide tubes and electrodes are required. This necessitates additional power sources and wire-feed systems; therefore, oscillation in the joint is preferred where it can be used.

The height of the joint has a definite relationship and must be considered. The process can be used for joints as short as 4" (102 mm) and as long or high as 20' (6.1 m). It is difficult to oscillate extremely long guide tubes because they become heated and flexible. When two guide tubes are used and properly secured together, oscillation is possible. However, as the number of tubes increases, the height of the joint must be decreased.

JOINT DESIGN

In electroslag welding, the basic type of weld is the square groove weld. However, the square groove weld can be used to produce butt joints, tee joints, corner joints, and even lap and edge joints. The square groove butt configuration is used for the transition joint where two thicknesses of plate are joined with a smooth contour from one thickness to the other. The transition can be in the weld metal. Bead or overlay welds can also be made with electroslag, and fillet welds can be made between thick plates by using a suitably shaped shoe.

In a square groove weld, there are only two dimensions, the thickness of the parts being jointed and the root opening between the parts. The root opening can be varied, but it is relative, based on the plate thickness. It is desirable to have the root opening as small as possible to use a minimum amount of weld metal.

In consumable-guide welding, a limiting factor to the minimum root opening is the size of the consumable guide tube and the insulators that are required to keep it from touching the sides of the joint. The guide tube must be of sufficient size to carry the welding current and must be structurally strong until it is consumed in the flux pool. The root opening must be large enough to provide sufficient volume of the molten flux to ensure stable welding conditions. This root opening size requirement becomes one of the limiting factors for making small welds.

The water-cooled retaining shoes are designed to accommodate the different types of joints. Shoes are available for the square groove with minor reinforcing. These are used for butt joints and for other joints where the surfaces of the plates to be

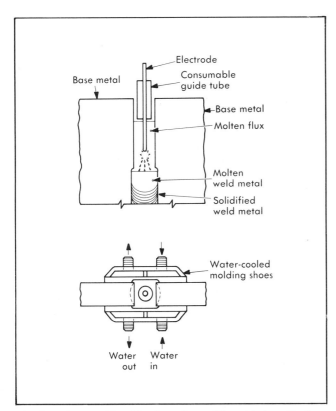

Fig. 9-46 Consumable-guide electroslag welding. (*Hobart Brothers Co.*)

ELECTROSLAG WELDING

joined are flush. For square groove welds involving corner or tee joints, fillet-type shoes are normally used.

PRINCIPLES OF OPERATION

Electroslag welding is done in the vertical position using molding shoes, usually water cooled, in contact with the joint to contain the molten flux and weld metal. In consumable-guide welding, the electrode is fed through a guide tube to the bottom of the joint. The guide tube, normally having a thick wall, carries the welding current and transmits it to the electrode.

At the start of the weld, granulated flux is placed in the bottom of the cavity. The electrode is fed to the bottom of the joint and for a brief period will create an arc. In a very short time, the granulated flux will melt from the heat of the arc and produce a pool of molten flux. The flux is electrically conductive, and the welding current will pass from the electrode through the molten flux to the base metal.

The passage of current through the conductive flux causes it to become very hot, and it reaches a temperature in excess of the melting temperature of the base metal. The high-temperature flux causes melting of the edges of the joint, as well as melting of the electrode and the end of the guide tube. The melted base metal, electrode, and guide tube are heavier than the flux and collect at the bottom of the cavity to form the molten weld metal.

As the molten weld metal slowly solidifies from the bottom it joins the parts to be welded. Shielding of the molten weld metal from atmospheric contamination is provided by the pool of molten flux. Surface contour of the weld is determined by the contour of the molding or retaining shoes.

The consumable-guide variation of electroslag welding normally uses fixed or nonsliding molding shoes. The welding head does not move vertically and is normally mounted on the work at the top of the weld joint. Multiple electrodes and guides may be employed for welds of larger cross section. It is also possible to oscillate the electrode and guide the tube across the width of the joint.

The surface of the solidified weld metal is covered with an easily removed thin layer of slag. The slag loss must be compensated for by adding flux during the welding operation. A starting tab is necessary to build up the proper depth of flux so that the molten pool is formed at the bottom of the joint. Runoff tabs are required at the top of the joint so that the molten flux will rise above the top of the joint. Both starting and runoff tabs are removed from the ends of the joint after the weld is completed.

When not using a consumable guide, the electroslag welding process utilizes a welding head that moves up the joint as the weld is made. Retaining shoes usually slide along the joint and rise with the head. Single or multiple-electrode systems can be employed, and they may be oscillated across the width of the joint. All of the other factors involved in operating the process are the same except that the guide tube is not used. As a result, the deposit weld metal is supplied entirely by the electrode.

The consumable-guide version of electroslag welding is applied as a machine operation. Once the process is started, it should be continued until the weld joint is completed. It is very difficult to restart the welding, and extensive cleaning is required prior to attempting the restart. The apparatus should be monitored by the welding operator, although little is done in guiding or directing it. Flux is added periodically, and the welding operator must monitor the depth of the molten flux pool. When oscillation is used or when sliding shoes are used, closer attention is required.

EQUIPMENT REQUIREMENTS

The equipment required for the consumable-guide electroslag welding process is shown in Fig. 9-47. A system can range from one electrode and guide tube assembly to systems utilizing six electrodes and guide tubes. The systems become more complex as additional electrodes are added. The use of lateral motion or oscillation provides greater latitude of the consumable-guide method. All the electrode wires are mounted on one oscillating assembly. As a result, only one oscillating device and control are required.

Power Source

The power source used for the consumable-guide electroslag welding process should be a direct-current welding machine of the constant voltage type. With d-c, the electrode is made positive (DCEP). In the normal electroslag welding process, without consumable guides, alternating current is often used, especially for three-wire systems. Both d-c and a-c power units must be rated at a 100% duty cycle because some electroslag welds take hours to complete.

The current capacity of the machine must exceed the current required for a single electrode according to the welding procedure schedule. The power source should have high voltage ratings because starting voltages as high as 55 V are sometimes required. High voltage is extremely important, especially when using long guide tubes. Welding current per electrode wire may range from as low as 400 A to as high as 800 A. Transformer-rectifier machines are best suited for electroslag welding. Primary contactors and provisions for remote control, including voltage adjustment, should be included.

Wire Feed

Normally, the wire-feed motor is mounted over the welding joint. However, it can be mounted elsewhere, and the electrode wire can be conducted to the joint by flexible conduits. With the constant-voltage d-c drive system, a constant-speed wire feeder is used. With a-c drive, an adjustable-speed wire feeder is used, and the characteristics of the power source are drooping.

Oscillation

An oscillation system is used to weld thicker steels. This requires a motor control for oscillating limit switches to adjust the width of oscillation and a control circuit for adjusting the oscillation speed and dwell at each end of the oscillation.

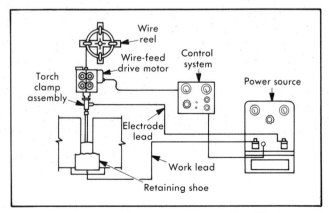

Fig. 9-47 Equipment requirements for consumable-guide electroslag welding. (*Hobart Brothers Co.*)

Shoes

When water-cooled shoes are used, a system for water circulation and heat removal is required. When running water is available and can be easily disposed of, this is the simplest solution. However, water-circulating systems that include heat exchangers can be used. The size of the heat exchanger must be sufficiently great to remove the heat generated in the weld.

Reusable Materials

In addition to the flux, electrode wire, and guide tubes routinely used for consumable-guide electroslag welding, there are several other materials used, including runoff and starting tabs. These are reusable and must be the same thickness and composition as the base metal.

Other reusable items are the strong backs used to hold the retaining shoes against the weld joint. Wedges are generally used to hold the retaining shoes in place. When more than one electrode is used, a steel-wool ball is placed at the bottom of the joint under the electrode wire to aid arc initiation. Steel wool also can be used for single-wire applications, although it is not normally required.

Insulation and Sealing Materials

Insulation material is used for certain applications. Insulators are sometimes required around the bare guide tube to avoid short-circuiting the system if the guide tube comes in contact with the retaining shoes or the face of the weld joint.

When the work surface is irregular, putty-like material must seal cracks between shoes and work. Commercial materials such as furnace-sealing compound can also be used.

Fluxes

Normal functions for an electroslag flux are:

1. Providing heat to melt the electrode and base metal.
2. Conducting the welding current.
3. Protecting the molten weld metal from the atmosphere.
4. Purifying or scavenging the liquid weld metal.
5. Providing stable operation.

There are two types of granular fluxes normally used for electroslag welding with a consumable guide tube, a starting flux and a running flux. The starting flux is designed to bring the electroslag process into quick stabilization. It melts quickly and wets the bottom of the sump to facilitate starting.

The running flux is designed to provide the proper balance for correct electrical conductivity, correct bath temperature and viscosity, and the proper chemical analysis. Running flux will operate over a wide range of conditions. Only a relatively small amount of flux is used, approximately 1/4 lb (100 g) per vertical foot (0.3 m) or height of the joint.

Electrode Wire

The electrode for consumable-guide electroslag welding supplies more than 80% of the deposited weld metal, the guide tube supplying the remainder. The electrode wire must match the base metal. Because an electroslag weld deposit is similar to a casting, it is essential that the properties of this as-cast metal overmatch the mechanical properties of the parts being joined. It is also important to consider the dilution factor provided by the base metal. In a consumable-guide weld, the dilution runs from a low of 25% to a high of 50% base metal. The amount of dilution of the base metal depends on the welding conditions.

The flux adds no alloys and has little effect on the weld deposit in relation to the analysis of the wire. In general, the same electrode wires designed for gas metal arc welding and submerged arc welding are employed for electroslag welding. A 3/32″ (2.4 mm) diam electrode size is the most common; it is the most easily used to feed through a guide tube and produces the highest deposition rate.

Guide Tube

The consumable guide tube melts just above the surface of the molten slag bath. A guide tube must be used whenever the length of the weld is 6″ (152 mm) or more, assuming that the head is stationary. When a bare guide tube is used, and if the weld is more than 12″ (305 mm) long, insulators should be placed on the tube to avoid the guide tube coming in contact with the side wall or face of the joint or the retaining shoes. Coated guide tubes are also available; the coating is an effective insulator, particularly when working in tight joints.

There are several variations of the consumable guide tube system. In some cases, bars are tack welded to the guide tube, or tubes are tacked to the edges of bars. These bars contribute metal to the weld deposit.

DEPOSITION RATES AND WELD QUALITY

Deposition rates for electroslag welding are among the highest of any welding process. Figure 9-48 shows the deposition rate versus welding current for 3/32″ (2.4 mm) and 1/8″ (3.2 mm) diam electrode wires.

Electroslag welding produces a high-quality weld metal deposit. The high quality of the electroslag weld metal is the result of progressive solidification that begins at the bottom of the joint or cavity. There is always molten metal above the

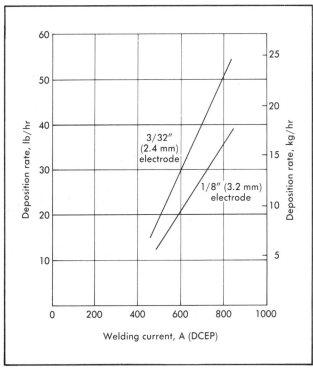

Fig. 9-48 Deposition rates for electroslag welding. (*Hobart Brothers Co.*)

ELECTROSLAG WELDING

solidifying weld metal, and the impurities, which are lighter, rise above the deposited metal and collect only at the very top of the weld in the area that is normally discarded.

Electroslag welding is a low-hydrogen welding process because hydrogen is not present in any of the materials involved in making the weld. Because of the slow cooling rate, any impurities that are in the base metal and are melted during the welding process have time to escape. Cooling rate for the electroslag weld is much slower than that for welds made by other arc welding processes. This slow cooling rate allows large grain growth in the weld metal and also in the heat-affected zone of the base metal. This minimizes the risk of cracking and reduces the high hardness in the heat-affected zone, sometimes found in conventional arc welds, but coarse grain size results in reduced toughness.

Weld metal produced by electroslag welding will generally qualify under the most strict codes and specifications, but normalizing is frequently required to refine the grain size and provide necessary impact values. Ductility of the weld metal is relatively high, in the range of 25 to 30%. Impact requirements for electroslag welds will meet those required by the AWS structural welding code. Charpy V-notch impact specimens producing 5-30 ft-lbf (6.8-40.7 N·m) at 0° F (-18°C) are normal and expected.

When joint toughness is an important factor, particularly for subzero temperature applications, the toughness of the large grains in the weld metal and heat-affected zone may be substantially lower than that of the parent metal or that obtained with conventional arc welding. Postweld normalizing may be necessary if toughness is a critical factor.

WELDING PROCEDURE SCHEDULES

Welding procedure schedules for electroslag welding with the consumable-guide method are generally the same as for electrogas welding (refer to Table 9-22). Welding procedure schedules are based on welding low-carbon steel under normal conditions, using water-cooled copper shoes and a 5/8" (16 mm) OD x 1/8" (3.2 mm) ID guide tube. The electrode diameter is 3/32" (2.4 mm) diam, and proprietary starting and running fluxes are used. Oscillation speed is based on the number of seconds per cycle, which is shown as a rate of speed. There is a dwell time at each end of oscillation that is normally 4 seconds.

OPERATING VARIABLES

Electroslag welding differs from the arc welding processes in that the base metal melting results from localized heat generated in the molten slag pool instead of from an arc. The heating involved in electroslag welding is concentrated in a volume of molten flux, which is the product of the metal thickness, the root opening, and the slag pool depth. In the arc welding processes, the localized heating is confined to the much smaller area of an arc and puddle, but the arc is at a much higher temperature.

Operation of electroslag welding is thus different from the arc processes. In electroslag welding, the metal surfaces to be melted (joint sidewalls) are parallel to the axis of the electrode. Thus, increasing the welding current does not increase the depth of fusion into the sidewalls of the base metal. The higher the welding current, the higher the deposition rate.

With all arc welding processes, an increase in arc voltage causes the weld bead to widen. In electroslag welding, this is also true, but the widening causes an increase in the depth of fusion into the sidewall. The increased voltage raises the slag bath temperature and causes more of the base metal or sidewall to melt. However, excessively high voltage will cause undercutting. Too low a voltage may result in arcing between the electrode wire and the molten weld metal at the bottom of the flux pool. The operator must be continually alert to make various adjustments as required during the welding operation. A good operating knowledge of electroslag welding is necessary because of the effects of changing the various parameters.

The depth of the molten slag pool should be checked if possible. When the pool is accessible to the operator, a dipstick can be used to determine its depth. Experience will quickly show that when the pool is quiet and the process is running without sparking or sputtering, the pool depth is correct. If the pool depth becomes too shallow, sparks will emit from the surface and can be seen by the operator. When this occurs, additional flux should be added to the pool.

If the retaining shoes leak and water gets into the weld cavity, the operation must be stopped. This can create a safety hazard and will create gross porosity in the weld metal. With respect to water-cooled shoes, the operator must ensure that the water flow is uninterrupted during the entire welding operation.

The major safety hazard in electroslag welding is the presence of a large mass of molten slag and weld metal. The high welding current creates a large mass of metal that must be contained within the weld cavity. If the retaining shoes should fail and allow the molten metal to escape, it is best to evacuate the area, turn off the equipment, and wait for the metal to solidify. Obviously, the surface under the welding operation should be noncombustible. The work being welded must be securely braced to eliminate the possibility of it falling.

RESISTANCE WELDING

Resistance welding (RW) is a group of welding processes that produces coalescence of metals with the heat obtained from the resistance of the work to electric current flowing in a circuit of which the work is a part, and by the application of pressure. There is no external heat source, and pressure is applied by the welding machine through electrodes. No flux, filler metal, or shielding is used, but in welding reactive metals, the process is sometimes performed in a vacuum or inert-gas environment.

The major types of resistance welding, all discussed in this section, are spot, seam, projection, flash, upset, percussion, and induction. Some of these processes are illustrated schematically in Fig. 9-49. Essential elements for resistance welding include a low-voltage, high-current welding transformer; electrodes for contacting the work; conductors connecting the electrodes with the welding transformer; means for exerting the electrode force (pressure) on the work; means to regulate current by changing the

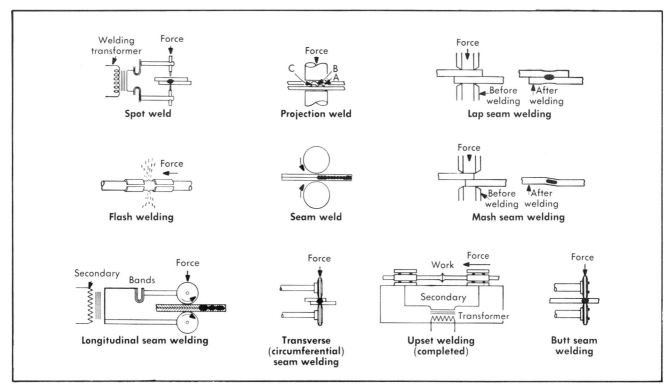

Fig. 9-49 Some of the basic methods of resistance welding.

transformer turns ratio or by electronic phase-shift heat-control unit; a power contactor to open and close the circuit to the welding transformer; and a welding timer to control energization and deenergization of the power contactor (see Fig. 9-50).

RESISTANCE SPOT WELDING

Resistance spot welding (RSW) produces coalescence at the faying surfaces in one spot. The size and shape of the individually formed welds (nuggets) are influenced primarily by the size and contour of the electrodes. Most spot welding is done by clamping the workpieces between a pair of electrodes and passing a low-voltage, high-amperage current through the electrodes and workpieces for a short cycle. Resistance heating at the joint contacting surfaces forms a fused nugget of weld material. The heat developed in spot welding depends on several variables, including the magnitude of the current, electrical resistance of the workpieces, time of current flow, conduction losses, and electrode force.

Applications

Spot-welded lap joints are used extensively to join sheet steels up to about 1/8" (3.2 mm) thick when gas or liquid-tight joints are not required. Sometimes, steel thicknesses to 1/4" (6.4 mm) are joined. With special equipment, 1" (25.4 mm) thicknesses or more can be welded, although these thicknesses are more suited for other joining processes.

Applications include the fabrication of containers and the attachment of braces, brackets, and similar components. The process is commonly used by mass production industries such as automotive, appliance, and furniture. The ease and speed of the welding operation also make the process suitable for the assembly of components that are to be subsequently brazed or bonded.

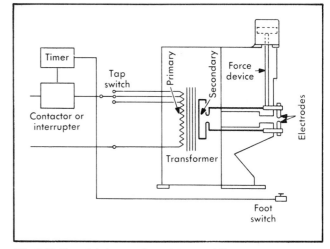

Fig. 9-50 Essential elements for resistance welding.

Advantages

A major advantage of resistance welding is its high speed. Also, the process is adaptable to mass production requirements, and equipment can be made an integral part of production lines. However, the process is also used for many job shop operations because it is faster than arc welding and can be performed with less skilled operators.

Because no flux, filler metal, or shielding gas are used with resistance welding, the composition of the base metal is not altered. Also, the application of electrode force refines the grain structure and makes it more uniform. With proper controls, the

RESISTANCE SPOT WELDING

process produces consistently sound, high-quality welds at high production rates and with low labor costs.

Other advantages include no limitations with respect to welding position; localized heating, which minimizes the possibility of distortion; and applicability to practically all steels and aluminum and copper alloys. The process is often more economical than using mechanical fasteners for assemblies that do not require gas or liquid-tight joints and where disassembly is not required.

Limitations

Equipment costs for resistance welding are generally higher than for arc welding, and the spot welds have lower strength. Because workpiece clamping is required, access to both sides of the joint is necessary. Special fixtures and material handling equipment are required for mass production applications. Another possible limitation is the high power demands of resistance welding, even though the duration of current flow per weld is short.

Process Variations

Spot welding is done by either the direct or indirect method. Parallel and series variations are used for multiple spot welding. Other variations include roll spot welding and weldbonding.

Direct welding. In this method, both the welding current and the pressure are applied by the electrodes (see Fig. 9-51, view *a*). All of the secondary current passes through the weld nugget(s). This results in indentations in both components of the assembly unless special provisions are made in electrode design.

Indirect welding. In this method, the welding current is applied to one of the workpieces through a contact located next to the electrode that applies pressure (see Fig. 9-51, view *b*). Indirect welding with two transformers, sometimes called push-pull welding, produces a higher voltage for welding metals having high electrical resistance (see view *c*).

Parallel welding. In this method, two or more spot welds are made simultaneously with current flowing parallel from a single transformer (see Fig. 9-51, view *d*).

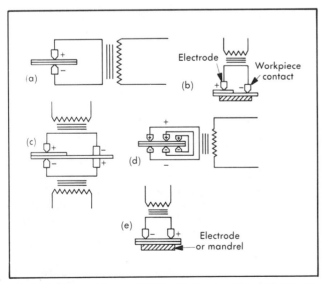

Fig. 9-51 Spot welding variations: (a) direct welding, (b) indirect welding, (c) indirect welding with two transformers, (d) parallel welding, and (e) series welding.

Series welding. In this method, current flows from one electrode into a third electrode or mandrel and then to the second electrode, producing two spot welds (see Fig. 9-51, view *e*).

Roll spot welding. In this method, a row of separate and spaced spot welds are made with a seam welding machine (discussed later in this section). The rotating electrode wheel is not retracted, and electrode force is continued between welds.

Weldbonding. This method is a combination of resistance spot or seam welding and adhesive bonding. The procedure used most commonly is to apply a structural adhesive to the area to be joined, followed by spot welding through the adhesive. Another method consists of applying tape or film adhesive, with holes cut in the adhesive where welds are required. Adhesives are discussed in Chapter 11.

Advantages of weldbonding over spot welding or adhesive bonding alone include improved fatigue life and durability, and better resistance to peel forces. Also, the adhesive acts as a seal in the joints to provide better corrosion protection and a generally tighter construction.

Welding Various Metals

Steels. Low-carbon steels have good weldability. However, medium and high-carbon steels, as well as alloy steels, are less weldable. They require precise sequencing control of the spot welding operation because they tend to harden and generally have to be heat treated after welding. High-strength sheet steels generally require less current for spot welding than mild steels, but higher electrode forces are needed because of springback of the material.

Ferritic and martensitic types of stainless steels have poor weldability. Austenitic stainless steels, however, are spot welded without problems by using short weld times, less current than for low-carbon steels, and high electrode forces.

Copper alloys. Copper is the least suitable metal for spot welding, but the weldability of different copper alloys varies with their electrical resistance. Alloys with low electrical resistance are more difficult to weld; those with high resistance are easier to weld. Spot welding of all copper alloys requires precise control of welding current and time, usually with higher currents and shorter times than for low-carbon steel and moderate electrode forces.

Copper-tin alloys (phosphor bronzes), copper-silicon alloys (silicon bronzes), and copper-aluminum alloys (aluminum bronzes) are relatively easy to weld because of their high electrical resistance. The higher the zinc content of copper-zinc alloys (brasses), the easier the alloy is to weld. Leaded brasses are difficult to weld, especially those with higher lead contents, because the welds produced are brittle.

Aluminum and magnesium alloys. All commercial aluminum and magnesium alloys in the form of sheet or extrusions may be spot welded, but the thickness of the sheets or extrusions and their number in a joint are limitations for producing satisfactory welds. Spot welding of these materials requires high welding currents, short welding times, fast electrode movement (low-inertia components), and precise controls because of their high electrical and thermal conductivity.

Titanium and alloys. Weldability of titanium and its alloys is similar to stainless steels because of their relatively low electrical and thermal conductivity. They can be spot welded more readily than aluminum and its alloys.

Coated steels. Sheet steel coated with corrosion-resistant metals such as zinc, aluminum, tin, or tin-zinc are commonly spot welded. Zinc-coated steels generally require higher currents, longer weld times, and higher electrode forces than for welding uncoated sheet steel. For aluminum-coated steels, welding current, time, and force are about the same or slightly higher than for uncoated steels. Steels with tin or tin-zinc coatings are generally welded in shorter times than uncoated steels.

Sheet steel with metallic coatings, such as nickel or chromium plate, are seldom spot welded because of the care required to avoid marking the plated surfaces. Sheet steel with conversion coatings such as phosphate are not generally spot welded without first removing the coating. Painted or plastic-coated sheet steel is seldom spot welded, but can be done with special electrodes and operating parameters.

Dissimilar metals. Low-carbon steels can be spot welded to most other ferrous metals and many nonferrous metals. This, however, requires correct *heat balance*—a condition in which the fusion zones in the pieces of material to be joined undergo approximately the same degree of heating.

When welding two equal thicknesses of the same metal with electrodes of the same analysis and diameter, heat balance is automatic. However, nearly half the practical applications do not experience this ideal condition. Heat balance may be affected by:

1. Relative electrical and thermal conductivities of the materials to be joined.
2. Relative geometry of the parts at the joint.
3. Thermal and electrical conductivities of the electrodes.
4. Geometry of the electrodes.

If it is desired, for example, to spot weld an equal thickness of a high-conductivity alloy (electrical and thermal) to an alloy of low conductivity, a correct heat balance could be obtained by the following techniques:

1. By using an electrode having a smaller contact area on the high-conductivity alloy than on the low-conductivity alloy to obtain approximately equal fusion. The electrode with the smaller tip area will produce a higher current density (concentrated) in the high-conductivity alloy, thus increasing the heat generated and minimizing the heat losses to the electrode from the contact area.
2. By using an electrode material or electrode facing of low conductivity on the high-conductivity alloy, which will lessen the heat losses in the electrode.
3. By use of a combination of items 1 and 2.

In very heavy metal stacking of dissimilar thicknesses, a long current flow or heating cycle permits a more uniform distribution of heat in the asymmetrical resistance path between the electrodes. A correct heat balance may be obtained by using multiple-impulse (pulsation) welding or a single impulse of continuous current flow for an equivalent time.

Joint Design

Spot welding is limited to lap joints of two or more metal thicknesses. The gap between parts to be joined should be as small as possible because any force required to close the gap reduces welding efficiency. The distance of spot welds from the edges of the joint must be sufficient to resist the welding pressure. Welds too close to the edges can cause overheating, upsetting, and possible expulsion of the molten metal. Joint overlap is generally restricted to twice the minimum edge distance.

When producing multiple spot welds along a joint, part of the secondary current flows through adjacent welds. This shunting of current increases with closer spaced welds. Closer weld spacing is possible by using shorter weld times, higher currents, and increased electrode forces.

Surface Preparation

Surface condition of the workpieces to be joined is critical for consistent weld quality. Good welding results require smooth, clean surfaces with a uniform and minimum electrical resistance. In general, the surfaces must be free of cutting fluids, drawing compounds, scale, thick oxides, heavy oil and grease, cleaning compounds, and paint.

The amount of surface preparation and cleaning required prior to welding varies with the materials to be joined. Adequate mechanical or chemical cleaning is essential for optimum quality in welding nickel, copper, magnesium, and aluminum alloys. Cold-rolled carbon steels do not generally require cleaning. Also, alloy and stainless steels are not usually cleaned unless it is necessary to remove excessive oil, grease, scale, or oxide films. Unpickled, hot-rolled carbon steels must be pickled or mechanically cleaned prior to welding.

Weld Quality and Strength

Weld quality depends primarily on the composition and condition of the metals to be joined, the design of the joint and workpieces, the type and condition of the electrodes, and the machine and controls used for welding. Weld quality is directly influenced by the available welding heat, and, because each welding variable is affected by the magnitude of the electrode force, force magnitude becomes a convenient measure of weld quality. It is advisable to determine the effect of electrode force and current on desired weld quality by experimentally welding a trial specimen.

Spot welds have low strengths in tension and are generally used for applications involving shear loading. The shear strength of a single spot weld depends on the cross-sectional area of the nugget; for multiple welds, the spacing and pattern also affect the strength.

Separation of the spot-welded components is sometimes a problem. Separation generally increases with increasing thicknesses of the components. Internal discontinuities may result from low electrode force, high welding currents, or other factors causing excessive heat. The appearance of spot welds is not generally critical, but they should be smooth and free from deep indentations or cracks. The use of large-diameter, flat-faced electrodes and indirect welding help minimize surface marking. Welds are inspected visually and sometimes by destructive testing with methods discussed in Chapter 7.

Spot Welding Machines

Among the types of spot welding machines as distinguished by general physical appearance and operating methods are the following:

1. Rocker-arm spot welders, foot or air operation (see Fig. 9-52 on page 9-106).
2. Press-type spot or projection welders, air or hydraulic operation (see Fig. 9-53 on page 9-106).
3. Transformer-gun package systems.
4. Multigun or ultra-high-speed spot welders.
5. Portable spot welders.

Further divisions of these machines are outlined under RWMA nominal kVa ratings (see Table 9-35). Pressure or, more properly, the electrode force, is supplied by either air or oil pressure through cylinders, by mechanical means such as cams,

RESISTANCE SPOT WELDING

TABLE 9-35
Spot Welder Standards of the Resistance Welder Manufacturers Association (RWMA)[8]

HORN TYPE:

	Single-Phase Transformer Available			Horn		
					Spacing, in. (mm)	
Size	kVa at 50% Duty Cycle, 60 Hz	Primary Potential, V	Cooling Medium	Diameter, min, in. (mm)	Minimum	Maximum
000	5	220 or 440	Air	1.25 (31.8)	4 (102)	8 (203)
00	7.5	220 or 440	Air	1.25 (31.8)	4 (102)	8 (203)
0	10	220 or 440	Air	1.50 (38.1)	4 (102)	8 (203)
1	15	220 or 440	Air or water	2.00 (50.8)	5 (127)	14 (356)
2	30	220 or 440	Water	2.25 (57.2)	6 (152)	15 (381)
3	50	220 or 440	Water	2.50 (63.5)	6 (152)	15 (381)

PRESS TYPE:

Type	Size	kVa at 50% Duty Cycle (Single-Phase Transformer, 60 Hz)	Nominal Throat Depth, in. (mm)	Nominal Electrode Forces, Hydraulic and Air,* lb (kN)	Platen Spacing,** in. (mm)
Projection	000	5	6 (152)	250 (1.11)‡	0.750-3.750 (19.05-95.25)
Spot			8 (203)		
Projection	00	20	6 (152)	550 (2.45)‡	1-4 (25.4-101.6)
Spot			8 (203)		
Projection	0	30, 50	6 (152)	1000 (4.45)‡	2-5 (50.8-127)
Spot			8 (203)		
Projection	1	30, 50, 75	12 (305)	2250 (10.0)	
			18 (457)	1550 (68.9)	
			30 (762)	1000 (4.45)	
Spot	1	30, 50, 75	18 (457)	2250 (10.0)	6-12 (152-305)
			24 (610)	1550 (68.9)	
			30 (762)	1000 (4.45)	

HORN TYPE:

Electrode Holders				Nominal Electrode Force at 12″ (305 mm) Throat Depth Operation, lbf (N)		Nominal Throat Depths Available, in. (mm)
Diameter, in. (mm)	RWMA Taper No.	Length, in. (mm) Upper	Lower	Manual	Air or Motor*	
0.75 (19.0)	4	6 (152)	8 (203)	75 (334)	100 (445)	8, 12, 16 (203,305,406)
0.75 (19.0)	4	6 (152)	8 (203)	100 (445)	150 (667)	8, 12, 16 (203,305,406)
0.875 (22.22)	4	6 (152)	8 (203)	150 (667)	200 (890)	8, 12, 16 (203,305,406)
1.00 (25.4)	4	8 (203)	12 (305)	200 (890)	300 (1334)	12, 18, 24 (305,457,610)
1.00 (25.4)	4	8 (203)	12 (305)	400 (1779)	800 (3558)	12, 18, 24, 30, 36 (305,457,610,762,914)
1.25 (31.8)	5	8 (203)	12 (305)	500 (2224)	1000 (4448)	12, 18, 24, 30, 36 (305,457,610,762,914)

PRESS TYPE:

Upper and Lower Platen Dimensions, in. (mm)	Horn Diameter, in. (mm)	Electrode Holder					
		Diameter, in. (mm)	RWMA Taper No.	Upper Length, in. (mm)	Lower Length, in. (mm)	Standard Ram Stroke,† in. (mm)
2 x 2 (51 x 51)	---	---	---	---	---	1 (25)
3 x 3 (76 x 76)	1.50 (38.1)	0.75 (19.0)	4	8 (203)	8 (203)	2 (51)
4 x 4 (102 x 102)	2.00 (50.8)	1.00 (25.4)	4	8 (203)	8 (203)	2 (51)
6 x 6 (152 x 152)	2.25-2.75 (57.2-69.8)	1.25 (31.8)	5	8 (203)	12 (305)	2 (51)

(continued)

RESISTANCE SPOT WELDING

TABLE 9-35—*Continued*

PRESS TYPE:

Type	Size	kVa at 50% Duty Cycle (Single-Phase Transformer, 60 Hz)	Nominal Throat Depth, in. (mm)	Nominal Electrode Forces, Hydraulic and Air,* lb (kN)	Platen Spacing,** in. (mm)
Projection	2	100, 150	12 (305)	4000 (17.8)	
			18 (457)	3000 (13.3)	
			30 (762)	2250 (10.0)	
Spot	2	100, 150	18 (457)	4000 (17.8)	6-12 (152-305)
			24 (610)	3000 (13.3)	
			36 (914)	2250 (10.0)	
Projection	3	150, 250	12 (305)	9000 (40.0)	
			18 (457)	6300 (28.0)	
			30 (762)	5000 (22.2)	
Spot	3	150, 250	18 (457)	5000 (22.2)	6-12 (152-305)
			24 (610)	5000 (22.2)	
			36 (914)	5000 (22.2)	
Projection	4	300, 400, 500	12 (305)	12,500 (55.6)	8-14 (203-356)
			18 (457)	12,500 (55.6)	
			30 (762)	9100 (40.5)	

Caution: Data in the above table are subject to revision by the RWMA, to whom readers should refer for possible revisions.

* Maximum values of electrode forces at other throat depths will vary inversely as the throat depth. Maximum electrode forces for air-operated welders are based on air-line pressure of 80 psi (552 ksi).

** Platen spacing of projection welders shall be measured with upper platen in down position and the range of platen spacing is that obtained by vertical adjustment of the lower platen.

† Standard ram strokes shown include adjustments.

‡ Air only.

PRESS TYPE:		Electrode Holder					
Upper and Lower Platen Dimensions, in. (mm)	Horn Diameter, in. (mm)	Diameter, in. (mm)	RWMA Taper No.	Upper Length, in. (mm)	Lower Length, in. (mm)	Standard Ram Stroke,† in. (mm)
8 x 8 (203 x 203)	2.75-3.00 (69.8-76.2)	1.50 (38.1)	7	8 (203)	12 (305)	3 (76)
9 x 9 (229 x 229)	3.00-3.50 (76.2-88.9)	1.50 (38.1)	7	8 (203)	12 (305)	4 (102)
12 x 12 (305 x 305)				Special		4 (102)

by manual means such as foot or hand levers through linkages, or by other means.

Rocker-arm spot welder. This type of welder controls the welding pressure and raises the upper electrode for loading and unloading work by the rocking action of the upper arm. It is adaptable to a wide range of work, usually in the lighter gages. The work clearance, particularly of the upper and lower arms, is excellent for welding odd sizes and configurations. Water-cooled arms and short electrodes allow maximum clearance of cylindrical work. Electrode length and arm clamping permit adjustment for various angles of electrode settings, and transformer tap switch and/or heat regulation provide a wide heat range for various thicknesses of stock to be welded.

The rocker-arm spot welder can be operated with a foot treadle (adjustable for position) which, when pressed down, brings the electrodes together. The welding pressure is then transmitted to the work through a compression spring on the rear rod. After a suitable amount of compression is obtained, the

RESISTANCE SPOT WELDING

welding circuit is closed by means of a mechanical switch. After a preset time, a timer stops the flow of current. Releasing pressure on the foot treadle opens the electrodes and resets the cycle.

The air-operated machine resembles the foot-operated welder except that a double-acting air cylinder is substituted for the

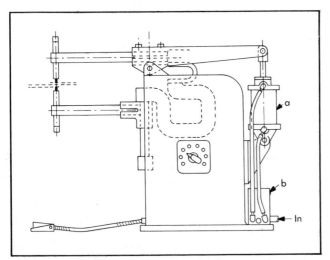

Fig. 9-52 Rocker-arm spot welding machine: (a) double-acting air cylinder, (b) four-way valve, either foot-operated or solenoid-operated.[6]

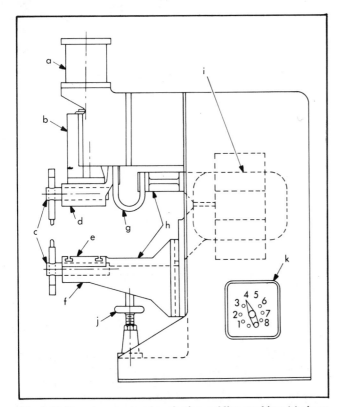

Fig. 9-53 Press-type spot and projection welding machine: (a) air or hydraulic cylinder, (b) welding head, (c) spot welding horns and electrodes, (d) upper table or platen, (e) lower table or platen, (f) lower knee, (g) flexible bands, (h) upper and lower terminals or connecting blocks, (i) transformer secondary, (j) knee support and jackscrew, and (k) primary tap switch.[7]

rear rod and compression spring. Welding pressure regulation is accomplished by regulating the air pressure to the air cylinder by a pressure-regulating valve; the machine is controlled by a solenoid-operated air valve initiated through a foot switch.

The air-operated spot welder with automatic sequence control of the rocker arm and of the flow of welding current is a very desirable production tool, and various sequence controls can be provided for single or continuous operation. This automatic welding cycle eliminates operating variables and synchronizes the heat and pressure.

Press-type spot or projection welders. These welders are available in sizes for welding material up to the heaviest gages that can be spot or projection welded. The name comes from the straight-line vertical stroke of the upper welding head so essential for projection welding.

The air-operated press welder generally has a direct-connected, double-acting air cylinder adjustably attached to the ram, which is guided by adjustable gibs and roller bearings in most designs; it carries the upper platen, usually insulated, in a slide base. This assembly provides for welding-stroke and welding-pressure application. The lower knee and the machine in general are designed for minimum deflection under the heavy range of pressure required for spot and projection welding.

Transformer-gun package systems. These transformer-gun (transgun) packages have been in use only since 1983, when transformer technology and microprocessor-based welding controls allowed transformers to shrink in size. With smaller transformers, it became possible to mount a welding gun directly onto the transformer while taking a space not much larger than a conventional gun. Because the secondary loop is small, the primary welding current has been reduced substantially, making the guns much more efficient than conventional systems. Transguns have not been used widely for portable guns because the standard transformers have relatively high voltage primaries, which would be in close proximity to an operator. The transgun is good for special machinery and robotic welding, performing any number of welds, because they are a complete modular package, easily replaceable and transportable.

Multigun spot welders. Multigun spot welders are usually fully automatic in operation and control and incorporate a multiplicity of electrodes and transformers. This type of equipment is usually designed and constructed for a single-purpose job and may have from two to as many as 100 or more spot welding electrodes arranged in their proper positions to make the required number of joints.

The welding guns are pneumatically or hydraulically operated, with the welding electrodes mounted directly under the cylinder assembly. These electrode assemblies may be controlled by solenoid valves that operate one or more welding stations in sequence or may be activated simultaneously with the transformers by sequences initiated by the welder control. Attached to the valve mechanism is a cam used to initiate the timing device through the proper switches. Workholding fixtures and clamps (see Fig. 9-54) to hold the work in position and to aid in loading and unloading the machine are sometimes essential.

Portable spot welders. The portable spot welder (see Fig. 9-55) is a welding tool rather than a welding machine. Its thermal capacity is determined by the transformer rating, length of water-cooled, current-conducting cable, and the size and shape of the portable gun used. The transformers are usually large because of the high duty cycle an operator can subject the unit to. Also, losses in the heavy, water-cooled cables require a large, high-voltage transformer. Portable spot welders are used as production tools where one operator can use several special configurations during one fixture setup.

Robotic Spot Welding

Spot welding of metal components in the automotive industry represents the largest use of industrial robots. Robotics have also been successfully integrated into the manufacturing process for welding appliances, cabinets, truck assemblies, and other sheet metal assemblies. Major reasons for these applica-

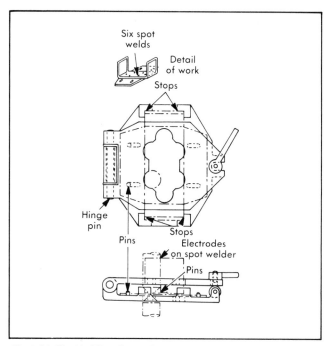

Fig. 9-54 Workholding fixture for making six spot welds.

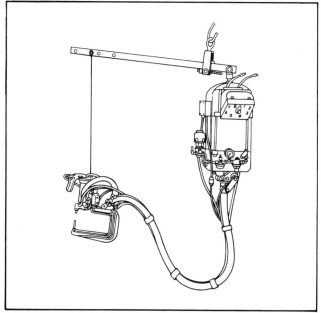

Fig. 9-55 Portable spot welder. (*Taylor-Winfield Corp.*)

tions are the increased flexibility and cost savings obtained. Even though a robotic system is expensive, it is not susceptible to obsolescence. Another important advantage is improved product quality. Robotic systems ensure uniform weld placement, accuracy in following welding procedures, and, if required, a feedback printout of every weld produced.

Typical applications. Robotic spot welding is done by two different methods. In one method, the robot holds the workpiece and passes it through a stationary welding gun. In the second method, which is more prevalent, the welding gun is attached to the robot and moves to the component to be spot welded.

In the automotive sector of robotic spot welding, there are two major categories of applications: respot line welding and subassembly buildup. In respot line welding, the body or subassembly is passed through special framing fixtures to locate the parts to one another and tack weld them together with stationary welding guns. The component is then passed downstream via a conveyor system or transfer bars to an area where the robots add the additional structural load-carrying spot welds. Typical component buildups that are done in this fashion are final body framing, front structure, underbody, and body sides. A typical assembly line for right and left-hand body sides is shown schematically in Fig. 9-56.

The other area of subassembly buildup generally uses smaller off-line groups of automation employing indexing lines, turntables, and stationary fixtures for part presentation. Typical components built up with this method are inner rails and package tray subassemblies, instrument panels, torque boxes, front apron assemblies, and bumper buildups. Figure 9-57 depicts an installation for the assembly of instrument panels.

Axes of motion. For spot welding, the robot arm requires an articulated structure to (1) position a welding tool in space relative to the robot base and (2) orient the welding tool to a particular workpiece to perform the welding operation. Normally, this is accomplished using six programmable axes of motion: three major axes to position the weld gun in space and three minor axes, out close to the weld gun, for final gun orientation. While it is true that for a given application six programmable axes may not be required to take advantage of the overall robot flexibility, six axes are recommended for a general-purpose, spot welding robot.

Coordinate systems. Depending on the design, robots operate within a system of coordinates that define their movements and, therefore, their working volumes. Some coordinate systems have advantages over others, depending on intended use. The three major coordinate systems are Cartesian (rectangular), cylindrical, and polar (spherical) coordinates. Other coordinate systems are defined by combinations of these three.

Cartesian coordinates. This system combines three linear displacement axes: the longitudinal X axis, the transverse Y axis, and the vertical Z axis. Any point in the robot's reach can be defined by the three linear coordinates (X, Y, and Z).

Cylindrical coordinates. This system combines two linear axes and one rotational axis, normally as follows: rotation R around the Z axis (turret movement); Y axis, moving along the radius of the cylinder; and Z axis, movement up and down the axis of the cylinder. Every point within the robot range is defined by an angle and two linear displacements (or two angles and one displacement).

Polar (spherical) coordinates. This system combines one linear axis and two rotations: rotation $R1$ around the Z axis (turret); rotation $R2$ around the X axis (elevation); and the Y axis, describing the radius of the spherical sector.

RESISTANCE SPOT WELDING

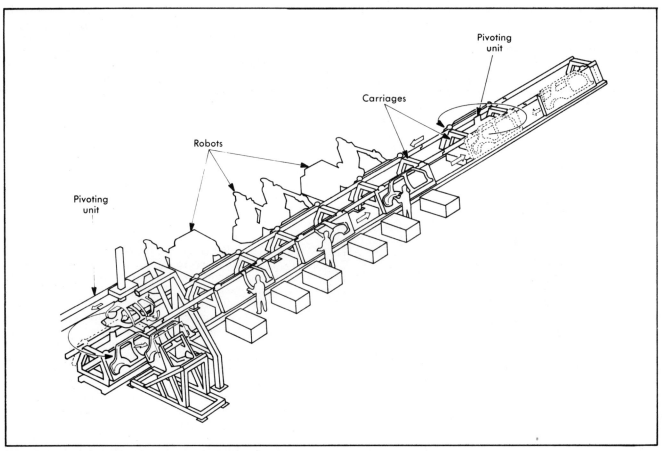

Fig. 9-56 Assembly line for robotic spot welding of right and left-hand automotive body sides. (*Sciaky Bros., Inc.*)

Combination system. There also exists another common combination of the polar coordinate system: three rotations of an articulated arm.

Based on the polar and combination coordinate systems, every point in the robot's reach can be defined by one linear displacement and two or three angles.

System selection. There is no hard and fast rule for selecting the best coordinate system because robots configured in each system are currently performing spot welding operations. Some general guidelines include the following:

- Normally, robots configured in the Cartesian coordinate system are somewhat restricted in their envelopes to perform complex spot welding programs.
- The same restriction also applies for cylindrical coordinate machines. While cylindrical coordinates are better than Cartesian coordinates in this respect, they still have too many shortcomings to be an all-purpose spot welder.
- The most common method used today for spot welding is the polar or spherical coordinate system robots. Those with two rotating axes and one linear axis are excellent for overall reach and deep penetration into vehicle bodies. Those with three rotating axes are better when it comes to complex moves in tight corners or when the robot must actually reach in back of itself.

In summary, it can be seen that each configuration has advantages and disadvantages. All of these considerations, plus the particular application, must be reviewed when selecting a style of robot to meet specific requirements.

Volume swept. The volume swept by a robot is a function of the mechanical arm and its configuration. Normally, industrial spot welding robots should have at least a 45″ (1143 mm) linear reach, be able to reach up from the floor 90″ (2286 mm), and rotate these motions through 200°. This size of swept volume for the three major positioning axes will supply sufficient volume for most polar or spherical coordinate spot welding robots.

Load-carrying capacity. The load-carrying capacity of a robotic spot welder is a feature that must be examined closely. Most robot manufacturers advertise their maximum capacity as a dead-lift figure. While this figure is an indicator of brute strength, it may not be adequate for the required payload at the last minor axis. Most load data is supplied as a torque rating around the three minor orientation axes. Normal values for these torque ratings should be in the range of 150 to 275 ft-lbf (203 to 373 N·m). This allows the designer of the weld gun flexibility for tradeoffs between weld gun center of gravity to total weight. Normally, an all-purpose spot welding robot should be able to handle from 100 to 225 lb (45.4 to 102 kg) of tooling payload. Those robots having under 70 lb (31.8 kg) of payload are usually too limited to be an all-purpose spot welding robot.

Speeds. Robot speeds are usually specified in linear inches (millimeters) per second; angular velocity is specified in degrees per second. Typical velocities for spot welding robots are:

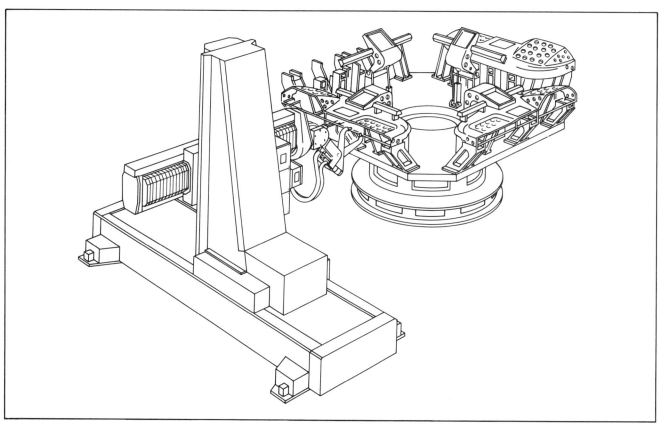

Fig. 9-57 Installation for robotic spot welding of instrument panels. (*Sciaky Bros., Inc.*)

For the three major axes:
    60 ips (1524 mm/s), linear
    65°/s, angular

For the three minor axes:
    110°/s, angular

The heavier the load, the proportionate overall slowdowns necessary in acceleration and deceleration to maintain reasonable levels of loading induced by tooling moments of inertia. This will slow overall cycle times.

Repeatability and accuracy. The performance of a spot welder is normally measured by the robot's accuracy and repeatability in returning to taught points. Repeatability is the tolerance in returning to a known taught point relative to the robot. The value for spot welding robots is normally 0.060-0.080″ (1.52-2.03 mm). Accuracy is the ability to achieve a position in space relative to the taught position. Normal tolerance levels for accuracy with spot welding robots is ±0.020-0.040″ (0.51-1.02 mm).

Peripheral equipment. The major peripheral equipment normally required to provide a complete spot welding system includes a weld gun and transformer, a weld controller, workpiece presentation equipment, external controls, automated dressing equipment for the electrode tip, and guarding and interlocks for operator safety.

Weld gun and transformer. The normal configuration for this equipment, with the operator handling the weld gun, has been to use an overhead-mounted transformer and air accessory package. The welding current is transmitted down large water-cooled cables to the weld gun. This weld gun cable assembly is supported by overhead balancers to assist in the manual movement of the gun to the weld zone. In some cases, the transformer assembly is mounted on the floor adjacent to the robot or hung on the robot itself. Some of the drawbacks that exist with this method are large electrical losses through the cable assemblies, restriction of robot motion due to the cables, excessive cable wear, and additional induced load to the robot to transport the cable assemblies.

To rectify these problems for robotic welders, welding guns with transformers built into them (discussed previously in this section) are becoming commonplace. With short leads from the transformer tap to the weld tips, weld current losses are cut drastically. Applications that required 75 kVa transformers previously can now utilize 22 kVa transformer-gun assemblies. Cable wear problems are reduced, and overall housekeeping is improved.

Weld controller. Proper welding controls, discussed subsequently in this section, increase the overall flexibility and efficiency of robotic spot welding.

Workpiece presentation. At present, robots do not have the capacity of intelligent mobility. As a result, the parts to be spot welded must be transferred into and out of the robot's envelope to complete the work. In automotive assembly plants, the normal methods used to present large subassembly components include indexing conveyor lines, overhead monorail systems, intelligent pallet systems, and automatic guided vehicle systems. In each case, a part is indexed in, positioned, and automatically clamped in place before the robot performs its welding task. Smaller subassembly buildups can use turntables to present

RESISTANCE SPOT WELDING

parts or even stationing fixtures that are manually loaded and unloaded. Considerations required before selecting a part presentation method include cycle rate, production needs, cost, and part location accuracies required.

External controls. Most robot welders, unless in a stand-alone application, require an external control system to coordinate the peripheral equipment for optimized work sequence. Initially, when robots were introduced to the industrial sector, they could communicate to anything external to the robot via approximately 12 discrete inputs and outputs. These signals would be programmed at specific steps in the program, and the robot would either signal other equipment to operate or await confirmation that something had occurred.

Now, current robots have expanded capabilities, with up to 64 inputs and outputs, and are able to monitor signals at all times and react instantaneously if so programmed. Even with this enhanced capability, multirobot installations require external controllers to coordinate the equipment, allow manual and semimanual operation, and provide system fault enunciation and diagnostics. System controllers can range from relay control panels with limited flexibility, to relatively inexpensive, yet flexible, programmable controllers, to overall master-computer control systems communicating to the robot.

Electrode tip dresser. A recent addition to automated robotic spot welding systems is the incorporation of electrode tip dressers. As a weld gun operates, metal residues, especially galvanization, build up on the tips. As this coating builds up, it increases the electrical resistance across the weld zone, causing weld quality to decrease. Now, with the flexibility to program the robot, it can be taught to move over to a tip dresser at regular intervals and have the tips cleaned. The overall effect of this is to ensure a better quality product.

Safety considerations. During the robot's tenure in industrial plants, it has come to be considered a very reliable product, and, in some instances, this reliability has caused a false sense of security. To help ensure that operators do not intentionally or inadvertently walk into a robot's path, safety barriers are required. Each robot or workcell should be enclosed with fencing, and all gates or access points should be monitored during automatic running of the system. Opening a gate must shut off the robot or at least signal it to stop motion. Monitoring can be done with limit switches at gates and multiple photoelectric light barriers at normal open access points.

Additionally, the robot's major position axes can usually be mechanically limited to its particular envelope requirements once a program sequence is determined. This will aid in alleviating pinchpoints between the robot and fence when a programmer or other person is within the system workcell. Deadman switches on the programming pendants, overhead beacons, warning signs, and robot-reach warning envelopes painted on the floor will assist in making a safe robotic spot welding installation.

Currents Used

In resistance spot welding, the machine transformer converts line power to low-voltage, high-amperage power. Both alternating and direct current are used for this process. Most applications, however, use single-phase alternating current having the same frequency as the line power. Direct current is used primarily for applications requiring high amperage.

Single-phase equipment. Transformers are normally rated on the basis of temperature-rise limitations. The standard kVa rating is based on a 50% duty cycle.

Alternating-current secondary circuit. Power factor corrections for these circuits are accomplished with series or shunt capacitors. Series capacitors in the primary circuit reduce the demand from the line power and improve the power factor. However, three-phase equipment has largely replaced single-phase capacitor installations. Shunt capacitors are seldom used except for long weld times and some seam welding applications.

Direct-current secondary circuit. By rectifying the secondary power to direct current, impedance losses are reduced. For a given transformer size and application, power demand is lower than for an alternating-current machine.

Direct-energy welding. In this method, single or three-phase, high-voltage, low-amperage alternating current from the power line is changed to low-voltage, high-amperage current that is fed directly to the electrodes.

Single-phase machines. On these direct-energy machines, the transformer has only one primary winding. The machines are used extensively because of their low cost and simple operation. Limitations include a low power factor and high power demand.

Three-phase machines. This direct-energy equipment is available in frequency converter and rectifier types. The frequency converter type has three primary windings. In the rectifier type, the secondary circuit supplies current to a rectifier bank that provides low-voltage, high-amperage direct current to the electrodes. Advantages of the rectifier type include a high power factor and low power demand. Limitations include high cost and high power dissipation in the diodes.

Stored-energy equipment. Machines of this type are of electrostatic design and are used to produce welding current pulses. They draw power from a single-phase supply, store it in a bank of capacitors and then discharge it. Machines of this type are generally confined to small units such as bench welders.

Throat Areas

The resistance welding machine is essentially a high-impedance, low power factor device. The magnitude of the current without any work present between the electrodes and in the throat is dependent on the value of the secondary voltage and the transformer coupling factor to overcome this impedance.

The introduction of magnetic material in the throat of such equipment causes a reduction of the welding current. The apparent loss of current arises from the more intense magnetic field or increase in flux leakages and from the core loss manifesting itself as heat generated in the steel sheet or other material, inherent because of the alternating magnetic field. Low-frequency converter and rectifier machines are less affected because of the more favorable electrical characteristics in the secondary circuit, such as isolation of the magnetic field outside the throat area. The magnitude of the magnetic field produced in the welder throat depends primarily on the magnitude of the welding current.

The smaller the throat area, the lower the secondary impedance; therefore, the more secondary current that can be produced by a given secondary voltage. As the throat area is enlarged, the impedance goes up and the secondary current will be lower with the same given secondary voltage. For example, a welding machine with a throat configuration 12" (305 mm) in depth and 8" (203 mm) horn spacings will deliver 36,500 A at 6 V; with a throat depth of 30" (762 mm), it will deliver only 17,600 A. For a given throat area, the secondary current is directly proportional to the open-circuit secondary voltage, less the percentage regulation in the welding transformer.

Machine Controls

Proper functioning of a resistance welding machine requires good controls to initiate and stop current flow, control its magnitude, and control the duration of current flow and the operating cycle. In spot welding, it is necessary to control the following time cycles:

1. Squeeze time: the time to close the electrodes and apply force.
2. Weld time: the time to initiate and maintain welding current.
3. Hold time: the time to turn off the current and maintain electrode force until the weld nugget solidifies.
4. Off time: the time to hold open the electrodes (in repeat mode only).

Resistance welding machines may be controlled mechanically, electrically, or electronically, but for optimum results, electronic controls are essential. With electronic control systems, the rate of current rise (upslope time) and fall (downslope time) can be programmed. Upslope control reduces or prevents overheating and expulsion of molten metal. Downslope control influences nugget solidification to prevent cracking and provides an annealing effect on some types of heat-treatable metals. Most controls are produced to requirements of the National Electrical Manufacturers Association (NEMA) Standard ICS 5.

Control systems are available with feedback circuits that monitor the development of a spot weld by sensing voltage, current, temperature, resistance, expansion, contraction, or other factors. Data from these circuits are transmitted to a microprocessor that adjusts parameters during the welding cycle.

Welding contactors. Most switches for making and breaking the electrical power circuits are now electronically operated. Electronic contactors are used most extensively because they can handle high currents at fast speeds. Those most commonly used include ignitrons or silicon-controlled rectifiers (SCRs).

Timing and sequencing controls. These units, which control each function of the operating cycle and duration of current flow, are now practically all of the synchronous type. Synchronous controls both start and stop current flow at precisely the same point on the voltage wave. As a result, they provide accurate timing and eliminate variations in initial current caused by power load transients.

Heat controls. Current outputs of resistance welding machines are controlled by tap switches on the primary circuits of their transformers or by electronic heat controls, or both. With electronic heat control, solid-state devices control firing of the contactors (usually ignitrons or SCRs) during each half cycle of the welding current. Electronic phase-shift heat controls adjust the current during the welding period.

Instrumentation. Dramatic improvements have been made in resistance welding instrumentation. Measurements are most often used for welder maintenance and increasingly for weld quality control. The most widely accepted methodology is the measurement of secondary current and time. Welding manuals provide plots of time versus secondary current used to obtain good nuggets—frequently called a lobe plot. Welds made with time and current that fall inside the lobe produce good nuggets.

Typically, a current-time analyzer is used for measuring the welding current and time. These meters can provide an accurate rms current value for welding times down to one-half cycle. Phased-back waveforms (seen at less than 100% heat) are also accurately measured down to less than one-half cycle. The analyzer measures the current in kiloamps and the time duration of current flow in half cycles. Both results can be displayed on digital readouts.

Quality control monitoring systems are available for use on critical welding processes. The typical monitor has a high and low current gage that is set to predetermined limits. When these limits are exceeded, the monitor signals an alarm condition, and the operator takes appropriate action. Monitor connections to the welding machine allow the monitor to stop the welder or mark the part when the monitor signals a suspected defective weld.

Electrodes

The shanks of spot welding electrodes must be of sufficient cross-sectional area to transmit the required current and have sufficient strength to withstand the forces applied at elevated temperatures. They generally range from 3/8 to 1" (9.5 to 25.4 mm) diam. Where practical, the electrodes are provided with internal water-cooling passages that extend close to their welding faces.

Some electrodes are of two-piece construction. This reduces maintenance costs because only the caps have to be replaced. However, resistance at the interface between the cap and adapter may cause overheating and wear. Tapered, threaded, or straight shanks on the electrodes are attached to holders that are clamped to the arms of the machine. The holders have provisions for water cooling, and some have ejector mechanisms for removing the electrodes. Holders are available in straight, offset, universal (adjustable offset), and multiple electrode designs.

Face shapes. Proper shape of the electrode welding face is essential to obtain the desired current and pressure densities. The shape used depends primarily on the composition, thickness, and geometry of the parts being joined. Radiused and domed contours are common, but flat-faced electrodes minimize surface marking.

The face areas of electrodes progressively increase in use because of mushrooming. As a result, the current and pressure densities decrease, and the welds produced become smaller. Also, there is a tendency for the electrodes to pick up metal from the workpieces during welding, which can cause overheating and faster mushrooming. To obtain consistent welds, the electrodes must be checked periodically and redressed when required.

Electrode materials. Standard resistance electrode materials are classified by the RWMA Bulletin No. 16, "Resistance Welding Equipment Standards." The materials are divided into two groups: copper-based alloys and refractory metal compositions. A number of proprietary alloys are also available from electrode manufacturers. For some applications, commercially available copper alloys (brasses or bronzes) or refractory powder composites are used.

Minimum properties for alloys that meet the RWMA classification are presented in Table 9-36. The specific compositions of the alloys are not specified as they vary among manufacturers. Both the copper-based alloys and the refractory metal compositions are each divided into five classes.

Class 1 material. This copper-based material is frequently used where conductivity is more important than the other material properties. Common applications include the welding of aluminum, brass, bronze, magnesium, and metallic-coated steels. The material is not heat treatable.

Class 2 material. This copper-based material has higher mechanical properties but somewhat lower electrical and thermal conductivity than Class 1 material. It is the most widely used electrode material for spot welding, especially for the

RESISTANCE SPOT WELDING

TABLE 9-36
Minimum Properties for Electrode Materials Used for Resistance Welding*

Electrode Material	Proportional Limit, Tension, ksi (MPa)			Hardness, R_B		
	Class 1	Class 2	Class 3	Class 1	Class 2	Class 3
GROUP A—COPPER-BASED ALLOYS						
Rod Diameter, in. (mm)	Round Rod Stock, Cold Worked					
Up to 1 (25)	17.5 (121)	35 (241)	50 (345)	65	75	90
Over 1 to 2 (25 to 51)	15 (103)	30 (207)	50 (345)	60	70	90
Over 2 to 3 (51 to 76)	15 (103)	25 (172)	50 (345)	55	65	90
Thickness, in. (mm)	Square, Rectangular, and Hexagonal Bar Stock, Cold Worked					
Up to 1 (25)	20 (138)	35 (241)	50 (345)	55	70	90
Over 1 (25)	15 (103)	25 (172)	50 (345)	50	65	90
Thickness, in. (mm)	Forgings					
Up to 1 (25)	20 (138)	22 (152)†	50 (345)	55	65	90
Over 1 to 2 (25 to 51)	15 (103)	21 (145)†	50 (345)	50	65	90
Over 2 (51)	15 (103)	20 (138)†	50 (345)	50	65	90
	Castings					
All sizes	---	20 (138)	45 (310)	---	55	90

Electrode Material	Proportional Limit, Tension, ksi (MPa)	Hardness, R_B
Class 4 alloys:		
Cast	60 (414)	33_C
Wrought	85 (586)	33_C
Class 5 alloys:		
Type H	16 (110)	88_B
Type S	12 (83)	65_B
GROUP B—REFRACTORY METALS		
Class 10—Rods, bars, and inserts		72_B
Class 11—Rods, bars, and inserts		94_B
Class 12—Rods, bars, and inserts		98_B
Class 13—Rods, bars, and inserts		69_B
Class 14—Rods, bars, and inserts		85_B

* Classified by the Resistance Welder Manufacturers Association (RWMA).
** International Annealed Copper Standard (IACS).
† Hot worked and heat treated but not cold worked.

Conductivity, %**			Ultimate Tensile Strength, ksi (MPa)			Elongation, %, in 2" (51 mm) or 4 diameters		
Class 1	Class 2	Class 3	Class 1	Class 2	Class 3	Class 1	Class 2	Class 3
GROUP A—COPPER-BASED ALLOYS								
Round Rod Stock, Cold Worked								
80	75	45	60 (414)	65 (448)	100 (689)	13	13	9
80	75	45	55 (379)	59 (407)	100 (689)	14	13	9
80	75	45	50 (345)	55 (379)	95 (655)	15	13	9
Square, Rectangular, and Hexagonal Bar Stock, Cold Worked								
80	75	45	60 (414)	65 (448)	100 (689)	13	13	9
80	75	45	50 (345)	55 (379)	100 (689)	14	13	9
Forgings								
80	75	45	60 (414)	55 (379)	94 (648)	12	13	9
80	75	45	50 (345)	55 (379)	94 (648)	13	13	9
80	75	45	50 (345)	55 (379)	94 (648)	13	13	9
Castings								
---	70	45	---	45 (310)	85 (586)	---	12	5

Conductivity, %**	Ultimate Tensile Strength, ksi (MPa)	Elongation, %, in 2" (51 mm) or 4 diameters
18 (average)	90 (621)	0.5
20 (average)	140 (965)	1.0
12	70 (483)	2
15	65 (448)	12
GROUP B—REFRACTORY METALS		
	Ultimate Compressive Strength, ksi (MPa)	
45	135 (931)	
40	160 (1103)	
35	170 (1172)	
30	200 (1379)	
30	---	

RESISTANCE SPOT WELDING

high-production welding of steels, nickel alloys, and some low-conductivity, copper-based alloys. The material is heat treatable, and maximum mechanical properties are developed in cold working wrought forms after heat treating.

Class 3 material. This copper-based material has higher mechanical properties but lower electrical conductivity than Class 2 material. It is used extensively for electrode shanks because of its strength. Another major application is spot welding of heat-resistant alloys. The material is heat treatable.

Classes 4 and 5 materials. These copper-based materials have lower conductivity than Classes 1, 2, and 3 and are not generally used for spot welding.

Classes 10, 11, and 12 materials. These refractory metal compositions are mixtures of copper and tungsten. When used as facings or inserts for electrodes, they provide exceptional wear resistance.

Classes 13 and 14 materials. These refractory metal compositions are commercially pure tungsten and molybdenum, respectively. They are sometimes used for spot welding non-ferrous metals having high electrical conductivity.

Special alloys. There are two copper alloys especially suited to welding coated materials. These two dispersion-strengthened coppers are more thermally stable than Class 2 material, helping prevent softening and minimizing alloying. Aluminum oxide and zirconium have both proven themselves to be effective alloys when welding coated materials or where high heats are used with working life up to six times that of Class 2 copper.

Operating Parameters

Recommended practices for resistance welding are detailed in AWS Publication C1.1. Typical schedules for single-impulse and pulsation spot welding of various thicknesses of SAE 1010 steel are presented in Tables 9-37 and 9-38. Electrode face

diameters given in these tables are suitable for most welding applications. Small variations in tip diameters can cause large variations in spot weld strengths because the tip diameters control spot sizes. The use of electrode faces having spherical radii provide long tip life and more consistent welds than electrodes with truncated faces.

RESISTANCE SEAM WELDING

Resistance seam welding (RSEW) produces coalescence at the faying surfaces by a series of overlapping spot welds made progressively along a joint by rotating wheel-like or roller electrodes. Seam welding has much in common with spot welding, discussed in the preceding section. Welds produced may be direct or indirect, similar to spot welding. The major difference is that seam welding uses rotating electrode wheels that maintain contact force during a succession of welds along a seam.

Applications

Seam welding is used for a variety of workpiece shapes. Applications include longitudinal welds and encircling welds on round, square, or rectangular parts. A major application is producing gas or liquid-tight joints on sheet metal tanks. Other applications include the welding of mufflers, cans, and other containers.

Advantages

Seam welding offers similar advantages to spot welding, previously discussed, with the additional benefit of being capable of producing continuous, leaktight welds. Also, overlaps can be less than for spot or projection welding, and seam widths can be less than the diameters of spot welds. Seam welding is generally practical for metal thicknesses ranging from 0.001 to 0.187″ (0.03 to 4.75 mm).

TABLE 9-37
Data for Single-Impulse Spot Welding of Low-Carbon Steel[9]

Thickness T of Thinnest Outside Piece, in. (mm) Note 1	Electrode Diameter and Shape Note 2		Net Electrode Force, lbf (kN)	Weld Time, Cycles Note 3	Welding Current, A
	D, min, in. (mm)	d, max, in. (mm)			
0.010 (0.25)	3/8 (9.5)	1/8 (3.2)	200 (0.89)	4	4000
0.021 (0.53)	3/8 (9.5)	3/16 (4.8)	300 (1.33)	6	6500
0.031 (0.79)	3/8 (9.5)	3/16 (4.8)	400 (1.78)	8	8000
0.040 (1.02)	1/2 (12.7)	1/4 (6.4)	500 (2.22)	10	9500
0.050 (1.27)	1/2 (12.7)	1/4 (6.4)	650 (2.89)	12	10,500
0.062 (1.57)	1/2 (12.7)	1/4 (6.4)	800 (3.56)	14	12,000
0.078 (1.98)	5/8 (15.9)	5/16 (7.9)	1100 (4.89)	17	14,000
0.094 (2.39)	5/8 (15.9)	5/16 (7.9)	1300 (5.78)	20	15,500
0.109 (2.77)	5/8 (15.9)	3/8 (9.5)	1600 (7.12)	23	17,500
0.125 (3.18)	7/8 (22.2)	3/8 (9.5)	1800 (8.01)	26	19,000

Notes:
1. SAE 1010 steel free from scale, oxides, paint, grease, and oil. Data applicable for total thickness of pileup not exceeding 4T. Maximum ratio between two thicknesses 3:1.
2. Electrode material: Class 2; minimum conductivity, 75% of copper; minimum hardness: R_B75.
3. Weld time is indicated in cycles of 60-cycle frequency.
4. Minimum weld spacing is that for two pieces for which no special precautions need be taken to compensate for shunted current effect on adjacent welds. For three pieces, increase spacing 30%.

Limitations

In addition to the same limitations discussed previously for spot welding, an additional limitation is that seam welds generally have to be in a straight or uniformly curved line, with no obstructions or sharp corners. The lengths of longitudinal seam joints are limited by the throat depths of the welding machines available.

Warpage of workpieces is a factor that must be considered in seam welding, but several techniques are used to minimize distortion. Metal thicknesses more than about 1/8" (3.2 mm) are more difficult to weld than with the spot or projection methods. Seam welding is not ordinarily used for joining large sheets because of the high amounts of electrical energy that are required.

Process Variations

Seam welding is performed in several ways, primarily depending on travel speed and timing of the welding current. In *continuous-motion welding*, the electrodes (or workpieces) are driven at a constant speed, and welding current is either interrupted or flows continuously. In either case, a continuous, leaktight seam is produced. This method is generally used for metals less than about 3/16" (4.8 mm) thick.

In *intermittent-motion welding*, rotation of the electrode wheels is automatically stopped to make a spot weld, then the electrodes are rotated to move the workpiece the required distance for the next weld. This method is often used for aluminum and steel alloys less than 3/16" (4.8 mm) thick and some metals more than 3/16" thick.

Seam welding. In this process (refer to Fig. 9-49), sometimes called stitch or roll spot welding, the on and off times of the current with continuously rotating electrodes determines the weld spacing. The minimum joint overlap is the same as for spot welding. There is generally no forging (mash-down) with lap seam welding.

Mash seam welding. In this process (refer to Fig. 9-49), the overlap is generally less than for lap seam welding, and there is more mash-down (electrode force) with continuous current. Joint thickness after welding usually varies from 120 to 150% of the sheet thickness. Continuous seams having a good appearance are produced in this way, but rigid workholding fixtures are required to minimize distortion.

Finish seam welding. In this process, mash-down is done on only one side of the joint, using an electrode wheel that is beveled on one side, to produce smooth surface finishes. Overlap is more than for mash seam welding, and higher current amperages and electrode forces are required.

Foil butt seam welding. In this process, metal foil is placed on one or both sides of a butt joint prior to seam welding. The foil distributes current to the edges of the sheet, provides additional electrical resistance, helps contain molten metal, and serves as a filler.

Welding Various Metals

Practically all steels—including low and high-carbon; low-alloy—high-strength, low-alloy (HSLA); stainless; and many coated steels—can be joined with seam welding. However, hardenable steels are not as weldable as low-carbon steels and may require post heat treatment (tempering). Austenitic types of stainless steels have higher coefficients of thermal expansion than carbon steels, and precautions are necessary to minimize distortion of the weldments.

Aluminum, nickel, and magnesium alloys can be seam welded. Welding of aluminum alloys generally requires the use of high currents and short cycles. Pure copper cannot be seam

Minimum Contacting Overlap, L, in. (mm)	Minimum Weld Spacing, ℄ to ℄, in. (mm) Note 4	Diameter of Fused Zone, in. (mm)	Ultimate Tensile Strength of Metal, ksi (MPa)	
			Below 70 (483)	Above 70 (483)
			Minimum Shear Strength, lbf (kN)	
3/8 (9.5)	1/4 (6.4)	0.10 (2.5)	130 (0.58)	180 (0.80)
7/16 (11.1)	3/8 (9.5)	0.13 (3.3)	320 (1.42)	440 (1.96)
7/16 (11.1)	1/2 (12.7)	0.16 (4.1)	570 (2.54)	800 (3.56)
1/2 (12.7)	3/4 (19.1)	0.19 (4.8)	920 (4.09)	1200 (5.34)
9/16 (14.3)	7/8 (22.2)	0.22 (5.6)	1350 (6.00)	
5/8 (15.9)	1 (25.4)	0.25 (6.4)	1850 (8.23)	
11/16 (17.5)	1 1/4 (31.8)	0.29 (7.4)	2700 (12.01)	
3/4 (19.1)	1 1/2 (38.1)	0.31 (7.9)	3450 (15.35)	
13/16 (20.6)	1 5/8 (41.3)	0.32 (8.1)	4150 (18.46)	
7/8 (22.2)	1 3/4 (44.4)	0.33 (8.4)	5000 (22.24)	

RESISTANCE SEAM WELDING

TABLE 9-38
Data for Pulsation Spot Welding of Low-Carbon Steel[10]

Combination of Thicknesses Welded Note 1		Electrode Diameter and Shape Note 2		Weld Time Cycles (60 Hz), on 20, off 5		
				Single Weld	Adjacent Weld, 2-4" (51-102 mm)	Adjacent Weld, 1-2" (25-51 mm)
T-1, in. (mm)	T-2, in. (mm)	D, min, in. (mm)	d, max, in. (mm)		Number of Pulsations	
1/8 (3.2)	1/8 (3.2)	1 (25.4)	7/16 (11.1)	3	4	5
1/8 (3.2)	3/16 (4.8)	1 (25.4)	7/16 (11.1)	3	4	5
1/8 (3.2)	1/4 (6.4)	1 (25.4)	7/16 (11.1)	3	4	5
3/16 (4.8)	3/16 (4.8)	1 1/4 (31.8)	1/2 (12.7)	6	14	20
3/16 (4.8)	1/4 (6.4)	1 1/4 (31.8)	1/2 (12.7)	6	14	20
3/16 (4.8)	5/16 (7.9)	1 1/4 (31.8)	1/2 (12.7)	6	14	20
1/4 (6.4)	1/4 (6.4)	1 1/4 (31.8)	9/16 (14.3)	12	18	24
1/4 (6.4)	5/16 (7.9)	1 1/4 (31.8)	9/16 (14.3)	12	18	24
5/16 (7.9)	5/16 (7.9)	1 1/2 (38.1)	5/8 (15.9)	15	23	30

Notes:
1. SAE 1010 steel with ultimate tensile strength below 70 ksi (483 MPa) and free from scale, oxides, paint, grease, and oil.
2. Electrode material: Class 2; minimum conductivity, 75% of copper; minimum hardness: R_B 75. Dome-shaped electrodes of 3" (76 mm) radius will produce about the same diameters, d and D, listed.

welded, but some copper alloys having high electrical resistance can be joined in this way. Many combinations of dissimilar metals can also be seam welded.

Joint Design

In most applications, the parts to be joined overlap each other and form lap joints. The amount of overlap can be made small, as in the mash seam welding variation discussed previously. However, parts that are to be overlapped, or flanged and welded, should have enough overlap, or flange width, to prevent excessive burning of the edges of the parts by the welding heat or too much ejection of hot metal. The overlap in seam welding is of great importance in making a satisfactory product. If the shape of the parts being welded makes it difficult for the machine operator to control the overlap, it should be fixed by prespot tacking to avoid warping, skidding, or creeping. In this operation, the overlap is first established and held in some suitable manner until several spot welds are made along the line of the future seam weld. Prespot tacking can be done on a seam welder with the welding electrodes not rotating, but it is more adequately done on a spot welder assigned for that purpose.

Parts should lie flat against each other so that no force from the electrode is required to make them touch each other. Improperly fitting parts will result in inconsistent and inferior welding and in excessive maintenance, such as replacing welding electrodes.

Parts to be circumferentially seam welded require adequate prior inspection and close assembly supervision. Press fits or other types of assembly permitting intimate metal-to-metal contact around the entire circumference at the zone to be welded should be used if at all possible; otherwise fewer good-quality welds will result.

To weld along a continuous curve, such as the flanged bottom of a cylindrical container, it is sometimes advisable to limit to a minimum diameter of 4" (102 mm) to allow suitable diameter of circular electrode and adequate working life. When the line of a weld proceeds at right angles by turning a corner, the minimum advisable radius is 2" (51 mm) for 0.031-0.050"

(0.79-1.27 mm) thick steel, 2 1/4" (57 mm) for 0.063" (1.59 mm) thick steel, 2 1/2" (63.5 mm) for 0.078" (1.98 mm) thick steel, and 3" (76 mm) for 0.094-0.125" (2.38-3.18 mm) thick steel.

Surface Preparation

To obtain high-quality welds, steel, whether low-carbon or stainless, should be free from rust, scale, paint, heavy grease, or oil and from any conversion coating such as phosphate. However, steels with zinc, tin, lead, or other metallic-coated surfaces are weldable. A light film of oil to prevent rusting usually has no bad effect on the weld, provided dust has not accumulated on the sheet surface during storage. Dust or dirt should be wiped off before welding applications.

In applications where the highest degree of weld quality and consistency is desired, it may be necessary to immunize or passivate the stainless steel before welding. On freshly machined, polished, or pickled articles, a thin oxide film can be made to form rapidly and uniformly by dipping in a cold 20% nitric acid solution for approximately 30 minutes. The oxide film can also be formed in a warm, about 150°F (65°C), 90% nitric acid solution for approximately 10 minutes. This passivating treatment forms a thin coating of oxide, but, of equal importance, it dissolves small particles of foreign material that may have become lodged in the surface as the result of contact with tools or polishing wheels. These particles of common steel will mar the stainless steel surface if not removed. The above procedure accomplishes good welding results, but is not always necessary.

Seam Welding Machines

Seam welding machines are similar to spot welding machines previously discussed except that one or two electrode wheels are used instead of spot welding electrodes. Press-type resistance welding machines are generally used. Three sizes of seam welding machines standardized by the RWMA are listed in Table 9-39.

The upper electrode wheel is mounted on a head moved by a cylinder, generally air, to apply the required force. The lower electrode, which can be a wheel, platen, or mandrel, is mounted

RESISTANCE SEAM WELDING

Net Electrode Force, lbf (kN)	Weld Strength, min, lbf (kN)	Welding Current, A	Diameter of Fused Zone, in. (mm)	Minimum Contacting Overlap, L, in. (mm)
1800 (8.01)	5000 (22.24)	18,000	3/8 (9.5)	7/8 (22.2)
1800 (8.01)	5000 (22.24)	18,000	3/8 (9.5)	7/8 (22.2)
1800 (8.01)	5000 (22.24)	18,000	3/8 (9.5)	7/8 (22.2)
1950 (8.67)	10,000 (44.48)	19,500	9/16 (14.3)	1 1/8 (28.6)
1950 (8.67)	10,000 (44.48)	19,500	9/16 (14.3)	1 1/8 (28.6)
1950 (8.67)	10,000 (44.48)	19,500	9/16 (14.3)	1 1/8 (28.6)
2150 (9.56)	15,000 (66.72)	21,500	3/4 (19.1)	1 3/8 (34.9)
2150 (9.56)	15,000 (66.72)	21,500	3/4 (19.1)	1 3/8 (34.9)
2400 (10.68)	20,000 (88.96)	24,000	7/8 (22.2)	1 1/2 (38.1)

on a supporting arm, table, or knee. The electrode wheel drive of a seam welder may be one of several forms. The upper or lower electrode may be directly gear driven through a gearbox and clutch by a motor, or both wheels may be driven by a knurl drive. The knurl drive utilizes a steel driving wheel formed to fit the electrode face and extending for a short distance up its side. The contact surface of the drive wheel is knurled to provide traction. The knurl type of driving mechanism is the one most generally used for seam welding.

In another application, a special clutch and brake drive is utilized to impart intermittent motion to the circular electrodes. This mechanism permits the electrode wheels to remain stationary during the passage of welding current, and spot spacing can be determined by correct gear selection.

TABLE 9-39
Standards for Seam Welding Machines Established by the Resistance Welder Manufacturers Association (RWMA)

Machine Size	kVa at 50% Duty Cycle (Single-Phase Transformer), 60 Hz	Nominal Throat Depth, in. (mm)*	Nominal Electrode Forces, lb (kN)	Standard Ram Stroke, in. (mm)**	Bushing Dimensions, in. (mm) Type	Bore	Combined Length	Electrode Sizes, in. (mm) Thickness	Diameter	Minimum Lower-Arm Work Clearance Diameter,† in. (mm) Knurl and Gear-Driven Electrodes	Idling Electrodes
1	50, 75	18, 24, 30 (457, 610, 762)	1000 (4.4)	4 (102)	Outboard	2 (51)	5 (127)	3/8 (9.5)	7 (178)	11 (279)	9 (229)
					Straddle	2 (51)	3 (76)				
2	100, 150, 200	18, 30, 42 (457, 762, 1067)	2200 (9.8)	5 (127)	Outboard	2 1/2 (64)	8 (203)	1/2 (12.7)	8 (203)	15 (381)	11 (279)
					Straddle	2 1/2 (64)	4 (102)				
3	250, 400	24, 36, 48 (610, 914, 1219)	3000 (13.3)	6 (152)	Outboard	3 1/4 (83)	9 (229)	3/4 (19)	10 (254)	18 (457)	14 (356)
					Straddle	3 1/4 (83)	5 (127)				

* The nominal throat depth shall be measured from the centerline of point of welding to the nearest point of interference for flat work or sheets. In the case of welders with universal upper heads, the above measurements shall be taken with the welder arranged for circumferential welding.

** Standard ram strokes shown include vertical adjustments of ram but no vertical adjustment of lower arm.

† The maximum length of work at the above minimum diameters shall be 6″ (152 mm) less than the nominal throat depth. These dimensions do not apply to the universal head type of seam welder.

RESISTANCE SEAM WELDING

Basic types of seam welding machines can be classified as circular, longitudinal, universal, portable, and special-purpose.

Circular machines. On these machines, the axes of rotation of the electrode wheels are perpendicular to the front of the machines (see Fig. 9-58, view *a*). These machines are used for circumferential welds, as well as for flat work requiring long seams.

Longitudinal machines. On these machines, the axes of rotation of the electrode wheels are parallel to the front of the machines (see Fig. 9-58, view *b*). They are used to produce short seams in flat work and for attaching components to assemblies.

Universal machines. These machines have a swivel-type upper head and interchangeable lower arms to permit the axes of electrode wheel rotation to be set for either circular or longitudinal operation. Such machines are desirable when a variety of welding operations are required, both circular and flat.

Portable units. These heads or guns are used for assemblies too large or heavy to be welded in machines. They are moved by motor-driven wheels over workpieces clamped in fixtures. An air cylinder provides force to the electrode wheels.

Special-purpose machines. There are several types of special-purpose machines available that have been designed to suit specific applications. One is a traveling electrode type on which workpieces are held on a fixed mandrel, which is the lower electrode, and the upper electrode wheel is moved along the seam. Another is a traveling fixture type on which the workholding fixture is moved under one or more upper electrodes that remain in fixed positions.

Workholding fixtures. Well-designed workholding fixtures are essential for resistance seam welding to ensure accurate position and minimize distortion. A typical two-station fixture for seam welding a cylindrical tank is shown in Fig. 9-59.

Currents Used

Transformers for seam welding machines are similar to those for spot welding machines, discussed previously, to supply low-voltage, high-amperage current. Most seam welding machines use alternating current, generally single-phase, but some machines use three-phase a-c and rectifier power supplies. Machines with stored-energy equipment are seldom used for seam welding.

Machine Controls

The controls for seam welding machines are also similar to those for spot welding machines except for the addition of controls necessary for relative motion between the workpieces and electrodes. Synchronous timing controls are generally necessary for seam welding because of the short on-off heating and cooling cycles. Automatic phase-shift heat controls to change the current during welding are also usually desirable.

Electrodes

The electrodes used for seam welding must be of the proper material and shape, and adequate cooling is mandatory. Cooling is generally done by flooding, usually with water jets directed to locations immediately before and after the electrode wheels. In some cases, internally cooled electrodes are used.

Size and shape. The size and general shape of the electrode will usually be determined by the shape of the parts to be welded, by the location of the welds, and by the need of a driving mechanism to keep the electrodes rotating. If welds are to be made on flanges, one end of the electrode face is often made practically flush with the side of the electrode, allowing the face to weld the flange with the minimum degree of clearance.

The contour of the electrode changes in welding, and the contacting electrode face becomes wider. It will eventually reach a point where the reduced unit welding current and unit force will not permit fusion, and the wheels should then be turned to their original width and contour before reaching this point. The maximum width can be determined by test. Automatic wheel dressers are used for some high-production applications.

Electrode face contours commonly used for seam welding are straight flat, single-bevel flat, double-bevel flat, and radiused. Electrodes with straight flat surfaces are difficult to set up and control, but are essential for some applications. Single and double-bevel flat faces minimize mushrooming. Radiused faces help guide the travel of the workpieces.

When the parts to be welded are of approximately equal thickness and it is desired to have as little surface marking as possible on one workpiece, the electrode in contact with the particular part should have a space width at least 50% greater than the widths given in welding data charts. Dome-face (radius crown) electrodes are recommended in the welding of stainless steel to minimize marking and indentation on the work. This is particularly desirable from a quality standpoint in stainless steel fabrication.

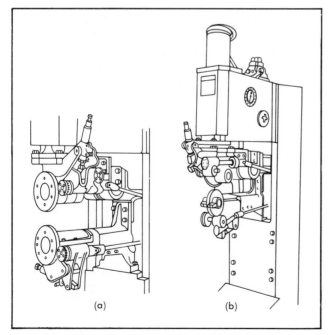

Fig. 9-58 Seam welding machines of the (a) circular and (b) longitudinal types.

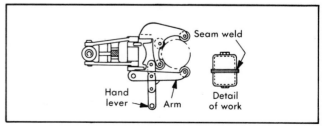

Fig. 9-59 Two-station seam welding fixture.

The diameters of circular electrodes used in seam welding are determined principally by the application. There must be an adequate mass of copper alloy to prevent excessive temperature rise and sufficient clearance to prevent the arms holding the welder bearings from interfering with the workpieces. If working conditions permit, the following sizes of circular electrodes are used:

1. For light work [electrode forces up to 1000 lbf (4.4 kN)]: 7" (178 mm) diam x 3/8" (9.5 mm) thick electrodes.
2. For medium work [electrode forces up to 2000 lbf (8.9 kN)]: 8" (203 mm) diam x 1/2" (12.7 mm) thick electrodes.
3. For heavy work [electrode forces up to 3000 lbf (13.3 kN)]: 10" (254 mm) diam x 3/4" (19 mm) thick electrodes.

Materials. Standard electrode materials for resistance welding as classified by the RWMA are discussed in the preceding section on spot welding (see Table 9-40). For seam welding aluminum and magnesium alloys, galvanized steels, and tin-plated steels, Class 1 electrode materials are recommended. For the high-production seam welding of carbon and low-alloy steels, Class 2 or 3 materials are used. Class 3 material is generally used for the seam welding of stainless steels.

Operating Parameters

Recommended practices for resistance welding are detailed in AWS Publication C1.1. Typical parameters for seam welding various thicknesses of low-carbon steel are presented in Table 9-40.

RESISTANCE PROJECTION WELDING

Projection welding is a resistance welding process wherein coalescence is produced by the heat obtained from the resistance to the flow of current through the work parts held together under pressure by electrodes. The resulting welds are localized at predetermined points by the design of the parts to be welded. Localization is accomplished by projections, embossments, or intersections that direct the flow of current from one workpiece to the other. The projected metal embossment is heated to a temperature sufficient to fuse the parts together. Force is always applied before, during, and after the application of current.

Applications

Projection welding is used principally to assemble blanked, stamped, formed, and machined parts. The process is especially useful for producing several welds simultaneously between two parts. Mechanical fasteners, brackets, pins, handles, clips, and similar components are attached to many products in this way. Cross-wire welding, discussed subsequently in this section, is used extensively for producing stove and refrigerator parts, fence wire, electronic connections, and grills. The process is generally used to join metal thicknesses ranging from 0.020 to 0.125" (0.51 to 3.18 mm).

Advantages

An important advantage of projection welding is that a number of welds can be made in a single cycle. Also, the welds require less overlap, can be spaced closer, and can be produced with narrower flanges than spot welds. Weld locations are more accurate, and nugget diameters and thicknesses are generally more consistent than those produced in spot welding.

Another advantage of projection welding is that thicker materials can be joined than with spot welding, including thickness ratios of six or more to one. Projection welding also uses larger diameter electrodes than spot welding, thus reducing the current density and maintenance requirements. Projections can be placed to minimize marking of critical surfaces.

Limitations

Projection welding is limited to joining two thicknesses in one operation, and the nugget sizes produced are limited by the sizes of the projections. In some applications, the projections have to be produced in a separate operation, thus adding to the cost. When several welds are made at once, the dimensional tolerances and alignment of the workpieces must be closely controlled.

Cross-Wire Welding

Cross-wire welding (see Fig. 9-60) is a variation of projection welding used extensively to produce wire products. The curved surfaces of two intersecting wires serves the function of a projection. The process is generally performed by welding a number of parallel wires perpendicular to one or more other wires. Any combination of wire sizes in a variety of metals can be joined. If the wires are closely spaced, a seam welding machine can be used.

Welding Various Metals

Projection welding is used most extensively for joining low-carbon steels. Free-machining steels that have high sulfur and phosphorus contents should not be welded because the welds produced are generally brittle and porous. The process is also used for welding some alloy steels, austenitic stainless steels, and coated metals, such as galvanized, tin-plated, and aluminized. It is not recommended for metals not strong enough to support the projections during welding. These metals include pure copper and some copper and aluminum alloys.

Joint and Projection Design

In applying projection welding to a job, the loads or stresses to which the welded assembly is subjected must be given careful consideration. Only sufficient projections should be used to resist these loads safely. The projections should be spaced over the maximum area available to avoid shunting-current loss caused by too-close spacing. Welding die life is short if the projections are too close to each other or too close to the limits of the die area.

In projection welding it is especially important that the parts to be welded be so designed that the proper fusing temperature is created at precisely the same instant in both elements being welded. For this reason, it is desirable that the projections be made in the thicker material so that these higher resistance

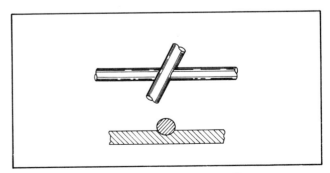

Fig. 9-60 General arrangement for cross-wire welding.

RESISTANCE PROJECTION WELDING

TABLE 9-40
Data for Seam Welding of Low-Carbon Steels

Thickness T of Each of Two Workpieces, in. (mm) Notes 1 and 3	Electrode Width and Shape D d Note 2 d, min, in. (mm)	D, min, in. (mm)	Electrode Force, lbf (kN) Note 6 Minimum	Normal	Minimum Contacting Overlap, L, in. (mm) Note 4
With full-wave continuous current:					
0.010 (0.25)	3/16 (4.8)	3/8 (9.5)	400 (1.78)	400 (1.78)	3/8 (9.5)
0.021 (0.53)	3/16 (4.8)	3/8 (9.5)	460 (2.05)	550 (2.45)	7/16 (11.1)
0.025 (0.64)	1/4 (6.4)	1/2 (12.7)	470 (2.09)	600 (2.67)	7/16 (11.1)
0.031 (0.79)	1/4 (6.4)	1/2 (12.7)	530 (2.36)	700 (3.11)	1/2 (12.7)
0.040 (1.02)*	1/4 (6.4)	1/2 (12.7)	600 (2.67)	900 (4.00)	1/2 (12.7)
With partial-wave continuous current:					
0.044 (1.11)	1/4 (6.4)	1/2 (12.7)	650 (2.89)	950 (4.23)	1/2 (12.7)
0.050 (1.27)	5/16 (7.9)	1/2 (12.7)	700 (3.11)	1050 (4.67)	9/16 (14.3)
0.062 (1.57)	5/16 (7.9)	1/2 (12.7)	750 (3.34)	1200 (5.34)	9/16 (14.3)

Data Common to All Welding Speeds

* Thicknesses above 0.040" (1.02 mm) are weldable with continuous current, but the results are not optimum as the weld surface is easily overheated.

Notes:
1. Low-carbon steel is hot rolled and lightly oiled, with an ultimate tensile strength of 42-45 ksi (290-310 MPa). Similar to SAE 1005-SAE 1010.
2. Electrode material is RWMA Class 2 alloy.
3. Surface is lightly oiled, but free from grease, scale, or dirt.
4. For large assemblies, the minimum contacting overlap should be increased by 30% for ease of guiding.
5. Large assemblies should be welded at the slower speeds for ease of handling and guiding.
6. Electrode force does not provide any force required to press poor fitting parts together.
7. Frequency of welding current is 60 Hz.

points will not be burned off before the other flat welding surface can be raised to proper fusion temperature.

The size and shape of the projections depends on the specific application, workpiece shape, and strength requirements. Some workpiece shapes eliminate the need for projections. Common projections include spherical, elongated, annular, and pyramidal, with spherical shapes generally offering advantages both in welding and simplicity in forming. The minimum spacing between projections is twice the projection diameter.

Experience indicates that projections of the form shown in Fig. 9-61, views a and b, are satisfactory for most joints on flat or irregular-shaped stampings. When welds are to be made in formed pieces that are circular and the projections contact the pieces, it may be desirable to elongate the projections for proper contact (see view c).

In the case of machined parts, care must be exercised to ensure a point contact instead of contacting two flat surfaces. This is often a possibility in welding a slender, cylindrical piece to a flat stamping. In such cases, a ring-type or radius projection (see Fig. 9-61, view d) is commonly used. The ring projection may also be embossed in sheet stock (see view e). This method is often used in preference to a machined part because of the lower cost of maintaining forming dies as compared with form-cutting tools.

Projection welding usually consists of welding a multiplicity of projections simultaneously. As a result, the tops of all

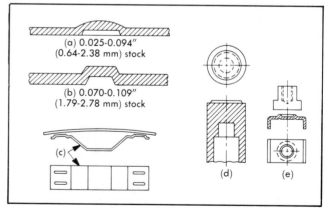

Fig. 9-61 Types of projections.

projections should be in the same plane. It is also important that the heights of all projections be the same, and every effort should be made to make the dimensions uniform.

Table 9-41 shows the general range of heights and diameters for projections. Projections of other shapes may be interpolated in terms of these data. It should be noted that for a given thickness of stock, there is an optimum height and diameter of

RESISTANCE PROJECTION WELDING

Maximum			Average			Minimum, Note 5		
Speed, ipm (mm/min)	Welds per in. (mm)	Current, A Note 7	Speed, ipm (mm/min)	Welds per in. (mm)	Current, A Note 7	Speed, ipm (mm/min)	Welds per in. (mm)	Current, A Note 7
480 (12 192)	15 (0.59)	14,000	240 (6096)	15 (0.59)	10,000	180 (4572)	20 (0.79)	8650
425 (10 795)	17 (0.67)	14,000	205 (5207)	17.5 (0.69)	10,000	155 (3937)	23 (0.91)	8700
405 (10 287)	18 (0.71)	14,200	100 (2540)	19 (0.75)	10,000	145 (3683)	25 (0.98)	8750
370 (9398)	20 (0.79)	15,000	175 (4445)	20.5 (0.81)	11,000	130 (3302)	28 (1.10)	9450
310 (7874)	23 (0.91)	18,000	140 (3556)	26 (1.02)	12,000	105 (2667)	34 (1.34)	10,400
285 (7239)	25 (0.98)	19,000	125 (3175)	29 (1.14)	12,000	95 (2413)	38 (1.50)	10,450
250 (6350)	29 (1.14)	21,000	108 (2743)	33.5 (1.32)	13,000	80 (2032)	45 (1.77)	11,200
190 (4826)	38 (1.50)	22,000	75 (1905)	48 (1.89)	15,100	60 (1524)	60 (2.36)	13,400

Recommended Welding Speed and Current for Pressure-Tight Joints

projection. If this height is exceeded, the metal at the edge of the projection is weakened, and the resulting weld strength is lessened. If the diameter, or area, is greatly increased, the current required is proportionally greater. It also becomes difficult to obtain uniform current distribution throughout the weld area, and the weld strength may be less than if the optimum dimensions were used.

Surface Preparation

Surface conditions of the workpieces to be joined by projection welding are not as critical as for spot welding. For optimum results, however, the surfaces should be clean. Also, any burrs around edges and holes should be removed.

Weld Quality and Strength

Variations in dimensions and properties of the workpiece materials, as well as the welding conditions, affect the quality of the joints produced by projection welding. As is the case with spot welds, projection welds have low tensile strengths, and assemblies are generally designed so that the joints are subjected to shear loading. Standard quality control measures for projection welds are presented in the AWS Publication C1.1, "Recommended Practices for Resistance Welding."

Projection Welding Machines

Press-type machines, the same as previously described in the section on spot welding machines (refer to Table 9-35), are generally used for projection welding. Rocker-arm machines are seldom used. Most machines are equipped with slotted or tapped platens for mounting the electrodes or welding dies. Electrode force is applied by a welding head that is hydraulically, pneumatically, spring, or magnetically actuated. Low-inertia heads are desirable.

Transguns have recently been used with great success for projection welding. As discussed previously, when the throat area increases, the current losses increase. Therefore, large, standard frame press welders have high primary-current draws. Also, with a large ram and tooling, the inertia is high, which hampers the fast response necessary for projection welding. Standard and special-application machines using transguns overcome these inherent problems.

Currents Used

Direct-energy equipment. As with spot welding and seam welding machines discussed previously, projection welding machines have a transformer to convert line power to low-voltage, high-amperage power. Both single and three-phase transformers are used, but for most applications, single-phase alternating current is employed. Direct current is sometimes used for high-amperage requirements.

Stored-energy equipment. In so-called pulse welding, energy is drawn from a capacitor or capacitor bank and discharged through a pulse transformer. Advantages of pulse welding include fast welding (cycles in the millisecond range), minimum distortion, and the capability for joining dissimilar metals and metals having high electrical and thermal conductivities. Pulse welding machines cost more than direct-energy machines, but they can reduce costs for certain applications, especially in joining small precision parts.

Machine Controls

Controls for projection welding machines are similar to those for spot welding machines discussed previously. The controls used are usually of the synchronous type and are generally equipped with phase-shift heat controls for precision timing.

Electrodes

As with spot welding, the electrodes for projection welding are used to conduct current to the workpieces and to apply the required forces. Dies used for projection welding hold and

RESISTANCE PROJECTION WELDING

TABLE 9-41
Sizes of Projections and Shear Strengths for Projection Welding[11]

Thickness T of Thinnest Outside Piece, in. (mm) Notes 1,2,3 and 4	Diameter D of Projection, in. (mm) Notes 7 and 8	Height H of Projection in. (mm) Notes 7 and 9	Tensile Strength Below 70 ksi (483 MPa)	Tensile Strength 70-150 ksi (483-1034 MPa)	Tensile Strength 150 ksi (1034 MPa) and Above	Diameter of Fused Zone, min (at Weld Interface), in. (mm)	Minimum Contacting Overlap, L, in. (mm) Notes 5 and 6
			Minimum Shear Strength (single projection only), lb (kN)				
0.010 (0.25)	0.055 (1.40)	0.015 (0.38)	130 (0.58)	180 (0.80)	250 (1.11)	0.112 (2.84)	1/8 (3.2)
0.012 (0.30)	0.055 (1.40)	0.015 (0.38)	170 (0.76)	220 (0.98)	330 (1.47)	0.112 (2.84)	1/8 (3.2)
0.014 (0.36)	0.055 (1.40)	0.015 (0.38)	200 (0.89)	280 (1.25)	380 (1.69)	0.112 (2.84)	1/8 (3.2)
0.016 (0.41)	0.067 (1.70)	0.017 (0.43)	240 (1.07)	330 (1.47)	450 (2.00)	0.112 (2.84)	5/32 (4.0)
0.021 (0.53)	0.067 (1.70)	0.017 (0.43)	320 (1.42)	440 (1.96)	600 (2.67)	0.140 (3.56)	5/32 (4.0)
0.025 (0.64)	0.081 (2.06)	0.020 (0.51)	450 (2.00)	600 (2.67)	820 (3.65)	0.140 (3.56)	3/16 (4.8)
0.031 (0.79)	0.094 (2.39)	0.022 (0.56)	635 (2.82)	850 (3.78)	1100 (4.89)	0.169 (4.29)	7/32 (5.6)
0.034 (0.86)	0.094 (2.39)	0.022 (0.56)	790 (3.51)	1000 (4.45)	1300 (5.78)	0.169 (4.29)	7/32 (5.6)
0.044 (1.12)	0.119 (3.02)	0.028 (0.71)	920 (4.09)	1300 (5.78)	2000 (8.90)	0.169 (4.29)	9/32 (7.1)
0.050 (1.27)	0.119 (3.02)	0.028 (0.71)	1350 (6.00)	1700 (7.56)	2400 (10.68)	0.225 (5.72)	9/32 (7.1)
0.062 (1.57)	0.156 (3.96)	0.035 (0.89)	1950 (8.67)	2250 (10.01)	3400 (15.12)	0.225 (5.72)	3/8 (9.5)
0.070 (1.78)	0.156 (3.96)	0.035 (0.89)	2300 (10.23)	2800 (12.45)	4200 (18.68)	0.281 (7.14)	3/8 (9.5)
0.078 (1.98)	0.187 (4.75)	0.041 (1.04)	2700 (12.01)	3200 (14.23)	4800 (21.35)	0.281 (7.14)	7/16 (11.1)
0.094 (2.39)	0.218 (5.54)	0.048 (1.22)	3450 (15.35)	4000 (17.79)	6100 (27.13)	0.281 (7.14)	1/2 (12.7)
0.100 (2.54)	0.250 (6.35)	0.054 (1.37)	4150 (18.46)	5000 (22.24)	7000 (31.14)	0.338 (8.58)	5/8 (15.9)
0.125 (3.18)	0.281 (7.14)	0.060 (1.52)	4800 (21.35)	5700 (25.35)	8000 (35.58)	0.338 (8.58)	11/16 (17.5)
0.140 (3.56)	0.312 (7.92)	0.066 (1.68)	6000 (26.69)	---	---	7/16 (11.1)	3/4 (19.1)
0.156 (3.96)	0.343 (8.71)	0.072 (1.83)	7500 (33.36)	---	---	1/2 (12.7)	13/16 (20.6)
0.171 (4.34)	0.375 (9.52)	0.078 (1.98)	8500 (37.81)	---	---	9/16 (14.3)	7/8 (22.2)
0.187 (4.75)	0.406 (10.31)	0.085 (2.16)	10,000 (44.48)	---	---	9/16 (14.3)	15/16 (23.8)
0.203 (5.16)	0.437 (11.10)	0.091 (2.31)	12,000 (53.38)	---	---	5/8 (15.9)	1 (25.4)
0.250 (6.35)	0.531 (13.49)	0.110 (2.79)	15,000 (66.72)	---	---	11/16 (17.5)	1 1/4 (31.8)

Notes:
1. Types of steel: low-carbon SAE 1010; stainless, AISI Types 309, 310, 316, 317, 321, 347, and 349 (nonhardenable; maximum carbon content 0.15%).
2. Material should be free from scale, oxides, paint, grease, and oil.
3. Size of projection normally determined by thickness of thinner piece, and projection should be on thicker piece where possible.
4. Data based on thickness of thinner sheet and for two thicknesses only.
5. Contacting overlap does not include any radii from forming.
6. Weld should be located in center of overlap.
7. Projection should be made on piece of higher conductivity when dissimilar metals are welded.
8. For diameter D of projection, a tolerance of $\pm 0.003''$ (0.08 mm) in material up to and including 0.050″ (1.27 mm) in thickness and $\pm 0.007''$ (0.18 mm) in material more than 0.050″ thickness may be allowed.
9. For height H of projection, a tolerance of $\pm 0.002''$ (0.05 mm) in material up to and including 0.050″ (1.27 mm) in thickness and $\pm 0.005''$ (0.13 mm) in material more than 0.050″ thickness may be allowed.

clamp the workpieces in proper alignment, and also serve as electrodes or holders for electrodes. Fixtures are auxiliary work-positioning devices that do not conduct current.

Electrodes for projection welding differ from those for spot welding in that a greater portion of the electrode material contacts the work. The dies in most applications are made to fit the pieces exactly over the entire surface. To minimize marking, the face diameter of an electrode for a single weld is generally made two or more times the diameter of the projection. Internally water-cooled electrodes or holders are frequently used.

Individual plugs may be press fit into the main die block, in which case a hole must be left in the main die for a driving pin to remove the plugs. This arrangement is shown in Fig. 9-62, view *a*. In view *b*, another arrangement is shown in which the individual dies may be removed without disturbing the main die block. Because the individual dies are held by the upper plate, different arrangements of projections may be used with the same main die block by changing only the locating plate.

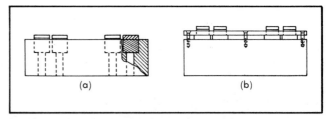

Fig. 9-62 Two designs for projection welding dies.

Materials used for projection welding electrodes include RWMA Classes 2, 3, or 4, with Class 2 being used most extensively. For some applications requiring harder electrodes, facings of Classes 10, 11, or 12 materials are applied to the electrodes. Details with respect to the RWMA electrode materials are presented in the preceding discussion on spot welding and in Table 9-36.

FLASH WELDING

Operating Parameters

Recommended practices for resistance welding are presented in AWS Publication C1.1. Recommendations for the projection welding of low-carbon and stainless steels are given in Table 9-42. The major variables, current, force, and time, must be maintained at constant values for optimum welds.

FLASH, UPSET, AND PERCUSSION WELDING

Flash welding (FW), upset welding (UW), and percussion welding (PEW) are related resistance welding processes. All three processes produce coalescence of metals by the application of electrical heating and pressure. They differ in the method of heating and the timing of the pressure application.

In flash welding, which is limited to the production of butt and miter welds, the abutting surfaces of the workpieces are heated prior to the application of pressure to forge the surfaces together. In upset welding, pressure is applied before the application of current and is maintained throughout the heating period to produce butt or seam welds. In percussion welding, coalescence of abutting surfaces is produced by heat from an arc established by the rapid discharge of electrical energy and pressure applied percussively during or immediately following the electrical discharge.

Similar equipment is used for flash and for upset welding. Flash welding is preferred in many industries because the resulting weld exhibits greater weld strength and a smaller upset. Power demand is less, more heat is evident at the welded surface and less in the body of the work, and less preparation of weld surface by machining is required. Dissimilar metals of widely varying fusion temperatures may be flash welded together because flashing (arcing) may be continued until the fusion temperature of each metal is reached. Successful flash welding of workpieces formed from relatively light gages of sheet aluminum is accomplished on a production basis.

TABLE 9-42
Data for Projection Welding of Low-Carbon and Stainless Steels[12]

Thickness T of Thinnest Outside Piece, in. (mm) Notes 1, 2, and 3	Minimum Electrode Face Diameter d, in. (mm) Note 4	Net Electrode Force, lb (kN)	Weld Time, Cycles (60 Hz Current)	Hold Time, Cycles (60 per s)	Welding Current at Electrodes, approx, A (60 Hz a-c)
Low-carbon steels:					
0.014 (0.36)	1/8 (3.2)	175 (0.78)	7	15	5000
0.021 (0.53)	5/32 (4.0)	300 (1.33)	10	15	6000
0.031 (0.79)	3/16 (4.8)	400 (1.78)	15	15	7000
0.044 (1.12)	1/4 (6.4)	400 (1.78)	20	15	7000
0.062 (1.57)	5/16 (7.9)	700 (3.11)	25	15	9500
0.078 (1.98)	3/8 (9.5)	1200 (5.34)	30	30	13,000
0.094 (2.39)	7/16 (11.1)	1200 (5.34)	30	30	14,500
0.109 (2.77)	1/2 (12.7)	1700 (7.56)	30	45	16,000
0.125 (3.18)	9/16 (14.3)	1700 (7.56)	30	45	17,000
Stainless steels:					
0.014 (0.36)	1/8 (3.2)	300 (1.33)	7	15	4500
0.021 (0.53)	5/32 (4.0)	500 (2.22)	10	15	4750
0.031 (0.79)	3/16 (4.8)	700 (3.11)	15	15	5750
0.044 (1.12)	1/4 (6.4)	700 (3.11)	20	15	6000
0.062 (1.57)	5/16 (7.9)	1200 (5.34)	25	15	7500
0.078 (1.98)	3/8 (9.5)	1900 (8.45)	30	30	10,000
0.094 (2.39)	7/16 (11.1)	1900 (8.45)	30	30	10,000
0.109 (2.77)	1/2 (12.7)	2800 (12.45)	30	45	13,000
0.125 (3.18)	9/16 (14.3)	2800 (12.45)	30	45	14,000

Notes:
1. Types of steel: low-carbon SAE 1010; stainless, AISI Types 309, 310, 316, 317, 321, 347, and 349 (nonhardenable, maximum carbon content 0.15%).
2. Material should be free from scale, oxide, paint, grease, and oil.
3. Data based on thickness of thinner sheet and for two thicknesses only. Maximum ratio between two thicknesses, 3:1.
4. Flat-faced electrodes and dies are normally used. Dimensions d shown are absolute minimum (d = 2 x projection diameter).

CHAPTER 9

FLASH WELDING

Flash Welding

In flash welding, the parts are loaded in the machine in very light contact with each other or slightly separated. After clamping by the electrodes (dies), current is applied and movement of the traveling platen is initiated practically simultaneously. Heating results from resistance of the workpiece contact surfaces to the flow of electric current and by arcs between the faying surfaces. Force applied by the platen expels molten metal from the joint and upsets the base metal. The flow of current is usually stopped during upsetting.

Applications. Flash welds are most commonly employed in joining two pieces of metal end to end or in welding one piece of metal to a projecting part of another piece. Some examples are the welding of strips end to end in steelmaking and processing to form a continuous strip; the welding of circled strips or bars to form rings for automobile wheel rims and ring gears; the welding of tubular sections end to end; the production of electrical motor and generator frames; and joining airframe and jet engine structural members.

Advantages. Flash welding is a fast and economical process for producing uniform, high-quality welds in many ferrous and nonferrous metals. A variety of shapes, including sheet, plate, rings, pipe, tubes, wire, and extrusions, can be joined. Little or no joint preparation is necessary and ejection of metal during upsetting helps remove impurities from the interface of the joint.

Limitations. Safety precautions are necessary when using flash welding because of the hot, molten metal particles ejected. Another possible limitation is that the parts to be joined must have cross sections that are practically identical. Also, for some applications, the upset material must be removed, thus adding to production costs.

Welding various metals. Flash welding is being used to weld many different ferrous and nonferrous metals, including carbon, alloy, stainless, and tool steels and copper, aluminum, magnesium, and titanium alloys. Low-carbon steels from 0.015 to 0.40" (0.38 to 10.2 mm) thick are commonly joined, and bars to 10" (254 mm) diam have been welded with special machines.

Flash welding of aluminum alloys in thicknesses below 0.050" (1.27 mm) is difficult and not recommended. Minimum pressures and short flashing times are necessary in joining copper and copper alloys. Flash welding of lead, zinc, tin, and beryllium alloys is not considered practical. Dissimilar metals can be joined if their flashing and upsetting characteristics are similar. Flash welding of titanium alloys, especially thick sections, may require inert gas shielding.

Product design considerations.[13] The following fundamental product design principles are recommended in flash welding:

1. Parts must be shaped so that both pieces will obtain the same degree of plasticity and the same depth of plastic zone during the flashing action and, hence, will weld properly during the forging action. This characteristic is generally designated as obtaining an even or good heat balance. For this reason it is necessary to weld sections of nearly identical shape and size.

2. The design must take into account the metallurgical changes that occur as the result of all welding processes. Air-hardenable steels are normally harder in the weld zone than in normalized parent metal. The copper dies that hold the parts during welding, and the metal behind the welding surfaces of the parts serve as cooling agents. Any additional strength given to a part by cold work before welding will be altered and often destroyed.

3. Parts must be designed so that the forging force exerted is resisted in the workpieces by forces that are parallel to the axis of the workpieces that are in the direction of the welding force.

4. Sections to be welded must be of such shape that they can be held in alignment by the clamping dies during the forging action. This implies sufficient clamping area to allow application of the necessary clamping force at parts of such shape that the reactive resistive forces do not tend to destroy alignment during the forging operation.

Surface preparation. While little or no joint preparation is necessary for flash welding, the ends of the workpieces are sometimes chamfered or tapered to increase current density. The surfaces of the workpieces that contact the dies (electrodes) must be clean, with no scale, rust, paint, or contaminants.

Machines. Flash welding machines are available for manual, semiautomatic, or automatic operation. Most machines resemble a horizontal press (see Fig. 9-63) and are equipped with a transformer and workholding dies (electrodes) mounted on two platens. One platen is stationary and the other is movable, with the movable platen traveling on electrically insulated ways.

Flash welders are usually classified according to method of clamping and driving mechanism. Clamping mechanisms may be operated manually, pneumatically, or hydraulically. Drives may be hand operated through a single or double-toggle mechanism to obtain the desired pressure, by a motor-driven cam shaped to give the proper rate of acceleration to the moving platen, or the drive may be hydraulic, usually controlled by a rotary valve that is in turn operated by cams profiled to accomplish the proper flashing acceleration. Standard flash welding machine sizes as classified by the RWMA are listed in Table 9-43.

Currents used. As with other resistance welding processes, flash welding requires a high-amperage, low-voltage source of power. Machines are usually equipped with single-phase a-c transformers, but the high demands for single-phase current can unbalance the three-phase power lines. For some applications, three-phase a-c, d-c, and frequency converters are used.

Machine controls. Electronic welding contactors of the silicon-controlled rectifier (SCR) type are used extensively for flash welding machines. Electronic contactors of the ignitron type are also used, especially for larger machines. Timing and sequencing controls are generally of the electronic synchronous type with phase-shift heat control. For some applications, adaptive controls sense the process parameters, compare them with preselected values, and modify them when required.

Dies, electrodes, and fixtures. In flash welding, the portions of the clamps that grip the workpieces are the current-carrying electrodes. For some workpieces, workholding fixtures are required in addition to the dies. For some applications, water cooling of the dies and/or fixtures is necessary.

Die materials. Dies (electrodes) for flash welding are often made of copper-based alloys, RWMA Classes 4 or 5, or refractory metal compositions, RWMA Classes 10, 11, or 12 (refer to Table 9-36). Steel electrodes are also used sometimes for the flash welding of aluminum alloys.

Tolerance requirements. The tolerance of axial alignment after welding is greatly enforced by the tolerance before welding. In normal clamping operations, a movable die clamps the workpieces against fixed dies. As an example, 0.500" (12.70 mm) diam tubing held to within ±0.005" (0.13 mm) will show the effects of welder adjustment. The dies must be bored to

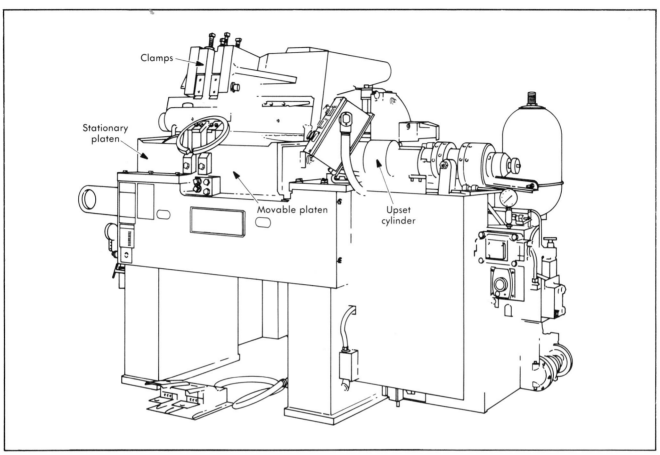

Fig. 9-63 Flash welding machine. (*Taylor-Winfield Corp.*)

0.505″ (12.83 mm) diam to hold the maximum diameter; they are accurately aligned with two pieces of 0.500″ diam tubing in place. When a piece of 0.505″ diam tubing is placed in one set of dies and another piece of 0.495″ (12.57 mm) diam in the other set of dies, the maximum runout will be 0.010″ (0.25 mm) after welding, equivalent to the tolerances before welding.

The tolerance of overall length of the parts after welding is influenced by the tolerance before welding. If pieces are located in the welder by touching the edges to be welded, tolerances after welding will equal the sum of the tolerances before

welding. Misalignment also results in reduction of material thickness (see Fig. 9-64). If backup locators are used, the tolerance after welding can normally be reduced to less than that of one part. The influence of tolerance (see Fig. 9-65) shows the importance of proper alignment design of the dies in the production of accurate work.

Material allowances for flash welding of solid round, hexagonal, and rectangular bars and of tubing and flat sheets, together with data to obtain proper heat balance, may be found by reference to AWS Publication C1.1, "Recommended Prac-

TABLE 9-43
Flash Welder Standards of the Resistance Welder Manufacturers Association (RWMA)[14]

Machine Size	Thermal Rating, 50% Duty Cycle, kVa	Nominal Upset Forces, max, lbf (kN)	Maximum Platen Opening, in. (mm)	Platen Size, in. (mm)	
				Width	Length
1	20	2250 (1.00)	2 (51)	12 (305)	12 (305)
2	50	4500 (2.00)	2 1/2 (63.5)	16 (406)	16 (406)
3	100	11,500 (5.12)	3 (76)	20 (508)	20 (508)
4	150	19,600 (8.72)	4 (102)	24 (610)	24 (610)
5	250	38,000 (16.90)	5 (127)	28 (711)	28 (711)

FLASH WELDING

tices for Resistance Welding." The various flash-upset-weld definitions, graphically expressed, may be obtained from the same publication.

Heat balance. A certain degree of sectional unbalance is permissible in flash welding, and for most materials a deviation of ±5% from recommended values for process factors will not cause objectionable variation in the physical properties of

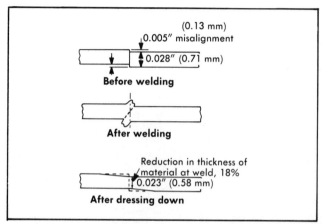

Fig. 9-64 Misalignment of workpieces results in reduction in material thickness.

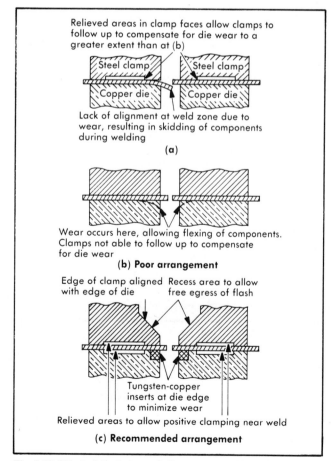

Fig. 9-65 Effect of die design and alignment on weld quality.

welds. These unbalances are sometimes made necessary by design consideration, such as when joining two members that must be in exact alignment (see Fig. 9-66). One piece can then be made with sufficient diameter to permit subsequent machining, thereby correcting diameter variations and alignment tolerances in welding.

In setting up for welding, excess thickness is distributed equally around the circumference. After welding, the assembly is machined until forging surface coincides with tubing surface, thus conforming to normal tolerances in dimensions and correcting misalignment. Variation in wall thickness of more than 10% at any point around the tube weld seriously hinders consistent weld quality. Such variation causes the weld plane to form at an angle to the centerline of the workpieces because of the difference of plasticity.

In flash welding where the thermal and electrical conductivities of the joint are asymmetrical because of joint geometry or alloys, a heat balance may be obtained by "projecting" the piece that has the higher conductivity farther from the clamping electrode so that the length of its resistance path is increased. The electrode, being nearer to the weld on the lower-conductivity side, removes heat from that piece. Differences in the melting points between the two alloys being welded will also affect the amount of projection. The proper distance each piece projects is determined experimentally.

Operating parameters. Recommended practices for resistance welding are presented in AWS Publication C1.1. The major variables for flash and upset welding are the clamping and upset pressures, and the currents, voltages, and speeds used.

Clamping pressures. Whenever practical, the workpieces should be backed up or placed so that their outer ends bear

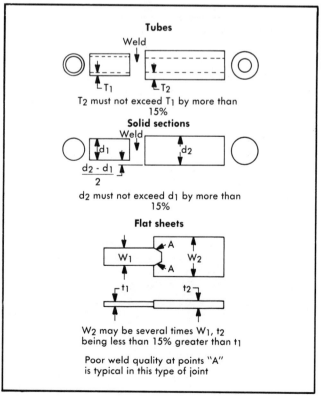

Fig. 9-66 Permissible section unbalance in flash welding.

against fixed stops on the platens of the welder, and the upset pressure is transmitted to the work by these fixed stops. Under this condition, the clamping pressure on the electrodes has only to be sufficient to provide a low-resistance contact to the welding current and to maintain alignment of the weld. When the work is backed up by means of fixed stops, the usual range of clamping pressure is from 3000 to 4500 psi (20.7 to 31 MPa) of the weld area.

Where it is not practical to back up the work, such as in circular rings or long pipes, the clamps have to grip the work with sufficient force to prevent slippage when the upset pressure is applied. This clamping pressure is far greater than that required for good contact and alignment purposes.

It has been common practice of welding machine designers to assume a ratio of 2 1/2 to 3 times the upset pressure for determining clamping pressures. Clamping pressures for stainless steel must be about 40-50% higher for contact purposes than on any other materials. This is because stainless steels are covered by a thin, high-resistance film of chrome oxide, and, unless sufficient clamping pressure is employed, there is a tendency for the current to break through this film and cause severe arcing between the work and the electrodes. However, this condition can be minimized by proper cleaning of the stainless steel.

Upset pressures. Upset or forging pressure is expressed in pounds per square inch or megapascals of weld area. For upset welds, this pressure varies from 2500 to 8000 psi (17.2 to 55.2 MPa). For flash welds it varies from 5000 to 25,000 psi (34.5 to 172.4 MPa), depending on the alloy welded. This pressure value may reach a maximum value of more than 35,000 psi (241 MPa) in the case of welding extra-high forging-strength steels.

Table 9-44 illustrates the upset pressures (forces) for flash welding different steels. The heat here is attained by flashing only. Welds made with insufficient pressure are characterized by porosity, inclusions, low strength, and poor impact resistance. Excessive upset pressures will produce poor welds also, as all

the metal in the plastic welding range may be forced out by the excessive pressure. Where excessive pressure has been used, the weld usually shows satisfactory tensile strength but has poor impact and fatigue resistance.

Heat of the upset is an important factor in making satisfactory welds. While the flashing action is going on, the weld is protected from contamination, but as soon as the upset starts, the flashing action ceases. Any time interval between cessation of flashing action and consummation of upset allows oxidation of the high-temperature weld surfaces again. The speed of upset cannot be overemphasized because many poor welds may be traced to low upset speed, even though all other welding conditions are satisfactory.

Welding currents, voltage, speeds. Welding currents ranging from 2000 to 5000 A/in.^{2} (3.1 to 7.8 A/mm^2) are used for slow upset butt welding of steel. In making flash welds in steel, currents range from 2000 to 5000 A/in.^{2} during the flashing period and 2000 to 50,000 A during the upset.

The selection of proper flashing current depends on the time needed to make the weld and to produce consistent flashing. Generally the low limit is the lowest value at which a stable flash may be maintained, about 2000 A/in.^{2} (3.1 A/mm^2) regardless of metal thickness. The upper limit is determined by the material being welded and the stock thickness. For stock more than 1/8″ (3.2 mm) thickness, relatively low current values must be used because slower heating allows the heat to run back from the weld faces to produce the wide zone of plastic metal necessary for proper upset.

In welding circular rings, such as wheel rims or other closed shapes of large diameter in relation to metal thickness, about 25% more current must be allowed. The shunting current is increased as diameter-to-metal thickness decreases. Where this ratio is very low (as in chain links), the shunting current is so great that a flash cannot be maintained between the ends, and an upset weld must be resorted to. Table 9-45 shows the open-circuit secondary-voltage range commonly used for various sizes of flash welders.

Upset Welding

Upset welding is a resistance welding process that produces coalescence simultaneously over the entire areas of abutting surfaces or progressively along a joint. Heating to welding temperature results from the resistance to electric current through the area where the surfaces are in contact. Pressure is applied before heating starts, is maintained throughout heating,

TABLE 9-44
Flash Welding Upset Pressures (Forces)
Used in General Practice

Workpiece Material	Thickness, up to, in. (mm)	Pressure Range, psi (MPa)
Aluminum and alloys	5/8 (15.9)	4500-5500 (31.0-37.9)
Copper and alloys	3/4 (19.1)	5000-7500 (34.5-51.7)
Carbon and alloy steels, SAE No.:		
1020	3/8 (9.5)	6000-8000 (41.4-55.2)
1020	1 (25.4)	7000-10,000 (48.3-68.9)
1020	2 (51)	9000-11,000 (62.1-75.8)
1020	4 (102)	10,000-12,000 (68.9-82.7)
2340	1 (25.4)	10,000-12,000 (68.9-82.7)
3140	1 (25.4)	10,000-12,000 (68.9-82.7)
4140	1 1/4 (32)	11,000-18,000 (75.8-124.1)
6145	1 1/4 (32)	11,000-18,000 (75.8-124.1)
Stainless steels	2 (51)	13,000-22,000 (89.6-151.7)

TABLE 9-45
Open-Circuit Secondary-Voltage Range Commonly
Used for Various Sizes of Flash Welders

Size of Machine, kVa	Voltage Range, V	
	From	To
10	0.75	2.5
25	1.25	3.5
50	2.0	5.0
100	3.0	7.0
300	4.0	8.5
500	6.0	11.5
1000	8.0	13.0
2000	10.0	20.0

PERCUSSION WELDING

and increases to upset the workpieces when the welding temperature is reached. Upset welding differs from flash welding, discussed previously, in that the heating results entirely from the resistance to current at the contact surfaces, and there is no flashing or arcing.

Applications. Upset welding is used extensively in the manufacture of continuously welded pipe and tubing and to join wire coils for continuous operations. The process is also employed to make many different products from wire, bar, strip, and tubing.

Advantages and limitations. Upset welding has advantages and limitations similar to flash welding except that safety precautions for flashing and arcing are not required. Upset welds are generally characterized by large symmetrical upsets. Capabilities of the process include joining wire and rod ranging from 0.05 to 1.25″ (1.3 to 31.8 mm) diam.

Process variations. The two major variations of upset welding are for making butt and seam joints. For butt joints, two sections having the same cross section are joined end to end. The seams of roll-formed products such as pipe and tubing are continuously welded with this process.

Materials joined. Upset welding is used to join many ferrous and nonferrous metals, essentially the same as those joined with flash welding.

Machines. Upset welding machines for butt joints are similar to flash welding machines. They have a transformer and workholding dies (electrodes) mounted on two platens, one stationary and the other movable. For seam welding, the machines are equipped with wheel electrodes that contact the edges of roll-formed pipe or tubes and upset the edges. Machine controls, currents, and electrodes used are also essentially the same as for flash welding.

Percussion Welding

Percussion welding is a resistance welding process that produces coalescence over the entire areas of abutting surfaces. Heat is supplied by a high-current arc produced by the rapid discharge of electrical energy between the two workpieces to be joined. Force is applied percussively during or immediately following the short pulse of electrical energy. The impact of one workpiece against the other extinguishes the arc, expels molten metal, and completes the weld. There are two major variations of the process: capacitor-discharge and magnetic-force percussion welding.

Applications. The use of percussion welding for butt joints (joining wires, rods, or tubes of equal cross section end to end) is generally limited to dissimilar metals and/or where minimum upsetting is required. This is because similar metals can be butt welded more economically by other processes. Major applications include the production of electrical and electronic connections and contact devices, and joining small components to other or larger parts.

Advantages. An important advantage of percussion welding is that the short time the arc exists limits melting of the base metal to a thin surface layer. This results in a shallow heat-affected zone and minimum upsetting, oxidation of the abutting surfaces, and alloying of dissimilar metals. Heat-treated and cold-worked metals can generally be welded without any softening, and prefinished metals are usually unaffected. Wires as small as 0.005″ (0.13 mm) diam can be joined with the capacitor-discharge process. The magnetic-force method can join flat workpieces with weld areas from 0.04 to 0.70 in.² (25.8 to 452 mm²).

Limitations. Flat parts have to be joined to flat surfaces and butt joints require parts of similar sections. As previously mentioned, butt welds of similar metals can be made more economically by other processes. Percussion welding requires two pieces to be joined; the ends of a single workpiece cannot be joined to produce a ring.

Welding various metals. Almost any similar or dissimilar metals and alloys, both ferrous and nonferrous, can be joined by percussion welding. This includes dissimilar metals having substantial differences in electrical conductivity and melting temperatures. Refractory and reactive metals can also be joined because the short weld cycles limit contamination.

Capacitor-discharge percussion welding. This process is similar to capacitor-discharge stud welding, discussed previously in this chapter under the subject of arc welding (refer to Fig. 9-33). Capacitor-discharge percussion welding is done in two ways: with a low-voltage, high-capacitance system or a high-voltage, low-capacitance system. Both systems use direct current from a capacitor or bank of capacitors charged by a rectifier or motor-generator set.

Low-voltage system. This method of capacitor-discharge percussion welding uses a low working voltage, generally 50-150 V, but sometimes higher. Arc starting with this method requires a nib or projection on one of the parts to be joined, special wire-end preparation, and a high-frequency, high-voltage pulse of alternating current.

High-voltage system. This method of capacitor-discharge percussion welding uses a high working voltage, generally 1000-3000 V, but sometimes higher. Arc starting with this method does not require nibs, projections, special wire-end preparation, or an auxiliary current circuit because the applied voltage is sufficiently high to ionize air in the gap between the workpieces and start the arc.

Machines. Portable, semiautomatic, and automatic machines are available for capacitor-discharge percussion welding. Methods used to apply force for welding include electromagnetic, electromechanical, cam drive, springs, and gravity. Handheld guns with portable power supply units are being used extensively for joining wires to terminals. The wires are held in movable jaws and the terminals in stationary jaws.

Magnetic-force percussion welding. This process is performed with a low-voltage (generally about 10-35 V) power supply from a transformer. Welds are made in less than one-half cycle of 60 Hz alternating current, and force is applied by an electromagnetic system. Arc starting is generally accomplished by providing a projection on one of the workpieces to be joined. The projection is vaporized with high current from the transformer.

Machines used for magnetic-force percussion welding are usually modified press-type resistance welding machines. They have two separate transformers, one for welding power and the other for electromagnetic power.

HIGH-FREQUENCY WELDING

With the high-frequency welding processes, the coalescence of metals is produced with the heat generated from the resistance of the workpieces to a high-frequency alternating current. In high-frequency resistance welding (HFRW), called the contact method, current is introduced to the workpieces by actual physical contact (see Fig. 9-67). An upsetting force is rapidly applied after heating is substantially completed.

In high-frequency induction welding (HFIW), called the induction method, current is induced in the workpieces by an external induction coil (see Fig. 9-68). There is no contact between the workpieces and the current.

Applications

The most common application for the high-frequency welding processes is the continuous seam welding of the edges of a single piece of metal in the production of metal pipe and tubing. Another application is the welding of butt joints between two parts, such as joining coil ends or sections and producing large strip and sheet blanks for forming. The processes are also used to produce structural shapes, spiral pipe and tubing, and helically and longitudinally finned tubing.

Satisfactory welds are normally produced in air, and the welds can be made with water or soluble-oil cutting fluids present. For some applications, such as the welding of titanium alloys, inert gas shielding is used. Flux is not generally required, but is helpful in welding some copper alloys.

Advantages

An important advantage of high-frequency welding is the narrow heat-affected zone produced. This limits oxidation and distortion and generally results in stronger joints. Concentration of the heating current at the work surfaces (shallow heating) permits welding temperatures to be reached with less power consumption than other resistance welding processes. High speeds make the processes suitable for high-production applications. Some pipes and tubes can be welded at rates to 1000 fpm (305 m/min).

Limitations

High-frequency induction welding requires a closed-loop path or a complete circuit for the flow of current entirely within the workpieces. This limits applications to flat, coiled, or tubular stock having a constant joint symmetry throughout the workpiece lengths. Equipment required is generally built into fully automated mills or production lines, necessitating a high capital investment.

Special precautions are necessary to protect personnel from the hazards of high-frequency current. Also, because the equipment operates near the radio-frequency range, care is necessary to avoid radiation interference and to meet regulations of the Federal Communications Commission.

Welding Various Metals

Some variations of the high-frequency welding processes, such as the finite-length resistance welding method, are generally limited to joining carbon steels and ferritic stainless steels. Other process variations are suitable for the joining of practically all metals, including ferrous and nonferrous metals, and dissimilar metals. Some aluminum alloys, however, have poor weldability.

Joint Design and Surface Preparation

Proper joint fitup and alignment, as well as correct vee preparation, are essential for optimum results with the HFRW and HFIW processes, especially in automated, continuous seam welding. When butt welding edges together, the edges must be parallel, and relative positions of the workpieces must be accurately controlled. Special surface treatments prior to welding are not generally necessary.

Power Supplies

The depths to which currents flow in the HFRW and HFIW processes depend on the frequencies of the currents used and the properties of the workpiece materials. At higher frequencies, the current flow is shallower and more concentrated near the work surfaces.

High-frequency power to about 10 kHz is usually produced by motor generators or solid-state inverters, with inverters becoming predominant. For frequencies of 100-500 kHz, vacuum-tube oscillators are generally used. Transformers and rectifiers convert plant line voltage to high-voltage direct current for use in the oscillators, which convert the direct current to high-frequency, high-voltage current for output transformers. The output transformers convert the high-voltage, low-amperage current to low-voltage, high-amperage current for welding.

High-Frequency Resistance Welding

The HFRW contact process differs from conventional resistance seam welding (discussed previously), which produces a series of overlapped nuggets, by producing a continuous weld

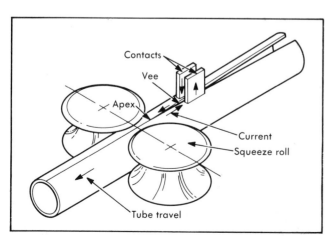

Fig. 9-67 High-frequency resistance welding. Current is applied to tube edges by two contacts. (*Fabricating Manufacturers Assn. and Thermatool Corp.*)

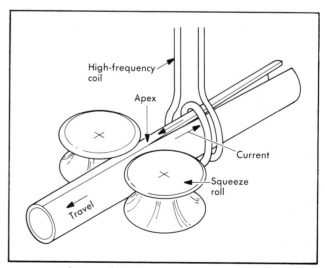

Fig. 9-68 High-frequency induction welding. Current is applied to tube by an external induction coil. (*Fabricating Manufacturers Assn. and Thermatool Corp.*)

HIGH-FREQUENCY WELDING

without nuggets and at much faster speeds. There are three major variations of the HFRW process: continuous seam, finite length, and melt welding.

Continuous seam welding. This variation of the HFRW process is used to produce pipe and tubing to more than 50" (1270 mm) diam, with wall thicknesses from 0.005 to 1" (0.13 to 25 mm). Sliding contacts are placed on either side of an open vee (4 to 7°) formed by the converging edges of strip stock, and pressure is applied by squeeze rolls (refer to Fig. 9-67). Coalescence of the metal is produced with the heat generated from the resistance of the workpiece to the flow of current, and the upsetting force completes the weld.

Finite length welding. In this variation of the HFRW process, usually limited to carbon steels and ferritic stainless steels, butt joints are welded between two parts, such as the joining of coil ends and producing large strip and sheet blanks for subsequent forming. Heating is produced along a seam already closed under light pressure. When the edges have been heated to fusion temperature, the pressure is increased to complete the weld.

Melt welding. In this variation of the HFRW process, high-frequency current melts a small volume of metal between electrodes that contact parts adjacent to each other. The molten metal flows together to produce a cast welded joint. One application consists of welding stacks of motor or transformer laminations together.

High-Frequency Induction Welding

In the HFIW process, high-frequency current flowing through an induction coil surrounding the work establishes a concentrated magnetic field. This field induces an electric potential causing a flow of current in the closed circuit provided by the workpiece. The resistance of the workpiece material to the flow of current provides the heat necessary for welding. Three major variations of the HFIW process are: continuous seam, butt end, and magnetic pulse welding.

Continuous seam welding. This variation of HFIW is used to produce longitudinal butt-seam tubing to 6" (152 mm) diam, with wall thicknesses to 0.375" (9.52 mm). An induction coil surrounds the tube at the open portion of the vee, some distance from the pressure (squeeze) rolls (refer to Fig. 9-68).

Butt end welding. Induction heating is used to provide welds between tubular-shaped pieces. Typically, the ends of the workpieces are prepared so that reasonably smooth surfaces are provided, and the tube ends are aligned end to end. An induction coil is placed around the joint, and, after a heat time of up to 60 seconds, pressure is applied to produce the weld. The process is used for tubes from 1 to 12" (25 to 305 mm) diam having wall thicknesses to 3/8" (9.5 mm).

Magnetic pulse welding. In this variation of HFIW, lap or sleeve joints between two tubes or pipes are welded. After the joint reaches welding temperature, a pulse of current from a capacitor bank is discharged through the inductor surrounding the joint. The current induced in the outer tube or pipe of the joint flows in a direction opposite to that in the coil. Magnetic forces thus produced repel each other and drive the heated outer component against the heated inner component, forging them together.

Process Selection for Tube and Pipe Production

Both the high-frequency resistance and induction welding methods have specific advantages. A major consideration in selecting one method over the other is the size of the pipe or tubing to be produced. The resistance process is more efficient and is therefore used more extensively for larger size pipe and tubing, where energy savings can be significant. The induction process is generally better for smaller diameter pipe and tubing.

High-frequency resistance welding is generally the choice for pipes more than 4" (102 mm) diam with wall thicknesses more than 3/16" (4.8 mm). High-frequency induction welding is usually preferred for producing tubes to 4" diam if the tube walls are not too thick. However, process selection is also influenced by the following specific advantages of each process.

Advantages of HFRW. An important advantage of the resistance method is high efficiency: less input power is required per unit of length produced. It is easier to weld thick-wall tubes, higher alloy metals, and profiled tubes with this process. There is also less induction heating of surrounding components. Another advantage is that the contacts can be used for all pipe and tube sizes produced.

The HFRW process is also used for joining two or more strips of material together to form special shapes, where there is no closed-loop path for the current to flow. Typical examples are the following:

- Helically finned, heat exchanger tubing where the base of the fin is continuously welded to the surface of the tube.
- Structural sections, such as H, I, T, and Z beams, where either one or two flanges are continuously welded to a web.
- Boiler-water wall tubing where two longitudinal fins are continuously welded to opposite sides of the tube.
- Automotive trim where a strip of stainless steel is welded to a strip of galvanized steel.
- Solar-absorber finned tubes where a copper tube is welded to a copper or aluminum fin.

Advantages of HFIW. Equipment required for the induction method is generally less expensive than for the resistance method. Thin-walled tubes can be welded easier with the induction process. Prefinished, polished plates and coated pipe or tubing can be welded in this way without surface marking or pickup of the coatings. Another advantage is that the induction coils have a longer life than the contacts used for resistance welding.

SAFETY IN RESISTANCE WELDING

Major hazards with resistance welding processes include the possibilities of electric shock, moving machine parts, and, in the case of flash, upset, and percussion welding, the ejection of molten metal particles. Because of the many variations in resistance welding processes, individual evaluations are required with respect to safety considerations. Recommendations for safety in welding are presented in ANSI/AWS Standard Z49.1.

General Requirements

Good housekeeping is essential for safety in resistance welding. Equipment and welding areas should be kept in good, clean, and dry condition, with frequent inspections and maintenance. Properly trained operators with skilled supervisors are also important for safety.

Machines and Mechanical Equipment

Machines for resistance welding should be equipped with guards and safety devices to prevent injury to operators. Initiating devices should be arranged or guarded to prevent inadvertent operation, with one or more emergency stop buttons provided. On press-type flash and upset welding machines, safety blocks or other means must be provided to prevent movement of the platen during maintenance or setup, and a fire-resistant shielding is required to protect the operator and other personnel from the expulsion of molten metal particles. Details with respect to machine safety are presented in Volume I, *Machining*, and Volume II, *Forming*, of this Handbook series.

Eye Protection

Eye or face shields or hardened lens goggles are recommended for most resistance welding processes. For flash, upset, and percussion welding, shaded lenses are required.

Skin Protection

Because burns can occur from contact with hot metal in some resistance welding processes, it is recommended that personnel wear nonflammable protective clothing, including aprons and gloves.

Electrical Shock

All electrical equipment, including controls, must be manufactured and installed in accordance with safety requirements of local, state, and national standards and codes, such as those issued by NEMA. The equipment must be grounded and high-voltage parts insulated and protected by enclosures with access doors that are electrically interlocked.

With resistance welding equipment that uses capacitors, the capacitors should be enclosed and insulated, and interlocks should interrupt the power and short-circuit the capacitors through a resistive load when the access door is opened. With high-frequency welding processes, precautions are necessary to prevent injuries from the power sources.

ELECTRON BEAM WELDING AND CUTTING

Electron beam welding (EBW) is a fusion joining process accomplished by impinging a high intensity beam of electrons on the joint to be welded. This results in precise melting and coalescence of the joint interface surfaces. This accurately controllable process provides a direct means of delivering high-energy densities.

In addition to their use for welding, electron beams are also employed for other processing operations, including machining, heat treating, and curing. Electron beam machining (EBM) for drilling and perforating small holes is discussed in Volume I, *Machining*, of this Handbook series. Electron beam cutting (EBC) is commented on later in this section. Electron beam heat treating for localized surface hardening and electron beam curing of paint films (organic coatings) by radiation are discussed in Volume III, *Materials, Finishing and Coating*, of this Handbook series.

PROCESS OVERVIEW

An electron beam welder operates in basically the same manner as do most EB devices commonly in use today, the best known of which is the cathode ray tube (CRT or picture tube) used in television sets and other video display units. In principle, some form of hot emitter is employed as a continuous source of thermal electrons. These emitted electrons are accelerated to speeds between 30 and 70% that of light, shaped into a collimated stream, and finally focused into a beam spot at a target.

In a CRT, the target is a screen coated with luminescent material. A relatively low-intensity beam spot is repetitively scanned over the entire screen area to produce visible images. In EBW, the target is a workpiece joint, and a relatively high-intensity beam spot is impinged on the joint to produce fusion welding. The fusion welding produced results from the kinetic energy of the beam electrons converting to heat when they impact with and penetrate into the workpiece.

This method of direct energy transferral provides a rapid, localized temperature rise, causing an instantaneous melting and vaporization of the workpiece material that results in the formation of a "keyhole" (a vapor channel with molten sides). When this keyhole is advanced along the joint, the molten material at the leading edge continuously flows around the sides, to the trailing edge, and solidifies to form a welded seam having a high depth-to-width ratio. Welds that are 10-40 times as deep as they are wide are not unusual in EBW. The keyhole formation process is a necessary and critical element for deep penetration welding. Without it, energy is only delivered to the top surface of the workpiece, and the heat must progress inward by thermal conduction, as in arc welding. There are several applications, however, in welding thin sections or delicate components where the electron beam is used to produce fine welds with depth-to-width ratios of 1:1.

APPLICATIONS

Electron beam welding is employed in a variety of precision and production applications. In the automotive industry, semiautomated and fully automated partial vacuum and non-vacuum EBW systems are being used to hermetically assemble die cast aluminum manifolds, steel torque converters, and catalytic converters, and for the fabrication welding of a large number of transmission components of varying materials. Other products joined by electron beam welding include solenoid valves, transducers, sealed bearings, diesel engine valves and injectors, and medical implants.

In the aerospace and nuclear industries, high-vacuum and partial-vacuum manual, semiautomated, and fully automated systems are used to perform a broad range of production assembly and repair procedure tasks on a wide variety of materials. In the saw blade industry, air-to-air mode, high-vacuum semiautomated and fully automated systems are used to produce the bimetallic (dissimilar metal) strip employed in making improved hack and bandsaw blades. Fast production of thin-walled tubing is another major application.

The various applications of electron beam welding cover a wide range of production rates, ranging from tens to hundreds of parts per hour. They involve making weld penetrations ranging from less than 0.050" (1.27 mm) to greater than 6" (150 mm) deep in a single weld pass.

With regard to the cost of employing the EBW process in production, figures given by various present users show a "total

ELECTRON BEAM WELDING

operating cost" experience that ranges from $0.05 to $0.95 per kilowatt of applied beam power per hour. This wide range in operating cost experience results from differences in the operating mode employed, the degree of vacuum and wire-feed assistance used, the level of preventive maintenance provided, and other factors.

ADVANTAGES

An important advantage of the EBW process is its capability for making high-quality welds that are deeper and narrower than arc welds and that are made with lower heat input. Very shallow welds with almost parallel sides can also be produced. Thick sections can be welded in a single pass, and the heat-affected zones (HAZs) are narrow, thus minimizing distortion. Welding speeds are fast, typically 30-100 ipm (762-2540 mm/min).

By projecting the electron beams, welds can be made in locations that are normally inaccessible. The beams can also be deflected to produce various shapes of welds and oscillated to improve quality and penetration. No filler metal, flux, or shielding gas are normally required, and welding can be done in any position. With the high-vacuum mode of operation, contamination of the metals being joined is minimized.

LIMITATIONS

Capital equipment costs for electron beam welding equipment are higher than for other welding processes, but operating costs are lower for many applications. Workpiece sizes that can be welded are limited by available vacuum chamber capacities. Many applications require precise edge preparation and alignment, and good fitup, which adds to costs.

When using the vacuum mode of EBW, production rates are limited by the time required to pump down the work chamber. With nonvacuum EBW, the distance that workpieces can be placed from the electron gun is limited. Electron beam welding also requires safety precautions for protection from X-ray and visible radiation.

WELDING VARIOUS METALS

The electron beam process can be used to join any metals that can be arc welded. Refractory and reactive metals can also be welded, as well as combinations of many dissimilar metals that cannot be joined by arc welding.

Thicknesses of metals joined vary from foil to plate stock. Steels joined by EBW include low and medium-carbon, alloy, tool, and stainless steels in thicknesses to about 12" (305 mm). Aluminum and magnesium alloys to 18" (455 mm) thick, and copper alloys to 4" (102 mm) thick are also welded. Molybdenum, tantalum, titanium, and beryllium can be joined by EBW, as well as silver, gold, and platinum. Finish-machined parts can be welded without marring the finish.

OPERATING PRINCIPLES

In electron beam welding, the beam of electrons is generated by an electron gun (see Fig. 9-69) operated in a vacuum environment of 1×10^{-4} mm of Hg (1×10^{-2} Pa) or less. The gun contains the following elements:

- A heated emitter element, which is often a directly heated wire or ribbon element, is referred to as the filament. It provides a continuous source of thermal electrons.
- A beam control element, which is the grid electrode and is often referred to as the bias grid. It controls the flow of electrons from the gun.

- A ground plane element, which is the anode electrode.

In operation, thermal electrons are emitted by the cathode, which may be either directly or indirectly heated. These electrons are simultaneously accelerated to a high velocity and shaped into a collimated stream by the electrostatic field geometry established from the particular gun electrode configuration employed.

The electron beam thus produced emerges from the gun through an exit hole in the ground plane anode. These exiting electrons contain the maximum energy input possible from the negative high voltage being applied to the cathode element. This is the operating (beam) voltage value, which is generally somewhere within the range of 30 to 200 kV.

The magnitude of the electron flow or operating (beam) current value in the exiting beam is easily altered (gated ON/OFF or raised/lowered in a ramped or stepped fashion) by simply varying the negative potential difference between the emitter and the grid.

There are electron beam guns commercially available having the capability to produce upward of 100 kW of beam power. Beam power is a comparative rating figure obtained by multiplying the operating beam voltage value by the output beam current value. These guns, some of which employ beam currents in excess of 1000 mA, can be ramped from zero to full power in a few milliseconds.

After exiting from the anode, the beam of electrons passes through electromagnetic focusing and deflection coils (see Fig. 9-69) on its way to the target. These coils allow a focused or defocused beam spot to be produced at the workpiece. The beam spot can be moved about in a fixed or oscillatory manner. With focusing, the capability to achieve beam spot intensities on the order of 10^7 W/in.^{2} (10^{10} W/m^2) is provided.

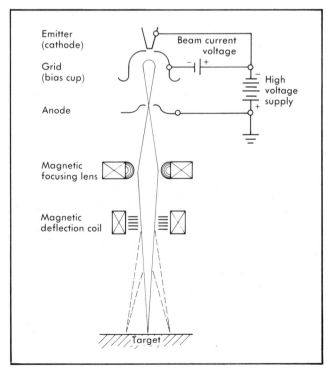

Fig. 9-69 Electron gun and optics system for electron beam welding. (*Leybold-Heraeus Vacuum Systems*)

ELECTRON BEAM WELDING

The electron beam produced may be used at the same level of vacuum environment in which it was generated or it may be brought out into a higher pressure region. Thus it can be used for various processes at any pressure level from high vacuum to above atmospheric (see Fig. 9-70).

The term "gun" describes the basic beam-generating elements (cathode, grid, and anode components), while the phrase "electron gun and optics assembly" describes an entire beam spot-producing system (beam generation and electron optical segments). However, it is common practice to use only the term "gun" when referring to an entire beam spot-producing system. Therefore, the terms "moving gun," "high-voltage gun," and similar terms generally mean a complete gun and optics assembly, not simply the basic gun elements.

OPERATIONAL MODES

Modern electron beam technology offers users of the process a variety of operational modes and provides a high degree of application versatility. Technology available allows EBW to be accomplished in or out of vacuum, at a high or low beam voltage, with a fixed or moving gun, and other possibilities.

High-Vacuum Welding

When EBW was first employed as a means for joining materials, welding was accomplished in the same vacuum environment as that required for beam generation, 1×10^{-4} mm of Hg (1×10^{-2} Pa) or less. This mode of operation, sometimes identified as high-vacuum electron beam welding (EBW-HV), produces the extremely high-quality welds for which EBW was initially developed.

A disadvantage of high-vacuum systems, however, is the time needed to evacuate the work chamber to the high-vacuum level required, which is unproductive time. The part geometry to be welded dictates the work chamber size and thus affects the time required to reach the high-vacuum level necessary for welding. Because the pumpdown time required depends on both work chamber size and the pumping system employed, this time can range anywhere from 15 seconds to as long as 1 hour.

Medium (Partial) Vacuum Welding

One solution for reducing the time needed to reach an acceptable weld-vacuum level has been the development of medium-vacuum electron beam welding (EBW-MV). In this mode of operation, commonly referred to as soft or partial-vacuum EBW, the welding is accomplished in a vacuum environment that is several orders of magnitude higher in pressure than that required for beam generation, generally somewhere in the range of 2×10^{-2} to 2×10^{-1} mm of Hg (2.6 to 26 Pa).

This method of EBW requires that the beam generation and work chamber regions be separated from each other by use of a vacuum divider. This is an aperture sized to impede gas flow without restricting beam passage. The two individual vacuum zones provided by employing such a device must each be evacuated by its own pumping system. Operating in this fashion, the beam can still be generated in a high-vacuum environment, while the workpiece surroundings need never be pumped to a vacuum level of any lower than 2×10^{-2} mm of Hg (2.6 Pa).

With partial-vacuum systems, the weld chamber can be custom designed to closely encompass the workpiece and any part fixturing involved. When this is done, it allows for the construction of a high-production repetitive-type system, where the cyclic pumpdown time required is typically in the range of only 3 to 30 seconds.

Nonvacuum Welding

The ultimate solution for reducing the time required to reach an acceptable vacuum level for welding has been the development of nonvacuum electron beam welding (EBW-NV). In this mode, welding is accomplished at or near atmospheric pressure.

This method of EBW requires that the beam generation and workpiece regions be separated by more than one vacuum divider. Also, the series of individual vacuum zones provided by employing several such apertures must each be evacuated by its own pumping system. Operating in this fashion, a graded pressure path is produced for the beam passage, ranging in value from a high vacuum level (where the beam is generated) to

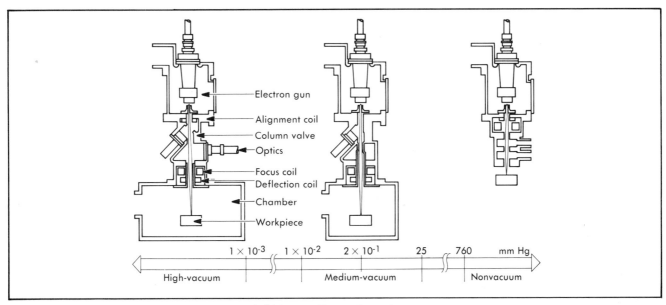

Fig. 9-70 Modes of operation for electron beams. (*Leybold-Heraeus Vacuum Systems*)

ELECTRON BEAM WELDING

atmospheric pressure (where the welding is performed). With this arrangement, the workpiece need never be exposed to a vacuum environment of any level, and a required time for achieving an acceptable weld-vacuum level is entirely eliminated. The nonvacuum system is limited, however, in that welding performed in air must be done within 3/4" (19 mm) and preferably 1/2" (12.7 mm) of the gun orifice.

Effect of Mode on Penetration

When either the partial-vacuum or nonvacuum mode of operation is employed, some loss in penetration capability will be incurred, compared to that attainable in the high-vacuum mode under similar operating conditions. The magnitude of this loss in penetration capability can vary from as low as a few percent to as high as nearly 100%.

Loss in penetration is caused by the fact that as the pressure surrounding the workpiece is increased above a high-vacuum level, the collision frequency between electrons in the beam and residual gas molecules also increases. This results in a beam dispersion action that causes both the beam and the focused beam spot to become larger, thereby reducing the effective beam power density being delivered to the workpiece.

Figure 9-71 gives a representative plot of how penetration can decrease with increasing pressure. This data is normalized to that achievable under high-vacuum conditions. The spread shown in this representative plot is because operating parameters other than pressure, such as beam voltage, distance traveled, residual gas composition, and other parameters, will also affect the beam penetration achievable at various pressure levels.

At pressures on the order of 5×10^{-2} mm Hg (6.5 Pa), both high and low-voltage electron beams can travel relatively long distances, 5-10" (127-254 mm), with only a minor reduction in penetration capability. At atmospheric pressure, even high-voltage electron beams will incur a drastic reduction in penetration capability over extremely short distances, 0.5-1" (12.7-25.4 mm).

Fusion Zone Profile

A representative comparison of the fusion zone profiles produced by the high-vacuum electron beam, laser beam, nonvacuum electron beam, and gas tungsten arc welding

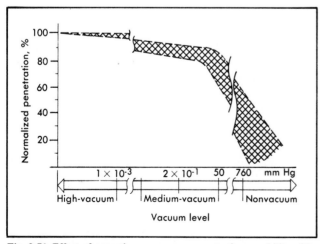

Fig. 9-71 Effect of operating pressure on penetrating capability with various operational modes of electron beam welding. (*Leybold-Heraeus Vacuum Systems*)

processes is presented in Table 9-46. The drawings also help to illustrate the degree to which beam scattering can affect final weld profile. They also indicate how much narrower the fusion zone of an energy beam process is when compared to an arc process. In addition, the operational data listed for the four processes, which are nominal values for penetration of an aluminum alloy of roughly 15/64" (6 mm) thickness, illustrates that the electron beam process is the most energy efficient.

LOADING AND UNLOADING METHODS

As a means of providing the capabilities attainable only with high-vacuum electron welding, but with minimum unproductive time, various methods have been developed to minimize pumpdown time per workpiece processed. These methods include batch, rotary index (dial feed) chamber, air-to-air, and tubular transfer loading and unloading systems.

Batch Loading and Unloading

In this method, a number of workpieces are loaded simultaneously during each vent cycle of the chamber. This allows a quantity of vacuum welds to be produced during each individual pumpdown time. By sizing work chambers and tooling to minimum volume requirements and using oversized pumps, production rates with a high vacuum approach those of medium-vacuum welding.

Rotary Index Chamber

In this method, a prepumped chamber is rotated to the welding station. Vacuum is maintained by using sliding face seals.

Air-to-Air Loading and Unloading

In this method, workpieces are passed, incrementally or continuously, through an arrangement of separately pumped pressure locks isolated from each other by sequencing valves or sliding seals. This allows vacuum welds to be produced without any pumpdown time. Several variations of this method are being used for a variety of high-production applications.

Special strip welders handle the raw material and welded product on stock reels outside the welding chamber. A typical machine has five or more separate cubicles in the chamber, each cubicle being separately pumped to a different level of vacuum. The strip stock is continuously fed through seals and the successive cubicles, with welding being performed in one of the cubicles. The welded product, such as bandsaw blade material, exits from the chamber and is wound on a takeup reel.

Rapid Transfer System

With this system, a conventional electron beam welder is fitted with a transfer tube that passes through the work chamber (see Fig. 9-72). The center section of the tube is cut away in the region of the beam and is rotated by a gear drive to allow access for welding. Workpiece carriers fill the tube and contain seals that maintain the vacuum in both the prepump position and the work chamber. The carriers are transferred sequentially under the beam for welding and ejected to the atmosphere for unloading. Carriers are then collected, reloaded, and recycled through the welder. Pre-evacuation is performed while another assembly is being welded.

ACCELERATING VOLTAGE

The operating (beam) voltage used for electron beam welding spans the range from about 30 to approximately 200

TABLE 9-46
Comparison of Various Fusion Processes

	Process			
	High-Vacuum Electron Beam Welding	Laser Beam Welding	Nonvacuum Electron Beam Welding	Gas Tungsten Arc Welding
Fusion zone profile				
Operating power, kW*	3.0	3.7	3.5	3.5
Speed, ipm (mm/min)*	100 (2540)	50 (1270)	75 (1905)	20 (508)
Power density, W/in.² (W/m²)*	10^7 (155 x 10^8)	10^6 (155 x 10^7)	10^5 (155 x 10^6)	10^4 (155 x 10^5)
Rate of energy input, kJ/in. (kJ/mm)*	1.8 (0.07)	4.4 (0.17)	2.8 (0.11)	10.3 (0.41)
Total energy consumption rate, kJ/in. (kJ/mm)*	6 (0.24)	45 (1.77)	10 (0.39)	18 (0.71)

(Leybold-Heraeus Vacuum Systems)

* Approximate values.

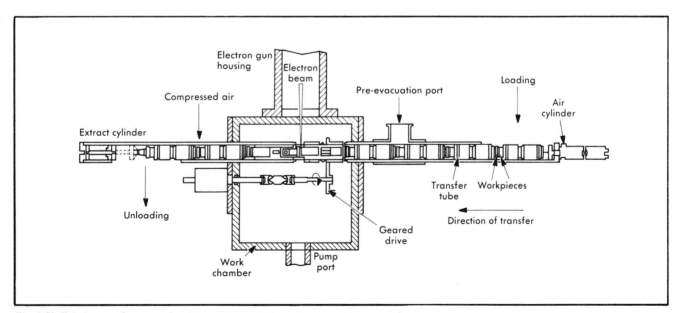

Fig. 9-72 Tubular transfer system for electron beam welding. (*Wentgate Engineers Ltd.*)

kV. By convention, systems operating at beam voltages of 60 kV or less are usually referred to as low-voltage EBW units; systems operating at beam voltages greater than 60 kV are generally called high-voltage EBW units.

Nonvacuum EBW machines are generally always high-voltage systems to help maximize their working distance capability (length of beam travel in atmosphere). High-vacuum and partial-vacuum EBW machines are normally either high or low-voltage

ELECTRON BEAM WELDING

systems. High power (30-100 kW) output levels are readily available from both high and low-voltage EBW systems.

Both high and low-voltage systems have certain advantages. These include the following:

- When required for a specific application, high-voltage beams can be focused to a smaller spot size than low-voltage beams at equivalent power levels.
- High-voltage beams are less affected by stray magnetic fields than are low-voltage beams.
- Low-voltage beams produce less intensive X-rays than do high-voltage beams.
- Systems producing low-voltage beams have more compact beam voltage generators than high-voltage systems.

Selection of the proper system, however, requires careful evaluation of the advantages applicable to the specific operation.

WELDING MOTION

To weld the entire length of a joint, the joint must be advanced under the beam or the beam must be advanced along the joint. Manufacturers of high-vacuum and partial-vacuum equipment offer systems capable of welding by either method. They supply fixed gun systems that weld by moving the workpiece, mobile gun systems that weld by moving the gun, or combination systems having simultaneous gun and workpiece movement. Mobile gun systems for the high-vacuum and partial-vacuum processes are normally always of the low-voltage variety, with the gun and its motion-producing mechanism mounted from an interior surface of the vacuum welding chamber. Fixed gun systems for the same processes are generally of either the high or low-voltage type, with the gun mounted on an exterior surface of the vacuum welding chamber.

In principle, to do an equivalent weld task, a fixed gun system could be expected to require a larger vacuum weld chamber than a mobile gun system. This is because of a need to provide added space to accommodate the workpiece when the joint is traversed under the beam. However, selection of a system type (fixed or moving gun) is generally determined by workpiece size, weld locations, tooling adaptation, and production requirements.

Systems for the nonvacuum process are predominately high-voltage units, employing either workpiece movement only or a combination of gun and workpiece movement to produce welding motion. Although no vacuum weld chamber structure is necessary in nonvacuum EBW, some type of protective radiation enclosure is required. This enclosure need only be large enough to encompass the workpiece, but it can be made large enough to encompass the entire system (beam-producing unit and workpiece tooling).

JOINT PREPARATION AND BEAM-TO-SEAM ALIGNMENT

In applying the electron beam welding process, regardless of the method of operation used, certain requirements have to be satisfied to achieve optimum results. For example, the proper degree of joint fitup and cleanliness must be provided, and the alignment of beam impact point and impingent angle must be properly established and adequately maintained for best end results to be achieved.

Joint Preparation

Cleaning. As with all types of welding processes, some care must be taken to ensure that the joint interface surface area and the region in the immediate vicinity are properly cleaned of any impurities. If impurities are absorbed into the weld zone, they could cause an adverse effect on the final quality of the weld seam produced. In addition, when high or medium-vacuum EBW is employed, the entire workpiece must be cleaned of any substances that could produce a heavy gas load (noticeably outgas) when exposed to vacuum. Otherwise, the time required to pump down the work chamber will become excessively long or the outgassing may cause blowholes and porosity in the weld zone.

Joint fitup. Because the high energy density achieved with EBW is produced by concentrating the beam power into a tightly focused spot, care must be taken to ensure that joint fitup is proper. In general, joint fitup provided must be such that no joint gap in excess of 10% of the beam spot diameter is present. When employing high-vacuum EBW, where a focused spot diameter in the range of 0.010 to 0.050" (0.25 to 1.27 mm) is generally obtainable, a joint gap greater than 0.001 to 0.005" (0.03 to 0.13 mm) is not recommended. When using nonvacuum EBW, where the beam spot at the workpiece may be as large as 0.250" (6.35 mm) diam, a joint gap between 0.020 and 0.030" (0.51 and 0.76 mm) can easily be tolerated. For both high-vacuum and nonvacuum EBW, larger gaps are possible using techniques that involve beam defocusing, beam oscillation, and the use of a wire-feed device.

Although not normally required for EBW because the process produces an autogenous weld, wire-feed devices may be employed if needed to provide material for either a filling or deoxidizing function. In addition, with both high and medium-vacuum EBW, "beam spot stirring" (deflecting the beam spot in an oscillatory manner) can also be used to help compensate for excessive joint gaps. Beam spot stirring also helps to eliminate gas entrapment by providing a mechanism that allows gas bubbles to move to the surface of the weld puddle.

Beam-to-Seam Alignment

The small spot area through which an electron beam applies its energy to the workpiece necessitates that a precise alignment be maintained between the beam spot and the joint seam over the entire seam path. The use of modern servodrives and computer controllers allows EBW machines to achieve this degree of precision motion control. With present day CNC/EBW-style equipment, instructions for multiple axes ($X/Y/Z/$ROTARY) of weld motion and varying parameter (power/focus/deflection) settings are easily input through conventional program entry procedures. Complex weld schedules can readily be executed in an automated manner.

A number of seam-tracking methods have been developed to maintain the degree of alignment required by the EBW process, even under most probable production conditions, such as errors in joint machining. These methods involve mechanical means, such as the use of a stylus to follow the joint groove; optical means, including the use of a photodiode array to sense the proximity of the beam spot to the joint groove; and electronic means, such as the use of "back-scattered electrons" to detect seam position.

A probe-type seam-tracing system is shown schematically in Fig. 9-73. It enables the movable gun to follow an irregular seam or contoured part while welding. The device can be arranged so that the gun can trace from an adjacent template. By the use of servocontrols, the seam-tracking device makes it possible to drive the weldment linearly on the X axis, while correcting for any misalignment on the Y axis simultaneously.

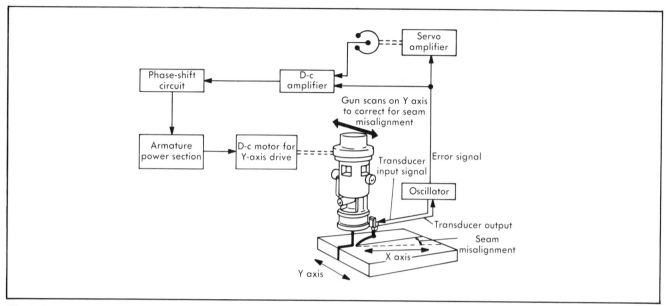

Fig. 9-73 Probe-type seam-tracing system for electron beam welding. (*Sciaky Bros.*)

The principle for a means of seam location and tracking using secondary electron emission is illustrated in Fig. 9-74. There is a variation in signal generated by detecting the secondary electrons produced from the primary electrons impinging on the workpiece. This signal variation is used as a means for accurately locating and/or following the weld seam.

In this seam-tracking method, the primary beam is alternately used to scan the area ahead of the weld puddle for seam location and to maintain the weld puddle for seam fusion. This requires that high deflection speeds be used to avoid any resulting discontinuities in the weld seam.

ELECTRON BEAM CUTTING

In electron beam cutting (EBC), an electron beam is focused to a beam spot intensity of approximately 10^{10} W/in.^{2} (1.55 x 10^{13} W/m^2). This intensity is several orders of magnitude greater than that employed for electron beam welding. When impinged on a workpiece, the electrons produce complete vaporization of material in the beam spot's path. The EBC process provides an effective method for severing (cutting or slitting) refractory-type materials with accurate control.

The EBC process is normally accomplished under fairly high-vacuum conditions. This mode of operation requires an optimum degree of beam focusing capability and beam control versatility to be achieved. Precisely contoured slitting or cutting of thin materials can be performed with minimal kerf and maximum processing speed. The beam is usually operated in a relatively high-frequency pulsed mode for this type of operation.

Electron beam cutting, however, is used to only a limited extent. More recently, laser beam cutting (LBC), discussed next in this chapter, has become a major competitor of EBC. This is primarily because LBC can be accomplished in the atmosphere and therefore can be used with or without a supplementary cutting gas. For applications requiring an extremely fast beam motion or a totally inert ambient atmosphere, however, the low-inertia, high-vacuum EBC process is still an ideal method. Another advantage of EBC over LBC is the ability to drill, trepan, or cut slots to more controllable and precise depths.

SAFETY IN ELECTRON BEAM WELDING AND CUTTING

In addition to the safety precautions required against the common welding hazards, discussed previously in this chapter, protection must be provided for the special dangers of high energy used in electron beam welding and cutting. These include radiation and possible electric shock from the high voltages used. Details with respect to safety precautions are presented in AWS Publication F2.1, "Recommended Safe Practice for Electron Beam Welding and Cutting," and ANSI Standard Z49.1, "Safety in Welding and Cutting." Regularly scheduled inspection and maintenance are important.

Radiation

Radiation hazards include both visible radiation and the radiation from X-rays. Visible radiation from the molten metal requires eye protection. Specifications for eye protection equipment are contained in ANSI Standard Z87.1, "Practice for Occupational and Educational Eye and Face Protection." Recommendations for filter lenses are presented in ANSI/AWS Standard Z49.1.

Steel walls of the work chambers generally provide protection from X-rays in low-voltage machines. Lead coverings are provided on high-voltage machines. Leaded glass windows are used for both low and high-voltage systems. For nonvacuum systems, radiation-tight enclosures are also provided.

Electrical Shock

To minimize the possibility of electrical shocks from the high voltages used, the machines should be manufactured and installed in accordance with national standards, such as those issued by NEMA.

Respiratory Protection

There is little danger from toxic gases or contaminants when using high-vacuum electron beam processes because of the

ELECTRON BEAM SAFETY

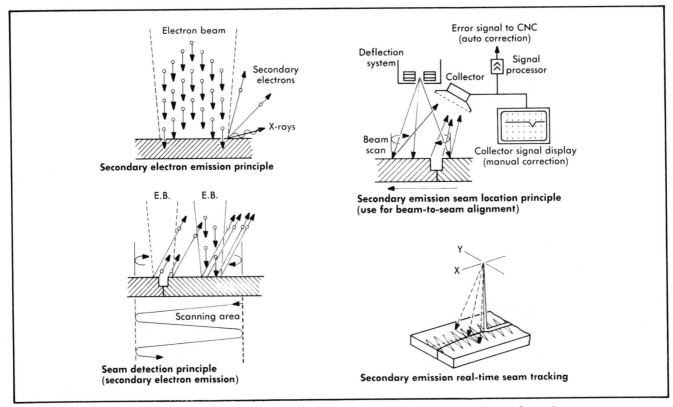

Fig. 9-74 Principle for seam location and tracking using secondary electron emission. (*Leybold-Heraeus Vacuum Systems*)

small amount of air left in the chambers. With medium-vacuum and nonvacuum systems, however, this can be a problem. The best protection against possible respiratory problems is to provide adequate and effective, positive ventilation by means of exhaust systems. Regulations issued by OSHA, as well as local codes, specify requirements with respect to ventilation.

In specialized applications such as welding toxic materials, such as beryllium or uranium, some danger exists that finely divided particles of vaporized, deposited materials may be agitated into suspension by the inrushing air when the chamber is vented to the atmosphere. Upon opening the chamber door, these particles can be released to areas adjacent to the machine. Care must be taken to confine such contamination or to render the machine functions harmless.

LASER BEAM WELDING AND CUTTING

Laser beam welding and laser beam cutting are both being used extensively for industrial applications. The word laser is an acronym for "light amplification by stimulated emission of radiation."

In addition to their use for welding, laser beams are also employed for other processing operations, including machining, marking, and the heat treatment of metals. Laser beam machining (LBM), including drilling operations, is discussed in Volume I, *Machining*, of this Handbook series. Laser beam cutting (LBC) is discussed later in this section. Discussions of the uses of lasers for selective surface-transformation hardening, deburring, and hard facing are presented in Volume III, *Materials, Finishing and Coating*, of this Handbook series. The use of lasers for inspection is discussed in Chapter 3, "Inspection Equipment and Techniques," of this volume.

LASER BEAM WELDING

Laser beam welding (LBW) is a fusion joining process that produces coalescence of metals with the heat generated by the absorption of a concentrated, coherent light beam impinging on the components to be joined. In the LBW process, the laser beam is focused to a small spot for high power density and directed by optical elements such as mirrors or lenses. It is a noncontact process, with no pressure being applied. Inert gas shielding is generally employed to reduce oxidation, but filler metal is rarely used.

While laser beam welding is similar to electron beam welding, discussed in the preceding section, there are important differences. Unlike electron beam welding, which often requires a vacuum, laser beam welding can be performed in air or in a controlled atmosphere. Laser beams do not penetrate sections much thicker than 3/4" (19 mm); electron beams can penetrate metal thicknesses of 2" (51 mm) or more in a single pass.

Applications

Most applications of laser beam welding can be grouped into one of four major categories: structural, assembly, sealing, and conduction welds. Structural welds are generally butt and fillet welds with metal thicknesses ranging from about 1/32 to 1/2" (0.8 to 12.7 mm) where maximum load-carrying efficiency is required per unit of joint length.

Assembly welds are usually lap, spot, or seam welds in thin metals, to about 1/8" (3.2 mm) thick, where strength is not a major consideration. Partial-penetration assembly welds, however, are made in thicker metals. Sealing welds are a special class of assembly welds for joining two parts (usually a cover to a container) and providing the joint with a specified level of hermeticity. Sealing welds are often made in a chamber filled with a special atmosphere that is contained in the product after sealing to improve component life or to permit detection of leaks in service.

Conduction welds are another special class of assembly welds for joining electrical wires or connectors. The main requirement is the establishment of sufficient joint area to pass the required amount of electricity with minimum disturbance to current flow.

Laser beam welding is being used for an extensive variety of applications. A number of welds are being made in the production of automotive transmissions and air-conditioner clutch assemblies. In the latter application, laser welding permits the use of a design that could not otherwise be manufactured. The process is also being used in the production of relays and relay containers and for sealing electronic devices and heart pacemaker cases. Other applications include the continuous welding of aluminum tubing for thermal windows and for refrigerator doors.

Advantages

Major advantages of laser beam welding include the following:

1. Heat input is close to the minimum required to fuse the weld metal; thus, metallurgical effects in adjacent material (heat-affected zones) are reduced, and heat-induced workpiece distortion is minimized. Materials that would be damaged by heat can be assembled close to laser welds.

2. Single-pass laser welding procedures have been qualified in materials more than 1/2" (12.7 mm) thick, reducing the time required to weld thick sections and reducing or eliminating the need for filler wire and elaborate joint preparation.

3. No electrodes are required; welding is performed with freedom from electrode contamination, indentation, or damage from high-resistance welding currents. Because LBW is a noncontact process, distortion is minimized and tool wear eliminated.

4. The laser can be located a convenient distance from the workpiece and redirected around tooling and obstacles in the workpiece, permitting welding in areas not otherwise accessible. Laser beams are readily focused, aligned, and redirected by optical elements.

5. The workpiece can be located and hermetically welded in an enclosure that is evacuated or that contains a controlled atmosphere.

6. The laser beam can be focused on a small area, permitting the joining of small, closely spaced components with tiny welds.

7. A wide variety of materials can be welded, including some combinations formerly considered "unweldable."

8. The laser can be readily mechanized for highly automated, high-speed welding techniques, including numerical and computer control.

9. Surface contaminants such as oxides, organic materials, and dirt from handling are evaporated when the beam is used at maximum intensity and thus may not cause unacceptable defects in some noncritical welds.

10. Welds in thin material and small diameter wires are less susceptible to burn-back than is the case with arc welding.

11. Laser welds are not influenced by the presence of magnetic fields, as are arc and electron beam welds.

12. Laser welds are somewhat more tolerant of poor joint fitup than are electron beam welds, but fitup should be as tight as possible.

13. The laser beam tends to follow the weld joint through to the root of the workpiece, even when not exactly aligned with it. Electron beams tend to penetrate straight through a part, regardless of alignment.

14. Although lasers generate a beam at low efficiency (about 10%), narrow, deep welds can usually be produced at an energy saving when compared to arc welds.

15. Metals with dissimilar physical properties, such as resistance, can be welded.

16. No vacuum or X-ray shielding are required.

17. Aspect (depth-to-width) ratios—up to 5:1—are attainable when the weld is made by forming a cavity in the metal, discussed later in this section under the subject of keyhole welding.

Some advantages are more important to one major application category than another. Table 9-47 relates the advantages of laser beam welding to the four major application categories.

Assembly welds exhibit the advantages of low heat input, minimum distortion, elimination of electrodes, and high speed offered by laser beam welding. Laser sealing welds take advantage of the fact that welding can be accomplished under conditions where the interior of the container is filled with a special atmosphere at or near ambient pressure. Advantages of laser beam welding for conductors include the ability to weld in crowded areas where electrodes would not fit, avoidance of marking or deformation of delicate conductors, and reliability for high-volume production.

Limitations

Laser beam welding has several limitations when compared to electron beam and conventional arc welding methods. These limitations include the following:

1. Joints must be accurately positioned laterally under the beam and at a controlled position with respect to the focal point of the beam. With short focal length lenses, the focus limits can be more critical than for electron beams; for long focal length lenses, the focus lengths can be comparable to limitations for electron beams.

2. If surfaces to be welded must be forced together

LASER BEAM WELDING

TABLE 9-47
Advantages of Laser Beam Welds with Relation to Application Categories

Principal Advantages of Laser Welds	Weld Application Categories			
	Structural Welds	Sealing Welds	Assembly Welds	Conduction Welds
Minimum heat input to heating thermally sensitive materials		X		
Minimum heat input to metal	X	X	X	
Rapid single pass	X		X	
No filler wire	X			
Noncontact weld			X	X
No electrodes			X	X
Workpiece in enclosure		X		X
Small welds in foils or thin wires				X
Wide variety of metals				X
Simple automation			X	

mechanically, the clamping mechanisms must ensure that the final position of the joint is correct with respect to limitation 1, compared to resistance welding, which can clamp and weld in one action.

3. Laser weld depth is generally less than that produced by electron beam welders. Laser beam welding is also limited with respect to the maximum metal thicknesses that can be joined.
4. Laser welds have lower depth-to-width ratios than electron beam welders operating above 100 kV.
5. Materials such as magnesium tend to evaporate, producing voids. Rimmed steels, when welded at high speeds, also exhibit voids. Killed or semikilled steels may have to be substituted when high-speed welding is required. The reflectivity and high heat conductivity of some materials, such as aluminum and copper alloys, reduces weldability.

Welding Various Metals

Laser beam welding can be used to join a wide variety of metals, both ferrous and nonferrous, as well as dissimilar metals that are metallurgically compatible. Low-carbon steels are readily weldable, but when the carbon content exceeds about 0.25% martensitic transformation may cause brittle welds and cracking; pulsed laser welding can minimize this. As mentioned previously under limitations, fully killed or semikilled steels are preferable, especially for structural applications, because rimmed steels may have voids. Steels having high amounts of sulfur and phosphorus may be subject to hot cracking during welding, but pulsed laser welding can minimize this. Also, free-machining steels containing sulfur, selenium, calcium, or lead may cause porosity.

Carburized steels and cast irons can only be welded with difficulty. Also, welds in such metals are generally porous and contain cracks. Occasionally, nickel shims are added to these metals and some alloy steels to increase weld toughness. Aluminum in small quantities has also been added to joints of rimmed steel to reduce gas porosity.

Many stainless steels are considered good candidates for laser welding. The low thermal conductivity of these metals permits making narrower welds and deeper penetrations than possible with carbon steels. Stainless steels in the 300 series, with the exception of free-machining Types 303 and 303 Se and stabilized Types 321 and 347, are readily weldable. Welds made in some of the 400 series stainless steels can be brittle and may require postweld annealing. Many heat-resistant nickel and iron-based alloys are being welded successfully with laser beams. Titanium alloys and other refractory metals can be welded in this way, but an inert atmosphere is required to prevent oxidation.

Copper and aluminum are not generally welded. However, copper and brass are often welded to themselves and other materials with the specialized joint designs used for conduction and assembly welding. Aluminum and its weldable alloys can be joined for partial-penetration assembly welds and are commonly joined by pulsed conduction welds for hermetically sealed electronic packages. Joint designs must retain aluminum in tension.

Refractory metals such as tungsten are often conduction welded in electronic assemblies, but require higher levels of power than other materials. Nickel-plated Kovar is often used in sealing welds or electronic components, but special care is required to ensure that the plating contains no phosphorus. There is phosphorus in the electroless nickel-plating process commonly on Kovar parts that are to be resistance welded.

Dissimilar metal joints are commonly encountered in conduction welds where the twisting of conductors forms a mechanical support that minimizes bending of potentially brittle joints. Dissimilar metals having different physical properties (reflectivity, conductivity, and melting points) are often formed in the welding of conductors. For example, extra turns of one material as opposed to the other material may be welded to the joint to balance the melting characteristics of the materials. Some of these concepts can also be applied to structural and assembly welds, but the possibilities are much more limited.

Weld Joint Design

A wide variety of joint designs can be used for laser welding. The specific design to be used depends on which major application category is intended.

Structural welds. Rules applicable to the design and placement of single-pass, arc-welded butt joints apply to structural laser welds. However, butt joints can be substantially thicker than for single-pass arc welds if the laser power is high enough to form a keyhole in the metal. The ability of the laser to produce a deep, narrow weld accounts for the unusual single-pass butt welding capacity of lasers.

Not all laser processes are operated at keyhole power levels. At lower power levels, welding takes place by conduction from the surface. The thickness of conduction-welded joints is much less than for keyhole processes.

When structural members are at an angle, arc processes employ a joint design where the stress is transferred from member to member through fillets at their intersection. In contrast, lasers can be directed into the root of intersecting members. The beam will follow the gap between plates and, with sufficient power, emerge from the opposite side of the joint. In this manner, the joint involves all or most of the root. Fillets may be present and help reduce stress concentration; however, they are not the principal stress-carrying elements in the laser joint.

Whenever possible, components should be fitted together tightly; however, gaps of 2% of the metal thickness can be tolerated provided the beam spot diameter is about three times larger than the gap and provided some loss of reinforcement is acceptable. Larger gaps may be fused but will exhibit underfill. Thin sections can tolerate somewhat greater gaps than plates. The amount is dependent on surface tension of the material and the size of the spot. Larger spots (or oscillated beams) can provide some added gap tolerance in thin sheets because edges need only be within one half of the incident beam diameter for some fusion to occur.

Assembly welds. Partial-penetration welds can be made with a laser using butt-weld designs similar to those used for structural welding. However, the root of the fusion zone frequently exhibits closely spaced, linear porosity. If such porosity is objectionable, a relief should be undercut in one or both faces of the butt joint at the desired depth of penetration. Thus, the weld will become a partial-thickness, full-penetration weld, and porosity will be minimized by allowing the keyhole to vent into the undercut portion.

The ability of a laser beam to follow a gap between two surfaces provides a skidding phenomenon that can be used to form a weld between the faces of overlapped sheets. Such so-called skid welds may be considered as substitutes for resistance spot welding in assembly operations. They are characterized by broad areas for good conductivity or load-carrying capabilities. Excess overlap can be eliminated because it is not required to contain expulsion when the nugget is formed. A flanged "mouth" may be required to collect the beam. Figure 9-75 compares the skid-weld design with a resistance weld and shows the low figuration of the skid weld. Potential material savings are shown in Fig. 9-76.

Alternatively, the beam can be directed through the top sheet and into (or through) underlying sheets to form a spike-like fusion zone that joins the sheets. The cross section of such welds at the interface is about the size of the beam diameter as it penetrated the sheets. Additional cross section is attained by forming a circle or line with the same weld or with a series of

spike-like welds. Considerable latitude in beam placement is possible with this joint configuration. Metal from the weld will bridge small gaps between the plys. The gaps, however, should not exceed one-half the weld cross section.

Sealing welds. The most frequently encountered joints for sealing welds are butt and formed-edge configurations. Components such as heat-sensitive, glass-to-metal seals can be placed within 0.050" (1.27 mm) of a properly made weld without damage. Conduction welds made by individual pulses are frequently used to minimize melting. In conduction pulsed welds, penetration cannot greatly exceed 0.125" (3.2 mm).

Overlaps of 80-90% are recommended in pulsed laser welding for the following two reasons:

1. Weld cross section tends to be thick at the center but thin at the edge. If weld centers are too far apart, the lower contour of the joint takes on a profile not unlike sawblades, with thin areas where leaks may occur.

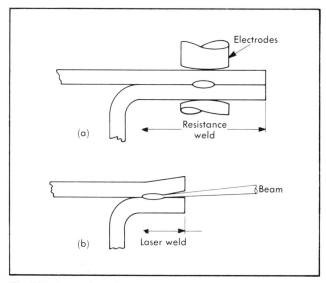

Fig. 9-75 Comparison of overlap required with conventional resistance weld (view *a*) and laser beam skid weld (view *b*). (*IITRI Laser Center*)

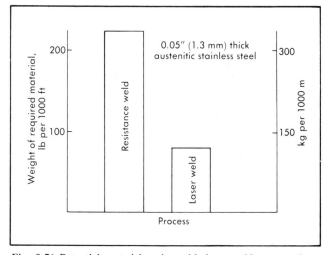

Fig. 9-76 Potential material saving with laser weld compared to resistance weld. (*IITRI Laser Center*)

LASER BEAM WELDING

2. Most materials have some small amount of contamination that can cause a blowhole in any given spot. However, there is a good chance that the blowhole will be refused by the overlapping spot if the degree of overlap is kept high.

Conduction welds. When welding wires or tubes, the joint is formed where the cylindrical surfaces touch. Touching occurs when parallel parts are clamped or when wires are twisted. Twisting or the use of special clamps can increase target size for very small wires. Because many welds involve metals with different thermal properties, joint design can be used to balance relative thermal masses. This might involve adding an extra turn of wire or changing the wire gage. The thermal mass rate should be as near to 1:1 as possible.

Operating Principles

Three types of information required to understand the energy source for laser welding are:

1. Characteristics of the laser energy source.
2. Manner in which the light energy is delivered.
3. Way in which the energy interacts with the metal to form a weld.

Characteristics of laser beam source. Any laser (see Fig. 9-77) has three fundamental parts: a gain medium, a pumping source, and a resonator. The gain medium is stimulated by an external source and emits the laser light. The resonator directs the light back and forth through the gain medium, causing light amplification. Lasers derive their classification—solid-state or gaseous—from the physical state of their gain media.

The generation of laser light from these sources is relatively inefficient. Solid-state lasers convert up to 5% of the input power to light; CO_2 lasers convert 5-15%. It is important to note that this is the efficiency inside the laser. It does not, however, mean that laser welding is necessarily less efficient than other forms of welding. In fact, lasers may conserve energy when compared to conventional welds. Some of the factors that can result in conservation of energy are:

1. Narrow welds involving only a fraction of the metal that is associated with a conventional weld.
2. Faster welds that minimize the heating of adjacent metal.
3. Reduced distortion that may eliminate energy consumption associated with postweld machining.

Solid-state lasers. In solid-state lasers, the gain medium is a solid—usually a pencil-sized rod of a host material. An active ion (a dopant) is added to the host material. Neodymium (Nd) ions are most commonly used in solid-state welders. The host solid can be either a carefully grown crystal of yttrium-aluminum-garnet (YAG) or a piece of very special optical glass or ruby (Al_2O_3). Chromium is used as a dopant for ruby. Solid-state lasers use flash lamps to provide energy to the neodymium. The host material must be capable of transmitting the resulting light (and heat) to that part of the system where the light is used and the heat can be disposed of. Solid-state lasers produce energy at a wavelength of 1.06 μm.

Gaseous lasers. In a gas laser, such as that using carbon dioxide (CO_2), gas atoms or molecules produce light after they absorb energy from an electric current passing through a mixture of gases. Gas lasers are available in one of two configurations. In one configuration, the gas flows axially along the beam, and the gas tubes are long, resulting in a relatively large laser (see Fig. 9-78). Gas may flow slowly or very rapidly. Slow flow permits enhanced power when pulsing. Rapid flow is more compact and efficient. In the other configuration, the gas flows across the beam in a transverse flow system. With the latter configuration, the laser source can be much more compact (see Fig. 9-79). Gas lasers produce energy at a wavelength of 10.6 μm.

Delivery of light energy. Laser light has qualities that make it useful for both industrial and scientific applications. These qualities include the following:

1. Monochromaticity.
2. Low divergence.
3. Low order mode (for most lasers).
4. Coherence.

Welding applications emphasize monochromaticity, low divergence, high output, and efficiency, all of which are provided by the neodymium-doped, solid-state and CO_2 gas lasers. Laser light is delivered in two quantitative forms: pulsed and continuous [continuous wave (CW)].

Pulsed light. With pulsed light, the generation of one pulse or a series of pulses is at a rate of up to 200 pulses per second for the YAG laser. Neodymium-doped glass and chromium-doped ruby lasers can pulse a few times each second. A welding pulse involves an initial peak rate of energy power that starts the melting, followed by a period during which power is delivered at

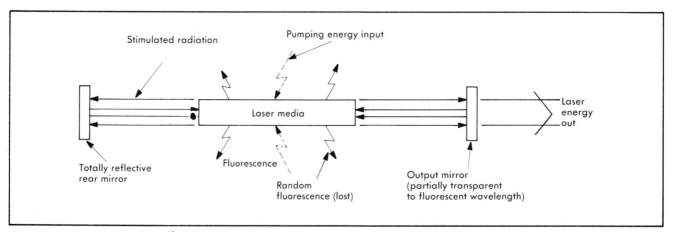

Fig. 9-77 Elements of a basic laser.[15]

a lower rate to allow the welding to continue. Such pulses are called enhanced pulses and permit small lasers to perform welding. Larger lasers may be pulsed without the peak of energy. These are called gated pulses and, if the laser is powerful enough, may also melt metal while exhibiting the heat input control associated with all pulsed processes.

Welding requires that the initial peak power be sufficient to initiate melting, but not so high that metal is vaporized, which leaves a rough, pitted surface. Welding also requires long pulses relative to pulsed cutting or drilling. Long pulses give the metal time to melt in sufficient quantity to ensure an adequate weld cross section.

A typical cross section for a pulsed laser weld that depends on conduction for melting has a 1:1 depth-to-width ratio. Higher ratios can be obtained with an increase in surface roughness as the power approaches power levels that favor the keyhole mode of melting. Welding pulse duration can be

controlled and varied with a maximum of 20 milliseconds, although the majority of pulsed welds are made in 3-8 milliseconds. Welding pulses are about 10 times longer than drilling pulses.

Pulsed welds are influenced by two laser characteristics. The energy per pulse (in joules) determines the depth of penetration, while the average power of the laser establishes how many times a second the unit can deliver a specific packet (pulse) of energy. This ability determines weld process speed.

Pulsed welds are best applied to thicknesses less than 0.125″ (3.2 mm). Each pulse forms a weld nugget. The nuggets may be used to form isolated spots of fusion, or they may be overlapped to form a seam. Weld nuggets made for leak tightness are often overlapped 80-90%, with a 50% overlap being considered minimum. Careful pulse selection permits the formation of exceptionally uniform, smooth beads [100 μin. (2.54 μm)].

Continuous energy. If welding energy is applied continuously, seam welds can be formed at a considerably higher speed, but penetration may have to be reduced because of thermal conductivity of the metals being welded.

Focusing beam energy. To produce a weld, the power density of the laser beam must be raised to a minimum level of 1 x 10^5 W/cm^2 (1.55 x 10^4 W/in.^{2}) and should not exceed 1 x 10^7 W/cm^2 (1.55 x 10^6 W/in.^{2}). The unfocused output beam generally does not provide these levels, and a beam focusing system is required. A simple lens (see Fig. 9-80) is used for beams up to about 1 kW. A focusing mirror system (Fig. 9-81) may be required for higher power levels. Several other configurations are being used.

The optical spot size (D_f) is the result of the relationship between the following:

Beam wavelength (γ), 1.06 μm (41.73 μin.) for YAG lasers; 10.6 μm (417.3 μin.) for CO$_2$ lasers.
Lens focal length (f).
Unfocused beam diameter at the lens (D_o).

The relationship between these elements can be expressed by the following equation:

$$D_f = \frac{2\,\gamma f}{\pi\,D_o} \approx \frac{f}{D_o} \qquad (6)$$

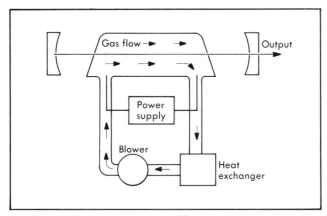

Fig. 9-78 Axial-flow gas laser system.[16]

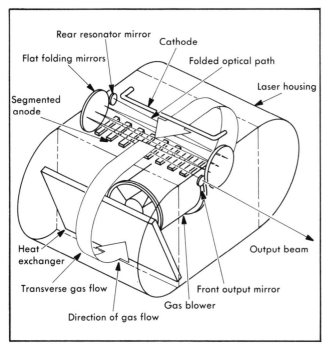

Fig. 9-79 Transverse-flow gas laser system. (*Spectra Physics Inc.*)

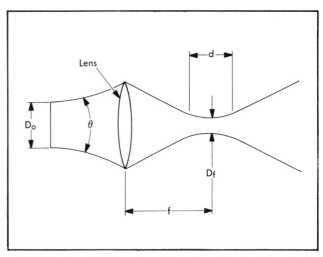

Fig. 9-80 Schematic illustration of laser beam focusing by a simple lens.[17]

LASER BEAM WELDING

The fraction f/D_o is often referred to as the f number of a focusing system. This number is important to spot size in several ways, including the following:

- Focus systems with low f numbers produce small spots.
- Changing the unfocused beam diameter, deliberately or as a consequence of lens movement along a diverging beam, causes a change in this number.
- Lasers with shorter wavelengths can potentially be focused to smaller spots.
- Average power density in the spot increases or decreases by the square of the radius of the spot size. Power density is greatest at the center of the beam for lasers operating in their lowest order mode.
- Small, intense spots increase penetration for any given power level and also reduce the heat-affected zone that results.

Achieving the smallest spot size is not the only consideration in welding, however. Variances in the position of the workpiece in the path of the laser require that the beam be focused to:

1. Provide a spot size that accommodates lateral variation in the joint.
2. Provide a focal depth that accommodates variances in the distance between focus system and workpiece.

The second condition is achieved by noting that there is a relationship between the diameter of the beam (spot size) and a region along the narrowest part of the beam, where there is virtually no significant change in spot size (refer to Fig. 9-80). Such a region could provide for variations in the relationship between the focus system and the workpiece. This constant diameter region is called the depth of focus (d) and increases as the square of the spot size:

$$d \approx \frac{D_f^{\,2}}{\gamma} \qquad (7)$$

A significant depth of focus is required when:

- The workpiece is not flat or will not stay flat during welding.
- Runout is expected in a rotating workpiece.

- Tooling required to meet the more stringent condition of a smaller spot would be impractical.
- Material is sufficiently thick, about 1/2" (12.7 mm), that a sharply focused beam is not efficient, and a beam with straighter sides is required.

The consequence of employing a large depth of field is a larger spot size, which in turn may call for a more powerful laser. Therefore, a tradeoff study that considers spot size, depth of field, required laser power, workpiece accuracy, and level of tooling is necessary and desirable for all laser applications.

Workpiece interactions. When beam energy strikes a work surface, some energy is sacrificed to reflectance, and the remainder is absorbed as light to a very shallow depth. This shallow film of metal heats until reflectance is reduced and normal heat transfer begins to occur. The amount of heat transfer is in direct relationship to the laser power, time of exposure, and spot size. Naturally occurring oxides and other films on the metal will influence the heat transfer initially.

Conduction welds. In conduction welding, laser energy is absorbed in sufficient quantities to melt the metal but not to vaporize it. The melt zone then expands by thermal conduction outward from the beam impingement point (see Fig. 9-82). At the same time, the melting process is progressing into the metal to form the joint. Because conduction is the same in both directions, penetration into the metal proceeds at the same rate that the area of the heated zone expands outward on the workpiece surface.

Both penetration and area expansion of the heated zone terminate at the end of the pulse, leaving a weld that is about as wide as it is deep. The depth can be increased in this ratio to 3:1 maximum by lengthening the pulse. However, excessively long pulses, or resorting to higher energy levels, cause vaporization that results in rougher surfaces. Conduction welds can be made by either continuous or pulsed power. For a given average power, however, enhanced pulsing produces deeper penetration because of the higher initial power "spikes" on each pulse.

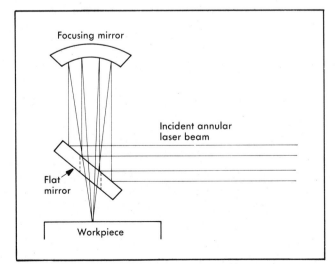

Fig. 9-81 Mirror system for laser beam welding.[18]

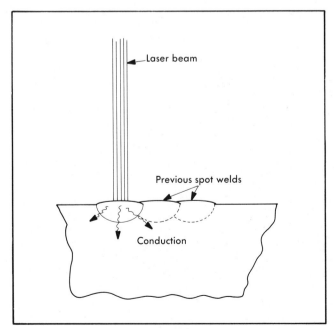

Fig. 9-82 Laser weld formed by conduction. (*IITRI Laser Center*)

LASER BEAM WELDING

Typical pulsed linear welding speeds are 20-60 (508-1524 mm/min), using an overlap of more than 50% on each spot. This requires very rapid pulsing. Increasing the rate of pulsing, however, requires a reduction in pulse duration, which determines penetration. Thus, fast welds made at high repetition rates are also shallow welds and vice versa. Most conduction welds are achieved with pulsed beams. Pulsed conduction welds are employed for their restricted heat-affected zone and uniform, smooth surfaces.

Deep-penetration keyhole welds. As laser power approaches or exceeds 1 kW, it is possible to generate vapor to form a cavity (keyhole) in the molten pool (see Fig. 9-83). With this mode, energy can be introduced to a much greater depth than is possible with conduction welding. However, considerably more energy and consequent disturbance of the metal are encountered. Weld depths of 5/8" (16 mm) are being routinely achieved at power levels of 15 kW using the keyhole method.

The molten mass acts as an efficient energy absorber; surface finish, intrinsic reflectivity, or the presence of absorbing films have little effect on the process. Keyhole welds are made with a continuous (CW) beam, and a minimum forward speed must be maintained to move molten metal around the cavity to the pool at the rear of the weld. Otherwise, the keyhole cannot be held open by the vapor, and the process is not effective. Periodic collapse of the cavity with attendant voids will occur if:

- the beam does not penetrate through the metal and exit from the underside,
- the process speed becomes irregular, or
- the process encounters a change in thermal conditions.

A change in thermal conditions is most often encountered when closing a circumferential weld. It is overcome by gradually increasing power as the weld is started so that a gradual increase in penetration occurs. Upon closeout, the process is carried past the startup region. Then the power is gradually reduced to the conduction-limited condition, where there is no cavity to form a void upon termination of the process. This increase and subsequent decrease of power is termed ramping.

Effect of focus. As the mode of welding changes from conduction to keyhole, the depth to which energy is delivered within the workpiece increases. Under keyhole conditions, the role of focal point placement becomes more important and less straightforward.

A survey of speed effects on penetration at several focal point placements provides a technique for establishing the best focal point (see Fig. 9-84). These are usually conducted on the basis of full-plate penetration. The presence or absence of penetration is noted for each condition. This permits an instant evaluation of the results of a specific speed-focus combination. Power, gas shielding, and material are held constant.

The most distinctive feature of such a survey is determining the maximum speed required to produce full penetration. This condition is represented by the apex of the full penetration zone. Because of its prominence in the survey, it has been called the benchmark test point. The benchmark condition represents the most efficient focal point placement, but not necessarily the most effective welding procedure.

At the benchmark condition, a tolerance for variance in focus placement is much too small for practical welding situations, and rapid freezing conditions may enhance any tendency to form porosity. The benchmark can serve as point of reference for other, more attractive settings. Knowing the benchmark for several laser systems greatly aids in the meaningful transfer of processes from one machine to another.

Successful procedures are usually based on focus-speed settings significantly below the benchmark, where there is greater latitude for focus placement variance. These are described as "off-mark" conditions. This latitude is accompanied by the introduction of some excess heat into the weld. Excess heat aids in bead contour formation and accommodation of minor inconsistencies in the weld joint.

Excess heat may also reduce porosity by providing the opportunity for impurities to float out of the weld while the metal is still molten. The excess heat may also reduce the detrimental effect of the heat-affected zone of the weld on such properties as toughness. Selecting a reduced speed must be balanced against increased distortion.

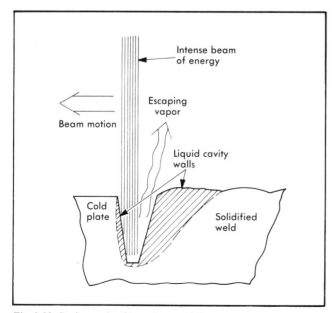

Fig. 9-83 Cavity mode of laser beam welding.

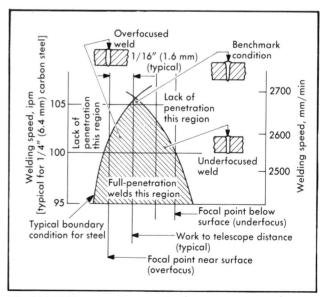

Fig. 9-84 Weld cross sections resulting from benchmark survey.

LASER BEAM WELDING

Selecting a focal point setting that tends to place the focus too near the workpiece surface produces the smoothest weld reinforcement and the least undercut. However, in materials with short freezing ranges, the resulting weld cross sections may freeze first near the top of the metal (see Fig. 9-85). A crack may appear below the surface as the molten metal at the bottom of the weld attempts to freeze in the absence of additional molten metal. Focal point placement high in (or above) the weld is sometimes referred to as overfocusing and is encountered on very thin material where the keyhole is not significantly deep.

A workpiece position that places the focal point further inside the keyhole results in a wedge-shaped weld (see Fig. 9-84). A wedge-shaped weld freezes from the bottom upward, and solidification cracks and some porosity are eliminated.

Interaction of metal with gas. Because laser processing usually occurs at atmospheric pressure, some gas is always present. Typical ambient conditions for industrial laser welding include the following:

1. Inert gas shielding in open air for maximum protection of the metal.
2. Active gas additions to enhance bead wetting.
3. Special gas mixtures in an enclosure:
   a. For extra protection of reactive metals such as titanium.
   b. To seal in a detectable gas such as helium.
   c. To fill the article being welded with a gas that protects components during service.

The sealing of electronic circuits in an enclosure filled with a mixture of gases, such as helium and nitrogen, is an example of the latter technique. The detection of the filling gas aids in finding leaks after the weld is complete.

The role of shielding gas. In all types of fusion welds, the use of shielding gas implies protection of the metal against reaction with the air. In laser welds, shielding gas also determines the amount of beam energy that reaches the work. Figure 9-86 shows the influence of several common gases on weld penetration. Practical shielding systems, except for special enclosures, are subject to some air leakage. Several common types of shields are illustrated in Fig. 9-87. Each must be carefully adjusted so that air ingestion is minimal and constant.

Several of the shields use jets of gas to displace the plasma plume that forms above the work surface. This allows more of the beam energy to reach the work without being absorbed in the plasma reaction that forms the plume. Plasma control must be carefully established and maintained during laser welding.

Selection of shielding gas. Gases used for shielding the weld surface at the point of beam interaction are helium, argon, nitrogen, and carbon dioxide, or mixtures of these gases.

Helium. This gas provides the best penetration for a given power level. It is particularly effective in thick section welds and for eliminating the plume that forms above keyhole welds and disturbs the beam path. However, helium is light and does not readily displace air. Additionally, helium is expensive and acts as a powerful coolant on the weld; excessive chilling increases undercut and porosity.

Argon. This gas provides the best displacement of air. It is used for general shielding purposes on conduction welds. A small percent of argon mixed with helium works well in shields for keyhole welds. The benefits of a small amount of argon to stop air ingestion under the shield skirt outweigh the disadvantage of the increased plume that forms with it. Welds made in argon exhibit less spatter than those in helium or CO_2.

Nitrogen. Nitrogen can be used as a shielding gas in a manner similar to CO_2 or air. Welds made with nitrogen as a shielding gas are relatively smooth and clean. However, because nitrogen is not a completely inert gas, it will be absorbed by some molten metals and can increase the strength and reduce the ductility of the metals, with possible cracking.

Carbon dioxide. This gas (CO_2) can be used with some sacrifice in penetration and an increase in spatter. It greatly enhances metal flow, which produces smooth beads without undercut. Welds shielded with carbon dioxide have a distinct oxide on them, and the gas should not be used on materials other than steel.

Air. Air can be used as a shield. The metal vapor surrounding the weld provides some protection from oxygen and nitrogen. However, this practice is not recommended except where metallurgical quality requirements are minimal.

Equipment Used

Carbon dioxide lasers with continuous wave (CW) delivery of the light are most common for structural welding. Pulsed equipment is frequently used to make assembly welds.

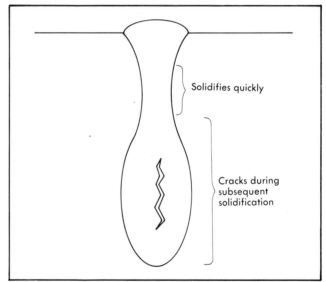

Fig. 9-85 Solidification cracks in overfocused weld.

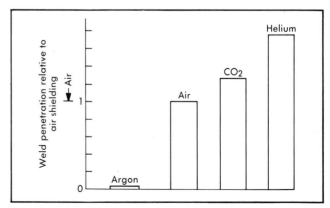

Fig. 9-86 Influence on weld penetration of several common shielding gases.

Both YAG and CO_2 lasers can be used for pulsed welding. When YAG lasers are used for CW welding, krypton-filled arc lamps are used. Carbon dioxide lasers, if equipped for pulsing, need no configuration changes to go from CW to pulsing.

Fiber-optic techniques for delivering the YAG beam are available. Up to four fibers from a single head are available for multiple spot welding. Fibers will transmit 100 or more average watts of power, but some power and beam quality are lost in the transmission. Additionally, the following conventional beam delivery systems are available:

1. Fixed beam, used for movable workpieces and for smaller joints.
2. Movable beam, used for fixed workpieces and flimsy or large, hard-to-fixture parts.

The YAG laser has a relatively large focal depth due to its wavelength and is frequently used for assembly welds. Under these circumstances, the relative beam-work motion does not have to be as accurately coordinated with the workpiece contour as might be the case for CO_2 systems.

Pulsed laser equipment is generally used for close-tolerance, high-quality sealing welds. The Nd:YAG laser systems are more common, perhaps because of the highly reflective materials often welded in sealing applications, but CO_2 lasers can be used for very rapid pulsing and higher welding speeds.

For hermetic sealing of hybrid and microelectronic components, considerable additional equipment may be required as follows:

1. Laser with the following special features:
   a. lens backspatter protection,
   b. ramp timer and ramp-down capability for closeout, and
   c. TV monitor and reticule generator.
2. Motion-package (two-axis minimum):
   a. capable of operating in an inert atmosphere and
   b. flame-retardant covers for ways.
3. Glove box:
   a. capable of establishing and maintaining an inert atmosphere with a less than 1 ppm level of contaminants,
   b. vacuum oven, 200° C (390° F), to prepare component,
   c. dust filters for solid contamination,
   d. moisture and oxygen analyzers, and
   e. antechamber that can be evacuated to permit part transfer.

When welding through glass enclosure for conduction welds (joining electrical wires or connectors), Nd:YAG or Nd:glass lasers are required because their wavelength can be transmitted through glass. These lasers are also preferred when beam manipulation involves fiber-optics or long extensions into confined areas. Otherwise, CO_2 (pulsed) lasers may also be considered. There are materials that can be used for CO_2 laser windows, but they are moderately expensive.

Beam-to-seam alignment. Allowing the centerline of the laser beam to move more than one-half the diameter of the focused beam can result in weld defects. To prevent such defects, careful control is essential. Various seam-tracking methods described for electron beam welding in the preceding section of this chapter may also be used for laser beam welding.

Wire Feed

Most laser welds, even structural types, are made without filler metal. However, as the thicknesses of butt welds increase from sheet metal to plate, the tendency for undercut increases. The surface tension of the pool causes the surface of the weld to pull the pool into a high crown, leaving a depression at the edge of the weld bead. Wire feed can be used in conjunction with a second pass to fill excessive undercut.

The focus of the second pass may be broadened. A ratio of one unit of wire to one unit of travel is typical. Wire diameter should not exceed focal spot diameter. Large diameter wire may be split by the beam if a fine spot is used. Otherwise, the large molten zone on the end of such wires acts as a variable reflector. This molten reflector makes control of the beam-weld interaction difficult.

Wire feed is rarely encountered in assembly welds because they do not usually involve sheet or plate thickness, where wire would be beneficial in overcoming undercut. Wire may be added when assembling tubes or rods. Braze material has been used as filler when joining cold drawn rods or wires. In such applications, lasers are employed to minimize annealing of the work-hardened material.

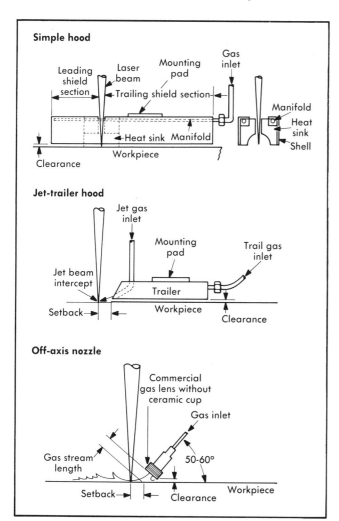

Fig. 9-87 Common types of shields for laser beam welding. (*IITRI Laser Center*)

LASER BEAM CUTTING

Because of reflection problems with wire feed, powder injection into the weld pool is being used for many applications.

Operating Parameters

Welding rate with the laser beam process depends on the relationship of three elements: travel speed, material thickness, and the power density used. The relationship of these three elements for welding carbon steel is shown in Fig. 9-88.

A single pulse of appropriate length is often used to produce conduction welds to join electrical wires or conductors. For automated processes, relative movement between the workpiece and beam limits the rate at which welds can be made. The beam must be held stationary on the workpiece so that the area of incidence is not blurred with a resultant loss of melting capability. Rates of 20 spots per second have been reported.

Short pulses appear to produce the least spatter. Apparently spatter is related to pool stirring, and short welds exhibit only a small, short-lived pool. If such welds are too small, more than one weld may be required. Multiple welds also serve to add stiffness to the joint.

LASER BEAM CUTTING

Laser beam cutting (LBC), like laser beam welding just discussed, uses a concentrated, coherent light beam impinging on the workpieces. The heat produced generally results in melting and vaporization of the material to be cut. However, with some materials, such as carbon, material removal is entirely by vaporization. For most applications, an externally supplied, pressurized gas is used. The process is also used for drilling holes, discussed in Volume I, *Machining*, of this Handbook series.

Applications

Laser beam cutting is being used for both straight and contour cutting of sheet and plate stock, as well as formed components, in a wide variety of materials. Complex contour

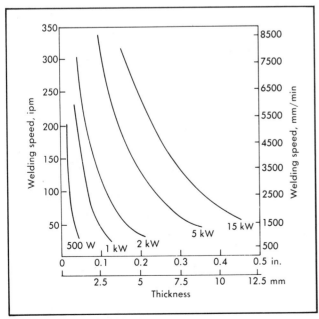

Fig. 9-88 Relationship of thickness, travel speed, and power for welding carbon steel with full penetration.[19]

cutting of cylindrical surfaces is being done by a combination of laser beam movement and workpiece rotation, using NC or CNC for control. Many lasers are being used as an integral part of or as attachments for CNC punch presses.

Advantages

Important advantages of laser beam cutting are that it produces a narrower kerf and a smaller heat-affected zone than other thermal cutting processes. This permits cutting fragile and intricate parts with minimum distortion and provides material savings. Other major advantages include fast speeds, the ability to cut a wide range of materials, and the capability of cutting in locations having limited accessibility. Being a noncontact process, there are no mechanical forces applied to the workpieces and no wear, as with mechanical cutting tools.

Generally, no special surface preparation is required for laser beam cutting, but heavily scaled or rusted metals may prevent cutting. Subsequent finishing of the cut surfaces is generally not required. The process is easily automated, and the use of CNC provides low tooling costs and flexibility in workpiece design.

Limitations

Equipment costs for laser beam cutting are high compared to oxyfuel gas and plasma arc cutting. However, the process is cost effective for many applications, especially if the same equipment can also be used for welding requirements. The process is also limited with respect to material thicknesses that can be cut. While 2″ (51 mm) thick steel has been cut in this way, most metal applications are for thicknesses of 1/2″ (13 mm) or less. Thickness capability depends on speed requirements and the quality of cut desired.

Most applications of laser cutting require the use of a high-velocity gas jet. Cutting speeds possible vary with the power density of the laser, the thickness of the cut, and the thermal properties of the workpiece material. Partial-depth operations, such as countersinking and pocketing, cannot be performed because the process cuts through the entire material thickness.

Cutting Various Materials

Lasers are being used to cut a wide variety of metals, ceramics, and many other materials. The process is especially useful for severing materials that are difficult to cut, such as titanium, tungsten, tantalum, and natural diamond. Plastics, fabrics, leather, and paper are cut faster and more cleanly than with other cutting methods. Rubber, wood, and composite materials are also cut in this way.

Stainless and alloy steels are easily cut, but at slower speeds than carbon steels. Most tool steels, except tungsten high-speed and hot-work grades, can be cut satisfactorily. Aluminum, copper, and other reflective metals are more difficult to cut. Aluminum alloys require more laser energy than steel because of their reflectivity and thermal dissipation. Pure copper is generally not cut with laser beams, but some copper alloys having lower electrical conductivities, such as brasses, can be cut. Beryllium copper and thin copper foil can be cut.

Quality of Cut

Kerf and edge taper. The minimum kerf produced with laser beam cutting is about 0.004″ (0.10 mm) wide in thin metals, and this width increases linearly with material thickness. Kerf width is generally about 0.010″ (0.25 mm) with materials up to about

3/8″ (9.5 mm) thick. Edge taper is usually about 0.5-2°, but this decreases with reduced cutting rates.

Edge finish. The finish of a laser machined edge differs from that produced by stamping. Whereas stamping produces areas of rounding, burnishing, and fracture, laser machining produces a more uniform finish. Typical edge finishes produced in laser cutting various metals are presented in Table 9-48.

Burrs produced. Burrs are produced by incomplete removal of molten metal and metal oxides from the kerf. The tendency for burr formation increases as the viscosity of the molten metal and metal oxides exiting the back surface of the cut increases. Burrs produced in laser cutting various metals are indicated in Table 9-48.

Dimensional repeatability. Part-to-part dimensional repeatability is determined by contributions from the interaction of the laser beam with the workpiece material, superimposed on those from the motion and control system. Molten-metal flow dynamics, residual stress condition of the work material, and cutting path sequence are all significant factors in determining dimensional repeatability. Repeatability in the range ±0.001 to ±0.005″ (0.03 to 0.13 mm) is attainable, depending on the material type and thickness, cutting conditions, and part size.

Mechanical properties. Laser beam cutting produces a thin recast layer with a minimal heat-affected zone. Mechanical properties are largely influenced by the base material properties. Characteristics of the recast layer and heat-affected zone are material and process dependent and influence the mechanical properties. For example, because of the absence of fracturing during laser cutting, the toughness of laser cut steels is higher than for their stamped counterparts.

Process Principles

The laser beam can be considered a small arc, about 0.004″ (0.10 mm) diam. The types used primarily for cutting are the CO_2 and Nd:YAG lasers. Characteristics of these lasers for cutting applications are summarized in Table 9-49. Continuous power is often used for cutting, and pulsed power is commonly used where heat load causes distortion or burnout.

In machining, high-intensity laser energy, greater than 10^6 W/cm^2 (6.45×10^6 $W/in.^2$), is directed onto the surface. A portion of this energy, determined by the material's surface reflectivity at the laser wavelength, surface temperature, and angle with respect to the beam, is absorbed. The absorbed energy is converted to heat, resulting in melting and vaporization. While room-temperature reflectivity values can be high, absorption increases rapidly with increasing temperature. At the melting temperature, absorption approaches 100%.

The relationship between reflectivity and surface temperature is the basis for a threshold effect associated with laser machining. Above a threshold intensity, absorbed energy is sufficient to produce heating necessary to substantially reduce reflectivity and, therefore, initiate surface melting.

Though most metals have sufficient absorption and sufficiently low threshold for efficient laser processing, good electrical conductors such as gold, silver, and copper have excessively high threshold intensities for CO_2 laser machining. Alloys of these metals, such as 2% beryllium copper and brass, which because of their composition have lower electrical conductivities, are candidates for CO_2 laser machining. Because absorption of the shorter wavelength Nd:YAG laser beam by metals, including the good electrical conductors, is substantially higher

TABLE 9-48
Burr Formation Tendency and Typical Edge Finishes Produced in Laser Cutting Various Metals

Material Cut	Thickness, in. (mm)	Burr Produced	Edge Finishes, R_a, μ in. (μ m)
Aluminum	0.3 (7.6)	Substantial burr	260 (6.6)
Brass	0.06 (1.5)	Substantial burr	200 (5.1)
Low-carbon steel	0.03 (0.8)	No significant burr for any thickness	50 (1.3)
	0.25 (6.4)		150 (3.8)
Alloy steel (AISI 4130)	0.1 (2.5)	No burr	110 (2.8)
Stainless steel	0.06 (1.5)	Oxidation resistance results in moderate burr	130 (3.3)
	0.18 (4.6)		250 (6.4)
Titanium, argon-assist	0.03 (0.8)	Substantial burr	180 (4.6)
Titanium, air-assist	0.03 (0.8)	Small burr	120 (3.0)

(*Laserdyne*)

LASER BEAM CUTTING

than for the CO_2 laser beam, the Nd:YAG laser is generally more effective.

Because most material in the cut is melted, in contrast to being vaporized, an assist gas jet is instrumental in removing molten material necessary to produce a quality cut, especially for deep cuts. The gas jet also protects the faces of lenses from backscattered material. For most metals, an oxygen assist gas is used to remove material from the cut. Exothermic reaction of molten metals such as iron and titanium with oxygen assist gas provides additional energy for faster cutting, especially on thicker metals. This not only maximizes cutting rate but improves edge finish. Air is sometimes used as the gas for cutting thin sections. To prevent embrittlement of the edge of materials, such as the refractory metals, or to produce an unoxidized, bright, finished edge, inert gases such as nitrogen, helium, or argon are used. However, in most metals the use of inert gases means reduced cutting rates.

Laser Cutting Equipment

The proper laser to be used depends on the range of applications required. The laser and assist gas must provide sufficient heat input for cutting through the required thicknesses at the necessary rates, while producing the edge, finish, and dimensional accuracy requirements. The beam delivery system for a laser includes the focusing lens, shielding gas delivery system, and joint alignment devices. Flexible, fiber-optic beam delivery systems are also available for Nd:YAG lasers.

Positioning systems. Laser systems for cutting straight, curved, or irregular shapes from flat stock are designed for positioning the workpieces beneath fixed beams. Such systems are often combined with punch presses to permit alternative cutting and punching. Additional information on laser punch presses is presented in Volume II, *Forming*, of this Handbook series. Other systems combine both workpiece and beam motions and can often be used for welding, heat treating, and drilling operations, as well as for cutting.

For some applications, industrial robots are being used for loading and unloading workpieces, manipulating the workpieces beneath fixed laser beams, or positioning the beams (mounted on the robot arms) over the workpieces. Computer control permits multidimensional contouring providing the control system meets the needs for high-speed processing of multiaxis data and for necessary programming, such as teach mode and CAD/CAM program generation.

Controls. Computer numerical controls (CNC) are becoming the predominant control method for laser cutting systems. These units are capable of simultaneous laser and motion system control at the speeds possible with laser machining. Such controls promote process repeatability and allow optimizing process parameters for a given part program. Also, programs can be quickly and easily changed, making the process economical for low-volume requirements.

Other equipment. Requirements for fixture, tooling, and workhandling devices vary with the workpiece configuration and the application. Adaptive control sensors are available for automatic focusing of the laser beam. Exhaust systems are generally required, especially when cutting plastics, to remove the smoke and fumes generated during cutting. Enclosures also must prevent the operator from having access to the focused laser beam or being exposed to direct or reflected laser light.

Operating Parameters

Cutting rates possible with lasers depend on many factors, including workpiece thickness and reflectivity (at the laser beam

TABLE 9-49
Characteristics of Metalcutting Lasers

Laser Characteristic	Type of Laser		Selection Considerations
	CO_2	Nd:YAG* (Pulsed)	
Wavelength	10.6 microns (0.0004")	1.06 microns (0.00004")	Absorption of various materials to be cut
Divergence	Low (2 mrad)	High (9 mrad) (varies with laser conditions)	Minimum focused spot size and location of focal point
Spatial energy distribution	Gaussian (smallest spot size with maximum intensity)	Multimode	Effective beam size and cut width; Gaussian distribution gives narrower cut
Output power	Up to 5 kW	Up to 600 W	Maximum thickness and feed rate capabilities
Peak power (pulsed)	Up to 8 times average level	Up to 40 times average level	Cutting reflective metals through threshold effect
Pulse rate (Hz)	1 to continuous	1 to 300	Cutting rates for given power level
Pulse duration	10 μs to continuous	50 μs to 20 m sec	Peak power

(Laserdyne)

* Information provided is for rod-type Nd:YAG laser.

wavelength), laser power (both peak and average), laser beam diameter, workpiece design, and edge, finish, and dimensional tolerance requirements. The diameter of the laser beam influences the cut width or volume of material melted and the beam intensity. The cutting rate decreases as the reflectivity of the workpiece material increases.

In general, cutting rates decrease exponentially with increasing material thickness. Maximum cutting rates for several metals of different thicknesses, using CO_2 lasers with 1 kW continuous wave output, are presented in Table 9-50. For higher quality edge finishes, the cutting rates must be reduced.

SAFETY IN LASER WELDING AND CUTTING

In addition to the safety precautions required against the hazards common to other welding and cutting processes, discussed previously in this chapter, protection must be provided against the specific hazards inherent with the use of lasers. These include eye damage, skin damage, respiratory problems, and electric shock. Details with respect to safety precautions are presented in ANSI Standard Z136.1, "Safe Use of Lasers."

Eye and Skin Protection

Safety glasses appropriate for the specific laser system used must be worn. Specifications for eye protection are contained in ANSI Standard Z87.1, "Practice for Occupational and Educational Eye and Face Protection." Recommendations for filter lenses are presented in ANSI/AWS Standard Z49.1 and the laser eyewear guide published by the Laser Institute of America. Protection against skin burns can be provided by proper enclosure of the laser beam.

Respiratory Protection

The best protection against possible respiratory problems is to provide adequate ventilation by means of an exhaust system. Regulations issued by OSHA, as well as local codes, specify requirements with respect to ventilation.

TABLE 9-50
Maximum Cutting Rates Using CO_2 Lasers with 1 kW Continuous Wave Output

Material Thickness, in. (mm)	Material Cut		
	Mild Steel (O_2-Assist)	Aluminum (O_2-Assist)	Titanium (Air-Assist)
	Cutting Rate, ipm (mm/min)		
0.014 (0.36)	---	493 (12 522)	---
0.019 (0.48)	516 (13 106)	---	---
0.029 (0.74)	359 (9119)	249 (6325)	563 (14 300)
0.060 (1.52)	171 (4343)	80 (2032)	348 (8839)
0.1 (2.5)	106 (2692)	36 (914)	250 (6350)
0.2 (5.1)	57 (1448)	---	150 (3810)
0.3 (7.6)	37 (940)	---	101 (2565)

(*Laserdyne*)

Electrical Shock

To minimize the possibility of electrical shocks from the high voltages, laser equipment should be constructed in conformance with national standards, such as those from NEMA.

THERMIT WELDING

Thermit, a term commonly used to identify aluminothermic welding processes, is a registered trademark of Th. Goldschmidt, AG, Essen, West Germany. In Thermit welding, coalescence (joining) of metals is produced by heating them with superheated molten metal from a reaction between a metal oxide and aluminum. Although termed a welding process, Thermit welding by definition actually more closely resembles metal casting.

The process offers advantages for certain specialized applications, especially for joining heavy and/or complex cross sections that very often are not weldable with conventional gas or electric arc processes. The most common application is welding rail sections into continuous lengths. Other applications include welding and splicing concrete-reinforcing steel bars together, welding electrical connections, and repairing large components.

PROCESS PRINCIPLES

When finely divided aluminum and iron oxide are blended and fired by means of a special ignition device, the alumino-thermic reaction is as follows:

$$Fe_2O_3 + 2\,Al \rightarrow Al_2O_3 + 2\,Fe + heat$$

It is the affinity of aluminum for the oxygen of the iron oxide compounds that sustains the aluminothermic reaction until completion.

Because no external heat source is required, but heat is generated during the chemical reaction between aluminum and iron oxide, the reaction is exothermic in nature. Because of the difference in density of the final components, Al_2O_3 (slag) and Fe (thermite iron), both components will automatically separate thin seconds (see Fig. 9-89), and the liquid iron can be used for various welding applications.

For technical purposes, alloying elements in granular form can be added to match the chemistry, as well as the physical properties, of the parts to be Thermit welded. The amount of heat generated by the aluminothermic reaction results in a superheated metal that fuses with the parent metal of the parts to be welded, resulting in a metallurgically pure bond after solidification. Besides iron oxide, there are various modifica-

THERMIT WELDING

tions of copper oxides commonly used for technical applications described later in this section.

Depending on the application, elements such as magnesium, silicon, or calcium can be substituted for aluminum. However, characteristics such as the low boiling point of magnesium and calcium, the hygroscopy of calcium, and the high melting points of calcium oxide and magnesium oxide severely restrict the technical use of these metals.

Depending on the size of the granules used, aluminothermic reactions can become violent. This requires the addition of nonreacting constituents. The maximum temperature should not exceed 4500° F (2480° C) to avoid losses due to vaporization of the individual components. Lower temperatures will lead to incomplete separation of metal and slag, with slag inclusions entrapped in the metal matrix.

In general, aluminothermic mixtures in granular form are not explosive and are nonhazardous. Depending on the grain size of the constituents, as well as the quantity of nonreacting components, the ignition temperature is in the area of 2700° F (1480° C). The mixture is ignited by an external heat source.

JOINT PREPARATION

The sections to be welded must be aligned properly, and the faces to be joined must be free of grease, dirt, rust, and scale. A proper gap between the two faces is mandatory, the gap size being determined by the cross section of the pieces to be welded. This gap is surrounded by a sand mold, either premanufactured or made at the job site. The preparation of molds on the job is discussed subsequently in this section under the subject of repair welding.

Common rules practiced by the foundry industry, such as proper venting and the correct dimensioning of risers and gates, are applied when determining the mold configuration. Extra liquid steel must be provided to compensate for volume shrinkage during solidification. Also, turbulence must be avoided as the metal fills the cavity formed by the inner surface of the molds and the end faces.

RAIL WELDING

The oldest and in many areas still the most common device for joining rail sections is the mechanical joint. However, because of low stiffness, the tendency to loosen, and high stress concentration in the bolthole area, such joints are exposed to accelerated damage. Battered rail ends accelerate the rate of track deterioration.

Welding of rail joints requires higher first-time installation costs, but results in substantially lower maintenance costs and longer life for the track structure. Thermit welding is being used by the railroad industry to convert bolted rail sections into

continuous track structures and by mines to convert haulage tracks. Crane rails of all types are also being welded to minimize maintenance and reduce vibration of buildings and structural elements. Furthermore, safer track conditions are being achieved with continuously welded rail.

Welding Without Preheat

Welding with no external preheat, the so-called "self-preheat process," is mainly applied when the joints have small cross sections. The rail ends are preheated by a portion of the molten metal produced by the Thermit reaction. Mold and crucible are of a two-piece design (see Fig. 9-90) and are premanufactured of sand bonded with phenolic resin. The molds are light, non-hygroscopic, and have unlimited shelf life.

After the Thermit reaction is completed, a metal plug melts, allowing the molten steel to automatically flow from the crucible section into the cavity formed by the mold section, thus filling the gap between the rail sections. The chamber at the bottom serves as a basin for the first metal passing through the gap, cleaning and preheating the rail ends. After the basin or preheat chamber is filled, the gap between the rail ends fills, while the aluminum oxide slag remains on top as an insulator.

Welding with Preheat

The Thermit process utilizing an external source for preheating is used for all larger cross section applications because of its greater economy. Depending on the application and the amount of time allowed for preheating, the rail ends are heated to approximately 1100-1800° F (595-980° C) before the steel enters the mold cavity. The Thermit reaction occurs in a separate refractory-lined crucible that is located above the centerline of the molds.

Aluminothermic welding applications with short preheat times require larger amounts of aluminum and iron oxide mixtures than those with long preheat times. The lack of sufficient preheat, which cannot be provided within a shortened preheating time, must be compensated for by additional superheated, liquid steel to provide effective preheating of the rail ends. Figure 9-91 shows the position of the crucible and the flow of material from it into the mold.

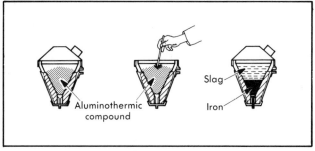

Fig. 9-89 Principles of aluminothermic welding. (*Orgo-Thermit Inc.*)

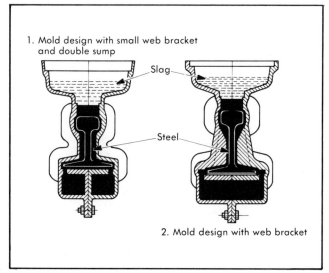

1. Mold design with small web bracket and double sump

Slag

Steel

2. Mold design with web bracket

Fig. 9-90 Self-preheat Thermit welding process. (*Orgo-Thermit Inc.*)

Weld Quality and Strength

Because of the stringent requirements applied to the quality and strength of rail welds, a number of test criteria have been developed to guarantee proper quality control. The most common static test is a slow bend test, where a welded joint rests on two supports and a two-point load is gradually increased until fracture occurs.

A second parameter, recorded during the load application, is the deflection at the center of the weld. This permits conclusions in reference to the ductility of the welded joint. The load arrangement of the slow bend test can also be applied to a dynamic fatigue test where the center of the weld is subjected to a pulsating or fluctuating load.

A simulation of the relative movement between the wheel of a railroad car and the rail itself is accomplished by a rolling load test. A cantilever arrangement subjects the head of the welded rail to repeated loadings from zero to maximum tension stress. The wheel load is adjustable and is determined by the size of the rail section to be tested.

A parameter crucial to the surface wear of the welded joint is the hardness in the weld and the adjacent heat-affected area. Because of the fact that rolled steel (rail) shows a greater work-hardening effect than cast steel (Thermit) under service, the hardness of the weld is set at slightly higher levels than the virgin rail. Under traffic conditions, this difference will eventually be balanced out, the weld and rail structure showing the same hardness and consequential wear characteristics. The narrow band of low hardness in the heat-affected rail section can be compensated for by the proper weld hardness.

All of the testing criteria discussed are designed for quality assurance in a laboratory environment. For testing of welds installed in a track structure, nondestructive testing methods, such as magnetic particle and liquid penetrant for surface defects, and ultrasonic inspection for inner structural defects are applied on a regular basis. Nondestructive testing methods are discussed in Chapter 6.

Finishing of Welded Rail Joints

Because a Thermit weld is comparable to a casting, excess metal such as risers and gates must be removed to obtain the required configuration of the structural parts welded together. Because of automation in the high-speed rail laying process, the manual procedure of hot cutting with special chisels has been largely replaced by special shearing devices. These devices remove the excess metal around the contour of the weld immediately after solidification of the Thermit steel.

With one commercially available machine, two double-activated shear blades approach the weld from opposite sides and shear off the red hot metal. After cooling to approximately 700° F (370° C), the contour of the rail head is ground to the required profile with a special grinder. For smaller applications, as well as all welding of special structures, the excess metal is removed by torch cutting, followed by manual grinding.

REPAIR WELDING

Thermit welding is being used extensively for specialty repair operations, especially those involving the joining of heavy cross sections. Parts repaired in this way include large diameter rolls and shafts; ingot molds; machine and mill frames and housings; and rudder and stern frames for ships. Because each of these applications is different, the molds and boxes, contrary to rail welding, are prepared at the job site to fit the individual joint.

Mold Preparation

With the parts to be welded properly aligned and having the correct gap, a wax collar is built around the gap, between the two weld faces. Once the wax collar is completed—its shape being identical to the final weld collar—a mold is rammed. The mold provides for the location of vents, risers, and running gates, identical to standardized foundry practices. Care must be taken that the wax collar will not be damaged during the preparation of the mold.

Molding Sand

The quality of the molding sand requires special attention. It must have high refractory characteristics, adequate permeability, and good shear strength. It also must be free of clay components having low melting points.

Wax Removal

Once the mold is completed (see Fig. 9-92), the inside of the mold and weld faces are preheated. The heat is slowly initiated to melt the wax first. The wax then drains through a special spout. Afterward, the spout is plugged with sand to prevent

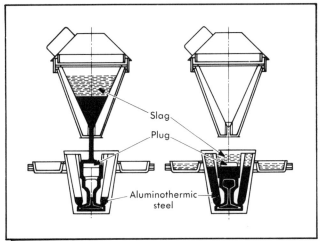

Fig. 9-91 Thermit welding without preheat. (*Orgo-Thermit Inc.*)

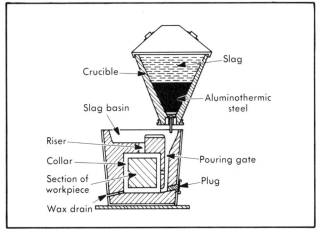

Fig. 9-92 Repair arrangement for Thermit welding. (*Orgo-Thermit Inc.*)

THERMIT WELDING

runout of liquid Thermit during the pour. After complete removal of the wax, the heat is gradually increased to preheat the faces until they reach a temperature range between 1500 and 1800° F (815 and 980° C).

Charging the Mixture

The Thermit mixture is charged into a special cone-shaped and refractory-lined container (see Fig. 9-93) called a crucible. The largest crucible commercially available can accommodate about 1800 lb (815 kg) of Thermit. This means that two or three crucibles must be used simultaneously if quantities exceeding this amount are required to make a weld. The liquid Thermit steel is poured from the bottom through a hole that is secured by special devices that prevent premature tapping.

REINFORCEMENT BAR WELDING

Continuous-welded reinforcement bars permit the design of complicated concrete structures smaller in diameter or thickness than those where unwelded bars would have been applied. Thermit full-fusion welding without preheat is one way of welding and/or splicing concrete-reinforcing steel bars together. Another means of utilizing the aluminothermic process for butt splicing that is finding widespread application consists of filling a metal sleeve with liquid Thermit steel. With this process, a mechanical rather than a welded splice is obtained.

The full-fusion method uses two mold halves, manufactured by either the CO_2 or shell mold process, that are positioned at the joint of the aligned bars and sealed to the bars to avoid the loss of molten metal. The aluminothermic welding mixture is placed in the crucible part of the mold, the mixture being separated from the interior cavity of the mold section by a set of tapping discs. After completion of the aluminothermic reaction, the liquid metal melts the tapping discs and flows into the mold cavity to fill the gap between the bar ends. Arrangements for horizontal and vertical welding are shown in Fig. 9-94. For the mechanical-sleeve bar splice, a graphite mold is substituted for most of the sand mold.

WELDING ELECTRICAL CONNECTIONS

For welding of electricity-conducting joints, the iron in the aluminothermic mixture is fully or partially replaced by copper,

resulting in the following reaction:

$$3 Cu_2O + 2 Al \rightarrow Al_2O_3 + 6 Cu + heat$$

This process is preferably used for welding cables and wires, as well as solid copper or steel conductors, against construction parts, such as steel rails that serve as grounding devices (see Fig. 9-95). Graphite is the most suitable material to use for the one-part crucible mold setup.

SAFETY CONSIDERATIONS

Any moisture present in the Thermit mix or crucible, or on the workpieces, can cause the formation of steam during the reaction. This can cause ejection of molten metal from the crucible. To prevent this, the mix, crucible, and workpieces should be kept dry.

The area in which Thermit welding is performed should be kept free of combustible materials and should be well ventilated. Operators and any other personnel in the area should wear protective clothing such as face shields with filter lenses and safety shoes. When preheating is used, the safety precautions discussed for oxyfuel gas equipment should be followed.

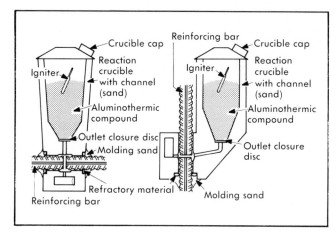

Fig. 9-94 Horizontal and vertical, full-fusion Thermit welding of reinforcement bars. (*Orgo-Thermit Inc.*)

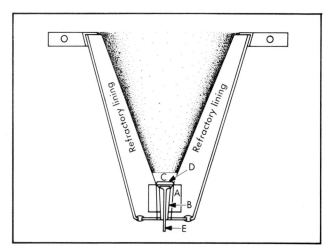

Fig. 9-93 Sectional view of a Thermit crucible: (a) refractory stone, (b) refractory thimble, (c) ground magnesite, (d) metal disc, and (e) tapping pin. (*Orgo-Thermit Inc.*)

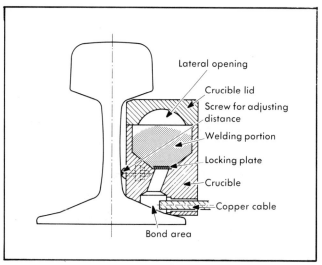

Fig. 9-95 Thermit welding of copper cable. (*Orgo-Thermit Inc.*)

DIFFUSION WELDING

Diffusion welding (DFW) is one of several solid-state welding processes discussed in the remainder of this chapter. As mentioned in the introduction to this chapter, with solid-state welding, workpieces are joined by the application of heat and usually pressure, or by the application of pressure only.

Temperatures produced in the solid-state welding processes are generally below the melting points of the materials being joined. As a result, there is usually no melting, and any liquid metal present is squeezed from the joint by the pressure exerted.

In diffusion welding, the surfaces to be joined are brought together under moderate pressure at an elevated temperature, generally in a controlled atmosphere. There is no melting of the materials being joined, and there is only minimum deformation of the workpieces. The primary mechanism for joint formation is solid-state diffusion.

APPLICATIONS

Diffusion welding is being used in the aircraft, aerospace, and nuclear industries to join high-strength materials. Applications include joining similar and dissimilar metals, often with a thin layer of a different metal (a diffusion aid) between them. In some applications, diffusion welding is being combined with superplastic forming to produce complex components, thus reducing the number of parts required and assembly costs. The process is generally most economical when close dimensional tolerances or special material properties are required.

ADVANTAGES

Advantages of diffusion welding include the following:

1. High-quality welds can be produced that have essentially the same physical, chemical, and mechanical properties as the base metal, with no impairment of the base material's properties.
2. Welds can be produced below the recrystallization temperature of nearly all metals, thus minimizing distortion and metallurgical damage and often requiring no subsequent operations.
3. Weldability is largely independent of material thickness.
4. Many dissimilar metals, not weldable by fusion processes, can be joined.
5. Continuous, leaktight welds can be produced.
6. Numerous welds in an assembly can be made simultaneously.
7. Joints with limited access can be welded.

LIMITATIONS

Diffusion welding is only capable of low production rates because weld cycles are longer than other processes. Equipment costs are high, and consumable material costs are also high if precious-metal fillers and/or inert gases are used. If the diffusion rate of one metal is considerably higher than the other metal, there is a possibility of porosity in the weld. Also, if the metals being joined have a large difference in thermal expansion, failure may occur during cooling of the weldment.

PROCESS VARIATIONS

Diffusion welding may be considered to be a two-stage process, even though the two stages may occur simultaneously.

The two stages are: (1) microscopic plastic deformation resulting in intimate metal-to-metal contact and (2) diffusion and grain growth to complete the weld. There are several variations of the process, the most common being combined forming and welding, and continuous-seam diffusion welding.

Combined Forming and Welding

Forming and welding of superplastic metals and alloys are being combined to produce complex shapes in the aircraft and aerospace industries. Two versions of this method are creep isostatic pressing and superplastic-forming diffusion welding.

Creep isostatic pressing. In this two-step process, creep forming of superplastic sheets is combined with hot isostatic pressing to produce one-piece, diffusion-welded structures. One sheet is creep-formed to the contour of a die, shaped inserts are placed on this sheet, and then a second sheet is creep-formed over the first sheet and the inserts. Diffusion welding of the formed sheets and inserts is then performed by hot isostatic pressing in an autoclave.

Superplastic-forming diffusion welding. In this process, superplastic forming and diffusion welding are combined in a single cycle, using identical process temperatures. Welding is done under low pressure conditions. Forming can be done first, followed by welding, or the steps can be reversed.

Continuous-Seam Diffusion Welding

In this process, workpieces positioned by tooling are fed through a machine having four rollers. Upper and lower rollers function like resistance seam-welding rollers. The side rollers maintain the shape of the workpieces. Rollers and workpieces are heated by electrical resistance, and the rollers apply pressure on the seam.

WELDING VARIOUS METALS

As previously mentioned, diffusion welding is being used to join both similar and dissimilar metals, but the metals must be compatible. The most common application is joining titanium and titanium alloys. Copper, iron, zirconium, and tantalum, which have a high solubility for interstitial contaminants such as oxygen, are also readily weldable with this process. Diffusion welding is also being used to join many composites.

Metals and alloys having low solubility for interstitial contaminants are more difficult to diffusion-weld. These include aluminum and aluminum alloys and iron, nickel, and cobalt-based alloys containing chromium, aluminum, and titanium. Nickel-based alloys having carbide formers and low carbon contents, however, are being successfully welded. Steels are not generally diffusion welded because of the ease with which they can be fusion welded, but they are diffusion welded for some applications.

JOINT DESIGN AND SURFACE PREPARATION

Some of the conventional joints used for fusion welding processes are satisfactory for diffusion welding. However, the surfaces to be joined and the fitup of the mating parts generally require greater care than other welding processes. Acceptable surface finishes require a combination of flatness and smooth-

DIFFUSION WELDING

ness. Cleanliness, including film removal, is essential, and the surfaces must be kept clean until they are welded. For welding, the surfaces must be brought into intimate contact.

DIFFUSION AIDS

The use of an interlayer of an alloy or metal differing from the base metals being joined is common in diffusion welding. Advantages of these so-called diffusion aids, in addition to increasing diffusivity, include scavenging of undesirable elements, providing a barrier layer that prevents brittle intermetallic formations, permitting welding in a less costly atmosphere, or lowering temperature, pressure, or time requirements.

Diffusion aids, however, must be chosen with care in relation to the material to be joined to avoid such disadvantages as decreased strength or stability. A purer form of the base metal is often used—for example, pure titanium for welding titanium alloys and pure nickel for nickel-based alloys.

The diffusion aids are seldom more than 0.010" (0.25 mm) thick. They can be preplaced as inserts or applied as powders or coatings. Coatings can be electroplated, evaporated, or sputtered on the surfaces.

EQUIPMENT USED

Equipment used for diffusion welding is generally built especially for a specific application. The equipment varies with the size and shape of the workpieces, the type of atmosphere to be used (a vacuum, an inert gas, or a reducing atmosphere), and temperature requirements.

One method of diffusion welding is through the use of the static pressure of gas in an autoclave. In this process, the components to be bonded are finished to final size, cleaned to an acceptable surface condition, and assembled in a container made of expendable sheet metal or formed by welding the edges of the parts with a fusion process such as electron beam welding. The container must be pressuretight and is usually evacuated. The whole assembly is then heated in an autoclave containing a high-pressure gas, and the static pressure of the gas is trans-

mitted uniformly throughout the assembly. The mating surfaces are held under pressure long enough to permit diffusion between the components. Excellent dimensional control can be achieved, and, because only a small amount of deformation is required, brittle materials can be bonded.

Diffusion welding is also done in presses equipped with means for heating (radiant, induction, or resistance heating, or heated platens) and often with a protective atmosphere chamber around the weldment. The process is also performed in conventional furnaces with loading applied by press platens in the enclosures. Diffusion spot welds are also produced between sheet metal parts on resistance welding machines.

Differential expansion is also used for diffusion welding. The components to be joined are enclosed in a material with a lower linear coefficient of thermal expansion, and the assembly is heated. Because the enclosing material expands less than the components, it produces pressure at the joint interface and causes bonding.

Diffusion welding of small areas is also performed in die sets. It may be difficult to keep the parts of a hot die aligned for large areas, but if a soft metal such as copper is used in one of the dies, it will produce uniform pressure over the bonding faces.

OPERATING PARAMETERS

Diffusion welding depends on three interrelated parameters: time, temperature, and pressure. All these parameters work together to achieve the intimate contact required for the diffusion process to take place. Elevated temperature also serves the important function of increasing the surface energy—hence the mobility—of the atoms. Each of the parameters can be varied and controlled to meet specific material and job requirements.

Time cycles for diffusion welding range from less than one minute to several hours, depending primarily on the materials being joined. Welding temperatures are generally equal to or greater than one-half the melting temperature of the metals being joined. Pressures vary from atmospheric to 30 ksi (207 MPa) or more.

FRICTION WELDING

Friction welding (FRW) is a solid-state joining process that produces coalescence in metals or nonmetals using the heat developed between two surfaces by a combination of mechanically induced rubbing motion and applied load. Mechanical energy is directly converted to thermal energy at the joint interface. Under normal conditions, the faying surfaces do not melt. Filler metal, flux, and shielding gas are not required with this process, but shielding gas is sometimes used for welding reactive metals.

APPLICATIONS

Friction welding has been established in all areas of metalworking. Typical applications include the following:

- Automotive industry:
    Engine valves, driveshafts, steering shafts, transmission shafts, gears, clutch components, turbochargers,

fan-clutch shafts, air conditioning clutch housings, and struts.
- Truck and agricultural industries:
    Track rollers, hydraulic piston rods, pin assemblies, cluster gears, axle housings, and power takeoff shafts.
- Aerospace and aircraft industries:
    Compressor rotors, fan shafts, cluster gears, rivets, driveshafts, propeller hub extensions, drag braces for landing gears, rocket-engine injector posts, helicopter main-rotor shafts, and fuel cell ports.
- Oil and gas industries:
    Drill pipe-to-tool joints, sucker rods, pump shafts, manifold or surface pipe to connections, and high-pressure valve flanges.
- Miscellaneous:
    Copper-aluminum electrical connectors, bimetallic electric motor shafts, bimetallic outboard motor shafts,

drills, reamers, hubs to pulleys, socket wrenches, bomb fuse housings, hydraulic pump pistons, bicycle forks, aluminum-steel anodes, steel-steel anodes, and printing press rollers.

ADVANTAGES

Important advantages of friction welding include the suitability of the process for joining a wide variety of dissimilar metal combinations, short cycle times, and adaptability to automation for mass production applications. Joints produced are generally as strong as the base metals, and, because the heat is localized at the interface, only a narrow heat-affected zone results. Surface preparation and cleanliness are less critical than for other solid-state welding processes, and power requirements are less than for flash welding.

Friction welding can sometimes be performed on finish machined parts, maintaining common manufacturing tolerances. The process is being used to replace large, long, costly forgings with bar stock welded to smaller forgings, thus reducing costs.

LIMITATIONS

A possible limitation to the use of rotational friction welding is that one of the components must be capable of being rotated about its axis, and the weld interface should generally be axially symmetric (circular). It is not necessary that both pieces be of the same cross-sectional shape throughout; for example, small diameter shafts can be welded to large square or rectangular plates or irregular-shaped forgings. Initial equipment costs for friction welders are generally higher than for flash or upset welders, but return on investment can be rapid. Also, alignment of workpieces after welding (axial displacement) can cause a problem if finished parts are to be welded.

PROCESS VARIATIONS

The friction welding process can be classified into two main energy variations and five motion variations (see Fig. 9-96). Historically, the most widely used system in the United States has been the inertia friction welding or flywheel friction welding process, while the direct-drive friction welding process has been used primarily in Europe, the USSR, and Japan; however, the direct-drive process is gaining in popularity in the U.S. Any energy system may be used with any motion system.

About 99% of all friction welding machines employ the rotational method. With this method, one component is rotated relative to and in contact with the mating face of the other component to generate heat. The other relative motion variations of friction welding are as follows:

- Radial. A method in which one component is rotated relative to and in contact with one or more other components. The contact faces or faying surfaces are the OD of one component(s) and the ID of the other component(s).
- Orbital. A method in which one component is moved in a small circular motion relative to and in contact with the mating face of another component. Either both components rotate about their own axis, with their axes displaced, or neither component rotates about its own axis, and the components move in an orbital motion to each other. This method allows the joining of nonround components and the radially oriented joining of round or nonround components.

- Angular oscillating. A method in which one component is moved in an angular oscillating motion about its own axis and in relative contact with the mating face of another component.
- Linear reciprocating. A method in which one component is moved linearly in a reciprocating motion relative to and in contact with the mating face of the other part.

OPERATING PRINCIPLES

The principles of operation for friction welding vary with the energy source (inertia, direct-drive, or hybrid) and the motions used (rotational, linear reciprocating, angular oscillating, radial, or orbital).

Rotational Friction Welding

Friction welding in production is normally an automatic welding process. The basic steps in rotational friction welding are illustrated in Fig. 9-97. First, one workpiece is rotated, and the other is held stationary (view *a*). The two workpieces are then brought together under an axial compressive force (friction welding force), as shown in view *b*.

Rubbing of the faying surfaces heats the workpieces locally, and upsetting (change in length) begins (Fig. 9-97, view *c*). Then, once the proper interface temperature is reached, the rotating piece is abruptly stopped to complete the process by forging the two pieces together. The forging phase is responsible for most of the upsetting of the material (view *d*). The weld produced is characterized by the absence of a fusion zone, the narrow heat-affected zone, and the presence of plastically

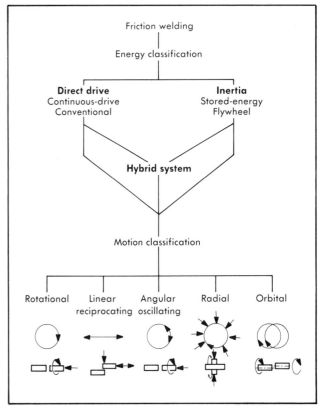

Fig. 9-96 Classification of friction welding process variations. (*Manufacturing Technology, Inc.*)

FRICTION WELDING

deformed material around the weld (flash). Weld quality is dependent on the proper selection of the material, joint design, welding variables, and postweld processes.

Inertia Friction Welding

In the inertia friction welding variation, one of the workpieces is connected to a flywheel, and the other is restrained from rotating. The flywheel is accelerated to a predetermined rotational speed, storing the energy required for welding. The drive motor is disengaged, and the workpieces are forced together by the friction welding force. This causes the faying surfaces to rub together under pressure.

Kinetic energy stored in the rotating flywheel is dissipated as heat, through friction at the weld interface, causing the flywheel speed to decrease. An increase in friction welding force (forge force) may be applied before rotation stops. The forge force is maintained for a predetermined time after rotation ceases. The relationship between the inertia friction welding parameter characteristics appears in Fig. 9-98.

Direct-Drive Friction Welding

In the direct-drive variation of friction welding, one of the workpieces is attached to a motor-driven unit, while the other is restrained from rotation. The motor-driven workpiece is generally rotated at a predetermined constant speed, and the workpieces to be welded are forced together by a friction welding force. For some applications, it is beneficial to vary the speed during welding. Heat is generated as the faying surfaces (weld interfaces) rub together. This continues for a predetermined time or until a preset amount of upset takes place.

The rotational driving torque is then discontinued, and the rotating workpiece is stopped by the application of a braking force. The welding force is maintained or increased to a forging force for a predetermined time after rotation ceases. The

relationship between parameter characteristics for direct-drive friction welding is shown in Fig. 9-99.

Hybrid Systems

Hybrid systems combine some features from both inertia and direct-drive welding processes. One method for a direct-drive friction welder is to vary the braking point or not to brake the spindle to zero before applying the forge force. In this way the rotating spindle chuck assembly dissipates its kinetic energy during the forge cycle in a similar fashion as an inertia friction welder. This rotating forging action can be increased by adding flywheels to the chuck assembly. Another method is to use a d-c drive system for a direct-drive friction welder and simulate, with a speed and power program, the inertia or power input during the forge phase.

Friction surfacing is a method in which a rod is rotated relative to and in contact with another component (see Fig. 9-100). Both components also move relative to each other in linear motion. As a result, a plasticized layer of rod material is deposited on the surface of the second component.

WELDING VARIOUS MATERIALS

Most of the metals and alloys that can be friction welded are listed in Table 9-51. Many more combinations can be welded with various degrees of success. As a general rule, materials that are good, dry bearing materials or that exhibit hot shortness

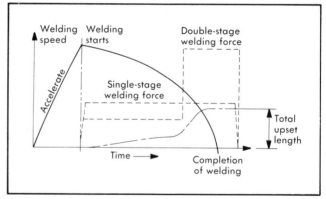

Fig. 9-98 Inertia friction welding using single or double-stage welding force.

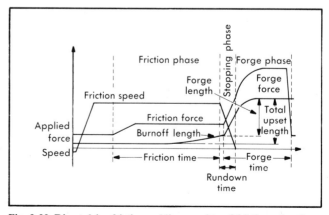

Fig. 9-99 Direct-drive friction welding consists of friction, stopping, and forge phases.

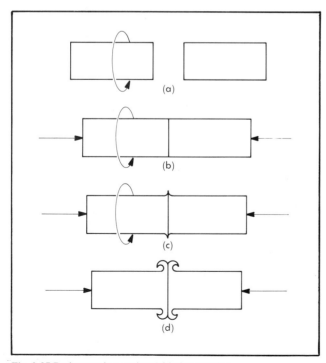

Fig. 9-97 Basic steps in rotational friction welding.

TABLE 9-51
Metals Joined by Friction Welding

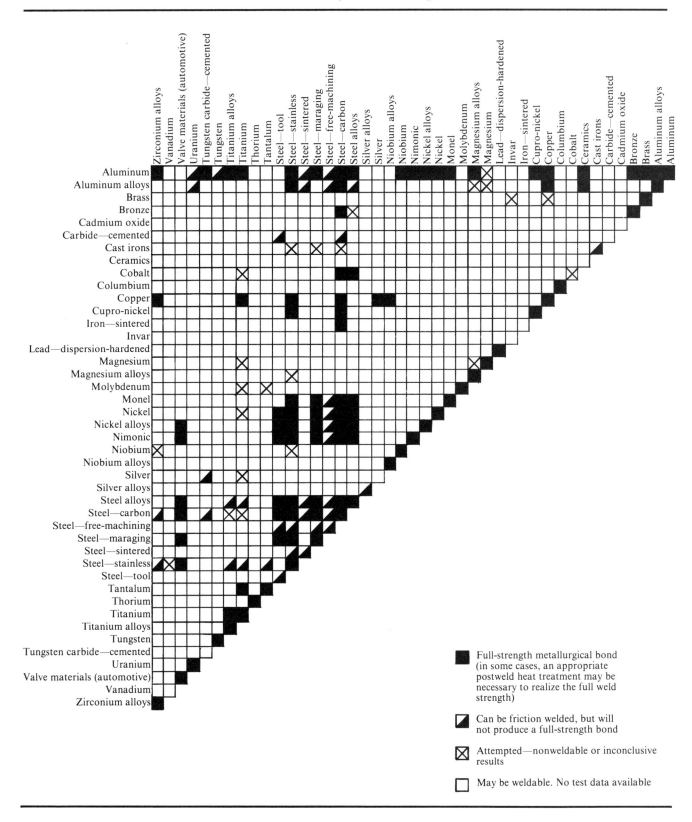

Full-strength metallurgical bond (in some cases, an appropriate postweld heat treatment may be necessary to realize the full weld strength)

Can be friction welded, but will not produce a full-strength bond

Attempted—nonweldable or inconclusive results

May be weldable. No test data available

FRICTION WELDING

cannot be friction welded. Cast iron, for example, cannot be friction welded because any incipient bonding that occurs is so brittle that it has no commercial value. Also, materials with high directional properties will produce poor welds.

Generally, at least one of the weld members must be forgeable at the welding temperature if it is to be successfully friction welded. Weld interface temperatures usually reach a value within a few hundred degrees of the melting temperature of the lower-melting metal. Some plastics are joined by the friction welding process.

JOINT DESIGN AND PREPARATION

The nature of friction welding requires that the joint face of at least one of the members to be joined be essentially round. Also, the revolving member should be somewhat concentric in shape, as it must be rotated at relatively high speed.

Basic joint designs consist of combinations of bars and tubes to themselves or to a plate as illustrated in Fig. 9-101. Some special joint designs, multiple concentric joints and taper joints, are shown in Fig. 9-102.

Noncircular members have been successfully welded, but the flash produced is very rough and unsymmetrical, presenting problems if it must be removed. For noncircular joints, the mating member must have a joint surface that encompasses the full interface of the noncircular member during rotation. Some welds between dissimilar metals of widely different forging temperatures or thermal diffusivity values require relative size adjustments at the interface to produce the proper balance of forging and upsetting of each member (see Fig. 9-103).

Joint surface preparation for most materials is not critical, because the original abutting surfaces for most welds are completely forged away in the process. Sheared, flame-cut, and sawed surfaces are usually satisfactory, provided that adequate weld energy is used to correct for out of squareness. Center projections such as those that are produced by cutoff tools present no problem.

Pilot holes or concave surfaces should be avoided, as they entrap air and oxides in the weld. Degreasing or removal of light oxide is not necessary, but heavy forge or mill scale should be removed. Scale acts as a bearing surface and sometimes cannot be flashed out of the weld interface. Similarly, carburized, nitrided, and plated surfaces should be avoided.

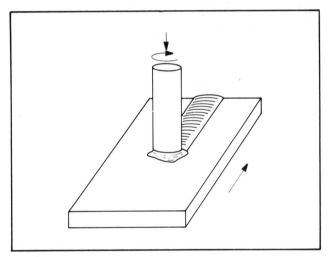

Fig. 9-100 Friction surfacing.

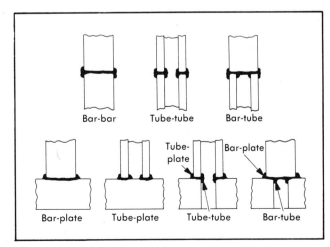

Fig. 9-101 Basic joint designs for friction welding.

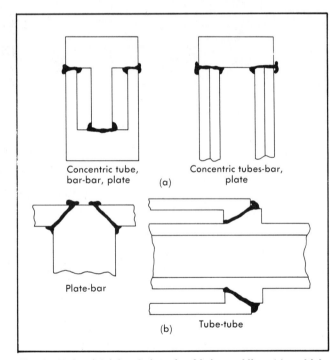

Fig. 9-102 Special joint designs for friction welding: (a) multiple concentric and (b) taper.

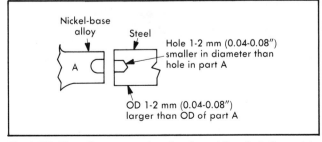

Fig. 9-103 Size adjustments at interface for welding dissimilar metals having different thermal diffusivity values.

When welding two different materials with widely varying mechanical properties, such as aluminum to steel or copper, joint preparation is critical. The weld contact face of the harder of the two materials must be machined prior to welding and must be square to its rotational axis. The softer material (aluminum in this example) must be cleaned either by normal or abrasive machining or by chemically removing the oxides and surface contaminations prior to welding.

WELD STRENGTH

Friction welds are not affected by some of the factors that lower weld strengths in fusion welds, such as cast structures, coarse grain size, and atmospheric contaminations. As a result, the fatigue strengths of friction welds will usually approach or match those of the weakest of the parent materials after the welds have received the recommended heat treatment.

Weld strength will decrease due to the reorientation of flow lines in the weld zone in materials that exhibit high directional properties, such as free-machining steels or steels containing large amounts of nonmetallic inclusions. Also, a reduction in strength is apparent if the weld zone is carburized and hardened or if carburized and hardened parts are welded to each other.

PREWELD AND POSTWELD HEAT TREATMENT

Good metallurgical judgment will generally dictate when preweld and postweld heat treatments are required. The friction weld zone is subject to "mass quench" effect, which may be as severe as a water quench. The need for postweld heat treatment is affected by several variables, including material hardenability, joint geometry, and weld parameters. Residual heat from the welding operation is normally considered beneficial to lessen the effect of mass quenching of hardenable steels. However, too much retained heat may present problems, such as with previously hardened bearing surfaces adjacent to the weld zone.

For a large class of ferrous materials, such as carbon, alloy, and tool steels, plus the 400 Series stainless steels, quenching develops hardness. Rapid cooling of this family of steels forms martensite. Stress relieving or tempering may be required to relieve residual stresses and/or to reduce hardness levels in the weld and heat-affected zone. This is normally done to create desired mechanical properties of the weld zone. When materials of this class are friction welded, hardness of the weld zone will be affected by carbon and alloy content, geometry of the weld interface and adjacent surfaces, and weld parameters. As a general guideline, stress relieving or tempering may be necessary for materials with hardenability greater than AISI 1035 steel.

Because friction welding is a solid-state joining process, the heat-affected zone responds to heat treatment in the same way that the non-heat-affected material remote from the weld zone responds. A postweld quench-and-temper heat treatment will produce uniform grain size and hardness through the weld area and parent material.

Age-hardening materials are in a soft condition after quenching. Normal heat treatment to produce high strength with useful ductility starts with solution heat treating, which includes quenching in air or liquid. A subsequent aging process develops strength and hardness. Included in this class of materials are:

Precipitation-hardening stainless steels, such as 17-4PH
Maraging steels, such as Vascomax 250, made by Vanadium-Alloys Steel Co.

Aluminum alloys, such as AA6061 and AA2024
Nickel alloys, such as Inconel 713C, made by International Nickel Co.
Alpha-beta titanium alloys, such as 6A1-4V titanium
Magnesium alloys, such as AZ80A

These materials may be friction welded before or after heat treatment, but in either case the weld zone will be in the soft solution-treated condition. To develop high strength, postweld aging is required.

With materials that are strengthened by cold working, the metal grains are permanently deformed without formation of new grains. The significant increase in hardness and strength can be related directly to the amount of cold working. Copper and copper alloys, cobalt-base alloys, and austenitic stainless steels are included in this class. Prior cold working is eliminated in the weld zone. When dissimilar materials are welded, joint geometry, chemical composition, and heat conductivity of all components must be considered to determine whether postweld treatment is needed.

Thermal treatment of friction welded joints is not always limited to postweld treatment. Component parts are sometimes heated before welding, usually for the purpose of slowing the cooling rate to help control the effect of mass quench after welding. This method can be used when component parts are of unequal mass, such as a high-hardenability, thin-wall tube to a thick plate section.

MACHINES USED

There is virtually no upper limit with respect to friction welding large sections. The limitations are commercial rather than technical. Present machine models come in many different sizes and configurations—horizontal, vertical, single-spindle, and dual or multiple-spindles, synchronized with or without workpiece orientation.

Available commercial machines have weld capacities ranging from 1 to 50 000 mm^2 (0.002 to 77.5 in.^{2}) of weld area, based on low-carbon steel, SAE 1018. Known direct-drive friction welders range from micro machines to ones with 300 ton (2670 kN) forge force. Known inertia friction welders range from micro machines to ones with 700 ton (6200 kN) forge force. There is no limit as to the size that can be produced for either direct-drive or inertia systems.

Machine monitors can range from simple upset or loss-of-length monitors, which measure the output of a friction welding machine, to a computer system that digitally checks, compares, records, and if necessary, makes a hard copy of all input and output variables of the welding machine. The choice of which monitor to use is based on the application. Highly critical parts for the aerospace industry obviously require all functions be monitored, while noncritical parts may require no monitor.

Monitoring of the rate of loss of length, which relates directly to the heat or energy input, is being used successfully in production for direct-drive friction welders. In inertia friction welding, the weld torque can be measured directly from the deceleration rate of the spindle or by monitoring the motor load.

OPERATING PARAMETERS

The basic parameters for inertia and direct-drive friction welding are listed in Table 9-52. Depending on the materials welded and/or the type of machine used, additional parameters may be important. For inertia friction welding, these additional parameters include forge force and dwell time (the time after

FRICTION WELDING

TABLE 9-52
Basic Variables for Inertia and
Direct-Drive Friction Welding Processes

Inertia	Direct-Drive
Input:	Input:
Spindle inertia (flywheel)	Spindle speed (rpm)
Spindle speed (rpm)	Force
Force	Reduction in length
Output:	Output:
Weld time	Weld time or upset*
Upset	

* If weld time is used as an input control, upset (loss of length) is an output; if upset is used as an input control, weld time is an output.

rotation has stopped and during which force is still applied). For direct-drive friction welding, additional parameters include preheat time, preheat force, and declutch and brake time.

All friction welding systems use relative velocity, axial pressure, and time for heating as the three principal parameters to control the weld quality. Sound welds can be produced with most material combinations using a wide range of process parameters. In particular, the welding of low-carbon steel is possible using surface speeds from 360 to 3000 sfm (110 to 914 m/min). Forge pressure for this material can vary from 10 to 25 ksi (69 to 172 MPa). The heating or friction pressure in direct-drive friction welding is usually 40-60% of the forge pressure.

Direct-Drive Friction Welding

The weld heating cycle in direct-drive friction welding is determined by the area and diameter to be welded. There are discrete pressures per unit area to be used during the heating cycle and a loss of length parameter that is controlled and monitored. The two fundamental variables are pressure (force) and loss of length. A third variable on some machines is rotary speed, but because most direct-drive machines are single-speed, this becomes a fixed parameter. Direct-drive friction welding can control the heating phase of the welding either by a timer or a preselected axial displacement distance. The terminology for these two selections is usually known as time or distance programming of the friction welding machine.

Inertia Friction Welding

In inertia friction welding, the flywheel inertia and angular velocity of the flywheel determine the weld energy. The weld force determines the rate of energy consumption. Heating time in inertia friction welding is an output or a resultant of the weld input variables: energy and weld force. Because the weld energy is a function of the moment of inertia and the square of the angular velocity of the flywheels, the flywheel is not a process variable because it cannot change during the weld cycle. Most inertia welding applications use only one welding force, similar in value to the forge force in direct-drive friction welding. Results with changes in variables are illustrated in Fig. 9-104.

Input Variables

Friction welding is a machine-controlled, repeatable process. After manufacturing has established optimum welds, the continued production of sound welds can only be ensured if all the material and machine variables are fixed. The friction welding machine cannot differentiate among incoming materials, and it is important to specify and eliminate variations on the input side. Specifications for materials to be friction welded should include the following:

- Chemical composition.
- Hardness range and heat treatment.
- Weld surface condition—sheared, saw-cut, machined, rusted, or forged.
- Geometric (OD/ID) tolerances.
- Allowable inclusions, such as cracks, laps, and slag.

SAFETY CONSIDERATIONS

Most friction welding machines are similar to lathes and presses and should be equipped with guards, shields, and safety devices. Recommended safety practices for lathes and presses should be followed. Operators should wear protective clothing and eyeshields.

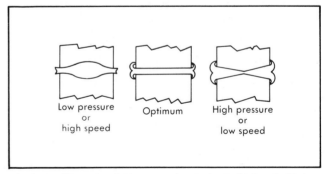

Fig. 9-104 Effect of variables on results obtained with inertia friction welding.

ULTRASONIC WELDING

Ultrasonic welding (USW) is the joining of materials induced by clamping the components together under a modest static force normal to their interface and applying oscillating shear stresses of ultrasonic frequencies approximately parallel to the plane of the interface. The combined static and vibratory forces cause oscillating, interfacial shear stresses between the workpieces, dispersing surface films and other foreign matter so that intimate contact and bonding of the component surfaces occurs. The solid-state ultrasonic welding process does not involve melting of metals nor does it involve the high pressures and large deformations characteristic of deformation welding; the process is accomplished in much shorter times and at lower pressures than those that are required for diffusion bonding.

APPLICATIONS

With increased understanding of the bonding phenomenon, with development of more efficient and powerful equipment, and with continued experience in solving diversified joining problems, the uses of ultrasonic welding have been expanded to encompass the joining of a broad range of similar and dissimilar materials in a variety of conventional and unusual geometric forms, including spot welds, line welds, ring welds, and continuous-seam welds. This versatility of ultrasonic welding makes the process valuable for joining applications that cannot be satisfactorily accomplished by other metallurgical joining techniques. Thus the process has been introduced into an increasing number of production operations in the electronics and electrical switchgear fields, in the fabrication of nuclear reactor components, in packaging, in wire and foil splicing, and in other areas.

Although many metals can be ultrasonically bonded, the easiest to weld are aluminum and copper alloys. Typical applications include foil welding in aluminum and copper mills, wire-to-wire wire terminations, tube-to-sheet welding for solar panels, power transformer wire terminations, field coils, motor armatures, and brush-wire terminal attachments.

Wire Termination and Splicing[20]

Both single and stranded wires are welded to terminals, providing a high-strength, low ohmic resistance joint and eliminating the need for crimping and soldering. Stranded or braided wires joined by ultrasonic welding provide substantial savings in both assembly time and materials and better conductivity than crimped, soldered, or resistance-welded joints. Many wire-to-wire splices and wire-to-terminal joints are made in assembling wire harnesses for automotive use.

Contact buttons for relays and circuit breakers, such as silver-tungsten or silver-cadmium oxide, can be welded to copper or brass arms. If a full area weld is necessary, the button size should be limited to about 9.5 mm (0.374″) diam or equivalent area.

Panel Assembly[21]

Successive ultrasonic spot welds are being used to assemble aluminum panels, replacing adhesive bonding, riveting, or resistance welding. The advantages of ultrasonic welding include minimum surface preparation, no added materials, no complex tooling or fixturing, and low energy requirements. Present equipment is available for ultrasonic spot welding of aluminum sheet up to about 2 mm (0.079″) thick. This limitation applies only to the sheet adjacent to the vibrating tip.

Solar Panels[22]

Ultrasonic welding equipment is now being used in the assembly of solar panels. A microprocessor-controlled stepper motor is used to transfer either the panel or the ultrasonic head. Successive spot welds, each about 23 mm (0.906″) long and 2 mm (0.079″) wide are made between a copper fin and copper tube. Ultrasonic welding is also being used in the manufacture of photovoltaic modules, where ultrasonic seam welding is replacing soldering and spot welding operations.

Transformers, Coils, and Armatures

Ultrasonics is being used for the welding of magnet wire to the terminals of power transformers. Magnet wires that can be ultrasonically bonded without prestripping include polyamid,

polyester, and polyamid-imide. Field coil assembly involves joints between stranded copper wire and aluminum ribbon, and joints between aluminum ribbon to itself and to copper ribbon. All these joints are being made ultrasonically, providing high strength and conductivity.

Automotive starter motor armatures are assembled using automated ultrasonic welding equipment.[23] The commutator has a slotted riser into which pairs of copper wire are inserted. The wires are welded to each other and to the sides and bottom of the slot in a single short (0.35 second) weld pulse. Each automated system permits a production rate of up to 180 armatures per hour.

Ultrasonic Weldbonding

A recent development is ultrasonic weldbonding (a combination of ultrasonic welding and adhesive bonding) used by the U.S. Air Force on aluminum panels for ground support aircraft.[24] Fatigue strength tests of ultrasonically weldbonded panels were superior to those produced by other methods, and the cost savings were considerable.[25] Weldbonding is preferred to either adhesive bonding or spot welding alone where structural strength is critical or watertight sealing is required.

An ultrasonic metal spot welder incorporating power and force programming is required for successful weldbonding. The major advantage of this machine is the potential for significant cost and weight reductions for use in aircraft assembly.[26] Consideration of relative factors such as weight, cost, and utility generates an overall comparison favorable to the use of ultrasonic weldbonding for panel assembly.

ADVANTAGES

In addition to the advantages cited in the applications just discussed, there are other benefits from the use of ultrasonic welding. Low heat input and no melting of the metals being joined results in minimum distortion, and there are no weak cast nuggets or brittle intermetallics formed, as with resistance spot welding.

Power requirements are considerably less than for resistance welding in joining aluminum, copper, and other metals having high thermal conductivity. Minimum surface preparation is required for ultrasonic welding, and welds can be made through certain surface coatings and platings. The absence of an arc and air pollution reduces the safety precautions that are necessary. No consumables such as solder and flux are required, and, because no cooling water is needed, the equipment can be lightweight and portable. Long tool life and consistently uniform quality are other important advantages.

LIMITATIONS

One possible limitation to the use of ultrasonic welding is that the workpiece next to the tip must be relatively thin. A thickness of 1/8″ (3.2 mm) or less is generally preferred, depending on the material and application. However, there is no thickness limitation on the other workpiece being joined. Another limitation is that the process is restricted to lap joints. Butt welds are not possible because there are no means of applying clamping forces and supporting the workpieces.

High capital equipment costs is another possible limitation to the use of ultrasonic welding, but the negligible cost of consumables and welding cycles that are faster than brazing or soldering often offset the initial costs. Ultrasonic welding is generally limited to soft metals; with ultrasonic welding of hard metals, tip wear is faster.

CHAPTER 9

ULTRASONIC WELDING

PROCESS PRINCIPLES

Ultrasonic welding of metals at room temperature produces a localized temperature rise at the weld interface from the combined effects of elastic hysteresis, localized interfacial slip, and plastic deformation. So far as is known, however, in no case involving a monometallic weld made under proper machine settings has there been evidence of melting of the weld-zone metal. Data obtained with thermocouples embedded near the weld interface show an initial rise in temperature followed by a leveling-off. Increased power increases the maximum temperature achieved at the interface; increased clamping force increases the initial rate of temperature rise, but suppresses the maximum temperature achieved. Thus the temperature can be controlled, within limits, by appropriate adjustment of machine settings.

The magnitude of the temperature rise is also associated with the thermal properties of the material being welded. Among one group of materials studied, the highest temperature was produced in the material of lowest thermal conductivity (iron), and the lowest temperature was produced in the high thermal conductivity materials (aluminum and copper).

Measurements made in welding a variety of materials indicate that the temperature does not approach the melting point of the workpieces, and oscilloscope traces show no clearly defined spikes indicative of extraordinarily high temperatures. Typical data for materials ranging from low-melting-point aluminum to high-melting-point tantalum are provided in Table 9-53.

On the other hand, ultrasonic welds in certain materials may show significant effects of the interfacial heat generated during weld formation, and recrystallization, precipitation, phase transformation, and diffusion may be evident. Recrystallization along the interfacial plane has been observed in welds in several structural aluminum alloys, beryllium, low-carbon steel, and other materials, even though the alloys were not in the cold-worked condition prior to welding.

Welds in various solution-treated and aged ferrous alloys show dissolution of the precipitate that is normally found at the grain boundaries. Diffusion between dissimilar metals may also characterize the heating effects. The weld between aluminum and stainless steel, for example, shows a thin interfacial boundary line identified as an iron-aluminum intermetallic.

TABLE 9-53
Measured Weld-Zone Temperatures in Several Metals with Ultrasonic Welding

Metal	Melting Point °C	Melting Point °F	Weld-Zone Temperature °C	Weld-Zone Temperature °F	Percent of Absolute Melting Temperature
Aluminum	660	1220	177	350	48
Copper	1083	1980	227	440	37
Iron	1539	2800	538	1000	45
Mo-0.5 Ti	2610	4730	777	1430	36
Nickel	1453	2645	354	670	36
Tantalum	2996	5425	1075	1965	41
Zircaloy-2	1830	3325	733	1350	48

WELDING VARIOUS MATERIALS

Ultrasonic welding has been used for many years to join thermoplastics. More recently, the process is being successfully applied to welding soft metals, especially nonferrous metals. It is also being used to join dissimilar metals, such as copper to aluminum and aluminum to stainless steel, as well as metals to nonconductive materials, such as the joining of aluminum to ceramics or glass.

Ultrasonic Welding of Metals

Most metals can be welded ultrasonically, but aluminum and copper alloys, as well as precious metals and other soft materials, are the easiest and most practical to weld. Leaded brasses are not suitable for ultrasonic welding. Satisfactory welds are being made in iron and steels of various types, but power requirements are generally higher than for joining aluminum and copper. Successful welding of metals requires the development of dedicated tooling for each specific application.

Joining Plastics

Ultrasonic welding of thermoplastics differs from the ultrasonic welding of metals in that the mechanical energy of vibration dissipated as frictional heat between the faces of the plastic parts is enough to raise the temperature of the plastic above its melting point at the interface. Coalescence of melted material is therefore an important part of ultrasonic plastics welding. Efficient ultrasonic welding of plastic depends on (1) material, (2) joint design, (3) the shape of the part, (4) the distance of the joint from the horn contact surface (near-field or far-field), (5) horn configuration, (6) part support, and (7) energy delivered to the part.

Plastics welded. Ultrasonic welding of plastics requires that at least one of the materials be thermoplastic. Thermoplastic materials that can be ultrasonically welded include acrylics, acetals, polyolefins, polyamides, polycarbonates, polystyrene, polysulfone, styrene acrylonitrile, and acrylonitrile butadiene styrene. Rigid material is usually easier to weld because ultrasonic vibrations are absorbed by a soft, flexible plastic. Filler materials that stiffen the parent plastic improve the weldability of the plastic; glass fiber is commonly used for this purpose, but should be limited to about 25 or 30% glass fiber content. Other additives, however, may detract from weldability either by lubricating the weld interface (mold-release agents) or absorbing the molten plastic that is generated (asbestos).

Joint design. More efficient plastics welding will result if the contact areas between the parts are reduced to a minimum to concentrate the welding energy. An energy-directing, triangular section in the joint area, as shown in Fig. 9-105, melts almost immediately and flows uniformly to form a sound joint. The optimum size of the energy director is a width equal to 25% of the joint width and a height equal to 15% of the joint width, with a minimum height of 0.010" (0.25 mm). If a height greater than 0.025-0.030" (0.64-0.76 mm) is indicated, two or more energy directors should be used instead, with the sum of their heights equaling the indicated height. Figure 9-106 shows several joint designs and design parameters.

Workpiece shape. Symmetrical plastic parts can be ultrasonically welded more efficiently and quickly because they transmit the vibratory energy uniformly to the joint area. Odd shapes can also be welded if they permit the optimum placement of the welding horn.

Workpiece support. Plastic parts to be welded must be held rigidly for good welds. Locating nests are used to place the part accurately under the horn and to provide proper support. Nests are usually made of aluminum or, if the parts are oddly shaped, of urethane-type mold materials.

Plunge welding. In this technique, the workpieces, usually rigid plastics, are placed in a fixture or nest under the horn. The horn either comes down onto the workpiece, or the workpiece is raised to make contact with the horn. This method is commonly used for the assembly of toys, appliance components, automotive lamp fixtures, and instrument cases.

Vibration welding. This process, which differs from ultrasonic welding in that it uses friction to join thermoplastic parts, is discussed under the subject of other solid-state welding processes at the end of this chapter.

Other operations. In addition to welding of plastics, ultrasonics are also used for other operations including staking or heading, insertion, and degating.

Staking or heading. Staking or heading is the process of forming a plastic boss or stud ultrasonically over and/or around other objects for the purpose of securing the two or more objects together. The other parts that are being secured may or may not be plastic material. This method is also used for joining dissimilar plastics. Assembly with this method usually takes less than one second.

Insertion. This is the process of encapsulating metal components into plastic materials by ultrasonics. A cavity slightly smaller than the metal component is either molded in the part or drilled in a nonmolded part. The part is ultrasonically driven into the cavity. During the process, plastic flows around undercuts, knurls, slots, or grooves in the metal component to join the two materials. Certain small cross-sectional metal components may be driven without the aid of a hole or cavity. Assembling in this method usually takes less than a second, and, in many cases, more than one component can be inserted

simultaneously. Screws may also be inserted ultrasonically. When the screw is removed, the threads in the plastic allow the screw to be refastened.

Degating. The process of degating consists of separating molded parts from their runners after molding. This process is well suited for ultrasonics. Many existing techniques used to remove gates have proven too costly and unreliable when a quality appearance is required.

SURFACE PREPARATION FOR METAL WELDING

Workpiece cleanliness is not critical for the ultrasonic welding of metals, but heavy scale and/or oxides must be removed. Welding can be done through some surface films, coatings, or platings, but increased ultrasonic energy is generally required; some films must be removed prior to welding. Readily weldable metals, such as aluminum and copper alloys, can be welded in the mill finish condition, but may require the removal of surface lubricants with a detergent. A good surface finish facilitates ultrasonic welding.

QUALITY AND STRENGTH OF METAL WELDS

Ultrasonic welds generally have a slightly roughened surface resulting from the stresses. Spot welds made in this way are usually elliptical because of tip displacement. A slight indentation is produced in joining flat sheets, especially those made of soft metals. When properly applied, ultrasonics produces welds of high strength, approaching that of the parent metal.

Some welds, such as those in molybdenum-0.5% titanium alloy, show substantial plastic flow in the vicinity of the weld interface. In such a case, the original interfacial plane is completely obliterated and is succeeded by a turbulent-flow pattern. Occasionally, such turbulence may result in expulsion

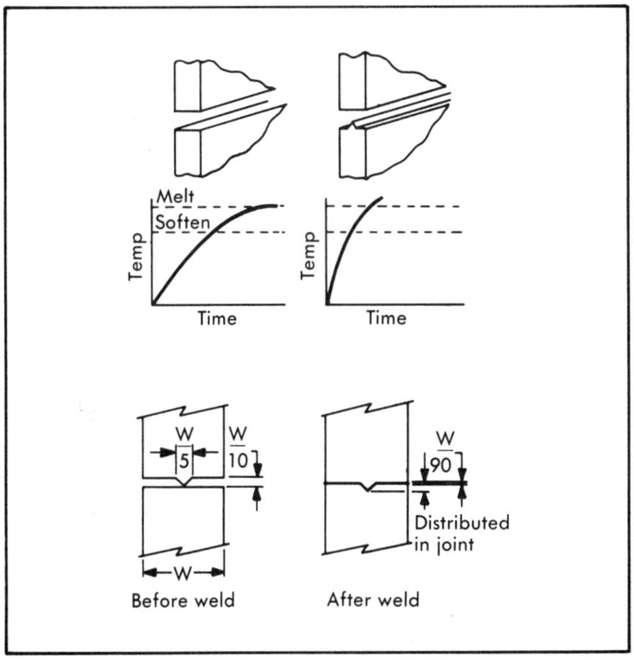

Fig. 9-105 Use of energy directors in ultrasonic welding of thermoplastics.

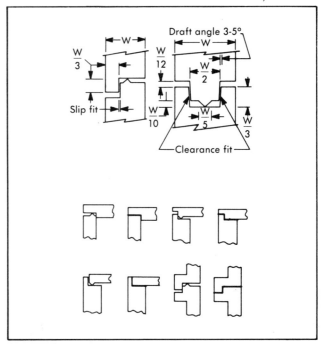

Fig. 9-106 Joint designs and parameters for ultrasonic welding of thermoplastics.

ULTRASONIC WELDING

of plastic metal from the bond zone between the sheets. This turbulence occurs at the weld interface; the areas of metal adjacent to the tip and anvil-contacting surfaces are usually not drastically affected.

ULTRASONIC WELDING EQUIPMENT

Ultrasonic welding equipment consists basically of a frequency converter that provides high-frequency electrical power and a transducer-coupling system that converts the electrical power to elastic vibratory power and delivers it to the weld zone. Associated apparatus includes the anvil, which serves as backing for the workpieces and provides the necessary reaction to clamping force; a force-application device, which may be hydraulic, pneumatic, spring-actuated, or deadweight-loaded; a timer to control the weld interval for pulse welding or a rotating and translating mechanism for continuous-seam welding of metals; and appropriate controls, which usually include a foot switch or palm buttons to actuate the weld cycle.

Frequency Converters

Ultrasonic equipment is usually powered by transistorized converters. The approximate energy required from power supplies (generators) to produce a simple lap-type spot weld between two monometallic sheets has been found to follow a 3/2-power law and is given by the equation:

$$E = KH^{3/2} t^{3/2} \qquad (8)$$

where:

$E =$ energy, J
$H =$ Vickers microindentation hardness number of weldment material
$t =$ thickness of sheet adjacent to sonotrode tip, in.
$K =$ a constant that incorporates other contributing factors

It is possible that K includes the effects of other factors as second-order variables, but it appears to be essentially constant for a given system.

Values of K in the order of magnitude of 100 are appropriate for calculating the approximate energy required from a frequency converter where an electrostrictive transducer is used to produce a simple lap weld between two sheets of similar material. Data obtained experimentally have confirmed the validity of this equation for approximating energy requirements for welding.

Transducers

High efficiencies for transducers are obtainable with the electrostrictive ceramic materials. Barium titanate, for example, with an efficiency of 60-75%, has been used in ultrasonic arrays for various purposes. However, it has not been used in ultrasonic production welding equipment because ceramic elements are fragile and difficult to install in coupling systems on a practical basis. Furthermore, its relatively low Curie point, 120°C (250°F), the temperature at which its electrostrictive properties are lost, introduces a major cooling problem to prevent overheating and subsequent depolarization.

Newer electrostrictive materials, including other titanates, zirconates, niobates, and tantalates, which will withstand high temperatures, have been developed. One of the most effective of these is lead zirconate titanate, which reportedly has a Curie temperature of 340°C (645°F) and an electromechanical conversion efficiency within the range of 70-90%.

Because ceramic transducer materials possess low tensile strength, they must be maintained under compressive stress so that the vibratory stress imposed during operation does not result in tensile strain on the ceramic. The power-handling capability of lead zirconate titanate in thin discs is about 6 W/cm³/kHz (100 W/in.³/kHz), although 3 W/cm³/kHz (50 W/in.³/kHz) is generally a practical design level. Assemblies of this type have been fabricated and evaluated by a calorimetric technique. Typical measurements on a 4.2 kW unit showed conversion efficiencies within the range of 67-89%.

Coupling Systems

A coupling system for an ultrasonic welder must be designed to transmit the vibratory energy from the transducer to the work with minimum energy loss. Such losses can occur within the couplers themselves and also at the interfaces between adjacent members. The coupler material is therefore important; the maximum power that can be delivered through a coupler depends on the mechanical and physical properties of the material of which it is made.

For ultrasonic welding application, it is desirable that the coupler material offer minimum internal friction losses in the transmission of vibratory energy in the frequency range of interest. Such losses are affected by both power level and frequency, with greater losses occurring at high power levels and frequencies more than 100 kHz. For small deformations (low power), the loss per cycle is low because essentially good elastic behavior prevails; at stress levels associated with high power delivery, the problem of internal friction and fatigue failure can be serious if the design is not sound. From tests to determine the energy dissipation in a coupler as a function of peak strain, the curves shown in Fig. 9-107 were obtained.

From the viewpoints of power-handling capability, minimum losses from internal friction, and impedance matching with lead zirconate titanate transducers, beryllium copper and aluminum bronze appear to exhibit satisfactory behavior as coupler materials for ultrasonic welding systems. More recent data indicate that 6Al-4V and 7Al-4Mo titanium alloys and 7075 aluminum alloy may also be superior for this purpose.

The shape of the coupler is another important factor in its ability to magnify the mechanical amplitude of the ultrasonic vibrations. Within an amplitude range of from 0.001 to 0.005″ (0.03 to 0.13 mm) at the coupler, or tip, amplification can be varied as desired by the choice of coupler shape. In practice, the

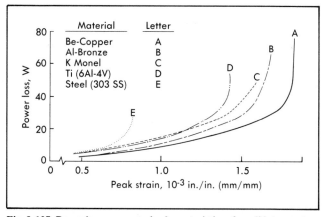

Fig. 9-107 Power loss versus strain characteristics of candidate coupler materials.

shapes, or horns, that are most often used are (1) step, (2) catenoidal, and (3) exponential. Although each of these basic shapes has a different amplitude-magnifying capability, another reason for the choice in horn design is reduction of stress.

Tremendous stresses, which depend on the horn shape as shown in Fig. 9-108, can be built up in the coupler horn. The horn designer must consider the yield strength of the coupler material and not exceed that strength or the horn will crack.

Horns and Tips

Aluminum is a popular choice for plastic welding horns because of its low cost and good machinability. Such horns are often chrome plated to provide better abrasive resistance and reduce marking on the parts being welded. Where high gain and high stress are present, the preferred material is titanium, selected for its higher mechanical strength and longer life. Common tip materials for welding metals are tool steels such as AISI Types A2 and D2.

All longitudinally vibrating tools have a resonant length, usually one-half the wavelength, but sometimes any integral number of half wavelengths. Tools also have a shape that serves to increase the vibration stroke (termed magnification) and to couple the mechanical vibration to a workpiece.

Sonotrodes (horns) are usually designed with the part to be welded in mind. Limitations of size and shape are important to efficient design. For example, sonotrodes greater than 3 1/2 to 4″ (89 to 102 mm) diam will crack or implode because of the stresses of their own vibrational energy. However, by the use of slotting, sonotrodes up to 9 1/2″ (240 mm) diam have been built. Applications of such large sonotrodes should be thor-

oughly evaluated before both the processes and the sonotrodes are designed.

MACHINES USED

An ultrasonic welding machine is designed to operate at a single frequency, which may be any frequency over a wide range but is usually within the range of 15 to 75 kHz. There is no critical frequency that causes welding of special materials or thicknesses. However, because of practical fundamentals of transducer-coupling system design, it is expedient to build delicate, low-powered welding machines to operate at high frequencies (50-75 kHz) and heavy, high-power equipment to operate at low frequencies (15-20 kHz).

Available ultrasonic welding machines are broadly classified according to the types of welds they produce—spot, ring, line, or continuous-seam welds. There are variations in design within each type, particularly with regard to size and power-handling capacity. In addition, designs may be varied for adaptation to specific applications, particularly when the equipment is to be incorporated in automatic or semiautomatic production lines.

Ultrasonic welding equipment is especially adaptable to automation. For example, the welding head without the anvil may be mounted on any rigid structure that will support the workpiece, because all the energy is usually introduced through the sonotrode. This welding head may be mounted in any position, with the tip contacting the workpiece from one side, above, or below. Moreover, because the electrical interconnection between the converter and the welding head consists of a small coaxial cable, the converter may be located at any reasonable distance up to approximately 150′ (45.7 m) from the welding unit. Because the process is carried out without excessive heating of the equipment or the workpiece, the welding head need not be insulated from adjacent processing stations, and the workpiece can be further processed immediately without cooling.

Spot Welding Machines for Metals

Basically, ultrasonic spot welding machines all operate on the same principle, with delivery of shear vibration through the sonotrode tip to the weld interface with a single pulse of high-frequency vibration. The transducing system may be of the wedge-reed or lateral-drive type (see Fig. 9-109), depending in large measure on the capacity of the machine.

Continuous-Seam Welding Machines for Metals

Continuous-seam machines usually operate with antifriction bearings and lateral-drive transducer-coupling systems, with provisions for rotating the entire transducer-coupling-tip assembly. A representative design is illustrated in Fig. 9-109, view d. Vibratory energy is transmitted through the lateral member to the periphery of a disc-shaped tip, which vibrates in a plane parallel to the weld interface. The rotating tip operates in rolling contact with the work along the desired path by a roller-roller system, a traversing-head system, or a traversing-bed system.

TIPS FOR WELDING METALS

The last link in the acoustic energy train is the sonotrode tip, which delivers the energy into the material being welded. Measurements have indicated that transmission across this interface, under suitable conditions, is within the range of 50-85% of the energy reaching the tip, depending in large part on

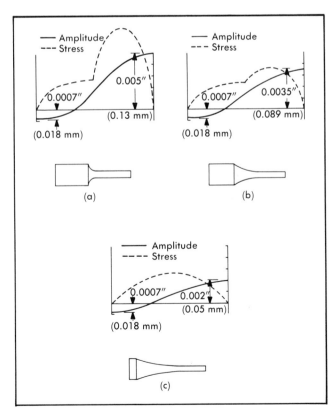

Fig. 9-108 Amplitudes and stresses developed in various coupler horn designs: (a) step, (b) catenoidal, and (c) exponential.

ULTRASONIC WELDING

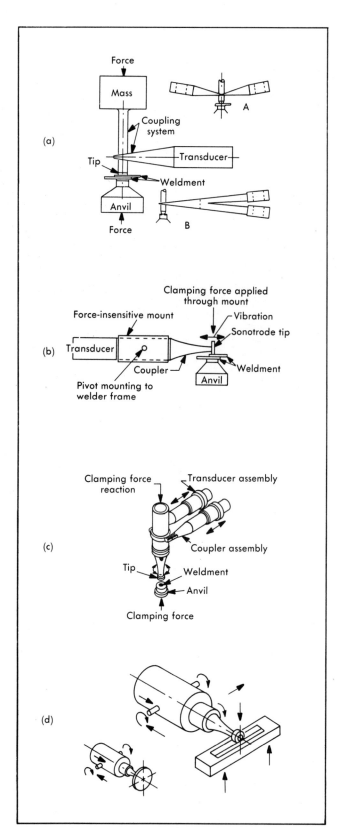

Fig. 9-109 Various ultrasonic welding machines: (a) wedge-reed spot welder, (b) lateral-drive spot welder, (c) ring welder, and (d) continuous-seam welder.

the properties of the weldment material. Impedance matching can be maximized by suitable selection of tip material and tip geometry, with clamping force playing a significant role. A survey of promising materials for sonotrode tips indicates the superiority of nickel-based superalloys.

Sonotode tip radius, while not highly critical as to specific values, is an important general consideration for it affects the weld area and thus the machine settings of clamping force, power, and pulse time or rolling rate. Photoelastic investigations have indicated that the most effective spot welds between flat sheets are obtained when the welding-tip radius is between 50 and 100 times the thickness of the sheet adjacent to the tip. Too large a tip radius results in large unwelded islands near the center of the weld spot and considerable variation in weld quality and reproducibility.

Tips for seam welds are generally provided with a crown radius that is less critical and is indicated in part by the desired weld width. For welding other than flat plane surfaces, such as joining wires to sheet, best impedance matching is obtained when the tips involved are matingly contoured.

OPERATING PARAMETERS FOR METAL WELDING

The important controllable variables of ultrasonic welding are (1) clamping force, (2) vibratory power, and (3) time. Selection of values for these machine settings depends on the weldment materials and material thickness, as well as on the weld geometry.

Clamping Force

The significance of clamping force in making an ultrasonic weld in no way resembles its effect in conventional pressure welding, wherein pressure causes the metal to extrude away from the die locale, greatly thinning the material and surface coatings before metal contact and metallurgical bonding occur. In ultrasonic welding, the static clamping force usually produces no substantial deformation or extrusion. Its function is to hold the workpiece in intimate contact, causing an interfacial stress in the material on which the oscillating interfacial shear stresses are superimposed.

Clamping force is not usually very critical per se, but a reasonably proper value is important for accomplishing a weld under conditions of minimum energy. For any particular welding problem, a proper clamping force permits weld formation at the minimum energy condition (lowest power and/or shortest weld interval). The clamping force operates to effect an impedance match and ensure coupling between the sonotrode tip and the weldment. Actual values of clamping force range from a few grams for welding fine wires to hundreds of pounds for heavier sheet materials.

Vibratory Power

Ordinarily, the power used in producing an ultrasonic weld is taken from a standard 60 Hz electric power line, from which it passes into the frequency converter. Power losses may occur anywhere within this energy train—within the frequency converter, in the transducer, in the coupling members, at the interfaces between these members, and at the tip-work interface. Actual specific values of power delivered during welding depend on the overall efficiency of the transducer-coupling system, the material being welded and its thickness, the electrical input power, and the clamping force.

Welding Time or Rate for Metal Welding

With spot welding of metals, the interval during which vibratory energy is transmitted to the workpieces is usually within the range of 0.01 seconds for very fine wires to about 1.0 seconds for heavier materials. Longer weld times usually indicate insufficient power. High power and short weld times usually produce results superior to those achieved with lower power and longer weld times. Poor surface appearance, internal cracks, and excessive heating result from long weld times.

Power-Force Programming

Ultrasonic spot welding has been carried out with single preset values and clamping forces, the values having been experimentally established for particular materials and material thicknesses. Measurements of the actual acoustic power delivered to the weld zone at any instant during the weld cycle show a variation in delivered power under such constant settings. At the initiation of the weld cycle, there is an induction period during which some slippage of the welding tip occurs in establishing coupling to the weldment. During this period, vibratory power is inefficiently utilized, and actual power delivery may be low. This period is followed by an interval during which power delivery is substantially higher, but toward the end of the cycle the delivered power gradually declines. This poor impedance matching between the tip and the workpiece, particularly at the beginning of the weld cycle, may be alleviated by suitably programming power and force. Power-force programming controls have been devised to provide variation of both power and force in increments of 10% of the maximum preset values, and to provide variation in time of 10% of the total preset weld time.

Energy Control Programming

Systems are available to automatically control the energy or time cycles in ultrasonic welding. With the so-called "energy control programming," the programmer dials in a preset power level, and the welding cycle is automatically shortened or lengthened as required to suit conditions. With a weld quality monitor, maximum and minimum cycle times are preset.

SAFETY CONSIDERATIONS

There are no unusual hazards to personnel in the operation of ultrasonic equipment for welding either metals or plastics. The high voltages involved, however, require proper machine design, installation, and operation, with adequate interlocks, insulation, and other safety precautions. Guards and/or other devices must also be provided to protect operators from clamping forces.

EXPLOSIVE WELDING AND CLADDING

Explosive welding (EXW) is a joining process in which the controlled energy of a detonating explosive is used to create a metallurgical bond between two or more similar or dissimilar metals. No diffusion occurs during bonding, no intermediate filler metal is needed to promote bonding, and no external heat is applied. The solid-state process is also commonly termed explosion or explosive cladding and explosive bonding.

APPLICATIONS

Explosive welding is being used for a wide variety of industrial applications. These include the production of chemical process vessels, conversion rolled billets, and transition joints. Other uses include electrical, marine, tube and pipe, and specialty applications, as well as buildup and repair operations.

Chemical Process Vessels

Explosion-bonded products are used in the manufacture of process equipment for the chemical, petrochemical, and petroleum industries, where corrosion resistance of an expensive metal is combined with the strength and economy of another metal. Typical applications include explosively clad titanium to Monel tube sheets and titanium to carbon-steel clad vessels for use in making chemical intermediates for man-made fibers.

Conversion-Rolled Billets

Large amounts of clad plate and strip have been made by hot and cold rolling of explosion-bonded slabs and billets. Explosion bonding is economically attractive for such conversion rolling because the capital investment for plating and welding equipment for conventional bonding methods is avoided. Highly alloyed stainless steels and some copper alloys that are difficult to clad by roll bonding are practical candidates for plate made by converting explosion-bonded slabs and billets.

Conventional hot rolling and heat treating practices are used when stainless steels and nickel and copper alloys are converted. Hot rolling of explosion-bonded titanium, however, must be restricted below about 1550°F (845°C) to avoid diffusion and the attendant formation of undesirable intermetallic compounds at the bond interface. Hot rolling of titanium also requires a stiff rolling mill because of the large separation forces required to accomplish reduction.

The most notable application of conversion-rolled, explosion-bonded clad material was in the production of United States coinage during the mid-1960s. After explosion bonding of triclad composites, consisting of 70 Cu-30 Ni bonded to copper and to 70 Cu-30 Ni, conventional hot and cold rolling methods were used to convert the clad billets to strip from which 10 and 25-cent coins were minted.

Transition Joints

Use of explosion-clad transition joints avoids the limitations involved in joining two incompatible materials by bolting or riveting. Many transition joints can be cut from a single large-area clad flat plate. Conventional fusion welding processes then can be used to attach the members of the transition joint to their respective similar-metal components.

Electrical Applications

Aluminum, copper, and steel are the most common metals used in high-current, low-voltage conductor systems. Use of these metals in dissimilar metal systems often maximizes the effects of the special properties of each material. However,

EXPLOSIVE WELDING AND CLADDING

joints between incompatible metals must be electrically efficient to minimize power losses. Mechanical connections involving aluminum offer high resistance because of the presence of the self-healing oxide skin on the aluminum member. Because this oxide layer is removed from the interface in an explosion-clad assembly, there is essentially no resistance to the current.

Welded transition joints cut from thick composite plates of aluminum to carbon steel or aluminum to copper permit highly efficient electrical conduction between dissimilar metal conductors. Sections can be added by fusion welding the aluminum side of the transition joint to the adjoining aluminum member. This concept is routinely employed by the primary aluminum reduction industry in anode rod fabrication.

Usually, copper surfaces are mated when joints must be periodically disconnected because copper offers low resistance and good wear. Joints between copper and aluminum bus bars are improved by using a copper-to-aluminum transition joint that is welded to the aluminum member. Deterioration of aluminum shunt connections by arcing is eliminated when a transition joint is welded to both the primary bar and the shunting bar.

Marine Applications

The use of aluminum as a superstructure material in the shipbuilding industry has highlighted the shortcomings of bolted or riveted dissimilar-metal combinations. In the presence of an electrolyte such as seawater, aluminum and steel form a galvanic cell, and corrosion takes place at the interface. When the aluminum superstructure is bolted to the steel bulkhead in a lap joint, crevice corrosion is masked and may go unnoticed until replacement is required. By using a transition joint cut from explosion-welded clad materials, corrosion can be eliminated. Because the transition joint is metallurgically bonded, there is no crevice in which the electrolyte can act, and galvanic action cannot take place. Steel corrosion is confined to external surfaces, where it can easily be detected and corrected by simple wire brushing and painting.

Joints between the aluminum superstructure of the ship and the explosively bonded aluminum cladding usually are made by gas metal arc welding. Mechanical testing, such as tensile, shear, impact, fatigue, and explosive-bulge, showed that the all-welded construction had equivalent or better properties than the more complicated riveted systems. Peripheral benefits include weight savings and perfect electrical grounding. In addition to lower initial installation costs, welded systems require little or no maintenance and, therefore, minimized life-cycle costs. Applications of structural transition joints include aluminum superstructures welded to decks of sophisticated naval vessels and commercial ships.

Tube and Pipe Applications

Explosion welding is a practical method for joining dissimilar-metal tubes and pipes, such as aluminum, titanium, or zirconium, to steel or stainless steel using standard welding equipment and techniques. The process provides a strong metallurgical bond that is maintenance-free throughout years of thermal and pressure-vacuum cycling. Explosion-welded tubular transition joints are used in many diverse applications in the aerospace, nuclear, and cryogenic industries.

Explosion-welded joints operate reliably through the full range of temperatures, pressures, and stresses normally encountered in piping systems. Tubular transition joints in various configurations can be cut and machined from explo-sion-welded plate, or they can be made by joining tubes by overlap cladding. Standard welding practices are used to make the final joints.

Tube welding and plugging. Explosion bonding is used to bond tubes and tube plugs to tube sheets in heat exchanger fabrication. The commercial process resembles the cladding of internal surfaces of thick-walled cylinders or pressure vessel nozzles. Countersinking of the tube entrance provides an angled surface of 10-20° at a depth of 0.5-0.6″ (12.7-15.2 mm). The exploding detonator propels the tube or tube plug against the face of the tube sheet to form the proper collision angle, which in turn provides the required metallurgical bond.

Tubes may be welded individually or in groups. Most applications of explosion welding in tube-to-tube sheet joints involve tube diameters of 0.5-1.5″ (12.7-38 mm). Metal combinations that are welded commercially include carbon steel to carbon steel, titanium to stainless steel, and 90 Cu-10 Ni to carbon steel.

Pipeline welding. Explosion welding methods have been developed to join sections of large-diameter pipe of the kind used in the construction of high-volume oil and gas pipelines. In one method, internal and external-band charges of welding explosive are simultaneously detonated adjacent to overlapped, telescoped pipe ends (see Fig. 9-110).[28] The welding charges are detonated simultaneously by high-detonation velocity initiation explosive charges placed along a leading edge of each welding explosive charge. The initiating explosive charges are each set off by a single detonator.

The velocity of detonation of the initiating explosive is selected so that welding charges are simultaneously detonated around the pipes while maintaining the detonation fronts at superimposed locations and at a large angle to the pipe axis. This avoids unbalancing forces on the pipes and minimizes the collision of circumferential shock waves, thus preventing pipe damage and imperfect welds.

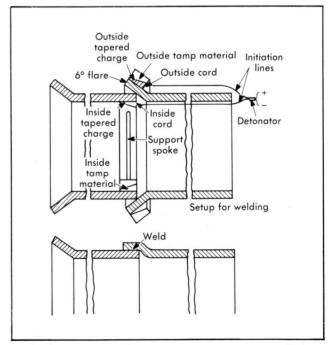

Fig. 9-110 Explosion welding of large-diameter pipe sections.[27]

EXPLOSIVE WELDING AND CLADDING

Specialty Applications

The inside walls of hollow forgings that are used for connections to heavy-walled pressure vessels are metallurgically bonded with stainless steel. These bonded forgings, or nozzles, range from 2 to 24″ (51 to 610 mm) ID and up to 3′ (0.9 m) long. Large clad cylinders and internally clad heavy-walled tubes are being extruded using conventional equipment. Figure 9-111 shows other explosive welding applications.

Buildup and Repair Operations

Explosion welding is also used for the repair and buildup of worn flat and cylindrical components. The worn area is clad with an appropriate thickness of metal and subsequently machined to the proper dimensions. In some cases, the repair can be made with a material that exhibits superior strength or abrasion and corrosion resistance in comparison with the original material. Explosion bonding to repair turbine-shaft bearing surfaces is one example of these operations.

OTHER ADVANTAGES

In addition to the advantages cited in the preceding discussion of applications—combining the desirable properties of dissimilar metals, reduced costs, weight savings, reduced corrosion of joint interfaces, improved electrical conductivity, increased reliability, and reduced maintenance—there are additional benefits that can be derived from explosive welding and cladding. Of major importance are the versatility of the process and the size capabilities.

Process Versatility

With explosive welding, high-quality metallurgical bonds can be formed not only between similar metals but also between those dissimilar metals classified as incompatible when fusion or diffusion joining methods are used. Brittle, intermetallic compounds that are formed in an undesirable continuous layer at the interface during bonding by conventional methods are minimized. More importantly, the compounds are isolated and surrounded by ductile metal in explosion clads. Titanium clad to steel is an example of such a system.

Metals with widely different properties, such as copper and maraging steel, can be joined explosively. Also, metals having widely different melting points, such as aluminum with a melting point of 1220° F (660° C) and tantalum with a melting point of 5425° F (2995° C), can be clad in this way. Metals having tenacious surface films that make roll bonding difficult, such as joining stainless steel to chromium-molybdenum steel, can be explosively welded.

High-quality wrought metals are clad without altering the chemical composition of the metals. Various clad metals can also be bonded to rolled plate that is strand-cast, annealed, normalized, or quenched and tempered.

Multiple-layered composite sheets and plates can be bonded in a single explosion. Cladding of both sides of a backing metal can be achieved simultaneously. When two sides are clad, the two prime or clad metals need not be of the same thickness or of the same metal or clad. A common tube-sheet composite contains titanium on one side, stainless steel on the other side, and carbon steel in the center.

Size Capabilities

Large clad-to-backer ratio limits can be achieved by explosion cladding. Stainless-steel clad components as thin as 0.001″ (0.03 mm) and as thick as 1 1/4″ (32 mm) have been explosion-clad. The thickness of the backing plate in explosion cladding is essentially unlimited. Backers more than 20″ (508 mm) thick and weighing 50 tons (45 t) have been commercially clad. Explosive cladding can be achieved over areas limited only by the size of the available cladding plate and the size of the explosion that can be tolerated. Areas as small as 0.02 in.^{2} (12.9 mm^2) and as large as 300 ft^2 (28 m^2) have been bonded.

LIMITATIONS

Possible limitations with respect to the use of explosive welding and cladding include the following:

- Problems with explosive welding and cladding include the inherent hazards of storing and handling explosives; the ability to obtain explosives with the proper energy, form, and detonation velocity; and the undesirable noise and blast effects.
- Metals to be explosively bonded must possess some ductility and resistance to impact. Brittle metals and metal alloys cannot be used because they fracture during bonding.
- In certain metal systems in which one or more metals to be explosion-clad has a high initial yield strength or a high strain-hardening rate, a high-quality bond may be difficult to achieve. This phenomenon is magnified when there is also a large density difference between the metals. Such combinations are often improved by using a thin, low-yield-strength interlayer between the metals.
- In general, the process is best suited to the bonding of flat and cylindrical surfaces that allow straight-line egression of the high-velocity jet emanating from between the metals during bonding.
- Backer thinness rather than thickness is a limiting factor. Thin backers must be supported, thus adding to manufacturing cost.
- The preparation and assembly of clads are not amenable to automated production techniques. Each assembly requires considerable manual labor.

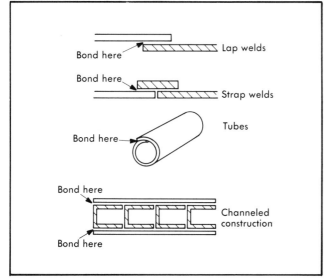

Fig. 9-111 Explosive welding applications.

EXPLOSIVE WELDING AND CLADDING

PROCESS PRINCIPLES

The principles of explosive cladding are illustrated in Figs. 9-112 and 9-113. Angle explosive cladding (Fig. 9-112) is limited to small workpieces. Large-area plates cannot be clad using this arrangement because the collision of long plates is so violent that metal cracking, spalling, and fracture occur. The parallel arrangement (see Fig. 9-113) is the simplest and most widely used in industry.

Jetting Phenomenon

With the parallel arrangement (see Fig. 9-114), a layer of explosive is placed in contact with one surface of the prime metal plate, which is maintained at a constant parallel separation from the backer plate. The explosive is detonated at a point or line and, as the detonation front moves across the plate, the prime metal plate is deflected and accelerated to velocity, V_P, thus establishing an angle between the two plates. The ensuing collision region then progresses across the plate with a velocity equal to the detonation velocity, D.

When the collision velocity, V_C, and angle are controlled within certain limits, high pressure gradients ahead of the collision region in each plate cause the metal surfaces to hydrodynamically flow as a spray of metal from the apex of the angled collision. The flow process and expulsion of the metal surface is known as jetting. The existence of a jet during explosion bonding has been verified by high-speed photography, plated-surface experiments, and witness plate results.

The ability to obtain good explosion bonds is directly related to jet formation. Typically, jet formation is a function of such variables as the plate collision angle, collision point velocity, cladding plate velocity, pressure at the collision point, and the physical and mechanical properties of the plates being bonded.

Experiments have established that there is a collision velocity below which no welding occurs. For jetting and subsequent cladding to occur, the collision velocity has to be substantially below the sonic velocity of the cladding plates. Some cladding, however, can be done at up to 120% of sonic velocity, but spalling is likely.

There is also a minimum and maximum collision angle below which no jetting occurs, regardless of the collision velocity. In the parallel plate arrangement shown in Fig. 9-113, this angle is set by the distance between the plates called the standoff distance. In the case of angle cladding, shown in Fig. 9-112, the preset angle determines the standoff distance and the attendant collision angle. The amplitude and frequency of the bond-zone wave structure vary as a function of the explosive used and the standoff distance.

Nature of the Bond

Explosively bonded metals made commercially generally exhibit a wavy bond-zone interface. Some combinations of metals, such as aluminum and stainless steel, however, exhibit a minimal wave pattern but have good physical properties. Aside from its technological importance, the wavy bond is noteworthy because of the regular pattern formed under violent conditions. It has been suggested that bond-zone wave formation is analogous to fluid flowing around an obstacle. When fluid

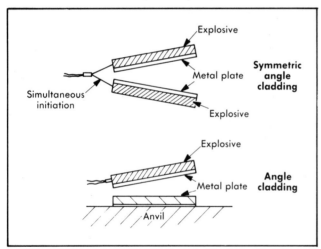

Fig. 9-112 Angle-explosive cladding.

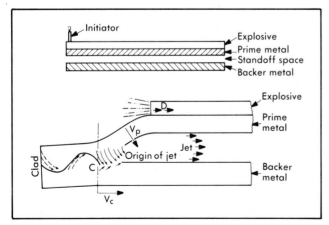

Fig. 9-113 Parallel-explosive cladding.

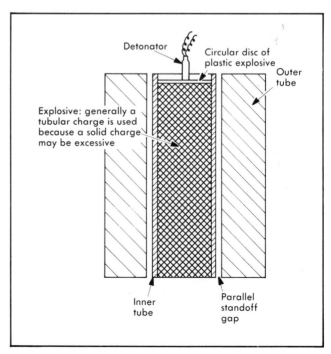

Fig. 9-114 Expansion method of explosively cladding cylindrical shapes.

velocity is low, fluid flows smoothly around the obstacle, but above a certain velocity, the flow pattern becomes turbulent.

The obstacle in the case of explosion bonding is the point of highest pressure in the collision region. Because the pressures in this region are many times higher than the dynamic yield strength of the metals, they flow plastically in a manner similar to fluids. Electron microprobe analysis across such plastically deformed areas shows that no diffusion occurs because of the extremely rapid, self quenching of the metals. The bond represents the frozen flow pattern of the plastic metal flow during bond zone formation.

Under optimum conditions, the metal flow around the collision point is unstable and oscillates, generating a wavy interface. Under the curl and behind the crest of the waves, small pockets of solidified melt are formed. Here, some of the kinetic energy of the driven plate is locally converted into heat as the system came to rest. These discrete regions are completely encapsulated by the ductile prime and base metals. The direct metal-to-metal bonding between the isolated pockets provides the ductility necessary to support stresses during routine fabrication.

The quality of bonding is related directly to the size and distribution of solidified melt pockets along the interface, especially for dissimilar-metal systems that form intermetallic compounds. The pockets of solidified melt in compound-forming systems are brittle and contain localized defects that do not affect composite properties. Explosion bonding parameters for dissimilar-metal systems normally are chosen so that melt pockets associated with the interface are kept to a minimum.

METALS WELDED AND CLAD

As previously discussed under applications and advantages, a wide variety of similar and dissimilar metals can be joined by explosive welding and bonding. Metals that are difficult or impossible to bond by other welding methods can be explosively welded. Flat plates, solid rods, and the outside and inside surfaces of cylinders and pipes can be explosively welded. Tubes can be machined from thick clads or made by overlap cladding. Explosion welding is employed for the joining of pipes, bonding tubes to tube sheets, and plugging leaking tubes in heat exchangers.

More than 300 dissimilar combinations of metals have been explosion welded, as well as numerous similar combinations. Many of these combinations were only in small sample configurations to demonstrate that a metallurgical bond could be achieved. The industrially useful combinations that are available in commercial sizes are shown in Table 9-54. The chart does not include triclads or combinations that corrosion or materials engineers or equipment designers may yet envision.

TABLE 9-54
Commercially Available Explosion-Clad Metal Combinations

	Zirconium	Magnesium	Stellite 6B	Platinum	Gold	Silver	Columbium	Tantalum	Hastelloy	Titanium	Nickel alloys	Copper alloys	Aluminum	Stainless steels	Alloy steels	Carbon steels
Carbon steels	•	•			•	•	•	•	•	•	•	•	•	•	•	•
Alloy steels	•	•	•					•	•	•	•	•	•	•	•	
Stainless steels			•		•	•	•	•		•	•	•	•	•		
Aluminum		•				•	•	•		•	•	•	•			
Copper alloys						•	•	•	•	•	•	•				
Nickel alloys		•		•	•			•	•	•	•					
Titanium	•	•				•	•	•		•						
Hastelloy								•	•							
Tantalum					•		•	•								
Columbium				•			•									
Silver						•										
Gold																
Platinum				•												
Stellite 6B																
Magnesium		•														
Zirconium	•															

(Detaclad Operations, E. I. du Pont de Nemours and Co.)

CHAPTER 9

EXPLOSIVE WELDING AND CLADDING

The combinations that explosion cladding can provide are virtually limitless.

Because explosion bonding is a cold process, thermal damage to the metals that may reduce corrosion resistance or impair other properties is avoided. Cladding and backing metals are purchased in the appropriate heat-treated condition, and the desired corrosion resistance is retained through bonding. Composites are customarily supplied in the as-bonded condition because hardening usually does not affect engineering properties. Occasionally, a postbonding heat treatment is used to meet required properties on specific combinations.

Vessel heads can be made from explosion-bonded clads either by conventional cold or hot forming techniques. The latter involves thermal exposure and is equivalent to a heat treatment. Backing-metal properties, bond continuity, and bond strength are guaranteed to equal the same specifications as the composite from which the head is formed.

METAL PREPARATION

Preparation of the metal surfaces to be bonded is usually required because most metals contain surface imperfections or contaminants that undesirably affect bond properties. The cladding faces are usually surface ground, using an abrasive machine, and then are degreased with a solvent to ensure consistent bond strength. In general, a surface finish that is smoother than 150 μin. (3.8 μm) is needed to produce consistent, high-quality bonds.

Fabrication techniques must take into account the metallurgical properties of the metals to be joined and the possibility of undesirable diffusion at the interface during hot forming, heat treating, and welding. Compatible alloys—those that do not form intermetallic compounds on alloying, such as nickel and its alloys, copper and its alloys, and stainless steel alloys clad to steel—may be treated by the traditional techniques developed for clads produced by other processes. Incompatible combinations such as titanium, zirconium, or aluminum to steel, however, require special techniques designed to limit the production of undesirable intermetallics that jeopardize bond ductility at the interface.

PRODUCT QUALITY

Products that are explosively welded or bonded are often subjected to nondestructive, destructive, and mechanical tests. Explosion-clad plates for pressure vessels are tested according to applicable ASME Boiler and Pressure Vessel Code Specifications. Unfired pressure vessels using clads are covered by ASTM Specifications A 263, A 264, and A 265.

Distortion

When the explosion bonding process distorts the composite so that its flatness does not meet standard flatness specifications, it is reflattened on a press or roller leveler (see ASME Specification SA-20). Press-flattened plates sometimes contain localized irregularities that do not exceed the specified limits, but which generally do not occur in roll-flattened products.

Nondestructive Testing

Nondestructive inspection of an explosion-welded composite is almost totally restricted to ultrasonic and visual inspection. Radiographic inspection is applicable only to special types of composites consisting of two metals having a significant mismatch in density and a large wave pattern in the bond interface. Details of nondestructive testing methods are presented in Chapter 6.

Destructive Testing

To determine the strength of the weld and the effect of the explosion cladding process on the base metals, destructive testing is sometimes used. Standard testing techniques can be used on many composites. However, nonstandard or specially designed tests often are required to provide meaningful test data for specified applications.

Chisel testing is a quick, qualitative technique that is widely used to determine the soundness of explosion-welded metal interfaces. A chisel is driven into and along the weld interface, and the ability of the interface to resist the separating force of the chisel provides a measure of weld ductility and strength.

Mechanical Testing

Tensile and shear strengths. Tensile tests of a composite plate having a thickness of less than 1 1/2″ (38 mm) require testing of the joined base metal and the clad. Strengthening does occur during cladding. As a result, tensile strengths are generally greater than for the original materials. Some typical shear strength values obtained for explosion-clad composites are presented in Table 9-55.

Hardness. Microhardness profiles on sections from explosion-bonded materials show the effect of strain hardening on the metals in the composite. In welding a strain-hardening, austenitic stainless steel to a carbon steel, the stainless steel is hardened adjacent to the weld interface by explosion welding, but the carbon steel is not hardened to a great extent. Similarly, aluminum does not strain-harden significantly.

Impact strength. Impact strengths can be reduced by the presence of hardened zones at the interfaces. However, low-temperature, stress-relief anneal decreases hardness and restores impact strength. Alloys that are sensitive to low-temperature heat treatments show differences in hardness that are related to explosion welding parameters.

Low welding-impact velocities do not develop as much adiabatic heating as higher impact velocities. Adiabatic heating anneals and further ages the alloys. Hardness traverses indicate the degree of hardening during welding and the type of

TABLE 9-55
Typical Shear Strengths for Explosion-Clad Composites

Cladding Metal on Carbon-Steel Backers	Typical Shear Strength, ksi (MPa)
Stainless steels	65 (448)
Nickel and nickel alloys	55 (379)
Hastelloys	56 (386)
Zirconium	39 (269)
Titanium*	35 (241)
Cupro-nickel	36 (248)
Copper	22 (152)
Aluminum (1100-H1)	13 (90)

* Stress-relief annealed at 1150° F (620° C).

EXPLOSIVE WELDING AND CLADDING

subsequent heat treatment required after explosion bonding. Explosion bonding parameters also can be adjusted to prevent softening at the interface.

OPERATING PROCEDURES

For explosive welding and cladding, the preset assembled composite is placed on an anvil of appropriate thickness to minimize distortion of the clad product. For thick composites, a bed of sand is usually a satisfactory anvil. Thin composites may require a support that is made of steel, wood, or other appropriate materials.

The air gap present in parallel explosion cladding can be maintained by metallic supports that are tack welded to the prime metal and backer plates, or by metallic inserts that are placed between the prime metal and backer. The inserts usually are made of a metal compatible with one of the cladding metals.

If the prime metal is so thin that it sags when supported by its edges, other materials such as rigid foam can be placed between the edges to provide additional support. The rigid foam is consumed by the hot egressing jet during bonding. A moderating layer or buffer such as polyethylene sheet, water, rubber, paints, or pressure-sensitive tapes may be placed between the explosive and prime metal surface to attenuate the explosive pressure or to protect the metal surface from explosion effects.

To minimize the problems of noise, air blast, and air pollution, cladding facilities should be located in areas remote from population centers. Using barricades and burying the explosives and components under water or sand lessens the effects of noise and air pollution. An attractive method for making small-area clads using light explosive loads employs a low-vacuum, noiseless chamber. Underground missile silos and mines also have been used as cladding chambers.

Explosive Cladding of Cylindrical Shapes

Explosive cladding of cylindrical shapes is often done with the parallel arrangement. The standoff gap is arranged in annular form between the surfaces of the components to be joined. Bonding is achieved in the following two ways:

1. By expansion of the inner component to collide with the outer component.
2. By implosion—collapsing of the outer component onto the inner component.

Expansion method. Figure 9-114 illustrates this technique in which the inner tubular component is expanded radially outward to impact the bore of the outer component. The explosive, generally a tubular charge, is contained within the bore of the inner tube and is initiated at one end by means of a disc of plastic explosive. A detonation front passes down the explosive, progressively deforming the tube to form a collision front with the outer component and traveling at an identical velocity. The selected explosive must therefore have a detonation velocity that travels at a subsonic rate.

Preferably, the outer component is of a substantial thickness sufficient to avoid its expansion on the impact of the inner component. Failure to withstand this impact without distortion may affect the bond quality. In such instances, a die is necessary to give external support to the outer tube. This can considerably increase the cost of the operation.

The disadvantage of this technique is that the inner tube bore dimension dictates the volume of explosive that can be accommodated within it. This imposes a lower limit to the tube diameter and wall thickness that can be successfully bonded.

Implosion method. In this technique (see Fig. 9-115), an external explosive charge collapses the outer tubular component onto the inner component. It is usual to support the inner component internally to prevent its collapse on impact of the outer tube.

The explosive, in annular form, is usually contained by an outer tube of suitable material such as cardboard or plastic. It is initiated at the upper end by means of a disc of plastic explosive. This causes a detonation front to pass progressively through the explosive charge. The inwardly collapsing outer component creates a collision front with the outer surface of the inner component, again traveling at a rate identical to the detonation velocity of the explosive. If the collision front velocity is to be subsonic, an explosive must be selected that has a detonation velocity below the sonic velocity of the materials.

The advantage of the implosion method is that there is virtually no lower limit to the diameter of the components that can be welded. There are, however, limits to the thickness of the outer components that can be successfully imploded. This is because greater thicknesses require larger standoff gaps over which they can be accelerated. If the gap becomes disproportionately large, the collapsing tube may wrinkle upon its inner surface prior to impact at the collision front.

Tube Joining Processes

Because the area of bond required in tube joining is usually limited, the angular arrangement is generally favored. This is because, in perhaps the majority of instances, the internal tube is expanded outward to form the bond. As the high-detonation-velocity explosive that can be used in conjunction with the angular geometry is dense and extremely powerful, lower volumes of explosive are required. This allows much smaller tube diameters and greater wall thicknesses to be bonded.

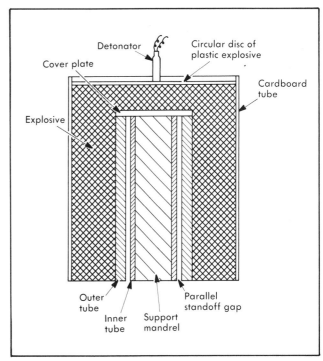

Fig. 9-115 Implosion method of explosively cladding cylindrical shapes.

EXPLOSIVE WELDING AND CLADDING

The most popular arrangement of the angular geometry in a typical application of this technique is shown in Fig. 9-116, view *a*. In this case, a heat exchanger tube is being bonded to a tubeplate joint. The angle is machined within the bore of the tubeplate hole. The explosive is initiated at the inner end of the charge, causing the detonation front to travel from the inside of the tubeplate hole outward. The final joint configuration gives an enhanced tube entry profile that assists in reducing erosive turbulence as the cooling medium enters the tube.

Alternative configurations shown in Fig. 9-116, views *b* and *c*, are frequently used for the repair of leaking heat exchanger tube/tubesheet joints that have been manufactured by more conventional techniques. Most repairs must be made in situations where any downtime of the plant must be minimized for economic reasons and where access to the joint is restricted. These particular geometries allow a tubular plug to be prefabricated from solid bar material. The plug is inserted into the leaking joint with a minimum preparation of the tubeplate hole being required.

EXPLOSIVES USED

The pressure, *P*, generated by a detonating explosive to propel the prime plate is directly proportional to its density, *p*, and the square of the detonation velocity, V^2_D. This pressure can be reasonably approximated by the following equation:[28]

$$P = 1/4 \, p \, V^2_D \qquad (11)$$

The detonation velocity is controlled by adjusting the packing thickness, density, and/or the amount of added inert material.

Types of explosives that have been used for explosive welding and cladding include:

High velocity, 14,750-25,000 fps (4496-9620 m/s):

- Trinitrotoluene (TNT).
- Cyclotrimethylenetrinitramine (RDX).
- Pentaerythritol tetranitrate (PETN).
- Composition B.
- Composition C4.
- Plasticized PETN-based rolled sheet and extruded cord.
- Primacord.

Low to medium velocity, 4900-14,750 fps (1494-4496 m/s):

- Ammonium nitrate.
- Ammonium nitrate prills (pellets) sensitized with fuel oil.
- Ammonium perchlorate.
- Amatol.
- Amatol and sodatol diluted with rock salt to 30-35%.

- Dynamites.
- Nitroguanidine.
- Diluted PETN.

SAFETY CONSIDERATIONS

Explosive welding and cladding should only be done by trained, experienced personnel because of the inherent dangers of handling and using explosives. Procedures must comply with applicable federal, state, and local regulations. Ear protection for all personnel is required.

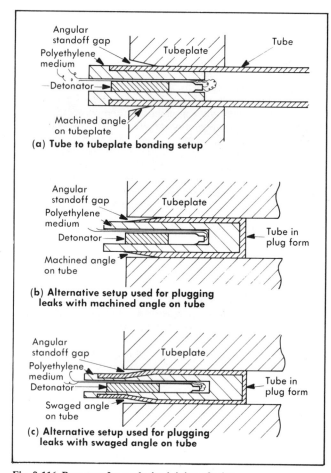

(a) Tube to tubeplate bonding setup

(b) Alternative setup used for plugging leaks with machined angle on tube

(c) Alternative setup used for plugging leaks with swaged angle on tube

Fig. 9-116 Processes for explosive joining of tubes.

OTHER SOLID-STATE WELDING PROCESSES

In addition to the solid-state welding processes discussed previously—diffusion, friction, ultrasonic, and explosive welding—there are several others of industrial significance that are mentioned briefly in the remainder of this chapter.

COLD WELDING

Cold welding (CW) is defined as a solid-state welding process in which coalescence is produced by the external application of mechanical force alone. A characteristic of the process is minimum heat. No heat is applied externally, and little is generated by the welding process itself. With extensive plastic deformation, however, some heat is generated, but this heat is not required to complete the weld and is not generally sufficient to cause any problems.

The welding operation is done at or near room temperature, and there is substantial deformation. A fundamental requirement

OTHER SOLID-STATE PROCESSES

for satisfactory cold welding is that at least one and preferably both of the metals to be joined be highly ductile and not exhibit extreme work hardening. As a result, the process is generally used for nonferrous materials.

Soft tempers of metals such as aluminum and copper are most easily cold welded. It is more difficult to use the process on cold-worked or heat-treated alloys of these metals because work hardening at the interface becomes pronounced, and ductility may become exhausted. The joining of copper to aluminum by cold welding is a common application of the process, especially when aluminum tubing or electrical conductor-grade aluminum is joined to short sections of copper to facilitate interconnection by soldering or brazing.

To make a cold weld, two pieces of metal are placed between a pair of dies or rolls, and force is applied to deform the metal. In sheet materials, a weld will be formed when a thickness reduction of about 50% has been reached, provided that the surfaces were reasonably clean at the start of the process.

Very simple tools may be designed for cold welding. For example, joints between wires may be formed manually with a pair of special pliers. Hydraulic and mechanical presses are also used for cold welding.

Although the welds are made at room temperature, the service temperatures of the welds must be considered, because mutually soluble materials may cause a brittle joint in service. This embrittlement is usually not a problem when cold welds are made between dissimilar metals that are not mutually soluble.

Clean metal faces on the workpieces are essential for strong cold welds. Dirt, oils, or oxide films must be removed to ensure metal-to-metal contact. Degreasing and wire brushing are commonly used for this purpose.

Butt Joints

Cold welding is used to produce butt joints in the ends of wire, rod, tubing, and extruded shapes. The workpieces are held securely in dies, with sufficient metal extending beyond the dies to permit upsetting during welding as the workpieces are pushed against each other. Distance between the dies should not be greater than four times the diameter or thickness of the workpieces. Multiple upsets are sometimes required, depending on the workpiece material and size.

Lap Joints

Cold welding is used to produce lap joints in ductile sheet or foil stock. Dies generally indent the metal and apply pressure to cause plastic flow at the interface. Pressures applied depend on the compressive yield strengths of the metals being joined and vary up to 500 ksi (3447 MPa) for some aluminum alloys.

Slide Welding

Slide welding is a less common form of cold welding in which the surfaces to be joined slide relative to each other, thus minimizing deformation during upsetting. Upsetting forces are less than for butt welding.

FORGE WELDING

Forge welding (FOW) is one of the earliest solid-state welding processes and was used extensively by blacksmiths to mount rims on wagon wheels. In this process, the components to be joined are heated to high temperatures below their melting points and are then forged together by dies, hammers, or rollers to cause permanent deformation at the interface. These processes are limited to special uses and have been largely replaced by the other welding processes described in this chapter. Details on the forging and hot rolling processes are presented in Volume II, *Forming*, of this Handbook series.

Related processes similar to forge welding include the following:

- *Roll welding (ROW)*. In this process, two or more heated sheets or plates are stacked together and passed through rolls until deformation produces a solid-state weld.
- *Hammer welding*. Forge welding is the preferred term for this process, which is performed with hammer blows.
- *Die welding*. Forge welding is the preferred term for this process, which is performed between dies, generally in a hydraulic press.
- *Thermocompression (hot pressure) welding*. This specialized deformation method is used for joining connections of ductile metals in electronic circuits. Resistance heating is generally used, with the heat being transmitted through an indentor tool.

Heating time is the major variable that affects joint quality in forge welding and related processes. With insufficient heating, welding does not occur; overheating results in low-strength, brittle joints. Low-carbon and some alloy steels in sheet, plate, tube, bar, or pipe form are joined by forge welding, with welding temperatures of about 2050° F (1120° C). Annealing is sometimes used to refine the grain size and improve the ductility of forge-welded joints. Fluxes are sometimes used in forge welding certain metals to prevent the formation of oxide scale.

COEXTRUSION WELDING

In this solid-state welding process, two or more metal parts are coextruded by heating and forcing the metals through an extrusion die. Some cold coextrusion welding has been done, but the metal parts are generally heated to reduce pressure requirements and improve the welding process.

Workpieces to be welded are generally placed in a tapered retort to facilitate extrusion. For reactive metals, the retort is usually evacuated. Coextrusion welding is used to join a variety of metals, including low-carbon steels, aluminum and copper alloys, nickel-based alloys, and reactive metals, such as titanium and zirconium.

PULSED MAGNETIC WELDING

Pulsed magnetic welding is a solid-state process similar in concept to explosive welding, previously discussed, but without the hazards of using explosives. Metallurgical bonding is produced by impacting metal parts against each other at high velocities using high-frequency, high-intensity pulsed magnetic fields. The process is used to join stainless steels, Inconel, and other metals. Dissimilar and crack-susceptible metals can be joined. Bond lengths of 5-10 times the cladding thickness can be produced.

A pulsed magnetic field in the range of 500,000 gauss exerts a force on the workpiece that translates into a magnetic pressure in excess of 100 ksi (690 MPa). The pressure accelerates the workpiece to a high velocity, up to 1000 fps (305 m/s). When the workpiece collapses on a tapered metal mandrel, high strain rates occur on impact, causing the mating surfaces of both materials to act like high-viscosity fluids. As the impact point of the workpiece moves along the tapered surface, a small layer of material is ejected. This self-cleaning action results in atomically

OTHER SOLID-STATE PROCESSES

clean surfaces that weld without reaching the melting temperature of the metal.

This process is used to weld end closures of nuclear fuel pins. The pin cladding (workpiece), with an OD of 0.230″ (5.84 mm) x 0.015″ (0.38 mm) wall thickness, is welded to a tapered end plug (mandrel) (see Fig. 9-117). The primary material used is Type 316 stainless steel, although other metals have been welded. A low-inductance, high-voltage capacitor bank is used for welding this low-conductivity material. Typical machine parameters are a charge voltage of 37.5 kV, stored energy of 26 kJ, a peak current of 1.25 MA, and a ringing frequency of 165 kHz.

VIBRATION WELDING

Vibration welding differs from ultrasonic welding, discussed previously, in that frictional heat from a small reciprocating linear motion is used to join thermoplastic and rubber parts. Frictional heat is generated by clamping two workpieces together under pressure and vibrating one workpiece at a preset amplitude and frequency (see Fig. 9-118). A continuous weld line is produced along the entire contact surface.

Frequencies commonly used for vibration welding are 120 and 240 Hz. Vibration amplitudes vary between 0.030 and 0.140″ (0.76 and 3.56 mm). The heat generated by the friction melts material at the interface. When the vibration stops, the workpieces are held under pressure until the melted material solidifies and the parts are bonded.

Bonds produced by vibration welding are strong and structurally sound, and operating costs are low. The process is being used to produce pressuretight joints in both small and large parts of circular, rectangular, or irregular shape. Total cycle times, including loading and unloading, average 6-15 seconds, and multicavity fixtures can be used.

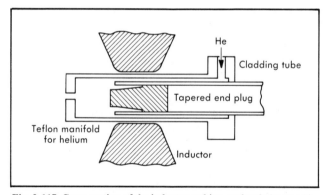

Fig. 9-117 Cross section of the inductor, tubing, and end plug used in making an end closure by magnetic pulse welding. (*Maxwell Laboratories, Inc.*)

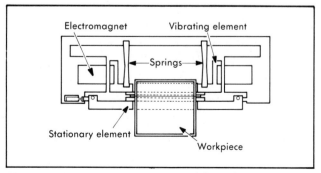

Fig. 9-118 Major components of vibratory welding equipment. (*Branson Sonic Power Co.*)

References

1. W. H. Kearns, ed., *Welding Handbook*, 7th ed., vol. 5 (Miami: American Welding Society, 1984), p. 287.
2. *Welding Aluminum* (Richmond: Reynolds Metals Co., 1958).
3. *Welding Handbook* (New York: Copper Development Association, 1972).
4. G. K. Hicken, N. D. Stucki, and H. W. Randall, "Application of Magnetically Controlled Welding Arcs," *Welding Journal* (April 1976).
5. Chet Shira, "Converter Power Supplies—More Options for Arc Welding," *Welding Design and Fabrication* (June 1985), pp. 52-55.
6. "Recommended Practices for Resistance Welding," Publication Code C1.1 (Miami: American Welding Society).
7. *Ibid.*
8. "Resistance Welding Equipment Standards," Bulletin 16 (Philadelphia: Resistance Welder Manufacturers Association).
9. "Recommended Practices for Resistance Welding," *loc. cit.*
10. *Ibid.*
11. *Ibid.*
12. *Ibid.*
13. Arthur L. Phillips, ed., *Welding Handbook*, 5th ed. (Miami: American Welding Society, 1963-1964).
14. "Resistance Welding Equipment Standards," *loc. cit.*
15. S. Bolin, "Laser Welding, Cutting, and Drilling—Part I," *Assembly Engineering* (May 1980).
16. George Schaffer, "Lasers in Metalworking," Special Report No. 679, *American Machinist* (July 1, 1975).
17. F. P. Gagliano, *Interaction of Laser Radiation with Metals to Produce Welds*, SME Technical Paper MR74-954 (Dearborn, MI: Society of Manufacturing Engineers, 1974).
18. T. R. Tucker and A. H. Clauer, "Laser Processing of Materials," MCIC Report 83-48 (Columbus, OH: Battelle Columbus Laboratories, November 1983).
19. K. Shinada, T. Ohmae, Y. Yoshida, S. Suzuki, and M. Tamura, "Basic Study on Laser Welding," Paper No. 3, *Proceedings—First International Laser Processing Conference*, held 16-17 November 1981, Anaheim, CA (Toledo, OH: Laser Institute of America).
20. J. Devine, "Joining Electric Contacts," *Welding Design and Fabrication*, vol. 53, no. 3 (1980), pp. 112-115.
21. J. Devine, "Ultrasonic Welding Helps Lighten Aircraft," *Welding Design and Fabrication*, vol. 51, no. 8 (1978), pp. 74-76.
22. T. J. Kelly, "Ultrasonic Welding of Cu-Ni to Steel," *Welding Journal*, vol. 60, no. 4 (1981), pp. 29-31.
23. F. R. Meyer, "Ultrasonics Produces Strong Oxide-Free Welds," *Assembly Engineering*, vol. 20, no. 5 (1977), pp. 26-29.
24. T. Renshaw, J. Curatola, and A. Sarrantonio, "Developments in Ultrasonic Welding for Aircraft," *SAMPE 11th National Technical Conference Proceedings* (Boston: 1979), pp. 681-693.
25. T. Renshaw, K. Wongwiwat, and A. Sarrantonio, "A Comparison of Properties of Single Overlap Tension Joints Prepared by Ultrasonic Welding and Other Means," *AIAA/ASME/ASCE 23rd Conference Proceedings* (New Orleans: 1983), pp. 1-8.
26. T. Renshaw and A. Sarrantonio, "Properties of Large Multi-spot Ultrasonically Welded Joints," *Journal of Aircraft*, vol. 18 (September 1981), pp. 761-765.
27. V. D. Linse and H. E. Pattee, Canadian Industries, Ltd., U. S. Patent 4,248,373, February 3, 1981.
28. M. A. Cook, *The Science of High Explosives* (New York: Reinhold Publishing Corp., 1966), p. 274.

Bibliography

Blazynski, T. Z., ed. *Explosive Welding, Forming and Compaction*. New York: Applied Science Publishers, 1983.

Cary, Howard B. *Modern Welding Technology*. Englewood Cliffs, NJ: Prentice-Hall, Inc., 1979.

Facts About Welding Titanium. Niles, OH: Reactive Metals, Inc.

Kearns, W. H., ed. *Welding Handbook*, 7th ed., vol. 2. Miami: American Welding Society, 1978.

_____ . *Welding Handbook*, 7th ed., vol. 3. Miami: American Welding Society, 1980.

_____ . *Welding Handbook*, 7th ed., vol. 4. Miami: American Welding Society, 1982.

_____ . *Welding Handbook*, 7th ed., vol. 5. Miami: American Welding Society, 1984.

Mazumder, J. "Laser Welding: State of the Art Review." *Journal of Metals* (July 1982), pp. 16-24.

MIG Welding Handbook. Florence, SC: L-TEC Welding & Cutting Systems, 1984.

Nippes, Ernest F., coord. *Metals Handbook: Welding, Brazing, and Soldering*, 9th ed., vol. 6. Metals Park, OH: American Society for Metals, 1983.

The Oxy-Acetylene Handbook. Florence, SC: L-TEC Welding & Cutting Systems, 1976.

Ready, John F. *Lasers in Modern Industry*, 1st ed. Dearborn, MI: Society of Manufacturing Engineers, 1979.

Rinehart, R. S., and Pearson, J. *Explosive Working of Metals*. New York: MacMillan, 1963.

Sacks, Raymond J. *Welding: Principles and Practices*. Peoria, IL: Chas. A. Bennett Co., Inc., 1976.

Seaman, F. D. *The Role of Focus in Heavy-Plate Laser Welding*. SME Technical Paper MR78-345. Dearborn, MI: Society of Manufacturing Engineers, 1978.

_____ . *The Role of Shielding Gas in High Power CO_2 (CW) Laser Welding*. SME Technical Paper MR77-982. Dearborn, MI: Society of Manufacturing Engineers, 1977.

Stauffer, Robert N. "Update on Noncontact Seam Tracking Systems." *Robotics Today* (August 1983), pp. 29-34.

_____ . "Weldbonding: Adhesives Add to Joint Quality." *Manufacturing Engineering* (December 1978), pp. 44-47.

Submerged Arc Welding Handbook. Florence, SC: L-TEC Welding & Cutting Systems, 1984.

Technical Guide for Flux-Cored Arc Welding. Troy, OH: Hobart Brothers Co.

Technical Guide for Gas Metal Arc Welding. Troy, OH: Hobart Brothers Co.

Technical Guide for Gas Tungsten Arc Welding. Troy, OH: Hobart Brothers Co.

Technical Guide for Shielded Metal Arc Welding. Troy, OH: Hobart Brothers Co.

TIG Welding Handbook. Florence, SC: L-TEC Welding & Cutting Systems, 1984.

Weisman, Charlotte, ed. *Welding Handbook*, 7th ed., vol. 1. Miami: American Welding Society, 1976.

Welding, Cutting, and Heating Guide. Denton, TX: Victor Equipment Co., 1977.

BRAZING AND SOLDERING

Brazing and soldering are joining processes that use heat and filler metals to produce metallurgical bonds. Unlike most of the fusion welding processes discussed earlier, brazing and soldering do not involve any melting of the base metals being joined. As a result, the mechanical and physical properties of the base metals are not generally duplicated at the joints. However, diffusion brazing can produce a strength equal to the base metal.

While both brazing and soldering use filler metals, the processes differ with respect to temper-

ature and bonding action. In brazing, the filler metals have liquidus temperatures *above* 840° F (450° C), but below those of the base metals, and the filler metals are distributed between the mating surfaces of the joints by capillary action. In soldering, the filler metals have liquidus temperatures *below* 840° F. Filler metals are distributed by both capillary action and wetting between the surfaces of the components that are being soldered, using the surface energies of the materials that are being joined.

BRAZING

Brazing is defined by the American Welding Society (AWS) as: "A group of welding processes which produces coalescence of materials by heating them in the presence of a filler metal having a liquidus above 840° F (450° C) and below the solidus of the base metal. The filler metal is distributed between the closely fitted faying surfaces of the joint by capillary action." Braze welding differs from brazing in that the filler metal is not distributed in the joint by capillary action.

APPLICATIONS

Applications for brazing are widely varied, and the process is used in practically every industry, from jewelry to aerospace. High-vacuum, refrigeration, and air-conditioning equipment manufacturers use the process extensively in making leaktight joints. Applications in the automotive industry include the production of accessories and steering wheels and in joining tubing. Aircraft and aerospace uses include making honeycomb structures, engine nozzles, tubing joints, and many other brazements.

Heating and plumbing manufacturers and contractors use brazing for joining pipe, tubing, and headers. Seams and spud connections for water heaters and tanks are made by brazing. Pasteurizers, separators, and tanks for dairy equipment are also brazed. Electrical wires, cables, and bus bars are joined by brazing, and the chemical industry uses the process for producing tanks, vats, and piping.

The selection of brazing versus welding or other joining processes depends primarily on the sizes of the components and the materials to be joined,

configurations of the joints, thicknesses of the sections, the number of joints to be made, and service requirements. Brazing is generally more suitable for joining smaller parts because of the difficulty in applying the required heat to larger components. However, parts as large as 70″ (1780 mm) diam and 15′ (4.6 m) long are brazed. The process is also usually preferred for joining thin sections to thick sections because reduced heat requirements minimize distortion.

Brazing is used extensively for joining many dissimilar material combinations and is often better for joints having interfaces with complex contours. When designed properly, applications satisfy requirements for permanent, strong joints. The process is generally not used for nonpermanent joints that require disassembly or for permanent, low-strength joints where other joining processes are generally more economical.

ADVANTAGES

Brazing is selected as a fastening process over other joining methods, such as welding, mechanical fastening, soldering, or adhesive bonding, because of the following characteristics:

1. Inaccessible joint areas that could not be made by gas metal arc, gas tungsten arc, and spot or seam welding can be joined by brazing.
2. Thin-walled tubes and light-gage sheet metal assemblies not joinable by welding can be joined by brazing.

*Contributors of sections of this chapter are: **Roy E. Beal**, Amalgamated Technologies, Inc.; **Tim Hirthe**, Technical Service Manager, Lucas-Milhaupt, Inc.; **Carl B. Miller**, Vice President-Engineering, U.S. Laser Corp.; **Robert L. Peaslee**, Vice President, Wall Colmonoy Corp.; **C. W. Philp**, Product Engineer, Brazing Products, Handy & Harman; **Bruce R. Williams**, Vice President, Fusion Inc.*

*Reviewers of sections of this chapter are: **Roy E. Beal**, Amalgamated Technologies, Inc.; **F. John Fuchs**, Applications Engineer, Blackstone Ultrasonics Inc.; **R. W. Gunkel**, Staff Engineer, Product Engineering Div., Aluminum Company of America, Alcoa Technical Center; **William B. Hampshire**, Assistant Manager, Tin Research Institute, Inc.; **Tim Hirthe**, Technical Service Manager, Lucas-Milhaupt, Inc.; **Joe Keller**, Solder and PWB Consultant; **A. V. Pajerski**, Product Engineering Div., Aluminum Company of America, Alcoa Technical Center; **Robert L. Peaslee**, Vice President, Wall Colmonoy Corp.; **C. W. Philp**, Product Engineer, Brazing Products, Handy & Harman; **Bruce R. Williams**, Vice President, Fusion Inc.*

TORCH BRAZING

3. Brazing can join dissimilar materials such as copper to stainless steels, brass to carbon steel, and ceramics to nickel alloys.
4. Leaktight joints for pressurized and vacuum systems are readily joined by brazing.
5. The joining of materials with filler metals at temperatures below 1300° F (705° C) can be performed.
6. The nickel-brazed joints in steel and the nickel alloy brazed joints in stainless steels are made for high-temperature service.
7. Multiple joints can be made at one time, as in furnace brazing, with potentially high production rates. Brazements produced in furnaces with protective atmospheres do not require cleaning or stress relieving after brazing.
8. Corrosion resistance can be provided for food-service equipment that employs silver or nickel filler metals for joining stainless steels. The chemical industry uses nickel filler metals for brazing stainless steels subject to corrosive service.
9. Less-skilled operators are required for high-production brazing.
10. Diffusion brazing can be used to join heat-resistant base metals for service temperatures far above the solidus temperature of the nickel filler metal.
11. Braze joints are ductile.
12. Brazing is readily automated, and high production rates are possible.

LIMITATIONS

Size limitation of the parts to be brazed is of major importance. Extremely large assemblies, although brazable, may often be made economically by welding, particularly if the linear distances to be joined are small, because of the cost and availability of large equipment such as brazing furnaces. By definition, brazing requires closely mating parts to ensure capillary flow of the filler metal. The cost of machining to attain the desired fit may rule out brazing as a joining process.

The general availability of equipment for either torch, induction, or furnace brazing in a plant or by a vendor may be a determining factor in selecting the process. The true worth of the process and determining factor in its use must be decided from its cost and desired joint characteristics on any particular joining operation. In such a case, a value analysis must be made to compare brazing accurately with any other joining process under consideration.

BRAZING PROCESSES

There are many brazing processes currently being used. They are generally classified by the method used to heat the assembly. In some applications, however, several methods of heating are used to produce brazed joints. Selection of a process depends primarily on the parts to be brazed, equipment available, and costs. Some brazing filler metals and base metals can be brazed by only one of the heating methods.

The most common brazing processes are torch, induction, dip, infrared, and furnace brazing. Other processes used less commonly include arc, diffusion, electron beam, exothermic, laser beam, resistance, block, blanket, and flow brazing.

Torch Brazing

A torch is the most common process of heating for brazing. Heat for the torch brazing operation is supplied by burning gas combinations such as air and natural gas, oxygen and acetylene, air and propane, and other mixtures, depending on heat requirements.

Handheld torch. By far the most easily used process is handheld torch brazing. The operator plays the torch flame on the parts, being careful to apply more heat to the heavier and more conductive sections first. A brazing flux applied to the joint area prior to heating prevents oxidation of the parts during heating. As the flux becomes molten, it protects the joint area from oxidizing and removes any residual oxides, thus preparing the surfaces for wetting by the filler metal. Parts should be clean and free of oxides and other foreign material before brazing. The brazing filler metal is usually hand-fed to the joint area as soon as the joint is up to temperature, but can also be preplaced in the form of rings, shims, and other shapes. In the case of paste alloys, both flux and filler metals are applied in a single step prior to heating. Figure 10-1 illustrates torch brazing with a handheld torch.

Prepositioned torch. By means of prepositioned torches and simple movement of the workpieces, it is often advantageous to preheat the entire assembly by one set of torches and make the final braze with a second set or, in some cases, a handheld torch, at which time the filler metal is hand or face-fed to the joint area. By using prepositioned torches, it is possible to preplace the filler metal in the form of paste alloy deposits or preformed rings or washers so that the operation proceeds fairly automatically. Shuttle machines are available to perform this type of brazing.

Semiautomatic brazing. Prepositioned torches for preheating and brazing can be arranged to heat large volumes of smaller parts passed through the heating stations in an in-line conveyor or rotary table machine. The last station or position in this case may be a cooling station to allow the filler metal to solidify completely and the part to cool. In the brazing of brass and steel parts by semiautomatic brazing, for example, the flux is sprayed on automatically, filler metal is preplaced, and then the joint is brazed. The final operation may consist of rinsing the still-warm part on the rotary table with water, which will in most cases remove the bulk of the brazing flux residue rapidly and economically and cool the part for operator removal.

High-production brazing of small assemblies by torch-heated, in-line, or rotary indexing machines has been designed to accomplish the following operations on an automatic basis:

1. *Assembly of details.* In many cases, small details can be fed from rotary or vibratory hoppers to fixtures that hold the parts during brazing.
2. *Slurry fluxing.* Slurry fluxes can be metered and deposited at the joint area after assembly.

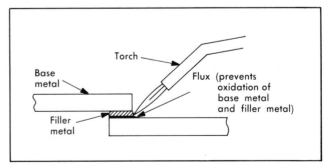

Fig. 10-1 Torch brazing.

3. *Preplacement of filler*. Rings or other preforms can be considered another detail in the prebraze assembly and included in or near the joint area.
4. *Paste brazing filler metal addition*. In many cases, brazing paste, consisting of a binder, powdered braze filler metal, and flux, can be applied directly to the joint area by automatic applicators.
5. *Gaseous-flux additions*. The addition of gaseous organic borate flux to the fuel gas in torch brazing will aid greatly in spreading the filler metal and reducing the requirements for paste brazing flux. In some cases, the gas flux by itself may be sufficient.
6. *Automated wire feeders*. Automated wire feeders apply the proper amount of the brazing filler metal to the heated joint.

Operating techniques. Torch brazing requires operating skill to produce satisfactory joints. The oxyacetylene flame, if used, should be adjusted so that it is neutral or slightly reducing. When a neutral flame is attained, the blue feather at the end of the flame cone has just disappeared (any more oxygen makes the flame oxidizing); with a slightly reducing flame, the blue feather is slightly apparent. Adjustment of other types of fuel gases may be more difficult, and it may be necessary to use accurate metering equipment to provide the neutral or reducing condition. It is important that all members of the assembly be brought to brazing temperature at the same time, particularly in the area of the joint, so that the filler metal may melt and wet all parts simultaneously. In this respect, torch brazing is particularly advantageous because the torch may be directed more on the heavier member or the member of greater thermal conductivity. In this manner, a joint of complex assembly can be brought to substantially the same temperature at the same time.

Another means of achieving uniform heating in torch brazing is the employment of multiflame or multitip torches. These multiple arrangements of tips and torches permit the placement of the flames at the most advantageous points. This principle is employed in mechanized torch brazing for the same purpose.

In heating an assembly for torch brazing, it is almost a universal practice to employ a flux. A possible exception would be the fluxless brazing of copper to copper with the BCuP filler metals. The flux can be used as an indicator of the temperature achieved, because flux should liquefy and turn clear just below the brazing temperature of the filler metal. Therefore, when the flux indicates that the joint is approaching the brazing temperature, the filler metal may be introduced in a trial attempt. Always melt the filler metal by the heat of the joint, not by the direct application of the flame. Filler metal is generally face-fed in manual torch brazing operations, and automatically fed or preplaced for mechanized torch brazing. However, preplaced filler metal may also be used in manual operation. Pastes are also used extensively with handheld automatic applicators.

Induction Brazing

Induction heating, applied widely in other operations such as heat treating, is ideally suited as a heat source for brazing, especially where rapid heating is required. In contrast to torch brazing, the immediate limitations are the necessity of locating the inductor precisely close to the workpiece and the selection of fixture materials for holding parts during brazing. The fixtures should be kept out of the induction field as much as possible to avoid excessive heating of fixtures or should be constructed of nonmagnetic materials such as ceramics.

Induction heating has a distinct advantage in that once properly set up, a very closely controlled heating area (generally smaller than that possible with torch brazing) can be obtained. In this manner, brazing can often be accomplished close to previously heat-treated areas without seriously lowering their hardness. Typical joint and coil designs used in induction brazing are shown in Fig. 10-2.

Generators. Induction brazing generators are of the following three principal types:

- Motor generators that have outputs from 3 to 10 kHz.
- Solid-state power supplies that produce output frequencies to 50 kHz.
- Vacuum-tube type units with output frequencies from 100 to 450 kHz. These generators are often referred to as RF or radio-frequency units.

For steel and ferrous alloys, the motor generator type is quite adequate because of the good magnetic coupling between the alternating field and the work. The heating pattern tends to be deeper, and this type is best if thorough heating of the parts to be brazed is indicated. Solid-state power supplies can be substituted for the motor generator units and have similar frequency and power applications for brazing. Radio-frequency generators operate at higher frequencies and tend to heat a shallower band of material close to the surface of the parts. They will, in addition, be more effective in heating copper, brass, and aluminum alloys. Power sources are available in output ranges from 1 to 50 kW.

Because power output and time at heat can both be precisely controlled in induction heating, the process has the distinct advantage of allowing setup for use by less-skilled operators. The filler metal is generally preplaced in the joint area. Induction heating is being used for semiautomatic and automatic brazing. Most or all of the features covered in the previous section on semiautomatic torch brazing will apply to induction brazing.

Operating techniques. A very important feature of induction heating equipment for brazing is the inductor coil, sometimes called a block or the work coil. Such coils may be constructed of copper tubing or machined from solid copper blocks. When the power input to the induction brazing unit is less than 3/4 kW (750 W), the coils may be air cooled. Water cooling is essential for larger capacity coils.

The coils must be fabricated for the workpiece, and the closer the coupling between the coil and the workpiece, the more efficient the operation. It is also possible to fabricate coils that will accommodate a range of similar sizes, although when the gap between the workpieces is large, efficiency is lower. This same factor of gap or couple may be employed to control the relative rates of heating of different parts of an assembly. A close couple (small gap) will give faster heating.

Induction brazing is particularly well suited to the assembly of elements by step brazing, discussed subsequently in this section. Filler metal for induction brazing is almost invariably preplaced in the form of rings, washers, and shims. It may also be in paste form with the flux and powder filler metal directly applied to the joint. Atmospheres may also be employed with induction brazing, which will eliminate the need for mineral flux and flux or oxide removal.

A two-station unit is commonly employed for induction brazing. While brazing is being done at one station, the other

INDUCTION BRAZING

one is being loaded. These stations usually handle a multiplicity of assembled units. The assemblies, previously cleaned, fluxed, and with the filler metal preplaced, are inserted in the locating fixture. By means of automatic timing devices, the high-frequency current flows for a predetermined period to produce the brazed joint.

Dip Brazing

In dip brazing, the heat required is furnished by a molten chemical or metal bath. When a molten chemical bath is used,

the bath may act as a flux. When a molten metal bath is used, the bath provides the filler metal. A cover of flux is provided over molten (filler) metal baths.

The principal use of dip brazing is in joining aluminum and its alloys using a molten bath of fluoride and chloride salts with melting points in the range of 660 to 9500°F (350 to 510°C). Essential features of the process include the following:

1. Precleaning is performed prior to brazing, usually in a chemical bath, to reduce aluminum oxide and prepare the surfaces.

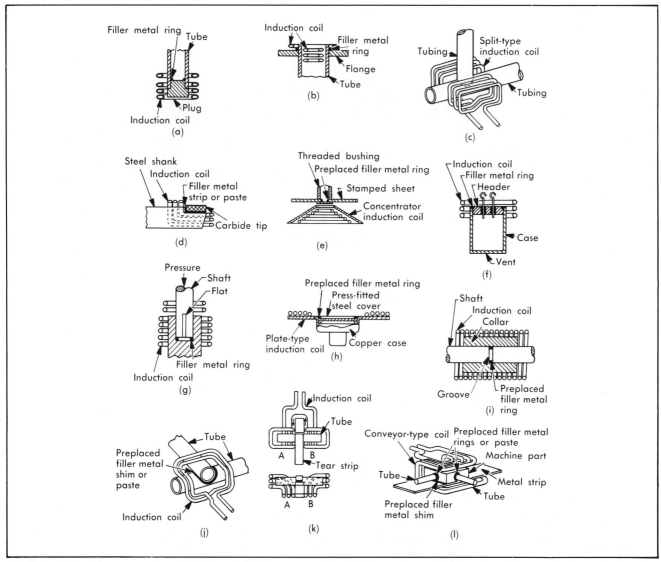

Fig. 10-2 Induction brazing coil and joint design: (a) Plug-to-tube. Turns of inductor coil may be spaced for suitable heat pattern depending on the materials being joined; minimum air gap between the inductor coil and workpiece is desirable for maximum energy transfer. **(b) Flange-to-tube.** Internal-external coil; flange chamfered to hold preplaced filler metal. **(c) Tube-to-tube.** T-split coil; filler metal ring preplaced internally to provide uniform fillet without excess joining filler metal along the sides of the tube. **(d) Carbide tip-to-shank.** Open-end coil; filler metal strip preplaced as shown. **(e) Threaded bushing-to-stamping.** Concentrator coil localizes heat; filler metal preplaced at base of bushing. **(f) Header-to-case seal.** Simple inductor coil for uniform heating; preplaced filler metal recessed; vent permits escape of expanded air to avoid leaky joint. **(g) Shaft-to-fitting.** Inductor coil with varying diameter; filler metal preplaced internally at base of recess; pressure used to seat shaft; small flat permits escape of gases. **(h) Formed-shape assembly.** Plate coil for localized heating; filler metal preform partially shielded from electromagnetic field by case. **(i) Shaft-to-collar.** Inductor coil; filler metal ring preplaced in machined groove. **(j) Tube-to-tube.** L-shaped pancake coil. **(k) Tear strip-to-tube with current reversal** between *A* and *B* to prevent overheating strip. Filler metal preplaced beneath strip. **(l) Component assembly.** Conveyor-type coil; filler metal shim preplaced between machine part and metal strip; filler metal rings preplaced on tubes.

2. Components are assembled, and the filler metal is placed in the joint area, often in the form of a paste or wire preform. Many assemblies incorporate sheet aluminum clad with the braze filler metal, a design used especially for dip brazing.

3. Because brazing operation takes place at temperatures in the range of 1040 to 1160° F (560 to 625° C), very close to the melting point of the parent metals, a means must be provided for supporting the assembly at these temperatures to prevent sagging or collapse of components. As far as possible, attempts should be made to make assemblies self-fixturing by such means as twist-tab crimping of sheet metal, swaging of tube connections, or spinning of one component to form the primary closure. When self-fixturing is not possible, lightweight nickel alloy fixtures can be used to restrain the parts. Springs and clips of Inconel X750 are frequently used, which maintain their usefulness over long exposure at temperatures in the 1000° F (540° C) area.

4. Any convenient means of preheating parts can be employed, but an air furnace is best suited. The assemblies or fixtured parts are preheated to about 1000° F and then transferred to the molten-salt bath for brazing. Preheating is required to:
   a. Avoid carryover of moisture into the molten salt that might result in steam generation and accidental explosion. Many aluminum dip brazing operations utilize a mixture of powdered braze filler metal and flux. This mixture is mixed with water to facilitate its application to the joint. The water, however, must be dried thoroughly before placing the assembly into the bath.
   b. Prevent localized freezing of the salt on the part.
   c. Minimize distortion in heating and prevent thermal shock.
   d. Promote uniform heating and better flow of the filler metal.

5. The preheated parts rapidly attain the temperature of the salt bath. It is seldom necessary to have the parts in the molten salt more than 1-6 minutes, depending on the size of the work. The filler metal melts and rapidly fills the joint areas. After brazing, the load is raised from the bath, and the excess flux is drained back into the bath. Joints should be designed properly to facilitate drainage of the flux.

6. As soon as the filler metal has solidified and while the parts are still hot—500° F (260° C)—the parts are immediately lowered into a hot water rinse. This rinse cracks and loosens the bulk of the flux residues. Subsequent warm and cold rinses remove the remaining flux and salt.

Flux residue. Extreme care should be taken to ensure removal of all remaining flux after brazing. Small pockets of flux remaining on the assemblies can cause severe corrosion problems if allowed to remain on the finished work. For critical work, this residue of flux is checked by dropping small quantities of the rinse water into a silver nitrate solution. The presence of chlorides or halogen compounds from the flux residues is immediately indicated by a cloudy appearance or precipitate of silver chloride. Often, continued rinsing and a final rinse with distilled water may be required. At this point, pollution control comes into consideration. Local regulations may restrict the nature of effluent, such as its salt content, from the rinse operation. In this case, secondary water treatment may be required to meet local codes and water contamination regulations.

Applications. Salt-bath dip brazing of carbon and alloy steels, tool steels, and other metals is being successfully carried out on a production basis. Copper, brass, silver, and nickel are some of the suitable filler metals. Molten-metal dip brazing is also used for small applications, such as the brazing of twisted electrical wire to ensure good conductivity.

Operating techniques. One method of dip brazing uses molten filler metal in an externally heated crucible. A layer of flux covers the surface of the filler metal, into which small assemblies are immersed. The metal is maintained at a temperature above the liquidus or within the brazing range by heat controls that compensate for heat transfer to the parts that are to be brazed.

Another method, referred to as the molten-chemical (flux) bath type, utilizes a suitable metal or ceramic pot containing dry powdered flux, which is a nonconductor of electricity. The flux is liquefied by torches or immersion heaters and in that state conducts electricity, which, suitably controlled, maintains the molten flux within the necessary brazing temperature range. This method is widely used for brazing aluminum sheet clad with filler metal and aluminum parts with preplaced filler metal. All parts must be clean and dry and assembled (preferably in jigs) before immersion in the flux bath. Flux adhering to a brazed assembly withdrawn from the bath should be drained from the assembly to facilitate cleaning operations after the brazing process.

Heat-treating salt baths are also used for dip brazing. These baths, discussed in Volume III, *Materials, Finishing and Coating*, of this Handbook series, are generally of the neutral chloride type.

Infrared Brazing

Infrared brazing primarily uses quartz-iodine incandescent lamps as a source of heat energy. The special lamps are tubular and can easily be focused to concentrate the heat at the area to be brazed. With this technique, it is not uncommon to obtain heat from ten 1000 W lamps (10 kW) concentrated at a joint area of less than 10 in.^{2} (64.5 cm^2) or wattage density of about 1000 W/in.^{2} (155 W/cm^2).

The United States Navy pioneered the use of equipment in making tubular brazed connections in shipboard piping. In this application, the heat source is a ring of high-powered lamps, and its holder or mounting is split in the middle and hinged. Its primary use was for high-pressure, copper alloy, silver-brazed pipe connections. Tests indicate it is one of the most reliable methods of silver brazing these connections, particularly in hidden or in inaccessible joint areas. The unit can be easily controlled through a silicon-controlled rectifier (SCR) master control that receives its primary signal from a thermocouple in the joint area. Timing and temperature are exactly reproducible in this manner, thus lowering the training requirements for operators performing the brazing.

Gas infrared heat sources are used to preheat assemblies for brazing to a temperature somewhat below the actual flow point of the filler metal, as in silver brazing. The final braze then can be performed easily and rapidly with torch heating. The preheating part of the cycle is particularly effective when large sections must be heated to brazing temperature.

FURNACE BRAZING

Furnace Brazing

Furnace brazing is the process most suited to mass-production brazing and for critical applications. This is particularly true in brazing small to medium-sized components of up to 3-4 lb (1.4-1.8 kg) each. This process probably accounts for the largest share of brazed hardware in the United States today. The following features distinguish furnace brazing:

1. The filler metal must be preplaced so that it will flow into the joints with no operator assistance after the parts have reached brazing temperature.
2. Fixturing of the parts must be kept at a minimum and best design makes the brazement self-fixturing. Large quantities of fixtures increase process cost and lower furnace productivity by adding deadweight.
3. An atmosphere protects the parts from oxidation at brazing temperatures, reduces trace oxides, and aids in the wetting of the filler metal on the parent metal.

Furnace types. Furnace brazing may be performed as either a batch or a continuous operation. Batch operations use retorts or cold-wall vacuum furnaces in which the load is stacked in rows on trays of nickel-chromium alloy. The entire load is then brought to brazing temperature, and all the parts braze at the same time. Vacuum furnaces are hermetically sealed, and the air is pumped out to produce a protective atmosphere. Semicontinuous vacuum furnaces are used for brazing aluminum automotive components such as radiators and air-conditioner heat exchangers. Continuous furnace brazing uses a conveyor mechanism that carries the parts through the heat zone and into a cooling zone on a mesh belt or on rolls driven by a chain and sprocket arrangement. The latter design is known as a roller-hearth furnace.

Figures 10-3 through 10-5 schematically illustrate the general arrangement of various types of furnaces used for furnace brazing. A vacuum furnace is shown in Fig. 10-5. Figure 10-4 illustrates the principle of continuous furnace brazing on a

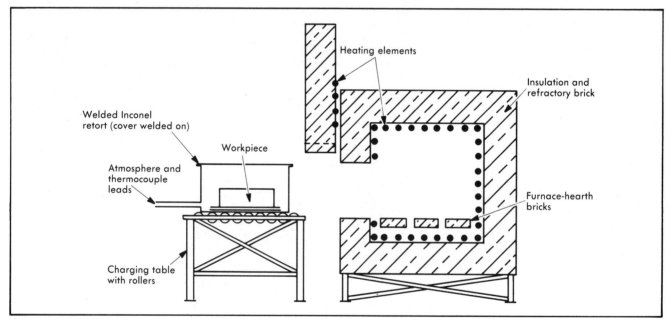

Fig. 10-3 Electric-fired box furnace for brazing. The welded retort shown can be replaced by a sand bottom seal.

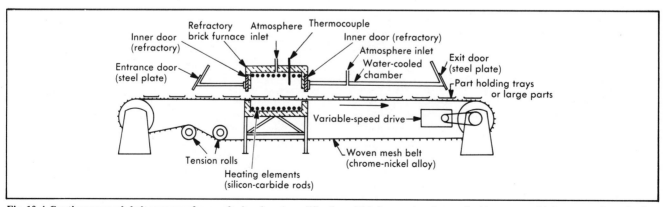

Fig. 10-4 Continuous mesh-belt conveyor furnace for brazing. A modification of this furnace type has a raised hot zone and is known as a humpback furnace.

mesh belt in which an exothermic or nitrogen-based atmosphere is used for copper brazing steel parts. If hydrogen were to be used as the atmosphere, the heating chamber would be raised above the entrance and exit level to contain the light gas, and the furnace would be known as a hump furnace. Additional information on the various types of furnaces and atmospheres used are presented in Volume III of this Handbook series.

Degree of oxidation. The metal-metal oxide graph shown in Fig. 10-6 helps to put into perspective the degree of oxidation or dissociation (reduction) that occurs at a given temperature and

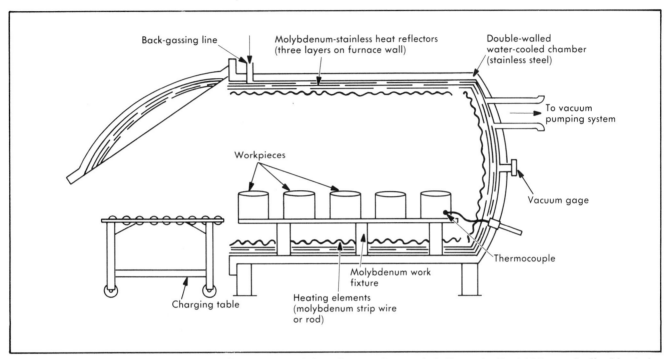

Fig. 10-5 Cold-wall vacuum furnace for brazing. There are many designs of vacuum furnaces, including top loading (pit), bottom loading (elevator), and side loading, shown.

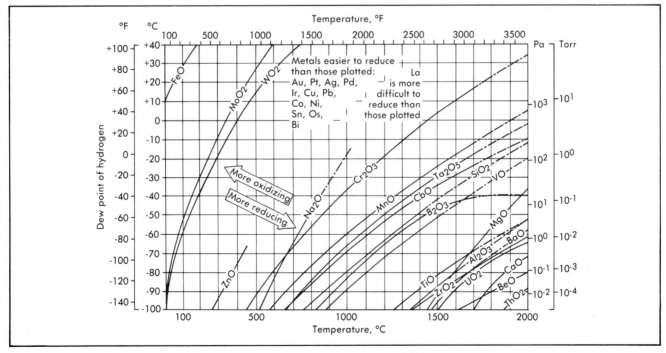

Fig. 10-6 Metal-metal oxide equilibria in pure hydrogen and vacuum atmospheres. (*Wall Colmonoy Corp.*)

FURNACE BRAZING

dew point or vacuum pressure. The curve for each element shown is the equilibrium curve; thus, it is necessary to move to the right of the curve to dissociate the oxides and bring the work out bright with a good braze. The curves for Al and Ti are to the far right of the graph; thus, when these elements are contained in a base metal, these elements will preferentially oxidize in an atmosphere that will produce bright, well-brazed, chromium-containing steels. To eliminate this problem, electrolytic nickel plating is employed.

Many of the oxides of elements are so readily dissociated that they fall to the left of the graph. These elements are indicated in the left triangle at the top of the graph. While not completely true for all atmospheres, this graph does indicate the greater or lesser degree of difficulty in dissociating the oxides of each element in a base metal.

Atmospheres. To meet the requirements of all the various metals that can and are furnace brazed, a further classification of furnace brazing is often made by the atmosphere used. Exothermic and endothermic atmospheres are produced in a separate generator by the controlled combustion of natural gas. They are suitable for brazing carbon steel, brass, copper, and other metals. The most common use of these atmospheres in industry is the brazing of appliance and automotive components made from steel, using copper as the filler metal—the so-called copper brazing process. Brass and copper are usually brazed with lower melting point, silver-bearing filler metals.

Dry hydrogen atmosphere, with a dew point of less than -80° F (-62°C), is available to industry as a byproduct of the chlorine gas industry, where it evolves during the electrolysis of sodium chloride in chlorine production. Another source is the partial combustion of natural gas with subsequent purification. It is available in compressed-gas cylinders and tanks and, in a few areas, as cryogenic hydrogen in the liquid form. Dissociated ammonia atmosphere is formed by the controlled cracking of ammonia gas in a cracking unit that yields a gas mixture of 75% hydrogen-25% nitrogen. Both dissociated ammonia and hydrogen are widely used in brazing cycles as reducing atmospheres to remove chromium oxide in stainless steel alloys. Only hydrogen or vacuum are satisfactory as an atmosphere with the boron-containing filler metals in the BNi series because the presence of nitrogen in the dissociated ammonia will interfere with filler-metal flow by tying up the boron as boron nitride and raising the melting point of the filler metal.

Nitrogen-based atmospheres are being used to replace exothermic and endothermic atmospheres. These atmospheres are mixtures of gasified liquid nitrogen and hydrogen gas or cracked methanol. When used for "copper brazing" of steel, moisture is added to remove carbon resulting from cracking of the brazing paste binder. When brazing steels, 2-10% hydrogen is used. Nitrogen-based atmospheres are also used to braze iron and chromium-nickel base metals. To braze stainless steels, the nitrogen-hydrogen atmosphere in the furnace must be very dry. Approximately 20% hydrogen is required to obtain suitable brazing results.

Other atmospheres that are on occasion used in brazing are nitrogen, argon, and other inert atmospheres. Argon or nitrogen is used to backfill a vacuum furnace during the brazing cycle to prevent vaporization of certain base metal or filler metal constituents and is used during the cool down period before removal of the parts from the furnace and exposure to air at room temperature.

The pumping systems of vacuum furnaces remove gaseous elements that would interfere with the brazing process. Because only minute amounts of oxygen or trace gases are present in a vacuum atmosphere, clean parts braze readily, and any oxides that might be present on the parts are immediately broken down as the temperature rises and the evolved oxygen is pumped out of the furnace.

Vacuum brazing is generally used when brazing materials containing titanium and aluminum from 0.05% and above, such as the alloys A-286 and Inconel X750.

For production brazing of base metals containing Ti, Al, and similar active elements, joints are usually plated with electrolytic nickel. The plating thickness ranges from 0.0005 to 0.0015″ (0.013 to 0.038 mm), depending on the percentage of Ti, Al, and other active elements; the brazing temperature; time at heat; and atmosphere quality. A high-quality vacuum atmosphere is also a satisfactory means of brazing titanium and its alloys.

Aluminum vacuum brazing. One of the critical problems in aluminum brazing by furnace or salt-bath methods has been the absolute removal of the last traces of brazing flux from the assembly after brazing. Washing flux residues is costly and is a serious pollution threat because of the large quantities of salts carried into streams and lakes as effluent from the wash and rinse operations. Furthermore, even a trace of residual flux can result in pitting or perforation of the brazement from corrosive attack as the flux trace pocket is exposed to moisture in use.

The addition of small quantities of magnesium in BAlSi filler metals permits fluxless vacuum brazing of aluminum, thus avoiding the flux removal problem. Large-scale vacuum furnaces have been developed for the process. The process is an intermittent, semicontinuous, vacuum-furnace brazing method. Chambers hold multiples of the fixtured assemblies ready for brazing. The brazing filler metal is clad on the surface of the parent metal, with a little extra filler metal required in some cases. A vacuum atmosphere is created for brazing, and, after completion, the chamber is then backfilled with pure, dry nitrogen.

The magnesium in the filler metal vaporizes and acts to break up the tenacious thin skin of aluminum oxides that still remains on the parts. After the oxide is broken up, the filler metal, which melts at a lower temperature than the parent material, flows readily into the joints by capillary action and creates fluxless brazed aluminum assemblies. The process takes place at about 1100° F (595°C). It is now adaptable to some types of assemblies and will, no doubt, become applicable to other designs as experience is gained by industry. Automotive radiators and air-conditioner heat exchangers are current examples of high-production brazements.

Operating techniques. Furnace brazing requires the proper control of temperature. Where brazing is to be performed in an atmosphere, the furnace must be specifically designed for this class of service. In the conveyor-type furnaces, the speed through the furnace must be controllable, because this governs the time the assembly will be subjected to the brazing temperature.

In producing joints by furnace brazing, the entire assembly is raised to brazing temperature. If one member is larger or heavier than another member, it may be slower in arriving at brazing temperature than the lighter member. The joint design must be such that the filler metal can be placed to flow only when both members of the joint are at brazing temperature.

Another factor is that of members having different coefficients of expansion or masses. If, for example, a cylindrical member having a high coefficient of expansion is placed outside another cylindrical member having a lower coefficient of expansion and raised to brazing temperature, the joint clearance at brazing temperature may be too wide to permit a properly brazed joint. This requires the adjustment of joint clearances at room temperature to achieve the proper clearance at brazing temperature.

Sometimes it is possible to compensate for this condition by employing a brazing filler metal that has a wide range between liquidus and solidus and exhibits a sluggish flow. This is not recommended, however, particularly for high-quality joints. When base metals with a higher coefficient of expansion are placed inside those having a lower coefficient of expansion, the conditions are reversed and may call for the opposite adjustment between room temperature and brazing temperature clearances.

Filler metals for furnace brazing should be preplaced in or adjacent to the joint. They may be in the form of rings, washers, shims, paste, powdered alloy, or, in some cases, a plating or coating of brazing filler metal on the base metal. Paste-type copper oxide or copper powders are commonly used and are applied adjacent to but touching the joint. Generally, an atmosphere is used in furnace brazing because the process lends itself so well to this technique and also because it eliminates the postbraze cleaning operation. The particular atmosphere involved is determined by the filler and base metals to be brazed. Only rarely when using atmospheres for brazing is it necessary to employ additions of suitable flux.

In utilizing a flux in a furnace, with or without an atmosphere, the brazing cycle is often a long one, and the flux selected should therefore be capable of performing under the extended brazing cycle. Fluxes, when used with an atmosphere, are to prevent excessive evaporation of higher boiling point elements such as zinc, or they are to prevent the oxidation of elements such as aluminum and titanium. Also, when an atmosphere is used with the flux, it extends the useful life of the flux, thus making it more effective.

The continuous-type furnace will normally be operated at a temperature of 50-150° F (28-83° C) above the liquidus of the filler metal or at the minimum value for the brazing temperature range of the filler metal to be used. The furnace should be brought up to temperature before any parts are processed through it. If an atmosphere is to be used, the furnace must be properly purged before admission of parts, and all safety regulations connected with that atmosphere should be observed.

The proper brazing time can be determined from experimental runs through the furnace. For small production runs, it is sometimes possible to watch the work through a door or peephole in the furnace. A more reliable means of checking brazing temperature at the joint is to place a thermocouple adjacent to the joint area. Provision must be made for cooling the parts after brazing. If brazing has been accomplished in an atmosphere furnace, be sure that the parts have cooled down in the atmosphere below the temperature at which oxides will form on the part.

Retort-type furnaces are commonly used for batch brazing. The retort must be adequately sealed and purged before being put into the hot furnace. This is for safety if the atmosphere is combustible, but is also required to expel the air to ensure the proper atmosphere around the parts.

Furnaces employing a vacuum atmosphere are suited to brazing all materials with the exception of those containing elements having high vapor pressures. These furnaces are best suited for processing high-quality brazements of difficult-to-braze materials such as aluminum, titanium, stainless and heat-resistant alloys, and similar metals. The vacuum atmosphere is obtained from two to four stages of vacuum pumps. Depending on the vacuum level required, the furnace may have a roughing pump and one or two stages of vacuum blowers, or it may have an additional pumping stage, such as an oil diffusion pump.

Resistance Brazing

Resistance brazing involves the use of low-voltage, high alternating-current power applied between two electrodes. The workpiece to be brazed is held between the electrodes under light pressure, and the heat developed in the workpiece from the resistance to the flow of electric current causes the filler metal to melt and flow into the joint. Two typical examples are brazing of electrical contacts and copper transformer leads. In the first case, the contact is clad on the back face with the filler metal, usually one of the BAg silver brazing filler metals. Heat is usually applied through the power supply of a resistance spot welder, with pressure adjusted carefully so that only enough pressure is applied to secure the position of the contact at brazing heat. The tips of the welder are generally shaped to the contour of the electrode. In some cases, it is advisable to use one of the lower conductivity electrode materials and let the electrode act as a heat source as it heats itself. Flux is employed and heating time is generally short.

In the joining of copper leads to large transformers, the ends of the power leads are equipped with carbon electrodes or faces that heat to a red heat. This additional heat source is required because of the high thermal conductivity of the metal. Filler metal is usually one of the BCuP series. No flux is required.

Power used. Resistance brazing is commonly applied to joints of a relatively small area because it is difficult to get uniform distribution of current in a large area or one in which the joint is discontinuous. It is necessary that access to the joints be possible from both sides to apply pressure. It is desirable to have the parts self-aligning or self-jigging to avoid the use of metal jigs within the secondary of the resistance welding circuit. Base metals having high electrical conductivity are best suited for resistance brazing.

Resistance welding equipment employs low voltages ranging from 2 to 25 V; the current will range from about 50 A for small parts to thousands of amperes for larger masses. The commercial equipment used for conventional resistance welding may be altered for use in resistance brazing; however, special commercial equipment is available for resistance brazing. Generally, resistance brazing calls for lower pressure and longer time of current flow than is necessary for usual spot, flash, or upset welding.

Electrode. The electrodes employed must be of high electrical resistance because the heat is generated principally in the electrodes and carried to the workpiece by conduction. It is unsatisfactory to use the resistance of the work as the sole source of heat. The current requirements are generally as high as those needed for spot welding in similar metals.

Carbon or graphite blocks, rods, or pencils are frequently used because filler metal will not readily wet these materials. However, they wear and waste away rapidly, necessitating frequent replacement. Tungsten or molybdenum stand up better in service. The time of current flow varies from about 1 second for small parts to several minutes for large, heavy work. The time of current flow is usually controlled manually by the operator, who determines when the filler metal has flowed and the joint is completed.

Filler metals and fluxes. Filler metals may be preplaced in the form of shims, washers, rings, or paste. In some cases, particularly when using the incandescent carbon-block tongs

CHAPTER 10

OTHER BRAZING PROCESSES

for heating copper and copper alloys to which the BCuP series are applied, it is possible to face-feed the filler metal. Fluxes are generally necessary with all the filler metals except the BCuP alloys, which when used on copper to copper are considered to be self-fluxing. Because dry fluxes are nonconductors of electricity, the fluxes should be moist when brazing is started.

Laser Brazing

The use of lasers (discussed in Chapter 9, "Welding and Cutting," of this volume) as a source of heat for brazing and soldering is a relatively recent development. A major advantage of using lasers is the capability of selectively applying heating energy to small areas without heating the entire component. Another advantage is close control of heat input and the ability to locate or position the heat accurately. The use of lasers also controls grain structure and intermetallic formations. Details with respect to the use of lasers are presented later in this chapter under the subject of soldering.

Because of their advantages, lasers are being used for the production of miniature and thin precision parts, to make joints near thermally sensitive connections, and for connections inside evacuated or pressurized vessels or containers. However, because of the high costs of laser equipment, the method is generally only being used when other brazing methods are not found to be adequate.

Diffusion Brazing

Diffusion brazing differs from other brazing methods in that a distinct layer of brazing filler metal is diffused into and with the base metal to change the physical properties of the joint. During diffusion brazing, the filler metal melts or a eutectic liquid forms from alloying between the two higher melting metals or alloys such as copper and silver-plated copper. Diffusion at the interface continues, and a layer of a new alloy may remain or the filler metal may disappear. As a result, the joint properties are nearly the same as those of the base metal. A limitation is that the cycles for diffusion brazing are longer than for other brazing processes. Depending on the variables of temperature, quantity of filler metal, and mutual solubility, the time at the brazing temperature can range from 10 minutes to many hours.

An example of diffusion brazing is high-temperature, nickel-based metal brazed with BNi-1a filler metal at 2150° F (1175° C) for 30 minutes at heat, with a joint clearance of 0.002" (0.05 mm). The filler metal has a solidus temperature of 1700° F (925° C). However, after the diffusion cycle, the remelt temperature is above 2500° F (1370° C). Thus, the brazement can operate in a 1900° F (1040° C) temperature for the life of the base metal and designed service.

Electron Beam Brazing

Electron beam welding equipment, discussed in Chapter 9, is only being used to a limited extent for brazing. Applications are generally restricted to small assemblies or the encapsulating of packaged devices. High vacuums in the work chambers permit the brazing of clean joints without the need for a flux or an atmosphere. The electron beams are defocused to reduce the power density and heating effect.

Exothermic Brazing

In exothermic brazing, the heat required is generated by the reaction of several chemical compounds. Solid-state or nearly solid-state metal-metal oxide reactions are used. Ignition of the exothermic mixture is by a flame, a hot spark, or a resistance heater. The preparation of the brazement, filler metal, flux, or atmosphere are similar to other brazing processes.

Other Brazing Processes

There are several other brazing processes, generally less commonly used than the methods that have been described.

Arc brazing. In this process, the heat required for brazing is obtained from an electric arc. In twin carbon arc brazing, the electric arc is established between two carbon electrodes.

Block brazing. In this process, the heat required for brazing is obtained from heated blocks applied to the parts to be joined.

Flow brazing. In this process, a molten nonferrous metal is poured over the joint until brazing temperature is attained.

Blanket brazing. In this process, a resistance-heated blanket is placed over the parts to be joined, generally using ceramic dies. Heat is transferred to the parts by conduction and radiation. This process is used frequently for brazed honeycomb fabrication.

Step brazing. In this method, which can be used with many of the brazing processes discussed, brazing of successive joints on an assembly is done with filler metals of successively lower melting temperatures. In this way, joining is accomplished without disturbing the joints previously brazed.

Brazing Automation

Brazing is being done automatically with various heating methods, including torches, furnaces (controlled atmosphere, including vacuum), resistance, induction, dip, and infrared methods. Accurate control of temperature and time at temperature is essential for any automated process. Filler metals are either preplaced at the joints during assembly of the components or, in some processes, are automatically fed into the joints at the brazing temperature.

Automatic applicators for paste alloys (mixtures of powdered filler metal and flux in a paste binder) have expanded the use of automatic brazing and soldering systems. Such systems include rotary index, in-line, fixed station, and shuttle machines.

Various degrees of automation are being used. Completely automated systems can include automatic fluxing (if paste alloys are not used), in-line inspection and cleaning, simultaneous brazing of multiple joints, and continuous brazing operations. The cost of automating is generally justified by increased productivity and, in many cases, by the material and energy savings.

BRAZING VARIOUS MATERIALS

Most materials, both metallic and nonmetallic, can be brazed with very few exceptions. The most common base metals are carbon steels, stainless and alloy steels, nickel and cobalt alloys, copper and brass alloys, and aluminum and some of its alloys. Refractory and precious metals, carbides, ceramics, and cermets are also brazed to themselves or to various materials.

Cast Irons

Most cast irons can be brazed, but white cast irons are seldom brazed. Special precleaning methods are required, however, to remove graphite from the workpiece surfaces. Also, brazing temperatures are kept as low as possible, with the filler metals used generally being silver based. Nickel filler metals containing chromium are used in brazing cast irons at higher temperatures. With these filler metals, special precleaning is not required.

Carbon and Low-Alloy Steels

Carbon and low-alloy steels can usually be brazed without difficulty. For some hardenable low-alloy steels, however, the required heat treatment must be taken into consideration when selecting the filler metal. In some cases, brazing and heat treating operations can be combined. Short brazing cycles are recommended for low-alloy steels to minimize the possibility of decarburization and grain growth. In furnace brazing, decarburization is controlled by changing the carbon potential of the atmosphere. This is most easily done by controlling the dew point of the atmosphere.

Stainless Steels

Surface contaminants and chromium oxide films, as well as base metal inclusions, can prevent optimum brazing of stainless steels, and brazeability varies with the type of stainless steel being joined. Chemical cleaning and immediate brazing in a protective atmosphere (including vacuum) is often required. Fluxes are also available that dissolve surface films during heating, but they should never be used in a vacuum furnace. When torch brazing, filler metals that melt at about 1100° F (595° C) help reduce oxidation, and prolonged brazing times at temperatures between 900 and 1600° F (480 and 870° C) should be avoided to minimize carbide precipitation.

Heat-Resistant Alloys

Nickel and cobalt-based, heat-resistant alloys (superalloys) often require chemical cleaning and sometimes mechanical cleaning prior to brazing. Controlled atmospheres, including vacuum, are used for high-quality brazing to prevent the formation of oxides and to reduce the oxides present on the workpiece surfaces.

Reactive and Refractory Metals

Reactive metals such as titanium, zirconium, and beryllium require cleaning to remove surface oxide films prior to brazing. Zirconium and titanium should be brazed immediately after cleaning. Brazing of all reactive metals must be done in a dry, inert-gas atmosphere or a vacuum atmosphere. Refractory metals such as molybdenum and tungsten can also be brazed in a vacuum atmosphere or in an argon or helium atmosphere having a low dew point.

Carbides and Cermets

Materials having a high percentage of tungsten and tantalum carbide are relatively easy to braze, but those with a high titanium carbide content are more difficult to braze. Care is necessary, however, in brazing all carbides and cermets because of the brittleness and low thermal expansion of these materials. When brazing to hard metal components such as toolholders, a layer of ductile metal (pure nickel or copper) is placed between the hard metal and the carbide or cermet. Filler metal shims with copper cores are available for this purpose.

Aluminum Alloys

Brazing of aluminum alloys is practical because of filler metals with suitable melting temperatures and properties and because of fluxes that disrupt the oxide film on these materials.

Fluxless brazing of aluminum in a vacuum is also being done, as discussed previously under the subject of furnace brazing.

Nonheat-treatable, wrought aluminum alloys in the 1XXX and 3XXX series, and low-magnesium alloys in the 5XXX series are brazed most successfully. However, heat-treatable wrought alloys in the 6XXX series are the most commonly brazed. Aluminum alloys having high magnesium contents of 1.0% or more are either difficult or impossible to braze. Aluminum alloys in the 2XXX and 7XXX series, with the exception of 7005 and 7072 alloys, are not usually brazeable because of their low melting temperatures. Most casting alloys are not brazeable; only casting alloys 100.0, 443.0, 710.0, 711.0, and 712.0 are considered brazeable with standard, commercial brazing procedures. Heat control is critical because the melting points of the aluminum alloys to be brazed are so close to the brazing temperatures.

Copper and Copper Alloys

Most coppers and copper alloys are brazeable, but some, such as aluminum bronzes, are more difficult to braze. Some lead-containing alloys form a dross that interferes with brazing. Also, alloys containing tin and silicon bronzes generally require stress relieving prior to brazing to avoid cracking. Tough-pitch coppers should not be brazed in the presence of hydrogen because it causes embrittlement.

Dissimilar Metal Combinations

Many combinations of metals can be brazed together. However, the filler metal used must be compatible with both base metals. Also, any differences in thermal expansions of the base metals must be taken into consideration to ensure proper joint clearances at the brazing temperature.

JOINT DESIGNS

Brazements should be designed so that the filler metal can be placed in the joint or on one side of the joint and pulled through the joint by capillary action. Design should preferably make allowance for preplacement or feeding of the filler metal into the joint area. Under some conditions, there is a limit to the distance filler metal will travel by capillary action. However, under most conditions, filler metal will flow a long distance by capillary action. Enough filler metal should be made available to fill the joint area completely.

Lap joints should be overlapped only enough to produce sufficient load-carrying capacity. This is usually four to six times the thickness of the thinner joint member. Tests should be made to determine the proper overlap. AWS Standard C3.2, "Standard Method for Evaluating the Strength of Brazed Joints in Shear," should be used for such tests.

Design Rules

The following are general rules to consider in any design for brazing. The design is correct if:

1. The assembly meets the physical and environmental criteria required for service.
2. The cost is considered to be acceptable from a manufacturing and end-use point of view.

In other words, any design is good if it is suitable for the purpose for which it is intended. Figure 10-7 illustrates some basic braze designs in use today. Note that all follow three basic concepts of joint-area geometry: (1) butt, (2) scarf, and (3) lap or

JOINT DESIGNS

Lap joint designs

Low stress

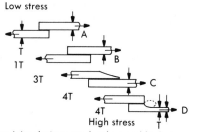

High stress

Lap joint designs used at low and high stresses. Note flexure of right member in C and D will distribute load through base metal

Butt joint designs

Low stress

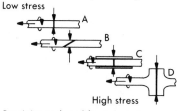

High stress

Butt joint and modifications to increase load-carrying capacity of joint under high stress and dynamic loading

Butt

Lap

Two basic types of joints used in brazements

Sheet metal joint designs—1

Butt flange joint

Butt joint and doubler

Designs useful with sheet metal brazements

Plate-to-plate or shaft-to-hub joint designs—1

Low stress

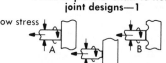

High stress

Sheet-and-plate or hub-and-shaft joint designs showing methods of removing stress concentration from edge of brazed joint. Note that grooves indicated in B and C may appear to weaken member; however, they actually increase overall brazement strength

Plate-to-plate or shaft-to-hub joint designs—2

Low stress

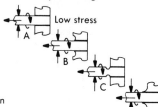

High stress

Sheet metal joint designs—2

Low stress

High stress

Joint designs for sheet metal brazements, including increasing ability to carry higher static and dynamic loading

Tube and header joint designs

Low stress

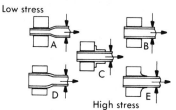

High stress

Designs for tube and header joints in a heat exchanger. High-velocity air across tubes, pulsations, and sonic stresses can vibrate tubes to destruction. In A and B, maximum stress is at header and thus tube will fail in fatigue at this point. C, D, and E distribute stresses, thus increasing allowance loading and service life

Tube-fitting joint designs

Low stress

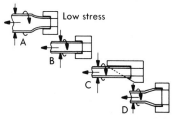

High stress

Joint designs for tube and fittings. Reducing tube sizing as indicated in A will produce a serviceable brazement for low stresses; however, multiple stress concentrations produced preclude its use in high-stressed dynamic loading. Expanding tube as indicated in D will produce best overall strength. Exact increase in diameter, contour of radii, and angle of expanded tube (as in C) will have to be developed for optimum service life with a specific design requirement

Tube and diaphragm joint designs

Formed metal fillet

Low stress   Gusset

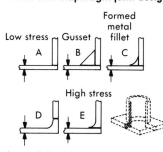

High stress

Represents tube and diaphragm section of an actual part where diaphragm was hydraulically loaded. Premature failure was encountered when designed as in A. The redesign stiffened the assembly to remove high stresses at one side of joint. Fillets such as in D and E, will also improve serviceability

Fig. 10-7 Joint designs used for brazing. (*Wall Colmonoy Corp.*)

shear. However, scarf joints are seldom used. Specifications for the design, manufacture, and inspection of critical brazed components are presented in ANSI/AWS Standard C3.3.

Clearances

For optimum conditions during brazing and for service requirements requiring highest strength, the clearance at brazing temperature should be as shown in Table 10-1. The reasons for these clearances are primarily to attain good capillary flow of the filler metal into or throughout the joint and to develop best tensile properties in the finished product. Joints made with too little or too much clearance will suffer in strength.

Types of Joints

Butt joints are used where the strengths of the brazed or diffusion-brazed joints are equal to, or nearly equal to, the base metal properties. When the filler metal used produces a weak butt joint, it is desirable to use a lap joint design where the overlap distance can be increased to give the required load-carrying capability.

In brazed lap joints, if t is the thickness of the thinnest member, the joint overlaps should be a minimum of $3t$. Following this principle with filler metals that are essentially equal to or above the base metal strength ensures that all joint strengths equal or exceed the strength of the parent metal being brazed. In designing critical joints, the strength should be tested using the shear test procedure specified in AWS Standard C3.2.

The following factors should also be considered in the design of brazements:

1. With a $3t$ design, the brazement may be looked on as one piece for stress-analysis purposes.
2. Locate the point of maximum stress in the design away from the edge of the braze joint.
3. Braze fillets are weak because the filler metal itself may be a weak material in this area of the joint. Excessively large fillets add nothing to the strength of the joint and are difficult and sometimes impossible to control.

Elevated Temperature Service Designs

Some filler metals can be used at relatively high service temperatures, depending on the joint properties. The materials most commonly considered for service above room temperature are the BAg group (silver brazing), 400-600° F (205-315° C); the BCu group (copper brazing), 700-900° F (370-480° C); the BAu group (gold brazing), 800-1000° F (425-540° C); and the BNi group (nickel brazing), 1400-2200° F (760-1205° C). Loss of filler metal from oxidation and creep and tensile strength of the filler metal at temperature are involved in the selection of material for elevated temperature service.

Gold and nickel alloy filler metals are widely used for brazing stainless steels for elevated temperature service on gas turbines. Copper filler metals are seldom used in joining carbon steels for service at elevated temperatures. In any program

TABLE 10-1
Recommended Joint Clearances at Brazing Temperature

Filler Metal, AWS Classification Group	Joint Clearance,* in. (mm)	Conditions
BAlSi	0.002-0.008 (0.05-0.20)	For length of lap less than 0.25″ (6.4 mm)
	0.008-0.010 (0.20-0.25)	For length of lap greater than 0.25″ (6.4 mm)
BCuP	0.001-0.010 (0.03-0.25)	For joint lengths less than 1″ (25 mm), with no flux and mineral fluxes
	0.007-0.015 (0.18-0.38)	For joint lengths greater than 1″ (25 mm) with no flux and mineral fluxes
BAg	0.002-0.005 (0.05-0.13)	Flux brazing (mineral fluxes)
	0.000-0.002 (0.05)**	Atmosphere brazing (gas phase fluxes)
BAu	0.002-0.005 (0.05-0.13)	Flux brazing (mineral fluxes)
	0.000-0.002 (0.05)**	Atmosphere brazing (gas phase fluxes)
BCu	0.000-0.002 (0.05)**	Atmosphere brazing (gas phase fluxes)
BCuZn	0.002-0.005 (0.05-0.13)	Flux brazing (mineral fluxes)
BMg	0.004-0.010 (0.10-0.25)	Flux brazing (mineral fluxes)
BNi	0.002-0.005 (0.05-0.13)	General applications (flux/atmosphere)
	0.000-0.002 (0.05)	Free-flowing types, atmosphere brazing

* Clearance on the radius when rings, plugs, or tubular members are involved. On some applications it may be necessary to use the recommended clearance on the diameter to assure not having excessive clearance when all the clearance is on one side. An excessive clearance will produce voids. This is particularly true when brazing is accomplished in a high-quality atmosphere (gas phase fluxing).

** For maximum strength, a press fit of 0.001 in./in. (mm/mm) of diameter should be used.

JOINT DESIGNS

involving elevated temperature, a test program to evaluate actual service on a prototype basis is mandatory.

Corrosive Service Design

Design for service in a corrosive environment is a vastly complex subject. Corrosion studies of base metals are further complicated by the introduction of a filler metal in a brazement. BNi filler metals can generally be considered to have much the same corrosion properties as found in stainless steel in an assembly of stainless steel and similar alloys, particularly when they have been adequately diffusion brazed. BAg filler metals are stable under certain conditions. Data are so sketchy when all the possible combinations and environments are considered that predictions are only tentative at best in any one set of circumstances. Mild corrosive attack is well resisted by silver alloy filler metals.

Specific examples may show that certain organic acids may corrode the joint area. Tapwater may corrode a silver-brazed joint in stainless steel using BAg-1 filler metal. BAg-21 and BAg-3 containing 2.5 and 3% nickel, respectively, will successfully resist such attack, which is known as crevice corrosion. The BAu filler metals and other filler metals containing the noble metals gold, platinum, and palladium have excellent resistance to chemical attack and are used for service in corrosive environments. Filler metals for the food industry must not contain cadmium, lead, or copper to meet most health code requirements.

Designing for Simplicity

Most efficient designs for brazing are self-fixturing for good reason: fixtures cost money to make, maintain, and use. In furnace brazing, for example, every attempt is made to make the parts self-fixturing. Fixtures add to the weight of the parts being brazed. Furthermore, a fixture will change dimensions in repeated runs through the furnace, requiring frequent rework to bring it to tolerance. In induction brazing, fixtures may frequently be required to maintain alignment of parts during the heat cycle. Areas of the fixture that approach the magnetic induction field must be made of nonmetallic materials. Torch brazing almost always requires fixtures of one type or another. These fixtures must be as simple as possible. Locating points must be kept away from the heating areas if possible. Dip brazing, particularly in the flux-bath brazing of aluminum, generally utilizes staking or self-fixturing because most fixture materials can contaminate the bath. Brazing of aluminum is generally performed at within 10 to 100°F (5.6 to 55.6°C) of the melting point of the parent metal.

SURFACE PREPARATION

Brazing will be performed satisfactorily only if and when the filler metal wets the surface of the metals to be joined. Any soil, oxides, coatings, oil, or other contaminants present on the surfaces prior to heating may interfere with this wetting and result in defective brazing. Because cleaning costs are high and are reflected in the overall cost of the operation, only that cleaning that is required should be performed. Keeping the parts to be brazed clean after the various operations that precede heating is the best assurance of a trouble-free operation. Cleaning can take all forms of operation from reasonable care in protecting parts from unnecessary contamination (as in copper brazing of carbon-steel parts in an atmosphere furnace) to ultrasonic cleaning to remove staining and fingerprinting (as in the case of brazed honeycomb panels for aerospace applications). Principal cleaning methods are discussed in Volume III, *Materials, Finishing and Coating*, of this Handbook series.

JOINT STRENGTH AND QUALITY

In some applications, brazing can provide higher joint strengths than fusion welding, without requiring the higher temperatures needed for fusion welding. In any analysis of brazing as a joining process, careful consideration must be given to the effect of the heating cycle on the properties of the base metal. Depending on the time of the brazing cycle and the temperatures reached during the process, many changes can take place in the original base metal properties. Among these are the following:

1. *Annealing.* Generally, brazing takes place above the annealing temperature of base metals, although there are exceptions. Details of the annealing process are presented in Volume III of this Handbook series. In furnace brazing, the entire assembly will be full-annealed, and for cold-worked sheet steel this may mean a reduction of tensile strength from more than 100 to less than 40 ksi (690 to less than 275 MPa). Spring-tempered components will lose their properties in the braze area. Localized heating, such as induction or torch heating, may restrict this annealing effect to a narrow area of the joint.

2. *Hardening.* In some cases, as in the air hardening of metals such as AISI 400 series stainless steels, simultaneous hardening with furnace or induction brazing can be accomplished. This effect is used in the furnace brazing of aircraft components. Postbraze treatment would require a tempering treatment. Localized heating for silver brazing can be accomplished on fully hardened components without seriously affecting the fully hardened condition, as in heat-treated 4140 steel tool shanks to which carbide inserts can be brazed under special conditions.

3. *Distortion.* Residual stresses in parts to be furnace brazed do not cause distortion. Uniform heating and cooling relieve the stresses equal and opposite, thus there is no distortion. The cause of distortion in general is the differential temperature in a given part during heating and cooling. Base metals that transform on heating or that are weak at temperature compound the problem. Care should be taken to develop the proper furnace brazing cycle. Localized heating can cause distortion if heating is not symmetrical.

Expansion

Materials expand during heating at rates determined by their linear coefficients of expansion. Caution must be used when calculating expansion, however, because the maximum temperatures covered in data tables often are not as high as the brazing temperature range. For this reason, the actual expansion that will take place when the brazing range is reached must be considered. For example, some typical materials encountered in brazing and their expansion curves are presented in Fig. 10-8.

Residual stresses. Because the brazing filler metal will solidify at a predetermined temperature, the materials will be joined prior to their cooling cycle from the brazing temperature. If their expansion characteristics vary widely, severe stresses will arise in assembly during the cooling cycle. Tungsten carbide changes dimensions only slightly during cooling compared with

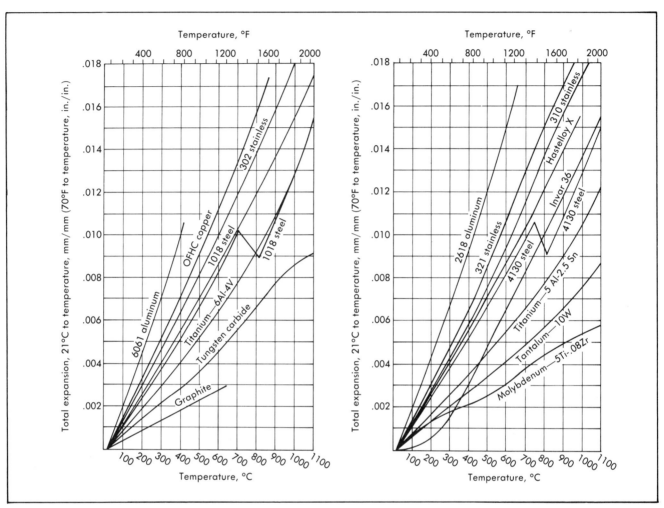

Fig. 10-8 Thermal expansion curves for several common materials.

the steel. For this reason, large carbide sections are a particular problem in brazing. Correction can be made by cooling slowly from the brazing temperature. A cooling rate of 50-100° F/hr (28-55° C/hr) will allow some creep to take place while the filler metal is still in the plastic range, thus minimizing distortion and possible cracking of the carbide. Special composite filler metals, such as clad sandwiches with copper cores, are also available to solve this problem.

Incorrect fitup. At room temperature, a steel plug to be silver brazed into a copper member may have correct clearance, but at brazing temperature the copper will expand more than the steel, enlarging the opening and resulting in excessive clearance for silver brazing, which may result in joint defects. In such a case, a press fit at room temperature may be needed for correct clearance at the temperature at which the filler metal flows into the joint. All assemblies should be designed so appropriate joint clearance is attained at the brazing temperature used.

Carbide Precipitation

Carbide precipitation is a phenomenon of the stainless steels. In such steels, when heated to between 900 and 1600° F (480 and 870° C), carbon combines with the chromium-forming carbides, which precipitate in the grain boundaries. The alloy material

adjacent to the carbide is depleted in chromium and, consequently, its corrosion resistance is reduced. This phenomenon does not influence the mechanical strength of the metal unless the part is subjected to prolonged corrosive attack, in which case it is eaten away. Further, this carbide precipitation is a time-temperature function, taking a longer time at the lower temperatures and occurring more rapidly at the high-temperature side. Correction of the precipitated carbide can be made only by heat treating the assembly to a temperature of 1850-2050° F (1010-1120° C), followed by rapid cooling (water quenching), but such treatment is not usually practical. The best solution to this problem is to perform the brazing as quickly as possible to minimize the time-temperature transition phase and to cool extremely rapidly if brazing is done in the higher temperature range of 1850-2200° F (1010-1205° C). Another solution is to use stabilized stainless steel containing columbium (AISI Type 347) or titanium (AISI Type 321) or to use a low-carbon grade, such as AISI Type 304L.

Stress Cracking

Stress cracking occurs more frequently in high-strength materials such as stainless steels, nickel alloys, and copper-nickel alloys. These metals tend to crack during brazing when

CHAPTER 10

JOINT STRENGTH AND QUALITY

the parts are in highly stressed condition and in contact with molten brazing filler metals. Materials that have high annealing temperatures, and especially those that are age-hardenable, are particularly subject to stress cracking. This condition may be corrected by brazing parts in the annealed or stress-relieved condition rather than in the hardened or residually stressed condition. Another approach is to remove the source of externally applied stress. While the base metals mentioned are more susceptible to stress cracking than others, all base metals are subject to stress cracking to varying degrees.

While residual stresses are most detrimental to base metals where brazing occurs below their annealing temperature, stress cracking can occur above the annealing temperature when stresses are produced by differential temperatures in the part or where a mechanical loading stress is produced by gravity or force exerted on the part. Cracking has occurred in large carbon-steel plates that were brazed with copper filler metal. Two 1″ (25 mm) thick plates, 40″ (1016 mm) wide by 60″ (1524 mm) long, cracked perpendicular to the outer edges when cooled too fast while liquid copper was still present on the part. Type 304 stainless steel plate, about the same size but about 6″ (152 mm) thick, also exhibited stress cracking when it was copper brazed.

Sulfur effects. Sulfur embrittlement is a problem with nickel and certain alloys containing appreciable amounts of nickel. If such metals are heated in the presence of sulfur or high-sulfur-content compounds, they may become embrittled. Material that is so embrittled must be scrapped. It is important that such alloys, when brazed, be clean and free of sulfur-containing materials such as oil, grease, paint, crayon marks, and drawing lubricants; heating must be done only in a reasonably sulfur-free atmosphere.

Phosphorus embrittlement. Phosphorus embrittlement is a condition created in certain metals by the formation of brittle compounds known as phosphides. Copper brazing filler metals containing phosphorus must not be used with any copper alloys, iron or nickel-based alloys, or alloys containing more than 10% of either component.

Nickel brazing filler metals containing phosphorus, however, have found extensive use when they are diffusion brazed. If the nickel-phosphorus filler metals are brazed for short times at low temperatures, their strength and ductility are low. However, at higher brazing temperatures with longer times at heat they can produce sufficient strength to tear the base metal. For example, BNi-7, when brazed at 1950° F (1065° C) for 60 minutes in tight-fitting joints of Type 304 stainless steel, is one example.

Quality Control

Prebraze inspection is highly important to ensure cleanliness and proper fitup between mating parts. Postbraze inspection is performed by several different methods. Details with respect to the inspection of critical brazed joints are presented in ANSI/AWS Standard C3.3.

Visual inspection. In an ideal situation, the filler metal is preplaced so that on melting it is pulled through the facing surfaces of the joint members by capillary action. Visual inspection will verify the extent of this pull-through. The joint fillet areas should be smooth and free of excess porosity and voids. Failure to show good wetting and good flow in the joint area is cause for rejection of a brazement.

The size of the braze fillet is not significant, and a radius of 0.010″ (0.25 mm) will generally provide as strong a joint as a radius of 0.030″ (0.76 mm). The radius is dictated by capillary action and cannot be increased to approach that used, for example, in welding.

Peel testing. A peel test is made by sawing through the brazed area and, with a wrench or pliers, attempting to pull the joined section apart. This will expose the joint area and show the extent of flow of the filler metal during brazing. Generally, the coverage that should be expected in a mineral-fluxed braze is a minimum of 80%. The remainder of the area will be voids caused by gas pockets or pockets of brazing flux. In a good peel test, the parent metal should be bonded tightly to the braze filler metal. Tearing of the parent metal indicates a high-quality joint. A few exceptions to this rule exist, such as brazing a very soft metal (copper) with a stronger filler metal (BAg-1), in which case it will be difficult to tear the filler metal from the base metal at all.

Joints brazed in a protective atmosphere (gas-phase flux) usually have filler metal coverage in the joint of nearly 100%. This assumes that the joint clearances at the brazing temperature and the brazing procedure are proper.

Load testing. The load test is based on the arbitrary selection of a load applied to one member of the brazed joint in either tension or compression. In the case of a plug brazed into a plate, the test might indicate "minimum pushout load permitted is 200 lb (90 kg) applied to the plug axially." Load testing is a very practical testing method, but must be tailored to each particular job to be effective.

Radiography. X-ray examination is sometimes useful. Such a test will show the extent of flow of the filler metal in the joint area. Interpretation may be difficult unless standards are available to evaluate the density of the image on the film.

Limitations of the X-ray process must be taken into consideration, as defects may not be discernible in a low-clearance joint, particularly as the thickness of the base metal increases. High silver or gold-containing filler metals have a higher X-ray density. As a result, voids are more visible than for copper, nickel, and other filler metals having X-ray densities similar to the base metal. Most X-ray processes have a 2% sensitivity and thus can only pick up a void in excess of 0.002″ (0.05 mm) in a steel joint of 1.000″ (25.4 mm) total thickness when brazed with copper filler metal. Radiography is discussed in Chapter 6, "Nondestructive Testing," of this volume.

Metallography. Preparation of a microsection of the joint area will reveal the flow of the filler metal, intermetallic compounds, extent of diffusion bonding in the filler metal, and the extent of penetration of the filler metal into the base metal.

Pressure testing. Vessels designed to contain fluids are often tested for leakage in the brazed-joint area by closing all openings in the assembly and pressurizing with low-pressure air as the part is immersed in water. Appearance of bubbles will quickly identify areas where leaks are present. With the proper safety precautions, pressure vessels can be tested by a similar method at pressures to 100 psi (690 kPa) to determine (1) the extent of leakage under high pressure and (2) the ability of the assembly to withstand the stated pressure without failure. Higher pressure testing and proof testing are accomplished hydrostatically. Additional information on leak testing can be found in Chapter 6.

Vacuum testing. Many brazed joints used in the vacuum, nuclear, and other industries must be far tighter than pressure testing will detect. As a result, they must be tested under vacuum, using helium as the testing gas and a mass spectrometer leak detector. The leak detector is very sensitive and will detect every minute leakage. Leak testing is discussed in Chapter 6.

BRAZING FILLER METALS

Ultrasonic inspection. Provided that the geometry permits and a suitable transmitting crystal head can be designed, ultrasonic inspection is effective as a nondestructive test for brazed joints. Evaluation is made semiquantitatively by comparing a known sample (with the extent of defect determined in advance to be acceptable) with an unknown part being inspected. A significant curve form is developed for each assembly and shown on a cathode-ray tube. Recent innovations include recording this information on a chart to give an accurate picture of the validity of any one section of the joint as the crystal traverses the joint area. These tests may or may not be performed under water. Ultrasonic testing is discussed in greater detail in Chapter 6.

Prototype sampling. When it is impossible to perform adequate nondestructive testing on a brazed joint, it is sometimes necessary to simulate the joint and then perform destructive testing such as peel tests and metallographic tests to verify the braze filler metal penetration into the joint area.

Other tests. If surface porosity and cracking of the filler metal are important, these parameters can be evaluated by fluorescent-penetrant inspection in a manner similar to the systems used for inspection of weld fillets for cracks in a weld. This method of inspection may give misleading results as fillets are cast structures and frequently have shrinkage porosity. Porosity indications must not be confused with cracking. Rate of heat transfer through a brazed joint in a heat exchanger is often tested by rating the completed exchanger to determine the Btu (J) output of the brazed heat-transfer section. This is in itself an indirect test of the brazed-joint area. Helium or freon leak testing is often performed on brazed joints for refrigeration and air-conditioning systems where low levels of freon leakage are specified.

Details of inspection equipment and techniques, nondestructive testing, and mechanical testing are presented in Chapters 3, 6, and 7.

BRAZING FILLER METALS

The AWS defines brazing filler metals as those to be added in making a braze. They are metals or alloys with liquidus temperature above 840° F (450° C). By the definition of brazing, the filler metal must melt below the melting point of the parts joined and must be capable of distribution in the closely fitted joint by capillary action. These filler metals were formerly identified as hard solders, silver solder, and brazing alloys, but these terms are now considered obsolete and, in their place, the term *brazing filler metal* is preferred.

The AWS *Brazing Manual* lists the following four properties as essential for brazing filler metal:[1]

1. Ability to wet the base metals on which it is used in order to make a strong, sound bond.
2. Proper melting temperature and flow properties that permit distribution in properly prepared joints by capillary action.
3. A composition of sufficient homogeneity and stability to minimize separation by liquation under the brazing conditions to be encountered, and free of excessively volatile constituents.
4. Desirable mechanical and physical properties in the joint, such as strength and ductility.

Brazing filler metal melting does not occur at one distinct temperature (except for pure metals and those of eutectic composition), but rather over a range. The lower temperature of the range is known as the *solidus*; the upper temperature of the range is known as the *liquidus*. The definitions of these points given in the AWS *Brazing Manual* are as follows: "Solidus is the highest temperature at which a metal or alloy is completely solid...Liquidus is the lowest temperature at which a metal or alloy is completely liquid." Brazing usually takes place at a temperature above the liquidus. However, certain alloys exhibit the peculiar property of being essentially molten below the true liquidus and, in consequence, brazing with these alloys may be performed at a temperature below the liquidus. To identify these points for a given alloy and not create confusion, each alloy is identified by its solidus and liquidus. A brazing temperature range is also provided that indicates the range of temperatures at which brazing is best performed.

Brazing filler metals are covered by "Specification for Brazing Filler Metal," AWS A5.8. Under this specification, provision is made for several groups of brazing filler metals. The classification numbers employ the letter B to identify brazing filler metals. Following this letter the classification employs the chemical symbols for the principal alloying element(s) found in the brazing filler metal. Next there follows a number(s) to differentiate the several compositions available in any one alloy group. Brazing filler metal designations with a letter V following the B refer to vacuum-grade filler metals for electronic devices. The following tables of filler metals list only the nominal chemistry; the A5.8 specification, however, lists the chemical range for each element.

Table 10-2 covers the aluminum-silicon brazing filler metals. Table 10-3 lists the copper-phosphorus brazing filler metals.

TABLE 10-2
Aluminum Brazing Filler Metals

AWS Classification	Nominal Composition, %				Temperature, °F (°C)		
	Si	Cu	Mg	Al	Solidus	Liquidus	Brazing Range
BAlSi-2	7.5	—	—	92.5	1070 (577)	1135 (613)	1110-1150 (599-621)
BAlSi-3	10	4	—	86	970 (521)	1085 (585)	1060-1120 (571-604)
BAlSi-4	12	—	—	88	1070 (577)	1080 (582)	1080-1120 (582-604)
BAlSi-5	10	—	—	90	1070 (577)	1095 (591)	1090-1120 (588-604)
BAlSi-7	10	—	1.5	88.5	1038 (559)	1105 (596)	1090-1120 (588-604)
BAlSi-9	12	—	0.3	87.7	1044 (562)	1080 (582)	1080-1120 (582-604)
BAlSi-11*	10	—	1.5	88.8	1038 (559)	1105 (596)	1090-1120 (588-604)

* Also contains 0.1 Bi.

BRAZING FILLER METALS

TABLE 10-3
Copper-Phosphorus Brazing Filler Metals

AWS Classification	Nominal Composition, %			Temperature, °F (°C)		
	Cu	Ag	P	Solidus	Liquidus	Brazing Range
BCuP-1	95	—	5	1310 (710)	1695 (924)	1450-1700 (788-927)
BCuP-2	92.75	—	7.25	1310 (710)	1460 (793)	1350-1550 (732-843)
BCuP-3	89	5	6	1190 (643)	1495 (813)	1325-1500 (718-816)
BCuP-4	86.75	6	7.25	1190 (643)	1325 (718)	1275-1450 (691-788)
BCuP-5	80	15	5	1190 (643)	1475 (802)	1300-1500 (704-816)
BCuP-6	91	2	7	1190 (643)	1450 (788)	1350-1500 (732-816)
BCuP-7	88.25	5	6.75	1190 (643)	1420 (771)	1300-1500 (704-816)

Note that BCuP-1 and 2 contain only copper and phosphorus, while classifications BCuP-3, 4, 5, 6, and 7 also contain silver. Certain of these filler metals have brazing temperature ranges below the liquidus indicated for the composition. These phosphorus brazing filler metals must not be used with any base metals containing iron or nickel and should not be used in environments with sulfur-bearing oil.

One of the most important groups of brazing filler metals is that based on silver. In Table 10-4 is a listing of the silver-based brazing filler metals. These are the filler metals that were formerly identified as "silver solders." They are widely used for joining similar metals and alloys and joining dissimilar metals of various compositions. In general, they are not suited for any dissimilar metal combinations involving aluminum or magnesium. Note in this table that all the brazing temperature ranges start at the liquidus. With the current emphasis on safety and health, the filler metals containing cadmium are being replaced with noncadmium silver filler metals.

Gold brazing filler metals are given in Table 10-5. These filler metals are used in the manufacture of electron tubes, aircraft jet engines, aerospace parts, and other components. Another significant group of brazing filler metals is known as the copper and copper-zinc group, as listed in Table 10-6. The copper brazing filler metal classification BCu is used almost exclusively in the furnace brazing process in which an atmosphere, usually containing some hydrogen, nitrogen, and frequently also carbon monoxide, is employed. The other classifications in this group are similar and in some cases identical to filler metals used in braze welding. Therefore, with these filler metals it is extremely important to identify the process to be employed, such as true capillary brazing or braze welding.

The nickel brazing filler metals are given in Table 10-7. These brazing filler metals are utilized for assemblies that must operate at elevated temperatures. Some filler metals of classification BNi are suitable for continuous service through 2200° F (1205° C) when properly diffusion brazed and will have remelt temperatures in excess of 2500° F (1370° C). These filler metals also find considerable use at room and cryogenic temperatures.

With few exceptions, all these filler metals are available and can be purchased to specifications with certifications if required. Most brazing filler materials are produced in wire, shim, sheet, powder, and paste. The availability of the BCuP series is sometimes limited because of the high hardness of these metals and the difficulty of forming them to certain sizes.

Filler metals in paste form are blends of finely powdered filler metals and fluxes held in suspension by paste-type binders.

Some pastes contain flux, and, in these types, the binders hold the filler metal and flux in suspension and prevent interaction between the filler metal and flux before heating to the brazing temperature. Different formulations available or custom blended change the rate at which they flow. Advantages of such products include eliminating a separate fluxing operation and ensuring a proper proportion of filler metal to flux. The filler metal pastes that contain no fluxing ingredients are used in furnaces containing atmospheres of vacuum, pure and dry hydrogen, or similar atmospheres that will dissociate metal oxides.

In certain forms of brazing, such as vacuum-tube joining and others, the level of minor impurities, such as higher vapor-pressure elements, in the filler metal is important and can affect the quality of the brazed vacuum tube in service. "Specifications for Brazing Filler Metal," AWS A5.8, contains a number of vacuum-tube filler metals not listed in this section.

BRAZING FLUX

The purpose of a brazing flux is to prevent oxidation of the joint and to promote wetting, flow, and the formation of a soundly brazed joint. A brazing flux, which is a mixture of chemical compounds, performs this function by combining with, excluding, or otherwise rendering harmless those products on the base metal surface that would retard or prevent the formation of a sound brazed joint. A brazing atmosphere provides a similar function as a flux and surrounds the part with an atmosphere that will generally prevent the formation of deleterious substances or that, as with an active gas such as hydrogen, may reduce the substances and render them harmless.

Brazing fluxes are not designed for, nor should they be used for, cleaning dirty base metals. All metal parts for brazing should be precleaned by appropriate techniques. Attempts to perform the cleaning function with the brazing flux usually cause the flux residue to load with oxide and other contaminants that will reduce or destroy the effectiveness of the flux. The flux must be employed only to handle such oxide as is formed during the heating operation.

Generally, the brazing flux must melt and cover the braze area at a temperature below that of the solidus of the filler metal employed. The lower melting point of the brazing flux should be such that it protects the metal during the period of heating and that it keeps the brazing flux fluid and active over the brazing cycle. The flux must not decompose and it must not, of itself, cause any contamination of the brazed area. In the molten

BRAZING FILLER METALS

TABLE 10-4
Silver Brazing Filler Metals

AWS Classification	Nominal Composition, %						Temperature, °F (°C)		
	Ag	Cu	Zn	Cd	Ni	Others	Solidus	Liquidus	Brazing Range
BAg-1	45	15	16	24	—	—	1125 (607)	1145 (618)	1145-1400 (618-760)
BAg-1a	50	15.5	16.5	18	—	—	1160 (627)	1175 (635)	1175-1400 (635-760)
BAg-2	35	26	21	18	—	—	1125 (607)	1295 (702)	1295-1550 (702-843)
BAg-2a	30	27	23	20	—	—	1125 (607)	1310 (710)	1310-1550 (710-843)
BAg-3	50	13.5	15.5	16	3	—	1170 (632)	1270 (688)	1270-1500 (688-816)
BAg-4	40	30	28	—	2	—	1240 (671)	1435 (779)	1435-1650 (779-899)
BAg-5	45	30	25	—	—	—	1250 (677)	1370 (743)	1370-1550 (743-843)
BAg-6	50	31	16	—	—	—	1270 (688)	1425 (774)	1425-1600 (774-871)
BAg-7	56	22	17	—	—	Sn 5	1145 (618)	1205 (652)	1205-1400 (652-760)
BAg-8	72	28	—	—	—	—	1435 (779)	1435 (779)	1435-1650 (779-899)
BAg-8a	72	27.8	—	—	—	Li 0.2	1410 (766)	1410 (766)	1410-1600 (766-871)
BAg-9	65	20	15	—	—	—	1240 (671)	1325 (718)	1325-1550 (718-843)
BAg-10	70	20	10	—	—	—	1275 (691)	1360 (738)	1360-1550 (738-843)
BAg-13	54	40	5	—	1	—	1325 (718)	1575 (857)	1575-1775 (857-968)
BAg-13a	56	42	—	—	2	—	1420 (771)	1640 (893)	1600-1800 (871-982)
BAg-18	60	30	—	—	—	Sn 10	1115 (602)	1325 (718)	1325-1550 (718-843)
BAg-19	92.5	7.3	—	—	—	Li 0.2	1435 (779)	1635 (891)	1610-1800 (877-982)
BAg-20	30	38	32	—	—	—	1250 (677)	1410 (766)	1410-1600 (766-871)
BAg-21	63	28.5	—	—	2.5	Sn 6	1275 (691)	1475 (802)	1475-1650 (802-899)
BAg-22	49	16	23	—	4.5	Mn 7.5	1260 (682)	1290 (699)	1290-1525 (699-829)
BAg-23	85	—	—	—	—	Mn 15	1760 (960)	1780 (971)	1780-1900 (971-1038)
BAg-24	50	20	28	—	2	—	1220 (660)	1305 (707)	1305-1550 (707-843)
BAg-26	25	38	33	—	2	Mn 2	1305 (707)	1475 (802)	1475-1600 (802-871)
BAg-27	25	35	26.5	13.5	—	—	1125 (607)	1375 (746)	1375-1575 (746-857)
BAg-28	40	30	28	—	—	Sn 2	1200 (649)	1310 (710)	1310-1550 (710-843)

TABLE 10-5
Gold Brazing Filler Metals

AWS Classification	Nominal Composition, %				Temperature, °F (°C)		
	Au	Cu	Ni	Pd	Solidus	Liquidus	Brazing Range
BAu-1	37.5	62.5	—	—	1815 (991)	1860 (1016)	1860-2000 (1016-1093)
BAu-2	80	20	—	—	1635 (891)	1635 (891)	1635-1850 (891-1010)
BAu-3	35	62	3	—	1785 (974)	1885 (1029)	1885-1995 (1029-1091)
BAu-4	82	—	18	—	1740 (949)	1740 (949)	1740-1840 (949-1004)
BAu-5	30	—	36	34	2075 (1135)	2130 (1166)	2130-2250 (1166-1232)
BAu-6	70	—	22	8	1845 (1007)	1915 (1046)	1915-2050 (1046-1121)

BRAZING FLUX

condition at the brazing temperature, the flux must have sufficient surface tension to maintain a film within the braze area; yet this film must be capable of being displaced by the molten brazing filler metal when it is introduced. Table 10-8 provides a summary of the principal types of brazing fluxes in commercial use.

Brazing fluxes, in general, contain fluorides or other halogen compounds. Because toxic effects may be produced by the inhalation of fumes produced by the halogens, AWS recommends that all fluxes containing these elements carry an appropriate caution notice that should be strictly observed.

Flux Specifications

The federal government has established specification O-F 499 for silver brazing flux. This document does not specify actual chemical analysis, but does define what chemicals shall be in the flux. Acceptance of a flux is based on performance and ability to function at certain temperatures and over certain time periods. Proprietary fluxes may or may not meet this specification. It would be wise for the user to secure representative samples of many fluxes and evaluate them on a specific job. One flux may actually perform better than another on any one job. Furthermore, certain fluxes perform better than others on specific types of heating operations. For example, one may be better in torch brazing and another may perform better in induction or furnace operations.

Flux Removal

After the flux has melted and been used in a brazing operation, the residue from fluxing can, in many cases, contain large percentages of oxides that are dissolved during the

TABLE 10-6
Copper and Copper-Zinc Brazing Filler Metals

AWS Classification	Nominal Composition, %						Temperature, °F (°C)		
	Cu	Zn	Sn	Ni	Fe	Pb	Solidus	Liquidus	Brazing Range
BCu-1	99.90 min	—	—	—	—	—	1980 (1082)	1980 (1082)	2000-2100 (1093-1149)
BCu-1a	99 min	—	—	—	—	—	1980 (1082)	1980 (1082)	2000-2100 (1093-1149)
BCu-2	86.5 min	—	—	—	—	—	1980 (1082)	1980 (1082)	2000-2100 (1093-1149)
RBCuZn-A	59.25	40	0.75	—	—	—	1630 (888)	1650 (899)	1670-1750 (910-954)
RBCuZn-C	58	40.3	1	—	0.7	—	1590 (866)	1630 (888)	1670-1750 (910-954)
RBCuZn-D	48	42	—	10	—	—	1690 (921)	1715 (935)	1720-1800 (938-982)

TABLE 10-7
Nickel Alloy Brazing Filler Metals

AWS Classification	Nominal Composition, %								Temperature, °F (°C)		
	Ni	Cr	B	Si	Fe	C, max	Mn	P	Solidus	Liquidus	Brazing Range
BNi-1	73.25	14	3.25	4.5	4.5	0.75	—	—	1790 (977)	1900 (1038)	1950-2200 (1066-1204)
BNi-1a	72.75	14	3.25	4.5	4.5	0.06					
BNi-2	82.4	7	3.1	4.5	3	0.06	—	—	1780 (971)	1830 (999)	1850-2150 (1010-1177)
BNi-3	90.9	—	3.1	4.5	1.5	0.06	—	—	1800 (982)	1900 (1038)	1850-2150 (1010-1177)
BNi-4	92.5	—	1.5	3.5	1.5	0.06	—	—	1800 (982)	1950 (1066)	1850-2150 (1010-1177)
BNi-5	70.9	19	—	10.1	—	0.06	—	—	1975 (1079)	2075 (1135)	2100-2200 (1149-1204)
BNi-6	89	—	—	—	—	0.06	—	11	1610 (877)	1610 (877)	1700-2000 (927-1093)
BNi-7	77	13	—	—	—	0.06	—	—	1630 (888)	1630 (1888)	1700-2000 (927-1093)
BNi-8	65.5	4.5	—	7	—	0.06	23	—	1800 (982)	1850 (1010)	1850-2000 (1010-1093)
BNi-9	81.5	14.5	3.6	—	—	0.5	—	—	1930 (1055)	1930 (1055)	1950-2200 (1065-1205)
BNi-10	77.5	12.5	2.5	3.5	3.5	0.4	—	—	1780 (970)	2020 (1105)	2100-2200 (1150-1205)
BNi-11	79.7	10	2.7	3.7	3.5	0.4	—	—	1780 (970)	2000 (1095)	2100-2200 (1150-1205)

TABLE 10-8
Brazing Fluxes

Brazing Flux, AWS Type No.	Base Metals on Which This Flux is Recommended for Use*	Filler Metals on Which This Flux is Recommended for Use	Lowest Useful Temp, °F (°C)	Highest Useful Temp, °F (°C)	Ingredients: May Contain Some or All of the Classes of Compounds Listed	Form as Supplied	Form of Application**
1	All brazable aluminum alloys	BAlSi	660 (350)	1160 (625)	Chlorides, fluorides	Powder	a, b, c, d
2	All brazable magnesium alloys	BMg	900 (482)	1200 (649)	Chlorides, fluorides	Powder	c, d
3A	All except those listed under 1, 2, and 4†	BAg, BCuP	1050 (566)	1600 (871)	Boric acid, borates, fluorides, fluoborates, wetting agent	Powder, paste, liquid	a, b, c
3B	All except those listed under 1, 2, and 4	BCu, BCuP, BAg, BAu, RBCuZn, BNi	1350 (732)	2100 (1149)	Boric acid, borates, fluorides, fluoborates, wetting agent	Powder, paste, liquid	a, b, c
4	Aluminum-bronze, aluminum-brass, and iron or nickel-based alloys containing minor amounts of Al and/or Ti‡	BAg (all), BCuP (copper-based alloys only)	1050 (566)	1600 (871)	Chlorides, fluorides, borates, wetting agent	Paste, powder	a, b, c
5	All except those listed under 1, 2, and 4	Same as 3B except BAg-1 through -7	1400 (760)	2200 (1204)	Borax, boric acid, borates, wetting agent	Paste, powder, liquid	a, b, c

* All metals must be clean before flux is applied.

** Form of application: (a) Sprinkle dry powder on joint region; (b) dip heated filler-metal rod in powder or paste; (c) mix with various vehicles such as water, alcohol, monochlorobenzene, or others to form a paste or slurry.

† Some Type 3A fluxes are specifically recommended for base metals listed under Type 4.

‡ Combinations of Type 1 and Type 3 fluxes may be used on these materials. In some cases, Type 1 may be used on base metals listed under Type 4.

operation. Warm or hot water soaking is probably the most widely used procedure for flux removal. For best results, this should be done immediately following brazing. Adjusting the acidity of the wash solution to make it basic (pH above 7.0) will aid in preventing the rusting of steel parts during this operation.

A flux residue is an anhydrous salt and may, at a later date, pick up moisture in service and contribute to corrosion of the brazed assembly. In cases where a brazement must serve at elevated temperatures, the residue may cause accelerated attack of the base metal. Subsequent painting or coating operations can be affected by flux remaining on the parts. Components are frequently electroplated after brazing. In this case, it is possible that the cleaning for plating, involving pickling, may be an effective method of removing the remaining residues of brazing flux. In some cases, mechanical cleaning may be required. This includes blast cleaning, wire brushing, or a steam jet spray.

ATMOSPHERES

Suitable atmospheres for brazing applications are listed in Table 10-9. The reaction of the atmosphere depends in part on the base metal, the brazing temperature, the composition of the atmosphere, and the condition of the atmosphere. Essentially all atmospheres permit brazing without flux. Atmospheres are most frequently used in furnace brazing, but may also be used in induction and resistance brazing. Vacuum is classed as an atmosphere because in all cases the essential element to be controlled is the partial pressure of oxygen in the atmosphere system. Oxygen may be measured as vacuum pressure, dew point, pH_2, pH_2O, or CO/CO_2. Aluminum and its alloys are usually vacuum brazed.

The following are the principal types of atmospheres and their uses:

1. *Type 1 exothermic*—used for copper and brasses because of its low hydrogen content. It is also noncombustible.
2. *Types 2 and 3 exothermic*—principal use is large-scale, mesh-belt furnace brazing of steel parts using copper filler metal, the so-called copper brazing process. Wet exogas is most common.
3. *Type 4 endothermic*—same as Types 2 and 3, but used where decarburization of steel parts must be prevented for any reason.
4. *Nitrogen-based atmospheres*—used for all base metals, as Types 1 through 4, as well as for chromium-containing steels when the furnace is specially modified.
5. *Type 5 dissociated ammonia*—used with stainless steels and tool steels, with all types of filler metals except the BNi series.

ATMOSPHERES

6. *Type 6 hydrogen*—available in cylinders, tube trailers, and, in some cases, as cryogenic hydrogen for all types of brazing with the exception of refractory alloys containing 4-5% combined titanium and aluminum in the base metal.
7. *Type 9 inert gas*—generally argon, helium, or nitrogen appropriately dried to keep moisture content to below -50° F (-45.6° C) dew point. This gas is often used as backfill in vacuum operations.
8. *Type 10 vacuum*—for brazing copper base metals with BCuP, BNi-6, and BAg filler metals.
9. *Type 10A vacuum*—used for copper and low-carbon steels when brazing with BNi-6, copper, or silver filler metals, except those containing Zn and Cd.

TABLE 10-9
Atmospheres for Brazing

Brazing Atmosphere, AWS Type No.	Source	Maximum Dew Point, Incoming Gas, °F (°C)	Approx. Composition, %			
			H_2	N_2	CO	CO_2
1	Combusted fuel gas (low hydrogen)	Room temp	0.5-1	87	0.5-1	11-12
2	Combusted fuel gas (decarburizing)	Room temp	14-15	70-71	9-10	5-6
3	Combusted fuel gas, dried	- 40 (- 40)	15-16	73-75	10-11	—
4	Combusted fuel gas, dried (carburizing)	- 40 (- 40)	38-40	41-45	17-19	—
5	Dissociated ammonia	- 65 (- 54)	75	25	—	—
	Nitrogen base		2-30 H_2 w/remainder N_2, or N_2 + methanol			
6§	Cylinder hydrogen	Room temp	97-100	—	—	—
7§	Deoxygenated and dried hydrogen	- 75 (- 59)	100	—	—	—
8	Heated volatile materials		Inorganic vapors (zinc, lithium, magnesium, volatile fluorides)			
9§	Purified inert gas		Inert gas (helium, argon, or other)			
10	Vacuum, above 2 torr (0.27 kPa)					
10A	Vacuum, 0.5-2 torr (0.07-0.27 kPa)					
10B	Vacuum, 0.001-0.5 torr (0.00013-0.07 kPa)					
10C	Vacuum, 0.001 torr (0.00013 kPa) and lower					

* Flux required in addition to atmosphere when alloys containing volatile components are used.
** Copper should be fully deoxidized or oxygen free.
† Heating time should be kept to a minimum to avoid objectionable decarburization.
‡ Flux must be used in addition to the atmosphere if appreciable quantities of aluminum, titanium, silicon, or beryllium are present.
§ Reduced pressures down to 2 torr (0.27 kPa).

10. *Type 10B vacuum*—for brazing of copper and carbon and low-alloy steels when brazing with BNi-6, BCu, and BAg filler metals, without Zn or Cd. The higher pressures prevent vaporization of the Cu and Ag from the filler metals.
11. *Type 10C vacuum*—used when base metals contain chromium, which requires lower pressure to dissociate its oxides. Alloys of titanium, zirconium, tantalum, and columbium are very active and are best processed in a vacuum atmosphere. If processed in a hydrogen-containing atmosphere, these base metals are embrittled.

SAFETY CONSIDERATIONS

Brazing may produce fumes that are hazardous to health. Brazing fluxes may evolve gases containing fluorides and

Filler Metals	Base Metals	Remarks
BAg*, BCuP, RBCuZn*	Copper, brass*	
BCu, BAg*, RBCuZn*, BCuP	Copper**, brass*, low-carbon steel, medium-carbon steel†, nickel, Monel	Decarburizes
Same as 2	Same as 2 plus high-carbon steels	
Same as 2	Same as 2 plus high-carbon steels	Carburizes
BAg*, BCuP, RBCuZn*, BCu, BNi	Same as 1, 2, 3, and 4 plus alloys containing chromium‡	
Same as 5	Same as 5; alloys containing Cr require special furnace considerations	
Same as 2	Same as 2	Decarburizes
Same as 5	Same as 5 plus cobalt, chromium, and tungsten alloys, and carbides‡	
BAg	Brasses	Special-purpose. May be used with 1 through 7 to avoid use of flux
Same as 5	Same as 5 plus titanium, zirconium, hafnium	Special-purpose. Parts must be very clean and atmosphere pure
BCuP, BAg	Copper	
BCu, BAg	Low-carbon steel, copper	
BCu, BAg	Carbon and low-alloy steels and copper	
BNi, BAu, BAlSi, Ti alloys	Heat and corrosion-resistant steels, Al, Ti, Zr; refractory metals	

(Applications)

SOLDERING

chlorides. Certain silver brazing filler metals containing cadmium or zinc will give off vapors. Adequate ventilation with a positive change of air is necessary under these conditions, and respiratory protection equipment may be needed. For specific details, the reader is referred to ANSI Standard Z49.1 for safety measures to be taken in the performance of brazing. Because cadmium is considered poisonous when vaporized from a cadmium-containing filler metal, many users are changing to filler metals not containing cadmium. Fluxes that give off

fluorides also require adequate ventilation to prevent hazardous health conditions.

For furnace brazing, safety precautions with respect to furnaces, discussed in Volume III, *Materials, Finishing and Coating*, of this Handbook series, should be followed. Precautions for the safe use of nitrate-nitrite salt baths for dip brazing are also discussed in Volume III. Safety precautions with respect to the use of electron and laser beams are presented in Chapter 9, "Welding and Cutting," of this volume.

SOLDERING

Soldering is defined by the American Welding Society (AWS) as:

"A group of welding processes which produce coalescence of materials by heating them to a suitable temperature and by using a filler metal having a liquidus not exceeding 840° F (450° C) and below the solidus of the base material. The filler metal is distributed between the closely fitted surfaces by capillary attraction."

Soldering is one of the oldest methods of joining metals and still finds varied and extensive use in industry. Most soldering operations produce a metallurgical intermetallic-type bond between the filler metal and the base material. Joints can be made to surfaces without this bond as in glass-to-metal joining, where surface activity and adhesion are the main mechanisms of joining.

Selection of soldering as a joining method over mechanical fastening, welding, brazing, or adhesive bonding depends primarily on end-use requirements with respect to joint strength, application, and operating temperature and environment, as well as production costs.

APPLICATIONS

Application areas of soldering vary widely. They include copper plumbing systems, automotive copper and brass radiators, aluminum refrigeration components, and electrical and electronic connections. The most sophisticated computers contain many thousands of soldered joints.

The methods of producing the soldered joints and the availability of a wide range of soldering alloys facilitates these uses. The technology is still changing, and new joining materials in the soldering group continue to appear and find application.

Electrical and electronic applications, including printed circuit boards, represent the major use for soldering. Common products produced by soldering include television and radio sets, car radiators, light bulbs, telephones, typewriters, and automotive fuel and ignition systems.

ADVANTAGES

Soldering offers many advantages for joining operations, including the following:

1. *Versatility*. The wide variety of solders, fluxes, and heating methods available make the process suitable for numerous applications. Multiple joints can be soldered simultaneously or sequentially.

2. *Reliability*. Reliable joints, impermeable to gases and liquids, can be produced consistently. The quality of most soldered joints can be evaluated by visual inspection, and unsatisfactory joints can be easily repaired and reworked. Low temperatures employed for soldering minimize distortion and heat damage to components being joined.

3. *Precise control*. The amount of solder and flux used, as well as the amount of heat applied, can be controlled accurately, thus ensuring consistent quality.

4. *Fast production*. The process is easily automated to attain high production rates.

5. *Low cost*. Soldering is generally an economical joining process, with minimal energy requirements.

LIMITATIONS

A possible drawback to the use of soldering is the limited mechanical strengths attained. However, joints strong enough for many applications can be made with proper joint designs, filler metals, and soldering procedures.

PROCESS PRINCIPLES

Generally, to obtain good soldered joints, the following steps are appropriate with most of the available methods used:

1. Preclean the workpiece surfaces to remove oxides and foreign materials such as grime, grease, protective waxes, and other contaminants and to remove surface tarnishes and absorbed air from the base metal surfaces. All surface contaminants adversely affect the execution of a good soldered joint or, at best, require a very strong fluxing action before joining can be performed. Cleaning can be done by chemical means, solvents, and aqueous methods.

2. An appropriate flux is selected for the materials to be joined. The flux is designed to clean and cover the area to be joined and prevent oxidation during the heating process. Depending on the component or alloy composition, the flux may be required to assist in the precleaning operation prior to reaching the soldering temperature.

   Fluxes are solvent or water based, containing halides, bromides, and organic or inorganic salts that are the main activators in producing good soldered joints. The initial heating process removes the carrier material and allows the salts to become molten immediately prior to the solder flowing over the metal surfaces.

3. The soldering operation is performed by bringing molten solders into contact with the prepared surfaces, and/or preplacing solid solder that is melted in position. Solders are generally heated to 100-150° F (55-85° C) above their melting point. The specific selection of temperature depends on both the solder and fluxes selected.

Correct solder, flux, and compatible base material will allow good wetting (adhesion of a liquid to a solid) and flow to occur over the metal surfaces to be joined. The joints are then allowed to cool without any disturbance that may cause internal or solidification cracking as the joint is formed.

4. The solder joint is then cleaned of any flux residues from the surfaces to ensure that subsequent corrosion of the joint will not be a problem.

Wetting occurs when a solder droplet applied to the surface of a base metal produces a contact angle of 90° or less. Normal contact angles in soldering are much lower than this, in the range of 3 to 10°, although some solder and base metal combinations do join satisfactorily with the higher contact angles. Preferably, wetting is considered satisfactory when the molten solder leaves a continuous permanent film on the base metal. Dewetting occurs where solder has wet a surface and subsequently withdrawn into high contact angle droplets.

Wetting can take place by the interaction of surface energies of the molten droplets and the base materials, without any further requirement. Wetting for soldering, however, is more often associated with the formation of an intermetallic compound at the advancing solder surface. This metallurgical interaction generally facilitates further wetting with most metals.

The flow of solder into narrow spaces by capillary action is a primary advantage of the soldering process. Many joints are prepared in this manner and depend, in addition to the wetting, on a fluid molten solder that readily spreads and fills the gap. The surface energies between materials can also promote or hinder this spreading action. Several tests have been devised by industry to measure the wetting, flowing, and capillary action capabilities of molten solder alloys.

SOLDERING METHODS

Soldering methods are generally classified by the method of heat application. Typical methods are conduction, convection, radiation, resistance, and induction. Ultrasonic energy may also be used as an aid to soldering. Selection of a heating method depends primarily on the cost and efficiency of the method, production requirements, and the sensitivity of the assembly to heat.

Conduction Heating

Conduction is the transmission of heat through, or by means of, a thermal conductor that is in physical contact with a body without appreciable displacement of the molecules of the material. In this type of heating, a soldering tip is heated, and the heat is transferred to the area to be soldered by direct contact. For example, a simple handheld soldering iron is a type of conduction heater. Consequently, it is of primary importance that the heat transmission area be kept clean and free from any insulating layers such as oxides that may be formed at elevated temperatures.

Soldering irons and guns. Heating of soldered joints with conventional soldering irons is the oldest soldering method. Soldering guns are electrical soldering irons with pistol grips and quick-heating, relatively small bits. A bit is that part of the iron or gun, usually made of plated copper, that transfers heat (and sometimes solder) to the joint. The most common electrical irons are heated by internal elements. Irons are also heated by direct flame or in ovens. Handheld irons are generally used when joints are few in number, when they can be made one at a time, or when they are so varied that another method is not sufficiently versatile.

Component and wiring layout for the irons must provide for easy soldering without damage to adjacent parts—either by conduction or by radiation. Heat sinks can be used to conduct heat away from sensitive parts. If wiring is complex or many closely spaced components are involved, the order in which joints are soldered can also be important. Temperature-controlled irons are available.

Large soldering irons with heating elements of several hundred watts can produce tremendous amounts of heat for soldering such items as large cans and similar assemblies. Soldering irons are not limited to electrical soldering.

Hot plates. Hot plates and similar surfaces are also used to conduct heat to the work. These heaters are simple and relatively low in cost, but usually require a certain amount of special fixturing. It is essential that all heat-transferring surfaces be kept absolutely clean, otherwise the temperature will vary as the surface oxidizes.

Oxidation is difficult to control at elevated temperatures. The hot plate heating method is quite suitable for automation, and the temperature of the hot plate itself can be used as a safeguard for the maximum temperature permissible for the total assembly operation.

The hot plate surface can be heated by flames or electric current. In some cases, the heating elements are built right into the fixture when the assemblies are prestacked and ready for soldering. The disadvantage of this method lies in the cooling time required for the solder joint. During this cooling time, if the fixtures are not adequate, microcracks can develop.

Dip soldering. In dip soldering, the solder and heat are applied simultaneously to the work by a molten metal bath. All prefluxed metallic surfaces coming into contact with the molten solder are rapidly wetted. This method allows high production volume at minimum cost of equipment and joint and permits soldering entire assemblies with any number of joints. Drawbacks of dip soldering include dross formation, the need for skimming, and requirements for jigs or fixtures.

Wave soldering. Wave soldering was developed to eliminate some of the drawbacks of dip soldering and to shorten soldering time by increasing the dynamic movement of the solder over the surface (a 75-80% reduction). This shorter time reduces warpage; air, flux, and vapor entrapments; and other disadvantages. With wave soldering, numerous connections on printed circuit boards are being simultaneously soldered in seconds. Automatic systems use a conveyor to transport the boards through fluxing, preheating, and wave soldering operations.

In wave soldering, solder is lifted to the connections by one or more standing waves of molten solder. All joints are formed during the passage of an assembly over the waves. The operation is continuous and limited in speed only by time and heat requirements. Because the wave is formed by continuously circulated, fresh, hot solder raised to the surface from the depths of the heater reservoir, drossing and local chilling are eliminated. At any given time, only a small band of the assembly is immersed in the wave, and excess heat exposure is therefore eliminated. Narrow, modular wave soldering stations can be inserted where they are needed in the production line.

Jet soldering. Wave soldering is not limited to the use of wide wave orifices. By restricting the flow of the solder from the nozzle, jets of special configuration can be aimed at various areas in the assembly, giving rise to the newer technique of jet soldering. This method is applicable to such items as the terminals of transformers and the lips of cans.

Solder waves and jets can be used with or without the addition of oil to change the surface tension of the solder and to alter soldering parameters by lowering soldering temperatures and allowing a fine, thin coating of solder. However, the use of oil always requires a postcleaning operation to remove any oil that may be left on the surfaces.

Convection Heating

Convection is the transfer of heat by moving masses of fluids or gases. With convection equipment, heat can be applied to the work by a stream of hot gases that may be either reducing or inert in nature. The heat-transfer medium is not limited to gases. Many liquids, such as oils, may be used to raise the work to the soldering temperature.

Torches. Soldering torches are used for solder preforms and paste alloys, and for line soldering of enclosures for hermetic sealing. Clearance must be allowed for the entire flame, and materials directly behind the joint must be able to withstand the temperature. Various fuel gases are burned with oxygen to provide the desired flame temperature.

Ovens (furnaces). Ovens or furnaces as sources of heat for soldering are another form of convection heating equipment that is well established in industry. Continuous ovens, with some sort of conveyor arrangement to carry the part through the heat zone, are used for production soldering. Various atmospheres can also be introduced into the oven to eliminate oxidation and the need for corrosive fluxes.

Vapor-phase soldering. In this process, a high-temperature vapor generated by boiling fluorinated hydrocarbons is used as the heat-transfer medium. The process is being used for reflow soldering with solder preforms in place and for joining small parts having unusual configurations. Soldering times generally range from 10 to 45 seconds, depending on the size of the assemblies.

Hot gas blankets. For small assemblies, especially in electronics, the use of large ovens or other equipment maintaining specific atmospheres is not always economical. The size of the assemblies and the varieties of operations to be carried out during soldering may make the use of hot gas blanket heaters attractive. Hot gas blanket soldering employs rather common equipment and concepts.

The atmosphere used is generally contained in a cylinder or other industrial container and is passed through a normal arrangement of regulators and flowmeters into an air heater, where the atmosphere is equal to the required soldering temperature plus the necessary increment of temperature for proper wetting. The assembly to be soldered is then passed under the hot-stream blanket of atmosphere, where it is heated and the solder connection is made.

Radiation Heating

Radiation is the total effect of emittance, transmittance, and absorptance of energy. Thermal radiation is electromagnetic

energy in transport. Soldering is concerned mainly with the radiation of heat. In practice, the three methods of heat transfer—convection, conduction, and radiation—are difficult to separate into the various types of equipment.

Unfocused radiation. The most common sources of radiant heat are light waves covering the spectrum from white light to the infrared range. The use of ordinary heat lamps is recommended for simple types of heating arrangements. The distance from the lamps and the speed with which the work passes through the lighted area will determine the temperature the assembly will reach. This is a clean form of heat application, because no physical contact with the work is required.

Focused radiation. Focused infrared light is often used for miniature soldering. The energy radiated by a source may be focused at desired location by an optical system. A light beam concentrated on a spot is a particularly suitable high-temperature soldering area at a difficult-to-reach location or even behind a glass cover. Laser soldering is a type in this category.

Laser soldering. Lasers, discussed in Chapter 9 with respect to their use for welding, are being used for brazing and soldering. An advantage is the capability of delivering the output light energy from a laser to a small spot, 0.002″ (0.05 mm) or less in diameter, resulting in the precise, selective application of heat. This makes the process desirable for microelectronic manufacturing and joining products having temperature-sensitive components. Other advantages include the reduced formation of intermetallic compounds and fine grain size because of rapid processing and fast solidification.

Possible limitations to the use of lasers include the high initial cost of equipment required, special fixturing needed for some applications, and safety precautions necessary, discussed in Chapter 9. Also, when improperly performed, laser soldering can result in reflected energy damage to components and charring of any flux residue.

Neodymium-doped, yttrium aluminum garnet (Nd:YAG) lasers provide a wavelength readily absorbed by conductive materials such as tin-lead, copper, beryllium copper, nickel, and other metals. Carbon dioxide (CO_2) lasers provide a wavelength more easily absorbed by insulative materials such as plastics, ceramics, and fiberglass.

Resistance Soldering

An electric current generates heat as it flows through a circuit. Contact soldering uses resistance heating elements to apply a preset amount of pressure to the feet of surface-mounted components. The current is programmed through the elements to reflow solder the components to printed circuit boards.

Electrodes vary from 0.078″ (1.98 mm) diam metal probes to large carbon blocks. Resistance soldering has the advantage of high joint production, no warmup requirements, and instant, controlled heat. Joints can be made in from 0.5 to 2 seconds, depending on wire size and materials involved. Another advantage is the degree of miniaturization possible; tiny electrodes can be used to connect modular circuitry components or other closely spaced components.

Induction Soldering

Electromagnetic induction soldering uses the part to be soldered as the heating element. Current induced in the part by an induction coil heats the joint to a depth that depends on current frequency. Because of skin effects, the higher the frequency, the more heat will be confined to the material surfaces—an extremely useful phenomenon in soldering because it minimizes distortion and oxidation of the base metal. Flux and solder are applied to the joints prior to joining, and preformed solder shapes can be used. A requirement for induction soldering is that the base metal be electrically conductive.

Ultrasonic Soldering

Cavitation induced by ultrasonic excitation of molten solder removes oxides from submerged metal surfaces to allow alloying of the molten solder with the base metal. Implosion of the cavitation bubbles creates a scrubbing action that fractures and dislodges oxides from the metal surfaces, and the oxides float to the surface of the molten solder.

This method eliminates the need for flux in many soldering operations and is used to join hard-to-solder metals such as aluminum. However, the ultrasonic action does not enhance wetting of the metal surfaces, as do fluxing agents, and there is no capillary flow of the molten solder. As a result, it is sometimes necessary to pretin one or both surfaces to be joined or place preformed or solid wire solder directly into the joint before or during ultrasonic excitation. However, it is not necessary nor desirable to pretin aluminum surfaces to be joined by ultrasonic soldering because this requires an extra operation and accelerates the rate of aluminum dissolution into the solder bath.

Two modifications of this process are used to produce aluminum tubular joints in air-conditioner coils. In the first technique, the joint components are solder coated in an ultrasonic solder bath. Then they are simultaneously heated to soldering temperature and pressed together to produce interference fits. The second technique involves immersing an assembled, air-conditioner coil having special joints into a molten solder bath excited by ultrasonic vibration energy.

Other Soldering Processes

There are several soldering processes in addition to those already discussed, most of which are used for specific applications.

Abrasion soldering. In this variation of soldering, sometimes called friction soldering, the faying surfaces of the base metals are mechanically abraded with the solder or other instrument during soldering.

Screen printing. Solder pastes (blends of powdered filler metals, fluxes, and paste binders) are being used with automatic applicators and screens, generally 60-80 mesh, to provide precise placement of solder dots, each containing a premeasured amount. The pastes provide tack retention for several hours, acting as temporary adhesives to hold components in place until they are reflow soldered. Heat for melting the solder is applied by electric hot plates, convection ovens, infrared, lasers, or vapor-phase systems.

Spray gun soldering. Gas-fired and electrically heated guns are being used to spray molten or semimolten solder from a continuously fed wire onto joints.

Step soldering. This process consists of soldering successive joints on an assembly with solders of successively lower melting temperatures to obtain joining without disturbing the joints previously soldered.

Sweat soldering. A process in which two or more parts that have been precoated with solder are reheated and assembled into a joint without the use of additional solder.

Automated Soldering Systems

Most automated systems for soldering are custom built for specific applications. With most systems, an operator loads and unloads components, and the application of solder, heat, and cooling is done automatically.

Rotary index machines. On these machines (see Fig. 10-9), an index table conveys fixtured parts through a timed sequence of operations, resulting in production rates to 1000 assemblies per hour. Fixtures at each station on the table facilitate loading and unloading and hold the components in proper alignment for soldering. The number of stations on a table depends on production requirements and the operator's ability to unload and reload each fixture during the index cycle. The loading and unloading can also be automated with vibratory feeders, pick-and-place units, robots, or other means. Unloading of soldered assemblies can also be done with ejection devices.

The application of solder and flux or paste is generally done at the first station adjacent to the loading and unloading position. Automatic applicators are frequently used for paste solders, with one or more guns mounted on a slide or slides. Heating is usually performed at several stations to progressively bring the parts to soldering temperature. Open-flame burners supplied with a natural gas and air mixture are a common means of heating, but radiant, induction, resistance, and oven heating are also used. Cooling is often done with compressed air jets or a water wash.

In-line systems. These systems, such as the one shown in Fig. 10-10, are generally desirable for high production rates and for soldering certain assembly configurations, such as long and narrow parts. They are generally designed for continuous operation with chain-driven fixtures that return to the operator or a mesh belt to carry self-locating parts. Methods of heating include gas-fired burners, heating chambers (gas or electric), or

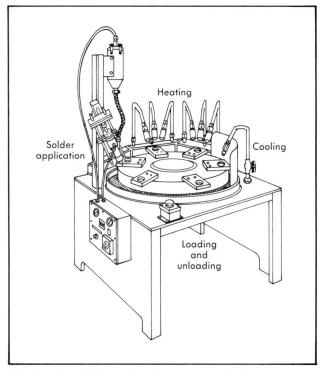

Fig. 10-9 Rotary index machine for automatic soldering. (*Fusion Inc.*)

CHAPTER 10

SOLDERING VARIOUS MATERIALS

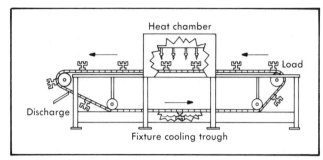

Fig. 10-10 In-line system for automatic soldering with chain-driven fixtures. (*Fusion Inc.*)

controlled atmospheres. Vacuum furnaces can be used for low vapor pressure metals.

Fixed-station machines. These machines, for soldering one assembly at a time, are often used for large assemblies and when production requirements are moderate.

Shuttle machines. These machines are generally designed to solder two assemblies simultaneously, with the parts being moved from the loading and unloading station to the heating station. They are suitable for low to moderate production requirements, with maximum production rates of about 200 assemblies per hour.

Workholding Fixtures

Requirements for workholding fixtures to be used in soldering vary with the specific application. Self-locating components generally do not require fixtures. When fixtures are necessary, the following general rules usually apply:

- Fixture rigidity is essential, especially in areas of high stress.
- Workpiece supports must provide precise alignment and should be located as far from the joint to be soldered as possible to minimize the heat-sink effect.
- The fixture should hold components in inclined positions for easier flux and filler metal location.
- Ample access should be provided to the joint area to facilitate the application of flux, filler metal, heat, and the cooling medium.
- When workpiece hold-down is required, quick-acting mechanical clamps or counterweights are preferable to springs, which lose their resiliency.
- The baseplates of fixtures should be secured to the soldering machines to ensure proper alignment.

When families of similar parts are to be soldered, the use of a common fixture with interchangeable inserts can reduce costs. Providing nests on the soldering machines for rapid changeover of fixtures can also cut costs. Fixture components are often made of Type 300 series stainless steels to resist corrosion during repeated heating and cooling cycles.

SOLDERING VARIOUS MATERIALS

The base metals to be joined by soldering are usually selected for mechanical, electrical, or other functional characteristics. For most industrial applications, cost is also a serious consideration. The base metal dictates which flux or solder to use for the joints to be made. Fluxes are formulated to react with specific base metal oxides, and care should always be taken to obtain a suitable flux. No one flux is ideal for all base metals.

Ferrous Metals

As with other metals, the solderability of ferrous metals varies with their chemical compositions.

Cast irons. Cast irons are generally difficult to solder. However, with adequate surface cleaning, gray, malleable, and nodular irons can be soldered. In some cases, precoating with a solder or a more solderable metal, such as copper or nickel, may be necessary. White cast irons are seldom soldered.

Carbon and alloy steels. Low-carbon steels are the most easily soldered steels. Medium-carbon steels are less readily soldered than low-carbon steels and require careful surface preparation and flux selection. High-carbon and alloy steels are seldom soldered, but adequate cleaning and precoating are generally necessary if this is done.

Stainless steels. These metals are readily solderable, but require the use of corrosive fluxes and lead alloy solders having high tin contents. Corrosive fluxes are necessary to remove the chromic-oxide surface layer that interferes with solder flow. For some applications, pretinning of the stainless steel parts to be joined is required.

Nonferrous Metals

Copper and copper alloys. Copper is one of the easiest metals to solder, and most copper alloys have good solderability. However, copper alloys containing beryllium, silicon, or aluminum require special acid fluxes.

Lead, tin, and their alloys. These materials are easily soldered, but care is necessary to prevent melting of the base metals.

Zinc and zinc alloys. Zinc is easily soldered, but zinc die casting alloys generally contain aluminum and other alloying elements that make the alloys difficult to solder.

Aluminum and aluminum alloys. The tenacious, refractory oxide layer formed on aluminum generally requires the use of active, corrosive fluxes for soldering. However, fluxless soldering of aluminum is being done ultrasonically, by precoating, and other means. Aluminum casting alloys are not solderable.

JOINT DESIGN

Because solders generally have lower strength properties than the materials to which they are generally joined, the joints must be carefully designed to fulfill service requirements. Solder joints rarely take pure shear loads. For high-load applications, the joints should be placed in low-stress areas, the joints may need to be supported mechanically, and high-strength solders should be used. Interlocking joints, edge reinforcements, rivets, spot welds, and other designs are used to increase joint strength and to take advantage of the mechanical properties of the base metal.

Types of Joints

Service requirements and the properties of the base materials to be joined influence the selection of the type of joint to be used for soldering. Also, the relative thermal expansions of the base materials and the solders must be considered.

Lap or sleeve joints are used most frequently for soldering and are generally preferable because they offer larger joint area for maximum strength when sufficient overlap is possible.

Joint Clearance

The amount of clearance in a lap joint is critical to successful soldering. Too little clearance results in flux entrapment, inadequate solder flow, and voids in the joint. Too much clearance impairs the capillary flow of the solder. For many applications, the proper clearance generally ranges from 0.003 to 0.006" (0.08 to 0.15 mm). However, when soldering precoated metals, clearances as low as 0.001" (0.03 mm) are sometimes used.

PRECLEANING AND PRECOATING

As previously discussed in this section, precleaning of the workpiece surfaces to be joined is generally required for successful soldering. Fluxing alone is not a satisfactory substitute for good precleaning. Common methods used for such precleaning include degreasing, acid cleaning or pickling, mechanical preparation, and etching. Details of these and other cleaning methods are presented in Volume III, *Materials, Finishing and Coating*, of this Handbook series.

Degreasing

Solvent degreasing is used to remove organic films such as oils and greases, which minimize the wetting action by the flux and solder. Vapor degreasing is generally preferable to immersion because of the minimum residual film left on the surfaces. However, immersion cleaning with the aid of ultrasonic agitation is satisfactory for many applications.

Acid Cleaning

Acid cleaning or pickling is used to remove rust, scale, and oxides or sulfides and provide chemically clean surfaces. Hydrochloric and sulfuric acids are the most common cleaning agents. The workpieces are then thoroughly washed with hot water and dried as rapidly as possible.

Mechanical Preparation

Abrasive methods commonly used for cleaning surfaces include grit or shotblasting, grinding, filing, and wire brushing. Care must be exercised in using such methods to prevent abrasive particles from becoming embedded in the surfaces being cleaned because such particles are not solderable. An etch treatment may be required after abrasive cleaning to remove such particles.

Etching

Etching is commonly used to clean nonplated copper surfaces. The etchants used include many inorganic salts and acids, depending on the metal to be cleaned.

Precoating

Coating of base metal surfaces with a more solderable metal or alloy prior to soldering is sometimes desirable, especially those metals having tenacious oxide films, such as aluminum alloys, highly alloyed steels, and cast irons. Precoating is often done by plating with tin, tin lead, tin zinc, tin copper, copper, cadmium, nickel, silver, and gold.

JOINT STRENGTH AND QUALITY

The properties of soldered joints can be significantly different than those of the bulk solders used. It is difficult to obtain reliable data for soldered joints because the properties of the joints are influenced by the compositions of the solders used and a number of soldering parameters. These parameters include the thickness of the joint, the solder temperature, the soldering time, and the quantity of solder in the joint. The only positive way to determine the properties of a joint is by testing.

A solder joint that has been adequately designed should be analyzed in a laboratory by testing to destruction. Cross-sectioning and metallurgical examination reveal joint properties and important data about metallurgical soundness of the joint, the amount of gases trapped in the process, inherent weaknesses in the assemblies that may be aggravated by heating during the soldering operation, damage to the surfaces to be soldered by metallurgical alloying, and intermetallic-compound formation.

Chemical tests involve checks on flux entrapment, thoroughness of cleaning procedures, and attack of fluxes on the assembly. Once this thorough investigation permits approval of the process, a situation that promises the highest degree of reliability through visual inspection is achieved.

As yet, no nondestructive test or instrument to evaluate the soldered connection replaces visual inspection. Electrical continuity of a recently made soldered connection can be deceiving in that a faulty joint may be indicated only with age. Most physical tests are destructive. However, ultrasonics and radiographic examinations have proved of value in particular applications.

Soldered joints in plumbing and other sleeve-type joints can be evaluated by radiographic and ultrasonic means. Selective destructive tests using tensile, peel, or shear of the joints can be applied as part of a quality control program with a statistical basis for making process adjustments and changes. This type of test is suitable for sleeve, capillary, or solder fillet joints.

One of the greatest advantages of soldering is the visual inspection with which the quality of most electronic and printed circuit solder joints can be evaluated. Good quality optical instruments are available to assist in this task.

Visual inspection is the main tool for the close control of electronic soldered joints. A visual examination requires proper inspector training, coupled with sound engineering design. Reliability is a long-term factor and certainly cannot be achieved through inspection alone; it must be designed into the solder connection.

Visual examination predominates in the electronic industries. Workmanship samples are preferably used to train inspectors in looking for solder joint characteristics and joint appearances. Examples of typical samples are:

- A cold solder with demarcation at the interface. So-called "cold-soldered joints" are joints with incomplete coalescence caused by insufficient application of heat to the base metal during soldering.
- A moved joint with crystalline or frosty appearance.
- Excess solder with large icicles or attached globules.
- Insufficient solder with small joints that are too resistive for electrical purposes.
- Flux entrapment showing areas with no solder or voids with flux in them.
- Solder bridging between conductor paths on circuit boards.
- Dewetting with gray surfaces, and solder globules not attaching to the parts to be joined.

Soldering quality can be qualitatively determined by detailed visual examinations to decide on rework needs or any process adjustments. Solder joints represent one of the most reliable assembly techniques available to industry amenable to automation and multiple joint manufacture. Component inspection

CHAPTER 10

SOLDERING FILLER METALS

ensures freedom from problems in production and ultimately in service of the soldered joints.

SOLDERING FILLER METALS

Table 10-10 lists the chemical compositions of some fairly common soldering filler metals, with some indication of their melting temperature ranges. A number of binary eutectics are presented. The solder filler metal selected depends first on its compatibility with the base metal and second on the maximum temperature of operation of the soldered joint. Many soldered joints are used for their electrical properties, and, therefore, conductivity of both base metal and filler metal are very important under this circumstance.

TABLE 10-10
Common Soldering Filler Metals*[2]

Solder Grade ASTM B32, Federal QQ-S-571E	Composition, %**							
	Tin	Lead	Antimony	Bismuth, max	Silver	Copper, max	Cadmium, max	Arsenic, max
Sn96	Rem.	0.10	0.20-0.50	0.15	3.3-3.7	0.08	0.005	0.05
Sn70	69.5-71.5	Rem.	0.50	0.25	0.015	0.08	0.001	0.03
Sn63	62.5-63.5	Rem.	0.50	0.25	0.015	0.08	0.001	0.03
Sn62	61.5-62.5	Rem.	0.50	0.25	1.75-2.25	0.08	0.001	0.03
Sn60	59.5-61.5	Rem.	0.50	0.25	0.015	0.08	0.001	0.03
Sn50	49.5-51.5	Rem.	0.50	0.25	0.015	0.08	0.001	0.025
Sn45	44.5-46.5	Rem.	0.50	0.25	0.015	0.08	0.001	0.025
Sn40A	39.5-41.5	Rem.	0.50	0.25	0.015	0.08	0.001	0.02
Sn40B	39.5-41.5	Rem.	1.8-2.4	0.25	0.015	0.08	0.001	0.02
Sn35A	34.5-36.5	Rem.	0.50	0.25	0.015	0.08	0.001	0.02
Sn35B	34.5-36.5	Rem.	1.6-2.0	0.25	0.015	0.08	0.001	0.02
Sn30A	29.5-31.5	Rem.	0.50	0.25	0.015	0.08	0.001	0.02
Sn30B	29.5-31.5	Rem.	1.4-1.8	0.25	0.015	0.08	0.001	0.02
Sn25A	24.5-26.5	Rem.	0.50	0.25	0.015	0.08	0.001	0.02
Sn25B	24.5-26.5	Rem.	1.1-1.5	0.25	0.015	0.08	0.001	0.02

Temperature Considerations

The critical nature of temperature in soldering must be addressed. Service requirements will dictate a minimum operating temperature at which the solder must still be solid and perhaps provide some mechanical property capability in addition. Sometimes soldering is carried out below a particular maximum temperature to protect the integrity of materials being joined.

Generally, soldering is performed at up to 150° F (85° C) above the melting range of the filler metal. Therefore, the soldering and not the melting temperature of the filler metal should be used to determine maximums that can be tolerated.

Freezing Ranges

Most solder filler metals have a freezing range. The freezing range is bounded by the solidus temperature at the lower end and the liquidus temperature at the high end. In between, the material is in a pasty range.

Many eutectic alloys also find use as solder filler metals. A eutectic material has a specific melting point with no freezing

Melting Range, °F (°C)		Mechanical Properties		Physical Properties		
Solidus	Liquidus	Tensile Strength, ksi (MPa)	Shear Strength, ksi (MPa)	Electrical Conductivity, % (IACS)	Expansion Coefficient, in./in./°F (mm/mm/°C)	Notes
430 (221)	430 (221)	4.67 (32.2)	2.68† (18.5)	6.0	NA	Used in the food processing industry because of nontoxic characteristics
361 (183)	377 (192)	7.8 (53.8)	5.0 (34.5)	12.5	12.0 (21.6)	Good pretinning alloy and used for soldering zinc and coating metals
361 (183)	361 (183)	7.7 (53.1)	5.4 (37.2)	11.5	13.7 (24.7)	Used for soldering printed circuit boards where temperature limitations are critical and for applications requiring short melting range
354 (179)	372 (189)					Used for soldering silver-coated surfaces, mainly in electronics and electrical work
361 (183)	374 (190)	7.6 (52.4)	5.6 (38.6)	11.5	13.3 (23.9)	Used for soldering electrical and electronic connections and for coating metals
361 (183)	421 (216)	6.2 (42.7)	5.2 (35.9)	10.9	13.0 (23.4)	Used for less critical electrical soldering and for joining sheet metal, pipe, tubing, and other structural shapes
361 (183)	441 (227)					A general-purpose alloy similar to Sn50
361 (183)	460 (238)	5.4 (37.2)	4.8 (33.1)	10.1	13.9 (25.0)	Frequently used for dip soldering and as a wiping solder. Can be used for same purposes as Sn50
365 (185)	448 (231)					Similar to Sn40A, but not recommended for use on galvanized iron
361 (183)	447 (230)					Similar to Sn35B, but with a lower antimony content
365 (185)	470 (243)					Higher antimony content promotes fine grain size and greater strength as a wiping solder
361 (183)	491 (255)					Used as an automobile radiator solder and for removing heat-strippable insulation during high-temperature tinning of wires
365 (185)	482 (250)					Used as an automobile body solder for filling dents and seams
361 (183)	511 (266)					For uses similar to Sn20 and Sn30
365 (185)	504 (262)					For uses similar to Sn20 and Sn30

(continued)

SOLDERING FILLER METALS

TABLE 10-10—*Continued*

Solder Grade ASTM B32, Federal QQ-S-571E	Composition, %**							
	Tin	Lead	Antimony	Bismuth, max	Silver	Copper, max	Cadmium, max	Arsenic, max
Sn20A	19.5-21.5	Rem.	0.50	0.25	0.015	0.08	0.001	0.02
Sn20B	19.5-21.5	Rem.	0.8-1.2	0.25	0.015	0.08	0.001	0.02
Sn15	14.5-16.5	Rem.	0.50	0.25	0.015	0.08	0.001	0.02
Sn10A	9.0-11.0	Rem.	0.50	0.25	0.015	0.08	0.001	0.02
Sn10B	9.0-11.0	Rem.	0.20	0.03	1.7-2.4	0.08	0.001	0.02
Sn5	4.5-5.5	Rem.	0.50	0.25	0.015	0.08	0.001	0.02
Sn2	1.5-2.5	Rem.	0.50	0.25	0.015	0.08	0.001	0.02
Sb5	94.0 min	0.20	4.5-5.5	0.15	0.015	0.08	0.03	0.05
Ag1.5	0.75-1.25	Rem.	0.40	0.25	1.3-1.7	0.30	0.001	0.02
Ag2.5	0.25	Rem.	0.40	0.25	2.3-2.7	0.30	0.001	0.02
Ag5.5	0.25	Rem.	0.40	0.25	5.0-6.0	0.30	0.001	0.02

* Reprinted with permission from ASTM Standard B32, "Solder Metal." Copyright ASTM.
** Other metals, %, max: aluminum, 0.005; iron, 0.02; and zinc, 0.005.
† Ultimate stress in joint.

Melting Range, °F (°C)		Mechanical Properties		Physical Properties		
Solidus	Liquidus	Tensile Strength, ksi (MPa)	Shear Strength, ksi (MPa)	Electrical Conductivity, % (IACS)	Expansion Coefficient, in./in./°F (mm/mm/°C)	Notes
361 (183)	531 (277)	4.8 (33.1)	4.2 (29.5)	8.7	14.7 (26.5)	Used as an automobile radiator solder; lower antimony content than Sn20B
363 (184)	517 (269)	5.8 (40)	4.71 (32.5)	9.8	14.7 (26.5)	Used as an automobile body solder and for general purposes such as protective coatings on steel sheets where a high tin content alloy is not required
437 (225)	554 (290)					Used for coating and joining metals, subject to hot-short working under stress
514 (268)	576 (302)					Used for coating and joining metals, such as radiator cores, and where soldered connections will be exposed to temperatures exceeding 400°F (204°C)
514 (268)	570 (299)					Similar to Sn10A, but minimizes the leaching of silver from silver alloy coated surfaces. Used for electronic applications where high service temperature is encountered
586 (308)	594 (312)	3.4 (23.0)		8.8	15.9 (28.7)	Used for coating and automobile radiators, and where soldered connections will be exposed to temperatures more than 475°F (246°C). Its wetting ability is not as good as Sn10A
601 (316)	611 (322)					Used to solder automobile heater cores
450 (232)	464 (240)	4.41 (31)				Used for electrical and electronic connections subjected to temperatures of about 465°F (241°C). Also used for sweating of copper tubing in solar heating, plumbing, and refrigeration equipment
588 (309)	588 (309)	2.86 (19.7)		14.0		Used interchangeably with Ag2.5, but has a better shelf life and does not develop a black surface deposit when stored under humid environmental conditions
580 (304)	580 (304)	4.4 (30.3)	2.9 (20.0)	8.8		Used on copper, brass, and similar metals with torch heating. It requires the use of a flux having a zinc chloride base to produce a good joint on untinned surfaces. Susceptible to corrosion under humid environmental conditions
580 (304)	716 (380)	4.55 (32)				Develops a shear strength of 1.5 ksi (10.3 MPa) at 350°F (177°C). When soldering hard-drawn brass or copper, the application temperature should not exceed 850°F (454°C). A typical application is on thermocouples for aircraft engines where relatively high operating temperatures will not affect strength of the solder. Precautions noted for Ag2.5 also apply

SOLDERING FLUXES

range. Only in a very few instances does the solder filler metal have a freezing range wider than 50° F (28° C). This is generally sound practice because if an assembly moves during this freezing period, then cracking of the solder can occur, producing a poor joint.

Mechanical Properties

Mechanical properties of tensile strength and shear strength for most of the filler metals are given in Table 10-10. These mechanical properties can be utilized to give a general indication of selection. However, most soldered joints are utilized for service where other mechanical properties such as creep and/or fatigue are involved, so that these factors must also be carefully considered. In addition, joint strengths are not necessarily similar to the values obtained when testing bulk solders.

Electrical Properties

Table 10-10 also presents electrical conductivity values and expansion coefficients for the solders. In electrical applications, these values are important and are generally related to solder joint shape and size to ensure current-carrying capacity of a joint is satisfied.

Other Characteristics

Solder filler metals can have the action of scavenging plating, such as gold and silver, from the surfaces of the components being joined. The ductility or brittleness of the interfaces between solder and base metals are important in some applications. Most metallurgical intermetallics formed, for example, tend to be brittle and should be minimized in formation by keeping the soldering temperature low and the soldering time short.

Commercial Forms

Commercial forms of solders include pig, cakes or ingots, bars, paste, foil, sheet, ribbon, wire (solid or flux cored), and preforms. Pig solder is available in 20, 40, 50, and 100 lb (9.1, 18.1, 22.7, and 45.4 kg) sizes. Cakes or ingots, rectangular or circular in shape, weigh 3, 5, and 10 lb (1.4, 2.3, and 4.5 kg). Bars are available in weights from 1/2 to 2 lb (0.23 to 0.9 kg).

Solder pastes, blended to suit specific requirements, contain finely powdered filler metal, flux, and a neutral paste binder to hold the flux and filler metal in suspension and to prevent metal-flux interaction before heating. Paste is generally supplied in amounts of 1 lb (0.45 kg) or more. Automatic paste applicators have a pressurized reservoir, two or more guns, and a control panel for precise application of the desired amount of paste in configurations such as dots or stripes.

Foil, sheet, and ribbon are supplied in various thicknesses and widths. Cored solder is solder wire or bar containing flux as a core. Both solid and flux-cored wire are available on spools, with diameters ranging from 0.010 to 0.250″ (0.25 to 6.35 mm). Wire or triangular bars cut into pieces or specified lengths are called segments or drops.

Solder preforms are available in a wide range of shapes, the most common being wire, punched parts, spheres, and flux-coated metal forms. When preplaced solder or precoated parts are used, the process is sometimes called reflow soldering.

SOLDERING FLUXES

All fluxes are chemically active to some extent to provide a solderable surface and protect both base metal and solder alloy during the heating process. Because corrosion is often a prime consideration in a completed joint, it is advisable to utilize the least aggressive flux to achieve the joint required. Fluxes for the whole range of metals that can be soldered are generally divided into three main categories: inorganic acids, organic acids, and rosin-based fluxes.

Inorganic Acids

Inorganic acid fluxes are commonly acids or salts, including such materials as zinc-ammonium chloride, hydrochloric acid, phosphoric acid, and similarly active and corrosive materials. These fluxes are mainly used for industrial-type soldering operations. Zinc-ammonium chloride is normally applied as an aqueous solution or made up into a paste, with a petroleum base that melts and flows during the soldering operation.

Organic Acids

A wide range of organic salts and organic acids can be utilized as soldering materials for various metals. Generally, they have less corrosive properties than the inorganic fluxes and yet, in many cases, are capable of providing satisfactory soldered joints. These fluxes too may be water based or solvent based, with a low percentage of the active compound or acid included in the flux material. Evaporation of a solvent and conversion of an active chemical to a passive chemical after the soldering operation is a desirable need for the electronics industry and has resulted in many varied compositions being offered for use.

Rosin-Based Fluxes

Rosin-based fluxes are generally considered noncorrosive, although mildly activated materials may have some corrosive effects under particularly severe exposure conditions. These fluxes are therefore generally divided into nonactivated rosin, which has no additive, and mildly activated rosin that is used for electronic and electrical circuits where a slight amount of activity is vital to increase wetting and provide good joining properties.

Some highly activated rosins are available for high-speed production lines that require very rapid fluxing capabilities to ensure joints are produced in time. Typical applications for these materials are in wave soldering and vapor-phase soldering of modern electronic components.

Flux Selection

A flux must be selected for a specific application on the basis of its compatibility with the base material and the solder. Full consideration must be given to the method of application, cleaning procedures, process used, soldering temperature, and, ultimately, the reliability desired in the completed joints.

For some of the lesser used metals in soldering, very few commercial fluxes are available. Often, specially made materials may be required before a product can be manufactured using the soldering process and a specific alloy. A list of metal surfaces that have been soldered with a general guide to their fluxing requirements is given in Table 10-11.

Flux Removal

After soldering, flux residues that may corrode the base metal or otherwise be harmful to the effectiveness of the joint must be removed or made noncorrosive. Noncorrosive flux residues need not be removed unless necessary for appearance,

TABLE 10-11
Soldering Flux Guide

Metal Surfaces	Inorganic Acid	Organic Acid	Organic-Rosin Base	
			Water White	Activated
Brass	1	1	2	1
Bronze	1	1	. . .	2
Cadmium	3	1	2	1
Copper	3	1	2	1
Gold	3	1	2	1
Lead	1	1	2	1
Nickel	1	1	. . .	2
Palladium	3	1	2	1
Platinum	3	1	2	1
Silver	3	1	2	1
Tin	3	1	2	1
Tin-lead (hot dip)	3	1	2	1
Tin-lead (plate)	3	1	2	1
Tin-nickel (plate)	3	1	2	1
Tin-zinc (plate)	3	1	2	1
Aluminum	. . .	. . .	Special solder and flux	
Beryllium copper	1	2	Special flux only	
Cast iron	1			
Copper alloys	1	2		
Germanium	1	2		
Inconel	2	. . .	Special flux only	
Kovar	1	2		
Magnesium	. . .	. . .	Special flux only	
Monel	2	. . .	Special flux only	
Nichrome	. . .	. . .	Special flux only	
Rhodium	1	2		
Rodar	1	2		
Steel	1	2		
Steel (galvanized)	1	2		
Stainless steel	1	. . .	Special flux only	
Zinc	1	2		
Zinc (die cast)	. . .	. . .	Special flux only	

Normally not soldered: beryllium, chromium, molybdenum, niobium, silicon, tantalum, titanium, tungsten, zirconium.
Code: 1 = normally used; 2 = used only under laborable conditions; 3 = not normally used.

testing, handling, or if the joint is to be subsequently covered with organic protective coatings. Cleaning aids visual examination.

Residues from self-neutralizing organic fluxes can generally be removed by washing in hot water, followed by rinsing. Removing the residues from reaction fluxes may require successive immersion in 2% sulfuric acid and 1% nitric acid solutions, followed by rinsing with warm water.

One method used to remove the residue from zinc chloride fluxes is to wash in hot water containing 2% concentrated hydrochloric acid, wash in hot water containing crystals of washing soda (sodium carbonate), and rinse with clear water. In some cases, mechanical scrubbing may be necessary, and, in others, deionized water rinses may be used.

SAFETY CONSIDERATIONS

Potential hazards with respect to soldering include heat, fumes, chemicals, and electricity. Details of safety precautions that are common to welding, brazing, and soldering are discussed in ANSI Standard Z49.1. The use of adequately trained personnel and competent supervision will minimize possible danger from the hazards. National safety standards shall be observed and kept in force.

Heat Hazards

In soldering, precautions are necessary to prevent burns from handling or contact with hot parts or equipment. Electric-heated soldering irons should be grounded and, when not in use, be kept in fireproof holders. Water should be kept away from molten solder to prevent expulsion of the solder.

Fumes

Solder, fluxes, and foreign materials on the surfaces of parts to be joined often produce fumes or smoke when heated that may be irritating or toxic. Fumes can be minimized by keeping soldering temperatures as low as possible. Adequate ventilation is essential to avoid any hazards from fumes. Eating and smoking in the work area should be discouraged.

CHAPTER 10

BIBLIOGRAPHY

Chemicals

The chemicals present in fluxes require careful handling and use to avoid contact with the skin and eyes, and they should not be ingested. Metals should be handled with care, and exposure should be kept to a minimum, below hazard levels.

Electrical Hazards

All electrical equipment used for heating in soldering should conform with NEMA standards. Contact must be prevented with current-carrying elements in soldering irons, ovens, resistance units, and induction equipment.

References

1. *Brazing Manual* (Miami: American Welding Society, 1976).
2. H. H. Manko, *Solder and Soldering* (New York: McGraw-Hill Book Co., 1964).

Bibliography

The Brazing Book. New York: Handy & Harman, 1983.

Brazing Manual. Miami: American Welding Society, 1976.

Kearns, W. H., ed. *Welding Handbook*, 7th ed., vol. 2. Miami: American Welding Society, 1978.

Krauskopf, Bruce. "Paste Brazing and Soldering: Automated Systems." *Manufacturing Engineering* (September 1982), pp. 70-73.

Nippes, Ernest F., coord. *Metals Handbook: Welding, Brazing, and Soldering*, 9th ed., vol. 6. Metals Park, OH: American Society for Metals, 1983.

Soldering Manual. Miami: American Welding Society, 1978.

Solders and Soldering. New York: Lead Industries Associ-ation, 1982.

Weymueller, Carl R. "How to Choose Brazing Filler Metals." *Welding Design & Fabrication* (July 1984), pp. 33-41.

ADHESIVE JOINING

While no universal theory of adhesion exists, the following definition explains the bonding or joining process: "The molecular force exerted across a surface of contact between unlike liquids or solids that resists interfacial separation. One surface is the adhesive while the other is the adherend."[1] The adhesive is a substance capable of holding materials together by surface attachment. The adherend is a body that is held to another body by an adhesive. Structural (engineering) adhesives are bonding agents used for transferring required loads between adherends exposed to service environments. Additional definitions are presented in ASTM D 907, "Standard Definitions of Terms Relating to Adhesives."

Curing is the changing of the physical properties of an adhesive by chemical reaction, which may be condensation, polymerization, or vulcanization. It is often accomplished by the action of heat and/or a catalyst and with or without pressure. Setting is the conversion of an adhesive into a fixed or hardened state by chemical or physical action.

ADVANTAGES AND LIMITATIONS

To benefit from adhesive-bonded construction, engineers must:[2]

- Understand the advantages and limitations of adhesive bonding.
- Be familiar with the more conventional methods of joining.
- Have a good grasp of economic factors and production practices.
- Be able to determine performance and material requirements as well as joint geometry.

There are many advantages, as well as several limitations, with respect to the use of adhesive joining.

ADVANTAGES OF ADHESIVE JOINING

Advantages with respect to the use of adhesive joining include the following:

1. Stresses are distributed uniformly over a large area, significantly reducing stress concentrations that cause fatigue and failure.
2. A wide variety of similar and dissimilar materials, as well as combinations of materials, can be joined, including those with vastly different thermal coefficients of expansion.
3. Very thin and fragile materials not suitable for mechanical fasteners or welding, as well as thick parts, can be fastened.
4. Components of all sizes and shapes can be joined.

5. Joints with smooth surfaces and contours can be produced.
6. Joints can be sealed against a variety of environments, heat transfer may be slowed, and electrolytic corrosion may be reduced.
7. Fatigue life is improved, vibration is damped, and thermal shock and impact are resisted.
8. Cures are effected at relatively low temperatures, avoiding the need for the high temperatures required for some other joining processes.
9. Costs are frequently less than for other fastening methods.
10. The weight of assemblies can be significantly reduced.
11. Joint design is simplified.
12. Some adhesives form flexible bonds that are tolerant of repeated cycling, resulting in improved fatigue life.
13. Special properties can be produced. Adhesive formulations are available to provide electrical insulation, conduction, or semi-conduction between members.

PROCESS LIMITATIONS

Possible limitations with respect to the use of adhesive joining include the following:

1. Careful adhesive selection is required to resist a specific environment. This may necessitate carefully planned testing with respect to the anticipated service of the assembly.

Contributors of sections of this chapter are: Girard S. Haviland, Manager, Engineering Center, Loctite Corp., Industrial Group; Dr. J. Dean Minford, Minford Consulting.
Reviewers of sections of this chapter are: D. D. Applegath, Adhesive and Sealant Development Lab, Dow Chemical U.S.A.; Ted J. Barnham, Materials Engineer, NAVAIR Engineering Support Office, Naval Air Rework Facility, Department of the Navy; Gary DeFrayne, Senior Materials Engineer, Adhesives Laboratory, Chrysler Corp.; Girard S. Haviland, Manager, Engineering Center, Loctite Corp., Industrial Group; Gerald J. Helmstetter, Technical Service Manager, Permabond International; Gerald R. Hurd, Field Engineer, Adhesive Systems Div., The B.F. Goodrich Co.; Fred A. Keimel, President, Adhesives and Sealants Consultants; Darrell A. Klemme, Laboratory Manager, Bostik Div., Emhart Fastening Systems Group; Dr. J. Dean Minford, Minford Consulting; Elizabeth A. Peterson, Manager, Technical Support, Morton Chemical Div., Morton Thiokol, Inc.; Denis J. Zalucha, Specialty Chemicals R&D, S.C. Johnson & Son, Inc.

APPLICATIONS

2. Rigid attention is demanded with respect to surface preparation and cleanliness prior to adhesive joining.
3. Heat and pressure or a relatively long cure period are sometimes required.
4. Jigs and fixtures are often necessary for good location of the parts to be assembled.
5. Maximum service temperatures of organic adhesives are low compared to the temperatures that can be withstood by many metals.
6. Nondestructive inspection of adhesive-bonded joints is difficult but desirable.
7. Many adhesive-bonded joints are not readily able to be disassembled.
8. Rigid process control is sometimes necessary.

TYPICAL APPLICATIONS

Adhesives have been used for thousands of years to join various materials. Their use for bonding metals in structural (load-bearing) applications, however, did not begin until World War II. Structural adhesives were first used in the aircraft industry, but are now being applied in a variety of industries.

Now, the major users of adhesive bonding are the automotive, aircraft, building products, and packaging industries. These four groups consume a major portion of the adhesive raw materials sold today. Other industries using adhesives include the shoe, apparel, furniture, bookbinding, electrical, railroad, shipbuilding, and medical industries. The following few specific examples serve to illustrate the importance of the adhesive joining process as an assembly technique.

AUTOMOTIVE USES

Beginning in 1960, automobile companies began to use heat-curing plastisol mastic adhesive to bond the inner and outer panels of hood and trunk compartment lids. This system eliminated the flutter and rattle of hood and trunk lid components over rough roads or at high speeds and reduced the weight of the lid assemblies. The adhesive is oil tolerant and can be dispensed from automated applicators in an assembly line operation.[3] Because the adhesive may be applied in conjunction with spot welding on the same part, it can be applied in a parts stamping operation and then heat cured later in the paint ovens.[4] The joining method combining structural adhesives and resistance spot welding, called weldbonding, is discussed later in this section.

Mastic adhesive is also used for bonding interior reinforcements to door panels and framing members to the inside of van-type vehicles. The automotive industry also uses adhesives for joining metal to fabric for interior trim, vinyl-to-metal exterior trim, improved performance of tire cords, adhering brake linings, and general fastening. For adhering the textured vinyl coverings to metal roof surfaces, the contact neoprene-phenolic cements have shown excellent resistance to exterior weathering conditions. Hot-melt adhesives are used to bond various carpet materials for floor mats and interior kick panels.

FOOD PACKAGING

In the food packaging industry, hot-melt adhesives are used for a large number of applications such as carton, can, and bag sealing, and the lamination of films, papers, and foils. The advantages of hot melts for such applications include rapid setup on cooling, which permits the use of high-speed fabrication machinery, and no volatile byproducts during the joining process, which permits their use on nonporous materials such as plastic film and metal foil. As a result, a number of rapid coating techniques have become feasible for manufacturing. In the heat sealing of plastic bags and containers, the plastic itself acts as the adhesive by sticking to itself in the melted state.

STRUCTURAL APPLICATIONS

Other major uses for adhesives include veneer and plywood laminated structures. In making wood particle boards, the adhesive is mixed uniformly with the particulate wood so it becomes the matrix holding the whole structure together. Similarly, epoxy adhesive is used as the binder material holding fiberglass, carbon, or boron fibers in composite structures. In the building construction industry, contact adhesives often replace nails and screws for attachment of paneling to studs.[5]

The sidewall construction for over-the-road trailers and motor homes is often a sandwich panel construction in which the exterior metal and interior metal, wood, or plastic facings are adhesively bonded directly to insulating plastic foam slabs. Similarly, the wall panels for commercial buildings and schools may consist of metal, wood, or plastic facings adhered directly to a wide variety of insulating foam core materials.[6]

WELDBONDING

Weldbonding is a joining method that combines structural adhesives and resistance spot welding. Advantages over spot welding alone include improved fatigue life and durability and better resistance to peel forces. Also, the adhesive can act as a sealant to provide better corrosion resistance. Possible problems include making good welds through an adhesive and preventing contamination of visible metal surfaces and the electrodes by the adhesive. Applications include aircraft construction, aluminum truck cabs and van body sidewalls, and aluminum body sheets for automobiles.

The predominant weldbonding method consists of applying a paste adhesive to the area to be joined, followed by spot welding through the adhesive. In another method, a tape or film adhesive is applied to the area to be joined, holes are cut in the adhesive where the spot welds are required, and then conventional spot welding is performed. Yet another method consists of spot welding the parts together, applying adhesive to the edges of the joint, and then heating to cause the adhesive to flow between the joined surfaces by capillary action.

BONDED SANDWICH CONSTRUCTION

One of the lightest and strongest constructions is the laminated or bonded sandwich consisting of thin, high-density facing members adhesively joined to a relatively thick, lightweight core. Both the facing and core materials can vary from metals like aluminum and steel to nonmetals such as wood, paper, and plastics. The basic elements of a bonded sandwich are shown in

Fig. 11-1. Many structural honeycomb panels are made with reticulating adhesive where surface tension causes the adhesive to move up or down the walls of the honeycomb and form a fillet of adhesive. Applications of adhesively bonded sandwich structures are ever increasing in number; some examples are listed in Table 11-1.

Use in Aircraft

The honeycomb sandwich structure used on a large military transport plane, the Lockheed C-5A, is shown in Fig. 11-2. It illustrates the strength-weight effectiveness of honeycomb by

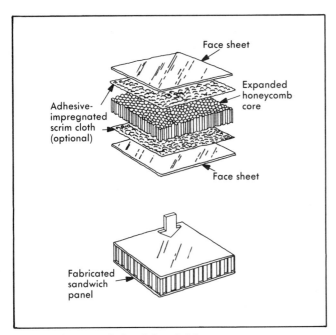

Fig. 11-1 Elements of a bonded sandwich.

the large area in this one craft of 24,000 ft^2 (more than half an acre), which equals 2230 m^2. A complete and comprehensive investigation of adhesive bonding in aircraft has been conducted by Douglas Aircraft Co. under an Air Force contract. In this investigation, a full-sized main fuselage of a large transport aircraft was entirely joined with adhesive and instrumented for every kind of test applicable to the service life of such an aircraft. The study is known today as the PABST program, which stands for Primary Adhesive Bonding Structural Technology.

Advantages

Advantages of sandwich structures include the following:

- High strength-to-weight ratios.
- High stiffness-to-weight ratios.
- Compound-contoured fabrications.
- High fatigue resistance as a result of the even distribution of stresses.
- Smooth exterior surfaces.

It should be of particular interest to manufacturing engineers to note an example of the ability of structurally bonded metal joints for resisting fatigue-type failures. For example, the PABST program showed that a deliberately machined crack in the adhesively bonded area did not propagate into catastrophic failure after all the fatigue testing was concluded. In contrast, it is common to find riveted aircraft construction in which catastrophic failures are induced by fatigue stresses radiating out from the drilled rivet hole.

Limitations

Possible limitations with respect to the use of sandwich structures include the following:

- Cost is usually higher than for conventional structures.
- Making attachments requires special attention.
- The thin skin provides poor resistance to punctures and dents.

TABLE 11-1
Applications of Bonded Sandwich Construction

Aircraft:	
Control surfaces	Doors (structural access, and entry)
Control tabs	Engine cowling
Bulkheads	Wing panels
Helicopter blades	Fairings
Flooring (cargo and passenger compartment)	Fan air ducts
Missile and spacecraft electronics and communications:	
Fins and control surfaces	Radomes
Structural shells	Shipping containers
Antenna reflectors	Intertank structures
Tankage	Electronic packaging
Heat shields	
Buildings:	
Prefab shelters	Partitions and doors
Curtain walls	
Miscellaneous:	House-trailer flooring
Desk tops	Boats
Scaffolding	Cargo containers

APPLICATIONS

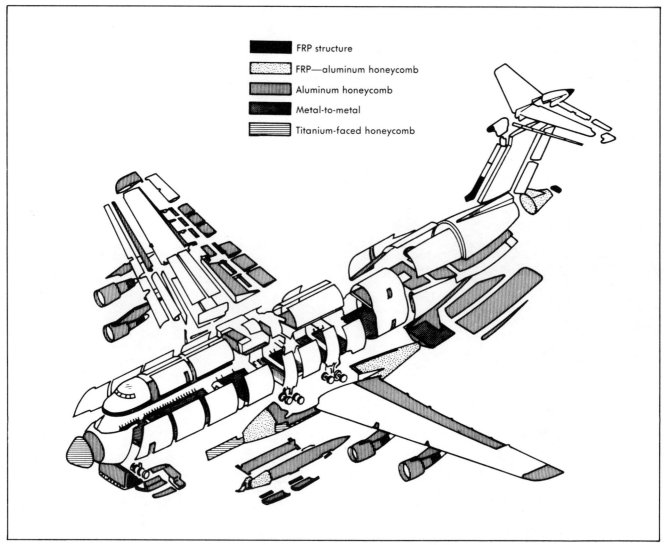

FRP structure
FRP—aluminum honeycomb
Aluminum honeycomb
Metal-to-metal
Titanium-faced honeycomb

Fig. 11-2 Honeycomb sandwich structures used on the Lockheed C-5A transport plane.

Design Requirements

Before adhesive-bonded sandwiches are applied, design data, inspection data, and producibility data should be obtained. The following basic requirements must be considered in sandwich design:[7]

1. The facings must have sufficient thickness and strength to withstand the tensile, compressive, and shear stresses induced by the design load.
2. The core must have sufficient strength to withstand the shear stresses induced by the service loading.
3. The core must be thick enough and have sufficient shear modulus to prevent overall buckling under the design load.
4. The stiffness of the core and the compressive strength of the facings must be sufficient to prevent wrinkling of the face sheets under the service requirements.
5. The core cells must be of proper dimension to prevent intracell buckling under the design load.
6. The core must have sufficient compressive strength to resist crushing by design loads acting normal to the panel facings or by compressive stresses induced through flexure.
7. The structure must have adequate strength in the flexural and shear modes to prevent permanent deflections under design load.
8. Ease of carving, forming, and tooling must be considered.
9. The type and weight of the adhesive must be considered. In extremely lightweight structures, face sheets 0.010″ (0.25 mm) or less in thickness, the weight of the adhesive becomes an important factor.
10. The operating environment must be considered, including temperature, moisture, vibration (fatigue), and expected length of service. The operating temperature of the assembly is important because adhesives degrade and creep at temperatures lower than metals.

The basic fabrication process for bonded sandwich construction is like that for any structural adhesive-bonded part.

PRINCIPLES OF ADHESIVE JOINING

When two flat, solid surfaces are brought together, only a small fraction of the total surface areas is actually in contact (see Fig. 11-3). If the microscopic voids that exist at the interface can be eliminated by careful polishing or by filling the voids with a fluid, joint strength is established that will require considerable energy to separate. In many adhesive systems, this liquid interlayer cures or hardens on cooling or chemical reaction to form a solid adhesive. If sufficient contact to both surfaces is maintained during this hardening process, a strong adhesive bond can be developed.

A variety of physical and chemical forces contribute to this total attraction between the adhesive and the adherend. Potentially the strongest forces are those attributed to actual chemical bonds of the covalent or ionic types. Other major contributors to adhesion, however, are due to physical interactions such as van der Waals forces, London forces, dipole-dipole interactions, and hydrogen bonding. While the type of forces that make up the bond strength are of importance to the adhesion scientist, the major considerations for the joining engineer are the practical performance and durability in service of the joined structure.

Another criterion for the development of satisfactory adhesion is that the adhesive chemically wet the adherend.[8] The magnitude of wetting or spreading on a surface is related to the relative surface free energies of the materials to be joined. Generally, metals and the oxides on their surfaces have high surface energies, while organic compounds, such as plastics, have low surface energies. Glasses have intermediate values. As a general rule, liquid adhesives have lower surface tensions and can be expected to spread if contacting higher surface tension solid adherends.

Even when all the criteria discussed have been met by a chosen adhesive joining process, it is necessary to make a judgment about the possibility of success from a practical viewpoint. Can the operation be carried out under adequately controlled conditions and the long-term or adequate service life potential of the joint be assured?

The term *satisfactory adhesion* has often been defined in textbooks as achieving one or both of two requirements. First, failure should occur within one of the adherends when excessive stress is applied to the bonded joint rather than at the interface or within the adhesive. Second, whatever stress is required to separate the joint should exceed any of the performance limits for the structure. From a practical standpoint, however, this definition may be inadequate in terms of assuring a durable-performing adhesive bond for long-term service. The two criteria are necessary and will indicate a satisfactory joint in the absence of adverse environmental factors. However, the joining engineer will also want to test joints for strength retention after simulated or actual exposure if the final manufactured product must survive under actual service conditions. As will be discussed in more detail later, the engineer should also consider that any of the service-life stresses that will operate on the bonded area must be taken into account in establishing an adequate test program for evaluating the permanence of the bonded structure.[9]

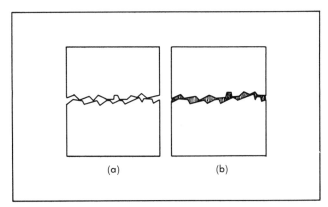

Fig. 11-3 Diagram of solid surface contact (a) without adhesive, and (b) with adhesive.

TYPES OF ADHESIVES

Just as a variety of materials can be bonded with adhesives, there are thousands of adhesive formulations available for bonding these materials.[10] Adhesives are available as liquids (pastes, solutions, and emulsions) and solids (films, tapes, rods, pellets, and powders). Formulations are often identified by brand name, but it is important to the user to be able to identify the chemical type as well. Suppliers are usually willing to provide such information, as well as pertinent data on the properties of the adhesive and test results on its performance in joints.

ADHESIVE MATERIAL CATEGORIES

The three main adhesive material categories are: (1) natural product raw materials, (2) inorganic raw materials, and (3) synthetic organic materials.

Natural Adhesives

Examples of natural product materials are gums and resins, starch, dextrin, casein, soya flour, and animal products such as blood and collagen. Adhesives made from these natural materials are most applicable to products where lower stresses are permissible. They are usually too weak for metal joints that may need to resist intermittent or steady stressing conditions. In many product applications, however, relatively large areas can be used so that the unit load is small. The number of such applications is large enough that natural-product-based adhesives still constitute the major poundage of adhesives used.

Inorganic Adhesives

The principal inorganic adhesives are sodium silicate and magnesium oxychloride. They have the advantage of low cost,

TYPES OF ADHESIVES

but have serious shortcomings in their low strength, negligible flexibility, and, in some cases, sensitivity to moisture.

Synthetic Adhesives

The synthetic organic adhesives are of primary interest to the manufacturing engineer. These adhesives have been developed in the laboratory to give high-strength bonds to wood, glass, plastics, and metals. Technical assistance is usually available from the adhesive manufacturers to fit one of these adhesives to a given assembly process. The synthetic organic adhesives fall into the raw material classes of elastomers and resins.

Resins may be further subdivided into thermoplastic and thermoset types. The most common individual members of these classes are styrene block copolymers; acrylic, polyolefin, nylon, and vinyl thermoplastic resins; and acrylic (anaerobics), epoxy, phenolic, polyurethane, and silicone thermosets. New technology also includes many hybrid types, which are alloys of the older classic types. Additional information about the variety of structural adhesives available is presented in several publications listed in the bibliography at the end of this chapter.

A summary of principal types of synthetic adhesives and their advantages, limitations, and major usage is given in Table 11-2. Although the manufacturing engineer need not, from a practical viewpoint, be familiar with the specific chemical structure of the materials in adhesives, an understanding of such structures is of primary importance to the adhesive formulator. They can be of interest to the user, as well, in explaining why a particular adhesive type is the best for the application. A study of the advantages, limitations, and current major usage from Table 11-2 is certainly pertinent for users who are choosing between adhesives because they will be aware of specifics about their application, which may not be obvious to the adhesive supplier. The synthetic adhesives listed in the table fall into six subclasses, indicated by Roman numerals, according to the method of setting or curing.

A polymer will serve as an adhesive if: (1) it adheres sufficiently to a particular adherend to give a useful bond and (2) it converts from a liquid to solid state during the actual bonding step. The latter requirement is not necessary for pressure-sensitive adhesives. Using these criteria, it is logical to classify adhesives by the manner in which they convert from the liquid state to the solid state during bonding.

CHEMICALLY REACTIVE ADHESIVES (CLASS I)

The chemically reactive adhesives all undergo a curing or crosslinking reaction within the adhesive. Most reactive adhesives provide high lap-shear strengths, to 7000 psi (48.3 MPa) or more, at room temperature. When crosslinked (thermoset), these adhesives retain properties well. Because many of these thermoset resins are relatively brittle, the peel strengths are frequently low. To improve the peel strengths, polymer alloys are commonly prepared from chemically reactive adhesives and various flexible thermoplastics and elastomers.

Plural Components (Class IA)

In this type of adhesive, the chemical reaction is initiated by mixing a reactive component or catalyst with the adhesive before application. The reaction then proceeds at some rate, depending on the particular curing agent or catalyst, until an inert-thermoset, chemically resistant resin develops. Heating will usually accelerate the cure rate as well as improve initial fluidity for better substrate wetting, resulting in improved bond durability. Epoxies are probably the most common resin bases for this class of adhesives, although polyester, polysulfide, polyurethane, and silicone resins are available in two-part mix formulations.

Soaring energy and labor costs and the need to improve productivity have made it increasingly advantageous in recent years to use adhesives that can cure rapidly at room temperature, adhere to a wide variety of adherends, and need no mixing or metering prior to application. In these respects, some modified structural acrylic adhesives can be mentioned as having such characteristics. While a curing catalyst or accelerator does not have to be premixed with resins in such adhesives, a separate component must be applied to one or both adherend surfaces before the joint is closed. Such adhesives are characterized as being two-step types, as opposed to two-part adhesives, where the ratio of parts and their mixing are important to their properties. The curing can be effected in a matter of minutes, and strong joints can be made with little or no surface preparation and, in some instances, on oily parts.[11]

Current commercial products are described as second or third-generation acrylics. The catalyst need only be applied to one adherend, while the resin is applied to the second adherend. Mating the surface automatically mixes the resin and catalyst, producing a thermoset bondline in a few minutes. As originally introduced in the marketplace, these adhesives lacked toughness and flexibility and required good surface preparation on metal adherends. The incorporation of polymeric elastomers and new acrylic resins have favorably altered these properties and made the adhesives highly tolerant of oil contamination.[12]

Epoxy resin formulations that cure at room temperature have been a mainstay of structural bonding in general manufacturing for many years. Details of many structural bonding applications with these adhesives are discussed in several of the publications listed in the bibliography at the end of this chapter. The most convenient commercial form of such epoxy adhesives has been the equal parts of A and B mix types; the ratio is not highly critical to achieving adequate curing, and the use of automated mixing and application equipment is easy.[13] A variety of inorganic fillers can be used to control the viscosity to fit a particular application. The rigidity and sensitivity of the bondline to crack propagation in earlier formulations has been eliminated by blending elastomeric rubber with the epoxy.[14]

Microencapsulated two-part epoxy adhesives, which are coated onto threaded fasteners to replace lock washers, remain dormant until the shearing action of engaging threads causes some of the capsules to break, thus allowing the adhesive to cure. The capsules that do not break on initial assembly allow the removal and reuse of the fastener several times with only a slight loss in break-loose, break-away, and prevailing torque.

Heat-Activated Adhesives (Class IB)— Epoxies, Urethanes and Phenolics

This class of adhesives is often referred to as the one-part heat-curing type. All of the necessary ingredients have been premixed by the adhesive supplier, but heating is required to initiate the chemical reaction. Because they are premixed, shelf life, even at room temperature, may be limited to a few months. Such adhesives can be stored at subambient temperatures to improve their shelf life. Every manufacturer of this type of adhesive tries to optimize shelf life, yet permit as rapid a cure as possible in the 180-350° F (82-177° C) temperature range.

While some industries will always prefer a room temperature curing system, certain major industrial markets, such as light fixtures, appliances, motors, speakers, metal furniture, hydraulic oil filters, and other high-volume consumer products will traditionally use a heat-cured adhesive. Material economics and durability of product are two of the most important reasons for using these products.

The phenolic resin materials are generally used as a modifying agent for imparting strength and water resistance to other resins. For example, blending a phenolic resin with a vinyl thermoplastic resin has produced a class of adhesives known as vinyl-phenolics, which have had one of the best histories of durable bonding of metals in aircraft. Similarly, the addition of phenolic to epoxy resin has produced a class of aircraft bonding adhesives known as epoxy-phenolics with high service temperature capability.

One of the first phenolic-modified adhesives for bonding aircraft was made by blending nitrile elastomer rubber with phenolic resin. Their resistance to high-humidity service environments when bonding metals is seldom equaled by any of the most modern adhesives in the marketplace.[15]

One-Part Specially Catalyzed Adhesives (Class IC)—Cyanoacrylates and Anaerobics

There are several types of adhesives that need neither on-site mixing nor heat to cure, including cyanoacrylates, anaerobics, and acrylics with surface activators.

Cyanoacrylates. One of these types of adhesives that has attracted considerable attention because of ease of use is a cyanoacrylate.[16] The picture of an elephant being supported by the strength developed by one drop of adhesive is familiar. It seems incredible that a tensile strength of 5000 psi (34.5 MPa) is developed without the benefit of adding a separate catalyst or heat. This high strength is developed within a minute after the bondline is closed. Polymerization of the cyanoacrylate only occurs rapidly in the presence of a weakly basic compound, such as an amine, an alcohol, or trace amounts of water on the surface. For this latter reason, some describe the cure as moisture induced.

Advantages of cyanoacrylates include: (1) ease of use, (2) rapid formation of bonds, (3) small quantity required, (4) adherence to dissimilar materials, (5) colorless bondlines, and (6) good resistance to many solvents.

General limitations exist and include the following: (1) poor gap-filling characteristics; (2) bonds have low shock resistance and low peel strength; (3) with some adherends, like glass and metals, the bonds have poor moisture resistance; (4) bonds lose strength after exposure to temperatures higher than 160° F (71° C); and (5) curing is sometimes accompanied by a white haze or halo adjacent to the bondline.

As with many adhesive evolutions, the manufacturers have developed systems or alloys that have overcome many of the limitations without losing the basic advantages of speed and strength. Cyanoacrylate alloys are available having temperature capabilities to 250°° F (120° C), having high impact and peel strength, or existing in a gel form for gap-filling capability. Unfortunately, all these characteristics are not as yet available in one formulation, but may soon be with continuing development.

Anaerobics. Also prominent in this one-part class are the anaerobic adhesives that achieve cure at room temperature only in the absence of oxygen.[17] As long as oxygen is available, the curing mechanism cannot proceed, which is why these adhesives are stored in oxygen-permeable containers. When oxygen is excluded, such as by confinement between surfaces to be joined, polymerization can start, and the adhesive becomes a thermoset plastic. These adhesives have important properties, including rapid cure at ambient temperature, no need for metering and mixing prior to application, and resistance to a wide variety of solvents and industrial fluids. From a purely chemical point of view, these properties are not always achieved optimally and simultaneously. Ingenuity in chemistry, however, has permitted remarkable tradeoff compromises in such properties.

Present-day anaerobic structural adhesives are the culmination of an evolution that began with the anaerobic machinery adhesives used for sealing and bonding of rigid parts.[18] While ideally suited to do the job of improving the strength and reliability of threaded fasteners and sealing leakage in connected parts, they lacked the flexibility and toughness of true structural adhesives. Sophisticated combinations of the former methacrylate chemistry with urethane chemistry has produced desirable structural characteristics, while retaining the property of curing in the absence of oxygen. Unlike the second-generation acrylic adhesives mentioned earlier, the anaeorobic-type acrylics should only be used to bond clean or specially surface-treated metal, glass, or ceramic surfaces. Some typical application areas for these improved anaerobics are the assembly of firearms and fuel pumps, electronic components for high-temperature service, bonding metal to glass, glass stemware, and honing stones.

Radiation-Curing Adhesives (Class ID)

Radiation curing of adhesives permits rapid curing, conserves energy, allows easy automation, and avoids air pollution by eliminating volatile products. Energy sources used for radiation curing are ultraviolet (UV) light, visible light, electron beam (EB), and gamma radiation. Gamma radiation has limited application, being restricted to a few specialized and electronic uses.

Ultraviolet light curing adhesives. Modified acrylics, anaerobics, and epoxies can be cured with UV light at 365 nm (3650 angstrom units) wavelength and 10,000 to 100,000 $\mu W/cm^2$ (64 500 to 645 000 $\mu W/in.^2$) intensity. They are prepared with photoinitiator chemicals that become active in the presence of the light. At the higher light intensities, cure takes place in 3-15 seconds, and air-exposed anaerobic material can be cured dry to touch. Obviously, the bondline must be visible to the light from at least one substrate to have direct activation. This would seem to limit their usefulness to glass and UV-clear plastics. However, in some cases, the formulations are made with dual or triple activation. As long as a fillet is visible, parts can be fixtured in seconds and strength developed anaerobically by surface activation or with heat at a more leisurely pace of minutes or hours.

The convenience and speed of UV curing has allowed many batch operations to be replaced by line curing. Mercury arc lamps are most widely used as the source of light. Because these light sources can be 10 times as strong as the UV intensity of sunlight, operator protection is essential. In the production of transformers, UV-cured adhesive coats and penetrates the laminations, reducing hum and insulating the components. Fast curing with this method eliminated the batch drying formerly required.

Electron beam curing. Electron beam (EB) curing adhesives are being used with flocking, metallized paper, plastics, and foil laminates. Applications include the manufacture of magnetic

TYPES OF ADHESIVES

TABLE 11-2
Principle Types of Synthetic Adhesives

Polymer Type	Identifying Chemical Structure	Classification*
Acrylic		II,VI I (A,D)
Acrylate diester, anaerobic		I (A,B,C,D)

Cellulosic:
  Ethers
  Esters
	
	(Derived from natural products)
		II,III

Cyanoacrylate		IC
Epoxy**		I (A,B,D),V

Olefin polymers:
  Copolymers of ethylene with
  vinyl acetate, acrylates, acrylic
  acid, or acid salt (ionomer)
		III,V

Phenolic**		IA,IB,II,V
Polyamide		II,III,IV

Polyaromatic:
  Polybenzimidazole
  Polyamide
		IB,V

Advantages	Limitations	Major Usage
Ultraviolet stability, clear	Heat resistance	Bonding of plastics, glass, and metals
Room temperature cure, rapid fixture, durable up to 400° F (205° C) service	Maximum gap 0.03″ (0.8 mm)	Bonding, sealing, retaining, impregnating
Good solubility and low cost	Moisture sensitivity	Bonding of leather, paper, wood, nonwoven fabrics, costume jewelry, and household cement
Fast-setting, adhesion to many hard-to-bond plastics	High-cost restricted glue-line thickness and area	Specialty adhesive for surgical suturing
Versatility, high strength, solvent resistance	Peel strength, cost	Structural bonding (high peel alloys available), concrete repair, construction industries
Flexibility, ease of handling as films or hot melts, cost	Creep, heat resistance	Laminating, packaging, bookbinding
Low cost, heat resistance, weatherability	Brittleness	Plywood, abrasive wheels, structural bonding
Flexibility, oil and water resistance	Cost	Can seam sealant, hot melt for shoes
Stability at 700° F (370° C) with good low-temperature properties, "ladder polymer" structure	Cost, handling, high temperatures required to form bonds	Aerospace applications, honeycomb sandwich assembly

(continued)

TYPES OF ADHESIVES

TABLE 11-2 Continued

Polymer Type	Identifying Chemical Structure	Classification*
Polyester	$$\text{www } R - CH = CH - \underset{\underset{O}{\|\|}}{C} - O - R' \text{ www}$$	IA,II,III
Polysulfide	HS www S —— S www SH	IA
Polyurethane	$$\text{www } R - \underset{\underset{H}{\|}}{N} - \underset{\underset{O}{\|}}{C} - O - R' \text{ www}$$	I (A,B,C, E),II
Resorcinol	(structure: resorcinol ring with HO, CH_2 www, www CH_2, OH)	IA,II
Rubber: Natural "Reclaim" Butyl Butadiene-styrene Neoprene Nitrile	$$\left[CH_2 - \underset{\underset{CH_3}{\|}}{C} = CH - CH_2 \right]_n$$ Isoprene polymer	II,V,VI ....
Silicone	$$R - \overset{\|}{\underset{\|}{Si}} - O - \overset{\|}{\underset{\|}{Si}} - O \text{ www}$$	I(A,B,C),VI
Urea	$$\text{www } NH - \underset{\underset{O}{\|\|}}{C} - NH - CH_2 - O \text{ www}$$	IA
Vinyl: Polyvinyl chloride (PVC) Polyvinyl acetate (PVA) Polyvinyl acetals Polyvinyl alkyl ethers	$$\text{www } CH_2 - \underset{\underset{R}{\|}}{CH} \text{ www}$$	II,III,IV,VI

* The Roman numerals in this column refer to the accompanying text, which lists six classes of adhesives according to the method of curing.

** These resins are frequently used in combination with an elastomer such as nitrile rubber, neoprene, or vinyl. The combination is referred to as an "alloy."

Advantages	Limitations	Major Usage
Flexibility, sharp melting point for hot melts	Cost, limited adhesion	Foils, plastics, shoe bonding
Weatherability, wide temperature range	Strength	Elastomeric adhesive or sealant for auto, construction, and aircraft applications
Cryogenic performance, versatility	Handling, heat resistance	Bonding of flexible to non-flexible substrates
Room temperature setting, weatherability	High cost	Marine plywood, tire cord adhesion
Elastomeric, high "tack"; the varieties below have special properties Weatherability Strength Oil resistance	Low tensile and shear strength, poor solvent resistance	Pressure-sensitive tapes, household adhesives, laminating adhesives, footwear Forms alloys with thermosets for structural adhesives
Performance at temperature extremes	Cost, strength	Sealants, pressure-sensitive tapes for aerospace electrical usage, coupling agents
Very low cost, room temperature curing	Moisture sensitivity	Plywood, furniture
Versatility, adhesion to glass, oil and grease resistance		Household glues (PVA), safety-glass lamination (acetals), furniture, footwear

CHAPTER 11

TYPES OF ADHESIVES

discs and tapes with thermoplastic hot-melt or polyurethane adhesives.

Moisture-Curing Adhesives (Class IE)— Polysulfides, Polyurethanes and Polysiloxanes (Silicones)

These are liquid or paste adhesives that react on exposure to atmospheric moisture. Moisture-curing polysulfides[19] are primarily used as adhesive/sealants, but polyurethanes[20] can be applicable for either true structural bonding or as adhesive/sealants. The silicones are also available in moisture-curing room-temperature-vulcanizing (RTV) formulations that are structural or adhesive/sealant in nature.[21]

True structural-strength silicone bonds are more frequently two-part catalyzed-type formulations that fall in the Class IA group previously discussed. The urethane adhesives in structural applications are also generally two-part catalyzed systems. Such adhesives have been used extensively for many years to bond polyester-fiberglass to itself or polyester-fiberglass to metals in automotive manufacturing. It is usually only necessary to remove a mold release agent from polyester-fiberglass surfaces to secure strong, durable bonds, but, on metal adherend surfaces, a special epoxy primer is often required to achieve water-durable bonds with polyurethane adhesives.

EVAPORATIVE ADHESIVES (CLASS II)

With evaporative adhesives, curing or setting occurs through the loss of solvent or water. Therefore, at least one of the adherends must be porous enough to absorb the solvent or water, or sufficient drying time must be allowed before assembly. Both thermoplastic and thermoset systems can be applied by this method. Soluble, nonreactive materials include rubber, vinyl resins, thermoplastic urethanes, acrylics, phenoxy resin, and natural materials such as cellulose esters, asphalt, starch, and casein. Many reactive resins, such as phenolics and urethanes, are also used in solvents. Some of these adhesives are flexible and have good peel strengths, some up to 100 lb/in. (17.5 N/mm) of width. Adhesion in shear or tension will generally be low and susceptible to more creep than the chemically reactive types. Latex (emulsion) adhesives are being used to bond impermeable surfaces when the required longer drying time can be tolerated or if forced drying is used.

There have been continuing environmental and economic pressures on organic solvent-based adhesive users in recent years, thereby increasing the market potential for water-based adhesives.[22] Some of the current uses of water-based adhesives are for labels, packaging, wood bonding, fabric bonding, panel lamination, high-pressure laminate bonding, construction mastics, bonding of floor and wall tile, and tapes.

If water-based adhesives are to be considered for any application, it is important to secure as much information as possible about their application, drying, and bonding capabilities. The difficulty of rapidly removing water from bondlines as compared with organic solvents has always favored the use of the organic solvent types. This has activated extensive research by adhesive suppliers to study water removal methods, with only modest results. It is still difficult to achieve production speeds equal to those with organic solvents.

HOT-MELT ADHESIVES (CLASS III)

Hot-melt adhesives[23] must be formulated with thermoplastic resins because by definition a thermoset resin will not form a melt condition upon reheating. Synthetic polymers used in hot-melt adhesives include ethylene vinyl acetate (EVA), polyethylene, styrene block copolymer, butyl rubber, polyamide, polyurethane, and polyester. Hot-melt adhesives must be applied in the molten state and depend on a rapid solidification for the development of bondline strength. Thus, polymer properties such as melting point, hot tack, melt viscosity, and heat stability are most important in determining the usefulness of resins in hot melts.[24] The apparent simplistic manner of applying and developing fast bond strength using hot melts would lead to the conclusion that they might be the perfect adhesive product, but there are both advantages and disadvantages that should also be recognized. Hot-melt adhesives are used extensively in the packaging industry and for product assembly applications to bond a variety of substrates, including metals, plastics, glass, fabrics, wood, and paper-related products.

Advantages

Advantages of hot-melt adhesives include the following:

1. Bonds form rapidly, resulting in high-speed assembly and short clamp time.
2. Variable gaps can be filled in joints.
3. Most materials can be bonded.
4. Clean, easy handling.
5. Cost is less per unit assembly than for many mechanical fasteners.
6. Easy recovery and repair of substandard assemblies.
7. No problems with solvent or fume flammability.
8. Simple materials inventory and storage.
9. Precise bond control through variations of the temperature and the quantity of adhesive.
10. Equipment available for hand or automated assembly.
11. Easily maintained equipment.
12. Minimal production-line space requirements.

Limitations

Because of their thermoplastic nature, there are several characteristics of hot-melt adhesives that may limit their use, including the following:

1. Bonds lose strength at elevated temperatures.
2. Some bonds may creep and fail with time (delamination).
3. Hot melts may be sensitive to some chemicals and solvents.
4. Some adherends may be sensitive to the hot-melt application temperature.
5. Sophisticated application equipment may be required for high-performance hot melts, which can be highly viscous.
6. Some hot melts have a tendency to degrade at application temperature unless protected from the air.
7. Some hot melts become brittle at low temperatures.
8. Controlled wettability on adherends that have high heat-conductivity properties (for example, metals) must be designed into the manufacturing operation.

DELAYED-TACK ADHESIVES (CLASS IV)

Delayed-tack adhesives are nontacky solids that are heat-activated to produce a state of tackiness that is retained upon cooling for periods of up to several days. Blends of a resin such as polyvinyl acetate, polystyrene, or polyamide, with a solid plasticizer give this characteristic.

FILM ADHESIVES (CLASS V)

Film adhesives[25] are related to the one-part heat-activated, chemically reactive adhesives (Class IB) discussed previously in that similar adhesives are used and similar bond properties are obtained. They may also be similar to Class III or Class VI adhesives. The advantage of film adhesives include: (1) controlled glue-line thickness, (2) ease of application, (3) freedom from solvents, and (4) the opportunity to prepare two-sided films, each side with different adhesive properties to bond dissimilar surfaces. Also, film adhesives may be supplied on a flexible carrier, such as cloth or paper, in sheet or tape form. The most serious disadvantage for the curing type is the requirement for precise heating of the parts for an extended length of time. The difficulty of automating the tape feeding and cutting limits the application of these adhesives to hand operations.

The most common use for structural film adhesives is in metal laminations where the film can be crosslinked and cured after assembly. For this reason, tape and film adhesives have dominated the airframe market for many years. The usage has increased from several hundred pounds of tape adhesive on early commercial jets such as the Boeing 707 to several thousand pounds on jumbo jets as the Boeing 747. (Note: 1 lb = 0.4536 kg).

In aerospace and aircraft applications, much of the adhesive is used in honeycomb construction, producing very lightweight assemblies with high peel strength, high impact strength, and cleavage and fatigue strength hitherto impossible. The interlayer in automotive safety glass is also based on a film adhesive made from polyvinyl butyral resin. Many other laminated structures are made with thermoplastic film adhesives. Thermoplastic films based on polyolefins are heat-laminated; films having pressure-sensitive adhesive on both sides are used to assemble without heat.

PRESSURE-SENSITIVE ADHESIVES (CLASS VI)

A pressure-sensitive adhesive[26] may be defined as a material capable of bond formation by the brief application of pressure on a coated adherend at room temperature. The adhesive is applied to one surface from solution, emulsion, or hot melt, and then the adhesive is dried to a permanently tacky state. The coated surface is then brought into contact with a second adherend, and light pressure is applied to flow the adhesive on to the surface.

Masking tape, surgical tape, and labels are the major uses for pressure-sensitive adhesives, which are collectively called PSAs in the trade. A variety of other products using PSAs include wall and shelf coverings, imitation wood grain coverings, ceiling and floor tile, disposable diaper tabs, medical and sanitary products, graphic artwork, and protective maskings.

PSAs consist of a combination of elastomers, tackifying resins, plasticizers, and fillers. Pressure-sensitive adhesives are usually identified by the chemical nature of the elastomer used, such as natural rubber, styrene-butadiene rubber (SBR), acrylic, and others. While most PSAs are still applied from organic solvent solutions, the industry is developing alternatives because of rising solvent prices and legislation aimed at reducing environmental pollution. This has led to the development of aqueous emulsion systems and hot-melt pressure-sensitive adhesives (HMPSAs).[27] Pressure-sensitive adhesives are also available in 100% solids formulation, where curing of block copolymer thermoplastic rubber has been effected by electron beam (EB) or ultraviolet (UV) light radiation.[28] Both cohesive strength and solvent resistance properties can be measurably improved by such a technique. Those grades of PSAs with high cohesive strength are now being used for assembly applications. Automotive applications include sound and vibration damping, roof tops, side moldings, emblems, and brake quadrant assemblies.

PRIMERS FOR STRUCTURAL ADHESIVES

Primers used for structural bonding function as adhesion promoters or surface protectors. Adhesion promoters are generally silane materials and provide little surface protection. Primers used for surface protection, which also generally promote adhesion, are comprised of a resin, a crosslinking agent, film formers, a corrosion inhibitor, and a solvent carrier.

DESIGN CONSIDERATIONS

When materials are to be joined with adhesives, initial design considerations must include not only the physical and chemical characteristics of the adherends and the adhesive, but also the service requirements and operational environment that the bonded parts will encounter in use. These include the amount and types of stresses anticipated, temperature extremes to be encountered, the frequency and rate of cycling between temperature extremes, environmental conditions that the bond will be exposed to (water, oil, salt, acid, and so on), and appearance. Maximum bond integrity can be realized only when the joining operation is carefully examined, particularly those factors related to the surfaces of the materials being bonded.

MATERIALS TO BE BONDED

A wide variety of materials is available today for manufacturing and many of them, especially thin and fragile materials, can be joined only with adhesives. Even high-strength materials can often be joined with adhesives more economically and will outperform assemblies made with other joining methods. Adhesive bonding is particularly advantageous for joining porous materials and nonmetallics and for bonding dissimilar substances. Two general parameters should be kept in mind when bonding materials with adhesives:

1. All parts must be clean and structurally sound. However, adhesives such as the second-generation acrylics and some special one-part heat-curing epoxy formulations can be bonded with poorly prepared or even oil-contaminated surfaces, but there are no reports in the literature with respect to durability under adverse environments. Clean surfaces are still preferred.
2. The adhesive employed should not seriously degrade either adherend.

CHAPTER 11

DESIGN CONSIDERATIONS

Similar Adherends

Generally, it is easier to select an adhesive and design a bonded joint when the adherends are identical or similar than when the adherends are different. In all cases, however, the nature of the surface, porosity, cleanliness, and surface preparation must be carefully considered before attempting to join materials or assemblies with adhesives.

Porous Materials

Porous materials bonded with adhesives include wood, paper, rubber, fabrics, leather, foamed plastics, some ceramics, and porous metals. Porosity will vary considerably within these general types. For example, hardwoods such as oak, maple, and walnut are not as porous as the less dense softwoods, such as cedar, pine, and fir. As porosity increases, the possibility of forming starved glue lines increases because the adhesive tends to be absorbed into the pores. Therefore, the hardwoods form somewhat stronger adhesive joints. However, the physical and chemical properties of different woods are different, and consideration must be given to such variables as moisture content, chemical properties of extractables, surface effects, density, hardness, and strength.

Bonding of porous surfaces requires special handling to prevent absorption of the adhesive, which causes a weak joint. Preventive measures that are usually effective include the following:

1. Using high-viscosity adhesives.
2. Formulating with high-molecular-weight resins and polymers.
3. Maintaining high solids contents.
4. Bonding or curing with minimum pressure. Sometimes, very high pressures can force adhesive into porous areas to create better bonds.
5. Incorporating fillers into the adhesive.
6. Partially reacting adhesive before application to adherend and before application of pressure.
7. Allowing a short presoak time for the adhesive to penetrate before mating adherends and applying pressure.

Porous adherends are particularly helpful in the elimination of residual solvents or volatiles produced during bondline curing. When joining dissimilar porous surfaces such as rubber and wood, special bonding systems are frequently required. The wood may need to be pretreated by a filler, sealer, or primer application to ensure good, uniform bondability, while the rubber surface may be cyclized by a chemical treatment. A porous material like wood can be effectively bonded to a nonporous metal with so-called contact cements like the neoprene-phenolic adhesives. Even with such applications, an extra coat of the contact adhesive on the wood prior to bonding can improve the durability of the joint. The precoat of adhesive not only serves to fill porosity in the wood surface, but will allow a wider range of bonding conditions in the manufacturing operation, thus ensuring a better bond.

Laminated sandwich panel manufacturing presents an example of the effective joining of porous to nonporous adherends. One high-volume laminated building panel, for example, consisted of an exterior-weathering aluminum facing with a bonded plywood, hardboard, or gypsum backup board as the exterior facing of the panel. The insulated core material bonded directly to the backup board is low-density polystyrene or polyurethane foam expanded core material.

The cores of such sandwich panels are laminated directly to almost any combination of boards constituting the exterior facing of the panels. All materials are joined with a neoprene-phenolic contact cement adhesive applied from solvent by spraying roller coating or curtain coating procedures. A final hot pressing of the fully assembled panel ensures a structure that has significantly exceeded the originally planned 20-year service life. Such panel constructions can also be made by applying a layer of two-part room-temperature-curing epoxy between each combination of adherends and assembling and curing the bondlines simultaneously.

Impregnation with Adhesives

The anaerobic sealing compounds have replaced many other sealing compounds such as linseed oil, varnish, sodium silicate, and epoxy or styrene polymers for impregnating castings and powder-metal parts.[29] This is because of their unique character of staying liquid in air and curing without heat when confined. Because the anaerobic sealing compounds are thin, they can penetrate almost any degree of microporosity encountered and plug all cavities 0.008″ (0.20 mm) or smaller. When powdered metal parts are so treated, the machinability may be improved by 500% because of the elimination of tool chatter. Impregnation can make it practical to metal plate porous parts because plating chemicals cannot be trapped under the plating. Polyesters and silicates are also used for impregnation.

Nonporous Materials

Metal adherends can be considered as nonporous materials, except for a few such as powder metal products or metal foams. Metal weldments are another possible porous metallic situation, and the anaerobic sealing adhesive compounds previously mentioned are often used to repair weld porosity. Other nonporous materials include laminates of various types, such as epoxy glass fabric, phenolic canvas, or melamine paper; cast, extruded, or molded plastic sheets; molded polyester fiberglass; and glass.

The usual procedure in bonding nonporous materials is to select an adhesive as nearly like the adherends as possible. Modified epoxy adhesives are frequently employed on reinforced thermosetting resinous materials. Most thermoplastic adherends require special adhesives and/or special surface treatments to produce satisfactory bonds. Adhesive bonding can compare favorably with a variety of other joining procedures for engineering thermoplastics such as ABS, acetal, nylon, polyphenylene oxide, polycarbonate, polyimide, polyphenylene sulfide, polysulfone, fluoropolymers, and polyesters.[30] Thermoset resin adherends such as epoxies and phenolics are also responsive to adhesive bonding.

A degreasing solvent is required as a first-step surface preparation for many plastics. An additional step, involving abrasion of the surface, is often required, and, in some instances, a final chemical etching procedure must be used. Because the elimination of volatiles is frequently a problem in bonding nonporous materials, glass fabric, chopped glass, or other fillers are often included in the adhesive to provide an escape path for volatiles, to enhance bond strength, and to control the bondline thickness.

Examples of bonding dissimilar nonporous materials include metal to rubber, metal foils to laminates or plastics, and metals to the same or different metals. Rubber-based adhesives have been developed that can produce rubber-tearing bonds to metals with a high degree of reliability. Usually, both adherends should be adhesive coated, and some heat and pressure are required to produce the highest resistance to severe service environments. High-strength bonds can also be expected with certain cyanoacrylates.

Usually, the preparation of rubber surfaces does not require anything beyond a wipe with a solvent such as acetone, alcohol, or methylethylketone (MEK). In some cases, vulcanized rubber must be cyclized or the surface chlorinated. Metal foils such as copper are bonded to phenolic-paper or epoxy-glass-fabric laminates with phenolic-polyvinyl acetal adhesives. Thin metal foils are bonded to plastics using hot-melt and polyvinyl-acetate adhesives.

Dissimilar Adherends

Special consideration must be given to the design of bonded joints of dissimilar materials. When different metals or plastic and metals are involved, the surface chemistry of each must be separately considered, and the preferred surface preparation for each adherend must be carefully followed.[31] In addition, the high modulus of materials like metals, coupled with differences in their rates of thermal expansion, can transfer high stresses into the joint area when the joint is thermally cycled. Plastics and metals have significant differences in coefficient of thermal expansion, and, as a result, they form joints that can be highly stressed. If the adhesive is low in modulus, such as with nitrile-rubber-phenolic adhesives, the adhesive in the bondline can act as a stress-relief interlayer. The incorporation of certain fillers in adhesive resins can alter the coefficient of expansion of the cured resin so that the adhesive is a closer match to the adherends.

Sometimes, a single adhesive system will not bond to two dissimilar adherends, and various primers have to be applied to one or both adherends to improve the reliability of the joint. For example, when joining metallic and plastic (polyester-fiberglass) components in automotive applications, the metal adherend is usually primed with a two-part room-temperature-curing epoxy when bonding with a two-part room-temperature-curing poly-urethane adhesive. In this case, the polyester-fiberglass need only be solvent wiped, or wiped and mechanically abraded, to secure reliable adhesion with the polyurethane adhesive. In aerospace applications, involving dissimilar adherends, a duplex adhesive film is used, with each side of the adhesive film showing optimum bonding to one of the two dissimilar surfaces.

Some adhesives are made with coupling agents or adhesion promoters. Silanes are used for glass and ceramic bonding, and sometimes metals. Joints using these are able to withstand high humidity and temperature. In effect, these materials are designed to form a link between two adherends by reacting with the surface atoms of the adherends and the adhesive.

JOINT DESIGN[32]

The four most common types of stress applied to adhesive bonds are illustrated in Fig. 11-4. These stresses result when the joints are simultaneously subjected to a combination of mechanical and thermal conditions. Structural adhesives are generally the strongest when the joint is loaded in shear or tension. Cleavage or peel stresses, in contrast, will cause bonded joints to fail in many cases at relatively low average loading levels.

It can be seen in Fig. 11-4 that the tension and shear forces are much more uniformly distributed over the area bonded as compared to cleavage, where one side of the joint supports most of the load, and to peel, where only one edge supports the load.

Because the bond area is not involved in peel, the peel strength is expressed in force per unit of bond width rather than in force per unit of bond area.

The most effective bonded structures are those designed to minimize the stress concentration of peel and cleavage and maximize the spreading of stress with tension and shear loading. Unfortunately, pure tension loading is almost impossible to obtain because of the practical tendency of joint components to get out of line and generate some cleavage or peel. Even when the most rigorous methods are used to maintain true alignment (as in standard ASTM test procedures for measuring tensile strength of joints), the values are only good estimates of the true tensile strength potential.

A simple overlap joint, resembling the diagram illustrating shear stresses in Fig. 11-4, is most commonly used to measure the shear strength potential of joints in standard test method ASTM D 1002. As the specimen is loaded, the adherends elongate and bend, subjecting the bondline to increasing peel stresses, leading to failure at an average calculated stress that is considerably less than the failure-inducing peel stress. Figures 11-5 through 11-10 illustrate some common joint designs used for various applications.

An extremely important step in the process of designing an adhesive joint is to state the performance expectations for the joint. The specifications must be as precise as possible, but with acceptable limits. Some of the properties to be specified include the following: (1) fatigue strength, (2) ultimate strength, (3) impact strength, (4) strength retention with aging at service temperature limits, (5) bondline thickness tolerances, (6) humidity resistance, (7) salt-spray resistance, (8) solvent resistance, and (9) cure time to give handling strength. Make the bonding areas as large as possible to minimize the strength requirements per unit of area.

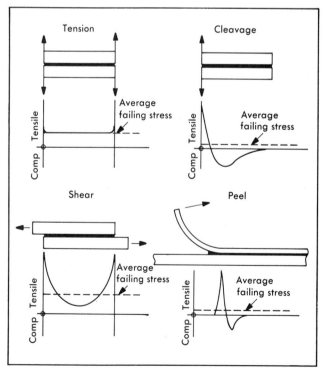

Fig. 11-4 Common joint stresses.

DESIGN CONSIDERATIONS

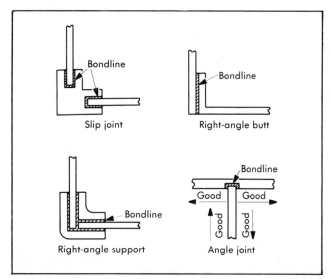

Fig. 11-5 Sheet metal corner joints. These joints usually require simple supplementary attachments.

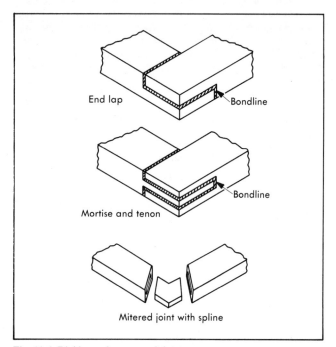

Fig. 11-6 Rigid-member corner joints.

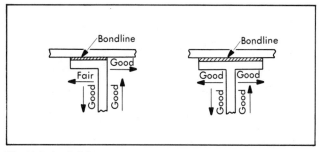

Fig. 11-7 Angle joints.

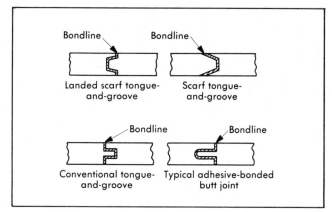

Fig. 11-8 Butt joints. Straight butt joints are weak in cleavage. Therefore, recessed butt joints, such as those illustrated, are recommended.

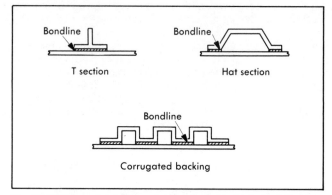

Fig. 11-9 Stiffener joints. These joints are used to minimize deflection and flutter of thin metal sheets.

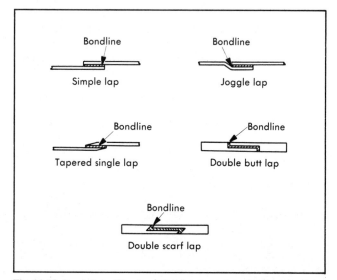

Fig. 11-10 Lap joints. The simple lap joint may be subject to cleavage and peel stresses under load because the shear forces are not in line. The joggle lap joint aligns the stress and can be formed by simple metal forming operations. The tapered single lap allows bending of the joint edge when distortion occurs under stress. The double butt lap and the double scarf lap are suitable for thicker materials, but require machining, which increases costs.

PRODUCT AND PROCESS SELECTION

The four basic requirements that should be considered when analyzing an adhesive application are as follows:

1. The type of material to be bonded is important, whether the adherends are metal, wood, paper, fabric, leather, plastic, elastomer, or ceramic. Are they bondable? Are they able to support the load under all conditions? Physical properties of the adherend such as size, flexibility, porosity, and heat distortion temperature should be considered. The design of the joint should be engineered around the weakest member of the system. Because the quality of the final assembly may be structural, the strength of the adherend itself is important.

2. All service conditions must be considered. A stress analysis is necessary to determine if the bond is within the stress limits for life expectancy. The stress cycle is important. Whether the type of loading is continuous or intermittent should be considered. Adhesive bonds should be downrated for conditions such as heat and heat aging, cold, water, humidity, chemicals, oil, and solvents. Test data should be found or developed to substantiate the suitability of any strength assumptions.

3. All possible process or bonding procedures should be thoroughly investigated. The most simple process that will satisfy the final requirements should be selected. All assembly steps, such as surface preparation, adhesive application, and curing or setting methods, should be reviewed with the performance requirements as a guide. Keep the procedure as simple as possible. Special equipment such as fixtures, ovens (drying and bonding), and applicators should be included in the evaluation.

4. As a final requirement, evaluate the economics of the system. The cost of the adhesive itself per unit usually is minor compared to the cost of the process. The cost of labor may prohibit the purchase of cheap but hard-to-apply adhesives. Automated equipment will reduce the cost of assembly.

PHYSICAL REQUIREMENTS

Bond strength is the measure of performance; however, the specification should cover the bond strength requirements under environmental conditions. Any evaluation program should include the temperature range, moisture conditions, stressing conditions, and any other condition related to the service performance of the assembly.

SETTING CHARACTERISTICS

The curing of a structural adhesive compound relies on polymerization or chemical reactivity with additive components. The reaction is accomplished by using a heat time cycle or a multiple-component system. For heat-activated adhesives, either of the solution or film type, the polymer or resin plus the curing agent are mixed in a single compound. Curing operation then requires an oven, platen press, autoclave, or some other heat source to complete the bond. Induction heating fixtures are being used to cure specially formulated adhesives in bonding automotive hoods, replacing the spot welds previously used. The cure of most adhesives is accelerated with heat, even when other cure mechanisms are predominant.

Epoxies, urethanes, and phenolics are often curable only at elevated temperatures in the range of 250 to 500° F (121 to 260° C). At these temperatures, the viscosity is sharply reduced, producing excellent wetting and displacement of oil and dirt. High-temperature-curing adhesives cannot be used if the substrates have low heat distortion temperatures. Solid film adhesives are always cured with heat to initiate wetting. With careful control of temperature and assembly pressure, excellent wetting without squeeze-out can be achieved. Aircraft skin bonding is predominately done this way.

The strength and durability advantages obtained with film adhesives and properly prepared surfaces will usually outweigh the disadvantages of the intensive use of energy used in autoclaves and fixturing. Cures are usually effected after the bondline has been at temperature for 1/2 to 4 hours. In all heat-curing adhesive processes, a time-temperature curve should be established for each application to attain the optimum properties in the joint. The highest bond strengths achievable with adhesives will be obtained using these procedures.

ROOM TEMPERATURE CURING

Adhesives that cure at room temperature make use of a multicomponent system. The polymer or resin is contained in one component, and the curing agent and catalyst are in the other. Proper mixing of the components will result in a compound that will cure at room temperature. Curing rates may be altered by varying the mix ratio or changing the catalyst. Epoxies and urethanes are often formulated in this way. Such adhesives are generally used where high strength is required, but the adherend does not lend itself to heat cycles.

Generally, the room-temperature-cured adhesives do not have as wide a cure temperature latitude as the heat-cured adhesives. Each formulation will have a limited pot life determined by its chemistry and temperature. The pot life in storage and manufacturing operations can sometimes be extended by chilling the mixture to -40 to -60° F (-40 to -51° C).

Anaerobic and Elastomer-Modified Acrylic Adhesives

Anaerobic and elastomer-modified acrylic adhesives fall in the two-part category of curing, although it is a two-step process for curing that does not involve the deliberate premixing of two components. These resins are made sensitive to activators or catalysts so that merely joining the resin and catalyst produces curing. In most applications, one surface is coated with the catalyst, the other surface with the resin, and the two are assembled quickly and firmly, with fixturing occurring in minutes or seconds. Both of these room-temperature-curing types of adhesive systems have been used in high-production automotive-type applications.

The two-part premix-type adhesives require mix and dispense equipment, with static mixers, just before the point of application. If a machine is stopped for any reason, it is programmed to dispense into a waste container to prevent adhesive setup in the mixing nozzle. Cure may take 60 seconds to 24 hours, depending on the formulation.

Anaerobic acrylics become unstable when air is excluded from the molecules, and this condition occurs when parts are

PRODUCT AND PROCESS SELECTION

assembled. This means on-part life before assembly can be extended considerably over other types of cure. It is possible to tumble parts, such as small screws, store them in thin layers in bags or trays for a few days before assembly, and still achieve cure in 4 hours after assembly. It is necessary that transition metals, such as iron, copper, zinc, cadmium, and titanium, or any combination of these elements with other metals, be present to start the cure. Anaerobic structural adhesives are seldom cured by exclusion of air alone. Generally, a primer/accelerator is used to introduce active metal radicals on at least one surface, which really makes the application a two-step process. An activator dip or spray remains effective even if done days before assembly. Cure time is 30 seconds to 120 minutes.

The anaerobic modified-acrylic adhesives fall into this two-step curing category because a separately applied resin and accelerator are automatically contacted when parts are assembled. Usually, each adherend will have had one of the two parts preapplied. However, if the gap between adherends is greater than 0.020" (0.51 mm), then more thorough and uniform curing will be achieved with the accelerator preapplied to both adherends.

Anaerobic acrylics and epoxies can have ultraviolet or visible light photoinitiators incorporated into their cure systems. Formulations thus made are stable, easy to dispense, and faster responding than all other cure systems except cyanoacrylates. Photoinitiators can be combined with other cure systems, making extremely versatile formulations. Cure times vary from 3 to 120 seconds.

Cyanoacrylates

Cyanoacrylates have setting characteristics that enable them to be considered as true one-part room-temperature-curing adhesives under one set of conditions, yet involving a two-step technique at other times. The most widely accepted theory of curing is that polymerization occurs rapidly in the presence of a weakly basic compound, which can be something as common as water.[33] The polymerization to a structural strength polymer is achieved as assembly pressure thins the bondline to a minimum, less than 0.003" (0.08 mm).

Thick sections and material in the open require an activator to achieve rapid setting in seconds. This two-step technique for setting cyanoacrylates is used extensively for tacking and securing of wires and screws in electronic assemblies. Except for such tacking applications, thick sections of cyanoacrylates are not used because of shrinkage (about 15%), which causes residual stresses in the bondline. A high-speed cure needs to be achieved to avoid a condition called blooming, which results from cyanoacrylate vapors condensing and curing nearby. Increased humidity or activator cure can help reduce this blooming. Cure times with cyanoacrylate resins are 3-120 seconds.

Room-Temperature-Vulcanizing Silicones

Single-package room-temperature-vulcanizing silicones (RTVs) are moisture curing and are being used for some structural applications. Their durability for hanging window glass and mirrors has increased their general acceptability for other structural bonding. They are not very strong, about 20 psi (138 kPa) design stress, for field application, but this strength can remain unchanged for many years. For factory applications when the substrates are properly prepared, the design stress can be 60 psi (414 kPa). In thick cross sections of single-package adhesives, the bond may take several days to develop strength

because the vapor must penetrate all the way through to achieve cure. Modern two-package silicones eliminate this limitation—they cure instantly on mixing part A with part B.

High-Tack Evaporation-Type Adhesive

Elastomers are often dissolved in solvents that must be flashed off before the bondline can be closed and the adhesive proceed to set up. The rate of evaporation of the solvent really controls the set time of the adhesive. The solvents may be organic or water-based, and the considerable difference in flash-off time of these respective solvents is most important in manufacturing procedures.

Organic solvents may take from 1 to 20 minutes to flash off, and good ventilation will be required for worker safety. Water-based latex and casein-type adhesives are much safer for workers when removing the solvent, but the rate of water loss is much slower unless intensive energy heating is used. Under equivalent energy heating conditions, the water might require minutes or hours to dry.

Pressure-sensitive adhesives fall in the category of evaporation-type adhesives, although the solvent removal is effected by the manufacturer in processing and preparing the adhesive for the customer. Such polymers will have high tack when dried and, in tape form, will be pressure-sensitive as received by the customer. Because of this permanent tackiness, the tape must be stored between release papers to which they have only slight adherence. The most general procedure for bonding with the evaporative-type adhesives is to coat both adherends with the solvent-dispersed adhesive and, after the solvent evaporates, to assemble the coated surfaces.

Hot Melts

Hot melts form a group of adhesives that have a different setting characteristic from any of the adhesives previously discussed. Most of them are purely thermoplastic materials that are set as a solid at room temperature. When heated above their melting point, they become fluid and are able to wet the adherends to which they are applied. Generally, a quantity of fluid hot melt is applied to one or both of the surfaces to be joined, and the surfaces are brought together and held until the adhesive has cooled below its solidification point.

Hot-melt adhesives give quick bonds and work well on automated assembly lines. An important limitation, however, is that they must be used at temperatures below their softening point. Some hot melts and pressure-sensitive adhesives have crosslinking capabilities, whereby their strengths slowly increase after initial solidification, and they are turned into a thermoset material as opposed to a thermoplastic.

INFLUENCE OF TEMPERATURE

All cure systems will increase in chemical activity with elevated temperature. In addition, some adhesives are formulated to have dual or triple-cure systems. For example, the anaerobic-radical materials are often made ultraviolet-light sensitive, in addition to their customary anaerobic-curing nature. Some will cure with ultraviolet or visible light, elevated temperature, and anaerobic-radical response (with or without an activator). Epoxies and some anaerobics have two-stage cures, which occur at distinctly different temperatures. They may partially cure at room temperature, but do not achieve their ultimate qualities until they are heated to some threshold temperature that starts further crosslinking. In all cases, the user should follow the formulator's instructions carefully to achieve best properties in the joint.

ADHESIVE LIFE

The application life of an adhesive must be considered from two points: first, the shelf life or aging characteristics of the adhesive; and second, the pot life or workable life of the adhesive. Adhesives can undergo slight curing in storage, resulting in gelling and loss of flowability. Refrigerated storage will delay such reaction and increase the storage life significantly. More-often, this applies to single-component adhesives. Usually, multiple-component curing systems are stable for rather long periods of storage and will not react until the components are mixed.

Normally, the shelf life of the evaporative and hot-melt adhesives are good, especially at room temperature. There are, however, a few polymeric materials that will change even while they are in solution, and the user needs to recognize this when trying to use such a material. The primary indication that such a change is occurring will be an increase in viscosity. The adhesive manufacturer should always be consulted for best storage recommendations.

Pot life is an important factor in multiple-component curing systems and in some evaporative adhesives. In the former, the pot life is dependent on the reactivity of the curing agent and catalyst. The workable life of the adhesive must be adjusted to the manufacturing production cycles. The pot life of the evaporative adhesives is not as critical as for the curing types because minor adjustments in workability can still be made by adding solvent. Sometimes, changing the solvent from faster to slower drying types will increase the open time to accommodate the production cycle.

CLEANABILITY

When selecting an adhesive, consideration of postapplication cleanup of the adherends and application equipment is important. Removal of excess adhesive on the bonded section could be difficult, especially when curing compounds have been employed. Well-designed application equipment will eliminate cleanup costs in most jobs.

APPLICATION CONDITIONS

Ideal conditions would be to install a strict temperature and humidity control, for example 77° F (25° C) and 50% relative humidity. A controlled environment will eliminate many of the variables in adhesive application in areas such as spraying and roller coating. The variation in temperature has a decided effect on curing adhesives and the rate of evaporation of solution adhesives. In high humidity, blushing or the condensation of atmospheric moisture at the bondline interface often occurs. If moisture is absorbed into the bondline, erratic bond strength can result.

SAFETY CONSIDERATIONS

Whenever organic materials are formulated and used on the production line, precautions are always necessary. Some of the curing agents, catalysts, resins, and pigments are irritants and may cause discomfort. A few are toxic and/or corrosive and many are flammable. With the help of proper equipment and ventilation, many of these hazards can be reduced to a minimum.[34] When choosing an adhesive for an application, be sure to read the handling instructions carefully before conducting

any testing trials. Very often, a careful examination of the manufacturer's label and accompanying instruction brochure will point to the best method for application of the adhesive.

All federal, state, and local regulations must be observed when storing, using, and disposing of adhesives. Proper training of personnel and adequate supervision are essential. The OSHA Safety Communication Standard requires that all in-plant containers holding hazardous materials be labeled, that safety data sheets be made available to all employees, and that an employee training program be in use.

Toxic Materials

Contact with, inhalation of, or ingestion of phenolic, cyanoacrylate, and epoxy adhesives, as well as some solvents, catalysts, and accelerators, may cause allergic reactions. Careful handling is required, and protective equipment may be needed to avoid skin contact.

Flammable Materials

Solvents and other flammable materials should be stored in sealed containers and used only in safe, well-ventilated areas where flames or sparks are not present. Solvent trays should have safety lids, and fire extinguishers should be provided.

Work Areas

A separate area for adhesive bonding is recommended. This area should be well ventilated and provided with a first aid kit, fire extinguishing equipment, an eye rinse fountain, and a sink with running water. Vent hoods should be provided for workstations and curing equipment. Because cyanoacrylate vapors are heavier than air, exhaust vents should be placed below the work area.

Personal Hygiene

Showers, wash basins, soap, towels, and protective creams and equipment should be provided and used regularly. Medical aid should be available for allergic reactions or burns. Cyanoacrylate adhesives can form strong bonds to skin almost instantly and attempts should not be made to pull the skin from the bond. By flexing the bonded area, the skin can generally be separated without damage. Soaking in hot soapy water can also help, but the use of solvents is not recommended.

Protective Devices

Plastic or rubber gloves should be worn when handling toxic adhesives, and contaminated gloves should be cleaned or discarded. Exposed skin should be coated with an ointment or cream, and the use of face shields, glasses, or goggles may be necessary. Protective clothing is also recommended.

Safety guards and protective devices are necessary for any machines or equipment used for adhesive application and curing. When a robot is used for adhesive application, protective fencing or a light curtain should be provided to stop operation of the robot when anyone enters the work area.

Environmental Protection

Precautions must be taken against the release of hazardous substances and pollutants or contaminants that may endanger public health or welfare. About 6000 chemicals subject to EPA regulations are banned from land disposal unless EPA determines that such prohibition is unnecessary.

APPLICATION METHODS

APPLICATION METHODS

Before choosing a method of applying the adhesive, the user should consider the following:[35]

1. Various methods for the best filling of the bondline and wetting of the adherends.
2. Economy of the application.
3. Production rate for the piece being fabricated.
4. Method of application from the viewpoint of simplicity.

The testing of the adherend should be initiated at the beginning of the investigation. The tests will likely reveal several suitable ways to apply the adhesive. Adhesives may be applied manually by roller, brush, extrusion and flow, and trowel. They can be applied semiautomatically with spray guns or high-pressure extrusion guns, or they can be applied automatically by machine methods that are usually geared for mass production of a particular part. Industrial robots are also being used for the application of adhesives and sealants.

MANUAL ROLLER APPLICATION

Rollers for manual application can be constructed from wood, paper, cork, metal mesh, rubber, or synthetic fibers. The length of nap on a roller determines the amount of material left on the coated surface.

SCREEN OR STENCIL PRINTING

Anaerobics are uniquely suited for screen or stencil application because of their stable nature in the presence of air. Accurate control of quantity is possible, and intricate patterns are applied in a second or two.

BRUSHING

Brush bristles for applying adhesives are made of various types of hair, synthetic fibers, wood, and metal. Compatibility with the adhesive may be important. The anaerobics, in particular, may require the use of all synthetic fibers so that the material does not cure in the bristles. Brushing is usually a manual operation, although sometimes the adhesive is fed to the brushes under pressure.

EXTRUSION AND FLOW

Extrusion and flow are general methods of applications used by operators equipped with caulking guns. Extrusion application is also used in curtain coaters, flow coaters, and high-pressure air-powered extrusion units. Rotary extrusion is a method similar to screen printing for applying precise patterns of hot-melt adhesive to continuous webs of various substrates. A rotating print cylinder and doctor-blade assembly forces adhesive from heated supply units through the patterned mesh opening of the cylinder onto the substrate. Hot-melt adhesives are also being applied with extruders having capillary rheometers that permit rapid measurement of melt viscosity.

TROWELING

A toothed trowel normally leaves a fairly constant amount of adhesive on the work surface. Small cutouts or teeth along one margin of the trowel allow a predictable amount of material to pass through and remain on the surface.

SPRAYING

The selection of spray equipment over other methods of application is usually predicated by economic considerations. This is particularly true when the products are large or of a complex shape. Spraying is fast and provides a means of reaching inaccessible areas easily. Furthermore, the drying time of the coating usually is reduced when it is sprayed because of the fine distribution of solvent into the airspace above the workpiece. When automated spray equipment is employed, particularly for long runs of identical objects, the optimum advantages of spray equipment are realized. Spray equipment can be classified by method: air spray or airless spray, depending on the technique used to project the liquid.

Air Spray

With this adhesive application method, low fluid pressure moves the material to the spray-tip area, where air is introduced to atomize the adhesive into an acceptable spray pattern. Figure 11-11 illustrates an equipment layout for air-spray applications.

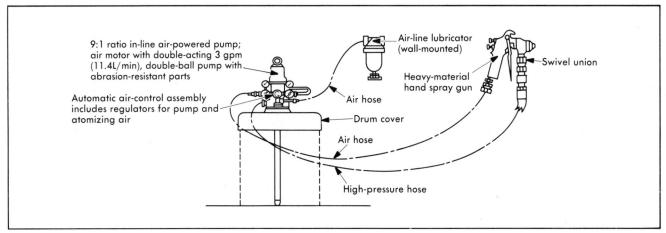

Fig. 11-11 Equipment layout for air-spray installation.

Airless Spray

Pressurized adhesive passing through a small opening atomizes. Once the liquid has left the nozzle, momentum is the only force that carries it forward because the only material emerging from the gun is the adhesive itself. The air between the nozzle and the target resists the motion of the particles, slowing them down appreciably, which reduces overspray. Figure 11-12 illustrates an equipment layout for airless-spray application.

Use of Heat

With either method of spray application, the adhesive can be heated prior to atomization to lower the viscosity and decrease the atomization energy required. This makes it possible to apply heavier films and reduce overspray losses. In addition, the use of the proper amount of heat can eliminate the effects of ambient humidity or temperature on the coating. Either can adversely affect the coating by the precipitation of water vapor or postthinning of the material on a relatively warm surface. Figure 11-13 compares spray patterns and energy requirements for hot and cold air and hot and cold airless sprays.

ROLL COATERS

More adhesives are applied with roll coaters than by any other single method. Roll coaters are very efficient, with waste as low as 2%. They may be used to coat webs or individual flat sheets or panels of materials such as paper, paperboard, plastics, synthetic rubbers, cloth, wood composition materials, and metals. Bench-type roll coaters are available in widths from 4 to 26″ (102 to 660 mm). Some models have open-end rollers that permit material larger than the rollers to be fed through the machine. Floor-mounted roll coaters are available in various types, including kiss-roll, pressure-roll, and reverse-roll coaters. Figures 11-14 through 11-18 illustrate some of the common types of roll coaters available.

VACUUM IMPREGNATION

Vacuum impregnation is commonly used, especially in applying anaerobic adhesives to powder metal, laminated, and die cast parts. Adhesive is pushed into microscopic pores after air

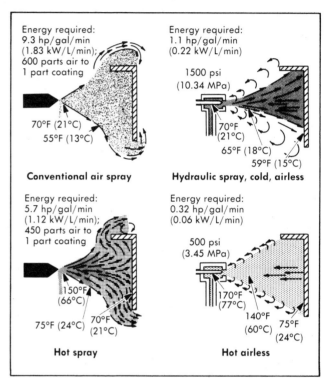

Fig. 11-13 Comparison of spray methods.

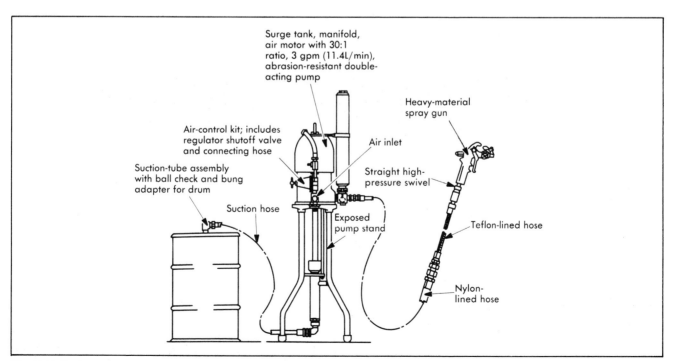

Fig. 11-12 Equipment layout for airless-spray installation.

APPLICATION METHODS

has been excluded by a vacuum cycle. This is done in a large mesh basket in a vacuum vat with the parts immersed. Excess adhesive is spun off, leaving a relatively clean surface.

MANUAL APPLICATORS

Adhesive applicators can be handheld or machine (or fixture) mounted. Handheld applicators include heavy-duty diaphragm-valve handguns and light-duty pinch-tube pencil applicators with fingertip lever actuators. With the actuator depressed, adhesive flows out of the nozzle; when released, flow stops. Pencil applicators are also available with poppet valves in the nozzles—when the nozzle is pushed against a surface, the valve opens and adhesive flows; when lifted, flow stops.

AUTOMATIC APPLICATORS

Machine or fixture-mounted adhesive applicators are available in a number of different designs.

Stationary Applicators

Stationary nozzle applicators are generally operated by depressing a foot switch. An operator or machine positions a part under the nozzle, and adhesive is dispensed onto the part.

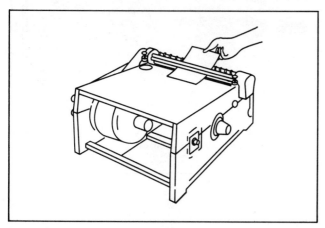

Fig. 11-14 Bench coater. Used for production rates from 200 to 300 pieces per day up to as many as 12,000 per day, depending upon the size of the individual pieces and the work flow conditions.

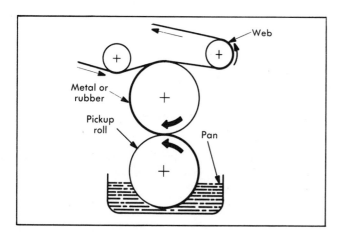

Fig. 11-15 Kiss-type roll coater. Most commonly used for web applications; the contact is controlled by web tension.

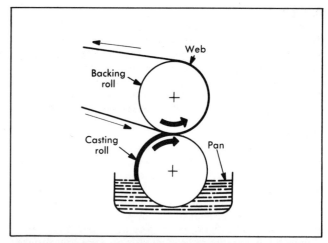

Fig. 11-16 Pressure roll coater. Used for both web and rigid panel applications, this style is particularly suited to panels because the rolls help move the panels through the machine. Some models can apply adhesive to both sides of the material simultaneously.

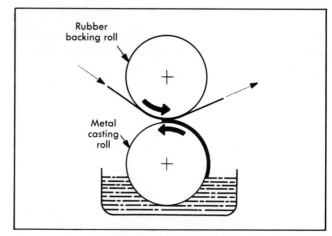

Fig. 11-17 Reverse roll coater. This type is used for precision web coating because the transfer roll, running in reverse to the surface being coated, provides excellent control of coating thickness.

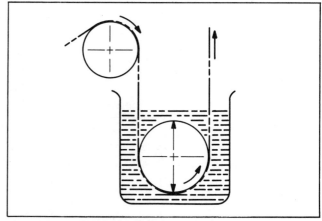

Fig. 11-18 Dip roll coater. Used for webs, the dip roll coater will coat either one side or both sides of the web depending upon the depth of immersion into the tank.

Touch Applicators

Touch applicators are operated by a switch located behind the nozzle. The operator places the part onto a custom-made dispensing nozzle, and the adhesive is deposited at a specific location on the part.

Advancing Nozzle Applicators

Advancing nozzle applicators are used where there must be a clearance between the moving parts and the nozzle, as on assembly machines. The applicator is operated by a foot switch or a machine-generated signal. When energized, the nozzle advances to the point of application, dispenses, and retracts. These applicators can dispense a drop, strip, or circular bead of adhesive.

Rotospray Applicators

Rotospray applicators are used where a 360° bead of adhesive is required inside a hole. These applicators consist of an adhesive valve, an air motor, and a revolving disc. They are usually mounted on a slide, and the disc is advanced into the hole. Adhesive is dispensed onto the revolving disc, where centrifugal force spins the adhesive from the disc and applies a bead at the selected location. If the rotospray is advanced while dispensing, a film of adhesive can be applied to the length of the hole.

Pressure-Time Vacuum Dispensing System

A pressure-time vacuum dispensing system consists of a disposable plastic syringe barrel that is filled with adhesive, an air regulator and gage to control the pressure, and an electrical timing circuit to control the dispense cycle. When the system is energized, a timed pulse of air is transmitted to the top of the syringe barrel and pushes a metered amount of adhesive out a nozzle attached to the bottom of the barrel. When the timer times out, the pressurized air in the barrel is exhausted, and an amount of vacuum is drawn on the adhesive to hold it suspended in the barrel and nozzle.

The amount of adhesive dispensed is controlled by the pressure and timer settings. Higher pressure and longer time will cause more product to be dispensed; lower pressure and shorter time will cause less product to be dispensed. With this type system, a dispense accuracy of 15% can be expected unless adjustments are made to either the timer or pressure settings to compensate for the adhesive volume change within the barrel as adhesive is used up.

Positive-Displacement Dispensing System

Another common system for dispensing anaerobic and modified-acrylic adhesives uses a ram-piston positive-displacement pump with a gravity-fed adhesive reservoir and an actuating device. Custom nozzles can be attached directly to the discharge outlet of the pump or an adhesive feedline connected to a remote applicator. Positive-displacement pump systems are capable of dispensing high-viscosity adhesives. They are unaffected by ambient temperature changes and viscosity and pressure fluctuations normally associated with pressure-time systems.

Adhesive is gravity-fed directly from a container, bottle, or tube into the inlet port of the pump to fill the metering chamber. When the pump is energized by the actuator, the pump piston, driven by an air cylinder, extends forward into the metering chamber to displace a predetermined amount of adhesive through a nonreturn check valve and out the dispensing nozzle.

When the actuator is de-energized, the air cylinder and pump piston retract, ready for another cycle. As the piston is retracting, the check valve closes, and a slight vacuum develops between the valve and the end of the piston so that the chamber refills with adhesive. The amount of adhesive dispensed is determined by the piston stroke length within the metering chamber, and this is controlled by a stroke adjuster, usually attached to the back of the air cylinder. Increasing piston diameter and lengthening stroke will allow larger amounts to be dispensed per cycle. Decreasing piston diameter allows small quantities to be displaced. Dispense accuracy of 2% is common with ram-piston pump applicators.

ROBOTIC APPLICATORS

Industrial robots are being used for the application of adhesives and sealants. The robots are generally used to manipulate the dispensing gun, but occasionally the parts to be joined are manipulated by the robots. Advantages of using robots for such applications include reduced labor requirements and costs, faster production, consistently high quality, and reduced adhesive usage. Adhesives can be applied to a number of parts simultaneously by using multiple guns on a single robot. A possible limitation is that high volumes are generally necessary for cost-effectiveness. However, the flexibility of robots permits handling a variety of different parts in small batches.

Robots Used

Selection of a robot for adhesive or sealant application depends on the specific application. For light-duty applications with small parts having flat or slightly contoured surfaces, robots having low payload, reach, and positioning capacity are often satisfactory. Speeds below 600 ipm (15 240 mm/min) are common for such applications. However, variable speed capability with fast, smooth acceleration and deceleration is generally desirable for most applications to increase flexibility. For heavy-duty applications and faster production, robots with increased capacity, often specially engineered for the specific application, are usually necessary.

Five-axis robots are generally adequate for most applications, but a sixth axis may be necessary for nonsymmetrical nozzles. Electric servocontrolled robots having a high degree of accuracy and repeatability are usually preferable to hydraulic units because of smoother motions and better repeatability. Dispensing speeds to 3000 ipm (76 200 mm/min) have been used for straight-line applications, but 1200 to 1800 ipm (30 480 to 45 720 mm/min) are more typical speeds, depending on bead-path complexity. Programming can be accomplished with a teach pendant, a programmable controller, or off-line CNC.

Automotive Application

One robot dispensing system being used by automotive manufacturers is of gantry design to allow the system to straddle production lines. Figure 11-19 illustrates a car-door assembly system. A programmable interface integrates the unit with the parts handling system.

Applying Various Adhesives

Hot melts, urethanes, and two-part epoxies are adhesives being applied extensively by robots. The hot-melt application equipment consists essentially of a melting and pumping unit, flexible hose or a pipe-hose system, and a heated gun and nozzle. An electronic control system is provided to vary the

APPLICATION METHODS

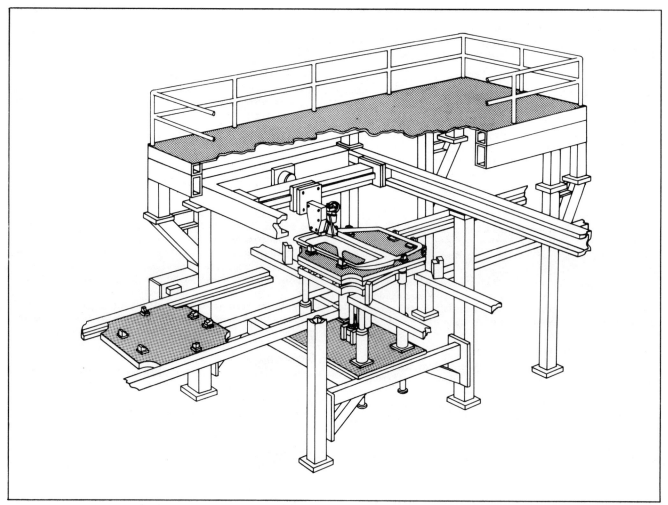

Fig. 11-19 Robotic door assembly system.

output of either the pump or the gun, or both, while the robot performs its program. Internal flow and bubble detection devices and external bead sensing units are also generally provided to ensure proper operation.

SELECTION OF EQUIPMENT[36]

The selection of equipment for dispensing of adhesives is the basis for the selection of a whole system to apply adhesives. If your adhesive supplier cannot address the whole system, then another may be chosen. The application equipment may dictate the type or at least the characteristics of the adhesive. It is imperative that a systems approach be taken right at the beginning, with the adhesive, process, and equipment all considered together. Broadly, the considerations include the following:

1. What adhesives can give satisfactory bond strength and life on the substrates?
2. Can these adhesives be handled and fed in the proper quantity and at the required speed to meet production requirements?
3. Can the equipment prevent operator exposure to improve safety?

4. Can the equipment provide automatic inspection of the quantity dispensed and inspection of the cured bond?
5. Will parts handling by machine ensure cleaner assemblies or perhaps perform cleaning as part of the assembly?
6. Will the conditions of cure be closely controlled by machine cycles of temperature, time, and humidity?

Once an adhesive and a method of application have been selected, the features of the equipment are still to be decided. Before buying any particular equipment, ask if the following considerations can be met:

1. Cleanup should be easy and any equipment parts with cured material easy and inexpensive to replace.
2. Control of adhesive quantity per part should be within the requirements of the specific application. If proportioning and mixing are required, how accurately is it done? Are there easy ways to check?
3. The life expectancy of the equipment and components should be known; replacement and overhaul are necessarily part of the future cost of manufacturing. Troubleshooting charts for the equipment are helpful because they aid early detection and quick repair.
4. Production rates for the equipment should be known,

as well as whether these rates are for continuous or intermittent production. Do not be trapped by average numbers; the machine rates and quantities must span all conditions and tolerances.

5. Does the machine have provisions for shutdown or power failure?

6. The control of adhesive temperature and the use of temperature indicators may be necessary for some adhesives.

7. Manual and setup operation should be possible.

8. Equipment operation should be as simple as possible. Simplicity makes training fast and avoids mistakes that hinder reliability.

9. When equipment breaks down, service backup will be necessary. Availability of a manufacturer's field service personnel, spare parts, schematic drawings, and parts lists all help shorten the amount of time the equipment is down.

10. Warranty coverage is important to anyone thinking of buying equipment. Are either or both the adhesive and equipment warranted to perform? Installation service should be available, as well as manuals for installation, repair, and operation.

11. Extreme care should be taken to make sure that the adhesive is fully compatible with all parts of the equipment. Adhesives can cause corrosion, swelling, and failure of certain types of metals, elastomers, and plastic parts. Anaerobic-radical curing adhesives can be destabilized by metals and impurities in plastics, which cause curing in lines and valves. Equipment for these materials should always be coordinated with the manufacturers.

SURFACE PREPARATION

Surface preparation is an important step in some bonding applications. However, many surfaces are bonded as received. The preparation of the adherend surface for adhesive bonding will largely determine the success or failure of the bond. In theory and under the most sophisticated laboratory preparation conditions, it is possible to bond two perfectly planar, clean surfaces when they are brought into solid-state contact without an intermediate adhesive. The theoretical magnitude of this bond strength will be sufficiently great that fracture failure of the joint will occur in the cohesively weaker adherend rather than at the interface.

In the real world of joining, however, the generation of perfectly clean surfaces is not feasible or affordable. The purpose of preparing the adherend's surface is to guarantee that, after the adhesive is applied, it will wet the surface of the adherend or tightly attached oxides. All loosely attached materials, such as reacted chemicals, water, oil, grease, or dirt, must be removed. No adherend surface can remain exposed to the atmosphere without accumulating some or even all of these contaminants. Water, either adsorbed or as a free film, is usually present in one or more monolayers thickness. Therefore, the immediate bonding of surfaces after preparation will minimize the possibility of contamination and should be emphasized in production.

When a delay in bonding a prepared surface is necessary, the prepared surfaces should be protected against contamination. Surfaces may be covered with clean paper, cheesecloth, or films. Primed surfaces must be protected, but cannot have contact with the coverings. Otherwise, the primer may transfer to the cover. Moisture and oil from handling can contaminate the prepared surfaces. Handlers should wear clean gloves and change them frequently. In most cases, washable cotton gloves are satisfactory. With cyanoacrylates, however, cotton gloves should never be used. Cotton is porous, allowing thin adhesives to penetrate and, in contact with cyanoacrylates, perform as an activator, bonding skin and glove alike. Polyethylene or rubber gloves should be used, and damaged gloves should be discarded as soon as they are punctured.

There are many degrees and methods of surface preparation. They can range from simple dusting or blowing away of loose dirt to complete removal of all materials that are foreign to the substrate itself. With some surface preparations, not only will the existing surface sometimes be wholly removed, but a new and different surface may be generated in its place. Methods may include the use of hand tools, chemicals, power brushes, steam, or abrasive blasting.

METALLIC SURFACES

Metal surfaces are rarely pure metal; surface contaminants include dirt, dust, grease, and oil, and, usually, oxides resulting from corrosion. Gases or acids commonly found in air may produce surface chlorides, sulfides, and other acid salts. Finally, because the oxides on the surface may be highly polar in their chemical nature, there will be layers of adsorbed water or other polar organic chemicals to interfere with adhesion. The grease or oil should be removed from the surface not only to obtain a more bondable surface, but also to permit further effective chemical or mechanical treating of the surface.

Vapor degreasing or a solvent wipe is the minimum surface cleaning required for all metals. After degreasing, a clean sandblast will enhance the adhesion, and machining or abrasion of the surface can be effective, but a wash or degreasing should follow to remove any debris from the mechanical processing. Particular attention must be paid to the cleaning process so that it does not become the source of further contamination.

Only long-term tests can determine the adequacy of cleaning. Initial ultimate strength can be good even though the surface may be susceptible to long-term moisture failure at a low value. A cleavage test conducted in a salt-spray atmosphere discussed in ASTM Standard D 3762 is one of the quickest ways to determine durability of surface preparation. It will show, for instance, that sandblasting of an aluminum surface is rather short-lived because of the oxides that form rapidly on clean aluminum. Because of the adhesive limitations of natural oxides, chemical coatings have been developed that assist adhesion.

Conversion Coatings

Conversion coatings are metal salts produced by chemical reactions on the surfaces of metals that produce tight bonds with the substrate and increase roughness and surface area for the adhesive to bond. Steel parts are pickled and zinc phosphated in strong acid baths. Aluminum is etched in a sulfuric acid and

SURFACE PREPARATION

sodium dichromate solution. After etching, additional aluminum processing may include alodizing or anodizing to build up bondable, corrosion-resistant surfaces. Copper may be treated in an alkali-hypochlorite-phosphate solution.

All of these processes require chemical tanks as well as parts handling and drying equipment. A supplier of adhesives or paints can be helpful in selecting among the many techniques and solutions available. Also, the metals supplier may have conducted testing of the adherend material with a variety of adhesives and finishes. Details with respect to metal cleaning, conversion coatings, and equipment requirements are presented in Volume III, *Materials, Finishing and Coating*, of this Handbook series.

Checking Surface Preparation

There are two quick tests that can be used to check the surface preparation of metals for production operations. The first is a water-break test for wettability, done before parts are assembled. If water wets the part and runs off in sheets instead of beading up on the surface, then the parts are free of oil, and the adhesive will probably wet the surface also. If the water beads, as on a waxed car, in any area, that area will likely be the site of poor bonding.

The other test is the cleavage or wedge test previously mentioned. It consists of the assembly of two 1" (25 mm) wide by 4" (102 mm) thick metal coupons (processed with the production parts) that have been pried apart with a thin wedge so that the split proceeds part way down the 4" length, as described in ASTM D 3762. The crack length is measured, and then the assembly is exposed to a warm, condensing humidity condition. The rate of crack growth encountered within minutes will offer a quantitative comparative evaluation of the surface preparation for most adhesives.

NONMETALLIC SURFACES

The fundamentals of surface preparation for nonmetallic materials are as follows:

1. Clean the adherend surface with solvent.
2. Abrade or etch.
3. Clean with solvent again.
4. Handle the prepared surfaces only with clean gloves.
5. Employ a protective covering to guard against airborne contaminants.
6. Bond as soon as possible after surface preparation to avoid oxidation, migration, and air contamination.

An important fact to remember when selecting the degree and method of surface preparation is that the service and life expectancy of the bond are directly proportional to the degree of surface preparation, assuming the adhesive will withstand the service conditions to which the bonded area is to be exposed.

Glass and Ceramics

These materials are often cleaned with a detergent wash and a clean rinse. For limited areas, an alcohol wipe or wash can follow the water wash to remove any soil generated by the washing and to assist in drying the surface.

Thermosetting Plastics

Many plastics, especially the thermosetting plastics, are easily bonded and require only a thorough surface cleaning by solvent wiping or abrading, and solvent wiping before bonding. The adequateness of such preparations for even long-term water-soaking or natural weathering exposures has been reported in the literature for epoxy and fiber-composite bonded structures.

Like metals and metal alloys, plastics are rarely pure. In addition to the mixtures of plastic that make up the base material, there may be uncombined plasticizer, lubricants, flame retardants, and mold-release agents that complicate the surface adhesion. Physically removing these is the easiest way, but tests must be done to detect, for instance, the continued bleed of a plasticizer, which can diminish bond strength with time.

Thermoplastics

These materials, which soften with heat, are also subject to chemical alterations when contacted by some cleaning chemicals. Solvents must be chosen for compatibility. Alcohols (ethyl, methyl, or isopropyl) are much less aggressive than a chlorinated solvent like trichloroethane, which is less aggressive than ketones such as methylethylketone (MEK) or acetone. A quick wipe with one of the stronger solvents, however, may be as effective as abrasion in cleaning a surface. The relative effectiveness of a simple alcohol wipe as compared to wiping and abrading a surface for fabricating durable joints has been reported in the literature for both polyester-fiberglass and engineering-grade styrene adherends.[37]

Cleaning the adherend and curing the adhesive should generally be accomplished as rapidly as possible to avoid continued liquid contact. Some liquid adhesives can have strong chemical action on thermoplastic adherends prior to curing and can release residual stresses that exist in all molded parts to one degree or another. This stress release may manifest itself as surface crazing or even instantaneous rupture of the part. High stresses require alteration of the molding process or stress relieving after molding by some heat treatment.

Polycarbonates and polystyrenes are particularly susceptible to stress cracking. Difficult-to-bond surfaces like acetal, polypropylene, and polyethylene are often treated with open flame, corona discharge, or plasma to enhance bondability. Such treatments alter the chemical and mechanical nature of the surface and are effective for bonding, painting, or printing.

INSPECTION, TESTING AND QUALITY CONTROL

Inspection and testing of adhesive-bonded joints are conducted to: (1) evaluate the quality or performance of adhesive bonded joints under specified loading or environmental conditions, and (2) establish manufacturing and quality control procedures on the basis of test results.

The selection of methods for the inspection and evaluation of joint quality depends on: (1) the complexity and cost of the adherends, (2) the type of adhesive, (3) the joint design, and (4) the expected service conditions. Methods that are suitable for use with adhesive-bonded metallic adherends are not necessarily useful when nonmetallic adherends are inspected. Similarly, tests used to evaluate the performance of simple lap joints are of little use in evaluating the soundness of adhesive-bonded sandwich structures. The usefulness and limitations of inspection and testing methods must be clearly understood before they can be successfully applied. With all tests, there is scatter among the data. For this reason, a statistical evaluation of adhesive bonded joints is strongly recommended.

Inspection and test methods for adhesive-bonded joints are detailed in documents issued by government agencies, by technical societies, and by industrial firms that use adhesives in production. All the available methods cannot be reviewed in this section; only the most widely used methods are emphasized. Most of the methods discussed are covered by ASTM specifications, and additional details on nondestructive testing are presented in Chapter 6, "Nondestructive Testing."

NONDESTRUCTIVE TESTING

The ability to determine bond strength and durability nondestructively is the goal of anyone using adhesives. Unfortunately, the best efforts to nondestructively determine these parameters are still a poor second to finding values using destructive test methods. The aircraft industry has been the leader in the development of nondestructive testing methods for practical production. Sophisticated and quantitative procedures are also being developed in academic institutions.

Appearance

Visual inspection can be used to a limited degree to determine the quality of adhesive-bonded joints. The usefulness of this method is dependent on joint design, the adhesive, and the adherends.

Tap Test

In this test, the inspector taps the structure lightly and analyzes the resulting tone. Tone differences indicate inconsistencies in the bonded area. As with any kind of nondestructive examination from the outside of the joint, it is beneficial to deliberately bond a structure with known defects in the bondline and ascertain how that imperfection is picked up by the test procedure. In this case, the difference in the tapping sounds from continuous bondlines and known defect bonds will be distinguishable. Even with experienced personnel, however, it has been shown that disbonds must be about 1.5″ (38 mm) or greater in diameter to be detected.

Ultrasonic Tests

Ultrasonic energy can be transmitted or echoed in an adhesive-bonded structure with defects detected by the alteration of the received results.[38] Pulses of ultrasonic energy are introduced on one side of the structure and detected on the other side; a void will prevent transmission of the energy. Pulses of energy can be introduced into the structure, and the echo produced by reflection at the bondline can be analyzed.

This procedure is widely used in the aircraft industry where frequency and amplitude changes are detected when an ultrasonic transducer is liquid-coupled to a bonded metal. Some of these testers claim to be able to detect bondline porosity as well as areas of disbond. In a tester developed at Fokker Aircraft (Fokker Bond Tester), a correlation has been claimed between ultrasonic measurements and lap-shear bond strengths.

Radiography

Radiographic inspection methods have proved successful in locating defects in adhesive-bonded metal-to-metal joints and metal sandwich structures. To be able to work in metal-to-metal joints, the adhesive must contain metal powder or some other filler to create enough contrast to make shadows discernible. Both voids and porosity in the bondline can be detected if the adhesive is X-ray opaque.

Eddy Current Tests

The eddy current technique uses an oscillating current in a probe to induce eddy currents in bonded metals. These induced currents result in a mechanical vibration in the metal that changes in acoustic response when an unbonded area is encountered. Voids must normally be at least 0.05″ (1.3 mm) diam to be detected.

Thermal Inspection[39]

In this method, heat-sensitive detectors are used to locate differences in surface temperature that occur over unbonded areas when the entire surface is heated. Ideally, the difference in thermal conductivity between the bonded metal and the adhesive should be as great as possible, in which case the disbond areas will appear as hot spots. Some of the infrared detectors that can be used include liquid crystals, heat-sensitive papers, and heat-sensitive dyes. Liquid crystal sensors are quite sensitive, but for making a permanent record, the thermal-sensitive papers are better.

Acoustic Emission Techniques

In this procedure, the bond may either be mechanically or thermally stimulated, and a detectable acoustic emission will result. A piezoelectric sensor and an amplifier are generally used to detect the acoustic emission level, which will vary if the conducting medium through the joint is variable.

Acoustic Holography

The acoustic holography approach to nondestructive testing uses pulse-echo ultrasound and focused transducers to produce a hologram of reflections from within the bond. While this technique has shown promise, the equipment is expensive, and the process is time-consuming.

DESTRUCTIVE TESTING

Numerous procedures have been developed to evaluate destructively the properties of adhesive-bonded joints and structures; most have been developed under the auspices of Committee D14 of the American Society for Testing and Materials and appear in the "Book of ASTM Standards," Part 15.06. This publication is revised frequently, and the current edition should be consulted for the latest information.

If a high degree of reliability is required, it will be necessary to proof or leak test a complete structure. A proof test should simulate actual service conditions insofar as joint loading is concerned. The stress level should be higher than that expected in service, and the test duration should reflect the expected life of the structure. The environmental conditions that will be encountered in service should also be considered in designing the test. Full-size testing is more conservative than modeling because of the area and mass effects, which give lower unit strengths on large parts than on smaller specimens. The reasons for this are conjectured to be the lack of complete fill, variations

INSPECTION AND TESTING

in cure, and unequal loading. For whatever the reason, specimens 10″ (254 mm) or more in span can be expected to give unit strengths 20% less than, for instance, 1/2″ (12.7 mm) shear specimens.

Care must be exercised in the accumulation and reporting of data on the mechanical testing of adhesive bonds. The data should include (1) the number of specimens tested, (2) specimen identification, (3) method of specimen preparation, (4) type of test, (5) testing conditions, (6) specimen design and dimensions, and (7) test results.

Tensile Tests

The relative tensile strength of adhesives can be determined with bar and rod-shaped specimens in accordance with ASTM Standard D 2095. A minimum of five specimens are tested for each test condition. Specimens except those in which both substrates are metal should be conditioned prior to testing for 40 hours at 73.4 ±2° F (23 ±1° C) and a relative humidity of 50 ±2%. Metal-to-metal joints can be tested as soon as the specimen reaches an equilibrium temperature of 73.4 ±2° F. Testing is done in a standard tensile testing machine. The loading rate is 2400-2800 psi (16.5-19.3 MPa) of bond area/min. The maximum load at which failure occurs is recorded, and the percentage of cohesion failure, adhesion failure, and substrate failure is estimated visually. The tensile strength is calculated.

The relative tensile strength of wood-to-wood and metal-to-metal joints can be determined with machined specimens and tested in accordance with the provisions of ASTM Standard D 897. Wood specimens must be conditioned before test for 40 hours at 73.4 ±2° F and a relative humidity of 50 ±2%. Specimens made with metal substrates need not be conditioned before testing. Special grips whose design is shown in ASTM D 897 are used for testing these specimens.

Shear and Lap-Shear Tests

The relative shear strength of adhesive-bonded joints that are loaded in compression can be determined in accordance with ASTM Standard D 905. This method is intended to evaluate adhesives for bonding wood. The testing machine should have a capacity of 15,000 lb (67 kN) in compression and should be equipped with a self-aligning shearing tool. Before testing, the specimens should be conditioned at 73.4 ±2° F and a relative humidity of 50 ±2% for seven days or until the specimens reach equilibrium. Data to be recorded include specimen identification, conditioning procedures, testing conditions, number of specimens tested, and shear strength (minimum, average, and maximum).

A similar procedure, ASTM Standard D 2182, has been developed to determine the relative shear strength of adhesive-bonded metal-to-metal joints by compression loading. The test machine should have a capacity of 10,000 lb (44.5 kN) and be capable of maintaining a uniform loading rate of 1200-1400 psi (8.3-9.6 MPa) per minute. The shearing tool is provided with a heating coil so tests can be made at room or elevated temperatures. The specimen should be placed in the shearing tool and loaded in compression until failure. Data to be recorded include specimen identification, bonding conditions, bond thickness, conditioning treatment, number of specimens tested, shear stress at failure, and nature of failure.

ASTM Standard D 1002 is used widely to determine the relative shear strength of adhesive-bonded metal-to-metal joints when loaded in tension. The testing machine should have a capacity such that the breaking load of the specimens falls between 15 and 85% of full-scale capacity. The specimens should be cut from test panels and be placed in the self-aligning tool of the testing machine and loaded in tension at 1200-1400 psi (8.3-9.6 MPa) per minute until failure. Data to be recorded are similar to those cited for ASTM Standard D 2182. Other ASTM standards for determining the shear strength of adhesive-bonded joints include D 906, D 2293, D 2294, and D 2339.

Peel Tests

The T-peel test (ASTM Standard D 1876) is designed to determine the relative peel resistance of adhesive bonds between flexible adherends. The tension-testing machine should be so selected that the maximum specimen load falls between 15 and 85% of the upper limit of the loading range. The rate of movement should be constant under fluctuating loads. During testing, a chart should be produced with inches or millimeters of separation as one coordinate and applied load as the other. Nonmetallic specimens should be conditioned before testing. The test should be conducted at a constant head speed of 10 ipm (254 mm/min). Data to be recorded include specimen identification, bonding conditions, conditioning treatment, test conditions, and peel strength (average, maximum, and minimum).

The climbing-drum peel test (ASTM Standard D 1781) is designed to determine the relative peel resistance between a relatively flexible adherend and a rigid adherend. It can also be used to determine the relative peel resistance of adhesives in sandwich structures. The peeling apparatus is shown in Fig. 11-20 together with a section of sandwich structure. The testing machine to which the peeling apparatus is attached should be so selected that maximum specimen load falls between 15 and 85% of the machine capacity. The rate of movement should be constant under fluctuating loads. Laminated specimens should be 1″ (25 mm) wide and at least 10″ (254 mm) long; sandwich-structure specimens should be 3″ (76 mm) wide and at least 12″ (305 mm) long. The peel resistance should be determined over at least 6″ (152 mm) of the bonded area by loading the peeling apparatus at a crosshead rate of 1.00 ±0.10 ipm (25.4 ±2.5 mm/min). Load versus distance peeled data should be recorded on a chart. Data to be recorded include specimen identification, bonding conditions, conditioning treatment, machine calibration procedure, number of specimens tested, average peel torque, and mode of failure.

Cleavage Test

ASTM Standard D 1062-51 is used to determine the comparative cleavage strength of adhesive-bonded metal-to-metal joints under tension loading. The specimens should be attached to the testing machine with self-aligning grips and loaded to failure at a rate of 600-700 lb (2.7-3.1 kN) per minute. Data to be recorded include specimen identification, bonding procedure, testing conditions, number of specimens tested, and cleavage strength (average, maximum, and minimum).

Environmental Temperature and Humidity

Any of the specimens specified in the previously mentioned standards or production parts can be used to determine the effect of the environment on strength. ASTM Standard D 1151 suggests some temperatures and humidity conditions that can be used; however, there is no consensus in this respect. The tests used should be determined by the expected field experience or, as second best, by duplicating the suppliers' tests so that a correlation between your results and theirs will be meaningful.

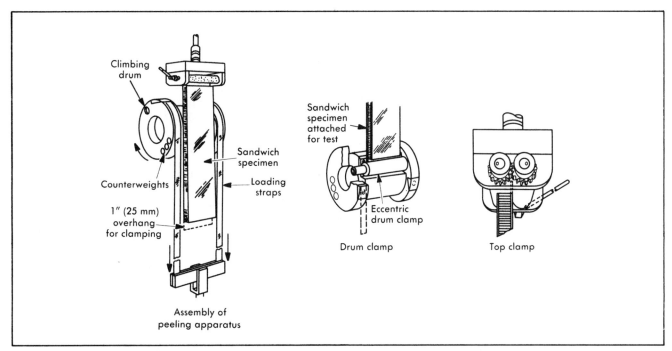

Fig. 11-20 Apparatus for peel test (ASTM Standard D 1781).

Most suppliers have aging data on representative specimens and may even have developed enough data to do predictive analyses, such as Arrhenius plots. These plots attempt to predict life of a bond under stated conditions and at varying temperatures according to chemical debonding equations and accelerated high-temperature data. They can be useful in the selection of adhesives, but are not substitutes for testing your own parts.

Both Underwriters' Laboratories (UL) and the Institute of Electrical and Electronic Engineers (IEEE) have developed extensive data on organic materials using accelerated temperature techniques. The same techniques are applicable to the long-term oxidization of adhesive bonds.

Stress Plus Environmental Conditions

The effect of simultaneously stressing and weathering on bond permanence is dramatically different from nonstressed weathering and needs to be included in the testing of any structure that will be subjected to stressing in its service environment.[40] The importance of simultaneous stress and weathering

went unnoticed for many years, and the scientific literature did not refer to it until about 1960. In tests, a steady stress was maintained, but in such a qualitative manner that the true sensitivity of bonded joints to significant stressing was still missed. By the mid 1960s, test methods were being used in which the stressing level was accurately known, and it was evident that the adhesives application engineer must not only consider how much stress is present, but whether it is steady or intermittent.

A number of testing methods have been proposed, ranging from simply attaching a weight to a test specimen and letting it hang to highly complicated and expensive loading devices capable of varying the loading and the cycling periodically. The lap joint specimen described in ASTM Standard D 1002 has been used in many test evaluations in which the joint is stressed in shear. Some investigations have also used peel stress specimens that place the adhesive in a particularly critical situation because the stress is now concentrated across a single line of the bond. The reader can refer to several general descriptions of this subject in the references and bibliography at the end of this chapter, from which the tests most appropriate to a specific structure can be selected.

References

1. D. H. Kaelble, *Physical Chemistry of Adhesion* (New York: Wiley & Sons, 1971).
2. E. J. Bruno, ed., *Adhesives in Modern Manufacturing* (Dearborn, MI: Society of Manufacturing Engineers, 1970), pp. 46-47.
3. J. D. Minford and E. M. Vader, *Adhesive Bonding of Aluminum Automotive Body Sheet*, Paper No. 740078, SAE Congress and Exposition, held February 1974, Detroit (Warrendale, PA: Society of Automotive Engineers, 1974).
4. J. D. Minford, F. R. Hoch, and E. M. Vader, *Weldbond and Its Performance in Aluminum Automotive Body Sheet*, Paper

No. 750462, SAE Congress and Exposition, held February 1975, Detroit (Warrendale, PA: Society of Automotive Engineers, 1974).
5. C. C. Booth, "A Guide to Building Construction Adhesives," *Adhesives Age* (February 1979), pp. 31-37.
6. J. D. Minford and E. M. Vader, "Aluminum Faced Sandwich Panels and Laminates," *Adhesives Age* (February 1975), p. 30.
7. C. V. Cagle, *Adhesive Bonding Techniques and Applications* (New York: McGraw-Hill Book Co., 1968), p. 71.
8. G. L. Schneberger, *Adhesives in Manufacturing*, ed. G. L. Schneberger (New York: Marcel Dekker, 1983), chap. 1, pp. 3-11.
9. J. D. Minford, *Treatise on Adhesion and Adhesives*, ed. R. L. Patrick (New York: Marcel Dekker, 1981), vol. 5, chap. 3.

CHAPTER 11

REFERENCES

10. I. Skeist, *Handbook of Adhesives*, 2nd ed. (New York: Van Nostrand Reinhold, 1977).
11. D. J. Zalucha, "New Acrylics Structurally Bond Unprepared Metals," *Adhesives Age* (February 1972), p. 21.
12. A. G. Bachmann, "Aerobic Acrylic Adhesives," *Adhesives Age* (August 1982), pp. 19-23.
13. K. A. Jacobs, "Adhesive Application Equipment for Two-Part Reactive Materials," *Adhesives Age* (May 1982), pp. 35-39.
14. A. F. Lewis and R. Saxon, *Epoxy Resins*, ed. H. Kahwichi (New York: Marcel Dekker, 1969), chap. 10.
15. J. D. Minford, *Durability of Structural Adhesives*, ed. A. J. Kinloch (London: Applied Science Publishers, 1983), chap. 4, pp. 173-200.
16. William F. Thomsen, *Adhesives in Manufacturing*, ed. G. L. Schneberger (New York: Marcel Dekker, 1983), chap. 12, pp. 305-323.
17. M. Hauser and G. S. Haviland, *Adhesives in Manufacturing*, ed. G. L. Schneberger (New York: Marcel Dekker, 1983), chap. 11, pp. 269-303.
18. G. S. Haviland, *Machinery Adhesives for Locking, Retaining and Sealing* (New York: Marcel Dekker), 1986.
19. M. E. Kimball, "Polyurethane Adhesives: Properties and Bonding Procedures," *Adhesives Age* (June 1981), pp. 21-26.
20. J. D. Minford, *Durability of Structural Adhesives*, ed. A. J. Kinloch (London: Applied Science Publishers, 1983), chap. 4, pp. 197-198.
21. J. V. Lindyberg, *Adhesives in Manufacturing*, ed. G. L. Schneberger (New York: Marcel Dekker, 1983), chap. 15, pp. 387-406.
22. W. A. Pletcher and E. J. Yaroch, *Adhesives in Manufacturing*, ed. G. L. Schneberger (New York: Marcel Dekker, 1983), chap. 16, pp. 407-423.
23. R. D. Dexheimer and L. R. Vertnik, *Adhesives in Manufacturing*, ed. G. L. Schneberger (New York: Marcel Dekker, 1983), chap. 13, pp. 325-352.
24. D. J. Hines, "Testing and Performance of Hot-Melt Adhesives," *Adhesives Age* (June 1980), pp. 27-32.
25. J. C. Bolger, *Treatise of Adhesion and Adhesives*, ed. R. L. Patrick (New York: Marcel Dekker, 1973), vol. 3, chap. 1, pp. 31-50.
26. J. W. Hagan and K. C. Steuben, *Adhesives in Manufacturing*, ed. G. L. Schneberger (New York: Marcel Dekker, 1983), chap. 14, pp. 353-386.
27. A. Zawilinski, "Formulation and Performance of Water-Based PSA's," *Adhesives Age* (September 1984), pp. 29-34.
28. R. Kardashian and S. V. Nablo, "Electron Beam Curing Equipment," *Adhesives Age* (December 1982).
29. T. S. Fulda, *Impregnation of Porous Metal Components with Anaerobic Sealants*, SME Technical Paper FC77-532 (Dearborn, MI: Society of Manufacturing Engineers, 1977).
30. I. Skeist, ed., *Handbook of Adhesives* (New York: Van Nostrand Reinhold, 1978), chap. 41.
31. J. D. Minford, *Physiochemical Aspects of Polymer Surfaces*, ed. K. L. Mittal (New York: Plenum Press, 1983), vol. 2, pp. 1139-1180.
32. G. L. Schneberger, *Adhesives in Manufacturing*, ed. G. L. Schneberger (New York: Marcel Dekker, 1983), chap. 4, pp. 67-82.
33. Thomsen, *loc. cit.*
34. P. J. McNulty, "Toxicity Testing and Reporting," *Adhesives Age* (June 1980), pp. 18-26.
35. "What's New in Machinery and Equipment," *Adhesives Age* (May 1979), pp. 38-43; (May 1980), pp. 16-22; (May 1981), pp. 24-29; (May 1982), pp. 23-29.
36. F. C. Herot, "What You Should Know About Engineered Dispensing Stations for Adhesives," *Adhesives Age* (May 1980), pp. 23-28.
37. J. D. Minford, *Physiochemical Aspects of Polymer Surfaces*, ed. K. L. Mittal (New York: Plenum Press, 1983), vol. 2, pp. 1139-1180.
38. J. L. Rose and P. A. Meyer, "Ultrasonic Procedures for Predicting Adhesive Bond Strength," *Materials Evaluation* (June 1973), pp. 109-114.
39. E. W. Kutzscher, K. H. Zimmerman, and J. L. Botkin, "Thermal and Infrared Methods for Nondestructive Testing of Adhesive Bonded Structures," *Materials Evaluation* (July 1968), pp. 143-148.
40. W. D. Bascom, "Stress Corrosion of Structural Adhesive Bonds," *Adhesives Age* (April 1979), pp. 28-37.

Bibliography

Bachmann, Andrew G. *"Aerobic" Acrylic Adhesives*. SME Technical Paper AD84-580. Dearborn, MI: Society of Manufacturing Engineers, 1984.

Baker, T. E., and Judge, J. S. "Control and Characterization of Adhesives in the Electronics Industry." *Adhesives Age* (April 1980), pp. 15-20.

Beck, R. H., and Yurek, D. A. "Structural Adhesive Bonding of the Automotive Body." *Body Engineering Journal* (October 1975).

Bittence, John C. "Engineering Adhesives." *Machine Design* (June 10, 1976), pp. 92-96.

Blomquist, Robert. *Cyanoacrylates—A Practical Guide to Their Chemical and Physical Properties*. SME Technical Paper AD85-777. Dearborn, MI: Society of Manufacturing Engineers, 1985.

Bluestein, C. "Radiant Energy Curable Adhesives." *Adhesives Age* (December 1982), pp. 19-22.

Bolger, J. C. "Epoxies for Manufacturing Cars, Buses and Trucks." *Adhesives Age* (December 1980), pp. 14-20.

Brenner, Walter. "Structural Adhesives Challenge Mechanical Fasteners." *Machine Design* (January 24, 1985), pp. 61-64.

Cagle, C. V. *Handbook of Adhesive Bonding*. New York: McGraw-Hill, 1973.

Chang, Y. F.; Tremonti, K. P.; Kish, T. G.; and Chun, W. *Induction Curing Adhesives for Automotive Hoods to Eliminate Spot Welds*. SME Technical Paper AD85-787. Dearborn, MI: Society of Manufacturing Engineers, 1985.

Cotter, R. J. *Systems Approach to Adhesive Bonding*. SME Technical Paper AD81-139. Dearborn, MI: Society of Manufacturing Engineers, 1981.

Cotter, Robert J. *How to Dispense Adhesives*. SME Technical Paper AD85-773. Dearborn, MI: Society of Manufacturing Engineers, 1985.

Davis, George E. *Precision Controlled Application of Continuous Patterned Hot-Melt Adhesive*. SME Technical Paper AD85-781. Dearborn, MI: Society of Manufacturing Engineers, 1985.

DeFrayne, Garry, ed. *High-Performance Adhesive Bonding*. Dearborn, MI: Society of Manufacturing Engineers, 1983.

DeSanti, E. A. "Drying Waterborne PSA's." *Adhesives Age* (September 1984), pp. 44-49.

Dietlein, John E. *Silicone Sealants as Adhesives*. SME Technical Paper AD84-585. Dearborn, MI: Society of Manufacturing Engineers, 1984.

Dollhausen, M., and Warrach, W. "Polyurethane Adhesives Technology." *Adhesives Age* (June 1982), pp. 28-33. Edwards, Bruce H. *Polyurethane Structural Adhesives*. SME Technical Paper AD85-775. Dearborn, MI: Society of Manufacturing Engineers, 1985.

Fries, John A. *Product Assembly with Pressure Sensitive Adhesives*. SME Technical Paper AD84-584. Dearborn, MI: Society of Manufacturing Engineers, 1984.

Harris, W. J., and Clauss, F. J. "Inspecting Bonded Structures by Laser Holography." *Metal Progress* (August 1971), pp. 63-66.

Hauser, M., and Loft, J. T. "Anaerobics and Modified Acrylics: How and What They Will Bond." *Adhesives Age* (December 1980), pp. 21-24.

Haviland, G. S. "Designing with Threaded Fasteners." *Mechanical Engineering* (October 1983), pp. 17-31.

—————. *Machinery Adhesives for Locking, Retaining and Sealing*. New York: Marcel Dekker, 1986.

Hegland, Donald E. "Adhesives—Production Cost Cutters." *Production Engineering* (February 1981), pp. 117-121.

Helmstetter, Gerald J. *The Anaerobic Advantage*. SME Technical Paper AD85-774. Dearborn, MI: Society of Manufacturing Engineers, 1985.

Hoenisch, Frank P., and Sanderson, F. T. *Aqueous Acrylic Adhesives for Industrial Laminating*. SME Technical Paper AD85-770. Dearborn, MI: Society of Manufacturing Engineers, 1985.

Houwink, R., and Solomon, G., eds. *Adhesion and Adhesives*. New York: Elsevier Publishing Co., 1967.

Hulstein, C. "Automatic Application of Anaerobic Adhesives." *Adhesives Age* (July 1979), pp. 25-29.

Kaye, I. "Troubleshooting Hot-Melt Adhesives Systems." *Adhesives Age* (August 1979), pp. 27-31.

Kilchesty, A. "Comparing Emulsion-Based and Solvent-Release Sealants." *Adhesives Age* (November 1981), pp. 40-42.

Kull, C. F., and Moody, D. J. "Solving Adhesive Application Equipment Problems." *Adhesives Age* (May 1979), pp. 35-37.

Larson, Melissa. "A Roundup—Update on Adhesives." *Assembly Engineering* (June 1983), pp. 9-12.

Lee, H., and Neville, K. *Handbook of Epoxy Resins*. New York: McGraw-Hill, 1967.

Loft, J. T., and Hauser, M. "Engineering Adhesives: New Tools for the Design Engineer." *Design Engineering* (May 1981), pp. 24-26.

MacIver, Gregory M. *Structural Urethane Adhesives for High-Speed Automotive Assembly*. SME Technical Paper AD81-151. Dearborn, MI: Society of Manufacturing Engineers, 1981.

Mahoney, L. C. "Structural Adhesives for Rapid Cure Applications." *Adhesives Age* (December 1979), pp. 26-30.

Marceau, J. A.; McMillan, J. D.; and Scardino, W. M. "Cyclic Stress Testing of Adhesive Bonds." *Adhesives Age* (April 1978), pp. 37-41.

McClain, R. R. "High Reactivity Epoxy Resins." *Adhesives Age* (February 1978), pp. 31-34.

Minford, J. D. *Durability or Permanence of Aluminum Adhesive Joints*. SME Technical Report ADR80-11. Dearborn, MI: Society of Manufacturing Engineers, 1980.

Mittal, K. L., ed. *Adhesive Joints*. New York: Plenum Press, 1984.

Murray, B. D. *Ultraviolet Curing Anaerobic Adhesives*. SME Technical Paper FC76-498. Dearborn, MI: Society of Manufacturing Engineers, 1976.

Nablo, S. V., and Tripp, E. P., III. "Electron Curing of Adhesives and Coatings." *Adhesives Age* (February 1979), pp. 24-28.

Pagel, H., and Luckman, E. R. "Emulsion Polymer Isocyanate, A Durable Water-Based Adhesive." *Adhesives Age* (October 1981), pp. 34-39.

Patrick, R. L., ed. *Treatise on Adhesion and Adhesives*. New York: Marcel Dekker, 1973.

Peace, R. "Evaluating Cyanocrylates for Product Assembly." *Adhesives Age* (September 1979), pp. 29-33.

Petrie, E. M. "Joining the Engineering Plastics: How Adhesives Compare with Other Bonding Methods." *Adhesives Age* (August 1980), pp. 14-24.

Pilarski, Richard J. "Robotic Adhesive Dispensing for Bonding and Sealing." *Robotics Today* (October 1984), pp. 35-37.

Rorabough, O. "Hot Melt Sealants: What are Their Advantages and Limitations." *Adhesives Age* (November 1980), pp. 23-30.

Saunders, Charles M. *Hot-Melt Applications with Flexible Auto-mation*. SME Technical Paper AD84-603. Dearborn, MI: Society of Manufacturing Engineers, 1984.

Schneberger, G. L. *Adhesive Bonding—Basic Concepts*. SME Technical Paper AD79-349. Dearborn, MI: Society of Manufacturing Engineers, 1979.

_____ . "Basic Concepts of Adhesive Bonding." *Adhesives Age* (January 1980), pp. 42-46.

_____ , ed. *Adhesives in Manufacturing*. New York: Marcel Dekker, 1983.

"Second Generation Acrylic Adhesives." *Adhesives Age* (September 1976), pp. 21-24.

Sehgal, Krishan C. *Fundamental and Practical Aspects of Adhesive Testing*. SME Technical Paper AD85-780. Dearborn, MI: Society of Manufacturing Engineers, 1985.

Silverman, B., and Norrbom, A. "Polysulfide Sealants in Aircraft Composite Structures." *Adhesives Age* (June 1983), pp. 28-32.

Slautterback, Fred A. *Hot-Melt Equipment—Applicator Equipment Through Simplification*. SME Technical Paper AD84-597. Dearborn, MI: Society of Manufacturing Engineers, 1984.

Stauffer, Robert N. "Weldbonding: Adhesives Add to Joint Quality." *Manufacturing Engineering* (December 1978), pp. 44-47.

Stoops, B., and Ferrier, P. "Merging Two Technologies: Robotics and Hot-Melt Adhesives." *Adhesives Age* (April 1983), pp. 22-25.

Thompson, Richard T. *Five Design Considerations for Adhesive Bonded Plastic Joints*. SME Technical Paper AD85-776. Dearborn, MI: Society of Manufacturing Engineers, 1985.

Thompson, R. T. "Improved Methods for Fastening Steel Parts in Aluminum Housings." SAE Paper 790503. *SAE Congress and Exposition Meetings*. Held 28 February-4 March 1979, Detroit. Warrendale, PA: Society of Automotive Engineers, 1979.

Toensmeier, P. A. "Hot Melt Compatability." *Adhesives Age* (November 1984), pp. 28-31.

Valitsky, R. A. "The Role of Adhesives and Sealants in Fitting Cylindrical Parts." SAE Paper 830667. *SAE Congress and Expositions Meeting*. Held 28 February-4 March 1983, Detroit. Warrendale, PA: Society of Automotive Engineers, 1983.

Wick, Charles. "Bonding Metals with Structural Adhesives." *Manufacturing Engineering* (October 1979), pp. 68-72.

Williamson, Donald. "Adhesives Go Automated—Boosting Speed, Accuracy." *Manufacturing Engineering* (July 1985), pp. 33-36.

AUTOMATED ASSEMBLY

Assembly in the manufacturing process consists of putting together all the component parts and subassemblies of a given product, fastening, performing inspections and functional tests, labeling, separating good assemblies from bad, and packaging and/or preparing them for final use. Assembly is unique compared to the methods of manufacturing such as machining, grinding, and welding in that most of these processes involve only a few disciplines and possibly only one. Most of these nonassembly operations cannot be performed without the aid of equipment, thus the development of automatic methods has been necessary rather than optional. Assembly, on the other hand, may involve in one machine many of the fastening methods, such as riveting, welding, screwdriving,

and adhesive application, as well as automatic parts selection, probing, gaging, functional testing, labeling, and packaging. The state of the art in assembly operations has not reached the level of standardization; much manual work is still being performed in this area.

Assembly has traditionally been one of the highest areas of direct labor costs. In some cases, assembly accounts for 50% or more of manufacturing costs and typically 20-50%. However, closer cooperation between design and manufacturing engineers has resulted in reducing and in a few cases eliminating altogether the need for assembly. When assembly is required, improved design or redesign of products has simplified automated (semiautomatic or automatic) assembly.

CONSIDERATIONS FOR AUTOMATED ASSEMBLY

Before automated assembly is adopted, several factors should be considered. These include practicality of the process for automation, simulation for economic considerations and justification, management involvement, and labor relations.

PRACTICALITY OF AUTOMATION

Determining the practicality of automated assembly requires careful evaluation of the following:

* The number of parts in the assembly.
* Design of the parts with respect to producibility, assemblability, automatic handling, and testability (materials, forms, sizes, dimensional tolerances, and weights).
* Quality of parts to be assembled. Out-of-tolerance or defective parts can cause production losses and increased costs because of stoppages.
* Availability of qualified, technically competent personnel to be responsible for equipment operation.
* Total production and production-rate requirements.

* Product variations and frequency of design changes.
* Joining methods required.
* Assembly times and costs.
* Assembly line or system configuration, using simulation, including material handling.

The best candidates for successful and economical automated assembly are generally simple, small products having a fairly stable design life. Such products are usually required in relatively large volumes and have a high labor content and/or a high reject rate because of their manual assembly. However, the development of flexible, programmable, and robotic assembly systems (discussed subsequently in this chapter) can decrease production and product-life requirements.

Potential Advantages

Potential advantages resulting from assembly automation include the following:

1. Improved product quality, consistent product repeatability with fewer rejects, and a high degree of production reliability as a

Contributors of sections of this chapter are: Steven A. Cousins, Development Engineer, DuPont Engineering Development Laboratory, E.I. duPont deNemours & Co., Inc.; Harold R. Marcotte, Staff Engineer, Automation Lab, Defense Systems Div., Honeywell, Inc.; Malcolm Mills, Manager-Electromechanical Assembly, GMF Robotics; Art Pietrzyk, Manager, Commercial Engineering, Programmable Controller Div., Industrial Computer Group, Allen-Bradley Co.; Charles K. Watters, President, Assembly Machines, Inc.

Reviewers of sections of this chapter are: Nathan D. Apkon, Sales Manager, Robotics Div., Design Technology Corp.; John R. Beatty, Manager-Training and Documentation Services, Robotics and Vision Systems Dept., General Electric Co.; R.G. Bradyhouse, Technical Manager-Producibility, The Black & Decker Corp.; William J. Bryant, Vice President, Cross Assembly Systems Div., Cross & Trecker Corp.; Matthew J. Burns, President, Automated Assemblies Corp.; Brian R. Carlisle, Chairman/Chief Executive Officer, Adept Technology; Steven A. Cousins, Development Engineer, DuPont Engineering Development Laboratory, E.I. DuPont deNemours & Co.; Paul H. Dixon, Dixon Automatic Tool Co.; Robert L. Douglas, President, Engineered Systems Div., Litton Automation Systems, Inc.; FMC Corp., Material Handling Equipment Div.; Philip H. Francis, Director, Advanced Manufacturing Technology, General Systems Group, Motorola, Inc.;

PRACTICALITY OF AUTOMATION

result of reducing or eliminating human errors. Component inspection and part testing during assembly prevents defective parts from being used. The consistently high-quality products obtained reduce liability and warranty costs.

2. Reduced manufacturing costs resulting from decreased labor requirements and increased productivity. Savings result from reductions in both direct and indirect labor.

3. Improved safety and better working conditions by removing operators from hazardous operations.

4. More efficient production scheduling (such as just-in-time techniques) and reduced inventory requirements because of the ability of automated assembly systems to respond immediately to production demands.

5. Reduced floor space requirements.

Possible Limitations

The high initial cost of automated assembly machines, systems, and equipment has been a deterrent to increased use, especially for smaller factories producing limited quantities of various products. However, the development of flexible manufacturing systems are expected to make automated assembly more economically justifiable.

Automatic assembly cannot be divorced from preceding operations because clean, consistently uniform, and high-quality parts are required for its success. The parts do not necessarily have to be held to closer tolerances, but uniformity from part to part is essential. Complete inspection of components on assembly machines is generally not practical or economical. It is usually better to inspect the parts prior to assembly; only their critical dimensions, locations, and presence on assembly machines need be checked.

In addition to problems caused by excessive variations in parts, random machine failures (occasional misfeeds or incomplete assemblies) may be due to the presence of chips or foreign material, poor hopper construction, misadjusted or worn transfer units, or erratic operation of tooling. When assembly is combined with machining operations, care must be taken to prevent chips from entering the assemblies. Burrs, flash, or distorted parts, as well as thin or fragile parts, can be troublesome because they might interfere with tracking or escapement. In some cases, trouble may be avoided by prestacking the parts on mandrels, inserting them in magazines on the assembly machine, and using a shuttle mechanism to transfer parts (one at a time) from the top or bottom of the stack.

Product Design

A major problem inherent in automating assembly is the incompatible design of the product and the resulting producibility of a given assembly. The design of products and their components will have more effect on their manufacturing costs than all the equipment and processing combined. Unfortunately, product design is usually concerned primarily with functional performance; the producibility of the product is secondary or neglected altogether. As technology advances, management must take steps to ensure that the optimum compromise between functionality and manufacturing costs is achieved.

Product designers working in close cooperation with manufacturing engineers in the initial design or redesign of a product and its components will play a major role in the success of automatic assembly. Parts should be designed for easy handling and orienting, with the provision of locating points, sufficient clearances for the assembly tooling, and realistic tolerances (including torque and press-fit tolerance ranges). In some cases, fasteners can be redesigned or even eliminated to facilitate assembly. Chamfered leads are desirable on closely fitting parts. Weight and shape characteristics should favor automatic feeding. Use of standardized components permits more flexible assembly machines that may be capable of handling families of similar products. Additional details with regard to product design for automated assembly are presented later in this chapter.

System Concept and Selection

Another important consideration in assembly automation is the system concept and selection. Many factors influence this consideration, such as volume of parts per unit of time, product life, frequency of design changes, available labor and costs, management attitudes, and competitive pressures. The suitability of automatic assembly for a specific product also depends on total production requirements, the complexity of the assembly, the number of parts in the assembly, and the cost of handling, feeding, orienting, inserting, and joining the parts. Assembly machine costs generally increase in proportion to the number of parts in the product. For example, with assemblies containing more than about 10 parts, special-purpose automatic machines using indexing transfer mechanisms become increasingly uneconomical as the number of stations increases. When one or more parts of a product are impossible or impractical to handle automatically, the assembly system must include manual workstations. However, manual stations in automated systems can limit production rates, and storage facilities must be provided to compensate for fluctuations in operator speed.

The variety of automation concepts continues to increase with technological development. Currently, assembly systems can be divided into two major subdivisions: continuous assembly, such as with bottling and cigarette manufacturing, and intermittent assembly, such as indexing units. Each of these categories offers the choice of a single station, multiple rotary stations, multiple in-line machines, multiple carousel lines, or

Reviewers cont.: Theodore R. Francis, President, Feeder Corporation of America; *LaRoux K. Gillespie*, Bendix Kansas City Div., Allied Bendix Aerospace; *Roger E. Gower*, President, Intelledex; *S. Neal Graham*, Vibromatic Co., Inc.; *Leopold M. Grant*, Manager Sales and Marketing, Kingsbury Assembly Machine Div., Kingsbury Machine Tool Corp.; *Roger Hevesey*, Feedmatic-Detroit Inc.; *Ray Hinson*, Manager, Manufacturing Technology Institute, Advanced Manufacturing Systems, Inc.; *Gerald W. Hock*, Project Manager, Engineering Consulting, Corporate Engineering and Manufacturing, General Electric Co.; *Bart Huthwaite*, Troy Engineering; *Terry King*, Sales and Marketing, Electronics Dept.; *Kanematsu-Gosho (U.S.A.) Inc.; *Gerald J. Lauer*, President, Automated Process Inc.; *Keith Lefebvre*, Product Manager, Programmable Control Div., Gould Inc.; *J. Roger Lembke*, Bendix Kansas City Div., Allied Bendix Aerospace; *Harold R. Marcotte*, Staff Engineer, Automation Lab, Defense Systems Div., Honeywell, Inc.; *Aaron Martin*, Sales Manager-Robotics, Hitachi America Ltd.; *Gary P. Maul*, Assistant Professor, Dept. of Industrial and Systems Engineering, The Ohio State University; *Frank H. McCarty*, Director of Manufacturing Engineering, Raytheon Co.;

the power-and-free conveyor design that permits accumulation of parts with a combination of intermittent and continuous operation. The degree of manual work in the process will strongly influence the concept selection because how the equipment paces the operator is important.

Early attempts at automatic assembly were not without minor setbacks and at times were complete failures. Some of these failures naturally caused management to be skeptical when further automation was considered. In some cases, this lack of management confidence was justified, but time, experience, and perseverance on the part of manufacturing engineers have led to a much greater understanding of automatic assembly and what it will and will not do for any producer of assembled products. Although generalized, the salient points that should be considered as part of any automatic assembly analysis are detailed in this section.

Prior to the actual selection of an assembly system, several basic steps must be taken. It cannot be overemphasized that the degree of success of any assembly system is primarily a function of the attention that goes into the preliminary engineering analysis. The following points set forth the items which should receive consideration.

Product review. Review the entire line of products from individual components through subassemblies to completed products. This review should be based on the following prime considerations:

1. Look for the highest-volume components in the product line. High volume is given such high priority because as the number of a specific component assembled per year increases, the yearly cost savings increase. This increase in savings then results in a high return on investment and a shorter payout period. To ensure the maximum benefit, the product review should include the product engineering activity because in many cases the actual volume of any product can be substantially increased by combining similar parts or assemblies into one basic part or assembly. This step alone, if properly coordinated, can reduce costs.

2. Product life must be considered one an area for automatic assembly has been selected. It is important to remember that the time between product selection and actual system introduction can be from eight months to two years. When one considers that the payout period does not start until the system is in operation, it is obvious that products should not even be considered for automatic assembly if product longevity is not substantial.

Quality level. Determine the importance of quality for the parts to be assembled. An automatic assembly system is an automatic inspector. Burrs on the edges of stampings might not cause problems in hand assembly or in the function of the end product, but these same burrs, from the standpoint of jamming, can reduce the efficiency of an automatic assembly machine by as much as 80%. Manual assemblers can also sort out defective parts, such as misformed or mistapped nuts, which would jam an automatic assembly machine. Consequently, in planning an automated system, the manufacturing engineer must recognize the fact that any lot of parts will contain some defective units plus some stamping or machining offal.

System design. Once the manufacturing engineer thoroughly analyzes the part to be assembled, it should be possible to design a manufacturing system that will function properly. It is very important to introduce system simulation at this point to accomplish the following:

- Validate material handling logistics.
- Reduce work in process.
- Reduce queuing problems, both human and equipment.
- Validate product mix to optimize processes.

It should be noted that the review might indicate a need for part redesign, changes to existing processes, flexible automation, or even facilities to presort parts before they are fed into an automatic assembly system.

Automation limits. The manufacturing engineer must also realize the importance of recognizing the statistical limitation of any automatic assembly system, again utilizing system simulation.

Efficiency. The statistical-limitation theorem simply means that the overall efficiency of a synchronous automatic assembly system is equal to the product of the gross efficiency of each element of the system when all working stations are tied into a common work-conveying system. For example, the element efficiencies of a dial index table with three working stations and an automatic unload station are given in Table 12-1. This analysis of machine downtime or efficiency provides only an approximation because stoppages cannot occur at one station of an indexing machine while another station is down.

TABLE 12-1
Element Efficiencies of a Dial Index Table

Description of Element	Efficiency, %
Station A	92
Station B	94
Station C	90
Table	98
Automatic unload	96

Reviewers cont.: **George S. McVeigh**, *Manager*, *Automation Systems*, *Hoppmann Corp.*; **Malcolm Mills**, *Manager-Electromechanical Assembly*, *GMF Robotics*; **William D. Moyer**, *President*, *Automation Associates*, *Inc.*; **Nicholas G. Odrey**, *Director of Robotics Laboratory*, *Institute for Robotics*, *Lehigh University*; **Art Pietrzyk**, *Manager*, *Commercial Engineering*, *Programmable Controller Div.*, *Industrial Computer Group*, *Allen-Bradley Co.*; **Don Ralston**, *General Manager*, *Automatron Engineering*, *Inc.*; **Jack Reece**, *California Vibratory Feeders*, *Inc.*; **Ron Ruhl**, *Automation Devices*, *Inc.*; **J. Schanstra**, *Feeder Technology*, *Inc.*; **Clyde W. Skaggs**, *Project Manager*, *Electronics Automation Application Center*, *General Electric Co.*; **Kenneth R. Treer**; **Kenneth E. Twinem**, *Senior Engineer*, *Material Handling Systems*, *GMF Robotics*; **Robert L. Vaughn**, *Director of Productivity*, *Lockheed Missiles & Space Co.*, *Inc.*; **Charles K. Watters**, *President*, *Assembly Machines*, *Inc.*; **Gordon Wescott**, *Tooling and Test Equipment*, *Equipment Div. Laboratories*, *Raytheon Co.*; **Richard E. Westlake**, *Mid-West Feeder Inc.*; **Richard D. Zimmerman**, *Spectrum Automation*.

PRACTICALITY OF AUTOMATION

Upon initial inspection of the individual element efficiencies given in Table 12-1, this machine seems to be one of rather high efficiency. However, when the law of system efficiency is applied, system efficiency = 0.92 x 0.94 x 0.90 x 0.98 x 0.96 = 73.21%. To the company that bought the machine, this means that during an 8-hour production shift, the machine will be down a total of 2 hours and 9 minutes. This fact often remains unnoticed because, in many cases, the 2 hours and 9 minutes of downtime per shift are comprised of individual downtimes of less than 10 seconds. Consequently, the machine creates the illusion of efficient operation. This engineering optimism is periodically shattered, however, when for a given shift, machine cycle capability is compared to the number of parts produced. The engineer can at times find this loss of production hard to explain because the machine apparently ran well throughout the day.

Design for efficiency. In all fairness to the manufacturing engineer, many companies have developed methods of determining automation efficiency and, as a result, know what an automated system will actually produce in an hour's time before it is built. To ensure that the manufacturing engineer designs an automatic assembly system that will ultimately produce at the required level of efficiency, the following procedure should be followed:

1. List each basic station of the proposed automatic assembly system.
2. Make a sublist of each motion or function (including nonstandard actions such as jams) that transpires during one machine cycle of each basic station as outlined in the list. An example of a usable format is shown in Table 12-2. It can be seen that the station described in this table, on the average, will be down 142.00 seconds for each hour

it is run; its efficiency is 96.06%. The basic equation for average downtime is:

$$X = Z \frac{V}{Y} \tag{1}$$

where:

X = average downtime, s/hr
Z = time to correct malfunction, s
V = machine cycle rate, cycles/hr
Y = life expectancy of components based on manufacturer's specifications or past maintenance records indicating frequency of downtime on identical components. This factor would also include the frequency of tool changes and jams. Life expectancy is expressed in terms of cycles between failures

Note that although the downtime in this example is projected in terms of seconds per hour, a particular function may fail as infrequently as once a week or even once a month. The ensuing downtime is prorated over each running hour between failure occurrences. In practice, the manufacturing engineer can use any base that is commensurate with the time base of information available.

The engineer should first make a downtime evaluation of the basic transfer portion of the machine, which will establish its efficiency. Then the efficiency of each station should be established. As each unit of efficiency is established, it should be multiplied by the product of the previous unit efficiencies. As each new station is calculated and multiplied by the previous efficiency, an ever-decreasing projection of the overall system efficiency is generated. An example of this type of data might appear as shown in Table 12-3. Note that this machine, as conceived with eight working stations, will be 65.2% efficient

TABLE 12-2
Sublist of Motions and Functions During One Machine Cycle of a Single Assembly Station

Motion or Function Description	Possible Failure Mode	Projected Downtime per Hour, s	Remarks
I. Part, on fixture, moves into first station and operates limit switch indicating part present	1. Limit switch malfunctions electrically	4.8	This time is based on the manufacturer's projected life of 15,000,000 cycles
	2. Limit switch malfunctions mechanically	2.4	
	3. Part not properly placed on fixture	120.0	This is industrial engineering estimate based on the parts involved
II. Fixtured part is clamped in station	1. Jaws worn or broken	0.0	This is a repair that could be done during scheduled downtime
III. Drill head is actuated and drills hole in part	1. Actuating-circuit failure	2.4	This is based on past maintenance data on this type of component
	2. Mechanical malfunction of the drill head	2.0	
	3. Replace worn and broken drills	7.0	This time is based on a drill usage of 1 each 12 hours of operation
IV. Release fixture from station	1. Circuit failure and mechanical malfunction	3.4	This is based on past maintenance data on type of component
		142.0 s/hr	

TABLE 12-3
Example of Overall System Efficiency for an Eight-Station Assembly Machine

Evaluated Unit	Unit Efficiency,%	Accumulated System Efficiency,%
Transfer and basic machine	96	96.0
Station 1	93	89.2
Station 2	98	87.4
Station 3	92	80.4
Station 4	97	77.9
Station 5	94	73.2
Station 6	96	70.2
Station 7	97	68.0
Station 8	96	65.2

or, stated differently, will be down because of malfunctions an average of 34.8% of the time. If this machine has a basic theoretical production rate of 1000 assemblies per hour, it would net 652 assemblies per hour on a day-to-day basis.

If, in this example, volume requirements are such that a minimum of 700 assemblies per hour are required, it is obvious that this machine, as proposed, will be inadequate. This assembly system, then, is overautomated for the job it must perform. Consequently, the following alternate approaches must be considered:

1. Incorporate the operations performed by stations 7 and 8, for example, into another assembly station that would yield a new system that is 70.2% efficient.
2. Review the elemental breakdown of the functions of each station to determine if designs of greater reliability could be introduced and, hence, could raise the overall system to the required level—in this case 70%.
3. Add standby workstations. For example, assume that an analysis of station 4, which assembles parts C and D, indicates a particularly low level of efficiency that cannot be corrected. One solution to this problem would be to add a second station 4 to the assembly line so that when the first station 4 malfunctions, the second station 4 will take over and prevent downtime. This problem evolves into a basic consideration that station 4 should be designed to the extent possible from a safety standpoint to allow its repair while the assembly system is running. In extreme cases, the complete station can be mounted on gibs or rollers and physically moved to and from the assembly system. Although this approach solves the efficiency problem, it can substantially increase the cost of the assembly system, especially if applied to several different stations in the system. Consequently, the manufacturing engineer must compare the added production yield afforded by this concept with the additional cost to produce it.
4. Try a different approach to automatic assembly, such as a nonsynchronous (power-and-free) system.

Nonsynchronous system. All the system analyses discussed have been predicated on a number of fixed workstations (which in reality are individual machines) being attached to a fixed transfer mechanism. Some types of fixed transfer mechanisms (or *synchronous systems*) are: (1) the dial index table, (2) the

in-line transfer machine, and (3) the carousel or over-and-under transfer machine, all discussed in more detail later in this chapter.

The single common entity of these general types of systems is that when any element of the total system (either workstation or transfer station) fails to operate, the total system is down, and production is stopped until the fault is corrected. This is not to say that these types of machines are poor choices. In fact, if a proper engineering analysis of the system requirements is made as outlined and a system is then purchased based on this analysis, many years of excellent service can be obtained.

If, however, because of economics, volume requirements, or other factors, none of these solutions are acceptable, then another approach is possible. This approach avoids the statistical limitations of series production systems. Very briefly, this nonsynchronous concept recognizes that any manufacturing system that is composed of individual work elements has inherent unavoidable downtime made up of individual component inefficiencies, jams, and tool changes. Conceptually then, each work element should be separated from the next by a material handling system of sufficient capacity that the next element can continue to operate with in-process parts in storage, or can float, while the previous work function is down.

Consequently, the overall system efficiency is only as low as the least efficient work element in the system. For example, in a particular standard synchronous system, efficiency approximates $0.92 \times 0.95 \times 0.90 \times 0.96 \times 0.88 \times 0.91 = 60.4\%$. In a nonsynchronous system composed of the same elements, system efficiency would be 88%, the efficiency of the least efficient element. This means that, with the same basic machine elements, the latter system will outproduce the standard system by 45.6%. However, it is seldom, if ever, practical or economical to completely insulate each station from the next because the buffer storage or floats would be too large.

In reality, the only basic difference between this system and the typical standard systems previously described is that the fixed transfer mechanism, which moves the production parts from one work function to another, is replaced by an automatic material control system that has built-in storage capacity (accumulators) plus a feature that allows the storage portion of the system to be bypassed. Another example of the way this type of system works is demonstrated by a work function that drills a hole in a part at a gross rate of 1000 parts per hour. Its projected inefficiency is shown in Table 12-4.

CHAPTER 12

PRACTICALITY OF AUTOMATION

TABLE 12-4
Projected Inefficiency of a Workstation That Drills a Hole in a Part at a Gross Rate of 1000 Parts per Hour

Component inefficiency	106.20 s/hr
Jams	77.50 s/hr
Drill changes	56.30 s/hr
Total	240.00 s/hr

The station efficiency is then 93.3%; therefore, its net average production is 933 parts per hour. Consequently, the next station in the process cannot produce at a net rate any greater than 933 parts per hour. However, the actual time required to change a drill in the preceding station is 4 minutes. This 4-minute downtime results in a production loss of 140 parts. Therefore, if the material handling and storage system between the two stations is designed to hold 140 parts plus a contingency of 25%, or a total of 175 parts, the station following the drill station can continue to run at its own level of efficiency while the previous station is down for its 4-minute drill change. For most automatic assembly applications, however, storage systems typically handle many fewer parts.

One additional factor must also be considered in the design of the automatic material handling and storage system. The second work function in the example given is a station that places a rivet in the hole drilled at the first station. At a prescribed interval, the rivet anvils must be changed, which takes 6 minutes. During this time, this station will not be handling 210 parts from the drilling station. Consequently, the automatic material handling and storage system must have capacity in addition to the 175-part float required for downtime on the drill station; 210 parts plus a 25% contingency is 262 parts. Therefore, the total float required between the drill and rivet stations is 437 parts. In actual operation, parts from the drill operation would go into the storage portion of the automatic handling system until it reached the 175-part level. At this point, the system would go into bypass and feed directly to the rivet operation. On a prescribed program basis, the bypass would shut off, and the 175-part float would be cycled to the rivet operation and replaced with new parts.

From a purely conceptual basis, the need for in-process float was recognized with the advent of the first power-and-free (nonsynchronous) assembly systems. Although these systems provide for variances in individual station efficiencies, their storage capacity, as such, is limited. The advantages of in-process float have been recognized by several of the major automatic assembly machine builders. Some of their new machines are of the fixed transfer type, but include integrated loops for storage and repair at strategic locations. Other builders have provided manual stations whereby partially completed assemblies can be removed from or introduced to various points in the assembly system. In any event, totally integrated assembly systems that include material handling and storage capabilities are in production today and are proving their worth on a daily basis.

Flexible Automation

All of the discussion to this point has dealt with fixed, dedicated, or hard automated systems—those not instantly adaptable to accommodate different manufactured products.

As an alternative, flexible manufacturing installations are being increasingly applied. Flexible manufacturing systems (FMSs) consist of robotic systems interacting with machine tools and other kinds of automation digitally networked together and controlled, often by an "intelligent" host computer.

Flexible manufacturing systems are generally best suited for mid-volume production and where high product mix or customization is desired. These systems enable the manufacturing environment to make on demand and to adapt to changes in parts inventories by spontaneously manufacturing other parts.

The design and implementation of flexible automation requires knowledge and is more difficult than for fixed automation. Among the most common obstacles are the following:

- Reliable digital communications among various system controllers.
- Line balancing in a dynamic, flexible environment.
- Design for high utilization of costly equipment.
- Proper use of sensors and self-diagnostics.

Details with respect to flexible and robotic assembly systems are presented later in this chapter.

Typical Applications

The predominant users of automated assembly systems are the automotive industry, appliance manufacturers, producers of electrical and electronic hardware, farm equipment builders, consumer product makers, the defense industry, and the pharmaceutical industry.

In one automotive application, needle bearings are being automatically assembled in automatic transmission pinions at a production rate of 1200 assemblies per hour. Cycle time per assembly is 3 seconds, an automatic greasing operation is performed on each assembly, and the machine handles 45,600 individual parts each hour. The machine can be modified to single or double-row bearings.

In another automotive application, a 98-station synchronous system assembles any of 64 pump configurations, consisting of as many as 37 different components, at the rate of 1000 assemblies per hour. The pumps are for automotive hydraulic steering units. The assembly system consists of two main lines and two auxiliary off-line dial machines, with all four components equipped with chain-driven workholding pallets. A data-code entry system is used to program the system for various pump configurations.

LABOR RELATIONS

Whether assembly is done manually, semiautomatically, or automatically, people playing the proper roles are essential to success. Properly trained and motivated personnel are especially important in automation to ensure the effective use of human resources. Education is necessary to demonstrate to everyone involved that automation is not a threat to their livelihood. Rather, automation is a vital means of survival for companies by increasing quality and productivity, and reducing costs. It also improves the work environment with respect to safety and health.

The best automation equipment, tooling, and components to be assembled will not guarantee success unless the personnel involved are prepared to accept automation. All employees should be notified immediately of the planned automation. To overcome negative attitudes, communications should stress the advantages. These communications should let the people know why it is being done, what they will be doing, and benefits to employees and the company, thereby eliminating potential problems.

Although automation can increase production and reduce costs by using less labor, it generally creates new jobs. Customer demands for higher quality, lower cost products result in increased sales and employment. These additional jobs often require different skills, which necessitate training. Benefits from such jobs usually include reduced physical effort and tedium, increased use of personnel capabilities, greater interest in participation, and restoration of pride in workmanship.

Proper training of factory personnel is necessary for the supervision, operation, and repair of automation equipment. Basic training is recommended at the machine builder's location and as many pertinent personnel as possible should be involved in system start-up and debugging.

The importance of good employee relations, personnel job satisfaction, and morale cannot be overemphasized. In some automation applications, assembly stations have been added to avoid making the operator task too difficult. There are many methods to improve job satisfaction, including increased management motivation, job rotation and enrichment, and transfers to new positions.

MANAGEMENT INVOLVEMENT

Involvement and support by all levels of management are essential to the success of automated assembly. Capital investment for the necessary equipment must be justified for automated manufacturing. Top management must be sold on the importance of the concept and support the belief that the financial investment will improve product quality, increase productivity, reduce costs, and result in increased profits. Realistic expectations must be established for equipment performance and its effect on both short and long-term planning for the company. Top management must also motivate other levels of management and all employees affected and encourage participation in decisionmaking and goalsetting.

A catalog of available techniques for automated assembly is not available, but if it were, it would run to many hundreds of pages. However, as interest in the field of automated assembly has grown, specialists have developed among suppliers. Today there are a number of equipment builders and some captive in-house organizations capable of planning and developing a complete automated manufacturing system by any of the known concepts and utilizing most of the established techniques. Decisions to make or buy often depend on whether competent technical people are available in the firm to design, build, and debug the proposed system.

Production Scheduling and Control

A production scheduling and control system specifies how the production resources of a manufacturing organization are to be employed. Assembly systems are a production resource, and as such, their operation must be scheduled and controlled. Scheduling and control of assembly systems cannot be divorced from the scheduling and control of any other part of the manufacturing operation. The demands placed on the final assembly will determine the demands placed on all facilities. A production scheduling and control system may be separated into a decisionmaking process and a data handling process.

Decisionmaking. The decisionmaking process determines how assembly needs may be fulfilled. Some of the techniques that can be used in decisionmaking are common sense, mathematical analysis, and simulation. For example, mathematical analysis may be used to determine lot size and machine loading of fabricated components, while simulation is used to select the sequence of components for final assembly.

Several factors must be considered in determining which technique is appropriate. The decisions that can be made and therefore the techniques that can be used are different if the assembly is customer-ordered, intermittent or batch, single-product continuous, or multiproduct continuous. Similarly, the number of alternative facilities available governs the type of decisions needed. If there are several assembly systems or lines to choose from, the control system must provide for selecting which line to use for which product.

If the assembly is made to customer order, the sequence in which the units should be assembled must be decided. The generally available techniques rarely apply to this type of decision. The primary difficulty in developing a standard technique for making assembly-sequence decisions is the problem of arriving at a common, acceptable description of the costs that the manufacturer encounters as a result of variations in product assembly. Most of the techniques that are employed fall into the category of common sense. Simulation can be used to evaluate and compare different sequences and is a technique that should be considered in this situation.

If the assembly system has intermittent or batch production, one decision to be made is the number of units in each batch or lot. Mathematical analysis, in the form of economic-lot-size formulas, can be used in making these decisions. The classical economic-lot-size model assumes a constant known demand and, considering the setup costs and inventory-carrying costs, determines the lot size that will result in the least overall cost. Extensions to the model include consideration of variable and uncertain demand. To obtain valid optimum results, it is necessary to include all relevant costs in the computation. Costs that are sometimes overlooked or understated include those associated with labor learning, with stocking the line, and with incompleted repair units at the end of the run. Not only is it necessary to consider all relevant costs, but it is necessary to review them periodically to determine if they are correct. Changes in the production process may change the setup costs, but all too often the economic order quantities are not recomputed.

Another decision needed for intermittent or batch production is the sequence in which the batches are produced. The changeover costs when product A follows product B may be different from the changeover costs when product A follows product C.

In a single-product continuous assembly, the question of production leveling may be of concern. The costs of increasing production include employment and training, additional service and staff activities, added shifts (with supervision and premiums), and overtime. The costs of decreasing production include unemployment compensation insurance, employee transfers, and idle time. There are several mathematical models for making production and labor-force decisions in successive time periods that minimize the expected value of total costs over a large number of periods. Among these models are those using linear programming, dynamic programming, and the transportation algorithm.

In multiproduct continuous production, if each product is assigned to a dedicated line, the problems are similar to those of single-product continuous operation, with possible additional flexibility because operators may be transferred to different lines. However, if this type of assembly is performed on mixed-

MANAGEMENT INVOLVEMENT

model assembly lines, the sequence in which the models are assembled must be selected. Simulation is also an appropriate tool for this type of decision process.

Before any decision process is included in a scheduling and control system, it should be established that:

1. The decisions that will be made will be appropriate for the specific assembly operation.
2. All relevant factors will be considered.
3. The information required by the decision process will be available and will be sufficiently accurate.

Data handling techniques. There are several different types of information required by a production scheduling and control system. Among these types of information are: (1) customer-demand information, (2) product-structure information (including components or bills of material and operating or routing information), (3) inventory status, and (4) facilities loading. Figure 12-1 illustrates how this information relates to a general production control system. There are a variety of ways to use and maintain this information, ranging from manually controlled charts and control boards to on-line computer systems.

Computers are now the predominant method of using and maintaining information required for production scheduling and control, as well as for other application functions. They have largely replaced the use of visual display charts, card files, punched cards, and control boards, even for small installations.

Software packages using production control languages are available to maintain such systems. With continuing advances in computer and communication technology, progress is being made in integrating office automation with computer-aided design (CAD), computer-aided manufacturing (CAM), and computer-integrated manufacturing (CIM).

Technical and Office Protocol (TOP) addresses the engineering and office environment and includes many application functions. This program maintains compatibility with Manufacturing Automation Protocol (MAP) discussed later in this chapter under the subject of controls for automated assembly.

Assembly Line Balancing

Line balancing is the assignment of assembly functions (work elements) in the required order (precedence relationship) to the individual stations in a system. The cycle for assembly functions performed at each station should be about the same because production is governed by the cycle of the slowest station. Assembly operations requiring long cycles should be divided among several stations whenever possible.

With manual assembly, operations are broken down into discrete tasks, with estimated times assigned to each task. The objective is either to minimize the number of operators required to meet a given demand or to maximize the production of a given number of operators. Precedence diagrams of work elements, such as the one shown in Fig. 12-2, are helpful in balancing. Several computer programs have been written to facilitate optimum balancing of assembly lines.

Synchronous assembly systems function as balanced, indexing occurring at regular intervals only when the functions at each station have been completed. With nonsynchronous systems, each station functions independently. Any imbalance among the stations is accommodated by buffer storage of parts between stations. As a result, production can continue when one or more stations are inactive for any reason, as long as sufficient buffer stock is available.

ECONOMIC CONSIDERATIONS FOR ASSEMBLY AUTOMATION

The manufacturing engineer is charged with the responsibility of selecting the most appropriate production equipment.

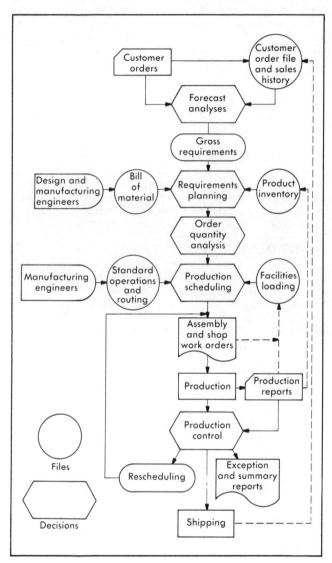

Fig. 12-1 Typical production model showing information requirements for control.

	Work element	Estimated operation time, s
	A	0.25
	B	0.45
	C	0.25
	D	0.50
	E	0.35
	F	0.20
	G	0.30
	H	0.40
	I	0.25

Fig. 12-2 Typical assembly-precedence diagram for nine work elements.

Any automated assembly system installed must provide the highest return for the least capital outlay. Automated assembly advantages of improved quality, increased productivity, and reduced costs help the manufacturer to secure a larger market share by supplying quality products at competitive prices.

Justification Methods

Justification of automated assembly is a major challenge, and there is no universal agreement on the best solution. The long-used analytical tools of conventional accounting practices, auditing, and tax rule guidelines for capital equipment decisions are no longer adequate. Most traditional return-on-investment examinations do not consider indirect cost reductions, quality improvement, and the impact on overall business. Discounted cash flow (DCF) techniques for investment analysis are still valuable if properly applied—taking into consideration better estimates of costs and benefits.

Efforts are under way to make significant changes in current accounting practices. Computer Aided Manufacturing-International, Inc. (CAM-I) of Arlington, TX, is heading up a consortium of approximately 35 organizations (government, industry, selected universities, and major accounting firms) in an effort identified as the Cost Management System (CMS) project. As described in a prospectus published by CAM-I, the objective of the project is to establish a standard body of knowledge about cost-management practices for an automated environment and to influence CMS practices in a wide range of companies. The project provides the foundation for transitioning the role of cost management from a passive historical review process to one that assists a company in optimizing daily manufacturing operations and meeting long-term business objectives.

Direct and Indirect Labor Savings

Direct labor reduction should receive initial consideration in justifying capital equipment expenditures. However, the manufacturing engineer must give attention to savings in projected labor costs, not just the savings from the historical labor base.

Mechanized assembly can reduce product cost to the lowest unit assembly cost. Because of low labor requirements, assembly systems can be placed in close proximity to major markets, thus reducing delivery time. Personnel hired for assembly operations to increase production become a liability with respect to future operating costs. Furthermore, cyclical hiring and firing involves training of new workers and retraining of reassigned workers; this incurs an economic penalty in poor assembly quality. Automatic assembly equipment, on the other hand, can be operated on demand and does not incur additional costs when not operating. Production surges can be met by placing assembly machines on additional shift operation instead of hiring new employees. Automated assembly systems reduce personnel turnover and stabilize employment levels.

Automated assembly can also provide indirect savings by reducing the need for supervisory personnel, part inspectors, and support personnel. These savings are sometimes difficult to identify because they are often buried in factory overhead costs.

Warranty and Product Liability Costs

Automated assembly generates an upgrading of overall product quality and permits 100% inspection without additional labor. Assemblies can be coded and identified for potential liability legislation requirements. This means of documenting product quality should be considered in overall justification.

Reduction of warranty costs as the result of inspection during assembly is another important benefit of automated assembly that should be considered in justification. Failure of a product sold for a few dollars can cost the manufacturer several hundred dollars for replacement in the field. Such product failures also result in loss of customer trust and deterioration of the manufacturer's competitive position.

Production and Inventory Control

Assembly automation enables marketing and sales personnel to take orders on the basis of rapid deliveries and high volumes. With automated equipment, production requirements can be rapidly attained without hiring or rehiring personnel. Part inventories can also be significantly reduced, eliminating the costs of batch manipulation and transport. Just-in-time methods are being increasingly applied to reduce inventories.

Cost-Effective Assembly Systems

Cost-effective assembly for some products often lies between manual and fully automated systems. Both the feasibility and cost of each proposed mechanized operation should be compared to manual assembly. It is sometimes preferable to load large components manually, as well as those with smooth or decorative surface finishes. In other cases, it is better to fabricate the components (for example, coil spring winding) on the assembly machine.

For complex products having many parts, it is generally preferable to divide the assembly operations among two or more machines. Combining too many parts and assembly functions on one machine can be inefficient, result in excessive downtime, or even cause failure of the entire system. While the initial cost of using more than one machine is higher, the increased efficiency and reduced downtime resulting from fewer stations on each machine generally provide more economical operation. The machines can be connected by conveyors and each machine operated individually. Accumulating banks for temporary storage and repair stations can be provided between machines.

In the case of flexible automation, the process of economic justification is more complex. The reason is that flexible automation often changes fundamentally the nature of the manufacturing process. To a degree, capital investment (automation) replaces expense (labor) and the usual financial analysis tools mentioned fail to account properly for the new approach to production.

Experience has shown that too often investment decisions based on payback and similar criteria result in rejecting proposals to adopt flexible automation. However, it often turns out that such investments are warranted when full and proper account is taken of issues including the following:

- The capability of performing product customization.
- Reducing inventory costs by adopting just-in-time strategies.
- Shortening product life cycles.
- Responding more rapidly to new product development opportunities.

Moreover, there is value, though difficult to measure, in learning to design and use new computer-integrated manufacturing (CIM) technology, which will be more common in all future manufacturing operations.

PRODUCT DESIGN FOR AUTOMATED ASSEMBLY

Optimum design or redesign of a product and its components is essential for successful, efficient, and economical automatic assembly. Considerable amounts of money are often spent to automate the assembly of existing product designs when it would be much more economical to redesign the products to facilitate automatic assembly. Design for assembly (DFA) is being increasingly practiced because of the realization of potential production savings and better quality and improved reliability in the product.

Close cooperation is required between design and manufacturing engineers in evaluating a product design for improved assembly. The inherent capabilities and limitations of assembly operations should be considered during the early design or redesign stages. At the earliest possible design stages, it is also best to assess the parts for the ease with which they can be supplied and oriented. Assembly of various designs should be evaluated and compared.

VALUE ANALYSES AND MOTION STUDIES

Value analysis programs are being used to determine simpler product designs for manufacturing methods that can reduce costs. The most effective technique for minimizing the cost of assembly is to reduce the number of parts to be assembled. The function of all parts in an assembly should be determined and consideration given to the possibility of combining the functions of several parts into a single component. When considering the economic aspects of parts count reduction and integration, also consider the total cost of each part (direct and indirect costs), not just a purchased or fabricated cost.

Motion time studies should be performed on all handling, feeding, orienting, inserting, and joining operations. This is generally done with prototypes of the products and their components. These studies are essential to determine the relative assembly time and cost of various designs.

USE OF COMPUTERS

Computer analyses with available software packages can be used to compare the economics of several designs, to compare the costs of manual versus automatic assembly, to eliminate subparts, and to automate manual design procedures. A design for assembly (DFA) analysis method was developed by Dr. G. Boothroyd when he was at the University of Massachusetts under a grant from the National Science Foundation. This method has been developed by Dr. Boothroyd and Dr. P. Dewhurst into a series of six interactive microcomputer software programs. Parts feeding and orienting problems can be scientifically evaluated using accepted guidelines for rating product designs.

DESIGN FOR SIMPLIFICATION

The optimum product design is one that eliminates the need for assembly or reduces the number of parts to be assembled to a minimum. One simple example is illustrated in Fig. 12-3, which shows a single stamping that replaces a two-part assembly. Use of the more modern forming processes, discussed in Volume II, *Forming*, of this Handbook series, may help in minimizing or eliminating components. Such designs usually reduce total product and assembly costs.

When single-component products are impossible or uneconomical, the number of parts required should generally be kept as low as possible, and their complexity should be minimized. There are rare occasions, however, where it may be more economical to manufacture two or more pieces to replace one. The reason for minimizing the number of parts is to improve the remaining, more functional parts and to eliminate nonfunctional ones. To determine if a part can be eliminated, the following three questions should be answered:

1. Does the part move with respect to other parts?
2. Is the part made from a different material than the other parts?
3. Will the part require removal for product servicing?

An affirmative answer to any of these questions generally indicates that the part is required. Negative answers to all three questions indicate that the part may not be necessary and any function it performs may be able to be transferred to a more essential component.

Assembly Sequence

A study of all possible alternatives with respect to the sequence of assembly is essential. The first operation is generally placement of the base component or main body of the assembly, usually a forged, cast, molded, stamped, or machined member. As previously mentioned, this may require the use of fixtures or work carriers, but in the case of some large components, handling and transferring can be done without fixtures or carriers. A graphical representation of the assembly sequence can be helpful in studying possible variations.

The ideal arrangement is one in which all assembly operations can be performed on one face of the product with short, straight-line motions, preferably vertically from above. If more than one side or face must be used, every effort should be made to keep the number of planes of access necessary to a minimum. Every additional direction from which assembly work must be performed creates additional problems and cost. Combined rotary and straight-line motions, if necessary, generally require two or more workstations.

Workholding

It is essential for automatic assembly to have a base component of the product onto which the other components are assembled. The base must have features, such as manufacturing

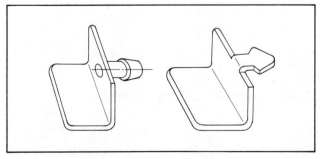

Fig. 12-3 Two-part assembly (left) is replaced by a single stamping.

DESIGN FOR EASE OF ASSEMBLY

holes or projections, for fast and accurate location on work carriers and/or fixtures. Location is often attained by providing tapered dowel pins on the carriers or fixtures. When locating with pins is not practical, it may be necessary to grasp the part in jaws and position it on the fixture. If grasping is impractical, vacuum pickup and transfer is another alternative.

If possible, fixtureless assembly is best. This requires that the base component or main body of the product be capable of handling for rapid transfer. Manufacturing holes are often provided in parts for pin location at the various assembly stations. When fixturing is necessary, consider design features of both product and fixture that will permit one fixture to serve instead of two. Product design strongly influences fixture design.

DESIGN FOR EASE OF AUTOMATIC ASSEMBLY

Parts to be assembled automatically should be designed for ease of handling, feeding, orienting, positioning, and joining. A design checklist to facilitate automatic assembly is presented in Table 12-5.

Part configurations that can be easily oriented include the following:

1. Completely symmetrical parts such as spheres, cylinders, pins, and rods. Figure 12-4 illustrates some examples of how parts can be made symmetrical. In general, the lengths of cylindrical parts should be at least 25% longer or shorter than their diameters to facilitate feeding.
2. Substantially disproportionate parts, either with respect to weight or with respect to dimensions, such as headed screws, bolts, and rivets. The center of gravity should be near one end of each part to produce a tendency to naturally feed in one specific orientation. If this natural

orientation is not the desired position, it is relatively easy to rotate the parts to the proper position.

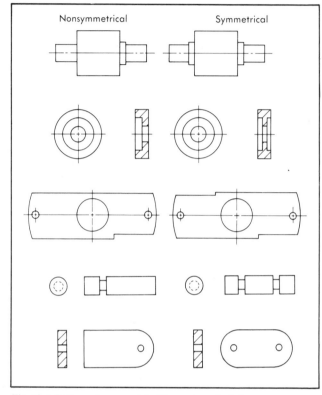

Fig. 12-4 Parts made symmetrical for easier orientation.

TABLE 12-5
Design Checklist for Automatic Assembly

Keep number of parts to be assembled to a minimum

Make product and component designs as simple as possible

Provide a base or main body on which other parts can be assembled or, if possible, that can serve as its own fixture or work carrier

Provide locating surfaces or holes, orientation characteristics, and accessibility to all assembly areas when fixtures or work carriers are required

Design for optimum sequencing, with each part added from above if possible

Avoid need for expensive and time-consuming joining operations

Design components for easy handling, feeding, orienting, positioning, and joining:

    Keep center of gravity low

    Minimize number of orientations required

    Avoid designs that cause nesting, tangling, shingling, jamming, or wedging

    Design parts to be stiff and rigid, but not brittle or fragile

    Avoid designs that are subject to variations in humidity, temperature, pressure, magnetism, and static electricity

    Eliminate burrs and flash or design into areas that do not interfere with assembly

    Provide adequate strength and rigidity to withstand forces of assembly without bending or distortion

    Provide chamfers, tapers, radii, or other guiding surfaces and locating surfaces for loading and positioning

    Minimize the number of smooth finished surfaces that cannot be scratched or damaged

    Provide clearances for assembly tooling

DESIGN FOR EASE OF ASSEMBLY

Parts that are nearly symmetrical generally present the greatest number of problems in feeding and orienting. Parts having features such as off-center holes or cavities are also difficult to orient and may require tooling outside the hopper or other storage device for orientation. Sometimes external features can be added to the parts (see Fig. 12-5) to permit easier orienting in the hopper. Such features should allow the feed tracks from the hopper to maintain orientation.

Weight distribution is an important consideration in part design because gravity is used extensively in feeding systems for automatic assembly. Designers should try to avoid instability in part feeding by providing the part with a low center of gravity. Unstable parts having a high center of gravity with relation to the tracking surface tend to topple. Increasing the size of the tracking surface may help in some cases. In some applications, it is effective to feed the part in an inverted position to that desired. By providing a twist in the feed track, the part can subsequently be brought into correct orientation.

Much work has been done at the University of Massachusetts, Massachusetts Institute of Technology, the University of Michigan, and elsewhere on the design of small parts for automatic handling. The work at the University of Massachusetts uses a special coding system similar to those developed for various group technology applications and issues a series of

questions regarding the symmetry and features of a component.[1] Depending on the answers to these questions, a three-digit code number is assigned to the component, indicating the ease or difficulty of feeding and orienting the part. The process of obtaining the code number indicates what design features can be changed to simplify handling problems.

Feeding Considerations

Commonly encountered feeding problems that can lead to jamming include tangling, nesting, and shingling. Tangling, caused by a protrusion on one part inserting itself into an opening in another part, makes it difficult to separate the parts for feeding and orienting. Retaining and snap rings, lockwashers, springs, and parts having lugs and recesses are subject to this problem. This condition can be alleviated by either eliminating protrusions and/or closing end openings. The redesign of retaining rings (see Fig. 12-6) is helpful in this regard.

Compression coil springs are particularly difficult to handle and feed automatically because they are basically unstable and tend to tangle. When heat treating and grinding of the coil ends are not required, it is sometimes preferable to wind the springs on the assembly machine itself. If the springs must be fed to the assembly machine, the coil ends should be closed (see Fig. 12-7). Increasing the wire diameter, as well as increasing or decreasing the pitch of the spring, also helps to alleviate this problem.

Parts with thin flat surfaces or tapered edges have a tendency to climb onto each other and overlap, called shingling, which can cause wedging of the parts in the tracks and jamming. This condition can often be eliminated by providing thicker contact surfaces or by making the edges vertical or of a steeper angle (see Fig. 12-8). For parts with very thin edges, the edges can be bent upward or upset. If flatness is required, the edges can be bent flat after feeding.

Nesting of cup-shaped parts can also cause jamming. This condition can be minimized by changing the cup diameters, adding ribs, or increasing or decreasing the angle of the sidewalls. A similar problem is the telescoping of hollow parts, particularly round ones, that are larger at one end than the other.

Distortion of parts due to handling and stacking can cause serious problems. Thin metal parts, as well as soft parts and those made of plastics, are especially susceptible to these conditions. Whenever possible, the parts should be made rigid and stable, but not brittle or fragile. Cutoff tabs, burrs, and flash should be removed prior to assembly or located on the parts so that they do not interfere with feeding, orienting, and positioning. Parts having ground or otherwise finished surfaces that cannot tolerate damage may not be able to be fed automatically. In some cases, however, such surfaces may be protected by designing the parts with flanges or other projections.

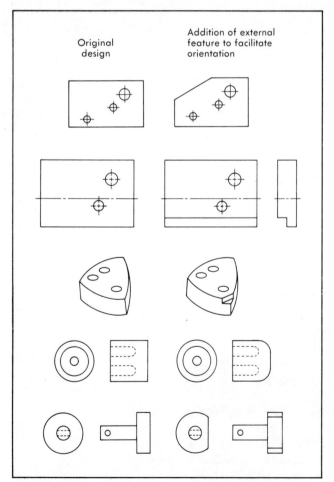

Fig. 12-5 Addition of external feature (chamfer, slot, shoulder, radius, or flat) can facilitate orientation.

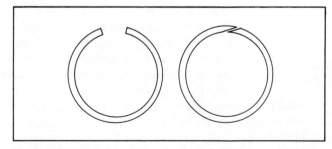

Fig. 12-6 Retaining rings such as the one at the left have a tendency to tangle. Design at right minimizes tangling.

Insertion Considerations

Providing chamfers, radii, tapers, or other guide surfaces on shafts and mounting holes and eliminating sharp corners whenever possible facilitates the insertion of components into assemblies. For example, cone and oval-point screws are easier to insert than rolled-thread or headed-point screws because they tend to centralize themselves in holes. Figure 12-9 illustrates some changes in design that facilitate insertion and mounting.

Orientation Considerations

Whenever possible, components to be automatically assembled that require orienting should be provided with external surfaces, cavities, or protrusions that will facilitate orientation. Features that are often nonfunctional but that serve this purpose include holes, slots, chamfers, grooves, or pads on external surfaces. Functional features that can be used to facilitate orientation include flanges and heads on cylindrical parts and threaded fasteners.

Joining Considerations

It is desirable to eliminate or minimize joining and fastening operations in automatic assembly whenever possible to reduce costs and increase productivity. When joining or fastening is required, select the easiest, fastest, and most economical

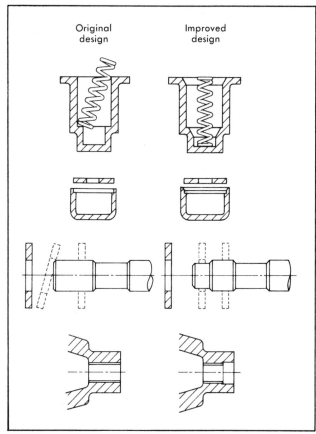

Fig. 12-9 Changes in design that facilitate inserting and mounting of components.

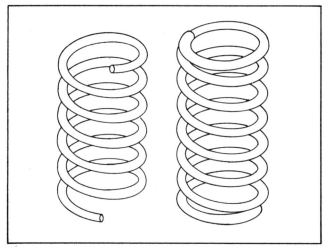

Fig. 12-7 Coil springs frequently tangle. Closing their ends, as shown at right, helps to minimize tangling.

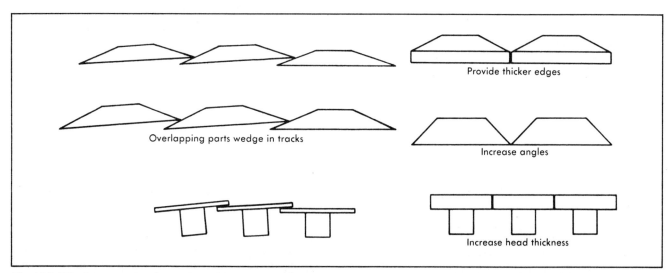

Fig. 12-8 Shingling or overlapping can be avoided by providing thicker contact edges or vertical or highly angled surfaces (right).

DESIGN FOR EASE OF ASSEMBLY

method possible. The best product designs for assembly are those that require simple, conventional tools and no special tooling for assembly. For example, the use of snap or interference fits is less costly and requires less time than fasteners. Staking, spinning, or welding are also often preferred to the costly feeding and driving of fasteners such as screws, bolts, and nuts. The use of clamps to hold parts in place while an adhesive cures should be avoided. Consideration should be given to using a faster curing adhesive that will provide the bonding strength needed.

Requirements for disassembly, maintenance, or repairability of a product limit the joining methods (discussed subsequently in this chapter) that may be used. When required, joining operations should be performed at separate stations, preceded by devices that automatically inspect the presence and position of the components needed.

MODULAR AND STANDARDIZED DESIGNS

Many assemblies are too complex to permit complete automatic assembly on a single machine. In such cases, it is efficient to break down the total assembly into a series of subassemblies that are subsequently joined together. Typically, 10-12 parts are all that should be assembled on a single machine without degrading machine reliability and throughput. Subassemblies can often be standardized for a family of products, resulting in substantial savings.

Standardizing components in both subassemblies and assemblies with respect to design and materials can reduce tooling costs. The functions performed by several parts should be combined in a single part whenever possible, thus reducing the number of components to be assembled.

RETAINING PRE-ESTABLISHED ORIENTATION

Consideration should be given to the possibility of retaining the orientation established during the manufacture of components for an assembly. Stampings are ideally suited for this. Stampings from the blanking or forming dies can be pushed into magazines by the motion of the punch. Savings over orienting parts at the assembly machine must be balanced against the cost of the magazines. It is also necessary to maintain sufficient banks of preoriented parts.

Taped and filmed carriers are also used to bring properly oriented parts to assembly machines. Thin stampings are often stamped in continuous strip stock without the strip or web being separated. The strip is wound into a coil, and the coil is placed in the assembly machine, which incorporates a mechanism for separating the individual parts as required. Retention of preoriented parts is often the only feasible method of handling fragile, easily damaged, or interlocking components. The other alternative is to perform forming operations on the assembly machine, as discussed subsequently in this chapter.

QUALITY REQUIREMENTS

Consistent and close dimensional tolerances and geometries are essential for parts to be assembled automatically. In many cases, the tolerances may have to be more stringent than those required for the function of the product to prevent jamming of the assembly machine or the production of defective products. Proper design of the components, however, may minimize or eliminate the need for tight dimensional requirements. Using the assembly machine to qualify parts prior to assembly needlessly complicates the machine design and masks the real problem—fabricating and delivering high-quality parts to assembly.

Tolerance Study

Once the parts to be automatically assembled are known, a complete correlative study must be made to ensure that engineering drawings, inspection gages, production tooling, and fixtures at workstations of the assembly machine use the same datum or points of reference for tolerance. In other words, if all dimensions of a part are taken from one face, then all production tooling, gages, and automatic assembly machine fixtures and tooling must be designed to operate from that same face so that all tolerances are in the same direction.

Quality Study

The ability of the assembly system to inspect its own work must be evaluated. For example, consider three parts that are to be riveted together at a particular station of an assembly machine. If the feed track of one part jams, hundreds of defective assemblies could be produced before the fault is noticed. This problem can be minimized by providing a sensor to measure the travel of the riveting head or a probe function after the operation. On a station-by-station basis, the manufacturing engineer must determine the various ways a defective part could be produced. Based on the probability of a defective assembly occurrence versus the cost in yield losses, quality qualification should be added to each station. It must be remembered, however, that the more complicated a station becomes, the less reliable it will be and hence the fewer good parts per hour it will produce on an average basis. Therefore, all peripheral equipment on any assembly station must be simple and reliable. Product designs should facilitate in-process inspection and verification.

Problems may be the fault of part suppliers who have different interpretations of tolerance and quality requirements. Die castings and plastic moldings produced in multicavity dies are often a source of problems because of deviations in the cavities. Low-cost fasteners commonly lack uniformity. Such possible problems have led to the increased use of automatic gaging equipment for 100% inspection of components. This type inspection, as well as in-process inspection of operations on the assembly machines, ensures high reliability.

The use of optical scanning methods, machine vision, and other inspection technologies is increasing, both for detecting bad parts and for use in computer-based process control. When properly applied, such approaches can reduce downtime by rerouting rejected parts. Also, any drift or trend away from nominal dimensions or necessary surface conditions can be detected automatically and their causes identified and corrected immediately.

Cleanliness

Clean parts free from chips, cutting fluids, lubricants, flash, and foreign matter are necessary for successful automatic assembly. The presence of such materials can clog feeder tracks, produce jams, and damage equipment.

Other Considerations

The sensitivity of parts to be assembled to moisture, static electricity, and residual magnetism must be considered. Moisture and humidity may cause distortion of the parts. For some applications, such as electronic assembly, the effects of static electricity and residual magnetism must be counteracted.

ASSEMBLY MACHINES AND SYSTEMS

A broad variety of machines and systems is available for automated assembly. A general outline of some of the concepts is shown in Fig. 12-10.[2] In addition, combinations of these basic systems and flexible, robotic, and electronic assembly systems are discussed subsequently in this section.

SELECTION FACTORS

Selection of the optimum assembly system often depends on careful consideration of many factors, including the following:[3]

1. Production rate requirements.
2. Size and weight of parts to be assembled.
3. Manual operations required, if any.
4. Number of automated operations.
5. Complexity of the operations performed.
6. Material handling and supply logistics.

The possibility of product and/or component design changes is another important factor to be considered.

Production Rate Requirements

Approximate production rates for various assembly system arrangements having single tooling are shown in Fig. 12-11.

Higher production rates can be realized with systems having multiple tooling. Physical size and weight of the parts to be assembled and the complexity and number of operations must be considered in determining the most efficient system.

Size and Weight of Parts

The size and weight of the parts to be assembled can present several problems, including difficulty with positioning accuracy and equipment necessary to physically move the parts if the parts are large. Single-station machines are generally best for precision location where few operations are required. Synchronous and nonsynchronous systems are used for more operations and/or when manual operations are necessary.

Manual Operations

Although it is generally desirable to eliminate all manual operations, this is not always possible. Dial-type (rotary) assembly machines are usually limited to one or two manual operations, in-line machines have space for a number of operators, and carousel systems allow even more manual operations. A number of manual operations can also be performed on synchronous and nonsynchronous systems. Continuous systems are generally almost fully automatic for the high-speed production of small assemblies and usually have many or all manual operations for the low-volume production of large assemblies.

Number of Automated Operations

The suggested number of automated operations for various assembly machine configurations is presented in Fig. 12-12. As the number of automated operations increases, the efficiency of the individual stations must be higher to maintain an acceptable machine efficiency because the overall machine efficiency is the product of individual station efficiencies. Combining too many assembly operations in one machine or system can sometimes

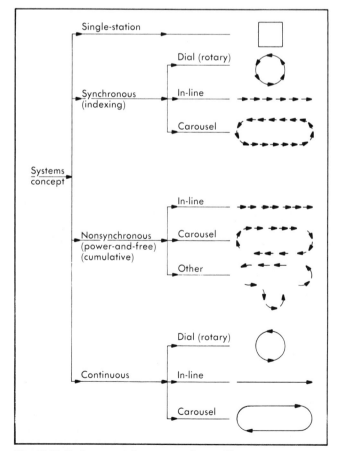

Fig. 12-10 Basic concepts for automated assembly systems.

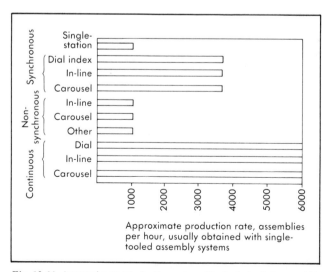

Fig. 12-11 Approximate production rates with single-tooled assembly systems.

ASSEMBLY MACHINES AND SYSTEMS

be inefficient; it may be better to divide the operations among several machines.

Complexity of Operations

The complexity of the individual operations to be performed must be carefully considered along with the efficiencies of the various assembly configurations possible in determining which type of automation arrangement is most suitable for the assembly task.

Material Handling and Supply Logistics

Floor space and additional equipment required for material handling and storage may possibly be greater than that needed for assembly itself. Synchronous and nonsynchronous in-line assembly systems permit spreading out equipment for the orderly handling of material and accessibility for operators and maintenance personnel. Concepts such as just-in-time inventory help minimize space requirements.

BASIC EQUIPMENT REQUIREMENTS

Most assembly machines and systems are specially designed for a special product or a family of products. They can be of continuous or intermittent operation, with intermittent transfer being the most common for automated assembly. Basic assembly machine components include workholding devices, transfer and/or indexing mechanisms, parts feeding, and orienting devices.

All assembly machines and systems must provide means for easy and rapid removal of jammed parts or defective assemblies. Safety interlocks, noise control devices, and environmental protection are also essential. General requirements for these factors are discussed in Volume I, *Machining*, and Volume II, *Forming*, of this Handbook series. Ample space should be provided around the system for material handling and storage as well as for access by maintenance and repair personnel. A good structural foundation and suitable lighting are also essential.

Workholding

Although some product housings or frames (to which parts are to be assembled) can be conveyed individually, it is more common to load them on pallets (special reusable fixtures) that

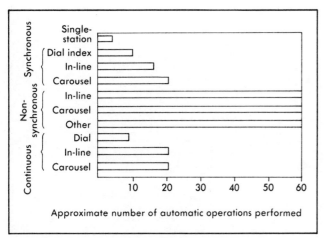

Fig. 12-12 Approximate number of automated operations that can be performed with various assembly systems.

are conveyed through the system. The pallets are generally loaded and unloaded manually, but this can be done automatically by dedicated automation, pick-and-place units, or robotic systems.

On indexing machines, the pallets are generally locked by clamps at each station to permit positive location for assembly. For some applications, it is advantageous to code the pallets mechanically, optically, or magnetically for proper placement. Pallets are often made from cast iron, but aluminum or plastics are sometimes used to reduce their mass. Ample space should be provided to facilitate loading and unloading and, when required, orienting.

Transfer and Index Mechanisms

Transfer and index mechanisms are required to move pallets or assembly components from one workstation to another. Mechanical feeds are most common with conveyors and slide motions, but air, hydraulic, and electric actuators are sometimes used. Cam and turret systems, Geneva motions, walking beams, roll-bar transfers, and rack-and-pinion units are also commonplace.

Modular Components and Machines

Many elements of assembly equipment can be purchased as standard items that can sometimes be used directly for specific requirements. Standard modules include machine bases, conveyors, dial index tables, drives, part transfer units, slide units, powered heads, parts feeders, tracks, chutes, tooling, and controls. Integral assembly machines use standard modules including a basic chassis that combines indexing and actuation of all tooling from a single power unit rather than having individually powered units.

Advantages of using modular components and machines include lower design and hardware costs, shorter development time, improved reliability, easier maintenance, and greater reusability to accommodate product design changes. In many cases, most standard modules can be adapted to new or different assembly operations by replacing certain tooling such as gripper jaws and orienting devices.

One type of standardized, interchangeable, cam-actuated station-movement unit that can be mounted anywhere along an assembly machine is shown schematically in Fig. 12-13. Each basic unit contains a slide mechanism (to which the required tooling is attached) that can be mounted horizontally, vertically, or at any angle in between. Movement is imparted to the slide mechanism by a chain or lever linkage that is actuated by a follower arm in contact with a cam. The piston rod of an air-counterweight cylinder maintains constant loading on the chain linkage and moves in and out of the cylinder as the cam imparts motion to the follower arm. In case of jamming, which would prevent movement of the slide mechanism, the 2:1 mechanical advantage of the chain linkage is overcome, and the cylinder itself is pulled downward away from its stop. This provides 100% overtravel protection and prevents damage.

Check switches are provided for both forward and return travel of the slide mechanism. If these switches are not actuated at the proper time during the cycle, the machine will stop and an individual light will pinpoint the location of the jam that prevented full travel or return.

A small lockout cylinder, with a pawl mounted on its piston rod, is also provided. When it is desired to lock out movement of the slide (by a selector switch or the machine's checking and memory system), the pawl is raised. As a result, the air-counterweight cylinder is merely pulled away from its stop, just as in the case of a jam. When the pawl is retracted, the slide is again free to move in response to cam actuation.

A single camshaft (extending the full length of the machine) actuates all transfer and slide motions, ensuring positive interlocking and synchronization for fast, accurate assembly. Double-movement units are available so that two independent motions can be provided at each station. To change the operations performed at any station, it is only necessary to retool the slide mounting block, change the plate cam, and adjust the feed mechanism.

Platens (and the possible workholding fixtures attached to them) can be of the free-floating type, being entirely unattached to any moving mechanism. They are transferred from station to station by means of fingers that, during each cycle, engage the platens, carry them to the next station position, and then retract. Side-acting shotpins enter bushings in the platens during each dwell period for precise location. Should any repairs be required, the platens can be lifted from the tracks and spares substituted. Also, platens can be left out of the system, and the memory-control circuit will automatically prevent the loading of parts onto the vacant spaces.

SINGLE-STATION ASSEMBLY

Machines having a single workstation are used most extensively when a specific operation has to be performed many times on one or a few parts. Assembling many parts into a single unit, like inserting blades or buckets into turbine or compressor wheels, is a common application. These machines may also be used when a number of different operations have to be performed, if the required tooling is not too complicated. These machines are also incorporated into multistation assembly systems.

SYNCHRONOUS ASSEMBLY SYSTEMS

Synchronous (indexing) assembly systems are available in dial (rotary), in-line, and carousel varieties. With these systems, all pallets or workpieces are moved at the same time and for the same distance. Because indexing intervals are determined by the slowest operation to be performed at any of the stations, operation time is the determining factor affecting production rate. Operators cannot vary the production rate, and a breakdown at any station causes the whole line to stop. By proper consideration to line balancing and parallel assembly operations, such downtime problems can be minimized.

The number of automatic operations that can be performed with synchronous systems is generally limited to a maximum of 20 for in-line machines and less for dial (rotary) systems. However, because the cycle times at the individual stations are generally low (3 seconds or less), production rates are high— 3600 assemblies per hour or more. Double or triple tooling provides higher production rates.

Synchronous systems are used primarily for high-speed and high-volume applications on small, lightweight assemblies where the various operations required have relatively equal cycle times. They are also generally used for fully or substantially automated operations because manual operations are not usually compatible with these systems. However, manual stations, both semiautomatic and completely manual, can be used on synchronous lines. Stations can also be bypassed and operators inserted if idle stations have been initially designed into the system. Dual palm buttons should be provided at manual stations to prevent transfer until operators are finished with their tasks.

The efficiency of synchronous systems can be increased by providing surge (buffer or banking) and repair loops. With some systems, certain operations are performed off-line to

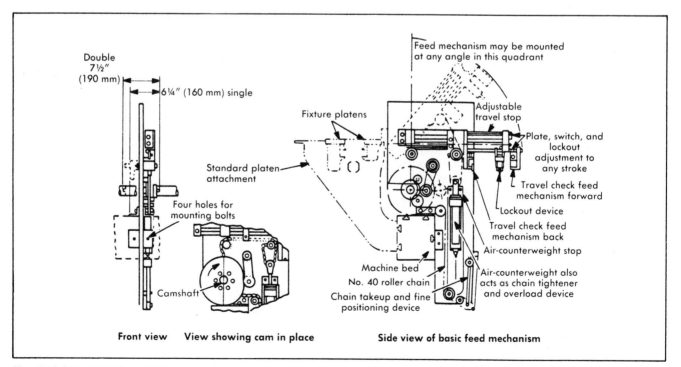

Fig. 12-13 Interchangeable station-movement unit contains slide mechanism that can be mounted at any angle between horizontal and vertical. (*Gilman Engineering & Manufacturing Co.*)

DIAL (ROTARY) ASSEMBLY

ensure that good subassemblies in the required amounts are presented to the final assembly system.

NONSYNCHRONOUS ASSEMBLY SYSTEMS

Nonsynchronous transfer (accumulative or power-and-free type) assembly systems, with free or floating pallets or workpieces and independently operated individual stations, are being widely used where the times required to perform different operations vary greatly and for larger products having many components. Such machines have slower cycle rates than synchronous machines, but slower stations can be double or triple tooled to boost production. One major advantage of these so-called power-and-free systems is increased versatility. The individually actuated, independent stations operate only when a pallet, supplied on demand, is present and when manual and automatic operations can easily be combined. Different methods can be used to meet line balancing needs. For example, multiple loading, joining, or testing stations can be banked or sent down multiple tracks for longer operations, while shorter operations are done on a one-at-a-time basis. Nonsynchronous machines often have a lower initial cost, but require more controls (a set at each station) and generally require more space.

With nonsynchronous systems, the workpieces or pallets can be stopped individually at any station for work to be done or can be queued at manual stations to allow for variations in operator speed. When one or more stations are down for any reason, other stations can continue to operate from their floats of partial assemblies, minimizing production interruptions. Such systems have been described as a series of single-station machines with an integrated, automatic part transfer and in-process buffering system. Practically any number of operations can be linked together, and standby stations and repair loops can be provided. A limitation with nonsynchronous systems is that they operate at slower speeds—generally at a maximum production rate of about 1400 assemblies per hour.

CONTINUOUS-MOTION SYSTEMS

With continuous-motion systems, assembly operations are performed while the workpieces or pallets move at a constant speed and the workheads reciprocate. High production rates are possible because indexing time is eliminated. However, the cost and complexity of these systems are high because the workheads have to synchronize and move with the product being assembled. Applications for continuous-motion automated assembly are limited except for high-production uses in the packaging and bottling industries. The systems are, however, used for the manual assembly of large and heavy products, such as automobiles and refrigerators, with the operators moving with the products while performing their functions.

DIAL (ROTARY) ASSEMBLY

Dial or rotary index machines of synchronous design, one of the first types used for assembly, are still used for many applications. Workstations and tooling can be mounted on a central column or around the periphery of the indexing table. These machines are generally limited to small and medium-sized lightweight assemblies requiring a relatively low number of operations that are not too complex; as the table diameter increases, its mass and complexity can become impractical. Another possible disadvantage is limited accessibility to the workheads and tooling. Also, servicing the indexing table and

mechanism, as well as the controls, is difficult with center-column designs.

Typical Application

A good example of a successful application of a 20-station dial index machine with two operators is the assembly of a furnace fan limit control that contains 11 parts, as shown in Fig. 12-14. A block diagram of the machine is seen in Fig. 12-15. At Station 1, the first operator drives a setscrew into the post of each cam assembly and places the post in an inclined track. A pickup mechanism at the bottom of the track automatically transfers the post into a nest on the index table. Stations 2, 4, 6, 8, 10, 12, 14, and 16 are all checking stations to ensure that each part has been placed into the nests correctly.

At Stations 3, 7, and 11, preplated coil stock is fed through a progressive die mounted in a punch press located at the side of the assembly machine. Here required cams are made in chain form

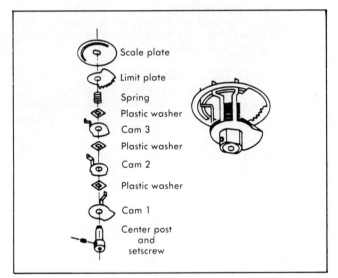

Fig. 12-14 Components and assembly of a furnace fan limit control produced on machine shown in Fig. 12-15.

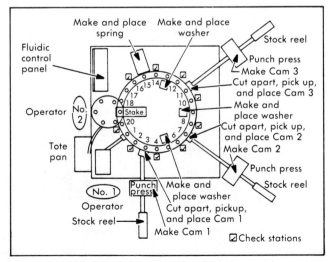

Fig. 12-15 Block diagram of a 20-station dial index machine used to assemble parts shown in Fig. 12-14.

and are fed to the assembly machine, where the chain is cut apart and the cams are automatically picked up and placed in the nest.

At Stations 5, 9, and 13, coiled plastic stock is fed through a two-stage progressive die. A hole is punched into the strip at the first stage, and the washer is cut off and pushed into the nest at the second stage. A spring winder at Station 15 produces one complete spring for each machine cycle. As the spring is cut off, it is blown through a plastic tube into the nest.

Stations 17 and 18 are open to allow for possible design changes in the cam assembly. At Station 19, a second operator manually places a limit plate and a scale plate into a nest on a small auxiliary index table. This table indexes the parts over the nest of the main table. The small table has a floating nest that allows a staking tool to push the two parts down on top of the post and stake the assembly together. As the staking tool is raised, the floating nest picks up the completed assembly, indexes it, and deposits it on an inclined track leading to a tote pan. A gage at Station 20 ensures that the nest is empty.

Advantages and Limitations

Advantages of dial machines include minimum floor space requirements because of their compact designs, high production rates—up to 3600 or more assemblies per hour, and the ease with which standard modules and tooling can be used. Cycle time, however, is limited by the slowest operation required. Dial machines are often tied together with transfer devices to other machines and systems. Limitations include practical physical size and space available for loading, unloading, tooling, maintenance, and repairs.

Versatility

Tables for rotary indexing machines are available in various sizes, with a maximum practical diameter of about 200" (5080 mm). Fixtures or nests are equally spaced around the tables, and standard tables usually have from 4 to 32 stations. The stations can be single or double tooled, depending on production requirements.

Double indexing is possible when it is desired to have a workpiece pass a manual operating station twice during assembly. Lift-and-carry devices can be provided to transport parts from station to station where they must be placed down into nests or fixtures.

IN-LINE SYSTEMS

In-line assembly machines are used in synchronous (indexing), nonsynchronous (accumulative or power-and-free), and continuous designs. In-line indexing assembly machines can be of the wraparound (circumferential) or over-and-under type (see Fig. 12-16) or of the conventional transfer-machine type described in Volume I, *Machining*, of this Handbook series. In the over-and-under type, workholding pallets or platens move horizontally in a straight path and when empty return to the loading station on a conveyor under the machine. In the wraparound type, the work moves around the periphery of the machine in an oval, rectangular, or square path.

Various methods of moving the workpieces from station to station are used on different assembly machines. On one over-and-under type, the platens are rolled over in two 90° rotations when they reach the end of the machine and are returned on a lower track to the starting end. In another type, for assembling smaller components, the platens are indexed along two sets of parallel tracks, with automatic operations performed as the

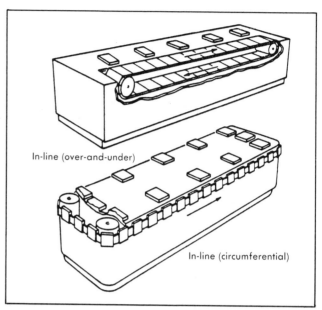

Fig. 12-16 In-line indexing assembly machine bases of the over-and-under and circumferential (wraparound) types.

platens are transferred along the back row and manual operations (if required) performed as the platens return along the front row. On one in-line wraparound type, a single indexing unit is provided at one end of the machine, with a flexible steel band that is driven by a drum wheel and rides around the edge of a built-up table to support the pallets for moving from station to station. The workholder pallets are attached to and indexed by the steel-band drive, with locator pins preventing shifting of the band on the drive drum. Another type of assembly machine is equipped with self-propelled pallets.

Typical Applications

A cam-operated nonsynchronous assembly system for producing rear drum-brake backing plates [12" (305 mm) diam and weighing 6 1/2 lb (3 kg)] at the rate of 900 per hour is illustrated in Fig. 12-17. Operations performed include piercing, welding, shaving, hot upsetting, and hollow milling, with automatic loading, assembling, and unloading on the one machine. Although this system operates on a 4-second cycle, several stations are capable of operating faster if needed because each station has its own drum cam. The drum cams are powered by continuously running electric motors and are driven through one revolution each cycle by alternately engaged air-operated clutch and brake units.

Workpieces are transported around the rectangular system on friction-driven pallet carriers by a power-and-free conveyor. The pallets are supported by an oil film on hardened-steel plates fastened to the roller-chain conveyor. With this floating transport system, pallets can be accumulated ahead of any of the independent stations if required.

Sensors at the independent stations actuate flags on the pallets if the required operations are not performed. The flags cause the pallets to bypass subsequent stations and thus prevent further work from being done on the assemblies. At the unloading station, incomplete assemblies are automatically rejected.

Hot upsetting requires more than 4 seconds. To compensate for this, two duplicate stations have been provided side by side in

IN-LINE SYSTEMS

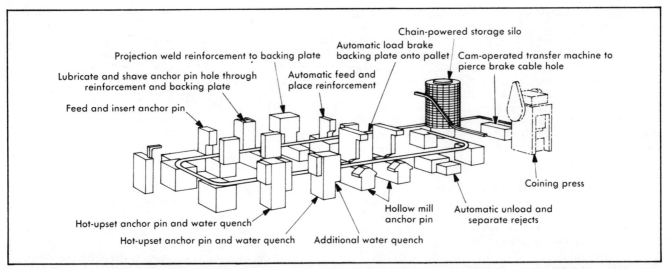

Fig. 12-17 Nonsynchronous system automatically assembles and machines 900 brake backing plates per hour.

the system. Production is shared by these two stations by means of signal flags on the pallets and counting units at each station.

Blank plates enter the system from a coining press. A cam-operated walking-beam transfer unit unloads the press and carries the parts through a station that pierces either a right or left-hand emergency brake cable hole in each blank. These parts are stored in a 600-piece capacity chain-powered silo ahead of the 10-station machine.

Brake backing plates are automatically loaded onto pallets at the first station. A reinforcement plate is automatically fed and placed on each part at the next station. These plates (as well as anchor pins added later) are fed from bowls by horizontal vibratory tracks. Vibratory presorting bowls ahead of the feeder bowls reject any misformed parts and stray material that might interfere with proper feeding.

Reinforcements are projection welded to the backing plates and anchor pin holes are shaved through both plates at the next two stations. Anchor pins are inserted and then hot-upset on either of two standard resistance welders. The final two working stations are used for hollow milling the anchor pins. Cycle time for this operation is only 4 seconds (including pallet indexing and clamping, rapid advance, machining, rapid return, and unclamping). As a result, one station can handle the full production of 900 parts per hour while cutting tools are being changed at the other station. An air cylinder in the cam-drive system lifts the milling unit for tool changes, allowing pallets to pass without interrupting production.

A machine for producing disc brake caliper assemblies at the rate of 1200 per hour is shown schematically in Fig. 12-18. It handles both left and right-hand assemblies for three different models or six different assemblies in all. The machine, monitored and partially controlled by a computer system, consists essentially of 24 individual automatic machines and three manual stations spaced around an elongated, oval-shaped power-and-free conveyor. The conveyor transports the workpieces around the system in pallet carriers, with a right and left-hand pair in each pallet. Automatic operations performed include loading, installing and torquing bleeder screws, placing rubber piston seals, cleaning the bores, pressing pistons into the bores, air-leak testing, installing rubber boots, torquing plugs, placing O-rings, probing, placing spacers, crimping flanges,

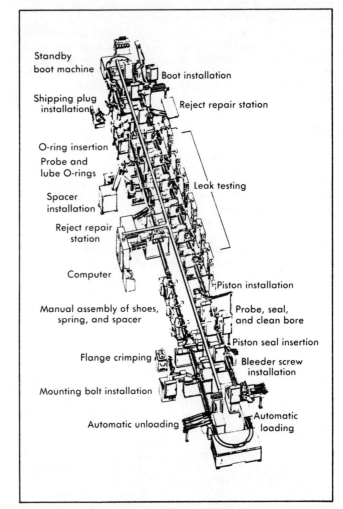

Fig. 12-18 System consists of 24 individual automatic machines and three manual stations spaced around a power-and-free conveyor for producing disc brake caliper assemblies at a rate of 1200 per hour. (*The Cross Co.*)

inserting mounting bolts, stamping, and unloading. The only manual operations required are positioning outer brake shoes in the caliper assemblies, adding a retainer spring, and inserting a plastic spacer.

Advantages

In-line indexing systems allow more operations and provide more accessibility than dial machines. They can also be used for heavier and more complex assemblies. Manual operations and automatic stations can be added anywhere along the line, and repair and storage loops can be provided as required. Virtually any number of operations can be tied together, subject only to mechanical limitations. Modular construction is possible because of the availability of standard transfer mechanisms, workstations, tooling, and other components.

Limitations

The inefficiency of in-line assembly systems becomes increasingly cumulative as additional stations are added. The slowest operation limits the production rate, but the use of multiple tooling increases the output. Nonsynchronous systems are more costly and have lower production rates than dial machines and synchronous systems and require more floor space.

CAROUSEL MACHINES

Similar to the synchronous in-line assembly systems just discussed, carousel machines consist of a series of fixtures or holding devices attached to a roller chain, precision chain, or steel belts or moved by fingers from one workstation to another. However, the carousel machine moves the work in a horizontal plane through a rectangular path, or some variation of the same, returning the pallets to their starting point. All parts are indexed at the same time for the same distance on either a timed or an on-demand basis.

Advantages of the carousel include utilization of all the fixtures in the system because none are returned below, possibility of more operations in the same space, operations can be performed on all sides of the machine, and workpieces are returned to the starting point.

FLEXIBLE ASSEMBLY SYSTEMS

Greater flexibility from automated assembly systems is essential because of continuing increases in product differences resulting from market demands and reductions in product life-cycles. Requirements for high-volume, long-running production are decreasing.

Considerable development work has been done and is continuing with respect to more flexible assembly systems for handling smaller lot sizes and a wider variety of products. The objectives of such systems include increased cost effectiveness and reduced obsolescence of capital equipment expenditures.

One developing concept is the use of automatic guided vehicles (AGVs), which are currently being applied to low-volume large assemblies such as automotive and appliance products. The vehicles are usually self-powered electrically or by compressed air. They electrically follow cables buried in the floor and are computer controlled for any required paths to various assembly stations. The cost of AGVs and their control systems limit their application to large assemblies required in low volumes. Combining AGVs with programmable workstations offers considerable flexibility.

Two major classifications of flexible assembly systems are programmable and adaptable. Programmable and adaptable systems include those using industrial robots, which are discussed next in this section.

Dedicated, Flexible and Adaptable Systems

Dedicated, special-purpose assembly systems are designed to assemble specific products with few or no modifications. They generally require high-volume production for economic justification. Flexible assembly systems are capable of assembling more than one product model or models. Truly flexible systems can assemble on demand from an ensemble of different but similar products without tooling changeovers. Other systems may require only extra fixtures or different pallets, changes in tooling, and, for some applications, extra stations. These systems can be economically justified with lower production requirements.

Adaptable systems that are totally automated and capable of assembling any variety of products are difficult to implement and are rare today, but they are expected to become more common in the future. They require both passive controls for programming and active controls (sensors) capable of decision and control tasks. A mixture of manual, dedicated, and flexible methods seems to be one promising solution for adaptable assembly systems.

Degrees of Flexibility

There are many ways of obtaining various degrees of flexibility in assembly, including the following:

- Increased use of manual operations.
- Design or redesign of products and components for commonality to facilitate flexible assembly.
- Use of standard components and subassemblies whenever possible.
- Use of modular systems for fast changeover and conversion to future requirements.
- Use of programmable workheads that can perform a number of operations, with different programs for each product to be assembled.
- Provision of redundant modules, with different combinations of modules activated to assemble various products.
- Provision of additional space and/or idle stations for possible future design changes and production requirements.
- Use of universal or adjustable workholders (pallets) to simplify changeover.
- Use of coded pallets with programmable controller or computer control.
- Provision of buffer storage and repair loops.
- Use of automatic guided vehicles (AGVs) for material handling because they are easier to reprogram than changing conveyors.
- Use of versatile feeding and orienting devices (discussed later in this chapter) that can be readjusted to handle different sizes and shapes of parts.
- Provision of interchangeable feeders; multiple feeders at required stations, with provisions for selecting the one needed; or interchangeable feeders that can be plugged into the assembly system.
- Use of more magazines, containing preoriented parts, that can be interchanged on assembly systems.

CHAPTER 12

ROBOTIC SYSTEMS

- Use of advanced controls, such as microprocessor-based programmable controllers or computer systems, instead of hard-wired inflexible controls.

ROBOTIC ASSEMBLY SYSTEMS

Robotic assembly (the use of industrial robots for assembly) is being increasingly applied. One major robot manufacturer has estimated that by 1990 more than 16,000 robots will be used in assembly systems. About 30% of these units will be dedicated to mechanical assembly applications, while the remaining 70% will be used in the electronics industry.

Industrial robots are programmable manipulators that perform a variety of tasks. An effective robotic assembly system requires careful consideration of the delivery of components to the workstations, component feeding and orienting, robot end effectors, sensing requirements, and system controls.

Robot characteristics that are especially suited for assembly applications include the following:

- High accuracy and repeatability in both point-to-point and path conformance.
- Reliability, flexibility, and dexterity.
- Capability for a large number of inputs and outputs.
- Sensory communications and system communications capability.
- Off-line programmability with adaptability to a high-level language.
- Memory capacity for program storage.

Accuracy is the precision with which the robot moves from its home position to a designated coordinate location. It is often expressed as a distance differential between the point where the robot manipulator actually is and the point that the controller indicates. Robot accuracy is affected not only by resolution of the controller and inherent mechanical inaccuracy of the robot, but also by speed, payload, and direction of approach and by position within the work volume. A claimed accuracy of $\pm0.004''$ (0.10 mm) is common and $\pm0.002''$ (0.05 mm) is becoming available.

Repeatability is a measure of the precision of the robot to return to a predefined, programmed point on demand, cycle after cycle. It is expressed as a distance differential when the robot arm returns to a taught point within a certain range of speeds and payloads. A repeatability of $\pm0.002''$ (0.05 mm) is common and $\pm0.001''$ (0.03 mm) is becoming available.

Advantages

Robots now available for assembly operations have more specialized features than general-purpose robots, including increased precision (better repeatability), faster speeds, better controls and operating systems, improved capability for interacting with other equipment, and more flexible and convenient programming. Major advantages of robotic assembly systems include the following:

- Consistently repeatable quality and predictable output.
- Flexibility—the ability to assemble multiple products on a single system and to reconfigure the system to perform a variety of tasks.
- Reduced costs per product assembled.
- Minimum obsolescence of capital equipment.
- Modular construction of systems permits adding capacity in required increments.

Possible Limitations

For successful and economical robotic assembly, the products may have to be designed or redesigned for compatibility with the process. Components to be assembled must be held to close tolerances and properly oriented. It is desirable to take advantage of gravity and assemble components vertically. Grippers and part presentation devices for these systems can sometimes cost as much or more than the robots. In many cases, retooling is required at additional expense to assemble a different product with the robot.

Robotic assembly is generally slower than with fixed, dedicated, or hard automated systems. Robotic systems are generally best suited for low to medium volume requirements. The robotic assembly of small products required in high volumes and large parts in low volumes is often not economically justifiable. Also, robots may sometimes be too costly for simple pick-and-place, three-axis transfer functions unless they are justifiable for other considerations such as unhealthy or unsafe working environments.

Future Requirements

Developments that can increase the applications for robotic assembly systems include the following:

- Improved design or redesign of product components to facilitate assembly.
- Classifying parts into families of similar parts (group technology) to reduce tooling requirements.
- Programmable feeders and universal grippers. The introduction of multiple-turret end effectors and quick-change wrists that enable automatic changing has facilitated the assembly of complex parts.
- Standardization of off-line programming capability, control hardware, and diagnostics.
- Remote center compliance (RCC) and instrumented remote center compliance (IRCC).

Typical Applications

Most current applications of robotic assembly systems involve small products in medium volume requirements, families of products, and products or production mixes that are likely to change significantly. Predominant users of such systems include the automotive, electronic, electromechanical, and precision mechanical industries. Electronic applications are discussed later in this chapter.

Automotive applications. Robotic systems are being used to assemble numerous automotive components. The assembly of universal joints involves the insertion of needles in bearings. Systems for engine cylinder heads (see Fig. 12-19) include the assembly of valves, tappets, and covers. Spot welding guns are positioned automatically by means of robots in the assembly of automobile bodies (see Fig. 12-20), as discussed in Chapter 9, "Welding and Cutting."

A vision-guided robot carrying pneumatic wrenches (see Fig. 12-21) is being used to tighten bolts on car underbodies being transported down a moving conveyor line at the Oldsmobile Div. of General Motors Corp. The robot is mounted on a carriage that is temporarily clamped to the car and travels with it. Solid-state cameras view the underbody and report the location of gage holes to the robot system, which then locates the position of the bolts. Cycle time is 53 seconds to find and torque the 12 fasteners on each body and return to the starting position.

ROBOTIC SYSTEMS

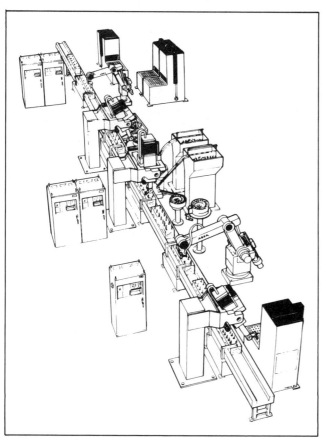

A robotic assembly system at the Fisher Body Div. of General Motors Corp. is being used to assemble 12 different door trim panels at a rate of more than 400 assemblies per hour. The system consists of a 37-station nonsynchronous conveyor with 13 robots. Three optical sensors at one station determine which car line and style of trim panels are to be assembled. Data are relayed to a master programmable controller that controls subsequent operations. A vision system with two cameras at another station scans the trim panels to determine locations of the studs. If the studs are improperly located, the vision system alters the robot program for proper location. The various robots install stamped nuts and plastic fasteners supplied from

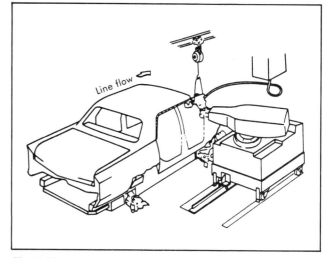

Fig. 12-19 Robotic assembly system for automotive engine cylinder heads. (*ASEA*)

Fig. 12-20 Spot welding guns are positioned accurately and automatically by means of robots in assembly of automobile bodies.

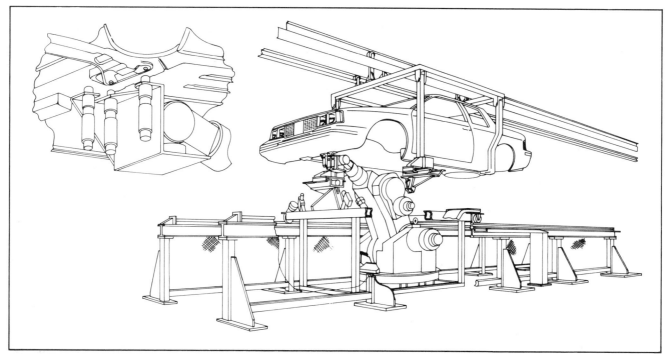

Fig. 12-21 Underbody bolt securing using a vision-guided robot.

overhead hopper bowls and spray adhesive onto the panels. A communications network system provides diagnostic information and production data.

Electrical applications. Westinghouse Electric Corp., with funding from the National Science Foundation, developed a programmable assembly system for the low-volume or batch production of small, fractional-horsepower electric motors having a number of variations. Called APAS (adaptable-programmable assembly system), the system consists of six computer-controlled workstations, robots at four of the six stations, part presentation equipment, fixtures and tools, transfer conveyors, and sensory devices in a complete assembly line (see Fig. 12-22).

A robotic cell for assembling electrical contactors is in use at the Allen-Bradley Co. A material handling robot in the center of the cell retrieves pallets of unassembled parts delivered from a warehouse. The pallets are individually presented to one of three assembly robots. Details of this application and the control hierarchy used are presented later in this chapter under the subject of controls.

Robot Power Sources

Industrial robots are available with electric, pneumatic, or hydraulic actuators to move the robot arms through desired paths. Servoelectric drive mechanisms are the most popular drive for assembly applications. However, pneumatic or hydraulic drives may be economically desirable for some applications if clean air or oil pressure sources are available.

Electric drives. Electric-drive robots commonly have an electric motor servocircuit with a potentiometer, transducer, optical encoder, or resolver to control the position of the arm. They are fast, accurate, quiet, adaptable to sophisticated controls, and relatively inexpensive. Possible limitations include hunting (overshooting), power limitations, and, sometimes, the need for a gear train or other means of transmitting power. However, direct drives that eliminate gear trains are becoming increasingly popular with many robot manufacturers.

Pneumatic drives. Pneumatic actuators for robots are relatively inexpensive and clean. They can develop moderately high forces at high speeds, but the compressibility of air limits the accuracy attainable. Positional accuracy and repeatability are also sensitive to changes in load. They may be noisy in operation because of the possible leakage of air. Pneumatic manipulators are most generally used for light-duty, two-positional, pick-and-place applications.

Hydraulic drives. Hydraulic-drive robots can develop high forces at moderate speeds and can be accurately controlled. However, they cost more than electric actuators, require filters, and are subject to fluid and noise pollution. They are used most often for moving heavy parts.

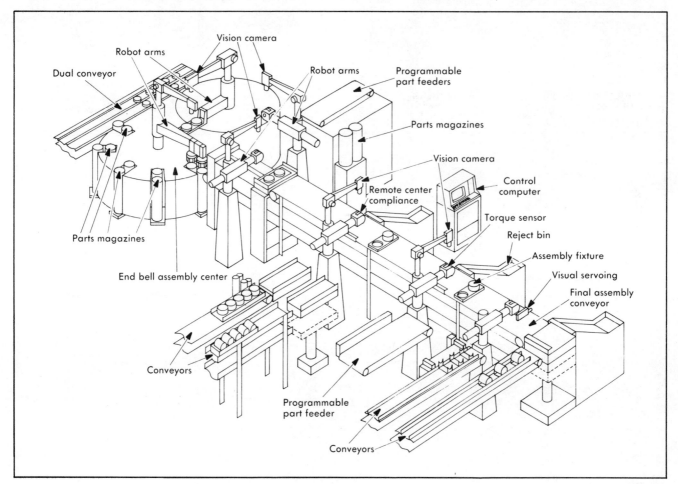

Fig. 12-22 Robotic assembly system for small electric motors.

ROBOTIC SYSTEMS

Manipulator Configurations

The manipulator configuration to be used for a specific assembly application will usually be determined by one or more of the following requirements:

- The work envelope needed. The envelope is the three-dimensional volume of spatial points in which the end of the robot arm can be moved.
- The weight (payload) of the components to be assembled.
- Cycle time, repeatability, and accuracy requirements.

The most popular manipulator configurations for robotic assembly systems include Cartesian coordinate, cylindrical coordinate, articulated arm, SCARA (Selective Compliance Assembly Robot Arm), and gantry.

Cartesian coordinate. With Cartesian coordinates, manipulator movement is linear along one of three perpendicular axes—X, Y, and Z. Robots with this type of manipulator are most popular for handling small parts in pick-and-place applications. When properly supplied with parts that can be easily oriented, the robots can be successfully integrated into assembly systems, providing a high degree of accuracy, repeatability, and speed.

Cylindrical coordinate. Robots with cylindrical coordinate manipulator configurations are among the most popular in use today. They can be supplied with three, four, or five axes of motion. For the assembly of small parts, tabletop units are available. These units generally have a useful load capacity of 2-7 kg (4.4-15.4 lb) and a work envelope of 300 mm (11.8") in R, 120 mm (4.7") in Z, and 300° in θ. Positional repeatability would typically be in the range of ±0.03 mm (0.001"). An advantage is the ability to move into small openings without interference.

For larger weight requirements, floor-mounted robots with greater payload capacities are available in the same configuration. The work envelope on such robots (see Fig. 12-23) would typically increase to 500 mm (19.7") for the R and Z axes. Positional repeatability would usually be in the range of ±0.05 mm (0.002").

Larger robots than those previously described are available to handle large parts, but positional repeatability is usually decreased to about ±1.0 mm (0.039"). These large robots have work envelopes up to 1200 mm (47.24") in the R axis and 1300 mm (51.18") in the Z axis. A disadvantage in using robots of this size is that the clearance for the rear of the robot arm must be considered when designing the workcell.

Articulated arm. Articulated arm robots (see Fig. 12-24) are among the most versatile available, but usually with some sacrifice in repeatability. They are available with up to six axes of motion and payload capacities from 2 to 80 kg (4 to 176 lb). Such robots are generally more expensive than other types, and their complexity can be a disadvantage. However, they are well suited for applications requiring simultaneous movement of all axes. Also, unlike the large cylindrical coordinate manipulators, they are more efficient with respect to space requirements.

SCARA configuration. The SCARA (Selective Compliance Assembly Robot Arm) robot was designed primarily for assembly applications and is gaining worldwide acceptance for use in such applications. It has an asymmetrical, horizontal work plane (see Fig. 12-25) and offers vertical axis insertion at the end of the wrist from any location within the work plane. Many models are available with symmetrical work planes. Joint configuration allows a multiaxis movement that is often faster than other robot kinematic designs.

Initially, the design intent of the SCARA robot was to position itself over the workpiece and then the drives would disengage so that the arm would be free to act as a compliant device in the R and U axes while the Z axis would be performing the assembly. Some manufacturers now offer SCARA-type horizontally articulated robots. The high positional repeatability of ±0.001" (0.03 mm) or less for some models and high motion speeds make this manipulator configuration very desirable for high-volume assembly applications.

High-speed SCARA robots are also gaining in popularity. These small tabletop units are capable of moving 700°/s in the θ, U, and α axes and 950 mm/s (37.4 ips) in the Z axis, carrying a

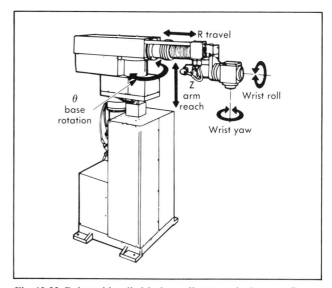

Fig. 12-23 Robot with cylindrical coordinate manipulator configuration. (*GMF Robotics Corp.*)

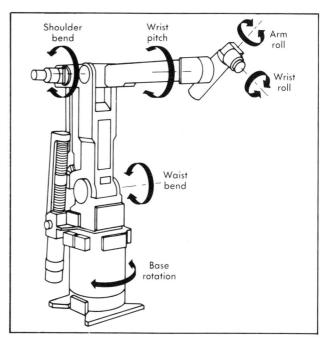

Fig. 12-24 Articulated arm robot. (*GMF Robotics Corp.*)

ROBOTIC SYSTEMS

1 kg (2.2 lb) payload. The work envelope for these small units is 300° in the θ and U axes and 150 mm (5.9″) in the Z axis. Arm lengths are typically 380 mm (15″) for θ and 225 mm (8.9″) for the U axis.

Larger high-speed SCARA robots are available with arm lengths of 410 mm (16″) for θ, 330 mm (13″) for U, and 500 mm (19.7″) for Z. With payloads of 7 kg (15.4 lb), maximum speeds are generally about 300°/s for the θ and U axes, 540°/s for the α axis, and 750°/s for the Z axis.

Gantry robots. A gantry robot (see Fig. 12-26) is essentially a Cartesian coordinate manipulator configuration with three translational axes and up to three rotational axes. It gets its name from the type of support mechanism that allows the manipulator to move above the workpiece.

Typically, the X carriage of a gantry robot travels along the structure on racks, while the Y carriage incorporates a rack-and-pinion drive and travels within the X carriage. The Z axis is mounted within the Y carriage. Depending on envelope requirements, the Z axis can be made telescoping, thus minimizing the overhead clearance for Z-axis operation.

End Effectors

End effectors (end-of-arm tooling) consist of grippers, hands, holders, and other tools for handling components to be assembled. They are not generally integral parts of robots and commonly have to be designed and built for specific applications. They should be designed to handle as many different components as possible. For example, multiple sets of jaws can possibly be used with a single end effector to handle several types of components. The end effectors can be provided with or without mechanical compliance or sensory devices and vision systems for more precise location. A safety device, such as the overload protection shown in Fig. 12-27, is necessary to protect the robot.

Mechanical clamping of workpieces is most common, with pneumatic, hydraulic, or electric operation. Grippers apply surface pressure on the components to be assembled. They are available with jaws, fingers, expansion-contraction devices, and anthropomorphic hands. Other types of flexible fixtures are coming into use for the robotic assembly of components having complex shapes, such as turbine blades. Both modular fixtures (in which the robot assembles the required fixture in the workspace) and phase-change fixtures (such as fluidized beds) have great potential for specialized assembly requirements.

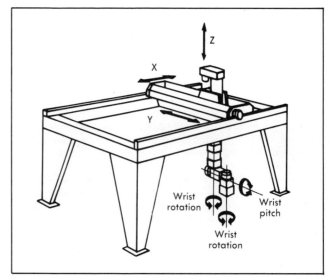

Fig. 12-26 Gantry robot with three translational axes and three rotational axes. (*GMF Robotics Corp.*)

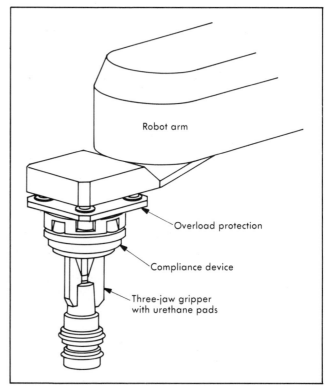

Fig. 12-27 Typical end-of-arm tooling. (*GMF Robotics Corp.*)

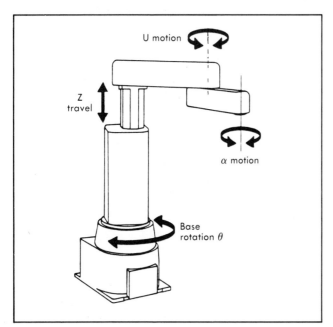

Fig. 12-25 SCARA (Selective Compliance Assembly Robot Arm) robot. (*GMF Robotics Corp.*)

Jaw motions can be of parallel or scissors action, with both jaws moving or one jaw fixed and the other moving. Finger-type grippers, with articulated, parallel, or angular motions, most commonly have two fingers, but three and four fingers are required for some applications. Gripping can also be done magnetically on ferrous parts, with vacuum (suction cups), air-inflated bladders, piercing grippers that puncture the components to lift them, or adhesive grippers equipped with tape.

Various methods of automatic gripper-jaw changeover are available that can use one robot gripper to deposit and retrieve a selection of jaws from a pallet, thus permitting the handling of a variety of components. Quick-change devices are available for mounting on wrists. Racks, magazines, rotary indexing units, and turret heads holding various interchangeable grippers within reach of the robot arm are also used. Programmable or universal grippers are also being developed.

Compliance Devices

Compliance devices that compensate for position errors can be built into robot wrists, workholding pallets, or both. The devices can be of passive or active types or a combination of both. Passive compliance devices react to forces and torques (generated by off-center position errors or angular errors encountered in insertion tasks) by being mounted on flexible mounts such as elastomer pads, shims, or springs. Active compliance is attained with electromechanical devices that move the grippers so that applied forces are zeroed out.

Sensors

Various sensors, both contact and noncontact, are used on robot grippers or workholding pallets for one or more of the following purposes:

- Locate and identify parts to be assembled.
- Ensure that the part is correctly oriented.
- Verify the presence and/or insertion of parts.
- Guide a robot.
- Determine forces and/or temperatures.
- Compensate for position errors.
- Control gripping forces.
- Provide overload protection.
- Recalibrate a robot.

The use of sensors is desirable for many assembly applications, especially those requiring precise positioning and inserting, because they can increase reliability, minimize cycle time, reduce costs, and prevent damage through incorrect assembly. Sensors can provide direct digital input to robot, workcell, or system controls.

Tactile (contact) sensing. Microswitches provide a simple binary method of determining the presence of parts. True tactile sensing, however, requires the continuous measurement of variable forces. A true tactile sensor may consist of a matrix of wires (force-sensing elements) covered by a plastic or other elastomeric material arranged into an array of conductive pads. Depending on the force, each pad responds to deflection and resulting change in electrical resistance. This force datum is typically used with pattern recognition techniques to provide information on forces and part geometry and orientation. Strain gages are also being used for measuring displacement forces and for monitoring the amount of torque applied in twist applications such as bolt tightening.

Noncontact sensing. There are a number of noncontact sensors being used for robotic assembly. The most common include pneumatic, ultrasonic, proximity, and optical sensors.

Pneumatic sensors. Part presence can be detected by the disturbance of air flow from jets directed across the path of the part.

Ultrasonic sensors. With these sensors, sound waves reflected from a part are analyzed. The reflected "signature" can be compared with one stored in the control memory. Typical applications include detecting part presence and recognition as well as part imperfections.

Proximity sensors. Proximity switches are noncontact sensors (capacitance or inductance types) that detect the approach or arrival of parts.

Optical sensors. Parts can be detected by breaking or reflecting a light beam that is directed across their paths. Fiber-optics can be used to place the light source in a difficult position.

Machine Vision Systems

Machine vision systems involve the use of cameras and processing computers to analyze images and make interpretations so that some action may be initiated. One approach is to use an array of photosensitive elements (photodiodes or pixels) arranged in a matrix where each element reacts to light rays reflected or emitted from a part, producing a two-dimensional digital pattern of the part. For correlation systems, recognition is achieved by comparing this pattern with one in the computer memory.

Machine vision systems are being increasingly applied for object recognition, guidance, and inspection operations. Advantages of these systems include reduced tooling (gripper) and fixture costs, increased flexibility because of their reprogrammability, reduced scrap and/or rework of assemblies, and improved product quality. Details with respect to cameras used, image interpretation, binary processing, and lighting are presented in Chapter 3, "Inspection Equipment and Techniques."

Controls

The control functions for a robotic assembly system may be broken down into levels or areas of responsibility: the robot controller and the workcell controller.

Robot controller. A robot controller contains the circuitry and memory required to operate the robotic system. The control circuitry directs the operation and motions of the robot and allows communication with external devices. For programming convenience, the robot controller should have a handheld teach pendant. A CRT display is a desirable option.

With electrically actuated robots, manipulator motion control is done through a servocontrol system that controls the drive motors that position the individual manipulator axes. Position control is accomplished with encoders or resolvers that monitor the position of the drive motor shaft.

Some robot systems use incremental positional encoders, while others use absolute encoders. The absolute encoders retain the positional information when the main power is interrupted. This eliminates the zeroing procedure required for incremental encoders.

The memory of a robot controller stores the operating system software and the information entered into the programming and operating systems. An erasable programmable read-only memory (EPROM) is a fixed memory whose contents can only be read and cannot be altered by the user. A random access memory (RAM) is used as the system's working memory. User programs that are stored in the robot controller must be loaded into the RAM to be executed. Because the RAM is a volatile memory, a battery backup should be provided to prevent loss of program information if power is interrupted. Batteries should be checked periodically to ensure that they have adequate power when needed.

Bubble memories are sometimes used to store programs and data that are not being executed by the systems. These memories are nonvolatile, and stored programs and data are retained when power is lost. Off-line memories provide backup and bulk storage for user programs and data in devices away from the robot controllers. Such storage devices may be digital cassettes or floppy disks.

Workcell controllers. The workcell controller has the responsibility for controlling sequencing operation and integrating all components of the cell. Depending on the purpose and scope of the cell, the components can include conveyors, automation equipment, vision systems, and other peripheral devices.

Programmable logic controllers, discussed subsequently in this chapter under the subject of controls for automated assembly, are being used extensively as the hardware for performing the control functions. More recently, personal computers (PCs) are being increasingly applied on shop floors for this purpose. Advantages of using a personal computer as a workcell controller include low cost, space savings, simplified programming, and many options.

Robot Programming

Industrial robots are programmed by either on-line or off-line methods.

On-line programming. One method of on-line programming consists of lead-through teaching in which the programmer manually moves the manipulator through the desired cycle. In another method, motion sequences are recorded in memory by depressing buttons on the teach pendant or control console. Disadvantages of on-line programming include the need to stop production for programming in some cases and, complex procedures may be required for some applications. When a CAD/CAM database exists, on-line programming often duplicates information already in the database and is not readily compatible with such databases.

Off-line programming. Advantages of off-line programming include eliminating the need for stopping production, the capability of moving programs from one robot to another of similar accuracy and programming language, and the ability to easily incorporate programs into automated assembly systems. A number of programming languages are being used. Some of these languages are complex, and most require a language processor on the robot, which is costly and generally used infrequently. Development work is being done with world modeling (automatic programming) in which a robot is assigned a task, develops a plan, and programs itself.

Program development. A robot program is typically developed with the following steps:

1. *Task analysis.* The first step in creating a program is to define the sequence of operations that the robot is to perform and the exact order in which they are to be performed. This includes defining control signals, computations, and special program logic. Program creation is usually best accomplished by developing a flowchart.
2. *Program language.* Once the flowchart is completed, the program logic is converted into the language to be used.
3. *Program entry.* Once the program is written, the next step is to enter it into the controller via the teach pendant or the keyboard with CRT display. If a software package has been developed to use a personal computer, the pro-

gram can first be written into the computer and then dumped into the robot controller.

4. *Program translation.* After entry, the program language file is converted into a file that can be understood by the operating system.
5. *Program loading.* After translation, the program can be loaded into the controller memory, where it awaits execution.
6. *Position teaching.* Next, the user teaches each position to which the robot will move in the program. This can be done either by jogging the robot with the teach pendant to the required positions and recording them or by entering positional coordinate data directly through the keyboard. The first attempt at writing a program is seldom successful.
7. *Program execution.* The program can now be run. This should be done at a slower-than-normal speed to test e program. When the program has been proven correct, it can be run at normal speed.

These program development steps apply to what is normally termed second-generation languages. Future-generation languages will have world modeling capability and include task-object programming. This would alleviate the need for a teach pendant to physically record each point in the program.

Safety

Safety precautions necessary for the use of industrial robots are discussed at the end of this chapter.

AUTOMATED ELECTRONIC ASSEMBLY

Most electronic assemblies consist of inserting components into or placing them onto printed circuit boards (PCBs) or substrates. Components assembled include the following:

- Axial lead components that have a wire lead extending out from the end(s) along its axis. These include resistors, capacitors, diodes, inductors, and other electronic devices normally supplied on lead tape.
- Integrated circuits (ICs) contained in dual in-line packages (DIPs). They have circuit leads or pins extending symmetrically downward from their bodies and are normally supplied in plastic stick magazines.
- Radial lead components that have their leads coming off the peripheries. These include transistors, disc capacitors, ICs, potentiometers, and light-emitting diodes (LEDs).
- Small outline transistors (SOTs) that have their three leads bent outward, the two outer leads bent in one direction and the center lead bent in the opposite direction.
- Odd-shaped electronic or electromechanical components such as connectors, transformers, relays, and switches.
- Surface-mounted devices (SMDs) are leaded or leadless electronic devices that are soldered directly to pads on the surfaces of PCBs, as opposed to through-hole insertion mounting.

Transistors that incorporate metal-oxide-silicon semiconductor layers are referred to as MOS devices. A microelectronic circuit fabricated from a single semiconductor IC having the equivalent of more than 10,000 individual gates or active circuit functions is called a medium-scale integration (MSI) chip. Arrays of ICs on a single substrate that comprise 100,000 or more individual active circuit functions or gates are referred to as large-scale integration (LSI) packages.

Automation of printed circuit board assemblies has progressed from manually formed component leads, with blueprint-guided insertion, to fully automatic insertion machines and robotic systems. All types of components are now being sequentially inserted through a continuous array of in-line machines or through groups of machines bridged by material handling equipment. Today's electronic manufacturing facility is also equipped with a wide range of automated test equipment, controlled by computers.

Historical Development

Automation of printed circuit board assembly production first occurred about 1950 and has progressed through five periods. The first generation, from about 1955 to 1965, had hard-tooled automation along a fixed conveyor to insert as many as 60 components simultaneously at fixed positions. A finished printed circuit board assembly could be produced every 2-3 seconds. This process was applicable only to mass production.

In the second generation, insertion tooling was mounted on numerically controlled X-Y positioning systems, allowing manufacturers to change the types of printed circuit boards to be assembled in minimum time. This generation lasted through 1974.

Computer-controlled equipment marked the third generation and extended through 1979. A minicomputer in a central processing configuration allowed the collection of production control information. On-line testing systems, which allowed for the verification of components, were developed. For the first time, the quality and quantity of production increased in the assembly process. On-line assembly testing allowed the user to reduce the indirect production costs of inspection and rework.

In the fourth generation, microprocessors on assembly machines created the first stand-alone pieces of equipment. In today's age of assembly, flexible automation is achieved through automated board handling, material handling technology, and data management systems. Feeder problems for regular electronic assembly are not too complicated because of the availability of components on carrier tapes or in magazines or trays, thus presenting the parts in proper orientation. Odd-shaped components (not axial or radial) sometimes present special problems.

Automation Capabilities

Full automation of the component insertion operation provides high throughput and productivity. Operators are manually able to make 100-500 component insertions on a board per hour; semiautomated systems, between 500 and 1000 components per hour; robots, 1000-2000 components per hour; and dedicated systems for DIPs, 4000 or more components per hour. Dedicated systems can insert 4000 radial components per hour, 7000-30,000 axial components per hour, and 2000-100,000 surface-mounted devices per hour. Speed and quality are considered the most important benefits of automation.

Additional benefits from automation include reduced labor and rework and a consistent production volume. Insertion machines offer expansion in production capabilities and have data communications for interfacing higher level computer systems.

Commercial equipment covers automated board handling and surface-mount pick-and-place or robotic systems. Figure 12-28 illustrates how both leaded and surface-mount compo-

nents can be placed by a robot. Some systems incorporate optical registration capabilities to correct board misalignment or pattern displacement automatically. Of today's automatic component insertion systems, a broad mix of equipment is available to satisfy both small and large-volume manufacturers. The goal of most equipment suppliers is to offer automation capable of suiting the widest range of companies and applications.

Board and Component Handling Equipment

A large variety of board and component handling equipment is available for printed circuit board assembly. There are machine loaders and unloaders, buffers and stackers that gather boards before loading or after unloading, turnovers that flip boards, and conveyors or automatic guided vehicles (AGVs) that transport boards and components directly between process machines. Many handlers combine several of these functions. Handling equipment can be used to build an automatic material throughput system that keeps an address for each printed circuit board in the assembly process.

There are two general approaches for board loading. In the first type of loading system (pass-through), boards are extracted from a magazine and loaded into a process machine. After the machine operation, the board is reloaded into a separate magazine at the opposite end of the machine. In the second approach (load-unload), the loading system extracts and loads boards into an assembly machine, then returns them into the exact same position in the originating magazine. Benefits from using the latter type of board loading system include the following:

- It reduces by 50% the floor space required for the machine loading function.
- It reduces the investment in board magazines, which are a process requirement.
- It decreases the number of transactions a material handling system must take.
- It allows individual boards to be identified through tracking of the magazine. Because the printed circuit board has a unique slot in the same magazine throughout the assembly process, each board can be located at any time.

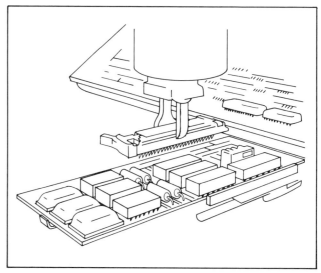

Fig. 12-28 Connectors and odd-shaped components, both leaded and surface-mount, can be placed by robots.

ELECTRONIC ASSEMBLY

Automatic guided vehicles are computer-controlled carts that are being used by some manufacturers to transport magazines of printed circuit boards throughout the system. Advantages include both random access and flexibility, and productivity is generally better than buffer transfers or conventional conveyor units.

Leaded Components

Automatic insertion equipment systems for leaded components, such as axial, radial, and DIPs, represent the most mature electronic assembly technology. This assembly equipment family is composed of reel packaging systems, sequencing systems, component verifiers, and the component insertion machine. The machine withdraws individual components from storage positions and transfers them to an insertion head in a preprogrammed sequence. At the insertion head, component leads are formed (if required) and inserted into correct locations in the PCBs. The machines then automatically trim and clinch the protruding leads. Figure 12-29 illustrates insertion of resistors sequenced on tape.

Axial lead component inserters offer the highest level of reliability of all placement systems with yields above 99%. Dedicated machines can insert 30,000 components per hour and feature high-speed rotary indexing, automatic board handling, and programmability. Axial lead inserters feature random or sequenced insertion. Components can be selected randomly from reels at the inserter. This feature provides repair capability by allowing a component to be reinserted automatically.

Automatic insertion of the varied body sizes and lead diameters of radial lead components is possible by handling components by the leads, not by the body. Standard spacing between leads on reel tapes makes automation possible. Inserters can handle DIP lead row spacings of 0.300, 0.400, and 0.600″ (7.62, 10.16, and 15.24 mm). Systems can also insert DIP sockets, DIPs into sockets, and mount decoupling capacitors. An automatic DIP insertion machine is illustrated in Fig. 12-30. Odd-shaped components (not axial, radial, or DIP) may be loaded manually or by robots.

After leaded components are inserted into printed circuit boards, an automatic vision system can detect missing components or leads not protruding through the board. After repair, the board proceeds to further processing steps such as wave soldering and cleaning.

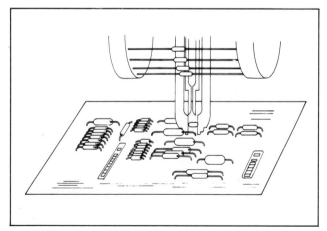

Fig. 12-29 Automatic axial lead component insertion is the most mature form of automated electronic assembly.

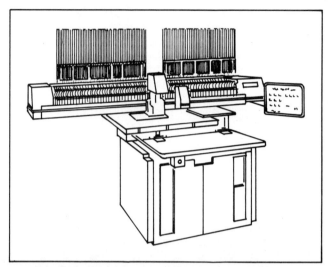

Fig. 12-30 Automatic inserting machine can place DIP sockets and DIPs into the sockets.

Surface-Mounted Devices

Surface-mount technology allows freedom in circuit design and further miniaturization of electronic assemblies. The smaller size of SMDs and elimination of through-holes make more effective use of the available substrate surface. Also, the smaller size of SMDs permits high horizontal and vertical component packing densities on boards, which provides weight and size advantages. Their smaller size and lighter weight make SMDs less susceptible to vibration and shock, resulting in board quality improvements.

Assembling SMDs onto substrates, however, does present difficulties. Because many circuit board designs that have SMDs also include leaded components, an additional process step is required. Surface-mounted devices are often expensive, and at present, there are only limited typical components available as standard forms. Conventional circuit-pattern registration tolerances are not acceptable for most SMD assembly. Problems can be caused by thermal incompatibility between the surface-mounted devices and the substrate (board) material, but suitable substrate materials are available to eliminate such problems.

Surface-mount assembly systems are available with broad performance capabilities. Many systems provide a recycling feature, whereby boards with missing elements are automatically returned to the proper station. Although at present SMDs comprise only about 10 to 15% of total component usage, it is expected that by the 1990s they could account for 50% of all printed circuit board assembly.

Process and Equipment for SMDs

A typical manufacturing process for the assembly of boards containing only SMDs is diagramed in Fig. 12-31. If the assembly does not contain any leaded components, then solder paste can be screen printed onto the printed circuit board at SMD locations as shown.

If the board contains leaded components, they should be automatically inserted into the printed circuit board before any SMDs are assembled. In the case of SMDs and leaded components, the SMDs are epoxied in place on printed circuit boards. Some machines apply epoxy to the bottom of the component

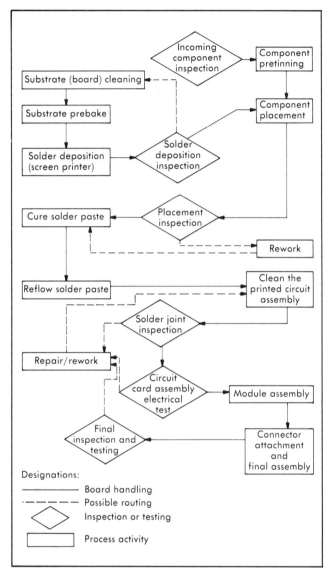

Fig. 12-31 Typical manufacturing flow for surface-mounted assemblies.

before placing it onto the board. Other machines have an epoxy application station that applies a metered amount to the surface of the board at the same time components are being applied onto another board downstream. The epoxy or solder must then be cured by ultraviolet (UV) or infrared (IR) energy systems. Cured epoxy or solder is strong enough to hold the SMDs in place during normal handling. Next, components are soldered into place. Wave, vapor-phase, and furnace reflow soldering are common techniques used with SMDs. The adhesive technique can also be used to assemble components to both sides of a board that contains through-hole components. In this case, vapor-phase soldering is used to reflow the components on the top side of the board after solder has been appropriately applied.

Component Soldering Equipment

Soldering is usually a necessary process step in the assembly of any electronic circuit. Some success has been attained by

attaching SMDs with electrically conductive epoxy adhesive, thus eliminating the need for soldering, but the process is slow and costly. Details of the soldering process are presented in Chapter 10, "Brazing and Soldering," of this volume. Different types of soldering units used for securing electronic components include the following:

- Dip-type soldering equipment is used for tinning resistors, capacitors, transistors, diode leads, and terminals. It is also used for tinning and soldering substrates; soldering small coils, relays, windings; and soldering miniature parts.
- Drag-type equipment is used when large quantities of uniform printed circuit boards are processed.
- Infrared (IR) equipment is used to change the porous electroplated tin-lead on a circuit into an alloy with a strong bond to the base copper.
- Laser equipment is used for soldering boards, DIPs, leadless chip carriers, hybrid packages, connectors, wire wrap pins, integrated circuits, lead frames, and chip capacitors.
- Roll-tinning equipment is used to solder-coat printed circuit boards to improve circuit solderability and shelf life.
- Ultrasonic equipment is used to solder DIPs, axial lead components, motors, transformers, connectors, terminal blocks, integrated circuits, and pretinned flat packs.
- Vapor-phase equipment is used for fusion of both flexible and rigid tin-lead electroplated printed circuit boards, microelectronic component assembly, and mounting chip carriers.
- Wave soldering equipment is used for through-hole and surface-mounted boards.

Automatic Test Equipment

Problems that arise during manufacturing of electronic assemblies include: printed circuit board shorts, component failures, process malfunctions, and assembly errors. Locating problems early in the assembly process can drastically reduce production costs. Testing of bare substrates, loaded substrates, and uninserted components plays a vital role in printed circuit production.

Bare board testing. The first part of circuit testing takes place before board population. Bare board testing ensures that the printed circuit is functional with no shorts or opens. These testers often use a so-called "bed-of-nails" fixture having spring-loaded contact pins that interface with the board surface conductors. Failures such as broken circuit paths, solder slivers, and unetched copper are detected and noted for repair. Other methods are available to eliminate costly tooling. One method consists of electronic scanning of all board circuits, with the results analyzed by computer to determine reliability.

In-circuit testing. Uninserted components are inspected prior to loading so that tests subsequent to board population can concentrate on assembly errors. Equipment is available to test components as they arrive from the manufacturer. After components have been inserted onto printed circuit boards and secured by soldering, the boards are tested again for open component-circuit values and short circuits.

In-circuit testing checks for proper placement and orientation of components and checks components on the board to ensure that they meet manufacturing specifications. In-circuit testers use a vacuum fixture with special spring-pin tooling. If loaded-board reliability is a major production fault, then a

ELECTRONIC ASSEMBLY

loaded-board tester is advantageous for inspection. It allows rapid test program development, but fault coverage is limited to shorts. In-circuit analyzers have the ability to detect most manufacturing errors on printed circuit boards and to detect some analog component faults. They are incapable of digital logic testing, however. In-circuit testers are capable of digital logic pin fault detection and are typical for production testing.

Most automatic test equipment in use is in-circuit test equipment to verify the operation of individual components on the printed circuit board, especially after soldering. Shorts or open circuits after wave soldering are common causes of assembly defects. When printed circuit boards have more than 1000 solder joints, a high soldering yield is necessary. The defective printed circuit boards discovered by automatic testing are sent for repair.

Functional board testing. Functional board testers are used for production testing. Functional testing increases the potential that a completed printed circuit board will correctly operate in the final product. If other forms of testing have been performed, failures detected at this time will primarily consist of interactional problems between components. Testers exercise the board under test by interfacing card edge connectors and/or integrated circuit probe clips. Faults are defined in user language.

In functional testing, fault analysis is done with either a fault dictionary or by guided-probe techniques. A fault dictionary, or footprint, is a memorization of the fault output pattern done by modeling or through circuit analysis. The guided-probe technique involves a record made of all test patterns on a known good board for comparison with the test board. This permits backward tracing of a fault on a bad board from the failing pin to the error source. Test program generation is done by a system programmer.

Completed printed circuit board manufacturers use a combination of in-circuit testers and functional test equipment, suited for the probable errors of their assemblies, for maximum inspection efficiency. In these automatic inspection systems, functional testing detects dynamic failures not detected by in-circuit testing. A failed functional test board can be returned to in-circuit testing for additional probing.

Using Robots for PCB Assembly

Industrial robots are widely used for component insertion, but their general role is for highly specialized product placement and for assembling components that are not automatically insertable by standard equipment. Robotic placement systems can automatically insert trimmer capacitors, potentiometers, headers, connectors, ceramic filters, DIP switches, crystals, and other odd-shaped devices.

Robotic stations for inserting odd-shaped components do not generally offer higher speeds than dedicated assembly machines. Robot cycle times are usually between 1 and 6 seconds. Robots have insertion rates one tenth those of axial component insertion machines, but they are approximately two to five times faster than humans. Increased quality by providing consistency to the insertion operation is a major benefit of using robots. Other advantages include quality and management information flow from the robot computers and sensors and from test equipment. To fit robots efficiently into an automated assembly line, a sufficient number are needed to match the throughput of dedicated machines.

In certain low to medium-volume assembly situations, robots are well suited for insertion of axial and radial leaded

components and placement of SMDs. Robots are much more flexible than dedicated equipment. They can especially be economically effective where board volume is low and the component mix is high. The greater the part variety, the greater the flexibility advantage of robots. Robots can be adequately suited for successful placement of a wide variety of SMDs through vacuum-assisted end-of-arm tooling. Figure 12-32 shows how a line of robots can be used in a flexible assembly system.

To use a robot for an electronic assembly function, the circuit board must be accurately indexed into the correct position. Robots are sometimes equipped with vision systems for improved accuracy. Parts feeders and lead preparation equipment are needed to correctly present components with properly formed leads to the robot. Components must also be available when the robot needs them. Components may be robot fed from trays, tapes, sticks, or vibratory feeders.

Many robotic applications for inserting odd-shaped components use robots of the SCARA type. These robots have asymmetrical, horizontal work planes and offer vertical motions from any point within their work planes. Multiple grippers handle a range of components, and built-in sensors detect component jamming and allow defective components to be replaced. Cartesian robots are also emerging for this application.

Although the overwhelming majority of robots in electronic assembly are being used for insertion tasks, they are well suited for other assembly functions. There are robot systems for dispensing adhesive or solder masks. There are also robot-directed laser discrete-point soldering systems. Other applications include piercing parts or subassemblies, disk media handling, and loading and unloading fixtures for automatic test equipment. Robots are also being used to do final packaging of electronic products—placing printed circuit boards into housings, fitting housings together, and boxing the finished product.

Circuit Design for Assembly Automation

The following guidelines for printed circuit board layout facilitate automatic insertion:

1. Provide substrates with locating features such as tooling holes for placement handling.

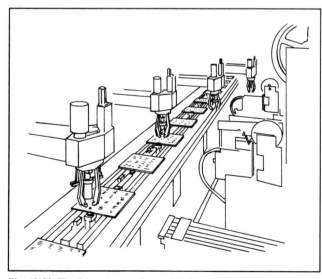

Fig. 12-32 Flexible automated assembly line equipped with robots for placing surface-mounted components.

2. Provide vision targets on substrates for optical alignment.
3. Use coordinate system to lay out electronic devices with respect to the location feature.
4. Use standardized components and lead spacing.
5. Allow for proper clearances between components and between components and tooling holes.
6. Provide tooling zones on every component to allow placement machine handling and board processing.
7. Select proper printed circuit board hole sizes. Component lead holes should be 0.018" (0.46 mm) larger than component lead diameter.

The Electronic Automation Application Center of General Electric Co. has developed a quantitative method of rating the ease of manufacture of printed board assemblies. This method, termed Manufacturability Rating System (MRS), identifies each manufacturing operation, asks questions related to the design, and assigns rating values. A review of a design indicates correctable problems that can reduce costs and improve quality.

Factory Automation

The major factory automation strategies involving component insertion and printed circuit board assembly are in-line systems and flexible assembly systems.

In-line systems. These systems use the production line concept, where individual machines are physically connected together to form a sequential process. Surface-mount technology offers an opportunity to use this approach to combine several processes. There is a balancing dilemma with the in-line approach; the wide range of placement equipment insertion rates, board designs, and component configurations make system balancing difficult.

Flexible assembly systems. These systems utilize separate islands or cells of automation where the destination of output from each cell can be programmed. The material transportation system can consist of power roller conveyor systems, automated guided vehicles, and automated storage and retrieval systems (AS/RS) for moving magazines containing printed circuit boards. Figure 12-33 diagrams the material flow in a flexible assembly system made possible by software programmed to take bad boards out and send them to repair stations.

A printed circuit board manufacturer with a high volume of a single type of board having a low component mix might best use a dedicated in-line production arrangement. However, a company that makes many types of boards using many components will be most efficiently served with a flexible assembly line. Table 12-6 lists the characteristics of assembly modules in the flexible arrangement.

Whether to include dedicated machines in flexible automated assembly is determined by the volume of components and the mix of axial and radial leads, DIPs, SMDs, number of pins, and sizes. A robot-only flexible system is proper for a highly mixed, low-volume (thousands of boards per month) operation. An assembly line setup with robots may be quickly reconfigured with an existing program to handle several different product mixes.

A flexible assembly system offers the following production benefits:

- Each machine operates at its maximum output potential.
- Routing of the assemblies through the system is software-controlled and can be modified based on what is actually occurring in the process.

TABLE 12-6
Flexible Automated Assembly Modules and Characteristics

Bare PCB Feeding

Magazine configuration
Supplied by assembly line manufacturers
Capacity of 150 lb (68 kg)
Up to 16 x 14 (405 x 380 mm) board sizes

Part Feeding

Current techniques include tray, tape, vibratory linear or bowl feeders, and magazines
Can use passive (gravity) techniques
Sequencing on tape utilized for chip, axial, and radial component. Also provides limited quality control tests. Available from machine suppliers and numerous other firms

PCB Storage Buffers

Magazine configuration
Same size as board feeders
About 50-board capability, 60 lb (27 kg)
Supplied by some system manufacturers
Provides means of keeping machines with different insertion rates running without stopping

Transfer Mechanism

Usually in-line conveyor utilizing guides and rollers
Board sizes compatible with feeders, 16 x 14" (405 x 380 mm)
Approximately 2-3 seconds to locate board
Other techniques include: roller conveyors, chain conveyors, rotary systems, X-Y positioners, vacuum pickups, and connecting conveyors

Component Placement Insertion Machines

Usually high-speed machine dedicated to single component type (axial, radial, DIP, chip)
Very short strokes in X-Y or X-Y table for positioning
Suppliers include assembly line manufacturers
Most suppliers addressing SMD
Insertion rates from 3000/hr for DIPs to 25,000/hr for axials
Multicomponent machines either very expensive and/or not perfected

(continued)

- There are no production line balancing problems.
- As production requirements increase, the manufacturer can expand capacity by adding new production cells.
- The assembly system can utilize different vendor's equipment in the various process operations.

Software is implemented on four hierarchical levels: machine control, supervisory, factory, and corporate. At the lowest level, the assembly machines generate production, consumption, and quality information. The data are collected and stored at the Assembly Supervisory System that monitors the process and communicates with a traffic management system. In the Factory Management System, all the various processes (inspection, storage, CAD, repair, and ATE) are integrated. Development of this

TABLE 12-6—Continued

Placement Robots

Two to four axes
Cartesian coordinate configuration favorite technique
Electronic or pneumatic
X and Y strokes comparable to board size, 10-20"
(254-508 mm)
Repeatability of 0.001" (0.03 mm)
One to two cycles per second necessary
Can be pick-and-place units
Handles odd-shaped components though there is movement
toward replacing component placement/insertion
Many suppliers

Multifunction Robots

Up to 6 axes
Articulated configuration
Longer strokes
Repeatability of 0.01" (0.3 mm)
Cycle time of 1.5-5 seconds
Handles operations such as screwdriver and larger
component (transformer) placement

PCB Off-Loading

Two approaches:
Slide cards into magazine and robot handling
Magazine dominates
Similar to buffers

Soldering

Supplied by assembly line manufacturers and independent
suppliers
Wave solder for leaded components, reflow or ultraviolet
and infrared curing for chips and SMDs, followed by
wave or reflow soldering
Conveyor speeds up to 24 fpm (7.3 m/min)
Board sizes up to 24" (610 mm)
Can be interfaced with most assembly lines

Automated Text Equipment

Numerous suppliers of in-circuit, functional, or combined
test systems
Bed-of-nails or edge connectors most common activation
techniques
Recent introduction of robot board handlers by several
manufacturers using articulated electronic robots
supplied by outside vendors
Board sizes to 24" (610 mm) and larger by special order
Currently not often interfaced to assembly line
Bar coded (tickets) board test results provide repair and fault
diagnosis information.

(CEERIS International, Inc.)

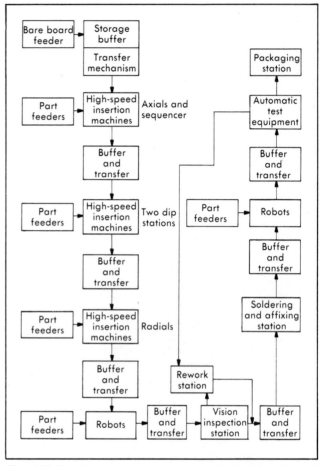

Fig. 12-33 Flexible automated electronic assembly flowchart. Printed circuit boards can be stuffed, tested, and packaged without any human contact. *(CEERIS International, Inc.)*

PARTS FEEDING, ORIENTING AND POSITIONING

The importance of automatic feeding, orienting, and positioning of parts to be assembled cannot be overemphasized. Without automation equipment to perform these functions, a large percentage of automated assembly would be economically impractical. Even when assembly systems are economically feasible, a major cost of tooling is for orienting, feeding, and placing components from a bulk condition.

Solving Problems

Many problems in parts feeding, orienting, and positioning can be avoided by the proper design or redesign of the components to be assembled, discussed previously in this chapter. Whenever possible, critical or complicated orientation should be eliminated. If this is not possible, the number of critical orientations at the assembly machine should be minimized. Even with optimum design, however, most parts require a comprehensive analysis and parts handling experience for successful automated assembly.

Because many phases of parts feeding, orienting, and positioning have become highly specialized and quite often involve proprietary techniques, the manufacturing engineer must rely heavily on manufacturers of equipment for guidance in plan-

system has been difficult because of the proliferation of computer systems, networks, and protocols. At present, no standard "off-the-shelf" Factory Management System exists. The highest level is the Corporate Management System, in which summary data collected through the Factory Management System are utilized by the financial and accounting systems.

ning. It is seldom necessary or economically feasible for the manufacturing engineer to undertake the actual design of a parts handling system, but it is important in the planning role to have at least elementary knowledge of the methods available for bulk storage, feeding, orientation, conveying, escapement, placement, and control.

Methods Used

Fundamental methods for providing prepositioned parts automatically include the following:

- Preoriented parts supplied to the assembly machine in stacks, magazines, reels, or trays.
- Manufacturing parts at the assembly machine.
- Orienting feeders or feeders with supplementary orienting devices.

The method used is determined by the geometry of the part (or family of parts) to be fed, available space, and the final orientation required at the assembly stations. Size, weight, shape, and other characteristics of the parts and production rate requirements are among the factors determining the type and complexity of optimum equipment. An orienting feeder system is preferred because it demands the least amount of manual involvement; however, many parts cannot be handled in bulk form because they are highly susceptible to damage or entanglement. Other parts have complex shapes, widely varying dimensions, or no distinctive external or internal geometric features for mechanical positioning and thus cannot be oriented economically. Still other parts are too large or too heavy or have unsatisfactory conveying characteristics for orienting feeders. In these cases, stack feeders or reel feeders may be applicable. In some cases the parts may best be supplied by manufacturing at the process.

Feeding and orienting. Most feeding and orienting of small parts from bulk is done with bowls or hoppers, discussed subsequently in this section. Vibratory bowl feeders are most common, but nonvibratory feeders are often required for large and oily components. Table 12-7 lists a variety of hopper feeder types and indicates characteristics of parts they are suited to handle. Such data can serve only as a rough guide because listed characteristics occur in various degrees. Parts can tangle or nest so hopelessly that feeding is almost impossible, or at such a slow rate as to be impractical, or else be so minor a problem that almost any type of feeder can handle them. Except for a few simple shapes, specific parts are not listed, but general characteristics of the feeders are related to those of the parts to assist in choice of the equipment.

Versatility. Increased flexibility can often be obtained by providing means for mechanically adjusting feeder tracks and orienting devices to handle different size parts. In some cases, sections of feeder bowls and tracks can be replaced or entire bowls interchanged. Some assembly machines are provided with multiple feeders at some stations for alternate use on different products, but this practice is not generally recommended. In other cases, different preoriented parts can be fed from different magazines.

Programmable parts feeding. The concept of programmable parts feeding is being actively pursued by many organizations. Most concepts require the establishment of a parts classification system and part families, and most will handle only less complex families. With some concepts, each part family requires a set of tools, such as tracks, rails, wipers, and other components, that are programmable and adjustable along the

bowl or other feeder. Some concepts employ a vision system to sense the parts and their orientation. Incorrect or improperly oriented parts are rejected back into the feeder.

One company has developed a programmable parts feeding system (see Fig. 12-34) that offers an economical alternative to traditional parts feeders with fixed tooling. It utilizes an optical scanning device and a microcomputer control to recognize parts for orientation and/or sorting. As a part passes the optical scanner, the microcomputer collects the optical information and compares it with data stored in its memory to determine the orientation of the scanned part, accepting only the desired part orientation. Other part orientations are reoriented to the desired orientation or diverted for recirculation. Foreign or undesired parts are rejected from the parts handling system.

This system enables many part types or part families to be handled in one system, and when part changes are made, the system is easy to reprogram. It can also be programmed for part sequencing applications, for example selecting in sequence a bolt, washer, and nut from a random mixture of those parts stored in a parts feeder bowl. This system also offers limited inspection capabilities by rejecting unacceptable parts such as broken parts.

Retaining Pre-Established Orientation

As previously mentioned during the discussion on designing parts for automated assembly, consideration should be given to the possibility of retaining the orientation of parts established during preceding manufacturing operations or by an outside supplier. Sometimes this is the only feasible and/or economical method of handling fragile, easily damaged, or interlocking parts. Methods of retaining pre-established orientation include guide tracks, magazines, reel and tape carriers, indexing devices, and trays.

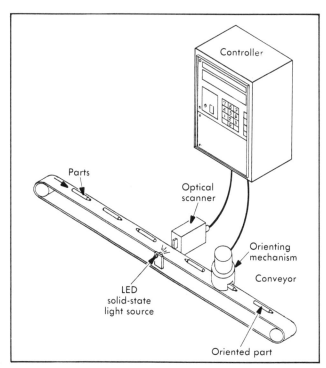

Fig. 12-34 Programmable parts feeder with vision system. (*FMC Corp., Material Handling Equipment Div.*)

PARTS FEEDING AND ORIENTING

TABLE 12-7
Suitability of Hopper Feeders for
Various Parts and Requirements*

	Types of Hopper Feeders				
Type of Part or Feeding Requirements	Drum or Tumble	Barrel	Vibratory	Centrifeed	Rotary
Headed parts	1	1	1	1	1
Washers............................	1	1	1	1	1
Pins	1	1	1	1	...
Long parts	...	...	...	...	...
Nesting parts	...	...	1	...	...
Tangling parts	...	...	1		
Fragile parts	...	...	1	1	
Dirty or oily parts	2	1	3	2	2
Scrap and foreign material present	3	...	1	...	...
Highly finished parts	...	...	1	1	2
Ground, hardened parts	...	2	1	1	2
High feed rate.......................	2	2	2	1	2
Complicated orienting.................	1	2	1		
Large capacity	1	4	4	4	3
Multiple chuting	...	...	1	...	...

Suitability ratings are (1) recommended, (2) sometimes used, (3) requires special design or consideration, and (4) usually supplied automatically from reserve hopper capacity.

Guide tracks. In some cases, guide tracks can transfer parts directly from a manufacturing process to the assembly machine. Some tracks invert the parts, with U-bends or other means, to ensure correct presentation at the assembly station.

Magazines. A magazine is a holding and dispensing device that is stacked with oriented parts. Designs of magazines vary depending on the parts to be held. Stacks of parts can be placed in or on inclined guide rails, tubes, rods, arbors, or other guide means.

Magazines are commonly filled at a preceding operation and placed on the assembly machine as required. Stampings from blanking or forming dies can generally be pushed directly into the magazines by the punches. Hopper feeders are sometimes used to feed parts that will not track edge to edge in vertical magazines. In some cases, magazines mounted on the assembly machines are manually loaded.

Magazines almost always present parts one at a time in exact position and are synchronized with the assembly machines. If there is little or no nesting of the parts, the parts have no burrs or flash, and the parts are not too thin or warped, a part can be pushed or stripped from the bottom of the stack by a reciprocating blade approximately the thickness of the part, using a suitable obstruction to prevent more than one part from moving. The stack moves downward by gravity or pressure. Similar means are used for stripping parts from the top of a magazine, with the stack of parts being pushed upward by a spring, counterweight, indexing motor, or servodrive mechanism.

A magazine feeder for nested covers is shown in Fig. 12-35, with the positioning blade in its outermost position. On the return stroke, slice blades separate one cover and allow it to drop through a relieved section to the lower slide level. Where nesting is a problem, stripping fingers or grips (see Fig. 12-36) or escapement means are used to separate the parts and drop them one at a time to a loading station or positioning slide.

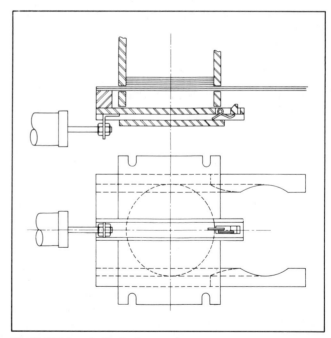

Fig. 12-35 Magazine feeder for nested covers.

Magazine feeders are useful for the high-volume assembly of many types of parts that are difficult to orient automatically, cannot be conveniently handled in a track, would require too long a track for practical storage, or that come in oriented stacks from some previous operation.

Typical parts fed from magazines include those large in area relative to the thickness, such as gaskets. Some parts, because of

TABLE 12-7—*Continued*

		Types of Hopper Feeders			
Leaf	Reciprocating	Elevating	Shaft	Brush or Pocket	Pocketed Drum
	1				
1	2	3	. . .	2	
1	2	1	. . .	1	
1	1	1	. . .	1	1
1	. . .	1	1	. . .	. . .
. . .	. . .	3			
2	3	2			
. . .	. . .	3			
2	2	2	1	1	1
2	1	1	1		
2	2	2	2	2	2
		3			
. . .	3	1	3		
. . .	. . .	3	. . .	. . .	

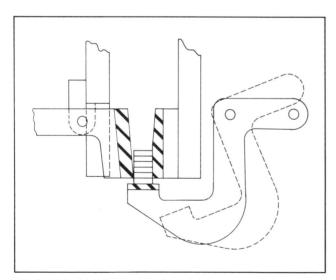

Fig. 12-36 Rubber-faced grips release the parts and regrip all but the one left on the transfer tong.

their fragile nature or easily damaged finish or edges, can be handled only by preorienting in a magazine.

Reel and tape carriers. Thin stampings are often produced in a continuous strip without separation. The strips are wound into coils for storage or placement on assembly machines, where the parts are sheared from the strip as required for assembly. This method of retaining components in strip form until assembly is often called bandoliering. It is a common method for feeding electrical connectors and other parts produced in progressive dies.

Reel feeding is also used for dispensing components mounted on continuous strips of adhesive tape or film. Electrical connectors are frequently supplied to an assembly operation on tape.

Tray feeders. Trays having individual compartments for holding oriented parts to be assembled are common, especially when parts cannot be stacked because of their delicate nature or because their configurations make stacking impossible. The trays, often vacuum formed, are generally loaded manually, but this can sometimes be done automatically. An unloading mechanism, pick-and-place unit, or robot is required to transfer parts from the tray to a conveyor or feeding device. Centerline to centerline parts spacing and proper tray location are essential.

Indexing devices. For many parts, handling without contact with adjacent parts is desirable. Parts with highly finished ground surfaces subject to damage or that will not stack because of shape, such as spark plugs, are handled individually in pockets in an indexing means to present them one at a time to an unloading position. The carrying means with the pockets is often interchangeable and circulates from operation to operation, being refilled and returned to the unloading or dispensing means.

Manufacturing at Assembly

Manufacturing of components on demand at assembly machines is often impractical or uneconomical for many applications. There are some parts, however, where this practice is desirable, thus eliminating the cost of handling, transferring, and orienting the parts.

Machining and grinding operations. Operations such as broaching, turning, boring, drilling, reaming, milling, threading, and grinding can be performed on automated assembly machines, but the practice is not generally recommended. This is because of possible problems caused by chips, abrasive grains, burrs, cutting fluids, and lubricants and contamination of feeders, nests, orienters, and the products being assembled. Also, machining cycles are generally longer than those required for assembly, and workholding pallets would have to be designed to withstand higher forces. In some applications, parts or partial assemblies are transferred to off-line metal-removal modules and then returned to the assembly line.

MANUFACTURING AT ASSEMBLY

The use of lasers and electron beams for cutting, drilling, and other machining operations, however, is practical for some automated assembly applications, with provisions for the removal of gaseous products.

Forming operations. Press operations performed on or adjacent to assembly machines are common, especially for thin, difficult-to-handle parts and those that tend to adhere to each other, such as shims, washers, gaskets, and springs. Provisions must be made for stock feeding and the handling of offal. Possible problems include the need for replacing stock and maintaining the dies, which cause downtime. Deep drawing and complex forming operations may make this practice impractical.

In some applications, parts can be blanked directly into the assemblies. In other cases, the formed parts must be transferred to the assemblies. Secondary forming of parts carried in a web or strip is sometimes desirable prior to or after separating the parts at assembly. Rollforming, burnishing, and spinning operations are sometimes performed on automated assembly machines.

Spring winding. Because of the difficulty in handling and feeding some springs that tend to tangle, they are sometimes made on assembly machines by coupling spring winders to the machines. Careful control of the wire material and diameter is essential, and buffer storage of the springs produced may be required. Periodic changing of the wire coils and tools is also necessary, resulting in downtime of the assembly machine.

Sometimes secondary forming operations can be performed on the springs after winding. Problems may be encountered if the springs require tempering, but this can sometimes be done by providing induction coils. Changing the material from which the springs are made may eliminate the need for tempering.

Wire terminations. Equipment is available to automatically strip insulation from wires and apply terminals. In some applications, the terminals are cut or removed from strips and clinched to the wires by swaging. In other cases, the terminals are soldered to the wires.

Supplementary operations. There are other operations sometimes performed integral with assembly and at other times subsequent to assembly. These include washing, painting or coating, lubricating, inspecting and testing (discussed later in this chapter), counting, weighing, marking, and packaging. Formed-in-place gaskets are being produced on assembly machines from hoppers of liquid silicone compounds or other materials. Liquids are readily metered by volume, and powders can be dispensed by volume or weight.

Serialized stamping, etching, or coding (identifying the shift, day, month, and year the assembly was produced) are frequently done to certify inspecting and testing operations. Such information can prove valuable for warranty verification and in case products have to be recalled.

Bulk-Storage Feeders

Bulk-storage feeders provide storage and maintain a supply of parts for orienting and feeding. Major types include overhead gravity-feed storage hoppers and elevating-belt bulk feeders. Selection of a specific type requires consideration of part size(s), production requirements, the method to be used for loading the bulk storage unit, floor space and height limitations, frequency of changeover if more than one part is involved, and the condition of the parts—dry or wet, clean or dirty, soft or hard, and the presence of burrs, flash, or chips.

After considering all pertinent factors, the minimum bulk-load capacity is recommended because excessive storage in

hoppers or bins can make maintenance and changeover cumbersome. Level sensors with warning signals or lights are available to detect a low quantity of parts in the hoppers or bins. Means for washing, cooling, or lubricating parts in the hoppers or bins are also available.

Gravity-feed storage hoppers. Gravity-feed hoppers offer an economical and simple method of supplying parts to orienting feeders having limited bulk capacity. Some units are equipped with vibrators that can be energized by a parts-level detector in the orienting feeder. Other units may be arranged to accept standard drop-bottom tubs. Parts feed by gravity from a bin as the orienting feeder conveys the parts away from the bin opening. Overhead hoppers are also available with a powered-belt base that can meter parts on demand to the orienting unit.

Elevating-belt bulk feeders. With these feeders, a cleated fabric or steel belt or chain conveyor lifts parts from a storage bin and elevates them to a discharge chute (see Fig. 12-37). These units provide storage near or on the floor and can be supplied with either manual or automatic controls actuated by a level detector. Units using magnetic belts rather than cleated belts are available for feeding fragile ferrous parts. Orienting or selecting of parts can take place during elevating or in the track or supplementary feeding unit.

Elevator bulk feeders are commonly used to supply large or heavy parts from storage. Some units can handle bars to 24" (610 mm) long and 15" (380 mm) diam. Standard storage capacities range from 1 to 70 ft^3 (0.03 to 2 m^3). Variable-speed drives are available.

Another type of elevator bulk feeder consists of a floor-mounted bin into which bulk parts are loaded. The bin is then elevated and dumps the parts into a stationary bulk hopper. This method is generally used when the parts cannot be handled reliably on a cleated belt or chain conveyor.

Vibratory Bowl Feeders

Vibratory bowl feeders are one of the most common types of devices for feeding and orienting small cylindrical, flat, or other shaped components. By the use of directional vibration, randomly oriented parts loaded in bulk into bowls are caused to climb gently ramped tracks attached to and encircling the inner

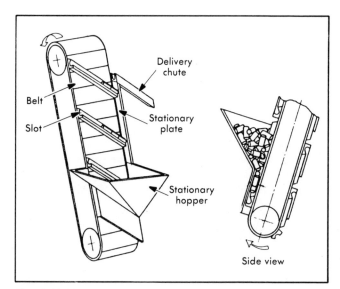

Fig. 12-37 Elevator hopper feeder.

walls of the bowls. The bowls are mounted on vibratory drive units (see Fig. 12-38) that cause the bowls to reciprocate vertically while oscillating horizontally. The bottoms of the bowls are generally made slightly convex or conical to assist the outward movement of the components as they rotate around the bowl under the influence of the vibration.

Parts in the vibrating bowls move uniformly, largely independent of adjacent parts. The fact that the parts are conveyed in a controlled manner, rather than by rolling or sliding, makes these feeders one of the most versatile types for orienting parts having relatively complex geometric shapes. The gentle feeding action permits many fragile parts to be fed and enhances separation of nested and tangled parts.

In many applications, bowls referred to as outside-tooled bowls are used where high feed rates and/or complicated orientations are involved. These bowls consist of an inside spiral track for elevating the parts from the inner storage area and an outside spiral track (attached outside the bowl wall) that travels around the bowl wall in a level or slightly downhill plane. The inner track is normally used for elevating parts in bulk, with the orientation being performed on the outside track. Rejected parts are returned to the inside storage area by a return pan encircling the outer bowl wall. Dual-bowl feeders having two bowls mounted on the same drive unit are available, each bowl handling a specific size part. Multilayered vibratory bowl feeders have been reported for supplying several different parts to assembly operations.

Bowl capacities. Vibratory bowl feeders are available with bowls as large as 72" (1829 mm) diam and will handle a wide variety of parts in different sizes one part at a time. For most applications, the vibratory bowls have a maximum diameter of 24" (610 mm). Sections subject to high wear are generally coated and sometimes hardened. They can be tooled with multiple tracks and outlets and be arranged with auxiliary storage hoppers to maintain an efficient level of parts in the bowls.

Feed rates of up to 500 ipm (12 700 mm/min) are common with vibratory bowl feeders. The feed rate used depends on the part shape, material, and weight and the required orientation. Feed rates to 800 ipm (20 320 mm/min) have been achieved with special bowl designs and tooling. Feed rates are usually adjusted by means of an electronic control device that varies the voltage to an electromagnetic vibrator. Techniques used to increase the overall output of a feeder include the following:

- Altering the vibration amplitude or frequency.
- Varying the spring angle of the drive unit.
- Using multiple tracks and feed chutes.
- Converging lines of feed.
- Merging multiple tracks into one.
- Stacking bowls two or more high.
- Preorienting and merging.
- Bonding rubber, oriental bristle rug, or other materials to the inner surfaces of the bowls and tracks to increase the frictional driving forces.

Orienting with inside-tooled feeders. A variety of selector and orientation devices (called tooling) are used to properly position parts supplied to or from vibratory bowl feeders. These include track projections and cutouts, spill or fan (strikeoff) rails, wiper cams or blades, changes in track widths, auxiliary selectors (rails or hooks), and air blowoffs. Most operate on the principle of returning unoriented parts back into the bowl for recycling and delivering properly oriented parts to an outlet chute at the top of the bowl. Some devices reorient parts to desired attitudes. Bowls are also available with programmable, optical, and sonic parts recognition systems that identify and discharge only correctly oriented parts. The first step in orientation is arranging parts in a single line. This is accomplished using wipers, pressure breaks, and dishouts.

One manufacturer's system identifies part position by optical recognition (see Fig. 12-39). It utilizes the principles of photoelectric detection to ensure the discharge of correctly oriented parts. This system reads part position by comparing the light/dark pattern from an arrangement of photodetectors with a reference pattern in a separate programmable controller.

As a part passes over the track plate, an infrared light activates the sensor's photodetectors to identify part position. This information is used by the controller to activate an air jet or similar device to eject a misoriented part from the feeder

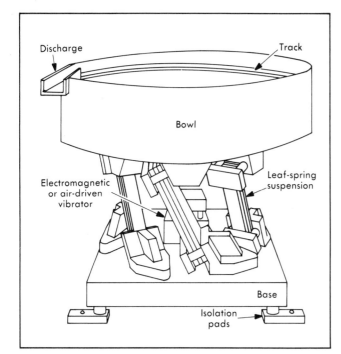

Fig. 12-38 Vibratory bowl feeder.

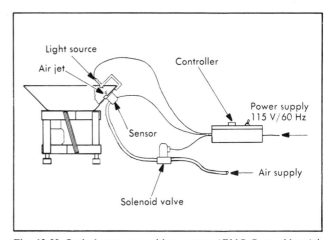

Fig. 12-39 Optical parts recognition system. (*FMC Corp., Material Handling Equipment Div.*)

VIBRATORY FEEDERS

track. For sorting or gaging purposes, rejected parts can be diverted to a secondary feed line or into an adjacent bin.

The simplest means of selecting, when applicable, is to remove sections of the track (see Fig. 12-40) to drop out or overbalance unwanted parts. Reduced supporting surfaces, called cutouts, are used to allow some parts to fall off. Obstructions, generally called wipers or cams, are sometimes placed on the tracks to interfere with unwanted parts, forcing them off the track and back into the bowl. Shaped tracks or profiling can be designed to accept only properly oriented parts, but this limits feed rates. Powered brush wheels or shaped, notched wheels, usually made of resilient material, are sometimes used when there is a possibility of jamming between stationary wipers or cams and the parts.

Typical applications. The versatility of vibratory bowl feeders has applications too numerous to discuss in the limited space available in this volume. The variety of applications possible are limited only by the ingenuity of the designer; only a few typical applications are discussed here. A single bowl can sometimes be used to sort different sizes of common family parts by providing adjustable tooling. Many fasteners are fed through vibratory bowl feeders and into thread-rolling machines.

Untangling clamps. Assembly of spring-type clamps to the ends of tie rod tubes for steering linkages eluded automation for some time because of tangling and interlocking of the clamps. In the bulk stage, the clamps were often severely tangled, with up to four clamps interlocked. This resulted in jamming of the feed tracks and subsequent downtime of the assembly machine.

Close cooperation between the supplier of the vibratory bowl feeders and the manufacturer of the assembly machines led to an ingenious solution. It involved use of a blade cam on each vibratory bowl. A ridge, projecting from the cam into the feed track, untangles the clamps and positions them in single file. Vibratory motion of the bowl causes the slots in the clamp to nest on a narrow, raised rail at the end of the track, thus providing proper orientation. Clamps not untangled and oriented fall back to the bottom of the bowl for recycling.

Ceramic substrates. Tiny white ceramic substrates present problems in that they have no external features to facilitate orientation mechanically. Measuring 0.68″ (17.3 mm) long by 0.16″ (4.1 mm) wide by 0.04″ (1.0 mm) thick, they do have a black stripe of electrically resistive material printed off-center on one face. The orientation problems presented by these parts was solved by using reflective photocells to identify the printed side of each substrate. Next, the offset direction of the printed stripe was identified for use on vibratory feeder bowls.

The first selector, shown at the top in Fig. 12-41 orients the parts so that their printed faces are all in one direction. A reflective-type photocell is normally kept actuated by a light source. When a part passes in front of the photocell with its unprinted face toward the photocell, the white surface reflects the light emitted by the photocell, thus maintaining its actuation. However, when a part passes with its printed face toward the photocell, the reflected light is reduced, causing photocell deactuation. This energizes a solenoid valve that allows a blast of air to blow the part onto its opposite face, as shown.

Parts exiting from this selector are merged into a single feed line, with the printed faces of the substrates up. The parts are

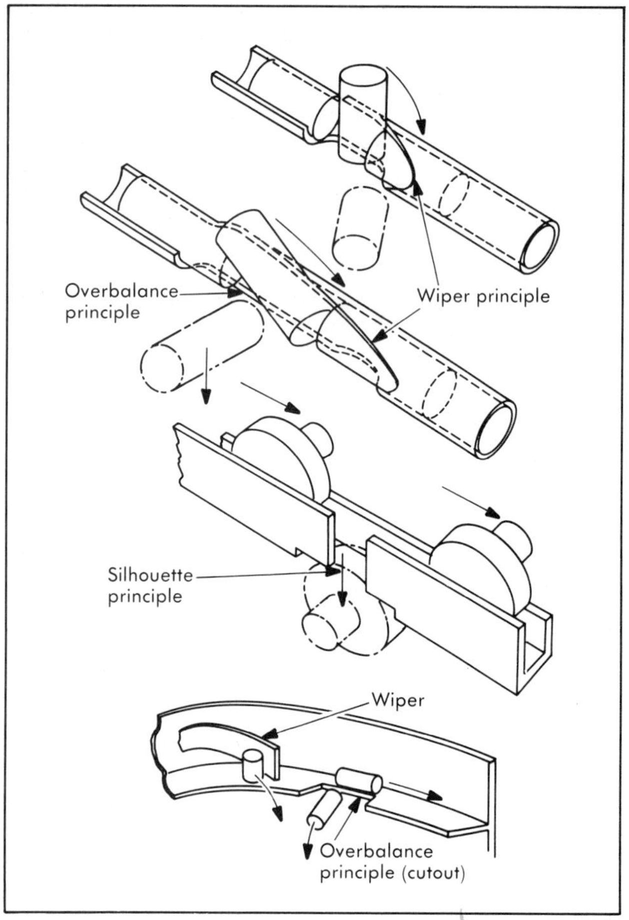

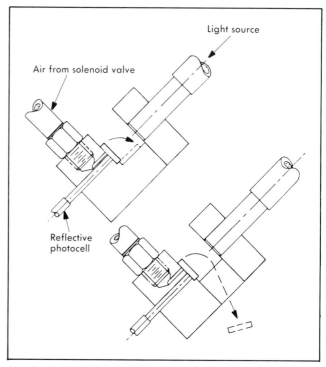

Fig. 12-40 Use of cutouts and wipers for vibratory feeder orienting.

Labels in Fig. 12-40: Overbalance principle; Wiper principle; Silhouette principle; Wiper; Overbalance principle (cutout)

Fig. 12-41 Photocell selector at top orients ceramic parts so that printed faces are all in one direction. Selector at bottom blows incorrectly oriented parts back into vibratory bowl.

Labels in Fig. 12-41: Air from solenoid valve; Light source; Reflective photocell then mechanically inverted so that they enter a second selector, seen at the bottom in Fig. 12-41, with their printed faces down. In this selector, the photocell will only see parts having a printed stripe that is below center. Such parts, being incorrectly oriented, will be blown from the track and into the vibratory bowl for recirculation.

Another vibratory bowl device developed to select oriented ceramic substrates is shown in Fig. 12-42. In this case, the parts may or may not be printed at the time of feeding. The only identifiable feature on each part is a 20° bevel on one of the longer edges.

When a correctly oriented part is fed onto the carbide knife edge of this selector, the vibratory action of the feeder causes the part to slide from the knife edge onto the lower rail because of its beveled edge. Misoriented parts feed the full length of the knife edge and fall from the end onto the lower track. Drop height is such that most of the parts rotate 90° during the fall. Those that do present a new edge to the next selector.

Two lines, each having four selectors, are used in the primary stage of the feeder. At 100% efficiency, the select-and-rotate action should result in orienting 50% of the parts fed. This reduces recirculation requirements because the number of parts correctly oriented in the first selector averages 12.5%.

The two lines of selected parts are merged into a single track, and the parts are passed through a final selector before discharge. Nonoriented parts are recirculated after passing through the fourth primary selector in each line. Using this system, oriented parts are fed at a rate of more than 180 per minute.

The vibratory bowl on which these selectors are used feeds the substrates through two separate printing operations. It can also be used to feed a high-speed sorter that inspects the parts for electrical resistance and continuity.

Feeding springs. Compression-type springs are among the most difficult components to feed automatically in high-volume applications, but several methods have been developed for untangling and feeding oriented springs. One system uses timed, pulsating air blasts to agitate and separate tangled springs that are bulk loaded into an upper bowl. The same air supply drives a number of springs through outlet nozzles and into plastic tubes. The tubes, which serve as magazines and are normally full, convey the springs, end to end, to manual opera-

tor pickoffs, portable escapements, or fully automatic escapement mechanisms. Periodic reversal of the airflow direction automatically clears the outlet nozzles of any tangled springs, driving them back into the bowl, thus eliminating downtime due to jamming.

Slight modifications of springs may be necessary to ensure successful feeding. It also helps to have two coils close together at each end of the spring or about three coils close together in the middle of the spring. On tapered diameter springs, the end of the wire at the larger diameter end should be drawn over the center of the spring axis to prevent tangling. Springs with two tapered ends should have at least three or four coils close together at both ends. It is also necessary that springs supplied to the bowl be dry and clean.

Another method of feeding springs is a unit that serves as a bulk feeder and preliminary untangler. It also maintains the level of parts in a vibratory bowl by means of a proximity control switch. On demand, the unit oscillates vertically to allow parts to pass through grids into the vibratory bowl, thus preventing the entry of large clumps of tangled springs. In cases of extreme interlocking problems, a mechanical separator can be incorporated in this system. Interlocked parts enter the separator and are ejected as single springs prior to feeding through the orienting and selecting mechanisms in the vibratory bowl.

Assembling within vibratory bowls. There are applications where certain parts can be assembled within the vibratory bowls themselves. When applicable, this approach can result in a considerable reduction in cost. One example is a system for assembling bolts and washers. Washers in one vibratory bowl are fed clockwise, while bolts in another bowl are fed counterclockwise. As the bolts pass through an assembly section, washers drop over their shanks.

Built into this system are checking devices to make sure that a washer, and not more than one, has been placed on each bolt. Washers that do not fall on the bolts are ejected back into the proper bowl for refeeding. Satisfactory assemblies are discharged to a placement station where they are positioned in nests on an assembly machine.

One manufacturer provides a similar type of assembly operation utilizing only one custom-built bowl. Bolts are fed upward on an inside track where they are hung by their heads. At the same time, washers are fed single file on the bowl's outside track. The two components then merge, and the bolts are assembled into the washers. Any bolt without a washer is rejected back into the bowl for refeeding.

Handling microcomponents. Microcomponents such as diodes, chips, dice, and ferrite memory cores used in the semiconductor industry present their own class of feeding/orienting problems. Some of these parts are as small as 0.010" (0.25 mm) square and many have to be oriented so that they leave the feeder with the proper side up.

Feeder bowls for such parts made by one firm are custom machined from aluminum bar stock. Precision machining of these compact bowls is difficult, but the surface finish produced is superior to that of conventional cast bowls. This provides gentler handling and less abrasion of delicate parts, especially semiconductor dice, integrated circuits, and similar items. Another advantage is that the bowls can be machined to whatever track width, helix angle, exit configuration, or orienting feature required for a specific application. The bowls are normally plated or anodized to resist wear.

Feeder drives for the vibratory bowls are of cup core design with fully enclosed coil and small magnetic gap. In addition,

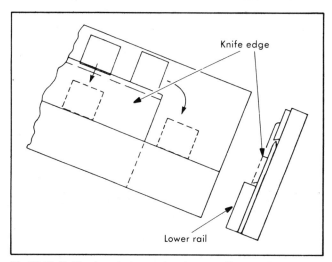

Fig. 12-42 Knife-edge selector uses bevel on one of longer edges on each ceramic substrate to properly orient the parts.

VIBRATORY FEEDERS

armature overhang provides shielding to eliminate stray magnetic fields. Feed rates are infinitely variable from less than 1 to more than 100 parts per second. Models are available for clockwise or counterclockwise movement of the parts.

Enlarged views of sections of these feeder bowls are shown in Fig. 12-43. In the top view, parts traveling clockwise have reached the end of the inclined portion of the track and are about to slide onto the final, level part of the track. The parts being fed are dice having a solder bump on one side. It is necessary to orient them with the bumps up.

Near the end of the inclined track, there is a groove running parallel to the track and near its left-hand edge. Dice with their bump surface up will slide over this groove and onto the level portion of the track. Those with their bumps facing down will get caught in the groove and be dumped back into the bowl for refeeding when they reach that portion of the groove interrupted by a cutaway section. Debris such as pointed slivers of silicon are also disposed of in this manner.

The bottom view shows the dice after they have traveled to the end of the level track. They are prevented from advancing farther by an externally mounted stop. Properly oriented dice are commonly removed from the track, one at a time, by a vacuum lifting device that transfers them from the feeder to a test or assembly station. Any dice reaching the level track that have climbed each other and overlap slide off onto an overflow track. This overflow track, which is slanted toward the outer edge of the bowl, carries the dice to a chute for return to the bowl and refeeding.

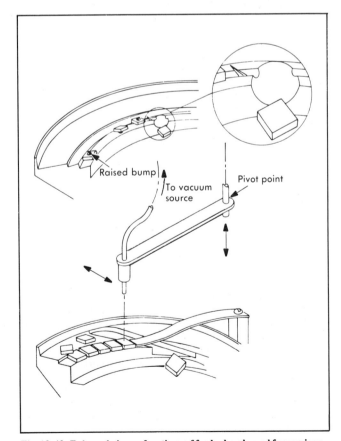

Fig. 12-43 Enlarged views of sections of feeder bowls used for semiconductor microcomponents.

In-Line Vibratory Feeders

In-line (linear or straight-line) vibratory feeders work on the same principle as vibratory bowl feeders and are made up of two vibratory conveyors (see Fig. 12-44). One conveyor acts as a reservoir and supplies the randomly oriented parts to the second conveyor, which is tooled to discharge a single line of oriented parts. Parts rejected by the orientation conveyor slide back onto a recirculating surface. Multiple in-line feeders are placed in tandem to supply odd-shaped parts. A pair of feeders can also be set side by side to move parts in opposite directions. Faster feeds are attained if the in-line vibratory feeders are inclined at an angle of about 5°.

Horizontal Belt Feeders

Horizontal belt feeders are similar in concept to the in-line vibratory feeders, but they are nonvibratory and used for parts having simple configurations. Belts are employed to convey the parts, as shown in Fig. 12-45. The belt in the bulk storage area, which is controlled by a parts-level detector, meters small quantities of unoriented parts to the recirculating belt, which conveys them onto the discharge belt. Wiper blades, air jets, and other tooling are mounted in the orientation area. Improperly positioned parts are rejected and fall back onto the recirculating belt. Extremely high feed rates are obtainable, and there is a minimum of part damage with this type of equipment.

Nonvibratory Hopper Feeders

A wide variety of nonvibratory hopper feeders is used for supplying parts to assembly operations. Some of the more common types are discussed in this section.

Centrifugal feeders. In this type of feeder, the centrifugal and gravity forces resulting from the rotation of a slightly conical disc in the bottom of a stationary hopper (bowl) causes the parts to slide to the periphery of the hopper. They are then carried by the disc to an escapement gate or profile where they are discharged in a single line. Smaller diameter centrifugal feeders now available are replacing some vibratory feeders.

On some feeders, parts are transferred from a rotating disc to an orienting rim that rotates around the disc independently and at a different speed (see Fig. 12-46). The size, shape, and feeding characteristics of the part being handled determine the opti-

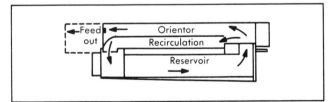

Fig. 12-44 In-line vibratory feeder.

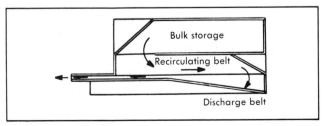

Fig. 12-45 Horizontal belt feeder.

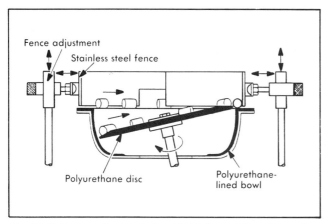

Fig. 12-46 Rotary orienting feeder. (*FMC Corp., Material Handling Equipment Div.*)

mum speed relationship, which is factory set. A variable-speed controller increases or decreases the desired parts-per-minute rate while still maintaining the speed ratio of the two rotating components. Because of their design, centrifugal-type feeders offer gentle handling, quiet operation, and much higher feed rates for a wide range of parts suited to this type rather than vibratory feeding.

Although centrifugal feeders are sometimes used for parts having simple configurations, such as bushings and bearing rollers, they can be tooled to handle more complex parts. Feed rates ranging from 20 to 2000 parts per minute are possible for a wide variety of applications. With the advent of high-speed, computerized, continuous-motion assembly machines, centrifugal feeders are being commonly used instead of vibratory feeders.

One feeder developed to feed forged steel, ball-joint sockets is shown schematically in Fig. 12-47. Attempts to handle these parts in overhead-mounted vibratory parts feeders with gravity delivery tracks proved to be unreliable, orientation was diffi-

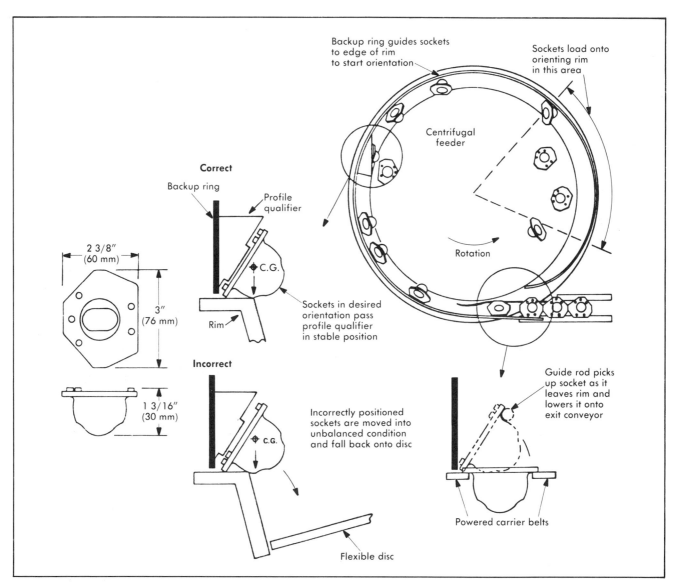

Fig. 12-47 Centrifugal feeder for ball-joint sockets simplified orientation and reduced the sound levels generated. (*Hoppmann Corp.*)

NONVIBRATORY FEEDERS

cult, and operation was very noisy. With the centrifugal feeder shown, orientation is simple, sound levels are maintained at or below 80 dB (A), and from 40 to 50 sockets are delivered per minute from random bulk.

The positions of five short projections on each socket flange with relation to a profile qualifier allow properly oriented parts to leave the bowl, while incorrectly positioned sockets fall back onto the disc. Guide rods at the feeder exit are positioned to pick up the flange lips and lower the sockets onto a powered delivery conveyor.

Another feeder, the rotary bowl feeder, uses gravitational and frictional forces to transfer parts (see Fig. 12-48). Parts are gravity fed down the slope of the cone-shaped bowl to the sloped bowl wall. The sloped wall efficiently transfers parts up a stationary ramp where they are discharged onto the rotating bowl rim. Here they are singulated and oriented. These feeders are noted for their high-speed feeding and orientation of a wide range of parts suited to this method of parts feeding.

Centerboard hopper feeders. With these feeders (see Fig. 12-49), a centerboard is arranged to be alternately raised and lowered through a fixed hopper, usually having its base sloping toward the centerboard. Some of the parts in the hopper, properly oriented to fit the shaped upper edge of the centerboard, will stay on and at the top position, slide or roll off into a

feed track. With a deeply slotted centerboard or two adjacent centerboards (spaced apart to receive the bodies of the parts), these feeders can handle long-headed pieces satisfactorily.

Bladed or hooked wheels. With these feeders, a rotary wheel with blades or hooks is used to feed parts from a fixed hopper. In the design shown in Fig. 12-50, a rotating bladed wheel (paddle wheel) causes some parts to fall into a shaped groove in the bottom of the hopper. These oriented parts are raised by the

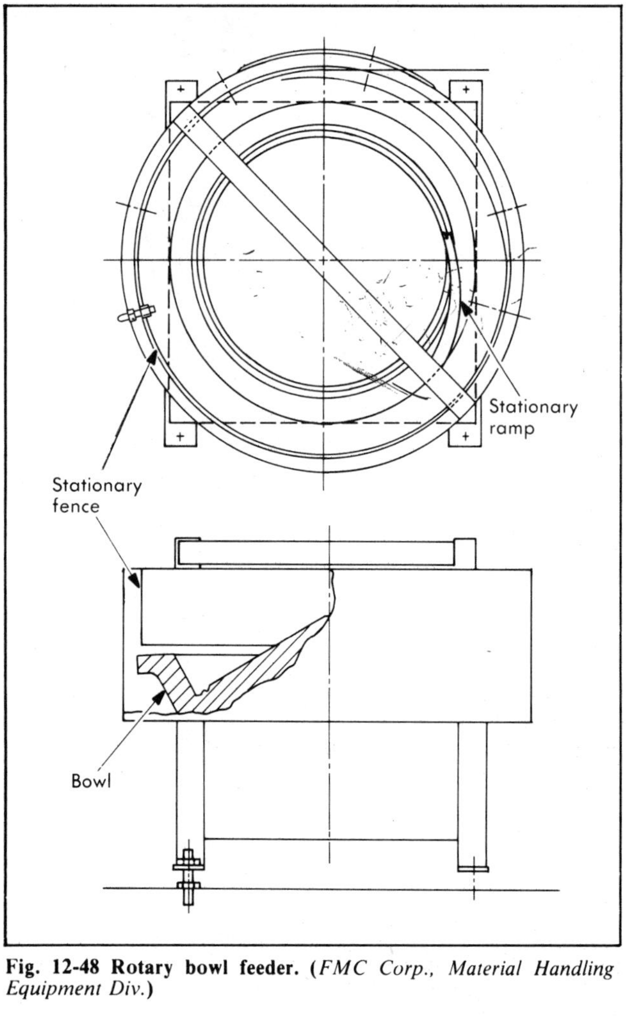

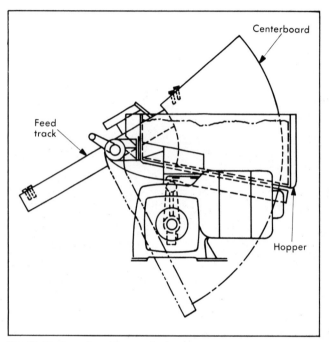

Fig. 12-49 Centerboard hopper feeder.

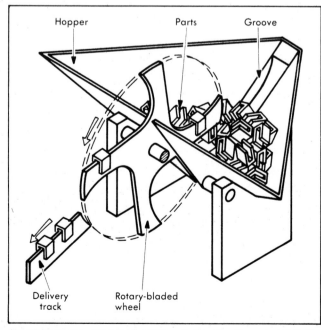

Fig. 12-48 Rotary bowl feeder. (*FMC Corp., Material Handling Equipment Div.*)

Fig. 12-50 Rotary-bladed wheel lifts parts from fixed hopper and drops them on track.

blades and slide onto a feed track. In some designs, the parts slide into tracks from the hoppers without being lifted. Other feeder designs have hooks projecting from the rotating wheel to enter the open ends of cup-shaped parts, lift the parts from the hopper, and drop them into delivery chutes.

Reciprocating feeders. These feeders (see Fig. 12-51) are used primarily for handling balls or symmetrical cylinders of small size, although end-for-end orienting is sometimes performed outside the hopper. Commonly, a tube exit chute is reciprocated through parts held in a funnel-shaped receptacle.

Often the tube is stationary and the parts holder is reciprocated (view *a*). Bearing balls and rolls are fed through multiple tubes for assembly. Reciprocating blade-type hoppers, such as the one seen in view *b*, pick up headed parts on the upper end of a reciprocating blade and elevate them to a stationary gravity track. As the blade stops at the top of its upward travel, the parts slide off onto the external chute where orienting is performed.

Rotary disc hoppers. These feeders usually have one feature in common. A rotating disc or sleeve carrying peripheral exit gates allows parts properly oriented to pass the gates to a chute section. The simplest of these is the pin gate—so called because the gates are pins, shaped or straight, as shown in Fig. 12-52. Pin gates are used for fast feeding or simple parts having diameters greater than their length. Rotary hoppers can be designed in endless variety. They may operate vertically, inclined, or horizontally; may have single or multiple rows of exit gates; and may be driven steadily or intermittently. Figure 12-53 shows a geneva-actuated pin design discharging from the bottom of an inclined tunnel gate and having a dejamming slide at the side that clears each gate as it stops. Magnets are sometimes placed in the rotating disc to lift components from the top of the pile in the hopper.

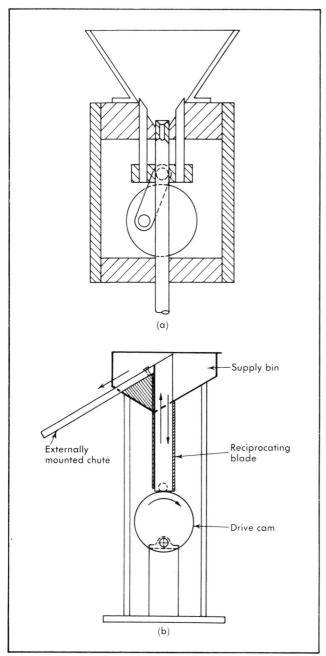

Fig. 12-51 Reciprocating feeders: (a) for reciprocating either the parts bin or the exit tube and (b) reciprocating-blade type for headed parts. (*FMC Corp., Material Handling Equipment Div.*)

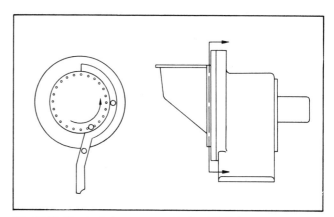

Fig. 12-52 Standard pin-gate rotary feeder. (*KDI Corp.*)

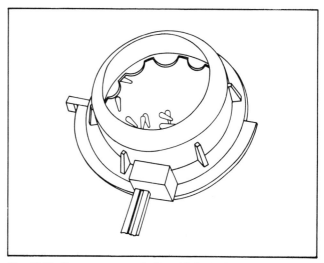

Fig. 12-53 Gate-type rotary feeder with intermittent geneva drive. (*KDI Corp.*)

AUXILIARY ORIENTING DEVICES

Pocket hoppers. Pocket hoppers (see Fig. 12-54) are frequently used to count batches of balls or small rollers and may be arranged with a rotating or indexing plate for automatic feeding. Pockets arranged on the periphery of a drum (see Fig. 12-55) are used to feed multiple chutes with a time succession of simple parts. As shown, mold cavities on a moving belt are loaded with pop sticks. Rotating discs with shaped pockets are often mounted at an angle so the pocket is moved through a pile of parts and then discharges at or near the high point of the revolution, either through an opening of the chute into which it falls or by being wiped off and guided into a side chute. Fast-feeding hoppers of the latter type are used in large quantities for feeding buttons.

Tumbling barrels and drums. These feeders are often used for parts susceptible to tangling or nesting and dirty parts, but they are not suitable for fragile parts or those that have been hardened and finish ground. The feeders carry parts in a rotating barrel or drum so arranged with vanes or buckets as to lift the parts and drop them on or into various orienting or chute arrangements. Basically, a drum feeder is a means to recirculate parts, but it is very versatile because special orienting means to suit most parts can be used. Parts are subject to a tumbling action and by use of a gap between drum and pan or by screen sections in the drum much debris such as dirt or chips can be eliminated in the hopper.

Drum hoppers have large capacity for their size and can be lined with plastic, fiberglass, or bonded neoprene. Although they can easily be baffled to reduce the dropping distance of parts, they are not advisable for fragile parts. Drum hoppers do not always provide uniformly high feed rates and tend to be noisy. They are recommended for tangling parts and for applications requiring multiple chutes, high delivery rates, complicated or positive orienting, and large capacity.

Auxiliary Orienting Devices

Although orienting of parts to be assembled is often done in the various feeders just discussed, auxiliary orienting devices are often needed, especially for parts having complex shapes.

Many orienting devices have been designed using rolls, rotating wheels, vacuum, magnets, probes, sensing units, and other means. It is recommended that such devices be arranged for fail-safe operation whenever possible. It is better to reject a few properly oriented parts with improperly oriented parts than to accept improperly oriented parts.

Orienting rolls. Tapered rollers are often fed into an auxiliary orienting device, such as the one shown in Fig. 12-56, in an end-to-end position, with either end leading. The device is equipped with orienting rolls to position the parts with their larger diameter ends facing upward.

Orienting rolls are also used to feed and orient parts at high rates. Such devices consist of ground rolls mounted at a slight angle and rotating in opposite directions (see Fig. 12-57). Tapered rollers for bearings are being fed and oriented at rates of 400 or more per minute with such devices.

Rotating wheels. Some parts can be sorted by allowing them to fall on rotating wheels fitted with pins or having shaped holes. Correctly positioned parts are guided off the wheel into

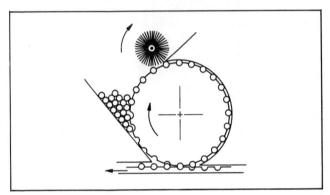

Fig. 12-55 Pop-stick feeder.

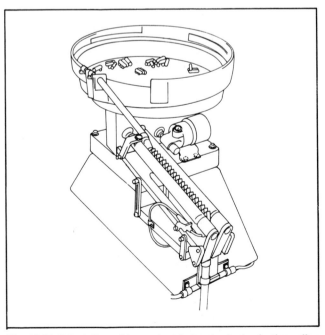

Fig. 12-56 Orientation of tapered parts by standard orienting rolls. (*FMC Corp., Material Handling Equipment Div.*)

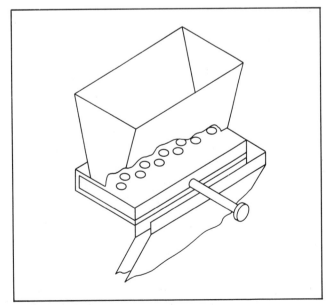

Fig. 12-54 Simple form of pocket hopper.

feed tracks or allowed to drop off into a return pan after being carried part way around. Wheels may be mounted vertically or at any angle.

Figure 12-58 shows the use of a flat wheel behind which is placed a magnet adjustable for position relative to the wheel. The device feeds symmetrical steel-backed silver contacts. If the contacts have the steel adjacent to the wheel face, they are carried past the dropoff into the outlet feed track. If the silver face is adjacent to the wheel face, the magnetic field is not strong enough to hold the part, and it slides off into the reject chute.

Probes. The use of a probe to orient cup-shaped cylindrical parts having a hole in one end is illustrated in Fig. 12-59. Components are fed down a vertical chute at random (their ends in different positions). If the closed end of the lowermost component faces the reciprocating probe, the component is pushed forward beyond the edge of a funnel-shaped chute and falls by gravity in the desired oriented position (with its open end leading). The wedge surface of a spring-mounted pawl guides the part to fall in the oriented position.

If the open end of a component faces the probe, the probe enters the hole and pushes the component across the entrance of the exit chute until it rests on a lip. This movement deflects the pawl, which strips the component from the probe as it returns. The component then falls with its open end leading, as required.

Vision systems. Orienting of difficult parts is sometimes done by using machine vision systems, discussed previously in this chapter under the section on robotic assembly systems, to sense the orientation of components. Then, mechanical handling devices, pick-and-place units, or robots are used to place each part into the required orientation and into the necessary position.

Feed Tracks

Feed tracks are used to deliver properly oriented parts into the proper positions to be assembled. They can also serve as a buffer storage of oriented parts to allow production to continue when a feeder jam or parts shortage exists. It is generally preferable to have straight feed tracks, and with proper machine planning, curved tracks can usually be avoided. The tracks are arranged to support and guide parts and to maintain their orientation. Some parts cannot be confined and fed by simple feed tracks because of thin edges wedging or overlapping tendencies, some parts can be moved only in a straight line and require transfer or other means to change direction or position, and some parts will not retain a preferred orientation while moving along feeder tracks. Parts transfer means are too often considered minor and unimportant segments of automated assembly systems; however, improperly designed tracks can make an otherwise efficient system a total failure. Before specifying feeder requirements, a comprehensive study should be made of part characteristics.

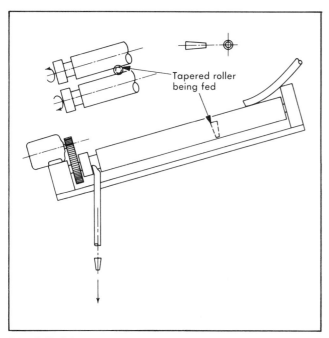

Fig. 12-57 Orienting rolls for tapered rollers.

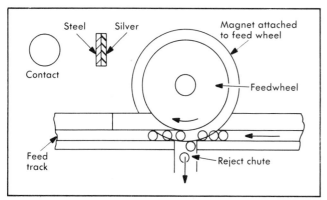

Fig. 12-58 Magnetic device arranged for orienting silver contacts.

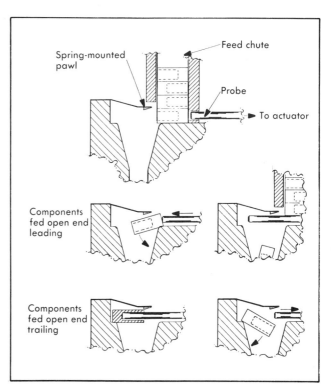

Fig. 12-59 Reciprocating probe and spring-mounted pawl are used to feed cylindrical parts with their open ends leading.[4]

FEED TRACKS

Gravity-feed track designs. Common designs for gravity-feed tracks are shown in Fig. 12-60. The versatile design illustrated in Fig. 12-61 can be modified to handle a wide variety of parts. Tracks of this design can be fabricated to any length with twists or turns of any kind when needed. Rods are welded or soldered to the intermittent spacers as the track is bent into position. The spacers are placed as needed, at some distance apart on straight sections and closer together on bends and twists. Where a rod ends, a spacer forms a coupling to start another rod. Standard adjustable tracks having flexible steel sides (see Fig. 12-62) are available for gravity feeding of basic part shapes.

Provision should be made in every case to drop out dirt and other extraneous material. Track clearances should be as liberal as possible, and constraining surfaces should be provided at the points where parts contact each other. It is usually good practice to localize possible jam points due to defective or oversize parts by a deliberate restriction at some easily accessible point. This point, by gate or other access means, should be arranged for easy removal of the offending piece. A track should never jam on a usable part, and provisions should be made to easily remove unusable parts that get into the track and jam. Light construction should be avoided, particularly if the construction is closed or semiclosed, to avoid damage by inexperienced personnel who are clearing jams.

Two zigzag track arrangements are shown in Fig. 12-63. Such construction is relatively expensive and is resorted to for several different reasons. Long parts such as rods, when being tracked side by side, will often jam because one end moves ahead of the other. With very short, straight runs and then a bend, this cannot happen, and the chute can run empty and refill without trouble. As a general rule, the shorter the part being fed, the shorter the straight run should be. Much longer straight runs are often used with reverse bends to control the speed of rolling or sliding down a large track drop to reduce damage to parts. Such track designs can be made to hold large numbers of parts as a storage means and frequently are combined with elevating devices to increase the drop and provide even more storage.

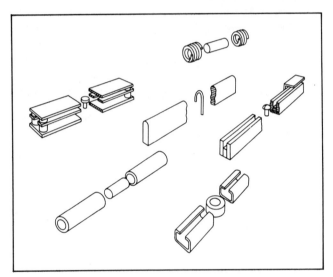

Fig. 12-60 Typical track sections.

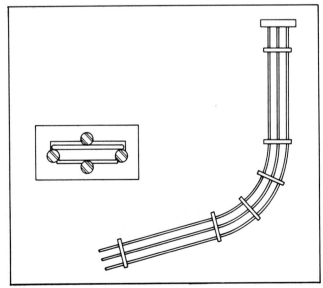

Fig. 12-61 Typical rod track construction.

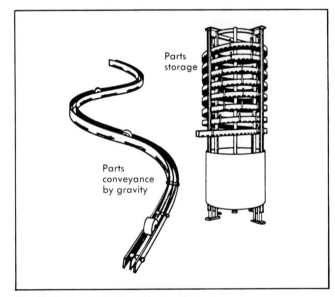

Fig. 12-62 Standard adjustable transfer tracks.

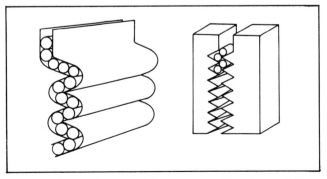

Fig. 12-63 Zigzag chutes used for parts control or storage of long cylindrical parts (left). Machined zigzag chute for short cylindrical or complex-shaped parts is seen at right.

Flexible feed tracks made of spring steel and wound wire (see Fig. 12-64) are sometimes used in place of rigid tracks. Their feeding and tracking qualities are good, but more importantly, they simplify the alignment to and connection between machines. They can be used to twist and turn oriented parts and also to feed parts to assembly stations. However, they may not be suitable for parts having critical details that might jam on the wires.

Powered feed tracks. Gravity is one means but not the recommended way of moving parts along a feed track. However, parts must often move up or horizontally. Powered feed wheels, intermittent pushing means, air blasts, moving belts, or controlled-direction vibration are all used to move parts. For thin parts that might overlap, a series of small air holes (at an angle of about 15° to the direction of feeding and in a horizontal plane) can be provided to move the parts along a close-fitting vibratory track. A track cover is also provided to prevent overlapping. Pneumatic tubes are used extensively for transferring screws from orienting feeders to screwdriving heads.

Means can be incorporated in the tracks to control the parts in various ways. Merging and diverging track connections are common. It is recommended, when possible, that positive-flow means be used whenever one track separates into two or more or when more than one track combines into a single track.

Escapement Devices

Escapements are mechanisms that release a single part or a preset quantity of parts at controlled intervals. They are generally located along the feed track or at its exit end and sometimes also serve as placement devices. The type of escapement used depends primarily on the part configuration and application requirements.

Some escapements are often not recognized as such. For example, fixtures on rotary indexing tables sometimes perform the function of escaping parts from magazines or feed tracks. Also, punches on presses may escape parts from tracks as the punches travel to perform their operation. Sometimes escapements reorient the parts or change their direction of feed, and orienting devices can sometimes act as escapements. Most escapements for automated assembly systems use ratchet, shuttle, drum, wheel, gate, or jaw devices (see Fig. 12-65).

Escaping and orienting. Figure 12-66 shows alternately reciprocating escapement rods being used to turn parts facing wrong. One correctly oriented part is dropped each cycle. The devices

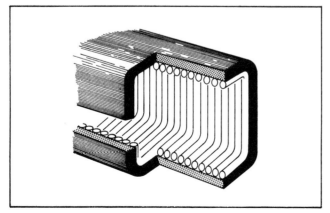

Fig. 12-64 Flexible feed track made of wound wire coated with heat-resistant plastic. (*Campbell Machines Co.*)

become more complicated as slides replace pins, but mechanical gaging of parts and rotation or discarding of unwanted orientations is very dependable, and the method can be used for multiple or series orienting. Cycle rates are usually less than 100 per minute for a single line of feed and are reduced considerably when handling large and/or intricate or fragile parts.

Nut escapement. An escapement mechanism for a nutrunning workhead is illustrated in Fig. 12-67. Hex nuts are fed from a vibratory feeder into a feed track. The leading nut falls into a cavity formed in fixed and pivoting jaws. A spring-loaded trip lever is displaced by the fixed jaw to allow the leading nut to enter the cavity. The slide on which the jaws are mounted is

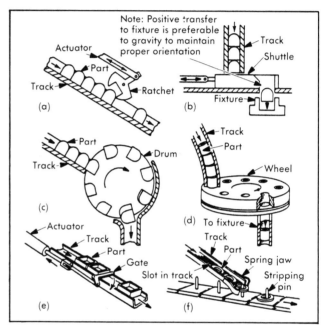

Fig. 12-65 Types of commonly used escapement devices: (a) ratchet, (b) shuttle, (c) drum, (d) wheel, (e) gate, and (f) jaw. (*Automation Devices, Inc.*).

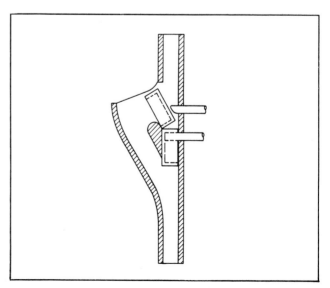

Fig. 12-66 Escapement-operated turnover device used for orienting.

ESCAPEMENT DEVICES

extended, bringing the nut into alignment with a probe and a mating stud. Nuts in the feed track are retained by the escapement finger. When the leading nut is supported on the probe, the pivoting jaw swings back, the slide retracts, the nutrunner advances, and the probe is withdrawn.

Escaping headed components. The escapement mechanism shown in Fig. 12-68 is suitable for releasing headed components such as bolts, screws, and other parts. The leading component is arrested by probe 2, which is extended by a pneumatic cylinder. When a component is required, probe 1 is first extended to catch under the head of the component immediately behind the leading component. Probe 2 is then retracted to release a single component to the work area. An air jet is sometimes used to ensure positive feed.

Escaping and performing assembly operations on stepped shafts. A mechanism for separating one stepped shaft at a time from a continuous supply of shafts is illustrated in Fig. 12-69. The shafts roll freely down inclined feed tracks toward the escapement device. The leading component enters cutout sections in the feed tracks and stops directly above an elevating block actuated by a pneumatic cylinder. When the block rises, the shaft is locked within a fixed clamp block. As the shaft is being elevated, the shaft ends deflect a pair of swinging pawls. After deflection, the pawls return to their normal positions against stop pins by means of gravity or spring loading.

An assembly operation is performed on the elevated shaft while it is clamped. During this period, the elevating block restrains other shafts in the feed tracks. When the assembly operation is completed, the elevating block is lowered, and the swinging pawls engage below the shaft ends to strip the shaft from the block. The shaft is then free to roll from the pawl surfaces onto feed tracks leading to a subsequent assembly station.

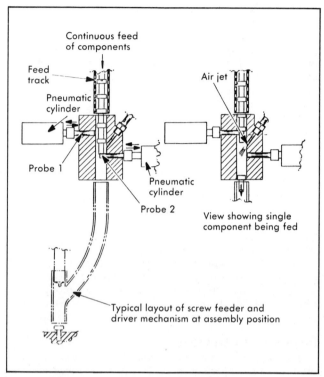

Fig. 12-68 Escapement mechanism for headed components such as bolts and screws.[6]

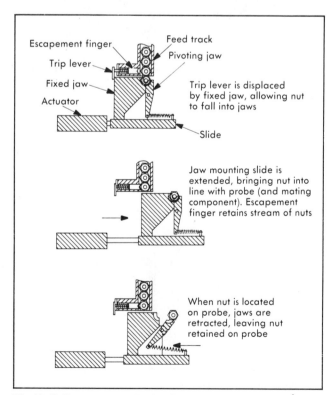

Fig. 12-67 Escapement mechanism for a nutrunning workhead.[5]

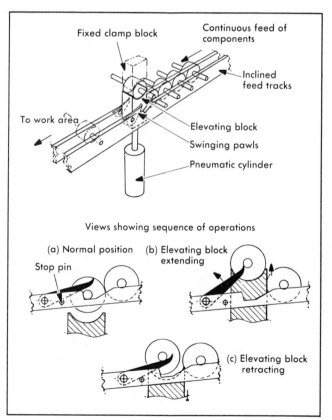

Fig. 12-69 Escapement mechanism for stepped cylindrical shafts.[7]

Noise Reduction

Noise levels in industrial plants must be controlled to meet OSHA requirements for safeguarding employees from the hazards of exposure. The sources of noise, OSHA noise standards, noise control methods, ear protection, and noise control programs are discussed in Volume I, *Machining*, and Volume II, *Forming*, of this Handbook series.

Several methods are available to reduce the noise from feeding and orienting units, feed tracks, escapement devices, and parts handling equipment. Lining feeder bowls with hard polyurethane, epoxy, or other material is used for some applications, but the linings may be short-lived and replacement can be costly.

Coating the outside of feeder bowls with damping material can help, but acoustical enclosures of noise insulation and absorption material are generally more effective. Some commercial units consist of a transparent plastic hemispherical dome mounted on a cylindrical side enclosure fitted with sound-absorbing material. Quick-opening clamps, hinges, or air-actuated means are available for ready access. Figure 12-70 shows hinged covers and enclosures on a combination storing, elevating, and orienting feeder to reduce noise levels.

Noise can be reduced by using conveyor belts made of fabric-laminated neoprene, urethane with a nylon core, urethane-coated cloth, or other materials, depending on the materials or parts being handled. Other means of reducing noise include the use of rubber, wood, or plastic chutes instead of metal; coating metal chutes with rubber, leather, or other sound-deadening material; or backing the metal chutes with wood or damping materials.

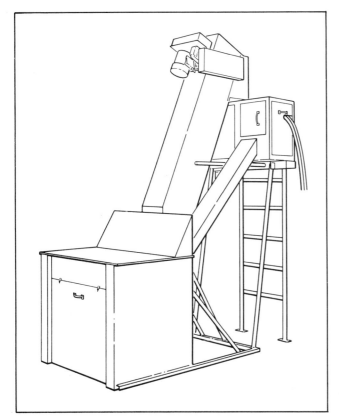

Fig. 12-70 Enclosures provided on combination storing, elevating, and orienting feeder to reduce noise levels. (*Campbell Machine Co.***)**

Metal conveyor rollers can be covered with rubber, plastic, or carpeting. Conveyor trolleys, trucks, and other material handling units can be equipped with rubber tires instead of metal wheels. Benches, tables, and other work surfaces should be covered with plywood and linoleum or other resilient material to reduce impact noise when metal parts or tools are dropped.

Tote pans and work containers can be made of plastic or wood instead of metal when practical. Some plants have developed hydraulic tippers for unloading large stock containers. Operators adjust the angular positions of the containers so that the workpieces slide instead of being dumped. Sound-damping material is applied to bottom and front outer surfaces as well as to the discharge chute.

Positioning (Placing) and Inserting Devices

Most automated assembly operations require that one properly oriented part, or possibly several parts, be transferred from a magazine, feed track, or conveyor to a predetermined point (nest, pallet, or previously assembled parts) where it is assembled. The placement mechanism may vary in complexity from a simple mechanical transfer device to a programmable industrial robot. Inserting can vary from simply dropping parts into place by gravity (generally unreliable) to the use of powered workheads. The type of placement device selected will depend on the size and shape of the parts, the distance the parts have to be transferred, the placement accuracy required, the complexity of the transfer motion, and production rate requirements.

Basic rules for efficient parts positioning include the following:

- Accurate and positive parts placement is preferable to gravity fall.
- Actuation means should be consistent and controllable.
- Checks for parts presence and completion of strokes are desirable to prevent jams and to minimize the production of improper assemblies.
- Synchronization with travel of nest, pallet, or assembly and the assembly operation.

One simple placement device is a dragoff mechanism in which a pallet pin or some part of the partial assembly engages a hole in a part in the feed track, drags it from the escapement device, and positions it on the pallet as the pallet moves under it. Pusher mechanisms, such as the one shown in Fig. 12-71, view *a*, are common. A ram, operating at 90° to parts traveling in the feed track, pushes a part through an escapement device into a nest or pallet. The ram holds back succeeding parts while loading one. Parts that have to be fed end to end can be handled as shown in view *b*. A shuttle escapes a part from a magazine and moves it into position under a pusher that inserts it into a nest.

A method of pressing steel dowel pins into bases is illustrated in Fig. 12-72. When a dowel pin is released from an escapement mechanism, it is drawn into vertical alignment by a permanent magnet. Then an air-actuated punch presses the pin into a base. Spring-loaded jaws may be preferable for holding the dowel pins because the magnets can collect metal particles. Air or vacuum systems are often used to blow or suck screws, rivets, nuts, bolts, and studs through tubes to the operating ends of automatic drivers.

Many standard pick-and-place units are available in various sizes and capacities. A nonstandard unit designed for placing flanged bushings with lift-swing-lift motions is shown in Fig. 12-73. The required motions of a pneumatically operated

POSITIONING AND INSERTING DEVICES

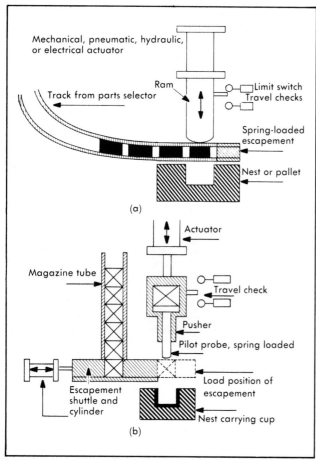

Fig. 12-71 Two types of placement devices.[8]

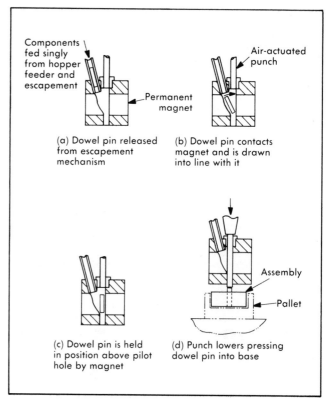

Fig. 12-72 Mechanism for inserting dowel pins into bases.[9]

radial arm are attained by a roller follower in a scroll cam. When the radial arm is partially elevated, a bushing is lifted clear of the feed rails by a placement pin, and the escapement block is released. When fully elevated, the radial arm indexes 90° and places the bushing vertically into a workhead.

A mechanism for transferring small coil springs from a spring winding machine to assembly mandrels or mating components is illustrated in Fig. 12-74. The rack and pinion is actuated by a pneumatic cylinder, and a finger on the end of a transfer arm retains the spring during transfer. A discussion of industrial robots and their use for positioning and inserting is presented in the preceding section of this chapter on automated robotic assembly.

Parts Detectors

To prevent jamming and provide optimum efficiency in automated assembly, the presence of components must be verified at the point of assembly. Various methods used for parts detection include electric, electromechanical, air or vacuum, optical, and other devices or sensors of both the contact and noncontact types. Various sensors are discussed in the preceding section on automated robotic assembly.

In-Process Storage

Many different devices are used for temporary in-process storage of parts. Elevating storage feeders commonly serve the storage function and also provide elevation to the parts for passing on to the next assembly operation in oriented condition. Spiral-type conveyors and vibrating banking towers are also popular because they retain orientation of the parts while providing a substantial float between operations and because they release parts to subsequent operations on demand. Stacker cranes, which can be made high to utilize overhead space and completely automatic to store or supply parts on demand, are also used.

JOINING AND FASTENING METHODS

As previously mentioned in this chapter, it is desirable to design or redesign products to facilitate automated assembly, reduce the number of components to be assembled, and, when possible, eliminate or minimize the need for joining and fastening operations. Although snap and press fits can often be made as part of the normal machine functions, many assemblies require the use of joining and fastening processes. When required, joining and fastening operations should generally be performed at separate stations, preceded by devices that automatically check the presence and position of the components.

Practically every known method of joining and fastening is being performed on assembly machines. Details of most of these processes are presented in preceding chapters of this volume, as follows:

Chapter	Title
8	Mechanical Fastening
9	Welding and Cutting
10	Brazing and Soldering
11	Adhesive Joining

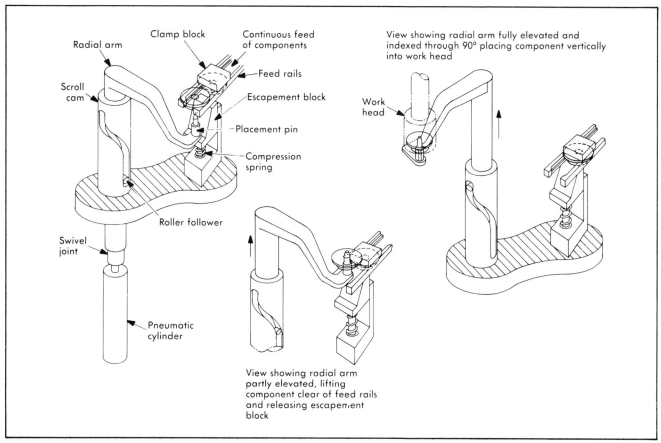

Fig. 12-73 Unit designed for placing flanged bushings with lift-swing-lift motions.[10]

Selection of a particular joining or fastening method for a specific application depends on several factors, including the following:

- The materials to be joined.
- Size, weight, and geometry of the components to be assembled.
- Joint designs and accessibility.
- Functional requirements of the assembled product, including strength, reliability, environment, appearance, and whether it has to be dismantled for maintenance or repair.
- Production requirements (rate and total).
- Edge and surface preparations necessary.
- Adaptability and compatibility of the joining method to automation, and effects on joint properties.
- Available equipment.
- Tooling requirements.
- Costs.
- Safety considerations.

Shrink and Expansion Fits

High joint strength and holding power are attained with shrink and expansion fits without the need for separate fasteners. Such fits are obtained by eliminating interference between two parts during assembly by heating or cooling the parts to change their dimensions. Various heating and cooling methods used are discussed in Chapter 8.

Induction heating units are commonly used to expand holes and arbors as pressure units or workhead mechanisms push mating components into the holes. Electrical resistance units are being used to heat and hot upset anchor pins to mating components. Magnetic pulse forming is being used to automatically shrink copper rings for retaining rubber seals on ball-joint housings for automotive suspension systems.

Integral Fasteners

Integral fasteners are formed in areas of components that interfere or interlock with other areas of assemblies, thus eliminating the need for separate fasteners. These fasteners are commonly used for assembling sheet metal products with lanced or formed tabs, extruded holes, embossed flanges and protrusions, seams, crimps, beads, and dimples (see Chapter 8).

Injected Metal Assembly

In injected metal assembly, discussed in Chapter 8, pressure die casting is used to inject molten metal for the permanent assembly of components. As cooling and solidification occurs, shrinkage locks the injected metal into undercuts, ridges, grooves, knurls, or keys in the parts being joined.

In a related process, thermoplastic resin (nylon mixed with chopped glass fibers) is being automatically injection molded on assembly machines to form bearing retaining rings on automotive propeller shafts. Vibratory bowls feed a predetermined amount of plastic pellets into the injection heads. The pellets are

JOINING AND FASTENING

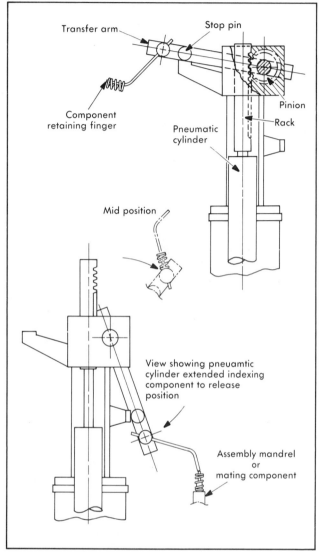

Fig. 12-74 Mechanism for transferring small coil springs from winding machine to assembly mandrel.[11]

then softened by electrical resistance heaters and injected into the workpieces.

Threaded Fasteners

Threaded fasteners include screws, bolts, studs, nuts, and similar components having external or internal threads. They are available in a wide variety of types, sizes, and strengths (see Chapter 8) to suit individual requirements for different joints and assembly designs. The required functions for threaded fasteners should be carefully evaluated in automated assembly. They are commonly used for load-carrying requirements and especially when disassembly and reassembly are necessary.

Selection of the proper type of threaded fastener can facilitate automated assembly. For example, cone and oval-point screws with symmetrical driving heads are easier to insert because they tend to centralize themselves in holes. With self-tapping screws, thread-forming types are generally better than thread-cutting types for automated assembly because they

do not produce chips that could interfere with feeding and orienting.

Assembly of threaded fasteners requires the application of torque and rotation. Proper tightening (tensioning) and control of torque is done in several ways, discussed in Chapter 8. Both hand and power-operated wrenches, nutrunners, and screwdrivers are used, the choice between hand and power depending primarily on production requirements. Multispindle nutrunners are used extensively for high-production applications. Industrial robots are also being used for the assembly of some threaded fasteners.

Riveting

Rivets are unthreaded, permanent fasteners available in solid, semitubular, tubular, compression, split, and special types (see Chapter 8). They are used for fastening two or more pieces together by passing their bodies through holes in the pieces and then clinching or forming a second head on the body end. Riveting is easily adapted to automated assembly, and the rivets can be installed economically and rapidly.

Clinching, setting, or driving of rivets is commonly done by impact peening with a succession of blows, compression squeezing, or a combination of compression and rolling or spinning. On automatic riveting machines, rivets are fed from hoppers and clinched between a driver and a die. Automatic drilling and riveting machines are being used by the aircraft industry, and industrial robots are employed for some riveting applications. Orbital, radial, and electromagnetic riveting are other methods discussed in Chapter 8.

Eyeleting

Eyelets are thin-walled, unthreaded, tubular fasteners having a flange or formed head on one end. They differ from rivets in that their bores extend completely through the fasteners. Eyelets are used to assemble light-gage parts and often serve the dual function of feeding wires through an assembly and holding the assembly together. They can be easily applied in automated assembly with low costs and high production rates.

Eyelets are set (clinched) by forcing their small diameter ends against dies that curl or funnel the edges and clinch the eyelets against the workpieces. Eyeleting machines are similar in operation to riveting machines. Semiautomatic and automatic machines are available with special positioning and feeding devices for single or multiple settings.

Stitching and Stapling

Stitching and stapling are used for many automated assemblies. Applications are broad with respect to the thickness and materials that can be joined. Wood, paper, fiberglass, plastics, cloth, and even thin metals can be joined by stapling. Stitches are formed on the machines that apply them, while staples are preformed and applied from strips, generally with pneumatic tools. Wire stitching machines feed accurate lengths of wire from a coil, cut and form the wire into U-shaped stitches, and drive them through the materials to be joined.

Other Mechanical Fasteners

Other mechanical fasteners often used in automated assembly include retaining (snap) rings, pins of various shapes and types, and washers—flat (plain), spring, and special-purpose. Details about these fasteners and assembly methods are presented in Chapter 8.

Welding

Many of the numerous welding methods discussed in Chapter 9 are used for automated assembly. These include both fusion and solid-state processes.

Arc welding. Arc welding processes commonly used for automated assembly include gas tungsten arc (GTAW or TIG), gas metal arc (GMAW or MIG), flux-cored arc (FCAW), submerged arc (SAW), stud (SW), and plasma arc welding (PAW). Possible problems include proper venting and removal of gases and fluxes and selection of proper heat-resistant materials for fixtures. Shields are generally required for protection from flash and spatter. Gas metal arc welding is the predominant process used for robotic assembly.

Resistance welding. Resistance welding is often desirable for automated assembly because it eliminates the need for filler metals, inert gases, and other materials. Possible problems include electrode and fixture wear and the need for good controls and monitoring. Demagnetizing may be necessary for some assemblies and workholding pallets. For electronic applications, surface cleanliness prior to welding is critical.

Resistance spot welding is especially adaptable to high-speed automated assembly. Fully automatic, multigun spot welders are used extensively for high-production applications. Industrial robots are being used to position and manipulate spot welding guns automatically. Projection welding is also very adaptable to automation and is used extensively to attach mechanical fasteners and when multiple welds must be made simultaneously.

Electron beam welding. Electron beam welding is adaptable to automated assembly, and both semiautomated and fully automated partial vacuum and nonvacuum systems are being used. Advantages include fast speeds, high-quality welds, and the capability of welding prefinished components with minimum distortion. Special shielding is required for operator protection, as discussed in Chapter 8.

Laser beam welding. The laser welding process is easily integrated into automated assembly systems. Advantages include the ability to generate localized, high-power densities without mechanical contact, thus eliminating contamination and tool wear. Robots equipped with lasers are being used to reach into difficult areas and to provide multiaxis capabilities. Possible limitations include space requirements and the need for properly guarding the laser path for operator protection.

Ultrasonic welding. In ultrasonic welding, vibration transmitted to the interface of parts to be joined causes friction and forms a bond. The process is easily automated and is being used to join similar and dissimilar metals, primarily aluminum and copper alloys, and thermoplastics. Other applications of ultrasonics include the following:

- Insertion—encapsulating metal components such as threaded inserts or studs into thermoplastics.
- Staking or heading—forming plastics over and/or around other components.
- Activating, reactivating, or curing adhesives.
- Cutting and/or sealing synthetic materials.
- Crimping or piercing two pieces to hold them together.

Soldering and Brazing

The soldering and brazing processes, discussed in Chapter 10, can be readily automated. Advantages include the capability of producing leaktight joints and joints in inaccessible areas. Possible limitations include the need for closely fitting joints with clean surfaces and close control of temperatures and time cycles. The use of preformed fillers and the automatic application of pastes and fluxes are common in automated assembly. Rotary index tables and in-line systems are used for such applications. Various methods of heating are described in Chapter 10. In the production of printed circuit boards, automated systems are equipped with conveyors to transport the boards through fluxing, preheating, and wave soldering operations. Robotic versions of these processes provide additional flexibility.

Adhesive Joining

Advantages of adhesive joining, discussed in Chapter 11, include the uniform distribution of stresses over large areas, the ability to join both thin and thick parts, and reduced assembly weights. Possible limitations include the need for carefully selecting an adhesive to suit the specific application, rigid process control, and safety precautions. Also, surface preparation and cleaning are generally required, and precautions must be taken to prevent contamination of fixtures, feed tracks, and placement units.

Heat, pressure, or long cure times are required with some adhesives, but most can be cured rapidly. Some adhesives cure at room temperature and others can be heat cured after assembly. Solvent and catalyst accelerators are also used to speed curing. The advent of radiation curing with ultraviolet (UV) light, electron beam (EB), or gamma radiation has reduced curing time, facilitated automation, and avoided air pollution.

Although adhesives and sealants are still being applied manually for many applications, semiautomatic and automatic machines are also being used. The development of improved dispensers has facilitated the use of adhesive bonding in automated assembly. Optical sensors are employed for some applications to detect the presence of adhesives or sealants. Industrial robot applicators are being used to manipulate dispensing guns and sometimes to move the workpieces. Multiple guns can be used on a single robot.

Auxiliary Operations

Secondary operations sometimes performed on automated assembly machines or systems include counting, lubricating, marking, and, in some cases, packaging. Marking is done by roll or magnetic means, stamping, the application of paint or ink, with lasers, or the application of labels. Packaging, often done separately, may consist of closing, sealing, vacuum packing, and wrapping operations. Unloading of automated assembly machines and systems commonly consists of ejection to bulk storage.

INSPECTING AND TESTING OPERATIONS

Inspection for automated assembly equipment is a critical and integral function that fills multiple roles. In addition to satisfying product assurance needs through dedicated inspection tests, an additional benefit from inspection is the monitoring of each function of the automated equipment. Every feeding operation and many of the work operations in automated assembly equipment must be tested immediately after the task is performed to ensure the effective operation of the assembly process. Furthermore, each machine motion that is not a mechanical link to the central driveshaft of the base machine should be considered as a candidate for a probable functional test point.

INSPECTING AND TESTING

A wide variety of equipment is used for inspecting and testing assembly machine operations. This category of equipment includes probes, mechanical and electromechanical switches, proximity and magnetic devices, capacitance and inductance units, and pressure and vacuum devices. More recently, optical and photoelectric gaging, eddy-current devices, lasers, robots, and machine vision have been increasingly applied for inspection. Details of many types of inspection equipment and techniques are presented in Chapter 3 of this volume. Various types of sensors are discussed previously in this chapter under the subject of robotic assembly.

Inspection for selective assembly is performed in some applications, with the gaging equipment used to select parts for assembly on the basis of fit rather than absolute size. In one application, the depths of pockets in pump bodies and the thickness of gears are automatically inspected, and the parts then segregated into one of six classes. Next, pivoting arms automatically transfer external gears of the proper thickness into position, where they are pressed into mesh with internal gears.

With quality control programs, there is a need for documentation of product parameters. This generally involves serialization or date coding to provide proof that the products meet specifications. The procedure reduces the possibility of product recalls and product liability lawsuits. Most modern inspection equipment provides an electrical signal for recording the appropriate parameters.

Quality of Incoming Parts

Although the ideal situation is to have 100% perfect parts received at the assembly machine, this is seldom the case. As a result, the machines (often the feeding devices) are equipped with mechanisms that accept satisfactory parts and reject nonconforming parts as well as those contaminated with debris. Inspection before parts are assembled prevents machine jams, part damage, and inoperative assemblies.

Presence and Position Probes

Immediately following or during the feeding of any component in an automated assembly system, it is necessary to probe or inspect each component's presence and/or position in the machine station. The information provided by these monitoring probes dictates the sequential activity of the assembly process. Unless an extenuating circumstance exists that would indicate immediate intervention by the machine operator, a detected fault should not stop the assembly equipment. Defective parts can be automatically ejected from the assembly system.

A common three-fault stop sequence is the normal procedure. In this sequence, an intermittent fault caused by either a misfeed or misoriented component results in the lockout of any further assembly of that device and its ultimate disposal at a reject station. If three consecutive faults at the same station occur, an indication message or signal is provided to direct the machine operator to make the proper correction. Typically, the quantity information on probe faults is not lost even though the machine does not stop. Memory storage can be utilized to retain this information, and with a printout, total fault information at all stations can be retained and checked later.

A simple probe device should be utilized to test that the installed components are properly positioned at their prescribed locations. This can be determined with dual-switch devices. In its simplest form, a probe head is mounted to a shaft. The probe head is held in a radial orientation so that its face can be configured to conform to the inserted component's topo-graphy. As the probe reference block is lowered to its preset position, the probe head contacts the installed component, lifting the switch actuation plate to the inspection position. A simple two-microswitch probe is illustrated in Fig. 12-75.

The tolerance zone (acceptable window) for such probes is established by adjusting the actuating screws that contact the microswitches. Both switches must be closed to provide an acceptable signal. If a component is not present, there is no actuation, and the switch wired normally open remains open. If a component is out of radial orientation or is not seated, or if there is more than one part present, there is actuation, and the normally closed switch is held open. This type of probe system can be used if a part-to-part tolerance of ±0.005″ (0.13 mm) is permissible.

When the possible tolerance buildups of assemblies in an assembly nest are such that the standard probe mechanism is inadequate, a probe system that references the base or datum point should be used. A reference probe with a light-emitting diode (LED) and micrometer adjustment is shown in Fig. 12-76. With this type of probe, the probe head or reference bushing determines the datum, irrespective of the buildup of part tolerances caused by a stack of parts. Optical switches are used in conjunction with notched flags, with the flags becoming the window dimensions. This probe concept can also be utilized with microswitches if the shaft connected to the probe pin is equipped with a microswitch actuation plate and the microswitches are mounted to the main shaft and move with the reference bushing.

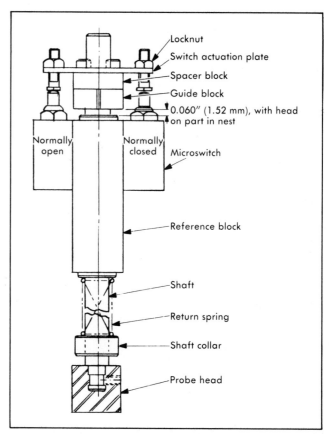

Fig. 12-75 Simple two-switch probe for detecting part presence and position.

Labels: Locknut, Switch actuation plate, Spacer block, Guide block, 0.060″ (1.52 mm), with head on part in nest, Normally open, Normally closed, Microswitch, Reference block, Shaft, Return spring, Shaft collar, Probe head

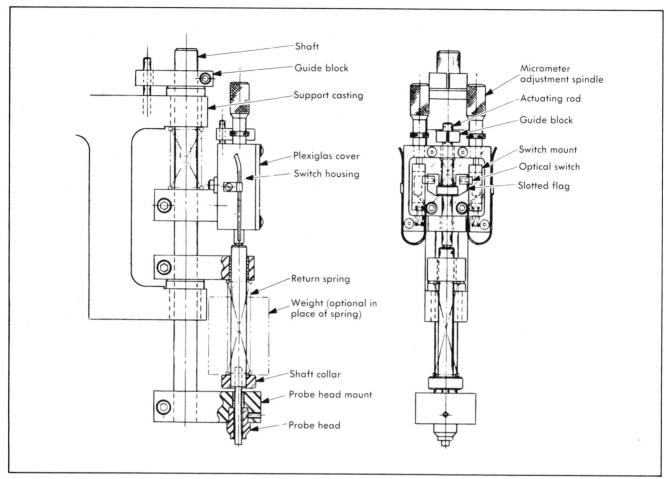

Fig. 12-76 Reference probe with a light-emitting diode (LED) and micrometer adjustment.

Another probe arrangement that serves the function of presence and position sensing with greater accuracy involves the use of either a switch device such as the one shown in Fig. 12-77 or a linear variable differential transformer (LVDT). An LVDT probe provides an additional feature in that it is not a GO-NOT GO device but rather an analog device that permits scaling or decisions based on continuous data. With this concept, trends in measurements can be gathered in the machine controller, with a printout provided when desired.

In addition to the probes and switches described to determine part presence and position, devices for detecting presence alone are satisfactory for many applications. Detection devices that can be used for such simple tasks include light-emitting diodes (LEDs), proximity switches, vacuum switch devices, and wand switches.

Inspecting During Assembly

Inspection stations for the purpose of ensuring quality standards are employed on many automated assembly systems. These stations can be complex or simple depending on the needs of the final product. These devices provide the manufacturer with a tool to improve and maintain consistent product quality.

Study results based on actual data shows the merits of automated inspection over other means (see Table 12-8). The data in this table are based on a product that required 100%

inspection. Initially this was done by an inspector without specific training. Then the inspectors were put through a comprehensive training program. The final column is based on redundant probes used on an automated assembly machine that performed the inspection task.

Redundant probes are sometimes recommended for those applications where product quality or process economics requires 100% acceptable assemblies. In the redundant mode, the first probe is set within acceptable limits, and the secondary unit is set at the same limits. Also, in this instance, both probe settings should be sealed to prevent indiscriminate alteration of the settings. To ensure 100% product output, it is common for the inspection department to place special gage masters in the machine nests at predetermined periods to establish functionability.

A wide variety of equipment is being used for automated inspection during assembly. Machine vision systems are becoming common for configuration analysis, lasers are used for accurate measurements, LVDTs for recording variable data, and wand switches for mechanical detection. Robot-based inspection systems are also being used with various sensors mounted on the robot wrists. The robot arms can reach inside the cavities of parts to measure reference datum points and planes. Databases for CAD/CAM systems can be integrated into the measuring system.

INSPECTING AND TESTING

TABLE 12-8
Relative Effectiveness Considerations of
Manual Versus Automated Inspection of Parts

Normal Inspection by Operators	Optimum Manual Inspection	Inspection on Automated Assembly Machine
	• Training, testing, and certification of operators • Periodic recertification	• Redundant automated probes • No operator fatigue • Positive assurance of product quality
90% effective	95% effective	100% effective

Machine vision is being used to analyze 14 features on 15 families of tie rods for an automotive steering linkage (see Fig. 12-78). The vision system operates at five stations of a multistation synchronous assembly machine. Each of the five stations uses two solid-state cameras coupled to one of two computers. Special lighting is provided at each station, and the computers make decisions based on the reflected light. At any station, a number is coded to the pallet holding a rejected part, and no further operations are performed on the part, which is removed at the end of the assembly machine.

The torque test station illustrated in Fig. 12-79 is used to ensure that the torque applied to a selector cap is above a minimum rating. As the workholding nest is indexed into position, the torque test station is advanced to a position where the torque actuator engages the selector cap slot. In the previous operation, where the selector cap was staked, the cap was retained in the proper position. The clutch is set to apply a preset torque to the actuator. After engagement, the torque drive cylinder advances, rotating the magnetic clutch housing.

If the selector cap is not staked properly, it will move, and the photo interrupter is blocked. This signal is typically stored within a memory storage device for control of disposal of the tested device. At the completion of the test phase, the clutch actuating assembly is retracted, and the torque drive is returned to its starting position. During the machine index time, the photodetector is read to test its functionality. A companion station for this minimum force check is a station that must move the selector cap under a maximum torque. The station is identical except that the photodetector must see a secondary slot if the tested component is satisfactory.

Inspecting Assemblies

Inspection of products after assembly generally involves functional tests to ensure that the products operate satisfactorily. Such tests often include balancing, leak testing, and calibration. Because many tests require considerable time, they sometimes have to be performed separately to avoid decreasing the productivity of assembly machines or systems.

Leak testing. A simple in-process leak test device that can be effectively installed on an automated assembly system is shown in Fig. 12-80. The device is remarkably fast and effective for finding leaks when the leak criteria is not severely critical. Tests must be made with sample test units that have established leaks built into them. The requirement is for a waterproof seal where

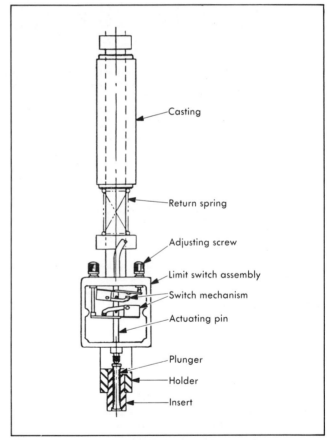

Fig. 12-77 Switch device used in a probe to detect part presence and position.

the nose cap of a small ordnance device has been crimped to a fuse body. A positive pressure is applied to the sealed area. If this pressure differential enters the device, it exits through the bottom and applies pressure on a free-moving ball within the detector unit. By altering the angularity of a device containing a photoelectric beam and the free ball, it is possible to vary the sensitivity of the test. Cycle rates of 30-50 parts per minute are possible with this test.

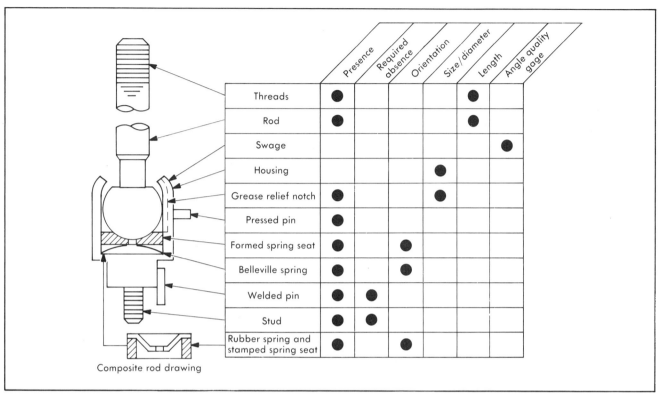

	Presence	Required absence	Orientation	Size/diameter	Length	Angle quality gage
Threads	●				●	
Rod	●				●	
Swage						●
Housing			●			
Grease relief notch	●			●		
Pressed pin	●					
Formed spring seat	●		●			
Belleville spring	●		●			
Welded pin	●	●				
Stud	●	●				
Rubber spring and stamped spring seat	●		●			

Composite rod drawing

Fig. 12-78 Table shows location of each feature on tie rod that is inspected by machine vision.

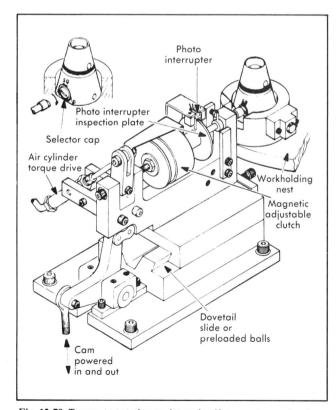

Fig. 12-79 Torque test station to determine if proper torque has been applied to a selector cap.

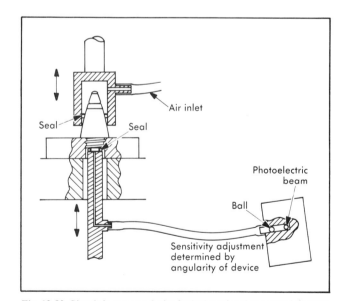

Fig. 12-80 Simple in-process device for leak testing that can be installed on automated assembly systems.

Other test methods for more sensitive leak testing include pressure loss or decay and the use of mass flowmeters and spectrometers. The pressure loss or decay method uses a sensitive pressure transducer to measure pressure changes in the part being tested. The transducer frequently consists of a strain gage mounted on a diaphragm that deflects under pressure. The mass flowmeter method uses the measurement of pressure drop

INSPECTING AND TESTING

across an orifice or a hot-cold anemometer. Either pressure or partial vacuum can be used. The mass spectrometer method requires more expensive equipment and is generally only used for detecting very small leaks. It involves enclosing the product to be tested in an airtight chamber and introducing a tracer gas. Detailed information on the subject of leak testing is presented in Chapter 6, "Nondestructive Testing."

Balancing. Static and/or dynamic balancing of assembled products, discussed in Chapter 7 of this volume, may be required. Balancing is sometimes done off-line from the assembly machine, but is frequently automated. In one application, an electronic system determines the amount and angle of dynamic unbalance for each end of an assembly. Then steel slugs of the proper length to correct the amount of imbalance are automatically sheared from coils, formed with projections, and resistance welded at correct angular positions on both ends of the assembly. Another method is to drill lightening holes to decrease the weight in heavy areas.

Surface flaw detection. A number of nondestructive tests (NDT), discussed in Chapter 6 of this volume, have been successfully applied on automated assembly and inspection machines. Both eddy-current and ultrasonic inspection instruments can be readily interfaced with computer-based machine controllers. Inspection for surface defects, hardness, and coating thickness can be accomplished using properly developed eddy-current test methods. Ultrasonic inspection, though somewhat more difficult to mechanize because of the need for a liquid coupler between the transducer and the part being inspected, can be utilized to detect subsurface inclusions and voids as well as defects that may be on the surface of the part. In any NDT inspection application, careful consideration must always be given to accurately positioning the part relative to the transducer to ensure complete and adequate inspection of the areas of interest on the part to be inspected.

Runout testing. Although runout can be checked on assembly machines for some applications, it is sometimes preferable and more economical to perform the testing on a separate machine. Figure 12-81 shows a small dial indexing machine

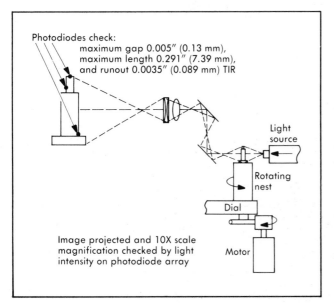

Fig. 12-81 Light source and lens system used on an automated machine to inspect gears and pinions.

developed for a required 100% test on runout, staking gap, and maximum length of a critical pinion and gear assembly.

The tested pinion assembly was rotated in front of the light source of a standard shadow-graph device. The shadow graph was altered with a specially developed screen mask having photodiodes mounted at critical positions on the projected screen locations. Dependent on whether the diode arrays are set to see or not see light, all critical tests can be accomplished at effective production rates. All diodes are set to reject at maximum conditions.

Inspecting for Safety

The need for and means of ensuring operator safety in automated assembly are discussed at the end of this chapter. Precautions are also necessary to protect the equipment. Many different types of sensors and switches are used to protect assembly machines and systems from damage, with output signals supplied to a control system. Monitoring the actions of the machine or system is desirable to ensure the proper completion of each operation.

Mechanical, hydraulic, or pneumatic motions that could cause tool breakage or process faults should be inspected for function during every index cycle of an automated system. There are many mechanical motions that are pneumatically actuated, and interference with basic mechanical motions can occur if the pneumatic devices become erratic or fail to function. In these instances, the motions should be monitored with either microswitches, proximity switches, or light-interrupted detection systems.

If the malfunction of a pneumatically actuated device would only result in nonfeeding of components or a simple work function not being completed, it is not necessary to monitor that motion because the part presence and position probe will detect that error. A detector should only be used if the malfunction could cause a machine to be shut down because of misalignment or broken components or if the safety of an operator is jeopardized.

CONTROLS FOR AUTOMATED ASSEMBLY

A variety of control products are being used for the automation of assembly operations. Primary objectives of the controls include maintaining or improving product quality, increasing output, reducing inventories and scrap, and creating and processing production information (database). Specific requirements of the controls for integrated automation include the following:

- Determine where (and what) each part to be assembled is, track the part from station to station, and know the specific operation to be performed at each station.
- Evaluate the overall quality of the parts, subassemblies, or assembled products at each station, with provisions for rejecting them if necessary.
- Verify the operations performed and product quality attained at each station.
- Prepare for and accommodate operational and/or product changes on-line.

Hierarchical Control Systems

Depending on the degree of sophistication needed or desired, automated control systems can be provided in a hierarchy of interactive levels. Cam-actuated assembly machines generally require a minimum of control sophistication. Power-

and-free machines having independent stations need more extensive control systems. Flexible assembly systems require programmable controls. Integrated automation systems involve the coordinated operation of multiple microprocessor-based controls and rely on computer-based production scheduling and data management linked by interactive communication networks.

Modern hierarchical control systems, exclusive of the actual mechanical elements, can include the following:

1. *Programmable logic controllers.* These microprocessor-based controllers, discussed in Volume I, *Machining*, of this Handbook series, are linked by discrete, analog, and intelligent input/output (I/O) devices to the actual physical operations (see Fig. 12-82). They can also be linked by proprietary networks to other intelligent devices such as computerized numerical control (CNC) units and robots. Although they were originally designed for sequential control, they are sometimes used to perform batch process operations, mathematical computations for selective assembly, or data gathering for maintenance, production quality, or management information systems.

2. *Motion or robot controls.* These controls cause drive systems, robots, precision metalcutting units, and other devices to perform one or more linear or rotary motions according to a prescribed pattern.

3. *Computers.* Minicomputers and mainframe computers are electronic devices used for all levels of supervisory functions and information processing. Personal computers have recently begun to be used for the control of manufacturing processes. They can perform the same type of I/O functions as programmable controllers, but usually at a slower processing rate. The personal computers have good data accumulation and reporting capabilities, and network communications are easily incorporated. The time required for software development for personal computers can vary widely depending on the complexity of the application.

4. *Communication systems.* These systems are integrated networks that permit the sharing of both proprietary (control-oriented, real-time) information and broadband (wide-based, data-oriented) information.

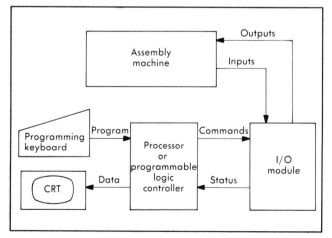

Fig. 12-82 Block diagram of a programmable logic controller used for an assembly machine.

Machine Controls

Essential to any automated assembly machine and forming the base for hierarchical control systems are real-time control devices that interface to programmable controllers and other control devices. These devices are generally connected via I/O modules that interface limit switches, pushbuttons, proximity switches, solenoids, motor starters, pilot lights, and other sensing and drive devices. The devices typically involve digital I/O points or on/off controls.

A more sophisticated category of I/O modules offers not only interface to real-time devices but also some conversion and communication capabilities. An analog input module in which a varying voltage or current is converted to a digital number is an example. New developments in analog I/O devices include modules that read, convert, and forward signals dealing with level, temperature, speed, light intensity, position, and wire faults and offer high levels of common-mode isolation. With the use of a concept called Block Transfer and a minimum of programming, large amounts of information can be quickly and efficiently transferred between I/O modules and the processors of programmable controllers.

Station Controls

Also essential to any automated assembly machine and forming a next higher level for hierarchical control systems are devices for real-time control at the station level. This is a more complex level and generally involves the use of intelligent I/O modules, real-time, logic-solving programmable controllers, and various motion control systems.

Intelligent I/O modules. These modules are called intelligent because they preprocess information—looking at input status, providing control algorithms and solutions, and directly controlling outputs, all as an integral part of a programmable controller system. Developments have increased the capabilities of intelligent I/O modules. These capabilities include the following:

- Motion control offering closed-loop servocontrol, open-loop stepper-motor positioning, and even specialized control of clutches and brakes for mechanical presses.
- Proportional-integral-derivative (PID) control implementation. Closed-loop controls can be executed independently of the programmable controller scans.
- High-speed logic control, providing high-speed throughput, reading inputs, making decisions, and controlling outputs independent of the scan.
- Direct communication capability. An intelligent I/O module can divide control among one or a number of processors on small programmable controllers that report to a larger (supervisory) controller.
- User-written BASIC programs can be run on specially designed intelligent I/O modules and implemented independent of processor memory.

Programmable logic controllers. Operation at the station level involves single or multiple programmable controllers performing real-time decisionmaking based on input from I/O modules. These devices are available in small, medium, and large sizes.

Even the smallest programmable controllers are now considered cost-effective replacements for many electromechanical relays, timers, hard-wired logic, and drum controllers. Advantages include the superiority of solid-state configuration, re-

CHAPTER 12

CONTROLS

duced wiring and panel space requirements, and increased flexibility and cost savings. In addition to ladder logic for machine control, they offer additional capabilities such as floating-point mathematics, interactive report generation, data manipulation instructions, and other features for performing computation and data acquisition functions. The devices also have peripheral interfaces such as CRTs and color graphics systems that allow interaction with the machine or process under the control of the programmable controller.

New capabilities are continually being incorporated into programmable controllers for station control. With controllers that often occupy only a single slot in an I/O rack, specific features can include the following:

- Sequential function chart programming. This supplement to ladder logic programming reduces scan times by partitioning a program into blocks, each with its own ladder logic rungs. Only those blocks specifically required at any point in the program are executed.
- Built-in communications interface for peer-to-peer communications, program uploading and downloading, remote programming, and networking functions, without the expense of additional external modules.
- Built-in remote I/O scanner/adapter capabilities that allow the programmable controllers to control the I/O points in either local or remote racks or to act as remote I/O adapters for use on remote I/O links.

Motion controls. Numerous developments in microprocessor-based motion controls allow many improvements in productivity, including reduced inventories, smaller lot sizes, and higher product quality. Some of the motion control systems used primarily for assembly stations include the following:

1. *One to three-axis motion controllers for velocity and position control.* These devices can be operated in a nonintegrated environment and are usually matched to stand-alone machines. Programming of these devices is typically done through keyboards integral with the units.
2. *Stepper or servopositioning modules.* These devices are integral parts of many programmable controller-based systems. They provide distributed control for point-to-point positioning applications. The units are typically located in the remote I/O racks of systems for distribution of a wide range of motion control functionality within the systems.
3. *Synchronized axis controllers.* This classification covers a large group of sophisticated velocity/position controllers with synchronized axis and multiaxis capabilities, often controlling several axes simultaneously. They include devices that can follow complex paths generated by either a host computer or taught to them by teach pendants; examples include CNCs and robot controls. They offer from 2 to 17 axes of control and generally feature color graphics displays of motion paths and a variety of operator interface functions. In addition to interfacing with power amplifiers and feedback devices, they communicate with programmable controllers, other control devices, and/or host computers via local area networks such as the Data Highway.
4. *Power amplifiers.* These controllers provide the power to drive servomotors for actual process motions. They are available in a wide range based on modularity, power conversion types, and ratings.

5. *Integrated controllers.* Integrated velocity/position controllers with power amplifiers are a combination of technologies for use on motors integrated into a system. These systems tend to be more application specific; a typical example is a single-axis slide position controller used for transfer functions.

Cell Controls

At the cell level, control emphasis shifts to the coordination of multiple stations, with the level of control moving upward from real-time operations to supervisory tasks. High-capability supervisory programmable controllers or computers use either Data Highway or peer-to-peer communications to direct the operations of station-level programmable controllers or computers. This is the basis for the concept of distributed control and computer-integrated manufacturing (CIM).

Distributed control. With distributed control, supervisory programmable controllers or computers oversee networks of smaller controllers located close to the actual operation over which they are exerting real-time control. Such a system reduces the severity of a particular station becoming inoperative and increases both system flexibility and fault-isolation time.

Beginning with the supervisory functions of the cell level, greater importance becomes placed on information generation and operator interface. Documentation of the program and I/O wiring, for example, is extremely critical. At the top of the cell level, the focus turns toward linking the databases that support plant management with the real-time activities that occur on the plant floor. This task represents the foundation of the concept called area management.

Area management. Area controllers are the tools through which the database-to-real-time link can be implemented. Cell-level industrial management systems are interfaced with station-level controllers. Designed to operate in industrial environments, area controllers gather data for transmission over local area networks (LANs) such as a Data Highway. They then interpret the collected data and communicate it, both horizontally to other area controllers and upward to assembly center and plant computers over a broad-band communications network. Information requirements and production directions are then sent back down from these computers to the appropriate controllers on the plant floor.

Assembly Center and Plant Levels

Above the cell level, computers at the assembly center and plant levels coordinate larger areas of intraplant activity. Planning and management functions are usually implemented at the assembly center level, while strategies and direction of the complete overall functions are generally done at the plant level.

At these upper levels of control, a prominent issue centers around high-level broad-band communications between diverse automated devices from various manufacturers. The issue is protocol standardization of the variety of schemes available for intraplant (multilevel) communications.

The Manufacturing Automation Protocol (MAP) standardization program is an international effort geared toward dealing with this issue. The MAP program is a multivendor communications standard that can reduce communication costs and increase the uptime of the application by effectively utilizing VLSI (very large scale integration) technology and communication standards. In a basic MAP scheme, communication between vendor's equipment is not routed through the central-level computer. Instead, the equipment is supported by the vendor's own gateway or a direct MAP interface module. The communication network between the plant computer and the gateway or MAP module is a multivendor open network.

Communications

A final requirement for a hierarchy of automation control (MAP) is a system of integrated communications. The basis for a system of communication networks is the integration of control automation functions both horizontally and vertically. Horizontal integration covers single-level communications between like and unlike devices such as programmable controllers, CNCs, robots, and computers. Vertical integration, using one or more networks, ties together the various levels of control. An integrated system of communication networks provides the link to and from the real-time, plant-floor level through multiple-station (supervisory) control and up to database management, scheduling, and administration.

At lower control levels, proprietary master-slave systems of local and remote I/O communications are most effective. Such a system can transfer information between a central processor and an I/O subsystem. For the next level of control, low-cost, general-purpose networks, often referred to as Data Highways, communicate through the station and cell levels. This is the ideal communications medium for moving blocks of data between stations (production profiles).

The next higher level of communications is a flexible, service-oriented system called mini-MAP. This network differs from the Data Highway in that it is more optimized for cell subnetwork applications. Demands placed on this network include fast, predictable response times and current or eventual compatibility with the industry's evolving communications standards. For the highest control level, the cell-level controllers communicate with the computers through a broadband system. A broad-band system carries communications capability from the cell level to the top of the automation control hierarchy.

An Example of Hierarchical Control

A computer-integrated flexible system is being used by the Industrial Control Div. of Allen-Bradley Co. to assemble, test, mark, and package electromechanical contactors and relays for electric motors at rates of about 600 units per hour. With the hierarchical control system shown in Fig. 12-83, the line can produce 125 variations of the products in two sizes.

This just-in-time process permits the fast production of small lot sizes and eliminates work-in-progress and finished parts inventories as well as direct labor. Only a few attendants are necessary to oversee operations. Color graphics interfaces permit human intervention at any stage in the process by means of on-line monitoring, diagnostics, and control. Warranty expenses have been lowered through improved quality. A possible problem with just-in-time methods is that a shortage of any part will stop production.

Center and plant-level controls. The foundation of the assembly system is a center-level computer into which customer orders are received and stored. This computer does all the necessary recording, accounting, and downloading of customer orders to a supervisory programmable controller at the cell level. Production of all products does not begin until an actual customer order has been received and processed. The accounting system is entirely automated. In addition to the initial logging of customer orders, shipping records and billings are entirely computer generated.

The computer at the center level has the ability to save and restore the memories of all programmable controllers with which it communicates, thus facilitating quick maintenance in the event of memory corruption. Overall planning and administrative information is received from a plant-level mainframe computer having two-way communications capability.

Cell-level control. A supervisory master programmable controller at the cell level receives order information from the center-level computer and implements the day's production. This controller coordinates the multiple assembly stations by providing an interface between the computer and real-time devices that perform more than 30 assembly operations at the various stations.

For example, the programmable controller can instruct one station to produce a specific armature and another station to begin work on a crossbar assembly for that armature. Using a local area network (Data Highway), the controller can communicate upward to the center and plant-level computers, pass instructions down to the station-level controllers, and interface with operations via printers and CRTs.

Station and machine controls. At the station level, both discrete and intelligent I/O modules are connected to more than 20 small and medium-sized programmable controllers. Machine-level control devices used include photoelectric sensors, transducers, bar code readers, limit switches, encoders, proximity sensors, drives, magnetic card readers, counters, printers, servopositioning modules, and CRT terminals.

The station-level programmable controllers communicate back and forth with the master controller at the center level by means of two Data Highways (proprietary local area networks). Information shared between the master controller and the station-level controllers includes the following:

- What is to be produced at each step of the operation.
- What parts currently exist at each station.
- The identities and quantities of rejects, if any.
- The status of alarms (part jams, low parts inventories, numerous rejects, and equipment failures), if any.
- Results of various testing/diagnostic procedures for statistical trending, analysis, and quality control.
- Repair records.

Controls of various operations. Space limitations prohibit a discussion of all control functions on this large computer-integrated assembly system. Only a few of the more interesting controls are described here.

Proximity sensors. An adjustable proximity sensor linked to a station-level programmable controller senses the thickness of stamped armature laminations fed from a magazine. Stacks of compressed laminations are also checked electronically for thickness. Another proximity sensor detects the presence and checks the supply of rivets that are inserted into the stacks of laminations.

Adaptive control. An adaptive control system is used for magnet grinding. A laser scanning gage measures the magnets, and information from the gage is fed back to the grinding machine. When the magnets start getting out of tolerance, the grinding wheel is automatically adjusted to produce magnets with acceptable tolerances. Tolerances measured by the laser gage are as small as one-sixth the diameter of a human hair.

Laser measurements and bar codes. A laser measuring unit checks the heights of yokes, and various types of sensors are used to verify the existence and proper alignment of components in the yoke-armature assemblies. Bar codes containing

DEBUGGING

the identity of the finished products are placed on the bottoms of the base housings. All stations through which the assemblies pass receive operating instructions from the bar codes.

Testing, packaging and marking. Quality checks performed include noise, electrical, and mechanical tests. Completed products are placed in boxes, the boxes are closed, bar code stickers are applied to the boxes, and an ink-jet printer applies the catalog numbers and ratings of the products.

DEBUGGING ASSEMBLY MACHINES AND SYSTEMS

Debugging or troubleshooting refers to the work required to obtain optimum production from a new assembly machine or system in the shortest possible time. Proper design, construction, and installation of the machine or system will minimize debugging needs; however, variations or changes in the parts to be assembled and the machine components and tooling generally necessitate varying degrees of debugging. Debugging should start with the design and construction of the machine and tooling and continue through the installation and operation. In many production systems, debugging is often a continuing process after initial operation. With custom-designed assembly machines, debugging may cost up to 25% of total machine cost.

Personnel Requirements

It is generally desirable to have a single engineer (task manager) in charge and responsible for all decisions. A setup person, under the supervision of the engineer, should have the responsibility for assembling and debugging the machine or system. The engineer, setup person, and all operators and maintenance personnel should be properly and adequately trained, preferably at the plant of the machine manufacturer.

Typical Procedures

Inspection of the accuracy and condition of the parts to be assembled is essential as the first step in any debugging proce-

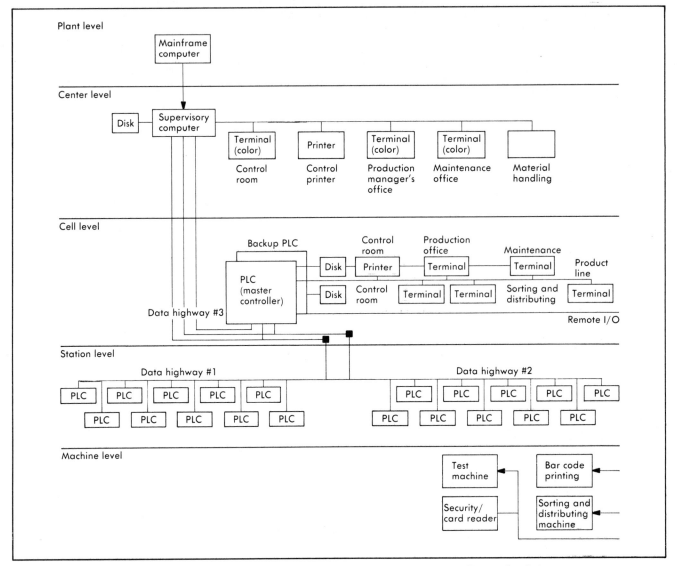

Fig. 12-83 Levels of control used in system for assembling contactors and relays for electric motors. (*Allen-Bradley Co.*)

dure. Sample parts, rather than product drawings, should be made available to the machine builder. Part quality should be corrected prior to assembly; successful assembly will not occur if part quality is poor. Necessary variations in the preassembly manufacturing and with the parts supply must be detected and corrected to ensure consistent quality. The accuracy and alignment characteristics of all machine components (index, transfer, fixture, and tooling) should be inspected.

When the inspection of product parts and machine components has been completed, individual stations should be individually cycled slowly, and any necessary adjustments or alterations should be made. Next a few stations can be cycled together. Then the entire machine or system is cycled for a specified time and adjustments made to attain the desired efficiency.

Each auxiliary control function, such as safety interlocks, automatic shutdown due to irregularities, and automatic parts ejection, should be checked by simulating malfunctions. During debugging, the machine should be cycled at high speed to detect the possibility of synchronization offset. The machine may work well at low cycle speeds because the synchronization error might be small, but at high speeds this error may be large compared to the machine cycle speed. Also, the problem of workpiece inertia becomes apparent at high machine speeds. Critical machine members may have to be strengthened to eliminate motion problems.

Debugging Aids

Debugging test data should be tabulated because this gives an overall view of system efficiency and pinpoints areas presenting maximum problems. Complex systems should be broken down into manageable modules to minimize debugging time.

Multipen strip recorders that simultaneously display motions and actions can be helpful in spotting function problems. Strobe lights are commonly used to study rotation or repetitive motion functions. Video and high-speed cameras are also used to detect malfunctions. Most computers and programmable controllers provide automatic diagnostics to detect failures of control devices.

SAFETY CONSIDERATIONS

The advent of automated assembly machines and systems in the workplace has reduced the number of human operators active in industrial assembly tasks and in many cases reduced the potential for human operator injury. The presence of automated systems in the factory, however, poses several safety issues that have not been present with older industrial machinery. In many cases, operators interface with an assembly machine for tasks that previously mandated contact with several human operators. In assembly systems, the operator may work with several cooperating machines, including robots. These machine motions, which are dictated by a computer, may at times appear unpredictable to the observer.

Generally, the safety rules that apply to any industrial machine (discussed in detail in Volume I, *Machining*, and Volume II, *Forming*, of this Handbook series) also hold true for assembly machines. In addition, characteristics unique to automated assembly systems and assembly machine interfaces demand special safety considerations. Safety issues must be given close attention when planning for automation, and accident prevention measures must be initiated. Manufacturing engineers must use their best judgment and experience to attain

a proper balance between safety systems and the access required to maintain good machine productivity.

Designing and Planning Stages

An assembly machine, robot, or series of machines and robots should not be installed without giving early consideration to how the arrangement will be inherently safe to operators and maintenance personnel. Designing and laying out automated assembly systems that provide for operator safety must be planned for in the earliest stages of design.

Designers and manufacturers of automation machinery are legally responsible for anyone who is injured by the equipment as long as the equipment is operational and regardless of how ill conceived the intentions of an injured party. It is in the best interest of everyone to give the automation equipment built-in features that prevent exposure to irregular hazards and that cannot be circumvented by inappropriate personnel.

Identifying hazards. The planner of an automated assembly installation must identify all of the major hazards that apply to the specific application and to the assembly equipment under consideration. This is the first step toward formulating a defense against personnel injury. Table 12-9 contains a list of hazards most often responsible for injury.

The planner should complete the hazards analysis by attempting to anticipate what can go wrong in the automated assembly application. Then the arrangement should be modified to prevent the unwanted events or to minimize their consequences. This can be accomplished by:

1. Specifying the basic elements of the assembly application.
2. Searching for hazards associated with these elements.
3. Specifying how the hazards have the potential for causing injury.

TABLE 12-9
Hazards Typical of Assembly Machinery

Hazard	Potential Causes
Tripping	Objects in operator's path
Slipping	Highly polished surfaces, oil drippings
Bumping of head	Low overheads, equipment protrusions
Electricity	Uncovered electrical leads
Burns	Uninsulated hot surfaces, hot process materials
Pinching	Catch points
Impact shock	Uncontrolled acceleration or oscillation of machine members
Noise	Rapid release of compressed gas, metallic impacts
Toxic substances	Degreasing solvents, process decomposition products
Pressure	Escaping gases, hydraulic forces
Radiation	Electromagnetic UV ionizing energy sources
Explosion or fire	Unmonitored flammable liquid and vapor sources

SAFETY

4. Determining how the arrangement for the application can be modified to eliminate or guard against the unwanted event.

This technique, sometimes known as idiot-proofing, is essential during the mockup phase of an automated assembly project. The most effective and inexpensive remedies to unsafe equipment situations are developed at this time. In the case of a straightforward purchase of an assembly machine, hazards can be eliminated in much the same way by a design review and a preacceptance inspection by the purchaser.

Table 12-10 contains a list of some specific safety-related design tasks. Table 12-11 stresses basic rules to make certain that automation equipment can be safely and conveniently maintained and repaired.

Applicable standards. Occupational Safety and Health Administration (OSHA) safety standards, as well as American National (ANSI) standards, should be reviewed as a major consideration during concept development of assembly systems. The planner is mandated to comply with OSHA standards. Conformance is a large part of the engineering, fabrication, and operating costs of automatic machinery. Important standards to review include the following:

NFPA 79 Electrical Standards for Industrial Machinery, available from the National Fire Protection Association, Quincy, MA 02269.

OSHA Safety and Health Standard 29 CFR, Part 1910:
  Subpart C: Occupational health and environmental control.
  Subpart H: Hazardous materials.
  Subpart M: Compressed gas and compressed air equipment.
  Subpart O: Machinery and machine guarding.
  Subpart S: Electrical.
  1910.212: General requirements for all machines.

American National Standards Institute standards:
  B15.1: Mechanical Power Transmission Apparatus.
  B11.19: Guards and Devices.
  B20.1: Conveyors and Related Equipment.
  B244.1: Lockout/Tagout of Energy Sources.

Machine safeguarding principles. OSHA regulations require the addition of guards, sound enclosures, electrical control features, and color schemes on assembly equipment that physically prevent the worker from contacting hazardous operations. Machine safeguarding should prevent accidental contact and impede deliberate access to operating dangers. Physical guarding and electrical controls on automation equipment must be designed to allow for legitimate operator access for adjustments, without creating exposure to hazards. This approach will preclude after-the-fact safety add-ons that are later removed because they are an inconvenience to operators.

Mechanical barriers. Guarding for the point of operation should be set so that any opening and the distance to the hazard point conform to the chart shown in Fig. 12-84. A general rule for assembly machines is that the operator should always have visual access to all workpieces, subassemblies, and assemblies in the machine. Mechanical barriers should be used only to restrict operators from areas of definite hazards, not from normal machine operation areas. Pinchpoints, sprockets, chains, belts, and pulleys are all hazardous areas. Color schemes in accordance with ANSI Standard 253.1 should be used to warn of hazards. Barrier guarding should be painted a different color than that of the machine.

If hazardous points on the assembly machine must be visible, then transparent guarding material, such as Lexan, can be used. Plexiglas is not an adequate guarding material for every application. A transparent guarding application is shown in Fig. 12-85.

Mechanical barriers over inspection probes, escapements, transfer units, and fixtures for operator interface are not effective because the frequent need to reach into these areas precludes the use of rigidly mounted guards. Guards that are not interlocked to the machine control circuit, yet that can be easily removed, are a detriment to the operator. If the machine can be run without them, then they will be removed. Therefore, safe operating conditions on assembly machines will not occur unless guarding does not frustrate the operator.

Optical and electrical barriers. A capacitive or radiation field generated by an antenna is an effective guard. Anything penetrating the field will change the field attributes and shut down the machine. This type of system is shown in Fig. 12-86. There are disadvantages to this system, however. Assembly

TABLE 12-10
Automation Planning Safety Checklist

- Safety measures should give preference to the following procedural order: the operator, assembly machines, peripheral machinery, assembly robots, and then workpieces and tooling
- Machine and assembly system should be designed so that it is impossible to gain access to a hazard point during operation
- All moving machine parts that could engage the operator should be covered
- Accidental unclamping of work (by operator or machine) should not propel the workpiece toward the operator. If this is possible, then shielding should be in place
- Operator should be shielded from any type of spray, chip, or broken tool ejection
- Operator should have safe, easy access to the workstations that must be interfaced with as part of the job
- Operators involved in a symbiotic relationship with an assembly machine should not be made to maintain an unrealistic workpace
- Moving parts should be designed to be fail-safe or to prevent operator injury should they fail
- Safety features should be designed so that they cannot be easily removed or circumvented
- Explosion-proof motors or fluid power should be used in explosive environments
- Power transmission and fluid drive mechanisms should preferably be an integral part of the machine or machine system

(continued)

TABLE 12-10—*Continued*

- There should be automatic overload and shutoff devices built into the machine
- The assembly machine should automatically shut down in the event of failure
- Mechanical devices should be used for directly feeding and rejecting parts on an assembly machine
- Motor drift and run-on times should be short
- Energy sources should diminish safely to zero energy state when machine goes down
- Access platforms or ladders should be provided for inspection and maintenance access in higher machine locations
- All standing, walking, and climbing surfaces around the equipment should be of good traction material
- Precautions and warnings should be clearly displayed
- Machine system emergency procedures should be clearly displayed
- Machine chassis and subsystems should be electrically grounded
- Controls should be located so that the operator will not be too close to the operation whenever activation is required
- Controls should be placed so that the operator will not have to reach excessively or be off balance
- Fail-safe interlocks should be present on automated assembly machinery to prevent production operation during operator or maintenance access. Key-accessed operation, which can defeat the interlocks, should only be possible for maintenance personnel
- The machine controls should be interlocked to ensure that the machine can only be operated in the sequence desired
- All control knobs and buttons should be clearly distinguishable
- Controls should be positioned or guarded so that they cannot be accidentally activated
- An emergency stop or panic button for operator shutdown of the automated assembly system should be present in an easily accessible location
- All possible sources of objectionable noise should be minimized
- Operator training and retraining is essential
- Periodic audit of conformance to safety is necessary

TABLE 12-11
Safety Concerns for Maintenance of the Automation Arrangement

- Frequently replaced parts of the automated assembly system should be arranged so that maintenance personnel have access with minimum effort
- There should be easy access to control protective devices such as fuses or breakers
- Specialized custom tools should not be required for routine maintenance
- The automation equipment should be modularized to aid in fast, easy replacement of major components
- Parts of machinery should be clearly identifiable
- The assembly machine system should be located so that there is sufficient clearance for maintenance. There should be appropriate spacing, especially in dangerous locations such as high-voltage sources
- Controls should be such that the machine system cannot be operated from some remote location while maintenance is being performed
- The assembly machine should have proper electrical grounding
- Assembly robots and machinery should be designed and situated for easy cleaning
- Grease and oil fittings should be accessible. Use pressurized lubrication for hard-to-access locations. Single-point lubrication is preferred
- Walking and standing surfaces should be of nonslip texture
- Maintenance personnel should have access to machine documentation, including arrangement drawings, electrical and pnuematic schematic diagrams, timing diagrams, maintenance instructions, and a list of replacement parts

machines have numerous moving elements, and the antenna will have to be placed so that it will not react to normal machine motion. Because the generated field is circular around the antenna, it is difficult to know if an effective field exists at any given point.

An operator can be protected when attempting to enter an assembly machine in motion through the use of light curtains and electrical circuits that sense human presence. A light curtain is an optical wall along a specific path created by a modulated light or infrared energy transmitter. If an operator violates

CHAPTER 12

SAFETY CONSIDERATIONS

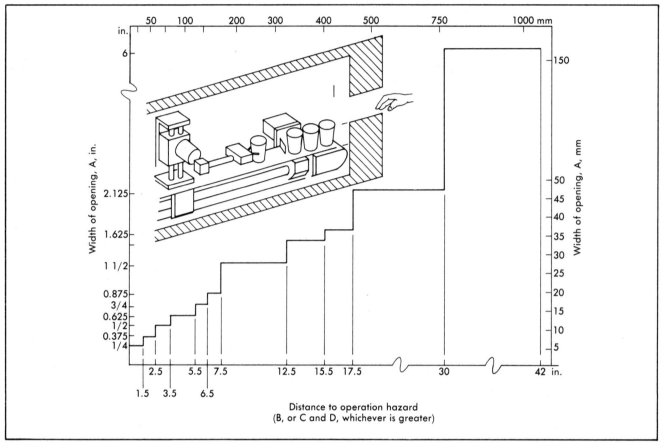

Fig. 12-84 Maximum suggested openings for uncovered areas of assembly machines.

Distance to operation hazard
(B, or C and D, whichever is greater)

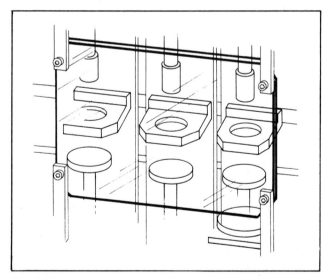

Fig. 12-85 A transparent guard restricts access but allows observation of operation.

the curtain and prevents the energy beam from reaching a reflector or receiver, then the ensuing change in current can be used in the machine control circuit to shut the machine down, thus protecting the operator from injury.

Light curtains are available in different dimensions. Advantages include allowing the operator to clearly observe machine motions, the capability of being placed close to the machine's moving elements, and knowing the exact curtain location. However, a clear, continuous visual path is required from transmitter to reflector or receiver. Light curtains should be considered in the initial layout of an assembly machine, not as an add-on feature. To minimize costs, a transmitter can send signals by mirrors to a receiver for protecting four sides of a machine. A disadvantage of light curtains is that the operator is not protected from parts or broken tools that are propelled from the machine. Also, the operator may trip the light curtain accidentally.

Electrical floor mats placed before an assembly machine can be used to shut down operation if anyone stands close enough to reach moving components. Mats are inexpensive and can be simply connected to the machine control circuit. On the negative side, they make close observations of assembly stations difficult. They do not discriminate whether an attempt is being made to violate safe practices, and they can be easily moved. Disadvantages of mats also include the possibility of persons tripping over them and interference with floor-cleaning operations.

Electrical controls. Assembly machine controls must include an emergency stop button to break all machine activity when engaged. Machine systems with multiple operator interfaces can have an emergency stop cord traversing the operator loca-

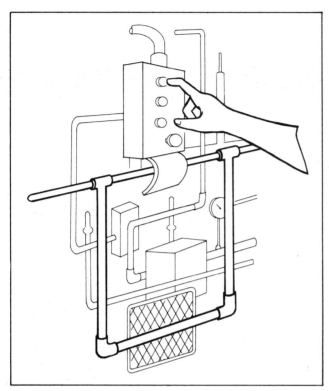

Fig. 12-86 Round tubes form an antenna that radiates a safety field.

tions or multiple emergency stop buttons. When assembly machines must be stopped for safety, braking action should occur as rapidly as possible. Separate control buttons should be provided for breaking the machine sequence in nonemergency cases, such as quality assurance problems. Once a reset button is activated, the machine must not restart automatically. The controls should be so designed that the start procedures must be implemented to reinitiate machine motion.

A "jog" or "inch" button should be included for troubleshooting purposes. The circuit should not permit machine actuation in the jog mode if safety interlocks are activated. The jog button must cause the machine to stop instantly when released.

Dual pushbutton stations or a walkaround control box are a good practice for large assembly machines. The control circuit must not allow an operator at one end to start the machine without concurrence by the other operator through a reset button. An audible horn and time delay relay provide a restart warning with withdrawal time allowance.

Sound enclosures. Because many workers resist any form of ear protection, mufflers and noise barriers should be used on automated assembly equipment to comply with OSHA standards. A maximum noise level of 85 dB is required for assembly machines where operators wear no ear protection. Noise should be contained in such a way as to allow efficient machine operation. Because sound enclosures may restrict visual and manual access, the planner of automated assembly systems should attempt to eliminate the source of high noise levels.

Attention to detail can reduce noise levels and minimize the presence of sound enclosures. For example, hoppers should have high-low level sensors to keep the minimum essential number of parts in transfer rails. If vibratory bowl feeders are too large, then

excess part movement will contribute to high noise levels. Orientation methods can be achieved more quietly in escapements or transfer devices, rather than in feeders. Mechanical action might be used to replace fluid power. Air jets should not be used to excess. Exhaust ports should be piped to a muffler.

Harmful wastes. Oil contamination can come from the exhaust ports of pneumatic components with lubricated compressed air. Vented oil fumes from these ports should be collected at a muffler. The automated assembly process should use lubrication application techniques other than spraying for subassemblies or assembly operations that require these coatings.

Assembly equipment that requires welding or laser drilling operations should have adequate ventilation systems to draw away vapors. Some base metals generate toxic gas wastes during welding, and the use of an inert environment is not unusual for these tasks. Toxic conditions must be avoided.

Proper documentation. The planner of an automated assembly system has to be certain that proper documentation is provided for all machinery, including the following:

1. Detailed operating procedures.
2. Precautions against deviating from procedures.
3. Maintenance procedures.
4. Personnel hazards present.

Multiple man-machine interfaces. An important aspect to the design of automated assembly systems is the worker interface. If the interface, or point where an operator makes direct contact with the assembly machines, is not seriously considered, then system performance, human efficiency, and safety are sacrificed. Poorly arranged equipment requires workers to compensate or overexert themselves unnecessarily. In designing an assembly equipment arrangement, the responsible planner must determine the following:

1. The objective of the system.
2. The environment in which it will operate.
3. The system maintenance concept.
4. The necessary assembly stations, machines, and the space they will occupy.
5. Equipment interconnections.
6. The number of operators and their function.

With this information, the planner will be able to optimize the arrangement of personnel functions and assembly robots and machines within the space constraints of the work area. Figure 12-87 illustrates a typical automated assembly system with man-machine interfaces.

Link analysis. Link analysis is a design tool that provides information needed to produce safe and efficient placement of operators and machines in an assembly arrangement. The idea behind link analysis techniques is that the safest arrangement can be found by optimizing different types of links (such as movement or communication) that are important to the automation application. A link analysis procedure for man-machine interfaces is as follows:

1. Draw a circle for each operator in the application and assign a number.
2. Draw a square for every robot or assembly machine and label each with a letter.
3. Draw connecting lines (links) between each operator and any other operator who interacts.
4. Draw connecting lines between each operator and the machine with which the operator interfaces.

CHAPTER 12

SAFETY CONSIDERATIONS

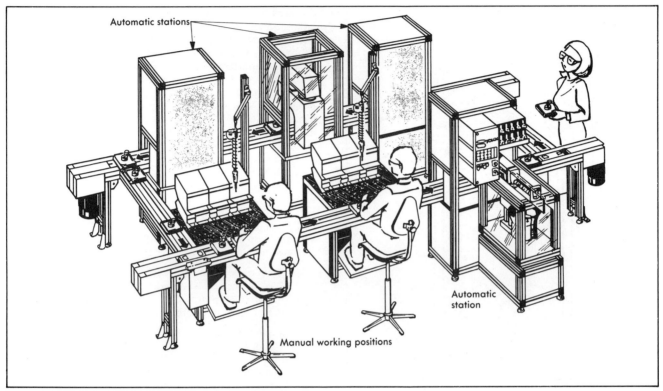

Fig. 12-87 Assembly system with man-machine interfaces.

5. Redraw the resulting diagram, minimizing the number of crossing lines to show the simplest possible arrangement. If robots are involved, utilize machinery as a part of the robot safety barriers if possible. Electrical and control panels should be conveniently and strategically located.
6. Rank each link according to importance by assigning high numbers to important links and low numbers to unimportant links. The high-ranking links should be the ones that are worked the most.
7. Optimize the diagram further, redrawing it so that the high-ranking links are shorter than the low-ranking links and minimize the number of crossing links.
8. Design the workspace to suit the shape of the diagram. Provide access for tool and setup changes, manual load and unload stations, arrival and removal of workpiece pallets, and maintenance activities.
9. Place the final link analysis diagram on a scale drawing, showing the actual positions of operators, machines, and open floor space. This drawing allows the planner to discover the difficulties of interfaces that may create equipment arrangements unsafe to the operators.
10. Review the scale drawing with production and maintenance personnel, the factory safety officer, and any other appropriate parties.

A number of factors should be considered to ensure safe operation when placing robots in automated assembly systems. The Robotic Industries Association (RIA) Safety Subcommittee, comprised of robot users, manufacturers, suppliers, and academians, spent several years developing a proposed standard for robot safety. This proposed standard was first presented at an RIA safety seminar in November 1984. The objective of this standard is to enhance the safety of personnel associated with industrial robot systems by establishing guidelines for the construction, installation, care, and use of industrial robots. Copies can be purchased from the Robotic Industries Association, P.O. Box 3724, Ann Arbor, MI 48106.

The guidelines presented here complement this standard and do not replace it in any way. The greatest responsibility for the safety of an assembly system that includes a robot rests on the user. It is the user who has the ultimate responsibility for proper installation, the presence of proper safeguards, and meeting the proper OSHA standards. The same rules that relate to other moving equipment apply to robots; however, because robots can initiate sudden, unsuspected motions in accordance with programming, the operator must be protected.

Robot hazards. The major hazard in using robots is the potential for injury due to the following:

1. Collision of the robot arm with a person inside the robot operating envelope.
2. Personnel becoming trapped between moving parts of the robot and fixed objects inside or close to the operating envelope.
3. Personnel being struck by tools or components dropped or ejected by the robot.
4. Collision between items being carried by the robot and personnel.
5. Chips and working media, such as paint or sealants, contaminating personnel.
6. Control errors that occur in hydraulic, pneumatic, or electrical systems that result in incorrect movement by the robot, thus affecting the operator.

7. Operator misunderstanding of the robot working envelope.

Occurrence of accidents. The greatest risk of accidents involving robots takes place during programming and maintenance. During these periods, personnel may be within the robot operating envelope. Many assembly applications call for an operator to teach the robot movements within close tolerance parameters. This calls for the operator to be very close to the robot's activity. Although teaching is done at a reduced speed, a hazard may arise if the robot moves in an unpredictable fashion. The highest percentage of robot-related accidents occur at this time because conventional safety systems, such as barriers, light curtains, and pressure mats, are incapable of providing protection. Special care needs to be taken in fashioning robot safeguards.

Robot safety barriers. A physical barrier should be placed around the robot operating area, thus prohibiting the curious outsider or other personnel from accidental or inadvertent entry into the robot work envelope. A fence structure is adequate for this purpose and can capture objects dropped or ejected by the robot. Figure 12-88 shows an appropriate physical barrier surrounding a robot workspace. Perimeter fencing is essential because:

1. Its presence is a warning, even to those unfamiliar with what it encloses.
2. It prevents material handling equipment and other plant vehicles from inadvertently moving into a robot danger zone.
3. Tampering with the equipment when it is not operating is minimized.
4. Authorized personnel are forced to enter the robot work area from the safest direction—an interlocked barrier gate.

The perimeter fence must be located outside the farthest extreme of the combined robot and tooling reach. Even then, there should be additional clearance to prevent a person from becoming trapped between the robot and fence. Restriction posts are not to be installed inside the work envelope. They create the hazard of an operator becoming pinned by the robot.

Access gates in the perimeter fence must be electrically interlocked to interrupt main drive power and stop the robot if they are opened during the automatic cycle of the robot. A manual restart switch at the main control panel outside of the perimeter guard should be used to return power to the robot. Closing the interlocked gate must not initiate the automatic cycle.

Sensing operator presence. For some applications, optical sensors or pressure-sensitive mats can be used as primary, secondary, or redundant safety interlocks. Other means of detecting intrusion into a hazardous robot envelope include auditory or sound monitors. Capacitance-type presence-detecting sensors can be mounted on the robot base and arm to stop it should something get too close.

Factors affecting robot safety. Ensuring safety when using industrial robots requires careful consideration of the following factors:

- If the assembly robot is not on an automatic guided vehicle (AGV), then it should be anchored in conformance with the manufacturer's specifications.
- All sources of energy (electric, pneumatic, hydraulic) to the robot should have locking-type disconnects for maintenance lockout.

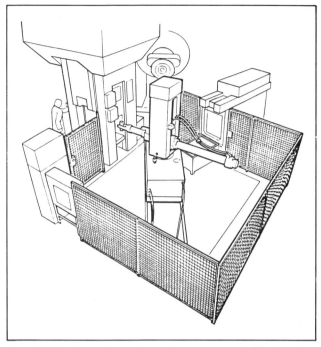

Fig. 12-88 Typical safety enclosure for robotic workcell. (*Machine Tool Trades Assn.*)

- Maintenance personnel should thoroughly understand all robot safety precautions.
- Proper lockout and testing procedures should be used before entering the operating envelope for work on a robot.
- All persons involved in the operation of a robot should be aware of the consequences of the control system and of the safety features provided.
- Control panels should be situated so that the robot can easily be seen during programming and production operation.
- During power lockout, stored energy should be released. This energy may be in the form of heavy robot loads, counterweights, flywheels, springs, and air or hydraulic accumulators. Servicing may take place after the robot is brought to the zero mechanical and electrical state.
- Solid-state electronic devices for controlling the robot should be shielded from potential radio frequency interference that could cause a loss of control.
- Robot teach pendants should have a "deadman" switch or emergency stop button to stop robot movement. The emergency stop should be wired directly into the drive-power stop circuit.
- While in the teach mode of operation, the speed of the farthest extremity of the robot arm should be limited to a maximum of 6 ips (152 mm/s). It should be even slower if this speed does not allow an operator to get out of the arm's way. The force behind the arm should not cause injury.
- An operator should not be able to place the robot into automatic production cycle using the teach pendant. This should be possible only from the master control panel after interlocked gates are shut.
- Operators inside the robot work envelope during programming should not place fingers and other body parts

SAFETY CONSIDERATIONS

in a position where injury could result in the event of a malfunction.

- A second person should be present when on-location programming and/or maintenance is being carried out.
- Programmers should consider incorporating safety features to assist operators and maintenance personnel. For example, a robot can be programmed so that during tool change the arm will go to a standard safe position first and reside for several seconds, thus allowing the operator time to move out of its path before it swings to the tool station.
- The direction of each robot axis should be marked on the stationary robot base to correspond with direction markings on the switches of control devices.
- A clearly visible amber light should be placed near the robot, and it should be energized anytime the robot is live, even when there is no motion.
- Warning signs should be placed on robot perimeter access gates to inform of existing hazards, such as overlapping robot work envelopes or other assembly machinery that may have movement in the work area. Figure 12-89 illustrates an application of overlapping robot operating envelopes.
- Install a fail-safe brake into the shoulder elbow and pitch axis of hydraulic robots. If hydraulic pressure is lost by accident or intentional shutdown, the spring-applied brakes engage and mechanically lock the robot joints, holding them until they are released by renewed hydraulic pressure.
- For welding applications, the robot and components should be electrically grounded, and the welding gun must not be insulated from the robot.

- Robotic assembly installations that participate with operators must match the capabilities and limitations of the workers. The robot pace should be operator dependent; the machines should wait on the humans.
- A glare-free light level of 50-100 ft-c (538-1076 lx) is recommended for a robot site.
- Floors at robot sites should be maintained in good repair with nonslip surfaces.
- Operators should remove packing crates, empty boxes, and containers; extraneous metal and wood; or anything that is not a necessary part of the work environment before applying power.
- Before starting any robot, the operator should make sure all safeguards are in place and all peripheral machinery is in cycle with the robot.

References

1. G. Boothroyd, C. Poli, and L.E. Murch, *The Handbook of Feeding and Orienting Techniques for Small Parts* (Amherst, MA: University of Massachusetts, Department of Mechanical Engineering, 1977).
2. Jack D. Lane, *Automated Assembly*, 2nd ed. (Dearborn, MI: Society of Manufacturing Engineers, 1986), p. 127.
3. *Ibid.*, pp. 157-174.
4. *Automated Assembly Data Memorandum*, Memo 680219 (London: The Institution of Production Engineers, 1984).
5. *Ibid.*, Memo 680593 (1971).
6. *Ibid.*, Memo 680321 (1984).
7. *Ibid.*, Memo 680351 (1984).
8. Lane, *op. cit.*, pp. 216-217.
9. *Automated Assembly Data Memorandum*, Memo 680529 (London: The Institution of Production Engineers, 1970).
10. *Ibid.*, Memo 680438 (1981).
11. *Ibid.*, Memo 680427 (1981).

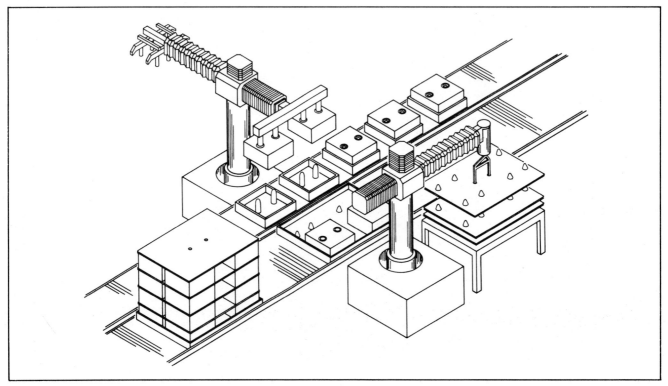

Fig. 12-89 Robots with overlapping work envelopes.

Bibliography

Andreasen, M. Myrup; Kähler, S.; and Lund, T. *Design for Assembly*. New York: Springer-Verlag, 1983.

Automated Assembling Data Memoranda. London: The Institution of Production Engineers, 1968-1984.

Bahn, Michael M., and Harned, John. *Flexible Dimensional Gauging System*. SME Technical Paper MS84-161. Dearborn, MI: Society of Manufacturing Engineers, 1984.

Bateson, John. "Comparison of Low Cost ATE Systems." *Electro-Onics*. Part 1 (November 1985), pp. 18-20; and Part 2 (December 1985), pp. 20-23.

Bergstrom, Robin P. "Automated Pump Assembly Pays Off." *Manufacturing Engineering* (June 1984), pp. 44-47.

Bertha, R. William. *Economics of High Volume Assembly*. SME Technical Paper AD74-414. Dearborn, MI: Society of Manufacturing Engineers, 1974.

_____ . *Road Blocks to Mechanized Assembly—People*. SME Technical Paper AD75-750. Dearborn, MI: Society of Manufacturing Engineers, 1975.

Boothroyd, Geoffrey. "Economics of Assembly Systems." *Journal of Manufacturing Systems* (vol. 1, no. 1, 1982), pp. 111-127.

_____ , and Dewhurst, P. *Design for Assembly*. Amherst, MA: University of Massachusetts, 1983.

_____ ; Poli, Corrado; and Murch, Lawrence E. *Automatic Assembly*. New York: Marcel Dekker, 1982.

_____ ; Poli, C.R.; and Murch, L.E. *Handbook of Feeding and Orienting Techniques for Small Parts*. Amherst, MA: University of Massachusetts, 1976.

Brisky, Michael. "Planning Your Surface Mount Manufacturing Line." *Circuits Manufacturing* (May 1985), pp. 77-82.

Burgam, Patrick M. "Integrating Vision in Tie Rod Assembly." *Manufacturing Engineering* (February 1984), pp. 53 and 54.

Cieslak, G.; Nesham, M.A.; Palmer, M.J.; and Schmidt, P.B. *Unattended Assembly Cell: Assembly of a Contactor*. SME Technical Paper MS85-736. Dearborn, MI: Society of Manufacturing Engineers, 1985.

Dallas, Daniel B. "Systems Engineering in Advanced Assembly." *Manufacturing Engineering* (October 1979), pp. 54-57.

Didocha, Robert J.; Lyons, Donald W.; and Thompson, J. Chris. *Integration of Tactile Sensors and Machine Vision for Control of Robotic Manipulators*. SME Technical Paper MS85-05. Dearborn, MI: Society of Manufacturing Engineers, 1985.

DiPietro, Frank A. *Organization of Assembling Cells by Robotics*. SME Technical Paper MS84-339. Dearborn, MI: Society of Manufacturing Engineers, 1984.

Essig, William E. *Computer-Integrated Electronic Assembly Using Robots*. SME Technical Paper EE85-140. Dearborn, MI: Society of Manufacturing Engineers, 1985.

Farnum, Gregory T. "Automating for Survival." *Manufacturing Engineering* (April 1985), pp. 45-48.

"Flexible Assembly: A Search for Economies of Scope." *Production Engineering* (December 1984), pp. 40-47.

Ghosh, Kalyan, and Leman, Claude. "Machine Interactions in Robotics and Their Effect on the Safety of the Workplace." *RI/SME Robots 9 Proceedings*. Dearborn, MI: Society of Manufacturing Engineers, 1985, pp. 19.1-19.8.

Goodrich, Jerry L. *Programmable Parts Feeders*. SME Technical Paper MF85-163. Dearborn, MI: Society of Manufacturing Engineers, 1985.

Graiser, Harlan N. *Automated Assembly Facility for Consumer Electronics Products*. SME Technical Paper MS84-365. Dearborn, MI: Society of Manufacturing Engineers, 1984.

Hastie, William M. "Board Handling Equipment." *Circuits Manufacturing* (March 1984), pp. 90-96.

Henderson, James A. *Westinghouse Technology Modernization for Electronic Assembly*. SME Technical Paper MS85-147. Dearborn, MI: Society of Manufacturing Engineers, 1985.

_____ , and Hosier, Robert N. *New Robotic Systems Change the Electronic Assembly Factory*. SME Technical Paper MS84-373. Dearborn, MI: Society of Manufacturing Engineers, 1984.

Hosier, Robert N. *A System Designed for Flexible Electronics Manufacturing*. SME Technical Paper EE85-139. Dearborn, MI: Society of Manufacturing Engineers, 1985.

Hoska, David R. *Design of Electronic Products for Automated Manufacture*. SME Technical Paper MS85-892. Dearborn, MI: Society of Manufacturing Engineers, 1985.

Howard, John M. "Focus on the Human Factors in Applying Robotic Systems." *Robotics Today* (December 1982), pp. 32-34.

Ioannou, Dr. Adrian. *Robotic Assembly of Printed Circuit Boards*. SME Technical Paper MS86-156. Dearborn, MI: Society of Manufacturing Engineers, 1986.

Kehoe, Ellen J. "Practical Robot Safety." *Robotics Today* (April 1985), pp. 38-41.

Kintner, Walter H., Jr. *Robots for Electronic Assembly*. SME Technical Paper MS85-559. Dearborn, MI: Society of Manufacturing Engineers, 1985.

Kreamer, William C. *Measuring Robot and Sensor Accuracy*. SME Technical Paper MS84-1038. Dearborn, MI: Society of Manufacturing Engineers, 1984.

Lane, Jack D. *Automated Assembly*, 2nd ed. Dearborn, MI: Society of Manufacturing Engineers, 1986.

Larson, Melissa. "Surface Mount Technology—An Overview." *Assembly Engineering* (April 1984), pp. 16-19.

Lee, Jay. "Robotic Safety—Analysis, Considerations, and Answers." *RI/SME Robots 9 Proceedings*. Dearborn, MI: Society of Manufacturing Engineers, 1985, pp. 19.49-19.53.

Mangin, Charles-Henri, and D'Agostino, Salvatore. "Flexible Automated Assembly Systems—An Approach for the Electronics Industry." *Assembly Engineering* (March 1984), pp. 30-33.

Markstein, Howard W. "Automatic Component Insertion/Placement Systems Ready for the Automated Factory." *Electronic Packaging Production* (August 8, 1984), pp. 106-112.

Murray, Jerry. "Automation in PCB Making." *Circuits Manufacturing* (September 1984), pp. 44-54.

Nof, Shimon Y., ed. *Handbook of Industrial Robotics*. Dearborn, MI: Society of Manufacturing Engineers, 1985.

Owen, Tony. *Assembly with Robots*. Englewood Cliffs, NJ: Prentice-Hall, Inc., 1985.

Peebles, John F. *Advancements in Electronic Assembly—The Automated Factory*. SME Technical Paper EE83-122. Dearborn, MI: Society of Manufacturing Engineers, 1983.

Potter, Donald D. *Safety for Robotics* (December 1983), pp. 19-21.

Rathmill, Keith, ed. *Robotic Assembly*. New York: Springer-Verlag, 1985.

Riley, Frank J. *Assembly Automation*. New York: Industrial Press, 1983.

_____ . "Building Flexibility Into Your Assembly Systems." *Assembly Engineering*: Part 1: (November 1983), pp. 22-24, Part 2: (December 1983), pp. 28-30, and Part 3: (February 1984), pp. 34-36.

Schreiber, Rita R. "Robots and Electronics Manufacturing." *Manufacturing Engineering* (December 1985), pp. 43-46.

_____ . "How to Teach a Robot." *Robotics Today* (June 1984), pp. 51-55.

Skaggs, Clyde W. *Design for Electronic Assembly*. SME Technical Paper MS85-893. Dearborn, MI: Society of Manufacturing Engineers, 1985.

Stauffer, Robert N. "High-Speed Production of Needle Bearing Assemblies." *Manufacturing Engineering* (September 1982), pp. 65 and 66.

_____ . "Robotic Assembly." *Robotics Today* (October 1984), pp. 45-52.

_____ . "Robot Accuracy." *Robotics Today* (April 1985), pp. 43-49.

_____ . "Robots Assume Key Role in Electronics Manufacturing." *Manufacturing Engineering* (April 1984), pp. 84-87.

_____ . "Progress in Tactile Sensor Development." *Robotics Today* (June 1983), pp. 43-49.

"The Advent of APAS," *Manufacturing Engineering* (April 1979), pp. 74 and 75.

VanderPlas, Thomas W. *A Vision-Guided Robot on the Automotive Final Assembly Line*. SME Technical Paper MS85-218. Dearborn, MI: Society of Manufacturing Engineers, 1985.

Waldman, Harry. "Automatic Assembly: Making Use of Probes and Vision Systems." *Manufacturing Engineering* (April 1983), pp. 91-93.

Walsh, Steve. "Gripper Design: Guidelines for Effective Results." *Manufacturing Engineering* (November 1984), pp. 53-55.

Wick, Charles. "Designing Parts for Automatic Assembly." *Manufacturing Engineering* (July 1980), pp. 46-50.

_____ . "Parts Feeding: Some Classic Cases." *Manufacturing Engineering* (July 1980), pp. 50-56.

Zimmerman, Richard D. *Fastener Feeding State of the Art*. SME Technical Paper AD83-862. Dearborn, MI: Society of Manufacturing Engineers, 1983.

INDEX

INDEX

INDEX

INDEX